The Oxford Handbook of
Diversity and Work

OXFORD LIBRARY OF PSYCHOLOGY

EDITOR-IN-CHIEF

Peter E. Nathan

AREA EDITORS:

Clinical Psychology
David H. Barlow

Cognitive Neuroscience
Kevin N. Ochsner and Stephen M. Kosslyn

Cognitive Psychology
Daniel Reisberg

Counseling Psychology
Elizabeth M. Altmaier and Jo-Ida C. Hansen

Developmental Psychology
Philip David Zelazo

Health Psychology
Howard S. Friedman

History of Psychology
David B. Baker

Methods and Measurement
Todd D. Little

Neuropsychology
Kenneth M. Adams

Organizational Psychology
Steve W. J. Kozlowksi

Personality and Social Psychology
Kay Deaux and Mark Snyder

OXFORD LIBRARY OF PSYCHOLOGY

Editor in Chief PETER E. NATHAN

Editor, Organizational Psychology STEVE W. J. KOZLOWSKI

The Oxford Handbook of Diversity and Work

Edited by

Quinetta M. Roberson

OXFORD
UNIVERSITY PRESS

OXFORD
UNIVERSITY PRESS

Oxford University Press is a department of the University of Oxford.
It furthers the University's objective of excellence in research, scholarship,
and education by publishing worldwide.

Oxford   New York
Auckland   Cape Town   Dar es Salaam   Hong Kong   Karachi
Kuala Lumpur   Madrid   Melbourne   Mexico City   Nairobi
New Delhi   Shanghai   Taipei   Toronto

With offices in
Argentina   Austria   Brazil   Chile   Czech Republic   France   Greece
Guatemala   Hungary   Italy   Japan   Poland   Portugal   Singapore
South Korea   Switzerland   Thailand   Turkey   Ukraine   Vietnam

Oxford is a registered trade mark of Oxford University Press
in the UK and certain other countries.

Published in the United States of America by
Oxford University Press
198 Madison Avenue, New York, NY 10016

© Oxford University Press 2013

First issued as an Oxford University Press paperback, 2014.

All rights reserved. No part of this publication may be reproduced, stored in a retrieval
system, or transmitted, in any form or by any means, without the prior permission in writing
of Oxford University Press, or as expressly permitted by law, by license, or under terms agreed
with the appropriate reproduction rights organization. Inquiries concerning reproduction
outside the scope of the above should be sent to the Rights Department, Oxford University
Press, at the address above.

You must not circulate this work in any other form
and you must impose this same condition on any acquirer.

Library of Congress Cataloging-in-Publication Data
  The Oxford handbook of diversity and work / edited by Quinetta M. Roberson.
    p. cm. – (Oxford library of psychology)
  ISBN: 978-0-19-973635-5 (hardcover); 978-0-19-938803-5 (paperback)
  1. Diversity in the workplace.   I. Roberson, Quinetta M.
  HF5549.5.M5O92 2013
  331.08—dc23
  2012023219

9 8 7 6 5 4 3 2 1

Printed in the United States of America
on acid-free paper

SHORT CONTENTS

Oxford Library of Psychology   vii–viii

About the Editor   ix

Contributors   xi–xiii

Contents   xv–xvi

Chapters   1–470

Index   471

OXFORD LIBRARY OF PSYCHOLOGY

The *Oxford Library of Psychology*, a landmark series of handbooks, is published by Oxford University Press, one of the world's oldest and most highly respected publishers, with a tradition of publishing significant books in psychology. The ambitious goal of the *Oxford Library of Psychology* is nothing less than to span a vibrant, wide-ranging field and, in so doing, to fill a clear market need.

Encompassing a comprehensive set of handbooks, organized hierarchically, the *Library* incorporates volumes at different levels, each designed to meet a distinct need. At one level are a set of handbooks designed broadly to survey the major subfields of psychology; at another are numerous handbooks that cover important current focal research and scholarly areas of psychology in depth and detail. Planned as a reflection of the dynamism of psychology, the *Library* will grow and expand as psychology itself develops, thereby highlighting significant new research that will impact on the field. Adding to its accessibility and ease of use, the *Library* will be published in print and, later on, electronically.

The *Library* surveys psychology's principal subfields with a set of handbooks that capture the current status and future prospects of those major subdisciplines. This initial set includes handbooks of social and personality psychology, clinical psychology, counseling psychology, school psychology, educational psychology, industrial and organizational psychology, cognitive psychology, cognitive neuroscience, methods and measurements, history, neuropsychology, personality assessment, developmental psychology, and more. Each handbook undertakes to review one of psychology's major subdisciplines with breadth, comprehensiveness, and exemplary scholarship. In addition to these broadly-conceived volumes, the *Library* also includes a large number of handbooks designed to explore in depth more specialized areas of scholarship and research, such as stress, health and coping, anxiety and related disorders, cognitive development, or child and adolescent assessment. In contrast to the broad coverage of the subfield handbooks, each of these latter volumes focuses on an especially productive, more highly focused line of scholarship and research. Whether at the broadest or most specific level, however, all of the *Library* handbooks offer synthetic coverage that reviews and evaluates the relevant past and present research and anticipates research in the future. Each handbook in the *Library* includes introductory and concluding chapters written by its editor to provide a roadmap to the handbook's table of contents and to offer informed anticipations of significant future developments in that field.

An undertaking of this scope calls for handbook editors and chapter authors who are established scholars in the areas about which they write. Many of the nation's and world's most productive and best-respected psychologists have agreed to edit *Library* handbooks or write authoritative chapters in their areas of expertise.

For whom has the *Oxford Library of Psychology* been written? Because of its breadth, depth, and accessibility, the *Library* serves a diverse audience, including graduate students in psychology and their faculty mentors, scholars, researchers, and practitioners in psychology and related fields. Each will find in the *Library* the information they seek on the subfield or focal area of psychology in which they work or are interested.

Befitting its commitment to accessibility, each handbook includes a comprehensive index, as well as extensive references to help guide research. And because the *Library* was designed from its inception as an online as well as a print resource, its structure and contents will be readily and rationally searchable online. Further, once the *Library* is released online, the handbooks will be regularly and thoroughly updated.

In summary, the *Oxford Library of Psychology* will grow organically to provide a thoroughly informed perspective on the field of psychology, one that reflects both psychology's dynamism and its increasing interdisciplinarity. Once published electronically, the *Library* is also destined to become a uniquely valuable interactive tool, with extended search and browsing capabilities. As you begin to consult this handbook, we sincerely hope you will share our enthusiasm for the more than 500-year tradition of Oxford University Press for excellence, innovation, and quality, as exemplified by the *Oxford Library of Psychology*.

Peter E. Nathan
Editor-in-Chief

ABOUT THE EDITOR

Quinetta M. Roberson
Quinetta M. Roberson is a Professor of Management in the Villanova School of Business at Villanova University. Professor Roberson earned her Ph.D. in Organizational Behavior, and undergraduate and graduate degrees in Finance, Accounting and Strategic Planning. Prior to getting her doctorate, Dr. Roberson worked as a financial analyst at CoreStates Bank in Philadelphia, PA serving in both the large corporate and small business commercial lending areas. Currently, Professor Roberson conducts research on organizational justice and strategic diversity management while teaching courses globally on human resource management at the undergraduate, graduate and executive levels.

CONTRIBUTORS

Evan P. Apfelbaum
Sloan School of Management
Massachusetts Institute of Technology
Cambridge, MA

Derek R. Avery
Fox School of Business
Temple University
Philadelphia, PA

Myrtle P. Bell
College of Business Administration
Department of Management
University of Texas at Arlington
Arlington, TX

Donna Chrobot-Mason
Center for Organizational Leadership
University of Cincinnati
Cincinnati, OH

Stephanie J. Creary
Carroll School of Management
Boston College
Chestnut Hill, MA

Bryan L. Dawson
Departments of Psychology and Sociology
North Georgia College and State University
Dahlonega, GA

Frank Dobbin
Department of Sociology
Harvard University
Cambridge, MA

Michelle M. Duguid
Olin Business School
Washington University in St. Louis
St. Louis, MO

Melissa J. Ferguson
Department of Psychology
Cornell University
Ithaca, NY

Michele J. Gelfand
Department of Psychology
University of Maryland, College Park
College Park, MD

Patricia N. Gilbert
Department of Psychology
Tulane University
New Orleans, LA

Matthew J. Goren
Department of Psychology
University of California, Berkeley
Berkeley, CA

Lindred L. Greer
Work and Organizational Psychology
University of Amsterdam
Amsterdam, The Netherlands

Michelle R. Hebl
Department of Psychology
Rice University
Houston, TX

Astrid C. Homan
Department of Psychology and Education
VU University Amsterdam
Amsterdam, The Netherlands

Karen A. Jehn
Melbourne Business School
The University of Melbourne
Malbourne, Australia

Karsten Jonsen
IMD International
Lausanne, Switzerland

Aparna Joshi
Smeal College of Business
Pennsylvania State University
State College, Pennsylvania

Alexandra Kalev
Department of Sociology
Tel Aviv University
Tel Aviv, Israel

Eden B. King
Department of Psychology
George Mason University
Fairfax, VA

Alison M. Konrad
  Richard Ivey School of Business
  University of Western Ontario
  London, Ontario, Canada
Carol T. Kulik
  School of Management
  University of South Australia
  Adelaide, Australia
Jason R. Lambert
  College of Business Administration
  Savannah State University
  Savannah, GA
Patrick F. McKay
  School of Management and Labor Relations
  Rutgers, the State University of New Jersey
  Piscataway, NJ
Carliss D. Miller
  Jindal School of Management
  University of Texas at Dallas
  Richardson, TX
Michàlle Mor Barak
  School of Social Work & Marshall School of Business
  University of Southern California
  Los Angeles, CA
Lisa H. Nishii
  School of Industrial and Labor Relations
  Cornell University
  Ithaca, NY
Laurie T. O'Brien
  Department of Psychology
  Tulane University
  New Orleans, LA
Mustafa Ozbilgin
  Business School
  Brunel University
  London, UK
Shanette C. Porter
  Institute for Policy Research
  Northwestern University
  Evanston, IL
Katherine W. Phillips
  Columbia Business School
  Columbia University
  New York, NY

Ray Reagans
  Sloan School of Management
  Massachusetts Institute of Technology
  Cambridge, MA
Orlando C. Richard
  Jindal School of Management
  University of Texas at Dallas
  Richardson, TX
Loriann Roberson
  Teachers College
  Columbia University
  New York, NY
Quinetta M. Roberson
  School of Business
  Villanova University
  Villanova, PA
Laura Morgan Roberts
  Ph.D. Program in Leadership and Change
  Antioch University
  Yellow Springs, OH
Hyuntak Roh
  School of Business
  Yonsei University
  Seoul, South Korea
Marian N. Ruderman
  Center for Creative Leadership
  Greensboro, NC
Eduardo Salas
  Department of Psychology
  Institute for Simulation and Training
  University of Central Florida
  Orlando, FL
Maritza R. Salazar
  School of Behavioral and Organizational Sciences
  Claremont Graduate University
  Claremont, CA
Samuel R. Sommers
  Department of Psychology
  Tufts University
  Medford, MA
Olca Surgevil
  Dokuz Eylul University
  Izmir, Turkey
Ahu Tatli
  School of Business and Management
  Queen Mary, University of London
  London, UK

Rae Yunzi Tan
Teachers College
Columbia University
New York, NY

Sherry M. B. Thatcher
Department of Management
Darla Moore School of Business
University of South Carolina
Columbia, SC

Kecia M. Thomas
Franklin College of Arts and Sciences
University of Georgia
Athens, GA

Melissa C. Thomas-Hunt
Darden School of Business
University of Virginia
Charlottesville, VA

Dnika J. Travis
School of Social Work
The University of Texas at Austin
Austin, TX

Jayaram Uparna
Kellogg School of Management
Northwestern University
Evanston, IL

Wendy P. van Ginkel
Rotterdam School of Management
Erasmus University
Rotterdam, The Netherlands

Daan van Knippenberg
Rotterdam School of Management
Erasmus University
Rotterdam, The Netherlands

Joana Vassilopoulou
Work and Organisation Research Centre (WORC)
Brunel Business School
Brunel University
London, UK

Sabrina D. Volpone
Fox School of Business
Temple University
Philadelphia, PA

CONTENTS

Part One • Introduction and Overview
1. Introduction   3
   Quinetta M. Roberson

Part Two • Conceptualization of Diversity
2. Diverse Forms of Difference   13
   Jason R. Lambert and *Myrtle P. Bell*
3. Understanding Diversity as Culture   32
   Eduardo Salas, Maritza R. Salazar, and *Michele J. Gelfand*
4. Moving Beyond a Categorical Approach to Diversity: The Role of Demographic Faultlines   52
   Sherry M. B. Thatcher

Part Three • Psychological Perspectives on Diversity
5. Navigating the Self in Diverse Work Contexts   73
   Laura Morgan Roberts and *Stephanie J. Creary*
6. An Examination of Categorization Processes in Organizations: The Root of Intergroup Bias and a Route to Prejudice Reduction   98
   Melissa Ferguson and *Shanette C. Porter*
7. The Social and Psychological Experience of Stigma   115
   Michelle R. Hebl and *Eden B. King*
8. Ideology: An Invisible yet Potent Dimension of Diversity   132
   Laurie T. O'Brien and *Patricia N. Gilbert*

Part Four • Interactionist Perspectives on Diversity
9. Diversity as Knowledge Exchange: The Roles of Information Processing, Expertise, and Status   157
   Katherine W. Phillips, Michelle M. Duguid, Melissa Thomas-Hunt, and *Jayaram Uparna*
10. Diversity as Disagreement: The Role of Group Conflict   179
    Karen A. Jehn and *Lindred L. Greer*
11. Demographic Diversity as Network Connections: Homophily and the Diversity–Performance Debate   192
    Ray Reagans

Part Five • Contextual Perspectives on Diversity

12. Understanding How Context Shapes Team Diversity Outcomes   209
    Aparna Joshi and *Hyuntak Roh*
13. Diversity Cognition and Climates   220
    Daan van Knippenberg, Astrid C. Homan, and *Wendy P. van Ginkel*
14. Considering Diversity as a Source of Competitive Advantage in Organizations   239
    Orlando C. Richard and *Carliss D. Miller*

Part Six • Practice Perspectives on Diversity

15. The Origins and Effects of Corporate Diversity Programs   253
    Frank Dobbin and *Alexandra Kalev*
16. Diversity Staffing: Inclusive Personnel Recruitment and Selection Practices   282
    Derek R. Avery, Patrick F. McKay, and *Sabrina D. Volpone*
17. Career Development   300
    Bryan L. Dawson, Kecia M. Thomas, and *Matthew J. Goren*
18. Leadership in a Diverse Workplace   315
    Donna Chrobot-Mason, Marian N. Ruderman, and *Lisa H. Nishii*
19. Effective Diversity Training   341
    Loriann Roberson, Carol T. Kulik, and *Rae Yunzi Tan*
20. Work–Life Interface and Flexibility: Impacts on Women, Men, Families, and Employers   366
    Alison M. Konrad

Part Seven • Systems Perspectives on Diversity

21. Socioeconomic Trends: Broadening the Diversity Ecosystem   393
    Michàlle E. Mor Barak and *Dnika J. Travis*
22. Global Diversity Management   419
    Mustafa Özbilgin, Karsten Jonsen, Ahu Tatli, Joana Vassilopoulou, and *Olca Surgevil*
23. Law and Diversity: The Legal–Behavioral Science Divide in How to Define, Assess, and Counteract Bias   442
    Evan P. Apfelbaum and *Samuel R. Sommers*

Part Eight • Conclusion/Integration

24. Conclusion: Future Directions for Diversity Theory and Research   461
    Quinetta M. Roberson

Index   471

PART 1

Introduction and Overview

CHAPTER

1 Introduction

Quinetta M. Roberson

Abstract

Diversity refers to differences among people. While such differences are characteristic of the human race, socio-cultural and economic trends have given rise to such variation in organizational workforces as well. To keep pace with society and the changing business environment, researchers across a number of disciplines have studied the phenomenon in an effort to understand its meaning, import, operation and consequences in organizations. The purpose of this chapter is to consider the environmental trends that have changed the composition of workforces and brought diversity to the forefront as an important management and research concern. In addition, it provides a tour of the structure of the volume and topics covered, which illustrate the diversity of this science and its application to work and organizations.

Key Words: diversity, demographic trends, globalization, multiculturalism, workforces

As predicted by "Workforce 2000" (Johnson & Packer, 1987), a report by the Hudson Institute that predicted that the U.S. labor force would become characterized by greater diversity, the 21st-century workforce is composed of people with a large variety of social and cultural differences. Propelled by changes in the demographic trends in society, public policy initiatives, and economic development, organizations saw an evolution in the "face" of their workforces. Representation of women, ethnic minorities, religions, and generations increased within the labor market and subsequently workforces, thus underscoring the need for organizations to understand how to manage such diversity. Twenty-five years since that initial report, business trends continue to make workforce diversity an important concern.

Driven by economic policy and technological innovation, world economies have become more interdependent. Referred to as "globalization," the amount of interaction and integration across societies and governments has increased exponentially since 1980. Primarily characterized by a confluence of economic and political factors, geographic boundaries have disappeared and an ever-developing set of connections between nations has been established. As a result, world economies are being propelled by the transnational flow of goods and services, information, and resources. With such international interconnectedness, organizational stakeholders are now more geographically dispersed than in traditionally collocated production models, presenting organizations with a greater array of operating challenges and opportunities. For example, although the internationalization of customer markets provides organizations with access to global consumers and thus larger market share, there is a concurrent need to understand regional differences in consumer values, preferences, and tastes. Similarly, although global supplier markets may enable more cost-effective resource procurement, they create a narrower set of operating parameters for organizations, given differences in trade legislation and business norms.

Fueled by deregulation, globalization has also increased competition between organizations. More specifically, the emergence of worldwide markets and access to global resources have reduced organizations' market power yet increased their need for strategic flexibility, innovation, and continuous improvement to remain competitive. In response to these needs, organizations have adopted new structures to enable such dynamic capabilities. For example, organizations have removed layers of management to reduce bureaucracy and push decision-making power to lower levels. In addition, work has become increasingly structured around interdependent arrangements (e.g., joint ventures, matrix organizations, teams) to pool complementary skills sets, with an overarching goal of developing more adaptive and innovative strategies.

Along with globalization, organizations have experienced a shift from a manufacturing economy to one characterized by services, niche markets, and knowledge exchange. As a result, a focus on workforces as strategic assets has become paramount to organizational effectiveness. Organizations have realized that their intangible resources are more likely to help them reach and sustain performance gains, given the challenges associated with competitors acquiring or replicating such nonphysical assets. Even more, organizational leaders have recognized the strategic value of human resources, given the unique compilation of abilities and competencies represented within workforces. Consequently, organizations have become increasingly focused on managing their knowledge assets—in particular, establishing processes to facilitate the creation, capture, and sharing of their knowledge, expertise, and learning.

Importantly, globalization has also brought about international labor markets. Flexible labor policies have given rise to greater worker mobility and migration, thus providing organizations with access to global talent. Further, whereas workforces have historically been derived from, or located in, each organization's country of origin, employees are now spread across the globe. Such cross-border movement of labor has produced workforces composed of a variety of nationalities, cultures, and languages; thus increasing the need for multicultural sensitivity and awareness. International demographic trends, such as aging workers and greater participation of women, have created additional complexities for organizations attempting to capitalize on the benefits of diversity.

To keep pace with the changing business environment, researchers have studied diversity from a number of disciplines, theoretical perspectives, and levels. As such, there is a substantive body of research that investigates the concept of diversity, its effects, and the mechanisms through which such effects occur. However, the findings and conclusions of this work are not very straightforward; questions regarding the what, why, when, and how of diversity remain. This handbook provides an overview and assesses the state of the field to highlight important areas for future research that will advance our understanding of the meaning, import, operation, and consequences of diversity in organizations. The contributors review current theory and research in certain topic areas, provide a summary of the conclusions that can be drawn from such work, and pose questions that indicate future directions for the field, difficult problems to be solved, and topics that remain to be addressed.

An overview of the handbook

The first step in studying a phenomenon is to understand what it is. Although diversity generally refers to any differences among employees in organizations, researchers have attempted to conceptualize and measure diversity in a number of ways. Some researchers have attempted to understand diversity and its effects using categorical approaches, such as observable and nonobservable characteristics; others have taken a more configural approach. Still, some researchers have adopted a broader and more generalizable perspective. Part Two explores such variability in the *conceptualization of diversity*.

Lambert and Bell (Chapter 2) provide an overview of different ways researchers have considered the construct of diversity. Like many diversity studies, they distinguish between surface- and deep-level characteristics as overarching categories of difference that are associated with different types of outcomes in organizations. They discuss the associated challenges, given the range of individual differences that exist and the underlying processes through which they influence attitudes, behavior, and other outcomes in organizations. Although recent typologies have attempted to match different forms of diversity with relevant explanatory mechanisms and measures to reflect such mechanisms, Lambert and Bell draw attention to additional concerns, including accounting for individuals' hidden identities and the appropriate level of analysis at which diversity should be conceptualized.

Although many conceptualizations of diversity are based on individuals' demographic attributes, Salas, Salazar, and Gelfand (Chapter 3) provide a complementary perspective by considering diversity as culture. Whereas this topic is particularly important given globalization and the increasing interdependence of world economies, it advances our understanding of diversity by considering its role in multicultural interactions. Moving beyond national origin as a proxy for culture, the authors discuss both objective and subjective components of culture and provide an overview of theory and research that explores their relative effects. Acknowledging the configurations of cultural identities within individuals, Salas and colleagues also draw attention to the contextual embeddedness and subsequent complexities of studying culture.

Recently, researchers have recognized the configural and contextual nature of diversity and put forth a theory to capture such multiplexity in the construct. Faultline theory, a multi-attribute perspective that considers the alignment of demographic attributes within groups or teams, accounts for both the multiple identity groups to which individuals belong and the interrelationships between in-group and out-group members. In Chapter 4, Thatcher reviews theory and research on the antecedents, consequences, and moderators of faultlines in groups and teams. In discussing the nuances of this conceptualization of diversity, including distinctions between latent and active faultlines and the identification of faultline triggers, she highlights challenges inherent in viewing diversity in terms of its structure in collective contexts. However, because faultlines represent the alignment of attribute dispersion within groups, Thatcher argues for faultlines as a useful tool for analyzing diversity in groups.

To fully understand diversity as a phenomenon, we must comprehend the mechanisms through which differences among people influence their attitudes and behavior. Although the meaning and import of diversity have come from a variety of theoretical foundations, much of the research has been rooted within psychology. Within this tradition, researchers have explored diversity and its effects at the intrapersonal level of analysis. Focused on individuals' perceptions and beliefs, such research has examined how individuals' cognitive processes influence their reactions to, and experiences with, others. Part Three reviews and discusses these *psychological perspectives on diversity*.

As diversity encapsulates people's membership in different identity groups and the nature of interactions between those groups, Roberts and Creary (Chapter 5) discuss theory and research related to how individuals navigate the self in diverse organizational contexts. Based on an assumption that through personal agency people can positively influence work environments, they consider identity construction and negotiation processes that unfold as people interpret and act on their differences. Specifically, the authors review several theoretical approaches, each of which has unique conceptualizations of identity itself, to the ways in which individuals actively participate in the co-construction of their identities and the motives that prompt such activity. In particular, they provide an extensive review of social identity theory and its proposed motives and tactics, which supplies the theoretical foundation for numerous other chapters in this volume. They also consider alternative perspectives on identity, including identity as a state of being versus a process and identity as an interaction between the self and environment, and how these varying identity-management perspectives offer important insights for navigating interpersonal interactions in diverse organizations.

Ferguson and Porter (Chapter 6) build upon this identity-as-self perspective by considering how people's category-based perceptions of others who belong to different social groups affect intergroup relations. Specifically, based on research findings that highlight people's preferences for the groups to which they belong, or their in-groups, they consider such intergroup bias as a foundation for a relative lack of diversity and inclusion in the workplace. As antecedents to prejudice, discrimination, and other forms of bias, Ferguson and Porter discuss automatic, nonconscious categorization processes and the conditions under which such categorical thinking occurs. Given that recent research suggests that bias is likely to be implicit, subtle, and unintentional, the authors largely focus on categorical antecedents to, and means of operationalizing, this specific type of bias. However, also recognizing the importance of reducing such bias in organizations, they discuss interventions aimed at social categorization processes and intergroup boundaries.

Following from a categorization approach to diversity and recognizing that some group memberships are imbued with negative social value, Hebl and King (Chapter 7) explore the intra- and interpersonal experiences of targets of stigma and their interaction partners. Drawing from stigma theory and research, they discuss how and why social value emerges, situating it in the nomologic network of stereotypes, prejudice, and discrimination. They also draw a link to work on identity, given that identity development and maintenance are complex processes for people with stigmas. Offering a comprehensive overview of stigmatization processes, Hebl and King summarize research from both the stigmatizer's and the target's perspectives, although research from the former perspective has been more extensive. In particular, they discuss the nature of stigmatized attributes, manifestations of stigma, and consequences of stigma for individuals and their organizations. Hebl and King also consider the range of coping strategies used to improve individuals' daily experiences.

Recently, ideology has emerged as an important topic of inquiry among psychologists because research has shown a link between people's ideological belief systems and their attitudes towards, and evaluations of, others. In Chapter 8, O'Brien and Gilbert explore how ideology can facilitate an understanding of diversity in the workplace. Conceptualizing ideologies as shared knowledge systems (similar to stereotypes) that describe the nature of the social world and how it operates, they examine theory and research concerning the structure, content, and functions of ideological beliefs. In doing so, they distinguish between hierarchy-enhancing ideologies, which are derived from motives to maintain the status quo, and the less-studied hierarchy-attenuating ideologies, which advocate social equality. Because individual differences in endorsement of ideology exist, O'Brien and Gilbert discuss the psychological functions that ideology performs for individuals. In addition, they consider the impact of ideology on intergroup relations and diversity attitudes.

Within the sociologic tradition, an interactionist perspective assumes that human behavior is a product of the way people interpret the social world around them. More specifically, as people attach meanings to their interactions with others, their behavior reflects socially constructed realities. Within the context of workplace diversity, this midrange point-of-view reasons that interindividual rather than intraindividual processes, as posited by psychological perspectives, drive attitudes and behavior. In other words, interactionist perspectives suppose that interpersonal processes between individuals belonging to different social groups influence individual-, group- and organization-level outcomes. Part Four discusses theory and research originating from *interactionist perspectives on diversity*.

Phillips, Duguid, Thomas-Hunt, and Uparna (Chapter 9) summarize the findings of empirical research from the information-processing perspective on diversity, which suggests that because heterogeneous groups are composed of a broader range of knowledge, skills, and abilities than homogeneous groups, they will subsequently have greater access to task-relevant information and expertise, which can enhance group decision making. However, they also discuss an expanded view of this perspective—the categorization elaboration model, which considers the interactive effects of social categorization and information elaboration on group performance. In this chapter, Phillips and her colleagues extend current knowledge-exchange perspectives on diversity by integrating research on majority and minority influence processes and examining how status may influence information processing, and subsequently performance, in diverse environments.

In Chapter 10, Jehn and Greer note that conflict is critical for understanding the impact of diversity on group effectiveness. Accordingly, a considerable amount of work has centered on relationships between team diversity, conflict, and team outcomes. In addition to reviewing such research, Jehn and Greer discuss how different types and configurations of diversity in workgroups influence the multilevel and potentially asymmetric process of intragroup conflict and how this in turn may help explain how diversity ultimately affects individual and team outcomes. Based on this review, they suggest that research needs to consider the asymmetry of perceptions of members of diverse groups to more thoroughly explain the effects of diversity and disagreement on group conflict and outcomes. To facilitate the study of these processes, they offer a framework for further exploration of diversity as disagreement in groups.

Reagans (Chapter 11) reviews and critiques research on how social networks influence the diversity–performance relationship. Because informal network connections have been shown to influence group processes, such as information processing and knowledge transfer, an understanding of the development and effects of such connections may provide insight into the operation of diversity in groups and teams. Accordingly, Reagans considers both the optimistic and pessimistic views of diversity (i.e., the "double-edged sword") and examines why its effect on team performance can vary from positive to negative. Reviewing the role of interpersonal dynamics, such as similarity attraction and in-group bias, as well as the role of propinquity, he offers a causal framework for future research on the development of strong ties and situational factors that facilitate such connections. In addition, he describes how a focus on diversity on social capital, which represents a more proximate outcome, may advance our understanding of the effects of diversity on team performance.

Although research demonstrate how people's diversity cognitions and interactions with diverse others influence individual- and group-level outcomes, such effects do not occur in a vacuum. Because employees are embedded within larger organizational structures, features of those structures are likely to affect the level and consequences of diversity. For example, an organization's strategy, culture, or climate may create norms and other patterns of social integration that shape attitudes and behavior and thus interrelationships between people. As such, researchers have given attention to the moderating influences of situational variables that shape whether diversity is likely to be associated with positive or negative outcomes and the larger effects on organizational performance. Part Five discusses this body of work that has adopted *contextual perspectives on diversity*.

Drawing attention to the mixed findings of diversity-performance research, Joshi and Roh (Chapter 12) suggest that accounting for context is important for maximizing the theoretical rigor and practical relevance of such research. Defining diversity context as the features of the surrounding environment that can enhance or constrain the meaning, occurrence, and effects of diversity, they offer a tripartite classification of diversity context including its structural, relational, and normative components. They also discuss a theoretical framework for identifying the effects of context on categorization and elaboration-based processes within work teams. To advance the field, they suggest cross-level, qualitative, temporal, and comparative research as methodologic directions for testing the framework, and for overcoming the challenges of, yet setting the stage for, conducting context-oriented research.

Also referencing the performance benefits and process challenges of diversity, van Knippenberg, Homan, and van Ginkel (Chapter 13) speculate that the role of diversity cognition and climates may be particularly promising for balancing these outcomes. Distinguishing between research focused on individual diversity beliefs and attitudes, research involving individuals' perceptions of team or organizational diversity climate (i.e., psychological climate), and research analyzing diversity climate as a shared team or organizational characteristic, they take stock of the state of current science and consider how such cognition and climates may moderate the effects of diversity. Based on this review, the authors discuss how bridging these different areas of research poses important questions for future research. In particular, they reason that research in diversity cognition and climates will benefit from more attention to diversity as a group characteristic to complement the dominant focus on demographic dissimilarity, and from more attention to the potential positive effects of diversity to complement the dominant emphasis on diversity's potential negative effects.

Although most studies of diversity in the workplace have explored the phenomenon at the individual, dyadic, and team levels of analysis, Richard and Charles (Chapter 14) review the findings of research focused on the relationship between diversity and firm performance. Based on an assumption that diversity represents a unique and valuable resource for organizations, the authors consider diversity as a source of competitive advantage. Specifically, they integrate psychological and interactionist perspectives on diversity with strategy theory to articulate how diversity at different levels of the firm creates value. They also rely upon contingency theory to highlight the conditions under which diversity might be most valuable. In particular, they consider the moderating effects of business strategy, organizational design and culture, and human resource practices, and offer general propositions regarding these effects.

Researchers and practitioners have acknowledged that although diversity's effects may naturally occur in organizations, proactive management of differences is necessary to capitalize on the benefits of diversity and minimize its challenges. Under the umbrella of "diversity management," organizations have implemented practices ranging from antidiscrimination and equal employment opportunity policies to more traditional human resource management practices. Although the overarching goal of these initiatives is to maximize the utilization of an organization's human capital, more specific goals include creating more diverse workforces, facilitating effective interactions between members of diverse groups, and building inclusive work environments. Research attention has been given to formal diversity management programs and their influence on individual, group, and organizational outcomes. Part Six reviews the findings of such research, which explores *practice perspectives on diversity*.

Dobbins and Kalev (Chapter 15) review the origins of equal opportunity and diversity programs, and their effects on workforces. They present a historical perspective on the evolution of diversity programs, highlighting innovations across each decade. Specifically, they review equal employment opportunity and antidiscrimination legislation in the United States and present data tracing the diffusion of diversity programs among U.S. firms. Because, as the authors note, data constraints drive much of the research in the field and subsequently what we know about the effects of diversity in organizations, they use a sociologic approach (i.e., attempt to explain labor market outcomes with organizational characteristics). They draw from empirical evidence that highlights the ineffectiveness of initiatives to quell managerial bias, yet indicates that innovations to address workforce integration have led to increased diversity at different levels. In addition, they review evidence on the effects of individual diversity practices and draw conclusions regarding the features of successful diversity programs.

Avery, McKay, and Volpone (Chapter 16) focus on why organizations should staff for diversity, who should recruit and select applicants, what messages should be conveyed to jobseekers, when organizations should prioritize diversity staffing, where organizations should recruit, and how to select for diversity. They note that although the reasons for staffing diversity are often based on stakeholder pressures or the recognition of the value of diversity, the acquisition and retention of personnel can be a potential source of competitive advantage by attracting and identifying candidates best suited to help the organization achieve its objectives. Given situational constraints to recruiting to diversity, Avery and his colleagues discuss the costs and benefits of different recruitment sources and media. In addition, they discuss selection tools that display useful validities and a markedly lower adverse impact against minorities.

Career development is considered a lifelong process that includes identification of a worker's career interests and needs; development of knowledge, skills, and abilities; and the ongoing assessment of interests and skills to achieve career mobility. However, the traditional concept of career development is changing, given environmental changes. In Chapter 17, Dawson, Thomas, and Goren focus on the importance of career development yet the external and internal barriers that exist for diverse employees, including stereotyping, occupational segregation, and demographic faultlines. They review drivers of career development decisions—specifically, factors that attract women and people of color to follow certain career paths, or deter them from doing so. In addition, they discuss mentoring (both formal and informal), a developmental relationship in which a more experienced or knowledgeable individual shares skills, information, and so forth to maximize the less experienced person's personal and professional growth and development. Because mentoring serves both career-related and psychosocial functions to protégés, Dawson and his colleagues review research on its benefits, which include effective socialization, lower turnover intentions, and increased job and career satisfaction. To provide a balanced view of the mentoring process, they also consider benefits to mentors.

Chrobot-Mason, Rudermanm and Nishii (Chapter 18) note that research on leadership in the context of diversity is sparse, but that leadership is evolving because of, and in response to, diversity. They consider three key areas of diversity and leadership: how leaders lead themselves, others, and the organization. In the first section, Chrobot-Mason and her colleagues discuss issues related to social identity, and how leaders' social identities interact with those of their employees in influencing what may be required for effective leadership. In the second section, they discuss the qualities that leaders are likely to need when managing employees from diverse backgrounds. Specifically, they focus on developing quality relationships, cultivating an inclusive climate, spanning boundaries, and framing of diversity initiatives. In the last section, they discuss research related to the role leaders play in setting formulating and implementing diversity strategy, policies and practices. They end by highlighting areas that could benefit from additional research to enhance our understanding of successful leadership in multicultural workplaces.

Roberson, Kulik, and Tan (Chapter 19) review theory and research on diversity training design, delivery, evaluation, and effectiveness. Because the relevant literature includes frameworks for pretraining needs assessment, learning models to guide diversity training design choices, and empirical evidence of diversity training's impact on training outcomes, they conclude that, in the past 10 to 15 years of research, advances have been made on several fronts. However, Roberson and her colleagues also note two major shortcomings. First, research has emphasized diversity training's effect on short-term changes in the trainee's knowledge and attitudes, neglecting longer-term changes in the trainee's skills and behavior. Second, research has emphasized diversity training's effect on individual-level learning outcomes, neglecting its impact on team- and organization-level outcomes. Given that these shortcomings are unlikely to be addressed unless scholars and practitioners engage in more research on diversity training, they offer directions for future research in this area.

Konrad (Chapter 20) defines the work–life interface as the activities and experiences occurring at the intersections between paid work and other life domains, and provides an overview of research on work–life flexibility and work–life interface experiences of paid workers. Although the field began with a focus on work–life conflict, the perspective evolved to work–life facilitation, which suggests that people can be more effective at work by bringing resources and skills developed in other domains. Accordingly, models were developed to predict the amount of conflict or facilitation and/or the relationship between the two. Yet, Konrad notes that there is still little empirical work as well as weak congruence between existing approaches. To address these limitations, Konrad proposes a dynamic, integrated (work–life conflict, facilitation, flexibility) model of work–life interface that incorporates contextual factors affecting individual experiences in the form of role demands and environmental munificence as well as incorporating psychological mechanisms linking experiences in different role domains.

Although research has examined the effects of diversity through different theoretical lenses, the related processes and outcomes do not take place discretely in organizations. Rather than occurring at one level or within one domain, diversity's effects are interrelated. For example, socioeconomic trends will determine the composition of organizational workforces, which will influence the bases on which social categorization occurs and the nature of social interactions between groups. Further, features of the internal and external environment may increase or decrease the salience of intergroup distinctions and subsequently enhance or hinder group processes and performance. In turn, the effectiveness of diversity programs will be based on the degree to which they address process and performance issues and facilitate group functioning. Given the connectedness of diversity processes and outcomes, some researchers have pursued the meaning and operation of diversity across different domains—in particular, the nature and pattern of interrelationships within a given environment. Part Seven discusses some of this work that has adopted *systems perspectives on diversity*.

Mor Barak and Travis (Chapter 21) identify major socioeconomic trends affecting the global workforce and examine challenges and opportunities embedded in broadening the diversity ecosystem, which refers to the amalgamation of people from different backgrounds, their attitudes and perceptions about diversity, and their physical and social context. In other words, they examine the social forces that have created a more diverse workforce worldwide. Trends that are discussed include advances in health care and growth in the world population, rising demand for migrant workers, employer migration, increased participation in the labor force by women, increased presence of racial and ethnic groups in the workplace, increased human rights efforts and national policies, regional differences in educational attainment, diversity of religion, rights and inclusion of differently abled persons, and technological innovations. Based on these socioeconomic trends, the authors conclude with a vision of inclusion for global diversity management.

Ozbilgin and his colleagues (Chapter 22) review theories and research related to global diversity management and in so doing note the challenges of transposing diversity and diversity management across national borders (as the concept of diversity management is traditionally rooted in North American conceptualization and import). They draw attention to the dearth of comparative, international and multinational global diversity management research, and discuss the drivers of global diversity management theory and practice, highlighting the overarching influence of the business case for diversity. Given different models of global diversity management (e.g., strategy, process, context, and intervention), Ozbilgin and his colleagues consider their related strengths and weaknesses. Based on this review, they present a framework for studying the meaning, operation, and management of diversity across national borders and emphasize a shift from normative- and process-based approaches to contextual and multifaceted understandings of diversity. Additional directions for future directions in research and practices are discussed.

Behavioral sciences, such as psychology and sociology, and the law approach diversity from different perspectives. As a result, most clear-cut, theoretical and empirical conclusions offered by behavioral science fail to be persuasive in the eyes of the legal system. To illuminate differences in the way behavioral sciences and the law conceptualize and treat racial bias, Apfelbaum and Sommers (Chapter 23) discuss their divergence in definition, assessment, and remediation. Although they note that the evolution of the legal perspective on discrimination has moved more slowly than in the behavioral realm, more specific distinctions include the definition and assessment of bias. Accordingly, they review seminal cases and standard legal practices alongside contemporary behavioral science research that offers a counterpoint to this perspective in each area. Apfelbaum and Sommers also discuss individual- and group-based approaches to counteracting bias as well as institutional and ideologic approaches to counteracting bias, and conclude with considerations for future work to bridge the legal–behavioral science divide.

PART 2

Conceptualization of Diversity

CHAPTER 2

Diverse Forms of Difference

Jason R. Lambert *and* Myrtle P. Bell

Abstract

The purpose of this chapter is to provide a review of the state of diversity in management literature, including the most recent conceptualizations and measures developed for studying diversity among individuals within organizations. Background on the theoretical and empirical development of surface-level and deep-level diversity is provided. Turning then to separation, variety, and disparity, the chapter will discuss the meaning, form, and assumptions underlying each type of diversity, and offers guidelines for conceptualization, measurement, and theory testing of each. The authors summarize the findings and suggest ideas for future research to move the diversity field forward.

Key Words: diversity, surface-level diversity, deep-level diversity, organizational behavior

Introduction

"Focusing on any individual difference, rather than differences having strong personal meaning and stemming from or coinciding with significant power differences among groups, would make all groups diverse, and would therefore make the entire concept of workplace diversity meaningless." (Konrad, 2003; p. 7)

Diversity refers to the variations of traits, both visible and not, of groups of two or more people (McGrath, Berdahl, & Arrow, 1995). It has been described using such terms as "heterogeneity," "relational demography," "organizational demography," "differences," "disparities," "distance," and "variation." Researchers have documented many challenges in conceptualizing diversity over the years (Harrison & Klein, 2007; King & Hebl, 2009; Milliken & Martins, 1996; Ragins & Gonzales, 2003; Williams & O'Reilly, 1998). These challenges are partly due to the different types of diversity in question and the various ways that diversity can be examined. Early researchers struggled to determine what should encompass diversity research because individuals may differ on any number of characteristics. As noted in the opening quote by Konrad (2003), however, differences having strong personal meaning and stemming from or coinciding with significant power differences among groups are distinct from some other types of differences.

In this chapter, we discuss some of the different conceptualizations used in diversity research. We first briefly review challenges of conceptualizing diversity. Secondly, we cover early conceptual and empirical research on similarity and attraction and social identity, which serve as the foundation for diversity studies. Next, we discuss various types (Milliken & Martins, 1996) and conceptualizations (Harrison & Klein, 2007; Harrison & Sin, 2006) of diversity and compare ways that the construct has been defined. We then offer guidelines for theory testing and measurement of diversity. Finally, we propose new ideas for future research in an effort to improve the understanding of the relationships between diversity and organizational outcomes.

Challenges of diversity research

One of the earliest and continuing challenges is the issue of defining race and ethnicity. Some scholars identify race as being composed of biological differences, whereas ethnicity refers to cultural differences (Betancourt & Lopez, 1993; Cox, 1990; Zuckerman, 1990). On the other hand, race is also a socially constructed term (Karsten, 2006) defined differently according to cultural norms and geography. Because groups are distinct from one another both biologically and culturally, the scope of examining the differences between groups is chosen at the discretion of the researcher (Betancourt & Lopez, 1993). Cox (1990) introduced the term "racioethnic research," which refers to both biological and cultural differences, to resolve the challenge of examining multiple distinctions in diversity research. Early investigations were limited to examining differences between Blacks and Whites, thereby ignoring the variance within and across racioethnic groups (Avery, 2003). The focus of many studies was the organizational effects of workplace diversity and organizational discrimination toward minorities, and some White researchers believed that diversity research was relevant only to minorities (Cox, 1990). Some of these challenges have been overcome as research has demonstrated the importance of diversity as it relates to better understanding organizational outcomes more broadly.

Despite relatively recent changes in research focus, for many years diversity research centered on differences based on race, sex, and, to a lesser extent, age, rather than less visible, less volatile, and less personal attributes such as attitudes or beliefs that are increasingly the areas of focus. The former attributes, referred to as "surface-level" diversity, are strong stimuli for prejudice, stereotyping, and discrimination, and the resulting negative individual, group, and organizational consequences that were the stimuli for much of the early diversity research. The latter attributes, referred to as "deep-level" diversity, have also been found to be stimuli for prejudice and bias, but over time may ameliorate negative outcomes resulting from surface-level differences. Understanding how surface-level and deep-level traits affect individual, group, and organizational outcomes both independently and interactively has become increasingly important.

Researchers have found that members of work units that are heterogeneous with respect to surface-level characteristics become less attached, are absent from work more often, and are more likely to quit (O'Reilly, Caldwell, & Barnett, 1989; Tsui, Egan, & O'Reilly, 1992). There is also evidence that diversity may produce conflict and employee turnover (Jehn, Northcraft, & Neale, 1999; Williams & O'Reilly, 1998). However, ethnically diverse groups cooperate better at tasks that require decision making (Cox, Lobel, & McLeod, 1991) and are more creative and innovative (Cox & Blake, 1991; Jackson, 1992; Tsui et al., 1992; Watson, Kumar, & Michaelson, 1993) than homogenous groups. Other research indicates that performance may be either improved or impaired, depending on the group composition and leadership of an organization (Jackson, 1992; Jehn et al., 1999; Richard, 2000). These mixed findings underscore the importance of continued research efforts investigating how to gain the benefits of heterogeneous groups while mitigating conflict between group members. Studies have also discovered that deep-level traits such as attitudinal similarity (Terborg, Castore, & DeNinno, 1976) and values (Harrison, Price, & Bell, 1998.) may affect group cohesion in ways that can either hinder or benefit organizations. Cox (1995, p. 235) proposed that "because existing research has shown that diversity can either enhance or hinder organizational performance, the core puzzle of diversity research is to discover under what conditions one may capitalize on the potential benefits of diversity while minimizing the potential for diversity-related phenomena to adversely affect performance." Understanding the social and psychological processes that affect "diversity-related phenomena" is an important first step for researchers.

Early theories in diversity research

Two theories commonly used to conceptualize diversity are the similarity-attraction paradigm and social identity. These theories have helped to set a foundation for both surface-level and deep-level diversity research.

Similarity-attraction paradigm

According to the similarity-attraction paradigm, the more similar individuals perceive themselves to be to each other, the more attracted they will be to one another and to the group (Byrne, 1971). Further, knowledge of a person's attitude or value similarity is an antecedent of liking (Lott & Lott, 1965). Studies indicate that antecedents to interpersonal attraction include personality type (Byrne, 1971; Chapman & Campbell, 1957; Fiedler, Warrington, & Blaisdell, 1952), music and recreational preferences (Bakagiannis & Tarrant, 2006), and socioeconomic status (Byrne, 1971; Hurwitz,

Zander, & Hymovitch, 1960; Seashore, 1954). Many of these antecedents to interpersonal attraction could be considered deep-level characteristics, as they are unobservable differences (Millikens & Martins, 1996).

Although surface-level characteristics such as race may create prejudicial attitudes between individuals, researchers have also found that once deep-level information about each other is obtained, those prejudices are weakened (Byrne & Wong, 1962). In numerous studies examining what attracts individuals to each other, Byrne and Wong (1962) discovered that nonprejudicial Whites were just as attracted to Blacks as they were to other Whites after discovering their similarity in attitudes or values. Furthermore, discrimination among prejudicial Whites against Blacks was reduced when similar values, beliefs, and attitudes that existed between them were revealed. The examination of how characteristics such as lifestyle attitudes and beliefs affect interpersonal attraction in early research (e.g., Byrne, 1971; Byrne & Wong, 1962; Lott &Lott, 1965; Seashore, 1954; Turner, 1987) provided insights on how interpersonal conflict and prejudices might be reduced. Although not termed as such, this early research combined surface- and deep-level research and highlights the complexity of conceptualizing diversity.

Social identity theory

Social identity theory (SIT) proposes that people assume different identities based on the salience of a social group or as they encounter different social groups at different moments (Tajfel & Turner, 1979). People's social identity provides them with self-esteem and self-definition through the perception of oneness with a social group (Ashforth & Mael, 1989). The strength and salience of one's social identity dictates how one expresses values, attitudes, and beliefs while interacting with others and how one perceives the values, beliefs, and attitudes of others.

Research stemming from SIT generally supports the idea that humans create initial categorizations of each other and groups of individuals they encounter (Turner, 1987). These categorizations can also be accompanied by perceptions of similarity or dissimilarity based on surface-level demographic data, but these perceptions change when deep-level information is obtained (Stangor, Lynch, Duan, & Glass, 1992; Turner, 1987). In early research, social identification was described as having three psychological processes that occur within a member of a group, two of which play an important role in diversity research. Tajfel (1978) identified the first process as social categorization, which was later more fully developed as a construct through the elaboration of SIT subsumed as self-categorization theory (e.g., Turner, Hogg, Oakes, Reicher, & Wetherell, 1987). Social categorization is the process by which individuals categorize others into groups in efforts to organize social information (Ellemers, De Gilder, & Haslam, 2004; Tajfel, 1978). According to Tajfel (1978), social categorization is the underlying process of social identification that is sufficient and necessary to induce forms of in-group favoritism and out-group discrimination.

The second process, social comparison, occurs when people make comparisons between the self-perceived categories of groups in relation to the group's perceived values and their own individual values (Tajfel, 1978). In social comparison, group members make comparisons to outside groups and define the norms of their group according to a particular situation (Ellemers et al., 2004). During the social-comparison process, individuals may perceive differences between and develop biases against out-group members.

In various experiments, Turner (1978a) demonstrated that when groups were created with minimal categorization, even when there was no salient category, participants artificially created in-group and out-group dynamics. In other words, individuals in groups will create artificial divisions between themselves and individuals from other groups just by being assigned to a group, even when no legitimate or observable differences exist. This finding has been helpful in understanding intergroup bias in the workplace.

The well-known Robbers Cave study (Sherif, Harvey, White, Hood, & Sherif, 1961, reprinted in 1988) demonstrates how groups with little or nothing more in common than their group membership can nonetheless perceive in- and out-groups between themselves and other groups. In the study, two groups of boys were camped out on different sides of the Robbers Cave campgrounds and were unaware of one another. Once each group became aware of the other, the groups each began to form artificial barriers between them, creating an in-group and out-group condition. However, once activities that required the cooperation of both groups of campers were introduced, intergroup harmony began to emerge. The results from this study converge with later findings that intergroup biases can emerge merely due to group categorization (Turner,

1978a, 1978b). Gaertner et al. (2000) later revisited the Robbers Cave study (Sherif et al., 1961) to demonstrate how the recategorization process occurs among group members.

Researchers have found that recategorization decreases intergroup bias by redefining how individuals understand their group membership at a higher level of category inclusiveness (Allport, 1954; Brown & Turner, 1981; Doise, 1978; Gaertner et al., 2000). The introduction of superordinate goals, such as cooperative activities, induces recategorization of groups and reduces conflict between groups (Gaertner, Dovidio, Anastasio, Bachman, & Rust, 1993; Gaertner et al., 2000). When group members are aware that they share membership qualities with members of another group on a different dimension, this can improve intergroup attitudes (Urban & Miller, 1998). Although categorization is not eliminated, intergroup bias is reduced because of the increased salience by group members of the crosscutting superordinate membership. As a result, the same biases and attitudes that produced in-group favoritism are redirected to the former out-group members, who now share a common superordinate group identity (Gaertner et al., 2000). Superordinate goals can be used as a tool to reduce biases among group members with both surface-level and deep-level differences (Brewer, 1995).

Diversity types and conceptualizations

Varied viewpoints guide diversity research (e.g., Harrison & Klein, 2007; Jackson & Ruderman, 1995; Lawrence, 1997; Milliken & Martins, 1996). Each may be guided by the level of examination or analysis (i.e., the firm or group level) and the relevant outcome (i.e., group functioning, cohesion, turnover, organizational attraction). An important point in the diversity literature was the specific identification and separation of outcomes related to surface level or deep level, yet mixed results remain with respect to their outcomes (Jackson, Joshi, & Erhardt, 2003). This suggests that diversity has not been fully defined as a construct (Harrison & Klein, 2007). The following section briefly covers types of diversity as a construct, and how it may be conceptualized.

Surface-level diversity

As mentioned earlier, "surface-level" refers to readily seen (and therefore useful for making immediate judgments) attributes of a member, such as race, sex, age, body size, or visible disabilities. Surface-level diversity research examines organizational outcomes that are associated with similarities and differences in those demographic characteristics (Lawrence, 1997; Milliken & Martins, 1996; Tsui, Egan, & Xin, 1995). Surface-level diversity research including dyads, groups and teams, or relationships between one member and the rest of a collective is sometimes defined as relational demography (Tsui et al., 1992). Much of this research examines performance outcomes such as group attachment (O'Reilly et al., 1989), cohesion (Harrison et al., 1998; Webber & Donahue, 2001), social integration (Ely & Thomas, 2001) and innovation (Cox & Blake, 1991; Jackson, 1991; Tsui et al., 1992). Surface-level diversity as it relates to individuals and the firm has also been studied, including examinations of how diversity affects organizational outcomes such as organizational attraction (Avery, 2003; Brown, Keeping, Cover, & Levy, 2006), absenteeism (Avery, McKay, Wilson, & Tonidandel, 2007), turnover (Jehn et al., 1999; Williams & O'Reilly, 1998), firm performance (Richard, 2000), reputation (Brown et al., 2006), and marketing (Cox & Blake, 1991). This research has produced mixed results that demonstrate both advantages and disadvantages to having a diverse workgroup (e.g., Cox, 1991; Cox & Blake, 1991; Harrison et al., 1998; Jackson, 1991; O'Reilly et al., 1989; Tsui et al., 1992).

Deep-level diversity

Deep-level diversity research considers similarities and differences in characteristics of employees such as attitudes, values, and beliefs (Harrison, et al., 1998; Jackson, May, & Whitney, 1995; Milliken & Martins, 1996). Deep-level diversity has been defined as a nonobservable type of diversity (Milliken & Martins, 1996) that is important to note because, unlike surface-level diversity, it does not readily evoke a response that is directly due to biases or prejudices (Milliken & Martins, 1996). Because of the numerous, unobservable differences that could be considered while examining deep-level characteristics, there is still confusion on what actually constitutes a deep-level characteristic (Harrison et al., 1998; Harrison & Klein, 2007). Some of the typically used attributes include attitudes, beliefs, and values (Harrison et al., 1998; Jehn et al., 1999; McGrath et al., 1995). Other research has examined network ties (Beckman & Haunschild, 2002), affect (Barsade, Ward, Turner, & Sonnenfeld, 2000), individual performance (Doerr, Mitchell, Schriesheim, Freed, & Zhou, 2002), pay (Pfeffer & Langton, 1988; 1993), and conscientiousness (Barrick,

Stewart, Neubert, & Mount, 1998). A deep-level attribute could also simply be one's perspective on a key issue based on one's own unique life experience (Jackson et al., 1991). Personality variables are also generally supported as being nonobservable characteristics (Milliken & Martins, 1996), although they may not be as deeply concealed as other characteristics. Work attitudes such as job satisfaction and organizational commitment are also deep-level traits that have been used in studies (e.g., Harrison et al., 1998).

Deep-level attributes of individuals are revealed based on verbal communication and nonverbal cues (Harrison, Price, Gavin, & Florey, 2002). Key to what distinguishes a deep-level trait from a surface-level trait is that the former is observed either through clues of its existence revealed over time through interaction or via verbal communication, as group members or two individuals begin to know one another better (Harrison et al., 2002), whereas surface-level differences are readily apparent. Deep-level diversity research has been shown to be more strongly related to group cohesion and interpersonal attraction than surface-level diversity over time (Harrison et al., 1998; Harrison et al., 2002).

Workgroup models

As a way to better understand trait differences between a member and the group and how those differences are manifested, McGrath et al. (1995) viewed attributes of differences in five clusters (McGrath et al., 1995):

Cluster 1: Demographic attributes (DEM) such as age, race, sex, sexual orientation, physical status, religion, and education. These attributes tend to have social meaning in both work and society.

Cluster 2: Task-related knowledge, skills, and abilities (KSA)

Cluster 3: Values, beliefs, and attitudes (VBA)

Cluster 4: Personality and cognitive behavior styles (PCB)

Cluster 5: Status within the organization (ORG), such as organizational rank, tenure, or department affiliation

Some clusters are more easily observable than others (McGrath et al., 1995). Cluster 1 (DEM), with the exception of education, religion, and sexual orientation, contains more surface-level differences. As mentioned earlier, surface-level differences prompt individuals to categorize others and develop perceptions of similarity or dissimilarity based on these attributes, which may result in bias or attraction. Clusters 2 (KSA), 3 (VBA), 4 (PCB), and 5 (ORG) are composed of deep-level traits. Although Cluster 5 (ORG) identifies traits recognized as being deep-level, some may actually be revealed over time or instantly, such as organizational rank and status. Signals of rank and status differences may include the location of employees' offices, assigned responsibilities, budget, or the number of employees a manager supervises. As a result, a hidden characteristic of an employee, such as status or rank, can easily become evident.

Using these clusters, McGrath et al. (1995) developed three models representing how diversity traits affect performance and group interaction (Fig. 2.1): the trait approach model A, the expectations approach model B, and the differential approach model C. They also proposed the integrative multicultural approach model (Fig. 2.2), which integrated the other three. We will briefly describe the first three models but will describe in full detail the integrative multicultural approach model and its theoretical process because it encompasses the three models that come before it.

The trait approach model A is based on the integration of research by Northcraft, Polzer, Neale, and Kramer (1995) and suggests that both the demographic characteristics (DEM) and other characteristics (KSA, VBA, and PCB) will directly affect and are related to member A's behavior, which will be related to group interaction and performance. This model is the simplest of all four and is based solely from the perspective of member A.

The expectations approach model B is based on expectations-states theory (Ridgeway, 1991) and suggests that demographic factors (DEM) of member A will influence the expectations that member B has of member A's KSA, VBA, and PCB. As a result, the behavior of both member A and member B will be affected, and this will directly relate to their group interaction and performance. In this example, member B forms expectations about member A by categorizing member A and forming perceptions of similarity or dissimilarity. These perceptions affect the way member A and member B work as a group.

The differential power approach model C suggests that based on DEM, member A may be perceived as having similar, different, or greater power and status relative to member B. The differential power associated with gender or race exemplifies this scenario. Research demonstrates that actual and symbolic power differences are indeed associated with demographic groups (Ely, 1995; Tolbert, Andrews, &

Figure 2.1 (with permission from McGrath, Berdahl, & Arrow, 1995)

Figure 1a: Trait Approach

Member A's DEM → Member A's KSA/VBA/PCB → Member A's Behavior → Group Interaction & Performance

Figure 1b: Expectations Approach

Member A's DEM → Member B's Expectations About Member A's KSA/VBA/PCB → Member A's & Member B's Behavior → Group Interaction & Performance

Figure 1c: Differential Power Approach

Member A's DEM → Member A's Power Relative to Member B → Group Interaction & Performance

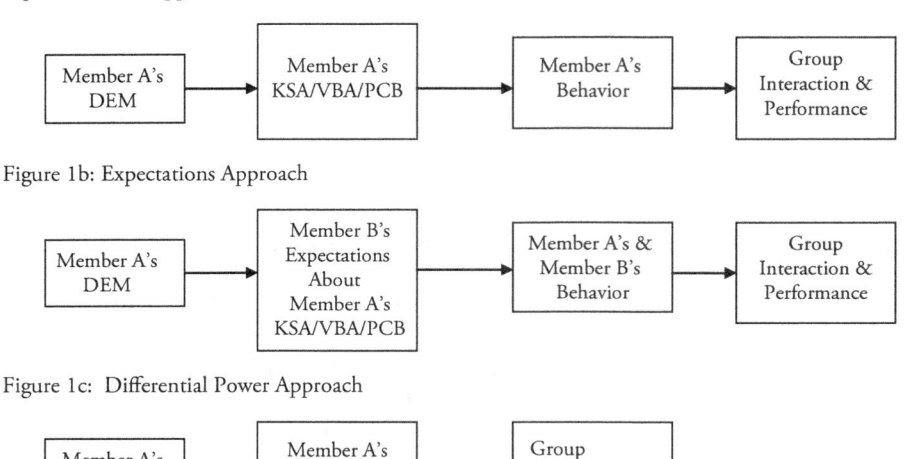

Figure 2.1. (a) Trait approach. (b) Expectations approach. (c) Differential power approach.
Source: McGrath, J. E., Berdahl, J. L., & Arrow, H. (1995). Traits, expectations, culture, and clout: The dynamics of diversity in work groups. In S. E. Jackson & M. N. Ruderman (Eds.), *Diversity in work teams* (pp. 17–45). Washington, D.C.: American Psychological Association.

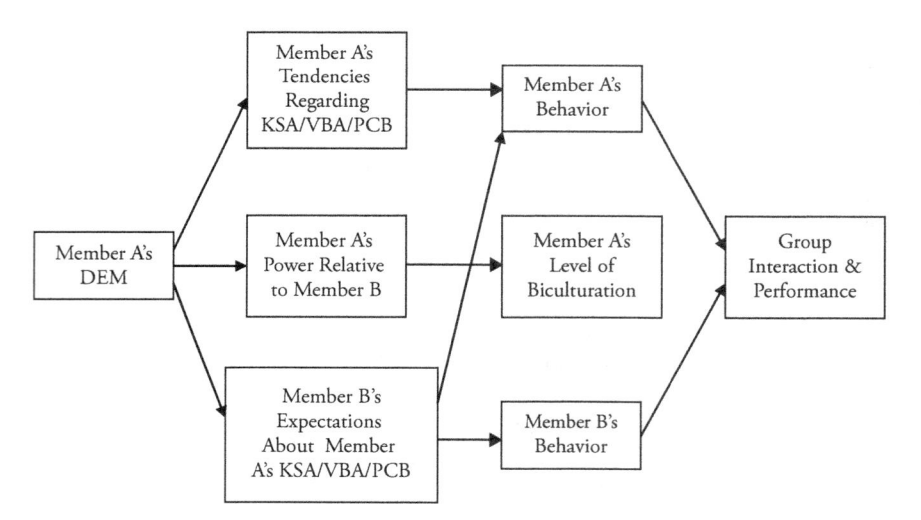

Figure 2.2. Multicultural approach.
Source: McGrath, J. E., Berdahl, J. L., & Arrow, H. (1995). Traits, expectations, culture, and clout: The dynamics of diversity in work groups. In S. E. Jackson & M. N. Ruderman (Eds.), *Diversity in work teams* (pp. 17–45). Washington, D.C.: American Psychological Association.

Simons, 1995). Consequently, these categorizations and perceptions among both member A and member B affect group interaction and performance.

The integrative multicultural approach (McGrath et al., 1995) incorporates all three models A, B, and C. In this view, when group members are diverse on demographic characteristics, they have differing cultural identities, which, through personal experiences and socioeconomic status, influence their level of expertise and deep-level attributes (KSA, VBA, PCB). This expertise affects their behavior and group interaction and performance (model A incorporation). Also, groups recognize these cultural identities and form expectations about each other's deep-level attributes (KSA, VBA, PCB) that affect their behavior as well as group interaction and performance (model B incorporation). Moreover, dominant group members may exhibit power over nondominant members because different demographic groups carry different status and differential power. This perceived power status differential will also affect group interaction and performance (model C incorporation). Although both demographic and perceived power differences may be observable, it is important to note that deep-level traits are always present, and perceived differences in status or power between individuals or groups will affect not only how deep-level traits such as KSA, PCB, and VBA are perceived, but whether or not they are expressed fully between members. Some DEM factors are perceived as having varying degrees of differential social status (Ely, 1995), which may create barriers to communication due to perceptions of social differences (Harrison & Klein, 2007).

The previous theoretical models help explain the role that diversity has in group interactions and outcomes. More importantly, the models demonstrate how surface-level diversity and deep-level diversity are connected. These interconnections may not always be able to be separated and may not allow surface- and deep-level diversity to be examined independently without regard to the other. All four models suggest that group members may always initially perceive deep-level traits like KSA, VBA, or PCB through a filter of surface-level traits. This is important for researchers to recognize because it may help reveal ways to circumvent surface-level filters of group members. Doing so may possibly encourage group interaction without the influence of prejudice, bias, or discrimination.

Diversity as separation, variety, and disparity

In their efforts to help researchers clarify the indistinct construct of diversity, Harrison and Klein (2007) proposed classifying diversity into three types: separation, variety, and disparity. Separation occurs when team members hold strong opposing viewpoints on a team task. Variety refers to the multiple approaches that team members may have to solve a problem. Disparity refers to either perceived or actual hierarchical difference in status or expertise between group members. The diversity typology is grounded in assumptions based on prior empirical and theoretical research.

Separation draws from the similarity-attraction paradigm model (Byrne, 1971) and SIT (Tajfel, 1978) discussed earlier. Separation diversity examines intergroup dynamics as it relates to conflict, cohesion, and morale based on differences in values, beliefs, or opinions. Variety focuses on differences in functional background, experience, education, or expertise and how these cognitive differences are related to group performance. Variety diversity is governed by the different information processes that individuals have and represents the group composition with respect to the differing background of expertise or knowledge of group members. Lastly, disparity draws from differences in status, hierarchy, or the distribution of resources and is grounded in distributive justice and equity perceptions relating to the proportion of socially valued resources or assets that group members hold. Along a continuum, disparity can exist as group members are perceived as having an abundance or deficit of a particular resource, with suppression of voice, interpersonal undermining, or internal competition as potential outcomes.

Theoretical implications for the three types of diversity. Diversity as a typology assists researchers in dealing with the challenge of conceptualizing, defining, and examining diversity. It enables researchers and managers to better understand why diversity yields different outcomes and to determine the best way to measure and analyze heterogeneity based on the research question to be answered. Harrison and Klein (2007) base their typology on the understanding that a group is not particularly diverse, but rather the group "is diverse with respect to one or more specific features of its members" (p. 1200). This description of diversity suggests that an attribute X may vary among group members for which a diversity researcher can examine myriad differing characteristics. As a result, it is important to identify the attribute X to be examined before conceptualization begins (Harrison & Klein, 2007; Harrison & Sin, 2006). Furthermore, the variation of the attribute may be examined in a variety of ways depending upon what process is being observed and what the potential outcome might be (Harrison & Klein, 2007). For example, there is more than one way to operationalize pay as an independent variable. A researcher could examine pay as variety diversity where the pay structure of a group focuses on how the degree of heterogeneity of pay within a group affects an outcome. Or, a researcher may wish to examine pay as disparity diversity, measuring the relative distance between two or more coworkers' salaries and how it relates to an outcome. The attribute can vary in its conceptualization as a diversity trait depending on how it is being examined and what outcomes are being predicted (Harrison & Klein, 2007). Each type of diversity is affected by the amount of diversity contained within the group and results in different predicted outcomes. Because the types of diversity are conceptualized differently with respect to their unique assumptions and traits, there are theoretical implications for each type of diversity, and each type of diversity can exist in one of three conditions: minimum, moderate, or maximum (Harrison & Klein, 2007).

Diversity as separation assumes that differences in values, beliefs, or opinions between group members are dichotomous in its maximum condition (Harrison & Klein, 2007). Along a spectrum of these traits within a group, some members will hold one set of values and beliefs at one end of the spectrum and other members will hold a different set of values and beliefs at the other end, resulting in a strong disagreement over values and beliefs. A recognizable feature of separation diversity is that in the maximum condition there is a bimodal distribution of beliefs and values among group members. This condition can result in interpersonal conflict, reduced cohesion, distrust, and decreased task performance: members are likely to diverge as two distinct subgroups if the diversity attribute is important for their team identity. In the minimum condition, all the members hold the same values and beliefs, thereby reducing interpersonal conflict and improving group cohesion (Harrison & Klein, 2007), but because the group is more homogeneous, reduced creativity and poor problem solving may emerge (e.g., Watson et al., 1993). In the moderate condition, members will be evenly distributed along the spectrum so they will disagree some, but not fully, regarding values and beliefs (Harrison & Klein, 2007).

Diversity as variety assumes that members of a group differ in their expertise, KSA, or experience, and these differences may or may not be equally distributed throughout the group (Harrison & Klein, 2007). There is no spectrum; rather there is a variety of categories that represent the members' individual differences. In the minimum condition, there are no individual differences among the group members, resulting in a homogenous group. This condition results in positive group outcomes such as strong group cohesion and efficiency. However, because there are no differences in expertise or viewpoints, negative outcomes such as groupthink (Janis, 1972) and lack of innovation may also exist. The moderate condition results in a heterogeneous group, but it lacks complete diversity because not all the members differ. Although heterogeneous groups are related to improved problem solving, innovation, and creativity (Tsui et al., 1992), there are implications for having a group that is not completely heterogeneous. For example, members who share similar characteristics may form alliances and cliques, resulting in conflict between perceived in-group and out-group members of those subgroups. Further, members may be apprehensive about "crossing" subgroup boundaries, which may result in less sharing of information and resources, and ultimately decreased task performance. Finally, the maximum condition suggests that every member is different with respect to knowledge, skills, or expertise. This results in a completely heterogeneous group where every individual differs. Heterogeneous groups are more creative, flexible, and innovative (Tsui et al., 1992), but they are also less efficient as group members must adapt and relate to each other's differences (Tsui et al., 1992). In the maximum condition, there is also less likelihood for coalitions and subgroups to form, members may be more receptive to others' viewpoints, and intragroup conflict can be better managed.

Disparity diversity refers to the perception that one or more group members possess an amount of a resource that others do not possess (Harrison & Klein, 2007), such as authority or wealth. In contrast to the other types of diversity, the direction of difference matters because it represents the relative distribution of a valued resource or asset (Harrison & Klein, 2007). In the maximum condition disparity is considered high, and it can represent either one group member possessing a resource compared to a larger number of members not possessing that resource, or a large number of members possessing a resource compared to a single member not possessing that resource. When disparity is in the minimum condition, disparity is low because all members possess the same amount of a particular resource, which is evenly distributed. In the moderate condition for disparity each member holds a different amount of a particular resource and no single person holds either the majority or minority of a resource, such as disparity in the maximum condition.

Mapping the diversity typology to surface-level diversity. According to Harrison and Klein (2007), it is important to note that an individual's demographic background such as gender, ethnic, racial, or cultural background will inform the deep-level attributes (e.g., values, beliefs, social power, etc.) exemplified in the typology. To map the diversity typology to surface-level diversity research appropriately, it is important to identify the construct being measured (Harrison & Klein, 2007). Individuals hold differing values and beliefs regarding race and gender equality. They propose that it is actually the difference in values and beliefs, not the difference in gender or race, that divides members of a group (Harrison & Klein, 2007). In this situation, the distance between opposing viewpoints regarding race or gender along a spectrum is what is being examined. Using the separation diversity type, surface-level traits can substitute for values and beliefs in the model when the researcher is measuring prejudicial attitudes or stereotype perceptions, for example, as they relate to racial or gender differences (Harrison & Klein, 2007).

Variety diversity refers to the differences in group members' perspectives and experience (Harrison & Klein, 2007). Based on the variety typology there is no spectrum but rather a variety of categories that each member falls into. As surface-level diversity relates to variety diversity, the assumption is that people's perspective is informed in part by their ethnic or racial heritage (Harrison & Klein, 2007). Research demonstrates that diverse workgroups are more creative, but also can be less cohesive (Tsui et al., 1992). The amount of heterogeneity (homogeneity) within a group is what the researcher examines as it relates to group performance outcomes when examining variety diversity. However, the categories in this instance are divided by race, gender, or any other visible trait differences instead of cognitive or functional individual differences.

Disparity diversity runs along a continuum that has a high and a low value (Harrison & Klein, 2007). This type of diversity can also be applied to race, gender, or other demographic traits to determine whether resources are distributed fairly among groups of people. The disparity of resource distribution is applied to demographic traits that can be observed by the researcher along a continuum as the resource and trait being examined relate to one another (Harrison & Klein, 2007). For example, by measuring the distance between levels of a resource such as a position within a company, one can then relate the distances to a demographic trait such as race. A company may employ a disproportionate number of White male executives as compared to the number of minority or female front-line employees. With the understanding that an executive position is higher than a front-line position (its distance), examining the racial or sex composition of those positions informs the researcher as to what extent positions of power have been (un)equally distributed among racial groups. This measurement of disparity can then be related to group outcomes.

The diversity typology helps inform the researcher how to approach diversity research in two ways. First, it assists the researcher in seeing how the diverse group to be examined is operationalized as an independent variable (Harrison & Klein, 2007). The researcher must determine whether the group is being examined for its members' differences in cognitive or physical abilities such as in variety diversity, differences in beliefs or attitudes such as in separation diversity, or differences in how resources are distributed or how group members are treated as in disparity diversity. Each type of diversity may be applied to the same workgroup. However, by doing so it changes the nature of the group as an independent variable.

Second, the typology informs researchers of the best way to measure diversity. If each type of diversity changes the independent variable, this changes the way diversity is measured and analyzed (Harrison & Klein, 2007). For example, variety diversity examines the level of heterogeneity (homogeneity) within a group, whereas disparity diversity measures the distance and dominance between members within a group. A measurement of variety diversity should produce a result that informs the researcher of the level of dispersion or number of distinctions of a trait among members, whereas a measurement of disparity diversity should produce a result that informs the researcher of the ratio or asymmetry of resources that exist between members. A method used to measure variety diversity that analyzes the variation of that group will not produce a result that can be used as the measurement of disparity diversity. Understanding what type of diversity is under examination becomes an important part of diversity research, and each type is treated uniquely regarding measurement and analysis. Otherwise, a researcher may conceptualize a variable as one type of diversity yet operationalize it as another, ending up with misleading results (Harrison & Klein, 2007).

Approaches to theory testing and measurement of diversity

Common analytical methods used in diversity research are standard deviation (SD), mean Euclidian distance (Harrison & Klein, 2007; Harrison & Sin, 2006), Euclidian distance also known as D-score (Harrison & Sin, 2006; Riordan & Wayne, 2008; Tsui et al. 1992), Blau's index (Blau, 1977), and the coefficient of variation (CV) (Allison, 1978; Williams & O'Reilly, 1998). Because diversity can be conceptualized differently, it should be measured differently based on its conceptualization. In fact, some of the differing research results that have been found over the years may be attributed to measurement problems, including using improper techniques for the type of diversity under examination (Harrison & Klein, 2007). Each method is uniquely appropriate for measuring a specific type of diversity because each has its own limitations and calculates the level of diversity based on the demographic distribution within a group (Riordan & Wayne, 2008). The following section will briefly review commonly used methods in diversity research, specifically tailored to the diversity types (e.g., see Harrison & Klein, 2007).

Measures of diversity as separation, variety, and disparity

Separation diversity can refer to the spectrum of either deep-level or surface-level differences between members of a group (Harrison & Klein, 2007). Standard deviation and mean Euclidian distance are best suited to analyze separation diversity because of the symmetry of the spectrum of traits within a group measured (Harrison & Klein, 2007). Both assume an interval scale of measurement and operationalize actual demographic similarity between all possible dyads. Standard deviation can measure the within-unit distance between members cumulatively. Its formula is $\sqrt{[\sum(X_i - X_{mean})^2/N]}$, where X_i is the score of the individual and X_{mean} is the average score of all the members of the group or unit. Euclidian distance measures the difference between one member and all the other members in a group, creating an individual-level value (Harrison & Sin, 2006; Riordan & Wayne, 2008). Its formula is $\sqrt{[\sum(X_i - X_j)^2/N]}$, where X_i is the score of the individual and X_j is the score of other members. To measure the cumulative distance between members, the mean Euclidian distance is used (Harrison & Sin, 2006). The average of the Euclidian distance between members is used instead of the sum because otherwise the result may be flawed due to the fact that a diversity measure that sums all possible dyads increases as team size increases (Harrison & Klein, 2007). A known limitation of using both SD and the mean Euclidian distance is they can be used to measure only one variable at a time (Harrison & Klein, 2007; Riordan & Wayne, 2008). In addition, one limitation to the mean Euclidian distance is that the directional information is masked due to the squaring of the difference between an individual and another person (Riordan & Wayne, 2008).

Diversity as variety refers to the heterogeneity of traits of members within a group and is not based along a spectrum of one trait (Harrison & Klein, 2007). Rather, different traits may be distributed equally or unequally throughout the workgroup or unit. Unlike separation diversity, which is conceptualized by the distance between members based on characteristics, qualitative distinctions between members are meaningful when conceptualizing diversity as variety (Harrison & Klein, 2007). Whereas the focus of separation is the degree of difference between members, variety examines the number of differences. Blau's index is one of the most widely used methods to measure categorical differences (Harrison & Sin, 2006). It is best applied to variety diversity because the values of Blau's index are bound by the number of categories where its computational formula is $1 - \sum_{pk}^{2}$, where p is the proportion of team members in the kth category (Harrison & Klein, 2007).

Because diversity as disparity runs along a continuum that has a low and high value, when operationalized, both the distance between group members and the value or amount of a resource the members possess are measured (Harrison & Klein, 2007). CV is best suited to measure disparity because it captures the asymmetry of a group. It is commonly used as a measurement in team-level demographic diversity (Williams & O'Reilly, 1998). It is calculated by dividing within-group SD by the group mean, $\sqrt{[\sum(X_i - X_{mean})^2/N]}/X_{mean}$.

Perceived versus actual diversity

Lawrence (1997) suggests that actual versus perceived characteristics may not always offer concrete explanations for a phenomenon under investigation because individual differences in perception exist. Researchers examine perceptions of diversity as a predictor of organizational and group outcomes (Harrison et al., 1998; Harrison et al., 2002; Jehn et al., 1999). Perceived diversity is operationalized by asking group members to what extent they believe another member possesses a particular trait instead of the researcher measuring the trait of group members.

Using perceptual diversity as a predictor in deep-level diversity research may help increase the understanding of group functioning because individuals perceive their environment differently (Harrison & Klein, 2007; Harrison et al, 2002; Lawrence, 1997). Even when actual diversity is not measured, the way individuals perceive the traits of others offers useful insight to understanding group and organizational outcomes in some instances (Harrison & Klein, 2007). If group members are not aware of each others' traits they may rely on their perceptions of one another to form attitudes toward group members. In this situation, perceptions of diversity may prove to be a more accurate predictor of group outcomes than actual trait differences as they "form the pivotal dimension for diversity's effects" (Harrison & Sin, 2006, p. 200).

Although it is theoretically sound to assume that over time individuals will exchange deep-level information between themselves (Harrison et al., 1998), it may be more precise to first determine what information individuals actually share and to then actually measure the perceptions of the degree to which individuals in a group believe they are similar (Harrison et al., 2002). To test this, Harrison et al. (2002) used deep-level diversity perception as a measure for dispersion and discovered that it can be used as an accurate measure of actual diversity for some traits but not for others. However, although measures of perceived diversity shed light on the understanding of group outcomes, perceived diversity lacks the construct validity needed to replace measures of actual diversity. Therefore, researchers should not substitute perceived diversity measures for actual diversity measures (Harrison & Klein, 2007; Harrison et al., 2002; Harrison & Sin, 2006).

Each conceptualization of diversity for a particular trait when examined as an independent variable can produce a different result for the dependent variable observed depending on whether the actual trait or the perceived trait is measured (Harrison & Klein, 2007; Harrison et al., 2002). For example, a group may be composed of members having certain actual deep-level traits. Disclosure about members' traits may or may not occur between the members. If those traits have not been disclosed, then when members are questioned they will report only their perceptions of what other members' traits might be. Perceptions among members can vary and may not be indicative of the actual trait (Harrison & Klein, 2007). Even if information about members' deep-level traits is shared, that information can potentially be processed differently due to biases stemming from attraction and social desirability (Byrne, 1971) or self-categorization (Turner, 1978a; Turner et al., 1987) and social comparison processes (Tajfel, 1978; Tajfel & Turner, 1979; Turner, 1978b). For example, some individuals may choose not to believe the disclosed differences between their coworkers and themselves if they are attracted to or identify with them. This may cause diversity to be perceived as less than it actually is (Harrison & Klein, 2007). On the other hand, some individuals may be keen to perceive differences, including those that they artificially create (Turner, 1978a). As a result, they may perceive more diversity than actually exists (Harrison & Klein, 2007). Also, as discussed in the following section, some surface-level traits may be disguised or invisible to group members in situations where other members purposely "pass" for a race or other surface-level attribute other than their own (Clair, Beatty, & MacLean, 2005).

Future research

In this section, we make recommendations for future diversity research. We specifically discuss research on hidden traits, mutable traits, and other construct dimensions.

Invisible social identities

Although diversity research has enabled researchers to better understand both surface-level and deep-level differences, scant attention has been paid to traits that are not only deep-level but may also be intentionally not disclosed by the individual. Clair et al. (2005) calls these hidden traits "invisible social identities" that create implications for managers in ways that are not usually discussed in diversity literature. In their article on "spirals of silence," Bowen and Blackmon (2003, p. 1395) argue that "managing 'invisible diversity' may be just as crucial as [managing] 'visible diversity' such as sex or ethnicity...but provides additional challenges" because of individuals' conscious choices to conceal their differences.

According to the integrative multicultural model cited earlier (McGrath et al., 1995), some deep-level traits listed within the DEM cluster can be considered invisible traits due to individuals' efforts to intentionally conceal them. Examples of traits that members may choose not to disclose are a hidden disability, sexual orientation, mixed racial identity, or socioeconomic status (e.g. Clair et al., 2005; Phillips, Rothbard, & Dumas, 2009). Workers may choose not to reveal some of these unobservable DEM characteristics because they fear being stigmatized by doing so (Clair et al., 2005; McLaughlin, Bell, & Stringer, 2004). Individuals with invisible social identities may choose to "pass" or "reveal" as a strategy for interacting with coworkers (Clair et al., 2005). Passing is associated with a host of negative individual consequences and related organizational consequences such as decrements to cohesion and attachment (Bell, Özbilgin, Beauregard, & Sürgevil, 2011).

Clair et al. (2005) called for developing an understanding of how invisible social identities affect group dynamics. We propose extending the literature of invisible identities by combining the model of the decision to pass or reveal (Clair et al., 2005) with the integrative multicultural approach (McGrath et al., 1995) to explain how invisible social identities affect interpersonal group behavior. It is important to integrate Clair et al.'s (2005) framework into current diversity frameworks and research so that researchers may better understand invisible social identities, recognize the distinction between invisible traits and deep-level traits, and pursue ways to operationalize invisible traits for future research. Further examination of the processes and outcomes associated with doing so would contribute to the stream of research.

Because there are noted distinctions between invisible, deep-level, and surface-level differences, we suggest that the examination of invisible social identities be categorized as its own type of research—namely, "hidden" diversity research. As a third type of diversity, hidden diversity may be examined through the lens of Harrison and Klein's (2007) diversity typology in the same way as other diversity research (i.e., surface-level, deep-level) and will differ in its conceptualization based on its minimum, moderate, or maximum condition similar to the conditions of separation, variety, and disparity diversity (Harrison & Klein, 2007). Applying the three conditions will aid researchers in theory building by reflecting the difference in the extent to which an identity is invisible and its implications. Mapping hidden diversity to the diversity typology (Harrison & Klein, 2007) will aid researchers in operationalization, measurement, and analysis.

Clair et al. (2005) discussed the implications of a person passing or revealing, which we classify as maximum and minimum hidden diversity respectively. Individuals may reveal to some but not all members (Clair et al., 2005), which we classify as a moderate condition for hidden diversity. The next section will briefly cover theoretical implications for each condition.

The minimum condition of hidden diversity stems from revealing processes (Clair et al., 2005). In this condition members reveal their invisible traits (e.g., sexual orientation or disability status), resulting in diversity being examined in a similar way as deep-level or surface-level diversity. When information about members' invisible identities is shared and not hidden, this can either create a foundation for trust and nonalienation, or barriers and biases due to attitude, value, or belief differences. In other words, because the minimum condition for hidden diversity is theoretically similar to the other types of surface-level diversity, it will share the same negative or positive consequences and should be examined in the same way. As a result, the group can be examined either as separation, variety, or disparity diversity in the minimum condition, depending upon the research question to be addressed.

The maximum condition of hidden diversity is grounded in passing behavior (Clair et al., 2005). In this condition members purposely do not share knowledge of their invisible trait with anyone within the group. Using passing tactics, members will hide their traits from other members, which results in negative consequences. Members who pass can experience psychological turmoil from being untruthful (Goffman, 1963). Because passing members feel different, they may also distance themselves from others to avoid situations that may coerce them to reveal (Clair et al., 2005). This may cause other members to become suspicious of them (Herek, 1996) and create a strain on working relationships (Kronenberger, 1991; Schneider, 1987). This situation may be examined best as separation diversity because barriers are formed between members. Furthermore, when individuals conceal their identity, suspicion among group members may cause them to perceive differences that may or may not exist, possibly resulting in measurement inaccuracies. Because the characteristics of the passing members are unknown, researchers must be aware that variety cannot be accurately measured using surface-level data if hidden traits exist among group members. Also, any measures of disparity can be misconstrued because disparity is conceptualized as both the distance or degree of difference between members and the distribution of a resource between members based on their distance (Harrison & Klein, 2007). If the trait of members is unknown, it is not possible to accurately calculate the level of disparity within the unit because it would be impossible for the resources to be distributed based on known attributes of group members.

In the moderate condition, members either reveal their invisible identities to some members but not others, or provide cues that not all members recognize. This condition partly stems from the passing tactic known as signaling (Clair et al., 2005). Signaling occurs when members offer cues to others about their invisible identity using symbols, gestures, and verbal and nonverbal messages (Clair et al., 2005). For example, someone who is gay might use slang that other gay men would recognize (Clair et al., 2005, p. 83). When signaling, it is possible that cues are recognized only by other members with similar invisible identities or those who have developed close relationships with such members and are very attuned to their signals. This can result in new expectations between some members but not others, because not all members are aware of the differences between the group members. Because some but not all members are aware of each others' invisible traits, some members may develop stronger ties than others within the group. This may reduce group cohesion and separate the group into factions, which can negatively affect group performance, thereby creating a condition of separation diversity as defined by Harrison and Klein (2007). Knowing the type of diversity and its condition will inform researchers how to best measure hidden diversity and which methods to use when investigating invisible social identities.

We suggest that the integrative model of the multicultural approach (McGrath et al., 1995) be adapted to demonstrate how invisible social identities (1) are not readily observable, (2) affect member A's KSA, PCB, and VBA in a unique manner different from deep-level differences, (3) and affect member B's and an additional member C's expectations about member A's KSA, VBA, and PCB based on member A's decision to pass or reveal. We also integrate into the framework the diversity typology conditions minimum, moderate, and maximum (Harrison & Klein, 2007) as discussed earlier.

For example, if member A chooses to pass, initially only member A is affected because member B is not aware of any difference between them. However, if member A reveals after initially passing, member B may form different expectations about member A and view member A differently. Member A must also deal with the consequences stemming from the reactions and new expectations of member B knowing member A's previously hidden trait. Member A may also choose to reveal only by offering cues that some (member C) but not other members may recognize. Or, member A may choose to reveal only to some (member C) but not all members. In this instance, member C may be aware of member A's traits while member B is not. This also may lead to different interpersonal and group outcomes because the dynamic of the relationships between group members now varies. By integrating research on invisible social identities (Clair et al., 2005) and workgroup diversity models (McGrath et al., 1995) and applying the minimum, moderate, and maximum conditions of diversity typology (Harrison & Klein 2007), we present a model of the hidden traits approach (Fig. 2.3) to help explain the process and ramifications of purposely passing and revealing as it pertains to group outcomes.

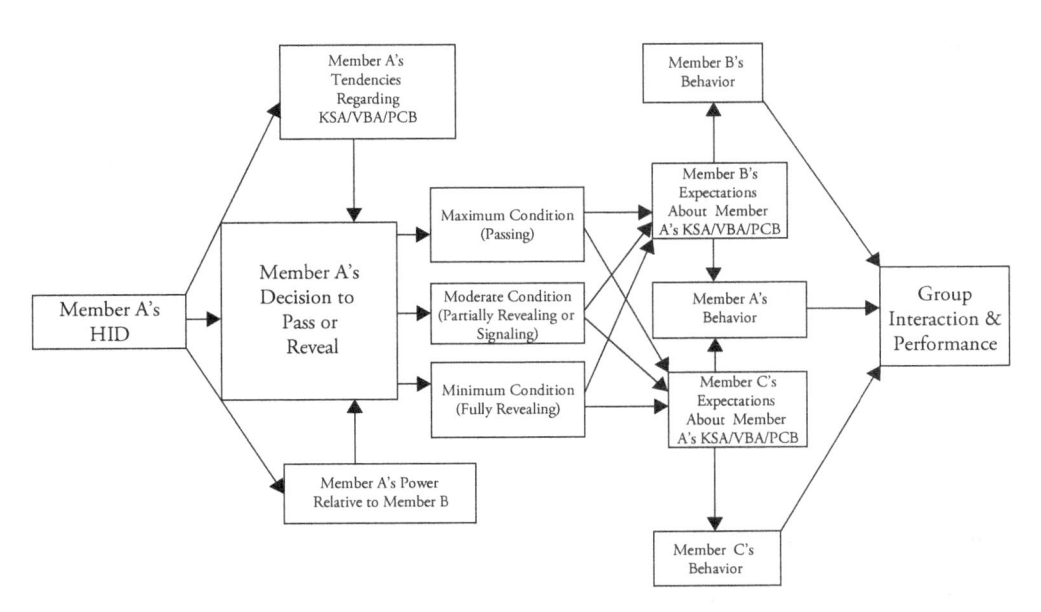

Figure 2.3. Hidden traits approach mapped to McGrath, Berdahl, and Arrow's (1995) multicultural approach model.
Adapted with permission from McGrath, J. E., Berdahl, J. L., & Arrow, H. (1995). Traits, expectations, culture, and clout: The dynamics of diversity in work groups. In S. E. Jackson & M. N. Ruderman (Eds.), *Diversity in work teams* (pp. 17–45). Washington, D.C.: American Psychological Association.

Hidden diversity differs from deep-level diversity because members choose to conceal or reveal their social identities purposely. As opposed to other types of diversity, with hidden diversity only one member—the member with the invisible identity or trait—is aware that diversity within the group or organization exists. Clair et al. (2005) suggest targeting interest groups outside the organization to find willing participants for researching the effect of social identities on organizational outcomes. This is because invisible traits are difficult or even impossible to observe or measure, even over time, as deep-level attributes can be. Confidentiality is an important issue for these members, so it may not be suitable to examine invisible identities using field studies that are conducted within a firm; members may believe confidentiality about their invisible social identity could be compromised (Clair et al., 2005). Further research in this domain may reveal more about interpersonal relationships between employees, as people with invisible identities are possibly privy to information not ordinarily shared between colleagues due to social desirability. For example, passing employees may overhear conversations that entail derogatory comments about their race, ethnicity, sexual orientation, or abilities only because the message sender is unaware of their identity. The ability to find research participants with invisible social identities may make information regarding these scenarios richer and more accessible.

Trait self-disclosure

Because invisible social identities may vary, each one may relate to a different outcome. Also, due to the perceived stigma associated with their hidden trait, respondents may not wish to reveal their invisible social identity. Consequently, measuring the extent to which the hidden trait is concealed may be more valuable to the researcher than identifying or measuring the trait itself.

We suggest measuring the degree of perceived disclosure using a Likert scale because unlike a diversity trait, the degree of perceived disclosure is a continuous variable rather than a categorical variable. Results from a study such as this may provide useful information for examining how the level of awareness of members' hidden traits is related to performance outcomes and the expectations that members have of one another. Further research is needed to construct valid scales to measure the degree of perceived disclosure of hidden traits. Qualitative methods such as face-to-face interviews or focus groups should also be used to further examine the attitudes, affective responses, and interactions experienced by members in the workplace who possess hidden traits.

More research is needed to address how the invisible identities of group members affect results in diversity research (Clair et al., 2005; Harrison & Klein, 2007). We can theorize as to how an invisible social identity of a group member affects group interaction, but in what ways does a hidden trait unknown to researchers affect their findings of outcomes related to surface-level traits? A researcher may conclude that certain outcomes are related to the type of surface-level or deep-level diversity being examined when possibly invisible social identities either act as confounding variables or are also unique predictors. Are there signals that researchers can search for to inform them of the existence of hidden diversity in a workgroup? This will assist researchers in controlling for the effects that hidden diversity has on an outcome. It will also inform managers of how to recognize and manage hidden diversity in a way that produces positive workgroup outcomes. Researchers also must consider how group members handle the revealing of hidden traits by other members. In this situation, the hidden trait becomes a mutable trait as the trait of the individual is perceived by other group members to have changed. What are the ramifications of that happening?

Mutable traits

Unless the study has a longitudinal design, much of diversity research examines surface-level and deep-level traits of individuals as constants when they are measured. The characteristics of group members, which are related to group functioning, are assumed tobe immutable. However, in reality, many characteristics are mutable and change over time. Employees age. A group member becomes very ill. Another gains or loses weight. What are the implications for group performance when the traits of group members change? How do the models and typologies of diversity apply to situations where traits are mutable? Research demonstrates that over time deep-level traits play an important role in group functioning (Harrison et al., 1998). If we can assume that deep-level traits have been shared between members over time, how does deep-level knowledge of a group member affect group functioning when another trait of that member changes?

Weight and body size

Weight is a mutable surface-level trait that is increasingly important but has received relatively little research attention when compared with race, sex, and age. Weight discrimination is widely accepted and is exacerbated by the fact that there are no federal laws to protect overweight people. Researchers have found that individuals experience weight discrimination similar to levels of racial discrimination (Puhl, Andreyeva, & Brownell, 2008). Overweight individuals are perceived as being unhealthy and less energetic (Crandall, 1994; Hebl, King, & Lin, 2004), and receive fewer employment opportunities, fewer promotions, and lower salaries than average-weight individuals (Pingitore, Dugoni, Tindale, & Spring, 1994). Overweight employees also drive a disproportionate amount of health-care costs for organizations, such as higher rates of absenteeism (Aldana & Pronk, 2001; Leigh, 1991; Tucker & Friedman, 1998) and work-related injuries (Bhattacherjee et al., 2003). Organizations are taking steps to reward employees for adopting or maintaining a healthy lifestyle in order to minimize those costs. When thin employees are ineligible to receive rewards for weight loss, does that affect their perception of equity about and attitude toward wellness programs and the organization? Do wellness programs that focus on health affect interpersonal relationships differently from those that focus on weight loss? Do organizations that hire overweight workers experience a competitive advantage similar to organizations that are diverse with respect to other differences (i.e., race and sex)? Future research should investigate what policies human resources managers can implement to improve organizational and interpersonal weight discrimination in the workplace. Also, researchers should examine more closely the effectiveness of organizational recruitment practices to determine whether hiring practices that discriminate based on weight are related to group outcomes.

Identifying other diversity construct dimensions

Although individuals have a limited number of surface traits, there are numerous deep-level traits to be examined. Through continued research, we may discover that lifestyle attitudes and personal beliefs revealed at work may have a stronger relationship with group cohesion than work attitudes because they may reveal more about a person's personality, an antecedent to interpersonal attraction and group cohesion (Byrne, 1971; Lott & Lott, 1965; Seashore, 1954). Deep-level diversity research conveys hope for positive group outcomes because with so many varying deep-level traits, which include a varying number of opinions, attitudes, values, and perspectives, group members in organizations should be able to discover similarities that bring them together.

Various psychological work characteristics have been used as variables when measuring differences between individuals in management research (e.g., Harrison et al., 1998; Jehn et al., 1999; McGrath et al., 1995). Researchers suggest that lifestyle attitudes such as the type of music someone enjoys are related to interpersonal attraction (Bakagiannis & Tarrant, 2006). It can be assumed that there are a seemingly infinite number of psychological differences between group members. Aside from work attitudes, other attitudes may exist that are unrelated to work and are expressed among members in the workplace.

Employees engage in many conversations at work that are unrelated to their tasks. Examples may include topics of conversation such as sports, politics, or other current events that convey the attitudes of employees. Those other attitudes that may be expressed in conversation at work serve as a reflection of possible antecedents to group functioning. Explorations of other dimensions of attitudes, values, and beliefs that may be revealed in the workplace may be fruitful. What types of conversations take place between group members in the workplace that serve as the medium for the exchange of lifestyle attitudes and beliefs? How does the information exchanged within these conversations between group members affect their group cohesion? What is the best way to capture the perceptions that group members have of one another about their group's deep-level characteristics?

Conclusion

There are many different lenses through which diversity is viewed. These perspectives inform researchers of innovative ways to address the role that individual differences play in the workplace. Surface-level diversity and deep-level diversity each have unique traits that affect organizational processes and outcomes, although they are constructed differently. Diversity research is diverse in its form, type, and level of analysis. Diversity research at the firm level informs managers of how to align the firm's strategy with goals of effective marketing, talent recruitment, innovation, and cost reduction. Individual- and group-level analysis inform managers how to improve and understand problem solving, group functioning, and conflict as more organizations become more diverse. Identifying a diversity type as being separation, variety, or disparity has unique implications for outcomes to be observed, and is important for operationalizing independent variables, theory building, conceptualization, and measurement. Some deep-level traits that are intentionally not revealed by some individuals and some unrecognizable demographic traits that are usually considered surface-level characteristics can be intentionally hidden. Overall, diversity affects individual, group, and firm outcomes, making it an important aspect of management.

There is a now a greater understanding of the difference between actual diversity and perceived diversity than in the past. Understanding the effect of time on diverse workgroups has proven to be useful, and relationships between surface-level diversity and deep-level diversity have been identified and are better understood. Some areas of diversity research remain limited, yet are evolving to address emerging issues such as the impact of overweight employees; discrimination against gays, lesbians, and transgender workers; and the inclusion of workers with disabilities. There is a continued need for research that recognizes differences and similarities among group members, and related behavioral processes that affect productivity and cohesion in workgroups and organizations and that can, ultimately, affect organizations' success. Lastly, we believe it is important, as noted by Konrad (2003), to acknowledge that differences having strong personal meaning and stemming from or coinciding with significant power differences among groups are distinct from other types of differences. A simplistic use of the term "diversity" that subsumes these important differences belies these different meanings and removes the opportunity to increase equality, minimize negative outcomes, and truly capture the benefits of increasing demographic diversity that initially spurred interest in diversity research.

References

Aldana, S. G., & Pronk, N. P. (2001). Health promotion programs, modifiable health risks, and employee absenteeism. *Journal of Occupational and Environmental Medicine, 43*(1), 36–46.

Allison, P. D. (1978). Measures of inequality. *American Sociological Review, 43,* 865–880.

Allport, G. W. (1954). *The nature of prejudice.* Cambridge, MA: Addison-Wesley.

American religious identification survey 2008 report: highlights. (2008). Retrieved from http://www.americanreligionsurvey-aris.org/reports/highlights.html.

Ashforth, B., & Mael, F. (1989). Social identity and the organization. *Academy of Management Review, 14,* 20–39.

Avery, D. (2003). Reactions to diversity in recruitment advertising—Are differences Black and White? *Journal of Applied Psychology, 88,* 672–679.

Avery, D., R., McKay, P. F., Wilson, D. C., & Tonidandel, S. (2007). Unequal attendance: The relationships between race, organizational diversity cues, and absenteeism. *Personnel Psychology, 60*(4), 875–902.

Bakagiannis, S., & Tarrant, M. (2006). Can music bring people together? Effects of shared musical preference on intergroup bias in adolescence. *Scandinavian Journal of Psychology, 47,* 129–136.

Barrick, M. R., Stewart, G. L., Neubert, M. J., & Mount, M. K. (1998). Relating member ability and personality to workteam processes and team effectiveness. *Journal of Applied Psychology, 83,* 377–391.

Barsade, S. G., Ward, A. J., Turner, J. D. F., & Sonnenfeld, J. (2000). To your heart's content: A model of affective diversity in top management teams. *Administrative Science Quarterly, 45,* 802–836.

Beckman, C. M., & Haunschild, P. R. (2002). Network learning: The effects of partners' heterogeneity of experience on corporate acquisitions. *Administrative Science Quarterly, 47,* 92–124.

Bell, M. P., Özbilgin, M., Beauregard, T. A., & Sürgevil, O. (2011). Voice, silence, and diversity in 21st-century organizations: Strategies for inclusion of gay, lesbian, bisexual, and transgender employees. *Human Resource Management, 50*(1), 131–146.

Betancourt, H., & Lopez, S. R. (1993). The study of culture, ethnicity, and race in American psychology. *American Psychologist, 48,* 629–637.

Bhattacherjee, A., Chau, N., Sierra, C. O., Legras, B., Benamghar, L., Michaely, J. P., et al. (2003). Relationships of job and some individual characteristics to occupational injuries in employed people: a community-based study. *Journal of Occupational Health, 45*(6), 382–391.

Blau, P. (1977). *Inequality and heterogeneity.* New York: Free Press.

Bowen, F., & Blackmon, K. (2003). Spirals of silence: The dynamic effects of diversity on organizational voice. *Journal of Management Studies, 40*(6), 1393–1417.

Brewer, M. B. (1995). Managing diversity: The role of social identities. In S. E. Jackson & M. N. Ruderman (Eds.), *Diversity in work teams* (pp. 47–68). Washington, D.C.: American Psychological Association.

Brown, D. J., Keeping, L. M., Cover, R. T., & Levy, P. E. (2006). Racial tolerance and reactions to diversity information in job advertisements. *Journal of Applied Social Psychology, 36,* 2048–2071.

Brown, R. J., & Turner, J. C. (1981). Interpersonal and intergroup behavior. In J. C. Turner & H. Giles (Eds.), *Intergroup behavior* (pp. 33–64). Chicago, IL: University of Chicago Press.

Byrne, D. (1971). *The attraction paradigm.* New York: Academic Press.

Byrne, D., & Wong, T. J. (1962). Racial prejudice, interpersonal attraction, and assumed dissimilarity of attitudes. *Journal of Abnormal and Social Psychology, 65,* 246–253.

Chapman, L. J., & Campbell, D. T. (1957). An attempt to predict the performance of three-man teams from attitude measurements. *Journal of Social Psychology, 46,* 277–286.

Clair, J. A., Beatty, J. E., & Maclean, T. L. (2005). Out of sight but not out of mind: Managing invisible social identities in the workplace. *Academy of Management Review, 30*(1), 78–95.

Cox, T., Jr. (1995). The complexity of diversity: Challenges and direction for future research. In S. E. Jackson & M. N. Ruderman (Eds.), *Diversity in work teams* (pp. 235–246). Washington, D.C.: American Psychological Association.

Cox, T., Jr. (1991). The multicultural organization. *Academy of Management Executive, 5*, 34–47.

Cox, T., Jr. (1990). Problems with research by organizational scholars on issues of race and ethnicity. *Journal of Applied Behavioral Science, 26*, 5–23.

Cox, T. H., & Blake, S. (1991). Managing cultural diversity: Implications for organizational competitiveness. *Academy of Management Executive, 5*, 45–56.

Cox, T. H., Lobel, S. A., & McLeod, P. L. (1991). Effects of ethnic group cultural differences on cooperative and competitive behavior on a group task. *Academy of Management Journal, 34*, 827–847.

Crandall, C. S. (1994). Prejudice against fat people: Ideology and self-interest. *Journal of Personality and Social Psychology, 66*(5), 882–894.

Doerr, K. H., Mitchell, T. R., Schriesheim, C. A., Freed, T., & Zhou, X. (2002). Heterogeneity and variability in the context of flow lines. *Academy of Management Review, 27*, 594–607.

Doise, W. (1978). *Groups and individuals: Explanations in social psychology.* Cambridge, England: Cambridge University Press.

Ellemers, N., De Gilder, D., & Haslam, S. (2004). Motivating individuals and groups at work: A social identity perspective on leadership and group performance. *Academy of Management Review, 29*, 458–478.

Ely, R. (1995). The role of dominant identity and experience in organizational work on diversity. In S. E. Jackson & M. N. Ruderman (Eds.), *Diversity in work teams* (pp. 161–186). Washington, D.C.: American Psychological Association.

Ely, R. J., & Thomas, D. A. (2001). Cultural diversity at work: The effects of diversity perspectives on work group outcomes. *Administrative Science Quarterly, 46*(2), 229–273.

Fiedler, F. E., Warrington, W. G., & Blaisdell, F. J. (1952). Unconscious attitudes as correlates of sociometric choice in a social group. *Journal of Abnormal and Social Psychology, 47*, 790–796.

Gaertner, S., Dovidio, J. F., Banker, B. S., Houlette, M., Johnson, K. M., & McGlynn, E. A. (2000). Reducing intergroup conflict: From superordinate goals to decategorization, recategorization, and mutual differentiation. *Group Dynamics: Theory, Research, and Practice, 4*(1), 98–114.

Gaertner, S. L., Dovidio, J. F., Anastasio, P. A., Bachman, B. A., & Rust, M. C. (1993). The common ingroup identity model: Recategorization and the reduction of intergroup bias. In W. Stroebe & M. Hewstone (Eds.), *European review of social psychology* (4, pp. 1–26). London: Wiley.

Goffman, E. (1963). *Stigma.* Englewood Cliffs, NJ: Prentice-Hall.

Harrison, D. A., & Klein, K. J. (2007). What's the difference? Diversity constructs as separation, variety, or disparity in organizations. *Academy of Management Review, 32*(4), 1199–1228.

Harrison, D. A., Price, K. H., & Bell, M. P. (1998). Beyond relational demography: time and the effects of surface- and deep-level diversity on work group cohesion. *Academy of Management Journal, 41*(1), 96–107.

Harrison, D. A., Price, K. H., Gavin, J. H., & Florey, A. T. (2002). Time, teams, and task performance: Changing effects of surface- and deep-level diversity on group functioning. *Academy of Management Journal, 45*(5), 1029–1045.

Harrison, D. A., & Sin, H. (2006). What is diversity and how should it be measured? In A. M. Konrad, P. Prasad, & J. K. Pringle (Eds.), *Handbook of workplace diversity* (pp. 191–216). London: Sage Publications.

Hebl, M. R., King, E. B., & Lin, J. (2004). The swimsuit becomes us all: Ethnicity, gender and vulnerability to self-objectification. *Personality and Social Psychology Bulletin, 30*(10), 1322–1331.

Herek, G. M. (1996). Why tell if you are not asked? Self-disclosure, intergroup contact, and heterosexuals' attitudes toward lesbians and gay men. In G. M. Herek, J. B. Jobe, & R. M. Carney (Eds.), *Out in force: Sexual orientation and the military* (pp. 197–225). Chicago: University of Chicago Press.

Hurwitz, J. I., Zander, A. F., & Hymovitch, B. (1960). Some effects of power on the relations among group members. In D. Cartwright & A. Zander (Eds.), *Group dynamics: Research and theory* (2nd ed., pp. 800–809). Evanston, IL: Row, Peterson.

Jackson, S. E. (1992). Team composition in organizational settings: Issues in managing an increasingly diverse workforce. In S. Worchel, W. Wood, & J. Simpson (Eds.). *Group process and productivity* (pp. 138–173). Beverly Hills, CA: Sage.

Jackson, S. E., Brett, I. F., Sessa, V. I., Cooper, D. M., Mulin, J. A., & Peyronnin, K. (1991). Some differences make a difference: Individual dissimilarity and group heterogeneity as correlates of recruitment, promotions, and turnover. *Journal of Applied Psychology, 76*, 675–689.

Jackson, S. E., Joshi, A., & Erhardt, N. L. (2003). Recent research on team and organizational diversity: SWOT analysis and implications. *Journal of Management, 29*, 801–830.

Jackson, S. E., May, K. E., & Whitney, K. (1995). Understanding the dynamics of diversity in decision-making teams. In R. A. Guzzo & E. Sales (Eds.), *Team decision-making effectiveness in organizations* (pp. 204–261). San Francisco: Jossey-Bass.

Jackson, S. E., & Ruderman, M. N. (1995). Introduction: Perspectives for understanding diverse work teams. In S. E. Jackson & M. N. Ruderman (Eds.), *Diversity in work teams* (pp. 1–13). Washington, D.C.: American Psychological Association.

Janis, I. L. (1972). *Victims of groupthink: A psychological study of foreign policy decisions and fiascoes.* Boston: Houghton Mifflin Company.

Jehn, K. A., Northcraft, G. B., & Neale, M. A. (1999). Why differences make a difference: A field study of diversity, conflict, and performance in workgroups. *Administrative Science Quarterly, 44*, 741–763.

Karsten, M. F. (2006). *Management, gender, and race in the 21st century.* Lanham, MD: University Press of America, Inc.

King, E. B., & Hebl, M. R. (2009). Conflict and cooperation in diverse workgroups. *Journal of Social Issues, 65*, 261–285.

Konrad, A. M. (2003). Defining the domain of workplace diversity scholarship. *Group and Organization Management, 28*(1), 4–17.

Kronenberger, G. K. (1991). Out of the closet. *Personnel Journal, 70*, 40–44.

Lawrence, B. S. (1997). The black box of organizational demography. *Organization Science, 8*, 1–22.

Leigh, J. P. (1991). Employee and job attributes as predictors of absenteeism in a national sample of workers: the importance of health and dangerous working conditions. *Social Science Medicine, 33*(2), 127–137.

Lott, A. J., & Lott, B. E. (1965). Group cohesiveness as interpersonal attraction: A review of relationships with antecedent and consequent variables. *Psychological Bulletin, 64,* 259–309.

McGrath, J. E., Berdahl, J. L., & Arrow, H. (1995). Traits, expectations, culture, and clout: The dynamics of diversity in work groups. In S. E. Jackson & M. N. Ruderman (Eds.), *Diversity in work teams* (pp. 17–45). Washington, D.C.: American Psychological Association.

McLaughlin, M. E., Bell, M. P., & Stringer, D. Y. (2004). Stigma and acceptance of persons with disabilities: Understudied aspects of of workforce diversity. *Group & Organization Management, 29,* 302–333.

Millikens, F. J., & Martins, L. L. (1996). Searching for common threads: Understanding the multiple effects of diversity in organizational groups. *Academy of Management Review, 21*(2), 402–433.

Northcraft, G. B., Polzer, J. T., Neale, M. A., & Kramer, R. M. (1995). Diversity, social identity, and performance: Emergent social dynamics in cross-functional teams. In S. E. Jackson & M. N. Ruderman (Eds.), *Diversity in work teams* (pp. 69–96). Washington, D.C.: American Psychological Association.

O'Reilly, C. A., III, Caldwell, D. F., & Barnett, W. P. (1989). Work group demography, social integration, and turnover. *Administrative Science Quarterly, 34,* 21–37.

Pfeffer, J., & Langton, N. (1993). The effect of wage dispersion on satisfaction, productivity, and working collaboratively: Evidence from college and university faculty. *Administrative Science Quarterly, 38,* 382–407.

Pfeffer, J., & Langton, N. (1988). Wage inequality and the organization of work: The case of academic departments. *Administrative Science Quarterly, 33,* 588–606.

Phillips, K. W., Rothbard, N. P., & Dumas, T. L. (2009). To disclose or not to disclose? Status distance and self-disclosure in diverse environments. *Academy of Management Review, 34*(4), 710–732.

Pingitore, R., Dugoni, B. L., Tindale, R. S., & Spring, B. (1994). Bias against overweight job applicants in a simulated employment interview. *Journal of Applied Psychology, 79,* 909–917.

Puhl, R. M., Andreyeva, T., & Brownell, K. D. (2008). Perceptions of weight discrimination: Prevalence and comparison to race and gender discrimination in America. *International Journal of Obesity,* 1–9.

Ragins, B. R., & Gonzales, J. A. (2003). Understanding diversity in organizations: Getting a grip on a slippery construct. In J. Greenberg (Ed.), *Organizational behavior: The state of the science* (pp. 125–163). Mahwah, NJ: Lawrence Erlbaum Associates.

Richard, O. C. (2000). Racial diversity, business strategy, and firm performance: A resource-based view. *Academy of Management Journal, 43,* 164–177.

Ridgeway, C. (1991). The social construction of status value: Gender and other nominal characteristics. *Social Forces, 70,* 367–386.

Riordan, C. M., & Wayne, J. H. (2008) A review and examination of demographic similarity measures used to assess relational demography within groups. *Organizational Research Methods, 11*(3), 562–592.

Schneider, B. E. (1987). Coming out at work: Bridging the private/public gap. *Work and Occupations, 13,* 463–487.

Seashore, S. (1954). *Group cohesiveness in the industrial work group.* Ann Arbor, MI: Institute for Social Research.

Sherif, M., Harvey, O. J., White, B. J., Hood, W. R., & Sherif, C. W. (1988). *Intergroup conflict and cooperation: The Robbers Cave experiment.* Hanover, NH: Wesleyan University Press, University Press of England.

Sherif, M., Harvey, O. J., White, B. J., Hood, W. R., & Sherif, C. W. (1961). *Intergroup conflict and cooperation: The Robbers Cave experiment.* Norman: University of Oklahoma Book Exchange.

Stangor, C., Lynch, L., Duan, C., & Glass, B. (1992). Categorization of individuals on the basis of multiple social features. *Journal of Personality and Social Psychology, 62,* 207–218.

Tajfel, H. (1978). Social categorization, social identity, and social comparison. In H. Tajfel (Ed.), *Differentiation between social groups: Studies in the social psychology of intergroup relations* (pp. 61–76). London: Academic Press.

Tajfel, H., & Turner, J. C. (1979). An integrative theory of intergroup conflict. In W. G. Austin & S. Worchel (Eds.), *The social psychology of intergroup relations* (pp. 33–47). Monterey, CA: Brooks-Cole.

Terborg, J. R., Castore, C., & DeNinno, J. A. (1976). A longitudinal field investigation of the impact of group composition on group performance and cohesion. *Journal of Personality and Social Psychology, 34,* 782–790.

Tolbert, P. S., Andrews, A. O., & Simons, T. (1995). The effects of group proportions on group dynamics. In S. E. Jackson & M. N. Ruderman (Eds.), *Diversity in work teams* (pp. 161–186). Washington, D.C.: American Psychological Association.

Tsui, A. S., Egan, T. D., & O'Reilly, C. A., III. (1992). Being different: Relational demography and organizational attachment. *Administrative Science Quarterly, 37,* 549–579.

Tsui, A. S., Egan, T. D., & Xin, K. R. (1995). Diversity in organizations: lessons from demography research. In M. Chembers, S. Oskamp, & M. A. Costanso (Eds.), *Diversity in organizations: New perspectives for a changing workplace* (pp. 191–219). London: Sage Publications.

Tucker, L. A., & Friedman, G. M. (1998). Obesity and absenteeism: An epidemiologic study of 10,825 employed adults. *American Journal of Health Promotion, 12*(3), 202–207.

Turner, J. (1978a). Social categorization and social discrimination in the minimal group paradigm. In H. Tajfel (Eds.), *Differentiation between social groups: Studies in the social psychology of intergroup relations* (pp. 101–140). London: Academic Press.

Turner, J. (1978b). Social comparison, similarity, and ingroup favouritism. In H. Tajfel (Eds.), *Differentiation between social groups: Studies in the social psychology of intergroup relations* (pp. 235–250). London: Academic Press.

Turner, J. C. (1987). *Rediscovering the social group: A self-categorization theory.* Oxford: Basil Blackwell.

Turner, J. C., Hogg, M. A., Oakes, P. J., Reicher, S. D., & Wetherell, M. (1987). *Rediscovering the social group: A self-categorization theory.* Oxford, England: Basil Blackwell.

Urban, L. M., & Miller, N. (1998). A theoretical analysis of crossed categorization effects: A meta-analysis. *Journal of Personality and Social Psychology, 74*(4), 894–908.

Watson, W. E., Kumar, K., & Michaelson, L. K. (1993). Cultural diversity's impact on interaction process and performance: Comparing homogenous and diverse task groups. *Academy of Management Journal, 36*, 590–602.

Webber, S. S., & Donahue, L. (2001). Impact of highly and less job related diversity on work group cohesion and performance: A meta-analysis. *Journal of Management, 27*, 141–162.

Williams, K. Y., & O'Reilly, C. A., III. (1998). Demography and diversity in organizations: A review of 40 years of research. *Research in Organizational Behavior, 20*, 77–140.

Zuckerman, M. (1990). Some dubious premises in research and theory on racial differences: Scientific, social, and ethical issues. *American Psychologist, 45*, 1297–1303.

CHAPTER 3

Understanding Diversity as Culture

Eduardo Salas, Maritza R. Salazar *and* Michele J. Gelfand

Abstract

Cultural diversity—the degree to which there are differences within and between individuals based on both subjective and objective components of culture—can affect individual and group processes. However, much is still unclear about the effects of cultural diversity. We review the literature on cultural diversity to assess the state of the art and to identify key issues for future research. This review emphasizes the importance of understanding different types of cultural diversity and their independent and combined effect on team performance. We identify key contributions to the study of cultural diversity and discuss frontiers for future research.

Key Words: diversity, teams, individuals, culture, cross-cultural, perceptions of dissimilarity, social distance, demography, cultural identity

Introduction

One of the most significant changes taking place in today's work environment is globalization (Arnett, 2002). Given the proliferation of multicultural corporations and the globalization of business, understanding the impact of cultural diversity on individual and team functioning in the work force is critical. Cross-cultural research addresses this need with a focus on the study of similarities and differences in processes and behaviors across cultures (Gelfand, Erez, & Aycan, 2007). Differences across cultures have been found to predict variation in key individual, team, and organizational processes and outcomes such as decision making, negotiation, conflict management, organizational citizenship behaviors, and innovation (Gelfand & Dyer, 2000; Gelfand, Erez, & Aycan, 2007; Kirkman, Lowe, & Gibson, 2006). In contrast, relatively little work has focused on the impact of diversity in multicultural interactions that occurs within multinational corporations and teams. Challenges to accessing multicultural teams and conceptualizations about how to measure culturally diverse teams may be some of the reason for the sparse research focused on multicultural interactions. In this chapter, we draw on organizational diversity research, cross-cultural comparative studies, and a few studies that examine multicultural teams to provide directions for the study of cultural diversity at multiple levels of analysis.

We provide an overview of the theoretical frameworks that tend to be used by diversity researchers. We do so to explore whether and how these frameworks can be leveraged to explain the effects of cultural diversity across and within people and teams. Throughout this chapter the relationship between cultural diversity and outcomes at the individual and team level will also be explored. We conclude with suggestions for future research. It is our aim to provoke diversity researchers to consider and conceptualize how culture affects perceptions and responses to diversity at multiple levels, the effects of cultural diversity on organizational behavior processes, and the contextual and social psychological condition under which cultural diversity may most affect key organizational outcomes.

Culture defined

Culture is a way of perceiving, thinking, and deciding that has endured over time and has become institutionalized by a social entity, such as a team or nation, guiding everyday behavior and practices (Gelfand, Erez, & Aycan, 2007). According to Triandis (1972), culture consists of two types of elements: (1) objective elements, which consist of visible aspects of culture such as language, religion, demography, social structures, and other political and social systems, and (2) subjective elements, which constitute more covert aspects such as values, beliefs, norms, and roles that characterize a culture and the way people experience their social world. Additionally, culture is considered to be a human part of the environment (Herskovits, 1955) that is transmitted across time and generations (Triandis, 1994).

Culture has also been defined as collective programming of the mind (Hofstede, 1991) that is shared among members (Shweder & LeVine, 1984). Following this logic, it is assumed that members of different cultures, who do not share a common meaning system, are more likely to respond to the same external stimuli in distinct ways. However, more recent advances challenge this notion of culture and suggest that it is also malleable and fragmented across individuals within the same culture (D'Andrade, 2001). For instance, Rohner (1984) suggests that many subcultures exist within a nation and that national culture may not be completely shared among fellow countrymen. Hofstede (1991) similarly described individuals as carrying several layers of culture within themselves.

Understanding the complexity of cultural diversity and measuring it appropriately is critically important for cross-cultural researchers who seek to understand how variation among people and societies affects a variety of social phenomenon. This chapter draws upon a generally accepted definition of diversity, which refers to the differences between individuals based on attributes that elicit the perception that another person is different from the self (Jackson, 1992; Triandis, Kurowski, & Gelfand, 1994; van Knippenberg, De Dreu & Homan, 2004; Williams & O'Reilly, 1998). From a cross-cultural perspective, individuals can answer the question "Who am I?" and teams can answer "Who are we?" based on a variety of both surface- and deep-level attributes that make them similar or different from others given their cultural heritage.

The next sections aim to identify various dimensions of cultural diversity that can exist within and across individuals and collections of individuals, ranging from small groups to societies. Scholars suggest that the culture exists at multiple levels of analysis (e.g., individual, team, organizational, and national levels) and that these different levels reciprocally influence one another (Erez & Gati, 2004). Empirical and theoretical research has focused on the cultural values and attitudes of individuals and on measuring these individual attributes using self-report measures (Hofstede, 1980; Schwartz, 1999). Culture has also been conceptualized and measured as a property of a team or larger collection of individuals, such as an organization or nation (Enz, 1988; Hofstede & Hofstede, 2005; Martin & Siehl, 1983; Schein, 1985; Weiner, 1988).

Through repeated social interaction, culture emerges within the collective and is believed to consist of "sets of rules and actions, work capability expectations, and members' perceptions that individuals develop, share and enact" after interaction together (Earley & Mosakowski, 2000, p. 27). Cultural differences across collectives tend to be measured by comparing similarities and differences among individuals within one collective and comparing them to members of others using aggregation techniques. Within collectives, culture emerges around a shared system of values and assumptions that tend to guide behavior, norms, rituals, and other cultural activities of members. Hence, variation in perceptions, attitudes, and behaviors across individuals and collections of individuals can often be attributed to their cultural differences.

In the remaining sections we talk about different sources of cultural diversity, when these differences affect behavior, measurement approaches, and implications for key organizational behavior outcomes at the individual and team level. This chapter focuses on understanding cultural diversity within and across individuals in teams. We conclude with recommendations for future directions.

Types of cultural diversity

The taxonomy of diversity as deep and surface level developed by Harrison, Price, and Bell (1998) is a useful starting point for classifying cultural differences, and we extend this classification system to introduce two ways of conceptualizing and measuring cultural diversity. First, we elaborate upon a type of deep-level diversity, subjective cultural diversity, which refers to the distribution of attributes that reflect culturally shaped values, attitudes, norms, roles, and beliefs that are not easily observed. Second, we discuss objective cultural diversity, which refers to the surface-level attributes of cultural difference that are readily detectable and easily perceived by individuals, such as one's age, gender, or ethnicity. Using this classification system, we outline and define various types of cultural diversity in the following section and also provide insight into how they are related. In doing so, we present connections to empirically supported findings linking these types of diversity to various individual- and team-level outcomes.

Objective attributes of cultural diversity

To differentiate one culture from another based on objective and subjective components, this chapter provides key insights into the means by which cultures of individuals and collections of individuals conduct everyday social processes. The degree to which cultures, either at the individual or collective level, are diverse can depend on how much variation there is based on the subjective and objective components of culture. Although not always the case, objective components of culture are used as a proxy for more deep-level differences that are associated with these visible features. In turn, subjective cultural components shape the way aspects of objective components of culture are perceived. The following elaborates on the connection between objective cultural components and subjective cultural components.

The focus on the relationship between objective and subjective components stems from a long tradition in psychology. Whiting and Whiting (1975) examined the effects of institutional differences on behavior by focusing on how children learn across societies. They characterized the institutional environment, and its effect on social processes, with the following categories: physical environment (e.g., climate and terrain), history (e.g., migrations), and maintenance systems (e.g., social structure). Previously, Berry (1966) explored the link between the different ecologic environments and their effect on social processes. His research demonstrated that individuals living in tightly structured agricultural settings displayed lower psychological differentiation and greater compliance in their childrearing practices than individuals from hunting and fishing communities. Extending this research further and connecting it to the field of modern cross-cultural psychology, Triandis (1972) further delineated a theoretical and methodologic framework for understanding how the subjective psychological experience of individuals is shaped by the objective human-made and physical, cultural components of their environment. Triandis' book, *Analysis of Subjective Culture*, catalyzed research that focused on understanding the association among deep-level, subjective culture (e.g., values, beliefs, expectations, norms, attitudes) across environments characterized by different objective components of culture.

In this chapter, we differentiate objective culture into two broad categories: (1) institutions at the macro level and (2) sociodemographic characteristics at the individual level. Characteristics of macro institutions include features such as language, political systems, physical setting, history, and social structure. Sociodemographic characteristics, such as race and ethnicity, are physical features of individuals within a collective that can differ across cultures due to different ancestry. Gender is also included as a biologic indicator because subjective experience of sex can vary across cultures. We elaborate on these classifications below.

Macro components of objective culture

Language Systems. One of the greatest barriers to cross-cultural collaboration is differences in the languages used to communicate. Drawing on the metaphor of a family tree, linguists have clustered languages around the world into families based on common sounds, syntax, and lexicon. Languages that are more similar are believed to stem from and be closely linked to a common ancestry, whereas distant languages may not have a common genealogy. They may be so far removed that comparison would demonstrate few similarities. Regardless, linguistic distance between two cultures can be discerned by locating the distance between these cultures on a map of these linguistic clusters. Strategies for communication can also vary cross-culturally, increasingly the likelihood of performance losses. This dimension of cultural diversity has also been explored in a study of multicultural teams. In particular, Ayoko, Hartel, and Callan (2002) found that discourse management strategies helped teams to avoid unproductive conflict and improve task performance in teams composed of people from different national cultures. In particular, discourse strategies that facilitated the use of explanation and mutual understanding were a major feature of productive conflict, whereas interrupting one another resulted in destructive conflict. Culturally diverse teams were also most effective when leaders assisted teams when communication breakdowns occurred and when all cultural subgroups were included in the discussion (Ayoko, Hartel, & Callan, 2002)

Social Structures. Social structures also distinguish nations and cultures from one another. Of particular interest are the patterns of social interaction that vary among people across cultures. Morris, Podolny, and Sullivan (2008) examined how social interactions among individuals are shaped by national culture and norms. These researchers examined informal ties among coworkers within American, Chinese, German, and Spanish cultures. Results suggest that employees' interaction with coworkers vary in terms of content and structure based on national norms. For instance, these researchers found evidence that the influence of a market transaction orientation in the United States led to less tie overlap among coworkers and to rather short-term connections. Chinese norms on filial responsibility, focused on the relationship between son and father, led to a greater tendency for instrumental exchanges to focus on subordinates, whereas an emphasis on formality in Germany led to more instrumental job-related connections at work compared to affective ties. Finally, Morris and colleagues (2008) found that norms of sociability tended to be associated with expressive content of communication, rather than on task-related topics, among the Spanish. This research provides evidence of how national culture and norms shape social structure in the form of interaction between people embedded within different countries.

Political Systems, Political scientists have identified various characteristics that differentiate one political regime from another and the factors that may lead to the use of various political systems around the globe (Bueno de Mesquita & Siverson, 1995). Forms of government across cultures are numerous, but political scientists have identified eight broad types of government, including full presidential republics, parliamentary republics, absolute monarchies, and single-party states. These political states vary in the extent to which participation of the population in developing policy is encouraged and allowed. Predictors of political structure and political decision making have been linked to differences in collectivist versus individualist orientation and to orientations regarding power (Schmitter, 1981). Research also demonstrates how the procedures used within one's national government can also shape everyday decision making. Specifically, Earley (1999) provides initial qualitative evidence of how American teams opt to use more democratic techniques, such as polling, whereas other countries leverage more authoritarian techniques, such as discussing the views of the leader, to reach collective consensus.

Physical Terrain and Climate. The physical features of the location where one once lived or currently lives have been found to have a strong association with cultural values (Berry, 1966; Triandis, 1972; Whiting & Whiting, 1975). Features of the physical environment can include climate, temperature, urban versus rural, region or country, latitude, or distance from water. Vliert, Huang, and Parker (2004) compared people in locations distinguished by their climate (hotter vs. colder) and found that people who have more wealth in cold climates tend to be less altruistic than those who are poor; the reverse is found to be true in hot climates. Examining geographic location, Little (1968) found that Mediterranean people prefer shorter distances for social interaction than do northern Europeans. Finally, societies that are more rural and rely on agriculture have been found to be more collectivist compared to industrial, urban societies, which are more individualistic (Kluckhohn & Strodtbeck, 1961; Triandis, 2009).

Sociodemographic Cultural Components. Similar cultures are likely to arise in a context where members share the same race or ancestry (Triandis, 1995). Race is considered to be one of the major divisions among humankind, revolving around physical or biologic features that are shared (Fernando, 1991). Ancestry is equated to the national origins of one's descendents, and these ancestors tend to share common physical features. Both race and ancestry may be considered a form of surface-level diversity, and these visible characteristics enable people to categorize others into social groups such as one's nation or country. Ethnic group differences have also been shown to be associated with deep-level differences in values and behaviors. For instance, Cox, Lobel, and McLeod (1991) provided results that suggest that different cultural norms among three distinct ethnic groups led to different behaviors on a group task. At an individual level, these scholars demonstrated that Asian, Black, and Hispanic individuals tend to have a more collectivist/cooperative orientation toward a task than their Anglo counterparts.

Gender is also tied to cross-cultural differences. Gender is a multidimensional phenomenon that not only is a sociodemographic characteristic, but also consists of other psychological aspects such as gender-role traits, attitudes, and values (Bem, 1993). Schwartz and Rubel (2005) suggested that men and women differ from one another across cultures in the degree to which they place importance on particular values. For instance, their study suggests that there are smaller sex differences for self-direction values across countries that are more autonomous (compared to embedded) and more individualistic (rather than collectivistic).Similar findings were found related to differences in the value of power and benevolence across nations depending on the degree to which there was gender equality within the country. These studies provide evidence of how gender, an objective component of culture, can affect differences in values across cultures.

Subjective attributes of cultural diversity

The subjective aspects of culture include one's beliefs, identities, values, norms, and attitudes that can be derived from the groups with which one is associated (Triandis, 1972). Specifically, individuals develop a sense of identity from the groups to which they belong (Tajfel & Turner, 1986). Individuals can belong to several groups, such as their families, religious organizations, political parties, or social clubs. From a social identity perspective, the answer to "Who am I?" is informed by a person's knowledge of the memberships he or she has in social groups and the value and emotional significance attached to those memberships (Tajfel, 1981). Identification with these associations can define the way people categorize others as in-group or out-group members and the values, norms, beliefs, and attitudes they hold (Deaux, 1996; Hogg & Abrams, 1988). For instance, defining oneself as a member of an organization has been shown to predict positive attitudes about the organization and the willingness to act in the organization's best interest (Mael & Ashforth, 1992).

One type of social identity is a cultural identity, which arises among individuals based on the deep tacit knowledge that is shared among members stemming from interpersonal interaction over time (Chao & Moon, 2005). Research has shown that people who identify strongly with their culture tend to endorse the culture's core values (e.g., Feather, 1994; Jetten, Postmes, & McAuliffe, 2002). A value has high perceived cultural importance when participants as a group believe that the average member in the group would strongly endorse it (Wan, Chiu, Tam, Lee, Lau, & Peng, 2007). Association with groups related to one's religion, family, profession, political interest, or avocation shapes and reinforces the values that members of these groups possess.

Data collected from different national groups provide evidence of how differences in values can distinguish people from different nations around the globe (Hofstede, 1980; Schwartz & Bilsky, 1987; Triandis, 1995). These national cultural value differences have been found to be associated with workplace behaviors, attitudes, and other organizational outcomes (e.g., Kluckhohn & Strodtbeck, 1961; Hall, 1976; Hofstede, 1980; Ronen & Shenkar, 1985; Schwartz, 1994; Trompenaars, 1993). Hofstede's (1980) extensive work classifying over 40 countries along four different dimensions of culture has strongly influenced cross-cultural research focused on investigating the effects of these national differences on individuals, teams, and organizational outcomes. Individualism versus collectivism, power distance, uncertainty avoidance, and masculinity versus femininity were the dimensions of culture that were found to distinguish one nation from another. Although Hofstede's (1980) research has been criticized for being oversimplified and ignoring cultural heterogeneity within countries (Sivakumar & Nakata, 2003), studies of cultural diversity tend to rely on the national value differences he outlined several decades ago to delineate the effects of cultural values on outcomes across countries (Taras, Kirkman, & Steel, 2010).

Values are not the only internalized aspect of the self that can be derived from group memberships. When a social identity is activated and made salient, it can induce conformity to in-group norms (Reicher, 1984; Spears, Lea, & Lee, 1990; Wilder & Shapiro, 1989). A recent study by Adarves-Yorno, Postmes, and Haslam (2006) found that the behavior of individuals on creativity tasks was informed by the normative context when their group identity was activated. Specifically, when operating as a member of a group, identification and belonging were found to be associated with adhering to the norms of the group when engaging in their work. Research elucidates that norms of tightness and looseness vary across countries, differentiating societies from one another (Gelfand, Nishi, & Raver, 2006; Pelto, 1968; Triandis, 1972). In particular, some can be characterized as "tight," imposing a high degree of constraint on behavior, whereas others evolve to be "loose," affording a high degree of freedom to determine one's own behavior (Gelfand, Nishii, & Raver, 2006). We suggest that the identification one has to one's culture or society can determine the extent to which one is likely to conform to the norms or deviate from them. The adherence or deviance from cultural norms will shape the predictability or the consistency of an individual's actions.

Individual-level cultural diversity

The construct of culture at the individual level is one that is evolving. Although individuals within the same nation or group continue to be lumped together as one homogeneous population in cross-cultural studies, research and theory advance the notion that a single individual can have various cultural influences within himself or herself (Sackmann, 1997). This point is best exemplified by research on bicultural individuals in the way that they are able to alter cultural frames depending on situational factors through the use of primes (Hong, Morris, Chiu, & Benet Martinez, 2000). Given the importance of culture as an antecedent to behavior, the knowledge that multiple cultural values can be simultaneously present within an individual requires new conceptualization and measurement techniques for the study of cultural diversity.

Chao and Moon (2005) classify the several cultural identities that exist within a single individual as being shaped by associative, demographic, and geographic factors from one's heritage and background. These authors draw on the metaphor of a mosaic and consider these three factors as different cultural "tiles" that make up an individual's cultural mosaic. They define demographic tiles of the cultural mosaic within a person as being physical in nature or inherited from one's parents, such as age, gender, race, and ethnicity. Geographic tiles can be connected to the notion of surface-level diversity because geography has to do with the natural or human-made physical features of a region that can shape an identity. Finally, associative tiles refer to the formal and informal groups that individuals choose to be a part of and with which they identify. We propose that associations with one group can be classified as deep-level diversity, as feelings of social identification, and as surface-level diversity, when people display their associations with groups through clothing or artifacts. Differences in core values across the many groups to which a person belongs can result in a variety of cultural identities that coexist within a person. In the following section, we expand on Chao and Moon's (2005) theoretical paper and explore how the structure and salience of cultural diversity can shape the cultural identity and behavior of individuals.

Configuration of cultural identities within individuals

To identify which cultural aspects of diversity will or will not be invoked, we suggest that the content of an individual's cultural identity; the importance of his or her cultural identities, values, and norms; and the broader context must be taken into account. As individuals move between the groups to which they belong to at home, school, and the workplace, different and multiple cultural values may coexist and have the potential to become simultaneously activated. These identities can merge in concordance or discordance with one another to affect the cohesiveness and strength of an individual's value set (Chao & Moon, 2005). If these identities are not in harmony, it can be a source of stress because conflicting values may be guiding behavior. Discordant cultural identities can enhance the salience of conflicting cultural identities. Drawing on social dissonance theory, dissonance may be aroused when people believe that there are discrepancies between their beliefs and behaviors, which can cause anxiety (Festinger & Carlsmith, 1959). Without coherence among values, behavior is likely to be less consistent, whereas harmonious cultural identities will be less salient to an individual and may more consistently shape behaviors.

The degree to which values drive behavior may depend on the importance or self-relevance one places on values. Values are conceptions of what is preferable, desirable, and important in a culture. Behaviors, preferences, and judgments can be justified or guided by values and they can also shape the affective evaluation of life experiences (Feather, 1996: Kluckhold, 1951; Rokeach, 1973; Schwartz & Bilsky, 1987). A value that is important culturally can be one that most members of that group consider to be important to the self or to their culture (Wan et al., 2007). The degree to which a cultural value is important to a particular person can vary across people (Schwartz & Sagie, 2000; Triandis & Gelfand, 1998). When cultural values have great self-importance and a person has high identification with his or her cultural identity, the accessibility of the practices, norms, meanings systems, and mental responses associated with this identity may be higher. With the use of the mosaic metaphor of Chao and Moon (2005), particular tiles of the mosaic may be activated more when particular cultural identities are highly self-relevant and there is great identification with a cultural group.

Through membership in a collective, individuals garner knowledge about the beliefs and behaviors of the groups to which they belong (for a review, see Cialdini & Trost, 1998). Descriptive norms about how to behave tend to be regarded as cognitions that individuals possess (Cialdini &Trost, 1998), but they can also be conceived of as a society-level construct as well (Durkheim, 1985; Pelto, 1968).

Descriptive norms about what is socially acceptable behavior can vary across nations and can be an expression of culture (cf., Tett & Burnett, 2003). Recent research suggests that differences in the perceptions of these norms can also affect psychological processes and behavior across cultures (Shteynberg, Gelfand, & Kim, 2009; Wan, Chiu, Tam, Lee, Lau, & Peng, 2007). Shteynberg, Gelfand, and Kim (2009) provide evidence that individuals with lower collectivist descriptive norms perceived a greater harm after rights violations than individuals with higher collectivistic descriptive norms. This research emphasizes the importance of considering norms as a subjective component of culture that can shape the way individuals perceive their environment.

The degree to which cultural identities affect behavior may be associated with the degree to which they are activated. The salience of cultural diversity categories or attributes is likely to depend on the degree to which the identity is meaningful and the extent to which the cultural identity is perceived depending on the social situation. We explore when cultural identities are made salient within individuals and the implications for predictable and normative behavioral outcomes.

Situational triggers of cultural identity salience

Cultural identities, or the tiles of the cultural mosaic, may also be activated by the triggers in the situational context. Much like social identities, cultural identities are malleable and can be activated when contextual conditions make a particular identity salient. For instance, Hong, Morris, Chiu, and Benet-Martinez (2000) demonstrate how situational attributions are activated through the use of cultural symbols (e.g., Chinese dragon and Statue of Liberty) across American and Chinese samples. They find that the activation of cultural knowledge through stimuli in the external environment depends on the extent to which it is cognitively accessible. They also demonstrate how cultural knowledge, when activated, can be a potent driver of behavior. Along related lines, Kitayama, Markus, Matsumoto, and Norasakkunkit (1997) elucidate how social situations, such as those that increase or decrease self-esteem, can elicit different cultural identities and responses across American and Japanese samples. These two studies underscore the importance of examining how the salience of cultural knowledge, identities, norms, and values can be sensitive to features of the sociocultural context, such as social artifacts, and shape behavior.

The activation of cultural identities can also be facilitated based on the extent to which similarities and differences between people are perceived. Perceived surface-level dissimilarity is an individual's perceptions of the differences between himself and herself and others in terms of overt, physically observable characteristics, whereas deep-level similarity perceptions are based on differences in terms of nonvisible characteristics such as personality, values, beliefs, norms, and attitudes. Drawing on the similarity-attraction paradigm (Byrne, 1971), similarities and differences between people can form the basis for interpersonal attraction. Research suggests that the degree to which one's cultural identity is made salient can affect subsequent team interaction. For instance, research by Randel (2003) finds that cultural identity salience can be triggered based on contextual conditions, such as whether team members share the same country of origin of a few or very many fellow team members, and that the dispersion of team members' cultural salience assessments are positively associated with team citizenship behavior. Van der Zee, Atsma, and Brodbeck (2004) provide further evidence that when one's cultural identity is salient in diverse teams, well-being and commitment to the team are both enhanced.

The social organization of different societies can affect systems of thought and how people from different cultures see aspects of the social world (Nisbett, Peng, Choi, & Norenzayan, 2001). For instance, Nisbett, Peng, Choi, and Norenzayan (2001) suggest that individuals from contexts characterized as being collectivist and holistic tend to be more tolerant of contradiction. Hence, when individuals from these contexts experience identity discordance, it may be the case that this conflict may not be perceived or attended to. It is possible that individuals who live in more culturally diverse environments may be less affected by the simultaneous presence of different cultural identities. We anticipate that these past experiences will also attenuate the effect of dissimilarity perceptions related both to deep- and surface-level cultural differences when interacting with culturally diverse others.

Contextual elements can also activate the salience of culturally derived norms and values. For instance, Gelfand and Realo (1999) found that the degree of accountability in the task environment can make descriptive norms salient. Specifically, accountability to constituents was found to enhance the propensity of collectivists to be cooperative and for individualists to be competitive in negotiation (Gelfand & Realo, 1999). Along related lines, other research demonstrates that when the individuals are held responsible to an in-group audience for their behavioral choices (Briley et al., 2000), their behavior is more culturally normative. Time pressure and need for closure, or the desire to reduce ambiguity in a social context, are additional contextual conditions that have been found to motivate individuals to use cultural knowledge to guide information processing. Researchers also provide evidence that cultural differences tend to be amplified when there is a high need for closure (Fu et al., 2007, Morris & Fu, 2001). Finally, cultural norms and values can also be brought to the surface in situations of uncertainty, such as uncertainty about the groups to which one belongs (De Cremer & Van Hiel, 2008; Van den Bos, 2005).

This section provides evidence that supports the notion that cultural identities are dynamic and subject to activation based on features of the broader social context in which people are embedded (Hong et al., 2000). In the section that follows, we explore the impact of the types, structure, and salience of cultural diversity within teams on team processes and performance. Just as cultural diversity can reside within an individual, cultural diversity can also be the characteristic of a social group that reflects the degree to which there are objective or subjective cultural differences between people within the group. Diversity within teams has been found to have a pervasive impact on both collective functioning and performance (e.g., Guzzo & Dickson, 1996; van Knippenberg & Schippers, 2007). Next, we discuss the complex influence of cultural diversity and the salience of this diversity in teams.

Team cultural diversity

A *team* refers to three or more individuals who interact for the accomplishment of a common goal (McGrath, 1984). Over the past decade, the use of teams across a variety of domains has increased (Wuchty, Jones, & Uzzi, 2007). Academicians and practitioners alike have struggled to understand how to improve the performance of teams, especially when they are composed of diverse members. Much of the empirical research on diversity in teams has focused on understanding the conditions that enable some diverse teams to effectively pool and use their differences to achieve optimal performance, while avoiding the dysfunctional processes often associated with heterogeneity.

Comparing national differences across teams

Cross-cultural studies comparing differences across nations elucidate many key insights about how collaboration and teamwork are enacted across nations (Gelfand & Dyer, 2000; Gelfand, Erez, & Aycan, 2007; Kirkman, Lowe, & Gibson, 2006). For instance, studies of teams with more collectivist orientation were found to view groups as having greater agency than teams composed of more individualist individuals (e.g., Chiu et al., 2000; Kashima et al., 2005; Morris et al., 2008). Team members' evaluations of their collective efficacy were also found to vary across teams where high-status members were present, depending on the mean level of power distance of members (Earley, 1999).

Differences with regard to the culture-specific meanings ascribed to interpersonal work styles across teams have also been found across nationalities. In particular, Sanchez-Burks, Nisbett, and Ybarra (2000) found that Mexicans attend closely to the interpersonal atmosphere of work relations whereas mainstream Americans tend to focus on task-specific concerns. For instance, Probst, Carnevale, and Triandis (1999) found that individualists tended to be least cooperative in a single-group dilemma and more cooperative in an intergroup dilemma in which personal outcomes were improved through group cooperation. In contrast, collectivists were found to be most cooperative in the single-group dilemma and less cooperative in the intergroup condition in which group outcomes were positively affected. Research also suggests that groups of decision makers from Japan were found to expect that others would share their similar orientations to collaboration and behave cooperatively much more than were Americans (Wade-Benzoni, Okumura, Brett, Moore, Tenbrunsel, & Bazerman, 2002).

Rewards motivating cooperation in culturally diverse teams also require consideration of cross-cultural differences given findings that suggest that collectives find personal credit embarrassing (Triandis, 1988; 1990), whereas individual recognition is highly desirable in achievement-oriented individualist cultures. Rewarding work that is interesting and opportunities for promotion are most attractive to American students, whereas rewards in the form of pay and bonuses were the preference among Chinese and Chilean students (Corney & Richards, 2005; King & Bu, 2005). These examples of the distinct motivations, expectations, and rewards for collaboration of culturally diverse members are examples of the differences and similarities between members that can cause them to clash during team interaction.

Culture also influences team processes associated with motivation. Collectivist samples in Israel were found to experience fewer performance losses when given a group goal compared to individualist samples that were told to do their best for the team (Erez & Somech, 1996). Earley (1989) found that the relationship between accountability and shared responsibility and performance in a team was moderated by collectivism. In particular, Earley (1999) found that individualist people performed worse when under conditions of shared responsibility and low personal accountability. In contrast, highly collectivistic people performed best under conditions of shared responsibility, regardless of the accountability.

Drawing upon foundational models of collective cognition theory (Gibson, 2001; Hinsz, Tindale, & Vollrath, 1997), cross-cultural research has elucidated how collective cognition can vary across cultures. For instance, Gibson and Zellmer-Bruhn (2001) found that metaphors about teamwork varied across four different nations. The divergent cognitive construal of teamwork across France, Puerto Rico, the Philippines, and the United States resulted in different expectations regarding team roles, membership, scope, and objectives. Likewise, the cognitive schemas for what constitutes a "successful" team can also vary across cultures. Sanchez-Burks, Nisbett, and Ybarra (2000) found that Mexicans perceived behaviors oriented toward interpersonal needs and harmony to be more important for success than Anglos, who perceived success to depend on the team's focus on the task. Taken together, these studies demonstrate that collective cognitions about work conducted in collectives can also vary across cultures.

Few scholars have addressed the special concerns that face multicultural teams (Gibson & McDaniel, 2010). However, working collaboratively in these culturally diverse teams can be quite a challenge. Differences in values, norms of behavior, cognitions about collaboration, and communication styles are frequent sources of irritation, conflict, and misunderstanding in teams composed of representatives from different nations (Brett, Behfar, & Kern, 2006). In fact, many multicultural teams can be characterized as having high levels of ethnocentrism (Cramton & Hinds, 2005) and task and/or emotional conflict (Elron, 1997; Von Glinow et al., 2004). Understanding how to leverage the cultural diversity within multicultural teams is critically important, especially considering the extent to which these teams are being leveraged within corporations across the globe. We explore these ideas in the following section.

Cultural differences within teams: multinational teams and cultural diversity salience

Within cultures, research has elucidated how collaboration within teams is shaped by largely similar cultural values, attitudes, norms, and cognitions. When individuals from different cultures come together to work within multicultural teams, both deep-level, subjective cultural differences and visible, surface-level features across cultures often hinder collaborative processes and outcomes. Drawing on social categorization and information-processing theories, we elaborate on how cultural differences that are both overt and concealed affect collaboration in multinational teams.

Multicultural teams can be leveraged to accomplish a broad variety of tasks, including execution, decision-making, and creativity tasks. Although individual team members may have the knowledge, skills, and ability to accomplish their shared goal, social processes can inhibit their ability to combine their collective resources and achieve their mission. When working in cross-cultural settings where objective components of cultural diversity are salient, anxiety and threat can arise and can narrow the focus of attention (Kahneman, 1973; Stephan & Stephan, 1985, 1996), restricting information processing (Staw, Sandelands, & Dutton, 1981). More recently, it has been argued that it is important to consider the salience of diversity when trying to understand the effect of diversity on team performance (van Knippenberg, DeDreu, & Homan, 2004). Along these lines, the salience of diversity in multinational teams is also likely to play a significant role in explaining the social identification and information processes that occur within these teams.

Various factors may influence when cultural differences become salient in multinational teams. Due to the overt nature of surface-level diversity, cultural diversity characteristics that are visible are more salient and activate social dynamics and information processing much sooner than deep-level characteristics. However, both time and the nature of the work may change the effects of diversity over time. For example, Pelled, Eisenhardt, and Xin (1999) found that the negative effects of surface-level diversity were weaker in teams with longer tenure. Extended tenure may lead group members to determine that their assumptions about holding similar attitudes and beliefs with like others may have been overestimated or underestimated. In addition, results from a study by Staples and Zhao (2006) suggest that reducing the salience of surface-level diversity in culturally diverse teams through virtual interaction can improve performance. This finding highlights the potential negative impact of cultural diversity salience on multicultural team processes and outcomes.

When a surface-level cultural characteristic is salient and individuals have this attribute in common, they are likely to assume that they hold more similar attitudes with one another compared to people who are different (e.g., Allen & Wilder, 1975, 1978, 1979; Chen & Kenrick, 2002; Holtz & Miller, 1985; Phillips, 2003; Tajfel, 1969; Wilder, 1984). The similarities and differences between team members can form the basis for categorizing oneself and others into in-groups and out-groups. From a social categorization perspective (Brewer & Brown, 1998), "we–they" distinctions are likely to arise in multicultural teams because people with the same cultural backgrounds tend to group together. However, the degree to which diverse groups experience subgroup categorization depends on the salience of these subgroups.

The salience of cultural diversity within a multinational team may not always trigger the same intensity of social categorization and social identity processes. The perceived social distance, or the degree to which two cultural groups are viewed to be similar or different, can vary (Triandis & Triandis, 1960). Determinants of perceived social distance include several factors such as in-group importance (Urban & Miller, 1998), personality (Liao, Chuang, & Joshi, 2008), or previous intergroup contact (Allport, 1954; Amir, 1969). In culturally diverse teams, history of war between nations, cultural orientation, and ethnocentrism (Triandis, 1992) may also predict social distance perceptions. These determinants are important to investigate because they can affect the magnitude of social distance perceptions, which could exacerbate subgroup tension, making the divide between cultural subgroups appear insurmountable. The degree to which diversity becomes salient and has an effect on team interaction processes and outcomes is likely to be determined by situational characteristics, including spatial arrangements, task requirements, and reward structure (Van der Vegt & Van de Vliert, 2005).

In contrast to the social categorization and social identity perspective, the information processing perspective emphasizes that the diversity of the team can enhance the elaboration of information and perspectives of the group to improve task performance (van Knippenberg, DeDreu, & Homan, 2004). Information-diverse teams are likely to possess a breadth and depth of task–relevant knowledge, skills, abilities, and perspectives that may be brought to bear on a task involving decision making, problem solving, or creativity. Research suggests that error detection (Davis, 1969), brainstorming (Paulus & Nijstad, 2003), and overall higher performance (Bantel & Jackson, 1989) tend to be associated with greater information diversity in teams. In culturally diverse teams working on problems related to the global marketplace, deep-level cultural knowledge, attitudes, and perspectives may be particularly relevant and useful to the functioning and performance of multinational teams.

Deep-level cultural components, such as values, norms, and cognitions, may alter social categorization and information processes in teams, and further investigation of these influences in multicultural teams is needed. For example, individualist societies are characterized by having a loose social framework where individuals are more likely to take care of themselves and their immediate families (Hofstede, 1980). Collectivist societies, on the other hand, can be described as having tight social frameworks where the distinction between in-groups and out-groups is quite clear and people expect that in-group members will take care of them and be loyal to one another (Hofstede, 1980). Research provides evidence that social categorization processes will likely be stronger in collectivist societies (Kirkman & Shapiro, 2001), suggesting that efforts to inhibit in-group favoritism and out-group derogation will be much more challenging in multicultural teams composed of both collectivists and individualists because of their different approaches to this collective interaction.

Social norms, cognitions, and values about various aspects of collaboration can vary across cultures (Gibson & Zellmer-Bruhn, 2001; Sanchez-Burks et al., 2000; Shteynberg, Gelfand, & Kim, 2009). These cultural differences can be exacerbated in situations of high ambiguity (Morris et al., 2008), such as working with dissimilar others in a multicultural team. Uncertainty, which can arise when in unfamiliar social environments, can lead individuals to be more likely to identify with groups (e.g., cultural groups) and to conform to group norms (Kruglanski, Pierro, Mannetti, & De Grada, 2006). In multicultural teams, team members may be more likely to engage in ways that are normative within their own cultures, yet discordant with others. For instance, ethnic groups in the United States have been found to use different conflict styles (Toomey, Yee-Jung, Shapiro, Garcia, Wright, & Oetzel, 2000).

For instance, Latino-Americans and Asian-Americans were found to use more avoiding and third-party conflict styles than African-Americans. When working together, culturally diverse team members may approach conflict in discordant ways, which may have a negative impact on the quality of team processes and outcomes.

It is also critical to investigate what types of diversity may facilitate these processes within multicultural teams. Research suggests that the diversity will affect social processes and outcomes only to the extent to which the diversity is meaningful to the parties involved (van Knippenberg & Schippers, 2007). In multicultural teams, many characteristics of cultural diversity among members may be present, such as ethnicity, language, and race. It is difficult to know which characteristics of diversity will shape group dynamics, especially given that some cultural diversity characteristics may have greater importance in some cultures than others, such as religion or age. Social judgments that vary cross-culturally, and that may influence how cultural differences are perceived and valued, are critically important to consider when studying the effects of social processing in culturally diverse teams.

One factor believed to shape the subjective perceptions of and reactions to particular cultural diversity characteristics within a multinational team is cultural intelligence. Earley and Ang (2003) identified the cultural intelligence factors that increase an individual's ability to effectively deal with cultural diversity from a sample of 51 individuals across six teams. These cultural intelligence factors were found to be associated with the integration of members into multinational teams (Flaherty, 2008). Other studies demonstrating the effects of personality and cognitive factors, such as openness to diversity and need for closure, also underscore the importance of examining the moderators that can explain the positive and negative effects of diversity on performance (Kearney, Gebert, & Voelpel, 2009; Homan, Hellenbeck, Humphrey, van Knippenberg, Ilgen, & van Kleef, 2008). Further research examining the moderators of the effect of cultural diversity on team performance is also essential for understanding how the impact of cultural diversity will affect team processes based on team members' diversity attitudes and personalities.

Contextualizing cultural diversity

The broader organizational context can shape the effect of diversity on behavior (Jackson, Joshi, & Erhart, 2003). Cultural diversity in teams may be more or less salient given the broader context in which work is conducted. One feature of the proximal environment that can affect collaboration in a culturally diverse team is its task. The team task is defined in terms of the nature of work performed by the team and can be characterized by a variety of different features, including the task type, task interdependency, and task complexity (McGrath, 1984). A complex task is one in which high cognitive demands are placed on the individuals completing a task (Campbell, 1988, p. 43; Jehn, 1995; Kankanhalli et al., 2006). The ability of a team to complete a complex task is further challenged by external stressors, such as time pressure or stressful work conditions. On the one hand, stress may activate cultural identities, facilitating in-group bias, and thus making it difficult for culturally diverse teams to work together. On the other hand, facing a stressful situation together might heighten a superordinate identity, facilitating effective collaboration. Drawing on pro-diversity attitude research, it may also be the case that a team climate that values diversity may further stimulate the integration of the members' heterogeneous information, viewpoints, and perspectives (Chen & Eastman, 1997; Ely & Thomas, 2001; van Knippenberg & Haslam, 2003) in culturally diverse teams. Furthermore, inclusive leaders can also shape the task environment by enhancing social harmony and reducing turnover in diverse teams (Nishii & Mayer, 2009). This research suggests that various characteristics of the proximal task environment can influence the performance of culturally diverse teams.

If a multicultural team is collaborating within an organization where diversity is characteristic of the broader workforce, interaction with people who differ along a variety of dimensions will be more frequent. The perceptions of differences may become less salient to individuals in these diverse work environments who become accustomed to interacting with diverse others compared to people who work in more culturally homogeneous organizations. Consequently, studies of multicultural teams must take into account not only factors internal to the team that might affect diversity salience, but the broader contextual environment as well.

Multicultural teams are often embedded in a broader world context. Studies show how the composition of the organization in which teams are embedded can reflect and reinforce power and status based on demographics (Pfeffer, 1983). Along these lines, international relations between countries may also influence social dynamics within teams where representatives from these nations are working together. For example, individuals from nations with greater power, resources, and stability may have greater external social capital to leverage. From a network perspective, this external social capital may provide a means to garner resources from groups, such as nationally based organizations, outside of the team to benefit team effectiveness (Ancona & Caldwell, 1992).

In multicultural teams, where cultural values, norms, and cognitions vary among team members, leaders may have the potential to shape team functioning and performance. Recent research by Klein, Knight, Ziegert, Lim, and Saltz (2011) demonstrates how leaders attenuated the effect of value diversity on team conflict when they engaged in task-focused leadership compared to person-focused leadership. Drawing on social identity theory (Brown, 2000; Tajfel, 1972; Hewstone, Rubin & Willis, 2002), team leaders may also be able to harness the benefits of cultural diversity in teams by shaping contextual conditions to make both superordinate (e.g., we are all on one team, we are all citizens of the same world) and subgroup (e.g., ethnic or national groups) identities salient. In doing so, members' need for distinctiveness will be satisfied (Brewer, 1991; 1993) and in-group favoritism will not be limited to those members contained within subgroup boundaries, but rather will be extended to out-group members from other cultural groups as well. We encourage future research to further explore how leaders may enable multicultural teams to leverage the virtues of their diversity to improve functioning and performance.

The association with a high- or low-status nation can also affect interaction. Drawing on social dominance theory, people with a higher social dominance orientation are likely to support and seek to maintain the hierarchical relationship between groups. Evidence suggests that racism and attitudes towards race-conscious policies are associated with people who have a greater social dominance orientation (Haley & Sidanus, 2006). In a team composed of individuals with high- and low-status cultural and country identities, it is important to examine how this orientation may trigger power and status dynamics between members affecting team processes and outcomes. Readers interested in the intersection of culture, status, and power should also see Chapter 9, which discusses these topics at length.

It is also critically important to take into account the role of social status and dominance when considering the effects of cultural subgroups on the outcomes of multicultural teams. Status is attributed to particular characteristics and associations (age, gender, education level). These status attributes are shaped by the broader sociocultural context and the meaning associated with or given to these characteristics. For instance, in the real world, groups often hold either majority or minority positions vis-à-vis each other (Farley, 1982; Tajfel, 1981). Across nations and within different cultures, particular parties enjoy higher status than others, and this can lead to variation in the ways that people from different societies may confer status. Earley (1999) found evidence of this variation in status hierarchies across societies when he asked managers from different countries to list the characteristics that would define someone of status within their country. This finding underlies the point that attributes of diversity will be perceived and interpreted differently across culturally diverse team members given their cultural backgrounds and the meaning attributed to various demographic characteristics.

Although cultural diversity can be composed of characteristics that are both objective and subjective, a considerable amount of research on the effects of diversity at the individual and team level has focused on cultural values, with a particular focus on the individualism and collectivist dimensions (Kirkman, Lowe & Gibson, 2006). Research on cultural values has demonstrated that it is valuable and important to examine each cultural value separately (see reviews of work in Gelfand, Erez, & Aycan, 2007; Kirkman, Lowe & Gibson, 2006; ; Tsui, Nifadkar, & Ou, 2007). Research that extends beyond the use of a single measure of deep-level culture is needed, as well as the consideration of other sociocontextual factors. In the following section, we discuss these issues in more depth and provide ideas about how research on cultural diversity can be advanced.

Key frontiers of cultural diversity research

The goal of this chapter was to provide a snapshot view of the trends, advances, and methodologic developments in the study of cultural diversity over the years. It is clear from this review that the study of cultural differences has been done at the individual and team level of analysis and is increasingly capturing the complexities and adaptable nature of culture. The overview of research also illustrates that cultural diversity research has focused primarily on comparative country analysis and that research on cultural diversity in multicultural teams is much more scarce. In the section that follows, our aim is to provide a summary of the areas and key themes that were discussed above and that may be fruitful for future research focused on cultural diversity.

Reviews of workplace diversity suggest that research has largely originated from the United States, using mostly North American samples (Tsui, Nifadkar, & Ou, 2007). Could the effects of different types of diversity of individual and team behaviors be biased by a reliance on a narrow, largely American sample? Might diversity types be perceived and responded to differently across societies with different social histories, economic structures, and political regimes? Cross-cultural studies examining the effects of diversity on key organizational behavioral outcomes, using both objective and subjective measures of diversity and perceived social distance, would provide a great deal of insight and narrow this research gap. Although great strides have been made over the years to resolve this dilemma, much of the literature on diversity has been primarily concerned with contemporary American society (Wise & Tschirhardt, 2000). Important questions about the effects of cultural diversity in teams remain to be explored and answered, especially given that some research on the effects of diversity conducted in the United States could not be replicated in other societies (Wiersema & Bird, 1993).

Researchers of organizational diversity have increasingly begun to examine context as a potential moderator of diversity effects (Joshi & Roh, 2009). A recent meta-analysis revealed the importance of considering the moderating effect of context on the relationship between diversity and a variety of performance outcomes, and further information about the effect of context can be found in Chapter 12 (Joshi & Roh, 2009). It is also desirable to consider some aspects of the contextual environment that may alter the effects of cultural diversity on key outcomes. Specifically, contextual features such as the composition of diversity within the social system where the unit of focus is embedded, the climate, the task environment, temporal conditions, and task characteristics may be important to examine as moderators in future research. Exploring this line of inquiry opens up interesting and unanswered questions, such as "What is the effect of perceptions of democracy on explaining cultural diversity in teams?" and "How might fatalism or psychological experiences tied to experiences of war or severe poverty shape interaction within multicultural teams?"

We speculate that certain dimensions of diversity will affect processes and outcomes differently depending on the broader national cultural context. This, in turn, may expand diversity research that has been conducted from a largely Western perspective. For example, status diversity might have different implications in high- versus low-power-distance cultures, and this question merits further investigation. Earlier in this chapter we also discussed the idea that discordant identities are problematic, but we encourage researchers to investigate whether this might be the case across all national contexts. Further motivating this question is research that suggests that individuals from societies that are more collectivistic and holistic might not be affected by this internal conflict due to their high tolerance for contradiction (Nisbett et al., 2001). Additional research is needed to explore this and other links that consider the relationship between national culture and diversity dynamics on individual, team, and organizational outcomes. Doing so creates the opportunity for discovering a new theoretical territory and advances our understanding about the contextual conditions under which diversity affects important processes and outcomes.

Studies of cultural diversity tend to be limited to a single level of analysis in their research design. If we draw from the view that cultures are nested or embedded (Erez & Gati, 2004), it is critical to consider the effects of cultural diversity across many different levels of analysis. Almost all multicultural interactions will possess features and aspects that cross the levels of analysis between individuals, work groups, organizations, and nations. Understanding the effects of cultural diversity at one level of analysis may be incomplete if characteristics of other levels of analysis are not taken into consideration (Kozlowski & Klein, 2000). For example, how might cultural diversity within an organization shape interaction processes and outcomes for individuals and teams nested within this organization? Furthermore, it would be particularly valuable to study whether the relationships between cultural diversity and outcomes at one level of analysis can be generalized to other levels of analysis. This multilevel approach would be useful for identifying the boundary conditions under which particular theoretical perspectives will be most predictive when examining the effects of cultural diversity.

In addition, national origin is often used as a proxy for the cultural values in cross-cultural research (Tsui, Nifadkar, & Ou, 2007). This approach can be problematic because national and deep-level culture do not completely overlap (Au, 1997). For this reason, it is important to better understand the psychological dimensions that demographic or proxy differences are associated with, if applicable (Beyer et al., 1997; Chattopadhyay et al., 1999; Cox et al., 1991). For example, variation in math performance on aptitude tests between boys and girls may not be directly caused by gender differences, but rather by the gender socialization practices employed by people in their surroundings that may expose them to different experiences and education, which ultimately affects performance outcomes (Eccles & Jacobs, 1986). Different socialization experiences among people who lived before or after World War II have also been shown to predict distinct values and attitudes about work among these groups (Fertig & Schmidt, 2001; Smola & Sutton, 2002). Given that societies change over time due to world events and modernization, relying on characterizations of national culture that were drawn from research conducted decades ago may be problematic and not generalizable today.

Much of the research done within cross-cultural teams is also focused on only one characteristic of diversity at a time, such as nationality. One downside of this approach is that we cannot explain how a combination of cultural characteristics influences teams simultaneously. To date, little research has investigated the interaction effects of cultural variables. The rarity of the interaction effects of culture is particularly striking given that there are no compelling theoretical reasons to suspect that cultural values operate independently to influence outcomes. One notable exception is the interest in conceptualizing collectivism and individualism in combination with other cultural variables, such as orientations to power (Chen et al, 1997; Singelis, Triandis, Bhawuk, & Gelfand, 1995). Research that conceptualizes the effects of cultural variables in combination with one another on team outcomes is both warranted and welcomed.

Recent advances in research suggest that nations differ in many aspects beyond cultural values, suggesting that differences in processes and outcomes in cross-cultural studies could stem from other sociocultural and situational factors (Busenitz, Gomez, & Spencer, 2000; Erez & Earley, 1993). We encourage scholars interested in understanding the effects of cultural diversity to broaden their studies to include aspects of the historical, political, social, geographic, and economic context of nations in order to identify how these factors affect perceptions and reactions to objective and subjective dimensions of diversity. Examining the effects of diversity across a variety of social situations will also provide insight about the conditions under which cultural variation in responses to diversity affect outcomes. For instance, what psychological factors may be driving the main effects of cultural differences identified in studies of rural location and climate? How might psychological factors and past societal history explain differences associated with ethnicity and race across different societies and the way that these differences are perceived and responded to?

Measurement of cultural diversity in teams may benefit from recent advances in that examines multiple dimensions of diversity in combination through the use of composite measures. Research on the diversity of organizations often relies on faultline measures that analyze the effects of many characteristics of diversity in combination with rather than in isolation from each other (Lau & Murnighan, 1998). Creating cultural profiles for each individual in a team based on demographic characteristics, as well as culturally relevant knowledge, values, and beliefs, would provide an opportunity to assess the alignment of multiple attributes of cultural diversity among team members. The outcome of using this method may be a better understanding of the complex relationship between diversity and performance in multicultural teams. Readers interested in this approach should also read Chapter 4 in this book.

Studies comparing teams across cultures also tend to use the mean score on cultural values scales, and this metric is considered to be a shared property of the group. Considering the within-country variation of cultural values that has been identified by cross-cultural scholars, it may be valuable to recognize the cultural differences among team members even when they share a common nationality. Recent advances in the measurement of diversity in organizations suggest the theoretical and empirical importance of examining difference as variation, separation, and disparity (Harrison & Klein, 2007). Drawing on this perspective, conceptualizations and assessments of cultural diversity must be updated to advance our empirical investigation of culturally diverse teams from the same nation or different nations.

Just as cultural differences among people within nations have been identified, the structure of cultural diversity within individuals and teams has also been conceptualized in more complex ways over recent years (Chao & Moon, 2005). The cultural profiles of individuals have attributes that reflect both objective and subjective aspects of their cultural backgrounds. When interacting with culturally diverse others, efforts to capture the interaction of this cultural diversity within and among individuals is particularly scarce. In sum, most research continues to focus on one particular type of diversity, such as nationality or collectivism and individualism, rather than using a multidimensional approach to assessing cultural diversity. Faultline theory, latent cluster analysis, and social network theory all provide new ideas about how to capture the multidimensionality of cultural diversity. To address the reliance on a unidimensional assessment of culture, research on cultural diversity at the various levels of analysis would benefit from the use of these methodologic tools.

This chapter aimed to motivate scholars to hypothesize about how various types and configurations of cultural diversity trigger and shape individual and team processes and outcomes. We posit that the social categorization and information processing at the individual and team level are mediated by psychological mechanisms, including cultural diversity and cultural identity salience, that are facilitated from the context and the cultural diversity inputs. We encourage researchers to draw on complex methodologic approaches to consider and test how and when various aspects of the contextual environment, such as social, physical, and political features, affect the relationship between cultural diversity and behavior at the individual and team level.

Much of this chapter has focused on the challenges that can arise in teams composed of culturally diverse individuals. However, we also encourage research that elucidates the factors that enable multicultural teams to leverage the benefits of their diversity. In particular, we hope that cultural researchers will engage in research aligned with the field of positive psychology, which is focused on studying the "conditions and processes that contribute to the flourishing or optimal flourishing or people, groups, and institutions" (Gable & Haidt, 2005, p. 104). For instance, multicultural teams have the potential to far surpass culturally homogeneous teams in their ability to prevent, detect, and manage errors because of their cultural diversity (Gelfand, Frese, & Salmon, 2011). Also, Mauro, Pierro, Mannetti, Higgins, and Kruglanski (2009) compared the performance of three groups composed of locomotors (individuals oriented toward action), assessors (individuals oriented toward evaluation) or both locomotors and assessors. These researchers found that groups containing a mix of locomotors and assessors were as fast and accurate as the teams composed only of locomotors or assessors. This finding motivates future studies that explore how the cultural diversity of team members within multicultural teams may generate outcomes that could counter the negative consequences of diversity to achieve outcomes that could not be attained by unicultural teams.

Conclusion

The focus on culture as values, beliefs, and attitudes has resulted in advancing our understanding of the perspectives, orientations, and assumptions that shape behavior across cultures. Although the values approach to understanding culture has made quite a contribution to cross-cultural research across nations, little attention has been paid to the factors that shape values and the relationship between multiple sources of values that coexist within a person or social unit. The variety of cultural values that coexist within an individual presents an opportunity to examine the conditions under which particular cultural values are invoked and shape cognition, affect, and behavior either individually or in combination with one another. Moreover, when several individuals, each with a multiplicity of cultural influences, or values, interact within a team, it is critically important to better understand the implications of cultural diversity structure and salience on individual and team outcomes.

Disclaimer

This work was partially supported by funding from the Army Research Office MURI Grant to Dr. Michele Gelfand, Principal Investigator, UMD (W911NF-08-1-014), subcontracted to UCF (Z885903). The views expressed in this work are those of the authors and do not necessarily reflect the organizations with which they are affiliated, their sponsoring institutions or agencies, or their grant partners.

References

Adarves-Yorno, I., Postmes, T., & Haslam, A. (2006). Social identity and the recognition of creativity in groups. *British Journal of Social Psychology, 45*(3), 479–497.

Allen, V. L., & Wilder, D. (1975). Categorization, belief similarity, and intergroup discrimination. *Journal of Personality and Social Psychology, 32,* 971–977.

Allen, V. L., & Wilder, D. (1979). Group categorization and attribution of belief similarity. *Small Group Behavior, 10,* 73–80.

Allen, V. L., & Wilder, D. (1978). Perceived persuasiveness as a function of response style: Multi-issue consistency over time. *European Journal of Social Psychology, 8,* 298–296.

Allport, G. W. (1954). *The Nature of Prejudice*. Cambridge, MA: Addison-Wesley.

Amir, Y. (1969). Contact Hypothesis in Ethnic Relations, *Psychological Bulletin, 71,* 319–342.

Ancona, D. G., & Caldwell, D. F. (1992). Bridging the boundary: External activity and performance in organizational teams. *Administrative Science Quarterly, 12,* 634–665.

Arnett, J. J. (2002). The psychology of globalization. *American Psychologist, 57,* 774–783.

Au, K. (1997). Another consequence of culture-intra-cultural variation. *International Journal of Human Resource Management, 8*(5), 743–755.

Ayoko, O., Härtel, C., & Callan, V. (2002). Resolving the puzzle of productive and destructive conflict in culturally heterogeneous workgroups: A communication accommodation theory approach. *International Journal of Conflict Management, 13*(2), 165–195.

Bantel, K., & Jackson, S. (1989). Top management and innovations in banking: Does the composition of the top team make a difference? *Strategic Management Journal, 10,* 107–124.

Bem, S. L. (1993). *The lenses of gender: Transforming the debate on sexual inequality.* New Haven, CT: Yale University Press.

Berry, J. W. (1966). Temne Eskimo perceptual skills. *International Journal of Psychology. 1,* 207–229.

Beyer, J. M., Chattopadhyay, P., George, E., Glick, W. H., Ogilvie, D. T., & Pugliese, D. (1997). The selective perception of managers revisited. *Academy of Management Journal, 40,* 716–737.

Brett, J., Behfar, K., & Kern, M., (2006). Managing multicultural teams. *Harvard Business Review.* November, pp. 84–91.

Brewer, M. B. (1993). Social identity, distinctiveness, and in-group homogeneity. *Social Cognition, 11*(1), 150–164.

Brewer, M. B., & Brown, R. J. (1998). Intergroup relations. In D. T. Gilbert & S. T. Fiske, eds. *Handbook of Social Psychology* (pp. 554–594). Boston: McGraw-Hill.

Brewer, M. B. (2003). Optimal distinctiveness, social identity, and the self. *Handbook of Self and Identity, 4,* 480–491.

Briley, D., Morris, M., & Simonson, I. (2000). Reasons as carriers of culture: dynamic vs. dispositional models of cultural influence on decision making. *Journal of Consumer Research, 27*(2), 157–178.

Brockner, J., Ackerman, G., Greenberg, J., Gelfand, M. J., Francesco, A. M., Chen, Z. X., & Kirkman, B. L. (2001). Culture and procedural justice: The influence of power distance on reactions to voice. *Journal of Experimental Social Psychology, 37*(4), 300–315.

Brown, R. (2000). Social identity theory: Past achievements, current problems and future challenges. *European Journal of Social Psychology, 30*(6), 745–778.

Bueno de Mesquita, B., & Siverson, R. (1995). War and the survival of political leaders: a comparative study of regime types and political accountability. *American Political Science Review, 89,* 841–855

Busenitz, L. W., Gomez, C., & Spencer, J. W. (2000). Country institutional profiles: Unlocking entrepreneurial phenomena. *Academy of Management Journal, 43,* 994–1003.

Byrne, D. (1971). *The attraction paradigm.* New York: Academic.

Campbell, D. J. (1988). Task complexity: A review and analysis. *Academy of Management Review, 13*(1), 40–52.

Chao, G. T., & Moon H. (2005). The cultural mosaic: a metatheory for understanding the complexity of culture. *Journal of Applied Psychology, 90,* 1128–1140.

Chattopadhyay, P., Glick, W. H., Miller, C. C., & Huber, G. P. (1999). Determinants of executive beliefs: comparing functional conditioning and social influence. *Strategic Management Journal, 20,* 763–789.

Chen, C. C., & Eastman, W. (1997). Toward a civic culture for multicultural organizations. *Journal of Applied Behavioral Science, 333,* 454–470.

Chen, C. C., Meindl, J. R., & Hunt, R. G. (1997). Testing the effects of horizontal and vertical collectivism: A study of rewards allocation preferences in China. *Journal of Cross-Cultural Psychology, 28,* 23–43.

Chen, F., & Kenrick, D. T. (2002). Repulsion or attraction? Group membership and assumed attitude similarity. *Journal of Personality and Social Psychology, 83,* 111–125.

Chiu, C., Gelfand, M., Yamagishi, T., Shteynberg, G., & Wan, C. Intersubjective culture: the role of intersubjective perceptions in cross-cultural research. *Perspectives on Psychological Science, 5,* 482–493.

Chiu, C., Morris, M. W., Hong, Y., & Menon, T. (2000). Motivated cultural cognition: The impact of implicit cultural theories on dispositional attribution varies as a function of need for closure. *Journal of Personality and Social Psychology, 78,* 247–259.

Cialdini, R. B., & Trost, M. R. (1998). Social influence: Social norms, conformity, and compliance. In D. Gilbert, S. Fiske, & G. Lindzey (Eds.) *The handbook of social psychology* (4th ed., vol. 2, pp. 151–192). New York: McGraw-Hill.

Corney, W. J., & Richards, C. H. (2005). A comparative analysis of the desirability of work characteristics: Chile versus the United States. *International Journal of Management, 22,* 159–165.

Cox, T., Lobel, S., & McLeod, P. (1991). Effects of ethnic group cultural differences on cooperative and competitive behavior on a group task. *Academy of Management Journal, 34,* 827–847.

Cramton, C., & Hinds, P. (2005). Subgroup dynamics in internationally distributed teams: Ethnocentrism or cross-national learning? *Research in Organizational Behavior, 26,* 231–263.

D'Andrade, R. G. (2001). A cognitivist's view of the units debate in cultural anthropology. *Cross-Cultural Research, 352,* 242–257.

Davis, K. C. (1969). *Discretionary justice: A preliminary inquiry.* CA, LA: Louisiana State University Press.

Deaux, K. (1996). Social identification. In E. T. Higgins & A. W. Kruglanski (Eds.), *Social psychology: Handbook of basic principles* (pp.42–47). New York: Guilford.

De Cremer, D., & Van Hiel, A. (2008). Procedural justice effects on self-esteem under certainty versus uncertainty emotions. *Motivation & Emotion, 32*(4), 278–287.

Durkheim, E. (1985). The rules of sociological method. In K. Thompson (Ed. and trans.), *Readings from Emile Durkheim.* Chichester: E. Horwood; London; New York: Tavistock.

Earley, P. C. (1989). Social loafing and collectivism: A comparison of the United States and the People's Republic of China. *Administrative Science Quarterly, 34,* 565–581.

Earley, P. C. (1999). Playing follow the leader: Status-determining traits in relation to collective efficacy across cultures. *Organizational Behavior and Human Decision Processes, 80,* 192–212.

Earley, P. C., & Ang, S. (2003). *Cultural intelligence: Individual interactions across cultures* Stanford business books. Stanford, CA: Stanford University Press.

Earley, P. C., & Mosakowski, E. (2000). Creating hybrid team cultures: an empirical test of transnational team functioning. *Academy of Management Journal, 43*(1), 26–49.

Eccles, J. S., & Jacobs, J. E. (1986). Social forces shape math attitudes and performance signs. *Journal of Women in Culture and Society, 11*(21), 367–380.

Elron, E. (1997). Top management teams within multinational corporations: Effects of cultural heterogeneity. *Leadership Quarterly, 8*(4), 393–412.

Ely, R. J., & Thomas, D. A. (2001). Cultural diversity at work: the effects of diversity perspectives on work group processes and outcomes. *Administrative Science Quarterly, 46*, 229–273.

Enz, C. (1988). The role of value congruity in intraorganizational power. *Administrative Science Quarterly, 33*(2), 284–304.

Erez, M., & Earley, P. C. (1993). *Culture, self-identify, and work.* New York: Oxford University Press.

Erez, M., & Gati, E. (2004). A dynamic, multi-level model of culture: from the micro level of the individual to the macro level of a global culture, *Applied Psychology: An International Review, 53*(4), 583–598.

Erez, M., & Somech, A. (1996). Is group productivity loss the rule or the exception? Effects of culture and group-based motivation. *Academy of Management Journal, 39*(6), 1513–1537.

Farley, F. H. (1982). The future of educational research. *Educational Researcher, 11*(8), 11–19.

Feather, N. T. (1996). Values, deservingness, and attitudes toward high achievers: Research on tall poppies. In C. Seligman, J. M. Olson, & M. P. Zanna (Eds.), *The Ontario symposium: The psychology of values* (pp. 215–251). Mahwah, NJ: Erlbaum.

Feather, N. T. (1994). Values and national identification: Australian evidence. *Australian Journal of Psychology, 46*, 35–40.

Fernando, S. (1991). *Mental health, race and culture.* London: Macmillan.

Fertig, M., & Schmidt, C. (2001). First-and second-generation migrants in Germany-what do we know and what do people think? *IZA Discussion Paper Series, 286*, 1–48.

Festinger, L., & Carlsmith, J. M. (1959). Cognitive consequences of forced compliance. *Journal of Abnormal and Social Psychology, 58*, 203–210.

Flaherty, J. E. (2008). The effects of cultural intelligence on team member acceptance and integration in multinational teams. *Handbook of Cultural Intelligence: Theory, Measurement, and Applications, 12*, 192–205.

Fu, H., Morris M., Lee, S., Chao, M., Chiu, C., & Hong, Y. (2007). Epistemic motives and cultural conformity: Need for closure, culture, and context as determinants of conflict judgments. *Journal of Personality and Social Psychology, 9*, 191–207.

Gable, S., & Haidt, J. (2005). What (and why) is positive psychology? *Review of General Psychology, 9*(2), 103–110.

Gelfand, M., Erez, M., & Aycan, Z. (2007). Cross-cultural organizational behavior. *Annual Review of Psychology, 58*, 476–514.

Gelfand, M., Frese, M., & Salmon, E. (2011) Cultural influences on error: prevention, detection & management. In D. Hofmann & M. Frese (Eds.), *Errors in organizations.* San Francisco: Jossey-Bass, Society for Industrial and Organizational Psychology (SIOP) Frontiers Series.

Gelfand, M. J., & Dyer, N. (2000). A cultural perspective on negotiation: progress, pitfalls, and prospects. *Journal of Applied Psychology, 49*, 62–99.

Gelfand, M. J., Nishii, L. H., & Raver, J. L. (2006). On the nature and importance of cultural tightness-looseness. *Journal of Applied Psychology, 91*, 1225–1244.

Gelfand, M. J., & Realo, A. (1999). Individualism-collectivism and accountability in intergroup negotiations. *Journal of Applied Psychology, 84*, 721–736.

Gibson, C. B. (2001). From accumulation to accommodation: The chemistry of collective cognition in work groups. *Journal of Organizational Behavior, 22*, 121–134.

Gibson, C. B., & McDaniel, D. (2010). Moving beyond conventional wisdom: advancements in cross-cultural theories of leadership, conflict & teams. *Perspectives on Psychological Science, 5*(4), 450–462.

Gibson, C. B., & Zellmer-Bruhn, M. E. (2001). Metaphors and meaning: An intercultural analysis of teamwork. *Administrative Science Quarterly, 46*, 274–303.

Guzzo, R. A., & Dickson, M. W. (1996). Teams in organizations: recent research on performance and effectiveness. *Annual Review of Psychology, 47*, 307–338.

Haley, H., & Sidanius, J. (2006). The positive and negative framing of affirmative action: a group dominance perspective. *Personality and Social Psychology Bulletin, 32*, 656–668.

Hall, E. T. (1976). *Beyond culture.* New York: Doubleday.

Harrison, D. A., Price, K. H., & Bell, M. P. (1998). Beyond relational demography: time and the effects of surface- and deep-level diversity on work group cohesion. *Academy Management Journal, 41*, 96–107.

Harrison, D. A., & Klein, K. J. (2007). What's the difference? diversity constructs as separation, variety, or disparity in organizations. *The Academy of Management Review Archive, 32*(4), 1199–1228.

Herskovits, M. J. (1955). *Cultural anthropology.* New York: Knopf.

Hewstone, M., Rubin, M., & Willis, H. (2002). Intergroup bias. *Annual Review of Psychology, 53*(1), 575–604.

Hinsz, V. B., Tindale, R. S., & Vollrath, D. A. (1997). The emerging conception of groups as information processors. *Psychological Bulletin, 121*, 43–64.

Hofstede, G. (1980). *Culture's consequences.* Beverly Hills, CA: Sage.

Hofstede, G. (1991). *Culture and organizations: Software of the mind.* New York: McGraw-Hill.

Hofstede, G., & Hofstede, G. J. (2005). *Cultures and organizations. Software of the mind* (2nd ed.). New York: McGraw-Hill.

Hogg, M. A., & Abrams, D. (1988). *Social identifications: A social psychology of intergroup relations and group processes.* London, United Kingdom: Routledge.

Holtz, R., & Miller, N. (1985). Assumed similarity and opinion certainty. *Journal of Personality and Social Psychology, 48*, 890–898.

Homan, A. C., Hollenbeck, J. R., Humphrey, S. E., Van Knippenberg, D., Ilgen, D. R., & van Kleef, G. A. (2008). Facing differences with an open mind: Openness to experience, salience of intragroup differences, and performance of diverse work groups. *The Academy of Management Journal Archive, 51*(6), 1204–1222.

Hong, Y., Morris, M. W., Chiu, C., & Benet-Martinez, V. (2000). Multicultural minds: A dynamic constructivist approach to culture and cognition. *American Psychologist, 55,* 709–720.

Jackson, S. E. (1992). Team composition in organizational settings: issues in managing an increasingly diverse work force. In S. Worchel, W. Wood, & J. A. Simpson (Eds.), *Group process and productivity* (pp. 136–180). Newbury Park, CA: Sage.

Jackson, S. E., Joshi, A., & Erhardt, N. L. (2003). Recent research on team and organizational diversity: SWOT analysis and implications. *Journal of Management, 29*, 801–830.

Jehn, K. A. (1995). A multimethod examination of the benefits and detriments of intragroup conflict. *Administrative Science Quarterly, 40,* 256–282.

Jetten, J., Postmes, T., & McAuliffe, B. J. (2002). "We're all individuals": Group norms of individualism and collectivism, levels of identification and identity threat. *European Journal of Social Psychology, 32,* 189–207.

Joshi, A., & Roh, H. (2009). The role of context in work team diversity research: A meta-analytic review. *The Academy of Management Journal Archive, 52*(3), 599–627.

Kahneman, D. (1973). *Attention and effort.* Englewood Cliffs, NJ: Prentice-Hall.

Kankanhalli, A., Tan, B. C. Y., & Wei, K. (2006). Conflict and performance in global virtual teams. *Journal of Management Information Systems, 23,* 237–274.

Kashima, Y., Kashima, E. S., Chiu, C.-Y., et al. (2005). Culture, essentialism, and agency: Are individuals universally believed to be more entities than groups? *European Journal of Social Psychology, 35,* 147–169.

Kearney, E., Gebert, D., & Voelpel, S. C. (2009). When and how diversity benefits teams: The importance of team members' need for cognition. *The Academy of Management Journal Archive, 52*(3), 581–598.

King, R. C., & Bu, N. (2005). Perceptions of the mutual obligations between employees and employers: a comparative study of new generation IT professionals in China and the United States. *International Journal of Human Resource Management, 16,* 46–64.

Kirkman, B. L., Lowe, K. B., & Gibson, C. B. (2006). A quarter century of culture's consequences: A review of empirical research incorporating hofstede's cultural values framework. *Journal of International Business Studies, 37*(3), 285–320.

Kitayama, S., Markus, H. R., Matsumoto, H., & Norasakkunkit, V. (1997). Individual and collective processes in the construction of the self: Self-enhancement in the United States and self-criticism in Japan. *Journal of Personality and Social Psychology, 72,* 1245–1267.

Klein, K., Knight, A., Ziegert, J. Lim, B. C., & Saltz, J. (2011). When team members' values differ: The moderating role of team leadership. *Organizational Behavior and Human Decision Processes, 114,* 25–36.

Kluckhohn, F., & Strodtbeck, F. L. (1961). *Variations in value orientations.* Evanston, IL: Row Peterson.

Kluckhold, C. (1951). Values and value orientations in the theory of action. In T. Parsons & E. A. Shils (Eds.), *Toward a general theory of action* (pp. 1–23). Cambridge: Harvard University Press.

Kozlowski, S. W. J., & Klein, K. J. (2000). *A multilevel approach to theory and research in organizations: Contextual, temporal, and emergent processes.* San Francisco, CA: Jossey-Bass.

Kruglanski, A. W., Pierro, A., Manetti, L. & DeGrada, E. (2006). Groups as epistemic providers: Need for closure and the unfolding of group centrism. *Psychological Review, 113,* 84–100.

Lau, D. C., & Murnighan, J. K. (1998). Demographic diversity and faultlines: The compositional dynamics of organizational groups. *Academy of Management Review, 23,* 325–340.

Liao, H., Chuang, A., & Joshi, A. (2008). Perceived deep-level dissimilarity: Personality antecedents and impact on overall job attitude, helping, work withdrawal, and turnover. *Organizational Behavior and Human Decision Processes, 106,* 106–124.

Little, K. (1968). Cultural variations in social schemata. *Journal of Personality and Social Psychology, 10*(1), 1–7.

Mael, F., & Ashforth, B. (1992). Alumni and their alma mater: A partial test of the reformulated model of organizational identification. *Journal of Organizational Behavior, 13,* 103–123.

Martin, J., & Siehl (1983). Organizational culture and counterculture: An uneasy symbiosis. *Organizational Dynamics, 122,* 52–65.

Mauro, R., Pierro, A., Mannetti, L., Higgins, T., & Kruglanski, A. (2009) The perfect mix: regulatory complementarity and the speed-accuracy balance in group performance. *Psychological Science, 20*(6), 681–685.

McGrath, J. E. (1984). *Groups: Interaction and performance.* Englewood Cliffs, NJ: Prentice-Hall.

Morris, M., Podolny, J., & Sullivan, B. N. (2008). Culture and coworker relations: interpersonal patterns in American, Chinese, German, and Spanish divisions of a global retail bank. *Organization Science, 19,* 517–532.

Morris, W., & Fu, H. (2001). *How does culture influence conflict resolution? A dynamic constructivist analysis.* Stanford University, Graduate School of Business.

Nisbett, R. Peng, K., & Choi, I., (2001). Norenzayan. Culture and systems of thought: holistic versus analytic cognition. *Psychological Review, 108*(2), 291–301.

Nishii, L. H., & Mayer, D. M. (2009). Do inclusive leaders help to reduce turnover in diverse groups? The moderating role of leader-member exchange in the diversity to turnover relationship. *Journal of Applied Psychology, 94*(6), 1412–1426.

Paulus, P. B., & Nijstad, B. (Eds.). (2003). *Group creativity: Innovation through collaboration.* New York: Oxford University Press.

Pelled, L. H., Eisenhardt, K. M., & Xin, K. R. (1999). Exploring the black box: An analysis of work group diversity, conflict, and performance. *Administrative Science Quarterly, 44,* 1–28.

Pelto, P. J. (1968). The difference between "tight" and "loose" societies. *Transaction, 5,* 37–40.

Pfeffer, J. (1983). Organizational demography. *Research in Organizational Behavior, 5,* 299–357.

Phillips, K. W. (2003). The effects of categorically based expectations on minority influence: The importance of congruence. *Personality and Social Psychology Bulletin, 29,* 3–13.

Probst, T. M., Carnevale, P. J., & Triandis, H. C. (1999). Cultural values in intergroup and single group social dilemmas. *Organizational Behavior and Human Decision Process, 77,* 171–191.

Randel, A. (2003) The salience of culture in multinational teams and its relation to team citizenship behavior. *International Journal of Cross-Cultural Management, 3*(1), 27–44. DOI: 10.1177/1470595803003001848.

Reicher, S. D. (1984). Social influence in the crowd: Attitudinal and behavioural effects of deindividuation in conditions of high and low group salience. *British Journal of Social Psychology, 23,* 341–350.

Rohner, R. P. (1984). Toward a conception of culture for cross-cultural psychology. *Journal of Cross-Cultural Psychology, 15,* 111–138.

Rokeach, M. (1973). *The nature of human values.* New York: Free Press.

Ronen, S., & Shenkar, O. (1985). Clustering countries on attitudinal dimensions: A review and synthesis. *Academy of Management Review, 10,* 435–454.

Sackmann, S. (1997). *Cultural complexity in organizations: Inherent contrasts and contradictions.* Thousand Oaks, CA: Sage.

Sanchez-Burks, J., Nisbett, R. E., & Ybarra, O. (2000). Cultural styles, relational schemas and prejudice against outgroups. *Journal of Personality and Social Psychology, 79,* 174–189.

Schein, E. H. (1985). *Organizational culture and leadership.* California: Jossey-Bass.

Schmitter, P. (1981). Interest intermediation and regime governability in contemporary western Europe and North America. In S. Berger (Ed.), *Organizing interests in Western Europe* (pp. 285–327). New York: Cambridge University Press.

Schwartz, S. H. (1994). Beyond individualism and collectivism: New cultural dimensions of values. In U. Kim, H. C. Triandis, C. Kagitcibasi, S.-C. Choi, & G. Yoon (Eds.), *Individualism and collectivism: Theory, method, and applications* (pp. 85–122). Newbury Park, CA: Sage.

Schwartz, S. H. (1999). A theory of cultural values and some implications for work. *Applied Psychology: An International Review, 48*(1), 23–47.

Schwartz, S. H., & Bilsky, W. (1987). Toward a universal psychological structure of human values. *Journal of Personality and Social Psychology, 53*(3), 550–562.

Schwartz, S. H., & Rubel, T. (2005). Sex differences in value priorities: cross-cultural and multimethod studies. *Journal of Personality and Social Psychology, 89*(6), 1010–1028.

Schwartz, S. H., & Sagie, G. (2000). Value consensus and importance: A cross-national study. *Journal of Cross-Cultural Psychology, 31,* 465–497.

Shteynberg, G., Gelfand, M., & Kim, K. (2009). Peering into the "Magnum Mysterium" of culture: the exploratory power of descriptive norms. *Journal of Cross-Cultural Psychology, 40,* 46–69.

Shweder, R., & LeVine, R. (1984). *Culture theory: Essays on mind, self, and emotion.* London: Cambridge University Press.

Singelis, T., Triandis, H. C., Bhawuk, D., & Gelfand, M. (1995). Horizontal and vertical individualism and collectivism: A theoretical and methodological refinement. *Cross-Cultural Research, 29* (3), 240–275.

Sivakumar, K., & Nakata, C. (2003). Designing global new product teams: optimizing the effects of national culture on new product development. *International Marketing Review, 20*(4), 397–445.

Smola, K. W., & Sutton, C. D. (2002). Generational differences: Revisiting generational work values for the new millennium. *Journal of Organizational Behavior, 23,* 363–383.

Spears, R., Lea, M., & Lee, S. (1990). De-individuation and group polarization in computer-mediated communication. *British Journal of Social Psychology, 29,* 121–134.

Staples, D., & Zhao, L. (2006). The effects of cultural diversity in virtual teams versus face-to-face teams. *Group Decision and Negotiation, 15,* 389–406. DOI: 10.1007/s10726-006-9042-x.

Staw, B. M., Sandelands, L., & Dutton, J. E. (1981) Threat-rigidity cycles in organizational behavior: A multi-level analysis. *Administrative Science Quarterly, 26,* 501–524.

Stephan, W. G., & Stephan, C. (1985). Ingroup anxiety. *Journal of Social Issues, 41,* 157–176.

Stephan, W. G., & Stephan, C. (1996). Predicting prejudice. *International Journal of Intercultural Relations, 20,* 1–12.

Tajfel, H. (1969). Cognitive aspects of prejudice. *Journal of Social Issues, 25,* 79–97.

Tajfel, H., & Turner, J. C. (1979). An integrative theory of intergroup conflict. *The Social Psychology of Intergroup Relations, 33,* 47.

Tajfel, H. (1981). *Human groups and social categories: Studies in social psychology.* Cambridge, England: Cambridge University Press.

Tajfel, H., & Turner, J. C. (1986). The social identity theory of intergroup behavior. In S. Worchel & W. Austin (Eds.), *Psychology of intergroup relations* (pp. 7–24). Chicago: Nelson-Hall.

Taras, V., Kirkman, B. L., & Steel, P. (2010). Examining the impact of culture's consequences: A three-decade, multilevel, meta-analytic review of Hofstede's cultural values dimensions. *Journal of Applied Psychology, 95*(3), 405–439.

Tett, R., & Burnett, D. (2003). A personality trait-based interactionist model of job performance. *Journal of Applied Psychology, 88*(3), 500–517.

Ting-Toomey, S., Yee-Jung, K., Shapiro, R., Garcia, W., Wright, T., & Oetzel, J. (2000). Ethnic/cultural identity salience and conflict styles in four US ethnic groups. *International Journal of Intercultural Relations, 24,* 47–81.

Triandis, H. C. (1972). *The analysis of subjective culture.* New York: Wiley.

Triandis, H. C. (1988). Collectivism and development. In D. Sinha & H. S. Kao (Eds.), *Social values and development: Asian perspectives* (pp. 285–303). Newbury Park, CA: Sage.

Triandis, H. C. (1989). The self and social behavior in differing cultural contexts. *Psychological Review, 96*(3), 506.

Triandis, H. C. (1990). Cross-cultural studies of individualism and collectivism. In J. J. Berman (Ed.), *Nebraska Symposium on Motivation, 1989: Cross-cultural perspectives. Current theory and research in motivation* (pp. 41–133). Lincoln, NE, US: University of Nebraska Press

Triandis, H. C. (1992). Cross-cultural research in social psychology. In D. Granberg & G. Sarup (Eds.), *Social judgment and intergroup relations: Essays in honor of Muzafer Sherif* (pp. 229–244). New York: Springer Verlag.

Triandis, H. C. (1994). Cross-cultural industrial and organizational psychology. In H. C. Triandis & M. D. Dunnette (Eds.), *Handbook of industrial and organizational psychology* (Vol. 4, pp. 103–172). Palo Alto, CA: Consulting Psychologists Press.

Triandis, H. C. (1995). *Individualism and collectivism.* Boulder, CO: Westview Press.

Triandis, H. C. (2009). Ecological determinants of cultural variations. In R. W. Wyer, C-Y. Chiu, & Y Hong (Eds.), *Understanding culture: Theory, research and applications* (pp. 189–210) New York: Psychology Press.

Triandis, H. C., & Gelfand, M. J. (1998). Converging measurement of horizontal and vertical individualism and collectivism. *Journal of Personality and Social Psychology, 74,* 118–128.

Triandis, H. C., Kurowski, L. L., & Gelfand, M. J. (1994). Workplace diversity. In H. C. Triandis, M. D. Dunnette, & L. M. Hough (Eds.), *Handbook of industrial and organizational psychology* (2nd ed., Vol. 4, pp. 769–827). Palo Alto, CA: Consulting Psychology Press.

Trompenaars, F. (1993). *Riding the waves of culture: Understanding cultural diversity in business.* London: Economist Books, London.

Tsui, A. S., Nifadkar, S., & Ou, Y. (2007). Cross-national cross-cultural organizational behavior research: Advances, gaps, and recommendations. *Journal of Management, 33,* 426–478.

Urban, L. M., & Miller, N. (1998). A theoretical analysis of cross categorization effects: A metaanalysis. Journal of Personality and Social Psychology, 74, 894–908.

Van den Bos, K. (2005). What is responsible for the fair process effect? In J. Greenberg & J. A. Colquitt (Eds.), *Handbook of organizational justice: Fundamental questions about fairness in the workplace* (pp. 273–300). Mahwah, NJ: Erlbaum.

Van der Vegt, G. S., & Van de Vliert, E. (2005). Effects of perceived skill dissimilarity and task interdependence on helping in work teams. *Journal of Management, 31,* 73–89.

Van der Zee, K., Atsma, N., & Brodbeck, F. (2004). The influence of social identity and personality on outcomes of cultural diversity in teams. *Journal of Cross-Cultural Psychology, 35*(3), 283–303. DOI: 10.1177/0022022104264123.

van Knippenberg, D., De Dreu, C. K. W., & Homan, A. C. (2004). Work group diversity and group performance: an integrative model and research agenda. *Journal of Applied Psychology, 89,* 1008–1022.

van Knippenberg, D., & Schippers, M. C. (2007). Workgroup diversity. *Annual Review of Psychology, 58,* 2.1–2.27.

van Knippenberg, D., & Haslam, S. A. (2003). Realizing the diversity dividend: Exploring the subtle interplay between identity, ideology, and reality. In S. A. Haslam, D. Knippenberg, M. J. Platow, N. Ellemers (Eds.), *Social identity at work: Developing theory for organizational practice* (pp. 61–77). New York, NY: Psychology Press

Vliert, E., Huang, X., & Parker, P. (2004). Do colder and hotter climates make richer societies more, but poorer societies less, happy and altruistic? *Journal of Environmental Psychology, 24,* 17–30.

Von Glinow, M. A., Shapiro, D. L., & Brett, J. M. (2004). Can we talk, and should we? Managing emotional conflict in multicultural teams. *Academy of Management Review, 29,* 578–592.

Wade-Benzoni, K. A., Okumura, T., Brett, J. M., Moore, D. A., Tenbrunsel, A. E., & Bazerman, M. H. (2002). Cognitions and behavior in asymmetric social dilemmas: A comparison of two cultures. *Journal of Applied Psychology, 87,* 87–95.

Wan, C., Chiu, C., Tam, K., Lee, S., Lau, I. Y., & Peng, S. (2007). Perceived cultural importance and actual self-importance of values in cultural identification. *Journal of Personality and Social Psychology, 92,* 337–354.

Weiner, Y. (1988). Forms of value systems: A focus on organizational effectiveness and cultural change and maintenance. *Academy of Management Review, 13,* 534–545.

Whiting, B., & Whiting, J. (1975). *Children of six cultures: A psycho-cultural analysis.* Cambridge: Harvard University Press.

Wiersema, M. F., & Bird, A. (1993). Organizational demography in Japanese firms: Group heterogeneity, individual dissimilarity, and top management turnover. *Academy of Management Journal, 36,* 996–1025.

Wilder, D. A. (1984). Intergroup contact: The typical member and the exception to the rule. *Journal of Experimental Social Psychology, 20,* 177–194.

Wilder, D. A., & Shapiro, P. (1989). Effects of anxiety on impression formation in a group context: An anxiety-assimilation hypothesis. *Journal of Experimental Social Psychology, 25,* 481–499.

Williams, K. Y., & O'Reilly, C. A. (1998). Demography and diversity in organizations: a review of 40 years of research. *Research in Organizational Behavior, 20,* 77–140.

Wise, L. R., & Tschirhart, M. (2000). Examining empirical evidence on diversity effects: How useful is diversity research for public-sector managers? *Public Administration Review, 60,* 386–394.

Wuchty, S., Jones, B. F., & Uzzi, B. (2007). The increasing dominance of teams in production of knowledge. *Science, 316,* 1036–1039.

CHAPTER 4

Moving Beyond a Categorical Approach to Diversity: The Role of Demographic Faultlines

Sherry M. B. Thatcher

Abstract
Recent research has suggested a conciliation of the different approaches to conceptualizing diversity through a theory of group faultlines, which are dividing lines that may split a group into subgroups based on the alignment of demographic attributes. This chapter will discuss the theory underlying faultlines and the findings of research in this area. Further, it will argue for how multi-attribute conceptualizations of diversity may be used to more accurately represent complex interactions between people and allow for more appropriate tests of the effects of heterogeneity in groups. This chapter concludes with a number of questions that faultline researchers may consider in the future.

Key Words: faultlines, demographic configuration, subgroups, groups, teams

Introduction

Because groups are central to organizational success (Devine, Clayton, Philips, Dunford, & Melner, 1999), managing group composition is one of the key challenges for organizations (Gruenfeld, Mannix, Williams, & Neale, 1996). Over the past three decades, diversity research has focused on the role of group composition in assessing group-level outcomes. Typically, group diversity research investigates the effects of micro-level individual differences such as age, tenure, and race on teams. In recent years, there has been acknowledgement that the effects of demographic diversity are neither clear nor consistent (Horwitz & Horwitz, 2007; Webber & Donahue, 2001). In an effort to understand the effects of group composition on teams, some researchers have suggested the value of aligning conceptualizations and operationalizations of different types of diversity (Harrison & Klein, 2007). Another approach is to investigate meso-level effects of group composition created as a result of individual psychological processes and social dynamics (Rousseau & House, 1994). One of the most compelling insights in this area of research is that the alignment of demographic attributes, known as demographic faultlines, may affect group processes and performance. Lau and Murnighan's (1998) seminal conceptual work on demographic faultlines has led to a plethora of research on this topic. Given the increasing interest in faultline-based subgroup formation and its impact on group outcomes, it is important to step back and review the literature on demographic faultlines. It is also crucial to assess how research on demographic faultlines has increased our understanding of group diversity.

Lau and Murnighan (1998) defined demographic faultlines as hypothetical dividing lines that split a group into two or more subgroups based on one or more demographic attributes. Faultlines vary in strength based on the overall homogeneity within the subgroups. For example, if the members of one subgroup are young, college-educated marketers and the members of another subgroup are older, high school-educated operations managers, the overall group contains a strong faultline (Lau & Murnighan, 1998).

The conceptualization of the faultline construct has expanded to include attributes that are not demographic in nature, such as personality or work attitudes. Despite this expansion, the majority of studies on faultlines have focused on faultlines based on demographic attributes such as race, sex, national heritage, age, education type, education level, functional background, and tenure. In this chapter I use the term *faultlines* to refer to faultlines based on any attribute, including demographic attributes, and the term *demographic faultlines* to refer to faultlines composed of only demographic attributes.

Demographic faultlines have been found to influence group processes and outcomes over and above those found by examining demographic diversity alone (Bezrukova, Thatcher, & Jehn, 2007; Lau & Murnighan, 2005; Li & Hambrick, 2005; Thatcher & Patel, 2012), suggesting that the structure of diversity is an important component in understanding groups. Researchers have studied the effects of demographic faultlines on a number of group processes and emergent states (e.g., conflict, trust, communication, psychological safety, and group cohesion) and outcomes (e.g., morale, team learning, team satisfaction, creativity, information sharing, top management team decision making, decision accuracy, and performance) (Barkema & Shvyrkov, 2007; Bezrukova, Thatcher, Jehn, & Spell, 2012; Bezrukova, Jehn, Zanutto, & Thatcher, 2009; Bezrukova et al., 2007; Gibson & Vermeulen, 2003; Lau & Murnighan, 2005; Li & Hambrick, 2005; Molleman, 2005; Pearsall, Ellis, & Evans, 2008; Polzer, Crisp, Jarvenpaa, & Kim, 2006; Rico, Molleman, Sanchez-Manzanares, & Van der Vegt, 2007; Sawyer, Houlette, & Yeagley, 2006; Thatcher, Jehn, & Zanutto, 2003; van Knippenberg, Dawson, West, & Homan, 2011). However, there is still much we can learn from exploring faultlines and group-related phenomena.

There are four main objectives of this chapter. The first objective is to clarify the relationship between demographic diversity and demographic faultlines. Second, I describe how theories that underlie faultlines are similar to and different from those underlying diversity. The third objective is to provide a brief review of the current state of faultlines research. From this discussion we can better assess how demographic faultlines may more accurately represent the complex mechanisms that guide interactions between group members, the fourth objective of this chapter. I conclude with a discussion of the gaps in faultline research and provide a set of research questions designed to guide future investigation in the area of faultlines.

Relationship between diversity and demographic faultlines

When groups are homogeneous there is no opportunity for diversity or demographic faultlines (Lau & Murnighan, 1998). Unlike diversity measures that tend to focus on the dispersion of a single attribute, faultlines focus on the *alignment* of one or more attributes (Bezrukova et al., 2007; Lau & Murnighan, 1998). Thus, even though groups may be heterogeneous (or diverse), the group may not contain a faultline if the attributes are not aligned. Consider two groups: Group A consists of three men who hold undergraduate marketing degrees and three women who hold master's degrees in education. Group B also consists of three men and three women. One man and one woman hold an undergraduate degree in education, one man holds a master's degree in education, one woman holds a master's degree in marketing, and one man and one woman hold an undergraduate degree in marketing. From a diversity perspective, Groups A and B are identical: each group contains three men, three women, three individuals with undergraduate degrees, three individuals with master's degrees, three individuals who majored in marketing, and three individuals who majored in education. However, from a demographic faultline perspective, these two groups are very different: the three demographic attributes in Group A are aligned and the same three demographic attributes in Group B are not aligned. Faultline strength is determined by the extent to which the subgroups are homogeneous. In this example, Group A would have a strong demographic faultline because both subgroups (male marketing undergraduates and female education master's graduates) are homogeneous (Lau & Murnighan, 1998).[1]

Some researchers interested in diversity on more than one demographic attribute use an additive model that aggregates the effects of multiple dispersion models (e.g., Jehn, Northcraft, & Neale, 1999; Schippers, Den Hartog, Koopman, & Wienk, 2003). For example, Schippers and colleagues (2003) were interested in how overall diversity on the attributes of gender, age, educational level, and team member tenure influenced team reflexivity and subsequent outcomes. Thus, they created a diversity score for each attribute and combined the scores to create an average group diversity score. Researchers interested in investigating how groups that have many differences (e.g., sex, race, background, AND age differences) differ from homogeneous groups (e.g., female Caucasian undergraduate marketing majors in their sophomore year) may find this approach useful. However, there are many limitations to using an aggregation approach (Harrison & Klein, 2007). From a theoretical point of view, it requires that each diversity attribute be conceived as having an equal impact on the outcome of interest (e.g., diversity on age has the same impact as diversity on race). The aggregation approach also assumes that an overall amount of diversity is what will influence actions or behaviors rather than a specific type of diversity (Harrison & Klein, 2007). From an operationalization point of view, the aggregation approach requires that all data be converted to the same format (e.g., raw age data be converted into categories). Thus, the aggregation approach requires that the researchers make a number of theoretical and measurement assumptions that may be unwarranted. In sum, although some diversity studies focus on the accumulative effects of demographic attributes, current aggregation approaches should be used with caution.

Because both demographic diversity and demographic faultlines are concerned with the group composition and the dispersion of demographic attributes, it is important to consider their relationship with one another. Two fairly recent developments in the area of diversity research have ramifications for the relationship between diversity and faultlines. The first development refers to the "type" of diversity that is important as groups perform a task. Researchers have distinguished between diversity that is based on social category (surface-level attributes such as race and sex), informational (knowledge attributes such as education and functional backgrounds), and value (deep-level attributes such as personality and beliefs) attributes (Harrison, Price, & Bell, 1998; Harrison, Price, Gavin, & Florey, 2002; Jehn, Chadwick, & Thatcher, 1997; Jehn et al., 1999; Pelled, Eisenhardt, & Xin, 1999; Phillips, Mannix, & Neale, 2004; van Knippenberg, De Dreu, & Homan, 2004). These distinctions are also relevant for faultline researchers because they may only want to consider the alignment of attributes that are central to the group task or context. The second development refers to the "form" of diversity (Harrison & Klein, 2007); these diversity forms are relevant for faultlines because they reflect the shape of attribute distribution. Faultlines capture one aspect of attribute distribution (alignment), and thus it is important to discuss the relationship between diversity forms and faultlines.

Diversity types and demographic faultlines

Many studies have examined the differential effects of diversity types on outcomes (e.g., Harrison et al., 1998; Jehn et al., 1999). Although a number of meta-analyses find surprisingly few effects linking diversity to performance (e.g., Bowers, Parmer, & Salas, 2000; Horwitz & Horwitz, 2007; Webber & Donahue, 2001), the majority of studies find that diversity on social category attributes leads to negative outcomes (e.g., Jehn et al., 1999; Murnighan & Conlon, 1991; Simons, Pelled, & Smith, 1999), diversity on informational attributes leads to positive outcomes (e.g., Ancona & Caldwell, 1992; Cox, Lobel, & McLeod, 1991; Dahlin, Weingart, & Hinds, 2005), and diversity on value-based attributes leads to generally negative outcomes that tend to disappear over time (e.g., Harrison et al., 1998; 2002). Researchers have not always made the distinction between the types of demographic attributes included in a demographic faultline, but some recent studies have begun to explore the role of specific types of demographic attributes and faultlines.

Following the lead of diversity researchers, some have argued that not all faultlines are equal (Bezrukova et al., 2009; Gibson & Vermeulen, 2003). The type of demographic attributes making up a faultline may be important in understanding how a faultline influences group processes and outcomes. A number of faultline researchers have found that distinguishing between social category, informational, and value-based characteristics provides a useful framework for investigating how different types of faultlines influence groups (e.g., Bezrukova et al., 2009; Molleman, 2005; Rico et al., 2007). Bezrukova and her colleagues (2009) investigated the extent to which social category faultlines (faultlines created based on members' alignment on social category characteristics such as age, race, and sex) differentially influenced performance relative to informational faultlines (faultlines created based on members' alignment of job-related attributes such as work and educational experiences). They found that social category faultline strength had a significant negative influence on performance but that informational faultline strength had no significant effect on performance. Other studies have found that social category faultlines (Choi & Sy, 2010; Molleman, 2005) and value (or personality-based) faultlines (Rico et al., 2007) led to negative group processes and outcomes. Choi and Sy (2010) found a positive association between informational faultlines and positive group processes. These findings confirm that faultlines based on different attributes are not equivalent. Alignment of racially similar subgroups does not have the same effect as alignment of educationally similar subgroups. However, there is still much work to be done to tease apart the differential effects of demographic attributes on the creation and effects of faultlines. Thus, one aspect of diversity that faultlines researchers need to be mindful of is the type of diversity that they are interested in studying.

Diversity forms and demographic faultlines

Another aspect of the relationship between diversity and demographic faultlines that must be considered is the relevance of the form of diversity when measuring faultline strength. A number of demographic characteristics have been used in the study and testing of faultlines, including, but not limited to, sex, age, race, ethnicity, functional background, educational background, organizational tenure, and team tenure (Barkema & Shvyrkov, 2007; Bezrukova et al., 2009; Li & Hambrick, 2005; Molleman, 2005; Thatcher et al., 2003). Because the characteristics represent different types of variables (e.g., categorical, ordinal), the level of diversity across these variables will have a differential effect on the strength of a faultline. At this point it is important to distinguish between latent, or potential, faultlines and active, or actual perceived, faultlines. Much of the faultline research, like that of the diversity research, has investigated latent faultlines. Researchers create a faultline score based on the distribution and alignment of the attributes of interest (e.g., values, sex, race). Because the majority of research on faultlines has focused on latent faultlines, we focus on latent faultlines unless otherwise stated. The distinction is crucial because there is likely to be a much stronger relationship between forms of diversity and *latent* faultlines than forms of diversity and *active* faultlines. For example, a high level of sex diversity occurs when there are equal members of the same sex on a team. Because there are only two ways to categorize someone with respect to sex, there is likely to be a strong correlation between sex diversity and latent faultline strength where one of the attributes of interest is sex. On the other hand, researchers interested in active, perceived faultlines may find that subjects actually perceive no faultline or perceive a faultline based on some attribute other than sex.

The diversity conceptualizations of separation, variety, and disparity proposed by Harrison and Klein (2007) are relevant to understanding the relationship between diversity forms and demographic faultlines. The concept of separation is defined as the "composition of differences in position or opinion among unit members, primarily of value, belief or attitude" (p. 1203), and when the distribution of this attribute is bimodal, there is maximum separation diversity. The "composition of differences in kind, source, or category of relevant knowledge or experience among unit members" (p. 1203) reflects variety diversity, and there is maximum variety diversity when the distribution of this attribute is uniform, such that no team member is alike on this attribute. Disparity diversity is defined as the "composition of (vertical) differences in proportion of socially valued assets or resources held among unit members" (p. 1203). Maximum disparity diversity occurs when the distribution of this attribute is positively skewed; for example, one member exists at the highest end of a continuum and all other members exist at the lowest end of the continuum.

All else being equal, demographic attributes that take the form of separation diversity are likely to have stronger effects on demographic faultline strength than demographic attributes that take the form of variety or disparity diversity.[2] Under conditions of *maximum separation* diversity, a group is split into two homogeneous subgroups; in other words, a strong demographic faultline is formed (Harrison & Klein, 2007). Thus, demographic attributes that by definition have a bimodal distribution (e.g., sex) or a limited distribution (e.g., race) are likely to play a central role in strong demographic faultlines. Because variety diversity refers to diversity of kinds, knowledge, or experiences, there may be unlimited categories of this attribute. *Maximum variety* diversity will not influence the homogeneity of a subgroup because each team member represents a different demographic attribute. For example, the demographic faultline of a group with six members who each have a different functional background (maximum variety diversity) will not be strengthened because the functional backgrounds of members will not align. However, in organizational contexts, groups are more likely to experience *moderate* variety diversity than *maximum* variety diversity, and moderate variety diversity will influence demographic faultline strength. Finally, disparity diversity is likely to influence faultlines only under conditions of moderate to maximum diversity, but the resulting subgroups are likely to be of unequal size and power. For example, when there is high disparity diversity, one or two individuals control all the power/resources and the remaining group members have little or no power/resources. The skewed nature of disparity diversity results in subgroups where one subgroup has the numerical majority but little in the way of power/resources and the other subgroup is a numerical minority with much in the way of power/resources. Therefore, demographic attributes reflecting distributions as described by separation, variety, and disparity diversity will affect demographic faultline strength, with separation diversity attributes having a stronger effect on faultline strength than variety or disparity diversity attributes.

Although researchers of faultline studies have begun to consider the types of demographic attributes that make up the content of faultlines, researchers have not yet examined how the form of diversity may affect the creation or strength of faultlines.

Theoretical underpinnings of demographic faultlines

To date, faultline researchers have tended to follow Lau and Murnighan (1998) and use social categorization (Turner, 1985; Turner, Hogg, Oakes, Reicher, & Wetherell, 1987), social identification (Bartel, 2001; Brewer, 2001), and similarity attraction (Byrne, 1971) theories to explain the potential effects of faultlines on group processes and outcomes. However, because diversity researchers also use the same theories to explain the underlying mechanisms of diversity on group processes and outcomes, it is important for faultline researchers to explain *why* faultlines have an effect above and beyond those of diversity. To that end, I discuss additional theories that can be used to explain why faultlines affect group processes and interactions. I will then introduce "faultline theory" as a conglomeration of the theories that explain the mechanisms underlying faultlines.

The theories that have been used to explain why diversity and demographic faultlines influence group processes and outcomes are social categorization theory (Turner, 1985; Turner et al., 1987), social identity theory (Tajfel, 1978), and the similarity-attraction paradigm (Byrne, 1971). The foundation of self-categorization theory (Turner, 1985) is that individuals classify themselves and others into categories based on demographic attributes and acquired skills (e.g., female, banker). This type of classification is useful in that it enables individuals to simplify their complex environment and make predictions about future interactions (Turner, 1985). The meaning one derives from these classifications is referred to as "social identity" (e.g., I see myself as a female banker, and this identity has meaning for me) (Hogg, 2006; Levine & Moreland, 1990; Linnehan, Chrobot-Mason, & Konrad, 2006; Tajfel, 1978). Social categorization theory and social identity theory are strongly related and are the basis for the formation of in-groups and out-groups. Byrne (1971) developed the similarity-attraction paradigm to explain that people form in-groups and out-groups on the basis of similarity. People are attracted to similar others, and past research has substantiated that demographic attributes provide a means for determining similarity, classification, and identification (Harrison et al., 1998; Horwitz & Horwitz, 2007; Tsui, Egan, & O'Reilly III, 1992). These theories together help explain why the structure of group demographic composition is important for group functioning.

Self-categorization theory, social identity theory, and the similarity-attraction paradigm explain why differences matter. We need additional theoretical guidance to explain why attribute alignment matters. Both self-categorization and social identity theories explain how subgroups are created, but they do not explain why having a greater distinction between subgroups may influence group processes and outcomes differently. The premise of optimal distinctiveness theory (Brewer, 1991; Brewer, Manzi, & Shaw, 1993; Hornsey & Hogg, 1999; Pickett & Brewer, 2001) is that individuals seek an optimal balance of uniqueness and similarity. Individuals desire to belong to a particular group, but they also desire to be distinctive from other groups. Every additional way that one group is differentiated from another makes this distinction stronger. This desire for distinctiveness explains why demographic faultlines influence group processes and outcomes over and above the influence of diversity alone.

Bezrukova and colleagues (2009) draw on work from social and social psychological distance theories (Hraba, Hagendoorn, & Hagendoorn, 1989; Jetten, Spears, & Postmes, 2004) to explain the desire for subgroups to be psychologically distant from one another. Social distance theories are used to explain that in-group/out-group formation entails an assessment of the extent to which out-groups are different from in-groups. Perceived distances between groups result from constructed social representations of nationality, ethnicity, or other demographic attributes (Hraba et al., 1989). Social psychological researchers (e.g., Jetten et al., 2004) have focused on the extent to which members of subgroups with overlapping memberships experience reduced psychological distance. In other words, perceived differences across subgroups diminish if there are other attributes that are shared by members of both subgroups. Alignment of multiple attributes increases the extent to which one subgroup perceives distance from the other subgroup.

The categorization-elaboration model (CEM) was developed to help explain why there have been both positive and negative effects of diversity (Van Knippenberg et al., 2004). One of the key facets of the CEM model is the extent to which categories are salient to individuals. CEM proposes that high levels of comparative fit, normative fit, and cognitive accessibility will make categories more salient. Comparative fit refers to the extent to which the categorization of differences reflects both high intragroup similarity and high intergroup differences, whereas normative fit reflects the extent to which a categorization matches an individual's belief systems (e.g., an individual who strongly believes in age-based stereotypes will see age as a salient difference). Finally, cognitive accessibility reflects the ease with which an individual retrieves the categorization from memory. Although all three facets of CEM are relevant to the study of faultlines, the idea of comparative fit is most central for latent faultlines. Comparative fit is greater when similarities are aligned, and thus the construct has great conceptual similarity to the faultline construct.

A *theory of faultlines* encapsulates the aggregation of these theoretical approaches. Individuals are attracted to those who are similar, they ascribe meaning to the groups to which they belong, and they categorize others into groups to which they do not belong. This process is easier to do and results in more strongly defined subgroups when multiple aligned differences create homogeneous subgroups. On this basis, individuals engage in behaviors and attributions that accentuate similarity to their own subgroup and distinction from those in other subgroups. As a result, the ability to operate as a unified group becomes increasingly difficult.

Current state of the research

In this section I provide a review of the literature on faultlines. I loosely organize the research into the following topic areas: faultline composition and antecedents of faultlines; latent faultlines, active faultlines, and active faultline triggers; the consequences of faultlines; moderators of the faultlines–outcomes relationship; and faultline endurance.

Faultline composition and antecedents of faultlines

One of the most discussed aspects of faultlines is the composition of the faultline. Because the idea of faultlines grew out of the mixed results of studies on demographic diversity, initial studies of faultlines focused on demographic faultlines (e.g., Lau & Murnighan, 2005; Shaw, 2004; Thatcher et al., 2003). For example, Thatcher and her colleagues (2003) focused on faultlines created from alignment on the attributes of years of work experience, type of functional background, education major, sex, age, race and country of origin and found curvilinear effects of demographic faultlines on group processes and outcomes. Researchers have expanded from a singular focus on the alignment of demographic attributes to more complicated conceptualizations of demographic alignment such as those described in the section labeled "Diversity types and demographic faultlines." Furthermore, some faultlines researchers have begun examining the effects of faultlines derived from attributes other than demographic attributes.

Molleman (2005) investigated faultlines created by demographic attributes as well as those created by abilities and personalities. He found that demographic faultlines (sex, age, part-time job) directly impaired the functioning of a team, whereas ability faultlines (ability in language, science, and human and social science) affected team functioning indirectly through an emphasis on similarities within subgroups. Furthermore, personality faultlines (extraversion, agreeableness, conscientiousness, emotional stability, and openness to experience) tended to accentuate dissimilarities between subgroups. However, the effect of ability and personality faultlines were present only in teams with high task autonomy. Molleman (2005) also looked at each potential faultline (e.g., demographic, ability, personality) separately. Rico and colleagues (2007) combined work experience (demographic variable) with conscientiousness (personality variable) into a potential faultline in their study and found strong, negative effects of faultlines on decision quality.

There are other potential sources of faultlines in organizational groups. The geographic distribution of groups may result in the creation of faultlines between subgroups of individuals operating in different locations (Cramton & Hinds, 2005). As explained by faultline theory, when group members work in different locations, an us-versus-them attitude develops across individuals at the different sites (Cramton, 2001; Hinds & Bailey, 2003).

Differences in geographic location result not only in access to different types of information but also in differences in assumptions, preferences, cultures, and constraints (Cramton & Hinds, 2005). Contextual situations that are understood in one location (e.g., use of siestas in the middle of a workday) may be misunderstood by group members in other locations (e.g., attributions of laziness because of a lack of understanding about traditional work structures). Polzer and his colleagues (2006) found empirical evidence for the creation of subgroups based on geographic location.

Latent faultlines, active faultlines, and active faultline triggers

There may be a difference between having latent faultlines and active faultlines in a group (Jehn & Bezrukova, 2010). In Lau and Murnighan's (1998) initial discourse on the topic they discussed the importance of task salience on faultline activation. For example, faultlines based on sex may become activated when a group's task is to develop gender equality initiatives in the workplace. Despite this awareness, the majority of the studies on faultlines are based on the assumption that created (latent) faultlines become activated without actually knowing whether participants experienced a faultline (Chrobot-Mason, Ruderman, Weber, & Ernst, 2009). One recent study that investigated the relationship between latent and activated faultlines found that groups with activated faultlines were more likely to have high levels of conflict, low levels of satisfaction, and low levels of group performance than groups with latent faultlines (Jehn & Bezrukova, 2010). Pearsall and colleagues (2008) found that sex-based faultlines influenced creativity only when the faultlines were activated (e.g., participants were asked to complete a task focused on a gender-specific item). Thus, both latent and active faultlines have been found to affect group processes and outcomes; however, there is still much work to be done in understanding the relationship between latent and active faultlines.

One way that faultlines may become active is through a "faultline trigger." A faultline trigger is an event or situation that makes a previously latent faultline salient. A number of experimental studies have manipulated conditions such that faultlines are triggered (Pearsall et al., 2008). Other studies have shown that there are consequences of faultlines even when faultlines are not triggered (e.g., Bezrukova et al., 2009; Lau & Murnighan, 2005). Another interesting conceptual and empirical development is the notion that faultlines may include a "trigger" variable. For example, Li and Hambrick (2005) investigated the role of factions in faultlines. Factions exist when individuals belonging to particular subgroups are forced to work together (i.e., organizational mergers, joint ventures, task forces, cross-cultural teams). Task content, as in the study referenced above by Pearsall and colleagues (2008), is one way that latent faultlines may be activated, but there are other potential triggers. Earley and Mosakowski (2000) describe how nationality became an active faultline for transnational teams that met face to face. Polzer and colleagues (2006) found that geographic distribution became an active faultline when group members had difficulties finding a time for chat meetings (due to time-zone differences). Once the faultlines became active, the group distributed tasks to subgroups based on location, resulting in decreased group communication and increased subgroup communication (Polzer et al., 2006). Chrobot-Mason, Ruderman, Weber, and Ernst (2009) conducted two qualitative studies to investigate the content of potential faultline triggers based on the perceptions of individuals working in a number of different countries. Their "trigger typology" consists of five categories: differential treatment, different values, assimilation, insult or humiliating action, and simple contact.

Other research has been conducted that reflects the difficulty of teasing apart the composition of the faultline from the faultline trigger. For example, Halevy (2008) shows how task structure can contribute to faultline formation. By giving team members different interests in a negotiation, he triggered faultlines within the group. Li and Hambrick (2005) investigated faultlines from the perspective of factions, whereby two or more social entities must come together to complete a common goal (e.g., the two sides of a merged company). They, like Halevy (2008), looked at the extent to which various interests are the basis for subgroup formation. Task or structural features have also been integrated with demographic differences to emphasize or create faultlines. Homan and colleagues (2008) manipulated faultlines such that reward structures (rewards for subgroups vs. no rewards for subgroups) were aligned with intragroup differences. Homan and colleagues (2007) used both experimental and spatial manipulations to ensure that faultlines based on sex, (bogus) personality feedback, and seating resulted in maximum faultline strength. The results of their study, like those from Polzer and colleagues

(2006), suggest that tangible spatial arrangements may be a contributor to faultlines.

Jehn and Bezrukova (2010) investigated the extent to which the configuration of team entitlement triggered latent faultlines to become active faultlines. The found that when entitled individuals—individuals who feel they deserve rewards regardless of their effort—were in different subgroups, latent faultlines were more likely to become active faultlines. This finding by Jehn and Bezrukova (2010) challenges some assumptions made by cross-cutting category theory. Theories of cross-categorization and cross-cutting (Deschamps, 1977; Gibson & Vermeulen, 2003; Jetten et al., 2004) suggest that when individuals with similar attributes are represented in different subgroups, the negative effects of subgroup categorization, namely biases, prejudice, and discrimination, will be reduced (e.g., Brewer, 2000; Marcus-Newhall, Miller, Holtz, & Brewer, 1993) and overall group cohesion will increase (e.g., Crisp & Hewstone, 1999). In the study by Jehn and Bezrukova (2010), the cross-cutting category of entitlement did *not* mitigate the effects of faultlines but actually triggered a latent faultline. In other words, it is not only the alignment of similarities and differences that matters; it is the content of those similarities and differences that are relevant to the study of faultlines and to group composition overall. These findings speak to the importance of understanding how different characteristics at all levels and contexts—individual personalities and abilities, subgroup characteristics, team attributes, and task variables—play a role in explaining the effects of both latent and activated faultlines.

The consequences of faultlines

The majority of studies on faultlines have focused on investigating and exploring the consequences of faultlines on group processes and outcomes. Faultlines have been linked to conflict, trust, communication, psychological safety, cohesion, morale, team learning, team satisfaction, group-level organizational citizenship behavior, creativity, information sharing, top management team decision making, decision accuracy, and performance (Barkema & Shvyrkov, 2007; Bezrukova et al., 2012; Bezrukova et al., 2009; Gibson & Vermeulen, 2003; Lau & Murnighan, 2005; Li & Hambrick, 2005; Molleman, 2005; Pearsall et al., 2008; Pelled et al., 1999; Polzer et al., 2006; Rico et al., 2007; Sawyer et al., 2006; Thatcher et al., 2003; van Knippenberg et al., 2011). The most commonly studied outcomes have been intragroup conflict, satisfaction, and performance.

Intragroup conflict is a group process variable that has consistently been found as a result of diversity in groups (Jehn et al., 1999; Williams & O'Reilly III, 1998). The two types of conflict most often examined in group research are relationship conflicts, which are disagreements over non–work-related interpersonal issues, and task conflicts, which are disagreements over work-related issues (Jehn, 1997; Pelled, 1996). Faultline theory and literature about coalitions (Brewer, 1996; Insko & Schopler, 1987; Polzer, Mannix, & Neale, 1998) suggests that when there are strong demographic faultlines, team members will tend to have pleasant interactions with members of the subgroup (Stevenson, Pearce, & Porter, 1985) but experience an increase in conflict and distrust between or across subgroups (Brewer, 2001; Choi & Sy, 2010; Hogg, Turner, & Davidson, 1990; Homan et al., 2007; Pearsall et al., 2008). For example, when faultlines are strong, information may be misinterpreted so that rather than being seen as constructive critiques, comments are viewed as criticisms, threats, or conflicts (Bartel, 2001; Lau & Murnighan, 2005). The desire for the subgroups to remain distinct from one another as well as superior to one another can also lead to conflict (Halevy, 2008; Insko, Schopler, Hoyle, Dardis, & Graetz, 1990). Within the faultline literature, some studies have reported that faultlines are positively and significantly related to relationship conflict (Bezrukova et al., 2007; Li & Hambrick, 2005; Pearsall et al., 2008; Polzer et al., 2006; Thatcher et al., 2003). For example, Choi and Sy (2010) found that faultlines on the basis of tenure–age, age–race, and tenure–age increased relationship conflict. However, not all of the empirical research has found that faultlines increase conflict. Lau and Murnighan (2005) found that strong faultlines actually decreased relationship conflict. Although Choi and Sy (2010) found that many types of faultlines increased the presence of relationship conflict, faultlines on the basis of tenure–race were actually negatively related to relationship conflict.

In contrast, a number of studies have shown that faultlines are positively and significantly related to task conflict (Bezrukova et al., 2007; Choi & Sy, 2010; Li & Hambrick, 2005). Molleman (2005) and Jehn and Bezrukova (2010) did not distinguish between types of conflict and found that demographic faultlines were strongly related to intragroup conflict. Overall, a recent meta-analysis on demographic faultlines shows that strong faultlines are associated with an increase in relationship and task conflict (Thatcher & Patel, 2011).

Faultline theory predicts that subgroup formation influences the overall performance of the group. As time and energy is spent bridging the chasm created by a strong faultline, there is less time and focus spent on meeting the group's goals (Li & Hambrick, 2005), and subgroups often become competitive with one another (Brewer, 1996; Halevy, 2008; Hornsey & Hogg, 1999; Polzer et al., 1998). Subgroups caused by faultlines hinder the negotiation processes that occur in groups (Clark, Anand, & Roberson, 2000) as communication and task interdependence are damaged (Halevy, 2008). Furthermore, the in-group versus out-group mentality that pervades groups with faultlines facilitates fragmentation and limits both the opportunities for information exchange as well as the desire to share relevant and important information (Lau & Murnighan, 2005; Phillips et al., 2004; Sawyer et al., 2006).

Most published studies predict and find that faultlines lead to low performance levels and low decision-making quality. Strong faultlines have been found to have a negative influence on group-level bonuses (Bezrukova et al., 2012; Bezrukova et al., 2007), group learning (Gibson & Vermeulen, 2003; Lau & Murnighan, 2005), group functioning (Molleman, 2005), quality of decision making (Rico et al., 2007), and group performance (Homan et al., 2008; Jehn & Bezrukova, 2010; Li & Hambrick, 2005; Thatcher et al., 2003). Top management teams in settings with strong faultlines were less likely to make bold strategic decisions (e.g., invest in new geographic areas) (Barkema & Shvyrkov, 2007) and had lower productivity than teams in settings with weak faultlines (Barkema & Shvyrkov, 2007; van Knippenberg et al., 2011). Sawyer and colleagues (2006) found that convergent groups (conceptually similar to groups with strong faultlines) had lower levels of decision accuracy than cross-cutting groups (conceptually similar to diverse groups). However, they found no difference between convergent groups and same-race groups (conceptually similar to groups with a weak faultline). Bezrukova and colleagues (2009) hypothesized that groups with informationally based faultlines would have positive direct effects on group performance due to their ability to synthesize ideas from the different subgroups, but they did not find support for this hypothesis.

Faultline theory also predicts that the relationship between faultlines and satisfaction is negative. Due to the identification tendencies of individuals, members of faultline-based subgroups feel a strong affinity and connection to one another and negative affect toward members of other subgroups (Hornsey & Hogg, 2000; Pickett & Brewer, 2001). In addition, competition between subgroups decreases the overall morale of group members (Murnighan, 1978). A number of studies report that strong faultlines result in decreased satisfaction of group members due to the conflict, decreased trust, and us-versus-them mentality that pervades the group (Cronin, Bezrukova, Weingart, & Tinsley, in press; Jehn & Bezrukova, 2010; Rico et al., 2007). In addition, faultlines have been found to have a direct negative effect on group cohesion (Cronin et al., in press; Molleman, 2005). Bezrukova, Thatcher, and Jehn (2007) found that members in groups with strong faultlines were less satisfied with the group experience and less satisfied with their group performance than members in groups with weak faultlines. However, Lau and Murnighan (2005) showed that subgroups with strong faultlines expressed more satisfaction with their groups than those with weak faultlines. Thatcher and Patel's (2011) recent meta-analysis found that the negative effects of faultlines on performance were stronger than the effects of faultlines on group satisfaction; they argue that the positive feelings engendered by being part of a subgroup offset some of the negative aspects of faultlines experienced at the group level.

Moderators of the faultlines–outcomes relationship

The study of moderators is crucial for understanding how context can influence the role of faultlines in workgroups (Li & Hambrick, 2005). Like research on diversity, the goal of this stream of research is to find moderators that may diminish the negative effects of faultlines and enhance the positive effects of faultlines. The moderators that have been studied in the context of the faultlines–performance or faultlines–group process relationships are team identification, superordinate identity, group entitlement configuration, openness to experience, salience of intergroup differences, informational diversity, pro-diversity beliefs, shared task objectives, communication technology use, and task autonomy (Bezrukova et al., 2012; Bezrukova et al., 2009; Cramton & Hinds, 2005; Homan et al., 2007; 2008; Jehn & Bezrukova, 2010; Molleman, 2005; Polzer et al., 2006; Rico et al., 2007; van Knippenberg et al., 2011).

Jehn and Bezrukova (2010) found that group entitlement configuration influenced faultline activation. Bezrukova and her colleagues (2009; 2010) investigated the extent to which team identification acts as a moderator of the relationship between faultlines and outcomes; they found that team identification enhanced performance for groups with strong information-based faultlines. Homan and colleagues (2008) found that faultline groups performed more poorly when they did not have a superordinate identity.

Homan and her colleagues (2008) explored the idea that the personality variable of openness to experience, salience of intergroup differences, and salience of openness to experience would moderate the effect of faultlines and other diversity configurations on performance. They found that groups with high averages of openness to experience as well as saliency of intergroup differences and openness to experience performed better than groups with low averages. In another study, groups with faultlines that had both informational diversity and pro-diversity beliefs performed better than faultline groups with informational diversity and pro-similarity beliefs (Homan et al., 2007). These studies suggest that there are important group-level moderator effects that may be crucial in determining whether the outcomes of faultlines are positive (e.g., openness to experience) or negative (e.g., pro-similarity beliefs).

Another variable that may act as a moderator in the relationships between faultline antecedents and faultlines as well as faultlines and their consequences is communication technology use. Many researchers predicted that distributed teams would work more effectively than face-to-face teams because technology hides the visible features of diversity (Desanctis & Monge, 1999), but results of this research have been mixed (Carte & Chidambaram, 2004). With respect to faultlines, preliminary findings suggest that distributed teams (who rely on communication technology) should be more wary of subgroups (especially two subgroups) caused by faultlines than overall diversity levels (Cramton & Hinds, 2005; Polzer et al., 2006). In fact, the use of communication technology may increase the presence and persistence of faultlines. Current technologies used in group communication (e.g., email) provide users with the ability to communicate easily with only a subset of the entire group, increasing the likelihood of faultline activation and endurance (Cramton & Hinds, 2005; Polzer et al., 2006). As a result of subgroup communication rather than overall group communication, faultlines may lead to poor levels of performance because group members do not have all of the relevant information to make a good decision. Furthermore, the use of communication technologies for interactions within faultline-based subgroups is likely to create a stronger sense of subgroup competition than might occur in face-to-face interactions (Giambatista & Bhappu, 2010). To improve communication among the entire group, team leaders may choose to take on the task of acting as a bridge between any faultline-based subgroups that result from technology use.

Task characteristics such as task assignments and task interdependence may also operate as moderators in the faultline-group process and performance relationships. Task assignments may be optimal when distributed across subgroups. Even when tasks are functionally focused (e.g., engineering), it may be optimal to include members from other subgroups (e.g., marketing, accounting) so that future interactions between subgroups proceed more smoothly. However, it may be more efficient to compartmentalize the tasks so that there is as little interaction as possible across strong-faultline subgroups (Lau & Murnighan, 2005). Rico and colleagues (2007) investigated the influence of team task autonomy on the relationship between faultlines and outcomes and found that task autonomy exacerbated the negative effects of faultlines on decision quality and social integration. Similarly, Molleman (2005) found that faultlines were more detrimental to team functioning when team autonomy was high than when team autonomy was low.

Faultline endurance

The concept of faultlines focuses on the differences across subgroups. Over time, differences in knowledge, views, and preferences are reduced, especially when groups interact over a period of months or years (Katz, 1982). Furthermore, interaction of group members over time has been shown to lead to a reduction in stereotyping and an increase in group cohesion (Chatman & Flynn, 2001; Watson, Kumar, & Michaelsen, 1993). Li and Hambrick (2005) examined whether there were diminishing effects of faultlines on group processes over time and found that group tenure had no impact on group processes. On the other hand, Barkema and Shvyrkov (2007) found that top management teams that were in existence for long periods of time had significantly diminished negative effects resulting from strong faultlines. Barkema and Shvyrkov (2007) suggest that the pattern of faultline effects they found (e.g., a decrease in detrimental effects occurred after 3.75 years of weekly interactions in their dataset of Dutch firms) may reflect cultural norms.

The role of demographic faultlines in capturing demographic complexity

As can be seen from this brief review, much work has been done to investigate the impact of faultlines in groups. Because the effect of faultlines on outcomes occurs over and above those of demographic differences (Bezrukova et al., 2009; Lau & Murnighan, 2005; Thatcher & Patel, 2012), when group researchers focus on *only* demographic diversity they miss an important aspect of group composition that affects group functioning. Because faultlines capture the alignment of attribute dispersion within groups, faultlines give us a more complex understanding of diversity within groups.

Faultline theory provides the rationale for why alignment on multiple demographic attributes (faultlines) may influence group outcomes more strongly than demographic diversity alone. As individuals engage in behaviors and attributions designed to simultaneously create similarity with members of one subgroup and distinctiveness from members of another subgroup, it becomes easier to do so when there are multiple attributes of similarity and difference. This is reflected in Gibson and Vermeulen's (2003) study: they found that individuals with crossover attributes were able to bridge differences across subgroups. When faultlines are very strong, there are likely to be no (or few) crossover attributes. Other studies suggest that the presence of crossover attributes does not automatically result in better outcomes (Jehn & Bezrukova, 2010). These findings illustrate that we still have a ways to go to understand the myriad of ways that faultlines affect groups.

A second way that demographic faultlines capture complexity in a way that demographic diversity does not is that faultlines enable researchers to evaluate the effects of strong faultlines on subgroup outcomes. A number of positive outcomes at the subgroup level have been found. For example, subgroups were found to have high levels of interpersonal attraction (Lau & Murnighan, 2005), increased communication (Polzer et al., 2006), increased cooperation (Bezrukova et al., 2010), and high levels of social support (Bezrukova et al., 2010). Thus, the study of faultlines creates another level of analysis that researchers have only begun to investigate. Faultline theory, then, to some extent, is a multilevel theory connecting an individual to a subgroup and ultimately to a group. Studies should be designed to test the multilevel complexity that the theory of faultlines offers.

Demographic faultlines also provide a more complex view of diversity in that it may bring to the forefront stereotypically incongruent groups. For example, research in the minority/token literature (Kanter, 1977; Niemann & Dovidio, 1998) has shown that when individuals work in jobs that are stereotypically incongruent (e.g., male nurses, female miners), there are specific implications of this incongruence (Ely, 1995). When faultlines create stereotypically incongruent subgroups (e.g., female Ph.D. chemists), the effects resulting from these types of subgroups may be much different than when the subgroups are stereotypically congruent. Understanding demographic alignments may provide micro-level insight into issues that have been conceptualized at more macro-levels of analysis.

Another interesting aspect about faultlines is to consider how different types of demographic attributes interact to form subgroups. For example, whereas there has been theorizing on the differences between social-category, informational, and value-based differences, faultline theory would suggest that any combination of differences that makes one group similar and the other group different would be problematic for overall group outcomes. However, we have yet to have any systematic test of various combinations of attributes in a faultline score to determine which faultlines might be more detrimental than others. For example, we know that diversity on social category characteristics (e.g., race, age, sex) tends to result in poorer group outcomes than diversity on informational characteristics (tenure, education, functional background). Because faultlines are the alignment of demographic attributes, we are able to investigate what happens when different types of diversity align. For instance, we could compare the alignment of race and functional background to the alignment of race and education. Choi and Sy (2010) do this for a few combinations of attributes, but more complex combinations could be investigated. When investigating various combinations of faultlines, it is important to know whether there is dependence between the attributes included in a faultline. The ability to precisely articulate the conditions under which faultlines are most likely to influence outcomes would give us great insight into the mechanisms underlying the effects of faultlines.

Some identification researchers suggest that organizationally relevant identifications are nested (e.g., team identifications are nested in departments, which in turn may be nested in organizations). However, faultline theory does not make such a presumption. Faultline theory suggests that individuals identify with their subgroups to the detriment of their overall group unless there is a strong group identity (Bezrukova et al., 2009; Jehn & Bezrukova, 2010). Subgroups formed by faultlines may present a new identification source for individuals. Because subgroups are, by definition, smaller than the overall group, they may be an attractive source for self-verification and identity comprehension (e.g., Swann Jr., Polzer, Seyle, & Ko, 2004; Thatcher & Greer, 2008) whereby individuals feel understood and accepted. Understanding the motivation behind an individual's identification with subgroups or the larger group, such as an individual's self-concept (Cooper & Thatcher, 2010), is another interesting path for future research. Thus, the study of demographic faultlines gives us the opportunity to study new questions about the relationship between identity and demographic differences.

Gaps in the study of faultlines

In addition to providing a more nuanced view of diversity, there are many ways to further the study of faultlines. In the following section I discuss some gaps in the current literature and provide some areas for future research.

Faultline composition and antecedents

With respect to faultline composition, focusing less on surface-level variables (e.g., race, sex) and more on deep-level variables (attitudes, beliefs, values) when looking at long-lasting work teams is consistent with approaches prescribed by diversity researchers (Harrison et al., 1998; Harrison et al., 2002). We may find that alignment of surface-level, informational, and deep-level attributes produces the worst type of faultlines, resulting in group fissions (breakups), as described by Hart and Van Vugt (2006). Expanding the type of characteristics in faultline composition to include personality and ability attributes may yield significant findings. Furthermore, as virtual teams become more common, there is increased potential for the development of geographic-, culture-, and language-based faultlines.

Work values reflected in aspects of temporal preferences, use of technology, and communication preferences may be interesting to investigate as components of faultline composition. For example, a faultline along the dimension of communication preferences such that half of the group likes discussing problems orally until a solution emerges and half of the group prefers to exchange emails to come to a solution may be more harmful to performance than demographic-based faultlines. On the other hand, these types of faultlines may have little impact on affective-based outcomes.

It is also important to consider the implications of group size for demographic faultlines because group size may facilitate the desire for subgroup interactions (Hart & Van Vugt, 2006). Group size is taken into account in many of the operationalizations of faultlines and is often used as a control variable (Barkema & Shvyrkov, 2007; Bezrukova, Spell, & Perry, 2010; Li & Hambrick, 2005). For example, Gibson and Vermeulen (2003) controlled for group size in their study of subgroup strength, and correlations reflected a strong relationship between group size and subgroup strength (reflecting faultline strength). Studies on faultlines have not directly considered the effect of group size on faultline strength. However, it is important to keep in mind that strong demographic faultlines require homogeneity of the individual subgroups. When the overall group is very large, it is unlikely that subgroups can be homogeneous across multiple attributes. Thatcher and Patel's (2011) meta-analysis showed that the relationship between group size and demographic faultlines is in the form of an inverted-U shape.

Active faultlines and faultline triggers

Future research should investigate the extent to which all faultline triggers can be classified into one of the five categories (differential treatment, different values, assimilation, insult or humiliating action, and simple contact) developed by Chrobot-Mason and colleagues (2009) or whether there are additional triggers that are important to workgroups. In addition, it would be interesting to explore whether some triggers are more harmful than others. For example, faultline triggers based on different values may not reflect ideal working situations but may be bearable. On the other hand, insults and humiliating actions may be more serious triggers that cause irreparable harm to the overall group. Furthermore, we do not know enough about how groups that begin their life with a pre-existing "triggered" faultline (e.g., negotiating parties with different interests, the two sides of a merged company) differ from groups that initially perceive no faultline but experience a trigger (e.g., racial equality task).

It is interesting to note that Lau and Murnighan (2005) found that higher levels of interpersonal connections existed in subgroups when there were strong faultlines; furthermore, these faultlines occurred even when groups undertook tasks that were not designed to trigger faultlines. Other researchers have also found that faultlines influence group processes and outcomes even when not activated (Bezrukova et al., 2009; 2007; Thatcher et al., 2003). These findings support Tajfel's (1982) arguments that merely being aware of subgroups (e.g., in-groups and out-groups) creates a dynamic that pits subgroups against one another. The findings from these studies suggest that we still know very little about the extent to which the effects of active faultlines differ from those of latent faultlines. We are also just beginning to understand what might trigger a faultline.

Another interesting avenue to explore is the role of individuals in triggering faultlines. Individuals have multiple identity structures (e.g., gender, race, age), and many individuals have intra-individual crossover attributes (e.g., mixed race, second-generation immigrant). The extent to which individuals identify with a particular aspect of their self, dis-identify with a particular aspect, or create an entirely new identity may have implications for faultline activation. In addition, the way in which others categorize an individual with crossover attributes may influence faultline activation. Imagine a six-person group consisting of three Caucasians, two Asians, and an individual who is biracial (Asian and Caucasian). There are three potential race-based faultline conditions: (1) one strong faultline resulting in two subgroups of three people each (biracial person aligns with the Asians); (2) one strong faultline resulting in two subgroups, with one subgroup consisting of four people and one subgroup consisting of two people (biracial person aligns with the Caucasians); (3) one strong faultline and one weak faultline resulting in three subgroups (Caucasian group of three, Asian group of two, biracial "group" of one). In the third condition described above, the biracial individual may be able to act as a crosscutter, thereby deactivating the racial faultline. The biracial individual may also act as a token individual by choosing not to identify with either of the other two subgroups. This example is not merely a theoretical exercise: many countries are becoming more diverse as different-race couples have children, age no longer defines an individual's opportunities, and gender roles become increasingly blurred. In addition, individuals may have multiple educational and functional experiences. Individuals with multiple degrees or many different job experiences may influence faultline configuration and the extent to which faultlines will be activated. A fruitful extension of faultlines research is to consider the implications of intra-individual crossover characteristics on faultline development and activation.

The consequences of faultlines

Although many group processes and outcomes have been examined by faultline researchers, there are some gaps in what has been studied. Cooperation was found to be higher within subgroups (Bezrukova et al., 2010; Hart & Van Vugt, 2006), but to date no studies have investigated how faultlines influence overall group cooperation. Affective integration (trust, respect, liking) was an effective mediator in the subgroup–performance relationship (Cronin et al., 2011), but more research on these and other group processes is needed with respect to faultline-based subgroups. Although the majority of faultline studies have focused on group-level outcomes, recent studies have begun exploring the effects of faultlines at other levels of analysis (Bezrukova et al., 2010).

There are additional outcomes that may be of interest to those studying faultlines. Creativity is one potential outcome where the presence of faultlines may certainly be felt. Pearsall, Ellis, and Evans (2008) found that when gender faultlines were activated, groups had fewer ideas and the overall creativity of ideas was diminished. Another area to explore is that of group-level organizational citizenship behaviors (GOCB). Choi and Sy (2010) found that faultlines on the basis of tenure and race positively related to GOCB. When they examined mediation effects, they found that faultlines affected GOCB positively through the task conflict mediator, and faultlines affected GOCB negatively through the relationship conflict mediator. Bezrukova and colleagues (2010) found that faultlines moderated the relationship between interpersonal injustice and individual psychological stress. Although faultlines acted as a moderator in this relationship, the study suggests that faultlines have an impact on individual-level perceptions. Other potential individual-level outcomes of faultlines include turnover, absenteeism, organizational commitment, and organizational identification. Potential group-level outcomes could include shared mental models (Mohammed & Dumville, 2001), group cross-understanding (Huber & Lewis, 2010), group-level communication (Wu & Keysar, 2007), group collaborative behaviors (Ng & Van Dyne, 2005), and group deviant behaviors (Bruk-Lee & Spector, 2006).

Moderators of the faultlines–outcomes relationship

There are a number of moderators that might influence the faultlines–outcome relationship that have not been fully investigated. Task characteristics such as task interdependence (Wageman & Baker, 1995), routineness, and task content may be relevant to the relationship between faultlines and outcomes (Lau & Murnighan, 2005; Rico et al., 2007) and should be investigated. Job type may be another moderator; groups in stressful jobs such as nursing, medicine, policing, and control tower dispatch may benefit from the positive social support and cognitive integration in faultline-generated subgroups. Future research on potential moderators such as training programs, proactive leadership, and member selection processes will help inform the boundary conditions under which faultlines are positive, negative, or insignificant to group process and outcomes.

Direct versus moderating effects of faultlines

Apart from moderators that might influence the relationship between faultlines and the outcomes of faultlines, some researchers have questioned whether faultlines are in fact a moderator of other relationships. Researchers should carefully consider when groups experience the effects of faultlines directly and when they experience them indirectly. Although a few studies have investigated the potential indirect effects of faultlines, the number of studies is scarce. Gibson and Vermeulen (2003) found that subgroup strength (which corresponds closely to the faultline strength concept) moderated the relationship between features of organizational design and team learning. Lau and Murnighan (2005) found that faultlines moderated the relationship between cross-subgroup communications and outcomes such that in weak-faultline groups, the frequency of communication across subgroups contributed to higher levels of group learning, group satisfaction, group performance, and psychological safety. In a study of workgroups, Bezrukova and colleagues (2009) found that faultline distance (or the degree of differences between subgroups) exacerbated the negative relationship between faultline strength and both perceived and objective performance. Faultlines were also found to weaken the positive relationship between interpersonal injustice and psychological distress (Bezrukova et al., 2010). These findings suggest that group faultlines act as both a direct antecedent of group functioning as well as an indirect context in group interactions and individual perceptions. However, much more work needs to be done in an effort to distinguish when the effects of faultlines influence teams and individual team members directly or when the effects of faultlines are felt indirectly.

Faultline endurance

Two studies have looked at the issue of faultline endurance, but more research needs to investigate this topic. For example, future researchers may want to investigate the formation and endurance of faultlines, as well as the role of culture in faultline endurance. Cultural views of individualism–collectivism and power distance may affect not only the extent to which faultlines occur but also the effects of faultlines on group functioning and the duration that faultlines are likely to persist. For example, in high power-distance countries, the formation of subgroups may revolve around the power status of individuals in the group. Time is unlikely to diminish the differences that exist from the power differential.

Team turnover may present an opportunity for seismic shifts in a particular faultline configuration and faultline endurance. Future research may want to explore how the departure or entrance of a particular team member may alter the dynamics caused by a fractured faultline. A carefully controlled longitudinal study might be able to assess whether the effects of faultlines decrease over time, as has been shown in diverse teams (Harrison et al., 2002; Watson et al., 1993), become more entrenched, or shift as the task and environmental context change (Kozlowski, 1998).

Faultline definition and measurement

Subgroup size may be an important issue to consider. Some researchers have controlled for the effects of the "evenness of group size" because groups with an odd number of members would be unable to split into two equal-sized subgroups, and uneven subgroups may affect overall group processes and performance (Li & Hambrick, 2005; O'Leary & Mortensen, 2010; Thatcher et al., 2003). Phillips and colleagues (2004), in a study of knowledge diversity, found that equal-sized subgroups (i.e., two members each) with incongruent knowledge outperformed groups with three members (and unequal subgroups). Polzer and colleagues (2006) specifically investigated the number and size of subgroups caused by faultlines on conflict and trust. They found that when groups consisted of two three-person subgroups (e.g., one faultline), the team members perceived more conflict and less trust between subgroups than when subgroups consisted of three two-person subgroups (e.g., two faultlines) or fully dispersed groups (e.g., no faultlines, maximum diversity). A deeper understanding of the myriad of ways that faultlines can split a group is crucial to furthering our understanding of faultlines in organizational groups.

Another important finding from Polzer and colleagues (2006) relates to both the definition and measurement of faultlines. A faultline is currently defined as being strong when a group is divided into two or more homogeneous subgroups (Lau & Murnighan, 1998). Polzer and colleagues (2006) found that the most negative consequences from faultlines did *not* occur when faultlines were strong, using Lau and Murnighan's (1998) definition. When only *one* of the subgroups caused by a faultline is homogenous, the effect of faultlines can be as destructive as when the faultline creates two homogeneous subgroups. This is also reflected in a meta-analysis of intergroup evaluations (Mullen, Migdal, & Hewstone, 2001); in-groups are viewed as significantly different from out-groups AND from cross-categorized groups. These findings have implications for both theorizing and measuring faultlines. Current methods of measuring faultlines (Bezrukova et al., 2009; Shaw, 2004; Thatcher et al., 2003) create faultline scores that reflect the homogeneity of potential subgroups. Although these scores may adequately reflect the operationalization of the faultlines construct first developed by Lau and Murnighan (1998), they may not adequately reflect the underlying mechanisms affecting group processes and outcomes. Researchers may want to adapt these measures so that they create scores based on the homogeneity of a single subgroup. Furthermore, one of the key premises of faultlines, the relative homogeneity of all subgroups, is called into question but promises to be a fruitful area for future research.

Crucial research questions in the study of faultlines

In the previous sections I distinguished between diversity and demographic faultlines, discussed the underlying theory of faultlines, reviewed the current literature, argued that the study of faultlines allows for a more complex understanding of the effects of multi-attribute diversity, and discussed some gaps in the current literature. Below I list ten specific research questions that, when answered, will further our understanding of the role of faultlines in groups.

1. What features (e.g., type of diversity, form of diversity) of demographic diversity are most likely to lead to latent and active faultlines?

2. What individual differences are most likely to lead to active faultlines? For example, how do personality, status, and other attributes (e.g., citizenship status, have vs. have-nots, telecommuters vs. non-telecommuters) affect active faultlines?

3. What combinations of attributes create a faultline composition that has the worst (or best) effect on group processes and outcomes? How does subgroup number and size influence the effect of faultlines on group processes and outcomes?

4. How do faultlines influence outcomes at different levels of analysis (individual, subgroup, group)?

5. What role does geographic and cultural distance play in the creation and outcomes of faultlines?

6. What triggers latent faultlines to become active faultlines?

7. What is the role of intra-individual crossover attributes (e.g., biracial, multiple degrees) for managing faultlines?

8. What other moderators influence the relationship between faultlines and outcomes? Are there moderators that actually transform the generally negative relationship between faultlines and outcomes into a positive relationship?

9. What is the role of multilevel identification in faultline research?

10. What is the lifespan of faultlines? If the effects of faultlines dissipate over time, at what point do they do so?

Conclusion

The effects of individual attributes from the micro-level to the group level have been extensively studied in the diversity literature, and a plethora of evidence exists on the effects of group-level dynamics on group-level outcomes. Faultlines, as a meso-level group variable, have become increasingly important in studying subgroup dynamics. Faultlines add an additional dimension to our study of diversity in groups. By integrating the burgeoning literature on the theoretical and empirical findings of faultlines, this chapter provides a roadmap for researchers interested in continuing the study of faultlines.

Notes

1. For a comparison of demographic diversity and demographic faultline scores in four-person groups, please refer to Table 1 in Thatcher, Jehn, and Zanutto (2003).

2. Harrison and Klein (2007) argue that demographic attributes may be conceptualized as different forms of diversity depending on the context. For example, functional background diversity could be conceptualized as separation, variety, and disparity diversity. In this section of the chapter I am focused on the shape of the attribute distribution and use demographic attributes as examples of that distribution.

References

Ancona, D. G., & Caldwell, D. F. (1992). Bridging the boundary: External activity and performance in organizational teams. *Administrative Science Quarterly, 37*(4): 634–665.

Barkema, H. G., & Shvyrkov, O. (2007). Does top management team diversity promote or hamper foreign expansion. *Strategic Management Journal, 28*(7), 663–680.

Bartel, C. A. (2001). Social comparisons in boundary-spanning work: Effects of community outreach on members' organizational identity and identification. *Administrative Science Quarterly, 46*(3), 379–413.

Bezrukova, K., Jehn, K. A., Zanutto, E. L., & Thatcher, S. (2009). Do workgroup faultlines help or hurt? A moderated model of faultlines, team identification, and group performance. *Organization Science, 20*(1), 35–50.

Bezrukova, K., Spell, C., & Perry, J. (2010). Violent splits or healthy divides? Coping with injustice through faultlines. *Personnel Psychology, 63*(3), 719–751.

Bezrukova, K., Thatcher, S. M. B., Jehn, K., & Spell, C. (2012). The effects of alignments: Examining group faultlines, organizational cultures, and performance. *Journal of Applied Psychology, 97*(1): 77–92.

Bezrukova, K., Thatcher, S. M. B., & Jehn, K. (2007). Group heterogeneity and faultlines: Comparing alignment and dispersion theories of group composition. In K. J. Behfar & L. L. Thompson (Eds.), *Conflict in organizational groups: New directions in theory and practice* (pp. 57–92). Evanston, IL: Northwestern University Press.

Bowers, C., Parmer, J. A., & Salas, E. (2000). When member homogeneity is needed in work teams: A meta-analysis. *Small Group Research, 31*, 305–327.

Brewer, M. B. (2001). Ingroup identification and intergroup conflict: When does ingroup love become outgroup hate? In R. D. Ashmore, L. Jussim & D. Wilder (Eds.), *Social identity, intergroup conflict, and conflict reduction* (pp. 17–41). New York, NY: Oxford University Press.

Brewer, M. B. (2000). Reducing prejudice through cross-categorization: Effects of multiple social identities. In S. Oskamp (Ed.), *Reducing prejudice and discrimination* (pp. 165–183). Mahwah, NJ: Lawrence Erlbaum Associates.

Brewer, M. B. (1991). The social self: On being the same and different at the same time. *Personality and Social Psychology Bulletin, 17*, 475–482.

Brewer, M. B. (1996). When contact is not enough: Social identity and intergroup cooperation. *International Journal of Intercultural Relations, 20*(3–4), 291–303.

Brewer, M. B., Manzi, J. M., & Shaw, J. S. (1993). In-group identification as a function of depersonalization, distinctiveness, and status. *Psychological Science, 42*(2), 88–92.

Bruk-Lee, V., & Spector, P. E. (2006). The social stressors-counterproductive work behaviors link: Are conflicts with supervisors and coworkers the same? *Journal of Occupational Health Psychology, 11*(2), 145–156.

Byrne, D. E. (1971). *The attraction paradigm*. San Diego, CA: Academic Press.

Carte, T., & Chidambaram, L. (2004). A capabilities-based theory of technology deployment in diverse teams: Leapfrogging the pitfalls of diversity and leveraging its potential with collaborative technology. *Journal of the Association for Information Systems, 5*(11–12), 448–471.

Chatman, J. A., & Flynn, F. J. (2001). The influence of demographic heterogeneity on the emergence and consequences of cooperative norms in work teams. *Academy of Management Journal, 44*, 956–974.

Choi, J. N., & Sy, G. (2010). Group-level organizational citizenship behavior: Effects of demographic faultlines and conflict in small work groups. *Journal of Organizational Behavior, 31*(7), 1032–1054.

Chrobot-Mason, D., Ruderman, M. N., Weber, T. J., & Ernst, C. (2009). The challenge of leading on unstable ground: Triggers that activate social identity faultlines. *Human Relations, 62*(11), 1763–1794.

Clark, M. A., Anand, V., & Roberson, L. (2000). Resolving meaning: Interpretation in diverse decision-making groups. *Group Dynamics: Theory, Research, and Practice, 4*(3), 211–221.

Cooper, D., & Thatcher, S. M. B. (2010). Understanding identification in teams: The role of individualist-collectivist cultural orientation. *Academy of Management Review, 35*(4), 516–538.

Cox, T. H., Lobel, S. A., & McLeod, P. L. (1991). Effects of ethnic group cultural differences on cooperative and competitive behavior on a group task. *Academy of Management Journal, 34*, 827–847.

Cramton, C. D. (2001). The mutual knowledge problem and its consequences for dispersed collaboration. *Organization Science, 12*(3), 346–371.

Cramton, C. D., & Hinds, P. J. (2005). Subgroup dynamics in internationally distributed teams: Ethnocentrism or cross-national learning? *Research in Organizational Behavior. An Annual Series of Analytical Essays and Critical Reviews, 26*, 231–263.

Crisp, R. J., & Hewstone, M. (1999). Differential evaluation of crossed category groups: Patterns, processes, and reducing intergroup bias. *Group Processes & Intergroup Relations, 2*(4), 307.

Cronin, M. A., Bezrukova, K., Weingart, L. R., & Tinsley, C. H. (2011). Subgroups within a team: The role of cognitive and affective integration. *Journal of Organizational Behavior, 32*, 831–849.

Dahlin, K. B., Weingart, L. R., & Hinds, P. J. (2005). Team diversity and information use. *Academy of Management Journal, 48*(6), 1107–1123.

Desanctis, G., & Monge, P. (1999). Introduction to the special issue: Communication processes for virtual organizations. *Organization Science, 10*(6), 693–703.

Deschamps, J. C. (1977). Effect of crossing category membership on quantitative judgment. *European Journal of Social Psychology, 7*, 517–521.

Devine, D. J., Clayton, L. D., Philips, J. L., Dunford, B. B., & Melner, S. B. (1999). Teams in organizations: Prevalence, characteristics, and effectiveness. *Small Group Research, 30*(6), 678–711.

Earley, P. C., & Mosakowski, E. (2000). Creating hybrid team cultures: An empirical test of transnational team functioning. *Academy of Management Journal, 43*(1), 26–49.

Ely, R. J. (1995). The power in demography: Women's social constructions of gender identity at work. *Academy of Management Journal, 38*, 589–634.

Giambatista, R. C., & Bhappu, A. D. (2010). Diversity's harvest: Interaction of diversity sources and communication technology on creative group performance. *Organizational Behavior and Human Decision Processes, 111*(2), 116–126.

Gibson, C., & Vermeulen, F. (2003). A healthy divide: Subgroups as a stimulus for team learning behavior. *Administrative Science Quarterly, 48*(2), 202–239.

Gruenfeld, D. H., Mannix, E. A., Williams, K. Y., & Neale, M. A. (1996). Group composition and decision making: How member familiarity and information distribution affect process and performance. *Organizational Behavior and Human Decision Processes, 67*, 1–15.

Halevy, N. (2008). Team negotiation: Social, epistemic, economic, and psychological consequences of subgroup conflict. *Personality and Social Psychology Bulletin, 34*(12), 1687.

Harrison, D. A., & Klein, K. J. (2007). What's the difference? Diversity constructs as separation, variety, or disparity in organizations. *Academy of Management Review, 32*(4), 1199–1228.

Harrison, D. A., Price, K. H., & Bell, M. P. (1998). Beyond relational demography: Time and the effects of surface-and deep-level diversity on work group cohesion. *Academy of Management Journal, 41*(1), 96–107.

Harrison, D. A., Price, K. H., Gavin, J. H., & Florey, A. T. (2002). Time, teams, and task performance: Changing effects of surface-and deep-level diversity on group functioning. *Academy of Management Journal, 45*, 1029–1045.

Hart, C. M., & Van Vugt, M. (2006). From fault line to group fission: Understanding membership changes in small groups. *Personality and Social Psychology Bulletin, 32*(3), 392.

Hinds, P. J., & Bailey, D. E. (2003). Out of sight, out of sync: Understanding conflict in distributed teams. *Organization Science, 14*(6), 615–632.

Hogg, M. A. (2006). Social identity theory. In P. J. Burke (Ed.), *Contemporary social psychological theories* (pp. 111–136). Stanford, CA: Stanford University Press.

Hogg, M. A., Turner, J. C., & Davidson, B. (1990). Polarized norms and social frames of reference: A test of the self-categorization theory of group polarization. *Basic and Applied Social Psychology, 11*(1), 77–100.

Homan, A. C., Hollenbeck, J. R., Humphrey, S. E., Van Knippenberg, D., Ilgen, D. R., & Van Kleef, G. A. (2008). Facing differences with an open mind: Openness to experience, salience of intragroup differences, and performance of diverse work groups. *Academy of Management Journal, 51*(6), 1204–1222.

Homan, A. C., van Knippenberg, D., Van Kleef, G. A., & De Dreu, C. K. W. (2007). Bridging faultlines by valuing diversity: Diversity beliefs, information elaboration, and performance in diverse work groups. *Journal of Applied Psychology, 92*(5), 1189–1199.

Hornsey, M. J., & Hogg, M. A. (2000). Assimilation and diversity: An integrative model of subgroup relations. *Personality and Social Psychology Review, 4*(143–156).

Hornsey, M. J., & Hogg, M. A. (1999). Subgroup differentiation as a response to an overly-inclusive group: A test of optimal distinctiveness theory. *European Journal of Social Psychology, 29*(4), 543–550.

Horwitz, S. K., & Horwitz, I. B. (2007). The effects of team diversity on team outcomes: A meta-analytic review of team demography. *Journal of Management, 33*(6), 987–1015.

Hraba, J., Hagendoorn, L., & Hagendoorn, R. (1989). The ethnic hierarchy in the Netherlands: Social distance and social representation. *British Journal of Social Psychology, 28*, 57–69.

Huber, G. P., & Lewis, K. (2010). Cross-understanding: Implications for group cognition and performance. *Academy of Management Review, 35*(1), 6–26.

Insko, C. A., & Schopler, J. (1987). Categorization, competition, and collectivity. *Group Processes, 8*, 213–251.

Insko, C. A., Schopler, J., Hoyle, R., Dardis, G., & Graetz, K. (1990). Individual-group discontinuity as a function of fear and greed. *Journal of Personality and Social Psychology, 58*, 68–79.

Jehn, K. A. (1997). A qualitative analysis of conflict types and dimensions in organizational groups. *Administrative Science Quarterly, 42*(3), 530–557.

Jehn, K. A., & Bezrukova, K. (2010). The faultline activation process and the effects of activated faultlines on coalition formation, conflict, and group outcomes. *Organizational Behavior and Human Decision Processes, 112*(1), 24–42.

Jehn, K. A., Chadwick, C., & Thatcher, S. M. B. (1997). To agree or not to agree: The effects of value congruence, individual demographic dissimilarity, and conflict on workgroup outcomes. *International Journal of Conflict Management, 8*(4), 287–305.

Jehn, K. A., Northcraft, G. B., & Neale, M. A. (1999). Why differences make a difference: A field study of diversity, conflict, and performance in workgroups. *Administrative Science Quarterly, 44*(4), 741–763.

Jetten, J., Spears, R., & Postmes, T. (2004). Intergroup distinctiveness and differentiation: A meta-analytic integration. *Journal of Personality and Social Psychology, 86*, 862–879.

Kanter, R. M. (1977). *Men and women of the corporation*. New York, NY: Basic Books.

Katz, R. (1982). The effects of group longevity on project communication and performance. *Administrative Science Quarterly, 27*, 81–104.

Kozlowski, S. W. J. (1998). Training and developing adaptive teams: Theory, principles, and research. In J. A. Cannon-Bowers & E. Salas (Eds.), *Making decisions under stress: implications for individual and team training* (pp. 115–153). Washington, D.C.: American Psychological Association.

Lau, D. C., & Murnighan, J. K. (1998). Demographic diversity and faultlines: The compositional dynamics of organizational groups. *Academy of Management Review, 23*(2), 325–340.

Lau, D. C., & Murnighan, J. K. (2005). Interactions within groups and subgroups: The effects of demographic faultlines. *Academy of Management Journal, 48*(4), 645–659.

Levine, J. M., & Moreland, R. L. (1990). Progress in small group research. *Annual Review of Psychology, 41*(1), 585–634.

Li, J., & Hambrick, D. C. (2005). Factional groups: A new vantage on demographic faultlines, conflict, and disintegration in work teams *Academy of Management Journal, 48*(5), 794–813.

Linnehan, F., Chrobot-Mason, D., & Konrad, A. M. (2006). Diversity attitudes and norms: The role of ethnic identity and relational demography. *Journal of Organizational Behavior, 27*(4), 419–442.

Marcus-Newhall, A., Miller, N., Holtz, R., & Brewer, M. B. (1993). Cross-cutting category membership with role assignment: A means of reducing intergroup bias. *British Journal of Social Psychology, 32*, 125–146.

Mohammed, S., & Dumville, B. C. (2001). Team mental models in a team knowledge framework: Expanding theory and measurement across disciplinary boundaries. *Journal of Organizational Behavior, 22*(2), 89–106.

Molleman, E. (2005). Diversity in demographic characteristics, abilities and personality traits: Do faultlines affect team functioning? *Group Decision and Negotiation, 14*(3), 173–193.

Mullen, B., Migdal, M. J., & Hewstone, M. (2001). Crossed categorization versus simple categorization and intergroup evaluations: A meta-analysis. *European Journal of Social Psychology, 31*, 721–736.

Murnighan, J. K. (1978). Models of coalition behavior: Game theoretic, social psychological, and political perspectives. *Psychological Bulletin, 85*(5), 1130–1153.

Murnighan, J. K., & Conlon, D. E. (1991). The dynamics of intense work groups: A study of British string quartets. *Administrative Science Quarterly, 36*, 165–186.

Ng, K. Y., & Van Dyne, L. (2005). Antecedents and performance consequences of helping behavior in work groups: A multilevel analysis. *Group and Organization Management, 30*(5), 514–540.

Niemann, Y. F., & Dovidio, J. F. (1998). Relationship of solo status, academic rank, and perceived distinctiveness to job satisfaction of racial/ethnic minorities. *Journal of Applied Psychology, 83*, 55–71.

O'Leary, M. B., & Mortensen, M. (2010). Go (con)figure: Subgroups, imbalance, and isolates in geographically dispersed teams. *Organization Science, 21*, 115–131.

Pearsall, M. J., Ellis, A. P. J., & Evans, J. M. (2008). Unlocking the effects of gender faultlines on team creativity: Is activation the key? *Journal of Applied Psychology, 93*(1), 225–234.

Pelled, L. H. (1996). Demographic diversity, conflict, and work group outcomes: An intervening process theory. *Organization Science, 7*(6), 615–631.

Pelled, L. H., Eisenhardt, K. M., & Xin, K. R. (1999). Exploring the black box: An analysis of work group diversity, conflict, and performance. *Administrative Science Quarterly, 44*(1), 1–3.

Phillips, K. W., Mannix, E. A., & Neale, M. A. (2004). Diverse groups and information sharing: The effects of congruent ties. *Journal of Experimental Social Psychology, 40*(4), 497–510.

Pickett, C. L., & Brewer, M. B. (2001). Assimilation and differentiation needs as motivational determinants of perceived in-group and out-group homogeneity. *Journal of Experimental Social Psychology, 37*(4), 341–348.

Polzer, J. T., Crisp, C. B., Jarvenpaa, S. L., & Kim, J. W. (2006). Extending the faultline model to geographically dispersed teams: How colocated subgroups can impair group functioning. *Academy of Management Journal, 49*(4), 679.

Polzer, J. T., Mannix, E. A., & Neale, M. A. (1998). Interest alignment and coalitions in multiparty negotiation. *Academy of Management Journal, 41*(1), 42–54.

Rico, R., Molleman, E., Sanchez-Manzanares, M., & Van der Vegt, G. S. (2007). The effects of diversity faultlines and team task autonomy on decision quality and social integration. *Journal of Management, 33*(1), 111.

Rousseau, D. M. & House, D. J. (1994). Meso organizational behavior: Avoiding three fundamental biases. *Journal of Organizational Behavior: Trends in Organizational Behavior, 1*, 13–30.

Sawyer, J. E., Houlette, M. A., & Yeagley, E. L. (2006). Decision performance and diversity structure: Comparing faultlines in convergent, crosscut, and racially homogeneous groups. *Organizational Behavior and Human Decision Processes, 99*(1), 1–15.

Schippers, M. C., Den Hartog, D. N., Koopman, P. L., & Wienk, J. A. (2003). Diversity and team outcomes: The moderating effects of outcome interdependence and group longevity and the mediating effect of reflexivity. *Journal of Organizational Behavior, 24*(6), 779–802.

Shaw, J. B. (2004). The development and analysis of a measure of group faultlines. *Organizational Research Methods, 7*(1), 66–100.

Simons, T., Pelled, L. H., & Smith, K. A. (1999). Making use of difference: Diversity, debate, and decision comprehensiveness in top management teams. *Academy of Management Journal, 42*, 662–674.

Stevenson, W. B., Pearce, J. L., & Porter, L. W. (1985). The concept of "coalition" in organization theory and research. *Academy of Management Review, 10*(2), 256–268.

Swann Jr., W. B., Polzer, J. T., Seyle, D. C., & Ko, S. J. (2004). Finding value in diversity: Verification of personal and social self-views in diverse groups. *Academy of Management Review, 29*(1), 9–27.

Tajfel, H. (1978). *Differentiation between social groups: Studies in the social psychology of intergroup relations*, Oxford, England: Academic Press.

Tajfel, H. (1982). Social psychology of intergroup relations. *Annual Review of Psychology, 33*(1), 1–39.

Thatcher, S. M. B., & Greer, L. L. (2008). Does it really matter if you recognize who I am? The implications of identity comprehension for individuals in work teams. *Journal of Management, 34*(1), 5–24.

Thatcher, S. M. B., Jehn, K. A., & Zanutto, E. (2003). Cracks in diversity research: The effects of diversity faultlines on conflict and performance. *Group Decision and Negotiation, 12*(3), 217–241.

Thatcher, S. M. B., & Patel, P. C. (2012). Group faultlines: A review, integration, and guide to future research. *Journal of Management, 38*(4), 969–1009.

Thatcher, S. M. B., & Patel, P. C. (2011). Demographic faultlines: A meta-analysis of the literature. *Journal of Applied Psychology, 96*(6), 1119–1139.

Tsui, A. S., Egan, T. D., & O'Reilly III, C. A. (1992). Being different: Relational demography and organizational attachment. *Administrative Science Quarterly, 37*(4), 549–579.

Turner, J. C. (1985). Social categorization and the self-concept: a social cognitive theory of group. *Advances in Group Processes, 2*, 77–121.

Turner, J. C., Hogg, M. A., Oakes, P. J., Reicher, S. D., & Wetherell, M. S. (1987). *Rediscovering the social group: A self-categorization theory*. Oxford, UK: Blackwell.

Van Knippenberg, D., Dawson, J. F., West, M. A., & Homan, A. C. (2011). Diversity faultlines, shared objectives, and top management team performance. *Human Relations, 64*, 307–336.

van Knippenberg, D., De Dreu, C. K. W., & Homan, A. C. (2004). Work group diversity and group performance: An integrative model and research agenda. *Journal of Applied Psychology, 89*(6), 1008–1022.

Wageman, R., & Baker, G. (1995). Incentives and cooperation: The joint effects of task and reward interdependence on group performance. *Journal of Organizational Behavior, 18*(2), 139–158.

Watson, W. E., Kumar, K., & Michaelsen, L. K. (1993). Cultural diversity's impact on interaction process and performance: Comparing homogeneous and diverse task groups. *Academy of Management Journal, 36*(3), 590–602.

Webber, S. S., & Donahue, L. M. (2001). Impact of highly and less job-related diversity on work group cohesion and performance: A meta-analysis. *Journal of Management, 27*, 141–162.

Williams, K. Y., & O'Reilly III, C. A. (1998). Demography and diversity in organizations: A review of 40 years of research. *Research in Organizational Behavior, 20*, 77–140.

Wu, S., & Keysar, B. (2007). The effect of information overlap on communication effectiveness. *Cognitive Science, 31*(1), 169–181.

PART 3

Psychological Perspectives on Diversity

CHAPTER 5

Navigating the Self in Diverse Work Contexts

Laura Morgan Roberts *and* Stephanie J. Creary

Abstract

Navigating the self is critical for working in a diverse world, in which different identities interact in social space. This chapter presents five theoretical perspectives on how individuals navigate the self in diverse organizational contexts—social identity, critical identity, (role) identity, narrative-as-identity, and identity work. We review these five prominent theoretical perspectives on identity processes in diverse contexts to explicate various ways in which individuals actively participate in the co-construction of their identities in diverse contexts. As a next step in research, identity, diversity, and relationship scholars are encouraged to inquire into the generativity of proposed tactics for navigating the self in order to identify pathways for cultivating more positive identities in diverse work settings. The examination of positive relational identities is considered a promising path for further inquiry in this domain.

Key Words: identity, positive identity, identity construction, identity work, image management, positive organizational scholarship, social identity

Introduction

Navigating the self is germane to working in a diverse world. Navigating the self refers to the identity construction and negotiation processes that unfold as people interpret and act on their differences. Navigating the self involves proactive identity construction that helps fulfill the need for dignity, recognition, safety, control, purpose, and efficacy (Rothman, 1997, p. 7). Diversity within a work setting shapes how people view themselves—as insiders, outsiders, powerful, powerless, conformists, or deviants, to name a few identities. Personal, interpersonal, and intergroup dynamics influence how people interpret and act on their differences in diverse work settings. This chapter presents an array of tactics, and the underlying motives that prompt tactic use, when an individual navigates his or her self in a diverse work setting.

As Booysen (2007, p. 6) writes, "tension and conflict between diverse social identity groups are major disruptive factors in nearly every country of the world." Societal power disparities between identity groups, manifested at the personal and interpersonal levels, often, but not inevitably, hinder the effective functioning of culturally diverse teams. Biases and ego defensive routines can deepen misunderstanding, heighten animosity, and undermine trust between people from different cultural groups in work settings. Some approaches to navigating the self exacerbate identity conflicts in an attempt to preserve an individual's sense of worth and esteem. However, as people interpret and act on differences in constructive ways, they open possibilities for differences to become sources of creativity and resilience. It is therefore important to identify which tactics for navigating the self constitute generative pathways for cultivating more positive identities in diverse work settings and building stronger relationships across dimensions of difference.

Despite its practical significance, the topic of navigating the self has not been featured as a coherent body of research or conceptual field within diversity scholarship. Much of the diversity scholarship and practical advice privileges a managerial perspective by linking diversity to processes and outcomes of managerial interest such as satisfaction and performance, and advising managers of the top-down actions they can take to improve the climate and outcomes of diverse work contexts (Pringle, Konrad, & Prasad, 2006). In contrast to this view, navigating the self represents a bottom-up, agentic view of individuals who proactively engage in motivated—and at times strategic—acts of identification with groups, roles, scripts, traits, narratives, and personae that may serve to create a more inclusive work environment, satisfying work experience, and/or productive work outcomes.

The phrase "navigating the self" implies some degree of personal agency in shaping and sustaining one's own identity as one confronts the complexities and possibilities that emerge in diverse organizations. In contrast, diversity scholarship that places greater emphasis on structural inequality often diminishes the visibility (and perhaps the possibility) of individual empowerment. Structural determinism poses considerable constraints for navigating the self capably within diverse contexts. In fact, some scholars have construed such acts of positive identity construction as manipulative (e.g., higher-status people defining themselves in self-enhancing ways that reinforce the existing power structure) or exploitative (e.g., marginalized group members who take on positive identities of "team members" or "citizens" that placate or pacify their concerns for equality) (Learmonth & Humphries, 2011). Yet, understanding the motives and tactics for navigating the self can help to disarm individual biases and dismantle structural inequalities.

This chapter aims to synthesize the research on navigating the self in diversity scholarship. To do so, we will review five prominent theoretical perspectives on identity processes in diverse work settings to explicate various ways in which individuals actively participate in the co-construction of their identities. We articulate the core assumptions that underlie each theoretical perspective as we present different viewpoints on why and how an individual navigates him or her self in a diverse work setting.

Five theoretical perspectives on navigating the self in diverse work settings

In this chapter, we review five theoretical perspectives on identity that highlight different ways in which people navigate their self-identities in diverse work organizations: the social identity perspective, the (role) identity perspective, the critical identity perspective, the narrative-as-identity perspective, and the identity work perspective. Each perspective puts forth a different view of the essence of identity and how it is shaped. For the sake of explicating various motives, tactics, and outcomes, we review each perspective as a separate theoretical tradition. However, these perspectives are not mutually exclusive; some studies of navigating the self draw upon multiple theoretical perspectives to explain the motive behind using certain tactics, the influence of a particular context, or the outcomes resulting from a given approach to navigating the self. In the sections that follow, we review the core assumptions of each theoretical tradition and discuss the featured processes for navigating the self in diverse work contexts. Table 5.1 summarizes each perspective's definition of identity, as well as the general approach to, motives for, and commonly featured tactics associated with navigating the self in diverse work settings.

Social identity theory

First, we review social identity theorists' core assumptions about identity. Social identity theoretical approaches include both social identity theory (Tajfel & Turner, 1979) and self-categorization theory (Turner, 1987), which are distinct but related approaches to understanding how social groups and categories shape one's sense of self, and are often referred to interchangeably. Here, we use the umbrella term "social identity theoretical approaches" to encompass both. The social identity theoretical approaches examine how people understand and position themselves and others in terms of social group categories.

Social identity theorists establish that people segment, classify, and order the social environment and their place in it based on categories (Turner, 1987). Through self-categorization into multiple groups, including race/ethnicity, gender, age cohort, and organizational groups, people identify similarities and differences between themselves and others. The existence of a social identity constitutes both a person's knowledge that he or she belongs to a social group or category (Tajfel & Turner, 1979) and the feelings associated with that membership. A social category is represented in the self-concept as a social identity

Table 5.1 Navigating the Self in Diverse Work Contexts: Five Theoretical Perspectives

	Social Identity Perspective	(Role) Identity Perspective	Critical Identity Perspective	Narrative-as-Identity Perspective	Identity Work Perspective
Definition of identity	Knowledge that one belongs to a social group or category and feelings associated with that membership	Self-meaning attached to multiple roles an individual performs and the meanings of an individual's behavior	Multiple, shifting, competing, temporary, context-sensitive, and evolving manifestations of the self that are shaped by socioeconomic, institutional, cultural, and historical boundaries between identity groups	An emergent, interpretive process of becoming that is captured by an individual's storied self-understandings	Reflects how an individual develops a self-understanding that is coherent, distinct, and positively valued within the context of complex, ambiguous, and contradictory experiences
General approach to navigating the self in diverse work contexts	Responding to identity threats through group memberships and identification	Reducing identity conflict and increasing complementarity between different role identities	Challenging the status and power relations that are embedded in identities	Constructing stories of interaction with one's social world to define who one is for oneself and for others	Proactively constructing a socially validated identity that reflects aspects one deems most central to one's sense of self
Motive(s)	Self-enhancement, belongingness and differentiation	Alignment	Emancipation	Sense making	Self-verification
Specific tactics	Making favorable, self-enhancing comparisons between groups through social mobility, social creativity, social competition, and superordinate categorization	Intrapersonal identity integration and segmentation	Mobilizing organizational discourses to resist regulation	Creating multiple self-narratives that explain critical processes in identity and career development, stories of resilience, or cultural scripts that appeal to different audiences	Identity negotiation processes and agentic identity performance that allow individuals to claim and others to grant desired identities

that both describes and prescribes how one should think, feel, and behave as a member of that social group (Hogg, Terry, & White, 1995; Tajfel & Turner, 1979). As members of a social group, individuals share some degree of emotional involvement in and degree of social consensus about the evaluation of their group and of their membership in it with other group members (Tajfel & Turner, 1979).

Organizational scholars have applied and extended social identity theories to explain diversity dynamics in organizations. Williams and O'Reilly (1998) provide an extensive review of how social identity theory has been applied to understand diversity dynamics. One of the popular areas of diversity research that applies social identity theory is that of bias. Categorization processes often lead to bias; for example, leadership categorization theory (Lord & Maher, 1991) explains how leadership prototypes (i.e., views of the standard example or typical leader) affect leadership perceptions for diverse groups. The leadership prototype is both gendered and raced; it is applied most consistently to male leaders (e.g., Heilman, Block, Martell, & Simon, 1989) and White leaders (Rosette, Leonardelli, & Phillips, 2008), and thus results in biased evaluations of female and non-White leaders.

Many scholars also emphasize how interactions with people who are different, such as those belonging to different social identity groups, can be difficult or even hostile in work organizations. For example, persons who are overweight experience a host of negative employment outcomes, including perceptions that they are lazy and incompetent, lack self-control and discipline, and are therefore responsible for their weight. They are less likely to be hired, earn less money, and are evaluated more harshly in performance reviews (see Bell & McLaughlin, 2006, for a review). People who are seen with (or are in close physical proximity to) obese people are also evaluated less favorably (Hebl & Mannix, 2003). Recruiters may have a conscious or unconscious bias against hiring obese people because they do not want to be associated with obese people (Bell & McLaughlin, 2006). Unattractive workers are likely to suffer similar job-related outcomes (see Bell & McLaughlin, 2006, for a review).

Another popular area of social identity research that relates to workplace diversity is based on the similarity-attraction paradigm (Byrne, 1971). According to this paradigm, people prefer and have an easier time interacting with similar others, such as those who belong to the same social identity groups. As a result, they may have less diverse networks. For example, Ibarra's studies of diversity and social networks support that White employees tend to have less racially diverse social networks than do minorities (Ibarra, 1993, 1995).

Social identity research also explains how demographic representation influences identification processes. Studies of work team dynamics and organizational demography support that heterogeneity (i.e., whether and on how many visible dimensions team members differ from one another) may lead to a lack of attachment and increased conflict in workgroups (e.g., Chatman & Flynn, 2001; Colquitt, Noe, & Jackson, 2002). At the same time, research shows that heterogeneity can increase attachment for typically underrepresented groups. For example, Ely's (1994) study of female attorneys compared those in sex-integrated versus male-dominated firms. Ely found that women in sex-integrated firms were more likely to experience common gender as a positive basis for identification with other women than those in male-dominated firms. All of these studies hold in common the assumptions that social context shapes group identification, and that group identification influences social behavior.

Social identity theoretical approaches to navigating the self in diverse work settings. According to social identity theorists, group memberships fulfill the needs for self-enhancement, belongingness, and differentiation. Self-enhancement or positivity strivings involve the need to be viewed favorably by the self and others (see Baumeister, 1999, for a review). Group memberships provide a basis for self-enhancement, as people identify themselves with favorably regarded groups. According to Tajfel and Turner (1979, p. 101), group identifications are "relational and comparative: they define the individual as similar to or different from, as 'better' or 'worse' than members of other groups." People also make favorable, self-enhancing comparisons between in-groups and out-groups to increase the positivity of their self-regard. Group memberships also provide opportunities for optimal distinctiveness (Brewer, 1991); people fulfill their needs for belongingness and differentiation simultaneously as they define themselves as similar to their in-group, yet distinct in positive ways from members of other groups. Members make favorable comparisons between their in-group and a relevant out-group to sustain their perception that the in-group is positively distinct from the out-group (Tajfel & Turner, 1979).

Diversity can create a challenging context for constructing or sustaining a positive sense of self. Stereotypes and power imbalances between groups at the societal level pose threats to people's social identity, primarily the threat of being misjudged or mistreated due to social identity group membership, or of being rejected from a valued social identity group altogether (for a review, see Steele, Spencer, & Aronson, 2002). Social identity threats are likely to occur in diverse work settings, during which both in-group and out-group members are more likely to challenge the positive distinctiveness of other social identity groups and question the legitimacy of social identity group membership. Members of socially devalued groups (i.e., groups that are generally characterized within society as possessing unfavorable defining characteristics, and are often stigmatized by negative stereotypes and low relative status in social hierarchies) face an unusual predicament in constructing positive identities; rather than belong to a positively distinct group, they belong to a group that may distinguish them on the basis of negative attributes.

With respect to navigating the self, social identity theorists have devoted most of their attention to how members of socially devalued groups respond to social identity threat. Research in this domain (not specific to diversity in the workplace) has uncovered three primary responses to social identity threat—social mobility, social creativity (which includes superordinate categorization), and social competition. Theorists argue, in accordance with Tajfel and Turner's (1979) early propositions and a host of empirical studies, that members of devalued groups will adopt one of the following tactics, based upon their beliefs about whether group boundaries are permeable and differences are legitimate.

The first is social mobility. If members believe they can exit the lower-status group, they will navigate the self by employing social mobility tactics in an attempt to join a higher-status group. Even if they cannot physically exit their own group, members of socially devalued groups might attempt to affiliate with a highly regarded group by portraying themselves as prototypical members of that group—demonstrating that they possess the defining characteristics of the valued group (rather than the devalued group) so that they will be viewed as legitimate members. For example, certain people attempt to suppress their invisible devalued identities (e.g., sexual orientation, physical illness) while in the workplace so they will be perceived as members of higher-status groups (Clair, Beatty, & MacLean, 2005; Ragins, 2008).

The second is social creativity. If they believe group boundaries are impermeable but the status-oriented differences between groups are legitimate, members of devalued groups will "navigate the self" through the use of cognitive tactics. They will reevaluate their in-group using a set of criteria that will reestablish positive distinctiveness. For example, individuals whose occupations involve dirty work (Hughes, 1951) use cognitive tactics to negotiate and secure social affirmation for their identities (Ashforth & Kreiner, 1999). Specifically, these individuals may transform the meaning of their marginalized work and tainted identities by devaluing negative attributions and revaluing positive ones to make the occupation more attractive to insiders and outsiders (Ashforth & Kreiner, 1999).

A related social creativity tactic for navigating the self is superordinate categorization, which involves categorizing oneself at a higher, meta-group level (e.g., Gadget employees, rather than Gadget engineers and Gadget accountants) to achieve intergroup cooperation (see Allison & Herlocker, 1994). Superordinate categorization may benefit organizations. Chatman, Polzer, Barsade, and Neale (1998) argued that promoting a collectivistic organizational culture may encourage demographically diverse members to categorize one another as having the organization's interests in common, and may therefore lead to increased creativity and productivity. However, superordinate categorization may also suppress important differences and undermine one's sense of distinctiveness, especially for minority-group members in majority contexts. Majority-racial-group members tend to prefer to downplay subgroup distinctiveness and expect minorities to adopt majority-group culture. On the other hand, minorities may prefer to integrate rather than assimilate, by respecting subgroup differences and preserving minority cultures within an overarching group (Ryan, Hunt, Weible, Peterson, & Casas, 2007). As a corollary, Whites also may prefer to discuss intergroup commonalities, whereas minorities may prefer to talk about intergroup distinctions and power differences (Dovidio, Gaertner, & Saguy, 2007). Thus, the preference for superordinate categorization may depend on whether one belongs to a majority or minority group within an organizational context.

The third tactic is social competition. Social identity theorists posit that if members believe boundaries are impermeable and differences are illegitimate, but their lower status is unstable, they will engage in social competition against the out-group. Competitive behaviors are often associated with conflict and hostility because they involve power contests between lower-status and higher-status groups. Advocacy groups within organizations in the broader community use social competition to challenge group status differences, and corollary differences in access to resources and positional power. Members of such advocacy groups navigate the self by proactively challenging negative views about their social identities and fighting for equal status. They navigate the self by pushing for a social, rather than personal, redefinition of their identity group and status. For example, Creed and Scully (2000) described how lesbian, gay, bisexual and transgendered (LGBT) employees' disclosure of sexual orientation mobilized social change. This examination of grass roots mobilizing demonstrates how an individual's approach toward navigating the self also has implications for collective action.

(Role) identity theory

Next, we review (role) identity theorists' core assumptions about identity. (Role) identity theory proposes that the self-concept is socially constructed, based on the identities attached to the multiple roles that individuals occupy in society (Hogg, Terry, & White, 1995). A multifaceted self, constructed of multiple roles, mediates the relationship between social structure and individual behavior (Hogg et al., 1995). The origins of (Role) identity theory lie in two different yet strongly related strands of identity research (Stryker & Burke, 2000). The first strand, rooted in traditional symbolic interactionism, claims that (a) social structures affect the self and (b) the structure of the self influences social behavior (Stryker & Burke, 2000; see also Stryker, 1980; Stryker & Serpe, 1982). In this regard, (role) identity theory reflects Mead's (1934) assertion that "society shapes self shapes social behavior" (quoted by Stryker & Burke, 2000, p. 285). Sluss and Ashforth (2007) expound upon this core premise in their work on relational identities in the workplace; they describe how individuals derive a sense of self from their various role-based interpersonal relationships and how relational identities shape patterns of interaction.

The second strand of (role) identity theory focuses on the internal dynamics of self-processes that affect social behavior (Stryker & Burke, 2000; see also Burke, 1991; Burke & Reitzes, 1981; Burke & Stets, 1999). (Role) identities are thought of as "self-meanings" that are attached to the multiple roles an individual performs and the meanings of an individual's behavior (Stryker & Burke, 2000). For example, Burke and Reitzes (1981) found that college students' self-views of academic responsibility (a dimension of the student identity) were a strong predictor of college plans, suggesting that individuals will align their behaviors with their sense of self when both factors share meaning. Both strands of (role) identity theory share the belief that external social structures and the structure of the self are inextricably linked (Stryker & Burke, 2000).

(Role) identity theoretical approaches to navigating the self in diverse work settings. Given that the self is multifaceted and that individuals have as many identities as they have social roles (Stryker & Burke, 2000), it is important for individuals to align their actions and sense of self with the expectations of a given role. (Role) identity theory focuses on the need to manage the diversity among the multiple roles (and corresponding expectations) that an individual holds. The focus here is on diversity within a person, rather than the differences between in-group and out-group members (as featured in social identity theory). This approach to navigating the self is important for reducing or preventing the internal identity conflicts that may arise when multiple identities are not mutually reinforcing (Stryker, 2000). The motives for navigating the self relate to reducing conflict and increasing complementarity between different role identities, in order to create a more positive identity structure.

(Role) identity theory calls attention to the conflicting social expectations that many role incumbents face. According to (role) identity theory, identities are organized in a salience hierarchy, such that an identity that is higher in the salience hierarchy is more likely to be invoked across a variety of situations (Stryker & Burke, 2000). The salience of an identity reflects commitment to the role relationships associated with that identity because an individual is more likely to behave in accordance with an identity that is higher in the salience hierarchy than one that is lower (Stryker & Burke, 2000). Given the multitude of role expectations, (role) identity theorists purport that role prioritization may be important for increasing clarity of relational identities and commitment to varied role expectations (Ashforth, Harrison, & Corley, 2008).

Role congruity research also explains why people would be motivated to fit into behavioral expectations for certain roles, given the negative social consequences of role violation. For example, many studies have documented how female leaders are disadvantaged by societal beliefs that agentic traits, typically ascribed to the prototypical leader role, are incongruous with the communal traits that are ascribed to the female gender role (Eagly, Makhijani

& Klonsky, 1992; Heilman, 2001; Rosette & Tost, 2010). Female leaders who exhibit agentic behaviors are often perceived less favorably, due to role incongruity (i.e., a violation of the communal gender role expectations) (Eagly et al., 1992; Rudman & Glick, 1999; 2001). Much of this role congruity research focuses on how others perceive and evaluate those who fit prototypes for gender and leadership, but doesn't examine how people navigate the self (i.e., proactively engage in identity construction) to respond to or avert these perceptions. For example, Rosette and Tost (2010) report that women leaders at senior levels, who demonstrate success in masculine positions (and get the credit for the success), may be evaluated favorably in ratings of agentic and communal traits. Rosette and Tost's (2010) conclusion is based on an experimental condition, and not an examination of how women leaders attempt to navigate themselves in various situations. However, this research does establish a strong motivational basis for mitigating tensions within one's own role identity composition.

Navigating the self, according to the (role) identity theoretical perspective, may be motivated by the need to align one's identity structure with preferences (via prioritization) and the need to reconcile competing expectations or role demands (i.e., role incongruity). The following section will address the latter set of tactics for navigating the self. Beyond prioritization, people also navigate the self in ways that will establish desirable relationships between their own role identities.

Diversity researchers have used (role) identity theory to explain how people navigate identity conflicts by cognitively structuring the multiple facets of their identities in ways that promote complementarity. Navigating the self may involve choices to "disidentify" (e.g., deny or discard a lower-status identity for a higher-status identity), segment (e.g., create boundaries between identities while remaining committed to each), or integrate multiple identities (e.g., merge the identities so that they are no longer viewed as separate) (Caza & Wilson, 2009; Rothbard & Ramarajan, 2009). Bell's (1990) study of Black professional women who managed the tensions of living between two cultural worlds (Black and White) revealed that the women developed various identity structures, ranging from segmentation to biculturalism. These identity structures permeated beyond the women's cognitive sense of self to shape their social environment, as they "create[d] dynamic, fluid life structures that shape[d] the patterns of their social interactions, relationships, and mobility, both within and between the two cultural contexts" (p. 462).

Segmentation and **integration** are both viable strategies for mitigating identity conflict (see Ashforth et al., 2008, for a review). Individuals who use segmentation tactics tend to present themselves as "partial selves" when in the company of non-similar others. For example, female scientists who struggle with having identities as both a woman and a scientist in a male-dominated work environment (Settles, 2004) may choose to compartmentalize (Ashforth, Harrison, & Corley, 2008; Roccas & Brewer, 2002) their identities, or activate only their scientist work identity while at work to prevent their gender identity from interfering with the performance of their scientist identity (Settles, 2004).

While compartmentalization may reduce the impact of stress in various life domains, it may also inhibit a person's ability to draw upon the psychological, social, and cognitive resources that accompany various role identities across domains. Dutton and colleagues (2010) conclude from their literature review that in low-stress situations, integration tactics may be most potent for enhancing the degree of complementarity that an individual experiences between his or her multiple identities. For example, Harrington and Hall (2007) propose that individuals who experience conflict between work and nonwork role identities can integrate and find balance between these identities by establishing "protean" careers. Protean careers are self-directed career models in which individuals define their own views of success versus those in which models of success are defined by organizations (Harrington & Hall, 2007). Protean careers demonstrate values of freedom and growth versus advancement, high versus low mobility, psychological success versus success based on position, level, and salary, and pride, work satisfaction, and professional commitment over organizational commitment (Harrington & Hall, 2007). Hall and Mirvis (1995) also argue that these new career forms are critical for continuous learning and development among older workers in diverse organizations. As another example, Reybold and Alamia (2008) found that female faculty members developed a more integrated identity that encompassed both their identities as teachers and researchers, after experimenting with a compartmentalized professional identity structure and finding the two identities to be more synergistic than segmented. Identity integration allowed these faculty members to feel a greater sense of "academic flow" (p. 119).

Segmentation and integration are cognitive tactics for structuring one's own identity to manage role conflict. Another tactic for navigating the self, **defining behavioral scripts**, helps to address role ambiguity. An experimental study on navigating the self in workplace interracial interactions examined how role identity shifts can help reduce anxiety. Avery, Richeson, Hebl, and Ambady (2009) provided White participants with well-defined and loosely defined social scripts for interacting with a Black stranger in a simulated work situation. The well-defined scripts provided norms that dictated expected interpersonal behavior (e.g., interview or applicant vs. conversation partner) and thus helped to attenuate the anxiety that Whites typically experience during cross-race interactions. These scripts helped the White participants to develop their role identities in relation to their Black counterpart, and thus increased the likelihood of smooth cross-race interactions. However, the authors also reported that Black participants' discomfort during the interracial interactions was not affected by the scripted or unscripted encounter. Thus, it is important to continue exploring the impact of various tactics for navigating the self on diverse groups.

Critical identity theory

Critical identity theorists' core assumptions about identity. Critical identity theorists treat identities as multiple, shifting, competing, temporary, context-sensitive, and evolving manifestations of subjective meanings and experiences in the social world (Alvesson, Ashcraft, & Thomas, 2008). Critical identity theory is largely concerned with issues of power that constrain individuals' abilities to freely construct and negotiate identities in work organizations. It challenges social identity theorists' assertion that individuals freely undertake processes of self-categorization and identification. Rather, critical identity theory purports that socioeconomic, institutional, cultural, and historical boundaries between identity groups in society are reflected in organizational boundaries; lower-status groups occupy lower-level positions and identity groups are formally segregated from one another (Konrad, 2003). Identity research from this perspective often locates the root causes of stigmatization and discrimination in intergroup interaction patterns that activate social categorization processes (Linnehan & Konrad, 1999). Scholars in this tradition devote less attention to individual differences in personality and behavioral style. They view identities as more than just a collection of personality traits or individualized differences; they are informed by institutional, political, and societal structures (Warner, 2008). They also emphasize how context, social meanings, power disparities, and historical intergroup conflict affect current diversity dynamics in work organizations. In contrast to social identity researchers, critical identity researchers rarely examine how threat and conflict emerge from difference in and of itself. Rather, in this tradition, difference is always contextualized in power relations.

Research on the gendering of organizations, meaning the persistent structuring of organizations along gender lines, also fits within a critical perspective. This research focuses on macro- rather than micro-levels of analyses, but does lend insight into the masculine orientation of abstract conceptions of "ideal workers" (Acker, 1990). Although the ideal worker does not exist, organization structures and job descriptions reinforce these unrealistic expectations that workers have full-time availability, mobility, high qualifications, and strong work orientation, and that outside-of-work responsibilities are secondary to the organization's requirements (Benschop, 2006). These expectations are associated with heterosexual men whose spouses assume complete responsibility for household affairs, thus freeing them to be fully available for the organization's needs and well suited to the masculine culture of the organization. This research is grounded in the conception of gender as an ongoing process rather than a category. West and Zimmerman's (1987) foundational work in this domain examined the dynamics of "doing gender." Doing gender involves verbal and symbolic acts that reproduce the symbolic order of gender and often reinforce systems of dominance and oppression. For example, many men constantly negotiate and reconstruct masculine selves in workplace interactions by drawing upon organizational resources, discourses, and practices, and engaging in competition with other men to display dominance and validate identity (Hearn & Collinson, 2006). These discussions of gender frame the context in which people attempt to construct and negotiate their identities. Yet, within critical identity theory, the emphasis is on how societal discourse, activism, and scholarship can change rigid social structures. The question of individual agency in shaping one's own identity or shaping social structures is contested heavily (Benschop, 2006).

Critical identity theorists also posit that intersections of race, class, and gender, in particular, influence the formation of personal and social identities (Cole, 2009; Holvino, 2010). *Intersectionality* refers to the meaning and consequences of belonging to multiple social categories (Cole, 2009). It acknowledges that identity is not the summation of the multiple social groups to which a person belongs (Warner, 2008). Rather, identity is composed of the qualitatively different meanings and experiences that arise from the interaction of the multiple social group memberships that cannot be explained by examining each identity alone (Warner, 2008). Intersectionality also acknowledges the status and power relations that are embedded in identities. In this respect, intersecting identities create both opportunity and oppression because they can signal advantage, disadvantage, or both at the same time, depending on the salience of a particular identity in a particular social context (Collins, 1990). For example, research has found that being heterosexual was a privilege for heterosexual Latino men, but being a person of color was associated with relative subordination (Hurtado & Sinha, 2008). Scully and Blake-Beard's (2006) review of research on class in organizational diversity research also emphasizes that class is "inextricably linked to other social identities in the lived experiences of employees" (p. 433). Scott's (2011) dissertation on intersectionality among African-American female senior executives on Wall Street describes how various identity experiences, including class background, country of origin (immigrant families), region of socialization (North vs. South), skin tone, religion (Catholic, Protestant), and maternal and paternal relationships (role identities), together shaped the value systems and career choices of these women. As these women described the construction of their professional identities, they emphasized the simultaneous influence of these intersecting aspects of their lives. However, Scott's (2011) research and Scully and Notably, Blake-Beard's (2006) discussion of class emphasize the role of individual agency in constructing identities. This agentic perspective is not as salient in many other writings on intersectionality and the matrix of oppression.

Critical identity theoretical approaches to navigating the self in diverse work settings. According to critical identity theorists, emancipation is a primary motive for navigating the self. These theorists describe processes by which organizations regulate individual identities, and thus compromise one's freedom to self-define. They argue against the pursuit of managerial interest at the expense of liberty, autonomy, and justice for lower-class workers. The primary argument that critical theorists present is the following. Identities in organizations are regulated by organizational elites such that "ways of seeing, being, and doing are imposed" (Alvesson, Ashcraft, & Thomas, 2008, p. 16). Although the organization is not necessarily the most influential institution in identity construction, identity regulation is a significant method of organizational control that is accomplished through discourse and social practices. Organizations regulate individuals' identities through active identity work practices such as induction, training, and promotion (Alvesson & Willmott, 2002). Managers may also engage in socialization practices (e.g., training and education) that encourage employees to identify with the organization but also facilitate social domination (Alvesson, Ashcraft, & Thomas, 2008). In another case, managers may regulate employees' identities through appeals to self-image, feelings, values and identifications (Alvesson et al., 2008; see also Kunda, 1992; Willmott, 1993) during the feedback process (Alvesson et al., 2008). In this case, organizations "seduce subordinates into calibrating their senses of self with a restricted catalogue of corporate-approved identities bearing strong imprints of managerial power" (Alvesson et al., 2008, p. 16). Other mechanisms for regulating identities within work organizations including defining a person directly (e.g., as a middle manager); defining a person by defining others (e.g., having a killer instinct); providing a specific vocabulary of motives (e.g., working in groups, having a sense of community); explicating morals and values (e.g., being a team player); constructing knowledge and skills (e.g., managers as "strategists"); group categorization and affiliation (e.g., a member of the corporate family); social positioning (e.g., informal rankings); establishing and clarifying a distinct set of rules of the game (e.g., defining what a "team player" is); and defining the conditions in which an organization operates (e.g., globalization) (Alvesson & Willmott, 2002).

According to critical identity theoretical approaches, people have a limited range of options for navigating the self in diverse work contexts, in which their status is structurally imposed and reified through systems of dominance. In the face of such constraining conditions, critical identity theorists propose that individuals resist identity regulation to achieve a more desired self-view.

Discourse plays an important role in processes of identity formation, maintenance, and transformation, and is therefore a central element of navigating the self and resisting dominance (Alvesson & Willmott, 2002). Individuals attend to and mobilize organizational discourses and engage other discourses to self-identify as separate and independent entities and to repair their sense of identity (Alvesson & Willmott, 2002). Prasad and Prasad (2000) suggest that **resistance** helps individuals to affirm their own identities as autonomous individuals by taking discursive ownership over resistance (i.e., labeling certain acts as forms of resistance) and by interpreting their own actions as resistance. For example, LGBT employees who are being open and self-affirming are said to engage in acts of resistance against systems of heterosexist oppression (Creed, 2006). Acts of resistance may help individuals construct ethical narratives about themselves that serve as a "strategic resource for identity work" (Kornberger & Brown, 2007, p. 497). Meyerson and Scully (1995) and Meyerson (2001) introduce the construct of a "tempered radical"—a person who carefully leads change as an outsider within his or her own organization (i.e., someone who differs from the mainstream culture of the organization). Tempered radicals use their own ambivalent identification with the organization as a platform for resisting the dominant culture and promoting more inclusiveness, sometimes subtly and other times directly.

David Thomas' studies of minority executives also highlight the role of race-related discourse in shaping power dynamics and career outcomes between majority supervisors and minority subordinates. For example, Thomas (1993) reported that the highest-quality cross-race supervisory relationships were those in which managers and subordinates had similar views on the relevance of race-related discourse. If both parties wished to directly confront (i.e., talk about) race or both parties wished to avoid race-related conversations, relationships were of a higher quality than if one party wished to discuss race but the other did not. Thomas and Gabarro's (1999) comparative study of successful and plateaued White and non-White executives also demonstrated the impact of race-related discourse: non-White executives who advanced to the most senior levels talked directly about race and race-related challenges with mentors early in their career.

Narrative-as-identity

Narrative-as-identity theorists' core assumptions core assumptions about identity are as follows. The narrative-as-identity approach views identity as an emergent, interpretive process rather than as a static structure. Social identity, role identity, and critical identity theories account for the situational influences on changing identities, yet their discussions of diversity and navigating the self tend to construe identity as a state of being. The narrative-as-identity approach, in contrast, features identity as a process of becoming and captures people's storied self-understandings as situated in the temporal arc of past (who they have been), present (who they are), and future (who they are becoming).

Narrative-as-identity scholarship refers to "the stories people construct and tell about themselves to define who they are for themselves and for others" (McAdams, Josselson, & Lieblich, 2006, p. 4). According to this perspective, an identity is composed of an individual's narratives or stories of interaction with his or her social world. Identity narratives contain key themes that situate one's existence within a plot of unfolding events. These narratives provide people with a sense of order and continuity in the midst of potentially disconnected or even conflicting life episodes. Narrating the self is an integrative mechanism for identity construction that provides a sense of unity and purpose (Erikson, 1959) and brings coherence to life (McAdams, 1985; 1997). Narrative-as-identity theorists caution against equating "integrating" with "simplifying" identity. Some theorists emphasize that integrative narratives are not simplistic; they contain many voices in dialogue with each other (Gergen, 1991). This "conversation among narrators" or "war of historians" (Raggat, 2006) accounts for the opposition that is inherent within selfhood (Gregg, 2006). Regardless of the degree of contradiction within one's life story, self-narration facilitates the construction of a coherent sense of self across time and circumstance by enabling individuals to simultaneously accommodate change and consistency (Ashforth et al., 2008).

Narrative-as-identity theoretical approaches to navigating the self in diverse work settings. Sense making is a primary motive for navigating the self in diverse work settings. Sense-making activities involve inquiring and interpreting one's embeddedness within a social context, and help people to derive meaning from challenging situations and to (re)construct a positive sense of self even through disappointment and unexpected changes (Ashforth et al., 2008). As people consider the differences between their own past, present, and future selves, they craft narratives to make sense of these internal changes. This sense-making mechanism promotes resilience and the imaginative pursuit of future possibilities, even in light of disappointment.

Narrative-as-identity scholarship unearths the process by which individuals craft stories of growth via sense-making activities. For example, growth is a central theme in the derivation of redemptive meaning from negative life stories (McAdams, 2006) and in reflection and sense making about traumatic events (Maitlis, 2009). Maitlis' (2009) research reveals how musicians who have suffered career-altering injuries compose self-narratives that enable them to make sense of who they are as professionals and humans after the injury. Narratives of hope also reflect anticipation of future growth (Carlsen & Pitsis, 2009).

Identity narratives also help people to deepen others' understandings of their (often unorthodox) career trajectories, thereby meeting their needs for self-verification (Swann, 1983). For example, during career transitions, self-narratives enable a person to bridge gaps between old and new roles and identities (Ibarra & Barbulescu, 2010). A coherent self-narrative allows an individual to explain career and identity transitions through stories that depict one's career trajectory as a series of purposive events. To appeal to different audiences, an individual may create multiple self-narratives such that each individual self-narrative becomes part of a larger and more varied narrative repertoire (Ibarra & Barbulescu, 2010).

Narrative identity theorists have not typically focused on issues of diversity *per se*; the contribution of this approach stems more from the narrative methodology itself and what it reveals about the career experiences of racioethnic minority groups. Scholars who use narrative methodologies for data collection assume that storytelling and life histories explain critical processes in identity and career development. As people share their narrative about their career trajectory, they inform researchers of the critical events and people that have shaped who they have become. Researchers do not often write about this process of self-narrating among minority professionals, but they do rely on the data gathered from narratives to explain career experiences. In this sense, navigating the self (in research interviews) lends insight into people's agentic approaches toward navigating their careers.

The emphasis on proactivity and resilience is similar to a focus on protean careers (Hall & Mirvis, 1995) and narratives of growth (Maitlis, 2009). Although typical career profiles have been based on the experiences of dominant groups, narrative analyses of minorities uncover the unique, contextualized ways in which they define themselves as professionals. Studies of career and identity development for minorities often extend beyond the immediate work context and socialization processes in organizations; these studies of diversity and identity reflect a holistic, life history examination of the multiple factors that shape a person's sense of becoming a professional. Many of these studies are also concerned with highlighting the challenges, personal characteristics (i.e., resilience, fortitude), and social support networks that account for the "success" (i.e., leadership promotions) of minority professionals. In this sense, navigating the self refers to the process of reconciling societal pressures, job assignments, family expectations, and personal choices over a long period of time. For example, Bell and Nkomo's (2001) in-depth analysis of the life experiences of Black and White professional women revealed how factors such as maternal and paternal relationships influenced career orientations and trajectories. Thomas and Gabarro's (1999) study of minority executives captured personal histories and career biographies and then illuminated patterns in the development of minority executives who reached the top echelons of corporate America.

Studies that use narrative analyses often explain how diverse professionals have become who they are, but offer less insight into how these professionals define themselves as works in progress who are still immersed in a growth process of becoming. As such, this view of narrative-as-identity remains relatively uncharted yet fruitful terrain for uncovering alternative pathways (via self-narrating) for navigating the self in diverse work settings.

Identity work

Last, we review identity work theorists' core assumptions about identity. The phrase "identity work" is often attributed to Snow and Anderson (1987), who defined it as "the range of activities individuals engage in to create, present, and sustain personal identities that are congruent with and supportive of the self-concept" (p. 1348). In many respects, the notion of "identity work" may be viewed as synonymous with navigating the self. Like the other four perspectives that lend insight into navigating the self, the identity work approach posits that the self emerges from the dynamism of interaction with one's social world. As such, scholars who study identity work will likely place their work under one or more of the banners of social identity, role identity, critical identity, or narrative-as-identity research traditions. Yet identity work research also captures the tension and dynamism involved with navigating the self in ways that the other four perspectives minimize. Therefore, we set these identity work studies apart from the other four identity theory traditions, given that the identity work tradition portrays individuals as proactive agents in constructing socially validated identities that reflect aspects they deem most central to their sense of self.

The empirical research on identity work provides intentional and detailed accounts of how individuals deal with their complex, ambiguous, and contradictory experiences at work by constructing an understanding of self that is coherent, distinct, and positively valued. Both cognitive and behavioral tactics that individuals use to navigate the self in diverse work settings are revealed. Cognitive approaches to identity work include shifting dimensions of comparison to evaluate one's own social identity more favorably (social identity theory) and making sense of past experiences to describe oneself in more positive ways (narrative-as-identity theory). In contrast, behavioral techniques focus on active and relational sense-making processes that help individuals construct and sustain more positive identities. This focus on self-authoring is similar to the orientation of narrative-as-identity scholarship. The emphasis on human agency and malleability in identity construction contrasts with other theorists' views that identities (and power differences) are structurally imposed and resistant to change (e.g., some critical theorists).

In this section, we will focus on distinct behavioral identity work tactics that are not explicitly addressed by the other four identity perspectives. We point to two prominent behavioral identity work approaches to navigating the self in diverse work contexts: **identity performance** and **identity negotiation**. Identity performance research details an actor's deliberate attempts to navigate his or her social context via self-expression and impression management. Research on identity negotiation establishes the iterative, interactive nature of identity construction in diverse work contexts.

Identity work theoretical approaches to navigating the self in diverse work settings. In the tradition of symbolic interactionism, the identity work perspective includes a broad body of research on the interpersonal nature of identity construction (Stryker, 1980). The anchor in symbolic interactionism is similar to the (role) identity theorists' emphasis on social roles and expectations and their influence on a person's sense of self. Identity work encompasses a range of agentic tactics that people employ to proactively shape the meaning or significance of their identity in a given context. Identity work research draws heavily upon self-verification theory (Swann, 1983), which argues that people desire to be seen by others in ways that are consistent with how they see themselves. Self-verification is beneficial for epistemologic and pragmatic reasons: it helps people to have a sense of who they are (as reflected to them by others), and how they should interact (according to their place in the social world). The pragmatic benefits of self-verification are similar to those presented by role identity theorists; others' perceptions and expectations help to create a script for social behavior. Identity work research takes these presumed motives as the backdrop for the rich accounts of various tactics people will employ to help others develop a more accurate, complex, and appreciative understanding of their own identities.

Like social identity theory, identity work research also illustrates the ways in which people respond to discrepancies or threats to their identities, such as those prompted by stereotyping, stigmatization, or legitimacy challenges (Ashforth & Kreiner, 1999; Branscombe, Ellemers, Spears, & Doosje, 1999; Ibarra, 1999). In the following section, we will describe the identity work tactics that people use to address these identity threats. Recent scholarship on positive identity also raises the possibility that "identity work...is inspired by an entity's desire to grow and evolve rather than a need to maintain social status or self-worth in the face of threat" (Roberts, Dutton, & Bednar, 2009, p. 510; see also Kreiner & Sheep, 2009). Yet the research on navigating the self in diverse work contexts has focused primarily on dealing with identity threat and its challenges to the self-verification motive.

Research reviews of identity performance help to build coherence and allow for comparisons and generalizations across population-specific studies. In their fervor to present an in-depth account of identity performance for a particular group within a particular context, scholars typically do not cite the broad range of tactics that have emerged from studies in different contexts or according to different theoretical traditions.

Identity performance involves proactively shaping others' perceptions of one's social group memberships and identification (Roberts & Roberts, 2007). Identity performance encompasses a range of disclosures and enactments. One medium for identity performance expression is through appearance, or surface-level display cues. Surface-level display cues signify group affiliations and associated ideologies, through physical appearance (e.g., hair, makeup, clothing, jewelry) and symbolic gestures that emphasize certain cultural orientations (displaying photos or cultural artifacts, engaging in public cultural rituals). Identity performance also involves disclosing feelings about group membership and involvement in social identity group activities. Such disclosures communicate how important certain identities are to one's self-concept and daily living (Bell & Nkomo, 2001; Meyerson & Scully; 1995; Roberts, Cha, Hewlin, & Settles, 2009). Display cues and disclosures also shape perceptions of competence and fit in a diverse organization (Bell, 1990; Clair et al., 2005; Roberts & Roberts, 2007).

As stated previously, much of the identity work research associates agentic identity performance with identity threat. In addition to symbolic interaction and self-verification, impression management and social identity theories have helped to provide a theoretical foundation for the identity performance tactics that people use in response to threats. Social identity theory has focused primarily on cognitive tactics for strengthening or weakening group identification, rather than individual self-presentation. The impression management frame helps to explain why navigating the self can be a particularly challenging task in diverse work contexts (Roberts, 2005). In diverse work contexts, people with marginalized social identities (e.g., women; gays or lesbians; or members of minority racial, ethnic, religious, or national groups) and people with privileged identities (e.g., men; heterosexuals; those in majority racial, ethnic, religious, or national groups) experience social identity threats that interfere with their desire for self-verification and positive professional image construction. In the section that follows, we focus on two types of social identity threats—devaluation threats and legitimacy threats—and explain how they obstruct professional image construction, and thus prompt different identity work tactics to repair one's image in the eyes of others.

Devaluation threats are "situations, events or encounters that people interpret as signaling social identity-based negative evaluations of them" (Ely & Roberts, 2008, p. 181) and that often lead people to worry that negative stereotypes will be applied to them. Some members of marginalized groups may experience chronic devaluation threat if they are tokens (Kanter, 1977) or are underrepresented in senior positions (Ely, 1994; 1995), or if the dominant culture is at odds with their identity group's interests (Meyerson & Kolb, 2000). **Legitimacy threats** are triggered by signals that people are failing to live up to the positive expectations or idealized images of their social identity group and thus are not considered to be fully legitimate members of that group (Ely & Roberts, 2008). Members of privileged groups are more likely to experience legitimacy threats than devaluation threats, but both groups can experience both types of threat. For example, many men seek to demonstrate their ability to embody masculinity in its idealized and stereotypical forms by showing strength, authority, and autonomy, and feel threatened when they do not receive affirmation of their masculine status (Barrett, 1996; Connell, 1995; Kerfoot & Knights, 1993). Navigating the self is particularly challenging in diverse contexts because of the likelihood that responding to a social identity threat may trigger yet another social identity threat for the other party. Moreover, members often monitor each other's actions to assess loyalty to the group or authenticity of identity (Anderson, 1999; Branscombe et al., 1999), thus complicating one's ability to mitigate devaluation and legitimacy threats.

Four of the most common strategies for "navigating the self" when responding to devaluation and legitimacy threats are distancing, dispelling, living up to idealized images, and feigning indifference (Ely & Roberts, 2008). Common strategies for responding to devaluation threats are distancing oneself personally from one's social identity group and its stereotypes and dispelling negative stereotypes about the group more generally. Distancing involves disassociating from one's social identity group and is the behavioral counterpart of social identity theory's social mobility strategy (Roberts, 2005; Tajfel, 1978). Marginalized group members use distancing to suppress their marginalized identity in hopes that they will avoid social rejection, harassment, or loss of social status. Members of privileged groups also use distancing tactics to reduce the likelihood that others will view them according to negative stereotypes.

In contrast, the strategy of dispelling negative stereotypes is driven by attempts to restore the group's positive distinctiveness while maintaining one's own affiliation with the group. People using this strategy may also educate others about the inaccuracies of group stereotypes, attempt to enlighten out-group members about cultural differences, or even hold themselves up as a positive exemplar who does not embody the stereotypes; play into group stereotypes to accrue social benefits; or even take the role of group representative, holding themselves to a standard of perfection in order to demonstrate the group's capabilities (Roberts, 2005;

Roberts, Settles, & Jellison, 2008). In accordance with this line of research, Bergsicker, Shelton, and Richeson (2010) conducted six studies of impression management goals in interracial interactions. They found that Whites and non-Whites diverge in their impression management goals: Whites seek to be liked and be seen as moral, to dispel negative stereotypes that they are biased, whereas minorities seek to be respected, to dispel negative stereotypes of incompetence. These divergent goals led Whites to engage in more ingratiation impression management behaviors during cross-race interactions than self-promotion, whereas Blacks and Latinos used more self-promotion during cross-race interactions (Bergsicker et al., 2010).

Legitimacy threats prompt people to prove that they are able to live up to idealized images of their group. Common reactions to legitimacy threats involve demonstrating that one can live up to the culture's idealized images of one's social identity groups. For example, male medical residents may take unnecessary risks, avoid asking for help, and cover up their mistakes to order to be seen as heroic and invulnerable (Kellogg, 2005).

The intensity of coping with devaluation and legitimacy threats leads some people to adopt a fourth strategy, feigning indifference, to portray the image of one who is unconcerned with others' perceptions (Schlenker & Weigold, 1992). People who feign indifference often adopt a detached, even antisocial stance in order to appear autonomous and independent, to signal that they are unwilling to invest their time or effort into making a good impression on others. Another way to create the image of indifference is to intentionally defy group norms by expressing one's willful deviance from the dominant culture (e.g., deviating in physical appearance or expressing controversial opinions). Ironically, the goal of feigning indifference is to shield oneself from the pain of rejection or devaluation that may result from failure to respond effectively to social identity threats (Ely & Roberts, 2008).

Beyond these four tactics for responding to social identity threat, a fifth identity work tactic of managing visibility is also pertinent for navigating the self in diverse work contexts. Members of marginalized groups often struggle with gaining the appropriate amount of attention from colleagues at opportune moments (Blake-Beard & Roberts, 2004). Marginalized group members, even those in senior leadership positions, believe that their contributions are often obscured and rendered invisible but their shortcomings are spotlighted and become hypervisible (Kanter, 1977). A case study of the Rev. Dr. Martin Luther King, Jr. reveals the process of strategically managing one's own visibility to promote social change (Roberts, Roberts, O'Neill, & Blake-Beard, 2008).

Another important insight from agentic identity performance research relates to how people navigate the disclosure process of invisible identities. People who belong to stigmatized or marginalized invisible identity groups (e.g., sexual orientation, disabilities, religion) must carefully consider whether and how to disclose their identity group membership during social interactions (Clair et al., 2005; Creed & Scully, 2000; Ragins, 2008). Creed (2006) writes the following about "passing," or the nondisclosure of sexual identity at work: "passing requires complex stratagems, making the management of others' knowledge of one's sexual identity almost a career in itself (Woods, 1994). The emotional, psychological and spiritual costs are great, making nondisclosure a source of stress in itself, with various work and life consequences (DiPlacido, 1998)" (p. 378). Stone-Romero, Stone, and Lukaszewski (2006) review a range of disclosure options for people with disabilities in work organizations, including passing as "normal," overperforming, and acknowledging the disability. Given the implications for bias and discrimination, identity disclosure choices vary from person to person and from situation to situation.

Identity performance research typically focuses on the actor rather than the perceiver; it emphasizes how people experience identity threats, and how they attempt to cope with, mitigate, or prevent such threats from recurring. The tactics that we reviewed in the previous section have been illustrated throughout various empirical studies of marginalization and stereotyping in organizations and professions: distancing, dispelling, living up to idealized images, feigning indifference, managing visibility of strengths and shortcomings, and disclosure decisions about invisible identities. However, the identity performance research is one-sided in its emphasis on the actor, to the exclusion of the perceiver. It focuses on strategies and intentions but offers less insight with respect to impact and unfolding processes of mutual influence on identities. The bridge between identity performance and identity construction is through identity negotiation processes. This area of identity work research has focused more on work-related identities and individual characteristics rather than diversity and cultural identities. However, it does help to map out a process by which identities are co-constructed through acts of **identity claiming and granting**.

Bartel and Dutton (2001) provide a useful framing of these identity negotiation techniques in their description of the claiming–granting processes by which identities are socially constructed. The claiming–granting perspective offers a dynamic account of the identity work that unfolds during interpersonal encounters. It emphasizes the interdependence of an actor and audience when constructing positive identities within a social context. Claiming occurs when individuals perform acts they believe embody their self-view. Granting occurs when others within the social environment engage in comparison processes that allow them to affirm or disaffirm the identity an individual desires.

Achieving social validation of identities is especially important in diverse work groups (Milton, 2009). Researchers on interpersonal congruence and identity confirmation, who have assessed the extent to which group members understand and validate one another's identities, have found that these measures of social validation are correlated with creativity and cooperation in diverse work groups. For example, Polzer, Milton, and Swann (2002) found that diversity enhances creative task performance in groups with high interpersonal congruence levels, but it undermines performance in groups with low levels. Interpersonal congruence also explains differences between diverse groups with higher versus lower levels of social integration, group identification, and relationship conflict (Polzer et al., 2002). Navigating the self through claiming and granting during the first 10 minutes of group interactions determined whether group members elicited self-verifying appraisals and predicted group outcomes four months later (Polzer et al., 2002). In another study, Milton and Westphal (2005) found that identity confirmation has a positive impact on cooperation in racially diverse groups, and therefore mediates the impact of race-based diversity on performance. Thus, the identity performance research helps to illustrate motives and tactics, whereas the identity negotiation research provides more data on the positive outcomes of self-verification.

Future inquiry and next steps

In this chapter, we have sought to expand and enrich understanding of the various ways in which people navigate the self by situating tactics within broader, theoretical frameworks of identity management. Within these frameworks, we have articulated the often taken-for-granted theoretical assumptions of various traditions or scholarly communities, and their unique implications for navigating the self in diverse contexts. We also provided a forum for comparison across theories and identity groups. Our theoretically inclusive review can serve as a platform for future research on patterns, processes, and outcomes related to the various approaches toward navigating the self.

Reviewing theoretical approaches to navigating the self in diverse work contexts unearths a host of tactics that individuals employ to construct, restore, and sustain a positive sense of self. These cognitive and behavioral tactics provide individuals with a myriad of options for how they might achieve self-validation and self-enhancement, even among diverse colleagues who may apply stereotypes and trigger social identity threats. Each of these theoretical approaches offers important insights for navigating interpersonal interactions in diverse organizations, which can be developed to further scholarship and practice in this domain. Social identity theorists call attention to intergroup dynamics, critical theorists examine the role of discursive resistance, role identity theorists study the effects of segmented versus integrated identity structures, narrative theorists reveal sense-making processes that yield coherence, and identity work theorists investigate behavioral practices of claiming and influencing the significance and meaning of identities in diverse work contexts.

Although this review treats each perspective separately to unearth key themes with optimal precision, many studies of "navigating the self" draw upon more than one theoretical tradition. For example, social identity theory helps to explain why people use certain tactics for navigating the self and not others. White employees' racial identity attitudes explain why some react more positively than others to interracial situations at work (Block, Roberson, & Neuger, 1995). The strength of female scientists' and Black medical students' identification with their gender, race, and chosen professions is significantly correlated with their agentic identity performance tactics. Those who identify more strongly with gender and race are more likely to use dispelling tactics and less likely to use distancing tactics (Roberts et al., 2008). Thus, these approaches should not be viewed as exclusive or competing frameworks; rather, they represent bodies of research that overlap in common interests and expand our explanatory power.

We have not presented an exhaustive review of acts that may be encompassed under the rubric of "navigating the self" in this chapter. The myriad of assumptions regarding identity creates a vast field of possibilities for navigating the self: intentional and unintentional, conscious and unconscious, cognitive, emotional, and behavioral. Yet this vast array of possibilities poses theoretical and empirical challenges for scholars and practitioners who seek to understand how people effectively navigate the often rocky, uncertain, awkward, and yet promising terrain of interpersonal interactions in diverse organizations. Many studies of navigating the self limit their theoretical references to a narrow field of identity scholarship; rarely do identity scholars engage in dialogue that crosses disciplinary and theoretical boundaries. As a result, many of the commonly held practices for navigating the self are underexamined but contrasting assumptions based on disciplinary fields are overstated. Our goal for this chapter was to shed light upon these assumptions, highlight the theoretical and empirical contributions of various traditions, and present a more balanced and theoretically inclusive account of the field's current knowledge base on navigating the self in diverse work contexts. This review also helps to reveal possibilities for future research on navigating the self, both within and across identity theoretical traditions. In the following section, we pose several questions that may guide future research on navigating the self.

Which self is being navigated? Understanding complex identities. We anchored our discussion in identity theory based on the assertion that an identity is a core element (although not the entire composite) of the self-system. Although the self-system encompasses a broad range of emotions, motivations, schemas, scripts, and self-construals, identity refers to self-definition. Common themes emerge from the five theoretical perspectives on identity:

• Identities are a set of self-imposed and externally imposed meanings that situate an entity within a social world through the construction of defining characteristics and relationships with other entities.

• Identities are multifaceted, with meanings that evolve from group categories and memberships (Hogg, Terry, & White, 1995; Tajfel & Turner, 1979; Turner, 1987), social roles (Burke & Stets, 1999; Hogg et al., 1995; Mead, 1934; Stryker, 1980; Stryker & Burke, 2000; Stryker & Serpe, 1982), self-narratives (Carlsen & Pitsis, 2009; Gergen, 1991; Ibarra & Barbulescu, 2010; Maitlis, 2009; McAdams, 2006; Raggat, 2006), reflected appraisals and interpersonal encounters (Mead, 1934; Stryker, 1980; Stryker & Burke, 2000; Stryker & Serpe, 1982), social structures (Alvesson et al., 2008; Alvesson & Willmott, 2001; Cole, 2009; Holvino, 2010; Konrad, 2003; Linnehan & Konrad, 1999; Prasad & Prasad, 2000; Warner, 2008), individuating traits and characteristics (Hogg, Terry & White, 1995; Tajfel & Turner, 1979; Turner, 1987), and values (Hitlin, 2003).

• Identities evoke a set of cognitions, feelings, and behaviors that are associated with these defining characteristics and relationships. The study of identity reveals the meaning and significance of such self-relevant constructions for individuals and organizations.

Yet there is a gap in theorizing on how individuals develop a shared understanding of one another as people who possess multiple identities (Roberts & Creary, 2011). Future research might examine which tactics for navigating the self enable people to construct more complex rather than simplified identities. For example, how does the use of segmentation tactics like disidentification (Steele, 1997) and compartmentalization (Roccas & Brewer, 2002) help people to navigate themselves in increasingly complex work environments that call forth the activation of multiple identities simultaneously (e.g., physician-administrator, working mother, social network "friend" and employer)? How do integration tactics like dual identification (Hornsey & Hogg, 2000), superordinate categorization (Chatman, Polzer, Barsade, & Neele, 1998; Hornsey & Hogg, 2000), and "hyphenation" (Roccas & Brewer, 2002) help people to navigate multiple identities? Although the role identity research is referenced most often in studies of managing competing demands, other traditions can also provide useful insight into this process. Critical identity theory's emphasis on intersectionality may be helpful, narrative identity's emphasis on sense making and coherence may lend insight, and identity work's thick descriptions of identity performance and claiming and granting may help to shed light on this topic. By drawing from these varied perspectives, we might learn how to foster a shared understanding that individuals belong to multiple groups and possess multiple roles, all of which are significant and related to one another. We might also be able to test how mutual understanding of multiple identities improves the value of interpersonal relationships in diverse organizations.

What are the implications of various tactics of navigating the self for actors, observers, and intergroup relations? The five theoretical perspectives present different possibilities and concerns associated with navigating the self, including status hierarchies, psychological well-being, and performance.

Some tactics for navigating the self are more likely than others to reinforce **status hierarchies** of dominance and submission, privilege and marginalization. For example, social identity theory's social mobility tactics reinforce status hierarchies of dominance. By exiting a lower-status group to join a higher-status group, members of devalued groups legitimize the notion that one social group is "better than" another. In this respect, claiming an identity (e.g., a "powerful leader") may have positive cognitive and emotional outcomes for the individual (e.g., increasing one's self-esteem) but negative outcomes for others (e.g., disempowerment, oppression) (Roberts & Creary, 2011). Further, social creativity tactics transform the meaning of one's social identity group but may not change the relative ranking of social groups on the dimension of comparison. On the other hand, certain tactics are more likely to increase the status of marginalized groups in diverse work settings. According to critical identity theorists, discursive resistance of identity regulation can increase consciousness of inequality and emphasize affirmation of workers' identities as autonomous beings. Future research might examine the broader impact of navigating the self on the status hierarchies that exist within organizations and societies.

Research on navigating the self can also help to explain how diversity influences **psychological well-being**. Some tactics for navigating the self may enhance psychological well-being, whereas others may undermine it. For example, identity prioritization enhances predictability in a complex social world, but simplifying one's sense of self may have negative psychological consequences. Role identity theorists have concluded that segmentation tactics can limit identity spillover of affect, attitude, and behavior from one domain to another and reduce identity conflict (Parasuraman & Greenhaus, 2002), but identity performance research shows that identity suppression can induce identity conflict (Roberts, 2005). Prominent agentic identity performance tactics—distancing, dispelling, living up to idealized images, and feigning indifference—can interfere with learning and performance, lead to poor self-regulation, increase tension and stress, and undermine autonomy and relationships (Ely & Roberts, 2008). The desire to validate one's own self-worth can lead one to assign blame and become preoccupied with oneself, missing the opportunity to learn from others and to improve oneself and one's outcomes (Ely & Meyerson, 2006).

The defensive, ego-protective nature of certain tactics for navigating the self can enable people to construct more positive self-views in the short term but may undermine social interactions in diverse organizations in the long term (Crocker & Park, 2004). On the other hand, stories of resilience, identified in narrative-as-identity research, may be helpful in facilitating individual growth and enhancing feelings of competence (Maitlis, 2009); these narratives may be particularly important for marginalized or minority groups who seek to uncover the multitude of ways in which they define themselves as professionals.

Tactics for navigating the self may also influence **performance** on work-related tasks. Research on stereotype threat, which draws from social identity theory and identity performance research, describes how people respond to fears of being seen and judged according to negative stereotypes about their group. Stereotype threat often raises concerns that one's performance on a particular task will inadvertently confirm a negative stereotype about one's lack of ability (Roberson & Kulik, 2007; Steele, 1997; Steele et al., 2002). Under stereotype threat, one also fears that one's poor performance will reflect negatively on the stereotyped group. These concerns can increase one's level of anxiety (Aronson, Quinn, & Spencer, 1998), and the desire to disprove stereotypes can lead people to invest too much time in independent task pursuit rather than seeking help (Steele, 2010; Steele & Aronson, 1995). Coping with identity threat may undermine individual and team performance because people lose focus on the task at hand while mitigating concerns of stereotyping (Baumeister, 1999; Baumeister, Bratslavsky, Muraven, & Tice, 1998; Steele, 1997). Ironically, this distraction often leads people to confirm the very stereotypes they had hoped to dispel (Steele & Aronson, 1995). For example, when women or African-Americans fear that their math test performance will confirm a negative stereotype of incompetence, they are less able to focus on the test itself and more likely to perform poorly than when they are less concerned about social identity threats (for review of relevant study results, see Steele et al., 2002). Roberson and colleagues have examined stereotype threat in the workplace. Roberson, Deitch, Brief, and Block (2003) report that Black managers who experience stereotype threat spend more time monitoring their performance through peer comparisons and are more likely to discount performance feedback they receive from the organization. These tactics for navigating the self in the face of stereotype threat may help Black managers protect a positive identity but may also undermine longer-term performance and relationship building.

A meta-analysis of the various tactics and related outcomes, at multiple levels of analysis, would be helpful to develop a theoretically inclusive understanding of when and how to navigate oneself in diverse work contexts, based on one's goals, the audience, and the nature of intergroup relations. Motive might be a moderating factor in determining whether a tactic for navigating the self leads to more positive or negative intergroup, psychological, and performance outcomes. Researchers might assess various motives for navigating the self, such as: advancing one's career, gaining power,, restoring one's dignity, or maintaining the right to self-author (particularly when labeled or categorized by others in disempowering or inhumane ways). An intense focus on navigating the self may also help to explain how people manage multiple interests, realities, and paradoxes in organizational life as they balance their own complex needs for inclusion, recognition, advancement, and competence.

How does cultural diversity influence positive identity construction and navigating the self? Recent identity scholarship has sought to deepen our understanding of positive identities at work (Roberts & Dutton, 2009). Yet cultural diversity has remained peripheral to the discussions of cultivating positive "work" identities such as functional role, department, or organizational membership. Cultural diversity refers to differences among people in race, ethnicity, gender, religion, nationality, or other dimensions of social identity that are marked by a history of intergroup prejudice, discrimination, or oppression (Ely & Roberts, 2008). Even in contexts that are diverse along these dimensions, race, gender, and class diversity are often invisible contextual features of the positive identity studies. The relative lack of attention to cultural diversity may be due to its associations with bias, discrimination, stigma, threat, and conflict in organizations—all of which seem to contradict an interest in cultivating positive identities and positive organizational scholarship more broadly (Roberts, 2006). A theoretical gap exists in identity scholarship regarding how people cultivate more positive work-related identities in culturally diverse contexts, because the dominant research on diversity and navigating the self features a limited set of tactics for coping with identity threat. The question of positive identity construction reaches beyond identity threat and invites a broader range of tactics for constructing, sustaining, and restoring positive identities. The review presented in this chapter supports that cultural diversity research has much to offer in terms of charting new pathways for cultivating positive identities at work.

As Dutton and colleagues (2010) noted, "the way in which individuals go about constructing a positive identity may vary depending on the culture in which they are embedded." The cultural influences of race, gender, and class likely shape each person's interpretation of proposed mechanisms for positive identity construction. According to the *virtue* perspective in Dutton and colleagues' (2010) typology, an identity is positive when it is infused with the qualities associated with people of good character, such as "master virtues" (Park & Peterson, 2003) like wisdom, integrity, courage, justice, transcendence, redemption, and resilience. Gendered constructions of virtue may influence the process of positive identity construction for male and female professionals; bravery, as a virtue, is often associated with traditionally male professions (e.g., firefighters), whereas compassion, as a virtue, is often associated with traditionally female professions (e.g., nursing).

The *evaluative* perspective on positive identity focuses on the regard in which individuals hold their personal identity (i.e., as an individual), relational identity (i.e., as a member of a relationship), and social identity (i.e., as a member of a social group). According to this perspective, an identity is positive when it is regarded favorably by the individual who holds it and/or by referent others who regard the identity favorably. Psychological research on self-evaluations shows that African-Americans who based their contingencies of self-worth on others' approval, physical appearance, being good at school, or outdoing others in competition suffered greater self-esteem losses than did their White American counterparts (Crocker & Park, 2003). Basing self-esteem on love and support from one's family, on God's love, or on being a virtuous, moral person was a more stable and generative path toward increasing positive evaluations for people of all backgrounds, but for African-Americans in particular (Crocker & Park, 2003). These differences may influence positive identity construction processes in diverse organizations. Yet research on self-esteem among White men shows that believing in affirmative action quotas (whether or not they actually exist) protects White men's self-evaluations from threatening performance feedback (e.g., being told they performed poorly on an intelligence test) by boosting their sense of self-competence (Unzueta,

Lowery, & Knowles, 2008). Thus, the diversity implications of positive identity construction are substantial.

The *developmental* perspective on positive identity focuses on changes in identity over time and assumes that identity is capable of progress and adaptation. The developmental perspective asserts that an identity is positive when it progresses toward a higher-order stage of development (for an example, see Hall's [2002] description of progress through distinct career stages). The developmental perspective also asserts that an identity is positive when the individual defines himself or herself in a way that generates fit between the content of the identity and internal or external standards (e.g., adapting to new roles at work, see Ibarra, 1999; resisting stigmatization and oppression, see Creed, DeJordy & Lok, 2010, and Meyerson & Scully, 1995). As referenced in this chapter, career research suggests that White men and women may follow different trajectories for assimilation and maturity in career development than do non-White men and women (e.g., Bell & Nkomo, 2001; Thomas & Gabarro, 1999). Further, cultural scripts and social discourses associated with group memberships dictate the parameters of interpersonal and intergroup relations and serve as "contextual resources" that individuals draw upon to construct narrative identities (Alvesson et al., 2008).

The *structural* perspective focuses on the ways in which the self-concept is organized. Research fitting this perspective asserts that an individual's identity structure is more positive when the multiple facets of the identity are in balanced and/or complementary relationship with one another, rather than in tension or conflict with one another (see Cheng, Sanchez-Burks, & Lee, 2008; Kreiner, Hollensbe, & Sheep, 2006; Greenhaus & Powell, 2006). Identity work research shows that in the face of complicated dynamics, marginalized individuals are proactive agents who employ nuanced tactics for constructing positive identity structures in diverse work contexts (e.g., Meyerson & Scully, 1995). We encourage more explicit research that bridges cultural diversity with positive identity construction through the examination of tactics for navigating the self.

How do people navigate the self to create positive relational identities? The theoretical exploration of varied approaches toward navigating the self also promotes the discovery of generative pathways for building high-quality relationships in diverse organizations. Our research review suggests that these generative pathways for building high-quality relationships in diverse organizations might begin with enriching understanding of how individuals from varied cultural backgrounds navigate their selves in ways that construct more positive identities in diverse work contexts. Rather than focus merely on the individual's sense of self, however, we propose that identity scholars reconceptualize the core elements of generative positive identity that serve both individual and social aims. That is, we propose that scholars shift identity paradigms in diversity research away from a focus on individual or collective identities to a focus on positive relational identities, and a focus on how people navigate these relational selves.

Building on the work of Sluss and Ashforth (2007), we define positive relational identities as self-views that reflect the ability to derive positive value from and enhance interaction patterns within interpersonal relationships. A positive relational identity can strengthen the individual's ability to cultivate social resources (Dutton et al., 2010), but also strengthens the quality of the tie between two or more people from culturally diverse backgrounds. The distinction between a positive individual identity and positive relational identity is as follows. A positive individual identity emphasizes whether one considers oneself to be virtuous, held in high esteem (by the self and others), growing and adapting in positive ways, and coherent or whole. A positive relational identity would involve building a more positive sense of self along these dimensions *for each party in the relationship*, and thus reduces the likelihood that one's own positive identity construction—and corollary tactics for navigating the self—will occur at the expense of the other (i.e., elevating one's own sense of self by diminishing another person or group). To shift to a focus on positive relational identities, scholars would need to consider the tactics for navigating the self that promote shared growth, enhancement, and empowerment, as individuals within a relationship come to view themselves *and each other* as more virtuous, worthy, evolving, adapting, balanced, and coherent. The focus on positive relational identities provides a counterpoint to the more egocentric tactics, often supported by social identity and identity performance theories, that involve elevating one's own identity by degrading another's, rather than mutual gain.

Further, an emphasis on positive relational identities may also raise questions regarding "positive" qualities that define the relationship itself and the identification processes of relating to one another as relational partners. The virtue perspective on positive relational identity in diverse organizations might emphasize principles of relating to others with dignity, humility, and respect. Navigating the self might involve claiming and granting such relational principles. However, research should examine whether certain relational identities (i.e., "helper," "caregiver," or "servant") reinforce a dynamic of powerlessness and dependence on the party who has more access to resources. These relational identities are often associated with virtuous behavior, but the impact of such "virtuous" identity construction in diverse contexts should be examined closely.

The evaluative perspective on positive relational identities might involve tactics for navigating the self that reinforce mutual regard, affirmation, and love. The developmental perspective on constructing positive relational identities might illuminate the growth trajectory of a relationship in which trust, transparency, and intimacy increase over time, despite differences. Tactics for navigating the self might involve sense making that supports such views of mutual worth. And the structural perspective on constructing positive relational identities could characterize the elements of a relationship in which differences remain salient and complexity is validated. Navigating the self might involve prompting complex categorizations that encourage group identifications based on optimal distinctiveness within a collective, not just within an individual.

Recent research on positive relationships at work may help to further this line of inquiry on navigating the self (e.g., Davidson & James, 2007; Dutton & Heaphy, 2003; Geiger, 2010; Milton, 2009). We propose building upon these initial discussions to fully address the power dynamics between parties. A deeper understanding of dominance, submission, oppression, victimization, voice, silencing, and differential access to resources is critical in developing this scholarly approach toward positive relational identity construction in diverse work contexts. This scholarly approach would also require drawing upon various insights from social identity, critical identity, (role) identity, narrative identity, and identity work approaches; a single theoretical approach is unlikely to generate the new insights that are needed to navigate the self and engage diversity in this increasingly complicated social world. We hope that these intellectual endeavors will not only illuminate the interplay between navigating the self, positive identity, diversity, and relationships in organizations, but will also serve as the conceptual landscape for developing more generative encounters with difference in work contexts.

Concluding thoughts

We encourage scholars to continue to engage in cross-disciplinary, theoretically inclusive dialogue on navigating the self in diverse work contexts. We focused our review on five prominent theoretical perspectives on positive identity construction, but there are certainly other theories that are relevant but were not part of the scope of this chapter. For example, status characteristics theory presents a resource-based view of social structure that explains how people who are systematically denied access to resources necessary for effectiveness are then viewed as inferior performers. In short, access to resources shapes societal consensus on the value of groups, which then influences social interactions. Diversity scholars have drawn upon status characteristics theory to explain social interactions and identities within diverse work contexts. Thus, it may be useful in identifying additional ways that people navigate the self.

We also believe that debates on agency and structure in navigating the self are useful for challenging assumptions and deepening understanding of the complex interplay of person and context in self-definition. Overly individualistic accounts of the self and identity construction diminish the importance of context and limit the ability to envision the long-term impact of self-strategies on individuals. Yet overly deterministic accounts of structural constraints diminish the role of personal agency in making sense of and defining a meaningful existence in a diverse work context.

Finally, we draw from critical theorists who view themselves as primary agents of identity change by raising consciousness and holding attention on structural inequalities and dominance. This view serves as a reminder that our scholarship itself can create possibilities or constraints on how people navigate themselves to construct positive identities in diverse work contexts. For example, Shapiro, Ingols, O'Neill, and Blake-Beard (2009) take ownership of their agency as diversity scholars in their article "Making sense of women as career self-agents," which recasts the discourse on women's careers from "opting out" of the conventional, gendered, work-is-primary model to a more empowered narrative of women as "free agents" and "agent[s] of their own career." We encourage diversity and identity scholars to recognize the work of various theoretical traditions in their efforts to explain how, why, and to what end people navigate the self in diverse work contexts.

References

Acker, J. (1990). Hierarchies, jobs, bodies: A theory of gendered organizations. *Gender & Society, 4,* 139–158.

Allison, S. T., & Herlocker, C. E. (1994). Constructing impressions in demographically diverse organizational settings: A group categorization analysis. *American Behavioral Scientist, 37,* 637–652.

Alvesson, M., Ashcraft, K. L., & Thomas, R. (2008). Identity matters: Reflections on the construction of identity scholarship in organization studies. *Organization Studies, 15,* 5–28.

Alvesson, M., & Willmott, H. (2002). Identity regulation as organizational control: Producing the appropriate individual. *Lund University School of Economics and Management Institute of Economic Research Working Paper Series, 15,* 5–28.

Anderson, E. (1999). The social situation of the black executive: Black and white identities in the corporate world. In M. Lamont (Ed.), *The cultural territories of race: Black and white boundaries* (pp. 3–29). Chicago: University of Chicago Press.

Aronson, J., Quinn, D., & Spencer, S. (1998). Stereotype threat and the academic underperformance of minorities and women. In Swim, J. K., & Stangor, C. (Eds.), *Prejudice: The target's perspective* (pp. 83–103). New York: Academic Press.

Ashforth, B. E., Harrison, S. H., & Corley, K. G. (2008). Identification in organizations: An examination of four fundamental questions. *Journal of Management, 34,* 325–374.

Ashforth, B. E., & Kreiner, G. (1999). How can you do it? Dirty work and the challenge of constructing a positive identity. *Academy of Management Review, 24,* 413–434.

Avery, D., Richeson, J., Hebl, M., & Ambady, N. (2009). It does not have to be uncomfortable: The role of behavioral scripts in black-white interracial interactions. *Journal of Applied Psychology, 94,* 1382–1393.

Barrett, F. J. (1996). The organizational construction of hegemonic masculinity: The case of the US Navy. *Gender, Work, and Organization, 3,* 129–141.

Bartel, C., & Dutton, J. E. (2001). Ambiguous organizational memberships: Constructing organizational identities in interactions with others. In M. A. Hogg & D. J. Terry (Eds.), *Social identity processes in organizational contexts* (pp. 115–130). Philadelphia: Psychology Press.

Baumeister, R. (1999). The self. In D. Gilbert & S. Fiske (Eds.), *Handbook of social psychology* (pp. 680–740). Boston: McGraw Hill.

Baumeister, R. F., Bratslavsky, E., Muraven, M., & Tice, D. M. (1998). Ego depletion: Is the active self a limited resource? *Journal of Personality and Social Psychology, 74,* 1225–1237.

Bell, E. (1990). The bicultural life experience of career oriented black women. *Journal of Organizational Behavior, 11,* 459–477.

Bell, E., & Nkomo, S. (2001). *Our separate ways: Black and white women and the struggle for professional identity.* Boston: Harvard Business School Press.

Bell, M., & McLaughlin, M. (2006). Outcomes of appearance and obesity in organizations. In A. Konrad, P. Prasad, & J. Pringle (Eds.). *Handbook of Workplace Diversity* (pp. 455–474). Thousand Oaks, CA: Sage.

Benschop, Y. (2006). Of small steps and the longing for giant leaps: Research on the intersection of sex and gender within work and organizations. In A. Konrad, P. Prasad, & J. Pringle (Eds.), *Handbook of workplace diversity* (pp. 273–298). Thousand Oaks, CA: Sage.

Bergsicker, H., Shelton, J. N., & Richeson, J. (2010). To be liked versus respected: Divergent goals in interracial interactions. *Journal of Personality and Social Psychology, 99,* 248–264.

Blake-Beard, S., & Roberts, L. M. (2004). *Releasing the double bind of visibility for minorities in the workplace.* Center for Gender in Organizations, Simmons School of Management, CGO Commentaries No. 4, September 2004.

Block, C. J., Roberson, L., & Neuger, D. A. (1995). White racial identity theory: A framework for understanding reactions toward interracial situations in organizations. *Journal of Vocational Behavior, 46,* 71–88.

Booysen, L. (2007). Societal power shifts and changing social identities in South Africa: Workplace implications. *Southern African Journal of Economic and Management Sciences, 10,* 1–20.

Branscombe, N. R., Ellemers, N., Spears, R., & Doosje, B. (1999). The context and content of social identity threat. In N. Ellemers, R. Spears, & B. Doosje (Eds.), *Social identity context, commitment, content* (pp. 35–58). London: Blackwell.

Brewer, M. B. (1991). The social self: On being the same and different at the same time. *Personality and Social Psychology Bulletin, 17,* 475–482.

Burke, P. J. (1991). Identities and social structure: The 2003 Cooley-Mead Award address. *Social Psychology Quarterly, 67,* 5–15.

Burke, P. J., & Reitzes, D. C. (1981). The link between identity and role performance. *Social Psychology Quarterly, 44,* 83–92.

Burke, P. J., & Stets, J. E. (1999). Trust and commitment through self-verification. *Social Psychology Quarterly, 62,* 347–366.

Byrne, D. (1971). The ubiquitous relationship: Attitude similarity and attraction: A cross-cultural study. *Human Relations, 24,* 201–207.

Carlsen, A., & Pitsis, T. (2009). Experiencing hope in organization lives. In L. M. Roberts & J. E. Dutton (Eds.), *Exploring positive identities and organizations: Building a theoretical and research foundation* (pp. 77–98). New York: Routledge.

Caza, B. B., & Wilson, M. G. (2009). Me, myself, and I: The benefits of work-identity complexity. In L. M. Roberts & J. E. Dutton (Eds.), *Exploring positive identities and organizations: Building a theoretical and research foundation* (pp. 99–123). New York: Routledge.

Chatman, J. A., & Flynn, F. J. (2001). The influence of demographic composition on the emergence and consequences of cooperative norms in groups. *Academy of Management Journal, 44,* 956–974.

Chatman, J. A., Polzer, J. T., Barsade, S. G., & Neale, M. A. (1998). Being different yet feeling similar: The influence of demographic composition and organizational culture on work processes and outcomes. *Administrative Science Quarterly, 43,* 749–780.

Cheng, C., Sanchez-Burks, J., & Lee, F. (2008). Connecting the dots within: Creative performance and identity integration. *Psychological Science, 19,* 1178–1184.

Clair, J., Beatty, J., & Maclean, T. (2005). Out of sight but not out of mind: Managing invisible social identities in the workplace. *Academy of Management Review, 30,* 78–95.

Cole, E. R. (2009). Intersectionality and research in psychology. *American Psychologist, 64,* 170–180.

Collins, P. H. (1990). *Black feminist thought: Knowledge, consciousness, and the politics of empowerment.* New York: Routledge.

Colquitt, J. A., Noe, R. A., & Jackson, C. L. (2002). Justice in teams: Antecedents and consequences of procedural justice climate in teams. *Personnel Psychology, 55,* 83–109.

Connell, R. W. (1995). *Masculinities.* Berkeley, CA: University of California Press.

Creed, D., DeJordy, R., & Lok, J. (2010). Being the change: Resolving institutional contradiction through identity work. *Academy of Management Journal, 53,* 1336–1364.

Creed, D., & Scully, M. (2000). Songs of ourselves: Employees' deployment of social identity in workplace encounters. *Journal of Management Inquiry, 9,* 391–412.

Creed, W. E. D. (2006). Seven conversations about the same thing: Homophobia and heterosexism in the workplace. In A. Konrad, P. Prasad, & J. Pringle (Eds.), *Handbook of Workplace Diversity* (pp. 371–400). Thousand Oaks, CA: Sage.

Crocker, J., & Park, L. E. (2003). Seeking self-esteem: construction, maintenance and protection of self-worth. In M. Leary & J. Tangney (Eds.), *Handbook of self and identity* (pp. 291–313). New York: Guilford Press.

Crocker, J., & Park, L. E. (2004). The costly pursuit of self-esteem. *Psychological Bulletin, 130,* 392–414.

Davidson, M., & James, E. (2007). The engines of positive relationships across difference: conflict and learning. In J. Dutton & B. Ragins (Eds.), *Exploring positive relationships at work* (pp. 137–158). Mahwah, NJ: Lawrence Erlbaum Associates.

DiPlacido, J. (1998). Minority stress among lesbians, gay men, and bisexuals: A consequence of heterosexism, homophobia, and stigmatization. In G. M. Herek (Ed.), *Stigma and sexual orientation: Understanding prejudice against lesbians, gay men, and bisexuals* (pp. 138–159). Thousand Oaks, CA: Sage.

Dovidio, J., Gaertner, S., & Saguy, T. (2007). Another view of "we": Majority and minority group perspectives on a common ingroup identity. In W. Stoebe & M. Hewstone (Eds.), *European review of social psychology* (Vol. 18, pp. 296–330). Hove, United Kingdom: Psychology Press.

Dutton, J. E., & Heaphy, E. (2003). Coming to life: The power of high quality connections at work. In K. Cameron, J. Dutton, & R. E. Quinn (Eds.), *Positive organizational scholarship* (pp. 263–278). San Francisco: Berrett-Koehler.

Dutton, J. E., Roberts, L. M., & Bednar, J. S. (2010). Pathways for positive identity construction at work: Four types of positive identity and the building of social resources. *Academy of Management Review, 35,* 265–293.

Eagly, A., Makhijani, M., & Klonsky, B. (1992). Gender and the evaluation of leaders: A meta-analysis. *Psychological Bulletin, 111,* 3–22.

Ely, R., & Roberts, L. M. (2008). Shifting frames in team-diversity research: From difference to relationships. In A. P. Brief (Ed.), *Diversity at work* (pp. 175–201). Cambridge University Press.

Ely, R. J. (1994). The effects of organizational demographics and social identity on relationships among professional women. *Administrative Science Quarterly, 39,* 203–238.

Ely, R. J. (1995). The power in demography: Women's social constructions of gender identity at work. *Academy of Management Journal, 38*(3), 589–634.

Ely, R. J., & Meyerson, D. E. (2006). *Unmasking manly men: the organizational reconstruction of men's identity.* Working Paper, Harvard Business School, Boston, MA.

Erikson, E. H. (1959). Identity and the life cycle: Selected papers. *Psychological Issues, 1,* 1–171.

Geiger, K. (2010). *Cross-race relationships as sites of transformation: Navigating the protective shell and the insular bubble.* Unpublished dissertation. Antioch University. www.ohiolink.edu/etd.

Gergen, K. J. (1991). *The saturated self: Dilemmas of identity in contemporary life.* New York: Basic Books.

Greenhaus, J., & Powell, G. 2006. When work and family are allies: A theory of work-family enrichment. *Academy of Management Review, 31,* 72–92.

Gregg, G. S. (2006). The raw and the bland: A structural model of narrative identity. In D. P. McAdams, R. Josselson, & A. Lieblich (Eds.), *Identity and story: Creating self in narrative. Narrative study of lives* (Vol. 4, pp. 63–88). Washington, D.C.: American Psychological Association.

Hall, D. T. (2002). *Careers in and out of organizations.* Thousand Oaks, CA: Sage.

Hall, D. T., & Mirvis, P. H. (1995). The new career contract: Developing the whole person at midlife and beyond. *Journal of Vocational Behavior, 47,* 269–289.

Harrington, B., & Hall, D. T. (2007). *Career management and work-life integration: Using self-assessment to navigate contemporary careers.* Thousand Oaks, CA: Sage Publications, Inc.

Hearn, J., & Collinson, D. (2006). Men, masculinities, and workplace diversity/diversion: Power, intersections, and contradictions. In A. Konrad, P. Prasad, & J. Pringle (Eds.), *Handbook of workplace diversity* (pp. 299–322). Thousand Oaks, CA: Sage.

Hebl, M. R., & Mannix, L. M. (2003). The weight of obesity in evaluating others: A mere proximity effect. *Personality and Social Psychology Bulletin, 29,* 28–38.

Heilman, M. (2001). Description and prescription: How gender stereotypes prevent women's ascent up the organizational ladder. *Journal of Social Issues, 57,* 657–674.

Heilman, M., Block, C., Martell, R., & Simon, M. (1989). Has anything changed? Current characterizations of men, women and managers. *Journal of Applied Psychology, 74,* 935–942.

Hitlin, S. (2003). Values as the core of personal identity: Drawing links between two theories of self. *Social Psychology Quarterly, 66,* 118–137.

Hogg, M. A., Terry, D. J., & White, K. M. (1995). A tale of two theories: A critical comparison of identity theory with social identity theory. *Social Psychology Quarterly, 58,* 255–269.

Holvino, E. (2010). Intersections: The simultaneity of race, gender, and class in organization studies. *Gender, Work, and Organization, 17,* 248–287.

Hornsey, M. J., & Hogg, M. A. (2000). Assimilation and diversity: An integrative model of subgroup relations. *Personality and Social Psychology, 4,* 143–156.

Hughes, E. C. (1951). *Group psychology and the analysis of the ego.* New York: Liveright.

Hurtado, A., & Sinha, M. (2008). More than men: Latino feminist masculinities and intersectionality. *Sex Roles, 59,* 337–349.

Ibarra, H. (1993). Personal networks of women and minorities in management: A conceptual framework. *Academy of Management Review, 18,* 56–87.

Ibarra, H. (1995). Race, opportunity and diversity of social circles in managerial networks. *Academy of Management Journal, 38,* 673–703.

Ibarra, H. (1999). Provisional selves: Experimenting with image and identity in professional adaptation. *Administrative Science Quarterly, 44,* 764–791.

Ibarra, H., & Barbulescu, R. (2010). Identity as narrative: Prevalence, effectiveness, and consequences of narrative identity work in macro work role transitions. *Academy of Management Review, 35,* 135–154.

Kanter, R. M. (1977). *Men and women of the corporation.* New York: Basic Books.

Kellogg, K. (2005). *Challenging operations: Changing interactions, identities, and institutions in a surgical teaching hospital.* Unpublished doctoral dissertation. Cambridge, MA: MIT Sloan School of Management.

Kerfoot, D., & Knights, D. (1993). Management, masculinity and manipulation: From paternalism to corporate strategy in financial services in Britain. *Journal of Management Studies, 30,* 659–678.

Konrad, A. M. (2003). Special issue introduction: Defining the domain of workplace diversity scholarship. *Group and Organization Management, 28,* 4–17.

Kornberger, M., & Brown, A. D. (2007). "Ethics" as a discursive resource for identity work. *Human Relations, 60,* 497–518.

Kreiner, G., & Sheep, M. (2009). Growing pains and gains: Framing identity dynamics as opportunities for identity growth. In L. M. Roberts & J. E. Dutton (Eds.), *Exploring positive identities and organizations: Building a theoretical and research foundation* (pp. 23–46). New York: Routledge.

Kreiner, G. E., Hollensbe, E. C., & Sheep, M. L. (2006). Where is the "me" among the "we"? Identity work and the search for optimal balance. *Academy of Management Journal, 49,* 1031–1057.

Kunda, G. (1992). *Engineering culture, control and commitment in a high-tech corporation.* Philadelphia, PA: Temple University Press.

Learmonth, M., & Humphreys, M. (2011). Blind spots in Dutton, Roberts, and Bednar's "Pathways for positive identity construction at work: 'You've got to accentuate the positive, eliminate the negative.'" *Academy of Management Review, 36,* 424–427.

Linnehan, F., & Konrad, A. M. (1999). Diluting diversity: Implications for intergroup equality in organizations. *Journal of Management Inquiry, 8,* 399–414.

Lord, R., & Maher, K. (1991). *Leadership and information processing.* New York: Unwin Hyman.

Maitlis, S. (2009). Who am I now? Sensemaking and identity in posttraumatic growth. In L. M. Roberts & J. E. Dutton (Eds.), *Exploring positive identities and organizations: Building a theoretical and research foundation* (pp. 47–76). New York: Routledge.

McAdams, D. P. (1997). The case for unity in the (post)modern self: A modest proposal. In R. D. Ashmore & L. Jussim (Eds.), *Self and identity. Fundamental* issues (pp. 46–78). New York: Oxford University Press.

McAdams, D. P. (1985). *Power, intimacy, and the life story: Personological inquiries into identity.* New York: Guilford.

McAdams, D. P. (2006). *The redemptive self: Stories Americans live by.* New York: Oxford University Press.

McAdams, D. P., Josselson, R., & Lieblich, A. (2006). *Identity and story: Creating self in narrative. Narrative study of lives, Vol. 4.* Washington, D.C.: American Psychological Association.

Mead, G. H. (1934). *Mind, self and society.* Chicago: University of Chicago Press.

Meyerson, D. (2001). *Tempered radicals: How people use difference to inspire change at work.* Boston: Harvard Business School Press.

Meyerson, D., & Scully, M. (1995). Tempered radicalism and the politics of ambivalence and change. *Organization Science, 6*(5), 585–600.

Meyerson, D. E., & Kolb, D. (2000). Moving out of the "armchair": Developing a framework to bridge the gap between feminist theory and practice. *Organization, 7,* 553–571.

Milton, L. (2009). Creating and sustaining cooperation in interdependent groups: Positive relational identities, identity confirmation, and cooperative capacity. In L. M. Roberts & J. E. Dutton (Eds.), *Exploring positive identities and organizations: building a theoretical and research foundation* (pp. 289–317). New York: Routledge Press.

Milton, L., & Westphal, J. (2005). Identity confirmation networks and cooperation in work groups. *Academy of Management Journal, 48,* 191–212.

Parasuraman, S., & Greenhaus, J. (2002). Toward reducing some critical gaps in work-family research. *Human Resource Management Review, 12,* 299–312.

Park, N., & Peterson, C. 2003. Virtues and organizations. In K. S. Cameron, J. E. Dutton, & R. E. Quinn (Eds.), *Positive organizational scholarship: foundations of a new discipline.* San Francisco: Berrett-Koehler.

Polzer, J., Milton, L., & Swann, W. (2002). Capitalizing on diversity: Interpersonal congruence in small work groups. *Administrative Science Quarterly, 47,* 296–324.

Prasad, P., & Prasad, A. (2000). Stretching the iron cage: The constitution and implications of routine workplace resistance. *Organization Science, 11,* 387–403.

Pringle, J., Konrad, A., & Prasad, P. (2006). Conclusion: Reflection and future direction. In A. Konrad, P. Prasad, & J. Pringle (Eds.), *Handbook of workplace diversity* (pp. 531–539). Thousand Oaks, CA: Sage.

Raggat, P. T. F. (2006). Multiplicity and conflict in the dialogical self: A life-narrative approach. In D. P. McAdams, R. Josselson, & A. Lieblich (Eds.), *Identity and story: Creating self in narrative. Narrative study of lives, Vol. 4* (pp. 15–35). Washington, D.C.: American Psychological Association.

Ragins, B. R. (2008). Disclosure disconnects: Antecedents and consequences of disclosing invisible stigmas across life domains. *Academy of Management Review, 33,* 194–215.

Reybold, L. E., & Alamia, J. J. (2008). Academic transitions in education: A developmental perspective of women faculty experiences. *Journal of Career Development, 35,* 107–128.

Roberson, L., Deitch, E., Brief, A., & Block, C. (2003). Stereotype threat and feedback seeking in the workplace. *Journal of Vocational Behavior, 62,* 176–188.

Roberson, L., & Kulik, C. (2007). Stereotype threat at work. *Academy of Management Perspectives, 21,* 24–40.

Roberts, D. D., Roberts, L. M., O'Neill, R. M., & Blake-Beard, S. D. (2008). The invisible work of managing visibility for social change: Insights from the leadership of Reverend Dr. Martin Luther King Jr. *Business & Society, 47,* 425–456.

Roberts, L. M. (2005). Changing faces: Professional image construction in diverse organizational settings. *Academy of Management Review, 30,* 685–711.

Roberts, L. M. (2006). Shifting the lens on organizational life: The added value of positive scholarship. *Academy of Management Review, 31,* 292–305.

Roberts, L. M., Cha, S. E., Hewlin, P. F., & Settles, I. H. (2009). Bringing the inside out: Enhancing authenticity and positive identity in organizations. In L. M. Roberts & J. E. Dutton (Eds.), *Exploring positive identities and organizations: Building a theoretical and research foundation* (pp. 149–169). New York: Routledge.

Roberts, L. M., & Creary, S. J. (2011). Positive identity construction: insights from classical and contemporary theoretical perspectives. In K. Cameron & G. Spreitzer (Eds.), *The Oxford handbook of positive organizational scholarship* (pp. 70–83). New York: Oxford University Press.

Roberts, L. M., & Dutton, J. E. (Eds.) (2009). *Exploring positive identities and organizations: building a theoretical and research foundation* (pp. 23–46). New York: Routledge.

Roberts, L. M., Dutton, J. E., & Bednar, J. (2009). Forging ahead: Positive identities and organizations as a research frontier. In L. M. Roberts & J. E. Dutton (Eds.), *Exploring positive identities and organizations: Building a theoretical and research foundation* (pp. 497–516). New York: Routledge.

Roberts, L. M. & Roberts, D. D. (2007). Testing the limits of antidiscrimination law: The business, legal, and ethical ramifications of cultural profiling at work. *Duke Journal of Gender Law & Policy, 14,* 369–405.

Roberts, L. M., Settles, I., & Jellison, W. (2008). Predicting the strategic identity management of gender and race. *Identity, 8*(4), 269–306.

Roccas, S., & Brewer, M. B. (2002). Social identity complexity. *Personality and Social Psychology Review, 6,* 88–106.

Rosette, A., Leonardelli, G., & Phillips, K. (2008). The white standard: Racial bias in leader categorization. *Journal of Applied Psychology, 93,* 758–777.

Rosette, A., & Tost, L. (2010). Agentic women and communal leadership: How role prescriptions confer advantage to top women leaders. *Journal of Applied Psychology, 95,* 221–235.

Rothbard, N. P., & Ramarajan, L. (2009). Checking your identities at the door: Positive relationships between non-work and work identities. In L. M. Roberts & J. E. Dutton (Eds.), *Exploring positive identities and organizations: Building a theoretical and research foundation* (pp. 125–148). New York: Routledge.

Rothman, J. (1997). *Revolving identity-based conflict in nations, organisations, and communities.* San Francisco: Jossey-Bass.

Rudman, L., & Glick, P. (1999). Feminized management and backlash toward agentic women: The hidden costs to women of a kinder, gentler image of middle managers. *Journal of Personality and Social Psychology, 77,* 1004–1010.

Rudman, L., & Glick, P. (2001). Prescriptive gender stereotypes and backlash toward agentic women. *Journal of Social Issues, 57,* 743–762.

Ryan, C. S., Hunt, J. S., Weible, J. A., Peterson, C. R., & Casas, J. S. (2007). Multicultural and colorblind ideology, stereotypes, and ethnocentrism among Black and White Americans. *Group Processes & Intergroup Relations, 10,* 617–637.

Schlenker, B., & Weigold, M. (1992). Interpersonal processes involving impression regulation and management. *Annual Review of Psychology, 4,* 133–168.

Scott, M. C. (2011). *Intersectionality: The outsider within "privilege" of maternal relationships and the empowerment of sustainable values.* Unpublished Dissertation. The George Washington University.

Scully, M., & Blake-Beard, S. (2006). Locating class in organizational diversity work: Class as structure, style and process. In A. Konrad, P. Prasad, & J. Pringle (Eds.), *Handbook of workplace diversity* (pp. 431–454). Thousand Oaks, CA: Sage.

Settles, I. H. (2004). When multiple identities interfere: The role of identity centrality. *Personality and Social Psychology Bulletin, 30,* 487–500.

Shapiro, M., Ingols, C., O'Neill, R., & Blake-Beard, S. (2009). Making sense of women as career self-agents: Implications for human resource development. *Human Resource Development Quarterly, 20,* 477–501.

Sluss, D., & Ashforth, B. (2007). Relational identities and identification: Defining ourselves through work relationships. *Academy of Management Review, 32,* 9–32.

Snow, D. A., & Anderson, L. (1987). Identity work among the homeless: The verbal construction and avowal of personal identities. *American Journal of Sociology, 92,* 1336–1371.

Steele, C. (2010). *Whistling Vivaldi and other clues to how stereotypes affect us.* New York: W.W. Norton & Company, Inc.

Steele, C. M. (1997). A threat in the air: How stereotypes shape intellectual identity and performance. *American Psychologist, 52,* 613–629.

Steele, C. M., & Aronson, J. (1995). Stereotype threat and the intellectual test performance of African Americans. *Journal of Personality & Social Psychology, 69,* 797–811.

Steele, C. M., Spencer, S. J., & Aronson, J. (2002). Contending with group image: The psychology of stereotype and social identity threat. In M. P. Zanna (Ed.), *Advances in experimental social psychology* (pp. 379–440). San Diego, CA: Academic Press, Inc.

Stone-Romero, E., Stone, D., & Lukaszewski, K. (2006). The influence of disability on role-taking in organizations. In A. Konrad, P. Prasad, & J. Pringle (Eds.), *Handbook of workplace diversity* (pp. 401–430). Thousand Oaks, CA: Sage.

Stryker, S. (1980). *Symbolic interactionism: A social structural version.* Menlo Park, CA: Benjamin Cummings.

Stryker, S. (2000). Identity competition: Key to differential social movement involvement. In S. Stryker, T. Owens, & R. White (Eds.), *Identity, self, and social movements* (pp. 21–40). Minneapolis: University of Minnesota Press.

Stryker, S., & Burke, P. J. (2000). The past, present, and future of an identity theory. *Social Psychology Quarterly, 63,* 284–297.

Stryker, S., & Serpe, R. T. (1982). Commitment, identity salience, and role behavior: A theory and research example. In W. Ickes & E. S. Knowles (Eds.), *Personality, roles, and social behavior* (pp. 199–218). New York: Springer-Verlag.

Swann, W. B., Jr. (1983). Self-verification: Bringing social reality into harmony with the self. In J. Suls & A.G. Greenwald (Eds.), *Social psychological perspectives of the self* (Vol. 2, pp. 33–66). Hillsdale, NJ: Lawrence Erlbaum Associates.

Tajfel, H. (1978). *Differentiation between social groups: Studies in the social psychology of intergroup relations.* New York: Academic Press.

Tajfel, H., & Turner, J. C. (1979). An integrative theory of intergroup conflict. In W. G. Austin & S. Worchel (Eds.), *The social psychology of intergroup relations* (pp. 33–47). Monterey, CA: Brooks-Cole.

Thomas, D. A. (1993). Racial dynamics in cross-race developmental relationships. *Administrative Science Quarterly, 38,* 169–194.

Thomas, D. A., & Gabarro, J. J. (1999). *Breaking through: The making of minority executives in corporate America.* Boston: Harvard Business School Press.

Turner, J. C. (1987). *Rediscovering the social group: A self-categorization theory.* New York: Blackwell.

Unzueta, M., Lowery, B., & Knowles, E. (2008). How believing in affirmative action quotas protects White men's self-esteem. *Organizational Behavior and Human Decision Processes, 105*(1), 1–13.

Warner, L. R. (2008). A best practices guide to intersectional approaches in psychological research. *Sex Roles, 59,* 454–463.

West, C., & Zimmerman, D. (1987). Doing gender. *Gender and Society, 1*(2), 125–151.

Williams, K. Y., & O'Reilly, C. A. (1998). Demography and diversity in organizations: A review of 40 years of research. *Research in Organizational Behavior, 20,* 77–140.

Willmott, H. (1993). Strength is ignorance; slavery is freedom: Managing culture in modern organizations. *Journal of Management Studies, 30,* 515–552.

Woods, J. D. (1994). *Corporate closets: The professional lives of gay men in America.* New York: Free Press.

CHAPTER 6

An Examination of Categorization Processes in Organizations: The Root of Intergroup Bias and a Route to Prejudice Reduction

Melissa J. Ferguson *and* Shanette C. Porter

Abstract

To understand how people experience diversity, researchers have focused on category-based perceptions of others who belong to different social groups and the subsequent impact on intergroup dynamics. Specifically, scholars have focused on the automaticity of such categorizations, including stereotyping and implicit bias. This chapter will discuss these automatic, nonconscious processes, including their antecedents and their association with and effects on individual, group, and organizational outcomes. Given the automaticity of such processes, measurement strategies and suggestions for their use in future research will also be discussed.

Key Words: social identity, categorization processes, intergroup bias, diversity

The study of intergroup bias has a long history in psychology. Our understanding of this phenomenon continues to evolve as the social cognitive, intergroup, and organizational literatures grow. In an increasingly global society, where diversity of gender, ethnicity, nationality, and culture is valued but not maximally taken advantage of, understanding group processes is essential. The United States is rapidly becoming more diverse; according to the U.S. Census Bureau, by about 2040, Latinos, Blacks, and Asians will constitute more than 50% of the population. The candidate pool for jobs in America is similarly becoming more diverse (e.g., Reskin & Bielby, 2005). Recent years have also brought increasing numbers of women qualified for competitive jobs in higher education, the corporate world, and the sciences (e.g., Fiske, 2010; Heneman, Judge, & Heneman, 1999; Offerman & Gowing, 1990). These changes in demographics offer increased opportunities for diverse work environments, which boast several positive outcomes (e.g., Boyett & Conn, 1991; Mannix & Neale, 2005; Reskin & Bielby, 2005).

In the literature, diversity can refer to a variety of types of heterogeneity, such as surface-level heterogeneity, in which visible characteristics differ within a group, or deep-level heterogeneity, in which invisible characteristics differ within the group, such as attitudes, opinions, or skills (e.g., Barrick, Stewart, Neubert, & Mount, 1998; Lawrence, 1997). Unless otherwise noted, here diversity is used to refer to surface-level, or social category, differences, such as gender, ethnicity, nationality, and so on. Understanding and supporting diversity in the workplace, on the one hand, and inclusion practices on the other, is important for a number of reasons. For one, understanding diversity within both organizations and teams is important for combating issues of historical injustice. Segregation within organizations is associated with unequal job outcomes for ethnic and gender groups, for example (e.g., Hellerstein & Neumark, 2008). Two recent lines of research highlight other important advantages of diversity in organizations and teams. First, there is evidence that diverse environments promote prosocial outcomes for both minority and majority members, such as reduced intergroup bias, and increased helping and support for out-group members (Allport, 1954; Hurtado, Dey, Gurin, & Gurin, 2003). Second, diversity can help an organization's bottom line: even with only one nonmajority group member, diversity is associated with the productive debate of unique ideas, which is particularly beneficial for creative problem solving (for a review, see Mannix & Neale, 2005). And although research on the productivity of diverse groups more generally is mixed, the take-home message from this pool of research seems to be that diverse groups can produce more unique ideas, innovative responses, and creative solutions than homogenous groups—but the extent to which the benefits of diverse groups are realized depends largely upon how diversity within groups is managed by both workgroup members and superordinates (e.g., Phillips, Kim-Jun, & Shim, 2010; Phillips, Liljenquist, & Neale, 2009; Mannix & Neale, 2005).

If diversity is so beneficial and potentially effective, then why are organizations still largely homogenous at both the organizational and team level? There is no single answer to this question, as evidenced by the sheer density of research on this topic. Among the explanations is that there are still large education gaps, divided along race and gender lines. Cognitive and behavioral psychologists tend to focus instead on the intrapersonal, interpersonal, and intergroup processes that occur within organizations that might result in a lack of diversity, unequal intergroup outcomes (e.g., the tendency for traditionally lower-status ethnic group members and women to achieve lower pay and job ranks than traditionally higher-status groups), and a lack of inclusiveness in the workplace. In particular, there is much research to suggest that a preference for one's in-group, or homophily, and anti–out-group stereotyping and bias play large roles in these outcomes (Bielby, 2000; Brown & Turner, 1981; Byrne, 1971). Many important theoretical and practical questions have been raised regarding these phenomena in this volume and elsewhere. In the following, we primarily examine just one of those questions: What are the antecedents and processes that produce intergroup stereotyping and bias in the workplace? In our examination of that question we also touch upon how understanding the antecedents of intergroup stereotyping and bias can be informative for understanding (1) the consequences of bias and the extent to which intergroup bias is inevitable, (2) what can be done to prevent, or ameliorate the consequences of, intergroup bias and prejudice in organizations, and (3) how organizations can capitalize on diversity. Note that although it has long been noted in a variety of fields that in-group preference, stereotyping, and prejudice can be explicit, overt, and intentional, it is far more common in recent decades in America for bias to manifest in subtler and perhaps unintentional, manners, and thus this chapter will largely focus on this latter type of stereotyping and bias (e.g., Greenwald & Banaji, 1995).

Categorical thinking

Prejudice is one of the most insidious issues still facing society. Although this phenomenon can be complex and multiply determined, research suggests that the root cause—that is, the most distal necessary antecedent from a social psychological standpoint—is social categorization (Allport, 1954; Bodenhausen & Macrae, 1998; Brewer, 1988; Tajfel, 1978). Categorization is the grouping of similar things (in the case of social categorization, types of people) together with other similar things, and apart from distinct things, in a way that makes sense to an individual either over time or in that moment (e.g., Bruner, 1957; Tajfel, 1970). Thus, groups are defined both in relation to one another and in the context of one's current situation. For example, depending on whether one is abroad, discussing the weather, or attending a baseball game, Americans versus Italians, Northerners versus Southerners, or New Yorkers versus Chicagoans might be deemed the appropriate categories. Given the complexity of our social environments, social categorization provides invaluable functions, such as organizing one's social environment, allowing one to engage in sense making, and preparing one to interact efficiently and cost-effectively with his or her environment (e.g., Bodenhausen, 1988; Tajfel, 1970). Social categorization also, however, lays the groundwork for prejudice.

As noted, social categorization is the momentary or stable grouping of subjectively similar people into groups, which are also differentiated from each other. Importantly, during social categorization, people also categorize the self (Hogg & Terry, 2000; Oakes, Haslam, & Turner, 1994)—that is, individuals orient themselves in their mapping of similarity and differentiation, thus creating a personal social identity and engendering a "we" (or "us") and "they" (or "them") distinction between relevant groups. For example, we are Americans versus they are Italians; we are Northerners versus they are Southerners, and so on. Note that these self and other categorizations denote a shift from the interpersonal to the intergroup. Wilder (1986) suggested that this *mere categorization* of the self and others into groups leads to a different set of outcomes than one might expect if individuals were not considered in relation to one another (also see Tajfel, Billig, Bundy, & Flament, 1971). Although this claim has in many ways stood the test of time, experiments conducted by these researchers and others have identified other important psychological factors related to the basic process of social categorization. First, a "we" versus "they" distinction is largely innocuous without a crucial finding in evolutionary and social psychology: namely, individuals tend to engage in social comparisons between self (in-group) and other (out-group) *automatically*—that is, without the effort or intention of the individual (Barkow, Cosmides, & Tooby, 1992; Tajfel, Billig, & Bundy, 1971; Tajfel & Turner, 1979). Second, these two processes of social categorization and social comparison produce intergroup bias is due to individuals' preferences for people who are perceived to be similar to them—a preference found to be largely based in the fundamental motivational need for self-esteem or self-enhancement, and specifically in this case, a positive social identity (Barkow, Cosmides, & Tooby, 1992; Tajfel & Turner, 1979). A positive social identity refers to the subjective favorability of one's in-group when compared to one's out-group, and thus when achieved through social categorization processes, fulfills one's basic need to feel good about oneself, given that the group offers both a general sense of belongingness and, importantly, a sense of belongingness to a group that is both distinctive and comparatively better than other groups.

Abrams, Hogg, and colleagues (e.g., 1988; 1990; 1999) have found that the preference for one's own in-group is also motivated by the need to resolve self-concept uncertainty (e.g., uncertainty about how to act, what to believe, and how this relates to others' behavior and beliefs). These researchers suggest that individuals resolve such uncertainty by subscribing to responses, beliefs, and so on that are subjectively prototypical of their group in a given situation (also see Schimel et al., 1999, and Greenberg et al., 1990). There are several factors influencing the extent to which uncertainty reduction is a motive in self-categorization. Of course, uncertainty reduction through group identification is most useful when one is experiencing a time of high uncertainty and/or is high in dispositional uncertainty and is most successful when one is highly identified with the group (e.g., Hogg, 2000; Mullin & Hogg, 1998). Thus, individuals are, for example, more likely to show evidence of prejudice when they face uncertainty about an important issue or when their group membership is otherwise not salient, thus conceivably inducing feelings of uncertainty (e.g., Grieve & Hogg, 1999; Hogg, 2000). Moreover, features of the group influence the extent to which uncertainty reduction is a motivational pull. For example, individuals are more likely to reduce uncertainty by identifying with groups that are high, versus low, in group entitativity—that is, the extent to which a group has clear boundaries, is homogenous, and generally holds together cohesively as a group. Finally, individuals low in status are more likely to seek uncertainty reduction through group identification than those with high status (Reid & Hogg, 2005).

Brewer (1991) offered a third motivational theory for intergroup bias: individuals contend with two opposing motivations, assimilation with an in-group and differentiation. Optimal distinctiveness is achieved when the needs are both perfectly satisfied. One way in which this might occur is when a group is large enough to promote belongingness but small enough to allow for distinctiveness. Intergroup bias, then, tends to occur when these competing needs are not met at optimal levels. As with the other motives described above, the extent to which optimal distinctiveness needs play a role in bias depends upon other factors, such as the status of the in-group and the individual's level of in-group identification (e.g., Leonardelli & Brewer, 2001; Leonardelli, Pickett, & Brewer, 2010). Recent work, for example, suggests that this motive might account for in-group bias evidenced by minority groups more than majority groups, except when group identification is high (e.g., Leonardelli & Brewer, 2001).

Taken together, these theories of intergroup bias suggest that individuals mentally divide others and the self into groups and, on comparison between one's own group and other groups, show a preference for—that is, bias toward—their in-group and for the individuals that make up the in-group. These categorizations and resultant bias have been shown to be in the service of self-esteem striving, self-esteem maintenance, uncertainty reduction, assimilation, and differentiation.

Consequences of social categorization processes

The social categorization and social comparison processes described above produce a host of intergroup outcomes, documented by years of research in this area. This chapter will focus primarily on just two of those consequences: stereotyping and prejudice. The relationship between social categorization and stereotyping has been examined in two ways.

The first type of this sort of research addresses the extent to which placing individuals into groups leads to the generation and application of stereotypes about out-groups. For example, early research found that dividing individuals into groups led to depersonalization wherein out-group members are seen as prototypical representatives of their respective groups rather than individuals with unique characteristics (e.g., Tajfel, 1969). Depersonalization is driven by accentuation, or the perception of increased similarity among individuals in any given out-group, as well as differences (exaggerated both in size and consistency) between groups (e.g., Tajfel, 1969). In many of the experiments demonstrating the phenomenon of accentuation, participants are first divided into groups based upon arbitrary shared characteristics, such as preference for paintings (i.e., a minimal groups paradigm). Next, all participants are asked to rate the degree to which out-group members share beliefs and attitudes on a variety of topics. Participants tend to believe that members of an out-group with a known similarity (e.g., preference for paintings) share opinions and attitudes with one another on both related (e.g., attitudes toward art) and unrelated (e.g., politics) topics, but not with members of other out-groups or the in-group (e.g., Allen & Wilder, 1979). These sorts of effects are pervasive in this literature (e.g., Hamilton, Sherman, & Rodgers, 2004; Hogg & Abrams, 1988; Jetten, Hogg, & Mullin, 2000). These similarity and dissimilarity accentuation effects occur primarily in characterizations of out-groups (e.g., Park & Rothbart, 1982). An exception is minority or low-status group members, who tend to view their own in-group as largely homogeneous, perhaps due to the strategic value of collective similarity in interacting with majority members (Brown & Smith, 1989; Simon & Brown, 1987).

The second manner of examining how social categorization influences stereotyping is to measure the extent to which existing cultural, or collective, stereotypes are endorsed or applied to out-group members when one is reminded of his or her in-group identity. Here, too, there is evidence for accentuation and depersonalization. For example, when White men are reminded of their own in-group, out-group members (e.g., women, African-Americans) are perceived as more similar to the prototypical out-group member than they are otherwise (Hogg & Turner, 1987). There is similarly extensive evidence that individuals are more likely to recall, endorse, and apply negative stereotypes to out-group members when in-group and out-group social identities are salient (e.g., Oakes, 1987; Oakes, Turner, & Haslam, 1991). For example, one study found that simply making normative groups salient (e.g., medical students with anti-alternative medicine vs. pro-alternative medicine attitudes) led to great activation of concepts associated with intergroup categorizations, such as "subject of study" (Blanz & Aufderheide, 1999). Moreover, Oakes and colleagues (1991) found that not only were group concepts activated, but people behaved in a way that suggested that the concept of group (rather than person) was activated. In their study, individuals who were presented with group information about normative academic groups (i.e., science students who endorsed hard work vs. a social life) were more likely to categorize people based on gender than were those who were presented with information about nonnormative groups. Finally, if in-group and out-group identities are apparent, in-group members will interpret out-group members' behaviors (e.g., kicking a tree) in line with dispositional attributes (e.g., X is violent) that are negative and/or known stereotypes associated with the group (e.g., Maass, Silvi, Arcuri, & Semin, 1989; Pettigrew, 1979; Taylor & Jaggi, 1974; also see Hewstone, Jaspars, & Lalljee, 1982).

The findings for the impact of social categorization on prejudice mirror those for stereotyping. Here again, minimal group paradigms have been used to demonstrate the impact of mere categorization on intergroup bias (Brewer, 1979; Hamilton & Trolier, 1986; Messick & Mackie, 1989). The primary finding is that when categorized into groups, individuals report more positivity toward their in-group (e.g., Otten & Moskowitz, 2000; Tajfel, 1969). Individuals also favor in-group members over out-group members on a variety of other measures of bias, such as resource or reward allocations, intergroup trust, prosocial helping, and evaluations of performance (e.g., Dovidio, Gaertner, Kawakami, & Hodson, 2002; Dovidio, Gaertner, Validzic, Matoka, Johnson, & Frazier, 1997; Mullen, Brown, & Smith, 1992; Tajfel, Billig, Bundy, & Flament, 1971). In-group members cooperate more with one another and work hardest when paired with other in-group members (Kramer & Brewer, 1984; Worchel, Rothgerber, Day, Hart, & Butemeyer, 1998).

Perhaps surprisingly, Brewer and colleagues (1981, 1999) have found that often the sort of outcomes described above do not reflect hostility toward the out-group. Instead, these researchers find that manifestations of intergroup bias commonly result from feelings of positivity toward the in-group (i.e., *absolute* liking), and comparatively less positivity (although not necessarily negativity) toward the relevant out-groups (i.e., *relative* disliking). In a practical sense, this means that although in-group bias is relatively common, hostility toward out-groups, especially when avoidable, is not. This has been illustrated empirically, for example, in Tajfel's rewards allocation studies, in which participants are asked to divvy up rewards between an in-group member and an out-group member. In the rewards allocation task, people tend to choose a strategy that favors their in-group member, regardless of whether this bias is at the expense of the out-group member or not (for a full description of the task and results, see Tajfel et al., 1971; Bigler, Jones, & Lobliner, 1997; Brewer, 1979). If one were truly concerned with penalizing the out-group, then the opposite strategy would be best—that is, to allocate the least amount of rewards to the out-group, regardless of the outcome for the in-group (i.e., even if it meant foregoing a net profit to the in-group). Moreover, the fact that researchers do not find evidence for either in-group favoritism *or* out-group negativity when one is asked to divvy up negative outcomes rather than rewards in this sort of task further suggests that intergroup bias is often the result of favoring the in-group rather than a desire to disparage the out-group (Mummendey, 1995).

Unfortunately, negativity or prejudice against out-groups that cannot be explained by a preference for one's own in-group does sometimes emerge, in certain contexts and for certain people. For example, some research suggests that individuals who are strongly identified with their in-group are more likely to exhibit bias against out-groups (e.g., Struch & Schwartz, 1989). Likewise, when one's in-group status is threatened, bias is evidenced on both the rewards *and* the punishment allocation tasks described above (Otten, Mummendey, & Blanz, 1996). In general, a threat to one's in-group's beliefs or values, fear of harm to an in-group member, recognizing that there is a lack of available resources, or otherwise engaging in a conflict-laden or competitive situation, increases the likelihood that out-group derogation and bias will be evidenced (Branscombe, Ellemers, Spears, & Doosje, 1999; Castano, Yzerbyt, Paladino, & Sacchi, 2002; Haslam, Turner, Oakes, McGarty, & Hayes, 1992; Sherif, 1967; Tajfel & Turner, 1979). Alternatively, reducing or eliminating the competitive or threatening nature of a situation reduces out-group hostility (e.g., Mummendey & Schreiber, 1984; Rabbie & Horowitz, 1988).

Early work on social identity responded to the focus on the individual in bias research—work that explicitly or implicitly relied on the assumption that prejudice is driven by one's motivation or affect in a given situation. At least partially in response to this work, Tajfel (1969), in his now-renowned précis on prejudice, *Cognitive Aspects of Prejudice*, underscored the banality of intergroup bias by highlighting its cognitive basis. In essence, Tajfel, and later others, suggested that across situations and people, and regardless of one's current motivation, social categorization processes will occur when there are multiple social groups. Was he correct, and if so, does this mean that intergroup bias is unavoidable? As noted above, the research conducted by Mummendey and colleagues (1995; 1999), for example, suggests that at least derogation of the out-group and extreme, blatant prejudice depend on the context and the person and thus are not inevitable. But whether social categorization processes themselves are automatic, even innate—and what the answer to this question means for the inevitability of bias that is the byproduct of in-group preference—are also important questions, to which this chapter turns next

Is intergroup bias inevitable?

Whether social categorization and social comparison processes are evolved, innate cognitive functions, or instead socially learned is not entirely clear; however, some have argued that evidence for the former has accumulated. For example, children as young as seven months old can distinguish between gender, and preschool-aged children distinguish among ethnicities and age groups (e.g., see Aboud, 1988; Baron & Banaji, 2006; Dunham, Baron, & Banaji, 2006, 2007; Miller, 1983). Also, research has found that a preference for similar others (i.e., one's subjective in-group) develops concomitantly with social categorization, and thus gender preferences develop earliest, followed by ethnic and age-group preferences (e.g., Aboud, 1988; Katz & Zalk, 1974).

The intergroup bias research conducted using infants as subjects is also informative for clarifying the processes that lead to in-group bias. Namely, this research suggests that while familiarity breeds liking, in-group preferences are not always explained by greater exposure to, or familiarity with, one group (Zajonc, 1968; also see Dasgupta, McGhee, Greenwald, & Banaji, 2000). That is, children under the age of one year develop in-group gender preferences, even though this cannot be due solely to familiarity with one or the other group. This contention has also been supported by research using minimal groups paradigms, wherein groups are formed by an experimenter based upon an arbitrary and/or randomly assigned distinction between groups, such as the color of one's shirt (e.g., Brewer & Silver, 1978; Tajfel, 1970). Evidence is increasing that suggests that social categorization processes appear to occur spontaneously and automatically, and that in-group preferences follow directly from these processes, and thus develop from an early age (see also Hardin & Banaji, in press).

These findings suggest that categorization processes occur quite easily, and there is plenty of evidence of implicit bias toward out-groups that would follow from such categorization processes, which we will review in the next section. Is there any way to combat these automatic categorization processes? A recent, intriguing line of work suggests that it is possible to undermine the prejudicial responses that follow from such early group-based processes. In a series of experiments, Moskowitz and colleagues (2000, 2005, 2011) found that for those for whom being egalitarian is a chronic goal, intergroup salience actually led to decreased implicit stereotyping of the out-group. In other words, *categorization processes occurred*, but an intergroup egalitarian response was enacted automatically rather than an intergroup bias one. Indeed, this appears to be an important lesson for bias reduction, more generally: if one wants to reduce intergroup bias, exploring and exploiting categorization processes (not stopping them) is one viable route. The ways in which this has been done, and potentially could be done, will be discussed in the context of organizations and workgroups next.

Intergroup bias in organizations

Intergroup bias has been measured both implicitly and explicitly. The meaning of implicit (i.e., automatic) and explicit (i.e., controlled) attitude measurement, and the various theoretical matters concerning this dichotomy, have been given much attention in recent years (e.g., Bargh, 1994; Devine, 1989; Fazio, Jackson, Dunton, & Williams, 1995; Greenwald, McGhee, & Schwartz, 1998; Jacoby & Witherspoon, 1982; Langer, 1975; McConnell & Leibold, 2001; Meyer & Schvaneveldt, 1971; Neely, 1977). The terms *implicit* (automatic) attitudes and *explicit* (controlled) attitudes have variously been used to refer to types of attitudes, the types of processes that produce attitudes and behaviors, and the ways in which attitudes are measured (e.g., De Houwer et al., 2009; Fazio et al., 1995; Ferguson & Fukukura, 2012; Greenwald & Banaji, 1995; Jacoby & Witherspoon, 1982; Petty, Fazio, & Brinol, 2007; Schacter, 1987; Squire, 1986; Wittenbrink & Schwarz, 2007). Keeping with recent literature, we use the terms *implicit* and *explicit* to refer to the processes that produce attitudes and behaviors. Explicit attitudes, then, are those produced by controlled, intentional regulation processes. Thus, individuals are aware of, and are able to self-report, these attitudes. Explicit attitudes tend to correlate with many overt behaviors, such as name calling and the use of slurs. Implicit attitudes tend to correlate with nonverbal behaviors, such as smiling, and the distance that one sits or stands from an out-group member. These attitudes are produced automatically—that is, without conscious intention, and sometimes without effort or awareness. As such, implicit attitudes are not directly self-reported but rather are measured with various tools, typically, but not always on the computer (for reviews see Fazio, 1995; Fazio & Olson, 2003; Greenwald & Banaji, 1995; Petty et al., 2007; Wittenbrink & Schwarz 2007). In many cases, these tasks assess attitudes toward an attitude object (e.g., studying, African-Americans, one's mother, animals, coworkers) by measuring how quickly people are able to categorize a positive or negative word (as positive or negative, respectively) after first seeing an attitude object. The more quickly one categorizes a positive word, and the more slowly one categorizes a negative word, after first seeing the word "mom," for example, is an indication of how positively one feels toward one's mother (for a description of other tasks, see Wittenbrink & Schwarz, 2007).

The Implicit Association Test, perhaps the most widely used tool for measuring implicit attitudes, assesses attitudes using a similar principle, but the task involves a pairing of attitude objects with attributes. For example, the categories of "women" and "men" (the attitude objects) are paired with the categories of "positive" and "negative" (the attributes), respectively, and then people are asked to quickly classify words (e.g., "Betty," "sunshine") associated with each attitude object and attribute. To the extent that it is easier to complete the categorization task when women and positive, and men and negative, are paired, versus the reverse pairing, is taken as evidence that one has a positive implicit bias toward women, and vice versa (e.g., see Greenwald et al., 2009; Greenwald, McGhee, & Schwarz, 1998).

Note that these categories of implicit and explicit are distinct from the in-group preference versus out-group hostility bias distinction discussed earlier—that is, implicit and explicit can reflect either in-group preference or out-group hostility. Nevertheless, one might expect that negative out-group attitudes are more likely to be spontaneously, explicitly expressed under the conditions that produce out-group hostility (i.e., threat or competition).

An added complexity to the implicit versus explicit attitudes is that there can be within-person dissociation in the two types of attitudes. Modern theories of prejudice, in fact, are largely based upon the phenomenon that people espouse egalitarianism or positive out-group attitudes explicitly, but display prejudice in their implicit evaluations, nonverbal behavior, and so on. Further, negative out-group behaviors seem to "leak out" when individuals can attribute their behavior to a nonprejudicial source, or otherwise rationalize or justify their behavior. For example, individuals may be equally likely to help in-group and out-group members during an emergency, but more likely to help an in-group than an out-group member when there is ambiguity in the degree to which the situation is a true emergency. Gaertner and Dovidio (1986) have termed this *ambivalence aversive racism* and note that it stands in contrast to the more overt, old-fashioned racism that was far more common in the United States prior to the 1970s or 1980s (see Duckitt, 1992). Other theories of contemporary prejudice have similarly suggested that under most conditions, prejudicial attitudes since 1980 tend to be expressed in unintentional, subtle, and indirect manners, rather than in explicit statements or overt behaviors (e.g., Crandall & Eshleman, 2003; Dovidio & Fazio, 1992; Dovidio & Gaertner, 2004; Greenwald & Banaji, 1995; Hardin & Banaji, in press; McConahay, 1983).

That attitudes have increasingly become more explicitly positive toward out-groups is in large part due to changes in official and unofficial legal and social policies, which in turn have shaped the norms for the intentional (explicit) expression of prejudice. Although a reduction in the explicit expression of prejudicial attitudes and behavior marks progress in efforts to reduce prejudice, as alluded to above, it is still the case that ethnic and gender out-groups face discrimination and prejudice at the individual, organizational, institutional, and societal level (e.g., see Bobo, 2001; Dovidio, 2001; Sniderman & Carmines, 1997). Moreover, it also has not been met with a concomitant decrease in implicit intergroup bias (see Fazio & Olson, 2003; Hardin & Banaji, in press). Plenty of recent studies have demonstrated implicit prejudice toward groups based on ethnicity and race (e.g., see Dovidio & Gaertner, 2004; Fazio et al., 1995; Nosek, Banaji, & Greenwald, 2002), gender (e.g., Banaji & Hardin, 1996), sexual orientation (e.g., Dasgupta & Rivera, 2009), and according to many other stigmatized characteristics (for a review see Olson & Fazio, 2004; Greenwald et al., 2009).

The importance of reducing implicit bias in the workplace cannot be overstated. Implicit intergroup bias has far-reaching negative effects in many organizational domains, including, but not limited to, selection, retention (including compensation and promotion issues), teams-related issues, general work environment, and worker self-esteem and well-being (Beckman & Phillips, 2005; Forman, 2003; Zatzick, Elvira, & Cohen, 2003). For example, processes important for working in teams, such as information exchange, suffer in diverse groups that are divided along racial lines (e.g., Lau & Murnighan, 2005; Li & Hambrick, 2005; Sawyer, Houlette, & Yealey, 2006). In other words, fostering harmonious intergroup interactions is at the crux of producing the best possible outcomes in organizational productivity, organizational climate, and social justice.

The following will focus primarily on groups with perceptually detectable differences such as ethnicity and gender rather than "invisible" differences (e.g., in political opinion or skills). Although much of the work discussed next will apply across types of diversity, the visibility of perceptually detectable differences, juxtaposed against the historical backdrop of tense relations in the U.S. workforce for these groups, provides a context that is perhaps uniquely suited for considering the robust effects of social categorization. Even relatively recent research finds evidence of interethnic and gender-based tension in the workplace. For example, compared with their White counterparts, African-Americans report feeling undervalued, as well as feeling that the workplace is less positive, with less access to opportunities (e.g., Reskin, 1998; for a review, see Smith, Brief, & Colella, 2010). Likewise, White Americans report lower job satisfaction and sociability in diverse work environments (Mannix & Neale, 2005; Riordan & Shore, 1997).

Fortunately, much progress has been made in the area of intergroup relations, and specifically on how modulating or exploiting the process of social categorization can reduce bias. From a social identity or self-categorization theory perspective, there are three potential ways in which intergroup bias has been reduced and cooperation has been increased: eliminating or deemphasizing distinctions between social categories (decategorization), creating or emphasizing an already existing higher-order category (e.g., factory worker or team member identity; recategorization), or retaining the social categories but revaluing the boundaries between the groups (mutual differentiation). As many scholars have noted, intergroup bias is multiply determined by cognitive, affective, and motivational causes. As such, it should be acknowledged that there are many other means to stereotyping and prejudice reduction; however, interventions aimed at social categorization processes and intergroup boundaries represent viable, often straightforward, and practical responses to a complex problem.

Decategorization

As prejudice reduction research began to take hold in the 1950s and 1960s, decategorization was quickly recognized as a method for achieving the goal of that research. Recall that social categorization processes engender a move from the individual to the group level of thinking (i.e., one categorizes self and other into groups). Although thinking at the group level itself is not necessarily problematic, one issue that arises is that group-level negativity towards out-groups can be, and often is, applied to individuals. Decategorization is anything that creates circumstances in which interpersonal, rather than intergroup, thinking is encouraged (Brewer & Miller, 1984; 1988). Decategorization has two possible benefits. First, otherwise negative interactions with an out-group member may be more positive if one is considering one's contact with an individual rather than one's cognitions or affect toward the group more generally. Second, just as stereotypes about, and affect toward, an out-group can influence experiences with an individual out-group member, experiences with an out-group member can generalize to group-level affect and beliefs. Of course, these positive outcomes are predicated on positive interpersonal experiences with out-group members.

Perhaps the best-known, and most elaborate, method of decategorization was proposed by Gordon Allport (1954) in his Contact Hypothesis, which details the optimal conditions needed to encourage positive interpersonal contact between members or out-groups. Allport, and later others, began to unpack the mechanisms through which the military might have provided a special situation in which intergroup conflict is reduced (see also Dovidio, Kawakami, & Gaertner, 2002; Hamberger & Hewstone, 1997; Pettigrew, 1997; Pettigrew & Troop, 2006; Richeson & Shelton, 2003; Rothbart & John, 1985; Shelton & Richeson, 2005). In short, the Contact Hypothesis suggests that prejudice can be reduced by repersonalizing individual out-group members in light of a shared, positive experience in which information about differentiated members is attended to (especially expectancy-inconsistent information) and subsequently used as a basis for guiding judgments about those individuals (e.g., Blair, 2002; Brewer & Miller, 1984; Erber & Fiske, 1984; Miller, Brewer, & Edwards, 1985). For attitude change to be generalized from attitudes toward the individual to attitudes toward the group, a higher threshold must be met. Rothbart and John (1995) suggested that the behavior of the out-group member must be inconsistent with a known stereotype, but that the out-group member should otherwise seem to be a typical member of the out-group rather than an exception. Contact must also happen frequently and across a variety of contexts.

Experimentally, a host of studies support the effectiveness of the Contact Hypothesis for changing the attitudes of both majority- and minority-group members (for a review, see Pettigrew & Tropp, 2006). The controlled circumstances under which the Contact Hypothesis creates attitude change, coupled with the constraints of the workplace, make the Contact Hypothesis somewhat challenging to implement in organizations; however, it is more promising than it might seem at first blush. For example, as mentioned, the military has institutionalized policies that by design encourage situations in which bias should be reduced. Moreover, it is not necessary to meet all of the optimal criteria outlined by the hypothesis in order to prompt attitude change. It a meta-analysis of studies, Pettigrew and Tropp (2006) found that although optimal conditions led to the greatest attitude change toward the individuals in the interaction, merely increasing contact between members of out-groups sometimes decreased prejudice. Finally, even indirect contact seems to confer benefits for intergroup relations. Learning that a member of one's in-group is friends with out-group members, observing positive cross-group interactions, and even imagining contact with out-group members has been shown to reduce prejudicial beliefs (Dovidio, Eller, & Hewstone, 2011; Mazziotta, Mummendey, & Wright, 2011; Wright, Aron, McLaughlin-Volpe, & Ropp, 1997). If mere contact with out-groups (or its observation) seems to improve intergroup relations, why do negative intergroup attitudes in organizations still persist? There are many answers to this question. One is that organizations can be contexts rife with conflict and competitiveness, both of which are inversely related to intergroup communication, as well as risk factors for exaggerated social categorization effects (e.g., Nelson, 1989; Richter, West, & van Dick, & Dawson, 2006). In other words, sometimes even in situations in which diversity exists, individuals can observe and experience a homogenous situation, and this is why the *opportunity* for intergroup contact (as opposed to actual intergroup contact) has a much smaller relationship with intergroup attitudes (e.g., Pettigrew, 2008). The critical element, then, seems to be encouraging intergroup contact, whether it is first-person or third-person, real or imagined. This intergroup contact also ought to be experientially positive (or neutral) in order to encourage personalization, and in turn for attitudes to improve, because aversive experiences can simply reinforce prejudicial attitudes.

Recategorization

Like decategorization, recategorization is a method of reducing the emphasis on boundaries between groups. Recategorization, however, encourages group-level thinking rather than personalization. In recategorization, old boundaries between groups are deconstructed, and a new, inclusive group is formed or emphasized (Brown & Turner, 1981; Doise, 1978; Sherif et al., 1961). In most cases, individuals are asked to form or attend to a higher-order identity that they share with their out-group, such as a work team identity or a shared organizational identity (e.g., Gaertner, Dovidio, Anastasio, Bachman, & Rust, 1993). A special case of recategorization occurs when individuals are given, or asked to attend to, information about a characteristic or attribute that their in-group and the out-group share (e.g., Urban & Miller, 1998). In these ways, recategorization exploits social categorization processes. That is, rather than attending to one's in-group or out-group status, one attends to an inclusive grouping of the in-group and out-group. As one might expect, the typical social categorization processes occur; however, in this case, positivity increases for the more inclusive group and group members (e.g., Mottola et al., 1997). One of the features of Allport's (1954) Contact Hypothesis was sharing an interdependent goal, and this point highlights the bidirectional relationship between cooperation and liking. That is, liking leads to increased cooperation, but cooperation can also lead to liking; these effects reinforce one another and thus have benefits that last far beyond the length of any intervention (Allport, 1954; Brown & Turner, 1981; Sherif et al., 1961).

Research on recategorization within the organizational field largely finds support for its effectiveness. Some studies, done in both educational and organizational settings, find that creating an inclusive "we" group is sufficient for reducing stereotyping and intergroup bias (Hogg & Terry, 2000). For example, Haslam and Ellemers (2005) summarize evidence suggesting that when individuals from different groups share an in-group identity, their expectations and motivations regarding the interaction differ from a situation in which no such identity is made salient. Notably, when individuals expect to share beliefs, cooperate, and reach an agreement, their behaviors are guided by these expectations. Thus, constructive disagreement, information sharing, use of adaptive persuasion techniques, and amount of communication are all greater in intergroup contexts in which a common in-group identity is made salient (Haslam & Ellemers, 2005). The expectations for interactions with a shared group, in essence, catalyze a self-fulfilling prophecy. Finally, individuals with a salient common in-group identity self-disclose more, build intimacy and trust, and are engaged in more cross-group helping (e.g., Archer & Berg, 1978; Dovidio et al., 1997).

Although recategorization is causally related to reducing discrimination within the context of the situation in which a common identity is formed, these effects may not generalize to attitudes and beliefs about the out-group. Forming a common group identity reduces bias through the de-emphasis on between-group divisions; thus, individuals may indeed become fond of out-group members with whom they share an in-group identity, but that affective positivity may be detached from the out-group members' out-group identity. In other words, a man may respect and fully cooperate with a woman who is on the same work team, but the attitudinal shift may be specific to the woman in the work team and may not translate to women with whom he does not share an in-group status. As a related point, these effects may be even further specified by the context. That is, even the positive attitudes toward targets achieved through a shared in-group status could be limited to the time that one shares an in-group status, particularly when the collective in-group salience is itself short-lived (e.g., Brewer, 1991). Finally, efforts at recategorization can sometimes be met with resistance, given that individuals may feel strongly tied to their already established social identity.

One final method for reducing bias at the workplace addresses these latter concerns by leaving intergroup boundaries intact but revaluing and recontextualizing those boundaries.

Mutual differentiation

Mutual differentiation differs from the other two types of interventions in that rather than deconstructing groups, boundaries within groups are maintained. The groups are recontextualized, however, to reduce the threat that might otherwise be present. Both self-categorization and social identity theory predict that individuals are threatened by ambiguous or weak boundaries between groups, as well as the fear that these boundaries might be reduced or eliminated. Hewstone and Brown (1986) suggested that one way to encourage intergroup positivity would be to affirm the boundaries between groups, or what they termed mutual differentiation. Similar to the other two types of interventions, the mutual differentiation model retains the use of a cooperative context in order to reduce the threat associated with interacting with out-group members. Because mere intergroup contact is sufficient for making category memberships salient in many cases, this theory lends itself to study in naturalistic settings (e.g., see also Brown & Hewstone, 2005).

The extent to which mutual differentiation reduces intergroup bias depends on the amount of intergroup contact. At high levels of (positive or friendly) contact, if social identities are salient, and if an out-group member is perceived to be typical of other out-group members, the amount of anxiety experienced by members of both groups should be lower, and the amount of empathy and positivity higher, than under any other conditions. Mutual differentiation seems to be especially effective for generalizing attitudes, and indeed is superior to the other two types of intervention under the conditions just outlined. For example, in one study, groups of four individuals, two from one social group and two from another social group, worked on a project. The results suggested that dividing the members' roles along the lines of their social groups (i.e., both members from one social group were responsible for one task, and both members from the other social group were responsible for a different task) created mutual differentiation and resulted in reduced negativity toward the out-group relative to groups in which roles were not divided along group lines (e.g., Brown & Wade, 1987; also see Deschamps & Brown, 1983). In addition, several studies have shown that counter-stereotypic, yet typical, members are essential for the generalization of positive attitudes toward the out-group, measured by both attitudes and behavior (e.g., Brown, Eller, Leeds, & Stace, 2007; Hewstone, 1994; Hewstone, Hassebrauk, Wirth, & Waenke, 2000). Like decategorization, cooperation is an antecedent for mutual differentiation. The major difference is that with mutual differentiation, cooperation is operationalized in a manner that highlights the distinctions between groups rather than minimizes them (e.g., Kenworthy, Turner, Hewstone, & Voci, 2005).

Capitalizing on diversity: multiculturalism versus colorblindness

There is no single best method for reducing bias in organizations. Moreover, the various methods for reducing bias are not entirely mutually exclusive. That is, to the extent that these types of interventions each offer maximum benefits under different conditions, they can each be used at different times to achieve optimal outcomes. To that end, researchers have offered integrative models for prejudice reduction (e.g., Brewer & Gaertner, 2001). Of course, what counts as an optimal outcome might also vary. For example, one might be concerned with promoting creative performance on a task, reducing majority-group bias, reducing minority-group bias, improving attitudes toward an individual, generalizing positive attitudes from a member of a group to the group more generally, or some combination of these outcomes. Thus, on the one hand, it is important to identify the relevant conditions and desired outcomes when developing a strategy for reducing bias. On the other hand, there is developing research to suggest that in cases of surface-level, demographic diversity, there is an intergroup *ideology* that seems to be superior for meeting most intergroup-related goals.

Regardless of the particular prejudice reduction strategy—decategorization, recategorization, or mutual differentiation—one could choose to either ignore between-group differences or recognize and acknowledge them. Multiculturalism is an ideology that promotes the recognition and acceptance of group differences (e.g., Lott, 2009). Color- (or gender-) blindness is an ideology that stresses ignoring group differences, and points to a lack of belief that racism still exists or is influential (Lott, 2009). Although multiculturalism is perhaps more obviously compatible with decategorization or mutual differentiation than with recategorization, the ideology could be employed for any of the strategies. For example, while emphasizing a common in-group identity, one could still recognize, value, and accept that differences exist between the groups. Alternatively, a strategy of colorblindness seems to be compatible only with either decategorization or recategorization.

Research on these two types of ideologies is in some ways still in its infancy, but several important findings have already emerged. First, for majority-group members, belief in a multicultural ideology leads to less bias than belief in a colorblind ideology (Neville, Lilly, Duran, Lee, & Browne, 2000; Richeson & Nussbaum, 2004). The opposite is also true: increasing adherence to colorblindness is associated with increasing levels of intergroup bias (Neville et al., 2000; Richeson & Nussbaum, 2004; Verkuyten, 2005). Second, minority-group members have a greater tendency to endorse a multicultural ideology, and among minority-group members, greater endorsement of multiculturalism is associated with stronger in-group identification as well as greater positivity toward the in-group (Verkuyten, 2005). Although an individual's endorsement of one or the other ideology predicts in-group identification and intergroup bias, experimental manipulations meant to encourage a multicultural or colorblind ideology also affect intergroup attitudes, stereotyping, and bias, suggesting that these ideologies are malleable (e.g., Richeson & Nussbaum, 2004). This research has been done in both experimental settings and naturalistic field settings (e.g., Plaut, Thomas, & Goren, 2009; van Knippenberg, Haslama, Alexander, & Platow, 2007).

Third, multiculturalism is more likely to facilitate organizations' desires to capitalize on diversity. Research on the influence of diversity in organizations on productivity and creativity is mixed, but the bottom line appears to be that well-managed and well-functioning diverse groups and environments can outperform homogenous groups and environments (e.g., Mannix & Neale, 2005; Pelled, Eisenhardt, & Xin, 1999). Multiculturalism influences many outcomes that in turn predict both the functionality of diverse groups and their ultimate productivity and performance. For example, Plaut and colleagues (2009) found that majority-group members' multicultural attitudes were negatively associated with minority-group members' perceptions of bias in the workplace and positively associated with minority-group members' psychological engagement at their organizations. Psychological engagement at the workplace is predictive of productivity, among other positive work-related outcomes. Taken together, these findings suggest that a multicultural ideology is more beneficial than a colorblind ideology for both majority groups and minority groups, and for multiple intergroup and work-related outcomes. Moreover, the linear relationships suggests that the more strongly one adheres to multiculturalism, the more adaptive the outcomes.

Further research is needed to fully understand the multiple mechanisms through which multiculturalism influences intergroup outcomes, as well as how multicultural ideologies interact with the strategies for prejudice reduction outlined earlier in the chapter to produce intergroup outcomes. So far, however, the existing research seems to underline the themes of this chapter: that social identity and social categorization processes are integral to understanding bias; that prejudice is rooted in basic cognitive processes but is not a foregone conclusion; and that the reduction of intergroup bias in organizations is important for promoting both social justice and work performance outcomes.

Future directions for research

We have reviewed a great deal of research that speaks to the ways in which prejudice and stereotyping can emerge, in the workplace or elsewhere. Today, intergroup prejudice and stereotyping are likely to emerge on an implicit rather than an explicit level, and thus may be somewhat more difficult to measure casually, even while their effects are significant, pervasive, and destructive at the individual and societal level. What are some of the directions that research might go in the future to understand how implicit bias exists and can be overturned in the workplace?

One important initial note is the need for continued examination, in the basic sciences, of the ways in which intergroup attitudes and relations unfold. As many scholars have argued (see Hardin & Banaji, in press), the area of implicit social cognition is a relatively new field, and there are still very fundamental questions to be addressed, including issues surrounding construct and predictive validity of implicit constructs. To be able to apply findings and research from social psychology to the workplace, and beyond, there needs to be continued special attention to the pressing issues and developments surrounding this topic in basic science.

For example, in the realm of predictive validity, there is a solid, and still burgeoning, amount of evidence showing the existence of implicit prejudice among "known groups" in the world (especially as measured by the IAT; see Greenwald et al., 2009). This means that groups that have a history of prejudice or intergroup rivalry or strife show correspondent preferences on the IAT, illustrating its sound construct validity. However, work is ongoing to fully understand the depth and boundaries of the predictive validity of implicit measures of prejudice and stereotyping. Although recent reviews and meta-analyses (Fazio & Olson, 2003; Greenwald et al., 2009) suggest that such implicit constructs can meaningfully predict both subtle as well as overt behavior—and even out-predict more traditional, explicit measures—there still needs to be careful work on when and how such implicit constructs shape and guide behavior.

Early research on implicit prejudice and stereotyping suggested that there is likely no way to avoid implicit bias (e.g., Bargh, 1999; Devine, 1989; Dovidio, Kawakami, Johnson, Johnson, & Howard, 1997). However, as we noted earlier, more recent work finds that implicit bias and implicit stereotyping are subject to various situational constraints (e.g., Lowery, Hardin, & Sinclair, 2001; Rudman, Ashmore, & Gary, 2001). Moreover, various researchers have shown that implicit bias can be experimentally changed through "retraining" procedures in which participants learn new automatic (and positively valenced) associations with stigmatized groups (e.g., Kawakami, Dovidio, Moll, Hermsen, & Russin, 2000; Kawakami, Dovidio, & van Kamp, 2005). This work shows numerous, interesting ways in which implicit bias and stereotyping can be altered, minimized, or altogether erased (at least temporarily), and future work will undoubtedly shed more light on the circumstances in which such modification is possible and durable.

One particularly interesting line of work comes from the laboratory of Moskowitz and colleagues and concerns the display of implicit egalitarianism (Moskowitz, 2000, 2005, 2011). In this research, participants who have shown a strong and chronic goal of avoiding prejudice and striving toward egalitarianism show no evidence of implicit stereotyping. Importantly, this work shows that such participants possess the knowledge about the specific stereotypes—it is not as though such participants simply somehow do not have the same knowledge as almost everyone else; it is just that their experience and motivation have allowed them to develop new kinds of implicit associations with stigmatized groups. It appears that they in fact show automatic *inhibition* of stereotypes associated with a group. This work essentially highlights a group of people according to a personality difference (i.e., those with a strong egalitarian motive) who have been able to "retrain" themselves. It is a nice parallel to the research showing that participants without such a motive can be retrained in the laboratory. Future research could continue to examine the ways in which implicit egalitarianism develops, generalizes, and shapes intergroup decisions and behavior.

A final note about future research concerns the increased interest in thinking and speculating about how implicit bias has consequences for the economic, labor, legal, and public policy realms (e.g., Ayres, 2001, Banaji & Bhaskar, 2000; Banaji & Dasgupta, 1998; Chugh, 2004; Greenwald & Krieger, 2006; Jost, Rudman, Bair, Carney, Dasgupta, Glaser, & Hardin, 2009; Kang & Banaji, 2006; Tetlock & Mitchell, 2009). Surely the growing and solid evidence for the existence of implicit prejudice means that thinking about its real-world applications is imperative. This line of theory and empirical research will have implications for the workplace, both in a direct manner as well as in terms of policies that influence the workplace. We strongly argue here for the importance of a constant dialogue between basic scientific research findings on implicit bias and their possible applications and implications for the world beyond academia.

References

Aboud, F. E. (1988). *Children and prejudice.* New York: Basil Blackwell.

Abrams, D., & Hogg, M. A. (1988). Comments on the motivational status of self-esteem in social identity and intergroup discrimination. *European Journal of Social Psychology, 4*, 317–334.

Abrams, D., & Hogg, M. A. (1990). Social identity, self-categorization and social influence. *European Review of Social Psychology, 1*, 195–228.

Abrams, D., & Hogg, M. A. (1999). *Social identity and social cognition.* Malden, MA: Blackwell.

Allen, V. L., & Wilder, D. A. (1979). Group categorization and attribution of belief similarity. *Small Group Behavior, 10*, 73–80.

Allport, G. W. (1954). *The nature of prejudice.* Reading, MA: Addison-Wesley.

Archer, R. L., & Berg, J. H. (1978). Disclosure reciprocity and its limits: A reactance analysis. *Journal of Experimental Social Psychology, 14*, 527–540.

Ayres, I. (2001). *Pervasive prejudice? Unconventional evidence of race and gender discrimination.* Chicago: University of Chicago Press.

Banaji, M. R., & Bhaskar, R. (2000). Implicit stereotypes and memory: The bounded rationality of social beliefs. In D. L. Schacter & E. Scarry (Eds.), Memory, brain, and belief (pp. 139–175). Cambridge, MA: Harvard University Press.

Banaji, M. R., & Dasgupta, N. (1998). The consciousness of social beliefs: A program of research on stereotyping and prejudice. In V. Y. Yzerbyt, G. Lories, & B. Dardenne (Eds.), Metacognition: Cognitive and social dimensions (pp. 157–170). Thousand Oaks, CA: Sage.

Banaji, M. R., & Hardin, C. D. (1996). Automatic gender stereotyping. *Psychological Science, 7,* 136–141.

Bargh, J. A. (1994). The Four Horsemen of automaticity: Awareness, intention, efficiency, and control in social cognition. In R. S. Wyer & T. K. Srull (Eds.), *Handbook of social cognition* (2nd ed., Vol. 1, pp. 1–40). Hillsdale, NJ: Erlbaum.

Bargh, J. A. (1999). The cognitive monster: The case against the controllability of automatic stereotype effects. In S. Chaiken & Y. Trope (Eds.), *Dual process theories in social psychology* (pp. 361–382). New York: Guilford.

Bargh, J. A., & Gollwitzer, P. M. (1994). Environmental control of goal-directed action: Automatic and strategic contingencies between situations and behavior. In W. Spaulding (Ed.), *Nebraska Symposium on Motivation* (Vol. 41, pp. 71–124). Lincoln: University of Nebraska Press.

Barkow, J. H., Cosmides, L., & Tooby, J. (1992). *The adapted mind: evolutionary psychology and the generation of culture.* New York: Oxford University Press.

Barrick, M. R., Stewart, G. L., Neubert, M. J., & Mount, M. K. (1998). Relating member ability and personality to work-team processes and team effectiveness. *Journal of Applied Psychology, 83,* 377–391.

Baron, A. S., & Banaji, M. R. (2006). The development of implicit attitudes: Evidence of race evaluations from ages 6, 10, and adulthood. *Psychological Science, 17,* 53–58.

Baron, J. N., & Pfeffer, J. (1994). The social psychology of organizations and inequality. *Social Psychology Quarterly, 57,* 190–209.

Beckman, C. M., & Phillips, D. J. (2005). Interorganizational determinants of promotion: Client leadership and the attainment of women attorneys. *American Sociological Review, 70,* 678–701.

Bielby, W. T. (2000). Minimizing workplace gender and racial bias. *Contemporary Sociology, 29,* 120–29.

Bigler, R. S., Jones, L. C., & Lobliner, D. B. (1997). Social categorization and the formation of intergroup attitudes in children. *Child Development, 68,* 530–543.

Blair, I. V. (2002). The malleability of automatic stereotypes and prejudice. *Personality and Social Psychology Bulletin, 6,* 242–261.

Blanz, M., & Aufderheide, B. (1999). Social categorization and category attribution: The effects of comparative and normative fit on memory and social judgment. *British Journal of Social Psychology, 38,* 157–179.

Bobo, L. D. (2001). Racial attitudes and relations at the close of the twentieth century. In N. J. Smelser, W. J. Wilson, & F. Mitchell (Eds.), *Racial trends and their consequences* (pp. 264–301). Washington, DC: National Academy Press.

Bodenhausen, G. (1988). Stereotypic biases in social decision making and memory: Testing process models of stereotype use. *Journal of Personality and Social Psychology, 55,* 726–737.

Bodenhausen, G. V., & Macrae, C. N. (1998). Stereotype activation and inhibition. In R. S. Wyer Jr. (Ed.), *Advances in social cognition* (Vol. 11, pp. 1–52). Mahwah, NJ: Erlbaum.

Boyett, J. H., & Conn, H. P. 1991. *Workplace 2000: The revolution reshaping American business.* New York: Dutton.

Branscombe, N. R., Ellemers, N., Spears, R., & Doosje, B. (1999). The context and content of social identity threat. In N. Ellemers, R. Spears, & B. Doosje (Eds.), *Social identity: Context, commitment, content* (pp. 35–58). Oxford, UK: Blackwell.

Brewer, M. B. (1988). A dual process model of impression formation. In T. K. Srull & R. S. Wyer Jr. (Eds.), *A dual process model of impression formation* (pp. 1–36). Hillsdale, NJ: Erlbaum.

Brewer, M. B. (1979). In-group bias in the minimal intergroup situation: A cognitive-motivational analysis. *Psychological Bulletin, 86,* 307–324.

Brewer, M. B. (1991). The social self: On being the same and different at the same time. *Personality and Social Psychology Bulletin, 17,* 475–482.

Brewer, M. B., Dull, V., & Lui, L. (1981). Perceptions of the elderly: Stereotypes as prototypes. *Journal of Personality and Social Psychology, 41,* 656–670.

Brewer, M. B., & Feinstein, A. (1999). Dual processes in the cognitive representation of persons and social categories. In S. Chaiken & Y. Trope (Eds.), *Dual process theories in social psychology* (pp. 255–270). New York: Guilford Press.

Brewer, M. B., & Gaertner, S. L. (2001). Toward reduction of prejudice: Intergroup contact and social categorization. In A. Tesser et al. (Eds.), *Blackwell handbook of social psychology: Vol. 3. Intergroup processes* (pp. 451–472). Oxford: Basil Blackwell.

Brewer, M. B., & Miller. N. (1984). Beyond the contact hypothesis: Theoretical perspectives on desegregation. In N. Miller & M. B. Brewer (Eds.), *Groups in contact: The psychology of desegregation* (pp. 281–302). New York: Academic Press.

Brewer, M. B., & Silver, M. (1978). Ingroup bias as a function of task characteristics. *European Journal of Social Psychology, 8,* 393–400.

Brown, R., Eller, A., Leeds, S., & Stace, K. (2007). Intergroup contact and intergroup attitudes: a longitudinal study. *European Journal of Social Psychology, 37,* 692–703.

Brown, R., & Hewstone, M. (2005). An integrative theory of intergroup contact. *Advances in Experimental Social Psychology, 37,* 255–343.

Brown, R. & Smith, A. (1989). Perceptions of and by minority groups: The case of women in academia. *European Journal of Social Psychology, 19,* 61–75.

Brown, R., & Turner, J. C. (1981). Interpersonal and intergroup behavior. In J. C. Turner & H. Giles (Eds.), *Intergroup behavior* (pp. 33–65). Oxford, England: Basil Blackwell.

Brown, R., & Wade, G. (1987). Superordinate goals and intergroup behavior: The effect of role ambiguity and status on intergroup attitudes and task performance. *European Journal of Social Psychology, 17,* 131–142.

Bruner, J. S. (1957). Intergroup contact and intergroup attitudes: a longitudinal study. *Psychological Review, 64,* 123–152.

Byrne, D. (1971). *The attraction paradigm.* Orlando, FL: Academic Press.

Castano, E., Yzerbyt, V., Paladino, M., & Sacchi, S. (2002). I belong, therefore, I exist: Ingroup identification, ingroup entitativity, and ingroup bias. *Personality and Social Psychology Bulletin, 28*, 135–143.

Chugh, D. (2004). Societal and Managerial Implications of Implicit Social Cognition: Why Milliseconds Matter. *Social Justice Research, 17*, 203–222.

Crandall, C., & Eshleman, A. (2003). A justification-suppression of the expression and experience of prejudice. *Psychological Bulletin, 129*, 414–446.

Dasgupta, N., McGhee, D. E., Greenwald, A. G., & Banaji, M. R. (2000). Automatic preference for White Americans: eliminating the familiarity explanation. *Journal of Experimental Social Psychology, 36*, 316–328.

Dasgupta, N., & Rivera, L. M. (2008). When social context matters: The influence of long-term contact and short-term exposure to admired outgroup members on implicit attitudes and behavioral intentions. *Social Cognition, 26*, 54–66.

De Houwer, J. (2009). The propositional approach to associative learning as an alternative for association formation models. *Learning and Behavior, 37*, 1–20.

Deschamps, J., & Brown, R. (1983). Superordinate goals and intergroup conflict. *British Journal of Social Psychology, 22*, 189–195.

Devine, P. G. (1989). Stereotypes and prejudice: Their automatic and controlled components. *Journal of Personality & Social Psychology, 56*, 5–18.

Doise, W. (1978). *Groups and individuals: explanations in social psychology.* Cambridge, UK: Cambridge University Press.

Dovidio, J. F. (2001). On the nature of contemporary prejudice: The third wave. *Journal of Social Issues, 57*, 829–849.

Dovidio, J., Kawakami, K., & Gaertner, S. L. (2002). Implicit and explicit prejudice and interracial interaction. *Journal of Personality and Social Psychology, 82*, 62–68.

Dovidio, J. F., Eller, A., & Hewstone, M. (2011). Improving intergroup relations through direct, extended and other forms of indirect contact. *Group Processes Intergroup Relations, 14*, 147–160.

Dovidio, J. F., & Fazio, R. H. (1992). New technologies for the direct and indirect assessment of attitudes. In J. Tanur (Ed.), *Questions about survey questions: Meaning, memory, attitudes, and social interaction* (pp. 204–237). New York: Russell Sage Foundation.

Dovidio, J. F., & Gaertner, S. L. (1986). Stereotypes and stereotyping: An overview of the cognitive approach. Prejudice, discrimination, and racism. *Prejudice, discrimination, and racism* (pp. 127–163). San Diego: Academic Press.

Dovidio, J. F., & Gaertner, S. L. (2004). Aversive racism. In M. P. Zanna (Ed.), *Advances in experimental social psychology, Vol. 36* (pp. 1–51). San Diego, CA: Academic Press.

Dovidio, J. F., Gaertner, S. L., Kawakami, K., & Hodson, G. (2002). Why can't we just get along? Interpersonal biases and interracial distrust. *Cultural Diversity & Ethnic Minority Psychology, 8*, 88–102.

Dovidio, J. F., Gaertner, S., Validzic, A., Matoka, K., Johnson, B., & Frazier, S. (1997). Extending the benefits of re-categorization: Evaluations, self-disclosure and helping. *Journal of Experimental Social Psychology, 33*, 401–420.

Dovidio, J., Kawakami, K., Johnson, C., Johnson, B., & Howard, A. (1997). The nature of prejudice: automatic and controlled processes. *Journal of Experimental Social Psychology, 33*, 510–540.

Duckitt, J. H. (1992). *The social psychology of prejudice.* New York: Praeger.

Ellemers, N., Rijswijk, W. v., Roefs, M., & Simons, C. (1997). Bias in intergroup perceptions: balancing group identity with social reality. *Personality and Social Psychology Bulletin, 23*, 186–198.

Erber, R., & Fiske, S. T. (1984). Outcome dependency and attention to inconsistent information. *Journal of Personality and Social Psychology, 47*, 709–726.

Fazio, R. H., Jackson, J. R., Dunton, B. C., & Williams, C. J. (1995). Variability in automatic activation as an unobtrusive measure of racial attitudes: A bona fide pipeline? *Journal of Personality and Social Psychology, 69*, 1013–1027.

Fazio, R.H., & Olson, M.A. (2003). Implicit measures in social cognition: Their meaning and use. *Annual Review of Psychology, 54*, 297–327.

Ferguson, M. J., & Fukukura, J. (2012). Likes and dislikes: A social cognitive perspective on attitudes. In S. Fiske, & C. N. Macrae (Eds.), *Sage Handbook of Social Cognition* (pp. 165–189). Los Angeles: SAGE Publications.

Fiske, S. T. (2010). *Social beings: Core motives in social psychology.* New York: Wiley.

Forman, T. A. (2003). The social psychological costs of racial segmentation in the workplace: A study of African-Americans' well-being. *Journal of Health and Social Behavior, 44*, 332–352.

Gaertner, S. L., & Dovidio, J. F. (1986). The aversive form of racism. In J. F. Dovidio & S. L. Gaertner (Eds.), *Prejudice, discrimination, and racism* (pp. 61–89). Orlando, FL: Academic Press.

Gaertner, S. L., Dovidio, J. F., Anastasio, P. A., Bachman, B. A., & Rust, M. C. (1993). The common ingroup identity model: recategorization and the reduction of intergroup bias. *European Review of Social Psychology, 4*, 1–26.

Greenwald, A. G., & Krieger, L. H. (2006). Implicit bias: Scientific foundations. *California Law Review, 94*, 945–967.

Greenberg, J., Pyszczynski, T., Solomon, S., Rosenblatt, A., Veeder, M., Kirkland, S., et al. (1990). Evidence for terror management theory II: The effects of mortality salience on reactions to those who threaten or bolster the cultural worldview. *Journal of Personality and Social Psychology, 58*, 308–318.

Greenwald, A. G., & Banaji, M. R. (1995). Implicit social cognition: Attitudes, self esteem, and stereotypes. *Psychological Review, 102*, 4–27.

Greenwald, A. G., McGhee, D. E., & Schwartz, J. L. K. (1998). Measuring individual differences in implicit cognition: The implicit association task. *Journal of Personality and Social Psychology, 74*, 1464–1480.

Greenwald, A. G., Poehlman, T. A., Uhlmann, E., & Banaji, M. R. (2009). Understanding and using the Implicit Association Test: III. Meta-analysis of predictive validity. *Journal of Personality and Social Psychology, 97*, 17–41.

Grieve, P., & Hogg, M. A. (1999). Subjective uncertainty and intergroup discrimination in the minimal group situation. *Personality and Social Psychology Bulletin, 25*, 926–940.

Hamberger, J., & Hewstone, M. (1997). Inter-ethnic contact as a predictor of blatant and subtle prejudice. *British Journal of Social Psychology, 36*, 173–190.

Hamilton, D. L., Sherman, S. J., & Rodgers, J. S. (2004). Perceiving the groupness of groups: Entitativity, homogeneity, essentialism, and stereotypes. In V. Yzerbyt, C. M. Judd, & O. Corneille (Eds.), *The psychology of group perception: Perceived variability, entitativity, and essentialism.* Philadelphia, PA: Psychology Press.

Hamilton, D. L. & Trolier, T. K. (1986). Stereotypes and stereotyping: An overview of the cognitive approach. In J. F. Dovidio & S. L. Gaertner (Eds.), *Prejudice, discrimination, and racism* (pp. 127–163). San Diego, CA: Academic Press.

Hardin, C. D., & Banaji, M. R. (in press). The nature of implicit prejudice: Implications for personal and public policy. In E. Shafir (Ed.), *The behavioral foundations of policy*.

Haslam, S. A., & Ellemers, N. (2005). Social identity in industrial and organizational psychology: Concepts, controversies and contributions. In G. P. Hodgkinson (Ed.), *International Review of Industrial and Organizational Psychology* (Vol. 20, pp. 39–118). Chichester: Wiley.

Haslam, S. A., Turner, J. C., Oakes, P. J., McGarty, C., & Hayes, B. K. (1992). Contex-dependent variation in social stereotyping 1: The effects of intergroup relations as mediated by social change and frame of reference. *European Journal of Social Psychology, 22*, 3–20.

Hellerstein, J. K., & Neumark, D. (2008). Workplace segregation in the United States: Race, ethnicity, and skill. *Review of Economics and Statistics, 90*, 459–477.

Heneman, H. G., Judge, T. A., & Heneman, R. L. (1999). *Staffing organizations*. Boston, MA: Irwin McGraw-Hill.

Hewstone, M. (1994). Revision and change of stereotypic beliefs: in search of the elusive subtyping model. *European Journal of Social Psychology, 5*, 69–109.

Hewstone, M., & Brown, R. (1986). Contact is not enough: An intergroup perspective on the "Contact Hypothesis." In M. Hewstone & R. Brown (Eds.), *Contact and conflict in intergroup encounters* (pp.1–44). Oxford, England: Basil Blackwell.

Hewstone, M., Hassebrauck, M., Wirth, A., & Waenke, M. (2000). Pattern of disconfirming information and processing instructions as determinants of stereotype change. *British Journal of Social Psychology, 39*, 399–411.

Hewstone, M. A., Jaspars, J. M. F., & Lalljee, M. (1982). Social representations, social attribution and social identity: the intergroup images of "public" and "comprehensive" schoolboys. *European Journal of Social Psychology, 12*, 241–269.

Hogg, M. A. (2000). Subjective uncertainty reduction through self-categorization: A motivational theory of social identity processes. *European Review of Social Psychology, 11*, 223–255.

Hogg, M. A., & Abrams, D. (1988). *Social identifications: A social psychology of intergroup relations and group processes*. London: Routledge.

Hogg, M. A., & Terry, D. J. (2000). Social identity and self-categorization processes in organizational contexts. *Academy of Management Review, 25*, 121–140.

Hurtado, S., E. L. Dey, P. Gurin, and G. Gurin. (2003). College environments, diversity, and student learning. In J. C. Smart (Ed.), *Higher education: Handbook of theory and research 18* (pp. 145–190). UK: Kluwer Academic Publishers.

Jacoby, L. L., & Witherspoon, D. (1982). Remembering without awareness. *Canadian Journal of Psychology, 36*, 300–324.

Jetten, J., Hogg, M. A., & Mullin, B.-A. (2000). Ingroup variability and motivation to reduce subjective uncertainty. *Group Dynamics: Theory, Research, and Practice, 4*, 184–198.

Jost, J. T., Rudman, L. A., Blair, I. V., Carney, D., Dasgupta, N., Glaser, J., et al. (2009). The existence of implicit bias is beyond reasonable doubt: A refutation of ideological and methodological objections and executive summary of ten studies that no manager should ignore. *Research in Organizational Behavior, 29*, 39–69.

Kang, J., & Banaji, M. R. (2006). Fair measures: A behavioral realist revision of "affirmative action." *California Law Review,* 1063–1118.

Katz, P. A., & Zalk, S. R. (1974). Doll preferences: An index of racial attitudes? *Journal of Educational Psychology, 66*, 663–668.

Kawakami, K., Dovidio, J. F., Moll, J., Hermsen, S., & Russin, A. (2000). Just say no (to stereotyping): Effects of training in the negation of stereotypic associations on stereotype activation. *Journal of Personality and Social Psychology, 78*, 871–888.

Kawakami, K., Dovidio, J. F., & van Kamp, S. (2005). Kicking the habit: Effects of nonstereotypic association training and correction processes on hiring decisions. *Journal of Experimental Social Psychology, 41*, 68–75.

Kenworthy, J., Turner, R. N., Hewstone, M., & Voci, A. (2005). Intergroup contact: When does it work, and why? In J. Dovidio, P. Glick, & L. Rudman (Eds.), *On the nature of prejudice: Fifty years after Allport* (pp. 278–292). Malden, MA: Blackwell.

Kramer, R. M., & Brewer, M. B. (1984). Effects of group identity on resource use in a simulated commons dilemma. *Journal of Personality and Social Psychology, 46*, 1044–1057.

Langer, E. (1975). The illusion of control. *Journal of Personality and Social Psychology, 32*, 311–328.

Lawrence, B. S. (1997). The black box of organizational demography, *Organizational Science, 8* 1–22.

Lau, D., and Murnighan, J. K. (2005). Interactions within groups and subgroups: The dynamic effects of demographic faultlines. *Academy of Management Journal, 48*, 645–659.

Leonardelli, G. J., & Brewer, M. B. (2001). Minority and majority discrimination: When and why. *Journal of Experimental Social Psychology, 37*, 468–485.

Leonardelli, G. J., Pickett, C. L., & Brewer, M. B. (2010). Optimal distinctiveness theory: A framework for social identity, social cognition and intergroup relations. In M. Zanna & J. Olson (Eds.) *Advances in experimental social psychology* (Vol. 43, pp. 65–115). New York: Elsevier.

Li, J. T., & Hambrick, D. C. (2005). Factional groups: A new vantage on demographic faultlines, conflict, and disintegration in work teams. *Academy of Management Journal, 48*, 794–813.

Lott, B. (2009). *Multiculturalism and diversity: A social psychological perspective*. West Sussex, UK: Wiley-Blackwell.

Lowery, B.S., Hardin, C. D., & Sinclair, S. (2001). Social influence on automatic racial prejudice. *Journal of Personality and Social Psychology, 81*, 842–855.

Maass, A., Salvi, D., Arcuri, L., & Semin, G. R. (1989). Language use in intergroup contexts: The linguistic intergroup bias. *Journal of Personality and Social Psychology, 57*, 981–993.

Mannix, E. A., & Neale, M. A. (2005). What differences make a difference? *Psychological Science in the Public Interest, 6*, 31–55.

Mazziotta, A., Mummendey, A. & Wright, C. S. (2011). Vicarious intergroup contact effects: Applying social-cognitive theory to intergroup contact research. *Group Processes & Intergroup Relations, 14*, 255–274.

McConahay, J. B. (1983). Modern racism and modern discrimination: the effects of race, racial attitudes, and context on simulated hiring decisions. *Personality and Social Psychology Bulletin, 9*, 551–558.

McConnell, A. R., & Leibold, J. M. (2001). Relations among the Implicit Association Test, discriminatory behavior, and explicit measures of racial attitudes. *Journal of Experimental Social Psychology, 37,* 435–442.

Messick, D. M., & Mackie, D. (1989). Intergroup relations. *Annual Review of Psychology, 40,* 45–81.

Meyer, D. E., & Schvaneveldt, R. W. (1971). Facilitation in recognizing pairs of words: Evidence of a dependence between retrieval operations. *Journal of Experimental Psychology, 90,* 227–234.

Miller, C. L. (1983). Developmental changes in male/female voice classification by infants. *Infant Behavior and Development, 6,* 313–330.

Miller, N., Brewer, M. B., & Edwards, K. (1985). Cooperative interaction in desegregated settings: A laboratory analogue. *Journal of Social Issues, 41,* 63–79.

Moskowitz, G. B., & Li, P. (2011). Egalitarian goals trigger stereotype inhibition: A proactive form of stereotype control. *Journal of Experimental Social Psychology, 47,* 103–116.

Moskowitz, G. B., Salomon, A. R., & Taylor, C. M. (2000). Implicit control of stereotype activation through the preconscious operation of egalitarian goals. *Social Cognition, 18,* 151–177.

Mottola, G., Bachman, B., Gaertner, S. L., & Dovidio. J. F. (1997). How groups merge: The effects of merger integration patterns on anticipated commitment to the merged organization. *Journal of Applied Social Psychology, 7,* 1335–1358.

Mullen, B., Brown, R., & Smith, C. (1992). Ingroup bias as a function of salience, relevance, and status: An integration. *European Journal of Social Psychology, 22,* 103–122.

Mullin, B. A., & Hogg, M. A. (1998). Dimensions of subjective uncertainty in social identification and minimal intergroup discrimination. *British Journal of Social Psychology, 37,* 345–365.

Mummendey, A. (1995) Positive distinctiveness and social discrimination: An old couple living in divorce. *European Journal of Social Psychology, 25,* 657–670.

Mummendey, A., Kessler. T., Klink, A., & Mielke, R. (1999). Strategies to cope with negative social identity: Predictions by social identity theory and relative deprivation theory. *Journal of Personality and Social Psychology, 76,* 229–245.

Mummendey, A., & Schreiber, H. J. (1984). "Different" just means "better": Some obvious and some hidden pathways to in-group favoritism. *British Journal of Social Psychology, 23,* 363–368.

Neely, J. H. (1977). Semantic priming and retrieval from lexical memory: Roles of inhibitionless spreading activation and limited-capacity attention. *Journal of Experimental Psychology, 106,* 226–254.

Nelson, R. E. (1989). The strength of strong ties: Social networks and intergroup conflict in organizations. *Academy of Management Journal, 32,* 377–401.

Neville, H. A., Lilly, R. L., Duran, G., Lee, R., & Browne, L. (2000). Construction and initial validation of the Color-Blind Racial Attitudes Scale (COBRAS). *Journal of Counseling Psychology, 47,* 59–70.

Nosek, B. A., Banaji, M., & Greenwald, A. G. (2002). Harvesting implicit group attitudes and beliefs from a demonstration Web site. *Group Dynamics, 6,* 101–115.

Oakes, P. J. (1987). The salience of social categories. In J. C. Turner (Ed.), *Rediscovering the social group: A self-categorization theory* (pp. 17–151). Oxford: Blackwell.

Oakes, P. J., Haslam, S. A., & Turner, J. C. (1994). *Stereotyping and social reality.* Oxford, UK & Cambridge, MA: Blackwell.

Oakes, P. J., Turner, J. C., & Haslam, S. A. (1991). Perceiving people as group members: The role of fit in the salience of social categorizations. *British Journal of Social Psychology, 30,* 125–144.

Offerman, L. R., & Gowing, M. K. (1990). Organization of the future: Change and challenges, *American Psychologist, 45,* 95–108.

Olson, M. A., & Fazio, R. H. (2004). Reducing the influence of extra-personal associations on the Implicit Association Test: Personalizing the IAT. *Journal of Personality and Social Psychology, 86,* 653–667.

Otten, S., & Moskowitz, G. B. (2000). Evidence for implicit evaluative in-group bias: Affect-biased spontaneous trait inference in a minimal group paradigm. *Journal of Experimental Social Psychology, 36,* 77–89.

Otten, S., Mummendey, A., & Blanz, M. (1996). Intergroup discrimination in positive and negative outcome allocations: The impact of stimulus-valence, relative group status and relative group size. *Personality and Social Psychology Bulletin, 22,* 568–581.

Park, B., & Rothbart, M. (1982). Perception of out-group homogeneity and levels of social categorization: Memory of the subordinate attributes of in-group and out-group members. *Journal of Personality and Social Psychology, 42,* 1051–1068.

Pelled, L. H., Eisenhardt, K. M., & Xin, K. R. (1999). Exploring the black box: An analysis of work group diversity, conflict and performance. *Administrative Science Quarterly, 44,* 1–28.

Pettigrew, T. (1997). Generalized intergroup contact effects on prejudice. *Personality and Social Psychology Bulletin, 23,* 173–185.

Pettigrew, T. F. (2008). Future directions for intergroup contact theory and research. *International Journal of Intercultural Relations, 32,* 187–199.

Pettigrew, T. F. (1979). The ultimate attribution error: Extending Allport's cognitive analysis of prejudice. *Personality and Social Psychology Bulletin, 5,* 461–476.

Pettigrew, T. F., & Tropp, L. R. (2006). A meta-analytic test of intergroup contact theory. *Journal of Personality and Social Psychology, 90,* 751–783.

Petty, R. E., Fazio, R. H., & Brinol, P. (Eds.) (2007). *Attitudes: Insights from the new implicit measures.* New York: Psychology Press.

Phillips, K. W., Kim-Jun, S. Y., & Shim, S-H. (2010). The value of diversity in organizations: A social psychological perspective. In D. De Cremer, R. van Dick, & J. K. Murnighan (Eds.), *Social psychology and organizations* (pp. 253–272). New York: Routledge.

Phillips, K. W., Liljenquist, K. A., & Neale, M. A. (2009). Is the pain worth the gain? The advantages and liabilities of agreeing with socially distinct newcomers. *Personality and Social Psychology Bulletin, 35,* 336–350.

Plaut, V. C., Thomas, K. M., & Goren, M. J. (2009). Is multiculturalism or color blindness better for minorities? *Psychological Science, 20,* 444–446.

Rabbie, J. M., & Horwitz, M. (1988). Categories versus groups as explanatory concepts in intergroup relations. *European Journal of Social Psychology, 18,* 117–123.

Reid, S. A., & Hogg, M. A. (2005). Uncertainty reduction, self-enhancement, and ingroup identification. *Personality and Social Psychology Bulletin, 31,* 804–817.

Reskin, B. F. (1998). *The realities of affirmative action in employment*. Washington, D.C.: American Sociological Association.

Reskin, B. F., & Bielby, D. (2005). A sociological perspective on gender and career outcomes. *Journal of Economic Perspectives, 19*, 71–86.

Richeson, J. A., & Nussbaum, R. J. (2004). The impact of multiculturalism versus color blindness on racial bias. *Journal of Experimental Social Psychology, 40*, 417–423.

Richeson, J. A., & Shelton, J. N. (2003). When prejudice does not pay: Effects of interracial contact on executive function. *Psychological Science, 14*, 287–290.

Richter, A. W., West, M. A., van Dick, R., & Dawson, J. F. (2006). Boundary spanners' identification, intergroup contact, and effective intergroup relations. *Academy of Management Journal, 49*, 1252–1269.

Riordan, C., & Shore, L. (1997). Demographic diversity and employee attitudes: Examination of relational demography within work units. *Journal of Applied Psychology, 82*, 342–358.

Rothbart, M., & John. O. P. (1985). Social categorization and behavioral episodes: A cognitive analysis of the effects of intergroup contact. *Journal of Social Issues, 41*, 81–104.

Rudman, L. A., Ashmore, R. D., & Gary, M. L. (2001). "Unlearning" automatic biases: The malleability of implicit stereotypes and prejudice. *Journal of Personality and Social Psychology, 81*, 856–868.

Sawyer J. E., Houlette, M. A., & Yealey, E. L. (2006). Decision performance and diversity structure: Comparing faultlines in convergent, crosscut, and racially homogeneous groups. *Organizational Behavior and Human Decision Processes, 99*, 1–15.

Schacter, D. L. (1987). Implicit memory: History and current status. *Journal of Experimental Psychology: Learning, Memory, and Cognition, 13*, 501–518.

Schimel, J., Simon, L., Greenberg, J., Pyszynski, T., Solomon, S., Waxmonsky, J., & Arndt, J. (1999). Stereotypes and terror management: evidence that mortality salience enhances stereotypic thinking and preferences. *Journal of Personality and Social Psychology, 77*, 905–926.

Shelton, J. N., & Richeson, J. A. (2005). Intergroup contact and pluralistic ignorance. *Journal of Personality and Social Psychology, 88*, 91–107.

Sherif, M. (1967). *Group conflict and cooperation*. London: Rgutledge & Kegan Paul.

Sherif, M, Harvey, O. J., White, B. J., Hood, W. R., & Sherif, C. W. (1961). *Intergroup conflict and cooperation: The Robbers Cave experiment*. Norman: University of Oklahoma Book Exchange.

Simon, B., & Brown, R. (1987). Perceived intragroup homogeneity in minority–majority contexts. *Journal of Personality and Social Psychology, 53*, 703–711.

Smith, A. N., Brief, A. P., & Colella, A. (2010). Bias in organizations. In J. F. Dovidio, M. Hewstone, P. Glick, & V. M. Esses (Eds.), *The Sage handbook of prejudice, stereotyping, and discrimination* (pp. 441–456). Thousand Oaks, CA: Sage.

Sniderman, P. M., & Carmines, E. G. (1997). *Reaching beyond race*. Cambridge, Massachusetts: Harvard University Press.

Squire, L. R. (1986). Mechanisms of memory. *Science, 232*, 1612–1619.

Struch, N., & Schwartz, S. H. (1989). Intergroup aggression: Its predictors and distinctness from in-group bias. *Journal of Personality and Social Psychology, 56*, 364–373.

Tajfel, H. (1969). Cognitive aspects of prejudice. *Journal of Social Issues, 25*, 79–97.

Tajfel, H. (1978). *Differentiation between social groups: Studies in the social psychology of intergroup relations*. London: Academic Press.

Tajfel, H. (1970). Experiments in intergroup discrimination. *Scientific American, 223*, 96–102.

Tajfel, H., Billig, M. G., Bundy, R. P., & Flament, C. (1971). Social categorization and intergroup behaviour. *European Journal of Social Psychology, 1*, 149–178.

Tajfel, H., & Turner, J. (1979). An integrative theory of intergroup contact. In W.G. Austin & S. Worchel (Eds.), *The social psychology of intergroup relations* (pp. 33–48). Monterey, CA: Brooks/Cole.

Taylor, D. M., & Jaggi, V. (1974). Ethnocentrism and causal attribution in a South Indian context. *Journal of Cross-Cultural Psychology, 5*, 162–171.

Tetlock, P. E., & Mitchell, G. (2009). Implicit bias and accountability systems: What must organizations do to prevent discrimination? In B. M. Staw & A. Brief (Eds.), *Research in organizational behavior* (vol. 29, pp. 3–38). New York: Elsevier.

Turner, J. C. (1987). Intergroup behaviour, self-stereotyping and the salience of social categories. *British Journal of Social Psychology, 26*, 325–340.

Urban, L. M., & Miller, N. (1998). A theoretical analysis of crossed categorization effects: A meta-analysis. *Journal of Personality and Social Psychology, 74*, 894–908.

van Knippenberg, D., Haslam, S. A., & Platow, M. J. (2007). Unity through diversity: Value-in-diversity beliefs as moderator of the relationship between work group diversity and group identification. *Group Dynamics, 11*, 207–222.

Verkuyten, M. (2005). Ethnic group identification and group evaluation among minority and majority groups: testing the multiculturalism hypothesis. *Journal of Personality and Social Psychology, 88*, 121–138.

Wilder, D. A. (1986). Social categorization: Implications for creation and reduction of intergroup bias. In L. Berkowitz (Ed.), *Advances in experimental social psychology* (Vol. 19, pp. 291–355). New York: Academic Press.

Wittenbrink, B., & Schwarz, N. (Eds.) (2007). *Implicit measures of attitudes: Procedures and controversies*. New York: Guilford Press.

Worchel, S., Rothberger, H., Day, A., Hart, D., & Butemeyer, J. (1998). Social identity and individual productivity within groups. *British Journal of Social Psychology, 37*, 389–413.

Wright, S. C., Aron, A., McLaughlin-Volpe, T., & Ropp, S. A. (1997). The extended contact effect: knowledge of cross-group friendships and prejudice. *Journal of Personality and Social Psychology, 73*, 73–90.

Zajonc, R. B. (1968). Attitudinal effects of mere exposure. *Journal of Personality and Social Psychology Monographs, 9*, 1–27.

Zatzick, C. D., Elvira, M. M., & Cohen, L. E. (2003). When is more better? The effects of racial composition on voluntary turnover. *Organizational Science, 14*(5), 483–496.

CHAPTER 7

The Social and Psychological Experience of Stigma

Michelle R. Hebl *and* Eden B. King

Abstract

In this chapter, focus is shifted from broad conceptualizations of diversity to the perspective that some differences are imbued with social value. Drawing from a rich tradition of stigma theory and research, we explore the intra- and interpersonal experiences of targets of stigma and their interaction partners. We review general theories about stigmatization, the nature of stigmatized attributes, manifestations of stigma, and consequences of stigma for individuals and their organizations. This synthesis guides important avenues for future research.

Key Words: stigma, dual perspectives

Introduction

Discussions among scholars and practitioners about diversity management often begin with the question, "What do we mean by *diversity*?" Diversity is sometimes defined broadly, referring to any characteristic that differs between people, including personality, values, and demographic attributes (see Harrison & Sin, 2005). Diversity can also be defined more narrowly as differences due to observable demographic characteristics such as gender, age, and ethnicity. We contend that one of the critical elements of such differences that is not necessarily captured by the construct of *diversity* is the relative value of these characteristics in society.

In this chapter, we shift the lens from general conceptualizations of difference to one in which certain differences are imbued with negative social value. Such devalued differences are often described as *stigmas* (Goffman, 1963), and attract stereotypes, prejudice, and discrimination (see Crocker, Major, & Steele, 1998; Jones et al., 1984). Our primary goal is to consider workplace diversity from the perspective of stigma theory and research and consider attributes that are *stigmatized* or devalued in the context of the workplace (e.g., Goffman, 1963). This lens directs focus on the intra- and interpersonal processes that emerge from the perspective of individuals who hold identities that are devalued, as well as the experiences of their interaction partners.

The importance of examining the often-negative social value that others place on particular diversity characteristics is, among other things, critical in understanding the challenges that particular sets of diverse individuals face. That is, being diverse in one particular way (e.g., being Asian) rarely holds the same experience for a person who is diverse in another way (e.g., being Black), even though the diversity characteristic may be similar (e.g., race). Simply put, not all groups are valued equally for their diversity, and differences between and among these valuations often emerge (Schaerer, 2010).

Understanding stigma theory and considering how diversity characteristics are often imbued with labels illuminate the challenges that some groups might face and others might not face, and other theoretical and practical implications also emerge in considering the social value of diversity characteristics. Theoretically, it is important to understand how and why social values emerge. Some of the theories we will discuss in this chapter (i.e., stereotype content model, intergroup emotions theory) help explain such origins, but there is much work to be done in understanding how imbued values can change and in ascertaining how to implement these changes. In terms of practical implications, a focus on stigma and the experiences that stigmatized individuals have produces individual- and organizational-level coping strategies and puts a critical emphasis on reinforcing successful diversity management. In sum, we believe an understanding of stigma allows for a more comprehensive understanding of diversity.

We begin by explaining the meaning of stigma and describe the nature of attributes that are stigmatized in the workplace. Next, we focus on the perspective of targets of stigma and review a rich and growing body of evidence regarding their common psychological and social experiences. We then turn to the perspective of those who enact stigma and a discussion of characteristics of people who may be most likely to stigmatize others, and the reasons underlying stigmatization. This is followed by a description of contemporary manifestations of stigma. Finally, drawing from our synthesis of existing literature, we describe what we see as critical directions for future research.

What does it mean to be stigmatized?

Stigma is defined by modern dictionaries as a "mark considered to be abnormal," a "mark of shame or discredit," and a "distinguishing mark burned or cut into the flesh." These views of stigma can be traced back to traditions in ancient Greece, when slaves, traitors, and criminals were literally marked or branded with physical cuts in their skin. Scholars of psychology, sociology, and management have been largely influenced by Goffman's (1963) conceptualization of stigma as an attribute that is discrediting and prevents an individual from full social acceptance. Building on these ideas, Crocker, Major, and Steele (1998) specified that stigma is an attribute that conveys a devalued social identity across most social contexts. Here, our interest is in the particular context of the workplace and the characteristics that may be devalued therein.

In the interest of clarity, the term "stigma" should be situated in a nomologic network of related constructs: stereotypes, prejudice, and discrimination. In their strictest sense, stereotypes represent *beliefs* or cognitions about the characteristics, attitudes, or behaviors of a group of people. Prejudice refers to an attitude or set of *attitudes* toward a person or group of people based on their group membership. Discrimination is *behavior* enacted toward an individual or group of people based on their group membership. The presence of one does not necessitate the existence of another; stereotypes do not always lead to prejudice, which does not always engender discrimination. Stigma refers to the attribute that defines the group membership of focus in these other concepts; a mark that conveys a devalued characteristic indicates that its holder is a member of a devalued social group. It follows that individuals who are stigmatized may be subjected to stereotypes, prejudice, and/or discrimination. Indeed, Crocker and colleagues (1998) argued that individuals who possess a stigma are typically targets of interpersonal rejection, negative stereotypes, discrimination, and economic disadvantage.

Who is stigmatized?

In his groundbreaking book, Goffman (1963) proposed that stigma may exist as a function of (a) moral flaws, (b) physical aberrations of the body, or (c) heredity-based factors. Moral flaws typically refer to behavioral expressions that are generally considered by society to be inherently "wrong," such as drug use, criminal activity, and nonheterosexual sex. Physical aberrations include literal marks on the body (e.g., port wine stains), disfigurements (e.g., missing limbs, cleft palates), or atypical physical characteristics (e.g., obesity, dwarfism). Hereditary-based stigmas are those characteristics that are devalued but considered to be genetically determined, such as a non-White racial background or (arguably) a non-male gender. Goffman's conceptualization of stigma has been very influential to scholars across disciplines, including psychology, sociology, and management.

Perhaps even more influential to scholarly research than Goffman's (1963) initial typology was the work that Jones and colleagues (1984) did in sorting stigmas along six important dimensions, each of which we will describe briefly. It is important to note that there are differences both between and within stigmas on these dimensions. First, stigmas differ in the extent that they are *concealable* or visible to others. Thus, reactions to a tattoo encircling one's eye (à la Mike Tyson's tattoo) may be different from reactions to a tattoo on the hip. Second, stigmas can vary with onset and the extent to which they *change over time*. An individual may be very obese during childhood and adolescence but thin during adulthood (or just the opposite). Also, what is stigmatized at one point in time may not be stigmatized as much at another (e.g., homosexuality). Third, stigmas differ in the extent to which they are *disruptive* to social interaction, or have a negative impact on face-to-face interactions. Engaging in conversation with an individual who stutters may be more disruptive than engaging in conversation with an alcoholic. Fourth, stigmas vary along a dimension of *aesthetics*, or how attractive/unattractive the stigma characteristics are. Because of attention placed on the face during social exchanges, for instance, someone who has a serious facial burn may find social interactions more difficult to navigate than someone who has had a criminal background. Fifth, stigmas show variation in the extent to which they are actually as well as perceived to be *controllable*, or preventable by the target. The same disability that is acquired through one's own fault versus at the hands of another may produce very different reactions. And sixth, stigmas differ in the extent to which they are *perilous* to others. An ex-convict who served time for assaulting others will likely be viewed as much more dangerous than will someone who served time for tax evasion. In sum, where a particular stigma falls along each of these dimensions has implications for the psychological and social experience of stigma. That is, the experiences that overweight, gay, physically disabled, and other stigmatized individuals have in interactions may be similar or very disparate.

Of Jones and colleagues' (1984) dimensions, *controllability* and *concealability* have captured the majority of variance in the relevant beliefs and experiences (Crocker et al., 1998). Controllability reflects the degree to which a stigma is perceived to be under the target's control. For people whose stigmas are perceived to be controllable (e.g., homosexuality, obesity, alcoholism), stigmatizers perceive them negatively and like them less than those with uncontrollable stigmas (Crandall, 1994; Hebl & Kleck, 2002; Weiner, Perry, & Magnusson, 1988). For people whose stigmas are perceived to be uncontrollable (e.g., physical disabilities, many medical conditions), however, stigmatizers show reactions comprising increased sympathy, empathy, desire for future interactions, and positive affect (DeJong, 1980; Weiner, 1995). Concealability refers to the degree to which a stigma can be hidden from observers. Targets who have concealable (vs. unconcealable) stigmas are burdened more heavily with stigma-management thoughts (Goffman, 1963; Major & Gramzow, 1999; Smart & Wegner, 1999), and stigmatizers often prefer to have targets keep concealable stigmas hidden (e.g., King, Reilly, & Hebl, 2008). Also, when targets are told that their stigma will be visible to stigmatizers, it activates targets to display different sets of behaviors to try to compensate (Crocker & Major, 1989; Miller, Rothblum, Felicio, & Brand, 1995). Given these considerations, we turn now to a discussion of the perspective of these targets of stigma.

Targets' perspectives

Until the early 1990s, research focused on questions related to the perspective of those who enact discrimination toward targets of stigma (see Swim & Stangor, 1998). In the past 20 years, however, a growing body of evidence has emerged that directly addresses the experiences of targets of stigma that are relevant to the workplace. This research can be classified into findings that focus on intrapersonal (or psychological) aspects of these experiences, and those that are more interpersonal (or social) in nature.

Overarching theories explaining what and why: intrapersonal experiences

People who possess a stigmatized characteristic are typically aware—and sometimes hyper-aware—that they are marked by social devaluation. When people know they are seen as abnormal and/or possess negative characteristics, and that they are being targeted with stereotypes, prejudice, and discrimination, they develop complex psychological processes related to self-esteem development, challenges (e.g., stereotype threat), and coping strategies. We discuss all of these constructs in more detail.

When targets possess characteristics that are devalued, they may first and foremost have concerns about their own worth, value, and capability. Basic human motivations include a desire for interpersonal belongingness (Baumeister & Leary, 1995) and a need to make sense of and understand the world in which one lives (Fiske, 2004). These motivations propel seemingly existential, but actually quite practical, questions regarding the self in relation to others such as "Who am I?" and "Who are my people?" When stigmatized individuals engage in this kind of introspection, they may encounter a dilemma of wanting to see themselves in a positive light (as suggested by self-esteem maintenance theory; Tesser, 2000) and wanting to understand themselves accurately (as proposed by self-verification theory; Swann & Ely, 1984). Both of these theories suggest that targets may choose to compare and surround themselves with similar others or people who nurture positive self-views.

Indeed, on the one hand, targets may develop, as a result of such identity processes, positive views of their in-group (Ellemers, Spears, & Doosje, 2002; Phinney, 1996). Consistent with this (and somewhat surprisingly, perhaps), many stigmatized individuals actually have higher self-esteem than do those who are not stigmatized. For example, the average level of self-esteem among ethnic minorities is higher than that of majority-group members (see Crocker, Major, & Steele, 1998). Crocker and Major (1989) described three explanations for this counterintuitive finding. First, ethnic minorities might gain self-esteem through the social support from their in-group. Second, attributing failure to external sources (like discrimination) rather than internal sources protects self-esteem. Third and finally, comparisons of relative value are likely to be to other in-group members; thereby, stigmatized targets may believe that they are doing well relative to their shifting comparison group. It is clear that stigma moderates the ability for individuals to feel favorably about themselves, such that generally stigmas that are uncontrollable (e.g., disability, race, gender) often result in greater within-group pride and association for their members, and decreased negativity (relative to those with controllable stigmas) from stigmatizers (e.g., just world beliefs; Lerner & Simmons, 1966).

On the other hand, targets may develop, as a result of identity processes, negative views of themselves, particularly when they continuously encounter evidence that their group is not valued in society. That is, the tendency to have higher self-esteem when one is stigmatized does not generalize to all groups; for example, women tend to have lower self-esteem than men (King, Hyde, Showers, & Buswell, 1999); heavy women have lower self-esteem than do thinner women (Crocker, Cornwell, & Major, 1993); and some gay and lesbian people hold negative views toward homosexuality (i.e., internalized homo-negativity; Mayfield, 2001). The negative impact of stigma on targets' self-esteem has been shown to be particularly heightened when targets are highly affiliated and identify strongly with their stigmatized in-group (Branscombe, Schmitt, & Harvey, 1999; Major, Quinton, & Schmader, 2003), when they are high in stigma consciousness (more acutely aware of stigmatization than others;

Pinel, 1999), or when they are high in rejection sensitivity (the extent to which others are likely to discriminate against them because of their stigma; Mendoza-Denton, Downey, Purdie, Davis, & Pietrzak, 2002).

In addition, most targets also have to deal with continuous threats to their self-esteem, particularly in domains where stereotypes about their abilities reside. Thus, awareness of negative beliefs about one's group influences not only views of the self, but also behavior. Stereotype threat refers to a phenomenon whereby negative stereotypes hinder targets' outcomes in stereotype-relevant domains (Steele, 1997). In their foundational work, Steele and Aronson (1995) found that the standardized test performance of African-American students suffered when the tests were described as diagnostic of intellectual ability. Shapiro and Neuberg (2007) argued that these stereotype threat effects could be explained by threats to one's (a) personal self-concept, (b) group concept, (c) own reputation, (d) group's reputation, (e) own reputation from the in-group's perspective, and/or (f) in-group reputation from the in-group's perspective. This wide range of threats corresponds to numerous potential behavioral consequences. Of particular importance to the workplace is the potential of stigmatized individuals to underperform in employment testing contexts (Brown & Day, 2006), which affect selection, compensation, and development decisions and therefore can be detrimental to stigmatized workers.

In sum, identity development and self-esteem maintenance is clearly a complex process for people with stigmas; sometimes trait levels of self-esteem are bolstered and other times trait level self-esteem is reduced. Interestingly, nonstigmatized group members may also find themselves in situations that decrease their *state* level self-esteem when they are similarly (to stigmatized individuals' experience) scrutinized, criticized, and objectified because of their stigmatized characteristics (Hebl, King, & Lin, 2004). But the repeated experience of this over time is what differentiates the experience between stigmatized and nonstigmatized individuals, and may lead stigmatized individuals to have lower self-esteem and/or eventually attempt to protect that self-esteem by disidentifying from the threat altogether (see Steele, 1997). In sum, this initial body of research shows that stigma can have both positive and negative implications for self-esteem. Now we turn to considering how stigma influences interactions with others.

Overarching theories explaining what and why: interpersonal experiences

Targets experience not only intrapersonal consequences as a result of being stigmatized but also *interpersonal* outcomes. In fact, a major contribution of Goffman's (1963) perspective is its focus on the experiences that individuals have in "mixed" interactions, which involve stigmatized and nonstigmatized individuals. Specifically, Goffman proposed that stigma is inherently an interpersonal process involving both targets and actors in dynamic, unfolding, and reflexive interpersonal interactions. Here we focus on the experiences that stigmatized individuals likely encounter in such interactions, including discrimination, meta-stereotypes, and identity management.

According to symbolic interactionist and "looking-glass self" perspectives (Shrauger & Schoeneman, 1979), people often wonder, "What do *they* think of *me*?" These questions can be classified as meta-perceptions, which refer to individuals' beliefs about how they are perceived by others (Laing, Phillipson, & Lee, 1966). Special types of meta-perceptions are **meta-stereotypes**, "a person's beliefs regarding that stereotype that outgroup members hold about his/her own group" (Vorauer et al., 1998, p. 917). Research has demonstrated that stigmatized individuals are aware of the stereotypes about their identity group and expect to be viewed in line with those stereotypes by out-group members (Vorauer, Hunter, Main, & Roy, 2000; Vorauer & Kumhyr, 2001), For example, in one experiment, participants who were privately assigned to a stigmatized identity believed that their interaction partners viewed them negatively (Santuzzi & Ruscher, 2002). Moreover, research has demonstrated that meta-stereotypes can interfere with mixed interactions (Frey & Tropp, 2006). Concerns about meta-stereotypes lead stigmatized individuals to behave defensively and to avoid interactions with those from other groups altogether (Hebl & Dovidio, 2005; Shelton & Richeson, 2006).

Unfortunately, meta-stereotypic concerns that interaction partners will discriminate against targets of stigma are often justified. Despite progress in the status of many stigmatized individuals, **discrimination** continues to emerge in organizations (see Dipboye & Collella, 2005). That is, research consistently documents the negative impact of stigma across the employment cycle, including career intentions (Gupta, Turban, & Bhawe, 2008), letters of recommendations written (Madera, Hebl, & Martin, 2009), hiring decisions (Rudolph, Wells, Weller, & Baltes, 2009), compensation (Judge & Cable, 2011), performance (Brown & Day, 2006; Nguyen & Ryan, 2008), quality of training (Shapiro, King & Quinones, 2007), and allocation of developmental experiences (King, Botsford, Hebl, Kazama, Dawson, & Perkins, in press). It is clear from a growing body of research that the traditional forms of overt and hostile prejudice are generally being supplanted by subtler negative interpersonal behaviors. Such behaviors have been labeled "interpersonal discrimination" (Hebl, Foster, Mannix, & Dovidio, 2002), "selective incivility" (Cortina, 2008), and "microaggressions" (Sue et al., 2007). The common element across these constructs is verbal, nonverbal, or paraverbal behavior that demeans stigmatized individuals. Although this subtle discrimination may seem to reflect progress, these subtle behaviors may have just as much, if not more, severely pernicious effects on self-efficacy (Stewart et al., 2010) and performance (Singletary & Hebl, 2010) at work. In particular, it may be relatively easy for targets to identify formal discrimination and attribute it to discriminatory others; however, targets' experience with daily micro-inequities (less smiling, less friendliness, rudeness) may leave them in a state of attributional uncertainty about others' intentions. This uncertainty may be cognitively taxing, as targets must constantly try to decipher others' behaviors (i.e., "Are they friend or foe?" "Are they discriminating or are they just rude?") rather than simply being able to quickly and accurately judge others as discriminatory on the basis of overt, clear behaviors. Such cognitive loads have been shown to at least partially mediate the relation between discrimination and decreased performance (Singletary & Hebl, 2010).

A central concern of workers, particularly those who are stigmatized, is to **manage the impressions** they make on their coworkers, supervisors, subordinates, and clients (Roberts, 2005). Stigmatized individuals uniquely weigh fears of rejection and discrimination with a desire to behave authentically and form genuine work relationships (King et al., 2008). Individuals with observable stigmas have to manage the potential negative stereotypes of their interaction partners and in some cases make decisions about whether to take advantage of resources that are available. For example, workers with observable disabilities have to decide whether to request and use accommodations. Individuals with a concealable stigma (such as a non-Christian religious affiliation or a history of mental disorder) have a different predicament: these individuals fear discrimination should their stigma be revealed (Goffman, 1963). These fears often translate into "disclosure dilemmas" about whether, how, when, to whom, and where to discuss this aspect of identity (e.g., Griffith & Hebl, 2002; Ragins, Singh, & Cornwell, 2007). Indeed, complex and weighty decisions about whether to reveal or conceal a stigmatized identity can emerge frequently in everyday workplace interactions (King, Mohr, Peddie, Kendra, & Jones, 2010).

Coping strategies

Recognizing these complex (and predominantly negative) interpersonal and intrapersonal experiences, research has also explored the ways in which targets of stigma cope. This research does *not* advocate that targets of stigma should be solely responsible for the burden of reducing prejudice and discrimination; instead, researchers point to the unconscious and intentional strategies that may improve the daily experiences of stigmatized targets.

First, research suggests that individuals sometimes unconsciously minimize or deny the extent to which they have faced discrimination (Crosby, 1984; Crosby, Cordova, & Jaskar, 1994). For example, women may admit that other women face discrimination but refuse to believe that they have personally encountered sexism. The theory guiding this research, referred to as relative deprivation, suggests that individuals maintain their self-esteem by denying that they, themselves, have been victims of discrimination (Crosby, 1984). Second, targets of stigma may react to fears of confirming stereotypes by devaluing success in relevant domains (Major & Schmader, 1998). For example, African-American students who are aware of negative stereotypes regarding their academic performance may construct beliefs that academic performance isn't important or valuable (Steele, 1997). Similarly, Black women who know that they are more likely to be heavy than White women may not negatively judge people on the basis of being heavy (Hebl, King, & Perkins, 2009). This strategy, referred to as disidentification, allows stigmatized targets to maintain their self-esteem despite continued threats—by simply disengaging their selves from the performance domain in which they are threatened, targets protect themselves (Steele, 1992).

Third, research suggests that targets of stigma sometimes consciously try to compensate for others' negative expectations (Kaiser & Miller, 2001). For example, participants who knew that their interaction partners could see that they were obese engaged in friendlier, more communicative behaviors than those who believed they could not be seen (Miller & Myers, 1998). Recent research shows that compensation can be successful in combating discrimination; specifically, "ostensibly gay and lesbian" job applicants who engaged in compensatory strategies (e.g., smiled more, were friendlier, used more eye contact, made positive comments) were targeted with less discrimination that gay job applicants who did not use such strategies (Singletary & Hebl, 2009). This strategy may be effective because it disrupts perceivers from confirming their stereotypes; in the face of wanting to make negative attributions toward targets, targets are being overly positive and nondefensive (see also Crandall & Eshleman, 2003).

Fourth, directly acknowledging a particular stigma can be a beneficial coping strategy on the part of stigmatized targets (Hebl & Kleck, 2002). The theory behind this coping strategy is that both stigmatized and nonstigmatized interactants are focused on the stigma that underlies much tension in an interaction. If not addressed, social norms prevent the nonstigmatized individuals from mentioning the stigma and they are placed in a state of thought suppression, in which they cannot mention the stigma and use complex cognitive resources to avoid doing so. Thus, acknowledgments on the part of targets can serve to "break through" (Davis, 1961) the interaction tension and alleviate thought suppression and anxiety on the part of both stigmatizer and target. Indeed, Singletary and Hebl (2009) found that both acknowledgment behaviors reduced discrimination toward gay and lesbian job applicants (see also Griffith & Hebl, 2002).

Fifth, directly contradicting negative stereotypes by providing additional stereotype-disconfirming information can reduce prejudice in what Fiske and Neuberg (1990) term individuation. This theory suggests that individuals are most likely to view others as stereotypical of their group in the absence of additional information. Thus, if one is choosing a leader in an initially leaderless group of individuals who do not know each other, a man will likely be selected (see Hebl, 1995). In one study, customers who appeared to be obese (i.e., wore an obesity prosthesis) were treated more positively when they claimed to be dieting and exercising than when they did not make such claims (King, Shapiro, Hebl, Singletary, & Turner, 2006). Sixth, another active form of coping that is available to members of legally protected groups (e.g., race, gender, national origin) is to make a formal claim of discrimination to their organization or legal agents. Making claims can be a challenging route to reducing discrimination, as some research suggests that making such claims can be met with backlash in the form of negative evaluations (Kaiser & Miller, 2001). However, the laws are in place to help reduce such discrimination, and recent evidence suggests that such laws have a strong impact on behavior—their presence reduces both formal (illegal types of) and interpersonal (legal types of) discrimination (Barron, 2009). Overall, there are a range of coping strategies that stigmatized individuals can and do enact in organizational settings.

Stigmatizers' perspectives

Unlike the more limited body of research focusing on the target's perspective, research examining the perspective of stigmatizers is much more extensive. In fact, the attention placed on this perspective has led to the development of overarching theories that attempt to explain who is likely to stigmatize and why. Another research approach has been to consider stigmatizers' perspective by considering different stages: antecedents to stigmatization, the experiences of the stigmatizer, consequences for stigmatizing, and remediation of stigmatizing from the stigmatizer's perspective. We review both the overarching considerations and the stages of the dynamic process of stigmatization.

Overarching theories explaining who and why

Although we cannot provide an exhaustive review of all theories that can explain the "who" and "why" of stigma, we briefly summarize five relatively overarching, comprehensive theories that differentially predict and explain stigmatization: stereotype content model, intergroup emotions theory, sociofunctional approach, system justification, and justification-suppression model.

The **stereotype content model** (SCM) is based on three beliefs. First, people respond to others on two basic dimensions of more and less socially desirable traits: warmth and competence (Cuddy, Fiske, & Glick, 2008). These two dimensions allow perceivers to accurately assess whether targets are "friends versus enemies" (the warmth dimension) and "if targets can effectively achieve things" (the competence dimension). Second, targets may generate ambivalent reactions. Although the model uses continuums, there are those who are perceived to be low on both dimensions (i.e., the poor, homeless), high on both dimensions (i.e., the middle class, Whites), high on competence but low on the warmth dimension (i.e., Asians, men), and low on competence but high on the warmth dimension (i.e., elderly, disabled). Reactions to those with mixed endpoints tend to be ambivalent.

Third, the locations of different target groups along the continuums follow from social structural variables. In general, high-status (vs. low-status) groups tend to be associated with more competence, and competition with groups is associated with low warmth and liking. Furthermore, the unique point at which a particular stereotype falls along the two dimensions of warmth and competence is associated with specific affective reactions (i.e., prejudices), such as admiration, contempt, envy, and pity. For instance, the associated emotional reaction to Asians and men would be envious prejudice, whereas the reaction to elderly and physically disabled individuals might be pity. According to the SCM, stereotypic perceptions related to warmth and competence give rise to affective experiences and behavioral patterns that make up stigmatization.

Another approach, **intergroup emotions theory**, considers emotions as sources of behavior in the process of stigmatization by combining appraisal and self-categorization theories (see Mackie, Devos, & Smith, 2000; Smith & Henry, 1996). That is, emotions become tied to events that individuals perceive to favor or harm their group. From this perspective, prejudice is driven by specific emotional reactions to an out-group that are generated by appraisals of the out-group. Generally, when individuals or groups have power relative to others, anger emerges as opposed to fear or contempt (Frijda, 1986). Anger, in turn, leads to offensive action tendencies such as attacking or confronting the out-group member (Mackie et al., 2000). Hence, when individuals feel that their in-group is more powerful than an out-group, their emotional response (i.e., anger) may lead to action tendencies that are manifested in discrimination toward members of that out-group.

Predictions from an intergroup emotions approach might be contradictory to those made by the SCM. For instance, both theories might predict negative emotional reactions to obese or gay individuals, but intergroup emotions theory might predict that anger would emerge, whereas the SCM might suggest that disgust should surface. The qualitative difference between these emotions may be subtle, but there may be important implications. For instance, strategies targeted at diminishing anger might differ significantly from strategies designed to lessen disgust. Nevertheless, intergroup emotions theory is similar to the SCM in that it implies that stigma will emerge as a function (in part) of emotional processes.

Whereas the SCM specifies the components of stigma and the accompanying emotional responses, the intergroup emotions approach goes deeper in an attempt to understand why specific emotions emerge as a function of intergroup relations. The **sociofunctional**, or biocultural, **approach** focuses even more intensely on addressing the question of why stigmatization occurs. This approach is grounded in the assumption that stigmatizing others can serve meaningful purposes to the stigmatizer (Neuberg, Smith, & Asher, 2000). Following an evolutionary line of reasoning, Neuberg and his colleagues argue that stigmatization is rooted in an inherent biological need to live in effective groups to promote the survival of their genetic makeup. Individuals or groups who are perceived to threaten the survival of one's in-group will be stigmatized. Neuberg further posits that individuals will attempt to minimize perceived threat from stigmatized out-groups with specific emotional (i.e., prejudice) and behavioral (i.e., discrimination) responses. Thus, the process of stigmatization may arise to ensure the "survival of the fittest."

Other evolutionary psychology explanations have also been used to explain stigmatization. One such theory, terror management, explains stigmatization by suggesting that making mortality salient leads individuals to ascribe to a worldview in which they accept what is similar and reject what is different (Rosenblatt, Greenberg, Solomon, Pyszcyzynski, & Lyon, 1989). In making these choices, they thereby respectively favor in-group members and stigmatize out-group members.

The final two theories that we describe focus more on cognitions (vs. emotions as the SCM and intergroup emotions theory specified, and vs. the evolutionary basis that the sociofunctional theory serves) and the particular use of these cognitions in justifying status quo and further discrimination. According to this approach, stigmatization can serve a **system justification** function (Jost & Banaji, 1994). In particular, "stereotypes serve ideological functions, in particular that they justify the exploitation of certain groups over others, and they explain the poverty or powerlessness of some groups and the success of others in ways that make these differences seem legitimate" (Jost & Banaji, 1994; p. 10). Also, Jost and colleagues (Jost & Banaji, 1994; Jost, Pelham, & Carvallo, 2002) suggest that there are cognitive reasons (e.g., need for cognitive closure, uncertainty reduction) as well as motivational reasons (e.g., belief in a just world, illusion of control) for participating in system justification. The system justification approach not only provides a rationale for stigmatizers but also proposes an explanation for why there is often widespread acceptance of a group's advantaged or disadvantaged status. That is, stigmatized targets often accept the legitimacy of their own disadvantaged status, and according to this theory, they may do this to minimize group conflict by believing that the system is just. If targets did not believe the system was just, they would be much more likely to feel their stigmatized status and realize how unjust and unfair their situation is. One example of this, for instance, is overweight individuals, who have been known to stigmatize themselves as well (Crandall & Biernat, 1990; Crocker et al., 1993). Clearly, however, stigmatizers (or those who clearly hold power and status) use system justification to secure results that are in line with their own interests.

The **justification-suppression model** (JSM), by Crandall and Eshleman (2003), distinguishes why the prejudice that people feel (attitudes) matches or does not match the prejudice that people behaviorally express (discrimination). Essentially, they suggest that individuals want to express their true emotions but also want to remain true to their egalitarian values. In the JSM, Crandall and Eshleman suggest three sources of variation (genuine prejudice, suppression, justification) that account for conditions under which prejudice may or may not be expressed. First, they propose that individuals harbor *genuine prejudice*, or "pure, unadulterated, original, unmanaged, and unambivalently negative feelings toward members of a devalued group" (p. 422). Second, because of egalitarian values and other motivations, individuals try to *suppress*, or "attempt to reduce the expression or awareness of prejudice" (p. 423). Third, because people possess genuine prejudice but must suppress it, they look for *justifications*, or reasons why they can hold targets responsible for their behaviors and negative outcomes. According to the JSM, then, displays of prejudice will be likely to occur when suppression is maximized and justification is minimized. Furthermore, the JSM specifies that suppression is likely with extensive practice, egalitarian goal commitment, and improved cognitive resources, and that justification can be reduced when there are no available reasons for prejudiced cognitions and behaviors.

Antecedents, manifestations, consequences, and remediation of stigmatization

Regardless of which theory one ascribes to in explaining stigmatization, there are some commonalities across stages in the stigmatization process that are also important to consider. For instance, certain factors may be particularly likely to lead stigmatizers to denigrate targets. Regardless of the particular theoretical explanations, stigmatizers also manifest similar sets of stigmatizing behaviors. Furthermore, there are consequences for stigmatization not only for the target but also for the stigmatizer. And finally, there are sets of behaviors that individuals and organizations can engage in to remediate stigmatizers' displays of discrimination. In this section, then, we consider antecedents of stigmatization, manifestations, consequences, and remediation of stigma.

Three particular sets of **antecedents** may be especially likely to influence stigmatizers' negative reactions toward targets, and these include personal factors, past experiences, and relational/situational factors. Each of these antecedent conditions has been discussed in more detail in Hebl and Dovidio (2005), but we summarize them here.

First, *personal factors* have been shown to lead individuals to hold prejudicial attitudes and express discrimination against others. For instance, some individuals may be more likely to have a "prejudiced personality" (Allport, 1954) and particular cognitive representations of, beliefs about, and experiences with members of stigmatized groups (Haddock, Zanna, & Esses, 1993). To name just a few, for example, stigmatization is more likely to emerge from individuals who embrace authoritarianism (Allport, 1954), Protestant work ethic ideologies (Crandall, 1994), and system-legitimizing beliefs (Jost & Major, 2001).

Second, the past experiences that individuals have had with targets can serve as antecedents to stigmatization. Stigmatizers who have had negative experiences in the past or have not had much experience at all may be particularly likely to stigmatize targets (Pettigrew & Tropp, 2000). Reflecting what has been called the "contact hypothesis," or the idea that under appropriate conditions contact can reduce prejudice between majority-group and minority-group members (see Allport, 1954; Pettigrew & Tropp, 2000, 2006), evidence consistently shows that increased contact with out-group members significantly decreases prejudice on the part of stigmatizers. At least under a given set of contingencies and circumstances (i.e., equal status), these studies reveal that mixed interactions can ultimately approximate "normal" relations. Importantly, this research shows that attitudes and behaviors are not immutable but are instead dynamic entities that change over time with repeated exposure to attitudinal objects or people.

The relational-situational setting is a third critical antecedent to consider in understanding why stigmatizers denigrate targets. That is, the physical, social, and selection characteristics of the setting can largely influence the way in which interactions proceed (see Patterson, 1982). For example, stigmatizers may react differently to targets in church rather than business settings, in formal rather than casual settings, in one part of the country than another (i.e., Deep South vs. California), and when scripted versus not scripted (see Richeson & Ambady, 2001a, 2001b; Rudman & Glick, 2001). Similarly, when interviews are structured (vs. unstructured), applicants are treated more fairly and discriminatory processes are less likely (Campion, Palmer, & Campion, 1997). Social norms and legal requirements differ across these and other situations, and thus they may produce very different interaction content and outcomes. Recent research has shown, for instance, that simply giving scripts for White individuals to follow in dyadic interactions with Black participants resulted in decreased anxiety (Avery, Richeson, Hebl, & Ambady, 2009). Consistent with the findings of most of the intergroup contact literature (Pettigrew & Tropp, 2000), the longer, deeper, and more interdependent the interaction/relationship between the stigmatizer and target is, the more likely it is to positively influence stigmatizers' behaviors. For example, stigmatizers whose interaction outcomes are interdependent perceive targets in more accurate, less stereotypical, individuated ways (e.g., Neuberg, Smith, Hoffman, & Russell, 1994). Similarly, stigmatizers whose livelihoods or even interaction goals involve catering to stigmatized targets (e.g., physical therapists, sales personnel) are also likely and motivated to stigmatize targets less (e.g., Snyder, 1992).

In addition to understanding why stigmatization occurs, researchers have investigated what behaviors stigmatizers express to targets (**manifestations**). It is clear that stigmatizers experience and manifest an array of (often negative) feelings toward targets, and researchers have documented these. Stigmatizers tend to display toward targets awkwardness and uncertainty about how to act (Hebl, Tickle, & Heatherton, 2000), ambivalence (Glick & Fiske, 1997), avoidance (Snyder, Kleck, Strenta, & Mentzer, 1979), suppression (Macrae, Bodenhausen, Milne, & Jetten, 1994), discomfort

(Devine, Evett, & Vasquez-Suson, 1996), and anger and aggression (Crosby, Bromley, & Saxe, 1980; Rüsch, Corrigan, Todd, & Bodenhausen, 2011). Stigmatizers also commonly exhibit mismatches or discrepancies between the attitudes/verbal behaviors (often more favorable) and nonverbal behaviors (often more negative) they express toward targets (see Devine et al., 1996; Hebl & Dovidio, 2005; Hebl et al., 2008). For instance, stigmatizers may verbally state and show on attitudinal measures very positive feelings toward physically disabled individuals; yet they prefer and show less anxiety in interactions in comparison with able-bodied individuals (for review, see Hebl & Kleck, 2000). Surprisingly, however, the pattern is sometimes the reverse. For instance, White stigmatizers who are racially biased (vs. those less so) might exert more effort at altering their nonverbal behaviors favorably, hence leading Black interactants to actually prefer (unbeknownst to them) the racially biased (vs. less biased) White interactant partners (Shelton, Richeson, Salvatore, & Trawalter, 2005).

A very large body of research has examined the content of attitudinal displays (prejudice) that stigmatizers exhibit toward targets. Some displays are still overt and "old-fashioned" (Swim, Aikin, Hall, & Hunter, 1995), but most have become much more subtle and/or ambiguous, and people are less willing to espouse extremely racist, sexist, or other "ist" statements (Gaertner & Dovidio, 1986). Similarly, researchers have differentiated between explicit forms (exemplified via traditional measures like self-report) and implicit forms of prejudice (exemplified by the Implicit Association Test [IAT] or other measures that do not involve the person's full awareness) that often show mismatches and predict different sorts of outcomes; see Dovidio, Kawakami, & Gaertner, 2002).

Like prejudice, displays of discrimination have also changed in recent years. One particularly useful taxonomy has distinguished between "formal" and "interpersonal" forms of discrimination (e.g., Hebl et al., 2002; King et al., 2006). Formal discrimination consists of behaviors toward targets that are prohibited by law (e.g., biases in selection, promotion, and salary procedures). Interpersonal discrimination consists of behaviors that are not illegal (e.g., decreased smiling, friendliness) but are socially isolating interaction-based behaviors that can accumulate over time to reveal profound differences in advantage (Martell, Lane, & Emrich, 1996). Recent accumulating research has shown that stigmatizers often withhold their displays of formal discrimination (perhaps because of authentically changing attitudes that are becoming more positive, social desirability, or laws that sanction such behaviors) but that stigmatizers display significant interpersonal discriminatory behaviors such as decreased smiling, eye contact, and friendliness; increased hostility, interest, and rudeness, and shortened interactions (Hebl et al., 2002; King et al., 2006).

Research has shown that stigmatizers may use interpersonal discrimination to reinforce what they believe is appropriate behavior and to extinguish what they believe is inappropriate behavior. That is, stigmatizers were more hostile toward pregnant woman applying for jobs than pregnant female customers; however, stigmatizers also displayed more benevolently sexist behavior (i.e., touching, overfriendliness) toward pregnant customers than pregnant job applicants (Hebl et al., 2007). Thus, stigmatizers may show ambivalence in their behavior, which is intended to reinforce the status quo and subservience of targets.

In an earlier description of the theoretical explanations for stigmatization, a number of reasons were mentioned as to why stigmatizers might wish to denigrate targets and may benefit from doing so. Indeed, stigmatizers gain self-esteem, can justify the status quo, express their true feelings, benefit in downward comparisons, and increase their sense of well-being. However, there are also some very negative **consequences** for stigmatizers that are only beginning to be realized. In fact, most of the attention on consequences of stigmatization focuses squarely (and perhaps rightly so) on the implications for targets; however, we believe it is also important to consider the impact that stigmatization has on the perpetrators themselves. First, recent research on perspective taking suggests that stigmatizers (vs. those who do not stigmatize others) may be more likely to experience psychological distress and lower levels of both psychological flexibility and general psychological health (see Masuda, Price, Anderson, Schmertz, & Calamaras, 2009). Essentially, Masuda and colleagues propose that undermining the distance between oneself and others, which is what stigmatizers do, may trigger avoidance mechanisms and an inability for stigmatizers to humanize others through perspective taking.

Additional research has shown that there may be financial costs for stigmatizers who discriminate against targets. For instance, research by King and colleagues (2007) found that employers and store managers who engaged in interpersonal discrimination toward their heavy customers were not successful in selling to these customers as much as the customers had initially intended to purchase. The customers who received interpersonal discrimination also recommended the store less to others and did not intend to return to the store as soon as did those who did not experience interpersonal discrimination. In a recent article, King and Cortina (2010) also articulate a financial imperative (at the organizational level) to providing stigmatized individuals with support rather than ostracism. It is easy to imagine how stigmatizers within an organization might hurt their organizations. If they send unwelcome messages to their employees in the context of interpersonal discrimination and/or more openly and formally discriminate against targets, they may lay themselves and their organizations open to expensive lawsuits, the loss of valuable employees, the loss of profits, and the absence of workplace equity.

Stigmatizers may also disadvantage themselves when it comes to receiving help from the targets they have denigrated. Research shows that targets are less willing to perform organizational citizenship behaviors when they experience (vs. do not experience) stigmatization (King et al., 2010; see also Singletary & Hebl, 2010). Stigmatizers may also be limiting their personal and professional development. In not acting in egalitarian ways that assist others in reaching their full potential, stigmatizers may be losing out on personal relationships that might otherwise be very meaningful. Similarly, stigmatizers might limit their professional or financial success by treating targets badly.

There are both individual- and organizational-level strategies that can reduce stigmatization and optimize social and professional interactions between stigmatizer and target. We begin by considering just a few, and not an exhaustive list of, individual-level strategies for **remediation**.

First, properly motivating the stigmatizer can lead to reducing stigmatization, or at least explicit displays of it. Indeed, researchers conclude that even though prejudice is ubiquitous, stigmatizers can make conscious efforts to avoid behavioral displays of prejudice and need not exhibit prejudice and/or discriminatory behaviors if they are motivated (e.g., Devine, 1989). Such forces may involve leading perceivers to believe that they will engage in future interactions with targets, that their outcomes will be inextricably linked together, that they will need each other for task completion, or that they will work on some superordinate goal (for reviews, see Gaertner et al., 2000; Oskamp, 2000). Not only can motivating forces influence stigmatizers' displays toward targets, but recent research has also shown that individuals have more trait-level levels of motivation for regulatory control of stigmatization. That is, individuals have different levels of both internal and external motivations to suppress stigmatization, and those with high levels of internal motivation and low levels of external motivation to respond without prejudice were most effective at regulating their prejudicial expressions (Devine, Plant, Amodio, Jones, & Vance, 2002; see also Shelton et al., 2005).

Second, stigmatizers can be taught to view interactions with stigmatized individuals to be challenging rather than threatening (Blascovich, Mendes, Hunter, Lickel, & Kowai-Bell, 2001). That is, if a stigmatizer views an interaction with a target as a threat, the stigmatizer will want to avoid or limit the interaction. But if the stigmatizer views an interaction with a target as a challenge, the stigmatizer may be motivated to approach and lengthen the interaction. Threat occurs when demands exceed one's resources, whereas challenge occurs when one's available resources meet demands. Blascovich and colleagues have shown that stigmatizers generally experience cardiovascular patterns associated with threat and perform worse when interacting with stigmatized than nonstigmatized targets. If stigmatizers can be trained to see such interactions as challenging instead of threatening, they may have more favorable physiologic and psychological reactions, which in turn will result in less threat and stigmatization (see also Mendes, Blascovich, Lickel, & Hunter, 2002).

Third, stigmatizers may actively suppress negative stereotypes (Crandall & Eshleman, 2003; McCrae et al., 1994) to avoid discriminatory behavior. That is, there are behaviors that targets can engage in that suppress the negative stereotypes held against them. For instance, King and colleagues (2006) found that obese individuals who held diet Cokes and talked about their exercise program were the targets of decreased discrimination relative to obese individuals in other conditions. The authors reasoned that the diet behaviors had worked to suppress and remove the justifications in the stigmatizer for expressing prejudice against heavy individuals. The JSM model suggests that this is particularly strategic and that discriminatory displays will be minimized when suppression is maximized and justifications for expressions are minimized. However, research by Macrae and colleagues (1994) has shown that suppressing stereotypes may later give way to a "stereotype rebound" in which a boomerang effect happens and more stereotypes are actually generated later. Thus, more research is needed to sort out when and how much suppression is beneficial for reducing the stigmatizers' denigration of targets.

We also consider just a few organizational-level strategies. Perhaps most importantly, laws can reduce the extent to which stigmatizers discriminate against targets. In fact, this may be one of the most effective strategies for shaping stigmatizers' behaviors and reducing stigmatization. Barron and Hebl (2010) suggest that laws serve both an instrumental and symbolic mechanism in reducing both formal and interpersonal discrimination. The instrumental effects involve the fact that behaviors that violate laws can be punishable; thus, stigmatizers do not discriminate because they will be punished. The symbolic effects involve moral codes of ethics; thus, stigmatizers do not discriminate because they believe that discrimination is societally unacceptable. Not only has research shown that laws reduce formal types of discrimination, but recent research shows that laws reduce interpersonal discrimination too (Barron, 2009).

Similarly, organizational policies and procedures can also limit the degree to which stigmatizers denigrate targets (Brief & Barsky, 2000; Button, 2001). Such polices and procedures might include preventive as well as compensatory policies for dealing with complaints of discrimination. Zero-tolerance policies may send a particularly loud and clear message to individuals that suppression is an absolute, that social norms are strongly in place, and that stigmatizers should be highly motivated to suppress stigmatization against targets. As was mentioned previously, however, these policies must be constructed carefully because they may invoke backlash and other negative feelings about being controlled.

Conclusions and future research directions

This chapter focused on the psychological and social aspects of stigmatization. We described how the current literature, amassed from sociology, psychology, and management perspectives, converges in suggesting that certain characteristics have negative value in our society. These values, known to those who hold them, have impacts on targets' self-esteem and other intrapsychic processes and significantly shape the social interactions that such targets have with their interactants. We reviewed a great deal of research that has transpired to explain processes of stigmatization, and these theories offer convincing emotional, cognitive, and evolutionary reasons for why certain characteristics in our society are imbued with negativity.

The current synthesis of research and theory regarding the social and psychological experience of stigma in organizations points to practical implications as well as several important areas for future research. First, it may be useful to approach our work with more diverse ideas about what diversity means. This recommendation is based on our conclusion that there is only a moderate degree of alignment in these traditional views of stigma and the focus of the majority of research on diversity in organizations. Much of the work on diversity management focuses on the observable and uncontrollable characteristics of race and gender. Indeed, the only characteristics for which employees are protected by federal legislation are race, color, religion, sex, national origin, disability, and pregnancy (Civil Rights Act of 1964; Americans with Disabilities Act of 1992; Pregnancy Discrimination Act of 1978). Although these characteristics are undoubtedly critical attributes in contemporary American society, researchers and practitioners may be overlooking a substantial set of targets of devaluation and disadvantage, such as those who hold stigmas that are perceived to be controllable or are concealable. Thus, we hope to inspire more research and action promoting overlooked populations of stigmatized individuals. Research has begun to identify some of these populations, such as those with accents (Gluszek & Dovidio, 2010) and transsexual individuals (Law, Martinez, Ruggs, & Hebl, in press), but there are many other overlooked populations who could benefit greatly by more research and research-based advocacy.

A second recommendation for future research is to increase consideration of dual perspectives of actual interactions in ongoing relationships. Research on stereotypes and discrimination has been heavily criticized for its reliance on laboratory studies in which participants rarely even meet ostensibly stigmatized targets (e.g., Landy, 2008). Indeed, it is often argued that prejudice and discrimination are less likely to emerge toward targets of stigma when positive, counter-stereotypic information about them is available. This raises the question of whether targets of stigma (and stigmatizers) are likely to encounter (or enact) different psychological and social processes when they apply for jobs compared to when they've been working at a job for years. The implications of relationship building for stigma and discrimination should be tested empirically. Whereas many researchers are interested in basic theory building, adopting their paradigms to also include more externally valid settings has the potential to seriously help the individuals being studied. Unlike basic researchers, who can turn off the laboratory lights at the end of the day, stigmatized targets are often in an immutable situation and can benefit immensely from more realistic and actionable research conducted within and outside of the laboratory confines.

Third, it may be helpful to explore the potential implications of the embedded nature of interpersonal interactions in organizations. The vast majority of existing research on stigma has focused on the perspective of individuals as presumed representatives of groups and organizations (see Oyserman & Swim, 2001). Research that explores the emergence and operationalization of stigma at the group and organizational levels could yield a more complex and nuanced view of stigma at work. For example, it would be interesting to explore the question of whether and how groups (e.g., top management teams, divisional workgroups) could enact stigmatization or be targeted by stigma. Integrating ideas about traditionally studied group phenomenon such as group polarization and group decision making might help to build new understanding about the meaning of stigma in organizations.

Fourth, it is important to note that the majority of the literature on stigma is based primarily on definitions of, assumptions about, and research concerning an American conception of stigma in organizations. Without a truly global perspective, we cannot know whether existing theory and evidence apply to other countries and cultures (Pettigrew, 1998). In understanding the experiences of women, for example, it is likely quite different to talk about advancement in Asian cultures than in Western cultures (Schein, 2001). We should not ignore the hugely different historical contexts that impinge on intergroup relations across cultures. Clearly, for instance, historical tensions between Israel and Palestine give rise to unique concerns about threat, competition, and discrimination (Semyonov, Raijman, & Yom-Tov, 2002). We must explore the manifestations and consequences of stigma in other countries and regions or limit our conclusions to the context in which our work has been conducted.

Conclusion

People in organizations are not merely different from one another. People differ with regard to socially meaningful attributes that sometimes convey severe devaluation. Consideration of markers of shame and discredit point to important intra- and interpersonal processes experienced by targets of stigma and the individuals with whom they interact. Moreover, the focus on stigma brings to light underexplored questions regarding workplace diversity. Organizations, employees, and the scholars who study them may gain unique insights by integrating stigma in their understanding of difference.

References

Allport, G. W. (1954). *The nature of prejudice*. New York: Addison-Wesley.

Avery, D. R., Richeson, J., Hebl, M., & Ambady, N. (2009). It doesn't have to be uncomfortable: The role of behavioral scripts in Black-White interracial interactions. *Journal of Applied Psychology, 94*, 1382–1393.

Barron, L. G. (2009). *The force of law: Effects of legislation on formal and interpersonal discrimination towards gay and lesbian job applicants*. Doctoral dissertation, Rice University.

Barron, L. G., & Hebl, M. (2010). Reducing "acceptable" stigmatization through legislation. *Social Issues and Policy Review, 4*, 1–30.

Baumeister, R. F., & Leary, M. R. (1995). The need to belong: Desire for interpersonal attachments as a fundamental human motivation. *Psychological Bulletin, 117*, 497–530.

Blascovich, J., Mendes, W. B., Hunter, S. B., Lickel, B., & Kowai-Bell, N. (2001). Perceiver threat in social interactions with stigmatized others. *Journal of Personality and Social Psychology, 80*, 253–267.

Branscombe, N. R., Schmitt, M. T., & Harvey, R. D. (1999). Perceiving pervasive discrimination among African-Americans: Implications for group identification and wellbeing. *Journal of Personality and Social Psychology, 77*, 135–149.

Brief, A. P., & Barsky, A. (2000). Establishing a climate for diversity: Inhibition of prejudice reactions in the workplace. In G. R. Ferris (Ed.), *Research in personnel and human resources management* (Vol. 19, pp. 91–129). Greenwich, CT: JAI Press.

Brown, R. P., & Day, E. A. (2006). The difference isn't black and white: Stereotype threat and the race gap on Raven's Advanced Progressive Matrices. *Journal of Applied Psychology, 91*, 979–985.

Button, S. B. 2001. Organizational efforts to affirm sexual diversity: A cross-level examination. *Journal of Applied Psychology, 86*, 17–28.

Campion, M. A., Palmer, D. K., & Campion, J. E. (1997). A review of structure in the selection interview. *Personnel Psychology, 50*, 655–702.

Cortina, L. M. (2008). Unseen injustice: Incivility as modern discrimination in organizations. *Academy of Management Review, 33*, 55–75.

Crandall, C. (1994). Prejudice against fat people: Ideology and self-interest? *Journal of Personality and Social Psychology, 66*, 882–894.

Crandall, C. S., & Biernat, M. (1990). The ideology of anti-fat attitudes. *Journal of Applied Social Psychology, 20*, 227–243.

Crandall, C. S., & Eshleman, A. (2003). A justification suppression model of the expression and experience of prejudice. *Psychological Bulletin, 129*, 414–446.

Crocker, J., Cornwell, B., & Major, B. (1993). The stigma of overweight: Affective consequences of attributional ambiguity. *Journal of Personality and Social Psychology, 60,* 218–228.

Crocker, J., & Major, B. (1989). Social stigma and self-esteem: The self-protective properties of stigma. *Psychological Review, 96,* 608–663.

Crocker, J., Major, B., & Steele, C. (1998). Social stigma. In D. Gilbert, S. Fiske, & G. Lindzey (Eds.), *Handbook of social psychology* (4th ed., pp. 504–553). Boston: McGraw-Hill.

Crosby, F., Bromley, S., & Saxe, L. (1980). Recent unobtrusive studies of black and white discrimination and prejudice: A literature review. *Psychological Bulletin, 87,* 546–563.

Crosby, F. J. (1984). The denial of personal discrimination. *American Behavioral Scientist, 27,* 371–386.

Crosby, F. J., Cordova, D. I., & Jaskar, K. (1994). On the failure to see oneself as disadvantaged: Cognitive and emotional components. In M. A. Hogg, & D. Abrams (Eds.), *Group motivation: social psychological perspectives* (pp. 87–104). New York: Harvester Wheatsheaf.

Cuddy, A. J. C., Fiske, S. T., & Glick, P. (2008). Warmth and competence as universal dimensions of social perception: The stereotype content model and the BIAS map. *Advances in Experimental Social Psychology, 40,* 61–149.

Davis, F. (1961). Deviance disavowal: The management of strained interaction by the visibly handicapped. *Social Problems, 9,* 120–132.

DeJong, W. (1980). The stigma of obesity: The consequences of naive assumptions concerning the causes of physical deviance. *Journal of Health and Social Behavior, 21,* 75–87.

Devine, P. G. (1989). Stereotypes and prejudice: Their automatic and controlled components. *Journal of Personality and Social Psychology, 56,* 5–18.

Devine, P. G., Evett, S. R., & Vasquez-Suson, K. A. (1996). Exploring the interpersonal dynamics of intergroup contact. In R. M. Sorrentino & E. T. Higgins (Eds.), *Handbook of motivation and cognition: Vol. 3. The interpersonal context* (pp. 423–464). New York Guilford Press.

Devine, P. G., Plant, E. A., Amodio, D. M., Harmon-Jones, E., & Vance, S. L. (2002). The regulation of explicit and implicit race bias: The role of motivations to respond without prejudice. *Journal of Personality and Social Psychology, 82,* 835–848.

Dipboye, R. L., & Collella, A. (2005). *Discrimination at work: The psychological and organizational bases.* Mahwah, NJ: Lawrence Erlbaum Associates.

Ellemers, N., Spears, R., & Doosje, B. (2002). Self and social identity. *Annual Review of Psychology, 53,* 161–186.

Fiske, S. T. (2004). *Social beings: a core motives approach to social psychology.* Hoboken, NJ: Wiley.

Fiske, S. T., & Neuberg, S. L. (1990). A continuum of impression formation, from category-based to individuating processes: Influences of information and motivation on attention and interpretation. *Advances in Experimental Social Psychology, 23,* 1–74.

Frey, F. E., & Tropp, L. R. (2006). Being seen as individuals versus as group members: Extending research on metaperception to intergroup contexts. *Personality and Social Psychology Review, 10,* 265–280.

Frijda, N. H. (1986). *The emotions.* Cambridge, England: Cambridge University Press.

Gaertner, S. L., & Dovidio, J. F. (1986). The aversive form of racism. In J. F. Dovidio & S. L. Gaertner (Eds.), *Prejudice, discrimination and racism: Theory and research.* (pp. 61–89). Orlando, FL: Academic Press.

Gaertner, S. L., Dovidio, J. F., Banker, B. S., Houlette, M., Johnson, K. M., & McGlynn, E. A. (2000). Reducing intergroup conflict: From superordinate goals to decategorization, recategorization, and mutual differentiation, *Group Dynamics: Theory Research and Practice, 4,* 98–114.

Glick, P., & Fiske, S. T. (1997). Hostile and benevolent sexism: Measuring ambivalent sexist attitudes toward women. *Psychology of Women Quarterly, 21,* 119–135.

Gluszek, A., & Dovidio, J. F. (2010). The way they speak: A social psychological perspective on the stigma of nonnative accents in communication. *Personality and Social Psychology Review, 14,* 214–237.

Goffman, E. (1963). *Stigma: Notes on the management of spoiled identity.* New York: Prentice Hall.

Griffith, K. H., & Hebl, M. R. (2002). The disclosure dilemma for gay men and lesbians: "Coming out" at work. *Journal of Applied Psychology, 87,* 1191–1199.

Gupta, V. K., Turban, D. B., & Bhawe, N. M. (2008). The effect of stereotype activation on entrepreneurial intentions. *Journal of Applied Psychology, 93*(5), 1053–1061.

Haddock, G., Zanna, M. P., & Esses, V. M. (1993). Assessing the structure of prejudicial attitudes: The case of attitudes toward homosexuals. *Journal of Personality and Social Psychology, 65,* 1105–1118.

Harrison, D. A., & Sin, H-S. 2005. What is diversity and how should it be measured? In A. M. Konrad, P. Prasad, & J. K. Pringle (Eds.), *Handbook of workplace diversity* (pp. 191–216). Thousand Oaks, CA: Sage Publications.

Hebl, M. (1995). Gender bias in leader selection. *Teaching of Psychology, 22,* 186–188.

Hebl, M., & Dovidio, J. F. (2005). Promoting the "social" in the examination of social stigmas. *Personality and Social Psychology Review, 9,* 156–182.

Hebl, M., Dovidio, J. F., Richeson, J. A., Shelton, J. N., Gaertner, S. L., & Kawakami, K. (2008). Interpretation of interaction: Responsiveness to verbal and nonverbal cues. In S. Demoulin, J. P. Leyens, & J. F. Dovidio (Eds.), *Intergroup misunderstandings: Impact of divergent social |realities* (pp. 101–116). New York: Psychology Press.

Hebl, M., Foster, J. B., Mannix, L. M., & Dovidio, J. F. (2002). Formal and interpersonal discrimination: A field study of bias toward homosexual applicants. *Personality and Social Psychology Bulletin, 28,* 815–825.

Hebl, M., & Kleck, R. E. (2002). Acknowledging one's stigma in the interview setting: Effective strategy or liability? *Journal of Applied Social Psychology, 32,* 223–249.

Hebl, M., & Kleck, R. E. (2000). The social consequences of physical disability. In R. E. Kleck, T. F. Heatherton, J. Hull, & M. Hebl (Eds.), *The social psychology of stigma* (pp. 419–440). New York: Guilford Publications, Inc.

Hebl, M., King, E., & Lin, J. (2004). The swimsuit becomes us all: Ethnicity, gender, and vulnerability to self-objectification. *Personality and Social Psychology Bulletin, 30,* 1322–1331.

Hebl, M. R., King, E. B., Glick, P., Kazama, S., & Singletary, S. (2007). Hostile and benevolent reactions toward pregnant women: Complementary interpersonal punishments and rewards that maintain traditional roles. *Journal of Applied Psychology, 92,* 1499–1511.

Hebl, M. R., King, E. B., & Perkins, A. (2009). Ethnic differences in the stigma of obesity: Identification and engagement with a thin ideal. *Journal of Experimental Social Psychology, 45,* 1165–1172.

Hebl, M. R., Tickle, J., & Heatherton, T. F. (2000). Awkward moments in interactions between nonstigmatized and stigmatized individuals. In T. F. Heatherton, R. E. Kleck, M. R. Hebl, & J. G. Hull (Eds.), *The social psychology of stigma* (pp. 273–306). New York: The Guilford Press.

Jones, E. E., Farina, A., Hastorf, A. H., Markus, H., Miller, D. T., & Scott, R. (1984). *Social stigma: The psychology of marked relationships.* New York: W. H. Freeman.

Jost, J. T., & Banaji, M. R. (1994). The role of stereotyping in system justification and the production of false consciousness. *British Journal of Social Psychology, 33,* 1–27.

Jost, J. T., & Major, B. (Eds.) (2001). *The psychology of legitimacy: Emerging perspectives on ideology, justice, and intergroup relations.* New York: Cambridge University Press.

Jost, J. T., Pelham, B. W., & Carvallo, M. R. (2002). Non-conscious forms of system justification: Implicit and behavioral preferences for higher status groups. *Journal of Experimental Social Psychology, 83,* 586–602.

Judge, T., & Cable, D. (2011). When it comes to pay, do the thin win? The effect of weight on pay for men and women. *Journal of Applied Psychology, 96,* 95–112.

Kaiser, C. R., & Miller, C. T. (2001). Stop complaining! The social costs of making attributions to discrimination. *Personality and Social Psychology Bulletin, 27,* 254.

King, E., Shapiro, J. L., Hebl, M., Singletary, S., & Turner, S. (2006). The stigma of obesity in customer service: A mechanism for remediation and bottom-line consequences of interpersonal discrimination. *Journal of Applied Psychology, 91,* 579–593.

King, E. B., Botsford, W. E., Hebl, M., Kazama, S., Dawson, J., & Perkins, A., Dawson, J. (in press). Benevolent sexism at work: Gender differences in the distribution of challenging developmental experiences. *Journal of Management.*

King, E. B., & Cortina, J. M. (2010). The social and economic imperative of lesbian, gay, bisexual, and transgendered supportive organizational policies. *Industrial and Organizational Psychology, 3,* 69–78. DOI: 10.1111/j.1754-434.2009.01201.x

King, E. B., Mohr, J., Peddie, C., Kendra, M., & Jones, K. (2010). *Everyday identity management of lesbian, gay, and bisexual newcomers.* Unpublished manuscript, George Mason University.

King, E. B., Reilly, C., & Hebl, M. (2008). The best and worst of times: Dual perspectives of "coming out" in the workplace. *Group and Organization Management, 33,* 566–601.

King, K. C., Hyde, J. S., Showers, C. J., & Buswell, B. N. (1999). Gender differences in self-esteem: A meta-analysis. *Psychological Bulletin, 125,* 470–500.

Laing, R. D., Phillipson, H., & Lee, A. R. (1966). *Interpersonal perception.* London: Tavistock.

Landy, F. J. (2008). Stereotypes, bias, and personnel decisions: Strange and stranger. *Industrial and Organizational Psychology: Perspectives on Science and Practice, 4,* 379–392.

Law, C. L., Martinez, L. R., Ruggs, E. N., & Hebl, M. (in press). Trans-parency in the workplace: How the experiences of transsexual employees can be improved. *Journal of Vocational Behavior.*

Lerner, M., & Simmons, C.H. (1966). Observer's reaction to the "innocent victim": Compassion or rejection? *Journal of Personality and Social Psychology, 4,* 2.

Mackie, D. M., Devos, T., & Smith, E. R. (2000). Intergroup emotions: Explaining offensive action tendencies in an intergroup context. *Journal of Personality and Social Psychology, 79,* 602–616.

Macrae, C. N., Bodenhausen, G. V., Milne, A. B., & Jetten, J. (1994). Out of mind but back in sight: Stereotypes on the rebound. *Journal of Personality and Social Psychology, 67,* 808–817.

Madera, J. M., Hebl, M. R., & Martin, R. C. (2009). Gender and letters of recommendation for academia: Agentic and communal differences. *Journal of Applied Psychology, 94,* 1591–1599.

Major, B., & Gramzow, R. H. (1999). Abortion as stigma: Cognitive and emotional implications of concealment. *Journal of Personality and Social Psychology, 77,* 735–745.

Major, B., Quinton, W. J., & Schmader, T. (2003). Attributions to discrimination and self-esteem: Impact of group identification and situational ambiguity. *Journal of Experimental Social Psychology, 39,* 220–231.

Major, B., & Schmader, T. (1998). Coping with stigma through psychological disengagement. In J. K. Swim & C. Stangor (Eds.), *Prejudice. The target's perspective* (pp. 219–241). San Diego, CA: Academic Press.

Martell, R. F., Lane, D. M., & Emrich, C. (1996). Male-female differences: A computer simulation. *American Psychologist, 51,* 157–158.

Masuda, A., Price, M., Anderson, P. L., Schmertz, S. K., & Calamaras, M. R. (2009). The role of psychological flexibility in mental health stigma and psychological distress for the stigmatizer. *Journal of Social and Clinical Psychology, 28,* 1244–1262.

Mayfield, W. (2001). The development of an internalized homonegativity inventory for gay men. *Journal of Homosexuality, 41,* 53–76.

Mendes, W. B., Blascovich, J., Lickel, B. & Hunter, S. (2002). Challenge and threat during social interactions with White and Black men. *Personality and Social Psychology Bulletin, 28,* 939–952.

Mendoza-Denton, R., Downey, G., Purdie, V., Davis, A., & Pietrzak, J. (2002). Sensitivity to status-based rejection: Implications for African American students' college experience. *Journal of Personality & Social Psychology, 83,* 896–918.

Miller, C. T., & Myers, A. M. (1998). Compensating for prejudice: How heavyweight people (and others) control outcomes despite prejudice. In J. K. Swim & C. Stangor (Eds.), *Prejudice: The target's perspective* (pp. 191–218). San Diego, CA: Academic Press.

Miller, C. T., Rothblum, E. D., Felicio, D. M., & Brand, P. A. (1995). Compensating for stigma: Obese and nonobese women's reactions to being visible. *Personality and Social Psychology Bulletin, 21,* 1093–1106.

Neuberg, S. L., Smith, D. M., & Asher, T. (2000). Why people stigmatize: Toward a biocultural framework. In T. F. Heatherton, R. E. Kleck, M. R. Hebl, & J. G. Hull (Eds.), *The social psychology of stigma* (p. 31–61). New York: The Guilford Press.

Neuberg, S. L., Smith, D. M., Hoffman, J. C., & Russell, F. J. (1994). When we observe stigmatized and "normal" individuals interacting: stigma by association. *Personality and Social Psychology Bulletin, 20,* 196–209.

Nguyen, H. D., & Ryan, A. M. (2008). Does stereotype threat affect test performance of minorities and women? A meta-analysis of experimental evidence. *Journal of Applied Psychology, 93,* 1314–1334.

Oskamp, S. (2000). Multiple paths to reducing prejudice and discrimination. In S. Oskamp (Ed.) *Reducing prejudice and discrimination* (pp. 1–19). Mahwah, NJ: Lawrence Erlbaum.

Oyserman, D., & Swim, J. K. (2001). Stigma: An insider's view. *Journal of Social Issues, 57,* 1–14.

Patterson, M. L. (1982). A sequential functional model of nonverbal exchange. *Psychological Review, 89,* 231–249.

Pettigrew, T., & Tropp, M. (2000). Does intergroup contact reduce prejudice? Recent meta-analytic findings. In S. Oskamp (Ed.), *Reducing prejudice and discrimination* (pp. 93–114). Mahwah, NJ: Lawrence Erlbaum.

Pettigrew, T. F. (1998). Intergroup contact theory. *Annual Review of Psychology, 49,* 65–85.

Pettigrew, T. F., & Tropp, L. R. (2006). A meta-analytic test of intergroup contact theory. *Journal of Personality and Social Psychology, 90,* 751–783.

Phinney, J. S. (1996). Understanding ethnic diversity: The role of ethnic identity. *American Behavioral Scientist, 40,* 143–152.

Pinel, E. C. (1999). Stigma consciousness: The psychological legacy of social stereotypes. *Journal of Personality and Social Psychology, 76,* 114–128.

Ragins, B. R., Singh, R., & Cornwell, J. M. (2007). Making the invisible visible: Fear and disclosure of sexual orientation at work. *Journal of Applied Psychology, 92,* 1103–1118.

Richeson, J. A., & Ambady, N. (2001a). When roles reverse: Stigma, status, and self-evaluation. *Journal of Applied Social Psychology, 31,* 1350–1378.

Richeson, J. A., & Ambady, N. (2001b). Who's in charge? Effects of situational roles on gender bias. *Sex Roles, 44,* 493–512.

Roberts, L. M. (2005). Changing faces: Professional image construction in diverse organizational settings. *Academy of Management Review, 30,* 685–711.

Rosenblatt, A., Greenberg, J., Solomon, S., Pyszczynski, T., & Lyon, D. (1989). Evidence for terror management theory I. The effects of mortality salience on reactions to those who violate or uphold cultural values. *Journal of Personality and Social Psychology, 57,* 681–690.

Rudman, L. A., & Glick, P. (2001). Prescriptive gender stereotypes and backlash toward agentic women. *Journal of Social Issues, 57,* 743–762.

Rudolph, C. W., Wells, C. L., Weller, M. D., & Baltes, B. B. (2009). A meta-analysis of empirical studies of weight-based biased in the workplace. *Journal of Vocational Behavior, 74,* 1–10.

Rüsch, N., Corrigan, P. W., Todd, A. R., & Bodenhausen, G. V. (2011). Automatic stereotyping against people with schizophrenia, schizoaffective and affective disorders. *Psychiatry Research, 186*(1), 34–39.

Santuzzi, A. M., & Ruscher, J. B. (2002). Stigma salience and paranoid social cognition: Understanding variability in metaperceptions among individuals with recently-acquired stigma. *Social Cognition, 20,* 171–197.

Schaerer, E. (2010). Intragroup discrimination in the workplace: The case for "race plus." *Harvard Civil Rights-Civil Liberties Law Review, 186,* 34–51.

Schein, V. E. (2001). A global look at psychological progress in management. *Journal of Social Issues, 57,* 675–688.

Semyonov, M., Raijman, R., & Yom-Tov, A. (2002). Labor market competition, perceived threat, and endorsement of economic discrimination against foreign workers in Israel. *Social Problems, 49,* 416–431.

Shapiro, J. R., King, E. B., & Quinones, M. A.. (2007). Expectations of obese trainees: How stigmatized trainee characteristics influence training effectiveness. *Journal of Applied Psychology, 92,* 239–249.

Shapiro, J. R., & Neuberg, S. L. (2007). From stereotype threat to stereotype threats: Implications of a multi-threat framework for causes, moderators, mediators, consequences, and interventions. *Personality and Social Psychology Review, 11,* 107–130.

Shelton, J. N., & Richeson, J. A. (2006). Interracial interactions: A relational approach. In M. P. Zanna (Ed.), *Advances in experimental social psychology* (Vol. 38, pp. 121–181). San Diego, CA: Academic Press.

Shelton, J. N., Richeson, J. A., Salvatore, J., & Trawalter, S. (2005). Ironic effects of racial bias during interracial interactions. *Psychological Science, 16,* 397–402.

Shrauger, S., & Schoeneman, T. J. (1979). Symbolic interactionist view of self-concept: Through the looking glass darkly. *Psychological Bulletin, 86,* 549–573.

Singletary, S. L., & Hebl, M. (2009). Compensatory strategies for reducing interpersonal discrimination: The effectiveness of acknowledgments, increased positivity, and individuating information. *Journal of Applied Psychology, 94,* 797–805.

Singletary, S. L. B., & Hebl, M. (2010). *The impact of formal and interpersonal discrimination on performance.* Unpublished manuscript, Rice University.

Smart, L., & Wegner, D. M. (1999). Covering up what can't be seen: Concealable stigma and mental control. *Journal of Personality and Social Psychology, 77,* 474–486.

Smith, E. R., & Henry, S. (1996). An in-group becomes part of the self: Response time evidence. *Personality and Social Psychology Bulletin, 22,* 635–642.

Snyder, M. (1992). Motivational foundations of behavioral confirmation. In M. P. Zanna (Ed.), *Advances in experimental social psychology* (Vol. 25, pp. 67–114). San Diego, CA: Academic Press.

Snyder, M. L., Kleck, R. E., Strenta, A., & Mentzer, S. J. (1979). Avoidance of the handicapped: An attributional ambiguity analysis. *Journal of Personality and Social Psychology, 37,* 2297–2306.

Steele, C. (1992, April). Race and the schooling of Black Americans. *The Atlantic Monthly, 269,* 68–78.

Steele, C. M. (1997). A threat in the air: How stereotypes shape the intellectual identities and performance of women and African Americans. *American Psychologist, 52,* 613–629.

Steele, C. M., & Aronson, J. (1995). Stereotype threat and the intellectual performance of African Americans. *Journal of Personality and Social Psychology, 69,* 797–811.

Stewart, K., King, E. B., Botsford, W., Gilrane, V., Hylton, K., & Jones, K. (2010). *A dark side of seemingly civil behavior? Consequences of benevolent sexism.* Unpublished manuscript, George Mason University.

Sue, D. W., Capodilupo, C. M., Torino, G. C., Bucceri, J. M., Holder, A. M. B., Nadal, K. L., & Esquilin, M. (2007). Racial microaggressions in everyday life: Implications for clinical practice. *American Psychologist, 62,* 271–286.

Swann, W. B., & Ely, R. J. (1984). A battle of wills: Self-verification versus behavioral confirmation. *Journal of Personality and Social Psychology, 46,* 1287–1302.

Swim, J. K., Aiken, K. J., Hall, U. S., & Hunter, B. A. (1995). Sexism and racism: Old-fashioned and modern prejudices. *Journal of Personality and Social Psychology, 68,* 199–214.

Swim, J. K., & Stangor, C. (Eds.). (1998). *Prejudice: The target's perspective.* San Diego, CA: Academic Press.

Tesser, A. (2000). On the confluence of self-esteem maintenance mechanisms. *Personality and Social Psychology Review, 4,* 290–299.

Vorauer, J., Hunter, A. J., Main, K. J., & Roy, S. (2000). Meta-stereotype activation: Evidence from indirect measures of specific evaluative concerns experienced by members of dominant groups in intergroup interaction. *Journal of Personality and Social Psychology, 78,* 690–707.

Vorauer, J. D., & Kumhyr, S. M. (2001). Is this about you or me? Self- versus other-directed judgments and feelings in response to intergroup interaction. *Personality and Social Psychology Bulletin, 27,* 706–719.

Vorauer,, J., Main, K. J., & O'Connell, G. B. (1998). How do individuals expect to be viewed by members of lower status groups? Content and implications of meta-stereotypes. *Journal of Personality and Social Psychology, 75,* 917–937.

Weiner, B. (1995). *Judgments of responsibility: A theory of social conduct.* New York: The Guilford Press.

Weiner, B., Perry, R. P., & Magnusson, J. (1988). An attributional analysis of reactions to stigmas. *Journal of Personality and Social Psychology, 55,* 738–748.

CHAPTER
8
Ideology: An Invisible yet Potent Dimension of Diversity

Laurie T. O'Brien *and* Patricia N. Gilbert

Abstract

Recently, ideology has emerged as an important topic of inquiry among social, personality, and political psychologists as research has shown a link between people's ideological belief systems and their attitudes toward, and evaluations of, others. This chapter will examine theory and research concerning the structure, content, and functions of ideological beliefs. In addition, the effects of such beliefs on diversity attitudes and intergroup relations will be considered. Directions for future research on ideology or worldview as an attribute of diversity will be offered.

Key Words: ideology, diversity

In the past two decades, there has been an increased interest in the study of ideology. Much of this interest was sparked by several influential papers published in the early 1990s highlighting the role of ideology in the maintenance of group-based inequality (e.g., Crandall, 1994; Jost & Banaji, 1994; Major, 1994, Pratto, Sidanius, Stallworth, & Malle, 1994). In the present chapter, we present key advances in the study of ideology with a focus on the ways in which ideology can help us to better understand issues of diversity in the workplace.

There are several key ways in which a focus on ideology can help us to better understand issues of diversity in the workplace. First, ideology can shed light on why people choose the careers they do and how group membership (e.g., gender, race) might shape those career choices (Sidanius, van Laar, Levin, & Sinclair, 2003; van Laar, Sidanius, Rabinowitz, & Sinclair, 1999). It can also help us to understand why people from different backgrounds might feel entitled to different salaries (O'Brien & Major, 2009; O'Brien, Major, & Gilbert, 2012).

Also, ideology can influence when people who experience negative work-related outcomes such as the failure to obtain a desired job or promotion will blame discrimination (Major, Gramzow, et al., 2002). Knowing an individual's ideological beliefs can also help us to predict his or her emotional responses to discrimination in the workplace (e.g., Foster, Sloto, & Ruby, 2006; Major, Kaiser, O'Brien, & McCoy, 2007). Finally, and perhaps most importantly, ideology can aid our comprehension of how people treat their colleagues from different ethnic and gender backgrounds and can suggest ways for helping people from diverse backgrounds work together more cooperatively and productively (e.g., Plaut, Thomas, & Goren, 2009).

The present chapter is divided into two sections. In the first section, we examine two different classes of ideology, distinguishing between ideologies that maintain the status hierarchy and ideologies that attenuate the status hierarchy, and describe several of the most commonly studied ideologies. In this first section, we also discuss the origins of individual differences in endorsement of ideology, with an emphasis on the psychological functions that ideology performs for the individual. We end the first section by describing research on the psychological structure of ideology.

In the second section of the chapter, we examine the implications of ideology for the self, intergroup relations, and diversity attitudes. With regards to the self, we discuss the implications of ideology for psychological well-being, vocational choice, entitlement to pay, and attributions to discrimination. Our analysis of the impact of ideology on intergroup relations stresses the importance of understanding how the group status of both the perceiver and the target affects the relationship between ideology and group-based evaluations. Finally, we end by offering evidence that ideology affects important diversity attitudes, including attitudes toward affirmative action, immigration, and work roles for women.

Part 1: Classes, origins, and structure of ideologies

For the purposes of the present chapter, we define *ideology* as an integrated system of beliefs that describes the nature of the social world and how it operates (see Jost, Federico, & Napier, 2009; Major et al., 2007). Ideological beliefs have both prescriptive and descriptive elements. That is, they both describe how the social world *should* operate and how it *does* operate. Ideologies serve a justification function in that they defend or uphold a particular worldview as righteous and good. Ideologies also have motivational force in that people are motivated to perceive the world in ways that reinforce the truthfulness and validity of their ideology.

The present chapter focuses on ideologies pervasive in Western cultures such as the Protestant Work Ethic (PWE; e.g., Katz & Hass, 1988; Mirels & Garrett, 1971; Weber, 1904–1905/1958) and the Belief in Just World (BJW; Furnham, 2003; Lerner, 1980; Rubin & Peplau, 1975).[1] Ideologies are culturally bound, and the cultural derivation of particular ideologies is a complex topic that is beyond the scope of this chapter. Ideologies such as PWE and BJW are ubiquitous in Western culture and pervade cultural artifacts such as books, movies, and other forms of media. Moreover, exposure to these cultural artifacts can activate a particular ideology, making them more salient in the minds of individuals. Once activated, these ideologies can color perception, affect, and behavior (e.g., Gutierrez & Unzueta, 2010; Katz & Hass, 1988; McCoy & Major, 2007; O'Brien & Major, 2009; Quinn & Crocker, 1999; Verkuyten, 2005; Wellman, Czopp, & Geers, 2009). Although cultural ideologies are a consensually shared form of knowledge (Jost et al., 2009), it is important to recognize that there are often individual differences in the extent to which individuals within a culture endorse a particular ideology (e.g., Furnham, 2003; Furnham & Proctor, 1989; Mirels & Garrett, 1971). Just as situational cues that activate an ideology can lead to situational differences in perception, affect, and behavior, individual differences in the endorsement of an ideology can lead to individual differences in perception, affect, and behavior (e.g., Katz & Hass, 1988; Major et al., 2002, 2007; Napier & Jost, 2008).

Two classes of ideologies

Most ideologies can be categorized into one of two classes—hierarchy-enhancing ideologies and hierarchy-attenuating ideologies (Sidanius & Pratto, 1999). Hierarchy-enhancing ideologies are ideologies that justify group-based inequality such as sexism, racism, ageism, and heterosexism. In contrast, hierarchy-attenuating ideologies are ideologies that justify social equality. To date, there has been more research conducted on hierarchy-enhancing ideologies, and so we discuss this class of ideologies first.

Hierarchy-enhancing ideologies. Human societies are structured according to group-based hierarchies, with some groups having greater access to material goods (e.g., land, money, and food) and psychological goods (e.g., political authority, power, and respect) than other groups (Sidanius & Pratto, 1999). Members of high status groups have a vested interest in maintaining this unequal distribution. In addition, people have an inherent motive to justify the status quo and current social system (Eidelman, Crandall, & Pattershall, 2009; Jost & Banaji, 1994; Lerner, 1980). As a result, ideologies develop that reinforce and enhance the current system of inequality. These ideologies are alternately called hierarchy-enhancing ideologies (Sidanius & Pratto, 1999), system-justifying ideologies (Jost & Banaji, 1994), and status-legitimizing ideologies (Major et al., 2002), depending upon one's theoretical perspective.[2] Other researchers eschew the word *ideology* altogether and prefer to refer to these belief systems as *worldviews* (e.g., Kaiser & Pratt-Hyatt, 2009; Koltko-Rivera, 2004).

Political conservatism is a classic example of a hierarchy-enhancing, system-justifying ideology (Jost, Glaser, Kruglanski, & Sulloway, 2003).

Political conservatism emphasizes the status quo and social stability, religion, the natural inequality of humans, liberty, and the sanctity of private property (Kerlinger, 1984, p. 17). According to Jost and colleagues, the ideological core of conservatism is resistance to change and justification of inequality (Jost et al., 2003). Political conservatism is related to prejudice against Blacks, Arabs, Asians, gay men, lesbian women, people of low socioeconomic status, and heavyset people (e.g., Crandall, 1994; Echebarria-Echabe & Guede, 2007; Lambert & Chasteen, 1997; Morrison & Morrison, 2002; Nail, Harton, & Decker, 2003; Reyna, Henry, Korfmacher, & Tucker, 2006; Son Hing, Chung-Yan, Hamilton, & Zanna, 2008).

The BJW is another often-studied hierarchy-enhancing ideology (e.g., Lerner, 1980; Rubin & Peplau, 1975). People who believe in a just world believe that good people are rewarded and bad people are punished. Thus, BJW implies that people in high status groups are being rewarded for their goodness whereas people in low status groups are being punished for their wickedness. Related to BJW, the PWE is a belief system that holds that hard work is rewarded with success (Mirels & Darland, 1990; Mirels & Garrett, 1971). BJW and PWE are depicted in cultural stories such as *The Little Engine that Could*, the prolific works of authors such as Horatio Alger, and movies such as *The Pursuit of Happiness*. While at times people may draw inspiration and strength from these messages (Dalbert, 2001; Tomaka & Blascovich, 1994), the flip side of the coin is that these messages imply that people and groups who have lower status in society deserve their position (e.g., Jost & Banaji, 1994). Thus it is not surprising that BJW and PWE are correlated with prejudice towards African Americans, women, heavyset people, people of low socioeconomic status, unemployed people, welfare recipients, gay men, and lesbian women (Biernat, Vescio, Theno, & Crandall, 1996; Christopher & Jones, 2004; Christopher & Mull, 2006; Crandall, 1994; Furnham, 1982a, 1982b, 1985; Katz & Hass, 1988; MacDonald, 1972; Malcomnson, Christopher, Franzen, & Keyes, 2006; Pratto, Sidanius, Stallworth, & Malle, 1994; Rubin & Peplau, 1975; Swim, Aikin, Hall, & Hunter, 1995).

The belief in meritocracy is another hierarchy-enhancing ideology that is closely related to PWE and BJW (Pratto, Sidanius, Stallworth, & Malle, 1994; Major et al., 2007). The belief in meritocracy is a belief that outcomes are distributed according to deservingness and that deservingness is a function of both hard work and talent (e.g., Major et al., 2007; McCoy & Major, 2007). The belief in meritocracy is associated with political conservatism, racist attitudes, and the denial of pervasive forms of racism (O'Brien et al., 2009; Son Hing et al., 2011). Furthermore, when individuals who strongly endorse meritocratic beliefs are presented with strong evidence of pervasive oppression, this worldview violation leads to decrements in self-esteem (Foster & Tsarfati, 2005; Foster et al., 2006; Major et al., 2007).

Recent research, however, suggests that there is an important distinction between descriptive and prescriptive meritocracy beliefs (Son Hing et al., 2011). People who endorse descriptive meritocracy beliefs believe that the current distribution of outcomes in society is meritocratic. In contrast, people who endorse prescriptive meritocracy beliefs believe that outcomes in society **should** be determined on the basis of merit. Although endorsement of descriptive and prescriptive meritocracy beliefs is modestly correlated, Son Hing and colleagues (2011) present compelling evidence that only descriptive meritocracy beliefs function in a hierarchy-enhancing capacity.

In recent years, scholars have also begun to investigate two additional hierarchy-enhancing ideologies—colorblindness (Apfelbaum, Sommers, & Norton, 2008; Gutierrez & Unzueta, 2010; Knowles et al., 2009; Norton, Sommers, Apfelbaum, Pura, & Ariely, 2006; Plaut et al., 2009; Richeson & Nussbaum, 2004; Ryan et al., 2007; Wolsko, Park, Judd, & Wittenbrink, 2000) and assimilationism (Sellers, Smith, Shelton, Rowley, & Chavous, 1998; Verkuyten, 2005; Wolsko et al., 2000). Although some scholars use the terms *colorblindness* and *assimilationism* interchangeably, a distinction between the two ideologies can be made. Whereas colorblindness is an ideology that emphasizes disregarding ethnic and racial categories and treating each person as a unique individual, assimilationism is more extreme in that it advocates that ethnic minorities abandon their cultural identity and conform to the dominant group's culture (Purdie-Vaughns, Steele, Davies, Ditlmann, & Crosby, 2008; Verkuyten, 2005). As with other hierarchy-enhancing ideologies, for White Americans, colorblindness and assimilationism are both related to increased levels of prejudice towards ethnic minority groups (Wolsko, Park, & Judd, 2006). Among minorities, the relationship between assimilationist ideologies and intergroup attitudes is more complicated; we return to this topic later in the chapter (Wolsko et al., 2006).

Hierarchy-attenuating ideologies. Although somewhat less studied than hierarchy-enhancing ideologies, there is another class of ideologies that advocate social equality. These ideologies promote the equal distribution of material and social goods and delegitimize social hierarchies. Political liberalism, which emphasizes individual freedom, participatory democracy, tolerance, equality, and positive government action to remedy social problems, is a classic example of a hierarchy-attenuating ideology (Kerlinger, 1984). Traditionally, egalitarianism (also known as humanitarianism; Katz & Hass, 1988) is one of the most frequently studied hierarchy-attenuating ideologies. Egalitarianism emphasizes adherence to democratic ideals of equality, social justice, and concern for other people's well-being (Katz & Hass, 1988).

More recently, there have been a number of papers published on multiculturalism as a hierarchy-attenuating ideology. Multiculturalism "promotes the value of diversity as a core principle and insists that all cultural groups be treated with respect and as equals" (Fowers & Richardson, 1996, p. 609). People who endorse egalitarianism and multiculturalism have more positive attitudes toward many traditionally oppressed groups, including Blacks, women, heavyset people, gay people, and other low status groups (e.g., Biernat et al., 1996; Case, Fishbein, & Ritchey, 2008; Glover, 1994; Katz & Hass, 1988; Monteith & Walters, 1998; Plant & Devine, 1998; Plant, Devine, & Peruche, 2010; Swim et al., 1995; Verkuyten, 2005).

Whereas egalitarianism and multiculturalism are focused on promoting equality and diversity for their own sake, other hierarchy-attenuating ideologies are more focused on promoting the recognition of the existence of pervasive, group-based oppression (e.g., Major et al., 2007; Sellers et al., 1998; Townsend, Major, Sawyer, & Mendes, 2010). We refer to these ideologies here as "oppositional" ideologies and they constitute a subclass of hierarchy-attenuating ideologies. For example, Major and colleagues discuss the rejection of meritocratic ideology as an alternative ideology that explains social status as a product of bias, discrimination, and/or favoritism (Major et al., 2007; see also Townsend, Major, Sawyer, & Mendes, 2010). Furthermore, they show that individuals who reject meritocratic ideology experience threat in response to information that challenges their worldview. More specifically, individuals who rejected meritocratic ideology showed a larger threat response when exposed to information that discrimination was rare as compared to when they were exposed to information that discrimination was pervasive (Major et al., 2007; see also Townsend et al., 2010).

Sellers and colleagues (1998) describe another oppositional ideology that they refer to as "oppressed minority ideology." This ideology emphasizes the similarities between the oppression of African Americans and other groups. "For some individuals, other oppressed groups with whom they identify as minority may consist of women, gay men, and lesbians; others may define minorities as only consisting of ethnic groups of color" (Sellers et al., 1998, p. 28). Regardless of which groups are considered fellow oppressed groups, individuals who endorse the oppressed minority ideology perceive the inequality of oppressed groups as unjust and advocate coalition building as the most appropriate strategy for achieving social equality. The nationalist ideology described by Sellers and colleagues (1998) also constitutes an oppositional ideology in that it recognizes the oppressed status of African Americans; however, it is distinct from oppressed minority ideology. Rather than focusing on the commonalities between oppressed groups, nationalist ideology stresses the uniqueness of Black people.

Although they have not traditionally been described as ideologies, there are elements of politicized collective identity (e.g., Simon & Klandermans, 2001) and group consciousness (e.g., Gurin, 1985) that bear marked similarity to the concept of oppositional ideology. Both group consciousness and politicized collective identity have been described as special forms of group identity that include a belief that the in-group's status is illegitimate and a motivation to use collective action to achieve political change (Gurin, 1985; Gurin & Townsend, 1986; Major, Quinton, et al., 2002; Simon & Klandermans, 2001). Thus, both group consciousness and politicized collective identity are similar to ideologies in that they include beliefs about how the social world does and should operate and that they defend or uphold a particular worldview as righteous. Group consciousness and politicized collective identity are distinct from ideologies, however, in their emphasis on identification as a member of a particular in-group.

We believe that the distinction between hierarchy-enhancing and hierarchy-attenuating ideologies is useful because it sheds light on the motivations that people have for endorsing a particular ideology. Thus, the distinction between hierarchy-enhancing and hierarchy-attenuating ideologies helps to predict who will endorse a particular ideology and in which situations he or she will endorse it. However, it is important to recognize that the distinction between these two classes of ideologies is not absolute. As we will discuss later, the same ideology may function at times in a hierarchy-enhancing capacity and at other times in a hierarchy-attenuating capacity.

Psychological origins and functions of ideologies

Like stereotypes, ideologies are social shared knowledge structures (Jost, Federico, & Napier, 2009). In this next section, we consider the processes by which ideologies come to be internalized by the individual and how the internalization of particular ideologies can be fueled by the psychological functions that ideologies serve. Undoubtedly, socialization practices are an important factor influencing the internalization of particular ideologies. Parents and other authority figures socialize children from a young age to adopt particular ideologies (Altemeyer, 1981, 1988, 1996; Rohan & Zanna, 1996; Sidanius & Ekehammar, 1979; Sidanius & Pratto, 1999). However, socialization processes do not offer a complete explanation of the psychological origins of ideology (Jost et al., 2003; Sidanius & Pratto, 1999).

Whereas socialization perspectives focus on the roles of parents and other authority figures in determining the origins of individual differences in ideology, functional perspectives on the origins of ideology focus on the psychological needs that are met by the adoption of particular ideologies. Perhaps one of the most straightforward functions that ideologies serve for the individual is a value-expressive function (Davey et al., 1999; Katz & Benjamin, 1960; Rokeach, 1973). Ideologies can also serve instrumental functions by prescribing particular paths to obtaining desired outcomes and epistemic functions by providing information about the world (Jost et al., 2003; Matthews, Levin, & Sidanius, 2009). In addition, to the extent that shared ideologies create a common sense of identity among individuals, ideologies may function as a mechanism to strengthen social bonds (e.g., Gurin, 1985, Gurin & Townsend, 1986; Simon & Klandermans, 2001).

Although some functions of ideologies are common to both hierarchy-enhancing and hierarchy-attenuating ideologies, there are other individual functions of ideologies that are unique to hierarchy-enhancing ideologies. For example, ideologies such as BJW and PWE often serve the function of control and predictability (Furnham, 2003; Lerner, 1980). BJW and PWE offer individuals reassurance about their ability to control their own outcomes—simply work hard and be a good person and one can obtain positive outcomes (e.g., Lipkus, Dalbert, & Siegler, 1996). Similarly, Jost and his colleagues have focused on the psychological needs and motivations that influence the adoption of political conservatism. According to this perspective, conservatism's emphasis on preserving the status quo and justifying inequality meets a particular profile of psychological needs. Based on the results of a meta-analysis, they identified several psychological variables that are proposed to motivate the adoption of conservatism, including death anxiety, dogmatism, and the needs for order, structure, and closure (Jost, Glaser, Kruglanski, & Sulloway, 2003; see also Hirsh, DeYoung, Xu, & Peterson, 2010). System instability is also associated with the adoption of politically conservative attitudes, which suggests that one function of conservatism may be to offer people reassurance in times of uncertainty (Jost et al., 2003).

In general, hierarchy-enhancing ideologies can serve to reduce anxiety over inequality in society and provide individuals with a sense of security (Janoff-Bulman, 1989; Jost et al., 2003; Matthews, Levin, & Sidanius, 2009; Napier & Jost, 2008). If people who obtain negative outcomes are bad people who deserve their fate, then one need not feel distress at their misfortune. For this reason, Jost and his colleagues have referred to these types of ideologies as palliative—they do not actually give individuals control over their outcomes or reduce injustice in the world, but they do make people feel better. The palliative nature of ideology may help to explain why BJW increases in times of greater income disparities—BJW may function to reduce the anxiety that would otherwise be caused by increased economic inequality (Malahy, Rubinlicht, & Kaiser, 2009). Compared to hierarchy-enhancing ideologies, there has been relatively less research on the unique psychological functions served by hierarchy-attenuating ideologies. We return to this issue later in the chapter.

Self-interest can motivate the adoption of particular ideologies that are perceived to benefit either the individual or the group to which the individual belongs (Bobo & Hutchings, 1996; Sears & Funk, 1981; Sidanius & Pratto, 1999). Compared to people from low status groups, people from high status groups are more likely to endorse hierarchy-enhancing ideologies that promote the interest of high status groups by justifying group-based inequality (e.g., Awad, Cokley, &

Ravitch, 2005; Bobo, 1999; Brug & Verkuyten, 2007; Cokley et al., 2007; Kluegel & Smith, 1986; Levy, West, & Ramireez, 2005; O'Brien & Major, 2005; Sidanius & Pratto, 1999; Verkuyten, 2005; Verkuyten & Yildiz, 2006; Wolsko et al., 2006). Furthermore, among high status groups, those individuals who are highly identified with the group (i.e., those who are the most motivated to promote the interests of the group) are the most likely to endorse hierarchy-enhancing ideologies and the least likely to endorse hierarchy-attenuating ideologies. In contrast, people from low status groups are more likely than people from high status groups to endorse hierarchy-attenuating ideologies that serve the interest of low status groups by promoting social equality (e.g., Brug & Verkuyten, 2007; Crocker, Luhtanen, Broadnax, & Blaine, 1999; Verkuyten, 2005; Verkuyten & Yildiz, 2006). Also, among individual members of low status groups, those who are highly identified with the group are the most likely to endorse hierarchy-attenuating ideologies and the least likely to endorse hierarchy-enhancing ideologies (Brug & Verkuyten, 2007; O'Brien & Major, 2005).

In the past few years, groundbreaking research has emerged from at least two different laboratories that has turned conventional research about the function of ideologies on its ear. This research suggests that the same ideology can serve different functions in different contexts and at different points in time (Knowles, Lowery, Hogan, & Chow, 2009; Levy, West, Ramirez, & Karafantis, 2006). For example, Levy and colleagues (2006) have shown that PWE can function in both a hierarchy-enhancing and a hierarchy-attenuating capacity. Levy and colleagues argue that although PWE can be used to justify the lower status of some groups as compared to others, it also has a more literal, surface meaning, which says that everyone can achieve equality through hard work. Among children, who tend to interpret PWE in a literal sense, PWE is positively related to social tolerance. However, among adults, who tend to interpret PWE as a justification for inequality, PWE is negatively related to social tolerance. In addition, adults' interpretation of PWE can be manipulated so that it functions as either a hierarchy-enhancing or -attenuating ideology depending upon the context.

Similarly, more recent research suggests that colorblind ideology can also serve in both a hierarchy-enhancing and -attenuating capacity (Knowles et al., 2009). According to Knowles and colleagues, when colorblindness is construed as a principle of distributive justice, it takes on an egalitarian meaning concerned with reducing inequality between groups. However, colorblindness can also be construed as a principle of procedural justice. When construed in this fashion, colorblindness functions as a justification for inequality between groups. Knowles and colleagues' research (2009) shows that anti-egalitarian White people are more likely to use colorblindness to justify inequality when they experience intergroup threat.

Most of the available research suggests that the default construal of both PWE and colorblindness, at least among adults, is a hierarchy-enhancing construal. However, research showing that these ideologies can function in a hierarchy-attenuating capacity in at least some contexts suggests that ideologies can be quite malleable. Researchers have also focused on another malleable aspect of ideologies—how ideologies can change over time in response to disconfirming evidence (Eccleston, Kaiser, & Kraynak, 2010; Levy, Freitas, Mendoza-Denton, & Kugelmass, 2006). Eccleston and colleagues examined people's endorsement of PWE and other hierarchy-enhancing ideologies before being presented with strong evidence that racism played a role in the federal government's response to the Katrina disaster (Eccleston, Kaiser, & Kraynak, 2010). They found that individuals who initially strongly endorsed hierarchy-enhancing ideologies lowered their endorsement of hierarchy-enhancing ideologies in response to evidence of the role of racism in the government's response. Ideologies appear to be subject to reality constraints, and at least under some circumstances, people will change their ideologies in response to disconfirming evidence (Jost et al., 2003; Levy et al., 2006).

Structure of ideologies

Do hierarchy-attenuating ideologies exist at the opposite end of a continuum from hierarchy-enhancing ideologies? Alternatively, are hierarchy-enhancing ideologies orthogonal to hierarchy-attenuating ideologies? Many researchers have treated various ideologies as bipolar. For example, many researchers measure liberalism/conservatism on bipolar scales (e.g., Robinson, Rusk, & Head, 1968; Wilson & Patterson, 1968). Similarly, Sidanius and colleagues have measured anti-egalitarianism by assessing an individual's belief in egalitarianism and then reverse-coding his or her responses. In this line of work, anti-egalitarianism is considered a hierarchy-enhancing ideology, but framed as egalitarianism it could be considered a hierarchy-attenuating ideology. To cite another example, Major and colleagues have tended to treat meritocratic beliefs as a bipolar construct, and their research suggests that endorsing meritocratic beliefs serves a hierarchy-enhancing function whereas rejecting meritocratic beliefs serves a hierarchy-attenuating function (Major et al., 2007; see also Townsend et al., 2010).

Although many researchers treat ideologies as if they have bipolar structure, some have argued that ideologies are unipolar (Conover & Feldman, 1981; Katz & Hass, 1988; Kerlinger, 1984). For example, Kerlinger argues that liberalism and conservatism are orthogonal, unipolar ideologies, and he uses factor analysis and cluster analysis to argue for the independent measurement of liberalism and conservatism (Kerlinger, 1984). However, his recommendations for independent measurement have not caught on in the literature, perhaps because his own distinct measures of liberalism and conservatism are correlated. Some of the apparent inconsistency in the literature may be explained by differences in ideological structure among the politically knowledgeable as compared to the politically unknowledgeable. Ideologies are more likely to have bipolar structure among the politically knowledgeable but unipolar structure among those who are not politically knowledgeable (Michaud, Carlisle, & Smith, 2009; Sidanius & Duffy, 1988).

A second important and related structural issue is the interrelationship among various ideologies of the same class. A number of studies have documented correlations between hierarchy-enhancing ideologies such as conservatism, BJW, and PWE (e.g., Christopher, Zabel, Jones, & Marek, 2008; Dittmar & Dickinson, 1993; Feather, 1984; Jones, 1997; Katz & Hass, 1988; Mudrack, 2004; O'Brien & Major, 2005; Wagstaff, 1983). Jost and his colleagues have argued that endorsement of political conservatism and other hierarchy-enhancing ideologies manifests out of various psychological needs, and thus the intercorrelation among hierarchy-enhancing ideologies may be a result of the fact that they serve similar psychological needs. (Jost, Glaser, Kruglanski, & Sulloway, 2003; see also Hirsh, DeYoung, Xu, & Peterson, 2010).

Social dominance theory also offers a useful perspective on the interrelatedness and structure of ideologies (Sidanius & Pratto, 1999). According to social dominance theory, individuals differ in the degree to which they "desire and support group-based hierarchy and the domination of 'inferior' groups by 'superior' groups" (Sidanius & Pratto, 1999, p. 48). This personality variable is known as social dominance orientation and is affected by factors such as group memberships and socialization experiences. In general, men and people from high status groups (e.g., White Americans) tend to have higher levels of social dominance orientation than women and people from low status groups. According to social dominance theory, endorsement of hierarchy-enhancing ideologies such as BJW and PWE will be correlated with each other because endorsement of these ideologies can manifest from a deeper-seated personality variable—social dominance orientation. A number of studies using path analysis and structural equation modeling suggest that (1) hierarchy-enhancing ideologies are intercorrelated and (2) this intercorrelation between hierarchy-enhancing ideologies can be explained by social dominance orientation (Sidanius & Pratto, 1999).

Importantly, the relationship between hierarchy-enhancing ideologies and social dominance orientation is weaker among individuals from low status ethnic groups than individuals from high status ethnic groups (Rabinowitz, 1999; Sidanius, Levin, & Pratto, 1996; Sidanius, Pratto, & Rabinowitz, 1994). Rabinowitz (1999) has offered a compelling explanation for this ideological asymmetry. He argues that some members of low status groups who are high in social dominance orientation support the hierarchy within which they currently live, even if it is a system that subordinates their in-group. In contrast, other members of low status groups who are high in social dominance orientation desire to see their own group in a dominant position. That is, they support the idea of a social hierarchy, but believe that the current system is unjust and should be altered so that their own group is at the top of the social hierarchy. Therefore, the first group of low status individuals who are high in social dominance orientation tend to endorse hierarchy-enhancing ideologies, whereas the second group of low status individuals who are high in social dominance orientation tend to oppose hierarchy-enhancing ideologies. Rabinowitz (1999) found that perceptions of injustice in the current social system moderated the relationship between social dominance orientation and endorsement of hierarchy-enhancing ideologies among individuals from low status groups in a manner consistent with his hypothesis. Among individuals from low status groups who perceived little discrimination against their group, social dominance orientation and hierarchy-enhancing ideologies were positively correlated; however, among individuals from low status groups who perceived high levels of discrimination against their group, social dominance orientation and hierarchy-enhancing ideologies were negatively correlated. An important implication of Rabinowitz's work is that the structure of ideologies may vary as a function of group status and beliefs about the prevalence of discrimination.

Comparatively speaking, there has been less research examining the interrelationships among various hierarchy-attenuating ideologies such as egalitarianism, multiculturalism, and liberalism. In contrast with hierarchy-enhancing ideologies, it is unclear whether there are specific personality variables that underlie endorsement of hierarchy-attenuating ideologies and create interrelationships among ideologies such as egalitarianism and multiculturalism (Jost et al., 2003), although there is evidence of a relationship between the personality trait of compassion and endorsement of liberal ideology (Hirsh et al., 2010). At this point, it is also unclear how oppositional ideologies such as the oppressed minority ideology relate to other hierarchy-attenuating ideologies. Research on the polarity of ideology has the potential to shed light on the personality factors underlying hierarchy-attenuating ideologies. For example, if liberalism and conservatism are at opposite ends of a bipolar continuum, then the personality traits that motivate adoption of a conservative ideology are by definition the same traits that lead to a rejection of liberal ideology.

Part 1 summary and implications for the workplace

Ideologies tend to fall into one of two classes: hierarchy-enhancing or hierarchy-attenuating. Hierarchy-enhancing ideologies serve to legitimize inequality in the social structure. Examples of hierarchy-enhancing ideologies include PWE, BJW, meritocracy, and colorblindness. Ideologies that promote social equality, on the other hand, are hierarchy-attenuating ideologies. Examples of these ideologies include egalitarianism, multiculturalism, rejection of meritocracy, and oppressed minority ideology. Applied to the context of the workplace, hierarchy-enhancing ideologies may function so as to maintain and enhance stratification in the workplace such that people in both powerful (e.g., managers) and powerless (e.g., custodial staff) positions are seen as deserving of those respective positions. Furthermore, hierarchy-enhancing ideologies may encourage the belief that people from high status groups such as men and Whites deserve to be in powerful positions whereas people from low status groups such as women and ethnic minorities deserve to be in powerless positions (Major, Gramzow, et al., 2002). In contrast, hierarchy-attenuating ideologies may function so as to reduce stratification in the workplace and increase equality and power sharing among diverse members of the workplace.

Individual differences in ideologies have their origins in socialization, personality, and the psychological functions they serve for the individual. In general, ideologies can serve the same types of functions as attitudes, including value expressive functions, instrumental functions, epistemic functions, and the strengthening of social bonds (e.g., Katz, 1960). In addition, there are unique functions served by particular ideologies. Hierarchy-enhancing ideologies frequently serve to reduce uncertainty and anxiety. Although there is less research on the particular functions of hierarchy-attenuating ideologies, they may also function to buffer feelings of distress caused by the perceptions of inequality by creating feelings of efficacy and empowerment (e.g., Molix & Bettencourt, 2010). Ideologies can also function to promote group interests—whereas hierarchy-enhancing ideologies promote the group interests of high status groups, hierarchy-attenuating ideologies promote the group interests of low status groups. Recent research suggests that ideologies are malleable. Not only can the same ideology serve different functions in different contexts, but ideologies can also change over time in response to disconfirming evidence.

One implication of research on the origins of ideologies is that people arrive in the workplace with ideological beliefs already in place. However, given the malleable nature of ideologies, these ideologies may change in response to different workplace experiences and contexts. Organizations have the power to shape how ideologies are expressed in a workplace context (Purdie-Vaughns et al., 2008). Moreover, expressions of ideology in the workplace can affect human behavior and work productivity (Plaut et al., 2009). For example, recent research suggests that simply displaying a poster on the wall depicting human diversity can increase helping behavior (Brauer & Er-rafiy, 2011).

Most researchers treat hierarchy-enhancing and hierarchy-attenuating ideologies as bipolar (i.e., at opposite ends of a continuum). However, there has been some limited research suggesting that ideologies are unipolar and orthogonal, at least among the politically unsophisticated. Ideologies are often intercorrelated. Personality variables such as social dominance orientation and compassion may underlie intercorrelations among hierarchy-enhancing and hierarchy-attenuating ideologies respectively. One implication of this research is that if a workplace organization attracts individuals who are high in social dominance orientation (such as law enforcement), then the workplace environment will consist of a large number of individuals who endorse a whole contingency of hierarchy-enhancing ideologies. In contrast, if a workplace organization attracts individuals who are low in social dominance orientation (e.g., social justice organizations, nonprofits), then the workplace environment will likely consist of many individuals who endorse a host of hierarchy-attenuating ideologies.

Part 2: Implications of ideology

One of the reasons scholars study ideology is because of the important implications that ideology has for the self, intergroup relations, and diversity attitudes. In the remainder of the chapter, we discuss the implications of ideology for these topics. With regards to the self, we discuss the implications for psychological well-being, vocational choice, entitlement to pay, and attributions to discrimination. Next, we break down the impact of ideology on intergroup relations by considering how the relation between ideology and group-based evaluations is moderated by both the group status of the perceiver and the group status of the target. We end by focusing on the bigger picture—how ideology affects attitudes toward various policies, including attitudes toward affirmative action, work roles for women, and immigration.

The self

Ideologies have implications for at least four different aspects of the self that are particularly relevant to diversity in the workplace: psychological well-being, vocational choice, entitlement to pay, and attributions to discrimination. To date, most research on the implications of ideology for the self has focused on the implications of ideology for psychology well-being. Among members of high status groups, endorsement of hierarchy-enhancing ideologies, which justify the position of high status groups, is associated with indices of well-being, including higher levels of self-esteem, happiness, positive affect, and life satisfaction and lower levels of anxiety, anger, and neuroticism (Jost & Thompson, 2000; O'Brien & Major, 2005; Quinn & Crocker, 1999; Rankin, Jost, & Wakslak, 2009). In comparison, endorsing hierarchy-enhancing ideologies tends to be associated with lower levels of well-being among members of low status groups, especially among individuals who highly identify with their group. In contrast to hierarchy-enhancing ideologies, there is some evidence that hierarchy-attenuating ideologies, such as multiculturalism, are associated with higher self-esteem for members of *both* high status and low status groups because they promote social acceptance and recognition of all cultural identities (Verkuyten, 2009a). Unfortunately, one drawback to most of the research on the relationship between ideology and psychological well-being is that it is correlational (although cf. Quinn & Crocker, 1999) and thus it is not possible to determine the causal direction of the relationship.

Sidanius and colleagues have examined the relationship between anti-egalitarianism and vocational choice in an ethnically diverse sample of college students (Sidanius et al., 2003). They divided vocations into hierarchy-enhancing careers and hierarchy-attenuating careers. Hierarchy-attenuating careers were defined as any career that implied help toward or sympathy with low status groups (e.g., social scientists, social workers, special education teachers) and hierarchy-enhancing majors were defined as any career that implied help toward or sympathy with high status groups (e.g., businesspersons, police, and military personnel). Students who were high in anti-egalitarianism were more likely to choose hierarchy-enhancing college majors and careers. Furthermore, students whose ideologies were congruent with their major and career choices had greater academic success (see also van Laar et al., 1999).

Investigators have also examined the relationship between hierarchy-enhancing ideologies and workplace entitlement (Hafer & Olson, 1989, 1993; O'Brien et al., 2012). Entitlement is an affectively laden cognitive judgment that people *should* receive a particular set of outcomes by virtue of who they are or what they have done (Major, 1994). Although the construct of entitlement can be applied to any number of outcomes, research on entitlement to pay has particularly important implications for salary and pay inequality between groups in society (Major, 1994).

Hierarchy-enhancing ideologies such as PWE and BJW explain group differences in the distribution of wealth in terms of group differences in effort and merit (Crandall, 1994; Furnham, 1990; Hafer & Olson, 1989; Hafer & Olson, 1993; Jost & Hunyady, 2002; Lerner, 1980; Major, 1994). Thus, hierarchy-enhancing ideologies imply that group differences in salaries, such as the salary gap that exists between men and women, are deserved. O'Brien and colleagues (2012) tested the hypothesis that hierarchy-enhancing ideologies would be associated with greater pay entitlement among men and lower pay entitlement among women. They found that when hierarchy-enhancing ideologies were measured as an individual difference variable (Study 1) or experimentally primed (Study 2), they were associated with significantly higher levels of pay entitlement among men. The relationship between hierarchy-enhancing ideologies and pay entitlement was in the opposite direction, but much weaker, among women. Although additional research is needed, the results of this study suggest that hierarchy-enhancing ideologies may contribute to the gender gap in salary by making men feel like they are entitled to more pay for their work.

Another interesting line of research examines the relationship between hierarchy-enhancing ideologies and attributions to discrimination. Major and colleagues (2002) hypothesized that if hierarchy-enhancing ideologies have a differential impact on feelings of entitlement and deserving among high status as opposed to low status groups, this could have important implications for the extent to which individuals blame discrimination when they fail to receive positive outcomes. More specifically, they hypothesized that when people feel they deserve positive outcomes but fail to receive them, they would be more likely to blame discrimination as compared to when people feel less deserving of positive outcomes. Two studies (one comparing men to women and the other comparing Whites to Latinos) assessed individual differences in endorsement of individual mobility, a hierarchy-enhancing ideology that espouses the notion that the status hierarchy is permeable and that individuals have the capacity to improve their own individual status. Consistent with hypotheses, when individuals belonging to high status groups were personally rejected by a member of a low status group, individual mobility beliefs were associated with greater attributions to discrimination (Major, Gramzow, et al., 2002, Studies 2 and 3). In contrast, when individuals belonging to a low status group were personally rejected by a member of a high status group, individual mobility beliefs were associated with fewer attributions to discrimination (see McCoy & Major, 2007, for a similar finding). Thus, hierarchy-enhancing ideologies may influence the situations under which individuals will make attributions to discrimination, and the relationship between hierarchy-enhancing ideologies and attributions to discrimination is moderated by group status (see also Thomsen et al., 2010).

Intergroup relations

In this section, we consider how ideologies affect the way that people evaluate others and the implications of those evaluations for intergroup relations. Ideologies affect evaluations made by perceivers from both high and low status groups of targets from both high and low status groups. Thus, to understand how ideology affects a perceiver's evaluations of others, it is necessary to take into account the group status of both the perceiver and the target.

High status perceivers/low status targets. The vast majority of the research on the relationship between ideology and intergroup relations has examined the impact of ideology on the attitudes of perceivers from high status groups toward people from low status groups. As mentioned previously, one of the most common findings is that, among individuals from high status groups, endorsement of hierarchy-enhancing ideologies is related to higher levels of prejudice against many low status groups, including Blacks, Arabs, Asians, women, gay men, lesbian women, people of low socioeconomic status, and heavyset people (e.g., Biernat, Vescio, Theno, & Crandall, 1996; Christopher & Mull, 2006; Crandall, 1994; Echebarria-Echabe & Guede, 2007; Katz & Hass, 1988; Lambert & Chasteen, 1997; MacDonald, 1972; Malcomnson, Christopher, Franzen, & Keyes, 2006; Morrison & Morrison, 2002; Nail, Harton, & Decker, 2003; Pratto, Sidanius, Stallworth, & Malle, 1994; Reyna, Henry, Korfmacher, & Tucker, 2006; Son Hing, Chung-Yan, Hamilton, & Zanna, 2008; Swim, Aikin, Hall, & Hunter, 1995; Wolsko et al., 2006). In contrast, endorsement of hierarchy-attenuating ideologies is related to lower levels of prejudice against low status groups (Biernat et al., 1996; Case, Fishbein, & Ritchey, 2008; Glover, 1994; Katz & Hass, 1988; Monteith & Walters, 1998; Plant & Devine, 1998; Plant, Devine, & Peruche, 2010; Swim et al., 1995; Verkuyten, 2005; Wolsko et al., 2006).

The effect of ideology on treatment of low status groups by high status groups has important implications for the workplace. In a field study conducted at a large health-care organization, Plaut and colleagues found that ethnic minorities who worked in departments where their White colleagues endorsed colorblindness were less engaged in their work than ethnic minorities who worked in departments where their White colleagues endorsed multiculturalism (Plaut et al., 2009). The effects of Whites' ideologies on their minority colleagues' engagement was mediated by the minority workers' perceptions of bias in their White colleagues.

A number of studies have experimentally examined the implications of activating particular ideologies for evaluations and treatment of members of low status groups (e.g., Biernat et al., 1996; Correll, Park, & Smith, 2008; Katz & Hass, 1988; Morrison, Plaut, & Ybarra, 2010; Richeson & Nussbaum, 2004; Verkuyten, 2005; Vorauer, Gagnon, & Sasaki, 2009; Wolsko et al., 2000). These experiments show a similar pattern as the correlational research described above. Activating multiculturalism generally leads to more positive out-group evaluations and treatment, whereas activating assimilationism/colorblindness leads to more negative out-group evaluations and treatment (Richeson & Nussbaum, 2004; Verkuyten, 2005, Studies 3 and 4; Vorauer et al., 2009; Vorauer & Sasaki, 2010; although see Morrison et al., 2010, for an exception to this general pattern). In contrast to scholars who argue that colorblindness inevitably leads to more negative evaluations of low status groups, Wolsko and colleagues argue that an emphasis on improving interethnic relations is common to both multicultural and colorblind ideologies (Wolsko et al., 2000). However, they argue that multiculturalism advocates a different path to improved intergroup harmony as compared to colorblindness. Specifically, colorblindness suggests that harmony can best be achieved by judging people as individuals, whereas multiculturalism emphasizes the importance of recognizing group differences. Therefore, multiculturalism should lead to greater and more accurate use of stereotypes than colorblindness.

Wolsko and colleagues found that, relative to control conditions, there was a reduction in prejudice in both the colorblind and multicultural conditions; however, the reduction in prejudice was greater in the multicultural conditions than the colorblind conditions (Wolsko et al., 2000, Studies 1 and 2). Furthermore, there was a significant increase in stereotyping in the multicultural conditions relative to the colorblind and control conditions (Wolsko et al., 2000, Studies 1, 2, and 3). It is important to note that participants used both negative and positive stereotypes more frequently in the multicultural conditions and that they also more accurately used these stereotypes in these conditions. The findings of the experiments by Wolsko and colleagues (2000) are particularly noteworthy because they show that multiculturalism can increase stereotyping while decreasing prejudice—a finding at odds with much of the traditional theorizing on the relationship between stereotyping and prejudice.

Other recent approaches to understanding the effects of ideology on high status perceivers' evaluations of low status targets have adopted nuanced approaches focusing on which members of low groups are most likely to be targeted by prejudice. These approaches emphasize that members of high status groups do not distribute their prejudice equally across all members of low status groups; that is, some individuals from low status groups are more disliked than other individuals (Gutierrez & Unzueta, 2010; Kaiser, Dyrenforth, & Hagiwara, 2006; Kaiser & Pratt-Hyatt, 2009). Gutierrez and Unzueta (2010) examined how the experimental activation of hierarchy-enhancing and hierarchy-attenuating ideologies affects preferences for stereotypic and counter-stereotypic minorities. When colorblind ideology was experimentally activated, participants liked a counter-stereotypic African American target more than a stereotypic African American target (Gutierrez & Unzueta, 2010). In contrast, when multicultural ideology was activated, participants liked a stereotypic African American target more than a counter-stereotypic African American target. These findings suggest that colorblindness may create a preference for individuals who permeate the boundaries of their ethnicity, whereas multiculturalism may create a preference for individuals who remain within the boundaries of their ethnicity.

Recent research by Kaiser and colleagues has examined the influence of hierarchy-enhancing ideologies on Whites' evaluations of ethnic minorities who make claims of discrimination and who are strongly identified with their group (Kaiser et al., 2006; Kaiser & Pratt-Hyatt, 2009). Among White individuals, endorsement of hierarchy-enhancing ideologies is associated with more negative evaluations of ethnic minorities who claim discrimination and who are strongly identified with their group. These effects appear to be due to perceived ideological dissimilarities between the White participants and the ethnic minorities who claim discrimination and who strongly identify with their group.

High status perceivers/high status targets. Although typically less researched than how ideologies affect evaluations of other groups, ideologies can also affect the way people evaluate their own groups (e.g., Green et al., 2009; Sidanius, Pratto, & Rabinowitz, 1994; Verkuyten, 2005). Understanding how people feel and act toward members of their own groups is a critical component of intergroup relations because discrimination against people from other groups is frequently more motivated by love for the in-group than hatred for the out-group (Brewer, 1999). In this next section, we consider how ideologies affect the attitudes of perceivers from high status groups toward their own group.

Among member of high status groups, endorsement of hierarchy-enhancing ideology is associated with higher levels of in-group identification and attachment, whereas endorsement of hierarchy-attenuating ideologies is associated with lower levels of in-group identification and attachment (Brug & Verkuyten, 2007; Levin, Sidanius, Rabinowitz, & Federico, 1998; O'Brien & Major, 2005; Sidanius et al., 1994; Verkuyten, 2005). Furthermore, activating hierarchy-enhancing ideologies such as assimilationism increases evaluations of the (high status) in-group, whereas activating hierarchy-attenuating ideologies such as multiculturalism decreases evaluations of the (high status) in-group (Verkuyten, 2005).

It is also important to note that in-group bias is particularly strong among members of high status groups who are high in social dominance orientation (Green, Thomsen, Sidanius, Staerkle, & Potanina, 2009; Kemmelmeier, 2005). A mock-jury study demonstrated that, among White jurors, social dominance orientation was associated with lower perceptions of guilt and shorter sentencing recommendations for a White male perpetrator who was charged with battering an African American woman (Kemmelmeier, 2005). When an African American man was charged with battering a White woman, however, social dominance orientation was associated with higher perceptions of guilt and longer sentencing recommendations. Although these studies did not directly assess endorsement of hierarchy-enhancing ideologies, because social dominance orientation is so closely related to endorsement of hierarchy-enhancing ideologies among White Americans, this study suggests there may be a relationship between endorsement of hierarchy-enhancing ideologies and in-group bias.

Low status perceivers/low status targets. Ideologies also affect the way members of low status groups evaluate members of their own group (e.g., Crandall, 1994; Jost & Banaji, 1994; Sidanius & Pratto, 1999; Wolsko et al., 2006). Members of low status groups who endorse hierarchy-enhancing ideologies are less identified with their in-group, whereas members of low status group who endorse hierarchy-attenuating ideologies are more identified with their in-group (Brug & Verkuyten, 2007; Levin & Sidanius, 1999; Levin et al., 1998; O'Brien & Major, 2005; Verkuyten, 2005). In addition, among members of some low status groups, including heavyset people and women, endorsement of hierarchy-enhancing ideologies is associated with more negative attitudes toward the in-group (Christopher & Mull, 2006; Crandall, 1994; Jost & Burgess, 2000). In contrast, endorsement of hierarchy-attenuating ideologies is associated with more positive attitudes toward the in-group (Swim et al., 1995). Furthermore, experimentally activating hierarchy-enhancing ideologies such as assimilationism decreases evaluations of the (low status) in-group, whereas activating hierarchy-attenuating ideologies such as multiculturalism increases evaluations of the (low status) in-group (Verkuyten, 2005). Finally, experimentally activating hierarchy-enhancing ideologies increases endorsement of negative stereotypes about one's own group (McCoy & Major, 2007).

Among members of low status groups, how does ideology influence evaluations of other low status out-groups? For example, do Latino Americans who endorse hierarchy-enhancing ideologies view African Americans more negatively? Unfortunately, this question is difficult to answer because there has been relatively little systematic research into how members of low status groups evaluate members of other low status groups, and these studies have not focused on the role ideology in these evaluations (cf. Levin, van Laar, & Sidanius, 2003; Shapiro & Neuberg, 2008; White & Langer, 1999). It is interesting to note that among women (a low status group), endorsement of ideologies is related to evaluations of ethnic minorities. For example, women who endorse PWE have more negative attitudes toward African Americans (Swim et al., 1995). Some research suggests that endorsement and activation of hierarchy-enhancing ideologies appears to be related to more negative evaluations of low status groups regardless of the group status of the perceiver (e.g., Swim et al., 1995; Verkuyten, 2005). Thus, endorsement or activation of ideologies among members of a particular ethnic minority group may also be correlated with attitudes toward other ethnic minority groups. This will be an important and interesting avenue for future research.

Low status perceivers/high status targets. According to system justification theory, endorsement of hierarchy-enhancing ideologies should increase evaluations made by people from low status groups of people from high status groups (Jost & Banaji, 1994; Jost & Hunyady, 2002). Likewise, endorsement of hierarchy-attenuating ideologies should decrease evaluations made by people from low status groups of people from high status groups. To date, however, the available literature on how ideology affects evaluations made by people from low status groups of people from high status groups is limited and often yields weak and nonsignificant findings (Verkuyten, 2005; Vorauer et al., 2009; Wolsko et al., 2006).

In research examining how multiculturalism and assimilationism affect intergroup relations, endorsement of multiculturalism was not associated with how members of a low status group (Turks) felt about members of a high status group (Dutch; Verkuyten, 2005, Studies 1 and 2). Furthermore, activation of assimilationism and multiculturalism did not affect Turks' evaluations of the Dutch relative to a control condition (Studies 3 and 4). These findings are noteworthy because, as discussed previously, assimilationism and multiculturalism were related to Turks' evaluations of the in-group, and Dutch evaluations of both the in-group and the out-group. Vorauer and colleagues' research has also yielded some surprising and nonsignificant findings. Across two studies, priming multiculturalism led Aboriginal Canadians to direct more positive comments at a White Canadian compared to a control condition. However, priming colorblindness led to an inconsistent pattern of effects across the two studies (Vorauer et al., 2009).

Finally, Wolsko and colleagues' (2006) research has also yielded mixed findings. Unfortunately for the present purposes, their measure of prejudice was a measure of in-group bias (preference for the in-group over the out-group), so it makes interpretation of attitudes toward the in-group a bit more complicated. In Study 1, they found that multiculturalism was associated with increased in-group bias among the low status group, but in Study 2, it was associated with decreased in-group bias among the low status group. Assimilationism was not associated with in-group bias among the low status group in either study. Thus, across multiple studies, ideologies are largely unrelated to evaluations of the high status group by people from the low status groups.

Diversity attitudes

In this section, we consider the relationship between ideology and attitudes toward diversity. There are many different diversity attitudes that could be examined. We chose to focus on attitudes toward affirmative action, the role of women in the workplace, and immigration because of their importance and the availability of empirical research on the relationship between ideology and these specific attitudes. We also discuss research on the relationship between social dominance orientation and diversity attitudes because social dominance orientation is so strongly related to endorsement of hierarchy-enhancing ideologies.

Affirmative action. According to the American Psychological Association, affirmative action refers to "voluntary and mandatory efforts undertaken by federal, state, and local governments; private employers; and schools to combat discrimination and to promote equal opportunity in education and employment" (cited in Crosby, 2004, p. 5). If the goal of affirmative action policies is to decrease group-based inequality, this would suggest that hierarchy-enhancing ideologies would decrease support for affirmative action and hierarchy-attenuating ideologies would increase support for affirmative action. Indeed, a number of studies have found support for this notion. For example, endorsement of colorblind and assimilationist ideology is related to greater opposition to affirmative action, whereas endorsement of multicultural ideology is related to greater support for affirmative action (e.g., Awad et al., 2005; Wolsko et al., 2006). Interestingly, the relationship between ideology and affirmative action attitudes was similar for African Americans, Asian-Americans, Latino Americans, and White Americans (Wolsko et al., 2006). Thus, there was no evidence of any ideological asymmetry between high status and low status groups.

Women in the workplace. Research has documented a relationship between attitudes toward women in the workplace and both hierarchy-enhancing ideologies and social dominance orientation (e.g., Christopher & Wojda, 2008; Hafer & Olson, 1993). For example, in a survey of working women, BJW was related to lower levels of discontent with women's lower status position in the workforce (Hafer & Olson, 1993). In addition, women who strongly endorsed BJW were less likely to engage in behaviors to improve the status of women in the workplace.

Recently, Christopher and Wojda (2008) carried out an investigation of the relationship between social dominance orientation, right-wing authoritarianism, and two specific attitudes toward working women: employment skepticism and traditional role preference. Employment skepticism refers to a belief that women lack the abilities required to succeed in the workplace, typically because they are seen as too nice or not tough enough (Valentine, 2001). Traditional role preference refers to the belief that women are better suited for traditionally feminine roles such as that of mother. Christopher and Wojda (2008) found that people who were high in social dominance orientation expressed higher levels of employment skepticism and traditional role preference, whereas right-wing authoritarianism was related only to higher levels of traditional role preference. The sample included both women and men; however, they did not test whether group status (in this case sex) moderated the relationship between social dominance orientation and attitudes toward women in the workplace. Thus, it is not possible to determine whether this study showed evidence of ideological asymmetry. That is, it is unknown whether the magnitude of the relationship between social dominance orientation and attitudes toward women in the workplace is weaker for women than men.

Immigration. Several studies have examined the relationship between ideologies and anti-immigration attitudes (Chandler & Tsai, 2001; Wolsko et al., 2006). For example, Wolsko and colleagues (2006) found that assimilationism was related to opposition to more lenient immigration policies, whereas multiculturalism was related to support for more lenient immigration policies. The relationship between ideological endorsement and attitudes toward immigration policies was similar for White, Asian, Black, and Hispanic participants. Thus, there was no evidence of any ideological asymmetry between high status and low status groups.

In an analysis of the data from the 1994 General Social Survey (GSS), Chandler and Tsai (2001) found that political conservatism was related to more negative attitudes toward immigrants' rights for both legal and illegal immigrants. There was not a significant difference between Whites and ethnic minorities in attitudes toward immigrants' rights. The authors did not examine whether ethnicity moderated the relationship between endorsement of conservative ideology and attitudes toward immigrants' rights, and thus this study is unable to offer a test of the ideological asymmetry hypothesis.

Consistent with research on the relationship between ideology and immigration attitudes, research has also shown that social dominance is related to lower levels of support for immigrant rights and more negative attitudes toward immigrants (Cohrs & Stelzl, 2010; Green et al., 2009; Sidanius et al., 1994). For example, Green and colleagues (2009) found that among French-speaking Swiss students, social dominance orientation was related to a desire to exclude immigrants who would not easily assimilate into Swiss culture and immigrants who were unhealthy, and a desire to decrease the percentage of immigrants allowed into the country. Similarly, Sidanius and colleagues (1994) found that social dominance orientation was related to a number of anti-immigration attitudes, including the belief that immigration results in higher crime rates and higher taxes. Participants who were high in social dominance orientation were also in favor of reducing the number of immigrants allowed into the country. More recently, Cohrs and Stelzl (2010) conducted a meta-analysis examining the relationship between social dominance orientation, right-wing authoritarianism, and immigration attitudes. This meta-analysis included nearly 40,000 participants from 155 samples in 17 countries. They found that both social dominance orientation and right-wing authoritarianism were moderately strong predictors of anti-immigration attitudes. Although a number of these studies included large numbers of ethnic minority participants, none of these studies reported whether the relationship between social dominance orientation and immigration attitudes was moderated by participant ethnicity, and therefore they do not allow for a test of the ideological asymmetry hypothesis.

Section 2 summary and implications for the workplace

In the second half of this chapter, we have reviewed the literature on the implications of ideology for the self, intergroup relations, and diversity attitudes. This literature review revealed that the implications of ideology for the self are largely dependent on the group status of the individual. Among members of high status groups, hierarchy-enhancing ideologies are related to greater levels of psychological well-being, entitlement to pay, and attributions to discrimination following personal rejections. In contrast, among members of low status groups, hierarchy-enhancing ideologies are related to lower levels of psychological well-being, entitlement to pay, and attributions to discrimination following personal rejections (e.g., Jost & Thompson, 2000; Major et al., 2002; O'Brien & Major, 2009).

The literature on the relationship between ideology and intergroup relations suggests the following: (1) among members of high status groups, endorsement and activation of hierarchy-enhancing ideologies is related to more negative evaluations of low status out-groups and more positive evaluations of the in-group, (2) among members of high status groups, endorsement and activation of hierarchy-attenuating ideologies is related to more positive evaluations of low status out-groups and more negative evaluations of the in-group, (3) among members of low status groups, endorsement and activation of hierarchy-enhancing ideologies is related to more negative evaluations of the in-group but is largely unrelated to evaluations of the out-group, and (4) among members of low status groups, endorsement and activation of hierarchy-attenuating ideologies is related to more positive evaluations of the in-group but is largely unrelated to evaluation of the out-group (e.g., Verkuyten, 2005; Wolsko et al., 2006).

Thus, whereas endorsement of ideologies is strongly linked to evaluations of low status groups by high status groups, endorsement of ideologies is weakly and inconsistently linked to evaluations of high status groups by low status groups. According to Levin and colleagues, this ideological asymmetry arises from the fact that ideological endorsement is more strongly related to social dominance goals among members of high status groups than members of low status groups (Levin et al., 1998; Sidanius, Levin, & Pratto, 1996; see also Mitchell & Sidanius, 1993; Rabinowitz, 1999; Sidanius et al., 1994). Therefore, endorsement of ideologies should be more strongly related to evaluations of the out-group among members of high status groups than members of low status groups. The findings reviewed here are largely consistent with this hypothesis.

Finally, the literature on the relationship between ideology and diversity attitudes demonstrates that social dominance orientation and endorsement of hierarchy-enhancing ideologies are related to more negative attitudes toward affirmative action policies, women in the workplace, and immigration (e.g., Christopher & Wojda, 2008; Pratto et al., 1994, Wolsko et al., 2006). Although the ideological asymmetry hypothesis has not been extensively tested with regards to the relationship between ideology and diversity attitudes, the available research suggests that the relationship between ideology and diversity attitudes may be similar for Whites and ethnic minorities (Wolsko et al., 2006).

The research reviewed in this section has important implications for diversity in the workplace. In addition to the direct impact of ideological beliefs on attitudes toward affirmative action, women in the workplace, and immigration, ideological beliefs may also have an indirect impact on a number of important workplace processes and outcomes. Through its impact on psychological well-being and entitlement to pay, ideological beliefs may influence work satisfaction and salary negotiations, respectively. Because ideological beliefs affect attributions to discrimination, ideological beliefs may also influence when employees will bring discrimination lawsuits against an employer. Because ideological beliefs affect evaluations of both in-group and out-group members, ideological beliefs may affect employee performance evaluations. Moreover, research points to the strong likelihood that the implications of these ideological beliefs for each of these workplace processes and outcomes is moderated by the social groups to which employees belong.

Directions for future research

Our review of the literature on the antecedents and consequences of ideology reveals several notable gaps in the literature. In this section, we pose five questions presenting future directions for the field. The first three questions pertain to the classes, origins, and structure of ideologies and the last two questions pertain to the implications of ideology.

What are the psychological functions served by hierarchy-attenuating ideologies?

Scholars have made good headway in uncovering the psychological functions served by hierarchy-enhancing ideologies. There is a fair amount of research suggesting that hierarchy-enhancing ideologies serve a unique profile of needs such as control, predictability, and the needs for order, structure, and closure (e.g., Hirsh et al., 2010; Jost et al., 2003; Lerner, 1980, Lipkus et al., 1996). However, there has been little systematic investigation into the psychological needs that are met by endorsing hierarchy-attenuating ideologies. It is possible that hierarchy-attenuating ideologies, such as multiculturalism with its emphasis on diversity, appeal to individuals high in needs for cognition, novelty, and sensation seeking. With its recognition of the situational constraints on individual behavior, liberalism constitutes a more cognitively complex ideology than conservatism and may therefore appeal to individuals who are high in the need for cognition and who enjoy complexity (Jost et al., 2003).

It is also possible that, like hierarchy-enhancing ideologies, hierarchy-attenuating ideologies serve to reduce distress over inequality in society, but in a different manner than hierarchy-enhancing ideologies. For example, perhaps ideologies such as the oppressed minority ideology described by Seller and colleagues serve the function of creating a common bond among members of oppressed groups and make people feel more efficacious about their ability to reduce group-based inequality. Consistent with this argument, Major and colleagues (2007) found that when people were presented with evidence of pervasive discrimination against their group, individuals who rejected a meritocratic worldview had higher self-esteem than those who endorsed a meritocratic worldview (see also Foster et al., 2006; Foster & Tsarfati, 2005). Thus, oppositional ideologies may serve as a buffer against distress in the face of oppression against one's group by providing external explanations for the low status of one's group (e.g., Crocker & Major, 1989). It is also important to recognize that oppositional ideologies could serve a need for predictability. That is, they may psychologically prepare individuals from low status groups for the very real possibility that they will face negative life outcomes.

When will ideological asymmetries emerge between high and low status groups?

According to social dominance theory, the motivations for endorsing hierarchy-enhancing ideologies are more complex and less closely related to social dominance motives among members of low status groups (Levin et al., 1998; Rabinowitz, 1999). The ideological asymmetry hypothesis states that the relationship between hierarchy-enhancing ideologies and various outcomes will be weaker among members of low status groups than members of high status groups. Some research has supported this hypothesis (e.g., Heaven, 1999; Levin et al, 1998; Rabinowitz, 1999), whereas other research has not (e.g., Wolsko et al., 2006).

Frequently, however, researchers do not report whether group status moderates the relationship between ideology and other variables (e.g., Chandler & Tsai, 2001; Christopher & Wojda, 2008; Cohrs & Stelzl, 2010; Green et al., 2010; Sidanius et al., 1994). As a result, it is difficult to know just how robust of a phenomenon ideological asymmetry is. One possible approach to further exploration of the ideological asymmetry hypothesis would be to conduct secondary data analyses on the large number of published datasets that include both high- and low status groups but do not test whether group status moderates the relationship between ideology and various outcomes. We recommend that researchers address the question of what types of outcomes (e.g., policy attitudes, out-group evaluations, etc.) are most likely to demonstrate ideological asymmetries. This research could yield valuable information about why members of low status groups endorse ideologies that are not in their financial interests (Jost & Banaji, 1994; Jost & Hunyady, 2002).

In addition, researchers should focus on whether some groups (e.g., ethnic groups) are more likely to show ideological asymmetries than other groups (e.g., gender). To date, most research on the ideological asymmetry hypothesis has been conducted by comparing ethnic groups; however, there are at least two studies showing that gender can also yield ideological asymmetries (e.g., Heaven, 1999; O'Brien et al., 2012). We suspect that ideological asymmetries are most likely to emerge for ethnicity when examining the relationship between ideology and ethnic attitudes and most likely to emerge for gender when examining the relationship between ideology and gender attitudes. However, to our knowledge this hypothesis has not been tested.

How malleable is ideology?

Most researchers generally assume that individual differences in ideological beliefs are relatively stable over time, and indeed some research supports this notion (e.g., Pratto et al., 1994; Kteily, Sidanius, & Levin, 2011). At the same time, it is clear that ideological beliefs can and do change over time. For example, two separate studies have shown evidence that the events surrounding Hurricane Katrina decreased people's belief in the PWE (Eccleston et al., 2010; Levy et al., 2006). Additional research is needed on the types of circumstances that lead to changes in ideological beliefs. Based on research on cognitive dissonance and attitude change (e.g., Batson, 1975), we suspect that mild challenges to ideological beliefs may have the effect of increasing their strength, whereas overwhelming challenges to ideological beliefs (such as the challenge to PWE beliefs posed by the events surrounding Hurricane Katrina) may result in weakening of ideological beliefs.

We believe that some of the most provocative research reviewed in this chapter is the research showing that the same ideological beliefs can serve in either hierarchy-attenuating or hierarchy-enhancing capacities depending on the context (e.g., Knowles et al., 2009; Levy et al., 2006). This research suggests that both colorblindness and PWE can serve in a hierarchy-attenuating capacity, although both ideologies appear to more frequently serve in a hierarchy-enhancing capacity. We encourage future researchers to investigate the factors that determine when a particular ideology will serve in either a hierarchy-enhancing or hierarchy-attenuating capacity and which ideologies are the most malleable.

Is colorblindness always harmful to ethnic minorities?

Most of the research reviewed in the present chapter suggests that colorblindness can be harmful to ethnic minorities (e.g., Apfelbaum et al., 2008; Vorauer et al., 2009; Vorauer & Sasaki, 2010). Recall, for example, that ethnic minorities who work in departments with colorblind White colleagues generally report lower levels of work engagement (Plaut et al., 2009). However, colorblindness can be used in a hierarchy-attenuating capacity, especially in low conflict situations (Correll et al., 2008) or when it is construed as a principle of distributive justice (Knowles et al., 2009). Furthermore, Wolsko and colleagues' (2000) research suggested that priming colorblindness reduced Whites' prejudice toward ethnic minorities relative to a control condition (although not as much as priming multiculturalism). Finally, African Americans appear to trust companies espousing colorblindness as much as companies espousing multiculturalism, at least when ethnic minority representation in the company is high (Purdie-Vaughns et al., 2008). Thus, it will be important for future researchers to delineate the precise conditions under which colorblindness is harmful as opposed to harmless or even beneficial to ethnic minorities.

Is multiculturalism a panacea?

In recent years, there has been an increase in the number of studies examining multiculturalism, and this particular hierarchy-attenuating ideology appears to hold an incredible promise for improving intergroup relations (Richeson & Nussbaum, 2004; Verkuyten, 2009b; Wolsko et al., 2000). We are very optimistic about the ability of multiculturalism to improve the status of ethnic minorities and other diverse groups. At the same time, we would caution against the temptation to view multiculturalism as a panacea. One paper suggests that multiculturalism may reduce prejudice against ethnic minorities for Whites who are not identified with their ethnicity, but may actually increase prejudice among highly identify Whites (Morrison et al., 2010). In addition, at least one study suggests that multiculturalism increases reliance on stereotypes (albeit accurate stereotypes; Wolsko et al., 2000). Furthermore, the finding that multiculturalism leads to a preference for stereotypic as opposed to counter-stereotypic minorities suggests that multiculturalism may benefit some ethnic minorities more than others (Gutierrez & Unzueta, 2010). Finally, the fact that companies espousing multiculturalism elicit feelings of trust from African Americans even when those companies have low minority representations suggests that multiculturalism could be misused (e.g., Purdie-Vaughns et al., 2008).

Conclusion

This chapter reviewed theory and research on the content, function, and structure of ideological beliefs as well as on the implications of ideological beliefs for the self, intergroup relations, and diversity attitudes. Borrowing a distinction from social dominance theory, we have argued that one of the most useful distinctions in the ideology literature is between ideologies that support and enhance group-based inequality (e.g., BJW, PWE, assimilationism) and ideologies that attenuate group-based inequality (e.g., egalitarianism, multiculturalism). This critical distinction between these two classes of ideologies helps to predict who will endorse particular ideologies, under what circumstances they will endorse them, and how these particular ideologies will influence important outcomes such as psychological well-being, intergroup relations, and diversity attitudes.

Notes

1. Unfortunately, there has not been a lot of psychological research on ideologies pervasive in non-Western cultures. One interesting possibility for future research might be to examine how beliefs about karma prevalent in some Eastern cultures relate to people's beliefs about the fairness of status hierarchies and caste systems.

2. A system-justifying ideology is an ideology that justifies the current social system. Technically, then, if one lived in a society where all people were equal, an egalitarian ideology would be considered a system-justifying ideology. However, because Western cultures all tend to be structured as group-based hierarchies, for all practical purposes the terms "hierarchy-enhancing," "status-legitimizing," and "system-justifying" are interchangeable.

References

Altemeyer, B. (1981). *Right-wing authoritarianism*. Winnipeg: University of Manitoba Press.

Altemeyer, B. (1988). *Enemies of freedom: Understanding right-wing authoritarianism*. San Francisco, CA: Jossey-Bass.

Altemeyer, B. (1996). *The authoritarian specter*. Cambridge, MA: Harvard University Press.

Apfelbaum, E. P., Sommers, S. R., & Norton, M. I. (2008). Seeing race and seeming racist? Evaluating strategic colorblindness in social interaction. *Journal of Personality and Social Psychology, 95*(4), 918–932. doi:10.1037/a0011990

Awad, G. H., Cokley, K., & Ravitch, J. (2005). Attitudes toward affirmative action: A comparison of color-blind versus modern racist attitudes. *Journal of Applied Social Psychology, 35*(7), 1384–1399. doi:10.1111/j.1559-1816.2005.tb02175.x

Batson, C. D. (1975). Rational processing or rationalization? The effect of disconfirming information on a stated religious belief. *Journal of Personality and Social Psychology, 32*, 176–184.

Biernat, M., Vescio, T. K., Theno, S. A., & Crandall, C. S. (1996). Values and prejudice: Toward understanding the impact of American values on outgroup attitudes. In C. Seligman, J. M. Olson, M. P. Zanna, C. Seligman, J. M. Olson, &

M. P. Zanna (Eds.), *The psychology of values: The Ontario symposium, Vol. 8* (pp. 153–189). Hillsdale, NJ: Lawrence Erlbaum Associates, Inc.

Bobo, L., & Hutchings, V. L. (1996). Perceptions of racial group competition: Extending Blumer's theory of group position to a multiracial social context. *American Sociological Review, 61*(6), 951–972. doi:10.2307/2096302

Bobo, L. D. (1999). Prejudice as group position: Microfoundations of a sociological approach to racism and race relations. *Journal of Social Issues, 55*(3), 445–472. doi:10.1111/0022-4537.00127

Brauer, M., & Er-rafiy, A. (2011). Increasing perceived variability reduces prejudice and discrimination. *Journal of Experimental Social Psychology, 47,* 871–881.

Brewer, M. B. (1999). The psychology of prejudice: Ingroup love or outgroup hate? *Journal of Social Issues, 55*(3), 429–444. doi:10.1111/0022-4537.00126

Brug, P., & Verkuyten, M. (2007). Dealing with cultural diversity: The endorsement of societal models among ethnic minority and majority youth in the Netherlands. *Youth & Society, 39*(1), 112–131. doi:10.1177/0044118X06297074

Case, K. A., Fishbein, H. D., & Ritchey, P. (2008). Personality, prejudice, and discrimination against women and homosexuals. *Current Research in Social Psychology, 14,* 23–38.

Chandler, C. R., & Tsai, Y. (2001). Social factors influencing immigration attitudes: An analysis of data from the General Social Survey. *Social Science Journal, 38*(2), 177–188. doi:10.1016/S0362-3319(01)00106-9

Christopher, A. N., & Jones, J. R. (2004). Affluence cues and first impressions: The moderating impact of the Protestant work ethic. *Journal of Economic Psychology, 25*(2), 279–292. doi:10.1016/S0167-4870(02)00196-4

Christopher, A. N., & Mull, M. S. (2006). Conservative ideology and ambivalent sexism. *Psychology of Women Quarterly, 30*(2), 223–230. doi:10.1111/j.1471-6402.2006.00284.x

Christopher, A. N., & Wojda, M. R. (2008). Social dominance orientation, right-wing authoritarianism, sexism, and prejudice toward women in the workforce. *Psychology of Women Quarterly, 32*(1), 65–73. doi:10.1111/j.1471-6402.2007.00407.x

Christopher, A. N., Zabel, K. L., Jones, J. R., & Marek, P. (2008). Protestant ethic ideology: Its multifaceted relationships with just world beliefs, social dominance orientation, and right-wing authoritarianism. *Personality and Individual Differences, 45*(6), 473–477. doi:10.1016/j.paid.2008.05.023

Cohrs, J., & Stelzl, M. (2010). How ideological attitudes predict host society members' attitudes toward immigrants: Exploring cross-national differences. *Journal of Social Issues, 66*(4), 673–694. doi:10.1111/j.1540-4560.2010.01670.x

Cokley, K., Komarraju, M., Pickett, R., Shen, F., Patel, N., Belur, V., & Rosales, R. (2007). Ethnic differences in endorsement of Protestant Work Ethic: The role of ethnic identity and perceptions of social class. *Journal of Social Psychology, 147,* 75–89.

Conover, P. J., & Feldman, S. (1981). The origins and mean of liberal-conservative self-identifications. *American Journal of Political Science, 25,* 617–645.

Correll, J., Park, B., & Smith, J. (2008). Colorblind and multicultural prejudice reduction strategies in high-conflict situations. *Group Processes & Intergroup Relations, 11,* 471–491. doi:10.1177/1368430208095401

Crandall, C. S. (1994). Prejudice against fat people: Ideology and self-interest. *Journal of Personality and Social Psychology, 66*(5), 882–894. doi:10.1037/0022-3514.66.5.882

Crocker, J., Luhtanen, R., Broadnax, S., & Blaine, B. (1999). Belief in U.S. government conspiracies against Blacks among Black and White college students: Powerlessness or system blame? *Personality and Social Psychology Bulletin, 25*(8), 941–953. doi:10.1177/01461672992511003

Crocker, J., & Major, B. (1989). Social stigma and self-esteem: The self-protective properties of stigma. *Psychological Review, 96*(4), 608–630. doi:10.1037/0033-295X.96.4.608

Crosby, F. (2004). *Affirmative action is dead: Long live affirmative action.* New Haven, CT: Yale University Press.

Dalbert, C. (2001). *The justice motive as a personal resource: Dealing with challenges and critical life events.* New York: Kluwer Academic/Plenum Publishers.

Davey, L. M., Bobocel, D., Son Hing, L. S., & Zanna, M. P. (1999). Preference for the Merit Principle Scale: An individual difference measure of distributive justice preferences. *Social Justice Research, 12*(3), 223–240. doi:10.1023/A:1022148418210

Dittmar, H., & Dickinson, J. (1993). The perceived relationship between the belief in a just world and sociopolitical ideology. *Social Justice Research, 6,* 257–272.

Eccleston, C. P., Kaiser, C. R., & Kraynak, L. R. (2010). Shifts in justice beliefs induced by hurricane Katrina: The impact of claims of racism. *Group Processes & Intergroup Relations, 13*(5), 571–584. doi:10.1177/1368430210362436

Echebarria-Echabe, A., & Guede, E. (2007). A new measure of anti-Arab prejudice: Reliability and validity evidence. *Journal of Applied Social Psychology, 37*(5), 1077–1091. doi:10.1111/j.1559-1816.2007.00200.x

Eidelman, S., Crandall, C. S., & Pattershall, J. (2009). The existence bias. *Journal of Personality and Social Psychology, 97*(5), 765–775. doi:10.1037/a0017058

Feather, N. T. (1984). Protestant ethic, conservatism, and values. *Journal of Personality and Social Psychology, 46*(5), 1132–1141. doi:10.1037/0022-3514.46.5.1132

Foster, M. D., Sloto, L., & Ruby, R. (2006). Responding to discrimination as a function of meritocracy beliefs and personal experiences: Testing the model of shattered assumptions. *Group Processes & Intergroup Relations, 9*(3), 401–411. doi:10.1177/1368430206064641

Foster, M. D., & Tsarfati, E. (2005). The effects of meritocracy beliefs on women's well-being after first-time gender discrimination. *Personality and Social Psychology Bulletin, 31*(12), 1730–1738. doi:10.1177/0146167205278709

Fowers, B. J., & Richardson, F. C. (1996). Why is multiculturalism good? *American Psychologist, 51*(6), 609–621. doi:10.1037/0003-066X.51.6.609

Furnham, A. (1982a). The Protestant work ethic and attitudes toward unemployment. *Journal of Occupational Psychology, 55*(4), 277–285.

Furnham, A. (1985). Just world beliefs in an unjust society: A cross cultural comparison. *European Journal of Social Psychology, 15*(3), 363–366. doi:10.1002/ejsp.2420150310

Furnham, A., & Proctor, E. (1989). Belief in a just world: Review and critique of the individual difference literature. *British Journal of Social Psychology, 28,* 365–384.

Furnham, A. F. (1982b). Why are the poor always with us? Explanations for poverty in Britain. *British Journal of Social Psychology, 21*(4), 311–322.

Furnham, A. F. (2003). Just World Beliefs are good for you. *PsycCRITIQUES, 48*(2), 179–181. doi:10.1037/000754

Furnham, F. (1990). A content, correlational, and factor analytic study of seven questionnaire measures of the Protestant Work Ethic. *Human Relations, 43*, 383–399.

Glover, R. J. (1994). Using moral and epistemological reasoning as predictors of prejudice. *Journal of Social Psychology, 134*, 633–640.

Green, E. G., Thomsen, L., Sidanius, J., Staerkle, C., & Potanina, P. (2009). Reactions to crime as a hierarchy regulating strategy: The moderating role of social dominance orientation. *Social Justice Research, 22*, 416–436.

Gurin, P. (1985). Women's gender consciousness. *Public Opinion Quarterly, 49*, 143–163.

Gurin, P., & Townsend, A. (1986). Properties of gender identity and their implications for gender consciousness. *British Journal of Social Psychology, 25*, 139–148.

Gutierrez, A. S., & Unzueta, M. M. (2010). The effect of interethnic ideologies on the likability of stereotypic vs. counterstereotypic minority targets. *Journal of Experimental Social Psychology, 46*, 775–784.

Hafer, C. L., & Olson, J. M. (1993). Beliefs in a just world, discontent, and assertive actions by working women. *Personality and Social Psychology Bulletin, 19*(1), 30–38. doi:10.1177/0146167293191004

Hafer, C. L., & Olson, J. M. (1989). Beliefs in a just world and reactions to personal deprivation. *Journal of Personality, 57*, 799–823. doi:10.1111/j.1467-6494.1989.tb00495.x.

Heaven, P. C. L. (1999). Attitudes towards women's rights: Relationships with social dominance orientation and political group identities. *Sex Roles, 41*, 605–613. doi:10.1023/A:1018851606423

Hirsh, J. B., DeYoung, C. G., Xu, X., & Peterson, J. B. (2010). Compassionate liberals and polite conservatives: Associations of agreeableness with political ideology and moral values. *Personality and Social Psychology Bulletin, 36*(5), 655–664. doi:10.1177/0146167210366854

Janoff-Bulman, R. (1989). The benefits of illusions, the threat of disillusionment, and the limitations of inaccuracy. *Journal of Social and Clinical Psychology, 8*(2), 158–175.

Jones, H. B. (1997). The Protestant ethic: Weber's model and the empirical literature. *Human Relations, 50*(7), 757–778.

Jost, J. T., & Banaji, M. R. (1994). The role of stereotyping in system-justification and the production of false consciousness. *British Journal of Social Psychology, 33*, 1–27.

Jost, J. T., & Burgess, D. (2000). Attitudinal ambivalence and the conflict between group and system justification motives in low status groups. *Personality and Social Psychology Bulletin, 26*(3), 293–305. doi:10.1177/0146167200265003

Jost, J. T., Federico, C. M., & Napier, J. L. (2009). Political ideology: Its structure, functions, and elective affinities. *Annual Review of Psychology, 60*, 307–337. doi:10.1146/annurev.psych.60.110707.163600

Jost, J. T., Glaser, J., Kruglanski, A. W., & Sulloway, F. J. (2003). Political conservatism as motivated social cognition. *Psychological Bulletin, 129*, 339–375.

Jost, J. T., & Hunyady, O. (2002). The psychology of system justification and the palliative function of ideology. In W. Stroebe, M. Hewstone, W. Stroebe, & M. Hewstone (Eds.), *European review of social psychology, Vol. 13* (pp. 111–153). Hove, England: Psychology Press/Taylor & Francis (UK).

Jost, J. T., & Thompson, E. P. (2000). Group-based dominance and opposition to equality as independent predictors of self-esteem, ethnocentrism, and social policy attitudes among African Americans and European Americans. *Journal of Experimental Social Psychology, 36*, 209–232.

Kaiser, C. R., Dyrenforth, P. S., & Hagiwara, N. (2006). Why are attributions to discrimination interpersonally costly? A test of system- and group-justifying motivations. *Personality and Social Psychology Bulletin, 32*(11), 1523–1536. doi:10.1177/0146167206291475

Kaiser, C. R., & Pratt-Hyatt, J. S. (2009). Distributing prejudice unequally: Do Whites direct their prejudice toward strongly identified minorities? *Journal of Personality and Social Psychology, 96*(2), 432–445. doi:10.1037/a0012877

Katz, I., & Hass, R. G. (1988). Racial ambivalence and American value conflict: Correlational and priming studies of dual cognitive structures. *Journal of Personality and Social Psychology, 55*, 893–905.

Katz, I. I., & Benjamin, L. L. (1960). Effects of white authoritarianism in biracial work groups. *Journal of Abnormal and Social Psychology, 61*(3), 448–456. doi:10.1037/h0043665

Kemmelmeier, M. (2005). The effects of race and social dominance orientation in simulated juror decision making. *Journal of Applied Social Psychology, 35*(5), 1030–1045. doi:10.1111/j.1559-1816.2005.tb02158.x

Kerlinger, F. N. (1984). *Liberalism and conservatism: The nature and structure of social attitudes.* Hillsdale, NJ: L. Erlbaum.

Kluegel, J. R., & Smith, E. R. (1986). *Beliefs about inequality: Americans' views of what is and what ought to be.* Hawthorne, NY: Aldine de Gruyter.

Knowles, E. D., Lowery, B. S., Hogan, C. M., & Chow, R. M. (2009). On the malleability of ideology: Motivated construals of color blindness. *Journal of Personality and Social Psychology, 96*, 857–869.

Koltko-Rivera, M. E. (2004). The psychology of worldviews. *Review of General Psychology, 8*(1), 3–58. doi:10.1037/1089-2680.8.1.3

Kteily, N. S., Sidanius, J., & Levin, S. (2011). Social dominance orientation: Cause or "mere effect"?: Evidence for SDO as a causal predictor of prejudice and discrimination against ethnic and racial outgroups. *Journal of Experimental Social Psychology, 47*, 208–214.

Lambert, A. J., & Chasteen, A. L. (1997). Perceptions of disadvantage versus conventionality: Political values and attitudes toward the elderly versus Blacks. *Personality and Social Psychology Bulletin, 23*(5), 469–481. doi:10.1177/0146167297235003

Lerner, M. J. (1980). *The belief in a just world: A fundamental delusion.* New York: Plenum Press.

Levin, S., & Sidanius, J. (1999). Social dominance and social identity in the United States and Israel: Ingroup favoritism or outgroup derogation? *Political Psychology, 20*(1), 99–126. doi:10.1111/0162-895X.00138

Levin, S., Sidanius, J., Rabinowitz, J. L., & Federico, C. (1998). Ethnic identity, legitimizing ideologies, and social status: A matter of ideological asymmetry. *Political Psychology, 19*, 373–404.

Levin, S., van Laar, C., & Sidanius, J. (2003). The effects of ingroup and outgroup friendship on ethnic attitudes in college: A longitudinal study. *Group Processes & Intergroup Relations, 6*(1), 76–92. doi:10.1177/1368430203006001013

Levy, S. R., Freitas, A. L., Mendoza-Denton, R., & Kugelmass, H. (2006). Hurricane Katrina's impact on African Americans' and European Americans' endorsement of the Protestant

Work Ethic. *Analyses of Social Issues and Public Policy (ASAP), 6*(1), 75–85. doi:10.1111/j.1530-2415.2006.00104.x

Levy, S. R., West, T. L., & Ramirez, L. (2005). Lay theories and intergroup relations: A social-developmental perspective. *European Review of Social Psychology, 16,* 189–220 doi:10.1080/10463280500397234

Levy, S. R., West, T. L., Ramirez, L., & Karafantis, D. M. (2006). The Protestant Work Ethic: A lay theory with dual intergroup implications. *Group Processes and Intergroup Relations, 9,* 95–115.

Lipkus, I. M., Dalbert, C., & Seigler, I. C. (1996). The importance of distinguishing the belief in a just world for self versus others. *Personality and Social Psychology Bulletin, 22,* 666–677.

MacDonald, A. P. (1972). More on the Protestant Ethic. *Journal of Consulting and Clinical Psychology, 39*(1), 116–122. doi:10.1037/h0033156

Major, B. (1994). From social inequality to personal entitlement: The role of social comparisons, legitimacy appraisals, and group membership. *Advances in experimental social psychology, Vol. 26* (pp. 293–355). San Diego, CA: Academic Press.

Major, B., Gramzow, R., McCoy, S. K., Levin, S., Schmader, T., & Sidanius, J. (2002). Perceiving personal discrimination: The role of group status and status legitimizing ideology. *Journal of Personality and Social Psychology, 80,* 782–796.

Major, B., Kaiser, C. R., O'Brien, L. T., & McCoy, S. K. (2007). Perceived discrimination as worldview threat or worldview confirmation: Implications for self-esteem. *Journal of Personality and Social Psychology, 92,* 1068–1086.

Major, B., Quinton, W. J., & McCoy, S. K. (2002). Antecedents and consequences of attributions to discrimination: Theoretical and empirical advances. In M. P. Zanna (Ed.), *Advances in experimental social psychology* (Vol. 34, pp. 251–330). San Diego, CA: Academic Press.

Malahy, L. W., Rubinlicht, M. A., & Kaiser, C. R. (2009). Justifying inequality: A cross-temporal investigation of U.S. Income disparities and just-world beliefs from 1973 to 2006. *Social Justice Research, 22*(4), 369–383. doi:10.1007/s11211-009-0103-6

Malcomnson, K. M., Christopher, A. N., Franzen, T., & Keyes, B. J. (2006). The Protestant Work Ethic, religious beliefs, and homonegative attitudes. *Mental Health, Religion & Culture, 9*(5), 435–447. doi:10.1080/13694670500264068

Matthews, M., Levin, S., & Sidanius, J. (2009). A longitudinal test of the model political conservatism as motivated social cognition. *Political Psychology, 30,* 921–936.

McCoy, S. K., & Major, B. (2007). Priming meritocracy and the psychological justification of inequality. *Journal of Experimental Social Psychology, 43,* 341–351.

Michaud, K. H., Carlisle, J. E., & Smith, E. N. (2009). The relationship between cultural values and political ideology, and the role of political knowledge. *Political Psychology, 30*(1), 27–42. doi:10.1111/j.1467-9221.2008.00679.x

Mirels, H. L., & Darland, D. M. (1990). The Protestant ethic and self characterization. *Personality and Individual Differences, 11,* 895–898.

Mirels, H. L., & Garrett, J. B. (1971). The Protestant Ethic as a personality variable. *Journal of Consulting and Clinical Psychology, 36,* 40–44.

Mitchell, M., & Sidanius, S. (1993). Group status and asymmetry in the relationship between ideology and death penalty support: A social dominance perspective. *National Journal of Sociology, 7,* 67–93.

Molix, L., & Bettencourt, B. (2010). Predicting well-being among ethnic minorities: Psychological empowerment and group identity. *Journal of Applied Social Psychology, 40*(3), 513–533. doi:10.1111/j.1559-1816.2010.00585.x

Monteith, M. J., & Walters, G. L. (1998). Egalitarianism, moral obligation, and prejudice-related personal standards. *Personality and Social Psychology Bulletin, 24*(2), 186–199. doi:10.1177/0146167298242007

Morrison, K., Plaut, V. C., & Ybarra, O. (2010). Predicting whether multiculturalism positively or negatively influences white Americans' intergroup attitudes: The role of ethnic identification. *Personality and Social Psychology Bulletin, 36,* 1648–1661. doi:10.1177/0146167210386118

Morrison, M. A., & Morrison, T. G. (2002). Development and validation of a scale measuring modern prejudice toward gay men and lesbian women. *Journal of Homosexuality, 43*(2), 15–37. doi:10.1300/J082v43n02_02

Mudrack, P. E. (2004). Job involvement, obsessive-compulsive personality traits, and workaholic behavioral tendencies. *Journal of Organizational Change Management, 17*(5), 490–508. doi:10.1108/09534810410554506

Nail, P. R., Harton, H. C., & Decker, B. P. (2003). Political orientation and modern versus aversive racism: Tests of Dovidio and Gaertner's (1998) integrated model. *Journal of Personality and Social Psychology, 84*(4), 754–770. doi:10.1037/0022-3514.84.4.754

Napier, J. L., & Jost, J. T. (2008). Why are conservatives happier than liberals?. *Psychological Science, 19*(6), 565–572. doi:10.1111/j.1467-9280.2008.02124.x

Norton, M. I., Sommers, S. R., Apfelbaum, E. P., Pura, N., & Ariely, D. (2006). Color blindness and interracial interaction: Playing the political correctness game. *Psychological Science, 17,* 949–953.

O'Brien, L. T., Blodorn, A., Alsbrooks, A., Dube, R., Adams, G., & Nelson, J. C. (2009). Understanding White Americans' perceptions of racism in Hurricane Katrina-related events. *Group Processes & Intergroup Relations, 12*(4), 431–444. doi:10.1177/1368430209105047

O'Brien, L. T., & Major, B. (2005). System-justifying beliefs and psychological well-being: The roles of group status and identity. *Personality and Social Psychology Bulletin, 31,* 1718–1729.

O'Brien, L. T., & Major, B. (2009). Group status and feelings of personal entitlement: The roles of social comparison and system-justifying beliefs. *Social and psychological bases of ideology and system justification* (pp. 427–443). New York: Oxford University Press.

O'Brien, L. T., Major, B. N., & Gilbert, P. N. (2012). Gender differences in personal entitlement: The roles of system justifying beliefs. *Basic and Applied Social Psychology.*

Plant, E., & Devine, P. G. (1998). Internal and external motivation to respond without prejudice. *Journal of Personality and Social Psychology, 75*(3), 811–832. doi:10.1037/0022-3514.75.3.811

Plant, E., Devine, P. G., & Peruche, M. B. (2010). Routes to positive interracial interactions: Approaching egalitarianism or avoiding prejudice. *Personality and Social Psychology Bulletin, 36*(9), 1135–1147. doi:10.1177/0146167210378018

Plaut, V. C., Thomas, K. M., & Goren, M. J. (2009). Is multiculturalism or color blindness better for minorities? *Psychological Science, 20,* 444–446.

Pratto, F., Sidanius, J., Stallworth, L. M., & Malle, B. F. (1994). Social dominance orientation: A personality variable predicting social and political attitudes. *Journal of Personality and Social Psychology, 67*(4), 741–763. doi:10.1037/0022-3514.67.4.741

Purdie-Vaughns, V., Steele, C. M., Davies, P. G., Ditlmann, R., & Crosby, J. R. (2008). Social identity contingencies: How diversity cues signal threat or safety for African Americans in mainstream institutions. *Journal of Personality and Social Psychology, 94*, 615–630.

Quinn, D. M., & Crocker, J. (1999). When ideology hurts: Effects of belief in the Protestant ethic and feeling overweight on the psychological well-being of women. *Journal of Personality & Social Psychology, 77*, 402–414.

Rabinowitz, J. L. (1999). Go with the flow or fight the power? The interactive effects of social dominance orientation and perceived injustice on support for the status quo. *Political Psychology, 20*(1), 1–24. doi:10.1111/0162-895X.00135

Rankin, L. E., Jost, J. T., & Wakslak, C. J. (2009). System justification and the meaning of life: Are the existential benefits of ideology distributed unequally across racial groups? *Social Justice Research, 22*, 312–333.

Reyna, C., Henry, P. J., Korfmacher, W., & Tucker, A. (2006). Examining the principles in principled conservatism: The role of responsibility stereotypes as cues for deservingness in racial policy decisions. *Journal of Personality and Social Psychology, 90*(1), 109–128. doi:10.1037/0022-3514.90.1.109

Richeson, J. A., & Nussbaum, R. J. (2004). The impact of multiculturalism versus color-blindness on racial bias. *Journal of Experimental Social Psychology, 40*, 417–423.

Robinson, J. P., Rusk, J. G., Head, K. B., Athanasiou, R., Shaver, P. R., & University of Michigan. (1968). *Measures of political attitudes*. Ann Arbor, MI: Survey Research Center, Institute for Social Research.

Rohan, M. J., & Zanna, M. P. (1996). Value transmission in families. In C. Seligman, J. M. Olson, M. P. Zanna, C. Seligman, J. M. Olson, & M. P. Zanna (Eds.), *The psychology of values: The Ontario symposium, Vol. 8* (pp. 253–276). Hillsdale, NJ: Lawrence Erlbaum Associates, Inc.

Rokeach, M. (1973). *The Nature of Human Values*. New York: Free Press.

Rubin, Z., & Peplau, L. A. (1975). Who believes in a just world? *Journal of Social Issues, 31*(3), 65–89.

Ryan, C. S., Hunt, J. S., Weible, J. A., Peterson, C. R., & Casas, J. F. (2007). Multicultural and colorblind ideology, stereotypes, and ethnocentrism among Black and White Americans. *Group Processes and Intergroup Relations, 10*, 617–637.

Sears, D. O., & Funk, C. L. (1981). The role of self-interest in social and political attitudes. *Advances in Experimental Social Psychology, 24*, 1–91.

Sellers, R. M., Smith, M. A., Shelton, J., Rowley, S. J., & Chavous, T. M. (1998). Multidimensional model of racial identity: A reconceptualization of African American racial identity. *Personality and Social Psychology Review, 2*(1), 18–39. doi:10.1207/s15327957pspr0201_2

Shapiro, J. R., & Neuberg, S. L. (2008). When do the stigmatized stigmatize? The ironic effects of being accountable to (perceived) majority group prejudice-expression norms. *Journal of Personality and Social Psychology, 95*(4), 877–898. doi:10.1037/a0011617

Sidanius, J., & Duffy, G. (1988). The duality of attitude structure: A test of Kerlinger's criterial referents theory within samples of Swedish and American youth. *Political Psychology, 9*(4), 649–670. doi:10.2307/3791532

Sidanius, J., & Ekehammar, B. (1979). Political socialization: A multivariate analysis of Swedish political attitude and preference data. *European Journal of Social Psychology, 9*(3), 265–279. doi:10.1002/ejsp.2420090305

Sidanius, J., Levin, S., & Pratto, F. (1996). Consensual social dominance orientation and its correlates within the hierarchical structure of American society. *International Journal of Intercultural Relations, 20*(3–4), 385–408. doi:10.1016/0147-1767(96)00025-9

Sidanius, J., & Pratto, F. (1999). *Social dominance: An intergroup theory of social hierarchy and oppression*. New York: Cambridge University Press.

Sidanius, J., Pratto, F., & Rabinowitz, J. L. (1994). Gender, ethnic status, and ideological asymmetry: A social dominance interpretation. *Journal of Cross-Cultural Psychology, 25*(2), 194–216. doi:10.1177/0022022194252003

Sidanius, J., van Laar, C., Levin, S., & Sinclair, S. (2003). social hierarchy maintenance and assortment into social roles: A social dominance perspective. *Group Processes & Intergroup Relations, 6*(4), 353–368. doi:10.1177/13684302030064002

Simon, B., & Klandermans, B. (2001). Politicized collective identity: A social psychological analysis. *American Psychologist, 56*, 319–331.

Son Hing, L. S., Bobocel, R., Zanna, M. P., Garcia, D.M., Gee, S. S., & Orazietta, K. (2011). The merit of meritocracy. *Journal of Personality and Social Psychology, 101*, 433–450. doi:10.1037/a0024618

Son Hing, L. S., Chung-Yan, G. A., Hamilton, L. K., & Zanna, M. P. (2008). A two-dimensional model that employs explicit and implicit attitudes to characterize prejudice. *Journal of Personality and Social Psychology, 94*, 971–987.

Swim, J. K., Aikin, K. J., Hall, W. S., & Hunter, B. A. (1995). Sexism and racism: Old-fashioned and modern prejudices. *Journal of Personality and Social Psychology, 68*(2), 199–214. doi:10.1037/0022-3514.68.2.199

Thomsen, L., Green, E.G., Ho, A.K., Levin, S., van Laar, C., Sinclair, S., & Sidanius, J. (2010). Wolves in sheep's clothing: SDO asymmetrically predicts perceived ethnic victimization among White and Latino students across three years. *Personality and Social Psychology Bulletin, 36*, 225–238. doi:10.1177/0146167209348617

Tomaka, J., & Blascovich, J. (1994). Effects of justice beliefs on cognitive appraisal of and subjective physiological, and behavioral responses to potential stress. *Journal of Personality and Social Psychology, 67*(4), 732–740. doi:10.1037/0022-3514.67.4.732

Townsend, S. M., Major, B., Sawyer, P. J., & Mendes, W. (2010). Can the absence of prejudice be more threatening than its presence? It depends on one's worldview. *Journal of Personality and Social Psychology, 99*(6), 933–947. doi:10.1037/a0020434

Valentine, S. R. (2001). Men and women supervisors' job responsibility, job satisfaction, and employee monitoring. *Sex Roles, 45*(3–4), 179–197. doi:10.1023/A:1013549710711

van Laar, C., Sidanius, J., Rabinowitz, J. L., & Sinclair, S. (1999). The three Rs of academic achievement: Reading, 'riting, and racism. *Personality and Social Psychology Bulletin, 25*(2), 139–151. doi:10.1177/0146167299025002001

Verkuyten, M. (2005). Ethnic group identification and group evaluation among minority and majority groups: Testing the multiculturalism hypothesis. *Journal of Personality and Social Psychology, 88*, 121–138.

Verkuyten, M. (2009a). Self-esteem and multiculturalism: An examination among ethnic minority and majority groups in the Netherlands. *Journal of Research in Personality, 43,* 419–427.

Verkuyten, M. (2009b). Support for multiculturalism and minority rights: The role of national identification and out-group threat. *Social Justice Research, 22,* 31–52.

Verkuyten, M., & Yildiz, A. A. (2006). The endorsement of minority rights: The role of group position, national context, and ideological beliefs. *Political Psychology, 27,* 527–548.

Vorauer, J. D., Gagnon, A., & Sasaki, S. J. (2009). Salient intergroup ideology and intergroup interaction. *Psychological Science, 20*(7), 838–845. doi:10.1111/j.1467-9280.2009.02369.x

Vorauer, J. D., & Sasaki, S. J. (2010). In need of liberation or constraint? How intergroup attitudes moderate the behavioral implications of intergroup ideologies. *Journal of Experimental Social Psychology, 46*(1), 133–138. doi:10.1016/j.jesp.2009.08.013

Wagstaff, G. F. (1983). Attitudes to poverty, the Protestant Ethic, and political affiliation: A preliminary investigation. *Social Behavior and Personality, 11*(1), 45–47. doi:10.2224/sbp.1983.11.1.45

Weber, M. (1958). *The Protestant ethic and the spirit of capitalism.* (T. Parsons, Trans.) New York: Scribner. (Original work published 1904–1905).

Wellman, J. A., Czopp, A. M., & Geers, A. L. (2009). The egalitarian optimist and the confrontation of prejudice. *Journal of Positive Psychology, 4*(5), 389–395. doi:10.1080/17439760902992449

White, J. B., & Langer, E. J. (1999). Horizontal hostility: Relations between similar minority groups. *Journal of Social Issues, 55*(3), 537–559. doi:10.1111/0022-4537.00132

Wilson, G. D., & Patterson, J. R. (1968). A new measure of conservatism. *British Journal of Social & Clinical Psychology, 7*(4), 264–269.

Wolsko, C., Park, B., & Judd, C. M. (2006). Considering the Tower of Babel: Correlates of assimilation and multiculturalism among ethnic minority and majority groups in the United States. *Social Justice Research, 19,* 277–306.

Wolsko, C., Park, B., Judd, C. M., & Wittenbrink, B. (2000). Framing interethnic ideology: Effects of multicultural and colorblind perspectives on judgments of groups and individuals. *Journal of Personality and Social Psychology, 78,* 635–665.

PART 4

Interactionist Perspectives on Diversity

CHAPTER 9

Diversity as Knowledge Exchange: The Roles of Information Processing, Expertise, and Status

Katherine W. Phillips, Michelle Duguid, Melissa Thomas-Hunt *and* Jayaram Uparna

Abstract

As part of an effort to understand diversity's influence on group processes and performance, some researchers have explored diversity from an information processing perspective. This perspective suggests that because individuals in heterogeneous groups have a broader range of knowledge, skills, and abilities than homogeneous groups, they will also have greater access to a variety of task-relevant information and expertise, which can enhance group decision making. This chapter summarizes the findings of empirical research from this perspective and extends the tenets of this perspective, acknowledging the limitations of the original formulation. Included in the review is research on minority and majority influence processes and the integration of expert knowledge in groups. Finally, the chapter integrates this new information processing view with work that focuses on the effect of status differences on the processing of information in diverse environments.

Key Words: diversity, knowledge exchange, information processing, expertise, status, team, group, categorization

Introduction

Why do organizations use teams to solve problems, create products, and make decisions? The answer to this question is varied, but an oft-cited refrain is that organizations use teams to leverage their people's unique information, knowledge, and skills to solve problems, innovate, and execute (e.g., Katzenbach & Smith, 1993). It is the potential of this knowledge exchange that helps make the idea of using groups exciting and potentially profitable in organizations. It is this same promise that generally undergirds the rhetoric behind the positive effects of diversity in teams (Jackson, 1992; Watson, Kumar, & Michaelson, 1993; Williams & O'Reilly, 1998). Thus, if individuals believe that diverse knowledge can be used to benefit the group, the idea of composing a group with a set of individuals with different backgrounds, experiences, and ways of looking at the world should reasonably yield significant enthusiasm (Cox, Lobel, & McLeod, 1991). This is the promise of diversity that comes with an information processing perspective. However, figuring out how to successfully integrate disparate knowledge and skills that are uniquely held by individual group members is a significant management challenge.

Teams permeate the work of organizations. Despite the difficulty of nailing down the exact extent to which organizations use teams, estimates on the prevalence of teams among Fortune 1000 companies dating back to the 1990s revealed that nearly all such companies used project teams for a defined period of time. About half were using permanent work teams and another 87 percent were found to be using parallel teams, where people were working on problem solving or quality improvement in parallel to their regular organizational position (Dumaine, 1994; Lawler & Cohen, 1992). Since that time, teams have become such an integral part of how work is accomplished that these surveys are not even conducted any longer. Teams are everywhere and organizations view them as essential to success (Devine, Clayton, Philips, Dunford, & Melner, 1990; Roomkin, Rosen, & Dubbs, 1998; Thompson, 2007; Wuchty, Jones, & Uzzi, 2007). Consequently, using teams in an organization has become a taken-for-granted aspect of the way work is done.

The growth of teams has been accompanied by a commensurate growth in the presence of diversity in organizations. Thus, as organizations found themselves moving to more team-focused structures for accomplishing work, they also found themselves considering how to manage the growth in racial, gender, national, and age diversity that has occurred in organizations. At the same time organizations also recognized the need to leverage those preexisting dimensions of diversity that were made more salient by the interdependence demanded of teams (i.e., functional, educational, and personality differences, tenure diversity, and differences in values and goals). This focus illuminates the critical importance of understanding diversity through a knowledge exchange perspective. Such a perspective clarifies not only if, but how, organizations might be able to benefit from the increasing diversity of the workplace through the exchange of knowledge in teams. Moreover, by using an approach that opens the black box of diversity and by examining the process of knowledge exchange in groups, researchers can contribute to organizations' understanding of how to capture the potential upsides of diversity while managing the downsides.

In this chapter we examine the original research on diversity from this information processing perspective and more recent instantiations, giving consideration to two other dominant diversity perspectives: social categorization theory and the similarity-attraction perspective. Furthermore, we examine the status differences that often accompany diversity characteristics and consider how such differences affect the ability of teams to capture their purported information processing benefits.

Defining diversity

We begin by adopting the definition of diversity used by Lambert and Bell (Chapter 2), which espouses that diversity is the variation of traits, both visible and not, of groups of two or more people (McGrath, Berdahl, & Arrow, 1995). Although this definition has been expounded upon in more recent reviews by van Knippenberg and Schippers (2007) and Mannix and Neale (2005), we adopt this simple definition because of its parsimony. This definition allows for consideration of research that examines a host of characteristics, such as race/ethnicity, age, gender, functional background, education, personality, values, and tenure in the workplace. Social psychological examinations of the impact of diversity even use minimal group distinctions that also aid in our understanding of the influence of diversity on team process and performance (Tajfel, 1981; Tajfel & Turner, 1986; for an empirical example see Lount & Phillips, 2007). Importantly, these minimal distinctions help us understand that the effects of diversity can be created by even the most seemingly insignificant cues in the environment (e.g., which floor is your office on in the building; which company did you originate from in the merger; or whether you are a married or single MBA student). These distinctions may seem irrelevant for the task at hand, yet they are psychologically important to the members and dynamics of the group.

In an effort to simplify the complexity that comes from the multiple sources of diversity in any given setting, researchers have introduced many ways of dividing these characteristics into their own categories (e.g., Cummings, Zhou, & Oldham, 1993; Harrison, Price, & Bell, 1998; Jackson, 1992; Jackson & Joshi, 2011). In many cases researchers make claims about the importance or relevance of a particular type of diversity for group process and performance based on the type of characteristic being considered. For instance, Jackson and Joshi (2011) state that *relations-oriented diversity* (as opposed to *task-oriented diversity*), defined as characteristics that are "instrumental in shaping interpersonal relationships," such as gender, age, ethnicity, nationality, religion, personality, and sexual identity, typically have "no apparent direct implications for task performance" (p. 653). This might lead to the conclusion that these types of diversity are irrelevant for understanding task-oriented behaviors in groups, such as knowledge exchange and information processing, and are only important for understanding *relations-oriented* dependent variables such as cohesion and liking. Yet, as we will see in this chapter, there are many sources of diversity that have relevance for both knowledge exchange and information processing in groups as well as social relations. Thus, we embrace an integrated view of diversity characteristics. We espouse that the information processing and social implications of various diversity characteristics are difficult to disentangle, and that relations-oriented processes and task-oriented processes in groups often work in tandem, or opposition, to influence processing of information and ultimate performance.

Defining our scope

Multiple methodologies have been used to conduct research on issues of diversity, ranging from experimental methodologies more familiar to psychologists, to the field work that characterizes much of the work of organizational researchers. In many reviews of the diversity literature you find one or the other's perspective more heavily emphasized. This is sometimes out of necessity as the literature is vast, and this is sometimes out of ignorance as the two areas of research operate in an only quasi-interdependent way. Our review will consider mostly research conducted in more controlled laboratory settings, in large part because the study of information processes needs a controlled environment in which close measure of exchanges may be made. Nevertheless, we will also include some research that has been conducted in the field (see Williams & O'Reilly, 1998, for more discussion on the importance of this distinction), as we believe it is critically important to try to integrate the two. To make our task manageable we focus on a common thread across these literatures, identifying work that directly provides insight into how information is being processed in group settings. This means that the task being completed by the participants in the study must require information processing to be included in our review. Thus, this is a selective review and is not meant to be comprehensive. Again, insight into this information processing perspective often comes from the laboratory or the controlled settings used by experimentalists where clear data about who has what information, and with whom and how that information is being shared and utilized, can readily be examined. When using a field approach it is often difficult to surmise how information is being utilized because processes are either not observable or are so embedded within a range of activities that researchers can only *infer* how information is being processed from the outcomes measured or observed. Also, within the field there is no *a priori* certainty about who does or does not possess critical information or opinions about the tasks at hand.

With this understanding and our definition of diversity in mind, we highlight a way of understanding the effects of diversity that relies on integrating the social category perspective with the information/decision-making perspective. The distinctions we use in the chapter embrace the complexities of diversity by highlighting the fact that variance in group settings, no matter which characteristics of diversity are being discussed, is accompanied by both some level of social categorization processes (i.e., *social category diversity*) *and* some potential differences in information and perspectives (i.e., *informational/opinion diversity*) (Phillips, Kim-Jun, & Shim, 2010). An important assumption we make throughout this chapter is that when groups of people come together to make decisions, there are likely to be differences in information and opinions among the group members. Groups are usually brought together to achieve targets that invariably require some form of information sharing among the members. Even when all group members possess the same information, they may not all come to the same conclusions after reading the information, as each one may *interpret* the same information differently or choose to recall or weight different parts of the information as being important. It is this situation where there are presumed informational or opinion differences within groups that is most interesting for this review.

We proceed by first briefly reviewing the predominant social categorization perspective and the information/decision-making perspective as described by Williams and O'Reilly (1998) and Van Knippenberg, De Dreu, and Homan (2004), and point out both their contributions and limitations. We also give consideration to minority influence (e.g., Brodbeck, Kerschreiter, Mojzisch, Frey, & Schulz-Hardt, 2002; Maass, West, & Cialdini, 1987; Nemeth, 1986) and social network perspectives (Burt, 1973, 2007; Reagans & McEvily, 2003) to explain the processes by which information is distributed. We then review research that uses an experimental approach to integrate social psychological research on information processing with the broader discussion of diversity in organizational workgroups (e.g., Homan, van Knippenberg, van Kleef, & De Dreu, 2007a; Phillips, 2003; Phillips & Loyd, 2006; van Ginkel & van Knippenberg, 2008). Next, we juxtapose this research with work that has focused on the integration of minority perspectives and expertise into groups and highlight work that has explicitly and implicitly considered the influence of status on the integration of knowledge. We also consider those studies that might have benefited from the use of a status lens.

Theoretical approaches to understanding diversity
Social categorization/similarity-attraction perspective

The social categorization perspective is the most prominent theoretical perspective adopted by diversity researchers (for reviews see Jackson & Joshi, 2011; Mannix & Neale, 2005; Milliken & Martins, 1996; Van Knippenberg & Schippers, 2007; Williams & O'Reilly, 1998). The language used around this perspective is sometimes confusing. First, we note that social categorization theory (Tajfel, 1981; Turner, 1987) goes hand in hand with social identity theory (Hogg & Abrams, 1988; Turner, 1982). The two theories were developed in parallel and together help us understand both the cognitive and motivational aspects of how and why people categorize one another into in-group and out-group. People have a desire to maintain a positive self-esteem, and they do this by comparing themselves to others around them. But first, people must define themselves and the others around them so they can engage in this social comparison process.

This perspective predicts that when individuals first walk into a room they take note of the social categories that are salient in the context. Researchers have argued that demographic or surface-level categories (i.e., those that are visible), such as age, gender, and race, serve as the most prominent sources of categorization. These characteristics help individuals simplify the social environment and make predictions about the presumed behavior, knowledge, and beliefs of others in the room (Harrison, Price, & Bell, 1998; Harrison, Price, Gavin, & Florey, 2002; Phillips, Northcraft, & Neale, 2006; Phinney, 1996). When individuals categorize people, they are most simply classified as being the same as themselves (in-group) or different from themselves (out-group). Having categorized people, individuals become motivated to view in-group members more positively than out-group members, as this bolsters their own self-esteem. Furthermore, such differential regard for in-group members and out-group members fosters behaviors that result in less collective communication, trust, cooperation, and cohesion, and more conflict in diverse compared to homogeneous settings (cf. Williams & O'Reilly, 1998). The process of categorization may also engender implicit beliefs that one's own group is superior to other groups (either on specific or diffuse dimensions, or both), infusing an inherent status differential, agreed upon or not, among in-group and out-group members.

Social categorization theory is especially powerful when coupled with the similarity-attraction paradigm (Berscheid & Walster, 1978; Byrne, 1971; Byrne, Clore, & Worchel, 1966), which helps account for *why* categorizations persist and shape judgments and behaviors accordingly. Specifically, the similarity-attraction paradigm argues that people are attracted to similar others and have a strong tendency to seek interaction with similar rather than dissimilar individuals (e.g., Blau, 1977; Lincoln & Miller, 1979; McPherson & Smith-Lovin, 1987). This homophily in social interactions is often also predicated on having first categorized people into in-group and out-group. Social categories help us understand who we are similar to and different from, and make it easier for us to find desired interaction partners.

Why do we seek similar others? One answer to this is that we want to find others whom we believe share our opinions, perspectives, and outlooks on life. To this end, one of the functions of categorizing people into in-group and out-group in workgroup settings is to predict who is likely to agree with and support our viewpoints. Thus, one immediate consequence of categorizing people is that individuals tend to assume that the members of their own social category are more likely to share the same information, opinions, and attitudes with them than are members of the out-group (e.g., Allen & Wilder, 1975, 1978, 1979; Chen & Kenrick, 2002; Phillips, 2003; Phillips & Loyd, 2006). That is, people assume that members of the in-group are going to agree with them and that out-group members will be more likely to disagree. This assumed similarity affects the way information is shared and processed in groups and makes the social categorization process critically important for understanding the information processing view of diversity (e.g., Phillips, 2003; Phillips, Mannix, Neale, & Gruenfeld, 2004; Phillips et al., 2006; Rink & Ellemers, 2007). Another explanation may be that by ensuring that the in-group contains individuals who are similar to self, there is less uncertainty and more predictability of how the group would react to stimuli. Thus, the individual may feel more in control of the situation merely because he or she can better predict what the members may feel or how they may act, and the individual is more in tune with what is considered normal or acceptable within the group.

Diversity has often been thought of as a double-edged sword, potentially improving performance on complex tasks but often accompanied by disruptions of group process (e.g., Guzzo & Dickson, 1996; Milliken & Martins, 1996; Williams & O'Reilly, 1998). Some researchers have argued that the best way to avoid the problems that accompany diversity and the categorization process is to minimize the salience of differences that make people unique and different, and instead emphasize the commonalities that bring individuals together (Gaertner, Mann, Murrell, & Dovidio, 1989; Kramer & Brewer, 1984; Polzer, Stewart, & Simmons, 1999). Still others argue that minimizing distinctiveness may undermine the very source of the potential benefits of diversity because people become less apt to acknowledge and leverage points of difference (e.g., Polzer, Milton, & Swann, 2002; Swann, Milton, & Polzer, 2000). In either case social categorization processes, especially early in the life cycle of a group, appear to be a predominant and important aspect of group life.

Information processing perspective

As much as the social categorization perspective makes salient the downside of diversity, the information processing/decision-making perspective of diversity highlights the upside of diversity. Put simply, the "value-in-diversity" hypothesis, often identified with this perspective, suggests that differences among group members will give rise to multiple perspectives and varied ideas, knowledge, and skills that can improve group problem solving and decision making (Williams & O'Reilly, 1998). Demographically different individuals are expected to have a broader range of knowledge and experiences than a group of homogeneous individuals. Researchers largely agree that functional or background diversity provides the range of knowledge, skills, and contacts that enhance problem solving (e.g., Ancona & Caldwell, 1992; Bantel & Jackson, 1989; Pelled, Eisenhardt, & Xin, 1999), but the empirical results are much more equivocal for other forms of social category differences such as race, gender, and age (cf. Mannix & Neale, 2005; Van Knippenberg & Schippers, 2007; Williams & O'Reilly, 1998).

However, there is some empirical support for the value-in-diversity hypothesis both from the field and from the laboratory (e.g., Cox, Lobel, & McLeod, 1991; Ely & Thomas, 2001; Herring, 2009; Jehn, Northcraft, & Neale, 1999; Phillips et al., 2006; van Knippenberg, Haslam, & Platow, 2004; Watson et al., 1993). For instance, Herring (2009) used data from the 1996 to 1997 National Organizations Survey and found that in his sample of 506 for-profit American work establishments there was a positive association between racial diversity and gender diversity and increased sales revenue, more customers, and greater relative profits. Herring concluded that "diversity is related to business success because it allows companies to 'think outside the box' by bringing previously excluded groups inside the box. This process enhances an organization's creativity, problem-solving, and performance" (p. 220). Also, Watson and colleagues (1993) examined cultural diversity among student workgroups over the course of a semester and found that, over time, differences in process and performance on case analyses that initially favored homogeneous groups disappeared. On two measures—range of perspectives and alternatives generated—culturally diverse groups were favored by the end of the 17-week period. Thus, social category diversity is thought to be valuable when it adds new information or ways of conducting work.

Diversity in social categories is presumed to be related to informational differences in one of two ways. First, consistent with the social network perspective, diversity in groups increases the likelihood that there will be access to different information in a group (Ancona & Caldwell, 1992). As individuals from different social categories are presumed to have less overlap in their social networks, they should be able to gain access to a broader range of information, allowing for the juxtaposition of unique knowledge, experiences, and ideas in groups (Burt, 2004; Granovetter, 1973; Reagans & McEvily, 2003). This should directly lead to improved outcomes in such groups. Second, the personal experiences of individuals from different social categories are also presumed to be different, such that individuals from different social categories are likely to have different preferences, experiences, information, work styles, and perspectives that they can bring to the group. For instance, men and women are thought to face fundamentally different normative expectations, and fill different societal roles when interacting with others that presumably might benefit the group's ability to be creative and innovative (e.g., Eagly, 1987; Hoffman, Harburg, & Maier, 1962; Hoffman & Maier, 1961). Cox, Lobel, and McLeod (1991) argued and found that Blacks, Hispanics, and Asians respond to prisoners' dilemma situations, where decisions about whether to compete or cooperate need to be made, differently than their White counterparts. They suggested that the difference in behavior exhibited could be attributed to the more collectivistic tendencies of non-Whites relative to more individualistically oriented Whites.

In reality, the linkage between social category diversity and informational/opinion diversity of the group varies across group contexts. Thus, recent research on the information/decision-making perspective suggests that social category diversity may be beneficial to group information processing even when people who hail from different social categories do not differ in their information, opinions, ways of thinking, and processing information. Consequently, we have modified the underlying assumptions of the information/decision-making perspective to take this into consideration. We discuss the expansion of the information processing perspective below.

Expansion of the information processing perspective

The notion that diversity is beneficial only because people who come from different social categories will have differences of information/opinion is an inherent assumption of the traditional information processing perspective of diversity (Phillips & Loyd, 2006). To assume that diversity's benefits only come from people who are socially different conflicting with one another presumes that these individuals necessarily have different opinions and information that are relevant to the current task, which may not be true (Phillips & Loyd, 2006). Further, it implies that people who belong to the same social category hold the *same* information and opinions and do not possess different information and perspectives from which a group might benefit (Phillips & Loyd, 2006). Recent expansion of the information processing perspective argues that being in a socially diverse environment, independent of the actual alignment between social category and informational/opinion diversity, may prompt greater critical thinking, the introduction and consideration of multiple perspectives, and the utilization of all available information and perspectives by all group members (e.g., Phillips & Loyd, 2006; Phillips et al., 2006).

The information processing benefits of diversity do not come solely from the contributions of social minorities (Antonio, Chang, Hakuta, Kenny, Levin, & Milem, 2004; Loyd, Wang, Phillips, & Lount, 2011; Phillips & Loyd, 2006; Phillips, Liljenquist, & Neale, 2009; Phillips et al., 2006; Sommers, 2006; Sommers, Warp, & Mahoney, 2008; Thomas-Hunt et al., 2003). For instance, Sommers and colleagues (2008) found that the mere anticipation of membership in a racially heterogeneous group can lead White individuals to exhibit more thorough information processing, even if the non-Whites do not bring a substantially unique perspective. Further, Phillips and colleagues (2009) studied four-person interacting groups, either socially homogeneous (all from the same sorority or fraternity) or diverse (with one member from a different sorority or fraternity), who had to solve a murder mystery. Diverse groups were found to outperform homogeneous ones, even when the differences of opinion present in the group were not aligned with social category differences. That is, when an out-group newcomer joined an otherwise socially homogeneous group to make it diverse, the group members processed information more effectively and were better able to solve the problem than when the newcomer was a fellow in-group member. Thus, Phillips and colleagues (2009) showed that social diversity has an impact on group performance above and beyond the introduction of minority viewpoints, as it actually makes people focus more on the task and process information more effectively (Loyd et al., 2011).

This more recent expansion of the information processing perspective of diversity builds on the original tenets to argue that the benefits of social category diversity may come from people who are different bringing unique perspectives, ideas, and ways of doing things to the table *and* by increasing the task focus and legitimacy of unique perspectives so that all group members are willing to think harder about the problems at hand (simply because of the presence of categorical differences). Research that directly integrates the social categorization perspective with the original and expanded information processing perspective explicitly attempts to understand how and why social category diversity affects individual and team information processing even when social category diversity and informational/opinion diversity are not congruent or aligned. Van Knippenberg, De Dreu, and Homans (2004) use the term "group information elaboration" to capture the exchange, discussion, and integration of task-relevant information and perspectives. In their 2004 theoretical paper they present the *categorization elaboration model* and argue, consistent with the expanded perspective of information processing presented below, that categorization processes and the information/decision-making perspective work hand in hand to help understand the effects of any and all types of diversity. We discuss the expanded perspective further and detail some of its findings and historical underpinnings below.

MINORITY INFLUENCE AND SOCIAL CATEGORIZATION

Minority influence research has a deep experimental tradition that has examined how the introduction of deviant viewpoints affects the cognitive processing of people in the numerical majority (Moscovici, 1976; Mugny, 1982; Nemeth, 1986; Wood, Lundgren, Ouellette, Busceme, & Blackstone, 1994). The introduction of minority viewpoints has been shown to lead to more divergent thinking, consideration of alternative perspectives, and greater information processing among the numerical majority (Nemeth, 1986; Tomasetto, Mucchi-Faina, Alparone, & Pagliaro, 2009; Van Dyne & Saavedra, 1996). Although minority opinion holders are rarely able to publicly influence group decisions, their presence is invaluable for prompting those in the social majority to seriously consider alternative views (Gruenfeld, 1995; Nemeth, 1986; Tomasetto et al., 2009) and generate more accurate perceptions (Sinaceur, Thomas-Hunt, Neale, O'Neill, & Haag, 2010). Furthermore, minority influence researchers have considered how social categorization might affect these processes, providing a potential point from which to launch the integration of what can be seen as competing perspectives.

The promising positive impact of minority influence on individual cognitions and performance, along with the aforementioned questions of congruence between social category and informational/opinion diversity, prompted the work developed by Phillips and her colleagues (e.g., Phillips, 2003; Phillips & Loyd, 2006; Phillips et al., 2004; Phillips et al., 2006). Phillips (2003) examined the role of "double minorities" in the processing of information in interacting workgroups. Double minorities are people who are in the numerical minority both in terms of their opinion or perspective and their category membership (i.e., they were out-group members) (Maass, Clark, & Haberkorn, 1982). This research expands the minority influence paradigm and allows for the explicit consideration of who has what information/opinions in the group and of which social categories they are a part.

First testing the assumptions that people might have in these diverse settings, Phillips (2003) found that MBA student participants who were in the numerical majority assumed they would hold more similar opinions with a fellow MBA student relative to a medical student. This assumption of congruence between social category and informational/opinion differences also emerged when asking undergraduate student participants how likely they were to share opinions about who committed a fictitious murder with fellow in-group members (i.e., same side of campus) as opposed to out-group members (i.e., different side of campus) (Phillips & Loyd, 2006). This finding suggests that although this shortcut of presumed agreement or congruence within social categories and differences between social categories may prove adaptive as a means of simplifying the world and making predictions about whom to trust, agree with, and listen to in group settings, people may over-rely on this assumption of congruence and miss opportunities to leverage the divergent information possessed by members of their own social category (Thomas-Hunt et al., 2003). The experience of surprise and frustration (especially when in-group members do not agree with them) when these assumptions are not maintained (Phillips, 2003; Phillips & Loyd, 2006) may ultimately have an impact on an individual's ability to process and integrate all available information in the group.

Second, Phillips (2003; Phillips et al., 2004) found that groups like it when this assumption of congruence between social categories and task-relevant information/opinions has been maintained. Groups with double minorities processed information more effectively and performed better than those with minority opinion holders who were part of the in-group. Rink and Ellemers' (2010) studies indicate that within diverse groups, congruence along deep-level dimensions can help teams overcome barriers that might otherwise thwart the efficient integration of their total information and hinder group decisions. Although there are notable papers that contradict these findings (e.g., Kooij-de Bode, van Knippenberg, & van Ginkel, 2008), this work integrating minority influence processes and social categorization suggests that social category diversity may actually help fuel the information processing benefits that occur in diverse settings.

BEYOND DOUBLE MINORITIES

The expanded information processing perspective suggests that even when the social category diversity introduced to a group is not directly congruent with the introduction of unique information and perspectives, it can still have an influence on the group. Unique information may be more effectively processed in diverse groups, even in those in which social category and information/opinion are incongruent, than it is in homogeneous groups. That is, as a consequence of assumed similarity within and differences between social categories, as well as the desire to maintain that congruence, the social category diversity of heterogeneous groups may enhance the likelihood that all available information and opinions, regardless of where they reside in the group, will be recognized and considered more thoroughly than in homogeneous groups (Phillips et al., 2006; Phillips et al., 2009; Phillips & Loyd, 2006; Loyd et al., 2011). To this point, Phillips and Loyd (2006) found that when groups had a minority opinion holder who belonged to the majority in-group, diverse groups spent more time processing the unique perspectives and information present than did homogeneous groups. Further, Phillips and colleagues (2006) found that racially diverse groups with two Whites and one non-White more readily recognized that they possessed unique information and used it more effectively for solving the problem at hand than did homogeneous groups composed of all Whites. Consistent with these findings, a mock jury study by Sommers (2006) showed that diverse juries of four Whites and two Blacks processed case facts more effectively and considered alternative judgments and potential explanations more thoroughly than did a jury of all Whites. Antonio and colleagues (2004) also found evidence consistent with this work.

Finally, integrating the information processing perspective with the social categorization approach highlights that diverse groups may often fail to recognize their information processing benefits because the conflict that they experience is more likely to be coded as negative or as interpersonal in nature (Lount, Sheldon, Rink, & Phillips, 2011; Simon & Peterson, 2000). These diverse groups also see conflict as more consequential, and managers may even see the conflict as intractable and provide fewer resources to the group (Lount et al., 2011). Moreover, homogeneous groups set themselves up to avoid these information processing requirements by not processing or even selecting unique information when it is available (Cao & Phillips, 2011; Loyd et al., 2011). Researchers have shown that the belief that diversity will be beneficial for a group's performance is critical for encouraging information processing (Homan et al., 2007a) and that with a strong belief in the value of diversity (which may come from past experiences, descriptions of the task, or other context variables, for instance), groups are more likely to actually benefit from that diversity.

Thus, there is accumulating support for an expansion of the information processing perspective and support for the notion that diverse groups have the potential to process more information more effectively than homogeneous groups. This potential occurs not just because people who are different can bring different perspectives to the table. On the contrary, socially diverse environments appear to affect the information processing abilities of all members of the group, creating a greater awareness, legitimacy, and desire for all group members to engage the task and utilize the information available to resolve discrepancies and come to an agreement when working in decision-making settings. Although these information processing benefits are not always recognized by diverse groups (Phillips et al., 2009), they nevertheless exist and contribute to the potential upsides of social category diversity.

We next discuss more explicitly the role of status and status differences in diverse environments. Thus far we have reviewed work that has not explicitly considered this factor. The linkage of diversity with status differentiation plays a critical role in understanding the knowledge exchange perspective of diversity and whether groups will be able to garner the purported benefits espoused by the information processing perspective detailed above.

Status differences in diverse groups

Consideration of status effects in groups has largely resided in the social psychological realm of sociology (Berger, Fisek, Norman, & Zelditch, 1977; Berger, Webster, Ridgeway, & Rosenholz, 1986; Ridgeway, 1988, 1991, 2001; Ridgeway & Berger, 1986; Ridgeway & Walker, 1995). It is work in this arena upon which students of knowledge exchange and influence in groups have been apt to draw (Thomas-Hunt & Phillips, 2004; Thomas-Hunt et al., 2003; Wittenbaum, 2000; Wittenbaum & Bowman, 2005). Although this work is not explicitly focused on diverse groups, these findings can add a more nuanced perspective to the integration of social category and information processing perspectives. Understanding the influence of status differentials that exist in everyday workplace settings should allow for even more sophisticated understandings of how social category diversity and informational/opinion diversity come together to influence a group's ability to effectively process information. Although some might argue that having higher status simply makes people immune to information processing concerns (Wittenbaum, 2000), a more integrated view of the entire group process sheds light on the complications that status differences engender in diverse groups. In this section, we take a step back and consider how a lens of status may inform the study of knowledge exchange in diverse groups.

Definitions and distinctions

"Status" refers to an entity's standing in a social hierarchy as determined by the respect, deference, or social influence accorded by others (Ridgeway & Walker, 1995). Status can be either an intragroup phenomenon, such that individuals within a group can be organized according to the amount of respect they receive from other group members, or an intergroup phenomenon, such that groups can be arrayed according to the respect that members of other social groups have for them. Power, on the other hand, is defined as an entity's (an individual's or group's) relative capacity to modify others' states by providing or withholding valued resources or administering unwanted punishments (Blau, 1977; Dépret & Fiske, 1993; Keltner, Gruenfeld, & Anderson, 2003; Pfeffer & Salancik, 1978).

Status and power are empirically and theoretically distinct constructs. Power is based on an individual's resources, which others may be dependent upon. In contrast, status is conferred upon individuals and hence exists entirely in the eyes of others. Thus, it is possible to have power without status. For example, a manager may control his employees' promotions and bonuses but may not be respected because they view him as unjust. Likewise, individuals can have high status without relative power; an emeritus professor may be well respected in her institution but have little impact on decision making.

Although the constructs of power and status are distinct, they are related in that they are potential determinants of each other and both are bases of hierarchical differentiation. An individual's status may be directly related to the type and amount of resources he is allocated, which then has implication for the power he holds (Blieszner & Adams, 1992; French & Raven, 1959; Kemper, 1991). Moreover, the resources that high-status individuals possess often may be seen as having greater value (Magee & Galinsky, 2008; Thye, 2000). In turn, powerful individuals tend to be respected and admired by others because of their control over resources, their formal position, or their assumed competence.

Expectations state and status characteristics theories

Expectations states theory explains the inequalities in participation and influence that occur in task-oriented groups and how the inequalities that emerge replicate the status hierarchies that exist in society (e.g., Berger, Webster, Ridgeway, & Rosenholz, 1986; Ridgeway, 2001). Group members' focus on the goals of the group generates pressure to anticipate the relative quality of each member's contributions. When members of the group anticipate that an individual will make more significant contributions to the group, they will be more likely to defer to that individual and give him or her more opportunities to participate (e.g., Berger, Fisek, Norman, & Zelditch, 1977; Meeker & Weitzel-O'Neil, 1985; Ridgeway & Berger, 1986). Performance expectations shape behavior in a self-fulfilling manner. A group member for whom greater performance expectations are held is more likely to be given the opportunity to perform in the group, to speak up and to offer task contributions, and thus is more likely to have these contributions positively evaluated and acted upon (e.g., Foschi, 1996, 2000, 2009; Foschi, Lai, & Sigerson, 1994)—moreover, the less likely he or she will be influenced by those who disagree with his or her suggestions (e.g., Thomas-Hunt & Phillips, 2004). In contrast, a group member with low performance expectations will be given fewer opportunities to perform, will speak less and in a more hesitant manner, will often have his or her suggestions ignored or evaluated poorly, and will be more likely to be influenced when his or her suggestions are challenged (cf. Loyd, Phillips, Whitson, & Thomas-Hunt, 2010; Thomas-Hunt & Phillips, 2004). Hence, relative performance expectations create and maintain a hierarchy of participation, evaluation, and influence among the actors that constitutes the group's status hierarchy.

Status characteristics theory builds upon expectations states with the premise that over time certain characteristics signal who will have the most positive impact during group decisions (Ridgeway, 1988, 1991). Status characteristics theory posits that through socialization in a broader culture, whether in society or in an organization, individuals learn to associate different personal characteristics with task competence or ability (for reviews, see Berger et al., 1977; Bunderson, 2000; Ridgeway & Berger, 1986). Those characteristics, such as gender and race, that have clearly established status value in our society are considered to be diffuse status cues (Berger, Webster, Ridgeway, & Rosenholtz, 1986; Ridgeway, 2001). Despite not being derived from past performance on specific tasks, these characteristics are believed to provide information about an individual's general aptitude, which is presumed to affect his or her competence on a variety of different tasks within some domain (Bunderson, 2003; Ridgeway, 1991). Individuals occupying a valued state of these characteristics (e.g., male) are bestowed more benefits, such as positive evaluations and influence over group decisions, than are those with less valued states of the characteristic (e.g., female). Unlike diffuse cues, which are assumed to be relevant to a variety of situations, specific status cues are relevant to particular situations. Specific status characteristics involve two or more states that are differentially evaluated, and associated with each state is a distinct specific expectation state. Possessing noted mathematical ability or creative writing ability, for example, generates distinct expectations about performance on specific future tasks in the relevant domains (Berger & Zelditch, 1985). Hence, possessing demonstrated mathematical ability enhances status if mathematical ability is in some way relevant to the future task, but if the future task does not require such mathematical ability, status will not accrue (Foddy & Smithson, 1996).

Empirical studies in psychology and sociology have consistently found that competence expectations can affect interactions within workgroups. For example, White men participate more, conform less, are less tentative in their speech, demonstrate less submissive nonverbal cues, and are interrupted and challenged less than their lower-status counterparts (Altemeyer & Jones, 1974; Eagly, 1983; Eagly & Carli, 1981; Pilavin & Martin, 1978; Smith-Lovin & Brody, 1989; Wood & Karten, 1986). The apparent behavioral validation of the social order creates a presumption of collective support for the social order (Ridgeway, 1988, 1991). Hence, group members construct collective norms that serve to legitimize the social order.

The influence of status on the processing of information in groups has been addressed by researchers as well. Wittenbaum (1998, 2000) argues and finds support for the notion that higher-status individuals are immune to the common information effect, focusing more evenly on commonly held and uniquely held information than their relatively lower-status counterparts. She purports that perceptions of competence afforded individuals with greater task experience (and hence, more specific task status) are responsible for the greater focus on uniquely held knowledge in comparison to actual task competence differences. Thus, just as mentioned earlier in this chapter, expectations and beliefs about who holds what information are just as or more important than who actually possesses that information for determining how information is processed in groups. The work by Wittenbaum considers the influence of task-relevant specific status cues and not the diffuse characteristics under consideration by diversity researchers, suggesting there is yet more to learn about the role of status in diverse groups.

If status buffers high-status individuals, making it easier for them to have their information and perspectives heard, then groups where important unique information is aligned with the status hierarchy should fare well (e.g., Bunderson, 2003; Thomas-Hunt & Phillips, 2004). Thomas-Hunt and Phillips (2004) found that groups with male experts performed better than groups with female experts on a task where individuals presumed that men were more capable than women. In a field study, Bunderson (2003) examined self-managed production teams in Fortune 100 companies and found that longer-tenured teams were able to use specific status cues to predict where expertise was held in the group, and when they predicted this well they performed better, suggesting that status cues are important for the processing of information. Given the benefits of aligning status cues and actual expertise in groups, it stands to reason that in diverse groups where social category differences and informational/opinion diversity are aligned (i.e., congruent groups), having a higher-status person introducing unique information may be beneficial for teams, as it would confirm expectations of where unique knowledge should exist (Thomas-Hunt & Phillips, 2004). However, it is those diverse groups where informational/opinion diversity and social category differences are *not* aligned (i.e., incongruent groups) where the study of status differentials become even more important to consider.

Status violations' influence on information processing

There are a number of studies that document the negative effects experienced by low-status members who behave in ways inconsistent with the status hierarchy (Fiske, Bersoff, Borgida, Deaux, & Heilman, 1991; Rudman & Glick, 1999; Sheldon, Thomas-Hunt & Proell, 2006). These include punishments and negative evaluations (Carli, 1991, 2001; Carli, LaFleur, & Loeber, 1995). Interestingly, high-status individuals who engage in questionable behavior may actually face higher penalties than their lower-status counterparts under some circumstances (Fragale, Rosen, Xu, & Merideth, 2009). However, there is research that suggests that individuals are more sensitive to members of low-status social groups who engage in stereotype-inconsistent behaviors than members of high-status groups who engage in counter-stereotypic behaviors (Duguid, 2011; Loyd et al., 2010). The vast majority of the literature on expectations violation involves the penalties women face for acting in ways that violate expectations of how they are supposed to communicate and act (for review see Eagly & Karau, 2002). Few studies have looked at other characteristics that are imbued with low status.

One set of studies, however, considers the impact of status inconsistencies between an individual's race/ethnicity and socioeconomic status on physiological responses and performance. Mendes, Blascovich, Hunter, Lickel, and Jost (2007) found that when individuals violate expectations, onlookers actually feel stressed. Specifically, when interacting with expectancy-violating partners (e.g., a Latino who described her family background as high socioeconomic status), participants exhibited biological responses consistent with threat, showed poorer task performance, and manifested negative and defeat-related behavior. Despite the absence of research within groups on physiological responses to status inconsistencies within groups, one can speculate that the divergence between individuals' status characteristics and their level of participation and influence behaviors might not only cause surprise, but might elicit threat reactions, which may further mitigate information processing within the group.

Given the growing knowledge we have about the influence of status on the processing of information in groups and our knowledge of the information processing issues faced in diverse settings, it would be beneficial to integrate this research more directly. Status cues abound in diverse group settings—both the specific and the diffuse. Little research has examined how these varying status cues come together to influence information processing in diverse group settings. For instance, will women benefit as much as men from task-specific status boosts, given their lower-status diffuse characteristic? Sociologists have considered the functions that best explain the combination of specific and diffuse status characteristics (e.g., Brandon, 1965), but relatively little empirical research exists that demonstrates how multiple status characteristics come together to influence individual and group behavior. Moreover, a direct integration of status expectations theory with work integrating the information processing and social categorization perspective might lead to the following question: How do low-status individuals who disagree with one another behave when one of them agrees with a higher-status group member? Does diversity have the same benefits over homogeneity when the diversity is instigated by the inclusion of a higher-status versus a lower-status out-group member? When the desire for increased diversity is discussed in organizations, it presumably means there is a desire to bring women, non-Whites, and other numeric minorities into the workplace. This would mean integrating low-status individuals into the organization and their workgroups. There is some research that has already worked towards the goal of integrating a status lens into the literature on diversity and information processing, and some work that would benefit from such a perspective. In the last section of this chapter we will highlight some of this work and suggest more directions for future research.

Future directions

In this section, we consider the potential power of research that uses a status lens to elucidate the impact of diversity on information processing in groups. To determine the landscape of existing work in this arena we conducted a systematic search for articles and categorized them based on their focus on status and information processing. First, we note work that exists at the intersection of status and information processing and discuss its merits and untapped potential. Then, we consider research that harnesses status and information processing perspectives in the examination of diverse teams, and note future directions for this research.

We began by searching four major databases: ABI Inform, JSTOR, PsycInfo, and Business Source Complete. We confined our search to articles published after Williams & O'Reilly's (1998) *Research in Organizational Behavior* "Diversity and Groups" chapter appeared in print and used the key words *groups* or *teams* AND each of the following diversity-relevant terms: *diversity, workplace diversity, race, gender, sexual orientation, national origin, motherhood, religious, SES (socioeconomic status), ethnic, multiculturalism, minority influence, majority influence, status and culture*. Despite our focus on knowledge exchange processes, we did not restrict the search to articles that explicitly considered expertise, communication, knowledge, or information exchange because we expected that numerous studies, with underlying information processing mechanisms, might not overtly categorize themselves as such. We only considered empirical studies, including meta-analyses, but excluded literature reviews or solely theoretical pieces. Finally, a study had to have dependent or independent variables that were measured at the group or team level and had some demonstrated focus on social category diversity to be included.

Our search yielded 51 studies (Fig. 9.1). We categorized the studies into nine categories, which captured (1) the degree to which they use a status lens (not at all, tacitly, explicitly) and (2) the degree to which communication or knowledge exchange is employed as a mechanism (not at all, tacitly considered, explicitly considered) (see Fig. 9.1). From our search we found 18 studies that had social category diversity as a focus but gave no consideration to status or information use or communication. In contrast, only 1 study explicitly considered both status and information use. Six studies employed an explicit status lens but gave no consideration to information use, and an additional 5 explicitly used a status lens and tacitly considered information processing. There were 11 studies that explicitly considered information use but gave no consideration to member status, and 7 that tacitly considered information use but not member status. One study tacitly considered status but did not consider information use, whereas the only other study that tacitly considered status also tacitly considered information use. Below we provide an overview of the types of studies that fall into each category that exhibited some focus on information use.

Before reviewing our findings, we must recognize that our insights were limited by our search constraints. We now conclude that our search was overly specified, only having captured those studies that explicitly list groups or teams as a keyword. In the sections below, we acknowledge some relevant work that did not show up in our search and acknowledge that more might exist. Status researchers often do not select *groups* or *teams* as a key word despite the fact that their research is focused at the group-level. Consequently, examinations of explicit status may be underreported.

Research at the frontier
NO STATUS/EXPLICIT INFORMATION PROCESSING

Studies in this category largely focus on communication, information exchange, and information elaboration in groups with social category diversity.

	No Status Focus	**Tacit Status Focus**	**Explicit Status Focus**
No Information Processing Focus	Baugh & Graen (1997) Dufwenberg & Muren (2006) Ely & Thomas (2001) Hobman et al (2003) Horowitz & Horowitz (2007) Kilduff et al (2000) Kirkman et al (2004) Knight et al (1999) Luijters et al (2008) Mohammed & Angell (2004) Pelled et al (1999) Pitts (2009) Randel & Earley (2009) Randel & Jaussi (2003) Rico et al (2007) Riordan & Shore (1997) Stewart & Johnson (2009) Tata (2000) Van der Zee et al (2004)	Jackson & Joshi (2004)	Butler (2006) Chatman & O'Reilly (2004) Earley (1999) Hirschfeld et al (2005) Karakowsky et al (2004) Knouse & Dansby (1999)
Tacit Information Processing Focus	Harrison et al (2002) McLeod et al (1996) Stahl et al (2010) Thomas (1999) Watson et al (1993) Watson et al (2002) Watson et al (2005)	Foschi (2009)	Kelsey (2000) Li et al (1999) Paletz et al (2004) Weisband et al (1995) Zhang, D. et al (2007)
Explicit Information Processing Focus	Bunderson et al (2002) Dahlin et al (2005) Homan et al (2008) Nam et al (2009) Pearsall et al (2008) Puck et al (2006) Sommers (2006) Stewart & Garcia-Prieto (2008) Umans (2008) Vallaster (2005) Van Dick et al (2008)		Bunderson (2003)

Figure 9.1. Categorization of articles based on information processing and status focus.

Investigation mostly remains at the group level, allowing for no real status-based differentiation of individual members' behavior. For example, research in this arena has focused on the influence of group diversity on information processing—ethnic diversity (Timurs, 2008), ethnic and national diversity (Dahlin, Weingart, & Hinds, 2005), cultural (Nam, Lyons, Hwang, & Kim, 2009), and functional diversity (Bunderson & Sutcliffe, 2002a). The findings of these studies are inconsistent, showing that group diversity sometimes aids information processing and other times impedes it. Additional work attempts to clarify the impact of group diversity by giving consideration to the factors that moderate and mediate the effects of group diversity on communication or information processing (Homan, Hollenbeck, Humphrey, van Knippenberg, Ilgen, & van Kleef, 2008; Stewart & Garcia-Prieto, 2008; Van Dick et al., 2008), giving particular emphasis to the salience of diversity and identification with the group. Although this work advances our understanding of diverse groups and their information processing activities, the lack of investigation of the differentiated behaviors of individual members as a function of status limits the ability to accurately interpret the use and communication of information in these groups. Sommers' (2006) study of racially homogeneous and diverse jury decision-making groups moves in the direction of decomposing the information-sharing activities of members by race. A status lens would suppose that the increased information-sharing behaviors of White jurors in diverse juries could be attributed to the higher status that they hold in the presence of Black jurors. Consistent with the findings of Thomas-Hunt and colleagues (2003), White jurors' increased relative status might heighten their contribution and emphasis of the information shared by others.

The work by Phillips and her colleagues (Phillips, 2003; Phillips et al., 2004, 2006, 2009; Phillips & Loyd, 2006) reviewed above in the section that integrates the social categorization perspective with the information processing perspective also falls into this category. This work could be furthered by adopting an explicit emphasis on status and the integration of status differences between in-group and out-group members, which might lend insight into how individuals would react to being in the numerical majority when they must coalesce with higher- or lower-status out-group members to do so. The tension created between concerns to gain or maintain higher status, concerns to be right, and concerns to maintain in-group relationships is ripe for further investigation.

Furthermore, Bunderson and Sutcliffe's (2002b) alternative conceptualization of functional diversity through their consideration of intrapersonal diversity is groundbreaking in that they differentiate individual group members. Nevertheless, they aggregate their findings to the group-level. Further insights might have been extracted through the consideration of the effects of intrapersonal diversity and the status configuration of those intrapersonal associations on members' information processing behaviors. Even at the group-level, the status configuration of members' dominant functional areas may provide further elucidation of the ways in which functional area diversity affects information processing. Are the diminished effects of dominant functional diversity due to similar status functional areas refusing to defer to one another, or an inherent hierarchy that minimizes contributions from those with lower status?

These studies bring an explicit information processing perspective to the study of diversity in teams. Their insights, however, would be augmented by consideration of the status of knowledge holders. Future research could extend existing findings by considering how unexpected expertise or knowledge becomes integrated in groups. How do groups treat knowledge contributed by low-status members who know things they are not expected to know? What happens when high-status members reveal knowledge of details they are not expected to know? Are they seen as being well informed and engaged, or overstepping boundaries? Do group members become fearful or threatened when others know what they know?

NO STATUS/TACIT INFORMATION PROCESSING

Studies that tacitly dealt with information processing and were without a status lens largely focused on the effects of diversity on group processes (Thomas, 1999; Watson, Barnir, & Pavur, 2005; Watson, Johnson, & Zgourides, 2002, Watson et al., 1993) and idea generation (McLeod, Lobel, & Cox, 1996; Stahl, Maznevski, Voigt, & Jonsen, 2010). These studies could benefit from a greater focus on both the effects of status on individual member behaviors and the information processes embedded in group dynamics. How does the status of group members affect their contribution of novel ideas and the adoption of those ideas by the group? How does the status afforded by social category shift member contributions and integration over time? Do groups in which social category distinctions convey differential status exchange information differently than those in which social categories afford equivalent status?

Furthermore, in an attempt to understand how these processes unfold, some researchers have examined these processes longitudinally (Harrison et al., 2002; Watson et al., 1993). Over a period of time, members in a group may form bonds of friendship and familiarity with each other. These bonds may affect the way in which individuals choose to share the unique information they possess (Phillips et al., 2004). Furthermore, as they become friends, the frequency of their interaction may not only lead them to exchange more and more information, but also increase their shared experiences and increase the similarity of information about a particular topic, especially if that topic is what brought them together in the first place (Polzer, Milton, & Swann, 2002).

Beyond the frontier

In this section of the chapter we delve more deeply into the seven studies that have pierced the frontier of team diversity research by integrating status and information processing lenses. We use these studies as a springboard for raising several directions for future research that arise from our review.

TACIT STATUS/TACIT INFORMATION PROCESSING

Foschi (2009) is the lone study in this category. Rather than solely studying the effects of gender in the absence of context, Foschi (2009) explicitly defines the context as masculine by indicating that the focal visual perception task was one in which men had proven to be far more accurate that women. Such a manipulation of the context affords men an explicitly higher status than women. Absent external standards, such a context has a negative impact on low-status members' self and others' perceptions of their competence and hence reduces low-status members' influence. The findings of Foschi (2009), however, give little insight into the way in which information exchange would be affected by self- versus experimenter-set competence standards in mixed-sex dyads. Might women performing at the same level as men be more likely to view themselves as less than competent and withhold their potential knowledge contributions? Evidence from one study not captured by our search suggests that the gender status of female members diminishes the ability of experts to assert influence and positively affect performance (Thomas-Hunt & Phillips, 2004). Future research should determine whether women withhold contributions or whether others in the group fail to acknowledge and integrate those contributions that they do make. What factors might increase the contributions made by low-status members and groups' acceptance of those contributions? Might solicitation of their ideas yield credibility to low-status members? Or, could the mere act of soliciting ideas from low-status members further erode perceptions of their ability to function on their own in the group?

EXPLICIT STATUS/TACIT INFORMATION PROCESSING

The studies in this category largely examined the impact of numerical status of social categories (i.e., percentage, proportion, varied composition) on members' exertion of influence. None of these studies explicitly discussed information processing; instead, they examined or employed tasks in which exerting influence inherently involved sharing or emphasizing information or knowledge. For example, Li, Karakowski, and Siegel (1999) investigated the impact of proportional representation on Asian men's participation in group discussions. In their study of videotaped face-to-face interactions of six-person groups interacting on a decision-making task that involved effectively ordering project management tasks, they manipulated the composition of the groups such that one third were all Asian men, one third were half Asian and half Caucasian men, and one third had one Asian and five Caucasian men. The findings revealed that Asian men in the numerical minority participated the least and received the lowest evaluations of leadership behavior. Unfortunately, no condition in which Caucasian men were in the minority was reported, making it difficult to assess whether Asian men relative to Caucasian men were differentially affected by numerical status.

In a related investigation, the composition of four-person groups was manipulated such that they were all Chinese, three Chinese and one American, one Chinese and three Americans, and all Americans (Zhang, Lowry, Zhou, & Fu, 2007). The experimenter varied who possessed a unique solution to a management problem presented to group members. When minority solution holders were Chinese, they were more likely to be influenced by the majority, indicating that numerical status does differentially interact with ethnic status. These effects were mitigated by computer-mediated communication.

Research by Kelsey (2000) provides further insight into the ways in which computer-mediated interactions may mitigate the effects of status. In an investigation of four-person all-male groups working on a project management decision-making task, Kelsey (2000) considered the way in which communication media affect the impact of ethnicity (Chinese vs. Caucasian) and numerical status cue participation and influence. The findings showed that in groups with social category diversity, the effects of numerical status are moderated by the status of members' social category and the communication medium used. Specifically, the results indicated that numerical minority status impedes the participation and influence of ethnically low-status group members in face-to-face but not computer-mediated groups.

Fortunately, the authors had the foresight to measure both actual and perceived influence and participation, giving the opportunity to see when perception and reality converge and diverge. Greater insight into knowledge exchange processes would have been afforded by text analysis that considered the nature of participation. Future research might consider the nature of the contributions. Do ethnic minorities and majorities attend to and contribute different types of information, or just more or less of the same type? Furthermore, the study design, in which all of the Chinese were non-native English speakers and face-to-face groups communicated verbally whereas those with group support systems communicated via written text, obscures the source of the status differential. Was it simply derived from ethnicity, or did language fluency affect perception of status? To what extent does language fluency contribute to perceived status? Does country of origin act as a status characteristic that drives information exchange processes over and above language fluency and ethnicity? Finally, might the nature of the task exacerbate or mitigate the status assigned to ethnicity? Had the task been more quantitative and less managerial, might Asian men have been perceived as having higher status? Increasing attention has been given to the effects of the gendered nature of tasks. How might the congruence of tasks with stereotyped competencies or deficiencies of group members activate or diminish status perceptions that affect knowledge exchange in diverse groups?

Interestingly, the findings of Zhang and colleagues (2007), Kelsey (2000), and Li and colleagues (1999) stand in some contrast to those earlier results of Weisband and colleagues (1995). In a study of the hierarchical status (i.e., undergraduate/graduate) effects on participation and influence within three-person groups, results showed that status-based decrements in evaluation persist in the face of computer-mediated exchanges. Also, in their investigation numerical status does not seem to affect the differential perceptions of low- and high-status members; however, masking the true identity of high-status group members labeled with low status reveals that the differential influence of low-status members may, in large part, be due to the biased perceptions of high-status members rather than lower contribution levels of low-status members. Unfortunately, the content of the participation was not considered, nor were other members' use of contributions from high- and low-status contributors. This research highlights the need for future studies to examine how multiple status characteristics come together to affect people's perceptions and behaviors in groups. Having multiple low-status characteristics—for example, being a woman and Black—has traditionally been thought to put people in a position of double jeopardy (Almquist, 1975; Beale, 1970), but recent work suggests that those individuals might be given great latitude. More research is needed as we try to understand how multiple characteristics drive status in groups. What happens when expectation-disconfirming situations occur—for instance, a functionally expert yet docile black man as compared to a mathematically challenged and aggressive Asian woman? Any number of such permutations could be investigated; we are not suggesting that merely studying these minutiae is important, rather that we can eventually attempt to uncover which factor(s) can better explain the behaviors and decisions that groups and individuals make by studying these crosscutting situations.

Finally, Paletz, Peng, Erez, and Maslach (2004) considered the impact of numerical status of ethnic minorities on idea generation within groups. The lack of variation in idea generation by ethnic status in their results may be a function of their aggregation of ideas at the group-level. Had they considered the idea contribution of members of each ethnicity, they might have seen effects. Furthermore, they might have considered not only contributions of ideas, but also the emphasis and attention given to ideas as a function of the numerical status of ethnic minorities. Nevertheless, they found additional evidence of divergent emotional experiences of low- and high-status minorities—specifically, that non-Asian minorities are more affected by the emotions in the group than are Asians. Future work might consider how this differential impact of emotions affects motivation and contribution behavior as well as members' willingness to accept the novel ideas of other members.

In general, these studies that focus on numerical status make a substantive contribution to understanding information processes in groups. Their insights might be furthered by a more nuanced consideration of how member status affects influence through actual information processing. At their best, these studies acknowledge that the impact of having a numerical minority depends on the status of other characteristics possessed.

EXPLICIT STATUS/EXPLICIT INFORMATION PROCESSING

Our search yielded only one study that employed a status lens to explicitly focus on leveraging the expertise or information possessed by members of groups with social category diversity (Bunderson, 2003). In this investigation, Bunderson drew upon status characteristics theory to explain the differential impact of diffuse and specific characteristics on expertise recognition and influence within groups. This investigation acknowledged that social category memberships have differential value that may affect perceptions of members and the way in which members' knowledge is able to be leveraged. It is one of the few examples of studies that link differentiated member status to knowledge use processes within groups. Two additional studies in this genre, not identified by our search because they did not select "groups" or "teams" as a key word, are that of Thomas-Hunt and colleagues (2003) and Thomas-Hunt and Phillips (2004). Thomas-Hunt and colleagues examined the effects of expert status and numerical status on the contribution and recognition of members' unique knowledge in groups with functional diversity. They found that those with solo status were far more likely to contribute unique knowledge than those with a similar other present. Furthermore, socially connected members gave greater attention to the unique knowledge contributions of isolates than to those of the member to whom they were socially connected. Finally, those with expert status were more likely than others to emphasize the unique knowledge contributions of other group members. Their results begin to elucidate the way in which status affects the complex information and influence patterns found in groups with members from multiple status-equivalent social categories (Phillips, 2003; Phillips & Loyd, 2006).

In addition to explicitly considering the impact of status on knowledge exchange processes within diverse groups, Bunderson's (2003) work highlights the importance of studying groups and teams *in situ*, as Williams & O'Reilly (1998) call for. Laboratory experiments, while illuminative and tightly controlled, often do not have the benefit of the complex and continued interpersonal relations that the workplace engenders. If the focus of organizational behavior is to better understand how groups evolve and exist in organizations, then it is imperative that field studies balance out and corroborate our laboratory findings. Furthermore, given our focus on knowledge exchange, we really need to employ field methods such as ethnography, which are poised to capture information and knowledge exchange in real time. We need to know who said what to whom, and in what context. Our understanding needs to reach beyond the actual words provided by transcription of the audio or video recordings now common in experimental settings. We need to capture gestures and other nonverbal signals that award and diminish credibility and give meaning to the actual words.

Conclusion

Despite the advances in understanding of diverse groups derived from the integration of social category and informational/opinion perspectives, this work has stopped short of fully specifying the factors at play in knowledge exchange in everyday workplace settings. In large part, the heavy reliance on the social category perspective has led to emphasis on the differentiation derived from membership in different social categories without significant consideration of the impact of the nature of the differentiation. In fact, Phillips, Rothbard, and Dumas (2009) argue that "status [distance] as a construct has heretofore been relatively ignored by diversity researchers and is an omitted variable that may help explain some of the behaviors we see in demographically diverse environments" (p. 714). Both the societal and local hierarchical ordering of characteristics may drive patterns of assertion and deference and affect if, how, and when information is shared and integrated into group discussions. Scholars should be mindful of the status differences that are associated with diversity when theorizing and making predictions and interpretations. These category differences are imbued with societal value, affording members of some social categories more respect, influence, and prominence (i.e., status) than those who belong to other social categories. Such regard is likely to further influence information processing by guiding expectations for not only who possesses similar and different perspectives, but also who possesses knowledge that will be most useful to the group. Not surprisingly, social identity theory and social categorization theory leave room for the status differentiation and resource inequity of groups, but diversity researchers in general, and those specifically focused on information processing, have largely not focused on this aspect of the theory (for exceptions, see Bacharach, Bamberger, & Vashdi, 2005; Chatman & O'Reilly, 2004; Chattopadhyay, 1999; Chattopadhyay, Tluchowska, & George, 2004).

Our hope is that this chapter highlights the progress that has been made and paves the way for future research that leverages a status lens in examining information exchange processes in groups with social category diversity. First, we mentioned the idea that integration of multiple demographic and status characteristics has been considered by researchers. However, a more thorough understanding of how various status-relevant characteristics, which may even have competing status implications (e.g., a female boss), come together to affect interactions in groups is critical for the integration of a status lens in this research.

Second, one could argue that even with the vast array of characteristics considered by diversity researchers, there is a set of important missing demographic characteristics, given the complexity of identity and status in society. Future research on diversity should include a broader array of social categories, including national origin, socioeconomic status, sexual orientation, and religion, among other characteristics. The growing importance of these characteristics in the workplace highlights the need for a better understanding of the nuanced differences in influence that may result depending on the salience and status of social categories. For instance, are religious differences just as salient and important to the knowledge exchange process as are other characteristics? Should all of these characteristics be considered equally important?

Third, we have focused here on the task-relevant communication and information exchange that occurs in groups; however, group members may also exchange information that is not task-relevant. This non–task-relevant information may be personal information about the self (i.e., self-disclosure) that may also have an influence on the broader knowledge exchange phenomenon. What is the role of self-disclosure in building trust, mitigating status threats, and creating opportunities for more thorough knowledge exchange in groups? Finally, future research on the knowledge exchange perspective should examine more closely not only what information is being exchanged in groups but what information is being withheld by group members. How much can we learn from understanding what information is purposefully being withheld from discussion? This approach is consistent with the spirit of group processes such as groupthink that are thought to infect homogeneous environments.

Traditionally social categorization processes have been thought of simply as generating the downsides of diversity, while the information processing perspective of diversity has been thought to undergird the positive side of diversity. The new information processing perspective of diversity works hand in hand with social categorization theory and suggests that in diverse environments, the benefits of information processing may not be possible with the potential downsides that accompany social categorization processes in these groups. In fact, the positive outcomes of diversity—let's refer to them as the pain of categorization and the gain of information processing—may not be possible without the double edge of the sword.

References

Allen, V. L., & Wilder, D. A. (1975). Categorization, belief similarity, and intergroup discrimination. *Journal of Personality and Social Psychology, 32,* 971–977.

Allen, V. L., & Wilder, D. A. (1978). Perceived persuasiveness as a function of response style: Multi-issue consistency over time. *European Journal of Social Psychology, 8,* 289–296.

Allen, V. L., & Wilder, D. A. (1979). Group categorization and attribution of belief similarity. *Small Group Behavior, 10,* 73–80.

Almquist, E. M. (1975). Untangling the effects of race and sex: The disadvantaged status of Black women. *Social Science Quarterly, 56,* 129–142.

Altemeyer, R. A., & Jones, K. (1974). Sexual identity, physical attractiveness and seating position as determinants of influence in discussion groups. *Canadian Journal of Behavioral Science, 6,* 357–375.

Ancona, D., & Caldwell, D. (1992). Demography and design: Predictors of new product team performance. *Organization Science, 3,* 321–341.

Antonio, A. L., Chang, M. J., Hakuta, K., Kenny, D. A., Levin, S. & Milem, J. F. (2004). Effects of racial diversity on complex thinking in college students. *Psychological Science, 15,* 507–510.

Bacharach, S. B., Bamberger, P. A., & Vashdi, D. (2005). Diversity and homophily at work: Supportive relations among White and African-American peers. *Academy of Management Journal, 48*(4), 619–644.

Bantel, K., & Jackson, S. (1989). Top management and innovations in banking: Does the composition of the top team make a difference? *Strategic Management Journal, 10,* 107–124.

Baugh, S., & Graen, G. (1997). Effects of team gender and racial composition on perceptions of team performance in

cross-functional teams. *Group & Organization Management, 22*, 366–384.
Beale, F. (1970). Double jeopardy: To be Black and female. In T. Cade (Ed.), *The Black woman* (pp. 90–100). New York: New American Library.
Berger, J., Fisek, H., Norman, R., & Zelditch, M. (1977). *Status characteristics and social interaction*. New York: Elsevier.
Berger, J., Webster, M., Ridgeway, C. L., & Rosenholz, S. (1986). Status cues, expectations, and behaviors. In E. Lawler (Ed.), *Advances in group processes* (Vol. 3, pp. 1–22). Greenwich, CT: JAI.
Berger, J., & Zelditch, M. (Eds.). (1985). *Status, rewards, and influence*. San Francisco, CA: Jossey-Bass.
Berscheid, E., & Walster, E. (1978). *Interpersonal attraction*. Reading, MA: Addison-Wesley.
Blau, P. (1977). *Heterogeneity and inequality: Towards a primitive theory of social structure*. New York: Free Press.
Blieszner, R., & Adams, R. G. (1992). *Adult friendship*. Newbury Park, CA: Sage
Brandon, A. C. (1965). Status congruence and expectations. *Sociometry, 28*, 272–288.
Brodbeck, F. C., Kerschreiter, R., Mojzisch, A., Frey, D., & Schulz-Hardt, S. (2002). The dissemination of critical, unshared information in decision-making groups: The effects of pre-discussion dissent. *European Journal of Social Psychology, 32*, 35–56.
Bunderson, J. S. (2000). *Perceived ideological divergence: Violating the psychological contracts of professional employees*. Working Paper, Olin School of Business, Washington University, St. Louis, MO.
Bunderson, J. S. (2003). Recognizing and utilizing expertise in work groups: A status characteristics perspective. *Administrative Science Quarterly, 48(4)*, 557–591.
Bunderson, J. S. (2003). Team member functional background and involvement in management teams: Direct effects and the moderating role of power centralization. *Academy of Management Journal, 46(4)*, 458–474.
Bunderson, J. S., & Sutcliffe, K. M. (2002a). Comparing alternative conceptualizations of functional diversity in management teams: Process and performance effects. *Academy of Management Journal, 45(5)*, 875–893.
Bunderson, J. S., & Sutcliffe, K. M. (2002b). Why some teams emphasize learning more than others: Evidence from business unit management teams. In H. Sondak (Ed.), *Toward phenomenology of groups and group membership* (pp. 49–84). New York: Elsevier Science.
Burt, R. (2007). Secondhand brokerage: evidence on the importance of local structure for managers, bankers, and analysts. *Academy of Management Journal, 50(1)*, 119–148.
Burt, R. S. (1973). The differential impact of social integration on participation in the diffusion of innovations. *Social Science Research, 2(2)*, 125–144.
Burt, R. S. (2004). Structural holes and good ideas. *American Journal of Sociology, 110(2)*, 349–399.
Butler, C. (2006). The influence of status cues on collective identity in teams of different national composition. *Academy of Management Proceedings*, A1–A6.
Byrne, B. (1971). *The attraction paradigm*. New York: Academic Press.
Byrne, D., Clore, G. L., & Worchel, P. (1966). Effect of economic similarity-dissimilarity on interpersonal attraction. *Journal of Personality and Social Psychology, 4*, 220–224.

Cao, J., & Phillips, K. W. (2011). *Team diversity and information acquisition: How homogeneous teams set themselves up to have less information than diverse ones*. Working paper, Northwestern University.
Carli, L. (1991). Gender, interpersonal power, and social influence. *Journal of Social Issues, 55(1)*, 81–99.
Carli, L. (2001). The female leadership advantage: An evaluation of the evidence. *Leadership Quarterly, 14(6)*, 807–834.
Carli, L., LaFleur, S. J., & Loeber, C. (1995). Nonverbal behavior, gender, and influence. *Journal of Personality and Social Psychology, 68(6)*, 1030–1041.
Chatman, J., & O'Reilly, C. (2004). Asymmetric reactions to work group sex diversity among men and women. *Academy of Management Journal, 47(2)*, 193–208.
Chattopadhyay, P. (1999). Beyond direct and symmetrical effects: The influence of demographic dissimilarity on organizational citizenship behavior. *Academy of Management Journal, 42*, 273–287.
Chattopadhyay, P., Tluchowska, M., & George, E. (2004). Identifying the ingroup: A closer look at the influence of dissimilarity on employee social identity. *Academy of Management Review, 29*, 180–202.
Chen, F., & Kenrick, D. T. (2002). Repulsion or attraction? Group membership and assumed attitude similarity. *Journal of Personality and Social Psychology, 83*, 111–125.
Cox, T. H., Lobel, S. A., & McLeod, P. L. (1991), Effects of ethnic group cultural differences on cooperative and competitive behavior on a group task. *Academy of Management Journal, 34(4)*, 827–847.
Cummings, A., Zhou, J., & Oldham, G. (1993). *Demographic differences and employee work group outcomes: Effects of multiple comparison groups*. Paper presented at the annual meeting of the Academy of Management, Atlanta.
Dahlin, K. B., Weingart, L. R., & Hinds, P. J. (2005). Team diversity and information use. *Academy of Management Journal, 48(6)*, 1107–1123.
Dépret, E. F., & Fiske, S. T (1993). *Perceiving the powerful: Intriguing individuals versus threatening groups*. Unpublished manuscript, University of Massachusetts at Amherst.
Devine, D. J., Clayton, L., Philips, J., Dunford, B., & Melner, S. (1990). Teams in organizations: Prevalence, characteristics, and effectiveness. *Small Group Research, 30(6)*, 678–711.
Dufwenberg, M., & Muren, A. (2006). Gender composition in teams. *Journal of Economic Behavior & Organization, 61(1)*, 50–54.
Dumaine, B. (1994, Sept. 5). The trouble with teams. *Fortune*, 86–92.
Duguid, M. M. (2011). Female tokens in high-prestige work groups: Catalysts or inhibitors of group diversification? *Organizational Behavior and Human Decision Processes, 116*, 104–115.
Eagly, A., & Carli, L. L. (1981). Sex of researchers and sex stereotyped communications as determinants of sex differences in influenceability. *Psychological Bulletin, 90*, 1–20.
Eagly, A. H. (1983). Gender and social influence. *American Psychologist, 38(9)*, 971–981.
Eagly, A. H. (1987). *Sex differences in social behavior: A social-role interpretation*. Hillsdale, NJ: Lawrence Erlbaum Associates.
Eagly, A. H., & Karau, S. J. (2002). Role congruity theory of prejudice toward female leaders. *Psychological Bulletin, 109(3)*, 573–598.

Earley, C. P. (1999). Playing follow the leader: Status-determining traits in relation to collective efficacy across cultures. *Organizational Behavior and Human Decision Processes, 80*(3), 192–212.

Ely, R., & Thomas, D. (2001). Cultural diversity at work: The effects of diversity perspectives on work group processes and outcomes. *Administrative Science Quarterly, 46*(2), 229–273.

Fiske, S., Bersoff, D. N., Borgida, E., Deaux, K., & Heilman, M. E. (1991). Social science research on trial: Use of sex stereotyping research in Price Waterhouse v. Hopkins. *American Psychologist, 46*(10), 1049–1060.

Foddy, M., & Smithson., M. (1996). Relative ability, paths of relevance, and influence in task-oriented groups. *Social Psychology Quarterly, 59*, 140–153.

Foschi, M. (1996). Double standards in the evaluation of men and women. *Social Psychology Quarterly, 59*, 237–254

Foschi, M. (2000). Double standards for competence: Theory and research. *Annual Review of Sociology, 26*, 21–42.

Foschi, M. (2009). Gender, performance level, and competence standards in task groups. *Social Science Research, 38*(2), 447–457.

Foschi, M., Lai, L., & Sigerson, K. (1994). Gender and double standards in the assessment of job applicants. *Social Psychology Quarterly, 57*, 326–339.

Fragale, A. R., Rosen, B., Xu, C., & Merideth, I. (2009). The higher they are, the harder they fall: The effects of wrongdoer status on observer punishment recommendations and intentionality attributions. *Organizational Behavior and Human Decision Processes, 108*, 53–65.

French, J., & Raven, B. H. (1959). The bases of social power. In D. Cartwright (Ed.), *Studies of social power* (pp. 150–167). Ann Arbor, MI: Institute for Social Research.

Gaertner, S., Mann, J., Murrell, A., & Dovidio, J. (1989). Reducing inter-group bias: The benefits of recategorization. *Journal of Personality and Social Psychology, 57*, 692–704.

Granovetter, M. (1973). The strength of weak ties. *American Journal of Sociology, 78*(6), 1360–1372.

Gruenfeld, D. H (1995). Status, ideology, and integrative complexity on the U. S. Supreme Court: Rethinking the politics of political decision making. *Journal of Personality and Social Psychology, 68*, 5–20.

Guzzo, R., & Dickson, M. (1996). Teams in organizations: Recent research on performance and effectiveness. *Annual Review of Psychology, 47*, 307–338.

Harrison, D, A., Price, K, H., & Bell, M. P. (1998). Beyond relational demography: Time and the effects of surface- and deep-level diversity on work group cohesion. *Academy of Management Journal, 41*, 96–107.

Harrison, D. A., Price, K. H., Gavin, J. H., & Florey, A. T. (2002). Time, teams, and task performance: Changing effects of surface- and deep-level diversity on group functioning. *Academy of Management Journal, 45*(5), 1029–1045.

Herring, C. (2009). Does diversity pay? Race, gender, and the business case for diversity. *American Sociological Review, 74*, 208–224.

Hirschfeld, R. R., Jordan, M. H., Feild, H. S., Giles, W. F., & Armenakis, A. A. (2005). Teams' female representation and perceived potency as inputs to team outcomes in a predominantly male field setting. *Personnel Psychology, 58*, 893–925.

Hobman, E. V., Bordia, P., & Gallois, C. (2003). Consequences of feeling dissimilar from others in a work team. *Journal of Business and Psychology, 17*(3), 301–325.

Hoffman, L., Harbiirg, E., & Maier, N. (1962). Differences and disagreements as factors in creative group problem solving. *Journal of Abnormal and Social Psychology, 4*, 206–214.

Hoffman, L. R., & Maier, N. R. F. (1961). Quality and acceptance of problem solutions by members of homogeneous and heterogeneous groups. *Journal of Abnormal and Social Psychology, 62*, 401–407.

Hogg, M., & Abrams, D. (1988). *Social identification.* London: Routledge.

Homan, A., Hollenbeck, J., Humphrey, S., Van Knippenberg, D., Ilgen, D., & Van Kleef, G. (2008). Facing differences with an open mind: Openness to experience, salience of intragroup differences, and performance of diverse work groups. *Academy of Management Journal, 51*(6), 1204–1222.

Homan, A. C., van Knippenberg, D. Van Kleef, G. A., & De Dreu, C. K. W. (2007a). Bridging faultlines by valuing diversity: Diversity beliefs, information elaboration, and performance in diverse work groups. *Journal of Applied Psychology, 92*, 1189–1199.

Horwitz, S., & Horwitz, I. (2007). The effects of team diversity on team outcomes: A meta-analytic review of team demography. *Journal of Management, 33*(6), 987–1015.

Jackson, S. E. (1992). Consequence of group composition for the interpersonal dynamics of strategic issue processing. In P. Shrivastava, A. Huff, & J. Dutton (Eds.), *Advances in strategic management* (8, pp. 345–382). Greenwich, CT: JAI Press.

Jackson, S. E., & Joshi, A. (2004). Diversity in social context: A multi-attribute, multilevel analysis of team diversity and sales performance. *Journal of Organizational Behavior, 25*(6), 675–702.

Jackson, S. E., & Joshi, A. (2011). Work team diversity. In S. Zedeck (Ed.), *APA handbook of industrial and organizational psychology* (1, pp. 651–686).

Jehn, K. A., Northcraft, G. B., & Neale, M. A. (1999). Why differences make a difference: A field study of diversity, conflict, and performance in workgroups. *Administrative Science Quarterly, 44*(4), 741–763.

Karakowsky, L., McBey, K., & Chuang, Y. (2004). Perceptions of team performance: The impact of group composition and task-based cues. *Journal of Managerial Psychology, 19*(5), 506–525.

Katzenbach, J. R., & Smith, D. K. (1993). *Wisdom of teams.* Boston: Harvard Business School Press.

Kelsey, B. (2000). Increasing minority group participation and influence using a group support system. *Canadian Journal of Administrative Sciences, 17*(1), 63–75.

Keltner, D., Gruenfeld, D. H., & Anderson, C. (2003). Power, approach, and inhibition. *Psychological Review, 110*, 265–284.

Kemper, T. D. (1991). Emotions from social relations. *Social Psychology Quarterly, 54*(4), 330–342.

Kilduff, M., Angelmar, R., & Mehra, A. (2000). Top management-team diversity and firm performance: Examining the role of cognitions. *Organization Science, 11*(1), 21–34.

Kirkman, L. B., Tesluk, E. P., & Rosen, B. (2004). The impact of demographic heterogeneity and team leader–team member demographic fit on team empowerment and effectiveness. *Group & Organization Management, 29*(3), 334–368.

Knight, D., Pearce, C. L., Smith, K. G., Olian, J. D., Sims, H. P., Smith, K. A., & Flood, P. (1999). Top management team diversity, group process, and strategic consensus. *Strategic Management Journal, 20*(5), 445–465.

Knouse, B. S., & Dansby, R. M. (1999). Percentage of work–group diversity and work–group effectiveness. *Journal of Psychology, 133*(5), 486–494.

Kooij-de Bode, H. J., van Knippenberg, D., & van Genkel, W. P. (2008). Ethnic diversity and distributed information in group decision making: The importance of information elaboration. *Group Dynamics: Theory, Research, and Practice, 12*(4), 307–320.

Kramer, R., & Brewer, M. (1984). Effects of group identity on resource use in a simulated commons dilemma. *Journal of Personality and Social Psychology, 46*, 944–1057.

Lawler, E. E., & Cohen, S. G. (1992). Designing pay systems for teams. *ACA Journal, 1*, 6–18.

Li, J., Karakowsky, L., & Siegel, J. (1999). The effects of proportional representation on intragroup behavior in mixed-race decision-making groups. *Small Group Research, 30*(3), 259–279.

Lincoln, J. R., & Miller, J. (1979). Work and friendship ties in organizations: A comparative analysis of relational networks. *Administrative Science Quarterly, 24*, 81–199.

Lount, R., & Phillips, K. (2007). Working harder with the out-group: The impact of social category diversity on motivation gains. *Organizational Behavior and Human Decision Processes, 103*, 214–224.

Lount, R. B., Jr., Sheldon, O. Rink, F., & Phillips, K. W. (2011). *How much relationship conflict really exists? Biased perceptions of diverse groups*. Working paper, Ohio State University.

Loyd, D. L., Phillips, K. W., Whitson, J., & Thomas-Hunt, M. C. (2010). Expertise in your midst: How congruence between status and speech style affects reactions to unique knowledge. *Group Processes and Intergroup Relations, 13*, 379–395.

Loyd, D. L., Wang, C. S., Phillips, K. W., & Lount, R. L. (2011). Social category diversity promotes pre-meeting elaboration: The role of relationship focus. Forthcoming in *Organization Science*.

Luijters, K., van der Zee, K., & Otten, S. (2008). Cultural diversity in organizations: Enhancing identification by valuing differences. *International Journal of Intercultural Relations, 32*(2), 154–163.

Maass, A., Clark, R. D., & Haberkorn, G. (1982). The effects of differential ascribed category membership and norms on minority influence. *European Journal of Social Psychology, 12*(1), 89–104.

Maass, A., West, S. G., & Cialdini, R. B. (1987). Minority influence and conversion. In Hendrick, C. (Ed.), *Review of personality and social psychology* (Vol. 8, pp. 55–79). Beverly Hills, CA: Sage.

Magee, J. C., & Galinsky, A. D. (2008). Social hierarchy: The self-reinforcing nature of power and status. *Academy of Management Annals, 2*, 351–398.

Mannix, E., & Neale, M.A. (2005). What differences make a difference? The promise and reality of diverse teams in organizations. *Psychological Science in the Public Interest, 6*(2), 31–55.

McGrath, J. E., Berdahl, J. L., & Arrow, H. (1995). Traits, expectations, culture, and clout: The dynamics of diversity in work groups. *Diversity in work teams: Research paradigms for a changing workplace* (pp. 17–45). Washington, D.C.: American Psychological Association.

McLeod, P. L., Lobel, S. A., & Cox, T. H. (1996). Ethnic diversity and creativity in small groups. *Small Group Research, 27*(2), 248–264.

McPherson, J. M., & Smith-Lovin, L. (1987). Homophily in voluntary organizations, status, distance and the composition of face to face groups. *American Journal of Sociology, 52*, 370–379.

Meeker, B. F., & Weitzel-O'Neil, P. A. (1985). Sex roles and interpersonal behavior in task-oriented groups. In J. Berger & M. Zelditch (Eds.), *Status, reward, and influence* (pp. 379–405). Washington, D.C: Jossey-Bass.

Mendes, W. B., Blascovich, J., Hunter, S., Lickel, B., & Jost, J. T. (2007). Threatened by the unexpected: Challenge and threat during inter-ethnic interactions. *Journal of Personality and Social Psychology, 92*, 698–716.

Milliken, F. J., & Martins, L. L. (1996). Searching for common threads: Understanding the multiple effects of diversity in organizational teams. *Academy of Management Review, 21*, 402–433.

Mohammed, S., & Angell, L. (2004). Surface- and deep-level diversity in workgroups: examining the moderating effects of team orientation and team process on relationship conflict. *Journal of Organizational Behavior, 25*(8), 1015–1039.

Moscovici, S. (1976). *Social influence and social change*. London: Academic Press.

Mugny, G. (1982). *The power of minorities*. London: Academic Press.

Nam, C., Lyons, J., Hwang, H., & Kim, S. (2009). The process of team communication in multi –cultural contexts: An empirical study using Bales' interaction process analysis (IPA). *International Journal of Industrial Ergonomics, 39*(5), 771–782.

Nemeth, C. J. (1986). Differential contributions of majority and minority influence processes. *Psychological Review, 93*, 10–20.

Paletz, S., Peng, K., Erez, M., & Maslach, C. (2004). Ethnic composition and its differential impact on group processes in diverse teams. *Small Group Research, 35*(2), 128–157.

Pearsall, M., Ellis, A., & Evans, J. (2008). Unlocking the effects of gender faultlines on team creativity: Is activation the key?. *Journal of Applied Psychology, 93*(1), 225–234.

Pelled, H. L, Eisenhardt, M. K., & Xin, R. K. (1999). Exploring the black box: An analysis of work group diversity, conflict, and performance. *Administrative Science Quarterly, 44*(1), 1–28.

Pfeffer, J., & Salancik, G. (1978). *The external control of organizations: A resource dependence perspective*. New York: Harper and Row.

Phillips, K., Rothbard, N., & Dumas, T. (2009). To disclose or not to disclose? Status distance and self-disclosure in diverse environments. *Academy of Management Review, 34*(4), 710–732.

Phillips, K. W. (2003). The effects of categorically based expectations on minority influence: The importance of congruence. *Society for Personality and Social Psychology, 29*(1), 3–13.

Phillips, K. W., Kim-Jun, S. Y., & Shim, S. (2010). The value of diversity in organizations: A social psychological perspective. In R van Dick & K. Murnighan (Eds.), *Social psychology and organizations* (pp. 253–272). New York: Routledge Press.

Phillips, K. W., Liljenquist, K. A., & Neale, M. A. (2009). Is the pain worth the gain? The advantages and liabilities of agreeing with socially distinct newcomers. *Personality and Social Psychology Bulletin, 35*, 336–350.

Phillips, K. W., & Loyd, D. L. (2006). When surface and deep level diversity meet: The effects of dissenting group members.

Organizational Behavior and Human Decision Processes, 99(2), 143–160.

Phillips, K. W., Mannix, E. A., Neale, M. A., & Gruenfeld, D. H. (2004). Diverse groups and information sharing: The effects of congruent ties. *Journal of Experimental Social Psychology, 40*(4), 497–510.

Phillips, K. W., Northcraft, G. B., & Neale, M. A. (2006). Surface level diversity and decision-making in groups: When does deep-level similarity help? *Group Processes and Intergroup Relations, 9*, 467–482.

Phinney, J. (1996), Understanding ethnic diversity. *American Behavioral Scientist, 2*, 143–152.

Pilavin, J. A., & Martin, R. R. (1978). The effects of sex composition of groups on style of social interaction. *Sex Roles, 4*, 281–296.

Pitts, D. W. (2009). Diversity management, job satisfaction, and performance: Evidence from U.S. Federal agencies. *Public Administration Review, 69*(2), 328–338.

Polzer, J., Milton, L., & Swann, W. (2002). Capitalizing on diversity. *Administrative Science Quarterly, 47*, 296–324.

Polzer, J. T., Stewart, K. J., & Simmons, J. L. (1999). A social categorization explanation for framing effects in nested social dilemmas. *Organizational Behavior and Human Decision Processes, 79*, 154–178.

Puck, J., Rygl, D., & Kittler, M. (2006). Cultural antecedents and performance consequences of open communication and knowledge transfer in multicultural process-innovation teams. *Journal of Organisational Transformation & Social Change, 3*(2), 223–241.

Randel, A., & Earley, P. (2009). Organizational culture and similarity among team members' salience of multiple diversity characteristics. *Journal of Applied Social Psychology, 39*(4), 804–833.

Randel, A. E., & Jaussi, K. S. (2003). Functional background identity, diversity, and individual performance in cross–functional teams. *Academy of Management Journal, 46*(6), 763–774.

Reagans, R., & McEvily, B. (2003). Network structure and knowledge transfer: The effects of cohesion and range. *Administrative Science Quarterly, 48*(2), 240–267.

Rico, R., Molleman, E., Sanchez-Manzanares, M., & Van der Vegt, G. (2007). The effects of diveristy faultlines and team task autonomy on decision quality and social integration. *Journal of Management, 33*(1), 111–132.

Ridgeway, C. L. (1988). Gender differences in task groups: A status and legitimacy account. In M. Webster, Jr., & M. Foschi (Eds.), *Status generalization: New theory and research* (pp. 188–206). Stanford, CA: Stanford University Press.

Ridgeway, C. L. (1991). The social construction of status beliefs: Gender and other nominal characteristics. *Social Forces, 70*, 367–386.

Ridgeway, C. L. (2001). Gender, status, and leadership. *Journal of Social Issues, 54*, 637–655.

Ridgeway, C. L., & Berger, J. (1986). Expectations, legitimation, and dominance behavior in task groups. *American Sociological Review, 51*, 603–617.

Ridgeway, C. L., & Walker, H. (1995). Status structures. In K. Cook, G. Fine, & J. House (Eds.), *Sociological perspectives on social psychology* (pp. 281–310). New York: Allyn and Bacon.

Rink, F., & Ellemers, N. (2007). Defining the common feature: Task-related differences as the basis for dyadic identity. *British Journal of Social Psychology, 46*, 499–515.

Rink, F., & Ellemers, N. (2010). Benefiting from deep-level diversity: How congruence between knowledge and decision rules improves team decision making and team perceptions. *Group Processes & Intergroup Relations, 13*(3), 345–359.

Riordan, C., & Shore, L. (1997). Demographic diversity and employee attitudes: An empirical examination of relational demography within work units. *Journal of Applied Psychology, 82*(3), 342–358.

Roomkin, M., Rosen, S., & Dubbs, N. (1998). *Human resources practices survey*. New York: Deloitte & Touche.

Rudman, L., & Glick, P. (1999). Feminized management and backlash against agentic women: The hidden cost to women of a kinder, gentler image of middle managers. *Journal of Personality and Social Psychology Bulletin, 77*, 1004–1110.

Sheldon, O. J., Thomas-Hunt, M. C., & Proell, C. A. (2006). When timeliness matters: The moderating effects of status on reactions to time delay within distributed collaboration. *Journal of Applied Psychology, 91*, 1385–1395.

Simon, T. L., & Peterson, R. S. (2000). Task conflict and relationship conflict in top management teams: The pivotal role of intragroup trust. *Journal of Applied Psychology, 85*(1), 102–111.

Sinaceur, M., Thomas-Hunt, M., Neale, M. A., O'Neill, O., & Haag, C. (2010). Accuracy and perceived expert status in group decisions: When minority members make majority members more accurate privately. *Personality and Social Psychology Bulletin, 36*(3), 423–437.

Smith-Lovin, L., & Brody, C. (1989). Interruptions in group discussion and the influence of women in mixed-sex groups. *American Sociological Review, 54*, 424–435.

Sommers, S. (2006). On racial diversity and group decision making: Identifying multiple effects of racial composition on jury deliberations. *Journal of Personality and Social Psychology, 90*(4), 597–612.

Sommers, S., Warp, L. S., & Mahoney, C. (2008). Cognitive effects of racial diversity: White individuals' information processing in hereogeneous groups. *Journal of Experimental Social Psychology, 44*(4), 1129–1136.

Stahl, G., Maznevski, M., Voigt, A., & Jonsen, K. (2010). Unraveling the effects of cultural diversity in teams: A meta-analysis of research on multicultural work groups. *Journal of International Business Studies, 41*(4), 690–709.

Stewart, M., & Garcia-Prieto, P. (2008). A relational demography model of workgroup identification: Testing the effects of race, race dissimilarity, racial identification, and communication behavior. *Journal of Organizational Behavior, 29*(5), 657–680.

Stewart M. M., & Johnson O. E. (2009). Leader–member exchange as a moderator of the relationship between work group diversity and team performance. *Group & Organization Management, 34*(5), 507–535.

Swann, W. B., Milton, L. P., & Polzer, J. T. (2000). Should we create a niche or fall in line? Identity negotiation and small group effectiveness. *Journal of Personality & Social Psychology, 79*(2), 238–250.

Tajfel, H. (1981). *Human groups and social categories: Studies in social psychology*. New York: Cambridge University Press.

Tajfel, H., & Turner, J. C. (1986). The social identity theory of inter-group behavior. In S. Worchel & L. W. Austin (Eds.), *Psychology of intergroup relations* (pp. 7–24). Chicago: Nelson-Hall.

Tata, J. (2000). The influence of national culture on work team autonomy. *International Journal of Management, 17*(2), 266–271.

Thomas, D. (1999). Cultural diversity and work group effectiveness: An experimental study. *Journal of Cross-Cultural Psychology, 30*(2), 242–263.

Thomas-Hunt, M. C., Ogden, T. Y., & Neale, M. A. (2003). Who's really sharing? Effects of social and expert status on knowledge exchange within groups. *Management Science, 49*(4), 464–477.

Thomas-Hunt, M. C., & Phillips, K. W. (2004). When what you know is not enough: Expertise and gender dynamics in task groups. *Personality and Social Psychology Bulletin, 30*, 1585–1598.

Thompson, L. (2007). *Making the team* (3rd ed.). Englewood Cliffs, NJ: Prentice-Hall.

Thye, S. (2000). A status value theory of power: Ratio level predictions for new exchange structures. *American Sociological Review, 65*, 407–432.

Timurs, U. (2008). Ethnic identity, power, and communication in top management teams. *Baltic Journal of Management, 3*(2), 159–173.

Tomasetto, C., Mucchi-Faina, A., Alparone, F. & Pagliaro, S. (2009). Differential effects of majority and minority influence on argumentation strategies. *Social Influence, 4*(1), 33–45.

Turner, H. (1982). Towards a cognitive redefinition of the social group. In H. Tajfel (Ed), *Social identity and intergroup relations* (pp. 15–40). Cambridge/Paris: Cambridge University Press.

Turner, J. C. (1987). The analysis of social influence. In J. C. Turner, M. A. Hogg, P. J. Oakes, S. D. Reicher, & M. S. Wetherell (Eds.), *Rediscovering the social group: A self-categorization theory* (pp. 68–88). Oxford, UK: Blackwell.

Umans, T. (2008). Ethnic identity, power, and communication in top management teams. *Baltic Management Journal, 3*, 159–173.

Vallaster, C. (2005). Cultural diversity and its impact on social interactive processes: Implications from an empirical study. *International Journal of Cross-Cultural Management, 5*(2), 139–163.

van der Zee, K., Atsma, N., & Brodbeck, F. (2004). The influence of social identity and personality on outcomes of cultural diversity in teams. *Journal of Cross-Cultural Psychology, 35*(3), 283–303.

Van Dick, R., van Knippenberg, D., Hägele, S., Guillaume, Y. R. F., & Brodbeck, F. C. (2008). Group diversity and group identification: The moderating role of diversity beliefs. *Human Relations, 61*(10), 1463–1492.

Van Dyne, L., & Saavedra, R. (1996). A naturalistic minority influence experiment: Effects on divergent thinking, conflict, and originality in work groups. *British Journal of Social Psychology, 5*, 151–168.

Van Ginkel, W. P., & van Knippenberg, D. (2008). Group information elaboration and group decision making: The role of shared task representations. *Organizational Behavior and Human Decision Processes, 105*(1), 82–97.

van Knippenberg, D., De Dreu, C., & Homan, A. (2004). Work group diversity and group performance: An integrative model and research agenda. *Journal of Applied Psychology, 89*(6), 1008–1022.

van Knippenberg, D., Haslam, S. A., & Platow, M. J. (2004). *Unity through diversity: Value-in-diversity beliefs as moderator of the relationship between work group diversity and group identification.* Paper presented at the Society for Industrial and Organizational Psychology 19th Annual Conference, Chicago.

van Knippenberg, D., & Schippers, M. C. (2007). Work group diversity. *Annual Review of Psychology, 58*, 515–541.

Watson, W., BarNir, A., & Pavur, R. (2005). Cultural diversity and learning teams: The impact on desired academic team processes. *International Journal of Intercultural Relations, 29*(4), 449–467.

Watson, W., Johnson, L., & Zgourides, G. (2002). The influence of ethnic diversity on leadership, group process, and performance: An examination of learning teams. *International Journal of Intercultural Relations, 26*(1), 1–16.

Watson, W., Kumar, K., & Michaelsen, L. (1993). Cultural diversity's impact on interaction process and performance: Comparing homogeneous and diverse task groups. *Academy of Management Journal, 36*(3), 590–602.

Weisband, S., Schneider, S., & Connolly, T. (1995). Computer-mediated communication and social information: Status salience and status differences. *Academy of Management Journal, 38*(4), 1124–1151.

Williams, K., & O'Reilly, C. (1998). Demography and diversity in organizations: a review of 40 years of research. *Research in Organizational Behavior, 20*, 77–140.

Wittenbaum, G. M. (1998). Information sampling in decision-making groups: The impact of member's task-relevant status. *Small Group Research, 29*(1), 57–84.

Wittenbaum, G. M. (2000). The bias toward discussing shared information: Why are high status group members immune? *Communication Research, 27*, 379–401.

Wittenbaum, G. M., & Bowman, J. M. (2005), Member status and information exchange in decision-making groups. In M. C. Thomas-Hunt (Ed.), *Status and groups* (Research on Managing Groups and Teams, Vol. 7, pp. 143–168). Emerald Group Publishing Limited.

Wood, W., & Karten, S. J. (1986). Sex differences in interaction style as a product of perceived sex differences in competence. *Journal of Personality & Social Psychology, 5*, 341–347.

Wood, W., Lundgren, S., Ouellette, J. A., Busceme, S., & Blackstone, T. (1994). Minority influence: A meta-analytic review of social influence processes. *Psychological Bulletin, 115*, 323–345.

Wuchty, S., Jones, B. F., & Uzzi, B. (2007). The increasing dominance of teams in production of knowledge. *Science, 316*, 1036–1039.

Zhang, D., Lowry, B. P., Zhou, L., & Fu, X. (2007). The impact of individualism-collectivism, social presence, and group diversity on group decision making under majority influence. *Journal of Management Information Systems, 23*(4), 53–80.

CHAPTER 10

Diversity as Disagreement: The Role of Group Conflict

Karen A. Jehn *and* Lindred L. Greer

Abstract

Conflict is critical for determining diversity's influence on group effectiveness. A considerable amount of work has amassed on the relationships between team diversity, conflict, and team outcomes. This chapter will briefly review recent findings and developments in this area. Three specific complexities needing future research will then be highlighted, with special attention to how diversity may promote not only conflict but also asymmetric experiences of conflict in teams. The three areas for future research are (1) the role of different conceptualizations and operationalizations of diversity in predicting the emergence and asymmetric experience of conflict in teams; (2) the impact of new and understudied forms of diversity, such as lifestyle diversity or power diversity, on conflict and conflict asymmetries; and (3) the role of the perception of diversity in activating the relationship between diversity and conflict asymmetries.

Key Words: conflict, disagreement, contagion, placement, group effectiveness, asymmetry, perception

Many questions remain about how diversity influences workgroup outcomes (cf. Horwitz & Horwitz, 2007). Numerous typologies of diversity characteristics have been created in an attempt to explain the varying effects of diversity on workgroup outcomes (e.g., visible vs. invisible; task-related vs. non–task-related; Pelled, 1996; social category vs. informational, Jehn, Northcraft, & Neale, 1999; surface- vs. deep-level, Harrison, Price, & Bell, 1998; Harrison, Price, Gavin, & Florey, 2002). However, recent reviews and meta-analyses (Jackson, Joshi, & Erhardt, 2003; Joshi & Roh, 2009; Mannix & Neale, 2005) suggest that there are no consistent direct effects of diversity on organizational performance, even when the different types are considered. More nuanced and context-dependent views of diversity are therefore needed to better understand how diversity affects group outcomes (cf. Joshi & Roh, 2009), and special attention is needed to the underlying processes that may explain how diversity affects group outcomes.

Conflict has been identified as a primary mediating process that has the potential to explain the effects of diversity upon important group outcomes, such as performance (cf. Jehn, Greer & Rupert, 2008; King, Hebl, & Beal, 2009; Lau & Murnighan, 1998; Williams & O'Reilly, 1998). In this chapter on diversity as disagreement, we focus on the multiple ways in which conflict may explain how and when diversity produces effective or ineffective outcomes in groups. This chapter will briefly review recent findings and developments in this area. Three specific complexities needing future research in the study of diversity and conflict in groups will then be highlighted, with special attention to how diversity may promote not only conflict but also asymmetric experiences of conflict in teams by diverse members. Areas for future research are the role of different conceptualizations and operationalizations of diversity in predicting the emergence and asymmetric experience of conflict in teams; the impact of new and understudied forms of diversity, such as lifestyle diversity or power diversity, on conflict asymmetries; and the role of the perception of diversity in activating the relationship between diversity and conflict asymmetries.

Group conflict

We begin by defining intragroup conflicts and discussing the different ways conflict can be conceptualized. Intragroup conflict has been defined as the process arising from perceived or real incompatibilities among group members (e.g., Boulding, 1962; De Dreu & Weingart, 2003; Thomas, 1992; Wall & Callister, 1995). The most common way researchers have approached the study of conflict in groups (i.e., intragroup conflict) is to examine the general level of conflict in groups (i.e. "how much conflict is there in this team?").

More recently, researchers have begun to examine the asymmetry of conflict within groups. Recent work (e.g., Coleman, Kugler, Mitchinson, Chung, & Musallam, 2010; Jehn, Rispens, & Thatcher, 2010; Jehn, Rupert, Nauta, & den Bosche, 2010; Thatcher & Phillips, 2010) has highlighted how members in a group may have different perceptions of the level, amount, and type of conflict in the group, and as a result may exhibit more or less conflict behaviors than their other group members (e.g., Jehn, Greer, Rispens, & Jonsen, 2012; Mannes, 2009). For example, in a study of 51 workgroups, Jehn and colleagues (2010) examined the consequences of asymmetric conflict perceptions on the effectiveness of individuals and groups. Group conflict asymmetry was defined as the degree to which members differed in their perceptions of the level of conflict in the group. They found that group conflict asymmetry decreased performance and creativity in the workgroups. They also examined individual conflict asymmetry, which was defined as one member perceiving more or less conflict than other group members. Whether a workgroup member was a high or low perceiver of conflict (compared to the other group members) determined his or her individual performance and satisfaction with the team. They suggested multiple mechanisms by which this could occur. Diversity between members in their perceptions of conflict in the team decreases their trust in and respect for one another; it also frustrates members and increases their cognitive load as they spend time and energy trying to make sense of their divergent perceptions of the conflict environment in the team.

We believe that this multilevel conceptualization and understanding of the process of intragroup conflict is important for diversity researchers to consider when examining the effects of workgroup diversity on individual and team effectiveness. Perhaps one of the reasons why the effects of diversity and conflict have been mixed is that past conceptualizations of these relationships have overlooked the ability of diversity to differentially affect certain members within the team and to feed conflict asymmetries. To facilitate this goal, following our review of the current state of the literatures on conflict and diversity, we will then discuss how different types and configurations of diversity in workgroups may influence the multilevel and potentially asymmetric process of intragroup conflict and how this in turn may help explain how diversity ultimately affects individual and team outcomes. We highlight new types of diversity categorizations (e.g., lifestyle diversity, power diversity), configurations (e.g., faultline placement), and perceptions that directly relate to our multilevel view of conflict in workgroups and may provide answers to how diversity affects individuals in groups via conflict and disagreement.

Types of intragroup conflict

Past research on intragroup conflict has primarily focused on conflicts arising from either task or relationship issues (Amason, 1996; Guetzkow & Gyr, 1954; Jehn, 1995). Task conflicts involve problems among group members about ideas and opinions relating to the job the group is performing (e.g., De Dreu & Weingart, 2003; Jehn, 1995, 1997), such as the focus for a major advertising plan. Relationship conflicts are about non–work-related issues between members, such as differences about politics, religion, environmental issues, or commuting that are often important to people but not necessarily related to the task they are working on (e.g., De Dreu & Weingart, 2003; Jehn, 1995, 1997). Process conflicts involve logistical issues within the group, such as disagreements about the delegation of resources and task responsibilities (Behfar, Mannix, Peterson, & Trochim, 2011; Greer & Jehn, 2007; Jehn, 1997).

Conflict and group effectiveness

When investigating the impact of diversity and conflict on group outcomes, the group outcomes typically studied fall into two general categories, those that are performance-related and those that are morale-related. Indicators of team performance can include departmental production records or supervisor ratings (e.g., Jehn, 1997; Pelled et al., 1999). Measures of morale typically focus on satisfaction with the group or member turnover intentions (Jehn, 1997; Murnighan & Conlon, 1991; Pelled et al., 1999). These indicators of morale are thought to represent team viability and are as important for group functioning and success as actual performance (Balkundi & Harrison, 2006; Hackman, 1987; Hackman & Wageman, 2005).

Research has shown that task conflict can improve performance under certain conditions (e.g., nonroutine tasks, open conflict norms) through improved consideration of different alternatives and group problem solving (e.g., Amason, 1996; Corseu & Schruijer, 2010; Greer et al., 2006; Jehn, 1997; Matsuo, 2006; Olson et al., 2007; Pelled, Eisenhardt, & Xin, 1999). Other research suggests that conflict interferes with the cognitive processing of group members (e.g., Carnevale & Probst, 1998). Task conflicts may impede a group member's ability to adequately process information. While the cognitive processing perspective has received support (see the meta-analysis by De Dreu & Weingart, 2003), De Dreu and Weingart do suggest, consistent with Jehn (1995, 1997), that under certain conditions task conflicts may still be able to increase group performance. Specifically, De Dreu and Weingart suggest that task conflict in groups performing nonroutine tasks in a trusting and psychologically safe environment can result in improved group performance.

The effects of task conflict on team viability (e.g., satisfaction, commitment, or willingness to work together again) are consistently negative (cf. De Dreu & Weingart, 2003; Jehn & Bendersky, 2003). In general, frustration and dissatisfaction are common reactions to any sort of disagreement or conflict among individuals (Ross, 1989). Therefore, relationship conflicts, as well as task conflicts, cause problems for team viability. If members are fighting, they are often unsatisfied and likely not to want to continue in the group, thus decreasing group morale. Relationship conflicts also interfere with successful group performance because of the misspent time and effort (Jehn & Bendersky, 2003) wasted on petty fighting over non–task-related issues or resolving the non–task-related issues, rather than on completing the task (e.g., Amason, 1996; Evan, 1965; Jehn, 1995; Li & Hambrick, 2005; Matsuo, 2006; Nibler & Harris, 2003; Pelled, 1997; Rau, 2005).

Regarding process conflict, some research has proposed that these disagreements in a team may improve group functioning as members' ability are fit to the task requirements (e.g., Goncalo, Polman, & Maslach, 2010; Jehn, Northcraft, & Neale, 1999). Other research shows that process conflict decreases members' cognitive abilities and distracts them from more important goal-related issues (e.g., Behfar et al., 2011; Greer & Jehn, 2007; Greer et al., 2006; Jehn & Mannix, 2001; Vodosek, 2007). Process conflict, as with the other types of conflict, is consistently found to decrease morale and satisfaction in the group due to the personal challenging and discomfort of individuals with conflict-filled interactions.

Past empirical findings on diversity and conflict

Social category heterogeneity and conflict

Social category heterogeneity has been shown to increase relationship conflicts in groups (e.g., Ayub & Jehn, 2010; Jehn et al., 1999; Mohammed & Angel, 2004; O'Reilly, Williams, & Barsade; 1997; Pelled et al., 1999). This is thought to be because social identity and social categorization processes in diverse groups lead to discomfort, hostility, and tension (e.g., Jehn et al., 1999; Tajfel & Turner, 1986) and dislike between members of different demographic categories (Byrne, 1971). Social category heterogeneity also influences task conflict in groups (Ayub & Jehn, 2010; Curseu & Schruijer, 2010; cf. Jehn, Bezrukova, & Thatcher, 2006): when group members have different social category characteristics, they are likely to have different experiences or values (Dougherty, 1992). These different "thought worlds" can cause task conflicts and can also lead to process conflicts regarding how best to coordinate the task at hand (Behfar et al., 2011; Jehn et al., 1999). In support of these ideas, Vodosek (2007) found all three forms of conflict to mediate the negative impact of cultural diversity on team outcomes. However, a recent meta-analysis by Stahl, Maznefski, Voigt, and Jonsen (2010) found that cultural diversity is positively related to task conflict, but is not significantly related to either relationship or process conflict.

Functional heterogeneity and conflict

Functional differences, just like social category differences, elicit in-group/out-group comparisons that result in tensions within groups that can escalate to relationship conflicts due to increased communication problems and resentment across different areas (Strauss, 1962). Functional heterogeneity also increases task conflict. Members of different functional backgrounds, by definition, bring different education, training, and experience to the group (e.g., Lovelace, Shapiro, & Weingart, 2001). These different perspectives, or "representational gaps" (Cronin & Weingart, 2007), lead to debates and disagreements about the group task (Pelled et al., 1999). Jehn, Northcraft, and Neale (1999) found that functional diversity increased improved performance when mediated by task conflict. Knight and colleagues (1999), in their study of 76 top management teams, showed that functional diversity's effects on goal consensus were mediated by relationship conflict and agreement seeking. Olson, Parayitam, and Bao (2007) showed that task conflict mediated the effect of cognitive diversity on team performance. In addition, members of different functional backgrounds rely on different working methods (Bantel & Jackson, 1989; Gruenfeld et al., 1996) and different views of how to coordinate a task (cf. Cronin & Weingart, 2007; Jehn et al., 1999) that can lead to process conflicts (Behfar et al., 2011; Jehn et al., 1999). Recent research by Klein, Knight, Ziegert, Lim, and Saltz (2011) contributed to this line of work by showing that the effects of functional diversity (operationalized as differences in work values) on team conflict depend on the style of the team leader. Work-value diversity was associated with team conflict only when leaders were person-focused rather than task-oriented.

Diversity faultlines and conflict

The concept of demographic faultlines (Lau & Murnighan, 1998) has arisen in response to critiques of the traditional conceptualization of diversity (see Chapter 4 in this book for a review). Demographic faultlines have been hypothesized to lead to increased levels of relationship conflict (e.g., Lau & Murnighan, 1998; 2005; Li & Hambrick, 2005; Thatcher et al., 2003). When faultlines occur in groups, the resulting subgroups, or coalitions, may increase the salience of in-group/out-group memberships, resulting in strain and polarization, and inter-subgroup competition (Lau & Murnighan, 1998). When group members align with others of similar demographics, they will see the others in the group as outsiders (Hogg, Turner, & Davidson, 1990), resulting in tensions that intensify relationship conflict within the group (Jehn, Bezrukova, & Thatcher, 2006). In addition, research indicates that aligned subgroups will have negative beliefs about members of the other subgroup, the "out-group," causing feelings of inequity and disrespect (Hogg, 1996), which increase experiences of relationship conflict. This can distract members from the task and can cause competition within the group based on non–task-related dimensions (e.g., "we older workers know more than you young members" or "those of us from the U.S. are more capable than you others"). These distinctions and splits within a common-goal workgroup can cause decreased performance and negative attitudes that, in the end, will decrease the effectiveness of the task performance of the group.

While demographic faultlines are likely to increase relationship conflict, their effects on task conflict within the group are less clear. On the one hand, when in-group and out-group identities are salient, subgroups may polarize (Lau & Murnighan, 1998) and talk less with each other about work issues. When communication between subgroups declines, task conflict is less likely to occur. On the other hand, when members have subgroup members to share their opinion with, they may be more willing to hold onto their own opinion during group discussions (Asch, 1952; cf. Lau & Murnighan, 1998). Task conflicts are therefore more likely because members backed up by representative subgroup members may be more willing to enter into task conflicts, given the support they feel based on their alignments. Task conflicts may become even more intense as subgroups each rally around their own unique point of view (Lau & Murnighan, 1998).

In addition, the different backgrounds that members of different functional subgroups have may lead members to approach process issues differently (Bantel & Jackson, 1989; Gruenfeld et al., 1996; Pelled, 1996). These differences may be accentuated by subgroup dynamics relating to equity and appropriate delegation of staff and resources. When subgroups form, inter-subgroup competition may take place as to who should get the overall group resources and how to delegate sought-after tasks (Lau & Murnighan, 1998). When subgroups feel compelled to compete for group resources, higher levels of process conflict may also result.

Findings so far on the effects of faultlines on conflict and performance have been mixed. Li and Hambrick (2005) found that strong faultlines (based on age, tenure, gender, and ethnicity) led to increased task conflict, relationship conflict, behavior disintegration, and decreased performance. The relationship between faultline strength and behavioral disintegration (decrease in interaction, exchange, and collective effort) was entirely mediated by relationship conflict, but not by task conflict. They found that relationship conflict had a negative influence on performance, but did not find an effect of task conflict on performance. The group processes (relationship conflict, task conflict, and behavioral disintegration) fully mediated the negative relationship between faultline size and performance. Lau and Murnighan (2005) found that faultlines (based on gender and ethnicity) explained more variance in perception of team learning, psychological safety, satisfaction, and expected performance than single-attribute heterogeneity indices. Lau and Murnighan also found strong faultlines to decrease relationship conflict. Thatcher, Jehn, and Zanutto (2003) found that diversity faultlines (based on years of work experience, type of functional background, degree major, sex, age, race, and country of origin) were linearly associated with lower levels of relationship and process conflict, but did not find a linear effect on either task conflict, performance, or morale. In curvilinear tests, they found that faultline strength had a curvilinear effect on relationship conflict, process conflict, performance, and morale. Groups with low faultline strength (where no subgroups existed; i.e., Asian male accountant, Black male manager, Native American male salesman, and Hispanic male secretary) and groups with very strong faultline strength (where subgroups cleanly align on the basis of multiple characteristics; i.e., two Black male managers and two White female assistants) had higher levels of process and relationship conflicts and lower levels of performance and morale than groups where medium faultline strength existed (i.e., one female Asian consultant, one White female consultant, one White male assistant, one Black male assistant).

Molleman (2005) found that both demographic faultline strength and distance (see Bezrukova, Jehn, Zanutto, & Thatcher, 2009; Thatcher, Jehn, & Zanutto, 2003, for overview of faultline strength and distance) increased general intragroup conflict (the average of task and relationship conflict items). He also found that faultlines formed on the basis of personality types significantly interacted with team autonomy in predicting intragroup conflict, such that when personality faultline distance was high and team autonomy was high, intragroup conflict was the highest, and when faultline distance was low and team autonomy was low, intragroup conflict was the lowest.

Furthermore, Pearsall, Ellis, and Evans (2007) found that relationship conflict mediated the relationship between activated gender faultlines and team creativity, such that faultlines were positively related to relationship conflict and relationship conflict was negatively related to team creativity. Choi and Sy (2010) found that social category faultlines, such as gender/age or age/race faultlines, were positively related to relationship conflict, which was indirectly negatively related to team performance. Lastly, Jehn and Bezrukova (2010) found that activated racial faultlines positively influenced general levels of conflict in the team, which negatively affected team outcomes.

In sum, research on faultlines and conflict has mixed results. Faultlines have been shown to both positively and negatively relate to general levels of intragroup conflict. We suggest by taking a more nuanced view of conflict, in terms of how it is asymmetrically perceived in groups, and investigating the effect of diversity and faultlines on conflict asymmetry, we may be able to gain better insight into how diversity and faultlines affect the conflict dynamics and ultimate outcomes of diverse groups. Therefore, we provide a new framework for understanding diversity and disagreement in groups using the conflict asymmetry perspective.

A new framework for understanding diversity and conflict: conflict asymmetry

We suggest that research needs to consider the asymmetry of perceptions by members of diverse groups to more thoroughly explain the effects of diversity and disagreement on group conflict and outcomes. Past conflict research often assumes that all members interacting on a work task perceive and experience the same amount of conflict (De Dreu & Weingart, 2003; cf. Jehn & Chatman, 2000). This assumption ignores the possibility that different parties involved in a conflict may perceive different levels of conflict. For example, one person in a workgroup may perceive a high level of conflict, while another may perceive little or no conflict. This view of asymmetric conflict perceptions has often been ignored in past research on conflict (e.g., Amason, 1996; Jehn, 1995; Pelled, 1996; cf. Jehn & Rispens, 2007). Similarly, research on organizational groups and teams in general often takes the view that groups possess *shared* team properties, or that experiences are commonly held by team members (Klein & Kozlowski, 2000; Mason, 2006), rather than *configural* team properties, or properties that reflect the differences in attitudes and perceptions among individuals working together (Chan, 1998; Klein & Kozlowski, 2000).

Recent research (Jehn et al., 2010) shows that group conflict asymmetry (the degree to which members differ in perceptions of the level of conflict in the group) decreases performance and creativity in groups. This effect was explained by the social processes (e.g., communication, cooperation) and the group atmosphere (e.g., trust, respect) that resulted from asymmetric perceptions. In addition, at the individual level, high perceivers of conflict reported lower performance and satisfaction with the team than did low perceivers of conflict. We therefore suggest that it is critical to assess individuals' different perceptions of conflict levels to accurately predict the effects of diversity on group and individual behavior and outcomes.

In addition to perceiving different levels of conflict, individuals may also respond or behave differently when conflict is perceived in a team. Individual conflict engagement is defined as an individual's behavioral confrontation of conflict issues (Greer & Jehn, 2010). This distinction between conflict perceptions and behaviors traces back to the classic work of Pondy (1967) on felt versus manifest conflicts. As an example of the differences between asymmetries in conflict perceptions and conflict engagement, imagine a team meeting in which a member perceives that others' opinions are in disagreement with her own, but has not yet expressed her own opinion. Perceptual conflict asymmetry may exist at this point. She may choose whether or not to verbally contradict the opinions of the others. If she does choose to express a contradictory opinion, this would be defined as conflict engagement. Similar to asymmetries in perceptions of conflict, individual engagement in conflict can also have negative outcomes for the individual within a team. Behaviorally engaging in relationship or process conflicts can distract individuals from the task and create tensions with other team members (Jehn & Bendersky, 2003), while behaviorally engaging in task conflict may help the individual to showcase his or her expertise on the issue and may increase the individual's intellective engagement with the issue as the individual formulates the argument. Therefore, by distinguishing between group-level and individual-level conflict perceptions and behaviors, more nuanced and clearer understanding of conflicts can be obtained (cf. Jehn et al., 2012; Korsgaard et al., 2008) and better insight gained into the exact process by which diversity influences team outcomes.

Given these different views of conflicts (asymmetry of perception and engagement), we suggest three areas for future research to move forward the study of diversity and disagreement in groups: (1) How do different conceptualizations of diversity affect these more nuanced conceptualizations of conflict in groups? (2) How do different understudied types of diversity (e.g., lifestyle and power) influence conflict perceptions and behaviors? (3) How does the perception of diversity add to or differ from the examination (as is common in much past research) of objective diversity when predicting multifaceted notions of conflict in teams?

Research question 1

As previously discussed in this chapter, the concept of demographic faultlines, wherein demographic characteristics align within a team in such a way as to create a clear dividing line between dissimilar team members (Lau & Murnighan, 1998), has generated a steady stream of research over the past decade. However, these studies have revealed contrasting results. We suggest that this is because past views of faultlines have been too simplistic and do not allow the possibility of understanding how different configurations of diversity differentially affect the conflict perceptions and behaviors of individual team members.

Recent work by O'Leary and Mortenson (2010) as well as by Polzer and colleagues (2006) and Greer, Jehn, Thatcher, and Van Beest (2010) all suggest that not all faultlines are created equal. Rather, the way in which faultlines divide a group (such as between two equally sized subgroups or between a larger subgroup and an excluded individual) may have not only important implications for group-level conflict (e.g., Polzer et al., 2006) but also important implications in that different faultlines may create important differences in the perception and expression of conflict between individuals within the same group. For example, Greer and colleagues (2010) show that when faultlines create a solo member, that solo member is more likely to perceive higher levels of conflict than other group members, but less likely to behaviorally engage in conflict. They show that this can then translate into impaired team climate and performance.

Future investigation of how different configurations of diversity can create differential experiences within the same team is therefore an important future research direction. The distinction between, for example, solo members or subgroup members based on demographic characteristics is theoretically and practically very relevant for the understanding of diversity and disagreement in groups. This is because in diverse teams, the solo members in particular need to share their opinions in order for the team to capitalize on the "value of diversity" within the team (Homan et al., 2007), but this is difficult as solos are likely to tend to conform to the dominant subgroup (Asch, 1952). Therefore, we suggest that it would be useful for future research to identify ways to make sure that all individuals on either sides of a faultline in a team have similar perceptions of conflict and feel empowered to speak about these perceptions when they are about the task. Research would benefit from both experimental designs that can create and compare different forms of subgroups in common-goal groups and also field research to examine the natural placement and perceptions of members based on their demographics and how they view the conflict in the group. For example, in a recent study of faultlines (Jehn & Bezrukova, 2010), members were placed into groups based on demographic alignment (e.g., Black males vs. White females). An interesting result of this research was that not all members perceived there to be a faultline and in turn did not perceive conflict or act in a conflict-filled way. The members who did perceive faultiness were more engaged in conflict and dissatisfied, thus leading to lower performance. This suggests that future research incorporate measures of both objective (calculated) and perceived demographic faultlines and relate these to individual perceptions of conflict to capture the asymmetry of conflict within the group that may exist.

Research question 2

We offer another line of inquiry challenging the assumptions often made in past diversity typologies. That is, we raise the question of whether there are non–task-related invisible characteristics that may be important. Much of the research assumes that all social category variables are visible and that all deep-level characteristics (often invisible) are task-related (e.g., personality traits, work values; Rink, 2005). We therefore seek to introduce a broader conceptualization of social category diversity. This is desirable because relying on prior conceptualizations of social category diversity has often led to contradictory results regarding conflict across studies. The typical troika of social category variables studied in the literature (age, sex, and ethnicity) could be classified as "visible" social category variables that often increase relationship conflict. While obviously a crude categorization (people do not always look their age, or look like they belong to a certain ethnic group), these features are usually more transparent to study than other potential social category variables (such as sexual orientation, marital status, social class, family background, whether one is a parent, whether one has a history of substance abuse, or whether one has changed his or her name), which may explain why they have been the focus of attention when examining conflict in organizational workgroups. Yet the knowledge that a group member falls into one of these latter categories is likely to activate the same categorization and comparison processes as occurs with the visible social category diversity variables. Thus, future research needs to more thoroughly examine what categories individual members are basing their behaviors and attitudes on (i.e., what is salient to them) in order to determine what type or level of conflict is likely to occur.

LIFESTYLE HETEROGENEITY AND CONFLICT

An interesting and potentially highly influential demographic characteristic in teams that has yet to receive much empirical investigation in the workgroup setting is lifestyle diversity. Lifestyle diversity, as we have defined it, could be considered a form of value diversity related to nonwork issues (e.g., marital status, sexual orientation). We propose that stigmas against sexual orientation, substance abuse, and certain social classes will affect stereotyping and prejudice (Brauer, 2001; Button, 2001; D'Emilio, 1983; Fussell, 1983; Hartmann, 1970; Herek, 1993; Newcomb, Mercurio, & Wollard, 2000; Plummer, 1975; Sorensen, 2000), and ultimately performance, as much or more than the traditional social category aspects examined (i.e., age and gender). In related, initial studies of this form of diversity, Jehn and colleagues (1999) introduced value diversity, a third type of diversity, distinct from social category or functional diversity. Value diversity represents differences in the values that members hold regarding work. Value diversity was found to increase all three conflict types and to decrease perceived and actual performance as well as morale. Research on various other lifestyle characteristics suggests that this form of diversity will also increase conflict in groups, but has been understudied within organizations for a number of reasons. First, it is very controversial to ask employees about these characteristics; however, a study on punk rock bands by Jehn, Conlon, and Greer (2010) demonstrated that these characteristics may have a larger influence on workgroup processes such as conflict and performance outcomes (e.g., productivity and morale) than the more traditional diversity characteristics (e.g., gender, race, work experience). In addition, the theory regarding these characteristics is underdeveloped. Therefore, more examination is required to determine how people who lead different lifestyles will perceive conflict differently, similar to the more visible social categories, and how this will influence the effects of conflict.

POWER DIVERSITY

Another form of diversity that is understudied and does not readily fit into past categorization schemes of diversity forms is diversity in power or status within teams. Initial research and theorizing in this area has suggested that differences in power or status within a team may have the potential to both benefit group interactions and to harm group interactions. On the one hand, power diversity offers a heuristic solution to problems of resource allocation (De Cremer, 2003; Keltner, van Kleef, Chen, & Kraus, 2008) and can facilitate order and coordination in groups (Magee & Galinsky, 2008). On the other hand, power diversity has the potential to make salient feelings of inequality and injustice (Henderson & Frederickson, 2001; cf. Lawler & Proell, 2009; Muller, 1985) and can breed rivalry and competition (Bloom, 1999; cf. Harrison & Klein, 2007). Greer and Van Kleef (2010) reconciled these viewpoints by showing that the effects of power dispersion depend on the amount of resources available to the group. When a group has low power, power dispersion is helpful, but when a group has high power, power dispersion leads to power struggles and conflict within the team. Further research into the potential moderators of power diversity and the exact underlying dynamics by which groups create and change power diversity within their team would be interesting.

Directly integrating work on power and status with work on traditionally studied demographic characteristics would also be an interesting pathway for future research. A potential mechanism by which differences in, say, gender exert their influence on group conflict may be through the instigation of power differences and inequalities within the team, which promote perceptions of conflict and are also likely to result in actual conflict behaviors, given their degree of personal importance to members. For example, Greer and colleagues (2006) found that status moderated the effects of demographic diversity, such that high-status demographic solo members in workgroups were less likely to perceive conflict, but more likely to act on conflict when perceived, than low-status solo members in teams. Therefore, integrating notions of power and status into research on diversity and conflict is important for future research.

Research question 3

One key direction in future research that has been largely neglected thus far is the distinction between actual diversity and perceived diversity (for exceptions, see Dooley, Freyxell, & Judge, 2000; Harrison et al., 1998, 2002; Jehn et al., 1999). Most past work on diversity has focused on objective demographic characteristics, such as gender, age, or race (cf. Williams & O'Reilly, 1998), that can *potentially* influence team processes, such as conflict, and team outcomes. However, as seen in the recent reviews and meta-analyses on diversity and group processes and outcomes (Jackson et al., 2003; Mannix & Neale, 2005; Stewart, 2006; Webber & Donahue, 2001; Williams & O'Reilly, 1998), findings on diversity have been largely inconsistent. We propose that one possible way of explaining these contradictory findings is by proposing that diversity affects group process and outcomes only when it is perceived or salient. Research has proposed and shown, for example, that individuals are not always accurate when assessing the degree of diversity in their work unit as compared to other work units (cf. Harrison & Klein, 2007).

Therefore, considering the perception, as well as the actuality, of diversity may help us better understand the effects of diversity on intragroup conflict and outcomes. In addition, as we mentioned before, members may have different perceptions of the level of conflict in the group, as well as different degrees of behavioral involvement. A member of a certain demographic category, when perceiving himself or herself to be in the minority, may be more likely to perceive the conflict as relationship-based rather than task-based, but less likely to engage in actual conflict behaviors while in a perceived minority position. If individuals feel that others are getting more resources or the best tasks within the group, they may be more likely to perceive process conflict rather than perceiving that it is a task conflict or based on task capabilities.

There is a conceptual distinction between objective and perceived demographic differences within groups (Garcia-Prieto, Bellard, & Schneider, 2003; Harrison & Klein, 2007; Zellmer-Bruhn, Maloney, Bhappu, & Salvador, 2008) that has been acknowledged in the empirical work on surface- and deep-level diversity (Cunningham, 2007; Harrison, Price, & Bell, 1998; Harrison, Price, Gavin, & Florey, 2002; Phillips &

Loyd, 2006; Phillips, Northcraft, & Neale, 2006), mentoring relationships (e.g., Lankau, Riordan, & Thomas, 2005), value and goal diversity (e.g., Jehn, Northcraft, & Neale, 1999; Mannix & Jehn, 2004; Rink, 2005), face-to-face versus computer-mediated communication (e.g., Bhappu, Griffith, & Northcraft, 1997), and perceived variability/homogeneity in in-groups and out-groups (e.g., Lee & Ottati, 1993). Research on supervisor–subordinate relations has suggested that perceived differences often have a greater effect on interactions than objective demographic differences (c.f., Riordan, 2000; Strauss, Barrick, & Connerley, 2001; Turban & Jones, 1988). Ashforth and Mael (1989) explain this by suggesting that the effect of demographic differences is through individuals' perceptions. Thus, we propose that these different perceptions of members' demographics and their difference in the group may also lead to different perceptions of conflict.

This same discrepancy between perceived and actual diversity is also a point of contention in the literature on demographic faultlines. Most work on faultlines conceptualizes faultlines based on objective demographic characteristics that can *potentially* influence team processes and team functioning (Gibson & Vermeulen, 2003; Lau & Murnighan, 2005; Li & Hambrick, 2005; but for an exception see Earley & Mosakowski, 2000). However, as Lau and Murnighan (1998) put forth in their original article on faultline theory, groups may have many potential faultlines, "each of which may activate or increase the potential for particular subgroupings" (p. 328). Since faultlines can remain inactive and go unnoticed for years without influencing the group process (Lau & Murnighan, 1998), it is important to take into account whether team members actually perceive or experience these subgroup splits and to what extent these faultline perceptions determine intragroup processes and outcomes. Recent work on faultline activation (the process by which objective faultlines become perceived within a group; Jehn & Bezrukova, 2010) suggests one possible route toward exploring the relationship between actual and perceived diversity and conflict experienced in a group. In this research, faultlines were activated when there were group members with certain personalities in each subgroup (e.g., narcissism, entitlement) that pulled the groups apart and made the faultlines salient, hence increasing perceptions of conflict. Future research should also examine other factors that may activate faultlines and pull the demographically aligned subgroups apart, such as specific demographic characteristics or perceptions and attitudes of group members. It is also important to note that certain group aspects can "deactivate" faultlines; that is, when groups had a superordinate group identity, the faultlines were less likely to be perceived, and conflict was decreased (Jehn & Bezrukova, 2010). By understanding this and other such factors that can lead to faultline activation, researchers can increase their understanding of the role of faultlines in the perceived conflicts of workgroups; that is, one subgroup may perceive all is fine while the other subgroup is experiencing large amounts of conflict. What this means for actual conflict behavior is also interesting. If there are asymmetric perceptions, conflict behavior may be potentially less manifest than if all subgroups perceived the conflict. However, this also means such conflicts may be more difficult to resolve and more negative for group outcomes.

Other work looking at identity salience as a mediator of the relationship between intragroup conflict and outcomes (e.g., Garcia-Prieto et al., 2003; Randel, 2002) may also represent another way to better understand the effects of diversity on conflict and group outcomes. Faultlines may become activated and instigate conflict only when identity salience relating to the faultlines is high—and identity salience may vary between members within the team, leading to individual differences in perceptual faultline activation and conflict perceptions and behaviors. We therefore propose that it is the workgroup members' perceptions that matter and that inform ultimate behaviors and group outcomes.

Conclusion

This chapter reviewed past research on diversity and disagreement in groups and proposed new frameworks to resolve the inconsistencies in past work and move the area forward. Three complex issues needing future research in the study of diversity and conflict in groups were presented, with special attention to how diversity may promote not only conflict but also asymmetric experiences of conflict in teams by diverse members. The areas for future research were the role of different conceptualizations and operationalizations of diversity in predicting the emergence and asymmetric experience of conflict in teams; the impact of new and understudied forms of diversity, such as lifestyle diversity or power diversity; and the role of the perception of diversity in activating the relationship between diversity and disagreement in teams. By examining these areas, we hope that research will continue to advance our understanding of diverse teams and how they interact, as well as providing suggestions for group leaders, members, and managers.

References

Amason, A. (1996). Distinguishing effects of functional and dysfunctional conflict on strategic decision making, Resolving a paradox for top management teams. *Academy of Management Journal, 39*, 123–148.

Asch, S. E. (1952). *Social psychology*. Englewood Cliffs, NJ: Prentice Hall.

Ashforth, B. E., & Mael, F. (1989). Social identity theory and the organization. *Academy of Management Review, 14*, 20–39.

Ayub, N., & Jehn, K. A. (2010). The moderating influence of nationalism on the relationship between national diversity and conflict. *Negotiation and Conflict Management Research, 3*, 249–275.

Balkundi, P., & Harrison, D. A. (2006). Ties, leaders, and time in teams: Strong inference about network structure's effects on team viability and performance. *Academy of Management Journal, 49*, 49–68.

Bantel, K. A., & Jackson, S. E. (1989). Top management and innovations in banking: Does the composition of the top management team make a difference. *Strategic Management Journal, 10*, 107–124.

Behfar, K., Mannix, E. A., Peterson, R. & Trochim, W. (2011). Conflict in small groups: The meaning and consequences of process conflict. *Small Group Research, 42*(2), 127–176.

Bezrukova, K., Jehn, K. A., Zanutto, E., & Thatcher, S. M. B. (2009). Do workgroup faultlines help or hurt? A moderated model of group faultlines, team identification, and group performance. *Organization Science, 20*, 35–50.

Bhappu, A. D., Griffith, T. L., & Northcraft, G. B. (1997). Media effects and communication bias in diverse groups. *Organizational Behavior and Human Decision Processes, 70*, 199–205.

Bloom, M. (1999). The performance effects of pay dispersion on individuals and organizations. *Academy of Management Journal, 42*, 25–40.

Boulding, K. (1962). *Conflict and defense*. New York: Harper and Row.

Brauer, M. (2001). Intergroup perception in the social context: The effects of social status and group membership on outgroup homogeneity and ethnocentrism. *Journal of Experimental Social Psychology, 37*(1), 15–31.

Button, S. B. (2001). Organizational efforts to affirm sexual diversity: A cross-level examination. *Journal of Applied Psychology, 86*, 17–28.

Byrne, D. E. (1971). *The attraction paradigm*. New York: Academic Press.

Carnevale, P. J., & Probst, T. M. (1998). Social values and social conflict in creative problem solving and categorization. *Journal of Personality and Social Psychology, 74*, 1300–1309.

Chan, D. (1998). Functional relations amongst constructs in the same content domain at different levels of analysis: a typology of composition models. *Journal of Applied Psychology, 83*, 234–246.

Choi, J. N., & Sy, T. (2010). Group-level organizational citizenship behavior: Effects of demographic faultlines and conflict in small work groups. *Journal of Organizational Behavior, 31*, 1032–1054.

Coleman, P. T., Kugler, K., Mitchinson, A., Chung, C., & Musallam, N. (2010). The view from above and below: The effects of power and interdependence asymmetries on conflict dynamics and outcomes in organizations. *Negotiation and Conflict Management Research, 13*, 283–311.

Cronin, M. A., & Weingart, L. R. (2007). Representational gaps, information processing and conflict in functionally diverse teams. *Academy of Management Review, 32*, 761–773.

Cunningham, G. B. (2007). Perceptions as reality: the influence of actual and perceived demographic dissimilarity. *Journal of Business and Psychology, 22*, 79–89.

Curseu, P. L., & Schruijer, S. G. L. (2010). Does conflict shatter trust or does trust obliterate conflict? Revisiting the relationships between team diversity, conflict, and trust. *Group Dynamics: Theory, Research and Practice, 14*, 66–79.

De Cremer, D. (2003). How self-conception may lead to inequality: effect of hierarchical roles on the equality rule in organizational resource-sharing tasks. *Group & Organization Management, 28*, 282–302.

De Dreu, C. K. W., & Weingart, L. R. (2003). Task versus relationship conflict, team performance, and team member satisfaction: A meta-analysis. *Journal of Applied Psychology, 88*, 741–749.

D'Emilio, J. (1983). *Sexual politics, sexual communities: the making of a homosexual minority in the United States, 1940–70*. Chicago, IL: University of Chicago Press.

Dooley, R. S., Fryxell, G. E., & Judge, W. Q. (2000). Belaboring the not-so-obvious: Consensus, commitment, and strategy implementation speed and success. *Journal of Management, 26*, 1237–1257.

Dougherty, D. (1992). Interpretive barriers to successful product innovation in large firms. *Organization Science, 3*, 179–202.

Earley, P. C., & Mosakowski, E. (2000). Creating hybrid team cultures: An empirical test of transnational team functioning. *Academy of Management Journal, 43*, 26–49.

Evan, W. (1965). Conflict and performance in R&D organizations. *Industrial Management Review, 7*, 37–46.

Fussell, P. (1983). *Class: A guide through the american status system*. New York, NY: Simon and Schuster.

Garcia-Prieto, P., Bellard, E., & Schneider, S. C. (2003). Experiencing diversity, conflict, and emotions in teams. *Applied Psychology, An International Review, 52*(3), 413–440.

Gibson, C., & Vermeulen, F. (2003). A healthy divide: Subgroups as a stimulus for team learning behavior. *Administrative Science Quarterly, 48*, 202–239.

Goncalo, J. A., Polman, E., & Maslach, C. (2010). Can confidence come to soon?: Collective efficacy, conflict and group performance over time. *Organizational Behavior and Human Decision Processes, 113*, 13–24.

Greer, L. L., & Jehn, K. A. (2007). The pivotal role of emotion in intragroup process conflict. *Research on Managing Groups and Teams, 10*, 23–45.

Greer, L. L., & Jehn, K. A. (2010). Individual engagement in conflict: Performance effects moderated by verbal style and influence tactic usage. University of Amsterdam working paper.

Greer, L. L., Jehn, K. A., & Thatcher, S. M. B. (2006). *Demographic faultline token splits: Effects on conflict and performance*. Presented at the Academy of Management, Atlanta, GA.

Greer, L. L., Jehn, K. A., Thatcher, S. M. B., & Van Beest, I. (2010). Faultline token splits. University of Amsterdam working paper.

Greer, L. L., & Van Kleef, G. A. (2010). Equality versus differentiation: The effects of power dispersion on social interaction. *Journal of Applied Psychology, 95*, 1032–1044.

Gruenfeld, D. H., Mannix, E. A., Williams, K. Y., & Neale, M. A. (1996). Group composition and decision making: How member familiarity and information distribution affect processes and performance. *Organizational Behavior and Human Decision Processes, 67*, 1–15.

Guetzkow, H., & Gyr, J. (1954). An analysis of conflict in decision making groups. *Human Relations, 7*, 367–381.

Hackman, J. R. (1987). The design of work teams. In J. W. Lorsch (Ed.), *Handbook of organizational behavior* (pp. 315–342). Englewood Cliffs, NJ: Prentice Hall.

Hackman, J. R., & Wageman, R. (2005). A theory of team coaching. *Academy of Management Review, 30*, 269–287.

Harrison, D. A., & Klein, K. J. (2007). What's the difference? Diversity constructs as separation, variety, or disparity in organizations. *Academy of Management Review, 32*, 1199–1228.

Harrison, D. A., Price, K., & Bell, M. (1998). Beyond relational demography, Time and the effects of surface- and deep- level diversity on group functioning. *Academy of Management Journal, 41*, 96–107.

Harrison, D. A., Price, K., Gavin, J., & Florey, A. T. (2002). Times, teams, and task performance. Changing effects of surface- and deep- level diversity on work group cohesion. *Academy of Management Journal, 45*, 1029–1045.

Hartman, G. (1970). Structuralism: The Anglo-American adventure. In J. Ehrmann (Ed.), *Structuralism* (pp. 137–158). Garden City: Doubleday

Henderson, A. D., & Fredrickson, J. W. (2001). Top management team coordination needs and the CEO pay gap: A competitive test of economic and behavioral views. *Academy of Management Journal, 44*, 96–117.

Herek, G. M. (1993). Sexual orientation and military service: a social science perspective. *American Psychologist, 48*(5), 538–549.

Hogg, M. (1996). Social identity, self-categorization, and the small group. In J. Davis & E. Witte (Eds.), *Understanding group behavior* (Vol. 2, pp. 227–254). Hillsdale, NJ: Lawrence Erlbaum Associates.

Hogg, M. A., Turner, J. C., & Davidson, B. (1990). Polarized norms and social frames of reference: A test of the self-categorization theory of group polarization. *Basic and Applied Social Psychology, 11*, 77–100.

Homan, A. C., Knippenberg, D. v., Kleef, G. A. v., & De Dreu, C. K.W. (2007). Bridging faultlines by valuing diversity: The effects of diversity beliefs on information elaboration and performance in diverse work groups. *Journal of Applied Psychology, 92*, 1189–1199.

Horwitz, S. K., & Horwitz, I. B. (2007). The effects of team diversity on team outcomes: A meta-analytic review of team demography. *Journal of Management, 33*, 987–1015.

Jackson, S. E., Joshi, A., & Erhardt, N. L. (2003). Recent research on team and organizational diversity, SWOT analysis and implications. *Journal of Management, 29*, 801–830.

Jehn, K. A. (1995). A multimethod examination of the benefits and detriments of intragroup conflict. *Administrative Science Quarterly, 40*, 256–282.

Jehn, K. A. (1997). Qualitative analysis of conflict types and dimensions in organizational groups. *Administrative Science Quarterly, 42*, 530–557.

Jehn, K. A., & Bendersky, C. (2003). Intragroup conflict in organizations, A contingency perspective on the conflict-outcome relationship. In B. Staw & L. L. Cummings (Eds.), *Research in organizational behavior* (25, pp. 189–244). Greenwich, CT: JAI Press.

Jehn, K. A., & Bezrukova, K. (2010). The faultline activation process and the effects of activated faultlines on coalition formation, conflict, and group outcomes. *Organizational Behavior and Human Decision Processes, 112*, 24–42.

Jehn, K. A., Bezrukova, K., & Thatcher, S. M. B. (2006). Conflict, diversity and faultlines in workgroups. In C. K. W. De Dreu & M. J. Gelfand (Eds.), *The psychology of conflict and conflict management in organizations* (pp. 177–204). New York: SIOP Frontier Series, Lawrence Erlbaum Press.

Jehn, K. A., & Chatman, J. A. (2000). The influence of proportional and perceptual conflict composition on team performance. *International Journal of Conflict Management, 11*, 56–73.

Jehn, K. A., Conlon, D., & Greer, L. (2010). *Lifestyle diversity in organizational groups*. Presented at the Academy of Management Meeting, Boston, MA.

Jehn, K. A., Greer, L. L., Rispens, S., & Jonsen, K. (2012). Conflict contagion: A theoretical model of the development and spread of conflict in teams. *International Journal of Conflict Management*, in press.

Jehn, K. A., Greer, L. L., & Rupert, J. (2008). Diversity and conflict. In A. Brief (Ed.), *Diversity at work* (pp. 166–219). Cambridge: Cambridge University Press.

Jehn, K. A., & Mannix, E. A. (2001). The dynamic nature of conflict. A longitudinal study of intragroup conflict and group performance. *Academy of Management Journal, 44*, 238–251.

Jehn, K. A., Northcraft, G. B., & Neale, M. A. (1999). Why differences make a difference, A field study of diversity, conflict, and performance in workgroups. *Administrative Science Quarterly, 44*, 741–763.

Jehn, K. A., & Rispens, S. (2007). Conflict in workgroups. In C. I. Cooper & J. Barlings (Eds.), *Handbook of organizational behavior* (pp. 262–276). Thousand Oaks, CA: Sage.

Jehn, K. A., Rispens, S., & Thatcher, S. M. B. (2010). The effects of conflict asymmetry on work group and individual outcomes. *Academy of Management Journal, 53*, 596–616.

Jehn, K. A., Rupert, J., Nauta, A., & Van Den Bossche, S. (2010). Crooked conflicts: The effects of conflict asymmetry in mediation. *Negotiation and Conflict Management Research, 13*, 338–357.

Joshi, A., & Roh, H. (2009). The role of context in work team diversity research: A meta-analytic review. *Academy of Management Journal, 52*, 599–627.

Keltner, D., Van Kleef, G. A., Chen, S., & Kraus, M. W. (2008). A reciprocal influence model of social power: Emerging principles and lines of inquiry. *Advances in Experimental Social Psychology, 40*, 151–192.

King, E. B., Hebl, M. R., & Beal, D. J. (2009). Conflict and cooperation in diverse workgroups. *Journal of Social Issues, 65*, 261–285.

Klein, K. J., Knight, A. P., Ziegert, J. C., Lim, B. C., & Saltz, J. L. (2011). When team members' values differ: The moderating role of team leadership. *Organizational Behavior and Human Decision Processes, 114*, 25–36.

Klein, K. J., & Kozlowski, S. W. (2000). From micro to meso: Critical steps in conceptualizing and conducting multilevel research. *Organizational Research Methods, 3*, 211–236.

Knight, D., Pearce, C. L., Smith, K. G., Olian, J. D., Sims, H. P., Smith, K. A., & Flood, P. (1999). Top management team diversity, group process, and strategic consensus. *Strategic Management Journal, 20*, 445–465.

Korsgaard, M. A., Jeong, S. S., Mahony, D. M., & Pitariu, A. H. (2008). A multilevel view of intragroup conflict. *Journal of Management, 34*, 1222–1252.

Lankau, M. J., Riordan, C. M., & Thomas, C. H. (2005). The effects of similarity and liking in formal relationships between mentors and protégés. *Journal of Vocational Behavior, 67*, 252–265.

Lau, D., & Murnighan, J. K. (2005). Interactions within groups and subgroups: The effects of demographic faultlines. *Academy of Management Journal, 48*, 645–659.

Lau, D. C., & Murnighan, J. K. (1998). Demographic diversity and faultlines: The compositional dynamics of organizational groups. *Academy of Management Review, 23*, 325–340.

Lawler, E. J., & Proell, C. A. (2009). The power process and emotion. In D. Tjosvold & B. Wisse (Eds.), *Power and interdependence in organizations* (pp. 169–185). Cambridge, UK: Cambridge University Press.

Lee, Y., & Ottati, V. (1993). Determinants of in-group and out-group perceptions of heterogeneity: An investigation of Sino-American stereotypes. *Journal of Cross-Cultural Psychology, 24*, 298–318.

Li, J., & Hambrick, D.C. (2005). Factional groups: A new vantage on demographic faultlines, conflict, and disintegration in work teams. *Academy of Management Journal, 48*, 794–813.

Lovelace, K. Shapiro, D., & Weingart, L. R. (2001). Maximizing cross-functional new product teams' innovativeness and constraint adherence: A conflict communications perspective. *Academy of Management Journal, 24*, 779–784.

Magee, J. C., & Galinsky, A. D. (2008). Social hierarchy: The self-reinforcing nature of power and status. *Academy of Management Annals, 2*, 351–398.

Mannes, A. E. (2009). Are we wise about the wisdom of crowds? The use of group judgments in belief revision. *Management Science, 55*(8), 1267–1279.

Mannix, E., & Jehn, K. A. (2003). Let's norm and storm, but not right now: Integrating models of group development and performance. In M. Neale, E. Mannix, & S. Blount (Eds.), *Research on managing groups and teams* (pp.11–37). Greenwich, CT: JAI Press.

Mannix, E. A., & Neale, M. A. (2005). What differences make a difference? The promise and reality of diverse teams in organizations. *Psychological Science in the Public Interest, 6*(2), 31–55.

Mason, C. M. (2006). Exploring the processes underlying within-group homogeneity. *Small Group Research, 37*(3), 233–270.

Matsuo, M. (2006). Customer orientation, conflict, and innovativeness in Japanese sales departments. *Journal of Business Research, 59*, 242–250.

Mohammed, S., & Angell, L. C. (2004). Surface- and deep-level diversity in workgroups: Examining the moderating effects of team orientation and team process on relationship conflict. *Journal of Organizational Behavior, 25*, 1015–1039.

Molleman, E. (2005). Diversity in demographic characteristics, abilities, and personality traits: Do faultlines affect team functioning? *Group Decision and Negotiation, 14*, 173–193.

Muller, E. N. (1985). Income inequality, regime repressiveness, and political violence. *American Sociological Review, 50*(1), 47–61.

Murnighan, J. K., & Conlon, D. E. (1991). The dynamics of intense workgroups: A study of British string quartets. *Administrative Science Quarterly, 36*, 165–186.

Newcomb, M. D., Mercurio, S. C. A., & Wollard, C. A. (2000). Rock stars in anti-drug-abuse commercials: An experimental study of adolescents' reactions. *Journal of Applied Social Psychology, 30*, 1160–1185.

Nibler, R., & Harris, K. L. (2003). The effects of culture and cohesiveness on intragroup conflict and effectiveness. *Journal of Social Psychology, 143*, 613–631.

O'Leary, M. B., & Mortensen, M. (2010). Go (con)figure: Subgroups, imbalances, and isolates in geographically distributed teams. *Organization Science, 21*, 115–131.

Olson, B. J., Parayitam, S., & Bao, Y. (2007). Strategic decision making: The effects of cognitive diversity, conflict, and trust on decision outcomes. *Journal of Management, 33*, 196–222.

O'Reilly, C., Williams, K., & Barsade, S. (1997). Group demography and innovation, Does diversity help? In E. Mannix & M. Neale (Eds.), *Research in the management of groups and teams* (Vol. 1, pp. 34–48). Greenwich, CT: JAI Press.

Pearsall, M. J., Ellis, A. P. J., & Evans, J. M. (2007). Unlocking the effects of gender faultlines on team creativity: Is activation the key? *Journal of Applied Psychology, 93*, 225–234.

Pelled, L. H. (1996). Demographic diversity, conflict, and work group outcomes: An intervening process theory. *Organization Science, 6*, 615–631.

Pelled, L. H. (1997). Relational demography and perceptions of group conflict and performance: A field investigation. *International Journal of Conflict Resolution, 22*(1), 54–67.

Pelled, L. H., Eisenhardt, K. M., & Xin, K. R. (1999). Exploring the black box: An analysis of work group diversity, conflict, and performance. *Administrative Science Quarterly, 44*, 1–28.

Phillips, K. W., & Loyd, D. (2006) When surface and deep-level diversity collide: The effects on dissenting group members. *Organizational Behavior and Human Decision Processes, 99*, 143–160.

Phillips, K. W., Northcraft, G. B., & Neale, M. A. (2006). Surface-level diversity and decision-making in groups: When does deep-level similarity help? *Group Processes & Intergroup Relations, 9*, 467–482.

Plummer, K. (1975). *Sexual stigma: An interactionist account.* London: Routledge.

Polzer, J. T., Crisp, B., Jarvenpaa, S. L. & Kim, J. W. (2006). Extending the faultline concept to geographically dispersed teams: How colocated subgroups can impair group functioning. *Academy of Management Journal, 49*, 679–692.

Pondy, L. R. (1967). Organizational conflict: concepts and models. *Administrative Science Quarterly, 12*, 296–320.

Randel, A. E. (2002). Identity salience, a moderator of the relationship between group gender composition and work group conflict. *Journal of Organizational Behavior, 23*, 749–766.

Rau, D. (2005). The influence of relationship conflict and trust on the transactive memory. *Small Group Research, 36*, 746–771.

Rink, F. (2005). *Diversity and small group decision making: Towards a social identity framework for studying the effects of task-related differences in dyads and groups*. Unpublished doctoral dissertation, Leiden University.

Riordan, C. M. (2000). Relational demography within groups: Past developments, contradictions, and new directions. *Research in Personnel & Human Resource Management, 19*, 131–173.

Ross, R. (1989). Conflict. In R. Ross & J. Ross (Eds.), *Small groups in organizational settings* (pp. 139–178). Englewood Cliffs, NJ: Prentice-Hall.

Sorensen, J. B. (2000). The longitudinal effects of group tenure composition on turnover. *American Sociological Review, 65*, 298–310.

Stahl, G. K., Maznefski, M. L., Voigt, A., & Jonsen, K. (2010). Unraveling the effects of cultural diversity in teams: A meta-analysis of research on multicultural work groups. *Journal of International Business Studies, 41*, 690–709.

Stewart, G. L. (2006). A meta-analytic review of relationships between team design features and team performance. *Journal of Management, 32*, 29–54.

Strauss, G. (1962). Tactics of lateral relationships. The purchasing agent. *Administrative Science Quarterly, 7*, 161–186.

Strauss, J. P., Barrick, M. R., & Connerley, M. L. (2001). An investigation of personality similarity effects (relational and perceived) on peer and supervisor ratings and the role of familiarity and liking. *Journal of Occupational and Organizational Psychology, 74*, 637–657.

Tajfel, H., & Turner, J. C. (1986). The social identity theory of intergroup behavior. In S. Worchel & W. G. Austin (Eds.), *Psychology of intergroup relations* (pp. 7–24). Chicago: Nelson-Hall.

Thatcher, S. M. B., Jehn, K. A., & Zanutto, E. (2003). Cracks in diversity research: The effects of diversity faultlines on conflict and performance. *Group Decision and Negotiation, 12*(3), 217–241.

Thatcher, S. M. B., & Phillips, K. W. (2010). Beauty is in the eye of the beholder: How asymmetric perceptions color our experience. *Negotiation and Conflict Management Research, 13*, 277–282.

Thomas, K. W. (1992). Conflict and negotiation process in organizations. In M. Dunette & L. Hough (Eds.), *Handbook of industrial and organizational psychology* (pp. 651–718). Palo Alto, CA: Consulting Psychologists Press.

Turban, D. B., & Jones, A. P. (1988). Supervisor-subordinate similarity: Types, effects, and mechanisms. *Journal of Applied Psychology, 73*, 228–234.

Vodosek, M. (2007). Intragroup conflict as a mediator between cultural diversity and work group outcomes. *International Journal of Conflict Management, 18*, 345–375.

Wall, J. A., & Callister, R. R. (1995). Conflict and its management. *Journal of Management, 21*, 515–558.

Webber, S. S., & Donahue, L. M. (2001). Impact of highly and less job-related diversity on work group cohesion and performance, a meta-analysis. *Journal of Management, 27*, 141–162.

Williams, K., & O'Reilly, C.A. (1998). Demography and diversity in organizations: A review of 40 years of research. In B. Staw & L. L. Cummings (Eds.), *Research in organizational behavior* (20, pp. 77–140). Oxford, UK: Elsevier Science Inc.

Zellmer-Bruhn, M. E., Maloney, M. M., Bhappu, A. D., & Salvador, R. (2008). When and how do differences matter? An exploration of perceived similarity in teams. *Organizational Behavior and Human Decision Processes, 107*, 41–59.

CHAPTER 11

Demographic Diversity as Network Connections: Homophily and the Diversity–Performance Debate

Ray Reagans

Abstract

Research documenting the influence of demographic diversity on informal social networks is reviewed and critiqued. I focus in particular on research describing the importance of demographic diversity in the development of strong interpersonal relationships. I also consider the importance of network connections between team members and with colleagues outside the team in mediating the association between demographic diversity and team performance. Internal and external relationships define a team's social capital, and I illustrate how a focus on a team's social capital helps to explain why the "diversity effect" on team performance varies from positive to negative. In my call for future research, in addition to a focus on demographic diversity, I emphasize the importance of considering more general dynamics and processes that either moderate or mediate the association between demographic diversity and important organizational outcomes.

Key Words: demographic diversity, identification, competition, propinquity, social networks, homophily, transactive memory systems

Introduction

Over the past 30 years, the U.S. labor force has become more diverse with respect to a number of demographic characteristics, including age, gender, race, and nationality. Changes in the U.S. labor force have quite naturally resulted in more diverse working environments. The increase in demographic diversity has coincided with a significant shift in the organization of work processes. Firms have replaced layers of bureaucracy and managerial control with more strategic and temporary forms of organization (e.g., cross-functional teams) that facilitate the transfer of knowledge, information, and expertise. Firms are focusing on more effective knowledge management because the ability to transfer knowledge effectively among individuals is critical to a host of organizational processes and outcomes, including the transfer of best practices (Szulanski, 1996), new product development (Hansen, 1999), learning rates (Argote, Beckman, & Epple, 1990; Darr, Argote, & Epple, 1995), and organizational survival (Baum & Ingram, 1998).

Network connections contribute to knowledge management by helping to surmount two significant barriers to knowledge transfer (Reagans & McEvily, 2003; Tortoriello, Reagans, & McEvily, 2011). In particular, while knowledge transfer can be beneficial, it is difficult to achieve when the source and the potential recipient do not overlap in their knowledge and expertise. Knowledge overlap facilitates knowledge transfer because individuals learn new ideas by associating those ideas with what they already know (Cohen & Levinthal, 1990; Simon, 1991). When knowledge overlap is low, successful knowledge transfer will require either more effort by the source and the recipient or a greater capacity for knowledge transfer. Prior research suggests that strong network connections increase the amount of effort individuals are willing to exert during the knowledge transfer process (Hansen, 1999; Reagans & McEvily, 2003, 2008; Sgourev & Zuckerman, 2011; Szulanski, 1996; Uzzi, 1997). Prior research also indicates that network range (i.e., maintaining a network that spans structural holes or disconnects) improves an individual's capacity for knowledge transfer (Reagans & McEvily, 2003; Tortoriello, Reagans, & McEvily, 2011).

Since informal network connections contribute to processes, such as knowledge transfer, that ultimately contribute to organizational performance, the value of informal network connections is increasing during a time period when the work environment is becoming more diverse. Consequently, a number of scholars and practitioners have asked how changes in the demographic composition of a firm or organization have affected the development of interpersonal network connections. In this chapter, I discuss and review two distinct lines of research that has considered the intersection between diversity and social networks. The first area of research considers how diversity affects the development of network connections between individual firm members. The second line of work considers how diversity affects team performance by influencing the relationships that team members develop with each other and with colleagues outside the team. I also discuss potential avenues for future research that would advance our understanding of how diversity affects network formation and team performance.

Diversity as connections: Homophily

Researchers with an interest in the network formation process have considered how an increase in diversity has affected the tendency for relationships in a firm or organization to exhibit *homophily*. Homophily exits when network connections, especially strong connections, are concentrated among individuals who share a demographic characteristic (Lazarsfeld & Merton, 1954). A network connection is strong when it connects individuals who feel emotionally attached to one another and/or communicate with each other frequently (Marsden & Campbell, 1984). In the general population, homophily has been documented across a large number of characteristics, including age (Burt, 1991; Marsden, 1988), education (Yamaguchi, 1990), gender (Brass, 1985; Ibarra, 1992, 1997), race (Ibarra, 1995; Marsden, 1987; Moody, 2001), and religion (Laumann, 1973). Inside of firms and organizations, researchers have found that organizational networks are often characterized by homophily. People who share a demographic characteristic are more likely to be connected to each other and are more likely to communicate with each other more frequently (Ibarra, 1992, 1995, 1997; Lincoln & Miller, 1979; Miller et al., 1981; Pfeffer, 1982, 1985; Kram & Isabella, 1985; Tsui & O'Reilly, 1989; Zenger & Lawrence, 1989). Homophily has been documented so frequently that it is often assumed to be a "law of interpersonal relationships" (McPherson et al., 2001).

Demographic similarity

The initial explanation for homophily focused on interpersonal dynamics in generating strong network connections. People who shared a demographic characteristic were assumed to also share life histories, experiences, and attitudes, which made it easier for them to interact. An easier and more pleasant encounter was more likely to result in a strong network connection (Byrne, 1971; Laumann, 1966; Schneider, 1987). While scholars focused on the positive effect that in-group membership had on tie strength, the positive effect was assumed to be a function of people who were similar on the "surface" (e.g., both women) also being similar with respect to "deep," or unobserved, behaviors, attitudes, and characteristics (e.g., both liberal).

Instead of assuming that demographically similar individuals will always be attracted to each other, more recent research grounded in social psychology gives priority to the broader social context in which similar individuals meet and interact with each other. In particular, social psychological explanations for homophily have highlighted the salience or social significance of the demographic characteristic two individuals have in common. Sharing a demographic characteristic will be of little consequence if the two individuals do not assign any weight or significance to the shared characteristic. Moreover, a demographic characteristic that is of little consequence in one situation could be socially significant in another situation. For example, sharing the characteristic "American" could result in a more positive interaction if two Americans meet one another on a street in Paris. But if the same two individuals were to meet on a street in Chicago, sharing that same characteristic would have little or no effect on their interaction, because almost everyone in Chicago is an American. In Chicago, the most important characteristic could be where an individual lives or was educated.

The salience of a demographic characteristic is important because individuals are more likely to identify with a salient characteristic, and identification with a characteristic generates positive affect for in-group members (Grieve & Hogg, 1999; Hogg, 1992, 1993; Hogg & Hains, 1996; Hogg & Hardie, 1991; Hogg & Turner, 1985). Prior research has established that two demographic factors can influence the salience of a characteristic and therefore the rate at which demographic similarity translates into homophily. One factor is the composition of the focal organizational unit or group. If an organizational unit contains a minority and a majority group, its composition is skewed (Kanter, 1977, p. 209). The demographic characteristic that defines minority status is more likely to be salient, while the characteristic that defines majority status is less likely to be salient (Brewer, 1991; Mullen, 1983; Tajfel & Turner, 1979; Turner, 1985). If women, for example, represent 10 percent of an organizational unit and men represent the remaining 90 percent, the category "female" will be salient for women but the category "male" will not be salient for men. As the composition of the unit becomes more balanced, the characteristics "female" and "male" become more salient. If men and women each represent 50 percent of a unit (i.e., the unit is balanced demographically), the category "male" will be salient for men and the category "female" will be salient for women.

A second demographic factor is the correlation among demographic characteristics. Salience increases when in-group membership with respect to one demographic characteristic is reinforced by in-group membership with respect to multiple characteristics (Blau & Schwartz, 1984; Lau & Murnighan, 1998). When multiple characteristics are "consolidated," the boundary between the in-group and the out-group is more clearly delineated. For example, if all the women on a team are young and all the men are older, membership in each in-group (i.e., young women and older men) will be salient. Thus, a demographic characteristic can be salient even for members of a numerical majority if those members share multiple demographic characteristics. The importance of being similar along multiple dimensions is not limited to demographic characteristics. If, for example, members of a numerical minority all perform the same task or activity in an organization, or if minority status in a firm corresponds with minority status in the general population, the characteristic that defines minority status will be more salient (Turner, 1987, Chapter 6).

The general idea is that two individuals will assign more weight to their demographic similarity when the shared characteristic is salient, and the increase in salience should increase the rate at which demographic similarity produces stronger network connections. The available empirical evidence is consistent with the two explanations for salience and the resulting homophily discussed above. Reported empirical results indicate that social similarity is more likely to produce a strong tie when people who share the focal characteristic (1) are part of a numerical minority (Mehra et al., 1998; Mollica et al., 2003; Reagans, 2005), (2) are assigned to a balanced organizational unit (Bacharach et al., 2005; Moody, 2001; Mouw & Entwisle, 2006), or (3) share consolidated characteristics (Blau & Schwartz, 1984).

NEGATIVE IN-GROUP BIAS

While most researchers have focused on the positive association between demographic similarity and tie strength, a small but growing number of scholars have focused on the conditions when demographic similarity will have a negative effect on the strength of a network connection (Duguid et al., 2010; Loyd, 2011; McGinn & Milkman, 2010; Reagans, 2005; Reagans & Burt, 2002). Indeed, while scholars emphasize the positive association between demographic similarity and tie strength, the available empirical evidence indicates that sharing a demographic characteristic increases, reduces, or has no effect at all on tie strength (Reagans, 2005, pp. 1379–1381). Elsewhere, arguments have been developed that sought to explain variation in the association between demographic similarity and tie strength as a function of three distinct causal mechanisms: (1) some baseline level of interpersonal attraction associated with sharing a demographic characteristic, (2) a positive effect due to in-group identification, and (3) a negative effect due to in-group rivalry and competition (Reagans, 2005; Reagans & Burt, 2002). In-group identification and competition vary with the relative frequency of the shared characteristic to define a predictable association between the effect that sharing a demographic characteristic has on tie strength and the relative frequency of the shared characteristic in the larger organizational unit. Sharing a demographic characteristic can be expected to have its most positive effect on tie strength when in-group members are part of a numerical minority. As members of the numerical minority increase in number the magnitude of the positive effect should start to decline (the positive effect that in-group identification has on tie strength is declining and the negative effect associated with in-group competition is rising). As the group continues to grow in size and starts to represent a plurality of individuals in the organizational unit, the effect associated with sharing a characteristic could turn negative (the negative rivalry effect is large enough to offset the baseline level of attraction and the positive identification effect). If group members represent a majority of the unit (and the characteristic defining in-group membership isn't consolidated with other demographic characteristics), sharing a demographic characteristic should have no effect on tie strength. Supporting evidence has been documented among investment bankers (Reagans & Burt, 2002), research scientists (Reagans, 2005), and teachers (Reagans, 2011).

This argument focused on status-based competition within a group in producing negative in-group connections. A related line of research focuses on the amount of status available to a group (Duguid, 2011; Duguid et al., 2010; Loyd, 2011). Not all demographic characteristics are the same: some confer more status (e.g., White, male, educated) than others (e.g., African-American, female, uneducated). An individual who belongs to a low-status group might avoid interacting with in-group members, especially if he or she has managed to exceed the status generally associated with his or her group (Duguid et al., 2010). For example, a female manager might avoid advocating for a female subordinate if she believes her female colleague is not as talented as she is (Duguid, 2011). The female manager could believe that the presence of a woman with less ability would undermine her standing in the group. Individuals could avoid strong in-group relationships even when quality is not an issue. For example, the female manager might avoid advocating for another woman out of concerns for appearing biased in the eyes of her male colleagues (Loyd, 2011).

Propinquity

A more sociologic explanation for homophily gives causal priority to being proximate in time and/or space (Feld, 1982, 1984; Festinger et al., 1950; Ingram & Morris, 2007; McPherson et al., 2001). The basic idea is that individuals are more likely to be connected to people they encounter more frequently. More frequent interactions could have a positive effect on tie strength either because repeated exposure provides individuals with an opportunity to discover mutual or compatible interests or because with repeated exposure individuals become more appreciative or tolerant of their differences. The positive effect that proximity can have on network connections has been established across a number of proximity indicators, including classrooms (Shrum et al., 1988), dormitories (Festinger et al., 1950), neighborhoods (Mouw & Entwisle, 2006), volunteer organizations (McPherson & Smith-Lovin, 1986, 1987), seating arrangements (Caldeira & Patterson, 1987), and break schedules (Reagans, 2011).

The proximity argument focuses on the formation of relationships in general. When used to account for homophily, sociologists focus on the opportunities that demographically similar individuals have to interact with each other. They maintain that institutional and structural forces provide demographically similar people with more opportunities to develop a network connection. For example, typecasting by employers segregates men and women at work (Bielby & Baron, 1986). As a result, men and women have more opportunities to develop relationships with members of their respective in-groups. The very same dynamics could just as well produce stronger ties between people who do not share a characteristic. For example, most of us are educated with people our own age, which generates strong ties between individuals who are similar in age. But because most schools are coed, the same process creates stronger cross-gender ties. Housing segregation by race in the United States generates strong ties among people who belong to the same racial group. Housing segregation by race can generate stronger network connections between individuals who have different education levels or who belong to different economic classes. Indeed, racial segregation makes it more difficult for middle-class African-Americans to maintain social closure with respect to class and avoid many of the social ills associated with poverty (Pattillo-McCoy, 1999).

Future directions: Diversity as connections

I have discussed the role of demographic similarity and propinquity in producing homophily. While the two mechanisms are distinct conceptually, organizational demography researchers often assume the two share demographic diversity as a common antecedent. In particular, it is generally understood that an increase in the demographic diversity of an organization or organizational unit will increase the salience of demographic similarity and the increase in salience will result in more homophily. However, the same increase in demographic diversity will

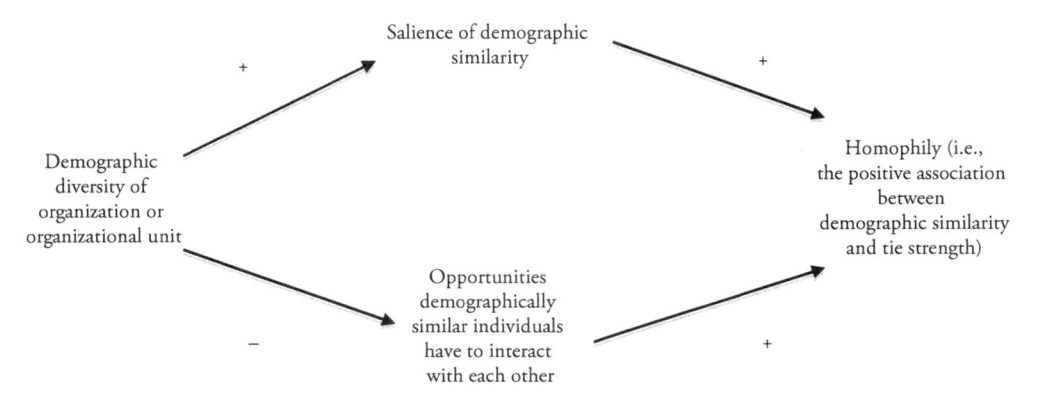

Figure 11.1. Demographic diversity and homophily.

make out-group members more proximate, thereby providing unit members with more opportunities to develop relationships with out-group members, which should reduce the tendency for relationships inside the organization or organizational unit to be characterized by homophily. The causal framework is illustrated in Figure 11.1. An increase in demographic diversity increases two mechanisms that have opposing implications for homophily (Blau & Schwartz, 1984; Brewer & Kramer, 1985; Hewstone et al., 2002; Moody, 2001). The positive effect that an increase in the salience of demographic similarity can have on homophily will be offset by the positive effect that opportunity can have on relationships between dissimilar individuals.

The causal framework in Figure 11.1 indicates that an increase in diversity has ambiguous implications for homophily. Given the directions of the link along the pathways, if the magnitudes of the coefficients are not known *a priori* it is impossible to know how an increase in demographic diversity will affect homophily. Figure 11.1 is not examined directly. Instead, scholars infer the relative magnitude of the coefficients in Figure 11.1 from the overall association between demographic diversity and homophily. For example, in an analysis of cross-race friendships among high school students, Moody (2001) found that an increase in racial diversity in a school reduced the likelihood that a student would be involved in a cross-race friendship. Moody concluded the salience effect was larger than the opportunity effect. When the association between diversity and homophily has been negative, scholars have concluded the opportunity pathway was larger than the magnitude of the similarity pathway (Rytina et al., 1988, pp. 650–652; Bacharach et al., 2005; Mouw & Entwisle, 2006).

Instead of using demographic diversity as a proxy for (salient) demographic similarity and the opportunities an individual has to interact with out-group members, future research should consider how demographic similarity and propinquity combine to produce strong network connections. Indeed, despite the large body of research, we do not know how much each mechanism contributes to tie strength. Organizational demography researchers have focused on the salience of demography similarity or propinquity or have used demographic diversity as a proxy for both mechanisms. As a result, we do not know how much demographic similarity and propinquity contribute to strong ties alone and when combined with each other.

While it seems reasonable to assume that propinquity will moderate the association between demographic similarity and tie strength, being in close proximity could either amplify or dampen any positive effect that demographic similarity has on tie strength. On the one hand, when demographic similarity is salient, two individuals could be more likely to take advantage of the opportunity that being in close proximity provides. Thus, being in close proximity should amplify any positive effect that demographic similarity can have on tie strength (Zeng & Xie, 2008). But on the other hand, more frequent contact between in-group members could reduce the positive association between demographic similarity and tie strength. In particular, recent research has shown that the positive association is a function of actual and expected similarity (Hogg & Hardie, 1991; Hogg et al., 1995). Expected similarity is a function of sharing a demographic or social characteristic, whereas actual similarity is a function of sharing unobserved attitudes, behaviors, and beliefs. When an in-group member meets or exceeds prior expectations with respect to unobserved attributes, his or her relationships with in-group members are stronger (Hogg et al., 1995). However, if two people who share a demographic or social characteristic are similar only on the surface, propinquity would provide them with more opportunities to discover how very little they actually have in common, which should reduce the positive effect that demographic similarity can have on network connections (Ziebro & Northcraft, 2009, pp. 148–149). For example, if a young person assumes all young people are liberal Democrats, more opportunities to interact with a young conservative Republican would make it more likely that their differences in political philosophies would be revealed and, consequently, the positive effect of being the same age would be diminished.

Recently, I analyzed how demographic similarity and proximity contributed to strong ties among elementary and middle school teachers. Network connections among teachers were a source of social support and were also conduits for knowledge transfer that allowed teachers to improve the quality of their instruction and ultimately the test scores of their students. The focus was on age similarity, especially considering that empirical analyses indicated that age was a primary source of demographic diversity in each school and therefore was likely to be salient or socially significant. Proximity was defined in terms of two teachers having a classroom on the same floor and overlap in their break schedules. Teachers with classrooms on the same floor were proximate in space and teachers who took breaks at the same time were proximate in time. Being proximate in time and/or space provided two teachers with more opportunities to develop a meaningful relationship.

The results showed that age similarity had a positive effect on tie strength and the positive age similarity effect was even more positive under the conditions that made age similarity more salient. In addition, the positive effect that age similarity had on tie strength was even more positive when teachers the same age had more opportunities to interact with each other (i.e., two teachers had a classroom on the same floor). These findings call into question the "trade-off" illustrated in Figure 11.1. Among the teachers analyzed, demographic similarity and propinquity had positive effects on tie strength, and the effects were even stronger when both mechanisms were present. Moreover, an increase in the salience of demographic similarity did not come at the expense of the opportunity to develop relationships with socially dissimilar colleagues. The correlations between the indicators of propinquity (i.e., the same-floor and break-overlap variables) and the age similarity variable were modest. However, the research findings did indicate that the negative effect that age dissimilarity had on tie strength was even more negative when age-dissimilar teachers were more aware of their differences and had classrooms on the same floor.

Thus, the empirical results are consistent with prior theorizing in the sense that the positive effect that proximity had on the strength of relationships between age-dissimilar individuals declined as their social differences became more salient. The decline in the proximity effect was not a function of age-dissimilar individuals' having fewer opportunities to interact with each other. As differences in age became more salient, age-dissimilar individuals were less likely to take advantage of the opportunity to build a strong tie. While statistically and theoretically significant, the decline should be considered in the context of the large and positive effect that propinquity had on tie strength. Among the teachers studied, proximity had the largest effect on tie strength, independent of demographic similarity. The results indicated that teachers did develop strong ties with age-dissimilar colleagues as their opportunity to develop a strong tie increased.

The research findings reported above illustrated how demographic similarity and proximity can combine in the production of strong interpersonal connections. I highlight *can* because while it was found that propinquity amplified the positive effect demographic similarity had on tie strength, it is not immediately clear that propinquity will always amplify the positive effect that demographic similarity can have on tie strength. In particular, if demographically similar individuals do not share important attitudes, behaviors, and beliefs, being in close proximity and encountering each other more frequently should provide them with an opportunity to learn how little they actually have in common and therefore reduce the positive effect that surface similarity can have on network connections (Ziebro & Northcraft, 2009). If people who share a demographic characteristic are only similar on the surface, the interaction between demographic similarity and proximity would be negative. If people who share a demographic characteristic are also similar with respect to deep characteristics, being in close proximity should provide them with more opportunities to reinforce what they have in common. When surface similarity and deep similarity are congruent, proximity should amplify the positive effect that social similarity can have on tie strength.

Among the teachers studied, the findings revealed that proximity amplified the positive effect that age similarity had on tie strength. Although it is possible that age-similar teachers were also similar in unobserved attitudes, behaviors, and beliefs, prior research has established that the association between surface and deep similarity is often weak (Harrison et al., 1998; Phillips & Loyd, 2006). Perhaps the critical issue is not what people actually have in common but what they believe they have in common. If an individual identifies with a demographic characteristic, perhaps he or she could assume that everyone who shares the characteristic also possesses the behaviors and characteristics that define in-group status (Hannan et al., 2007, Chapter 5). Identification with a salient characteristic could increase the tendency to give in-group members the benefit of the doubt during interactions. If in-group members are assumed to possess certain behaviors and characteristics, an individual is more likely to notice those behaviors and characteristics when they are exhibited. Individuals often see what they expect to see and do not see what they do not expect to see. If, however, individuals are motivated to draw distinctions between themselves and members of their in-group, perhaps because they compete against members of their in-group for status and attention (Reagans, 2005) or because they are concerned about how ties to in-group members will affect their standing in the larger group (Duguid et al., 2010), proximity would provide them with more opportunities to individuate in-group members.

Focusing on identification and competition in future research will be worthwhile as they can help explain how propinquity moderates the association between demographic similarity and tie strength. Propinquity provides an individual with an opportunity to learn more about an in-group member, but concerns about status can affect which behaviors an individual is more likely to notice. When in-group identification is high, being in close proximity with in-group members could provide an individual with more opportunities to discover and observe positive in-group characteristics. When an individual is concerned about his or her status, being in close proximity with an in-group member could provide him or her with more opportunities to discover and observe individuating characteristics.

Finally, throughout this review, the importance of situational and contextual factors in generating strong ties in general and homophily in particular has been emphasized. However, we must recognize that individuals do not respond to situational factors in the same way. For example, some individuals have spent more time as a member of a numerical minority, and experience in the minority condition could affect how much an individual identifies with current members of a minority (Smith & Moore, 2000). In an analysis of network connections at a large Midwestern university, Smith and Moore (2000) found that Black college students who were educated at predominantly White high schools were less likely to be connected to other Black students. Or some individuals are more collective in their orientation, while others are more individualistic. Adopting a more collective orientation could amplify how much identification and competition shape an individual's interactions with demographically similar colleagues, while the same situational factors could matter very little for a person with a more individualistic orientation. Future research should focus on how individual differences influence the link between contextual factors and the network formation process.

Diversity as connections: Team performance

Diversity researchers have also considered how a team's demographic composition affects its performance. The available empirical evidence has been mixed (Williams & O'Reilly, 1998). Reported research findings indicate that an increase in demographic diversity could increase, decrease, or have no effect at all on team performance. Despite the ambiguous research findings, scholars have maintained that demographic diversity is either beneficial or harmful for team performance. Given the ambiguous research findings, the two positions are often described as either being "pessimistic" or "optimistic" about the performance implications of demographic diversity (Mannix & Neale, 2005; Reagans & Zuckerman, 2001). In this section, I summarize the rationale underlying each stance and focus in particular on the importance of social networks in mediating the association between demographic diversity and team performance. I also describe a conceptual framework that is, at least implicitly, shared by both sides of the diversity–performance debate. The framework is used to motivate future research questions.

Diversity–performance debate

Scholars who are "pessimistic" about the performance implications of demographic diversity have argued that an increase in demographic diversity will be problematic for team performance because increasing diversity introduces social divisions that fragment interpersonal relationships inside the team (McCain, O'Reilly, & Pfeffer, 1983; O'Reilly, Caldwell, & Barnett, 1989; Pfeffer, 1985). Strong internal connections are important because they provide a foundation for a number of performance-enhancing processes and dynamics. For example, a team is more likely to be successful when team members are motivated to do well, share their knowledge and expertise, and develop a division of labor that utilizes whatever knowledge and expertise is available on the team. Each outcome is more likely when team members are connected by strong network connections (Balkundi et al., 2007; Cummings & Cross, 2003; Oh, Chung, & Labianca, 2004). Thus, by introducing social divisions, an increase in demographic diversity reduces the likelihood that team members will develop work structures and processes that ultimately contribute to superior performance outcomes.

Scholars who are more "optimistic" about diversity have focused on the knowledge and information individuals bring to a team. Individuals who share a demographic characteristic are assumed to be more similar with respect to unobserved characteristics such as frameworks, opinions, and worldviews. As a result, diverse teams are more likely to be characterized by a wider array of frameworks and perspectives, which should promote more critical debate during group discussions. By introducing divergent thoughts and opinions into internal team discussions, an increase in demographic diversity should also promote learning and creative problem solving, which contribute to superior performance outcomes (Ancona & Caldwell, 1992; Bantel & Jackson, 1989; Pelled, Eisenhardt, & Xin, 1999).

Diversity and social networks
Closure and collective action

While the two sides of the diversity–performance debate predict different performance outcomes, the two positions actually have a great deal in common. Diversity researchers are in relative agreement about the social networks that mediate the association between demographic diversity and team performance (Reagans & Zuckerman, 2001; Reagans, Zuckerman, & McEvily, 2004). The importance of social relationships is explicit in the so-called pessimistic position. An increase in diversity is assumed to be problematic because it will fragment relationships inside a team, thereby undermining a team's capacity to achieve collective goals and objectives. A large body of research has established that the focus on internal cohesion is warranted. Strong interpersonal relationships (both direct and indirect) inside a community help to align individual behavior with collective goals and objectives, and therefore allow communities to overcome collective action problems (Ingram & Roberts, 2000). In any group or community, conflicts of interest can develop between what is best for the community and what is best for each individual member of the community. For example, the successful transfer of knowledge between individuals has a positive effect on a host of organizational processes and outcomes. Knowledge transfer can be beneficial for the organization, but sharing knowledge is costly for the source. At a minimum, sharing knowledge requires time and effort. Moreover, anyone who shares what he or she knows with colleagues reduces the extent to which he or she can monopolize and therefore benefit from controlling valuable knowledge and information.

Explanations for the network closure effect are often grounded in rational choice theory (Coleman, 1990; Grief, 1989). When relationships in a community are characterized by closure (i.e., strong direct and indirect third-party ties), information travels more quickly (Coleman, 1988), and as a result community members hear about uncooperative behavior more quickly. The dense web of connections also means that community members are in a better position to sanction offending community members (Grief, 1989). Thus, individual members of a community cooperate out of a desire to protect their reputation and standing in the larger community. The origins of trust and cooperation could be grounded in rational choice, but once a strong tie has been developed, it is more likely to be maintained, even when commitment is not "rational" (Sgourev & Zuckerman, 2011). The empirical evidence supports the idea that the strong ties (both direct and indirect) defining network closure facilitate pro-social behaviors (e.g., knowledge transfer, extra effort) that allow collectivities (e.g., dyads, teams, or communities) to achieve outcomes that would be difficult to achieve otherwise.

Brokerage and creative problem solving

Network connections play an important role for "optimists" as well. Instead of focusing on relationships between team members, optimists focus on the pattern of relationships between contacts outside of the team. People who do not share a demographic characteristic are assumed to possess different knowledge and expertise, but they are also assumed to travel in different network neighborhoods, which helps to maintain those differences. Social capital researchers have established the importance of being exposed to diverse knowledge and information. The issue is most often discussed in terms of the benefits associated with maintaining network connections that span "structural holes" or disconnects between communities (Burt, 1992, 2005; Reagans & Zuckerman, 2008). When network connections are conduits for information diffusion and knowledge transfer, knowledge and information is more likely to be redundant within versus between communities (Granovetter, 1973). As a result, individuals with relationships that span communities have access to more diverse knowledge and information, hear about new developments more quickly, and have support in more social circles (Burt, 1992).

Initial "structural hole" research focused on network connections in facilitating the more rapid diffusion or transfer of knowledge and information. More recent arguments have focused on how being exposed to more diverse ideas and frameworks changes an individual (Burt, 2005; Reagans & McEvily, 2003). Being exposed to a wider array (and therefore potentially conflicting) of knowledge and information promotes the kind of learning that improves an individual's capacity for knowledge transfer and creative problem solving (Burt, 2005; Reagans & McEvily, 2003). Thus, scholars who expect for diversity to have a positive effect on team performance assume that a team will be more productive when the team assumes the position of a "broker" in an organization's information and knowledge network.

Thus, while the two sides of the diversity debate expect for an increase in diversity to have different performance outcomes, each side emphasizes the importance of network connections in producing team performance. Pessimists focus on the presence of relationships *inside* the team, while optimists give priority to the absence of connections between contacts *outside* the team. Each side even acknowledges the importance of the network feature emphasized by the other side. For example, Pfeffer and his colleagues (McCain, O'Reilly, & Pfeffer, 1983) warn that diversity can be problematic for team performance, but Pfeffer (1985) also advises managers to develop network connections that cut across tenure cohorts because of the information and learning benefits that boundary-spanning ties can create. And while Ancona and Caldwell (1992) expect for diversity to have a positive effect on team performance, they fully acknowledge that diverse teams will have a difficult time developing relationships and coordinating their behavior.

Teams that are internally cohesive and have range in their relationships with colleagues outside the team have more social capital, and diversity researchers are also in agreement about how and why diversity affects a team's social capital. Each side assumes that network connections in an organization are characterized by homophily. As a result, as demographic diversity increases on a team, team members are less likely to be connected by a strong interpersonal relationship. If the organizational network is characterized by homophily, people who do not share a demographic characteristic are less likely to be connected to each other and are also less likely to be connected to the same third parties (White, 2002). As a result, as diversity increases, individuals who are added to the team are less likely to be connected to the same people outside the team.

Thus, at least with respect to the social networks that mediate the relationship between diversity and team performance, there is (at least implicitly) agreement about which network connections matter and how changes in diversity will affect those connections. The underlying conceptual framework is illustrated in Figure 11.2. The coefficients in the "causal" chain indicate that an increase in demographic diversity is expected to reduce internal cohesion and increase external range, and each network feature is expected to have a positive effect on team performance. Figure 11.2 was tested in a small research and development firm (Reagans, Zuckerman, & McEvily, 2004). The teams performed a number of tasks, including process improvement, scientific analysis, and product/material development. Analysis indicated that demographic diversity had the predicted effect on a team's social capital, and social capital had the predicted effects on a team's performance.

With so much agreement, one has to wonder what the "debate" has been all about. Researchers who study diversity might disagree about the performance implications of introducing diversity, but they agree about the network factors involved; they simply emphasize different parts of the framework. Pessimists focus on the upper pathway, while optimists give causal priority to the lower pathway. Despite differences in perspective, one would have imagined that the agreement about the underlying conceptual framework would have resulted in more consensus, or at least a less protracted debate. It is possible that the debate has persisted because scholars have tested their arguments indirectly. In particular, instead of estimating the coefficients in Figure 11.2, scholars have regressed team

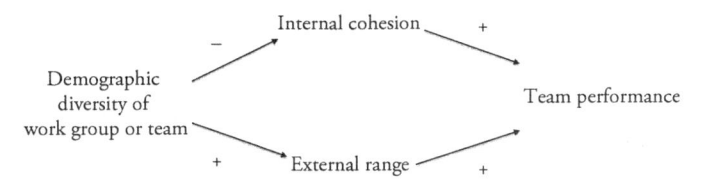

Figure 11.2. Demographic diversity and team performance.

performance on demographic diversity. If the estimated diversity effect was negative, they have concluded that whatever benefits diversity introduced were not large enough to offset the negative effect diversity had on internal relationships. If the estimated effect was positive, they have concluded that whatever difficulties in internal processes diversity introduced were not large enough to offset the benefits associated with having access to a wider array of knowledge and information. The diversity–performance debate has persisted because the research strategy has allowed diversity researchers to be ambiguous about the causal mechanisms underlying their position and so has obscured just how much both sides have in common.

Figure 11.2 illustrates how diversity affects a team's social capital and how social capital affects performance. One can draw two opposing implications from the figure. If an individual cares only about the overall diversity effect, Figure 11.2 suggests that he or she can ignore the intervening social capital variables and focus on the overall association between demographic diversity and performance. Initial research adopted this empirical approach. The strategy is based on two very strong assumptions. First, diversity will have the predicted effects on a team's social capital only when the broader organizational network is characterized by homophily. And the second assumption is that people who are similar on the surface are also similar with respect to important knowledge and expertise. Empirical evidence calls both assumptions into question (Harrison et al., 1998; Lawrence, 1997). Moreover, an exclusive focus on diversity can result in the wrong conclusions being drawn. For example, in the research and development firm studied, diversity didn't have a direct effect on team performance, and one could have concluded that diversity didn't matter. But it did: diversity had the predicted effects on a team's social capital, and a team's social capital had the predicted effect on team performance. The overall diversity effect was zero because the two pathways offset each other in the firm studied—but diversity clearly mattered.

A second implication is that one can ignore diversity and focus on the social capital variables because they are the more proximate determinants of team performance. Not only do the social capital variables have a predictable effect on team performance, but one can imagine they are easier to manage. For example, consider a manager who is charged with increasing a team's capacity for creativity. In an attempt to introduce more divergent thoughts and opinions, a manager could either increase diversity or could staff the team optimizing the holes between external contacts. When the network is characterized by homophily, if a manager decides to increase diversity, the manager must consider the relative change in each pathway in Figure 11.2 because increasing diversity will increase range and reduce cohesion. The overall effect that diversity will have on performance is difficult to predict without an appreciation for the relative magnitude of coefficients in Figure 11.2. A focus on external range will result in a more predictable outcome and will not necessarily come at the expense of the benefits provided by internal cohesion.

There is value in remaining mindful of the effects that diversity can have on the network variables and how much those variables contribute to performance. In particular, focusing on the links in the framework helps to explain systematic "variation" in what might appear initially to be ambiguous research findings. Given the direction of the links in the causal chain, the effect that an increase in diversity will have on team performance can vary from positive to negative as a function of the relative magnitude of the links in the chain. If the coefficients in the lower pathway are larger than the coefficients in the upper pathway, the overall diversity effect will be positive, but if the coefficients in the upper pathway are larger than the coefficients in the lower pathway, the overall diversity effect will be negative. And if the two pathways are equal, or if diversity has no effect on the network variables, the diversity effect will be zero. Focusing on the big picture allows us to understand that the "mixed" or "ambiguous" empirical results documented across prior studies have emerged from a systematic process (Chatman et al., 1998; Kochan et al., 2003; Mannix & Neale, 2005, p. 33).

Future directions: Diversity and team performance

Figure 11.2 illustrates how a team's social capital mediates the relationship between a team's composition and its performance. Future research should focus on the factors that shape the value of a team's social capital. For example, one explanation for the mixed diversity effects observed across previous studies is that the value of diversity is contingent upon a team's primary objective (Tsui & Gutek, 1999, pp. 96–97). Diversity introduces divergent thoughts and opinions but also makes it more difficult for team members to coordinate their activity. Divergent thoughts and opinions are beneficial when the primary objective is creativity or innovation, but the fact that diversity makes it more difficult for team members to coordinate their activity looms large when the team's primary objective is efficiency. Therefore, the managerial implications seem clear. Since diversity introduces divergent thoughts, a manager should introduce diversity when creativity or innovation is the primary objective. But since diversity makes it more difficult for team members to work with each other, diversity should be avoided when efficiency or cost reductions are the goal. The contingency approach speaks to the magnitude of the coefficients on the right side of Figure 11.2. The positive effect that each network variable can have on team performance, however, suggests that the contrast, while appropriate, is also too stark. All teams need to innovate and coordinate their behavior (Hackman & Morris, 1975). Even teams that are concerned with efficiency can benefit from creative and innovative solutions, and teams that are concerned with innovation need to cooperate with each other. That being said, the magnitudes of the network effects could vary with the team's primary objective (Rowley, Behrens, & Krackhardt, 2000). Therefore, a potential area for future research is to consider how the value of internal cohesion and external range varies as the primary goal of the team changes, either overall or at different points in time.

The previous discussion suggests that teams that have a specific level of social capital do not experience a constant increase in performance. And the value of a team's social capital could very well be contingent upon internal team dynamics that help determine how much network connections contribute to a team's performance. For example, internal cohesion helps to align individual behavior and team goals. Cohesion generates consistency in behavior, and consistency is important when team members value achievement or performance. If team members have low aspirations or performance goals, increases in cohesion will undermine team performance. In addition to aspiration levels, there is value in analyzing a team's social capital and internal work structures and processes in a more dynamic framework. In particular, future research should consider the interplay between a team's transactive memory system (TMS) and its social capital. A team has a well-defined TMS when work roles and responsibilities exploit team members' knowledge and expertise (i.e., knowing and doing are matched on the team) and when team members have developed frameworks that facilitate coordination across their specialized assignments. Internal cohesion increases the likelihood that a team will develop a TMS because when team members are connected by strong ties, they have a better sense for who knows what (Reagans & McEvily, 2003), and as a result team members are more likely to have developed work roles and responsibilities that exploit team members' knowledge and expertise (Liang, Moreland, & Argote, 1995; Reagans, Argote, & Brooks, 2005). Once a team has developed a TMS, the positive effect that internal cohesion has on team performance could increase. For example, Linda Argote, Ella Miron-Spektor, and I (Reagans, Argote, & Miron-Spektor, 2011) considered how the presence of a shared language interacted with specialized work roles to determine team performance. Sharing a language allowed team members to coordinate their behavior more effectively. Effective coordination was important, but it was especially important when team members had been assigned to work roles and responsibilities that took advantage of what they know (Reagans, Argote, & Miron-Spektor, 2011). Internal cohesion provides a foundation for the development of performance-enhancing work structures and processes, but once established the same structures and processes could increase the positive effect that internal cohesion has on team performance.

The development of a TMS could also increase the positive effect that external range can have on team performance. External range affects the likelihood that a team will have access to diverse knowledge and expertise and therefore defines a team's capacity for creativity and innovation. How team members use the knowledge and information at their disposal is also important, and quite often diverse knowledge and information is underutilized. For example, prior research on knowledge transfer and communication inside of teams has shown that team members are more likely to share common knowledge and information (Wittenbaum & Stasser, 1996). And even when a divergent thought or opinion is shared with other team members, it is less likely to be accepted. A divergent or minority opinion is more likely to be accepted if the person with the divergent opinion is viewed as credible and is viewed by others to be proposing a course of action that is consistent with the interests of the team and not his or her personal interests (Argote, 1999, pp. 121–122). Moreover, divergent thoughts and opinions are more likely to influence team processes when the person expressing the "minority" or dissenting views is also different demographically (Loyd, 2011; Phillips, 2003), unless the characteristic that defines his or her difference also indicates that he or she is less able (Thomas-Hunt & Phillips, 2004). This line of research has established that diverse knowledge and expertise is more likely to be beneficial when experts are willing to share what they know and when their team members are willing to evaluate team members' knowledge and expertise objectively and critically. When team members are willing to objectively engage in critical debate and discussion, the best work routines and practices are more likely to be developed and implemented (Jehn, 1995, 1997).

The proceeding discussion suggests that developing a TMS could make external range more valuable. When a TMS has been developed, knowledge experts are more credible, and as a result they are more willing to share what they know, and what they share is more likely to be critically engaged. External range could also affect the quality of the TMS that develops on a team. As external range increases, team members are less likely to overlap in their knowledge and expertise and are more likely to have developed an ability to combine what they know. Both factors should increase the odds of a team developing a TMS. Moreover, the value of external range should be higher when expert status on a team is reinforced by an information and knowledge advantage in the larger network outside the team.

Multiple teams

While this discussion has focused on a single team, organizations are often concerned about the performance of multiple teams, and those teams are often interdependent: the performance of one team often affects the performance of another. Recent theoretical models have focused on the kind of organizational network that would increase team performance on average. Initial research findings illustrate the importance of a "small-world" network structure. A global network is a small world when network neighborhoods are internally cohesive and when those neighborhoods are connected by a small number of bridges or shortcuts. A small world network structure provides teams with an opportunity to learn from each other, which would raise the performance of every team (O'Leary, Woolley, & Mortensen, 2011; Uzzi & Shapiro, 2005). Learning from the experience of others can also be detrimental. Indeed, the rapid diffusion of knowledge and information across teams can be beneficial when performance metrics emphasize the short term (Fang, Lee, & Schilling, 2010; Lazer & Friedman, 2007). Rapid information diffusion can undermine longer-term and more dramatic improvements in performance because dramatic improvements are more likely when individuals and teams are exploring different parts of a knowledge space. Global network structures that maintain system-wide diversity for a longer period of time increase the odds that teams will find the maximum peak in a problem space (Lazer & Friedman, 2007). The results are based on computational and simulation techniques but in my opinion represent some of the most promising research in the field (Hong & Page, 2004). The research is informative but also limited. Teams in the simulation are often performing the same task or working in the same problem space; it seems more likely that teams will have divided their efforts and are working on complementary but distinct parts of a problem. What we need are more theoretical models and empirical analyses assuming that the teams in an organization are interdependent but have also specialized their efforts.

References

Ancona, D. A., & Caldwell, D. F. (1992). Bridging the boundary: External activity and performance in organizational teams. *Administrative Science Quarterly, 7*(4), 634–665.

Argote, L. (1999). *Organizational learning: Creating, retaining and transferring knowledge.* New York, NY: Kluwer Academic Publishers.

Argote, L., Beckman, S., & Epple, D. (1990). The persistence and transfer of learning in industrial settings. *Management Science, 36*(2), 140–154.

Bacharach, S. B., Bamberger, P. A., & Vashdi, D. (2005). Diversity and homophily at work: Supportive relations among white and African American peers. *Academy of Management Journal, 48,* 619–644.

Balkundi, P., Kilduff, M., Barsness, Z., & Michael, J. H. (2007). Demographic antecedents and performance consequences of structural holes in work teams *Journal of Organizational Behavior, 28,* 241–260.

Bantel, K. A., & Jackson, S. E. (1989). Top management and innovation in banking: Does the composition of the top team make a difference? *Strategic Management Journal, 10,* 107–124.

Baum, J., & Ingram, P. (1998). Survival-enhancing learning in the Manhattan hotel industry, 1898–1980. *Management Science, 44*(7), 996–1016.

Bielby, W. T., & Baron, J. N. (1986). Men and women at work: Sex segregation *and statistical discrimination. American Journal of Sociology, 91,* 759–799.

Blau, P. M., & Schwartz, J. E. (1984). *Crosscutting social circles.* Orlando, FL: Academic Press.

Brass, D. J. (1985). Men's and women's networks: A study of interaction patterns and influence in an organization. *Academy of Management Journal, 28,* 327–343.

Brewer, M. (1991). The social self: On being the same and different at the same time. *Personality & Social Psychology Bulletin, 17,* 475–482.

Brewer, M., & Kramer, R. (1985). The psychology of intergroup attitudes and behavior. *Annual Review of Psychology, 36,* 219–243.

Burt, R. S. (2005). *Brokerage and closure.* London: Oxford University Press.

Burt, R. S. (1991). Measuring age as a structural concept. *Social Networks, 13,* 1–34.

Burt, R. S. (1992). *Structural holes: the social structure of competition.* Cambridge, MA: Harvard University Press.

Byrne, D. (1971). *The attraction paradigm.* New York: Academic Press.

Caldeira, G. A., & Patterson, S.C. (1987). Political friendship in legislature. *Journal of Politics, 4,* 953–975.

Chatman, J. A., Polzer, J. T., Barsade, S. G., & Neale, M. A. (1998). Being different yet feeling similar: The influence of demographic composition and organizational culture on work processes & outcomes. *Administrative Science Quarterly, 43,* 749–780.

Cohen, W., & Levinthal, D. (1990). Absorptive capacity: A new perspective on learning and innovation. *Administrative Science Quarterly, 35,* 128–152.

Coleman, J. S. (1988). Social capital in the creation of human capital. *American Journal of Sociology, 94* (Supplement: Organizations and Institutions: Sociological and Economic Approaches to the Analysis of Social Structure), S95–S120.

Coleman, J. S. (1990). *Foundations of social theory.* Cambridge, MA: Harvard University Press.

Cummings, J. N., & Cross, R. (2003). Structural properties of work groups and their consequences for performance. *Social Networks, 25*(3), 197–210.

Darr, E., Argote, L., & Epple, D. (1995). The acquisition, transfer and depreciation of knowledge in service organizations: Productivity in franchises. *Management Science, 44,* 1750–1762.

Duguid, M. (2011). Female tokens in high-prestige work groups: Catalysts or inhibitors of group integration? *Organizational Behavior and Human Decision Processes, 116*(1), 104–115.

Duguid, M., Loyd, D. L., & Tolbert, P. S. (2012). The impact of categorical status, numeric representation and work group prestige on preference for demographically similar others: A value threat approach. *Organization Science, 23*(2), 386–401.

Fang, F., Lee, J., & Schilling, M. A. (2010). Balancing exploration and exploitation through structural design: The isolation of subgroups and organizational learning. *Organization Science, 21*(3), 625–642.

Feld, S. (1982). Structural determinants of similarity among associates. *American Sociological Review, 47,* 797–801.

Feld, S. (1984). The structured use of personal associates. *Social Forces, 62,* 640–652.

Festinger, L., Schachter, S., & Bach, K. (1950). *Social processes in informal groups.* Stanford, CA: Stanford University Press.

Granovetter, M. (1973). The strength of weak ties. *American Journal of Sociology, 78*(6), 1360–1380.

Grief, A. (1989). Reputation and coalitions in medieval trade: Evidence on the Maghribi traders. *Journal of Economic History, 49,* 857–882.

Grieve, P., & Hogg, M. (1999). Subjective uncertainty & intergroup discrimination in the minimal group situation. *Personality & Social Psychology Bulletin, 25,* 926–940.

Hackman, J., & Morris, C. G. (1975). Group tasks, group interaction process, and group performance effectiveness: A review and proposed integration. In L. Berkowitz (Ed.), *Advances in experimental social psychology* (Vol. 8, pp. 1–55). New York: Academic Press.

Hannan, M., Polos, L., & Carroll, G. R. (2007). *Logics of organization theory: audiences, codes & ecologies.* Princeton, NJ: Princeton University Press.

Hansen, M. T. (1999). The search-transfer problem: The role of weak ties in sharing knowledge across organization subunits. *Administrative Science Quarterly, 44,* 82–111.

Harrison, D. A., Price, K. H., & Bell, M. P. (1998). Beyond relational demography: Time & the effects of surface- and deep-level diversity on work group cohesion. *Academy of Management Journal, 41,* 96–107.

Hewstone, M., Rubin, M., & Willis, H. (2002). Intergroup bias. *Annual Review of Psychology, 53,* 575–604.

Hogg, M. (1993). Group cohesiveness: A critical review and some new directions. *European Review of Social Psychology, 4,* 85–111.

Hogg, M. (1992). *The social psychology of group cohesiveness: From attraction to social identity.* Hemel Hempstead, UK: Harvester Wheatsheaf.

Hogg, M., & Hains, S.C. (1996). Intergroup relations and group solidarity: Effects of group identification and social beliefs on depersonalized attraction. *Journal of Personality & Social Psychology, 70,* 295–309.

Hogg, M., & Hardie, E. A. (1991). Social attraction, personal attraction & self-categorization: A field study. *Personality & Social Psychology Bulletin, 17,* 175–180.

Hogg, M., Hardie, E. A., & Reynolds, K. J. (1995). Prototypical similarity, self-categorization, and depersonalized attraction: A perspective on group cohesiveness. *European Journal of Social Psychology, 25,* 159–177.

Hogg, M., & Turner, J.C. (1985). Interpersonal attraction, social identification, and psychological group formation. *European Journal of Social Psychology, 15,* 51–66.

Hong, L., & Page, S. (2004). Groups of diverse problem solvers can outperform groups of high-ability problem solvers. *PNAS, 101*(46), 16385–16389.

Ibarra, H. (1992). Homophily and differential returns: Sex differences in network structure and access in an advertising firm. *Administrative Science Quarterly, 37,* 422–447.

Ibarra, H. (1995). Race, opportunity, and diversity of social circles in managerial networks. *Academy of Management Journal, 38,* 673–703.

Ibarra, H. (1997). Paving an alternative route: Gender differences in managerial networks. *Social Psychology Quarterly, 60,* 91–102.

Ingram, P., & Morris, M. (2007). Do people mix at mixers? Structure, homophily and the life of the party. *Administrative Science Quarterly, 52,* 558–585.

Ingram, P., & & Roberts, P. W. (2000). Friendships among competitors in the Sydney hotel industry. *American Journal of Sociology, 106,* 387–423.

Jehn, K. (1995). A multimethod examination of the benefits and detriments of intragroup conflict. *Administrative Science Quarterly, 40,* 256–282.

Jehn, K. (1997). A qualitative analysis of conflict types in dimensions in organizational groups. *Administrative Science Quarterly, 42*(3), 530–557.

Kanter, R. (1977). *Men and women of the corporation.* New York: Basic Books.

Kochan, T., Bezrukova, K., Ely, R., & Jackson, S. (2003). The effects of diversity on business performance: Report of the Diversity Research Network. *Human Resource Management, 42*(1), 3–21.

Kram, K., & Isabella, L. A. (1985). Mentoring alternatives: The role of peer relationships in career development. *Academy of Management Journal, 28*(1), 110–132.

Lau, D. C., & Murninghan, J. K. (1998). Demographic diversity and faultlines: The compositional dynamics of organizational groups. *Academy of Management Review, 23,* 325–340.

Laumann, E. O. (1966). *Prestige and association in an urban community.* Indianapolis, IN: Bobbs-Merrill.

Laumann, E. O. (1973). *Bonds of pluralism: The form and substance of urban social networks.* New York: Wiley.

Lawrence, B. (1997). The black box of organizational demography. *Organization Science, 8*(1), 1–22.

Lazarsfeld, P. F., & Merton, R. K. (1954). Friendship as social process: A substantive and methodological analysis. In M. Berger, T. Abel, & C. H. Page (Eds.), *Freedom and control in modern society* (pp. 18–66). Toronto, Canada: Nostrand.

Lazer, D., & Friedman, A. (2007). The network structure of exploration & exploitation. *Administrative Science Quarterly, 52,* 667–694.

Liang, D. W., Moreland, R. L., & Argote, L. (1995). Group versus individual training & group performance: The mediating role of transactive memory. *Personality and Social Psychology Bulletin, 21,* 384–393.

Lincoln, J. R., & Miller, J. (1979). Work and friendship ties in organizations: A comparative analysis of relational networks. *Administration Science Quarterly, 24,* 181–199.

Loyd, D. L. (2011). *Undermining diversity: How favoritism threat alters evaluations of similar others by women.* Working paper, MIT Sloan School of Management.

Mannix, E., & Neale, M. (2005). What differences make a difference? The promise and reality of diverse teams in organizations. *Psychology in the Public Interest, 6*(2), 31–55. (Abbreviated version reprinted in *Scientific American,* August 2006, pp. 32–40.)

Marsden, P. V. (1987). Core discussion networks of Americans. *American Sociological Review, 52,* 122–131.

Marsden, P. V. (1988). Homogeneity in confiding relationships. *Social Networks, 10,* 57–76.

Marsden, P. V., & Campbell, K. E. (1984). Measuring tie strength. *Social Forces, 63,* 482–501.

McCain, B., O'Reilly, C., & Pfeffer, J. (1983). The effects of departmental demography on turnover: The case of a university. *Academy of Management Journal, 26*(4), 626–641.

McGinn, K. L., & Milkman, K. L. (2010). *Shall I stay or shall I go? Cooperative and competitive effects of workgroup sex and race composition on turnover.* Working paper, Harvard Business School.

McPherson, J. M., & Smith-Lovin, L. (1987). Homophily in voluntary organizations: Status distance & the composition of face-to-face groups. *American Sociological Review, 52,* 370–379.

McPherson, J. M., & Smith-Lovin, L. (1986). Sex segregation in voluntary associations. *American Sociological Review, 51,* 61–79.

McPherson, J. M., Smith-Lovin, L., & Cook, J. M. (2001). Birds of a feather: Homophily in social networks. *Annual Review of Sociology, 27,* 415–444.

Mehra, A., Kilduff, M., & Brass, D. J. (1998). At the margins: A distinctiveness approach to the social identity and social networks of underrepresented groups. *Academy of Management Journal, 41,* 441–452.

Miller, J., Lincoln, J. R., & Olson, J. (1981). Rationality and equity in professional networks: Gender and race as factors in the stratification of interorganizational systems. *American Journal of Sociology, 87,* 303–386.

Mollica, K. A., Gray, B., & Trevino, L. K. (2003). Racial homophily and its persistence in newcomers' social networks. *Organization Science 14,* 123–136.

Moody, J. (2001). Race, school integration, and friendship segregation in America. *American Journal of Sociology, 107,* 679–716.

Mouw, T., & Entwisle, B. (2006). Residential segregation & interracial friendship in schools. *American Journal of Sociology, 12,* 394–441.

Mullen, B. (1983). Operationalizing the effect of the group on the individual: A self-attention perspective. *Journal of Experimental Social Psychology, 19,* 295–322.

Oh, H., Chung, M-H., & Labianca, G. (2004). Group social capital and group effectiveness: The role of informal socializing ties. *Academy of Management Journal, 47,* 860–875.

O'Leary, M. B., Mortensen, M., & Woolley, A. W. (2011). *Multiple team membership: A theoretical model of its effects on productivity and learning for individuals and teams.* Tepper School of Business. Available at: http://repository.cmu.edu/tepper/577

O'Reilly, C. A., III, Caldwell, D. F., & & Barnett, W. P. (1989). Work group demography, social integration, and turnover. *Administrative Science Quarterly, 34,* 21–37.

Pattillo-McCoy, M. (1999). *Black picket fences: Privilege and peril among the black middle class.* Chicago: University of Chicago Press.

Pelled, L. H., Eisenhardt, K. M., & Xin, K. R. (1999). Exploring the black box: An analysis of work group diversity, conflict, and performance. *Administrative Science Quarterly, 44*(1), 1–28.

Pfeffer, J. (1982). Organizational demography. In L. L. Cummings & B. M. Staw (Eds.), *Research in organizational behavior* (Vol. 5, pp. 299–357). Greenwich, CT: JAI Press.

Pfeffer, J. (1985). Organizational demography: Implications for management. *California Management Review, 28,* 67–81.

Phillips, K. W. (2003). The effects of categorically based expectations on minority influence: The importance of congruence. *Personality and Social Psychology Bulletin, 29,* 3–13.

Phillips, K. W., & Lewin Loyd, D. (2006). When surface & deep-level diversity collide: The effects on dissenting group members. *Organizational Behavior and Human Decision Processes, 2,* 143–160.

Reagans, R. (2005). Preferences, identity, and competition: Predicting tie strength from demographic data. *Management Science, 51,* 1374–1383.

Reagans, R. (2011). Close encounters: Analyzing how social similarity and propinquity contribute to strong network connections. *Organization Science, 22*(4), 835–849.

Reagans, R., Argote, L., & Brooks, D. (2005). Individual experience & experience working together: Predicting learning rates from knowing what to do & knowing who knows what. *Management Science, 51,* 869–881.

Reagans, R., Argote, L. & Miron-Spektor, E. (2011). *The two wonders of working together: How specialization and coordination influence team performance.* Working paper, MIT Sloan School of Management.

Reagans, R., & Burt, R. S. (2002). *Homophily, legitimation, and competition: Bias in managerial peer evaluations.* Unpublished manuscript.

Reagans, R., & McEvily, B. (2003). Network structure and knowledge transfer: The effects of cohesion and range. *Administrative Science Quarterly, 48,* 240–267.

Reagans, R., & McEvily, B. (2008). Contradictory or compatible? reconsidering the "trade-off" between brokerage and closure on knowledge sharing. *Advances in Strategic Management, 25,* 275–313.

Reagans, R., & Zuckerman, E. (2008). Why knowledge does not equal power: the network redundancy trade-off. *Industrial & Corporate Change, 17*(5), 903–944.

Reagans, R., & Zuckerman, E. W. (2001). Networks, diversity, and productivity: The social capital of corporate R&D teams. *Organization Science, 12*(4), 502–517.

Reagans, R. E., Zuckerman, E. W., & McEvily, B. (2004). How to make the team: Social networks vs. demography as criteria for designing effective projects in a contract R&D firm. *Administrative Science Quarterly, 49,* 101–133.

Rowley, T., Behrens, D., & Krackhardt, D. (2000). Redundant governance structures: An analysis of structural and relational embeddedness in the steel and semiconductor industries. *Strategic Management Journal, 21,* 369–386.

Rytina, S., Blau, P., Blum, T., & Schwartz, J. (1988). Inequality and intermarriage: A paradox of motive and constraint. *Social Forces, 66,* 645–675.

Schneider, B. (1987). The people make the place. *Personnel Psychology, 40,* 437–453.

Sgourev, S., & Zuckerman, E. (2011). Breaking up is hard to do: Irrational inconsistency in commitment to an industry peer network. *Rationality & Society, 23*(1), 3–34.

Simon, H. A. (1991). Bounded rationality and organizational learning. *Organization Science, 2*(1), 125–134.

Shrum, W., Cheek, N. H. Jr., & Hunter, S. M. (1988). Friendship in school: Gender and racial homophily. *Sociology of Education, 61,* 227–239.

Smith, S., & Moore, M. (2000). Intraracial diversity and relations among African-Americans: Closeness among black students at a predominately white university. *American Journal of Sociology, 106*(1), 1–39.

Szulanski, G. (1996). Impediments to the transfer of best practice within the firm. *Strategic Management Journal, 17,* 27–44.

Tafjel, H., & Turner, J.C. (1979). An integrative theory of intergroup conflict. In W. G. Austin & S. Worchel (Eds.), *The social psychology of intergroup relations* (pp. 33–47). Monterey, CA: Brooks-Cole.

Thomas-Hunt, M., & Phillips, K. W. (2004). When what you know is not enough: Expertise and gender dynamics in task groups. *Personality & Social Psychology Bulletin, 30*(12), 1585–1598.

Tortoriello, M., Reagans, R., & McEvily, B. (2011). Bridging the knowledge gap: The influence of strong ties, network cohesion, and network range on the transfer of knowledge between organizational units. *Organization Science, forthcoming.*

Tsui, A., & O'Reilly, C. A. III (1989). Beyond simple demographic effects: The importance of relational demography in superior-subordinate. *Academy of Management Journal, 32*(20), 402–423.

Tsui, A. S., & Gutek, B. A. (1999). *Demographic differences in organizations: Current research and future directions.* Lexington, MA: Lexington Books.

Turner, J. C. (1987). *Rediscovering the social group: A self-categorization theory.* Oxford, UK: Basil Blackwell.

Turner, J. C. (1985). Social categorization and the self-concept: A social cognitive theory of group behavior. In E. J. Lawler (Ed.), *Advances in group processes 2* (pp. 77–122). Greenwich, CT: JAI Press.

Uzzi, B. (1997). Social structure and competition in interfirm networks: The paradox of embeddedness. *Administrative Science Quarterly, 42*(1), 35–67.

Uzzi, B., & Spiro, J. (2005). Collaboration and creativity: Big differences from small world networks. *American Journal of Sociology, 111,* 447–504.

White, H. (2002). *Strategies and identities by mobilization context.* Working paper, Department of Sociology, Columbia University.

Williams, K. Y., & O'Reilly, C. A. III. (1998). Demography and diversity in organizations: A review of 40 years of research. In B. M. Staw & L. L. Cummings (Eds.), *Research in organizational behavior* (Vol. 20, pp. 77–140). Greenwich, CT: JAI Press.

Wittenbaum, G. M., & Stasser, G. (1996). Management of information in small groups. In J. L. Nye & A. M. Brower (Eds.), *What's social about social cognition? Research on socially shared cognition in small groups* (pp. 3–28). Thousand Oaks, CA: Sage.

Yamaguchi, K. (1990). Homophily and social distance in the choice of multiple friends: An analysis based on conditionally dymmetric log-bilinear association model. *Journal of the American Statistical Association, 85,* 356–366.

Zeng, Z., & Xie, Y. (2008). A preference-opportunity-choice framework with applications to intergroup friendship. *American Journal of Sociology, 114,* 615–648.

Zenger, T., & Lawrence, B. (1989). Organizational demography: The differential effects of age and tenure distributions on technical communication. *Academy of Management Journal, 32,* 353–376.

Ziebro, M., & Northcraft, G. (2009). Connecting the dots: Network development, information flow, and creativity in groups. In E. Mannix, J. A. Goncalo, & M. A. Neale (Eds.), *Creativity in groups. Research on managing groups and teams 12* (pp. 135–162). Stamford, CT: JAI Press.

PART 5

Contextual Perspectives on Diversity

CHAPTER 12

Understanding How Context Shapes Team Diversity Outcomes

Aparna Joshi *and* Hyuntak Roh

Abstract

The study of diversity context offers many opportunities and also represents many challenges. In this chapter we present a research agenda that exploits some opportunities and attempts to overcome the challenges in conducting contextualized diversity research. We offer a tripartite definition of diversity context comprising its structural, relational, and normative components, and discuss a theoretical framework for identifying the effect of context on categorization and elaboration-based processes within work teams. We conclude by suggesting directions for future research that we hope will be a road map for future research in this area.

Key Words: diversity, teams, context, cross-level research, demography

The study of context has gained prominence in organizational research. Scholars have noted that organizational phenomena are complex, and not accounting for the role of context in our research minimizes its theoretical rigor and practical relevance (Bamberger, 2008; Johns, 2006). The study of context is important and offers many opportunities for future diversity research. Opportunities arise because of the mixed nature of findings that have emerged in this area. Overall, team diversity effects on workplace outcomes such as effectiveness and performance have ranged from positive to negative to nonsignificant. Indeed, past reviews on this topic revealed that 20 percent of studies report positive effects, 20 percent report negative effects, and about 60 percent report null effects (Joshi & Roh, 2009). Even within single studies, researchers have found that some aspects of diversity have positive effects, some have negative effects, and others account for no variance in outcomes of interest (Ely, 2004; Jehn, Northcraft, & Neale, 1999; Kochan, Bezrukova, Ely, Jackson, Joshi, & Jehn, 2003; Leonard, Levine, & Joshi, 2004; Van der Vegt, Van de Vliert, & Huang, 2005). These mixed findings set the stage for the study of diversity context and indicate that contextual considerations are critical in our research.

Studying context also represents challenges. These challenges are illustrated by the scant attention paid to context in past diversity research. Less than 20 percent of the studies in the area of work team diversity have provided information regarding environmental context, such as organizational structure, strategy, or the nature of the industry or occupations represented in the research, that may be relevant to focal diversity variables (Joshi & Roh, 2007, 2009). In part, these challenges emerge because scholars coming from a single disciplinary domain may not sufficiently engage theoretical considerations outside that discipline. For example, an industrial/organizational psychologist may not account for macro environmental features that can shape the outcomes of individual demographic differences in organizations. A sociologist may focus on structural features of the organization and not acknowledge the role of individual differences in shaping employment outcomes. Since the development of context-oriented theories may require building bridges across macro–micro disciplinary domains, these disciplinary silos can present a barrier. In studying context, researchers often have to develop and test multilevel or cross-level models, which can impose more stringent requirements for data and sampling that can be daunting for researchers relying on a survey-based methodology. On a more practical note, gaining broad and deep access to organizations may be necessary but also more challenging for researchers interested in probing organizational context.

Despite these challenges, we contend that diversity research can be enriched both theoretically and empirically by accounting for context. Prevalent theories framing diversity research, such as social categorization theory, the attraction-selection-attrition framework, and information processing theory (see Jackson & Joshi, 2010; Van Knippenberg & Schippers, 2007, for reviews), have been applied to offer broad generalizations across various dimensions of diversity and across a wide array of work group and organizational outcomes. But extant applications of these theories do not account for the role of context, which could reconcile some of the mixed findings discussed earlier. Consider studies that have reported positive gender diversity effects and negative ethnic diversity effects on team performance (e.g., Kirkman, Tesluk, & Rosen, 2004; Kochan et al., 2003; Pelled, Eisenhardt, & Xin, 1999). Based on prevalent theoretical perspectives in the area, we should expect that these diversity attributes should have similar effects on process and performance outcomes. Yet, why does ethnic diversity emerge as a significant predictor of negative outcomes while gender diversity is either nonsignificant or positively associated with group process outcomes? Frequently, researchers answer these questions as an afterthought. For instance, to account for their results, Kochan and colleagues (2003) surmised that gender diversity is less problematic than ethnic diversity in organizations and the positive effects of gender diversity reflected more conducive relationships between white men and women in gender-balanced groups (Kochan et al., 2003). While these explanations offer some understanding of the mixed results, a fuller inquiry into various aspects of the research context in which these studies were conducted could shed more light on these findings. More specifically, the representation of white women rather than ethnic minorities at higher levels across these research settings may offer additional explanations for the findings reported. As we discuss in subsequent sections, in organizations with greater representation of women at all levels, gender-based social categorization may be minimized. On the other hand, if the organizations included in these studies did not employ ethnic minorities at higher levels, ethnicity-based social categorization may prevail, accounting for the discrepant findings for gender versus ethnic diversity. However, because these attributes of the context were not explicitly accounted for in the research, we cannot be sure which of these explanations are relevant to the findings reported.

In what follows we outline a framework that exploits some opportunities and tries to overcome the challenges in conducting contextualized diversity research. The tripartite definition of diversity context discussed below outlines the relational, normative, and structural features of diversity context. In the following section we offer a theoretical framework that combines this operationalization of diversity context with categorization and elaboration-based outcomes in teams. We conclude by suggesting directions for future research that we hope will be a road map for future research in this area.

Diversity context: A theoretical framework

Taking a compositional approach, we define diversity as the distribution of personal attributes, such as gender, race, or age, of a work unit such as a team or a department within an organization (Tsui & Gutek, 1999). We focus on two broad categories of team diversity outcomes: categorization-based and elaboration-based processes (Van Knippenberg, De Dreu, & Homan, 2004). Van Knippenberg and colleagues (2004) proposed that various aspects of team diversity can jointly or independently influence performance based on either categorization- or elaboration-based processes. Categorization-based processes involve the social categorization of dissimilar individuals as out-group members, which leads to intergroup bias that can have deleterious effects on team performance. Elaboration-based processes include the exchange of information and perspectives among group members, individual-level information processing, gaining feedback, and integrating information and perspectives; these processes explain the positive outcomes of workgroup diversity (Van Knippenberg et al., 2004). Our theoretical framework addresses the role of specific contextual factors in shaping either categorization- or elaboration-based outcomes of diversity. Outcomes such as emotional conflict, commitment, and social integration are considered categorization-based outcomes. Outcomes such as communication, task-based conflict, and reflexivity are considered elaboration-based outcomes.

Defining diversity context

Context has been defined in different ways. Capelli and Sherer (1991) define context as the environment that shapes phenomena of interest and exists at a level above the focal variables. For example, the context for individual attitudes or behaviors would be the group in which the individual is embedded, and the context for the group would be the organization in which the group is nested. Mowday and Sutton (1993) also define context as external stimuli that may constrain or enhance individual actions and consider context as an environment outside the focal phenomenon. Johns (2006) integrates these views to define context as "situational opportunities and constraints that affect the occurrence and meaning of organizational behavior as well as functional relationships between variables. Context can serve as a main effect or interact with personal variables such as disposition to affect organizational variables" (p. 386). We adopt this broad definition of context to defining various aspects of diversity context below.

Based on this definition of context (Johns, 2006), we define *diversity context* as the specific features of the environmental context that might enhance or constrain the occurrence and meaning of diversity in groups or teams and the relationship between diversity and attitudinal, behavioral, and performance outcomes. To further clarify the nature of diversity context, we distinguish between its *structural, relational,* and *normative* features. While the constructs studied under each component of diversity context may not be orthogonal, they represent analytically distinct features of the organizational context that are relevant to the study of diversity and its outcomes.

The conceptualization of *relational diversity context* is rooted in past theorizing in the area of social capital theory and social networks research (Granovetter, 1992; Nahapiet & Ghoshal, 1998). Granovetter (1992) describes "relational embeddedness" as the interpersonal relationships that individuals develop with each other through prolonged interactions over time. Based on this conceptualization, Nahapiet and Ghoshal (1998) define the relational aspects of social capital in terms of trust, trustworthiness, and identification with other actors in a social system. Drawing on this view, we define the relational aspects of diversity context as the nature of interpersonal interactions among organizational actors and the extent to which these interactions are inclusive, dense, and based on trust and positive affect. Although research has not taken into account this aspect of diversity context, we propose that the content and pattern of interactions among organizational actors has important implications for diversity outcomes in workgroups.

Normative diversity context is conceptualized in terms of the organizational culture, history/tradition, climate, and management practices. Together, these aspects of the context represent the norms, values, and behavioral expectations in an organization with implications for diversity and its outcomes. Based on the situational strength perspective we argue that the normative context can serve as a constraint on relationships among focal variables (Mischel, 1968). In the past, scholars have distinguished between "strong" and "weak" organizational situations (Bowen & Ostroff, 2004; Joshi, Dencker, Franz, & Martocchio, 2010). Strong contexts are characterized by explicit norms and values, extensive socialization, and a clear and consistent set of guidelines that reduce variance in individual attitudes and behaviors within the specific setting. On the other hand, weak contexts are characterized by inconsistent norms and lack of consensus regarding expected behaviors and values in the organization. We propose that diversity outcomes are likely to differ depending on the embeddedness of teams in a strong or a weak normative context.

The *structural aspects of diversity context* can be defined as the overall heterogeneity of the organization (i.e., the representation of demographic groups in the organization) and the level of structural integration (i.e., the representation of minority groups at higher levels in the organization) (see Cox, 1993; Joshi, 2006). The degree to which an organization is structurally segregated can be a powerful influence on social category-based identification and conflict among demographic groups (Cox, 1993; Ely, 1994; Wharton, 1992). In structurally segregated organizations, the balance of power and status is skewed in favor of the dominant demographic group; these status and power differentials in this context can undermine intergroup harmony and cooperation within the workgroup (Cox, 1993). Team diversity researchers have seldom taken into consideration the role that structural aspects of diversity play in shaping both the occurrence and the outcomes of

Table 12.1 A theoretical framework for understanding the effects of context on team diversity outcomes

Diversity Context	Theoretical Perspective	Categorization-Based Outcomes	Elaboration-Based Outcomes
Relational context	Social capital theory	In organizations with dense, homophilous, and centralized formal and informal networks	In loosely coupled, decentralized formal organizational networks with dense, trust-based informal networks
Normative context	Situational strength perspective	In weak normative contexts, which rely on inconsistent, reactive, short-term, and isolated programs regarding diversity and inclusion	In strong normative contexts, characterized by consistent and proactive norms/values, policies, and long-term tradition associated with diversity and inclusion
Structural context	Status-based/organizational demography perspectives	In structurally segregated homogeneous organizations	In demographically integrated heterogeneous organizations

diversity in organizations (see Joshi, Liao, & Roh, 2011, for a detailed discussion). Theoretically, considerable sociological literature in the area of organizational demography helps explicate the effects of structural context on team diversity outcomes (see DiTomaso, Post, & Parks-Yancy, 2007; Skaggs & DiTomaso, 2004).

Taking together the broad aspects of diversity context along with the categorization- versus elaboration-based outcomes discussed earlier, Table 12.1 outlines our theoretical framework for understanding the effects of context on team diversity outcomes.

Categorization- and elaboration-based effects of relational context

We contend that diversity phenomena are often rooted in the organization's relational context. The relational embeddedness of diversity phenomena has implications for individual interactions within teams and for team-based outcomes. Social capital theory suggests that networks of relationships provide access to resources and influence social interactions among members such as communication, information sharing, and knowledge combination (Nahapiet & Ghoshal, 1998). For example, researchers have argued that networks of social relations, particularly those characterized by weak ties or structural holes, facilitate information diffusion and communication among members by minimizing redundancy (Burt, 1992). Sparse networks, characterized by loosely coupled network ties, provide more informational benefits to members by providing better access to diverse information sources for the same "cost" as closed, dense formal network ties (Burt, 1992; Coleman, 1990). Within these sparse networks, diverse team members will be able to generate links between people with different skills, information, and experience and to bridge structural holes between unconnected members (Reagans & Zuckerman, 2001). Utilizing relatively loose and decentralized network ties, diverse members can also reach outside the team and seek boundary-spanning interactions with various external stakeholders who may contribute to the team's effectiveness (Ancona & Caldwell, 1992; Westphal & Milton, 2000). Some researchers have argued that the extent to which a diverse team is able to utilize expertise within the team also depends on the team's ability to utilize its external social capital (Joshi, 2006; Joshi et al., 2011). We also surmise that the extent to which a team can draw on its external social capital will depend on the overall relational context of the organizational environment. If the relational context provides access to diverse networks, it is more likely that a diverse team would be able to maximize the benefits of its external social capital.

In contrast, in organizations with closed and dense formal networks, we would expect that diverse members may be less able to develop relational ties with other members and are limited in utilize external social capital. Researchers have argued that network closure, often characterized by high level of density of network ties and a sense of strong homogeneous community, is a feature of social relationships that is conducive to the development of high level of internal social capital within a team (Coleman, 1990; Nahapiet & Ghoshal, 1998). However, researchers have also noted that network closure is a key mechanism by which inequality is perpetuated in organizations (Ibarra, 1992, 1995; Kanter, 1977). As demonstrated in Ibarra's seminal work in this area, social network closure elicits categorization among diverse members by imposing a strong sense of common identity that distinguishes out-group from in-group members (Etzioni, 1996) and thus prevents women and minorities (who are underrepresented in positions of organizational authority) from obtaining access to social networks that are important for gaining access to information and support in organizations (Ibarra, 1992; 1995). Assuming that social interactions tend to be homophilous, we surmise that strong network closure can inhibit the development of internal social capital among diverse members and strengthen categorization-based aspects of diversity in a team.

Based on Nahapiet and Ghoshal's (1998) framework, we further posit that when diverse team members have frequent friendship-based informal contacts outside the team and develop trust based on these ties, categorization-based effects of diversity would be less prevalent in teams. For instance, researchers have noted that frequent and positive interactions outside of formal requirements of the job provide opportunities to counteract stereotypes and minimize biases against underrepresented groups (Cox, 1993). There is also a considerable amount of research evidence demonstrating that where parties trust each other, they are more likely to engage in information sharing and cooperative activities through which further trust may be generated (Fukuyama, 1995; Putnam, 1995; Tyler & Kramer, 1996). Thus, we would expect that in organizations with dense *informal* network ties based on trust and positive affect among members, specific demographic groups would be less marginalized and thus diverse teams would obtain informational benefits by elaborating diverse knowledge, information, and experience. Taking these arguments together, we propose that in relational contexts that embody loosely coupled, decentralized, formal organizational networks and dense, trust-based informal networks, team diversity will be associated with elaboration-based outcomes. In relational contexts that are characterized by dense, homophilous, and centralized formal *and* informal networks, team diversity will be associated with categorization-based outcomes.

Categorization- and elaboration-based effects of normative context

The situational strength perspective argues that the psychological meaning of situations exerts a powerful influence on individual perceptions and behaviors, and thus a strong situation induces conformity among people while a weak situation allows ambiguous interpretation and less uniformity in behaviors (Mischel, 1973, 1997). According to this perspective, we propose that, in organizations with a strong normative context, there could be strong norms regarding inclusivity, and consensus around these norms may be fostered by regular diversity training and overall organizational socialization. In this setting, within-team effects of diversity are less likely to be salient. On the other hand, in organizations with inconsistent messages and lack of consensus regarding the value of diversity and inclusion, diversity effects may be less constrained and more likely to manifest in workgroup outcomes. As elements of normative aspect of diversity context, in this chapter we consider organizational culture, diversity management practices and climate, and organizational history/tradition.

Organizational culture refers to the specific norms, values, and beliefs that are prevalent in organizations (Cox, 1993). In past research, specific aspects of organizational culture have had important implications for diversity outcomes. For example, Chatman and colleagues found that the positive effects of demographic diversity were more likely in organizations that emphasize a collectivistic orientation than in organizations that emphasize individualism and distinctiveness (Chatman, Polzer, Barsade & Neale, 1998). In their qualitative study of three culturally diverse organizations, Ely and Thomas (2001) also found that employees in organizations that emphasized integration and learning perspective were more likely to view their racial diversity as a valuable resource and achieve sustainable benefits from diversity even while performing race-neutral tasks. Apart from the content of organizational culture, we further posit that the *strength* of these aspects of the organization's normative context will have implications for diversity effects in teams.

Furthermore, like organizational culture, the organization's diversity climate and diversity management practices also represent the normative diversity context because these practices reflect the values and approach of the organization toward diversity as well as rewards and sanctions with respect to inclusive behaviors (Ely & Thomas, 2001). Like other human resource management practices, diversity management practices exert influence on employees' perceptions and behaviors related to diversity by creating an organizational diversity climate (Bowen & Ostroff, 2004). The strength of the diversity climate, which is closely associated with the implementation of these practices, may then influence variability in people's interpretation and acceptance of organizational messages toward diversity. For example, we would expect that an organization that places emphasis on inclusion and learning would adopt diversity management practices such as flexible work schedules, cross-gender/race mentoring program, or diversity management committees that create a strong diversity climate that can send a signal to employees about the organization's emphasis and values regarding diversity. We surmise that employees in such an organizational climate are more likely to embrace differences, more willing to create norms of tolerance and open communication, and more willing to solve problems collectively (Hopkins & Hopkins, 2002; Nemetz & Christensen, 1996). On the contrary, in weak situations where an organizational climate fails to deliver consistent messages and consensus regarding the value of diversity and inclusion, categorization-based diversity effects would be less constrained and would be more prevalent at the team level. Despite its direct influence on employees' attitudes and behaviors, to date, not much research attention has been focused on the effects of diversity management practices and climate on employees and work teams.

An organization's history or tradition with regard to diversity-related issues can also be viewed as a normative context that represents its current and future approach to diversity. Applying a genealogical perspective, Phillips (2005) found that gender inequality is transferred from parent law firms to progeny law firms through the replication of routines engendered by the movement of founding partners. Organizational history can, therefore, be viewed as a replication of routines across generations of employees, and the extent to which organizational founders focused on rectifying inequality and discrimination may be replicated across generations of employees. In organizations where women and minorities have historically had a voice and access to resources, gender- or race-based diversity may have more positive outcomes in comparison to organizations where women and minorities have historically been in subordinate positions. From an institutional perspective, in organizations where women and minorities have historically held leadership positions, their equal status in the organization would be legitimized (Ridgeway, 1997). These perspectives suggest that an organization's history with diversity-related issues can shape the overall stability of status differentials among demographic groups and potentially have an impact on interactional dynamics within diverse groups. Thus, organizations with a more progressive history pertaining to gender-, race-, or age-based diversity are more likely to represent "strong contexts" and facilitate elaboration-based processes within workgroups.

As Rousseau and Fried (2001) noted, considering a combination of stimuli, rather than a single stimulus in isolation, often yields more meaningful theoretical insights into organizational behavior. In support of this view, research on the effects of human resources management practices indicates that a well-combined bundle of these practices can be more conducive to organizational effectiveness than a single practice, and the performance effects of these practice bundles often exceed the additive effects of the separate practices (MacDuffie, 1995). Similarly, a set of diversity management practices that organizations implement can exert significant normative contextual influence on the occurrence of diversity effects. For instance, in a study of the efficacy of various diversity management practices in U.S. firms, Kalev and colleagues (2006) found that while the effects of certain diversity management practices (e.g., diversity training) were not significant in increasing diversity among managerial employees, the effects became significant when accompanied by the use of responsibility structures within organizations (e.g., diversity management committee, diversity staff position).

Extending these views, we surmise that while the effect of a single aspect of normative context, such as culture, may not be sufficient and instrumental enough, when bundled with other aspects such as climate, diversity management practices, and organizational tradition, synergetic effects can occur and influence diversity-related effects at the team level. Thus, in strong normative contexts, characterized by consistent and proactive norms and values, policies, and long-term tradition associated with diversity and inclusion, we are likely to see elaboration-based outcomes in diverse teams. In weak normative contexts, which rely on inconsistent, reactive, short-term, and isolated programs regarding diversity and inclusion, team diversity will predict categorization-based outcomes.

Categorization- and elaboration-based effects of structural context

The organization's structural context represents a related but distinct feature of the overall context shaping team diversity outcomes. We define the structural context in terms of organizational demography as a way to understand the impact of status and relative proportions on interactional processes between demographic groups. We consider two specific aspects of organizational demography as objective characteristics of structural context—the overall heterogeneity of the organization (in terms of the representation of demographic groups in the organization) and the level of structural integration (the representation of minority groups at higher levels in the organization) (see Cox, 1991; Joshi, 2006).

Ely's (1994, 1995) seminal work on the social construction of gender identity in organizations highlights the powerful influence that the structural context can have on perceptual processes related to gender-based identification. These studies and others (e.g., Ridgeway, 1997) show that, in organizations where subordinate groups are underrepresented, negative stereotypes and biases toward these groups are higher. A more recent study by Joshi, Liao, and Jackson (2006) found that organizational unit management demography and workgroup demographic composition influenced pay differences based on ethnicity and gender in a large sales organization. Martins and colleagues (2003) compared the effects of racio-ethnic diversity in a homogeneous and a heterogeneous organization. Results showed that the outcomes of racio-ethnic diversity were more negative in racio-ethnically homogeneous contexts than in more heterogeneous contexts.

Together these findings suggest that the degree to which an organization is structurally segregated and/or homogeneous can be a powerful influence on social category-based identification and conflict among demographic groups (Cox, 1993; Ely, 1994; Pfeffer, 1992; Wharton, 1992). In structurally segregated homogeneous organizations, the balance of power and status is skewed in favor of the dominant demographic group; these status and power differentials in this context can undermine intergroup harmony and cooperation within the workgroup (Cox, 1993). Thus, in structurally segregated homogeneous organizations, we expect that categorization-based outcomes will be more likely. On the other hand, in demographically integrated heterogeneous organizations, status cues are less likely to be correlated with demographic attributes, and the possibility of elaboration-based outcomes at the team level may be higher.

Directions for future research

We began by noting that the study of diversity context is rife with both challenges and opportunities. Below we discuss ways to overcome the challenges and pursue several lines of research that might set the stage for more context-oriented diversity research. We offer four broad methodological directions for testing the theoretical framework outlined above.

Cross-level research

The notion that context is a higher-level construct that impinges on focal phenomena at lower levels is germane to the theoretical framework developed in the previous sections (Capelli & Sherer, 1991; Mowday & Sutton, 1993). Past research on the effects of diversity context on individual- and group-level outcomes has adopted a cross-level approach (e.g., Jackson & Joshi, 2004; Joshi et al., 2006). For instance, structural features of diversity context (i.e., proportion of female and ethnic minority managers) influenced the relationship between team gender and ethnic diversity and performance outcomes (Jackson & Joshi, 2004). In addition, other aspects of the diversity context outlined above may also shape lower-level diversity outcomes. For example, with respect to normative context, the diversity climate at a firm or business-unit level can also influence the relationships at the group level. Past research has shown that in organizations with greater emphasis on a collectivistic orientation (Chatman et al., 1998) or an emphasis on learning and integration (Ely & Thomas, 2001), team diversity is more likely to have a positive impact. Similar arguments can be made with regard to the firm-level diversity climate. In firms or business units with more inclusive diversity climates, categorization-based processes based on team ethnic diversity are likely to be mitigated and the negative effects of team ethnic diversity on team performance are likely to be weaker.

While a few studies have considered cross-level context effects in diversity research, we expect that with the increasing adoption of multilevel analytic methods, this will be a fruitful area for future research. For example, applying a cross-level approach, research could test whether strength of normative context, operationalized as the unit-level variance in diversity perceptions, moderates the effects of team diversity on performance outcomes. The relational attributes of context such as the level of multiplexity, density, and reciprocity of ties in the organization may also be an interesting cross-level moderator to consider. In general, cross-level modeling procedures, such as hierarchical linear modeling, offer many possibilities to test these models.

These procedures account for the nestedness of focal phenomena in higher-level constructs and examine whether the slope coefficients within a higher-level unit are explained by its structural, normative, or relational attributes (see Joshi et al., 2011, for more details).

Qualitative research

Ethnographic and case study methodologies would be particularly important for studying some aspects of diversity context as well as for identifying specific diversity attributes that may be relevant in an organizational setting. For example, an ethnographic analysis may examine how extra-organizational events such as race riots can shape intergroup conflict and power and status differentials in organizations, as well as their effects on outcomes such as turnover and performance. Alderfer's (1987) embedded intergroup relations approach suggests that intergroup encounters in organizations mirror intergroup relationships in the larger social structure. Therefore, in identifying diversity attributes and hypothesizing about diversity effects, researchers should pay attention to community and organizational intergroup relations (Alderfer, Tucker, Morgan, & Drasgow, 1983). Furthermore, qualitative measures can be combined with quantitative methods to obtain a fuller picture of the meaning and the outcomes of diversity in organizations. For example, researchers may begin by conducting in-depth interviews and/or focus groups to identify the meaning of diversity in a particular context and develop an initial research model. Next, they may draw on existing theory to develop a more fine-grained research model and test it using survey methods. They may then return to the field to validate their findings through further qualitative probing into the phenomena. Based on these efforts, researchers may further refine and retool the initial theoretical model and pose newer research questions and extend the model to other organizational contexts. Such an approach allows for a more holistic view of organizational phenomena in general and diversity-related effects in particular.

Temporal effects

Past research on temporal effects in organizations (see Ancona, Okhyusen, & Perlow, 2001) would suggest that societal and organizational events serve as an important context shaping focal phenomena. With regard to diversity context, we might consider specific events within the organization or society as being relevant. For example, race riots in the community and civil rights legislation have received attention in past research as a basis for the formation of minority caucus groups (Alderfer & Tucker, 1996). These events mobilized the formation of an African-American identity within an organization, ultimately leading to the development of the first caucus groups in U.S. employment history (Friedman, 1996).

National events such as the September 11, 2001, terrorist attacks or Hurricane Katrina can also be viewed as important for shaping diversity dynamics. Studies in educational settings conducted in the aftermath of the 9/11 attacks found an increase in levels of inclusion and intergroup cooperation along with renewed institutional efforts to address bias and prejudice in campus communities (e.g., Miele, 2004). Thus, it is possible that certain significant events such as a war or national catastrophes might have an "inclusivity effect" and serve to minimize intergroup conflict and shape the outcomes of diversity within teams. Further research might help us understand in more detail how these events would shape intergroup relations in the workplace. In addition, events within organizations such as the appointment of a new CEO, restructuring and layoffs, corporate scandals, or a discrimination lawsuit can possibly trigger intergroup dynamics that shape team diversity outcomes. Thus, context may manifest in the form of an event with structural, normative, or relational implications and significant effects for team-level outcomes.

Temporal effects can also be examined by longitudinally modeling the effects of diversity over time. For example, researchers may examine whether changes in a firm's business strategy over time or continuous investments in diversity management (i.e., changes in the normative context) influence the effects of workforce diversity on firm performance by measuring and analyzing variables in a longitudinal timeframe. Similarly, changes in diversity effects on decision-making patterns or cooperation in dynamic business environments (e.g., the same top management team experiencing relatively munificent vs. resource-scarce environments) would also be better examined by adopting a longitudinal research design (see Joshi et al., 2011, for more details).

Comparative cross-national research

In the United States, gender, ethnicity, and age are the most widely studied aspects of diversity: over 70 percent of the studies conducted in U.S. settings have accounted for these diversity attributes (Joshi & Roh, 2007). These diversity attributes have a unique place in the legislative, cultural, and historic context in the United States. However, across countries some of these attributes are less likely to be meaningful and other attributes may gain more meaning. Trends in worker migration and immigration have made diversity-related considerations fairly prevalent across the globe. In countries like South Africa, India, and Japan and in the European Union, various aspects of culture and history can shape specific aspects of diversity (Mor-Barak, 2005). In a study of the transfer of diversity management practices from U.S. parent companies to the United Kingdom, Ferner, Almond, and Colling (2005) found that the transfer and implementation of diversity management practices were complicated by the differing meanings of diversity within the United States and United Kingdom.

As another illustration, in a Dutch context, when Schippers and colleagues examined the effects of an overall diversity measure (including age, gender, education, and team tenure) on team outcomes, neither the overall diversity measure nor each aspect of diversity emerged as significant (Schippers, Den Hartog, Koopman, & Wienk, 2003). Research on the meaning of diversity in the Netherlands suggests that the Dutch associate the term "diversity" with "ethnic differences" or "immigrants" (see Mor-Barak, 2005). The diversity attributes considered by Schippers and colleagues may be less salient in the Dutch setting than perhaps national origin- or ethnicity-based diversity. These findings suggest that geographic location can alter the nature of the structural, normative, and relational aspects of diversity context and thus the very meaning of diversity in organizations.

Our review of diversity research suggests that, to date, the research has taken a United States-centric perspective both in the conceptualization of diversity, leading to the inclusion of certain diversity variables over others, as well as in terms of the type of dependent variables considered. Cross-national comparative approaches to the study of diversity would offer new theoretical insights and allow us to reframe research questions. For example, in the U.S. context it is often hypothesized that age-based differences in teams serve as a basis for social categorization and conflict. Therefore, researchers expect that age diversity would be detrimental to team performance. However, in many Asian settings, age diversity may *not* translate into conflict at the team level because of prevalent age-related cultural norms that dictate deferential intergenerational interactions. In fact, age-diverse teams in these contexts would represent greater cohesion and fewer process losses than teams that are homogeneous in terms of age. Thus, a cross-cultural comparison of various diversity attributes may yield new insights and highlight relevant boundary conditions regarding diversity effects in workgroups. With the growing internationalization of the management research community, taking into account the unique aspects and outcomes of diversity in non-United States settings may change the nature of the debate around the pros and cons of diversity that has evolved in the United States.

Conclusion

The study of diversity has a long history, but academic efforts to understand diversity outcomes in the workplace have generated mixed empirical evidence. We argue that this mixed terrain of findings indicates the importance of contextual considerations in diversity research. We argue that to better understand the influence of diversity context, a tripartite conceptualization of diversity context in terms of structural, relational, and normative attributes is necessary. Our theoretical framework proposed that the structural, relational, and normative features of diversity context have key implications for categorization versus elaboration outcomes in teams. To set the stage for more context-oriented diversity research, we also suggest several methodological directions for future studies to examine the many manifestations of diversity context, such as research examining the cross-level effects of various aspects of diversity context on outcomes at lower levels of analysis, qualitative research, studies considering temporal factors in accounting for diversity outcomes, and comparative cross-national research. We hope that the theoretical framework and methodological guidelines presented in this chapter can open new avenues and be a road map for future context-oriented research endeavors.

References

Alderfer, C. P. (1987). An intergroup perspective on group dynamics. In J. W. Lorsch (Ed.), *Handbook of organizational behavior* (pp. 190–222). Englewood Cliffs, NJ: Prentice-Hall.

Alderfer, C. P., & Tucker, R. C. (1996). A field experiment for studying race relations embedded in organizations. *Journal of Organizational Behavior, 17,* 43–57.

Alderfer, C. P., Tucker, R. C., Morgan, D. R., & Drasgow, F. (1983). Black and white cognitions of changing race relations in management. *Journal of Occupational Behavior, 4,* 105–136.

Ancona, D. G., & Caldwell, D. F. (1992). Bridging the boundary: External activity and performance in organizational teams. *Administrative Science Quarterly, 37*, 634–665.

Ancona, D. G., Okhuysen, G. A., & Perlow, L. A. (2001). Taking time to integrate temporal research. *Academy of Management Review, 26*, 512–529.

Bamberger, P. (2008). Beyond contextualization: Using context theories to narrow the micro-macro gap in management research. *Academy of Management Journal, 51*, 839–846.

Bowen, D. E., & Ostroff, C. (2004). Understanding HRM-firm performance linkages: The role of the "strength" of the HRM system. *Academy of Management Review, 29*, 203–221.

Burt, R. S. (1992) *Structural holes*. Cambridge: Cambridge University Press.

Capelli, P., & Sherer, P. (1991). The missing role of context in OB: The need for a meso-level approach. In L. L. Cummings & B. M. Staw (Eds.), *Research in organizational behavior* (Vol. 13, pp. 55–110). Greenwich, CT: JAI Press.

Chatman, J. A., Polzer, J. T., Barsade, S. G., & Neale, M. A. (1998). Being different yet feeling similar: The influence of demographic composition and organizational culture on work processes and outcomes. *Administrative Science Quarterly, 43*, 749–780.

Coleman, J. S. (1990). *Foundations of social theory*. Cambridge: Harvard University Press.

Cox, T. (1993). *Cultural diversity in organizations: Theory, research and practice*. San Francisco: Berrett-Koehler Publishers.

Cox, T. (1991). The multicultural organization. *Academy of Management Executive, 5*, 34–47.

DiTomaso, N., Post, C., & Parks-Yancy, R. (2007). Workforce diversity and inequality: Power, status, and numbers. *Annual Review of Sociology, 33*, 473–501.

Ely, R. (1994). The effects of organizational demographics and social identity on relationships among professional women. *Administrative Science Quarterly, 39*, 203–238.

Ely, R. (1995). The power in demography: Women's social constructions of gender identity at work. *Academy of Management Journal, 38*, 589–634.

Ely, R. (2004). A field of group diversity, participation in diversity education programs, and performance. *Journal of Organizational Behavior, 25*, 755–780.

Ely, R., & Thomas, D. (2001). Cultural diversity at work: The effects of diversity perspectives on wok group processes and outcomes. *Administrative Science Quarterly, 46*, 229–273.

Etzioni, A. (1996). The responsive community: A communitarian perspective. *American Sociological Review, 61*, 1–11.

Ferner, A., Almond, P., & Colling, T. (2005). Institutional theory and the cross-national transfer of employment policy: The case of "workforce diversity" in US multinationals. *Journal of International Business Studies, 36*, 304–321.

Friedman, R. (1996). Defining the scope and logic of minority and female network groups: can separation enhance integration? In K. M. Rowland & G. R. Ferris (Eds.), *Research in personnel and human resource management* (Vol. 9, pp. 307–349). Greenwich, CT: JAI Press.

Fukuyama, F. (1995). *Trust: The social virtues and the creation of prosperity*. New York: Free Press.

Granovetter, M. S. (1992). Problems of explanations in economic sociology. In N. Nohria & R. Eccles (Eds.), *Networks in organizations: Structure, form and action* (pp. 25–56). Cambridge, MA: Harvard University Press.

Hopkins, W. E., & Hopkins, S. A. (2002). Effects of cultural recomposition on group interaction processes. *Academy of Management Review, 27*(6), 521–553.

Ibarra, H. (1992). Homophily and differential returns: Sex differences in network structure and access in an advertising firm. *Administrative Science Quarterly, 37*, 422–447.

Ibarra, H. (1995). Race, opportunity, and diversity of social circles in managerial networks. *Academy of Management Journal, 38*, 673–703.

Jackson, S. E., & Joshi, A. (2004). Diversity in social context: A multi-attribute, multi-level analysis of team diversity and sales performance. *Journal of Organizational Behavior, 25*, 675–702.

Jackson, S. E., & Joshi, A. (2010). Work team diversity. In S. Zedeck (Ed.), *APA handbook of industrial and organizational psychology* (Vol. 2, pp. 651–686). Washington, D.C.: American Psychological Association.

Jehn, K. A., Northcraft, G. B., & Neale, M. A. (1999). Why differences make a difference: A field study of diversity, conflict, and performance in workgroups. *Administrative Science Quarterly, 44*, 741–763.

Johns, G. (2006). The essential impact of context on organizational behavior. *Academy of Management Review, 31*, 386–408.

Joshi, A. (2006). The influence of organizational demography on the external networking behavior of teams. *Academy of Management Review, 31*, 583–595.

Joshi, A., Dencker, J. C., Franz, G., & Martocchio, J. J. (2010). Unpacking generational identities in organizations. *Academy of Management Review, 35*(3), 392–414.

Joshi, A., Liao, H., & Jackson, S. E. (2006). Cross-level effects of workplace diversity on sales performance and pay. *Academy of Management Journal, 49*, 459–481.

Joshi, A., Liao, H., & Roh, H. (2011). Bridging domains in workplace demography research: A review and reconceptualization. *Journal of Management, 37*, 521–552.

Joshi, A., & Roh, H. (2007). Context matters: A multilevel framework for work team diversity research. In J. J. Martocchio (Ed.), *Research in personnel and human resources management* (pp. 1–48). Greenwich, CT: JAI.

Joshi, A., & Roh, H. (2009). The role of context in work team diversity research: A meta-analytic review. *Academy of Management Journal, 52*(3), 599–627.

Kalev, A., Dobbin, F., & Kelly, E. (2006). Best practices or best guesses? Assessing the efficacy of corporate affirmative action and diversity policies. *American Sociological Review, 71*, 589–617.

Kanter, R. M. (1977). *Men and women of the corporation*. New York: Basic Books.

Kirkman, B. L., Tesluk, P. E., & Rosen, B. (2004). The impact of demographic heterogeneity and team leader-team member demographic fit on team empowerment and effectiveness. *Group and Organization Management, 29*, 334–368.

Kochan, T., Bezrukova, K., Ely, R., Jackson, S., Joshi, A., Jehn, K., et al. (2003). The effects of diversity on business performance: Report of the Diversity Research Network. *Human Resource Management, 42*, 3–21.

Leonard, J. S., Levine, D. I., & Joshi, A. (2004). Do birds of a feather shop together? The effects on performance of employees' similarity with one another and with customers. *Journal of Organizational Behavior, 25*, 731–754.

MacDuffie, J. P. (1995). Human resource bundles and manufacturing performance: Organizational logic and flexible production systems in the world auto industry. *Industrial and Labor Relations Review, 48*, 199–221.

Martins, L. L., Miliken, F. J., Wiesenfeld, B. M., & Salgado, S. R. (2003). Racioethnic diversity and group member's experience. *Group and Organization Management, 28,* 75–106.

Miele, C. (2004). Building community by embracing diversity. *Community College Journal of Research and Practice, 28,* 133–140.

Mischel, W. (1968). *Personality and assessment.* New York: Wiley.

Mischel, W. (1973). Toward a cognitive social learning conceptualization of personality. *Psychological Review, 80,* 252–283.

Mischel, W. (1997). Personality dispositions revisited and revised: A view after three decades. In R. Hogan, J. Johnson, & S. Briggs (Eds.), *Handbook of personality psychology* (pp. 113–132). New York: Academic Press.

Mor-Barak, M. E. (2005). *Managing diversity: Toward a globally inclusive workplace.* Thousand Oaks, CA: Sage Publications.

Mowday, R. T., & Sutton, R. I. (1993). Organizational behavior: Linking individuals and groups to organizational contexts. *Annual Review of Psychology, 44,* 195–229.

Nahapiet, J., & Ghoshal, S. (1998). Social capital, intellectual capital, and the organizational advantage, *Academy of Management Review, 23,* 242–266.

Nemetz, P. L., & Christensen, S. L. (1996). The challenge of cultural diversity: Harnessing a diversity of views to understand multiculturalism. *Academy of Management Review, 21,* 434–462.

Pelled, L. H., Eisenhardt, K. M., & Xin, K. R. (1999). Exploring the black box: An analysis of work group diversity, conflict, and performance. *Administrative Science Quarterly, 44,* 1–28.

Pfeffer, J. (1992). *Managing with power: Politics and influence in organizations.* Boston, MA: Harvard Business Press.

Phillips, D. J. (2005). Organizational genealogies and the persistence of gender inequality: The case of Silicon Valley law firms. *Administrative Science Quarterly, 50,* 440–472.

Putnam, R. (1995). Bowling alone: America's declining social capital. *Journal of Democracy, 6,* 65–78.

Reagans, R., & Zuckerman E. W. (2001). Networks, diversity, and productivity: The social capital of corporate R&D teams. *Organization Science, 12,* 502–517.

Ridgeway, C. L. (1997). Interaction and the conservation of gender inequality: Considering employment. *American Sociological Review, 62,* 218–235.

Rousseau, D. M., & Fried, Y. (2001). Location, location, location: Contextualizing organizational research. *Journal of Organizational Behavior, 22,* 1–13.

Schippers, M. C., Den Hartog, D. N., Koopman, P. L., & Wienk, J. A. (2003). Diversity and team outcomes: The moderating effects of outcome interdependence and group longevity and the mediating effect of reflexivity. *Journal of Organizational Behavior, 24,* 779–802.

Skaggs, S., & DiTomaso, N. (2004). Understanding the effects of workforce diversity on employment outcomes: A multidisciplinary and comprehensive framework. *Research in the Sociology of Work, 14,* 279–306.

Tsui, A. S., & Gutek, B. (1999). *Demographic differences in organizations: Current research and future directions.* Lanham, MD: Lexington Books.

Tyler, T. R., & Kramer, R. M. (1996). Whither trust? In R. M. Kramer & T. R. Tyler (Eds.), *Trust in organizations: Frontiers of theory and research* (pp. 1–15). Thousand Oaks, CA: Sage.

Van Der Vegt, G. S., Van De Vliert, E., & Huang, X. (2005). Location-level links between diversity and innovative climate depend on national power distance. *Academy of Management Journal, 48,* 1171–1182.

Van Knippenberg, D., De Dreu, C. K. W., & Homan, A. C. (2004). Work group diversity and group performance: an integrative model and research agenda. *Journal of Applied Psychology, 89,* 1008–1022.

Van Knippenberg, D., & Schippers, M. C. (2007). Workgroup diversity. *Annual Review of Psychology, 58,* 2.1–2.27.

Westphal, J. D., & Milton, L. P. (2000). How experience and network ties affect the influence of demographic minorities on corporate boards. *Administrative Science Quarterly, 45,* 366–398.

Wharton, A. (1992). The social construction of gender and race in organizations: A social identity and group mobilization perspective. In P. Tolbert & S. Bacharach (Eds.), *Research in the sociology of organizations* (Vol. 10, pp. 55–84). Greenwich, CT: JAI Press.

CHAPTER 13

Diversity Cognition and Climates

Daan van Knippenberg, Astrid C. Homan *and* Wendy P. van Ginkel

Abstract

Demographic diversity at work can yield performance benefits but also invite psychological disengagement and be a source of interpersonal tension. In managing this double-edged sword of demographic diversity, the role of diversity cognition (beliefs, attitudes) and climates seems particularly promising, and in this chapter we take stock of the state of the science in this area. We conclude that research in diversity cognition and climates will benefit from more attention to diversity as a group characteristic to complement the dominant focus on demographic dissimilarity, and from more attention to the potential positive effects of diversity to complement the dominant emphasis on diversity's potential negative effects. This is a conclusion that by and large holds across the study of individual diversity beliefs and attitudes, individual diversity climate perceptions, and shared diversity climate perceptions.

Key Words: diversity, diversity beliefs, diversity climate, diversity attitudes, group norms, relational demography, shared cognition, teams, workgroups

---

Societies and organizations are becoming increasingly diverse. As a result, diversity at work is on the agenda of science and practice more than ever before (Harrison & Klein, 2007). As research evidence regarding the influence of diversity in the workplace is accumulating, it has become abundantly clear that diversity at work is no trivial matter. Diversity can be associated with worrisome outcomes like interpersonal tensions and discrimination, but also with synergetic outcomes such as increased creativity and team performance (van Knippenberg & Schippers, 2007; Williams & O'Reilly, 1998). The recognition that diversity thus is not only a fact of organizational life, but also a double-edged sword (Milliken & Martins, 1996) that requires careful management has given rise to the question of how the potential benefits of diversity can be harvested and its potentially harmful effects addressed.

A strong theme in this respect is that diversity is more likely to be associated with positive outcomes and less likely to be associated with negative outcomes the more individuals, teams, and organizations are favorably disposed toward diversity—the more favorable individual diversity beliefs and attitudes, and the more favorable team and organizational diversity climates, the more favorable the effects of diversity (Avery, 2011 Avery & McKay, 2006; Cox, 1993; Ely & Thomas, 2001; van Knippenberg & Haslam, 2003). This focus on diversity cognition and climates seems to hold particular promise from the perspective of applied science, because cognitions and climates more than many other moderators of the effects of diversity (cf. van Knippenberg, De Dreu, & Homan, 2004) should be *manageable*. That is, an understanding of the contingencies of diversity's influence in terms of cognition and climates should yield more actionable knowledge than some of the alternative angles on the issue (cf. van Knippenberg, Dawson, West, & Homan, 2011). In view of this promise of the focus on diversity cognition and climates, in this chapter we take stock of the state of the science in research in diversity beliefs, attitudes, and climates, both to determine where we currently stand and to identify where we might consider going.

In reviewing this literature, it becomes apparent that a division can be made between research focused on individual diversity beliefs and attitudes, research involving individuals' perceptions of team or organizational diversity climate (i.e., psychological climate), and research analyzing diversity climate as a shared team or organizational characteristic. We structure our review of the empirical research in diversity cognition and climate accordingly. After taking stock of the empirical evidence, we outline not only what may be concluded from the accumulated evidence in these areas but also how bridging these different areas of research invites important questions for future research. Before we proceed to this review, however, we first present a concise discussion of the team diversity literature more broadly to clarify the backdrop against which research in diversity cognition and climates is played out.

What is the issue? The double-edged sword of diversity

Diversity refers to a characteristic of a social group (team, organization); it is the extent to which there are differences between group members on any given attribute (Jackson et al., 1992; van Knippenberg & Schippers, 2007; cf. Harrison & Klein, 2007). While the number of attributes for which diversity is studied is gradually growing, the vast majority of diversity research can be classified as studying either the demographic attributes of gender, cultural background (i.e., ethnicity, race, nationality; Stahl, Maznevski, Voigt, & Jonson, 2010), and age, or the more job-related attributes of functional background and tenure (van Dijk, van Engen, & van Knippenberg, 2012). This division in demographic and job-related attributes also reflects a division in the issues that are typically understood to be on the agenda. Job-related diversity is more typically seen as speaking to the potential benefits of diversity (even when evidence suggests it may also have detrimental effects; van Knippenberg & Schippers, 2007), whereas demographic diversity more typically is understood to represent the double-edged sword of diversity in full, with the potential to be disruptive as well as beneficial. As research in diversity cognition and climate revolves around demographic diversity, we focus our analysis on demographic diversity. We do note, however, that a strong case can be made that what holds for demographic diversity by and large also holds for job-related dimensions of diversity, even when the latter may be more easily associated with positive rather than negative outcomes than the former (van Knippenberg et al., 2004).

The double-edged sword of demographic diversity is captured by the two perspectives on team and workgroup diversity that have dominated much of diversity research: the social categorization (and similarity-attraction) perspective and the informational resource perspective (van Knippenberg & Schippers, 2007; Williams & O'Reilly, 1998). The social categorization perspective points to diversity's potential to invite subgroupings along demographic lines, both in terms of "us versus them" perceptions (cf. diversity as separation; Harrison & Klein, 2007) and in terms of behavioral patterns that favor interaction with demographically similar others over interaction with demographically dissimilar others. Such subgroupings may invite a number of undesirable consequences. For one, it may reduce the attractiveness of the team or workgroup to its members, resulting in lower group cohesion and lower identification with and commitment to the team and organization (cf. Chattopadhyay, Tluchowska, & George, 2004). Subgroup thinking may also render interpersonal tensions more likely between demographically different team members, giving rise to interpersonal conflicts (Jehn, Northcraft, & Neale, 1999), and ultimately potentially to discrimination against dissimilar, "out-group," others (Tajfel & Turner, 1986; Turner, Hogg, Oakes, Reicher, & Wetherell, 1987). The tendency to see dissimilar others as not part of one's own (sub)group also invites a closing of the mind to communication with dissimilar team members, thus imposing a major obstacle to achieving the synergetic performance outcomes that could also derive from diversity (van Knippenberg et al., 2004). Team demographic homogeneity, in contrast, would make it easier to experience a sense of identity as one group and to collaborate in interpersonal harmony. The social categorization understanding of diversity thus first and foremost sees diversity as a potentially disruptive influence (Williams & O'Reilly, 1998) and raises the question of how diversity can be managed to prevent this negative impact from materializing.

The informational resource (or information/decision making; Williams & O'Reilly, 1998) perspective, in contrast, sees diversity as a source of task-relevant information, expertise, and perspectives (cf. diversity as variety; Harrison & Klein, 2007) and therefore as an asset to teams. By virtue of the larger pool of informational resources that diverse groups as compared with homogeneous groups are proposed to have at their disposal, diverse groups have greater ability to solve complex problems, reach high-quality decisions, and produce creative ideas and innovative products. Put differently, viewing groups as information processing systems (De Dreu, Nijstad, & van Knippenberg, 2008; Hinsz, Tindale, & Vollrath, 1997), diversity is proposed to add to the raw material available to the group. The informational resource perspective thus points to the positive performance effects of diversity (whereas it does not speak to the more attitudinal and interpersonal outcomes of diversity) and raises the question of how diversity may be managed to realize these performance benefits.

Some researchers tend to see the informational resource quality of diversity primarily in job-related dimensions of diversity and not so much in demographic diversity, and indeed the evidence in favor of the performance benefits of job-related diversity is stronger and more consistent (Joshi & Roh, 2009). There is a persuasive case for the informational value of demographic diversity too, however (Cox, 1993; Earley & Mosakowski, 2000; Ely & Thomas, 2001; Tsui & O'Reilly, 1989). Moreover, there is reason to believe that disruptive social categorization processes are more of a concern in realizing the synergetic potential of demographic diversity as an informational resource than for job-related diversity (van Knippenberg et al., 2004; cf. Fiske, 1998; Roberson & Block, 2001). In combination, this suggests that the double-edged sword of diversity is particularly salient for demographic attributes.

Not surprisingly, perhaps, demographic diversity, and first and foremost cultural diversity and gender diversity, for which these concerns may loom particularly large, is the primary working field of research in diversity cognition and climates. In the following, we review research in diversity cognition and climates following the distinction introduced earlier between individual diversity beliefs and attitudes, individual perceptions of diversity climate, and diversity climate as team or organizational characteristic. In reviewing this literature, we prioritize the overarching issue of the double-edged sword of diversity, considering how diversity cognition and climates may moderate the relationship between diversity and positive as well as negative outcomes of diversity.

Individual diversity beliefs and attitudes

A longstanding proposition in psychology is that people's perceptions and actions at least in part are shaped by their beliefs and attitudes (Eagly & Chaiken, 1993; Fishbein & Ajzen, 1975). From the perspective of a desire to understand influences on people's engagement with diversity, it is therefore a straightforward extension of this body of research to the prediction that beliefs about diversity and attitudes toward diversity shape individuals' responses to diversity. Accordingly, the more favorable individuals' beliefs and attitudes are toward diversity, the more likely diversity would be associated with positive outcomes and the less likely it would be associated with negative outcomes. The available research does seem to support this prediction (Stegmann & van Dick, 2009), but the evidence is less abundant and less robust than one might like (and think).

Conceptualization and measurement of diversity beliefs and attitudes: More than psychometrics to consider

One of the main themes in past research in diversity beliefs and attitudes has been to develop their measurement (e.g., De Meuse & Hostager, 2001; Hostager & De Meuse, 2002; Linnehan, Konrad, Reitman, Greenhalgh, & London, 2003; Montei, Adams, & Eggers, 1996). A first and important thing to note in reference to these measures is that they vary quite a bit in the understanding they convey of what it means to have favorable beliefs about or attitudes toward diversity. This variation is reflected both in the implied understanding of what is favorable and in the implied understanding of what diversity refers to. Indeed, the main issue to consider regarding measures of diversity beliefs and attitudes would not seem to be their psychometric properties, but rather the implied understanding of diversity and favorability. In short, it seems that the field has invested in measurement of constructs that are not conceptualized in a consensually shared way.

For some, favorability seems to revolve in whole or part around the absence of negative outcomes, whereas for others favorability explicitly refers to positive effects of diversity. Moreover, in some measures "diversity" primarily refers to demographically dissimilar others—accepted "code" in everyday language, but not the group characteristic diversity is understood to be in applied psychology—whereas other measures refer to diversity as a group characteristic. Moreover, whereas from the perspective of research in applied psychology measurement would ideally target beliefs and attitudes concerning diversity in the workplace in particular, some measures take a more general or explicitly societal perspective on diversity or demographic dissimilarity (e.g., Stanley, 1996).

At the one extreme lies research in diversity beliefs that is rooted in van Knippenberg and Haslam's (2003) analysis (Homan, Greer, Jehn, & Koning, 2010; Homan, van Knippenberg, Van Kleef, & De Dreu, 2007a; van Dick, van Knippenberg, Hägele, Guillaume, & Brodbeck, 2008; van Knippenberg, Haslam, & Platow, 2007). This line of research defines diversity beliefs as attribute-specific beliefs (e.g., gender diversity beliefs) about the value of diversity to workgroup functioning, and understands these to range from belief in the value of diversity (e.g., group performance benefits from gender diversity) to belief in the value of similarity (e.g., group performance suffers from gender diversity). Indeed, in their initial measurement in this research line, diversity beliefs were simply measured with two questionnaire items to this effect (van Knippenberg et al., 2007). Clearly, diversity is understood here as a group characteristic and not as referring to the quality of being demographically dissimilar.

At the other extreme is research that relies on discrimination scales to measure attitudes toward diversity (e.g., Dickson, Jepsen, & Barbee, 2008). Such measures at best can reflect the absence of discrimination as a favorable outcome, and concern attitudes toward demographically dissimilar others much more than toward diversity as a group characteristic. Most measures (and thus most analyses of diversity beliefs and attitudes) seem to lie somewhere in between these two extremes. Many studies seem to be closer to the study of prejudice and discrimination (e.g., Linnehan et al., 2003; Strauss & Sawyerr, 2009) than to inclusion of beliefs in the positive effects of diversity (e.g., De Meuse & Hostager, 2001). What is being studied in research in diversity beliefs and attitudes may thus vary more than the common usage of the labels "diversity beliefs" and "diversity attitudes" suggests.

This is no minor point. As outlined by van Knippenberg and Haslam (2003; van Knippenberg et al., 2007) in their development of the diversity beliefs concept, there are two key issues here. First, one's beliefs about demographically dissimilar others cannot be equated with one's beliefs about diversity. As an illustration, consider a Swedish person who does not speak any other language than Swedish. This person may hold no biases whatsoever against, say, Italians who do not speak Swedish and hold nothing close to a belief that speaking Swedish is superior to speaking Italian. Yet, this person may hold a strong belief that team diversity through a combination of Swedish members who only speak Swedish and Italian members who do not speak Swedish would be very bad for performance. That is, this individual may hold no negative stereotypic beliefs about or prejudiced attitudes toward Italians or toward an inability to speak Swedish, yet have strong beliefs in the value of similarity in language abilities when it comes to team composition. As this example illustrates, diversity introduces considerations that demographic dissimilarity *per se* does not, and attitudes toward the one cannot be equated with attitudes toward the other.

Whereas this is perhaps an obvious example, there is no reason why the same could and would not hold for the relationship between people's attitudes toward other demographic groups and people's beliefs about team diversity in those demographic attributes. The point here is that while it may not be unreasonable to expect that prejudiced attitudes are more likely to go hand in hand with negative than with positive attitudes toward diversity, the one cannot be treated as a proxy for the other. As a case in point, van Knippenberg and Haslam (2003) discuss evidence that diversity beliefs and intergroup bias can be independent, illustrating that it would be advisable to treat beliefs and attitudes about diversity as a group characteristic as different from beliefs and attitudes concerning demographically dissimilar others.

Second, from the absence of negative attitudes (e.g., prejudice), the presence of positive attitudes cannot be concluded. Empirical research in diversity beliefs suggests, for instance, that beliefs in the value of diversity are only quite modestly negatively correlated with beliefs in the value of similarity (van Knippenberg et al., 2007; cf. Stegmann & van Dick, 2009). This is no measurement problem, but rather reflects the fact that while believing in the value of, for instance, gender diversity to team performance would be at odds with believing in the value of gender similarity to team performance, not believing in the value of gender diversity does not automatically imply believing in the value of similarity; one could also believe that gender diversity is irrelevant for team performance (cf. van Knippenberg & Haslam, 2003). Positive beliefs and attitudes reflecting the perceived value in diversity thus need to be assessed in their own right and cannot be assumed from the absence of negative attitudes toward diversity.

These observations regarding the measurement of diversity beliefs and attitudes may be important because they should reflect on the predictive value of diversity beliefs and attitudes. As outlined by Fishbein and Ajzen (1975), beliefs and attitudes should be more predictive of the behavior of interest the more they specifically concern the behavior of interest (i.e., your attitude toward going out for dinner to a seafood restaurant should be more predictive of whether or not you actually have dinner at a seafood restaurant than your attitude toward going out for dinner more generally). If the diversity cognition in question is about diversity rather than about demographically dissimilar others, it should be more predictive of responses to diversity, and if the diversity cognition in question actually concerns positive effects of diversity or positive engagement with diversity, it should be more predictive of positive diversity outcomes than when favorability is only understood as the absence of a negative belief or attitude.

Of course, this is not to say that attitudes toward demographically dissimilar others are not important. They may be tremendously important, and in a desire to understand worrisome outcomes like discrimination at work they are likely to play a key role. By implication, through their relationship with such issues as prejudice and discrimination they may also play an important role in shaping the experience of being in a demographically diverse team or organization. Importantly, however, if one's aim is not so much to (only) understand discrimination and the psychological experience of being demographically dissimilar, but to (also) understand the performance of diverse teams, beliefs and attitudes regarding demographically dissimilar others will capture only part of the issue. In that sense, a focus on dissimilarity rather than diversity may be misspecified when one's focus is on the influence of team diversity (cf. the difference between diversity and relational demography; Chattopadhyay et al., 2004; van Knippenberg & Schippers, 2007).

The issue here is perhaps best captured by the Categorization-Elaboration Model (CEM) of workgroup diversity and performance (van Knippenberg, De Dreu, & Homan, 2004). Integrating and extending social categorization and informational resource perspectives on diversity, the CEM outlines how intergroup biases engendered by diversity may disrupt the group information elaboration (i.e., exchange and integration) that is core to realizing the synergetic benefits of diversity as an informational resource (e.g., Homan, Hollenbeck, Humphrey, van Knippenberg, Ilgen, & Van Kleef, 2008; Homan, van Knippenberg, Van Kleef, & De Dreu, 2007b; Kooij-de Bode, van Knippenberg, & van Ginkel, 2008; for a review, see van Knippenberg & van Ginkel, 2010). Preventing intergroup biases thus is an important element in realizing the potential benefits of diversity. Importantly, however, the CEM also outlines how preventing intergroup biases in and of itself is not enough to stimulate information elaboration. Benefiting from diversity as an informational resource is an effortful and deliberate process that requires active engagement with diversity and does not occur automatically in the absence of disruptive influences. Engendering information elaboration requires more than just the absence of intergroup biases; it is also contingent on such factors as team members' motivation and ability to engage in group information elaboration (van Knippenberg et al. 2004).

Illustrations of this issue can be found in research in decision-making groups with distributed information (i.e., informational diversity). To make high-quality decisions on the basis of distributed information, group members need to exchange and integrate their unique information and perspectives—information elaboration is key. Yet, the "base rate" finding in research in distributed information is that groups are poor users of their distributed informational resources. They exchange distributed information less than they should, and to the extent that they do exchange it, they integrate it less in final group products (e.g., decisions) than they should (Stasser, 1999). A study by van Ginkel and van Knippenberg (2008) explains how this is often due to the fact that group members lack the understanding of the importance of information elaboration to high-quality group performance and thus the motivation to engage in this effortful process. Rather, group members tend to focus on reaching consensus with minimal disagreement along the way, which leads groups to underuse distributed information that could argue against emerging group consensus. In an experimental demonstration of this process, van Ginkel and van Knippenberg showed that groups that were educated about the importance of information elaboration were more likely to engage in information elaboration (as evidenced in behavioral coding of group interaction) than control groups that lacked this understanding. The end result was that the former groups outperformed the latter in terms of the quality of the decision reached. In a similar vein, Scholten, van Knippenberg, Nijstad, and De Dreu (2007) looked at the role of process accountability, which is an influence increasing the motivation to form accurate judgments and decisions (Lerner & Tetlock, 1999). Scholten and colleagues experimentally showed that groups with distributed information collectively processed this information to a greater extent and reached higher-quality decisions when they were held accountable for the decision-making process than when they were not held accountable. Establishing similar motivational influences in the field, Kearney, Gebert, and Voelpel (2009) studied the moderating role of team members' need for cognition. Need for cognition is an individual difference variable capturing the motivation to carefully process information and form accurate judgments and decisions, and Kearney and colleagues showed that diversity was more likely to stimulate information elaboration when team members had a higher need for cognition. In short, information elaboration requires the motivation to actively engage in the process (cf. De Dreu et al., 2008).

Diversity beliefs and attitudes that are associated with reduced intergroup biases may thus set the stage for the positive performance outcomes of diversity, but in and of themselves may not be enough to engender the information elaboration process required to realize these synergetic benefits. We do note, however, that in terms of the more affective-evaluative outcomes associated with diversity (e.g., cohesion, commitment), beliefs and attitudes associated with reduced bias may be closer to the target than for diversity's effects on team performance, as they speak more directly to the psychological experience of being in a diverse group than to the process required to realize diversity's performance benefits. The importance of beliefs and attitudes that actually include the value of diversity as compared with beliefs and attitudes (only) capturing issues related to intergroup biases may thus be more evident in the performance outcomes of diversity than in the more attitudinal and perceptual outcomes associated with diversity. Indeed, the latter are also more closely associated with demographic dissimilarity (i.e., relational demography) than the former (cf. Chattopadhyay et al., 2004). Even so, we should be open to the possibility that a focus on stimulating the positive effects of diversity is more effective in preventing the negative effects of diversity than a focus on (only) the potential negative outcomes associated with diversity (van Knippenberg & van Ginkel, 2010; van Knippenberg, van Ginkel, & Homan, 2008).

To summarize, there is great variety in the understanding of what it means to have favorable diversity beliefs and attitudes. We propose that from the perspective of the understanding and management of diversity as a group characteristic, it is essentially that conceptualizations and associated measurement refer to diversity as a group characteristic, and understand favorability to refer to positive effects of diversity. This is not to say that there is no place for consideration of the negative effects of diversity or of demographic dissimilarity, but if diversity beliefs and attitudes do not include reference to diversity's potential positive effects, there seems to be an important disconnect between the proposition that there is value in diversity (cf. Cox, 1993) and the conceptualization and operationalization of the beliefs and attitudes that are proposed to be conducive to realizing this value.

Consequences of diversity beliefs and attitudes

As will be clear from the discussion so far, the one key reason to be interested in diversity beliefs and attitudes is that the potential negative effects of diversity should be less likely and the potential positive effects of diversity should be more likely to occur the more that diversity beliefs and attitudes are favorable to diversity. In considering the evidence speaking to this hypothesis, a methodological note of caution is in order as several studies assess consequences of diversity cognition in single-source surveys relying on percept–percept relationships. Such common method assessment may inflate relationships (Podsakoff, MacKenzie, Lee, & Podsakoff, 2003). Moreover, in many cases these outcome ratings arguably are closer to being part of diversity cognition than to being their consequence. Linnehan and colleagues (2003; cf. Linnehan, Chrobot-Mason, & Konrad, 2006), for instance, assessed behavioral intentions associated with dissimilar others as a consequence of diversity attitudes. Arguably, however, behavioral intentions are conceptually and empirically closer to attitudes than to the actual behavior they target. In a related vein, Tropp and Bianchi (2006) assessed how valuing diversity predicts interest in contact with culturally dissimilar others, but again this may be conceptually and empirically closer to being part of diversity cognition than to the actual behavior implied. That being said, there also is evidence that does not suffer from the drawbacks of relying on single-source, percept–percept relationships.

Across a survey and an experimental study, van Knippenberg and colleagues (2007) found that individuals' beliefs in the value of diversity (gender diversity in the survey, personality diversity in the experiment) moderated the relationship between team diversity and individuals' identification with the team: diversity was positively related to identification for individuals believing in the value of diversity, whereas it tended to be negatively related to identification for individuals believing in the value of similarity. Homan and colleagues (2007a) extended these findings to team performance, showing that gender-diverse teams made better use of team informational diversity when team members believed in the value of gender diversity rather than gender similarity, and moreover showed that this effect was mediated by team information elaboration. Speaking to some of the intergroup processes underlying the influence of value-in-diversity beliefs, Homan, Greer, Jehn, and Koning (2010) showed that diversity beliefs moderate the relationship between the extent to which team composition potentially invites subgroup perceptions (i.e., includes diversity faultlines; Lau & Murnighan, 1998) and actual subgroup perceptions, such that "us–them" perceptions were less likely to obtain the more team members believed in the value of diversity.

Speaking more to attitudes toward demographically dissimilar others than to diversity, and corroborating our earlier observations regarding different understandings of favorability of diversity attitudes, there is also evidence that not all favorable attitudes toward demographically dissimilar others are created equal when it comes to their effects. Research in intergroup relations makes a distinction between colorblind and multicultural perspectives on how best to approach racially dissimilar others (e.g., Park & Judd, 2005). Colorblindness essentially implies downplaying racial and ethnic differences—acting as if they are not there and do not matter—whereas multiculturalism implies recognizing and celebrating group differences. In reference to our earlier discussion, we may note the parallels between approaching demographically dissimilar others primarily from the perspective of preventing discrimination versus approaching demographically dissimilar others from the perspective of a belief in the value in diversity. In line with this earlier discussion, research in colorblind and multicultural beliefs shows that colorblindness is associated with more racial bias than multiculturalism (Richeson & Nussbaum, 2004; Wolsko, Park, Judd, & Wittenbrink, 2000). Bringing this research explicitly to diversity in the workplace, Plaut, Thomas, and Goren (2009) showed that majority White multicultural beliefs positively predicted minority members' psychological engagement with the job, while majority colorblind beliefs negatively predicted minority engagement.

In combination, then, these findings suggest that beliefs and attitudes concerning the value in diversity more than concerning the absence of discrimination are important in the psychological experience of being part of a diverse team or organization for oneself and fellow team members as well as for the performance of diverse teams. At the same time, we may note that the evidence is more modest than perhaps we should like, and more research is clearly needed to bolster the confidence in the current conclusions. Of particular importance here would be research contrasting (1) beliefs and attitudes concerning diversity versus demographic dissimilarity, (2) beliefs and attitudes concerning positive versus negative effects of diversity, and (3) affective, evaluative, and attitudinal outcomes versus team performance outcomes.

Determinants of diversity beliefs and attitudes

Research in the determinants of diversity beliefs and attitudes is relatively abundant compared with research in their consequences. A key theme in this respect, and of clear importance, is that women's and cultural minorities' diversity attitudes tend to be more positive (Kossek & Zonia, 1993; Linnehan et al., 2003; Mor Barak, Cherin, & Berkman, 1998; Strauss & Connerley 2003; Strauss, Sawyerr, & Oke, 2008). One reading of this is one of instrumentality (Linnehan et al., 2003): the unfortunate reality of organizational demography is that women and minorities have more to gain from favorable perspectives on diversity than Caucasian men, and therefore they may hold more favorable diversity attitudes. In line with this reading, Sawyer, Strauss, and Yan (2005) found that Whites held more positive diversity attitudes the higher they scored on the individual difference measure of self-transcendence, which captures the disposition to move beyond selfish concerns, whereas minority group members' attitudes were relatively positive irrespective of self-transcendence (i.e., this would be consistent with the reading that for Whites it is the "other" that benefits from favorable perspectives on diversity).

An alternative reading is that members of demographic groups that typically find themselves in minority positions (i.e., cultural minorities, women) as a consequence learn through their greater experience with diversity and demographically different others to appreciate diversity more than members of majority groups (cf. Tsui, Egan, & O'Reilly, 1992). Providing indirect support for this line of reasoning, Kossek and Zonia (1993) and van Knippenberg and colleagues (2007) reported that gender diversity in one's work environment is positively related to one's diversity attitudes and value-in-diversity beliefs (cf. McKay & Avery, 2006; van Knippenberg & Haslam, 2003). Or put differently, these studies provide direct support for the conclusion that experience with diversity is positively related to diversity beliefs and attitudes.

Of course, the one does not exclude the other in that the influences of instrumentality and experience may be at least partly independent and co-occur. Moreover, experience and instrumentality may feed into each other. Instrumental considerations regarding diversity may invite or discourage experience with diversity, and experience with diversity may change one's thinking about the instrumentality of diversity practices or diversity itself. Even so, one may wonder whether the operationalizations of diversity attitudes in these studies might speak to the matter in that they could have distinct "instrumental" or "experience" content that renders the one or the other interpretation more likely. The Kossek and Zonia (1993) measure, for instance, includes attitudes toward measures that would at least at first blush seem to benefit minorities more than majorities, such as recruiting minority group members. At the same time, however, the very same measure also yields a gender diversity influence that is perhaps easier to understand in terms of experience than in terms of instrumentality. The measure used by Strauss and colleagues (Sawyerr et al., 2005; Strauss & Connerley, 2003; Strauss et al., 2008) seems to include both instrumental and experience (e.g., whether or not one seeks out diverse encounters speaks to experience but potentially also to instrumentality). Other studies include measures that tap into the perceived value of diversity for the collective (group, organization) and thus could be understood to reflect instrumentality, but rather instrumentality for the team or organization rather than for the self or one's own demographic group (Mor Barak et al.'s, 1998, personal diversity value factor; van Knippenberg et al.'s, 2007, diversity beliefs). Sampling from these different measures, then, if anything it would seem that different measures do not uniquely tap into instrumental or experience influences on diversity attitudes, but rather are subject to both influences.

In a sense complementing the notion of learning from experience is the issue of more formal training and education as determinants of diversity attitudes. One of the more frequently adopted actions in managing diversity seems to be diversity training (Rynes & Rosen, 1995), and an obvious question is whether such training is able to change diversity attitudes. There seems to be surprisingly little evidence either way in this respect (cf. Pendry, Driscoll, & Field, 2007; Roberson, Kulik, & Pepper, 2001). In a similar vein, one may raise the question of whether diversity attitudes may be shaped by formal education. While indeed there is some evidence to that effect (Hostager & De Meuse, 2008), here too we seem to know surprisingly little. Given that training and education may speak relatively directly to the issue of managing diversity beliefs and attitudes, there would seem to be a clear need for more systematic study of the role of diversity training and diversity education (e.g., as part of a management curriculum) in fostering pro-diversity beliefs and attitudes.

The other main theme in research in the determinants of diversity beliefs and attitudes is the study of personality and individual differences. The "Big Five" personality factors agreeableness and openness to experience have, for instance, been linked to favorable diversity attitudes (Strauss et al., 2003; Strauss & Connerley, 2003), as have tolerance for ambiguity (Chen & Hooijberg, 2000; Strauss et al., 2003; cf. Strauss & Sawyerr, 2009) and self-transcendence (Sawyerr et al., 2005; Strauss et al., 2008). Authoritarianism (Strauss et al., 2003), self-enhancement (Sawyerr et al., 2005), and religious fundamentalism (Strauss & Sawyerr, 2009) have been linked to less favorable attitudes. It is less clear why these personality traits feed into diversity attitudes—are they relatively independent of experience with diversity, or are they more likely to evolve through the interplay of personal disposition and experience? We should at least be open to the possibility that individual difference variables relate to diversity cognition because they both predict experiences with diversity and the subjective interpretation of these experiences (van Knippenberg et al., 2008). For instance, individuals with greater openness to experience may be more likely to seek out experiences in demographically diverse teams, may because of their greater openness have more positive experience with the team's diversity, and may be more likely to interpret these experiences in ways that contribute to positive attitudes toward diversity. These issues are important to consider also because they would point to possible integrations of research in the personality determinants of diversity cognition and research in diversity training and education.

Individual diversity climate perceptions

Research in diversity beliefs and attitudes revolves around the individual's own beliefs or attitudes. Research in diversity climate, in contrast, revolves more around the perceived perspective of the organization (or team). In that sense, it need not be a perspective that is shared by the individual himself or herself; indeed, it may for some purposes even be construed as something that the individual is "subjected to" by virtue of working in the organization.

Organizational climate is "the atmosphere that employees perceive is created in their organizations by practices, procedures, and rewards" (Schneider, Gunnarson, & Niles-Jolly, 1994, p. 18). As an organizational (or team) characteristic, climate is a perception shared by the team or organizational membership (more on this below), but perceived climate can also be studied at the individual level, and is then also called psychological climate rather than organizational (or team) climate (Glick, 1985; Schneider & Reichers, 1983). Diversity climate thus refers to a specific subset of the more general climate construct, and can refer to either individual perceptions of the organization's or team's diversity climate (psychological diversity climate) or perceptions that are shared by the members of the organization or team in question (organizational or team diversity climate). Our concern in this section is with psychological diversity climate.

Consistent with this general perspective on climates, Gelfand, Nishii, Raver, and Schneider (2005) defined diversity climate as "employees' shared perceptions of the policies, practices, and procedures that implicitly and explicitly communicate the extent to which fostering and maintaining diversity and eliminating discrimination is a priority in the organization" (p. 104). While this definition recognizes diversity itself as a part of the diversity climate, like conceptualizations of diversity attitudes, it stresses preventing discrimination as a negative outcome more than stimulating positive outcomes of diversity, and these emphases are also reflected in the measurement of diversity climate—be it psychological or organizational.

Conceptualization and measurement of diversity climate perceptions: Again, more than psychometrics

Measures of diversity climate may be used to assess individual and socially shared climate perceptions with equal ease—assessing shared climate merely has the additional requirement of justifying aggregation of individual perceptions empirically (Klein & Kozlowski, 2000). In that sense, the current discussion of the measurement of psychological diversity climates by and large holds for the measurement of organizational diversity climates.

In considering measurement of diversity climates, the same key issues encountered for the measurement of diversity beliefs and attitudes arise. Diversity climate measures often seem concerned more with demographic minorities than with diversity, and with the prevention of negative outcomes (unfairness, discrimination) more than with the realization of the value in diversity. A common element of several measures is, for instance, the assessment of human resources policies targeted at minorities, such as equality in support for women and minorities (e.g., in terms of release time and graduate assistant support in an academic department; Kossek & Zonia, 1993), equal opportunity policies (Hicks-Clarke & Iles, 2000), and policies prohibiting discrimination on the basis of sexual orientation (Button, 2001). As a case in point regarding the emphasis on minorities and discrimination in these measures, Walsh, Matthews, Tuller, Parks, and McDonald (2010) propose a measure of equal opportunity climate that explicitly targets the occurrence of discrimination at work, for which the questionnaire items do not appear to be so different from many items used to assess diversity climate. As per Walsh and colleagues' discussion, equal opportunity climate should be different from diversity climate in that central to diversity climate should be harnessing the value in diversity more than the absence of discrimination. Again, we would definitely not argue with the importance of preventing unfairness and discrimination, but if one's interest also includes an understanding of how to realize the value in diversity in full, these measures seem to lack a clear focus on diversity and positive outcomes (cf. Ely & Thomas, 2001).

Another issue that is worth noting in this respect is that a number of diversity climate measures in fact are a mix of the perceived organizational perspective on diversity (e.g., human resources policies, the organization's attitude toward diversity) and the individual's own diversity attitudes (Hicks-Clarke & Iles, 2000; Kossek & Zonia, 1993; Mor Barak et al., 1998). When aggregated to the team or organizational level, this is reasonable when considering a shared attitude as part of the team or organizational climate (even though it shifts the referent away from the organization to the self), but when focusing on individual climate perceptions, it confounds two different issues: own attitude and perceived perspective of the organization. This is an important issue both from the perspective of conceptual clarity and on empirical grounds, as research in the determinants of attitudes and perceived climates shows that some determinants may have opposing relationships with the two: women and cultural minorities tend to have more favorable attitudes toward diversity (or more often demographic dissimilarity), but less favorable perceptions of diversity climate (see below).

It is also interesting to note that the emphasis in research in diversity climate is on organizational climate, whereas the vast majority of studies in diversity are concerned with team and workgroup diversity. Given that climate can also be meaningfully considered at the team level (e.g., Anderson & West, 1998), an obvious implication for research in diversity climate would be to study diversity climate at the team level more. For one, this would include determining whether there is meaningful between-team variation in diversity climate within the same organization to establish that diversity climate too can be considered to be a team-level influence. This would be an important step in bringing diversity climate research closer to the study of the team diversity–performance relationship that lies at the core of much of the research in diversity. As it is, research in diversity climate speaks more to issues of organizational demography (i.e., the experience of different demographic groups within the organization) and relational demography (i.e., the influence of demographic dissimilarity) than to issues of diversity. As noted before, we fully recognize that diversity in this sense has somewhat of a double meaning in that in practice it often refers not only to diversity as a group characteristic but also to issues of organizational and relational demography. Again, however, we contend that truly valuing diversity revolves around engaging with diversity as a group characteristic and not only with addressing issues of organizational and relational demography.

Whereas the majority of diversity climate studies indeed target the organization, an exception is work on perceived group openness to diversity by Hobman, Bordia, and Gallois (2003, 2004). While the concept naming may suggest otherwise, openness to diversity is conceptualized as climate and refers to the team rather than the organization. The shift from the organizational level to the team level also implies, however, that the emphasis inevitably is less on "systemic," formal human resources practices, and more on behavioral practices—recurrent or typical patterns of interaction that capture the group's climate. This has led Raver, van Knippenberg, Mayer, Nishii, and Vestal (2010) to understand this measure to capture descriptive group norms more than climate, as descriptive norms (i.e., what is typical behavior; Cialdini, Bator, & Guadagno, 1999) may be closer to what this measure captures than the notion of climate as including more formal practices and procedures. Regardless of whether one favors the climate or norm label, Hobman and colleagues' measure captures the perception that group members make extra efforts to listen to dissimilar others in the group and enjoy doing jobs with dissimilar others in the group (interestingly, the measurement developed by Hobman et al. also seems to have a more positive "tone" than other climate measures). Considering this inevitable shift away from formalized practices and procedures when one moves from the organizational to the team level of analysis, it would also seem important for future research to carefully consider the possibility that team and organizational climate may have different effects at least in part because typically only organizational climate would capture the more formalized, systemic aspect of climates.

In sum, then, our observations here echo our earlier observations regarding the conceptualization and measurement of diversity beliefs and attitudes. Conceptualizations and operationalizations of diversity climate tend to emphasize organizational demography more than diversity, and the prevention of negative effects more than the pursuit of positive effects. Interestingly, and also a bit worrisome, is that this seems to reflect organizational practice. In an insightful qualitative analysis of team diversity *perspectives* (arguably overlapping with the climate concept, but lacking the emphasis on more formalized practices), Ely and Thomas (2001) describe three types of perspectives they encountered. The discrimination and fairness perspective with its emphasis on preventing discrimination and unfairness to minority groups essentially is the perspective that seems to be captured most by existing diversity climate measures (and diversity attitude measures, for that matter). It is also the perspective that Ely and Thomas note was most common among the organizations they encountered. The access and legitimacy perspective views diversity as a means to connect with minority group markets (i.e., gain access and establish legitimacy in these markets). The integration and learning perspective views diversity as an informational resource for learning that may help improve team performance. The integration and learning perspective in that sense is more of a true diversity perspective rather than an organizational demography perspective. Interestingly and importantly, Ely and Thomas conclude that it is also the only perspective that was associated with performance benefits of diversity.

While we are careful not to base too bold conclusions on qualitative research like that by Ely and Thomas, we do note that their conclusions are highly supportive of the more general argument that diversity climates (and diversity beliefs and attitudes) are more conducive to the realization of the potential benefits of diversity when they include a focus on positive effects of diversity and focus more on diversity than on demographic dissimilarity. As for diversity beliefs and attitudes, it would thus seem important for future research to complement existing measures with measures with a stronger focus on diversity and its positive effects. Indeed, as with diversity beliefs and attitudes, quantitative research systematically contrasting the influence of climate aspects concerning positive versus negative effects, and concerning diversity versus demographic dissimilarity would be highly valuable.

Consequences of perceived diversity climate

In taking stock of research in the consequences of individual perceptions of diversity climates, we run into some of the same problems as for diversity beliefs and attitudes. A first is the fact that a number of studies concern percept–percept relationships from single-source surveys (e.g., Mor Barak & Levin, 2002). Another problem is the study of perceived climate "main effects" rather than climate as a moderator of the influence of diversity or demography (e.g., Hicks-Clarke & Iles, 2000; cf. Stegmann & van Dick, 2009). The issue here is that this does not establish a link between the influence of diversity climate and diversity. That is, direct relationships between perceptions of climate and outcomes of interest could also reflect the influence of the overall positivity of the climate that would equally inspire a more homogeneous or a more diverse workforce. In a related vein, studying only minority group members (e.g., Buttner, Lowe, & Billings-Harris, 2010; Button, 2001) makes it impossible to conclude that findings are diversity-related. What is needed to establish that the influence of diversity climate is associated with diversity are climate-by-diversity interactive influences on outcomes.

Fortunately, there is such evidence for interactions of climate and demography. Avery, McKay, Wilson, and Tonidandel (2007), for instance, show that the greater absenteeism observed among African-Americans was less pronounced the more the organization was perceived to value diversity, and McKay, Avery, Tonidandel, Morris, Hernandez, and Hebl (2007) found that African-Americans' commitment was higher and turnover intentions were lower with a more favorable diversity climate. Tropp and Bianchi (2006) found that while minority group members were less likely to perceive that diversity is valued than majority group members, the extent to which they perceived that diversity was valued was more predictive of their interest in out-group contact.

Providing a more indirect link with diversity or demography, Triana and García (2009) found that perceptions of support for diversity moderated the relationship between racial discrimination and procedural justice perceptions such that the perception of a favorable diversity climate buffered against the negative impact of the experience of discrimination. Shifting the referent from the organization to coworkers, Cunningham and Sartore (2010) showed that coworker support for diversity predicted self-reported extra-role behavior aimed at ensuring the success of diversity initiatives. In a related vein, Linnehan and colleagues (2003) observed that subjective norms of referent others (i.e., not limited to or necessarily including coworkers) predict behavioral intentions concerning demographic dissimilarity.

The available evidence thus supports the hypothesis that the favorability of a psychological diversity climate moderates the relationship between demographic background and outcomes, such that outcomes for minority group members are more positive as a diversity climate is perceived to be more favorable. Future research extending these findings more explicitly to the experience of diversity and relational demography and not only demography *per se* would be important in developing the study of psychological diversity climate.

Determinants of perceptions of diversity climate

As already alluded to, research in the determinants of psychological diversity climates provides an important counterpoint to research in the determinants of diversity beliefs and attitudes. Whereas diversity beliefs and attitudes are more positive for women and cultural (racial, ethnic) minority members than for Caucasian men, women and minority group members tend to have less positive perceptions of climate (Kossek & Zonia, 1993; Mayhew, Grunwald, & Dey, 2006; Mor Barak et al., 1998; Mor Barak & Levin, 2002; Tropp & Bianchi, 2006). These findings make perfect sense when one realizes that the daily realities of an organization's diversity climate are likely to be most salient to underrepresented groups, whereas majority group members may either be less aware of these realities or more favorable in their assessment as they are less affected themselves. In addition, one may also view it as a direct consequence of the more favorable attitudes of women and minority group members: the same climate would seem subjectively less favorable the higher one's standard for how it should be (i.e., as reflected in one's diversity beliefs and attitudes). In that sense, the disparity between findings for diversity beliefs and attitudes on the one hand and psychological diversity climate on the other also begs the question to what extent they reflect differential reactions to what is objectively the same experience and to what extent they reflect reactions to objectively different experiences. In part, this suggests studying the relationship between diversity beliefs and attitudes, and psychological diversity climate while taking demographic group membership into account.

In a different take on the same issue, Rau and Hyland (2003) presented experimental evidence from a study of college recruitment brochures that women and cultural minority group members are more attracted to organizations espousing valuing diversity than men and cultural majority group members. That is, if an organization is seen to value diversity, it elicits responses from women and cultural minority group members that are consistent with their more positive attitudes toward diversity and demographic dissimilarity. In a related line of research, Avery (2003) showed that Black students more than White students are attracted to racially diverse (Black and White) as compared with White organizations, especially when the organization's management is also diverse.

These findings thus suggest that if an organization is truly supporting diversity, women and minority group members do respond more positively, in line with findings for diversity attitudes. Viewed through this lens, the robust finding that women and minority groups typically have less favorable diversity climate perceptions could be taken to imply that many organizations do not meet the expectations of underrepresented groups in this respect.

Shared diversity climate

As we observed above, much of what is on the agenda in diversity research actually concerns processes and outcomes at the team and workgroup level rather than the individual level of (relational) demography. This renders the study of shared diversity climate—team rather than psychological climate—particularly relevant, as this connects most directly with the primary level of analysis in diversity research. That is, when we focus on the moderating role of diversity cognition and climate in the diversity–performance relationship, the primary level of analysis is the group. Accordingly, the primary level of analysis of diversity cognition and climates is that of the group or team (Raver et al., 2010). Whereas the study of individual diversity beliefs and attitudes and psychological diversity climate thus connects primarily with issues of organizational and relational demography, the study of shared diversity cognition and climate is the "natural home" of the study of diversity.

The measurement of shared climates is not an issue warranting separate consideration, because it relies on the same measures as those used for psychological climate and as only addition includes statistically legitimizing aggregation of individual perceptions to the group or organizational level through statistics testifying to the sharedness of perceptions (Klein & Kozlowski, 2000). Even so, related to this issue of aggregation is the fact that teams and organizations may differ in the extent to which climate perceptions are shared, and this is a variable worthy of consideration for more than methodological reasons. As Schneider, Salvaggio, and Subirats (2002) outline, sharedness of climate perceptions may be conceptualized as reflecting climate *strength*, and stronger climates can be expected to exert a stronger influence. A very similar argument is made about the social sharedness of task-relevant cognition, where greater sharedness of team and task cognition is associated with stronger effects of these cognitions (Tindale & Kameda, 2000). Sharedness of diversity cognitions and climates thus would also be a factor worth considering, on the expectation that diversity cognition and climate exert a stronger influence on team process and performance the greater the level of social sharedness (i.e., the stronger the climate; van Knippenberg et al., 2008). We are not aware of any empirical study of this issue for diversity cognition or climate specifically, however.

Consequences of shared diversity climates

"Research in shared diversity climate also has it share of studies focused on climate main effects that offer no basis for the conclusion that the climate effects are related to the effects of diversity (e.g., Gilbert & Ivancevich, 2001). There are also a number of studies, however, yielding support for the hypothesis that the relationship between diversity and outcomes is more positive with more favorable diversity climates. Cunningham (2009) found that the interaction between racial diversity and diversity climate predicted performance such that the relationship between diversity and performance was more positive with a more favorable diversity climate. Similarly, Gonzalez and DeNisi (2009) observed that diversity climate moderated the relationship between cultural and gender diversity and unit performance such that these relationships were more positive with a more favorable climate. Providing the shift to the effects of diversity at the team level that is important for a more direct connection with the main body of research in diversity, Raver and colleagues (2010) showed that gender diversity norms (or climate; operationalized with the Hobman et al., 2004, measure) moderated the relationship between gender diversity and team information elaboration and performance (and that information elaboration mediated this interactive influence on performance).

In addition, there is cross-level evidence that minority and majority demographic groups are differentially affected by diversity climate. McKay, Avery, and Morris (2008) showed that minority group sales performance lagged behind majority group performance at the store level, but less so the more favorable the store diversity climate. That is, a favorable diversity climate was more important to minority group than to majority group members. Gonzalez and DeNisi (2009) study also yielded modest evidence for cross-level interactions of shared diversity climate and relational and categorical demography on commitment, identification, and intention to quit, suggesting that a favorable climate is more important for members of underrepresented groups. These findings in a sense complement and extend the findings for psychological climate discussed earlier. At the same time, however, they raise some questions. As research in psychological climate suggests that demographic groups differ in their climate perception, one may wonder whether these cross-level findings reflect differential responses to the same perceived climate, or differences in climate perceptions not captured by the shared climate measures.

In sum, then, whereas the current evidence does not qualify as overwhelming, the available evidence does support the conclusion that shared diversity climate does indeed moderate the influence of both diversity and (relational) demography. Findings for psychological climate discussed in the previous section do, however, beg the question of what exactly sharedness reflects in a diverse organization. The evidence from research in psychological climate is quite robust in showing that perceptions of diversity climate differ as a function of minority versus majority status. This suggests the possibility that statistical evidence pertaining to levels of sharedness is dominated by the majority group (i.e., which, after all, typically is the largest demographic group within the organization). That is, "hidden" within shared climate measures might be a lack of sharedness of perceptions between demographic groups. It would therefore be highly worthwhile to study shared climate not only from the perspective of the organization or team as a whole, but also from the perspective of different demographic groups nested within the larger whole. Providing evidence for the potential value of such a "subgroup climate" approach, McKay, Avery, and Morris (2009) showed that considering subordinates' and managers' climate perceptions in interaction added to the explanatory value of their diversity climate model. Clearly, subordinates versus managers is a qualitatively different subgrouping within the organization than distinguishing demographic groups, but the study by McKay and colleagues study does show that there may be value added in a "subgroup climate" approach.

Determinants of shared diversity climates

Gelfand and colleagues' (2005) definition of diversity climate indicates that creating and maintaining diversity itself can be seen as part of a favorable diversity climate, and research in psychological climates by Avery (2003) and Rau and Hyland (2003) showed that more diverse organizations are more attractive to members of underrepresented groups. Research in diversity beliefs and attitudes also provides modest evidence that experience with organizational or workgroup diversity can render one more favorably disposed toward diversity. It stands to reason, then, that organizational diversity is a predictor of organizational diversity climate (McKay & Avery, 2006). The available evidence seems to both support and qualify this proposition.

Pugh, Dietz, Brief, and Wiley (2008) found that the proportion of racial minority employees predicted diversity climate, but less so with a higher proportion of racial minority members in the environment in which the organization is embedded (i.e., which would presumably reflect lack of choice in establishing organizational diversity, or which would require higher diversity to stand out favorably). Related to the notion of creating and maintaining diversity, Herdman and McMillan-Capehart (2009) conceptualized human resources actions such as diversity programs as precursors rather than as part of the diversity climate (which they understood more as the attitude of the organization toward diversity), and showed that such human resources actions are predictive of diversity climate, and more so when management is diverse and holds relational values that emphasize the value of human resources. The findings by both Pugh and colleagues (2008) and Herdman and McMillan-Capehart (2009) may thus be understood as suggesting that diversity and diversity-related human resources practices may indeed be positively associated with the perceived diversity climate, but more so when they are perceived to reflect the organization's genuine intention to embrace diversity.

While these determinants of diversity climate in a sense are implied by the definition of diversity climate (i.e., human resources practices, diversity), a separate question that yet needs to be considered is what leads to sharedness of perceptions of diversity climate. Following from the current discussion, we may note that there are at least two components to this question. The first is the question of what makes diversity climates strong (cf. Dickson, Resick, & Hanges, 2006). The second and perhaps at least as important question is what leads different subgroups within the organization (e.g., demographic groups, subordinates vs. management) to agree or disagree in their climate perceptions.

Conclusion and future directions: Toward integration across levels and literatures

Our review of the empirical evidence regarding the role of diversity beliefs and attitudes, psychological diversity climates, and shared diversity climates yields some consistent conclusions both in terms of the state of our knowledge and in terms of what we would deem the more important avenues for future research. A first and obvious conclusion is that the available evidence supports the hypothesis that diversity cognition and climates moderate the relationship of diversity and demographic dissimilarity with outcomes of interest. At the same time, we may note that the number of studies that actually tested diversity by diversity cognition or climate interactions, or demography by diversity cognition or climate interactions, is less substantial than one would expect on the basis of the frequency with which diversity attitudes and climates seem to be invoked in discussions of diversity management. In view of the importance that diversity cognition and climates seem to be accorded in diversity discourse, it would seem appropriate—if not to say wise—to increase the empirical knowledge base in which this discourse can be grounded.

In further developing the study of diversity cognition and climates, the issue that consistently stands out in all three areas reviewed—diversity beliefs and attitudes, psychological diversity climate, and shared diversity climate—is that the field currently pays more attention to demographic dissimilarity than to diversity in the assessment of cognition and climates and to influences that fall within the fields of organizational and relational demography more than in the field of diversity. Probably at least in part as a consequence, the potential negative effects of diversity and demographic dissimilarity are also emphasized much more in the conceptualization and measurement of cognitions and climates as well as in the study of their consequences than their potential positive effects. Perhaps the most obvious extension of this line of research thus is the systematic study of the influence of cognition and climates focusing on diversity versus demographic dissimilarity and focusing on positive outcomes versus negative outcomes. Directly related to this, the outcomes studied (i.e., as a consequence of diversity and diversity climate) should ideally also contrast outcomes where the absence of negative effects would be favorable (e.g., discrimination) and outcomes where positive effects of diversity can actually be expected (e.g., creativity). Exploring these issues would also imply bridging levels of analysis by focusing on both team-level outcomes (e.g., performance) and individual-level outcomes (e.g., identification). By implication, such efforts would also help bridge the research fields of diversity, relational demography, and organizational demography.

An issue that stands out as warranting at least further attention to determine whether or not it is important is the disparity between diversity attitudes and psychological climates (i.e., members of underrepresented groups have more favorable diversity attitudes, but less favorable assessments of diversity climate). In short, we need to know whether attitudes color assessments of climates, climates are more objectively different for minority group and majority group members, or both. Interestingly, there are also hints that truly favorable diversity climates (e.g., those characterized by a high level of diversity across the hierarchy and genuine embracing of diversity as a positive influence) may be assessed more favorably by members of minority groups than by members of majority groups. In short, it would be important to know if and how diversity climates can be created that are truly appreciated by all.

For research to develop answers to this question, an obvious starting point would seem to be the assessment of both diversity attitudes and diversity climate perceptions. This would allow for the examination—for majority group members as well as for minority group members—of the relationship between the two, as well as for the analysis of the demographic determinants of the one controlling for the other. While clearly this is not enough to address the issue in full, it is a start in determining to what extent attitudes color climate perceptions. To address that particular issue, ideally research would disentangle organizational practices as objective givens (i.e., the absence or presence of a formalized human resources practice) from their subjective evaluations (i.e., which could be an outcome of the interactive effect of diversity attitude and practice). Research could also assess the influence of variations in different climate aspects (i.e., particular practices) on majority and minority group perceptions to perhaps identify types of practices that are especially associated with diverging minority and majority group perceptions. Insights from such research would provide the building blocks to develop theory regarding the requirements of diversity climates to appeal to minority and majority group members alike.

In this respect, we would also hazard the proposition that the "perfect climate" is unlikely to be found in today's organizations, and that it is not just a matter of identifying the ideal combination in a series of studies assessing current organizational practices. The tentative suggestion that what makes climates more appealing to minority group members may make it less appealing to majority group members implies that we may need new theory and innovative approaches to diversity to create climates that would appeal to all demographic groups involved. Research therefore also should include experimental tests to investigate the influence of approaches to diversity that may not yet be (common enough) practice in the field (cf. Homan et al., 2007a; Rau & Hyland, 2003). One issue that seems to be on the agenda here is that diversity may become more subjectively "threatening" to majority group members (cf. van Knippenberg et al., 2004) with greater representation of minority group members in the organization (cf. Tsui et al., 1992). As organizations develop toward climates that are more favorable toward diversity in the sense that they are more diverse, organizational practices may increasingly also need to cater to the concerns of traditional majority groups to keep all organizational members positively engaged. For obvious reasons, this has not been the key concern in research in diversity cognition and climates, but it seems it would be a positive development in more than one way if it became more of a concern in future research. Based on the current analysis, we would expect that part of addressing this issue would be greater emphasis on diversity (i.e., as a group characteristic) and its positive effects and less on demography and discrimination.

Another issue to emerge from an integrative view across the subfields of inquiry reviewed is the issue of sharedness of diversity climate perceptions. Findings for psychological climate suggest this is an issue not only of climate strength, but also of agreement between subgroups within the organization. At the least, we would need to know whether indicators of sharedness truly reflect sharedness of perceptions across the board, or predominantly sharedness among majority group members. That is, research in shared climates would need to include assessment not only of overall sharedness, but also of within-subgroup sharedness and of between-subgroup differences in climate perceptions. Directly related to this, it would be valuable to explore the determinants and consequences of sharedness of perceptions between subgroups. The question of determinants here probably links directly back to the issue of differences in diversity attitudes and climates between demographic groups, and opens up the possibility that what makes climates more subjectively favorable for minority group members may sometimes make them less subjectively favorable for majority group members. The question of the determinants of between-subgroup sharedness thus directly connects with the question of what would be perceived to be a favorable climate by all.

Where the consequences of inter-subgroup sharedness are concerned, the issue may be quite complex too. From a climate strength or shared cognition perspective, the most obvious expectation would be that greater sharedness results in stronger climate effects. However, from a psychological climate perspective, the prediction could actually be that the sharedness of perceptions within the own subgroup may be more important in predicting outcomes than the climate experienced by other subgroups, as the former would reflect the socially shared reality of the demographic in-group and may be a more proximal influence on individuals' attitudes and behavior (cf. Turner et al., 1987). As the experience of diversity as well as dissimilarity most likely is contingent on experience interacting with dissimilar others, however, a third proposition may be that inter-subgroup sharedness of climate perceptions may actually be more predictive of outcomes than intra-subgroup sharedness of perceptions. That is, given that perceptions will vary somewhat from individual to individual, it may be particularly important that there is no systematic influence of demographic background in these variations for positive outcomes of diversity and dissimilarity to obtain. Of course, the possible influences of between-subgroup sharedness outlined here may co-occur. Moreover, the consequences of between-subgroup sharedness need not be limited to these three possibilities. We advance them here as perhaps the more obvious starting points to explore this issue rather than suggesting that these considerations are likely to capture the issue in full.

To these three issues that emerge as key themes from our review of the field, we may add a fourth not suggested by any of the subfields reviewed in particular. There is a tendency to understand diversity cognition and climate in a way that implicitly sees diversity or demographic dissimilarity as a uniform thing. Some conceptualizations focus only on one diversity attribute (typically cultural diversity, but not exclusively; e.g., Button, 2001), others on more than one attribute (cultural and gender), but treating these as essentially the same in the sense that what holds for the one would hold for the other. Yet, it seems the case that there is not only between-organization variation in how supportive they are of diversity, but also within-organization variation in how supportive they are of different dimensions of diversity. In terms of explicit attention to diversity in organizational discourse and human resources practices, gender diversity and cultural diversity seem to receive the most attention, and for instance diversity in age or sexual orientation substantially less so. One may point to a variety of reasons for these variations, and our issue here is not to argue with the policies or politics behind such differences in emphasis. We do note, however, that from a multi-attribute perspective on diversity, the potentially important question is how such within-organization variations affect the experience of diversity and dissimilarity and their consequences.

Several considerations may be relevant in this respect. For one, individuals may be minority group members in terms of more than one attribute. It may be hard for an individual to experience the organization's climate as positive if the climate is supportive of the one attribute (e.g., gender) but not the other (e.g., cultural background), especially when the individual is a minority group member on both attributes (e.g., an Asian woman). Moreover, organizational members may approach organizational diversity practices with some cynicism in that they may be enforced by external regulations rather than intrinsically motivated, and thus reflect legislation more than organizational commitment to diversity. Policies against discrimination, for instance, frequently seem informed by the legal reality to a substantial degree (cf. Ely & Thomas, 2001). This raises the possibility that individuals respond more favorably to such policies when they are also accompanied by policies regarding diversity attributes that are less represented in the legal domain (cf. Eisenberger, Cummings, Armeli, & Lynch, 1997). Such considerations suggest that if in research we differentiate climates more to be attribute-specific (i.e., gender diversity climate, cultural diversity climate, etc.), we may find that there are climate-by-climate interactions in predicting outcomes.

In conclusion, we can end on an upbeat note. Clearly, diversity cognition and climate is a field of inquiry where substantially more work needs to be done to develop our understanding of what shape diversity cognition and climate would ideally take to be conducive to positive outcomes for all individuals involved. Even so, the available evidence clearly speaks to the promise of a focus on diversity cognition and climate. In that sense, the current state of the science extends a clear invitation to research in diversity and relational demography to engage more fully with diversity cognition and climate, and we hope the current chapter is understood as the call to arms it is intended to be.

References

Avery, D. R., & McKay, P. F. (2006). Target practice: An organizational impression management approach to attracting minority and female job applications. *Personnel Psychology, 59*, 157–187.

Anderson, N. R., & West, M. A. (1998) Measuring climate for work group innovation: Development and validation of the team climate inventory. *Journal of Organizational Behavior, 19*, 235–258.

Avery, D. R. (2003). Reactions to diversity in recruitment advertising—are differences black and white? *Journal of Applied Psychology, 88*, 672–679.

Avery, D. R. (2011). Support for diversity in organizations: A theoretical exploration of its origins and offshoots. *Organizational Psychology Review, 1*, 239–256.

Avery, D. R., McKay, P. F., Wilson, D. C., & Tonidandel, S. (2007). Unequal attendance: The relationship between race, organizational diversity cues, and absenteeism. *Personnel Psychology, 60*, 875–902.

Buttner, E. H., Lowe, K. B., & Billings-Harris, L. (2010). Diversity climate impact on employee of color outcomes: Does justice matter? *Career Development International, 15*, 239–258.

Button, S. B. (2001). Organizational efforts to affirm sexual diversity: A cross-level examination. *Journal of Applied Psychology, 86*, 17–28.

Chattopadhyay, P., Tluchowska, M., & George, E. (2004). Identifying the ingroup: A closer look at the influence of demographic dissimilarity on employee social identification. *Academy of Management Review, 29*, 180–202.

Chen, C. C., & Hooijberg, R. (2000). Ambiguity intolerance and support for valuing-diversity interventions. *Journal of Applied Social Psychology, 30*, 2392–2408.

Cialdini, R. B., Bator, R. J., & Guadagno, R. E. (1999). Normative influences in organizations. In L. L. Thompson, Levine, J. M., & Messick, D. M. (Eds.), *Shared cognition in organizations: The management of knowledge* (pp. 195–211). Mahwah, NJ: Erlbaum.

Cox, T. H. (1993). *Cultural diversity in organizations: Theory, research and practice.* San Francisco, CA: Berrett-Koehler.

Cunningham, G. B. (2009). The moderating effect of diversity strategy on the relationship between racial diversity and organizational performance. *Journal of Applied Social Psychology, 39*, 1445–1460.

Cunningham, G. B., & Sartore, M. L. (2010). Championing diversity: The influence of personal and organizational antecedents. *Journal of Applied Social Psychology, 40*, 788–810.

De Dreu, C. K. W., Nijstad, B. A., & van Knippenberg, D. (2008). Motivated information processing in group judgment and decision making. *Personality and Social Psychology Review, 12*, 22–49.

De Meuse, K. P., & Hostager, T. J. (2001). Developing an instrument for measuring attitudes and perceptions of workplace diversity: An initial report. *Human Resource Development Quarterly, 12*, 33–51.

Dickson, G. L., Jepsen, D. A., & Barbee, P. W. (2008). Exploring the relationships among multicultural training experiences and attitudes towards diversity among counseling students. *Journal of Multicultural Counseling and Development, 36*, 113–126.

Dickson, M. W., Resick, C. J., & Hanges, P. J. (2006). When organizational climate is unambiguous, it is also strong. *Journal of Applied Psychology, 91*, 351–364.

Eagly, A., & Chaiken, S. (1993). *The psychology of attitudes.* Fort Worth, TX: Harcourt Brace Jovanovich.

Earley, P. C., & Mosakowski, E. (2000). Creating hybrid team cultures: An empirical test of transnational team functioning. *Academy of Management Journal, 43*, 26–49.

Eisenberger, R., Cummings, J., Armeli, S., & Lynch, P. (1997). Perceived organizational support, discretionary treatment, and job satisfaction. *Journal of Applied Psychology, 82*, 812–820.

Ely, R. J., & Thomas, D. A. (2001). Cultural diversity at work: The effects of diversity perspectives on work group processes and outcomes. *Administrative Science Quarterly, 46*, 229–273.

Fishbein, M., & Ajzen, I. (1975). *Belief, attitude, intention, and behavior.* Reading, MA: Addison Wesley.

Fiske, S. T. (1998). Stereotyping, prejudice, and discrimination. In D. T. Gilbert, S. T. Fiske, & G. Lindzey (Eds.), *Handbook of social psychology* (4th ed., pp. 357–411). Boston: McGraw-Hill.

Gelfand, M. J., Nishii, L. H., Raver, J. L., & Schneider, B. (2005). Discrimination in organizations: An organization-level systems perspective. In R. L. Dipboye & A. Colella (Eds.), *Discrimination at work: The psychological and organizational bases* (pp. 89–116). Mahwah, NJ: Erlbaum.

Gilbert, J. A., & Ivancevich, J. M. (2001). Effects of diversity management on attachment. *Journal of Applied Social Psychology, 31*, 1331–1349.

Glick, W. H. (1985). Conceptualizing and measuring organizational and psychological climate: Pitfalls in multilevel research. *Academy of Management Review, 10*, 601–616.

Gonzalez, J. A., & DeNisi, A. S. (2009). Cross-level effects of demography and diversity climate on organizational attachment and firm effectiveness. *Journal of Organizational Behavior, 30*, 21–40.

Harrison, D. A., & Klein, K. J. (2007). What's the difference? Diversity constructs as separation, variety, or disparity in organizations. *Academy of Management Review, 32*, 1199–1228.

Herdman, A. O., & McMillan-Capehart, A. (2009). Establishing a diversity program is not enough: Exploring the determinants of diversity climate. *Journal of Business and Psychology, 25*, 39–53.

Hicks-Clarke, D., & Iles, P. (2000). Climate for diversity and its effects on career and organisational attitudes and perceptions. *Personnel Review, 29*, 324–345.

Hinsz, V. B., Tindale, R. S., & Vollrath, D. A. (1997). The emerging conceptualization of groups as information processors. *Psychological Bulletin, 121*, 43–64.

Hobman, E. V., Bordia, P., & Gallois, C. (2003). Consequences of feeling dissimilar from others in a work team. *Journal of Business and Psychology, 17*, 301–325.

Hobman, E. V., Bordia, P., & Gallois, C. (2004). Perceived dissimilarity and work group involvement: The moderating effects of group openness to diversity. *Group & Organization Management, 29*, 560–587.

Homan, A. C., Greer, L. L., Jehn, K. A., & Koning, L. (2010). Believing shapes seeing: The impact of diversity beliefs on the construal of group composition. *Group Processes & Intergroup Relations, 13*, 477–493.

Homan, A. C., Hollenbeck, J. R., Humphrey, S. E., van Knippenberg, D., Ilgen, D. R., & Van Kleef, G. A. (2008). Facing differences with an open mind: Openness to experience, salience of intra-group differences, and performance of diverse work groups. *Academy of Management Journal, 51*, 1204–1222.

Homan, A. C., van Knippenberg, D., van Kleef, G. A., & De Dreu, C. K. W. (2007a). Bridging faultlines by valuing diversity: Diversity beliefs, information elaboration, and performance in diverse work groups. *Journal of Applied Psychology, 92*, 1189–1199.

Homan, A. C., van Knippenberg, D., van Kleef, G. A., & De Dreu, C. K. W. (2007b). Interacting dimensions of diversity: Cross-categorization and the functioning of diverse work groups. *Group Dynamics, 11*, 79–94.

Hostager, T. J., & De Meuse, K. P. (2002). Assessing the complexity of diversity perceptions: Breadth, depth, and balance. *Journal of Business and Psychology, 17*, 189–206.

Hostager, T. J., & De Meuse, K. P. (2008). The effects of diversity learning experience on positive and negative diversity perceptions. *Journal of Business and Psychology, 23*, 127–139.

Jackson, S. E., et al. (1992). *Diversity in the workplace.* New York: Guilford Press.

Jehn, K. A., Northcraft, G. B., & Neale, M. A. (1999). Why differences make a difference: A field study of diversity, conflict, and performance in workgroups. *Administrative Science Quarterly, 44*, 741–763.

Joshi, A., & Roh, H. (2009). The role of context in work team diversity research: A meta-analytic review. *Academy of Management Journal, 52*, 599–627.

Kearney, E., Gebert, D., & Voelpel, S. C. (2009). When and how diversity benefits teams: The importance of team members' need for cognition. *Academy of Management Journal, 52*, 581–598.

Klein, K. J., & Kozlowski, S. W. J. (2000). *Multilevel theory, research, and methods in organizations.* San Francisco: Jossey-Bass.

Kooij-de Bode, H. J. M., van Knippenberg, D., & van Ginkel, W. P. (2008). Ethnic diversity and distributed information in group decision making: The importance of information elaboration. *Group Dynamics, 12*, 307–320.

Kossek, E. E., & Zonia, S. C. (1993). Assessing diversity climate: A field study of reactions to employer efforts to promote diversity. *Journal of Organizational Behavior, 14*, 61–81.

Lau, D. C., & Murnighan, J. K. (1998). Demographic diversity and faultlines: The compositional dynamics of organizational groups. *Academy of Management Review, 23*, 325–340.

Lerner, J. S., & Tetlock, P. E. (1999). Accounting for the effects of accountability. *Psychological Bulletin, 125*, 255–275.

Linnehan, F., Chrobot-Mason, D., & Konrad, A. M. (2006). Diversity attitudes and norms: The role of ethnic identity and relational demography. *Journal of Organizational Behavior, 27*, 419–442.

Linnehan, F., Konrad, A. M., Reitman, F., Greenhalgh, A., & London, M. (2003). Behavioral goals for diverse organizations: The effects of attitudes, social norms, and racial identity for Asian Americans and whites. *Journal of Applied Social Psychology, 33*, 1331–1359.

Mayhew, M. J., Grunwald, H. E., & Dey, E. L. (2006). Breaking the silence: Achieving a positive campus climate for diversity from the staff perspective. *Research in Higher Education, 47*, 63–88.

McKay, P. F., & Avery, D. R. (2006). What has race got to do with it? Unraveling the role of racioethnicity in job seekers reactions to site visits. *Personnel Psychology, 59*, 395–429.

McKay, P. F., Avery, D. R., & Morris, M. A. (2008). Mean racial-ethnic differences in employee sales performance: The moderating role of diversity climate. *Personnel Psychology, 61*, 349–374.

McKay, P. F., Avery, D. R., & Morris, M. A. (2009). A tale of two climates: Diversity climate from subordinates' and managers' perspectives and their role in store unit sales performance. *Personnel Psychology, 62*, 767–791.

McKay, P. F., Avery, D. R., Tonidandel, S., Morris, M., Hernandez, M., & Hebl, M. R. (2007). Racial differences in employee retention: Are diversity climate perceptions the key? *Personnel Psychology, 60*, 35–62.

Milliken, F., & Martins, L. (1996). Searching for common threads: Understanding the multiple effects of diversity in organizational groups. *Academy of Management Review, 21*, 402–433.

Montei, M. S., Adams, G. A., & Eggers, L. M. (1996). Validity of scores on the Attitudes Towards Diversity Scale (ATDS). *Educational and Psychological Measurement, 56*, 293–303.

Mor Barak, M. E., Cherin, D. A., & Berkman, S. (1998). Organizational and personal dimensions of diversity climate: Ethnic and gender differences in employee perceptions. *Journal of Applied Behavioral Sciences, 31*, 82–104.

Mor Barak, M. E., & Levin, A. (2002). Outside of the corporate mainstream and excluded from the work community: A study of diversity, job satisfaction, and well-being. *Community, Work & Family, 5*, 133–157.

Park, B., & Judd, C. M. (2005). Rethinking the link between categorization and prejudice within the social cognition perspective. *Personality and Social Psychology Review, 9*, 108–130.

Pendry, L. F., Driscoll, D. M., & Field, S. C. T. (2007). Diversity training: Putting theory into practice. *Journal of Occupational and Organizational Psychology, 80*, 27–50.

Plaut, V. C., Thomas, K. N., & Goren, M. J. (2009). Is multiculturalism or color blindness better for minorities? *Psychological Science, 20*, 444–446.

Podsakoff, P. M., MacKenzie, S. B., Lee, J., & Podsakoff, N. P. (2003). Common method biases in behavioral research: A critical review of the literature and recommended remedies. *Journal of Applied Psychology, 88*, 879–903.

Pugh, S. D., Dietz, J., Brief, A. P., & Wiley, J. W. (2008). Looking inside and out: The impact of employee and community demographic composition on organizational diversity climate. *Journal of Applied Psychology, 93*, 1422–1428.

Rau, B. L., & Hyland, M. M. (2003). Corporate teamwork and diversity statements in college recruitment brochures: Effects on attraction. *Journal of Applied Social Psychology, 33*, 2465–2492.

Raver, J. L., van Knippenberg, D., Mayer, D. M., Nishii, L. H., & Vestal, A. (2010, August). *Gender diversity norms and beliefs: Influences upon group information elaboration and performance.* Paper presented at the Academy of Management 2010 Annual Meeting, Montreal.

Richeson, J. A., & Nussbaum, R. J. (2004). The impact of multiculturalism versus color-blindness on racial bias. *Journal of Experimental Social Psychology, 40*, 417–423.

Roberson, L., & Block, C. J. (2001). Racioethnicity and job performance: A review and critique of theoretical perspectives on the causes of group differences. *Research in Organizational Behavior, 23*, 247–325.

Roberson, L., Kulik, C. T., & Pepper, M. B. (2001). Designing effective diversity training: Influence of group composition and trainee experience. *Journal of Organizational Behavior, 22*, 871–885.

Rynes, S., & Rosen, B. (1995). A field survey of factors affecting the adoption and perceived success of diversity training. *Personnel Psychology, 48*, 247–270.

Sawyerr, O. O., Strauss, J., & Yan, J. (2005). Individual value structure and diversity attitudes: The moderating effects of age, gender, race, and religiosity. *Journal of Managerial Psychology, 20*, 498–521.

Schneider, B., Gunnarson, S. K., & Niles-Jolly, K. (1994). Creating the climate and culture for success. *Organizational Dynamics, 23*, 17–29.

Schneider, B., & Reichers, A. E. (1983). On the etiology of climates. *Personnel Psychology, 36*, 19–39.

Schneider, B., Salvaggio, A. N., & Subirats, M. (2002). Climate strength: A new direction for climate research. *Journal of Applied Psychology, 87*, 220–229.

Scholten, L., van Knippenberg, D., Nijstad, B. A., & De Dreu, C. K. W. (2007). Motivated information processing and group decision making: Effects of process accountability on information sharing and decision quality. *Journal of Experimental Social Psychology, 43*, 539–552.

Stahl, G. K., Maznevski, M. L., Voigt, A., & Jonson, K. (2010). Unraveling the effects of cultural diversity in teams: A meta-analysis of research on multicultural groups. *Journal of International Business Studies, 41*, 690–709.

Stanley, L. S. (1996). The development and validation of an instrument to assess attitudes toward cultural diversity and pluralism among preservice physical educators. *Educational and Psychological Measurement, 56*, 891–897.

Stasser, G. (1999). The uncertain role of unshared information in collective choice. In L. L. Thompson, J. M. Levine, & D. M. Messick (Eds.), *Shared cognition in organizations* (pp. 49–69). Mahwah, NJ: Erlbaum.

Stegmann, S., & van Dick, R. (2009, August). *Does it matter what we think about diversity? A meta-analysis on the effects of diversity beliefs*. Paper presented at the Academy of Management Annual Meeting, Chicago, IL.

Strauss, J. P., & Connerley, M. L. (2003). Demographics, personality, contact, and universal-diverse orientation: An exploratory examination. *Human Resource Management, 42*, 159–174.

Strauss, J. P., Connerley, M. L., & Ammermann, P. A. (2003). The "threat hypothesis," personality, and attitudes toward diversity. *Journal of Applied Behavioral Science, 39*, 32–52.

Strauss, J. P., & Sawyerr, O. O. (2009). Religiosity and attitudes towards diversity: A potential workplace conflict? *Journal of Applied Social Psychology, 39*, 2626–2650.

Strauss, J. P., Sawyerr, O. O., & Oke, A. (2008). Demographics, individual value structure, and diversity attitudes in the United Kingdom. *Journal of Change Management, 8*, 147–170.

Tajfel, H., & Turner, J. (1986). The social identity of intergroup behavior. In W. G. Austin & S. Worchel (Eds.), *Psychology and intergroup relations* (pp. 7–24). Chicago: Nelson-Hall.

Tindale, R. S., & Kameda, T. (2000). Social sharedness as a unifying theme for information processing in groups. *Group Processes & Intergroup Relations, 3*, 123–140.

Triana, M. D. C., & García, M. F. (2009). Valuing diversity: A group value approach to understanding the importance of organizational efforts to support diversity. *Journal of Organizational Behavior, 30*, 941–962.

Tropp, L. R., & Bianchi, R. A. (2006). Valuing diversity and interest in intergroup contact. *Journal of Social Issues, 62*, 533–551.

Tsui, A. S., Egan, T. D., & O'Reilly, C. A. (1992). Being different: Relational demography and organizational attachment. *Administrative Science Quarterly, 37*, 549–579.

Tsui, A. S., & O'Reilly, C. A. (1989). Beyond simple demographic effects: The importance of relational demography in superior-subordinate dyads. *Academy of Management Journal, 32*, 402–423.

Turner, J. C., Hogg, M. A., Oakes, P. J., Reicher, S. D., & Wetherell, M. S. (1987). *Rediscovering the social group. A self-categorization theory*. Oxford, UK: Blackwell.

van Dick, R., van Knippenberg, D., Hägele, S., Guillaume, Y. R. F., & Brodbeck, F. C. (2008). Group diversity and group identification: The moderating role of diversity beliefs. *Human Relations, 61*, 1463–1492.

van Dijk, H., van Engen, M. L., & van Knippenberg, D. (2012). Defying conventional wisdom: A meta-analytical examination of the differences between demographic and job-related diversity relationships with performance. *Organizational Behavior and Human Decision Processes, 119*, 38–53.

van Ginkel, W. P., & van Knippenberg, D. (2008). Group information elaboration and group decision making: The role of shared task representations. *Organizational Behavior and Human Decision Processes, 105*, 82–97.

van Knippenberg, D., Dawson, J. F., West, M. A., & Homan, A. C. (2011). Diversity faultlines, shared objectives, and top management team performance. *Human Relations, 64*, 307–336.

van Knippenberg, D., De Dreu, C. K. W., & Homan, A. C. (2004). Work group diversity and group performance: An integrative model and research agenda. *Journal of Applied Psychology, 89*, 1008–1022.

van Knippenberg, D., & Haslam, S. A. (2003). Realizing the diversity dividend: Exploring the subtle interplay between identity, ideology, and reality. In S. A. Haslam, D. van Knippenberg, M. J. Platow, & N. Ellemers (Eds.), *Social identity at work: Developing theory for organizational practice* (pp. 61–77). New York: Psychology Press.

van Knippenberg, D., Haslam, S. A., & Platow, M. J. (2007). Unity through diversity: Value-in-diversity beliefs as moderator of the relationship between work group diversity and group identification. *Group Dynamics, 11*, 207–222.

van Knippenberg, D., & Schippers, M. C. (2007). Work group diversity. *Annual Review of Psychology, 58*, 515–541.

van Knippenberg, D., & van Ginkel, W. P. (2010). The categorization-elaboration model of work group diversity: Wielding the double-edged sword. In R. Crisp (Ed.), *The psychology of social and cultural diversity* (pp. 257–280). Malden, MA: Wiley-Blackwell.

van Knippenberg, D., van Ginkel, W. P., & Homan, A. C. (2008, April). *Diversity mindsets: What you believe diversity does makes a difference*. Paper presented at the 23rd Annual Conference of the Society for Industrial and Organizational Psychology, San Francisco.

Walsh, B. M., Matthews, R. A., Tuller, M.D., Parks, K. M., & McDonald, D. P. (2010). A multilevel model of the effects of equal opportunity climate on job satisfaction in the military. *Journal of Occupational Health Psychology, 15*, 191–207.

Williams, K. Y., & O'Reilly, C. A. (1998). Demography and diversity in organizations: A review of 40 years of research. *Research in Organizational Behavior, 20*, 77–140.

Wolsko, C., Park, B., Judd, C. M., & Wittenbrink, B. (2000). Framing interethnic ideology: Effects of multicultural and color-blind perspectives on judgments of groups and individuals. *Journal of Personality and Social Psychology, 78*, 635–654.

CHAPTER 14

Considering Diversity as a Source of Competitive Advantage in Organizations

Orlando C. Richard *and* Carliss D. Miller

Abstract

This chapter serves as a research framework for academics and practicing managers interested in understanding the conditions in which diversity, especially visible attributes such as race, gender, age, and nationality, positively or negatively affects organizational performance. This chapter differs from previous articles and books with a predominantly micro approach because the focus shifts from the individual, dyadic, and team diversity levels of analysis to diversity in large groups, subunits, and organizations. The key assumption throughout this chapter is that diversity represents a unique and valuable resource for organizations. The chapter concludes with suggestions for future research on other contextual factors that might aid in unleashing a "diversity advantage."

Key Words: visible attribute diversity, resource-based view, diversity advantage

In the new global age, workforce diversity has become widespread, drawing attention to not only previous studied dimensions of diversity such as functional background, educational background, and tenure but also more salient workforce diversity features such as national culture, race, gender, and age. Although this chapter provides a broad framework for how diversity influences performance, its major thrust is how more salient, visible dimensions of diversity affect organizational processes and ultimately firm performance. The rationale for the coverage is twofold. First, although previous diversity research within a business context has provided a wealth of findings of how diversity in functional background, education, and tenure affects organizational performance (Hambrick & Mason, 1984), there is still much left to be understood as to when, how, and why the demographics of top management teams and/or groups lead to strategic actions and firm outcomes (Carpenter, Geletkanycz, & Sanders, 2004). Secondly, although the seminal upper-echelons work by Hambrick and Mason (1984) provides some theoretical guidance as to how any dimension of diversity may operate, the jury remains out on salient dimensions of diversity such as race, gender, age, and national culture. Future research should continue to explore how diversity affects strategic outcomes and firm performance at multiple levels of analysis, through multiple theoretical lenses, and by examining multiple dimensions of diversity (Joshi, Liao, & Roh, 2011; Nielsen, 2010).

Globalization and global competition has expedited the demographic trends to where we now work in organizations that are drastically heterogeneous. Given the obvious trend toward more differences in age, race, gender, and national culture, it is increasingly important for companies to be in position to manage these differences in a positive and proactive fashion instead of allowing these differences to manage the organization in a way that could prove to be disadvantageous. By integrating theoretical perspectives from strategic management and organizational demography, we can best understand how workplace diversity is a source of sustainable competitive advantage. Answers to the following research questions are provided throughout this chapter:

1. What are the organizational performance effects of workforce diversity, especially the visible attribute dimensions?

2. What are the business strategies and organizational cultures that transform workforce diversity into a competitive advantage?

3. What are the strategic and human resource management practices that managers can implement to maximize the positive effects of diversity while minimizing the potential negative effects?

The next section will review previous research on workplace diversity effects and conclude with recent theoretical tenets.

From diversity disadvantage to diversity advantage

Within the social sciences, a host of theories attempt to explain how and why workforce diversity affects organizational processes and outcomes. Below we briefly discuss the theories that focus on the negative consequences of diversity, or what we refer to as "diversity disadvantage." Next, we present the opposing theories from the relevant theories in strategic management that propose positive consequences of diversity ("diversity advantage"). We introduce a conceptual framework for studying workforce diversity effects that encourages cross-cutting across multiple dimensions and attributes of diversity. By first highlighting the micro-level behavioral aspects of diversity, we can then show the macro-level effects on firm performance and competitive advantage.

Diversity disadvantage

Social identity theory has been a key framework used to explain the negative effects of workforce diversity (Cunningham, 2009). According to this paradigm, people categorize themselves and others into groups based on numerous factors—especially salient demographic traits such as race, gender, and culture (Tajfel & Turner, 1979). People with similarities are grouped into the in-group, while those who are dissimilar are considered the out-group. This process leads to in-group bias and favoritism whereby in-group members elicit more positive attitudes, trust, and liking toward members of the in-group over the out-group (Gaertner & Dovidio, 2000). Empirical findings on various demographic attributes lend credence to the theory by showing that diversity in groups relates to increased conflict (Jehn, Northcraft, & Neale, 1999; Pelled, Eisenhardt, & Xin, 1999), poor social integration (O'Reilly, Caldwell, & Barnett, 1989), and increased turnover (Jackson, Brett, Sessa, Cooper, Julin, & Peyronnin 1991), thus illustrating the potential for diversity disadvantage (for an example, see Sacco & Schmidt, 2005).

The organizational demography literature also highlights some of the negative implications of group and team diversity on group processes and outcomes. There is evidence to support the indirect effect of demography on performance, and the direct effect of demography on the adaptability of group and team members (Pfeffer, 1983). Heterogeneous groups face a higher likelihood for miscommunication, increased unproductive conflict, and more time and energy invested for group cohesion to develop (Jehn, Northcraft, & Neale, 1999; Kochan et al., 2003). Thus, workplace diversity can create additional monitoring, coordination, and control costs for the firm (Dwyer, Richard, & Chadwick, 2003). Despite the potential costs for managing diversity, if unmanaged and unevaluated, diversity can surely lead to a competitive disadvantage (Kochan et al., 2003).

Diversity advantage

Another school of thought espouses the notion that diverse groups should outperform homogeneous ones because they possess a broader range of knowledge, skills, and abilities (van Knippenberg, De Dreu, & Homan, 2004). Diverse groups, including visible attributes such as race, gender, or sex, can afford more productive task conflict, creative ideas and innovative solutions, and improved decision making (Ancona & Caldwell, 1992; Bantel & Jackson, 1989; Jehn, Northcraft, & Neale, 1999; Phillips, Northcraft, & Neale, 2006) by raising divergent ideas and opinions about how best to improve group or organizational effectiveness (Zellmer-Bruhn, Maloney, Bhappu, & Salvador, 2008). Indeed, van Knippenberg and colleagues (2004) emphasize that diversity of information promotes the elaboration of beneficial task-related knowledge to assist with solving complex problems consistent with "value-in-diversity" notions (Milliken & Martins, 1996).

In terms of visible attribute diversity specifically, Cox, Lobel, and McLeod (1991) found that groups composed of racially diverse members provided more innovative solutions than those that were more homogeneous. The idea is that there is "value-in-diversity" in that the diverse knowledge acquired from a diverse workforce enriches organizations by providing greater resources for problem solving, creativity, flexibility, and target marketing (Cox, 2001). Based on this stream of research, McLeod, Lobel, and Cox (1996) also found that racio-ethnic diverse groups produced higher-quality solutions during brainstorming tasks, which ultimately relates to higher effectiveness. Also, research reveals that gender diversity relates to creativity (Hoffman & Maier, 1961). While most of the previous research has focused on work groups, another stream of research predicting similar diversity effects involves exclusively the top management team (Hambrick & Mason, 1984).

According to upper-echelons theory, top management teams (TMTs) have a stronger impact on organizational strategic behaviors and performance than any single member, including the chief executive officer, because decision making in an organization is a shared activity and a collection of cognitions, capabilities, and interactions among team members (Hambrick, 2007). Numerous studies have found that TMT heterogeneity affects organizational strategic and performance outcomes (Bantel & Jackson, 1989; Boeker, 1997; Carpenter & Fredrickson, 2001; Eisenhardt & Schoonhoven, 1990; Smith, Smith, Olian, Sims, O'Bannon, & Scully, 1994). The general tenet of upper-echelons theory is that TMTs have a stronger impact on performance than individual actors (Hambrick, 2007). Current research in the human resource management domain argues that the entire human capital pool has much stronger effects on performance than TMTs (Richard, Ford, & Ismail, 2006). Going beyond both previous workgroup and the upper-echelons unit of analysis is research that focuses on the entire human capital pool (Richard, 2000; Wright et al., 1995). Building on the information and decision-making or "value-in-diversity" approach, research has invoked the resource-based view or knowledge-based view of the firm to study how not only invisible but also salient dimensions of diversity such as racial diversity and/or gender diversity affect firm performance (Richard, 2000; Richard, Murthi, & Ismail, 2007).

Diversity as competitive advantage—Resource-based/knowledge-based view

It is a popular conception among business practitioners and scholars to consider a firm's employees to be its most valuable assets. The coordination and combination of employees' knowledge, skills, and abilities become the firm's human resources and capital, and a source of competitive advantage to the extent to which the resources are valuable, rare, hard to imitate, and strategically difficult to substitute (Slater, Weigand, & Zwirlein, 2008). This perspective represents the resource-based view (RBV) of the firm, the theoretical framework that defines the conditions for when a firm's resources can be a source of competitive advantage (Barney, 1991). Barney (1991) classified firm resources into three main categories: physical capital resources, organizational capital resources, and human capital resources—the umbrella from which workplace diversity emerges as a source of competitive advantage. A firm's resources "include all assets, capabilities, organizational processes, firm attributes, information, knowledge, etc. controlled by a firm that enable the firm to conceive of and implement strategies that improve its efficiency and effectiveness" (Barney, 1991, p. 191). Physical capital resources include the firm's technology, equipment, and location; organizational capital resources include the firm's planning, coordination, and control systems; and human capital resources include the intelligence, experience, insights, and relationships of a firm's employees.

From a human capital perspective, workplace diversity operates as a source of sustained competitive advantage because it creates value that is both difficult to imitate and rare due to its subjectivity, complex ambiguity, and creativity (Richard, 2000). Barney (1991) provides three reasons firm resources can be "imperfectly imitable": (1) obtaining the resource is dependent on "unique historical conditions," as is the case with cultural and racio-ethnic diversity; (2) the resource–competitive advantage link is causally ambiguous, as evidenced by the mixed results from diversity and firm performance studies (McMahon, 2010); and (3) the social complexity of the resource (Barney, 1991, p. 107). Diversity as a resource is considered socially complex because it possesses knowledge barriers and a unique mix of talent and insights that are difficult to capture and understand, and extremely difficult to transfer across organizations (Richard, 2000)—thus the competitive advantage. The social complexity of the knowledge barriers manifested through workplace diversity is further explored from the knowledge-based view of the firm.

The knowledge-based view of the firm (KBV), an extension from RBV, considers knowledge and the transferability and application of knowledge within the firm as the most strategically significant resource of a firm to enable a competitive advantage (Grant, 1996; Richard, Murthi, & Ismail, 2007). The KBV argument extends from the imitability attribute of RBV: because knowledge-based resources are socially complex, and thus difficult to imitate, diverse bases of knowledge, capability, and insights within firms are the key determinants of sustainable competitive advantage and superior firm performance (Grant, 1996). The resource-based perspective and the knowledge-based perspective are both useful in examining the strategic complexity of diversity in the workplace because they incorporate the bottom-line implications of strategic management, the social welfare concerns of diversity and inclusion, and the value of diversity in the creation and application of knowledge within the firm.

According to Wright and McMahan (1992), firms can develop sustainable competitive advantages by using the human capital pool of valuable, rare, and inimitable resource pool. The entire "value-in-diversity" notion discussed earlier rests on the assumption that workforce diversity adds value to the organization by providing different types of knowledge, skills, and abilities (Herring, 2009; van Knippenberg, De Dreu, & Homan, 2004; Williams & O'Reilly, 1998). Richard (2000) describes how the value from diversity appears necessary but not sufficient for organizations to gain sustainable competitive advantage. Diversity must also appear inimitable and rare, and it should not be limited to only a few hierarchical levels or specific occupations (McMahan, Bell, & Virick, 1998).

According to Richard (2000), the value obtained from workforce diversity would be hard to imitate. In most cases, a given firm's mix of human resources in terms of diversity (e.g., culture, race, gender, age, functional background) would be almost impossible for competitors to imitate. Intangible resources, such as a diverse workforce, can produce competitive advantage because the social complexity that exists cannot be imitated easily by competitors (Barney, 1991; Peteraf, 1993). Also, the social dynamics within particular firms cannot be copied across organizations and are essentially beneficial only to the organization where the dynamic relationships developed. For example, the organizational culture, human resource management systems, and managing diversity practices/processes that transform diversity into value added cannot be immediately imitated, and as Miller and Shamsie (1996) note, by the time they are imitated, the imitated firm will have further developed its skills. More important, the capabilities gained from the diverse workforce will likely remain firm-specific knowledge that will not be as valuable outside of the firm and thus can act as a critical ingredient for competitive advantage (Grant, 1996). In sum, it would be quite a challenge to imitate another firm's demographic composition (especially when considering multiple dimensions of diversity) as well as its organizational culture and practices. Finally, a resource must also be rare in order to offer sustainable competitive advantage (Barney & Wright, 1998).

When considering workforce diversity in organizations, among the rarest in organizations appears to be culture and race (Richard, 2000). While there is plenty of gender diversity (also age diversity) in organizations, this diversity does not exist at various levels and across various occupations (Richard, Barnett, Dwyer, & Chadwick, 2004). Therefore, gender diversity and age diversity also appears a rarity. For example, if we investigate TMTs across a nation, we might see a considerable amount of TMT personality diversity, functional background diversity, or tenure diversity across most firms, but we would rarely find diversity across more salient dimensions such as national culture, race, gender, and age. Because these salient dimensions not only provide the value and imitability that less salient dimensions such as personality produce but also appears a rarity, diversity in terms of national culture, race, gender, and age should afford a sustainable competitive advantage. In this chapter, we discuss the organizational, structures, strategies, and practices that help sustain workforce diversity's value. Hence, we offer in the sections to come a number of internal factors that moderate the diversity–performance relationship.

Moderation model findings

What we consider to be the ultimate solution to gaining a diversity advantage involves adopting a moderation model of diversity (Joshi & Roh, 2009; Joshi, Liao, & Roh, 2011). As noted earlier, consistent with an RBV of the firm assumptions, workforce diversity can provide value that might contribute to organizational performance but it can become sustainable as a resource only when it also appears inimitable and rare. Scholars have called for the consideration of the contexts within which various kinds of resources will offer the most value, thereby more likely contributing to sustainable competitive advantage (Jayne & Dipboye, 2004; Miller & Shamsie, 1996; Richard, 2000; Richard, Murthi, & Ismail, 2007). For example, Jayne and Dipboye's (2004) review of the literature concludes that diversity alone does not guarantee higher individual, group, or organizational performance; rather, effective "diversity management" is what matters. Joshi and Roh (2009) found that racial, gender, and age diversity effects on performance were twice as strong when accounting for context, such as industry and occupation type. Their findings are consistent with recent theory and findings on diversity in organization (Jackson, Joshi, & Erhardt, 2003; Richard, Murthi, & Ismail, 2007). The moderation model of diversity below accounts for the factors that contribute to maintaining diversity's inimitability so that competitors cannot easily duplicate those factors which are on the road to sustainable competitive advantage.

Contingency theory provides an ideal framework to study diversity because it allows diversity to be examined in conjunction with other internal and external contextual factors (Richard, Kochan, & McMillan-Capehart, 2002). We adopt the strategic choice theoretical approach instead of the institutional theory perspective by assuming that managers have the ability to alter particularly internal factors. For example, top executives in both homogeneous and heterogeneous organizations can revise the business strategy, create a particular type of organizational culture, implement various human resources policies, and change leadership using their own discretion. While top executives have less influence over external factors such as industry characteristics and national culture, they can use their judgment about what country to operate subsidiaries and market the firm's products and/or services, and how the firm will engage in the local community.

Fresh insights from the moderation model and the current state of research

Strategic management is concerned with how to compete within the environment a company resides, and how well a strategy is implemented has implications on performance (Herbert & Deresky, 1987; Mintzberg, 1978; Pfeffer & Salancik, 1978). The benefits of a diverse workforce depend on not only the organizational members' appreciation for the variety that different subgroups bring but also the nature of the task to be accomplished (Harrison & Klein, 2007). Inappropriate internal alignment between the human capital pool and the organizational strategy can prevent or impede the formulation and implementation of missions, goals, and objectives, thereby hindering organizational performance (White, 1986). Put another way, for organizations to be effective, they must specify the type of strategy they intend to employ and acquire the proper human resources to implement the strategy. For example, Skaggs and Youndt's (2004) study of service organizations reveals that fit between an organization's business strategy and their human capital related to higher levels of performance. Similarly, Hitt, Bierman, Shimizu, and Kochhar (2001), in a sample of law firms, found that human capital interacted with strategy to affect firm performance, supporting contingency theory. There is also some research revealing that entrepreneurial orientation moderates the relationship between both racial and gender diversity, and firm performance (Richard et al., 2004), finding that innovativeness positively, and risk taking negatively moderated the nonlinear relationship between cultural diversity in management and firm performance.

The empirical research on the workplace diversity–performance relationship has been quite scarce. In one of the first articles of the decade to examine the main effect of diversity on firm performance, Richard (2000), while not finding support for the main effect, found that business strategy positively moderated the relationship between racial diversity and performance (measured as productivity, market performance, and return on equity). Since the breakthrough article in 2000, research along this vein was silent until 2003. From 2003 to the present, there has been an average of one empirical study examining racio-ethnic/gender diversity and firm performance published per year in the leading management journals, excluding meta-analyses (Gonzalez & DeNisi, 2009; Jayne & Dipboye, 2004; Joshi, Liao, & Jackson, 2006; Kochan et al., 2003; Lau & Murnighan, 2005; Miller & Del Carmen Triana, 2009; Richard et al., 2004; Richard, Murthi, & Ismail, 2007).

Kochan and colleagues (2003) presented a summary of their results from a large five-year field-based study examining the "business case" for diversity. The authors studied the effects of race/gender diversity and firm performance in case studies of four large firms and found few direct effects (positive or negative) on firm performance, but they did find evidence for the moderating role of organizational context and group processes. For instance, in the case study of a large information processing firm, no direct effects for race or gender diversity were captured for team performance measures, but gender had a positive impact on group processes and race had a negative impact. Race was found to have a negative impact on performance when the organizational culture was competitive and the firm had a growth-oriented business strategy. In this same study, training and development reduced the negative effects of racial diversity and enhanced the positive effects of gender. In a recent multilevel study of a regional restaurant chain, Gonzalez and DeNisi (2009) identified the diversity climate as an important contextual moderator. Their results showed that at the organizational level, racio-ethnic and gender diversity had a negative impact on performance (captured as return on income and productivity) when the diversity climate was unfavorable, but in a supportive diversity climate, racio-ethnic and gender diversity was positively related to performance. The state of the research today no longer expects a simple linear relationship between diversity and firm performance, but a complex, curvilinear relationship where mediators play a significant role (e.g., firm reputation, innovation, human resources policies, training and development, entrepreneurial orientation), as do contextual considerations (i.e., industry and environmental stability), and the moderating roles of organizational culture and business strategy (for a conceptual illustration of the workplace diversity–firm performance relationship model, see McMahon, 2010).

MODERATING VARIABLES: BUSINESS STRATEGY

Miles and Snow (1978) offer a typology with four types of business strategy: prospectors, analyzers, defenders, and reactors. Prospectors constantly exploit new market opportunities and consistently develop new products. They therefore focus on effective product design and growth through research, development, and innovation. Innovation refers to an organization's tendency to engage in and support novel ideas, creative processes, and experimentation with the goal of producing new products or offering new services (Lumpkin & Dess, 1996). Previous research has shown that diversity relates to more variety in idea, novel approaches, and consideration of alternatives (Bantel & Jackson, 1989; Wiersema & Bantel, 1992). For example, Watson, Kumar, and Michaelson (1993) found that cultural diversity was related to more creative solutions in a brainstorming task. The creativity and innovation gained from diversity appear most beneficial in organizations pursing a prospector strategy.

Defenders produce a limited product line and target a narrow market segment. Their goal is to protect their turf from intrusion by competitors. Analyzers are considered to be stuck in the middle between prospectors and defenders. Reactors' strategies involve copying competitors' actions and involve no proactive behavior. Wright, Smart, and McMahan (1995) shed light on how creativity gained from human capital might benefit one strategic type (e.g., prospector) over another (e.g., defender). A culturally diverse workforce can offer diversity in ideas, novel approaches, and alternatives (Bantel & Jackson, 1989; Wiersema & Bantel, 1992), all of which seem beneficial for firms that pursue a prospector strategy. Research has shown that minority viewpoints can invoke consideration of non-obvious alternative options in work settings (Nemeth, 1992). Because prospectors need heterogeneity in decisions and problem solving to offer cutting-edge products and services, we expect benefits from a workforce consisting of cultural diversity. In contrast, a defender strategy reduces the demand for innovation.

General Proposition: *Workforce diversity will have more positive and significant effects on group, subunit, or organizational effectiveness when a firm possesses a prospector business strategy compared to an analyzer, defender, or reactor strategy.*

MODERATING VARIABLES: ORGANIZATIONAL CULTURE

Organizational culture represents the pattern of shared values that provide behavior norms for organizational members and serves as an organizational control mechanism (Deshpande & Webster, 1989). Organizational culture typologies exist that vary along the cooperation and interdependence dimensions of human interaction (Chatman & Barsade, 1995; McMillan-Capehart, 2005; Richard, Kochan, & McMillan-Capehart, 2002). Williams and O'Reilly (1998) propose that organizational culture acts as a powerful mechanism to manage diversity, and it can encourage either solidarity or divisiveness. We employ the Competing Values Framework (Deshpande & Webster, 1989; Deshpande, Farley, & Webster, 2000) to explain the role of organizational culture in unleashing "diversity advantage." The framework takes into account the dominant attributes that distinguish organizational culture types and is operationalized across two dimensions: formal–informal organizational processes (human resource flexibility vs.

control) and internal–external focus (internal integration vs. environmental interaction). There are four culture types derived from the two-by-two typology based on the two dimensions:

1. The **clan culture** is considered to be a friendly place to work due to its informal governance and internal orientation. It emphasizes the development of human resources, employee participation in decision making, teamwork, and cohesiveness.

2. The **adhocracy culture** also supports informal governance but also has an external orientation. Thus, it creates a dynamic and creative context and encourages employees to take risks. This culture thrives on human resources that offer flexibility and variety.

3. The **hierarchy culture** adopts an internal orientation but emphasizes formalization and mechanistic governance that reduce flexibility and variety. Clearly defined goals seem crucial for this culture.

4. The **market culture** supports a formal governance structure but with an external orientation toward the environment. The culture promotes individual achievement and seeks individuals motivated by competition and not cooperation.

Mounting evidence exists that for diversity to provide advantage, there must be a context in place that emphasizes cohesiveness, participation, and teamwork (Dwyer, Richard, & Chadwick, 2003; Pless & Maak, 2004; Richard, Kochan, & McMillan-Capehart, 2002). For example, Swann, Polzer, Seyle, and Ko (2004) describe how a group atmosphere that encourages freedom of expression should facilitate openness among diverse members. Pless and Maak (2004) emphasize how an organizational culture of inclusion that allows people with different backgrounds, mindsets, and ways of thinking to work together cooperatively is critical to unleash any potential "diversity advantage." Empirical research by Dwyer, Richard, and Chadwick (2003) found that clan organizational culture positively moderated the relationship between gender diversity in management and firm performance.

General Proposition: Workforce diversity will have more positive and significant effects on group, subunit, or organizational effectiveness when a firm possesses a clan organizational culture compared to an adhocracy, hierarchy, or market culture.

MODERATING VARIABLES: HUMAN RESOURCE MANAGEMENT PRACTICES

To facilitate team functioning to attain the benefits of diversity, it is necessary to create a work setting that is cooperative rather than competitive (Schippers, Hartog, Koopman, & Wienk, 2003). While diversity practices deal exclusively with diversity issues in organizations, the human resource management function oversees all people management processes. Therefore, it seems essential to discuss diversity management and human resource management in accord with one another. Diversity management falls under the umbrellas of human resource management. Past research reveals that human resource practices broadly and diversity practices more specifically affect organizational effectiveness goals such as workplace creativity among diverse personnel (Kirby & Richard, 2000). Various components of the human resource management system can facilitate outcome interdependence, which furthers organizational members' willingness to cooperate and allows diversity to contribute to increased innovation. Below we discuss training and development and reward systems, and how each has an impact in managing diversity, but more importantly how all should be used simultaneously to create a "diversity advantage."

According to Blau (1977), the greater the opportunity for mobility within an organization, the more positive associations among diverse members. If formulated and implemented appropriately, diversity initiatives should reinforce key organizational development practices (Agocs & Burr, 1996). Barry and Bateman (1996) put forth diversity training as a prime contingency factor between the workplace diversity and performance relationship. Hopkins, Hopkins, and Gross (2005) argue that effective diversity training should create norms of tolerance, open communication, and acceptance that facilitate cooperation among diverse members.

Reward systems should also be considered. Instituting outcome interdependence also creates a setting where all group or organizational members share a goal and rewards are group-based versus individual-based (Wageman, 1995, 2001). Outcome interdependence further facilitates each group member's willingness to cooperate and should thus enhance knowledge sharing and innovation (Saavedra, Earley, & van Dyne, 1993; Wageman, 2001) and should be beneficial to diversity workforces.

General Proposition: Workforce diversity will have more positive and significant effects on group, subunit, or organizational effectiveness when a firm provides diversity-related training and development throughout all hierarchical levels within the organization.

General Proposition: *Workforce diversity will have more positive and significant effects on group, subunit, or organizational effectiveness when a firm institutes outcome interdependence in its reward system.*

MODERATING VARIABLES: DESIGN FEATURES

Organizational design refers to the managerial decision making that determines the structure and processes that coordinate and control a firm's jobs. Two extremes of organizational designs offered in the literature are mechanistic versus organic. The mechanistic model gained prominence in the early 1900s based on the work of Henry Fayol and Max Weber (Weber, 1946). Henry Fayol suggested that organizations be designed in a highly specialized fashion to make the most efficient use of people. Max Weber proposed that the organization function in a machine-like manner to maintain efficiency through high formalization and centralization. In other words, jobs are standardized with specific procedures on how to do it, and all decision making takes place at a single point in the organization (e.g., top management ranks). Furthermore, a mechanistic structure limits the information network by initiating mainly downward communication from top managers to middle- and/or lower-level managers and limits the level of cross-level participation across hierarchical levels.

Current demographics reveal that women and minorities have minimal representation at the top management ranks as well as in the board of directors (Hillman, Cannella, & Harris, 2002; Hillman, Stropshire, & Cannella, 2007; Richard et al., 2004). Because many members of this talent pool work in middle to lower levels of the organization, a mechanistic design would not allow for the knowledge, abilities, and skills to be shared vertically as well as horizontally across organizational levels. Formal structures often create less flexibility and more rigidity, making it more challenging to acquire and utilize knowledge (Lin & Germain, 2003; Zaltman, 1979). In addition, formalization reduces innovativeness and restricts interaction across organizational levels. While a mechanistic structure should reduce the level of intergroup conflict that often occurs in diverse settings by limiting human interaction, it also limits the knowledge-sharing capabilities that are essential for "diversity advantage." Only uniqueness, rarity, and knowledge acquired from interaction among diverse organizational members can confer "diversity advantage." Thus, the organic design seems to offer a more compatible context for a diverse workforce.

A "diversity advantage" emanates when all group, department, or organizational members are included in the deliberations that accompany key decisions. Bunderson (2003) found that power decentralization positively related to the involvement in making decisions of management team members. Unless all members are allowed to influence decision formulation and implementation, it is unlikely any "diversity advantages" will accrue. An organic organizational design encourages great use of human capital and open communication flow through decentralization and less formalization, allowing knowledge sharing and flexibility in decision making (Burns & Stalker, 1961; Courtright, Fairhurst, & Rogers, 1989). Scholars such as Joan Woodward found that an organic design facilitated a firm's flexibility and ability to adapt (Woodward, 1965). The organic model promotes use of cross-hierarchical as well as cross-functional teams, in addition to low formalization of rules and procedures.

A decentralized organizational design downplays the idea of formalization by proposing knowledge, information, and competencies to be distributed across and up the hierarchical structure (Bunderson, 2003). This setting allows for the real benefits of diversity to be realized as put forth by academic scholarship. For example, Cox and Blake's (1991) multicultural model notes how managing diversity works in systems that are less determinant, less standardized, and more fluid. Organic organizational designs allow for communication downward, upward, horizontally, and diagonally, creating an appropriate setting for knowledge sharing across diverse organizational members (Grimes & Richard, 2003). The organic organizational design should also allow for less conformity with the past and promote a wider range of perspectives. Thomas (1990) puts forth similar arguments by stating how diversity thrives in a nonhierarchical, collaborative, and flexible design that values differences while tolerating individuality.

General Proposition: *Workforce diversity will have more positive and significant effects on group, subunit, or organizational effectiveness when a firm adopts an organic design rather than a mechanistic design.*

Future research directions

Throughout this chapter, as part of our "moderating model perspective," we have offered several contextual factors that can facilitate a "diversity advantage," such as business strategy, organizational culture, and human resource policies. What we have *not* addressed specifically is the role of external contingency factors. The following questions represent issues for future research:

1. How does the internal and external social networks of organizations and organizational members impact the relationship that workforce diversity has on organizational performance? For example, can organizational diversity be more advantages when there are strong network or weak network ties? Also, do network ties allow for more knowledge flow or organizational learning in diverse versus heterogeneous workforces?

2. How does environmental turbulence affect the relationship between workforce diversity and organizational performance? Do diverse workforces provide more advantages in a turbulent or a stable environment?

3. Does the impact of diversity on performance vary by geographic area? For example, does diversity have more detrimental effects in companies located in states or regions with a history of racial segregation, power struggles, and lack of inclusion? (For instance, one might expect different effects of racial, gender, nationality, and age diversity in organizations located in California compared to Mississippi as well as in heterogeneous versus homogeneous communities.)

4. What are the important mediating factors that connect workforce diversity to firm performance? Research could benefit from including a host of potential mediating factors such as conflict, elaboration of task-relevant information, strategic consensus, competitive actions, strategy-making processes, cohesion, knowledge-based information, and organizational learning.

Complementary to considering the external context, future research should also consider the entire umbrella under which the "diversity advantage" resides. We have highlighted the role of social networks and the community; however, future research should expand investigate the effects of supplier diversity on firm performance: Do firms that diversify their supplier base actually experience a competitive advantage? In addition, most research to date has employed cross-sectional research designs. Studies have shown the possibility for temporal contingencies for the diversity–performance relationship (Richard et al., 2007), so future research should use longitudinal designs to flesh out the actual effects of workplace diversity.

We conclude with final recommendations concerning the role of leadership. In a changing world, ignoring the demographic changes and issues related to managing diversity that demand attention can lead to subnormal performance. Executives who develop the diversity management skills and implement the ideal setting for a diverse workforce should be in position to reap a "diversity advantage," while others will suffer a "diversity disadvantage." The personal commitment of leaders from the executive suite to the line-management level determines how much attention and resources are devoted to diversity issues (Richard, Kochan, & McMillan-Capehart, 2002). For example, Dass and Parker (1996) emphasize how top decision makers must believe that diversity issues are relevant for them take managing diversity serious. Not only should decision makers have positive beliefs concerning diversity, but they must also instill similar views into their followers through effective leadership and policy development.

We put forward transformational leadership as the ideal kind of inspirational leadership to maximize the potential of a diverse workforce. Such leaders emphasize a common vision as well as a shared identity and inspire all members in such a way to meet organizational objectives (Bass, 1998; Bass & Avolio, 1994). During the decision-making process, the leader should make sure that all members maintain an impartial stance during the deliberations and explorations and avoid granting credibility and authority to one perspective over another (Harrison & Klein, 2007). The leader should implement nominal group techniques, brainstorming, and other participative methods that maximize inclusiveness (Sutton & Hargadon, 1996). The goal of the leader should be to minimize any power and status differences based on history or formal organizational structure so that all members can participate, thereby contributing to a "diversity advantage." An effective leader can initiate changes within the organization that can transform a diverse workforce into a valuable resource that is difficult for competitors to imitate. Creating an inclusive, participative context or diversity climate where diverse members can have input into the organizational decision making should provide more creativity, enhanced problem-solving capabilities, and ultimately increased firm performance (McKay, Avery, Liao, & Morris, 2011; Shore, Randel, Chung, Dean, Ehrhart, & Singh, 2011).

References

Agocs, C., & Burr, C. (1996). Employment equity, affirmative action and managing diversity: Assessing the differences. *International Journal of Manpower*, 17(4/5), 30–45.

Ancona, D. G., & Caldwell, D. F. (1992). Demography and design: Predictors of new product team performance. *Organization Science*, 3(3), 321–341.

Bantel, K., & Jackson, S. (1989). Top management and innovations in banking: Does the composition of the team make a difference? *Strategic Management Journal*, 10(S1), 107–124.

Barney, J. B. (1991). Firm resources and sustained competitive advantage. *Journal of Management*, 17(1), 99–120.

Barney, J. B., & Wright, P. M. (1998). On becoming a strategic partner: The role of human resources in gaining competitive advantage. *Human Resource Management*, 37(1), 31–46.

Barry, B., & Bateman, T. S. (1996). A social trap analysis of the management of diversity. *Academy of Management Review*, 21(3), 757–790.

Bass, B. M. (1998). *Transformational leadership: Industrial, military, and educational impact.* Mahwah, NJ: Lawrence Erlbaum.

Bass, B. M., & Avolio, B. J. (1994). *Improving organizational effectiveness through transformational leadership.* Thousand Oaks, CA: Sage Publications, Inc.

Blau, P. M. (1977). *Inequality and heterogeneity.* New York: Free Press.

Boeker, W. (1997). Strategic change: The influence of managerial characteristics and organizational growth. *Academy of Management Journal*, 40(1), 152–170.

Bunderson, J. S. (2003). Team member functional background and involvement in management teams: Direct effects and the moderating role of power centralization. *Academy of Management Journal*, 46(4), 458–474.

Burns, T., & Stalker, G. M. (1961). *The management of innovation.* London: Tavistock.

Carpenter, M. A., & Fredrickson, J. W. (2001). Top management teams, global strategic posture, and the moderating role of uncertainty. *Academy of Management Journal*, 44(3), 533–546.

Carpenter, M. A., Geletkanycz, M. A., & Sanders, W. G. (2004). Upper echelons research revisited: Antecedents, elements, and consequences of top management team composition. *Journal of Management*, 30(6), 749–778.

Chatman, J. A., & Barsade, S. G. (1995). Personality, organizational culture, and cooperation: Evidence from a business simulation. *Administrative Science Quarterly*, 40(3), 423–443.

Courtright, J. A., Fairhurst, G. T., & Rogers, L. E. (1989). Interaction patterns in organic and mechanistic systems. *Academy of Management Journal*, 32(4), 773–802.

Cox, T. (2001). *Creating the multicultural organization: A strategy for capturing the power of diversity.* San Francisco: Jossey Bass.

Cox, T. H., & Blake, S. (1991). Managing cultural diversity: Implications for organizational competitiveness. *The Executive*, 5(3), 45–56.

Cox, T., Lobel, S., & McLeod, P. (1991). Effects of ethnic group cultural differences on cooperative and competitive behavior on a group task. *Academy of Management Journal*, 34, 827–847.

Cunningham, G. B. (2009). The moderating effect of diversity strategy on the relationship between racial diversity and organizational performance. *Journal of Applied Social Psychology*, 39(6), 1445–1460.

Dass, P., & Parker, B. (1996). Diversity: a strategic issue. In E. Kossek & S. Lobel (Eds.), *Managing diversity. Human resource strategies for transforming the workplace* (pp. 365–392). Cambridge: Blackwell Publishers.

Deshpandé, R., Farley, J. U., & Webster, F. E. (2000). Triad lessons: Generalizing results on high performance firms in five business-to-business markets. *International Journal of Research in Marketing*, 17(4), 353–362.

Deshpandé, R., & Webster Jr, F. E. (1989). Organizational culture and marketing: Defining the research agenda. *Journal of Marketing*, 53(1), 3–15.

Dwyer, S., Richard, O. C., & Chadwick, K. (2003). Gender diversity in management and firm performance: The influence of growth orientation and organizational culture. *Journal of Business Research*, 56(12), 1009–1019.

Eisenhardt, K. M. & Schoonhoven, C. B. (1990). Organizational growth: Linking founding team, strategy, environment, and growth among US semiconductor ventures, 1978–1988. *Administrative Science Quarterly*, 35(3), 504–529.

Gaertner, S. L., & Dovidio, J. F. (2000). *Reducing intergroup bias: The common ingroup identity model.* Philadelphia, PA: Psychology Press.

Gonzalez, J. A., & DeNisi, A. S. (2009). Cross-level effects of demography and diversity climate on organizational attachment and firm effectiveness. *Journal of Organizational Behavior*, 30(1), 21–40.

Grant, R. M. (1996). Toward a knowledge-based theory of the firm. *Strategic Management Journal*, 17(10), 109–122.

Grimes, D. S., & Richard, O. C. (2003). Could communication form impact organizations' experience with diversity? *Journal of Business Communication*, 40(1), 7–28.

Hambrick, D., & Mason, P. (1984). Upper echelons: The organization as a reflection of its top managers. *Academy of Management Journal*, 9(2), 193–206.

Hambrick, D. C. (2007). Upper echelons theory: An update. *Academy of Management Review*, 32(3), 334–343.

Harrison, D. A., & Klein, K. J. (2007). What's the difference? Diversity constructs as separation, variety, or disparity in organizations. *Academy of Management Review*, 32(4), 1199–1228.

Herbert, T. T., & Deresky, H. (1987). Generic strategies: an empirical investigation of typology validity and strategy content. *Strategic Management Journal*, 8(2), 135–147.

Herring, C. (2009). Does diversity pay? Race, gender, and the business case for diversity. *American Sociological Review*, 74(2), 208–224.

Hillman, A. J., Cannella, A. A., & Harris, I. C. (2002). Women and racial minorities in the boardroom: How do directors differ? *Journal of Management*, 28(6), 747–763.

Hillman, A. J., Shropshire, C., & Cannella, A. A. (2007). Organizational predictors of women on corporate boards. *Academy of Management Journal*, 50(4), 941–952.

Hitt, M.A., Bierman, L., Shimizu, K., & Kochhar, R. (2001). Direct and moderating effects of human capital on strategy and performance in professional service firms: A resource-based perspective. *Academy of Management Journal*, 44(1), 13–28.

Hoffman, L. R., & Maier, N. R. F. (1961). Quality and acceptance of problem solutions by members of homogeneous and heterogeneous groups. *Journal of Abnormal and Social Psychology*, 62(2), 401–407.

Hofstede, G. (1991). *Cultures and organizations: Software of the mind*. London: McGraw.

Hopkins, W. E., Hopkins, S. A., & Gross, M. A. (2005). Cultural diversity recomposition and effectiveness in monoculture work groups. *Journal of Organizational Behavior, 26*(8), 949–964.

Jackson, S. E., Brett, J. F., Sessa, V. I., Cooper, D. M., Julin, J. A., & Peyronnin, K. (1991). Some differences make a difference: Individual dissimilarity and group heterogeneity as correlates of recruitment, promotions, and turnover. *Journal of Applied Psychology, 76*(5), 675–689.

Jackson, S. E., Joshi, A., & Erhardt, N. L. (2003). Recent research on team and organizational diversity: SWOT analysis and implications. *Journal of Management, 29*(6), 801–830.

Jayne, M. E. A., & Dipboye, R. L. (2004). Leveraging diversity to improve business performance: Research findings and recommendations for organizations. *Human Resource Management, 43*(4), 409–424.

Jehn, K., Northcraft, G., & Neale, M. (1999), Why differences make a difference: A field study of diversity, conflict and performance in workgroups. *Administrative Science Quarterly, 44*(4), 741–764.

Joshi, A., Liao, H., & Jackson, S. (2006). Cross-level effects of workplace diversity on sales performance and pay. *Academy of Management Journal, 49*(3), 459.

Joshi, A., Liao, H., & Roh, H. (2011). Bridging domains in workplace demography research: A review and reconceptualization. *Journal of Management, 37*(2), 521–552.

Joshi, A., & Roh, H. (2009). The role of context in work team diversity research: A meta-analytic review. *Academy of Management Journal, 52*(3), 599–627.

Kirby, S. L., & Richard, O. C. (2000). Impact of marketing work-place diversity on employee job involvement and organizational commitment. *Journal of Social Psychology, 140*(3), 367–377.

Kochan, T., Bezrukova, K., Ely, R., Jackson, S., Joshi, A., Jehn, K., Leonard, J., Levine. D., & Thomas, D. (2003). The effects of diversity on business performance: Report of the diversity research network. *Human Resource Management, 42*(1), 3–21.

Lau, D. C., & Murnighan, J. K. (2005). Interactions within groups and subgroups: The effects of demographic faultlines. *Academy of Management Journal, 48*(4), 645–659.

Lin, X., & Germain, R. (2003). Organizational structure, context, customer orientation, and performance: Lessons from Chinese state-owned enterprises. *Strategic Management Journal, 24*(11), 1131–1151.

Lumpkin, G. T., & Dess, G. G. (1996). Clarifying the entrepreneurial orientation construct and linking it to performance. *Academy of Management Review, 21*(1), 135–172.

McKay, P. F., Avery, D. R., Liao, H., & Morris, M. A. (2011). Does diversity climate lead to customer satisfaction? It depends on the service climate and business unit demography. *Organization Science, 22*(3), 788–803.

McLeod, P. L., Lobel, S. A., & Cox, T. H. (1996). Ethnic diversity and creativity in small groups. *Small Group Research, 27*(2), 248–264.

McMahan, G. C., Bell, M. P., & Virick, M. (1998). Strategic human resource management: Employee involvement, diversity, and international issues. *Human Resource Management Review, 8*(3), 193–214.

McMahon, A. M. (2010). Does workplace diversity matter? A survey of empirical studies on diversity and firm performance, 2000–09. *Journal of Diversity Management, 5*(2), 37–48.

McMillan-Capehart, A. (2005). A configurational framework for diversity: Socialization and culture. *Personnel Review, 34*(4), 488–503.

Miles, R., & Snow, C. (1978). *Strategy, structure, and process*. New York: McGraw Hill.

Miller, D., & Shamsie, J. (1996). The resource-based view of the firm in two environments: The Hollywood film studios from 1936–1965. *Academy of Management Journal, 39*(3), 519–543.

Miller, T., & Del Carmen Triana, M. (2009). Demographic diversity in the boardroom: Mediators of the board diversity–firm performance relationship. *Journal of Management Studies, 46*(5), 755–786.

Milliken, F., & Martins, L. (1996). Searching for common threads: Understanding the multiple effects of diversity in organizational groups. *Academy of Management Review, 21*(2), 402–433.

Mintzberg, H. (1978). Patterns in strategy formation. *Management Science, 24*(9), 934–948.

Nielsen, S. (2010). Top management team diversity: A review of theories and methodologies. *International Journal of Management Reviews, 12*(3), 301–316.

Nemeth, C. J. (1992). Minority dissent as a stimulant to group performance. In S. Worchel, W. Wood, & J. Simpson (Eds.), *Productivity and process in groups* (pp. 95–111). Newbury Park, CA: Sage Publications.

O'Reilly III, C. A., Caldwell, D. F., & Barnett, W. P. (1989). Work group demography, social integration, and turnover. *Administrative Science Quarterly, 34*(1), 21–37.

Pelled, L., Eisenhardt, K., & Xin, K. (1999), Exploring the black box: An analysis of work group diversity, conflict, and performance, *Administrative Science Quarterly, 44*(1), 1–28.

Peteraf, M. A. (1993). The cornerstones of competitive advantage: A resource-based view. *Strategic Management Journal, 14*(3), 179–191.

Pfeffer, J. (1983). Organizational demography. *Research in Organizational Behavior, 5*(1), 299–357.

Pfeffer, J., & Salancik, G. R. (1978). *The external control of organizations*. New York: Harper & Row.

Phillips, K. W., Northcraft, G. B., & Neale, M. A. (2006). Surface-level diversity and decision-making in groups: When does deep-level similarity help? *Group Processes & Intergroup Relations, 9*(4), 467–482.

Pless, N., & Maak, T. (2004). Building an inclusive diversity culture: Principles, processes and practice. *Journal of Business Ethics, 54*(2), 129–147.

Richard, O. C. (2000). Racial diversity, business strategy, and firm performance: A resource-based view. *Academy of Management Journal, 43*(2), 164–177.

Richard, O. C., Barnett, T., Dwyer, S., & Chadwick, K. (2004). Cultural diversity in management, firm performance, and the moderating role of entrepreneurial orientation dimensions. *Academy Of Management Journal, 47*(2), 255–266.

Richard, O. C., Ford, D., & Ismail, K. (2006). Exploring the performance effects of visible attribute diversity: the moderating role of span of control and organizational life cycle. *International Journal of Human Resource Management, 17*(12), 2091–2109.

Richard, O. C., Kochan, T. A., & McMillan-Capehart, A. (2002). The impact of visible diversity on organizational effectiveness: Disclosing the contents in Pandora's black box. *Journal of Business and Management, 8,* 265–291.

Richard, O. C., Murthi, B. P. S, & Ismail, K. (2007). The impact of racial diversity on intermediate and long-term performance: The moderating role of environmental context. *Strategic Management Journal, 28*(12), 1213–1233.

Saavedra, R., Earley, P. C., & Van Dyne, L. (1993). Complex interdependence in task-performing groups. *Journal of Applied Psychology, 78*(1), 61–72.

Sacco, J. M., & Schmitt, N. (2005). A dynamic multilevel model of demographic diversity and misfit effects. *Journal of Applied Psychology, 90*(2), 203–231.

Schippers, M. C., Hartog, D. N., Koopman, P. L., & Wienk, J. A. (2003). Diversity and team outcomes: The moderating effects of outcome interdependence and group longevity and the mediating effect of reflexivity. *Journal of Organizational Behavior, 24*(6), 779–802.

Shore, L. M., Randel, A. E., Chung, B. G., Dean, M. A., Ehrhart, K. H., & Singh, G. (2011). Inclusion and diversity in work groups: A review and model for future research. *Journal of Management, 37*(4), 1262–1289.

Skaggs, B. C., & Youndt, M. (2004). Strategic positioning, human capital, and performance in service organizations: A customer interaction approach. *Strategic Management Journal, 25*(1), 85–99.

Slater, S. F., Weigand, R. A., & Zwirlein, T. J. (2008). The business case for commitment to diversity. *Business Horizons, 51*(3), 201–209.

Smith, K., Smith, A. Olian, J. Sims, H. O'Bannon, D., & Scully, J. (1994). Top management team demography and process: The role of social integration and communication. *Administrative Science Quarterly, 39*(3), 412–438.

Sutton, R. I., & Hargadon, A. (1996). Brainstorming groups in context: Effectiveness in a product design firm. *Administrative Science Quarterly, 41*(4), 685–718.

Swann Jr., W. B., Polzer, J. T., Seyle, D. C., & Ko, S. J. (2004). Finding value in diversity: Verification of personal and social self-views in diverse groups. *Academy of Management Review, 29*(1), 9–27.

Tajfel, H., & Turner, J. C. (1979). An integrative theory of intergroup conflict. In W. Austin & S. Worchel (Eds.), *The social psychology of intergroup relations* (pp. 33–47). Monterey, CA: Brooks-Cole.

Thomas, R. R. Jr. (1990). From affirmative action to affirming diversity. *Harvard Business Review*, March-April, 107–117.

van Knippenberg, D., De Dreu, C. K. W., & Homan, A. C. (2004). Work group diversity and group performance: An integrative model and research agenda. *Journal of Applied Psychology, 89*(6), 1008–1022.

Wageman, R. (1995). Interdependence and group effectiveness. *Administrative Science Quarterly, 40*(1), 145–180.

Wageman, R. (2001). How leaders foster self-managing team effectiveness: Design choices versus hands-on coaching. *Organization Science, 12*(5), 559–577.

Watson, W. E., Kumer, K., & Michaelsen, L. K. (1993). Cultural diversity's impact on interaction process and performance: comparing homogeneous and diverse task groups. *Academy of Management Journal, 36*(3), 590–602.

Weber, M. (1946). *From Max Weber.* H. H. Gerth & C. W. Mills (Eds.). New York: Oxford University Press.

White, R. E. (1986). Generic business strategies, organizational context and performance: an empirical investigation. *Strategic Management Journal, 7*(3), 217–231.

Wiersema, M. F., & Bantel, K. A. (1992). Top management team demography and corporate strategic change. *Academy of Management Journal, 35*(1), 91–121.

Williams, K. Y., & O'Reilly, C. A. (1998). Demography and diversity in organizations: A review of 40 years of research. *Research in Organizational Behavior, 20,* 77–140.

Woodward, J. (1965). *Industrial organization: Theory and practice.* New York: Oxford University Press.

Wright, P. M., & McMahan, G. C. (1992). Theoretical perspectives for strategic human resource management. *Journal of Management, 18*(2), 295–320.

Wright, P. M., Smart, D. L., & McMahan, G. C. (1995). Matches between human resources and strategy among NCAA basketball teams. *Academy of Management Journal, 38*(4), 1052–1074.

Zaltman, G. (1979). Knowledge utilization as planned social change. *Science Communication, 1*(1), 82–105.

Zellmer-Bruhn, M. E., Maloney, M. M., Bhappu, A. D., & Salvador, R. (2008). When and how do differences matter? An exploration of perceived similarity in teams. *Organizational Behavior and Human Decision Processes, 107*(1), 41–59.

PART 6

Practice Perspectives on Diversity

CHAPTER 15

The Origins and Effects of Corporate Diversity Programs

Frank Dobbin *and* Alexandra Kalev

Abstract

Corporations have implemented a wide range of equal opportunity and diversity programs since the 1960s. This chapter reviews studies of the origins of these programs, surveys that assess the popularity of different programs, and research on the effects of programs on the workforce. Human resources managers championed several waves of innovations: corporate equal opportunity policies and recruitment and training programs in the 1960s; bureaucratic hiring and promotion policies and grievance mechanisms in the 1970s; diversity training, networking, and mentoring programs in the 1980s; and work/family and sexual harassment programs in the 1990s and beyond. It was those managers who designed equal opportunity and diversity programs, not lawyers or judges or government bureaucrats, thus corporate take-up of the programs remains very uneven. Statistical analyses of time-series data on the effects of corporate diversity measures reveal several patterns. Initiatives designed to quash managerial bias, through diversity training, diversity performance evaluations, and bureaucratic rules, have been broadly ineffective. By contrast, innovations designed to engage managers in promoting workforce integration—mentoring programs, diversity taskforces, and full-time diversity staffers—have led to increases in diversity in the most difficult job to integrate, management. The research has clear implications for corporate and public policy.

Key Words: diversity programs, diversity taskforces, mentoring, diversity training, workforce diversity

Diversity management traces its origins to the civil rights movement and the subsequent antidiscrimination measures adopted by President John F. Kennedy and Congress in the 1960s. From their inception federal antidiscrimination laws were mute on how firms should achieve equality of opportunity. The programs firms adopted, from race relations training to sexual harassment grievance procedures to culture audits, were devised not by Congress or by the executive branch, but by personnel experts keen to expand their purview in the firm. From the early 1980s, when the Reagan administration expressed doubts about the continued need for federal regulation of employment discrimination, employers recast their equal opportunity programs as part of the new diversity management initiative. Firms adopted a host of diversity programs designed to promote exchange between different groups and to facilitate career development for people who had long been left out of the tournament. Soon a wide range of government and private groups were describing these programs as ways to improve group relations and prevent discrimination (EEOC, 1998, p. 197; Glass Ceiling Commission, 1995; SHRM, 1999). Today these programs are the main channel through which antidiscrimination legislation is implemented, yet we know surprisingly little about their effects.

This chapter chronicles the programs that personnel managers promoted under the banners of equal opportunity and diversity management, charts their spread across American firms between the early 1960s and the early years of the new millennium, and reviews extant evidence of their effects on workforce composition. We address two questions: What have firms been doing to promote diversity? What effects have their efforts had?

Origins and outcomes of diversity programs

Antidiscrimination regulations from the early 1960s stimulated corporate America to develop the precursors to today's diversity programs. John F. Kennedy's Executive Order 10925 from 1961 required federal contractors to take "affirmative action to ensure that applicants are employed, and that employees are treated during employment, without regard to their race, creed, color, or national origin" (Executive Order 10925,26 Fed. Reg. 1961). The year after Kennedy's assassination, Lyndon Johnson signed the Civil Rights Act into law, outlawing employment discrimination based on race, creed, color, national origin, and sex, throughout the private sector. In the meantime, Congress had made it illegal to pay men and women different wages for the same work in the Equal Pay Act of 1963 (Boyle, 1973, p. 86; Nelson & Bridges, 1999).

Lacking hints from Congress on how to comply with laws against employment discrimination, personnel experts crafted programs based on weapons in their professional arsenal. Civil rights law stimulated what Lauren Edelman terms "endogenous" compliance: those being regulated helped to define the terms of compliance (Edelman, 2002; Edelman, Uggen, & Erlanger, 1999). This happened in part because Congress had decided not to create a independent regulatory agency to set compliance standards (Chen, 2009). Executives saw quickly that the law was a moving target, and many hired full-time equal opportunity experts, or created new departments, to track changes in the law and in judicial interpretation (Meyer & Scott, 1992). Judges and bureaucrats in local, state, and federal governments played roles in determining which employer-initiated programs would stand. The system of regulation was "porous;" citizens could appeal to various public authorities to interpret and reinterpret laws (Kelly 2003; Lieberman, 2002), shopping for the venue most likely to support their causes, be it the San Francisco city bureaucracy or the Supreme Court. In this context, companies came to rely on personnel professionals to predict which way the judicial wind would blow. Judges in turn came to accept the "best practices" of leading firms as evidence of good faith (Bisom-Rapp, 2001; Edelman et al., 1999; Krawiec, 2003). What personnel made popular gradually became lawful (Dobbin, 2009). Employer programs came to define fair employment and discrimination in the American mind, for the workplace is where Americans came face to face with fair employment laws.

The public's legal consciousness, and its ideas about what discrimination and diversity mean, evolved over time as social scientists, politicians, and management experts promoted new understandings of the world of inequality in dialogue with the courts (Dobbin & Sutton, 1998; Ewick & Silbey, 1998; Liberman, 2005; Lieberman, 1998; Stryker, forthcoming). Personnel experts promoted one round of diversity innovations after another. In the 1960s, they wrote nondiscrimination policies based on union contract clauses designed to prevent discrimination against union leaders, and developed new recruitment programs and skills and management training systems to bring in more women and minorities and prepare them for advancement. In the 1970s, as the profession more than doubled in size and as the proportion of women rose from a third to nearly a half, personnel experts created formal hiring and promotion systems designed to create a rulebook for personnel decisions, and thereby deny managers the chance to exercise bias.

When the Reagan administration mounted an assault on fair employment regulations, personnel experts argued that the new hiring and promotion practices helped to rationalize "human resources management" and rebranded their efforts under the heading of diversity management. Equal opportunity experts now argued not that the law required employers to hire and promote women and minorities, but that the market required it. Firms would not remain competitive if they could not figure out how to use the talents of all kinds of workers. Soon race relations workshops became diversity training programs, equal opportunity attitude surveys became corporate culture audits, and affirmative action officers became diversity managers. After 1990 the increasingly feminized human resources profession focused on women's issues, pushing for the expansion of work and family programs and anti-harassment programs. In each period, changes in corporate practice altered the meaning of fair employment in the American mind. Some changes altered workforce composition as well.

To date, there have been few rigorous studies of the efficacy of different diversity programs, but we are able to draw a few conclusions from the studies that exist. On average, the programs designed to diversify the pipeline through active recruitment and programs designed to upgrade extant female and minority workers (through training), have succeeded. Yet programs designed to quell managerial bias, such as diversity training and diversity performance evaluations, have failed to increase workforce diversity. The same is true for bureaucratic personnel procedures designed to stop managers from exercising bias. Programs that assign responsibility for diversity to managers (diversity taskforces, diversity managers, mentoring) have helped, while programs designed to increase networking within groups that are not well represented in management (affinity networks or employee resource groups) have not increased managerial diversity. Overall, efforts to interfere with the exercise of managerial bias have failed while efforts to make managers responsible for advancing diversity and efforts to recruit and upgrade women and minorities have succeeded.

The Sociological Approach

While most of the chapters in this volume report the results of behavioral studies, based in laboratory research or in field research on individual organizations, we review studies using an approach that has become common among sociologists who seek to explain labor market outcomes with organizational characteristics. Our own studies employ data from national samples of hundreds of U.S. employers, over several decades. A number of sociologists employ similar methods (Baron & Bielby, 1986; Edelman, 1992). Such data allow us to use advanced statistical techniques that permit evaluation of the effects of diversity programs on workforce composition over time. Because of the large number of organizations in these samples, and the long time spans they cover, we can isolate the effects of a new diversity program in the years that follow its introduction from the effects of changes in the environment and firm. We can establish whether, on average, mentoring programs lead to changes in the composition of the workforce. We are aided in the task by the availability of time-series data on workforce composition that allow us to observe the baseline level of diversity, and the rate of change, before innovations are introduced.

Behavioral studies, such as those reviewed in Chapter 19, "Effective Diversity Training," typically examine the consequences of diversity innovations in terms of individual behaviors or attitudes. The studies we discuss examine, for the most part, effects of diversity program innovations on workforce composition. They cannot identify the effects of diversity programs on behavior or cognition, but some of these studies help to fill important lacunae in the behavioral literature. For instance, Roberson, Kulik, and Tan report that little research has been done on the long-term behavioral effects of diversity training, or on the group or organizational effects. We report below that diversity training programs have had negligible effects on workforce composition. In addition to establishing the organizational effects of programs, the approach we take can thus help to determine whether behavioral and cognitive effects of innovations translate into changes in the makeup of the workplace.

In the process of reviewing sociological findings about the efficacy of diversity programs, we present graphs tracing the diffusion of different diversity programs among U.S. firms. The data for these graphs come from a retrospective survey Dobbin and Kalev conducted together in 2002, and from surveys Dobbin conducted in 1986 with John W. Meyer, W. Richard Scott, and John Sutton, and in 1997 with Erin Kelly. They cover 829, 279, and 389 employers respectively. Each survey was stratified by industry to cover a broad swath of the U.S. economy (Dobbin et al., 1993, 2007; Kalev & Dobbin, 2006). We spoke to human resource managers, asking whether and when they had used each employment practice (Dobbin, Edelman, Meyer, Scott, & Swidler, 1988). We also report some data from Lauren Edelman's (1992) exemplary retrospective survey from 1989. These surveys cover middle-sized to large U.S. employers and have high response rates, and thus are more representative than most cross-sectional studies of corporate practice (see Esen, 2005). To fill in the blanks we report some results from cross-sectional surveys conducted by the Bureau of National Affairs (BNA), the Conference Board, and the Society for Human Resources Management.

Where possible, to evaluate the effects of diversity programs on workforce composition we rely on survey data we collected and merged with data on employment composition generously provided to us by the Equal Employment Opportunity Commission (EEOC) for confidential use under an Intergovernmental Personnel Act agreement (Kalev et al., 2006). We report findings from some other studies that use employer-provided data on workforce composition (e.g., Castilla & Benard, 2010; Edelman

& Petterson, 1999; Holzer & Neumark, 2000). Data constraints drive much of the research in this field and consequently limit what scholars and policymakers know about the effects of diversity innovations.

The 1960s: The attack on Jim Crow

From the time John F. Kennedy signed Executive Order 10925 outlawing discrimination by federal contractors, private firms took the lead in defining discrimination. The President's Committee on Equal Employment Opportunity, an inter-agency committee with no means to discipline firms, was to oversee compliance. But the privately organized "Plans for Progress" subcommittee, the brainchild of Atlanta lawyer Robert Troutman, did the most to establish standards for fair employment. Within a year Troutman had signed up nearly 100 leading companies that would collaborate in devising strategies for promoting fair employment (Graham, 1990, pp. 33–59). Many of these Plans for Progress firms were military contractors, who faced the threat of contract cancellation that came with Kennedy's affirmative action order of 1961. The fair employment measures they developed spread far and wide in the 1960s, notably corporate nondiscrimination policies, special recruitment programs for minorities, and programs to train new minority recruits and upgrade current workers (Graham, 1990, p. 49; Sovern, 1966, p. 109).

Corporate nondiscrimination policies

Kennedy's Executive Order required federal contractors to post a notice stating: "The contractor will not discriminate against any employee or applicant for employment because of race, creed, color, or national origin" (*New York Times*, 1962, p. 29). A company version might have seemed redundant, but contractors soon wrote nondiscrimination policies of their own for inclusion in their Plans for Progress pledges, personnel manuals, and job advertisements, which now ended with the tag line, "An Equal Opportunity Employer in the Plans for Progress Program" (Bethlehem Steel, 1968, p. 3).

By mid-1965, most of the 300 companies that had signed on with Plans for Progress had their own nondiscrimination policies in place. By 1967, 71 percent of medium and large employers surveyed by the BNA had nondiscrimination policies (BNA, 1967, p. 10). These spread to smaller employers after 1970. In the 1986 survey (Fig. 15.1), one in five employers reported that they had a written policy protecting minorities by 1970, but nearly half reported that they had one by 1980 (Dobbin et al., 1993; Edelman, 1990). Policies covering women lagged behind those covering minorities, for Kennedy's 1961 affirmative action order did not cover sex discrimination. By the turn of the century, policies mentioning race and sex were found in more than 90 percent of medium and large employers, according to our 2002 survey (Kalev et al., 2006).

Once the policies were widespread, officials endorsed them. Thus, when the Allen-Bradley Company of Milwaukee was challenged by the Department of Labor in 1968 for discriminating against blacks, Secretary of Labor George P. Shultz

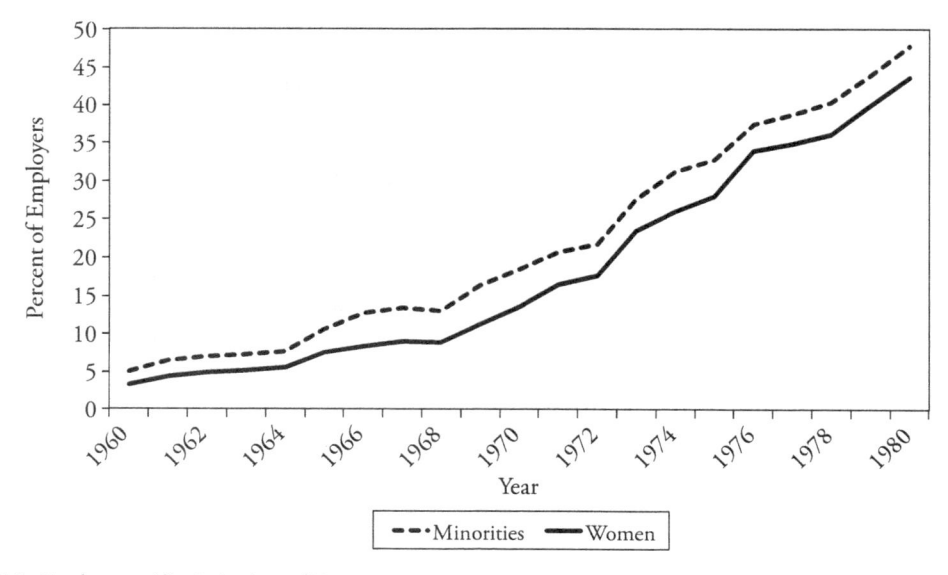

Figure 15.1. Employer antidiscrimination policies.
Source: Survey of 279 employers in 1986 (Dobbin et al., 1993)

said that the company must do as other companies had done and announce a nondiscrimination policy (Shaeffer, 1973).

Despite adopting written antidiscrimination policies, firms continued to treat groups differently. Many continued to advertise jobs for men and women separately, to ban pregnant women from work, and to exclude mothers from certain jobs. In 1966, the EEOC decreed that employers could not ban married women and those with small children, but it let segregated job ads and pregnancy bans stand (Pedriana, 2006). The newly formed National Organization for Women fought the EEOC on these issues, sending picketers to EEOC offices and suing the agency (Danovitch, 1990). By 1969 the EEOC had come out against separate job ads, except where a "bona fide occupational qualification" (BFOQ) limited the job to one sex (Abbott, 1994; Costain, 1992; Harrison, 1988; Pedriana, 2004). According to the guidelines that EEOC lawyer Sonia Pressman drafted, "the only jobs for which sex could be a BFOQ were sperm donor and wet nurse" (1990).

New recruitment programs

The company recruitment program was the second pillar of the early equal opportunity program. Many leading firms had longstanding recruitment programs targeting white men. They visited the Big Ten to find management trainees and trekked to vocational schools for skilled workers. In 1961, Lockheed established a program to recruit at Atlanta's segregated black high schools and at historically black colleges (Raskin, 1961). Personnel director Hugh Gordon argued that a firm that had practiced Jim Crow had to go the extra mile; "In the South...blacks who had been denied jobs just didn't have the confidence...to apply for jobs in companies where they thought they were not wanted. So it's understandable we had to make an effort to get the applicants" (2000). Lockheed brought busloads of black college students from Tuskegee Institute in Alabama on recruitment visits (Mattison, 1965, pp. 151–152). By 1963, the *New York Times* reported that "Personnel officers are taking a new look at their recruiting methods and seeking advice from Negro leaders on how to find and attract the best-qualified Negroes" (Stetson, 1963, p. 1).

America's historically black colleges now faced an onslaught of recruiters. Fisk College in Nashville saw recruitment visits rise from 27 to 78 between 1963 and 1964. Howard had 400 recruitment visits in 1964 and again in 1965 for a graduating class of 450 (Grove, 1965, p. 32). A 1967 BNA survey (Fig. 15.2) found that among leading employers, 31 percent had created new recruitment systems for blacks between 1965 and 1967 (BNA, 1967, p. 1). More than half of the firms were now advertising through organizations like the NAACP and the Urban League. A third sent recruiters to "predominantly Negro high schools and colleges," and a fifth were recruiting at women's colleges (BNA, 1967, p. 10).

Some executives resisted. One told the BNA that active recruitment of minorities would constitute reverse discrimination: "I have given instructions as of 1965...that if any good Negro applicants appear and if we have any openings, hire them. We have had none during this period...to go outside our area and recruit them would discriminate against local applicants" (BNA, 1967, p. 3). Resistance was rare among leading firms. A national survey of Fortune

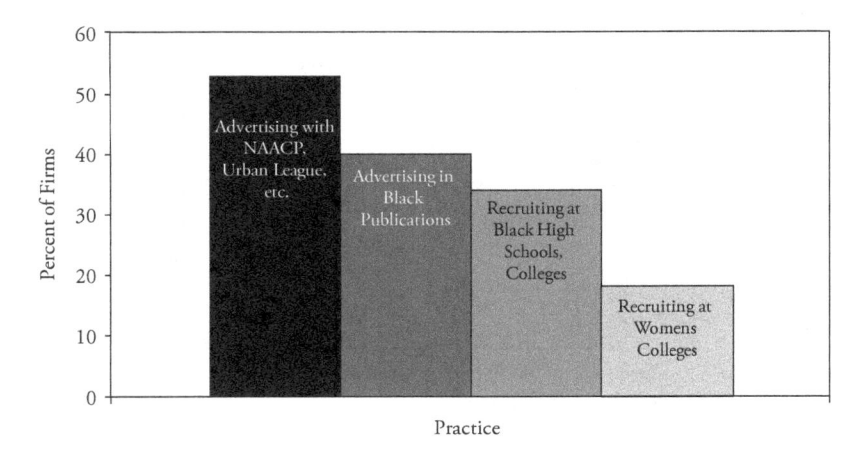

Figure 15.2. Targeted recruitment programs for Blacks, women, 1967.
Source: Bureau of National Affairs, 1967.

750 companies in 1969 found that top executives universally believed in special recruitment and training programs, and that just over half of line managers agreed with them (BNA, 1967, 1976). Yet these programs did not become widespread outside of the biggest firms: only one in 10 of the firms in our 2002 national sample had a special recruitment program.

Training for opportunity

Targeted recruitment programs would not help unskilled African-Americans and Latinos move into skilled jobs. Personnel experts now built on the training schemes devised to address wartime labor shortages, setting up programs to train minorities for clerical and manufacturing jobs they had been excluded from before (Braestrup, 1961). Employers with ongoing skill training and management training programs now pledged to enroll blacks (McFarland, 1965). Others created training programs for the first time, with the goal of upgrading women and minorities, and special programs to attract women and minorities to training.

As of 1960, most companies had not enrolled any women or minorities in management training, according to the BNA studies, but by 1966, 31 percent of large employers offered management training and 21 percent had special programs to enroll minorities in training (BNA, 1967). Between 1967 and 1985, the number of employers enrolling women and minorities in management training and apprenticeships grew steadily (Fig. 15.3). By 2002, our own study shows, 68 percent of firms offered management training and 20 percent of all firms targeted women or minorities for inclusion in management training.

Do equal opportunity policies and targeted recruitment and training work?

The innovations that were popularized in the 1960s were designed to increase integration of jobs that had been the exclusive province of white men. Perhaps the best measure of the efficacy of these programs, across firms, is whether they are followed by increases in the integration of management jobs, all else being equal. We know of no published research that examines the effect of equal employment opportunity statements on the subsequent employment of women and minorities. However, an unpublished analysis of our own 2002 survey data indicates that the adoption of such statements has not led to change in the demographic composition of management jobs. In models identical to those reported by Kalev and colleagues (2006), we examined the effect of the implementation of an equal opportunity policy on composition of the managerial workforce, in a sample of 814 corporations over the period 1971–2002. Statements are not followed by significant increases in white women in management, or in black, Hispanic, or Asian-American men or women. We suspect that this is because policy statements do not, by themselves, lead to changes on the factory floor. Managers may not know how to ensure equality of opportunity, or they may not be inclined to hire and promote workers from different backgrounds (Kanter, 1977).

The literature provides more evidence on the effects of targeted recruitment, management training, and recruitment into management training. Regarding recruitment efforts, Holzer and Neumark (2000) analyze data from the Multi-City

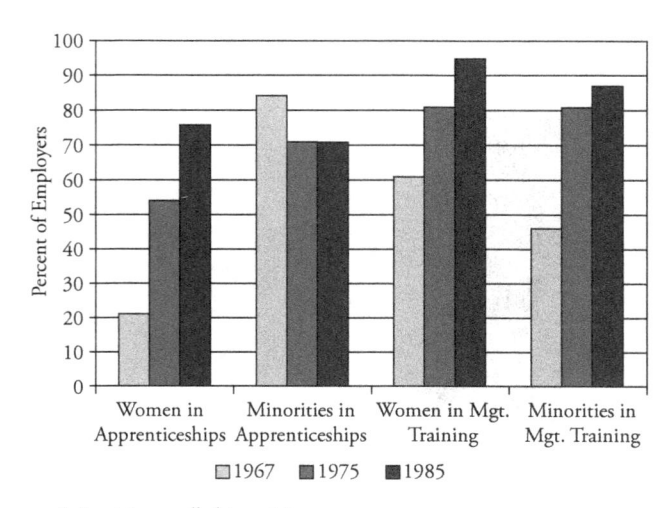

Figure 15.3. Firms with women/minorities enrolled in training.
Source: Bureau of National Affairs, 1986b, p. 14. Percentage of employers who enroll some women or minorities, conditioned on having the program.

Study of Urban Inequality, finding that firms that make special efforts to recruit women and minorities are more likely to hire them. Both Edelman and Petterson (1999) and Konrad and Linnehan (1995) find that active recruitment and special promotion programs are associated with increased diversity.

Evidence on management training programs points to a different pattern. Despite being hailed early on as a strategy for remediating inequality, research suggests that employer-provided training may have worked against equality. Participation in management or skills training does not harm women or minorities, but the groups continue to be enrolled in those programs at lower rates than white men. And training is a stepping stone to advancement. Thus, the 1995 report of the federal Glass Ceiling Commission listed lack of management training as a key barrier in career progression for women, and Knoke and Ishio (1998, p. 162) show that there are significant gender differences in access to company training even within occupations. Employers seem to view training more as an investment in human capital than as a means of equalizing opportunity. They tend to provide training for more educated and higher-status workers (Hight, 1998; Lynch & Black, 1998), and for those they expect to have continued employment and high productivity not affected by family obligations (Knoke & Ishio, 1998). These criteria result in statistical discrimination against women (Knoke & Ishio, 1998) and minorities (Yang, 2007). Thus, employer-provided training has not lived up to its potential to iron out pre-labor market disadvantages faced by women and minorities (Appelbaum & Berg, 2001). Yet, most existing evidence comes from research that collapses management training with skill training, and this may conceal effects of management training (Bills & Hodson, 2007). We need more fine-grained analyses of different types of training.

The 1970s: Expanding the labor relations model

Slow progress on integration in the 1960s spurred the administration, the courts, and Congress to turn up the heat. In 1970 and 1971 the Department of Labor required new workforce reports and new affirmative action plans from federal contractors, and stepped up compliance reviews. In 1971, in *Griggs v. Duke Power* (401 U.S. 424, 1971), the Supreme Court defined discrimination to include employer practices that were not explicitly exclusionary but that had a "disparate impact" on women or minorities. In 1972 Congress expanded the coverage of Title VII and gave the EEOC the authority to sue employers. In the context of recent racial strife in big cities, and the establishment of the National Organization for Women, these changes emboldened personnel experts to propose new compliance measures.

Equal opportunity specialists and departments: Creating organizational responsibility

From the early 1960s, new workplace regulations of all sorts stimulated firms to hire a variety of compliance experts (Kochan & Cappelli, 1984, p. 146). Whereas the Department of Labor enforced 16 statutes and executive orders in 1940 and 50 in 1960, by 1977 it enforced more than 130, including affirmative action regulations (Foulkes & Morgan, 1977, p. 171). The Department recommended that firms appoint affirmative action officers to handle compliance, and consultants insisted that middle-sized to large firms would need their own departments (Boyle, 1973). A 1977 article in the *Harvard Business Review* advised: "The various requirements of state and federal regulations...make increasing demands on both profit and nonprofit organizations.... Compliance with the laws relating to OSHA, EEOC, and ERISA demands expertise;" only specialists could keep track of "what is happening in the outside world" in terms of regulation and employer response (Foulkes & Morgan, p. 160). More and more companies followed General Electric, which had set up a separate equal opportunity office in 1968, with subcommittees to handle everything from compliance reviews to "social awareness" training (Schofer, 1971).

Organizational scholars have long recognized that firms create departments to mirror the players they face in the regulatory environment (Lawrence & Lorsch, 1967; Thompson, 1967). Jeffrey Pfeffer described department creation as a form of "protest absorption," which could allow unionists to appeal to labor relations departments and minorities to pursue "their interests through affirmative action offices" (Pfeffer & Salancik, 1978). John Meyer and W. Richard Scott (1992, p. 275) describe this pattern as uniquely American, for the fragmented character of the federal regulatory environment leads to distinct corporate departments to "symbolize safety, the environment, affirmative action" and so on.

A study from the late 1980s of 141 Tennessee manufacturers with at least 100 workers found

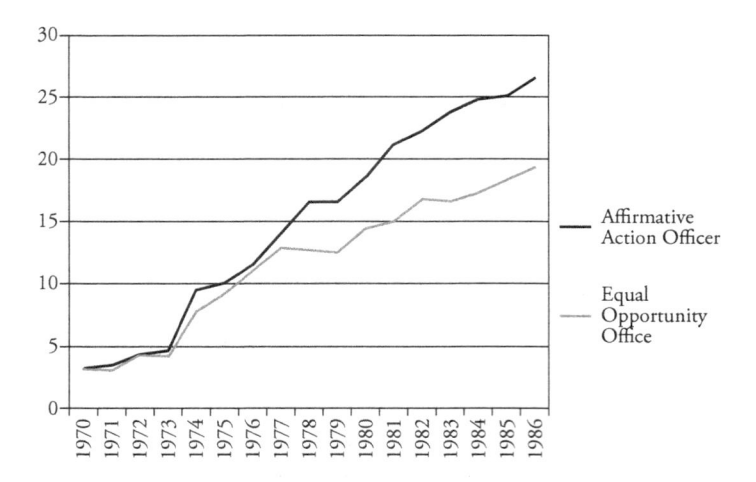

Figure 15.4. Antidiscrimination departments and officers.
Source: Survey of 279 employers in 1986 (Dobbin et al., 1993). Some organizations were not in operation at the beginning of the period. The denominator varies over time.

that over half had affirmative action offices (Johns & Moser, 1989). In Dobbin's collaborative 1986 survey of middle-sized to large employers, only 4 percent had equal opportunity offices or affirmative action officers by 1972. By 1986 these numbers rose to 20 percent and 25 percent respectively (Fig. 15.4). A similar pattern is evident in Lauren Edelman's national survey from 1989 (1992, p. 1555).

Equal opportunity performance evaluations: Monitoring individual managers

Once firms had specialists charged with developing antidiscrimination programs, they turned to the task of bringing line managers on board. Industrial psychologist Theodore Purcell championed the General Electric model, in the *Harvard Business Review* in 1974, of making managers accountable through a "measurement system with rewards and penalties designed to produce behavioral changes" (1974, p. 99). The equal opportunity performance evaluation was modeled on the merit rating systems that unions had lobbied for, and lined up nicely with the new financial performance systems conglomerates were using to judge managers (Baron, Jennings, & Dobbin, 1988; Jacoby, 1985).

Every one of the 20 leading firms that the Towers-Perrin consultancy studied in 1973 made equal opportunity part of the formal annual performance evaluation (Fretz & Hayman, 1973). A company president argued that firms must "place responsibility for achieving equal opportunity objectives where it rightfully belongs, with operating management, with each of us" (Ackerman, 1973, p. 94). In the BNA's 1975 study of leading firms, four in ten manufacturers, three in ten service firms, and two in ten nonprofits had equal opportunity performance evaluations (Bureau of National Affairs, 1976). In our 2002 survey, with a more representative sample that includes some smaller firms, only 4 percent of the sample had evaluations by 1985, but by 2002 nearly one in five firms had them.

Does responsibility breed diversity?

The 1970s brought to life two mechanisms for assigning responsibility: one created an organizational structure, a department or a position, and the other took the individualized form of evaluating managers' diversity efforts. Evidence suggests that the structural approach has been significantly more effective. Edelman and Petterson (1999) show that while equal opportunity departments do not increase gender and racial diversity on their own, they do expand diversity recruitment programs, which in turn improve diversity. In our analysis of data on more than 800 employers between 1971 and 2002 (Kalev et al., 2006), we find that the hiring of an equal employment opportunity specialist has significant positive effects on the subsequent share of women and minorities in management. Figure 15.5 shows that the appointment of a full-time diversity staffer leads, in the average firm, to a 10 percent increase in the proportion of white women in management and a 15 percent increase in the proportions of both black men and black women. These effects take place over about 5 to 7 years.

Diversity performance evaluations show weak and mixed effects on managerial diversity according

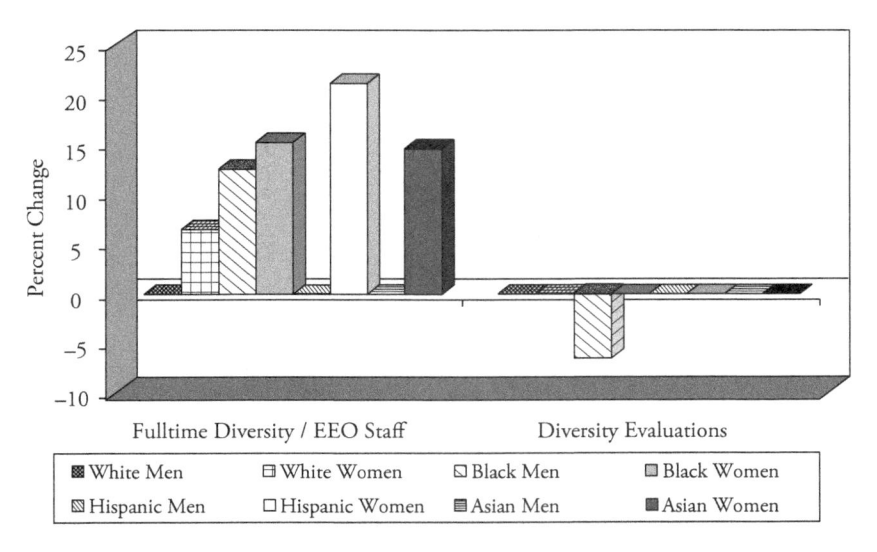

Figure 15.5. Effects of diversity staff and diversity performance evaluations.

to the same study. Firms that create diversity performance evaluations see small decreases in the share of black men. However, in the presence of formal oversight, through a full-time diversity staffer or taskforce, diversity performance evaluations exhibit no negative effects (Kalev et al., 2006). Diversity performance evaluations may have adverse effects because they alienate managers, but monitoring can prevent those effects.

Bureaucratic hiring and promotion: Tying the hands of managers

In the early 1970s, federal courts and Washington regulators identified hiring and promotion practices as a source of discrimination. The Supreme Court's 1971 Duke Power decision, challenging seemingly neutral job tests, led firms to scrutinize personnel routines generally. Then EEOC-brokered civil rights consent decrees called for modernization of hiring and promotion. In settlements with some of America's leading firms, across industries ranging from banking to steelmaking to trucking, the EEOC secured pledges to formalize salary assignment and promotion (Fehn, 1993; Shaeffer, 1975).

Personnel experts responded by developing a civil rights compliance arsenal based on the labor relations model. Unions had lobbied for bureaucratic procedures, from job posting to promotion rules, to prevent discrimination against unionists (Jacoby, 1985). Many of the same procedures might help to fight racial, ethnic, and gender discrimination. Formal personnel systems would also leave a paper trail, which would be useful in the case of lawsuits and would help employers meet reporting requirements (Thorpe, 1973, p. 649).

Some experts argued that **job tests** could prevent discrimination, but cautioned that employers should not use popular tests that served as high school equivalency exams, because inequality in educational opportunity left many blacks disadvantaged by such tests (Skrentny, 1996, p. 97). In 1960, 35 percent of white adults but only 23 percent of blacks had finished high school (Bureau of the Census, 1975, p. 380, Part I). Moreover, segregated black schools were chronically underfunded. Tests should therefore be tightly linked to job content. In 1966, *Personnel Psychology* championed validation of job tests to ensure that they predicted performance and did not simply exclude applicants who had attended inferior schools or dropped out (Dugan, 1966; Lopez Jr., 1966; Parrish, 1966). Later that year, the EEOC issued guidelines specifying that tests should be statistically validated to predict job performance (Thorpe, 1973, p. 647).

After 1971, when the Supreme Court found that general tests of academic skills could be discriminatory if they were not predictive of job performance (*Griggs v. Duke Power*, 401 U.S. 424 1971), personnel experts advised employers to either validate tests or get rid of them (Campbell, 1973; Gavin & Toole, 1973; Gorham, 1972; National Civil Service League, 1973; Slevin, 1973). Some employers validated, although many, including some of the largest police and fire departments, continue today to use unvalidated tests. Yet the ruling had a chilling effect on test creation. Both job and promotion tests languished after 1971, making tests the exception

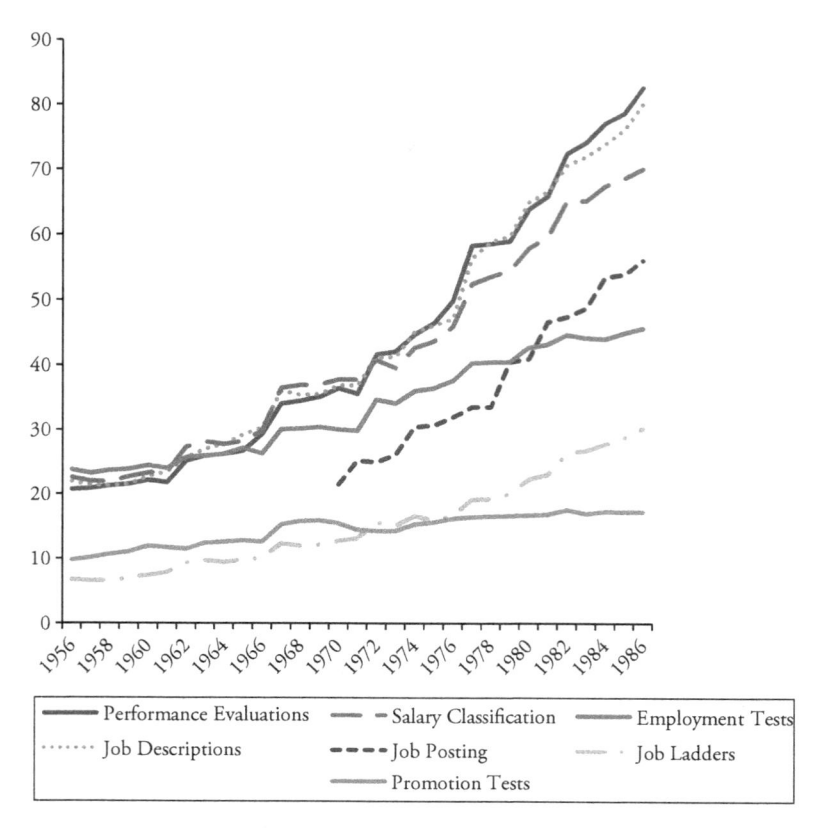

Figure 15.6. Bureaucratic hiring and promotion practices.
Source: Survey of 279 employers in 1986 (Dobbin et al., 1993). Job posting is taken from our 2002 survey (Kalev et al., 2006).

that proves the rule that employers adopted bureaucratic procedures to comply with equal opportunity laws. Job tests were one of the two early bureaucratic personnel practices that did not spread rapidly (Fig. 15.6), for they were not part of the "equal opportunity" prescription.

Personnel experts had mixed advice about **job ladders**, which specified promotion trajectories from entry-level jobs. Women and blacks were often crowded in jobs with no rungs above them, and so experts advised firms to abolish existing ladders and restructure them so that female- and minority-dominated jobs had gateways that led upward (DiPrete, 1989, p. 197). Another remedy was to replace job ladders with open bidding, "so that all employees are aware of vacancies as they occur and that promotion into these vacancies is based on qualifications, not sex" (Slevin, 1973, p. 30). Dobbin and colleagues' 1986 survey shows that the pattern of diffusion of job ladders looks more like job tests than like the other bureaucratic procedures (see Fig. 15.6). This was the second bureaucratic personnel procedure that did not spread apace.

Executives read that the EEOC favored **job posting**, and that it could prevent cronyism (Fulmer & Fulmer, 1974, p. 492). They also began to hear complaints that supervisors kept news of openings from women and minorities in the workforce. Unions had long demanded formal job posting systems to prevent managers from blackballing unionists (1974, p. 493). Equal opportunity experts now proposed open job posting on the union model. According to our 2002 survey, two in ten companies had policies requiring posting of jobs as of 1971 and nine in ten companies had them three decades later (see Fig. 15.6 for the trend from the 2002 data up to 1986).

In 1962 it came out that supervisors at several Louisiana oil refineries had excluded blacks from skilled jobs by inflating educational prerequisites for jobs. Personnel experts recommended written **job descriptions**, specifying prerequisites, that would be available to jobseekers (Boyle, 1973, pp. 94–95). Among the medium-sized and large employers in the 1986 survey, the use of job descriptions had risen gradually between 1956 and 1966, from 22 percent to 28 percent (see Fig. 15.6). But over the next 20 years, job descriptions caught on. Eight out of ten of these firms used written job descriptions by 1985.

Since the 1930s, management and personnel journals had extolled annual, written **performance evaluations** for use in promotion, pay, and disciplinary decisions (Cunningham, 1936; Drum, 1960; Patton, 1960; Rock & Grela, 1960). In the early 1970s, several firms were charged with employment discrimination for letting managers' informal views taint promotion decisions (*Rowe v. General Motors Corp.*, 457 F.2D 348, 359, 5 Cir 1972). Experts now argued that a written annual performance evaluation, with objective output measures, could fight prejudice (Peskin, 1969, p. 130). A 1974 article in *Personnel* suggested: "Performance reviews should...be based on solid criteria available to all concerned parties," to ensure that promotion decisions were based on ability—which, "coincidentally," conforms to the EEOC's guidelines (Froehlich & Hawver, 1974, p. 64). The BNA (1967, p. 16) found that companies were creating performance evaluations to stem discrimination. The 1986 survey shows that between 1956 and 1966, the prevalence of evaluations rose from 20 percent to 25. At that rate, 35 percent of firms would have had them by 1986. Instead, 80 percent of employers had installed them by then (see Fig. 15.6).

The Equal Pay Act required employers to pay the same wages to men and women doing the same work, and the Civil Rights Act outlawed discrimination in the terms and conditions of employment. Yet firms continued to pay different wages for the same work. In 1974, the Supreme Court ruled that employers could not pay women less than men by assigning them different job titles "simply because men would not work at the low rates paid to women" (*Corning Glass Works v. Brennan*, 1974). Union-inspired **salary classification** systems established skill, education, and experience requirements, placing like jobs into wage bands. Discrimination plaintiffs now asked for salary classification systems in their settlement negotiations (*Shultz v. Wheaton Glass Co.*, 421 F.2d 259 3rd Cir 1970).

Personnel experts advised firms to classify all jobs to ensure that pay rates were not discriminatory (Chayes, 1974, p. 81; Giblin & Ornati, 1974). About one third of employers reported that they had salary classification systems in the early 1970s, and some 70 percent had them by the mid-1980s (see Fig. 15.6). For comparison, employment tests started at about the same place but reached only 45 percent of employers by the mid-1980s.

When the administration, the courts, and Congress stepped up enforcement of fair employment laws in the early 1970s, personnel experts promoted a new round of compliance strategies. The picture drawn by national surveys confirms that the union personnel model was now used as a civil rights antidiscrimination system, and spread across firms despite the fact that unionization was declining. Seventy to eighty percent of employers had put in performance evaluations, job descriptions, and salary classification systems by the mid-1980s, up from 30 percent or less at the beginning of the 1970s. Job posting systems and centralized hiring and firing were not far behind. These practices left Americans with new ideas about workplace fairness. Bureaucratic rules governing hiring and promotion were supposed to quash bias and create a level playing field.

Does bureaucracy promote diversity?

Theorists offer conflicting predictions about the effects of formal hiring and promotion practices. Feminist scholars have argued that bureaucratic rules may reinforce the status quo in organizations. In *The Feminist Case Against Bureaucracy*, Kathy Ferguson (1984, p. 7) argues that bureaucracy creates a "scientific organization of inequality." Joan Acker (1990) argues that "rational-technical, ostensibly gender neutral, control systems [in organizations] are built upon and conceal a gendered substructure." Hiring and promotion procedures can codify disadvantage in formal organizational structure rather than reduce inequality by, for instance, formalizing selection criteria that advantage white men. Thus, job descriptions that require a decade of continuous service tend to advantage men, because women more often experience career disruptions following childbirth. Yet some social psychologists expect formal personnel procedures to quash discrimination by reducing managerial discretion and the operation of cognitive bias (Bielby, 2000; Reskin, 2000).

Evidence of the effects of bureaucratic practices is scant, indirect, and inconsistent. Most studies rely on cross-sectional data from employers, or short panel series, and use counts of formal personnel practices, failing to differentiate effects of particular practices. Several cross-sectional studies suggest that bureaucratic practices may promote equality, but it is difficult to know whether the bureaucratic practices are the cause or the consequence of workforce integration, or whether both are a consequence of a third factor. Reskin and McBrier (2000) find that large employers with formal personnel procedures have more women in management, and Walker (1990) finds that they have more black men on the job. Anderson and Tomaskovic-Devey (1995) find lower wage disparities among employers with more formal personnel procedures. In one of the few studies using longitudinal data, Baron, Hannan, Hsu, and Koçak (2007) find that firms founded with bureaucratic personnel systems have more women workers 6 years out. Elvira and Zatzick (2002) find that some minorities fare better when personnel decisions are bureaucratized.

Other studies have found that formal personnel systems are not associated with greater equality, notably those by Edelman and Petterson (1999), Konrad and Linnehan (1995), and Huffman and Velasco (1997). Yet others have identified mechanisms through which bureaucratic practices may thwart equality of opportunity. Next we discuss some of these studies in the process of reviewing evidence about the effects of individual practices.

Despite the Supreme Court decision in *Griggs v. Duke Power Company*, many employers continue to use **job tests** that have not been validated. The human resources director at a medium-sized New Jersey manufacturer, without a federal contract, reported in an interview we conducted in 1999 that he used an unvalidated test to assess math skills: "We'll throw ourselves on the mercy of the court if anything happens." Research by psychologists shows that cognitive ability tests disadvantage minorities, particularly blacks and Hispanics (Roth, Huffcutt, & Bobko, 2003; Hough & Oswald, 2000). In a study of employer selection methods in Canada, based on survey data from 154 organizations, Ng and Sears (2010) find that cognitive ability testing is associated with lower minority employment in general and in management. They also find that firms covered under employment equity legislation were less likely to use such tests.

DiPrete (1989, p. 197) argues that the problem with **job ladders** is that they often exclude from promotion lines the entry-level jobs dominated by women and minorities. Such exclusionary job ladders help to explain the gender gap in promotion in the federal civil service in the 1970s (DiPrete & Soule, 1988). In their analysis of promotions in an insurance company between 1971 and 1978, Spilerman and Petersen (1999) find that women were handicapped by being in jobs with short promotion ladders. The EEOC's 1974 consent decrees with the leading steelmakers recognized that constrained job ladders had harmed blacks, and mandated the replacement of department- with plant-level career systems and seniority. Blacks had been relegated to departments without skilled jobs, and hence had nowhere to move from the entry-level laborer jobs. Ichniowski's study shows that the switch to plant-wide promotion systems, which ended constraining job ladders, led to significant increases in the share of minorities in skilled jobs (Ichniowski, 1983).

Job posting systems require managers to notify existing workers, through posting, of job openings within the firm. Reskin and McBrier (2000) find more women in management in organizations that use open recruitment methods, including job posting. But job posting systems can be thwarted by managers who favor white men. Pager, Western, and Bonikowski (2009) show that managers make biased hiring decisions when sorting applicants who respond to job advertisements. Whites are more likely to receive callbacks or job offers, and blacks and Hispanics who do receive job offers are relegated to lesser jobs. Job posting thus may not reduce inequality.

Some consultants caution that **job descriptions** can hamper women and minorities by setting prerequisites that favor white men (engineering degrees, long uninterrupted service) but that are not essential to job performance (Boyle, 1973, p. 91). Job descriptions have also been linked to slow advancement of women and minorities bunched in narrowly defined jobs outside of promotion ladders (Baron & Bielby, 1986, pp. 479–495; Strang & Baron, 1990; Tomaskovic-Devey & Skaggs, 1999). Proliferation of narrow job titles, which is associated with job descriptions, may also reduce the perception of unfair treatment and thereby "cool out" ambitious women and minorities (Baron & Pfeffer, 1994).

Performance evaluations have been subjected to perhaps the closest scrutiny. Field and laboratory studies challenged "objective" performance evaluations, suggesting that they cannot prevent raters from exercising race and gender bias (Hamner, Kim, Baird, & Bigoness, 1974; Kraiger & Ford, 1985; Nieva & Gutek, 1980; Oppler, Campbell, Pulakos, & Borman, 1992; Pulakos, White, Oppler, & Borman, 1989; Tsui & Gutek, 1984). Meta-analyses show a persistent gap in ratings of black and white workers (Roth, Huffcut, & Bobko, 2003; McKay & McDaniel, 2006). Some of the racial gap is due to the race of raters—whites tend to give higher ratings to other whites, blacks to other blacks (Kraiger & Ford, 1985)—and most real-world managers are white (Elvira & Town, 2001). Both laboratory and field studies also find gender bias in performance ratings (Bartol, 1999).

Research also shows that firms may ignore ratings and make personnel decisions based on stereotypes (Auster & Drazin, 1988; Castilla & Benard, 2010; Elvira & Zatzick, 2002) or apply different standards when evaluating ratings of white men and others (Castilla & Benard, 2010; Roscigno, 2007, Chapter 8). Louise Roth's (2003, p. 180) analysis of the gender pay gap on Wall Street shows that compensation based on performance evaluations harms women, whose contributions are often underestimated (see also Kanter, 1977). Auster and Drazin (1988) and Castilla and Benard (2010) find that when men and women have identical performance ratings, men receive larger raises. Elvira and Zatzick (2002) find that blacks' performance scores were significantly lower than whites', controlling for lagged performance, tenure, salary, job, position, and personal characteristics. Roscigno's (2007) analysis of civil rights complaints data shows that minority workers are judged more severely than their white counterparts for sub-par performance. Castilla and Benard (2010) find, in a laboratory study, that bonus pay based on performance evaluations is biased in favor of men when a meritocratic organizational culture is emphasized. The authors term this finding "the paradox of meritocracy." Susan Bisom-Rapp's (1999) analysis of defense attorneys' advice to employers shows that performance evaluations are treated as a "preventative tool" (1999, p. 995), wherein managers learn how to write performance evaluations that will support their promotion and discharge decisions and prevent legal liability. Taken together, performance rating systems may create the appearance of meritocracy without actually undermining discrimination. Against these studies there is Dencker's (2008) examination of promotions during corporate restructurings, which shows that firms that base their personnel decisions on performance evaluations, rather than seniority, promote more women.

Experts have argued that **salary classification** systems sometimes formalize, and perpetuate, wage and rank differences based on the race and gender composition of jobholders (Boyle, 1973, p. 89). The little evidence we have suggests that salary classification systems devalue work done by women and minorities. Plaintiffs in a number of civil rights cases have claimed that salary classification systems have systematically ranked male-dominated jobs higher than comparable female-dominated jobs (Nelson & Bridges, 1999, p. 43). Nelson and Bridges further argue that court rulings in favor of employers in such cases have helped to institutionalize salary classification systems as equal opportunity compliance measures, despite a lack of evidence that they fight wage inequality. Moreover, while salary classification systems are touted for the capacity to eliminate managerial bias in wage-setting, in practice they typically permit managerial discretion. In one service sector firm studied by Towers-Perrin consultants, "authorized officers of a certain accountability and responsibility level were in the annual salary range of $14,000–$21,000. There were two exceptions—both females—who were placed in the $12,000–$18,000 range, and, to make matters worse, they were paid $10,600 and $10,900 respectively" (Fretz & Hayman, 1973, p. 137).

Despite the evidence that formal salary systems may not eradicate wage inequality, some research suggests that they reduce inequality relative to compensation systems that rely entirely on supervisory discretion. Elvira and Graham (2002) look at data for more than 8,000 employees in a finance firm, finding that the remuneration disparity between men and women is greater for bonuses and incentive pay, distributed without formal rules, than for base salary and merit raises, subject to formal rules, even after actual performance is controlled.

Taken together, the extant evidence on the effects of formal personnel procedures on workplace equality of opportunity confirms most of the misgivings personnel consultants had about these programs in the 1970s, as well as predictions made by feminist scholars of bureaucracy. None of the bureaucratic procedures has shown a consistently positive effect on workforce integration, and negative effects are commonly observed. We need more systematic research on the workings of each of these procedures and on the institutional and organizational conditions that mediate their effects on the workforce.

The 1980s: Reagan and the rebranding of equal opportunity

Ronald Reagan campaigned in 1980 on a promise to dismantle the federal regulations he blamed for the stagflation of the 1970s, and fair employment regulations were high on that list. Less than a decade after the Nixon administration worked out the contours of affirmative action compliance, the system was under attack. Reagan criticized affirmative action's "bureaucratic regulations which rely on quotas, ratios, and numerical requirements" (Blumrosen, 1993; McDowell, 1989, p. 34; Skrentny, 1996). His three main assaults on affirmative action floundered, but they signaled that the days of affirmative action enforcement were numbered (Edelman, 1992, p. 1541). He proposed to relieve three quarters of federal contractors from the obligation to write affirmative action plans in 1981, but his deputies balked. He proposed to close the Office of Federal Contract Compliance Programs, which monitors affirmative action, but faced opposition once again from some on his own staff (DuRivage, 1985, p. 368). Then he proposed to end Nixon-era goals and timetables for private firms, but moderates killed that proposal as well (Belz, 1991; Detlefson, 1991, p. 151; *Harvard Law Review*, 1989, p. 662; McDowell, 1989). Clarence Thomas, the new EEOC head, did curtail enforcement (Blumrosen, 1993, p. 270; Skrentny, 1996). At the same time, Department of Labor oversight of federal contractors was cut back, and both regulatory agencies saw budget and staff cuts (Anderson, 1996; DuRivage, 1985; Edelman, 1992; Fox, 1981; Leonard, 1989; Mayer, 1981; Skrentny, 1996).

Personnel experts responded by rebranding equal opportunity programs in two ways. They folded some programs (performance evaluations, salary classification) into the new "human resources management" paradigm, which looked a lot like classical personnel administration. Other programs they rebranded as part of "diversity management," designed to create "strategic advantage by helping members of diverse groups perform to their potential" (Conference Board, 1992, p. 11; Kossek & Lobel, 1995; Leach, George, Jackson, & LaBella, 1995; Miller, 1994).

Equal opportunity experts became diversity management consultants (Thomas, 2004). Leading firms had created race relations workshops in the early 1960s, and these now became diversity training seminars. Soon experts were promoting new programs, such as affinity networks and mentoring programs, as part of the diversity management system (Edelman, Fuller, & Mara-Drita, 2001; Kelly & Dobbin, 1998).

From equal opportunity policies to diversity mission statements

By the end of the 1970s, one in two medium-sized firms had an equal opportunity policy in place. New diversity mission statements of the 1980s touted the business necessity of managing diversity and added some new categories of workers to the list of race, color, creed, sex, and age, or left out mention of the categories altogether. Over half of the large firms sampled for a 1991 Conference Board survey had a diversity mission statement (Conference Board, 1992, p. 21). In our 2002 national sample, 40 percent of medium and large firms had one (Fig. 15.7). Firms added these on top of their equal opportunity statements to signal that they were not just interested in legal compliance.

From race relations workshops to diversity training

Plans for Progress employers added race relations sessions to their management training curricula at the dawn of the 1960s (Boyle, 1973, p. 87). Soon

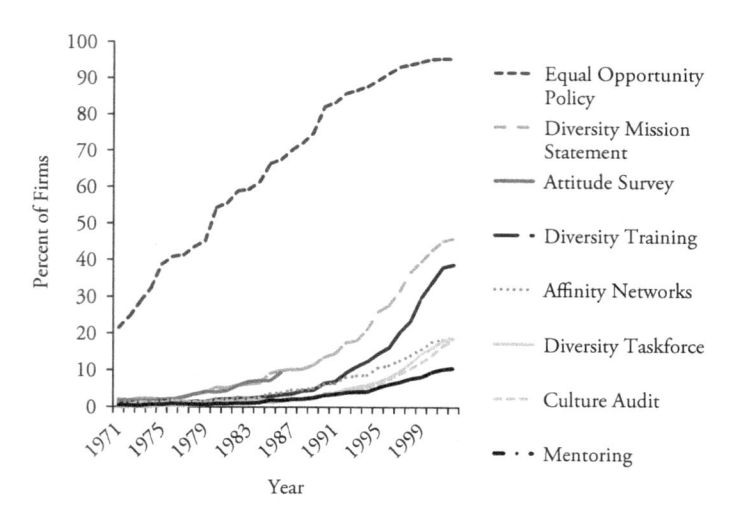

Figure 15.7. Diversity and equal opportunity programs compared.
Source: Survey of 829 firms in 2002 (Kalev & Dobbin, 2006). Attitude surveys are from survey of 279 employers in 1986 (Sutton, Dobbin, Meyer, & Scott, 1994).

federal agencies hired the same trainers to enlighten federal employees. By 1972, 50,000 Social Security Administration staffers had completed similar workshops. When the BNA surveyed industry leaders in 1976, it found that nearly 70 percent offered equal opportunity training for managers (BNA, 1976, p. 9).

In the 1980s, consultants distanced fair employment training from its origins in the law with the new moniker "diversity training" (Edelman, Fuller, & Mara-Drita, 2001). By 2006, a North Carolina food processing executive we interviewed told us that his trainings did not focus on race and sex: "Differences—that was the biggest thing that they taught. Not necessarily white/black, female/male. It was more about everybody is different. Tall, short, some people wear glasses. Some are bald." Yet in the late 1990s human resources managers still listed legal protection as the prime reason for using diversity training (Jordan, 1998). By 2002 only 20 percent of companies in our national sample used training that was devoid of legal or procedural content.

A 1991 Conference Board survey found that 63 percent of big firms offered diversity training (Winterle, 1992, p. 21). Surveys that included medium-sized firms arrived at a number of about 30 percent by the early 1990s and about 40 percent 10 years later (Rynes & Rosen, 1994). In the broad national sample from 1997, nearly half of employers had diversity training. Our 2002 study shows that they continued to spread, although in that later sample, the firms were smaller and hence less likely to have diversity training in place by 1997 (see Fig. 15.7).

From attitude surveys to diversity culture audits

Attitude surveys had been a mainstay of personnel management since the 1920s. In the 1960s, Harold Guetzkow (1965) argued that they expand efficiency by improving communication between workers and management. Federal contractors used surveys of attitudes on race relations from the early 1960s to identify problems at work, and now diversity managers relabeled these as "diversity culture audits," adding questions about gender culture and harassment (Cross, 1996; Lynch, 1997; MacDonald, 1993; Rowe & Baker, 1984, p. 33; Thomas, 1991). In the 1986 survey, nearly 10 percent of employers were using attitude surveys, and in our 2002 survey, nearly 20 percent of firms were using culture audits (see Fig. 15.7).

From equal opportunity taskforces to diversity taskforces

By the late 1960s, several large military contractors had established interdepartmental equal opportunity taskforces to devise strategies for promoting workforce integration (Schofer, 1971). By the early 1980s, diversity experts heralded diversity taskforces (Gant & Gentile, 1995). Some companies simply renamed the equal opportunity taskforce. The idea was to hold regular meetings among people from different departments who would talk over problems faced by the firm, brainstorm for solutions, and then implement those solutions in their own departments (Sturm, 2001).

By 1991, a survey by the Conference Board showed that one third of America's biggest firms had taskforces (Conference Board, 1992, p. 21). The 2002 survey shows that taskforces began to spread in the wider population of firms in the late 1980s (see Fig. 15.7).

Diversity management innovations: Mentoring and networking programs

Network theorists in sociology argued from the early 1970s that people find jobs through network contacts, and that promotions depend as much on who you know as on what you know (Baron & Pfeffer, 1994; Castilla, 2005; Granovetter, 1974; Kanter, 1977). While white men often have ties to other white men in positions of advantage (Burt, 1998; Reskin & McBrier, 2000), women and minorities are often stymied in job search and advancement by poor contacts with those in power (Blair-Loy, 2001; Burt, 1998; Ibarra, 1992, 1995; McGuire, 2000; Petersen, Saporta, & Seidelm, 1998). From the early 1980s, diversity managers and workers themselves called for affinity networks, each of which brought together members of one identity group for counsel and support.

Management psychologists had argued for formal mentoring programs that could extend the advantages of mentoring to the historically disadvantaged (Lunding, Clements, & Perkins, 1979; Roche, 1979). Formal mentoring programs match aspiring managers with volunteer mentors (Burke & McKeen, 1997; Burt, 1998; Moore, 2001; Neumark & Gardecki, 1996; Thomas, 2001). A study from the early 1980s of nine firms famed for their commitment to fairness found that every one promoted mentoring (Vernon-Gerstenfeld & Burke, 1985, p. 67). By the early 1990s, two studies showed that 20 to 30 percent of America's biggest firms had formal mentoring programs (Conference Board,

1992). In our broader sample of American firms, only 2 to 4 percent had networking and mentoring for women and minorities by 1990, but 10 percent had mentoring and 18 percent had networking by 2002 (see Fig. 15.7).

In the 1980s, the language of affirmative action gave way to a rhetoric of diversity management. Yet a Conference Board researcher argued: "Although there is a strong sentiment that diversity moves far beyond compliance, at this point, practices demonstrate a strong link between the two" (Wheeler, 1994, p. 7). Many core diversity management programs were born of efforts to conform with antidiscrimination programs.

Diversity programs and workforce diversity

Extant statistical analyses suggest that the diversity management revolution brought a number of new programs to leading American firms, but that those programs had modest effects on workforce diversity (see Figure 15.8). In particular, what was arguably the flagship practice, diversity training, did not lead to increases in managerial diversity. Similarly, the much-celebrated networking programs, labeled "affinity groups" or "employee resource groups," did not foster inclusion in the management ranks. By contrast, diversity taskforces, one of the least costly and least prevalent measures, show strong positive effects on the share of women and minorities in management. Mentoring programs as well have been effective.

In studies of a national sample of 830 employers between 1971 and 2002, we find that **diversity training** (offered either to all employees or to all managers) has little aggregate effect on workforce diversity (see Fig. 15.8). Training programs show statistically significant, yet substantively negligible, effects on two groups. Training is followed by a 7 percent decline in the proportion of black women and a 10 percent increase in the proportion of Hispanic women in management (Dobbin, Kalev, & Kelly, 2007). Previous studies had similarly found little effect of diversity training, although most focused on short-term changes in attitudes and self-reported behavior, not on workforce composition over decades (Kraiger, Ford, & Salas, 1993; Kulik & Roberson, 2008). These studies are discussed in Chapter 19 by Roberson, Kulik, and Tan.

In contrast to the apparent failure of diversity training to boost diversity, **diversity taskforces** show strong positive effects on diversity. An analysis of our 2002 survey data shows that following the establishment of diversity taskforces, firms see significant increases, among managers, in white women, and in black, Hispanic, and Asian men and women (Dobbin et al., 2007). Furthermore, the presence of a diversity taskforce in an organization improves the operation of most other diversity programs.

The finding that both diversity staff members and diversity taskforces have positive effects on managerial diversity, and that each of these innovations tends to improve the operation of other diversity programs, suggests that assigning responsibility for managing diversity to a full-time manager or a group of managers is more effective than measures that individualize blame for disparities, such as diversity performance evaluations or diversity training.

In interviews we conducted with human resources and line managers at 64 workplaces in Atlanta, Boston, San Francisco, and Chicago, respondents reported that taskforces are effective because they identify specific problems and remedies. If the taskforce sees that the company has not been recruiting African-American engineers, it will suggest sending recruiters to historically black colleges. If a company has trouble retaining women, the diversity manager may talk to women at risk of leaving and try to work out arrangements that will keep them on the job. Managers and taskforces monitor quarterly employment data to see if their efforts are paying off. Taskforces may be so widely effective, some diversity managers tell us, because they cause managers from different departments to "buy into" the goal of diversity.

Of the two programs designed to compensate for disadvantages in social capital, **networking programs** show little direct effect on the share of women and minorities in good jobs. In our analysis of the 1971–2002 data we find that networking programs are followed by significant rises in the odds of white women, and declines in the odds of white men and black men, in management, with no effects on other groups (Dobbin et al., 2007). The negative effect on black men is anticipated by qualitative research showing that whites can develop negative attitudes toward African-American organizing efforts (Carter, 2003; Friedman & Craig, 2004). Some studies, however, suggest that employee mobilization efforts can shape corporate diversity programs (Briscoe & Safford, 2008; Dobbin, Kim, & Kalev, 2011,), and thus networking programs may have indirect effects.

Mentoring programs, by contrast, show strong positive effects on black women, and Hispanic and

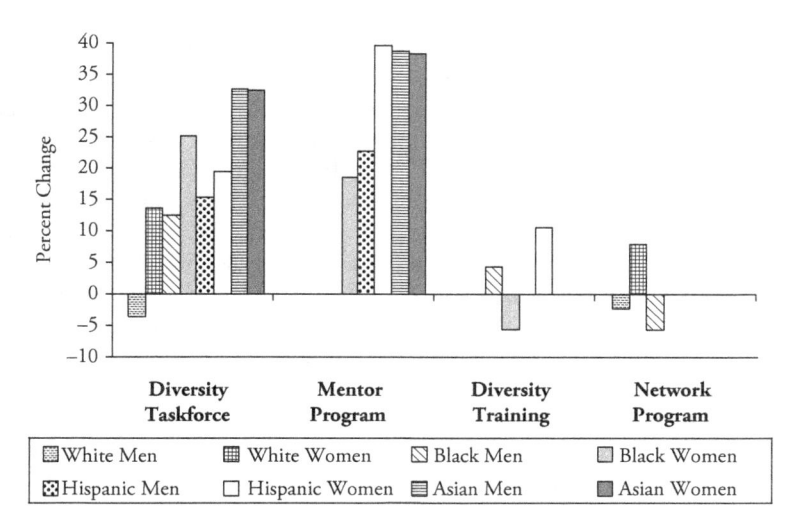

Figure 15.8. Diversity program effects on management diversity.

Asian men and women, in management (Dobbin et al., 2007). In a report prepared for a taskforce of the National Academies of Science, we examined the effects of mentoring programs in different industries, finding that in industries with significant numbers of college-educated non-managerial workers, who are eligible for promotion to management jobs, mentoring programs led to increases in all seven historically disadvantaged groups in management (white women, and black, Hispanic, and Asian-American men and women) (Dobbin & Kalev, 2006, p. 3).

Taken together, these findings suggest that personal guidance and support by mentors at work can facilitate career development for workers from all historically disadvantaged groups (Castilla, 2005), while the effect of affinity networks is limited to white women. Perhaps networking advantages white women because female networks are more likely than minority networks to include managers, who can serve as mentors. White women make up over 20 percent of managers, whereas no other race by gender group makes up more than 5 percent. Others have looked at related outcomes and found generally positive effects of mentoring on African-Americans and women. This research is reviewed in Chapter 17 on career development.

The 1990s and beyond: The rise of women's issues

When the Civil Rights Act of 1964 was passed, half of America's leading employers had formal policies requiring pregnant workers to resign (National Industrial Conference Board, 1964). Employers routinely barred women from management, refused to hire women with small children, and excluded married women. While women faced barriers similar to those faced by minority men, early corporate equal opportunity programs were focused on racial integration, following the agenda of the civil rights movement of the 1950s. Kennedy's 1961 affirmative action order had not covered sex, but advocates in government, including the President's Commission on the Status of Women created in 1961, championed women's workplace rights, and so sex was covered in the Civil Rights Act of 1964 (Goldin, 1990; Pedriana, 2004, 2006). By 1966 the President's Commission on the Status of Women had spawned 48 state-level commissions, and in that year the National Organization for Women was founded.

In the 1970s, women's rights advocates gained more of a voice and fought for maternity protection and protection against harassment at work (Fretz & Hayman, 1973; Kelly & Dobbin 1999; Mansbridge, 1986). Meanwhile, the civil rights focus had fueled both rapid growth in the ranks of personnel managers, which increased sixfold between 1960 and 1980 while the labor force grew by only 50 percent (Jacoby, 1985), and the feminization of its workforce. Women were nearly unknown in personnel as of 1960, but they held half of specialist and manager jobs by 1980, and 70 percent by the late 1990s (Roos & Manley, 1996). Whether due to the legacy of the women's movement, to the growing numbers of women in the workplace, or to the growing presence of women in personnel, women's issues came to assume a larger role in corporate diversity programs. While work–family coordination and sexual harassment prevention are matters that touch men and women alike, women in personnel management carried the torch for new programs.

Work–family programs

In the early 1970s, federal law did not require employers to offer **maternity leaves**, which guaranteed that women could have their jobs back after childbirth, but personnel offices began to create programs in the face of Congressional interest. Forty percent of major employers altered their maternity leave policies between 1972 and 1975 (BNA, 1975). The number of firms offering maternity leave nearly tripled between 1969 and 1978 (Kamerman, Kahn, & Kingston, 1983). Five states outlawed pregnancy discrimination between 1972 and 1981, but even where pregnancy discrimination was not outlawed, personnel managers created maternity leave policies (Ruhm & Teague, 1997). In Figure 15.9 we compare three states with different legal regimes. California had mandated maternity leave, New Jersey offered disability insurance to women on maternity leave, and Virginia had no legal protections. Private-sector employers created new maternity leave programs in all three states.

In 1993, Congress required employers to offer 12 weeks of unpaid leave to new mothers and fathers (Wisensale, 1997). Because personnel experts had already put maternity and medical leaves in place by 1993, the main effect of the law on program adoption was to popularize workplace leave policies for paternity and for the care of sick family members: the prevalence of each kind of program doubled overnight (Dobbin, 2009).

The women who advocated work–family programs from their positions in human resources departments also promoted flexible work and childcare programs from the 1970s (Didato, 1977; Packard, 1995; Swart, 1978). **Flextime programs** typically establish a core set of hours and allow employees to select their own start and end times with supervisory approval (Georgetown University Law Center, 2006; Swart, 1978). By 1978, a handful of leading companies had created flextime programs (Swart, 1978). Congress encouraged part-time career options and flexible hours through demonstration projects in the federal civil service (Rosenberg, 1980). Human resources experts argued that flextime could be part of a "good faith effort strategy" to show the firm's commitment to equal opportunity for women (Marino, 1980, p. 25).

One study found that flextime programs doubled in popularity to 29 percent between 1977 and 1986 (Fenstein, 1986). A 1984 survey of industry leaders found that 32 percent had created flextime programs since 1980 (BNA, 1986a). Kathleen Christensen's (1989) study for the Conference Board found that by 1987 46 percent of large firms surveyed had flextime programs, and another

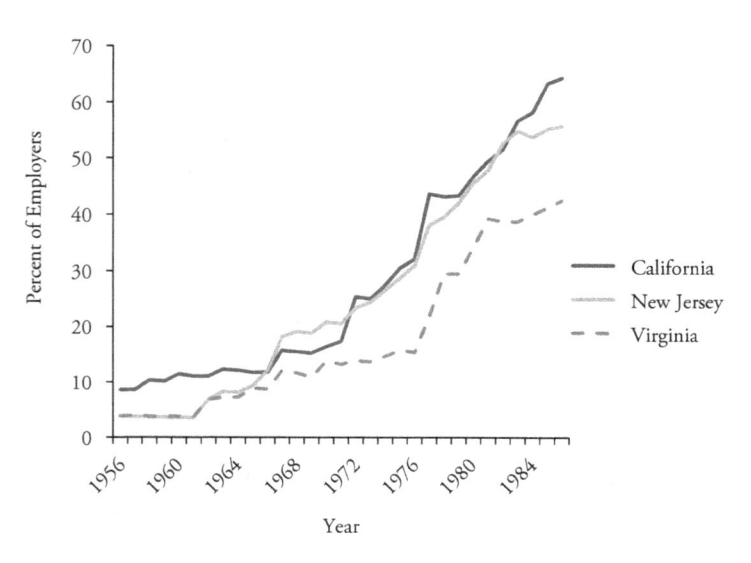

Figure 15.9. Maternity leave by state.
Source: Survey of 279 employers in 1986 (Dobbin et al., 1993).

7 percent were looking into them. A 1986 survey of 1,618 leading companies found that 35 percent had flextime, 34 percent had part-time career programs, 11 percent had job-sharing programs, and 10 percent had work-at-home programs (Kanter, Summers, & Stein, 1986). A 1994 study showed that 62 percent of leading companies had flexible work hours, 44 percent had job-sharing or part-time programs, and 25 percent had work-at-home programs (Miller, 1994).

Our 2002 survey, which includes smaller employers that were less likely to formalize work–family programs, showed that about one third of firms had flextime programs, and nearly as many had part-time-to-full-time transition policies. About one in five had a work-at-home program (Fig. 15.10). Job sharing was still spreading as of 1997 (Rapoport & Bailyn, 1996). Unlike maternity leave, which was legally mandated by 1994, flexible scheduling policies were discretionary. Employees could apply to use these programs, but supervisors had to approve their use (Kelly & Kalev, 2006).

From the early 1980s, human resources consultants promoted **child-care programs**, arguing that they could increase employee commitment and decrease turnover while helping employers to demonstrate a "good faith" effort to foster gender equality (Kossek & Nichol, 1992). Personnel consultants invented the most popular child-care benefit today, the dependent-care expense account, by building on 1981 legislation designed to encourage onsite child care (Kelly, 2003). Consultants convinced the Internal Revenue Service to allow expense accounts under the law, to extend the tax benefit to workers without access to onsite child care (Kamerman & Kahn, 1987, pp. 276–277).

Dependent-care expense accounts took off in the mid-1980s, and they appear to have given a boost also to referral services, onsite child care, and vouchers (Solomon, 1988). A 1998 survey found 50 percent of employers offering expense accounts and 9 percent offering onsite child care (Galinsky & Bond, 1998). Joanne Miller's 1994 survey of leading employers found 19 percent with onsite child care (1994b). By 2002, two thirds of firms in our sample offered dependent-care expense accounts, about a quarter had child-care referral services, and less than one in ten offered onsite child care or vouchers (see Fig. 15.10).

Do work–family programs increase opportunities for women and minorities?

There is limited research on the effects of corporate work–family programs on workplace inequality, and most studies use cross-sectional data that make it difficult to establish causality. Studies document employee perceptions that work–family arrangements improve productivity (Eaton, 2003) but may impair workplace attainment (Estes & Michael, 2005; see Kelly et al., 2008, for a review). Other findings suggest that family leaves

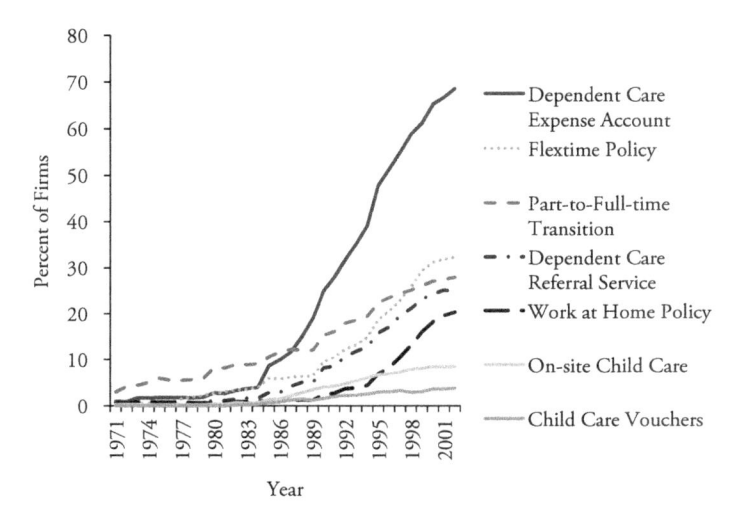

Figure 15.10. Flexible scheduling and child-care programs.
Source: Surveys of 829 employers in 2002 and 389 employers in 1997 (Dobbin & Kelly 2007; Kalev et al., 2006).

may reduce discontinuities in women's labor force participation but may lead to the segregation of women in lower-level jobs or in certain departments (Estes & Glass, 1996; Glass & Riley, 1998; Waldfogel, 1998). One study shows that users of parental leaves are less frequently promoted than other employees (Judiesch & Lyness, 1990). This pattern has also been seen in some European countries (Mandel & Semyonov, 2005).

There is evidence that men pay a higher penalty for using family leave. Allen and Russell (1999) find that men taking parental leaves were less likely to be rewarded than men who eschew leaves and women who take them (see also Stafford & Sundstrom, 1996; Wayne & Cordeiro, 2003). These differentials may not show up in aggregate data because leave use by men remains low.

We know even less about the effects of flexible scheduling and child-care programs on women's and men's careers, and little about how the effects of work–family programs vary across racial, ethnic, and occupational groups. Research in this area is discussed in Chapter 20.

Sexual harassment grievance systems and training

As the human resources profession became feminized, it directed attention to the issue of sexual harassment as well. Harassment had not been mentioned in the Civil Rights Act, but feminist law professor Catharine MacKinnon argued that harassment at work should be treated as sex discrimination under Title VII (Saguy, 2003). The courts did not immediately agree, but in 1976 and 1977 three federal courts found that *quid pro quo* harassment constitutes sex discrimination. The rulings did not outline compliance measures, but personnel experts revived an old standard from the personnel playbook: they proposed law-like procedures to remedy complaints that were designed to appeal to both judges and executives (Spann, 1990, p.57). Grievance procedures, they argued, could intercept harassment complaints and simultaneously telegraph the firm's no-tolerance policy on harassment (Hoyman & Robinson, 1980, pp. 14–15; Linenberger & Keaveny, 1981a, 1981b).

Few employers had harassment procedures in place before the federal judicial decisions of 1976 and 1977, but by the time of our 1986 survey, one in five firms had them. The Supreme Court ruled in 1986 that hostile environment harassment was covered by the Civil Rights Act and in dual rulings in 1998 suggested that employers who trained workers in company anti-harassment policies, and offered workers effective grievance mechanisms, might be protected against liability for harassment. Many observers claimed that these decisions moved the court into the territory of making law (Greenhouse, 1998, p. A20). But these practices were already ubiquitous in American firms, thanks to the advocacy of human resources experts (*Nation's Business*, 1998, p. 15). By 1991, the *Wall Street Journal* reported, harassment training had nearly saturated the Fortune 500 (Lublin, 1991). *Glamour* magazine reported that 86 percent of the Fortune 500 had training in place by the end of 1992 (Trost,

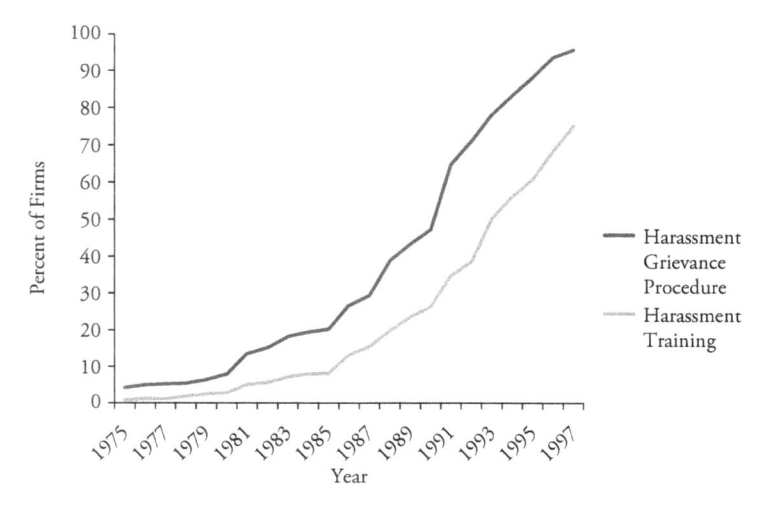

Figure 15.11. Anti-harassment programs.
Source: Survey of 389 employers in 1997 (Dobbin & Kelly, 2007).

1992). As Figure 15.11 shows, according to the 1997 survey Dobbin and Kelly (2007) conducted, in advance of the dual 1998 Supreme Court rulings, sexual harassment grievance procedures and training were widespread.

Do grievance procedures and training tame harassment?

While the Court accepted the theory that anti-harassment training programs and grievance procedures can prevent harassment and resolve complaints, there is little evidence to that effect. Legal scholar Susan Bisom-Rapp (2001) reviews the scholarly studies of anti-harassment training and finds no evidence that it actually reduces the incidence of harassment. As for grievance procedures, Lauren Edelman and colleagues (Edelman et al., 1999) look at time-series data from a national sample of firms and find no evidence that corporate grievance procedures reduce the incidence of harassment claims made to the government. Of course it may be that sexual harassment grievance procedures and training raise awareness about harassment and hence increase the number of complaints. In an analysis of evidence from workplace ethnographies, Lopez, Hodson, and Roscigno (2009) find that grievance mechanisms reduce sexual harassment but have no effect on general harassment. All in all, the jury is still out on whether anti-harassment training or harassment grievance procedures actually reduce the incidence of harassment.

Conclusion

Over the years personnel managers have put into place a series of different equal opportunity and diversity management programs. These measures were initially stimulated by the civil rights movement and John F. Kennedy's 1961 order requiring federal contractors to take "affirmative action" to end discrimination. Many of the strategies personnel managers developed came from their profession's kitbag. Each wave of measures redefined discrimination in the American mind.

In the 1960s, managers created corporate nondiscrimination policies. They expanded on traditional recruitment programs for skilled workers, now targeting historically black colleges and urban high schools. They built on conventional skill and management training practices, establishing programs designed for blacks and women. In the process they defined nondiscrimination as a matter of forbidding managerial bias and righting past wrongs through recruitment and training.

When Washington strengthened civil rights regulations in the early 1970s, personnel experts championed new equal opportunity programs built on the foundation of classic personnel administration. New practices were designed to bureaucratize hiring and promotion and thereby prevent bias: test validation, salary classification, job posting, and performance evaluations. These policies depicted structural flaws in the hiring and promotion process as the source of employment discrimination, and redesigned bureaucratic hiring and promotion systems as the remedy. These changes were to prevent managerial bias from tainting hiring and advancement, and they defined the formalization of personnel practices as the best way to prevent discrimination.

When Ronald Reagan moved into the White House in 1981 and threatened to turn the clock back on civil rights regulations, personnel experts fought back by developing business arguments for these programs. They dropped the language of legal compliance for a language of "diversity management." This language redefined discrimination as the result of managerial ignorance, to be addressed through training, and inequality as a result of the propensity of identity group members to stick together, to be addressed through mentoring and networking programs.

As the human resources profession became feminized, between 1970 and 1990, diversity programs became more oriented to women's issues. Work–family programs received renewed attention and spread broadly. New programs were put into place to fight sexual harassment at work. These innovations defined sex inequality at work as a consequence of conflicts between gender roles and work roles.

Research on the effects of these programs is ongoing, but we know that a number of them did little to promote gender and racial diversity. The innovations of the 1960s and 1970s appear to have had mixed effects. Targeted recruitment efforts have brought more women and minorities into the workplace, and skill and management training programs helped women and minorities to move up where they had access to those programs, but they were often denied access. Firms that hired full-time diversity officers, or created special departments, saw increases in diversity. Yet evidence to date suggests that bureaucratic hiring and promotion systems may have done more harm than good, institutionalizing patterns of inequality rather than challenging them. The diversity management movement of the

1980s popularized some ineffective diversity initiatives, such as diversity training and diversity performance reviews, and spawned some quite effective initiatives, such as diversity taskforces and mentoring programs. When it comes to work–family programs, extant research suggests that parental leaves have increased both participation of women in the workforce and job segregation, but we are still in the dark regarding the effects of flexible work schedules and child-care arrangements.

Our survey of research on the effects of these programs leads to several conclusions about the features of successful programs. The first is that corporations that put managers in charge of promoting diversity typically see results. Making managers a part of the solution, by appointing a full-time diversity manager, creating an interdepartmental taskforce, or assigning managers as mentors, helps to promote diversity. Moreover, diversity programs that otherwise have null or negative effects work better in the context of these practices. Similarly, regulatory oversight has been shown to improve the effects of certain diversity programs (Kalev et al., 2006). The second conclusion is that innovations designed to quash managerial bias have been broadly ineffective. Bureaucratic practices designed to eliminate managerial discretion from the hiring and promotion process have not led to increases in diversity; nor have diversity training programs designed to make managers aware of their own unconscious biases; neither have diversity performance evaluations that give managers feedback and career incentives to improve diversity. All three innovations point to managers as the problem to be solved, rather than as the source of the solution. All three are designed to change individual managers' behavior. The evidence suggests that this approach can have modest positive effects in the presence of managerial oversight of diversity efforts, but that it typically fails.

Research on diversity management and the remediation of workplace inequality is in its infancy. We still have understand little about how diversity programs influence workforce composition. Next we suggest several lines of future inquiry to deepen the field's understanding of corporate diversity efforts.

A better understanding of failure

Why do certain innovations consistently fail to bring about change? We need better theories of what makes broad classes of managerial innovations effective, as proponents of evidence-based management have pointed out (Pfeffer & Sutton, 2005). To begin with, we need better data on the mechanisms by which innovations shape behavior. Two specific domains of future research surface. On the one hand, we need to better understand why bureaucratic hiring and promotion systems designed to standardize personnel decisions have failed to promote diversity. Is it, as feminists argue (Acker, 1990), because bureaucracy formalizes traditional bases of exclusion by, for instance, establishing length-of-service requirements for management jobs that exclude mothers who have taken time off for childbirth? Is it because performance evaluations and salary classification systems are used selectively by managers in making promotions and assigning wages (Nelson & Bridges, 1999; Roscigno, 2007)? Is it because bureaucratic procedures create an appearance of equality and fairness, which has the effect, as Castilla and Benard (2010) suggest, of dampening managers' scrutiny of their own behavior? A second set of questions is suggested by the failure of diversity training and diversity performance evaluations to foster workforce diversity. Do these programs lead to adverse reactions from managers? Do they somehow reduce the motivation of managers to hire women and minorities? Organizational theory largely treats failure to change as an instance of decoupling, wherein formal structures are ignored in the everyday practice of the organization. As this list of questions suggests, failure may be caused by any number of processes other than decoupling.

A better understanding of success

Why do certain classes of innovations consistently succeed in bringing about change? We have noted that managerial and regulatory oversight of diversity efforts fosters success, but we know little about the underlying mechanisms. For example, do managers with hiring and promotion authority invest additional cognitive effort in processing data when they know they may need to explain their decisions (Lerner & Tetlock, 1999)? Does assigning responsibility simply ensure that someone takes charge of the task? Or does cognitive dissonance lead to greater commitment among managers assigned responsibility for diversity? And what are the mechanisms that transform the commitment of diversity managers, and taskforces, into substantive organizational change? Understanding the mechanisms underlying positive effects promises to help us to design better diversity programs, and tweak those already in place.

A broader understanding of diversity

How do diversity efforts affect the age distribution of the workforce, the utilization of disabled workers, and workforce composition by sexual orientation and immigration status? Does the effect of diversity effort vary at the intersection of social categories? Most research on diversity program effects focuses on gender, race, or ethnicity. We need more theory and research on other dimensions of disadvantage, as well as on the intersection of social categories. The findings we have outlined suggest some open questions concerning the intersection of race and gender. Why is it that black men see negative effects from networking programs while white women see positive effects? Why does diversity training appear to help black men but hurt black women? It is possible that differences in relational dynamics and in the content of gender and racial stereotypes (Browne & Misra, 2003; Moss & Tilly, 2001; Roscigno, 2007) lead to different program outcomes across the intersection of gender and race. We expect there are unplumbed program effects across other intersections as well. Thus, salary classification systems that emphasize skills over tenure, for instance, may advantage women with careers interrupted by maternity, but disadvantage older men with greater seniority. The intersection of race and immigration status is also unexplored. Thus, criminal record checks may expand hiring of blacks by countering the employer tendency to assume that all black men have criminal records (Holzer, Raphael, & Stoll, 2006), but do they also deter undocumented immigrants from applying for jobs?

A better understanding of context

How do organizations moderate wider contextual changes that influence workforce diversity? Most studies of corporate diversity efforts examine them in isolation from broader social changes, but many other changes in the organizational environmental have occurred in recent decades. We know, for instance, that elements of the new high-performance management paradigm have driven increases in diversity, even though they were not designed to (Kalev, 2009). Decades of studies suggest that minorities lose a disproportionate number of jobs in recessions (Wilson & Branch McBrier, 2005), but we know little about the effects of the downsizing and outsourcing fads on workforce composition and on corporate diversity efforts (Dencker, 2008).

Many firms have joined the performance-based compensation bandwagon, but we have scant knowledge of whether this trend has affected workforce composition. The literature on tokenism suggests that minorities who reach the top face extra scrutiny and stress (Kanter, 1977), but we do not know whether women and minorities on boards of directors stimulate growth in diversity in the lower ranks. We know that legal immigrants sometimes face labor market discrimination, but have raids on factories employing illegal immigrants had a further chilling effect on hires of legal immigrants? And has the "corporate social responsibility" movement affected corporate diversity efforts and workforce composition?

A better understanding of the bottom line

In the civil rights era, the great promise of equal opportunity programs was that they could increase social justice in America. The great promise of the diversity management movement today is that workforce diversity can also contribute to the corporate bottom line. But as yet, research has not produced clear evidence of the effect of diversity on performance. Cross-sectional studies suggest that diversity is positively correlated with a number of performance measures (Herring, 2009). But early studies showing a positive correlation between corporate *board* diversity and performance (Catalyst, 2007) were thrown into doubt by sophisticated time-series studies (Adams & Ferreira, 2009). Putting together the kind of rich longitudinal data required for exploring this question is a challenge, but several groups of sociologists are now at work on that.

All of these areas for future research require richer data from a variety of sources. For instance, the challenge of studying the effects of diversity policies and programs on workforce characteristics beyond sex, race, and ethnicity is substantial, for the most revealing studies use federal data (Kalev et al., 2006; Leonard, 1990), and the federal government does not collect systematic data on age, immigration status, disability, or sexual orientation. Perhaps the best hope for obtaining time-series data at the firm level lies in career data collected by firms themselves for internal use, such as those used by Fernandez (2001) and Castilla and Benard (2010).

To achieve a fuller understanding of program effects on careers, the ideal dataset would match time-series data from a large number of employers with data on individual employees. A longitudinal version of the National Organizational Survey

(Kalleberg, Knoke, Marsde, & Spaeth, 1996), which surveys individuals and then turns to their employers, would help us to understand how program effects vary across employee characteristics. Do networking programs lead to declines in black men in management by increasing quit rates, by facilitating promotions for white women that leave black men behind in the labor queue, or by some other mechanism? Perhaps the solution is to merge existing longitudinal data on individuals, from a source such as the National Longitudinal Survey of Youth, with retrospective data from the firms that employed them. Case studies, ethnographic research, and depth interviews can help us to understand how inequality is reproduced, or challenged, on the ground in firms (Kellogg, 2009; Kelly, Moen, & Tranby, 2011). Such data can shed light on the real-world experiences of workers, and on the relational dynamics that mediate the implementation of diversity program innovations.

References

Abbott, A. D. (1994). Review by Harrison White of "Identity and Control: A Structural Theory of Social Action." *Social Forces, 73*, 895–901.

Acker, J. (1990). Hierarchies, jobs, bodies: a theory of gendered organizations. *Gender & Society, 4*(2), 139–158.

Ackerman, R. (1973). How companies respond to social demands. *Harvard Business Review, 51*(1), 88–98.

Adams, R. B., & Ferreira, D. (2009). Women in the boardroom and their impact on governance and performance. *Journal of Financial Economics, 94*(2), 291–30 9.

Allen, T. D., & Russell, J. E. A. (1999). Parental leave of absence: Some not so family friendly implications. *Journal of Applied Social Psychology, 29*, 166–191.

Anderson, B. E. (1996). The ebb and flow of enforcing Executive Order 11246. *American Economic Review, 86*(2), 298–301.

Anderson, C. D., & Tomaskovic-Devey, D. D. (1995). Patriarchal pressures: an exploration of organizational processes that exacerbate and erode gender earnings inequality. *Work and Occupations, 22*(3), 328–356.

Appelbaum, E., & Berg, P. (2001). High-performance work systems and labor market structures. In Ivar Berg & Arne L. Kalleberg (Eds.), *Sourcebook of labor markets: Evolving structures of processes* (pp. 271–293). New York: Kluwer Academic/Plenum.

Auster, E. R., & Drazin, R. (1988). Sex inequality at higher levels in the hierarchy: An intraorganizational perspective. *Sociological Inquiry, 58*, 216–227.

Baron, J. N., & Bielby, W. T. (1986). The proliferation of job titles in organizations. *Administrative Science Quarterly, 31*, 561–586.

Baron, J. N., Hannan, M. T., Hsu, G., & Koçak, Ö. (2007). In the company of women: gender inequality and the logic of bureaucracy in start-up firms. *Work and Occupations, 34*(1), 35–66.

Baron, J. N., Jennings, P. D., & Dobbin, F. (1988). Mission control? The development of personnel systems in U.S. industry. *American Sociological Review, 53*, 497–514.

Baron, J. N., & Pfeffer, J. (1994). The social psychology of organizations and inequality. *Social Psychology Quarterly, 57*(3), 190–209.

Bartol, K. M. (1999). Gender influences on performance evaluation. In Gary N. Powell (Ed.), *Handbook of gender and work* (pp. 165–178). Thousand Oaks, CA: Sage.

Belz, H. (1991). *Equality transformed: A quarter-century of affirmative action*. Brunswick, NJ: Transaction.

Bielby, W. T. (2000). Minimizing workplace gender and racial bias. *Contemporary Sociology, 29*(2), 120–129.

Bills, D. B., & Hodson, R. (2007). Worker training: a review, critique, and extension. *Research in Social Stratification and Mobility, 25*, 258–272.

Bisom-Rapp, S. (1999). Bulletproofing the workplace: symbol and substance in employment discrimination law practice. *Florida State University Law Review, 26*, 959–1049.

Bisom-Rapp, S. (2001). Fixing watches with sledgehammers: the questionable embrace of employee sexual harassment training by the legal profession. *University of Arkansas at Little Rock Law Review, 24*, 147–168.

Blair-Loy, M. (2001). It's not just what you know, it's who you know: technical knowledge, rainmaking, and gender among finance executives. *Research in the Sociology of Work, 10*, 51–83.

Blumrosen, A. W. (1993). *Modern law: The law transmission system and equal employment opportunity*. Madison, WI: University of Wisconsin Press.

Boyle, M. B. (1973). Equal opportunity for women is smart business. *Harvard Business Review, 51*(3), 85–95.

Braestrup, P. (1961, June 5). U.S. unit presses for job equality. *New York Times*, p. 22.

Briscoe, F., & Safford, S. (2008). The Nixon in China effect: activism, imitation, and the institutionalization of contentious practices. *Administrative Science Quarterly, 53*, 460–491.

Browne, I., & Misra, J. (2003). The intersection of gender and race in labor markets. *Annual Review of Sociology, 29*, 487–513

Bureau of the Census (1975). *Historical statistics of the United States: Colonial times to 1970*. Washington, DC: U.S. Government Printing Office.

Bureau of National Affairs (1967). *A current look at: (1) The Negro and Title VII (2) Sex and Title VII* (No. 82). Washington, DC: Bureau of National Affairs.

Bureau of National Affairs (1976). *Equal employment opportunity: Programs and results* (PPF Survey No. 112). Washington, DC: Bureau of National Affairs.

Bureau of National Affairs (1975). *Paid leave and leave of absence policies* (Personnel Policies Forum Survey No. 111). Washington, DC: Bureau of National Affairs.

Bureau of National Affairs (1986a). *Work and family: a changing agenda*. Washington, DC: Bureau of National Affairs.

Bureau of National Affairs (1986b). *Affirmative action today: a legal and practical analysis*. Washington, DC: Bureau of National Affairs.

Burke, R. J., & McKeen, C. A. (1997). Not every managerial woman who makes it has a mentor. *Women in Management Review, 12*(4), 136–139.

Burt, R. S. (1998). The gender of social capital. *Rationality and Society, 10*(1), 5–46.

Campbell, J. T. (1973). Tests are valid for minority groups too. *Public Personnel Management, 2*, 70–73.

Carter, J. (2003). *Ethnicity, exclusion and the workplace*. London: Palgrave Macmillan Press.

Castilla, E. J. (2005). Social networks and employee performance in a call center. *American Journal of Sociology, 110*(5), 1243–1284.

Castilla, E. J., & Benard, S. (2010). *The paradox of meritocracy: an experimental approach to study why merit-based performance systems fail.* Paper presented at the annual meeting of the American Sociological Association, August, Boston, 55, 543–576.

Catalyst (2007). *The bottom line: Corporate performance and women's representation on boards.* New York: Catalyst.

Chayes, A. (1974). Make your EEO program court-proof. *Harvard Business Review, 52*(5), 81–89.

Chen, A. S. (2009). *The fifth freedom: Jobs, politics, and civil rights in the United States, 1941–72.* Princeton, NJ: Princeton University Press.

Christensen, K. E. (1989). *Flexible staffing and scheduling in U.S. corporations.* New York: The Conference Board.

Conference Board (1992). *In diversity is strength: Capitalizing on the new work force.* 75th Anniversary Symposia Series. Report Number 994. New York.

Costain, A. N. (1992). *Inviting women's rebellion: A political process interpretation of the women's movement.* Baltimore, MD: Johns Hopkins University Press.

Cross, E. Y. (1996). Letters to the editor: Managing diversity. *Harvard Business Review, 74*(6), 177–178.

Cunningham, R. M. (1936). Some problems in measuring performance of industrial salesmen. *Harvard Business Review, 14*(1), 98–113.

Danovitch, S. (1990). Interview conducted December 27, 1990, as part of an oral history project to commemorate the EEOC's 25th Anniversary. Retrieved from http://www.utoronto.ca/wjudaism/contemporary/articles/history_Eeoc.htm

Dencker, J. C. (2008). Corporate restructuring and sex differences in managerial promotion. *American Sociological Review, 73*, 455–476.

Detlefson, R. R. (1991). *Civil rights under Reagan.* San Francisco: ICS Press.

Didato, S. (1977, May 22). Problems cut by flexitime. *Washington Post*, p. D6.

DiPrete, T. (1989). *The bureaucratic labor market: The case of the federal civil service.* New York: Plenum.

DiPrete, T. A., & Soule, W. T. (1988). Gender and promotion in segmented job ladder systems. *American Sociological Review, 53*(1), 26–40.

Dobbin, F. (2009). *Inventing equal opportunity.* Princeton, NJ: Princeton University Press.

Dobbin, F., Edelman, L. B., Meyer, J. W., Scott, W. R., & Swidler, A. (1988). The expansion of due process in organizations. In Lynne G. Zucker (Ed.), *Institutional patterns and organizations: Culture and environment* (pp. 71–100). Cambridge, MA: Ballinger.

Dobbin, F., & Kalev, A. (2006). *Diversity management and managerial diversity.* Special report to the National Academies Committee on Women in Academic Science and Engineering.

Dobbin, F., Kalev, A., & Kelly, E. (2007). Diversity management in corporate America. *Contexts, 6*(4), 21–28.

Dobbin, F., Kim, S., & Kalev, A. (2011). You can't always get what you need: why diverse firms adopt diversity programs. *American Sociological Review, 76*(3), 386–411.

Dobbin, F., & Kelly, E. (2007). How to stop harassment: the professional construction of legal compliance in organizations. *American Journal of Sociology, 112*(4), 1203–1243.

Dobbin, F., & Sutton, J. R. (1998). The strength of a weak state: the employment rights revolution and the rise of human resources management divisions. *American Journal of Sociology, 104*(2), 441–476.

Dobbin, F., Sutton, J. R., Meyer, J. W., & Scott, W. R. (1993). Equal opportunity law and the construction of internal labor markets. *American Journal of Sociology, 99*(2), 396–427.

Drum, R. S. (1960). Performance evaluation. *Personnel Journal, 38*(2), 338–340.

Dugan, R. D. (1966). Current problems in test performance of job applicants: II. *Personnel Psychology, 19*(1), 18–24.

DuRivage, V. (1985). The OFCCP under the Reagan administration: affirmative action in retreat. *Labor Law Journal, 36*, 360–368.

Eaton, S. (2003). If you can use them: Flexibility policies, organizational commitment and perceived performance. *Industrial Relations, 42*, 145–167.

Edelman, L. B. (1992). Legal ambiguity and symbolic structures: organizational mediation of civil rights law. *American Journal of Sociology, 97*, 1531–1576.

Edelman, L. B. (1990). Legal environments and organizational governance: the expansion of due process in the American workplace. *American Journal of Sociology, 95*, 1401–1440.

Edelman, L. B. (2002). Legality and the endogeneity of law. In Robert A. Kagan, Martin Krygier, & Kenneth I. Winston (Eds.), *Legality and community: on the intellectual legacy of Philip Selznick* (pp. 187–203). Lanham, MD: Rowman and Littlefield.

Edelman, L. B., Fuller, S. R., & Mara-Drita, I. (2001). Diversity rhetoric and the managerialization of the law. *American Journal of Sociology, 106*(6), 1589–1641.

Edelman, L. B., & Petterson, S. M. (1999). Symbols and substance in organizations' response to civil rights law. *Research in Social Stratification and Mobility, 17*, 107–135.

Edelman, L. B., Uggen, C., & Erlanger, H. S. (1999). The endogeneity of legal regulation: grievance procedures as rational myth. *American Journal of Sociology, 105*, 406–454.

EEOC (1998). *Best practices of private sector employers.* Washington, DC: Equal Employment Opportunity Commission. Retrieved April 19, 2004 (http://www.eeoc.gov/abouteeoc/task_reports/practice.html).

Elvira, M. M., & Graham, M. E. (2002). Not just a formality: pay system formalization and sex-related earnings effects. *Organization Science, 13*(6), 601–618.

Elvira, M. M., & Town, R. J. (2001). The effects of race and worker productivity on performance evaluations *Industrial Relations, 40*, 571–590.

Elvira, M. M., & Zatzick, C. D. (2002). Who's displaced first? The role of race in layoff decisions. *Industrial Relations, 41*(2), 329–361.

Esen, E. (2005). *Workplace diversity practices survey report.* Alexandria, VA: Society for Human Resource Management.

Estes, S. B., & Glass, J. (1996). Job changes following childbirth: are women trading compensation for family-responsive work conditions? *Work and Occupations, 23*, 405–436.

Estes, S. B., & Michael, J. (2005). Work-family policies and gender inequality at work. *Sloan Work Family Research Network Encyclopedia.*

Ewick, P., & Silbey, S. S. (1998). *The common place of law: stories from everyday life.* Chicago: University of Chicago Press.

Fehn, B. (1993). "Chickens come home to roost": Industrial reorganization, seniority, and gender conflict in the United

Packinghouse Workers of America, 1956–1966. *Labor History, 34*(2 & 3), 324–341.

Fenstein, S. (1986, June 10). Labor Letter. *Wall Street Journal*, p. 1.

Ferguson, K. E. (1984). *The feminist case against bureacracy*. Philadelphia: Temple University Press.

Fernandez, R. M. (2001). Skill-biased technological change and wage inequality: evidence from plant retooling. *American Journal of Sociology, 107*(2), 273–320.

Foulkes, F. K., & Morgan, H. M. (1977). Organizing and staffing the personnel function. *Harvard Business Review, 55*(3), 142–177.

Fox, J. R. (1981). Breaking the regulatory deadlock. *Harvard Business Review, 59*(5), 97–120.

Fretz, C. F., & Hayman, J. (1973, September–October). Progress for women? Men are still more equal. *Harvard Business Review*, 133–142.

Friedman, R. A., & Craig, K. M. (2004). Predicting, joining and participating in minority employee network groups. *Industrial Relations, 43*(4), 793–816.

Froehlich, H., & Hawver, D. (1974). Compliance spinoff: better personnel systems. *Personnel, 51*(1), 62–69.

Fulmer, R. M., & Fulmer, W. E. (1974). Providing equal opportunities for promotion. *Personnel Journal, 53*, 491–497.

Galinsky, E., & Bond, J. T. (1998). *The 1998 business work-life study*. New York: Families and Work Institute.

Gant, S. B., & Gentile, M. C. (1995, March 13). Kurt Landgraf and Du Pont Merck Pharmaceutical Company. *Harvard Business School Press*.

Gavin, J. F., & Toole, D. L. (1973). Validity of aptitude tests for the "hardcore unemployed." *Personnel Psychology, 26*, 139–146.

Georgetown University Law Center (2006, spring). *Workplace flexibility 2010 legal memo: The Federal Employees Flexible and Compressed Work Schedules Act (FEFCWA)*. Georgetown University School of Law.

Giblin, E., & Ornati, O. (1974). A total approach to EEO compliance. *Personnel, 51*(5), 32–43.

Glass Ceiling Commission (1995). *A solid investment: making a full use of our nation's human capital*. Washington, DC: U.S. Department of Labor Glass Ceiling Commission.

Glass, J. L., & Riley, L. (1998). Family-responsive policies and employee retention following childbirth. *Social Forces, 76*(4), 1401–1435.

Goldin, C. (1990). *Understanding the gender gap: an economic history of American women*. New York: Oxford University Press.

Gordon, H. L. (2000). Cobb County Oral History Series No. 75. *Interview with Hugh L. Gordon conducted by Joyce A. Patterson*. Kennesaw State University.

Gorham, W. A. (1972). New answers on employment tests. *Civil Service Journal, 13*, 8–12.

Graham, H. D. (1990). *The civil rights era: origins and development of national policy 1960–1972*. New York: Oxford University Press.

Granovetter, M. (1974). *Getting a job: a study of contracts and careers*. Chicago: University of Chicago Press.

Greenhouse, L. (1998, April 23). Sex harassment seems to puzzle Supreme Court. *New York Times*, pp. A1–A20.

Grove, G. (1965, September 18). When a "No. 2" applies for a job. *New York Times*, p. SM32.

Guetzkow, H. (1965). Communications in organizations. In James G. March (Ed.), *Handbook of organizations* (pp. 534–573). Chicago: Rand McNally.

Hamner, W. C., Kim, J. S., Baird, L., & Bigoness, W. J. (1974). Race and sex as determinants of ratings by potential employers in a simulated work-sampling task. *Journal of Applied Psychology, 59*(6), 705–712.

Harrison, C. (1988). *On account of sex: the politics of women's issues 1945–1968*. Berkeley, CA: University of California Press.

Harvard Law Review (1989). Rethinking Weber: the business response to affirmative action. *Harvard Law Review, 102*, 658–671.

Herring, C. (2009). Does diversity pay? Race, gender and the business case for diversity. *American Sociological Review, 74*(2), 208–224.

Hight, J. E. (1998). Young worker participation in post-school education and training. *Monthly Labor Review, 121*, 14–21.

Holzer, H. J., & Neumark, D. (2000). What does affirmative action do? *International Labor Relations Review, 53*, 240–271.

Holzer, H. J., Raphael, S., & Stoll, M. (2006). Perceived criminality, criminal background checks and the racial hiring practices of employers. *Journal of Law and Economics, 49*, 451–480.

Hough, L. M., & Oswald, F. L. (2000). Looking toward the future—remembering the past. *Annual Review of Psychology, 51*, 631–664.

Hoyman, M., & Robinson, R. (1980). Interpreting the new sexual harassment guidelines. *Personnel Journal, 43*(4), 996–1000.

Huffman, M. L., & Velasco, S. C. (1997). When more is less: sex composition, organizations, and earning in U.S. firms. *Work and Occupations, 24*(2), 214–244.

Ibarra, H. (1992). Homophily and differential returns: sex differences in network structure and access in an advertising firm. *Administrative Science Quarterly, 34*, 422–447.

Ibarra, H. (1995). Race, opportunity and diversity of social circles in managerial networks. *Academy of Management Journal, 38*, 673–703.

Ichniowski, C. (1983). Have angels done more: the steel-industry consent decree. *Industrial and Labor Relations Review, 36*(2), 182–198.

Jacoby, S. M. (1985). *Employing bureaucracy: managers, unions, and the transformation of work in American industry, 1900–1945*. New York: Columbia University Press.

Johns, H., & Moser, H. R. (1989). Where has EEO taken personnel policies? *Personnel, 66*(9), 63–66.

Jordan, K. (1998). Diversity training in the workplace today: a status report. *Journal of Career Planning and Employment, 59*(1), 46–51.

Judiesch, M. K., & Lyness, K. S. (1990). Left behind? The impact of leaves of absence on managers' career success. *Academy of Management Journal, 42*, 641–651.

Kalev, A. (2009). Cracking the glass cages? Restructuring and ascriptive inequality at work. *American Journal of Sociology, 114*(6), 1591–1643.

Kalev, A., & Dobbin, F. (2006). Enforcement of civil rights law in private workplaces: the effects of compliance reviews and lawsuits over time. *Law and Social Inquiry, 31*(4), 855–879.

Kalev, A., Dobbin, F., & Kelly, E. (2006). Best practices or best guesses? Diversity management and the remediation of inequality. *American Sociological Review, 71*, 589–617.

Kalleberg, A. L., Knoke, D., Marsden, P. V., & Spaeth, J. L. (1996). *Organizations in America: analyzing their structures* and *human resource practices*. Thousand Oaks, CA: Sage Publications.

Kamerman, S. B., & Kahn, A. J. (1987). *The responsive workplace: employers and a changing labor force*. New York: Columbia University Press.

Kamerman, S. B., Kahn, A. J., & Kingston, P. (1983). *Maternity policies and working women*. New York: Columbia University Press.

Kanter, R. M. (1977). *Men and women of the corporation* (2nd ed.). New York: Basic Books.

Kanter, R. M., Summers, D. V., & Stein, B. A. (1986). The future of workplace alternatives. *Management Review, 75*(7), 30–34.

Kellogg, K. C. (2009). Operating room: relational spaces and microinstitutional change in surgery. *American Journal of Sociology, 115*(3), 657–711.

Kelly, E., & Dobbin, F. (1999). Civil rights law at work: sex discrimination and the rise of maternity leave policies. *American Journal of Sociology, 105*, 455–492.

Kelly, E., & Kalev, A. (2006). Managing flexible work arrangements in U.S. organizations: formalized discretion or "a right to ask." *Socio-Economic Review, 4*(3), 379–416.

Kelly, E. A. (2003). The strange history of employer-sponsored childcare: interested actors, uncertainty, and the transformation of law in organizational fields. *American Journal of Sociology, 109*(3), 606–649.

Kelly, E. A., & Dobbin, F. (1998). How affirmative action became diversity management. *American Behavioral Scientist, 41*, 960–984.

Kelly, E. L., Moen, P., & Tranby, E. (2011). Changing workplaces to reduce work-family conflict: schedule control in a white-collar organization. *American Sociological Review, 76*, 265–290.

Kelly, E. L., Ellen E. K., Hammer, L., Durham, M., Bray J., Chermack, K., & Murphy L. 2008. "Getting There from Here: Research on the Effects of Work- Family Initiatives on Work-Family Conflict and Business Outcomes." *Academy of Management Annals*, 2 (1), 305 – 340.

Knoke, D., & Ishio, Y. (1998). The gender gap in company job training. *Work and Occupations, 25*(2), 141.

Kochan, T. A., & Cappelli, P. (1984). The transformation of the industrial relations and personnel function. In Paul Osterman (Ed.), *Internal labor markets* (pp. 133–162). Cambridge, MA: MIT Press.

Konrad, A. M., & Linnehan, F. (1995). Formalized HRM structures—coordinating equal-employment opportunity or concealing organizational practices. *Academy of Management Journal, 38*(3), 787–820.

Kossek, E. E., & Lobel, S. A. (1995). *Managing diversity: human resource strategies for transforming the workplace*. Cambridge, MA: Blackwell.

Kossek, E. E., & Nichol, V. (1992). The effects of on-site child care on employee attitudes and performance. *Personnel Psychology, 45*, 489–509.

Kraiger, K., & Ford, J. K. (1985). A meta-analysis of ratee race effects in performance ratings. *Journal of Applied Psychology, 70*, 56–65.

Kraiger, K., Ford, J. K., & Salas, E. (1993). Application of cognitive, skill-based, and affective theories of learning outcomes to new methods of training evaluation. *Journal of Applied Psychology, 78*, 311–328.

Krawiec, K. D. (2003). Cosmetic compliance and the failure of negotiated governance. *Washington University Law Quarterly, 81*(2), 487–544.

Kulik, C. T., & Roberson, L. (2008). Common goals and golden opportunities: evaluations of diversity education in academic and organizational settings. *Academy of Management Learning and Education, 7*(3), 309–331.

Lawrence, P. R., & Lorsch, J. W. (1967). Differentiation and integration in complex organizations. *Administrative Science Quarterly, 12*(1), 1–47.

Leach, J., George, B., Jackson, T., & LaBella, A. (1995). *A practical guide to working with diversity: the process, the tools, the resources*. New York: AMACOM (American Management Association).

Leonard, J. S. (1990). The impact of affirmative action regulation and equal employment opportunity law on black employment. *Journal of Economic Perspectives, 4*(4), 47–63.

Leonard, J. S. (1989). Women and affirmative action. *Journal of Economic Perspectives, 3*(1), 61–75.

Lerner, J. S., & Tetlock, P. E. (1999). Accounting for the effects of accountability. *Pyschological Bulletin, 125*(2), 255–275.

Lieberman, R. (2005). *Shaping race policy: The United States in cmparative perspective*. Princeton, NJ: Princeton University Press.

Lieberman, R. C. (1998). *Race and state in the United States, Great Britain and France: employment discrimination policy in comparative perspective*. Paper presented at the Annual Meeting of the American Political Science Association.

Lieberman, R. C. (2002). Weak state, strong policy: paradoxes of race policy in the United States, Great Britain, and France. *Studies in American Political Development, 16*, 138–161.

Linenberger, P., & Keaveny, T. J. (1981a). Sexual harassment: the employer's legal obligations. *Personnel, 58*(6), 60–68.

Linenberger, P., & Keaveny, T. J. (1981b). Sexual harassment in employment. *Human Resource Management, 20*(1), 11–17.

Lopez Jr., F. M. (1966). Current problems in test performance of job applicants; I. *Personnel Psychology, 19*(1), 10–18.

Lopez, S. H., Hodson, R., & Roscigno, V. (2009). Power, status and abuse at work: general and sexual harassment compared. *Sociological Quarterly, 50*, 3–27.

Lublin, J. S. (1991, December 2). Sexual harassment is topping agenda in many executive education programs. *Wall Street Journal*.

Lunding, F. S., Clements, C. E., & Perkins, D. S. (1979). Everyone who makes it has a mentor. *Harvard Business Review, 56*(3), 89–101.

Lynch, F. R. (1997). *The diversity machine: the drive to change the white male workplace*. New York: Free Press.

Lynch, L. M., & Black, S. E. (1998). Beyond the incidence of employer-provided training. *Industrial & Labor Relations Review, 52*(1), 64.

MacDonald, H. (1993, July 5). Cashing in on affirmative action: the diversity industry. *New Republic, 209*, 22–25.

Mandel, H., & Semyonov, M. (2005). Family policies, wage structures, and gender gaps: sources of earning inequality in 20 countries. *American Sociological Review, 43*, 949–967.

Mansbridge, J. J. (1986). *Why we lost the ERA*. Chicago: University of Chicago Press.

Marino, K. (1980). Conducting an internal compliance review of affirmative action. *Personnel, 57*(2), 24–34.

Mattison, E. G. (1965). Integrating the work force in Southern industry. In Herbert R. Northrup & Richard L. Rowan (Eds.), *The Negro and employment opportunity: problems and practices* (pp. 147–154). Ann Arbor, MI: Burea of Industrial Relations, Graduate School of Business Administration, University of Michigan.

Mayer, C. E. (1981, November 15). U.S. relaxing enforcement of regulations. *Washington Post*, p. F1.

McDowell, G. L. (1989). Affirmative inaction: the Brock-Meese standoff on federal racial quotas. *Policy Review, 48*, 32–50.

McFarland, H. S. (1965). Minority group employment at General Motors. In Herbert R. Northrup & Richard L. Rowan (Eds.), *The Negro and employment opportunity: problems and practices* (pp. 131–136). Ann Arbor: Burea of Industrial Relations, Graduate School of Business Administration, University of Michigan.

McGuire, G. M. (2000). Gender, race, ethnicity, and networks: the factors affecting the status of employees' network members. *Work and Occupations, 27*(4), 500–523.

McKay, P. F., & McDaniel, M. A. (2006). A reexamination of black-white mean differences in work performance: more data, more moderators. *Journal of Applied Psychology, 91*(3), 538–554.

Meyer, J. W., & Scott, R. W. (1992). *Organizational environments: ritual and rationality* (2nd ed.). Beverly Hill, CA: Sage.

Miller, J. (1994). *Corporate responses to diversity*. New York: Center for the New American Workforce, Queens College.

Moore, P. C. (2001). *The transfer of human and social capital: employee development through assigned peer mentoring.* Unpublished Ph.D. dissertation, Stanford Graduate School of Business, Stanford, CA.

Moss, P. I., & Tilly, C. (2001). *Stories employers tell: race, skill, and hiring in America.* : New York: Russell Sage Foundation.

National Civil Service League (1973). *Training and testing the disadvantaged*. Washington, DC: Consortium.

National Industrial Conference Board (1964). *Personnel practices in factory and office: manufacturing* (Personnel Policy Study No. 194). New York.

Nation's Business (1998, December). The Supreme Court issued two sexual-harassment rulings last summer that should both worry and hearten employers. *Nation's Business*, 15.

Nelson, R. L., & Bridges, W. P. (1999). *Legalizing gender inequality: courts, markets and unequal pay for women in America*. New York: Cambridge University Press.

Neumark, D., & Gardecki, R. (1996). *Women helping women? Role-model and mentoring effects on female Ph.D. students in economics*. Cambridge, MA: National Bureau of Economic Research.

New York Times (1962, July 27). U.S. cites 2 pacts to end race bias. *New York Times*, p. 29.

Ng, E. S. W., & Sears, G. J. (2010). The effect of adverse impact in selection practices on organizational diversity: a field study. *International Journal of Human Resource Management, 21*(9), 1454–1471.

Nieva, V., F., & Gutek, B. A. (1980). Sex effects on evaluation. *Academy of Management Review, 5*, 267–278.

Oppler, S. H., Campbell, J. P., Pulakos, E. D., & Borman, W. C. (1992). Three approaches to the investigation of subgroup bias in performance measurement: review, results, and conclusions. *Journal of Applied Psychology, 77*, 201–217.

Packard, D. (1995). *The HP way: how Bill Hewlett and I built our company*. New York: HarperBusiness.

Pager, D., Western, B., & Bonikowski, B. (2009). Discrimination in a low-wage labor market: a field experiment. *American Sociological Review, 74*, 777–799.

Parrish, J. A. (1966). The industrial psychologist: selection and equal employment opportunity. A symposium. *Personnel Psychology, 19*(1), 1–2.

Patton, A. (1960). How to appraise executive performance. *Harvard Business Review, 38*(1), 63–70.

Pedriana, N. (2006). From protective to equal treatment: legal framing processes and transformation of the women's movement in the 1960s. *American Journal of Sociology, 111*(6), 1718–1761.

Pedriana, N. (2004). Help wanted NOW: legal resources, the women's movement, and the battle over sex-segregated job advertisements. *Social Problems, 51*(2), 182–201.

Peskin, D. B. (1969). Building groundwork for affirmative action EEO program. *Dean B Peskin Personnel Journal (pre-1986) ABI/INFORM Global, 48*(000002), 130–149.

Petersen, T., Saporta, I., & Seidelm, M. D. (1998). Offering a job: meritocracy and social networks. *American Journal of Sociology, 106*(3), 763–816.

Pfeffer, J., & Salancik, G. R. (1978). *The external control of organizations: a resource dependence perspective*. New York: Harper and Row.

Pfeffer, J., & Sutton, J. R. (2005). Prescriptions are not enough. *Academy of Management Review, 30*(1), 32–35.

Pulakos, E. D., White, L. A., Oppler, S. H., & Borman, W. C. (1989). Examination of race and sex effects on performance ratings. *Journal of Applied Psychology, 74*, 770–780.

Purcell, T. V. (1974). How G.E. measures managers on fair employment. *Harvard Business Review, 52*(6), 99–104.

Rapoport, R., & Bailyn, L. (1996). *Relinking life and work: toward a better future: a report to the Ford Foundation based on a collaborative research project with three corporations*. New York: Ford Foundation.

Raskin, A. H. (1961, June 18). Negro makes job gain in South under initial drive at Lockheed. *New York Times*, pp. 1, 50.

Reskin, B. F. (2000). The proximate causes of employment discrimination. *Contemporary Sociology, 29*(2), 319–328.

Reskin, B. F., & McBrier, D. B. (2000). Why not ascription? Organizations' employment of male and female managers. *American Sociological Review, 65*(2), 210–233.

Roche, G. R. (1979). Much ado about mentors. *Harvard Business Review, 57*(1), 14.

Rock, M. L., & Grela, J. J. (1960). Basing bonus payments on opportunity and performance. *Personnel Journal, 38*(2), 330–340.

Roos, P., & Manley, J. E. (1996). Staffing personnel: feminization and change in human resource management. *Sociological Focus, 99*(3), 245–261.

Roscigno, V. (2007). *The face of discrimination: how race and gender impact work and home lives*. New York: Rowman and Littlefield.

Rosenberg, G. S. (1980, February 13). "When less is more…" *Washington Post*, p. F1.

Roth, L. M. (Ed.). (2003). *Selling women short: gender and money on Wall Street*. Princeton, NJ: Princeton University.

Roth, P. L., Huffcutt, A. I., & Bobko, P. (2003). Ethnic group differences in measures of job performance: a new meta-analysis. *Journal of Applied Psychology, 88*(4), 694–706.

Rowe, M. P., & Baker, M. (1984). Are you hearing enough employee concerns? *Harvard Business Review, 62*(3), 127–138.

Ruhm, C. J., & Teague, J. L. (1997). Parental leave policies in Europe and North America. In Francine D. Blau & Ronald G. Ehrenberg (Eds.), *Gender and family issues in the workplace* (pp. 133–156). New York: Russell Sage Foundation.

Rynes, S., & Rosen, B. (1994). What makes diversity programs work? *HR Magazine, 39*(10), 67.

Saguy, A. (2003). *What is sexual harassment: from Capitol Hill to the Sorbonne.* Berkeley, CA: University of California Press.

Schofer, A. (1971). *General Electric's 1970 Report for the US Commission on Civil Rights, Exhibit No. 2U Before the United States Commission on Civil Rights, Clarification and Rebuttal of Staff Report: The Civil Rights Implications of Suburban Freeway Construction.* Retrieved from http://www.law.umaryland.edu/marshall/usccr/documents/cr12h8112_C.pdf.

Shaeffer, R. G. (1973). *Nondiscrimination in employment: changing perspectives, 1963–1972.* New York: The Conference Board.

Shaeffer, R. G. (1975). *Nondiscrimination in employment, 1973–1975: a broadening and deepening national effort.* New York: Conference Board.

SHRM (1999). *Workplace diversity.* VA: Alexandria: Society for Human Resource Management.

Skrentny, J. D. (1996). *The ironies of affirmative action: politics, culture and justice in America.* Chicago: University of Chicago Press.

Slevin, D. (1973). Full utilization of women in employment: the problem and an action program. *Human Resource Management, 12,* 25–32.

Solomon, J. (1988, September 7). The future look of employee benefits. *Wall Street Journal,* p. 29.

Sovern, M. I. (1966). *Legal restraints on racial discrimination in employment.* New York: Twentieth Century Fund.

Spann, J. (1990). Dealing effectively with sexual harassment: some practical lessons from one city's experience. *Public Personnel Management, 19*(1), 53–82.

Spilerman, S.,, & Petersen, T. (1999). Organizational structure, determinants of promotion, and gender differences in attainment. *Social Science Research, 28,* 203–227.

Stafford, F. K., & Sundstrom, M. (1996). Time out for childcare: signalling and earnings rebound effects for men and women. *Labour, 10,* 609–629.

Stetson, D. (1963, November 12). More salaried positions are opening to Negroes. *New York Times,* p. 2.

Strang, D., & Baron, J. N. (1990). Categorical imperatives: the structure of job titles in California state agencies. *American Sociological Review, 55,* 323–335.

Stryker, R. (Ed.). (Forthcoming). *The scientific mediation of civil rights law in Droit et Regulations d' Activites Economiques: Perspectives Sociologiques et Institutionnalistes.* Edited by Christian Bessy, Thierry Eelpeuch, and Jérôme Pélisse. Paris: La Decouverte.

Sturm, S. (2001). Second-generation employment discrimination: a structural approach. *Columbia Law Review, 101*(3), 459–568.

Sutton, J. R., Dobbin, F., Meyer, J. W., & Scott, R. (1994). The legalization of the workplace. *American Journal of Sociology, 99,* 944–971.

Swart, J. C. (1978). *A flexible approach to working hours.* New York: AMACOM (American Management Association).

Thomas, D. A. (2001). The tuth about mentoring minorities: race matters. *Harvard Business Review, 79,* 99–107.

Thomas, D. A. (2004). Diversity as strategy. *Harvard Business Review, 82*(9), 98–108.

Thomas, R. R., Jr. (1991). *Beyond race and gender: unleashing the power of your total work force by managing diversity.* New York: AMACOM (American Management Association).

Thompson, J. D. (1967). *Organizations in action.* New York: McGraw Hill.

Thorpe, C. D., Jr. (1973). Fair employment practices: the compliance jungle. *Personnel Journal, 52,* 642–649.

Tomaskovic-Devey, D. D., & Skaggs, S. L. (1999). Degendered jobs? Organizational processes and gender segregated employment. *Research in Social Stratification and Mobility, 17,* 139–172.

Trost, C. (1992, October 13). Labor letter. *Wall Street Journal,* p. A1.

Tsui, A. S., & Gutek, B. A. (1984). A role set analysis of gender differences in performance, affective relationships, and career success of industrial middle managers. *Academy of Management Journal, 27*(3), 619–635.

Vernon-Gerstenfeld, S., & Burke, E. (1985). Affirmative action in nine large companies: a field study. *Personnel, 62*(4), 54–60.

Waldfogel, J. (1998). The family gap for young women in the United States and Britain: can maternity leave make a difference? *Journal of Labor Economics, 16,* 505–546.

Walker, J. T. J. (1990). *Relative black male employment among business establishments: Relation to management orientation toward affirmative action, organizational context, and organizational characteristics.* Unpublished Doctoral Dissertation, University of Michigan, Ann Arbor.

Wayne, J. H., & Cordeiro, B. L. (2003). Who is a good organizational citizen? Social perception of male and female employees who use family leave. *Sex Roles, 49,* 233–246.

Wheeler, M. L. (1994). *Diversity training* (Conference Board Report No. 1083–94-RR). New York: Conference Board.

Wilson, G., & Branch Mc Brier, D. (2005). Race and loss of privilege: African American/White differences in the determinants of job layoffs from upper-tier occupations. *Sociological Forum, 20,* 301–321.

Winterle, M. J. (1992). *Workforce diversity: corporate challenges, corporate responses* (No. 1013). New York: Conference Board.

Wisensale, S. K. (1997). The White House and Congress on child care and family leave policy: from Carter to Clinton. *Policy Studies Journal, 25*(10), 75–86.

Yang, S. (2007). Racial disparities in training, pay-raise attainment, and income. *Research in Social Stratification and Mobility, 25,* 323–335.

CHAPTER
16
Diversity Staffing: Inclusive Personnel Recruitment and Selection Practices

Derek R. Avery, Patrick F. McKay *and* Sabrina D. Volpone

Abstract

In this chapter, we discuss the research literature on diversity staffing to shed light on a topic that is increasingly important to both researchers and practitioners. To navigate the literature in this area, we organize our discussion around six basic questions confronting organizations as they pursue diversity during the recruitment and selection processes: (1) *why* should organizations staff for diversity, (2) *who* should recruit and select applicants, (3) *what* messages should organizations convey to job seekers, (4) *when* should organizations prioritize diversity staffing, (5) *where* should organizations recruit applicants, and (6) *how* should organizations select for diversity. We also discuss several existing gaps in the literature and identify directions for future research and practice.

Key Words: diversity recruitment, personnel selection, minority employees, minority recruiters, recruitment messages, recruitment locations, recruitment sources, recruitment mediums

Introduction

Although there are a number of means by which companies may attain a competitive advantage over their competitors, one of the most direct and sustainable is to create and leverage differences in human capital (Pfeffer, 1998). That is, when companies acquire and retain personnel possessing greater knowledge, skills, and abilities than their competitors, they are better positioned to prosper (Aragon-Sanchez, Barba-Aragon, & Sanz-Valle, 2003). The first step toward gaining this competitive advantage is through strategic employee staffing initiatives. For instance, organizations can use recruitment, defined as "organizational practices and decisions that affect either the number, or types, of individuals that are willing to apply" (Rynes, 1991, p. 429), as a strategy to attract the most desired applicants available (Taylor & Collins, 2000). Subsequently, they can tailor their personnel selection systems to identify those candidates who are best suited to help the organization achieve its various objectives.

Toward this end, organizations aim to accomplish three things during the staffing process (Thomas & Wise, 1999). First, they hope to generate significant applicant interest in applying (Newman & Lyon, 2009). Second, they aim to maximize qualifications within the applicant pool (i.e., possess the knowledge, skills, and abilities desired). Third, companies seek to select the best employees available within their applicant pools. These goals are discussed thoroughly throughout a number of articles, book chapters, reviews, and meta-analyses that cover the past three decades of recruitment and selection literature (e.g., Breaugh & Starke, 2000; Chapman, Uggerslev, Carroll, Piasentin, & Jones, 2005; Hausknecht, Day, & Thomas, 2004; Highhouse & Hoffman, 2001; Le, Oh, Shaffer, & Schmidt, 2007; McDaniel, Whetzel, Schmidt, & Maurer, 1994; Rynes & Cable, 2003; Saks, 2005;

Taylor & Collins, 2000; Zottoli & Wanous, 2000). Nevertheless, with only a few exceptions (e.g., Avery & McKay, 2010), authors have yet to systematically consolidate the scattered literature detailing how organizations can recruit and select demographically diverse workforces.

As societal demographic diversity in the United States and other developed nations continues to increase (Finkelstein, 2010; Holvino, & Kamp, 2009; Toossi, 2006), so too does the need for a comprehensive understanding of diversity staffing. Specifically, as the proportion of members of traditionally underrepresented groups grows larger, the competition among organizations for talented, diverse employees will escalate. Companies cannot expect to rely on (a) traditional homogeneous applicant sources or (b) traditional staffing approaches to prove successful in attracting and selecting applicants from previously underrepresented groups (Avery & McKay, 2006; Ployhart & Holtz, 2008) if they hope to remain competitive. Today and tomorrow's best employees are diverse in a number of ways, and organizations need to consider diversity staffing strategies designed to access, entice, and identify talent among this diverse applicant pool (Ng & Burke, 2005).

However, many organizations have trouble adapting their policies and practices in response to changing labor market demographics (Riccucci, 1997; von Bergen, Soper, & Foster, 2002). This is unfortunate because researchers and practitioners need to rethink staffing from a more inclusive perspective if diversity recruitment and selection activities are to produce the desired results (Benschop, 2001; Breaugh & Starke, 2000, van Hooft, Born, Taris, & van der Flier, 2006). Many of the contemporary recruitment, selection, and placement strategies were developed decades ago, when the workforce in the United States and many other countries was considerably more demographically homogeneous. To be successful, organizations must consider alternative staffing strategies. Therefore, the purpose of this chapter is to integrate the existent research in the areas of recruitment and selection to shed light on diversity staffing for both researchers and practitioners. Through this detailed discussion, we aim to clarify existing findings, identify empirically based best practices, and provide an agenda for future research.

The remainder of this chapter is organized as follows. First, we review the diversity staffing literature. To consolidate this research, we organize our discussion around six basic questions facing organizations and researchers: (1) *why* organizations should staff for diversity, (2) *who* they should deploy to recruit and select applicants, (3) *what* messages should be conveyed to job seekers, (4) *when* organizations should prioritize diversity staffing, (5) *where* organizations should recruit, and (6) *how* they can select for diversity. Second, we emphasize the conclusions discussed in the literature review and describe the significant gap that exists between research and practice. Finally, we provide suggestions for future research and practice. We now turn to a review of the existing diversity staffing literature.

Diversity staffing: A review of the literature

Although we aim to examine diversity staffing in as comprehensive of a manner possible, the research conducted thus far tends to focus more on certain groups than on others. For instance, most diversity recruitment research has examined racio-ethnic, sex, or age diversity (Stone, Stone-Romero, & Lukaszewski, 2007). Moreover, much of the literature on maximizing the inclusivity of selection processes is limited to race and sex (Ployhart & Holtz, 2008). As such, a larger portion of our review focuses on these three types of diversity. Nevertheless, we make every possible effort throughout the review to incorporate any available research covering other types of identity-based diversity (e.g., disabled, gay) and generalize findings across types of diversity where appropriate.

Why should organizations staff for diversity?

The most logical opening for this discussion is a concise consideration of why organizations should seek diversity through their recruitment and selection processes. Firms typically view diversity as a means to (a) be fair, (b) attract a wider range of clientele, or (c) create a broader internal pool of human resources that should facilitate intra-organizational learning (Ely & Thomas, 2001). From an organizational staffing perspective, these three motives essentially simplify to two. On the one hand, companies may seek to attract diversity because they feel obliged to do so. This could entail actual or perceived pressures from internal or external stakeholders (e.g., employees, customers, business partners, government) or might reflect realities associated with shifting labor pool demographics. On the other hand, companies could elect to staff a diverse workforce voluntarily, based on beliefs that it will enhance their competitiveness. We now briefly take a closer look at each reason.

Extrinsic motivation for corporate diversity can be attributable to a number of different sources. First, many countries have enacted legislation prohibiting discrimination on the bases of various identity markers. One way to lessen the likelihood of litigation or other legal action is to diversify. Second, organizational decision-makers may perceive a moral obligation not to discriminate against individuals (Demuijnck, 2009). Third, the market often rewards companies for engaging in effective diversity management in the form of higher stock prices and greater financial returns (Roberson & Park, 2007; Wright, Ferris, Hiller, & Kroll, 1995), which could create a strong incentive for firms to seek diversity. Fourth, there simply aren't enough high-quality workers of any one particular demographic background in many instances to meet labor needs (Rynes & Barber, 1990). This means companies that resist diversity simultaneously may be restricting their own access to the employees they need to survive (Thomas, 2008). Finally, customers may compel companies to increase the representation of underrepresented groups (Reskin, McBrier, & Kmec, 1999). For instance, one recent study involving law firms (Beckman & Phillips, 2005) found that clients sometimes successfully pressured their legal representation to do a better job promoting female attorneys. Thus, it is clear that external stakeholders can have a significant impact on companies' desires to diversify.

Beyond feeling coerced to do so, firms also might opt for diversity because they believe in its potential to enhance organizational effectiveness. Although the literature is riddled with inconsistent findings concerning the link between organizational diversity and performance, some notable findings have shown that effects can be positive (e.g., Herring, 2009; Richard, 2000; this issue is covered in depth in Chapter 14 of this handbook). It seems that effective diversity management is a vital key to unlocking the prospective benefits of diversity. For instance, Gonzalez and DeNisi (2009) observed interactive effects between organizational diversity (race and sex) and diversity climate, or the shared perspective concerning the organizational value attached to fairness and inclusion (Mor Barak, Cherin, & Berkman, 1998), when predicting performance. Simply put, when climates were more supportive of diversity, its impact on the bottom line was positive. Thus, companies may view diversity as a potential source of sustained competitive advantage because a well-managed diverse workforce is relatively rare and potentially difficult to imitate.

Irrespective of whether companies are coaxed by their stakeholders to diversify or intrinsically recognize the potential value of diversity, there are clearly a number of legitimate reasons for companies to engage in diversity staffing. However, because most companies lack experience in this regard (i.e., they've never been very demographically diverse), they may be uncertain as to how to proceed in pursuit of this end. Fortunately, there is a considerable body of empirical literature to help guide diversity staffing efforts. In the next section, we review some of this work to shed some light on who companies should assign to be responsible for diversity staffing initiatives.

Who should recruit applicants?

We now turn our attention to focusing on the role of recruiters and interviewers, who often represent jobseekers' first contact with prospective employers. As such, both recruiters and interviewers strongly influence applicants' first impressions of the company (DeBell, Montgomery, McCarthy, & Lantheir, 1998; Larsen & Phillips, 2002). This influence is based on the tendency for applicants to view these individuals as organizational representatives and, therefore, to place particular emphasis on the characteristics of their interactions with them to draw conclusions about the organization (Highhouse & Hoffman, 2001; Rynes, 1991). Interestingly, applicants may infer attributes about the organization based on seemingly unrelated information. In fact, the mere outward appearance of a recruiter or interviewer often conveys a message to applicants about the types of current employees as well as the types of employees an organization is interested in recruiting (Hurley-Hanson & Giannantonio, 2006). Thus, recruiter and/or interviewer differences may cause jobseekers to perceive contrasting views of a company (Aselage & Eisenberger, 2003; Goltz & Giannantonio, 1995).

For instance, applicants may perceive a recruiter or interviewer's demographics as indicative of those of the typical employee. Based on this tendency, minority applicants often seek diverse organizational representatives and react positively (e.g., increased organizational attractiveness) during recruitment and selection processes when they encounter those whose demographics match their own (Knouse, 2009). Indeed, one study looking at the effects of campus recruiting during 293 interviews found that male applicants who were interviewed by male recruiters were more attracted to firms than men interviewed by women (Turban & Dougherty, 1992). Likewise, research demonstrates that racio-ethnic similarity between recruiters and applicants relates to the applicant's level of attraction to the company and actual job choice decisions (Goldberg, 2003). However, the racio-ethnicity of the applicant and recruiter need not be identical. Rather, it seems that what is important to minority jobseekers is that the recruiter also belongs to a racio-ethnic minority group (Avery et al., 2004). Therefore, applicants, especially those who are of minority groups, seem to seek recruiters and interviewers who are similar to them demographically.

To further explain the effects of recruiter–applicant and interviewer–applicant similarity on recruitment and selection outcomes, organizational representatives' perceptions of the applicant also must be considered. During recruitment, not only do applicants appear to prefer demographic similarity in the recruiters they encounter, it is also the case that recruiters seek applicants who are similar to them (Hurley-Hanson & Giannantonio, 2006). Similarity is sought on the basis of age, skin color, gender, education, or even club membership (Hellwig, 1985; Hurley-Hanson & Giannantonio, 2006; Ibarra, 1992; Judge & Ferris, 1992; Shah & Kleiner, 2005). In particular, research shows that during the hiring process, (a) people tend to assign positive ratings to those like themselves and (b) recruiter–applicant race similarity positively influences selection decisions (Goldberg, 2005; Heilman, Martell, & Simon, 1988; Wiley & Eskilson, 1985). Therefore, employing minority recruiters may lead to higher proportions of minorities among the new hires selected.

Interviewers' perceptions of the applicant are important as well. For example, research shows that interviewers routinely base judgments about applicants on factors such as perceived similarity to the applicant (e.g., Frank & Hackman, 1975; Gousie, 1993; Graves & Powell, 1995; Howard & Ferris, 1996; Huang, 2009; Rand & Wexley, 1975), which can contribute to biased decisions (Arvey & Campion, 1982). Further, résumé reviewers also exhibit a similarity bias, as job applicants with unconventional names (e.g., of Arabic origin or uncommon among the demographic majority) are reviewed more negatively than those with more mainstream names (Bertrand & Mullainathan, 2004; Derous, Nguyen, & Ryan, 2009; King, Mendoza, Madera, Hebl, & Knight, 2006). Therefore, having some diversity among those responsible for reviewing and interviewing candidates may also lead to higher proportions of minorities among the new hires selected.

The similarity-attraction paradigm (Byrne, 1971) explains why minorities are attracted to companies with minority recruiters and interviewers and minority recruiters/interviewers are more likely to recruit minority applicants than are White recruiters (Goldberg, 2005; Thomas & Wise, 1999). Specifically, this paradigm posits that similarity on the basis of values, beliefs, and experiences facilitates interpersonal attraction (Byrne, 1971). In the case of selection, minority recruiters and interviewers likely signal to minority applicants that the organization contains employees who are similar to themselves on the surface (Avery et al., 2004), which is a common proxy for deeper-level similarity such as values and beliefs (Cunningham, 2007). As such, employing diverse recruiters and interviewers should facilitate interpersonal attraction between organizational representatives and applicants, thereby enhancing both applicant attraction and likelihood of selection.

In sum, it seems clear that corporations' decisions concerning who will represent them during recruitment and selection procedures play an important role in determining who gets recruited and subsequently hired.

What messages should organizations send during staffing?

Next, we examine the literature describing how message content influences diversity staffing. During recruitment, ads contain messages that shape applicant attraction because the content presented commonly provides information on an organization's values and priorities (Highhouse & Hoffman, 2001; Rubaii-Barrett & Wise, 2007). Organizational values are communicated whether or not organizations explicitly intend to express them in job ads (Rubaii-Barrett & Wise, 2007). As such, jobseekers make assumptions about the organization based on the messages presented in recruitment material (Hurley-Hanson & Giannantonio, 2006; Rafaeli & Oliver, 1998). It is important, therefore, that the messages presented make all applicants feel comfortable and welcomed (Avery & McKay, 2006; Perkins, Thomas, & Taylor, 2000).

Unfortunately, this seems lost on many companies. Several studies show that corporate websites in the United States and abroad rarely communicate a clear message that demonstrates commitment to diversity (Antun, Strick, & Thomas, 2007; Rubaii-Barrett, & Wise, 2007; Singh & Point, 2006).

For example, Singh and Point (2004) examined over 200 websites that belonged to top-performing companies in Europe. On a positive note, they found that the one third of these companies acknowledged diversity as a competitive advantage. Unfortunately, approximately 20 percent of the companies did not explain why they felt that diversity is important. Further, only 10 percent demonstrated that they respect diversity. As such, mixed messages often are presented to applicants via organizations' discussions of diversity on their websites.

Evidence indicates that applicants respond favorably to message content signaling an inclusive and engaging workplace. Although information related to the characteristics of the job (e.g., pay, promotion opportunities) is the most important determinant of applicant attraction (e.g., Barber & Roehling, 1993; O'Reilly & Caldwell, 1980; Thomas & Wise, 1999), including messages about diversity initiatives helps to recruit a broader spectrum of jobseekers (Knouse, 2009; Smith, Wokutch, Harrington, & Dennis, 2004). For instance, the literature shows that diversity messages are particularly important to women and minorities, who, compared to majority jobseekers, are more likely to rely on information from recruitment materials than connections with current employees (Giscombe & Mattis, 2002; Kirnan et al., 1989). In particular, minority group members appear to respond positively to affirmative action statements, diversity management policies, descriptions of diversity philosophies, and diversity awards (Avery & McKay, 2006; Goldberg & Allen, 2008; Knouse, 2009; Ng & Burke, 2005; Rau & Hyland, 2003). They are often not alone in this tendency, as many White jobseekers also gravitate toward companies expressing value for diversity (Williamson, Slay, Shapiro, & Shivers-Blackwell, 2008), particularly if they are higher in ethnic identity, other-group orientation, or racial tolerance (Avery, 2003; Kim & Gelfand 2003; Meyers & Dreachsli, 2007). Further, minority group members not only respond to diversity messages during recruitment, but also seek out information on diversity practices when making job choice decisions (Ng & Burke, 2005). Thus it seems apparent that organizations expressing diversity-focused statements during recruitment should be better positioned to attract applicants across demographic groups.

In addition to verbal or written statements, the images (e.g., pictures) presented during recruitment also convey messages to applicants. Research suggests that the images used should be representative of the various demographic groups employed within the organization (Meyers & Dreachsli, 2007). Images containing members of a racio-ethnic minority, women, or handicapped people can signal to applicants that the company employs members of these groups and that they are visible within the organization (Avery, 2003; Kim & Gelfand, 2003; Perkins et al., 2000; Rau & Hyland, 2003). Not surprisingly, minority candidates often respond positively to images of minority employees in recruitment advertisements or brochures in the form of heightened attraction and intentions to pursue employment (Avery & McKay, 2006; Knouse, 2009).

Many of these issues discussed in the context of recruitment are equally applicable during selection. Overall, it seems that minorities look for signals indicating that selection decisions are made fairly (Ryan & Ployhart, 2000). Messages promoting fair and bias-free procedures are essential because, historically, a variety of commonly used selection procedures (e.g., interviews, testing) have discriminated against minority groups. For example, research has shown that interviews can be biased toward minorities. Specifically, religious minorities who wear religious clothing (e.g., Muslim women who wear Hijabis) report lower expectations of receiving a job offer than Muslim women who do not wear religious clothing (Ghumman & Jackson, 2010). Further, cognitive ability tests are often biased against minority racio-ethnic groups (Chung-Yan & Cronshaw, 2002). As such, communicating standards of fairness during selection is likely to be highly important to minority applicants.

When minorities perceive selection procedures to be unfair, the outcomes are negative. Specifically, research demonstrates that minority applicants are more likely than majority applicants to drop out of the selection process (Arvey, Gordon, Massengill, & Mussio, 1975; Ryan & Ployhart, 2000). However, when applicants perceive selection procedures to be fair, they are more likely to (a) hold positive views of the organization, (b) accept job offers, and (c) recommend the organization (Hausknecht, Day, & Thomas, 2004). The type of selection procedure used has some influence over applicants' perceptions. For example, interviews and work samples are perceived more positively than cognitive ability tests. Further, cognitive ability tests are perceived more favorably than are personality inventories and honesty tests (Hausknecht et al., 2004). Therefore, the literature describes the importance of fairness perception during selection. Consequently, messages of fairness should be communicated to applicants throughout the selection process.

When is it the right time to staff for diversity?

One area in which the literature hasn't proven particularly clear is identifying those situations in which diversity staffing efforts are apt to be more or less beneficial. It seems that many authors make the *de facto* assumption that all companies should always seek all types of diversity. In questioning this assumption, it is not our contention to say that companies should ever discriminate against members of any demographic groups. Rather, there are instances where it may not be in an organization's best interest to make concerted efforts to attract a demographically diverse applicant pool. For instance, available labor market pools may be deficient in certain types of diversity. Is it sound strategy in such instances for a small company to recruit outside of its labor market for the expressed purpose of attracting a more diverse applicant pool?

In combing the literature for research on this topic, it seems as though many organizations have drawn their own conclusions about when diversity staffing should become a more pressing organizational priority. One seemingly important determinant is human resource dependence, which is "a firm-level construct describing the degree to which an organization has difficulty procuring and maintaining supplies of human resources" (Fields, Goodman, & Blum, 2005, p. 167). In essence, the more challenging an organization finds it to recruit, select, and retain high-quality personnel, the more likely it is to employ higher proportions of members of underrepresented groups (i.e., women and minorities; Blum, Fields, & Goodman, 1994; Fields et al., 2005). Apparently, some organizations see diversity staffing as a last resort and are more willing to pursue nontraditional applicants only when they lack confidence in their ability to meet their labor needs within the supply of traditional jobseekers (Rynes & Barber, 1990).

The preceding conclusion suggests that perceived labor market shortages may increase the emphasis organizations place on diversity staffing. Nevertheless, there are other more legitimate reasons beyond this myopic approach that companies might prioritize or deprioritize goals for attracting and selecting diverse employees. For instance, one of the premier influences on the diversity of an organization's personnel is the demographic composition of its available labor pool (Reskin et al., 1999). If a firm that draws locally is situated in a community with little demographic heterogeneity along a dimension such as racio-ethnicity, it seems unwarranted to expect a high degree of racio-ethnic diversity among the organization's personnel. Likewise, if there is a *legitimate* (as opposed to merely perceived) shortfall in the representation of a particular group in the pool of available candidates, it may be counterproductive for a firm to invest significant resources strictly to recruit a more diverse pool. Consequently, although it is generally a good idea for firms to employ as inclusive of a recruitment strategy as possible, it is important to recognize that there are prospective situational constraints that may be beyond the organization's immediate control.

Where should organizations recruit?

If an organization is to engage in diversity staffing, a preeminent question involves where diversity recruitment should focus. Specifically, we examine the different locations that have been investigated as places to recruit minority applicants. The term "recruitment source" is often used in the literature to describe the places organizations choose to deploy their recruitment efforts. Broadly speaking, there are two types of recruitment sources (Meyers & Dreachsli, 2007; Taber & Hendricks, 2003). The first type are formal sources that include recruiting at places such as employment agencies, trade unions, school placement bureaus, campus fairs, radio, television, newspapers, the Internet, professional journals, and professional conferences. The second are informal recruitment sources, including employee referrals, referrals by friends or relatives, self-initiated applications, walk-ins or write-ins, and social networks (Kirnan, Farley, & Geisinger, 1989; Meyers & Dreachsli, 2007). Prior inquiry has demonstrated the importance of considering the source, as studies have shown that this variable can explain up to 5 percent of the variance in the quality of applications an organization receives (Kirnan et al., 1989).

One common finding within this literature involves the superiority of informal sources, as the quality of employees obtained from informal sources often exceeds that of those recruited from formal recruiting activities (Breaugh, 1981; Decker & Cornelius, 1979; Gannon, 1971; Kirnan et al., 1989). The reasoning behind these findings is that the applicants referred from informal sources have inside knowledge of the company obtained from their personal contacts employed there. This information helps them to formulate reasonable organizational expectations, which facilitates job adjustment and satisfaction (Knouse, 2009; Moser, 2005; Ryan & Tippins, 2004; Zottoli

& Wanous, 2000). Unfortunately, however, organizational reliance on informal sources may have a detrimental effect on diversity recruitment initiatives. For example, if current employees are mostly homogeneous, so too will be the personal contacts they are apt to refer. Therefore, using informal recruitment should cause any existing organizational homogeneity to be replicated (Giscombe & Mattis, 2002; Kirnan et al., 1989; McDonald, Lin, & Ao, 2009; Meyers & Dreachsli, 2007; Taber & Hendricks, 2003). A mix of both informal and formal recruiting sources seems optimal to attract a heterogeneous applicant pool unless the company's incumbent personnel are considerably diverse.

In examining the efficacy of particular recruiting sources in diversity recruitment, one that has demonstrated considerable potential is college recruitment. Many colleges and universities are filled with diverse talent, thereby making them an excellent source for quality applicants (Roach, 2006). Most literature suggests recruiting at minority-focused institutions (i.e., universities that historically have a large minority student body; e.g., Howard University for Black applicants; Roach, 2006). However, organizations have enjoyed success recruiting for diversity at large, heterogeneous public universities as well (Roach, 2006). To maximize the return on diversity recruitment efforts on college campuses, recruiters must be strategic. For example, they can contact minority-focused professional organizations (e.g., National Society of Black Engineers), attend minority-focused events at professional conferences (Newman & Lyon, 2009), and sponsor activities with these groups (Roach, 2006).

Beyond institutions of higher learning, other sources also appear useful for recruiting diversity. The U.S. Office of Personnel Management suggests that outreach programs, minority job fairs, and résumé banks are effective places to recruit minority applicants (Pitts, 2006). This could entail building and maintaining relationships with diverse communities that, ultimately, may become a fruitful labor source. In discussing *where* companies should recruit, it is also important to consider the location of information posted concerning job vacancies. Although newspaper ads and recruitment brochures have been used for decades and may seem outdated, companies have found creative ways to use these mediums to recruit talented applicants. Creative job advertising strategies such as this not only recruit talented applicants, but by placing these advertisements in locations frequented more often by certain populations than others, organizations can bolster their diversity recruitment efforts (Doverspike, Taylor, Shultz, & McKay, 2000; Newman & Lyon, 2009; Perkins et al., 2000).

One stark recruitment reality is that both organizations and applicants increasingly are turning to the Internet (Allen, Mahto, & Otando, 2007; Cober, Brown, Blumental, Doverspike, & Levy, 2000; Kuhn & Skuterud, 2000; Perkins et al., 2000; Rubaii-Barrett & Wise, 2007). In fact, some companies plan to stop printing recruitment brochures altogether to become more environmentally friendly and rely instead on cyberspace (McPartland, 2009). Internet recruiting provides a number of benefits to organizations over traditional recruitment practices (e.g., brochures, newspaper), such as the capacity to communicate a greater amount of information, reach a large number of jobseekers, and easily store, track, and screen résumés (Cober, Brown, Blumental, Doverspike, & Levy, 2000; Cober, Brown, Keeping, & Levy, 2004; Hogler, Henle, & Bemus, 1998; Lievens Harris, Keer, & Bisqueret, 2003; Van Hoye & Lievens, 2007; Walker, Feild, Giles, Armenakis, & Bernerth, 2009).

The use of the Internet in recruiting diverse applicants presents endless possibilities. For example, the literature shows that organizations can record recruiters from underrepresented groups in video presentations to influence recruitment outcomes (Ployhart & Holtz, 2008). Research by Knouse (2009) showed that participants were more attracted to organizations that included testimonials on recruitment websites. Some organizations have even gone so far as to use their sites to give applicants email addresses of current minority employees (Phillips, 1998). Also, providing job applicants access to job postings and other information online can be a tool to help disabled applicants (e.g., those with vision problems). Fonts can be enlarged and zoom-in options are available on images, which is a possibility on computers but not via other mediums. Therefore, the use of the Internet to recruit diverse applicants is potentially promising.

Organizations should exercise caution, however, in relying too heavily on Internet recruiting due to possible detrimental effects on diversity recruitment efforts. For example, Internet availability is often limited for minority groups (e.g., racial minorities, women, and older workers; Hogler, Henle, & Bemus, 1998). In fact, Black residents of rural areas have the lowest rate of computer ownership (6.4 percent) followed by Hispanic (12 percent) and Native American (15.3 percent) groups (Hogler et al., 1998). Further, Internet use differs by age. Specifically, 20- to 34-year-olds use the Internet more than other age groups (Bureau of Labor Statistics, 2006). As a result, the use of certain mediums can disadvantage some demographic groups during the recruitment process. This does not imply that these mediums should not be used by organizations during recruitment; rather, companies should consider the potential costs and benefits associated with using each medium.

How to select for diversity

The extent that organizations are successful in selecting for diversity is a function of their selection goals. If a firm's primary goal is to maximize the utility or economic value of selection decision making, then it is prudent to utilize selection methods that result in the highest predicted job performance among the job candidates who are selected. The utility of selection methods is directly and positively related to the validity of selection procedures, which refers to the extent that scores derived from selection tests/assessments are significantly correlated with subsequent job performance (Schmidt & Hunter, 1998). In particular, top-down selection using valid selection measures, wherein top-scoring job applicants are selected in a descending fashion until all available jobs are filled, is the selection strategy associated with the greatest utility. An additional concern with the use of various selection methods is the degree to which subgroup differences in scores result from their usage. The magnitudes of subgroup differences in scores is directly related to the extent of adverse impact (AI) against members of lower-scoring groups when a given selection technique is used to make hiring decisions. AI occurs when a selection method results in members of a particular minority or disadvantaged group (e.g., Blacks or women) having disproportionately lower selection rates (or likelihood of being hired) than those of a majority or advantaged group (e.g., Whites or men). AI is defined specifically as a minority selection rate that is less than 80 percent of the majority group's selection rate (i.e., "the 4/5ths rule"). Therefore, organizations that wish to diversify their workforces should be cognizant of the extent of AI associated with the selection/assessments included in their selection systems.

Next, we review the literature to shed light on the extent that various selection methods are predictive of job performance and the level of AI associated with their use. To begin with, of the various selection methods, cognitive ability tests (CATs) have been identified as the single most valid procedure for predicting job performance (Schmidt & Hunter, 1998). CATs measure individuals' general mental abilities and reasoning, and while they are highly valid predictors of job performance, Whites have been shown to earn markedly higher scores on these tests than their Black and Hispanic counterparts (Roth, Bevier, Bobko, Switzer, & Tyler, 2001). Accordingly, the use of CATs for selection purposes will result in substantial AI against Blacks and Hispanics. Thus, for organizations whose goals are to maximize racio-ethnic diversity within their workforces, the use of CATs will undermine such efforts. We focus our attention here on racio-ethnic subgroup disparities in selection method scores, as these have been the most studied and represent the largest differences between groups evident in the personnel selection literature (Hough, Oswald, & Ployhart, 2001).

The competing goals of maximizing the validity of selection systems and the racio-ethnic diversity of employees selected led Ployhart and Holtz (2008) to label this phenomenon the "diversity–validity dilemma." In addressing this issue, the authors reviewed literature pertaining to means by which firms can select a highly qualified and diverse workforce. An exhaustive coverage of Ployhart and Holtz's (2008) conclusions is beyond the scope of this chapter; however, we will briefly review strategies they identified as most likely to minimize subgroup differences in selection method scores, yet maintain useful levels of predictive validity.

Resulting from the fact that the job performance domain has broadened beyond cognitive constructs, personnel research has investigated alternative predictor methods by examining the predictive validities and AI associated with alternative selection methods. Below, in our review of these alternative selection methods (e.g., personality measures, integrity tests, employment interviews, and situational judgment tests), we focus attention on a number of widely used selection methods that display useful validities and markedly lower AI against minorities than CATs do. Other alternative selection methods, such as job knowledge tests, biodata, work samples, and assessment centers, are not reviewed because although they are valid selection techniques, their usage results in moderate to high levels of AI against minorities (Dean, Roth, & Bobko, 2008; McKay & McDaniel, 2006; Potosky, Bobko, & Roth, 2005; Roth, Bobko, McFarland, & Buster, 2008). Furthermore, these selection methods are most applicable for selecting experienced job applicants, thus limiting their feasibility in entry-level selection contexts (Schmidt & Hunter, 1998).

First, theoretical advances in the personality domain (e.g., Goldberg, 1993) led to the establishment and verification of the "Big Five" model of personality, which conceptualizes personality in regard to five global dimensions (i.e., emotional stability, extraversion, agreeableness, openness to experience, and conscientiousness). Meta-analytic research has shown that measures of conscientiousness predict performance across all jobs (Hurtz & Donovan, 2000), and useful validities have been obtained for the emotional stability, extraversion (for sales jobs), and agreeableness dimensions as well (Hurtz & Donovan, 2000). Furthermore, personality dimensions have been shown to predict job performance incrementally beyond cognitive ability (Schmidt & Hunter, 1998) and display negligible relations with CATs. Accordingly, the conscientiousness personality dimension results in negligible AI against minorities.

Second, two forms of integrity tests, clear-purpose tests (i.e., those that measure attitudes toward honesty directly) and disguised-purpose tests (i.e., those that measure dispositional traits related to honesty) have been used as alternative selection methods (Ones, Viswesvaran, & Schmidt, 1993). Ones and colleagues (1993) provide evidence for the predictive validity of integrity tests for predicting job performance and counterproductive work behaviors such as absenteeism, tardiness, and rules infractions. In addition, Schmidt and Hunter (1998) found that integrity tests predict job performance beyond CATs. Moreover, they result in minimal differences when the scores of minority groups (i.e., Black, Hispanics) are compared to majority groups (i.e., Whites).

A third alternative selection procedure, the employment interview, is the most commonly used selection method (McDaniel, Whetzel, Schmidt, & Maurer, 1994). Interviews can vary in format from largely informal, unsystematically administered and scored unstructured interviews to highly structured interviews that are based upon job analyses, include standard questions asked across jobseekers, and are scored using a standardized scoring form. Also, interviews are flexible in the sense that they can be developed to measure a variety of job-relevant constructs, including cognitive ability, job knowledge, personality, and applied social skills (e.g., interpersonal sensitivity; Huffcutt, Conway, Roth, & Stone, 2001). Although interviews are moderately correlated with CATs (Huffcutt, Roth, & McDaniel, 1996), they result in markedly lower AI against minorities than CATs. Moreover, the extent of AI is moderated by interview structure, such that structured interviews are associated with lower levels of AI against minorities than unstructured interviews (Huffcutt & Roth, 1998). Further, some researchers caution that prior meta-analytic estimates of racio-ethnic mean differences in interview scores may be underestimated due to range restriction (Roth, van Iddekinge, Huffcutt, Eidson, & Bobko, 2002). Corroborating their suspicions, Roth and colleagues (2002) found that while structured interviews result in much lower AI against Blacks and Hispanics than CATs, these measures are associated with larger subgroup differences within applicant samples.

Fourth, situational judgment tests (SJTs) measure job applicants' judgment and decision-making skills in job-related situations. SJTs have a number of favorable attributes, including their (a) broader sampling of job-relevant content, and by extension, expected criterion-related validity, (b) flexibility in tapping various work-related constructs (e.g., job knowledge, problem solving), and (c) possibility for lower AI relative to CATs. Despite some evidence that SJTs are moderately correlated with CATs (McDaniel et al., 2001), Whetzel, McDaniel, and Nguyen (2008) found SJTs to result in minimal subgroup differences when minority groups (i.e., Blacks, Hispanics) were compared with Whites.

A second strategy for selecting a qualified and diverse workforce is to use selection systems that combine and manipulate scores (Ployhart & Holtz, 2008). This tactic is designed to achieve varying selection goals, such as increased diversity in hiring while minimizing losses in the utility of selection systems. A major subject of research associated with this strategy has been the validities and AI that result from selection systems that combine cognitive and noncognitive (low AI) selection methods. The logic here is that selection system utility can be maintained by the use of CATs, whereas the AI related to their use can be offset by combining CAT scores with lower AI selection methods (e.g., structured interviews, personality tests). Simulation-based and meta-analytic research in this vein has shown that the AI that occurs from utilizing CATs can be somewhat obviated by including other low-AI predictors such as personality, structured interviews, and biodata in selection batteries (Bobko et al., 1999; De Corte, Lievens, & Sackett, 2007). Nonetheless, the AI reductions observed are small at low selection ratios commonly used in practical selection contexts

(Finch, Edwards, & Wallace, 2009; Ryan, Ployhart, & Friedel, 1998). Consequently, substantial losses in selection system utility occur under such conditions (De Corte et al., 2007; Finch et al., 2009).

Another method devised to resolve the "diversity–validity dilemma" is to use banding to interpret selection/assessment scores. Generally, in top-down selection contexts involving CATs, relatively few Blacks and Hispanics earn top scores compared to White job applicants, thus reducing their likelihood of hire. In response, the use of banding is considered a viable means to increase the likelihood that minorities will be selected. Banding is a technique of interpreting test scores that considers similar scores as equivalent (e.g., 90–100) because small differences in assessment scores might result from unreliability of measurement, as opposed to "real" differences in standing on the construct of interest (Campion et al., 1991; Henle, 2004). Research on banding has shown that it is most effective at increasing minority applicant selection rates when hiring decisions are made with minority preference, meaning that minority job applicants are hired preferentially from within score bands rather than White jobseekers (Aguinis, 2004; Sackett & Roth, 1996). Henle (2004) further demonstrated that minority preference banding methods are defensible in court cases only when used in concert with job-relevant bases for making selection systems (i.e., consideration of various qualifications such as work experience and relevant training and education).

A final viable strategy related to the interpretation of selection scores consists of the varying ways of weighting job performance criteria (Ployhart & Holtz, 2008). This tactic follows from Borman and Motowidlo's (1993, 1997) theory that job performance consists of task performance and contextual performance measurement, and that CATs and disposition are most predictive of task performance and contextual performance, respectively. Extending from this theory, several researchers proposed that the AI associated with selection systems might be reduced if contextual performance is weighted more strongly than task performance (Hattrup, Rock, & Scalia, 1997; Murphy & Shiarella, 1997). Simulation study results suggest slight reductions in AI against minorities occur when contextual performance and/or noncognitive selection methods (e.g., conscientiousness dimension of personality) are given greater weight than task performance and/or CATs in selection systems (Hattrup et al., 1997; Murphy & Shiarella, 1997); however, observed levels of AI satisfied the "4/5ths rule" only at extremely high selection ratios of 80 percent, which is indicative of a very lenient, low-utility hiring scheme.

In summary, selection for diversity will be largely contingent on an organization's selection goals. Decades of personnel selection research indicates that an organization's selection system utility is maximized by the use of CATs to make selection decisions. Use of CATs, however, will result in few Blacks and Hispanics being hired relative to Whites. As means of reconciling this apparent conflict between validity and diversity goals (Ployhart & Holtz, 2008), our review suggests the use of alternative predictors such as personality inventories, integrity tests, structured interviews, and situational judgment tests in selection systems. These selection methods have useful validities and result in relatively low AI against racio-ethnic minorities. Another viable yet somewhat less effective option is to combine CATs with other noncognitive selection tools (e.g., personality) in selection systems. Several of these alternative (noncognitive) predictors, such as conscientiousness, integrity, and structured interviews, show evidence of incremental validity in predicting job performance beyond CATs, which will enhance the overall validity of the selection system (Schmidt & Hunter, 1998). Readers should note that sizable reductions in the AI of these combined cognitive and noncognitive selection batteries occur only at very high selection ratios. Test score banding represents a third option for selection for diversity premised upon treating as equivalent test scores that are relatively similar in magnitude. Research shows that banding is effective at reducing AI against minorities only when selection decisions from within score bands are made with minority preference (Aguinis, 2004; Sackett & Roth, 1996). Finally, methods that differentially weight job performance criteria provide some reduction in AI against minorities, but only at extremely high selection ratios that diminish the utility of selection decisions (Hattrup et al., 1997; Murphy & Shiarella, 1997).

Conclusions

We believe that the research discussed here provides important information on the processes of recruiting and selecting a diverse workforce. First, we explored *why* organizations should staff for diversity. In doing so, we identified two reasons that organizations recruit and select minorities: companies are either pushed by their stakeholders to diversify, or they intrinsically recognize the potential value of diversity. Second, we examined *who* organizations should deploy to recruit and select applicants.

Based on the similarity-attraction paradigm (Byrne, 1971), we suggested that organizations employ diverse recruiters and interviewers (i.e., those belonging to both the demographic majority and minority groups) to interact with applicants. Third, we investigated *what* messages should be conveyed to jobseekers. The literature detailed that the information presented in job ads (i.e., written and pictured) and the perceived fairness of selection procedures affect selection outcomes in minority applicants (Highhouse & Hoffman, 2001; Rubaii-Barrett & Wise, 2007). Fourth, we examined *when* organizations should prioritize diversity staffing. While acknowledging that organizations have differing types of diversity available in their labor pools, we argued that organizations should practice inclusive selection strategies whenever possible. Finally, we questioned *where* organizations should recruit. Colleges and universities were identified as excellent sources for quality applicants (Roach, 2006). In identifying and answering these five basic questions (i.e., who, what, when, where, and why), we discussed how organizations can recruit and select demographically diverse workforces.

Although the existing literature on diversity recruitment is informative for researchers and practitioners, a research–practitioner gap still exists. Specifically, a gap exists between the existing diversity recruitment research and current organizational recruitment practices (Kravitz, 2010; Taylor & Collins, 2000). For example, though multiple researchers highlight a need for organizations to focus on the recruitment of diverse employees (Benschop, 2001; Ployhart, 2006; Stone, Stone-Romero, & Lukaszewski, 2007), researchers' findings and suggestions are not typically integrated into organizational practices. For example, in a survey of human resource managers, only half were aware that recruitment sources affected organizational outcomes such as turnover (Rynes, Colbert, & Brown, 2002; Ryan & Tippins, 2004). An additional study by Carrell and Mann (1993) demonstrated that when human resource managers were questioned regarding their organization's diversity practices, only 33 percent responded that their organization had written diversity policies and programs. Therefore, in the area of diversity recruitment, a gap exists between research and organizational practices. This is unfortunate, as managing diversity is considered one of the main challenges for human resources in modern organizations (Benschop, 2001). Moreover, despite no shortage of "best practices" offered in the popular literature, practitioners often lack empirically based guidance when designing their diversity recruitment and selection procedures (Kravitz, 2007).

Concerning recruitment, Avery and McKay (2006) provided research-based suggestions to help practitioners. Using an organizational impression-management framework, they concluded that there are several tactics firms might employ to create an impression that they value diversity. Namely, strategies like employing a female or minority recruiter, presenting inclusiveness policy statements in ads, and recruiting at predominantly minority or female institutions of higher education will convey to jobseekers that the firm values diversity.

Likewise, a few other scholars (e.g., Ryan & Tippins, 2004) provided a number of practical suggestions for applicant attraction based on the research literature. For example, as previously discussed, research demonstrates that the type of recruitment source used influences applicant attraction. As such, organizations should use sources such as referrals from current minority employees to attract diverse and qualified applicants. Further, research suggests that applicants who have multiple job opportunities (presumably more desirable applicants) are attracted by early recruitment activities more so than applicants who do not have as many opportunities. Consequently, organizations should ensure that initial recruitment activities (e.g., websites, brochures) are as attractive to candidates as later recruitment activities can be.

Regarding selection, a couple of papers (Kravitz, 2008; Ployhart & Holtz, 2008) recently provided excellent examples of this type of scholarship in their discussions of how organizations might minimize race- and sex-based AI. Both appeared in the scientist-practitioner forum section of *Personnel Psychology*, immediately following a detailed yet reader-friendly discussion of the diversity–validity dilemma (Pyburn, Ployhart, & Kravitz, 2008), which describes how organizations often must choose between less valid selection instruments with less AI and more valid instruments with more AI. Basically, this research details a number of viable strategies (e.g., work samples, diversity hire auditing, situational judgment tests, and interviews) companies may use to minimize bias when selecting employees and provides insightful suggestions for choosing the right approach. Additional research supports the use of these strategies to minimize bias in selection. For example, Sackett and colleagues (2001) suggest that interviews, as compared to paper-and-pencil tests, can reduce AI. This likely occurs because during an interview, an applicant can be judged wholly, as opposed to being judged as a one-dimensional test score. Similarly, work samples can reduce AI (Hattrup, Rock, & Scalia, 1997; Sackett & Ellington, 1997). When using work samples, organizations can measure applicants' overall performance rather than simply examining their cognitive abilities.

Future Directions

In this section, we suggest several potentially fruitful avenues for future research. To begin, researchers should examine the role of theory in future diversity recruitment research. At present, the diversity recruitment literature suffers from a lack of theoretical frameworks (see McKay & Avery, 2006, for an exception). This is alarming when one considers that 30 years have passed since Rynes and colleagues (Rynes, Heneman, & Schwab, 1980) lamented the general lack of recruitment theory. As such, the literature on diversity and recruitment lacks unity and cohesion (Pitts, 2006; Wise & Tschirhart, 2000). Moreover, researchers have tended to rely on general social psychological theories (e.g., social identity theory, similarity-attraction paradigm) that do not always neatly fit the phenomena of interest. Introduction of new diversity-focused theories would help to delineate and explicate underlying processes that may be specific to job choice. As such, they also stand to provide clarity regarding what is known and potentially stimulate further empirical investigations.

A second important consideration for future research involves the expansion of our research designs to be more inclusive and descriptive of the staffing process. For instance, most research on diversity recruitment has relied too heavily on lab studies and employed primarily undergraduate and nonprofessional samples (Chapman, Uggerslev, Carroll, Piasentin, & Jones, 2005; Thomas & Wise, 1999). Also, scholars have devoted more attention to understanding the earlier phases of staffing (e.g., generating applicant interest), while focusing considerably less on understanding how to maintain applicant interest throughout the process (Barber, 1998). It is entirely plausible that steps taken early in the process to convey the organization's commitment to diversity may be undermined subsequently if seemingly contradictory information becomes available, thereby creating a diversity mixed message (Avery & Johnson, 2007; Volpone & Avery, 2010). Consequently, we recommend that scholars consider longitudinal field research designs involving participants who are actively engaged in the job search process. Though these are more time-consuming and logistically challenging, they stand to provide much greater insight into the temporal nature of diversity staffing procedures.

Future research also should attempt to investigate the interactive effects of diversity tactics across various demographic groups. In the current diversity recruitment literature, recruitment tactics tend to be investigated singularly (Breaugh & Starke, 2000), and their impact is typically evaluated with respect to only a particular type of diversity (e.g., racio-ethnicity or sex). The result is a body of work that is commonly described as "piecemeal" and "compartmentalized" (Rynes, 1991). Contrary to this trend, researchers (e.g., Saks & Uggerslev, 2010) have started to investigate the simultaneous impact of various human resource interventions in what are known as "recruitment bundles." Unfortunately, however, we could not find any studies that (a) assess the impact of bundles within the context of diversity staffing or (b) consider diversity staffing more holistically as opposed to restricting the focus to a specific type of diversity. We hope that future inquiry in this area adopts more comprehensive approaches.

Another potentially fruitful line of investigation might involve paying greater attention to the influence of benefits offered by the company, as these often become more apparent (and potentially influential) as a jobseeker progresses through the staffing process. The existing literature demonstrates that benefits influence an applicant's job pursuit intentions (García, Posthuma, & Quiñones, 2010; Kendall & Ryan, 2009). However, the possibility that certain benefits are differentially attractive has not garnered sufficient scholarly attention. For example, the current implicit assumption seems to be that members of all demographic groups are equally attracted to the same benefits packages. Nevertheless, research shows that work–life benefits emphasizing child-care options can influence women's job choices (Thompson & Aspinwall, 2009), and there is reason to doubt that the effect on men would be similar. Further, domestic partner benefits can affect a gay applicant's impression of an organization (Barron & Hebl, 2010; Davis, 2007) but might not have the same effect on straight jobseekers. Thus, research should take into account how benefits might influence the diversity of new hires.

Future research also would benefit from examining diversity selection in cultures other than the United States. As it stands now, the selection literature does not adequately cover the topic of recruitment and selection practices across cultures (Ployhart, 2006). Specifically, thus far, a vast majority of the diversity recruitment and selection literature has been conducted in the United States, by American researchers, using American subjects and employees (e.g., Turban & Cable, 2003). Additional lines of research demonstrate that culture can affect selection outcomes (Johnson & Droege, 2004; Posthuma, Joplin, & Maertz, 2005). As such, future research should investigate the possible effect of cultural values on recruitment and selection outcomes, as research that is based primarily on a single culture will not be as helpful to researchers or practitioners as organizations become increasingly global.

Beyond these more general suggestions, we have three specific suggestions for future research on staffing diverse organizations. First, scholars should apply the strategic human resource management (SHRM) literature to delineate the prospective influence of corporate policies and procedures on the attraction and selection of a heterogeneous workforce. SHRM work underscores the role of human resource policies and procedures as contributing to the organizational bottom line, to the extent that they are aligned with a firm's strategic objectives (Barney & Wright, 1998; Lepak, Liao, Chung, & Harden, 2006). A key implication from SHRM theory and research is that organizations that pursue demographic diversity as a strategic initiative must develop a human resource architecture that is supportive of diversity. In this regard, theory building and subsequent research are needed to determine which human resource practices and/or configurations of practices will be serve diversity as a firm strategy. In our view, this is a key omission in the diversity domain, as there is virtually no existing guidance to firms on how to develop human resource systems that will support diverse staffing. Diversity theory and research suggest that the development of fair human resource policies and procedures could be a useful starting point in building such a diversity-supportive human resource system (Avery & McKay, 2006; Cox, 1994). However, companies must be aware that cognitive ability-based selection systems are likely to undermine diversity staffing initiatives targeted to minority personnel (McKay & Davis, 2007). Overall, we encourage a melding of the SHRM and diversity literatures to uncover ways that firms can create human resource systems supportive of diverse staffing.

Second, we call for greater integration of recruitment and selection research. With little exception, these two streams have developed independently of one another. This is particularly disheartening because it is probable that occurrences during one process have considerable bearing on what takes place during the other. For instance, choices of selection procedures and means of implementing them can influence whether or not jobseekers opt to continue pursuing employment opportunities or self-select out of the process (Hausknecht et al., 2004; Ryan & Ployhart, 2000). This illustrates the importance of organizations continuing to recruit and entice their applicants well beyond the initial attraction phase and throughout the duration of selection. With respect to diversity, theory and scholarship should explore the connections between the two processes. It may be that organizations are undermining the success of their diversity recruitment efforts by employing selection tools that result in adverse impact or are perceived to be biased, thereby creating chilling effects. To avoid such occurrences and shed greater light on how to employ a diverse workforce, models need to take a more comprehensive approach to staffing.

Third, there is an implicit assumption within the literature (and probably among many practitioners as well) that minority and female applicants are a homogeneous group. In actuality, underrepresented groups contain as much within-group heterogeneity as majority groups, and that variance may prove particularly important to organizations. For instance, some research indicates that diversity factors are less important than more general information about the job itself when making job pursuit decisions (Thomas & Wise, 1999). Though this may be true in general, it is likely less applicable among the highest-caliber minority jobseekers. Highly qualified female and minority jobseekers are apt to have a variety of prospective suitors, which permits them greater discretion when choosing their employer. Accordingly, diversity factors may take on greater importance among this group, who seek to be evaluated on the basis of their competency as opposed to having their identity work to their detriment (i.e., discrimination). We suspect that human capital likely moderates the impact of diversity cues during recruitment and selection and believe that empirical work testing this proposition stands to benefit theory and practice considerably.

References

Aguinis, H. (2004). *Test-score banding in human resource selection: Technical, legal, and societal issues.* Westport, CT: Praeger Publishers/Greenwood Publishing Group.

Allen, D., Mahto, R., & Otondo, R. (2007). Web-based recruitment: Effects of information, organizational brand, and attitudes toward a web site on applicant attraction. *Journal of Applied Psychology, 92,* 1696–1708.

Antun, J., Strick, S., & Thomas, L. (2007). Exploring culture and diversity for Hispanics in restaurant online recruitment efforts. *Journal of Human Resources in Hospitality & Tourism, 6,* 85–107.

Aragón-Sánchez, A., Barba-Aragón, I., & Sanz-Valle, R. (2003). Effects of training on business results. *International Journal of Human Resource Management, 14,* 956–980.

Arvey, R., & Campion, J. (1982). The employment interview: A summary and review of recent research. *Personnel Psychology, 35,* 281–322.

Arvey, R., Gordon, M., Massengill, D., & Mussio, S. (1975). Differential dropout rates of minority and majority job candidates due to time lags between selection procedures. *Personnel Psychology, 38,* 175–180.

Aselage, J., & Eisenberger, R. (2003). Perceived organizational support and psychological contracts: a theoretical integration. *Journal of Organizational Behavior, 24,* 491–509.

Avery, D. (2003). Reactions to diversity in recruitment advertising—Are differences Black and White? *Journal of Applied Psychology, 88,* 672–679.

Avery, D., Hernandez, M., & Hebl, M. (2004). Who's watching the race? Racial salience in recruitment advertising. *Journal of Applied Social Psychology, 34,* 146–161.

Avery, D. R., & Johnson, C. D. (2007). Now you see it, now you don't: Mixed messages regarding workplace diversity. In K. M. Thomas (Ed.), *Diversity resistance in organizations: Manifestations and solutions* (pp. 221–247). Mahwah, NJ: Lawrence Erlbaum Associates.

Avery, D. R., & McKay, P. F. (2010). Doing diversity right: An empirically based approach to effective diversity management. In G. Hodgkinson & J. K. Ford (Eds.), *International Review of Industrial and Organizational Psychology* (Vol. 25, pp. 227–252), West Sussex, England: Wiley.

Avery, D. R., & McKay, P. F. (2006). Target practice: An organizational impression management approach to attracting minority and female job applicants. *Personnel Psychology, 59,* 157–187.

Barber, A. E. (1998). *Recruiting employees: Individual and organizational perspectives.* Thousand Oaks, CA: Sage Publications.

Barber, A. E., & Roehling, M. V. (1993). Job postings and the decision to interview: A verbal protocol analysis. *Journal of Applied Psychology, 78,* 845–856.

Barney, J. B., & Wright, P. M. (1998). On becoming a strategic partner: The role of human resources in gaining competitive advantage. *Human Resource Management, 37,* 31–46.

Barron, L., & Hebl, M. (2010). Extending lesbian, gay, bisexual, and transgendered supportive organizational policies: Communities matter too. *Industrial and Organizational Psychology: Perspectives on Science and Practice, 3,* 79–81.

Beckman, C. M., & Phillips, D. J. (2005). Interorganizational determinants of promotion: Client leadership and the attainment of women attorneys. *American Sociological Review, 70,* 678–701.

Benschop, Y. (2001). Pride, prejudice and performance: relations between HRM, diversity and performance. *International Journal of Human Resource Management, 12,* 1166–1181.

Bertrand, M., & Mullainathan, S. (2004). Are Emily and Greg more employable than Lakisha and Jamal? A field experiment on labor market discrimination. *American Economic Review, 94,* 991–1013.

Blum, T. C., Fields, D. L., & Goodman, J. S. 1994. Organizational-level determinants of women in management. *Academy of Management Journal, 37,* 241–268.

Bobko, P., Roth, P. L., & Potosky, D. (1999). Derivation and implications of a meta-analytic matrix incorporating cognitive ability, alternative predictors, and job performance. *Personnel Psychology, 52,* 561–589.

Borman, W. C., & Motowidlo, S. J. (1993). Expanding the criterion domain to include elements of contextual performance. In N. Schmitt & W. C. Borman (Eds.), *Personnel selection in organizations* (pp. 71–98). San Francisco: Jossey-Bass.

Borman, W. C., & Motowidlo, S. J. (1997). Task performance and contextual performance: The meaning for personnel selection research. *Human Performance, 10,* 99–109.

Breaugh J. A. (1981). Relationships between recruiting sources and employee performance, absenteeism, and work attitudes. *Academy of Management Journal, 24,* 142–147.

Breaugh, J. A., & Starke, M. (2000). Research on employee recruitment: So many studies, so many recruiting questions. *Journal of Management, 26,* 405–434.

Bureau of Labor Statistics (2006). Employment and earnings, Table 28-Unemployment by reason for unemployment, race, and Hispanic or Latino ethnicity. *Current Population Survey.* Retrieved on September 30, 2010 from http://www.bls.gov/cps/cpsa2005.pdf

Byrne, D. (1971). *The attraction paradigm.* New York: Academic Press.

Campion, M. A., Outtz, J. L., Zedeck, S., Schmidt, F. L., Kehoe, J. F., Murphy, K. R., & Guion, R. M. (2001). The controversy over score banding in personnel selection: Answers to 10 key questions. *Personnel Psychology, 54,* 149–185.

Carrell, M., & Mann, E. (1993). Defining workforce diversity programs and practices in organizations. *Labor Law Journal, 44,* 755–764.

Chapman, D. S., Uggerslev, K. L., Carroll, S. A., Piasentin, K. A., & Jones, D. A. (2005). Applicant attraction to organizations and job choice: A meta-analytic review of the correlates of recruiting outcomes. *Journal of Applied Psychology, 90,* 928–944.

Chung-Yan, G., & Cronshaw, S. (2002). A critical re-examination and analysis of cognitive ability tests using the Thorndike model of fairness. *Journal of Occupational & Organizational Psychology, 75*(4), 489–509.

Cober, R. T., Brown, D. J., Blumental, A. J., Doverspike, D., & Levy, P. E. (2000). The quest for the qualified job surfer: It's time the public sector catches the wave. *Public Personnel Management, 29,* 479–495.

Cober, R. T., Brown, D. J., Keeping, L. M., & Levy, P. E. (2004). Recruitment on the net: How do organizational Web site characteristics influence applicant attraction? *Journal of Management, 30,* 623–646.

Cox Jr., T. H. (1994). *Cultural diversity in organizations: Theory, research, & practice.* San Francisco: Berrett-Koehler.

Cunningham, G. B. (2007). Perceptions as reality: The influence of actual and perceived demographic dissimilarity. *Journal of Business and Psychology, 22,* 79–89.

Davis, D. (2007). Designing benefits for domestic partners. *Journal of Pension Benefits: Issues in Administration, 15,* 56–57.

Dean, M. A., Roth, P. L., & Bobko, P. (2008). Ethnic and gender subgroup differences in assessment center ratings: A meta-analysis. *Journal of Applied Psychology, 93,* 685–691.

DeBell, C. S., Montgomery, M. J., McCarthy, P. R., & Lantheir, R. P. (1998). The critical contact: A study of recruiter verbal behavior during campus interviews. *Journal of Business Communication, 35,* 202–224.

Decker P. J., & Cornelius, E. T. III. (1979). A note on recruiting sources and job survival rates. *Journal of Applied Psychology, 64,* 463–464.

De Corte, W., Lievens, F., & Sackett, P. (2007). Combining predictors to achieve optimal Trade-offs between selection quality and adverse impact. *Journal of Applied Psychology, 92,* 1380–1393.

Demuijnck, G. (2009). Non-discrimination in human resources management as a moral obligation. *Journal of Business Ethics, 88,* 83–101.

Derous, E., Nguyen, H., & Ryan, A. (2009). Hiring discrimination against Arab minorities: Interactions between prejudice and job characteristics. *Human Performance, 22,* 297–320.

Doverspike, D., Taylor, M. A., Schultz, K. S., & McKay, P. F. (2000). Responding to the challenge of a changing workforce: Recruiting nontraditional demographic groups. *Public Personnel Management, 29,* 445–457.

Ely, R., & Thomas, D. (2001). Cultural diversity at work: The effects of diversity perspectives on work group processes and outcomes. *Administrative Science Quarterly, 46,* 229–273.

Fields, D. L., Goodman, J. S., & Blum, T. C. (2005). Human resource dependence and organizational demography: A study of minority employment in private sector companies. *Journal of Management, 31,* 167–185.

Finch, D., Edwards, B., & Wallace, J. (2009). Multistage selection strategies: Simulating the effects on adverse impact and expected performance for various predictor combinations. *Journal of Applied Psychology, 94,* 318–340.

Finkelstein, M. (2010). Diversification in the academic workforce: The case of the US and implications for Europe. *European Review, 18,* 141–156.

Frank, L., & Hackman, J. (1975). Effect of interviewer-interviewee similarity on interviewer objectivity in college admissions interviews. *Journal of Applied Psychology, 60,* 356–360.

Gannon, M. J. (1971). Sources of referral and employee turnover. *Journal of Applied Psychology, 55,* 226–228.

García, M., Posthuma, R., & Quiñones, M. (2010). How benefit information and demographics influence employee recruiting in Mexico. *Journal of Business & Psychology, 25,* 523–531.

Ghumman, S., & Jackson, L. (2010). The downside of religious attire: The Muslim headscarf and expectations of obtaining employment. *Journal of Organizational Behavior, 31,* 4–23.

Giscombe, K., & Mattis, M. C., (2002). Leveling the playing field for women of color in corporate management: Is the business case enough? *Journal of Business Ethics, 37,* 103–119.

Goldberg, C. (2005). Relational demography and similarity-attraction in interview assessments and subsequent offer decisions. *Group & Organization Management, 30,* 597–624.

Goldberg, C., & Allen, D. (2008). Black and white and read all over: Race differences in reactions to recruitment Web sites. *Human Resource Management, 47,* 217–236.

Goldberg, C. B. (2003). Applicant reactions to the employment interview: A look at demographic similarity and social identity theory. *Journal of Business Research, 56,* 561–571.

Goldberg, L. (1993). The structure of phenotypic personality traits: Author's reactions to the six comments. *American Psychologist, 48,* 1303–1304.

Goltz, S. M., & Giannantonio, C. M. (1995). Recruiter friendliness and attraction to the job: the mediating role of inferences about the organization. *Journal of Vocational Behavior, 46,* 109–118.

Gonzalez, J., & DeNisi, A. S. (2009). Cross-level effects of demography and diversity climate on organizational attachment and firm effectiveness. *Journal of Organizational Behavior, 30,* 21–40.

Gousie, L. (1993). Interview structure and interviewer prejudice as factors in the evaluation and selection of minority and non-minority applicants. *Applied H.R.M. Research, 4,* 1–13.

Graves, L., & Powell, G. (1995). The effect of sex-similarity on recruiters' evaluations of actual applicants: A test of the similarity attraction paradigm. *Personnel Psychology, 48,* 85–98.

Hattrup, K., Rock, J., & Scalia, C. (1997). The effects of varying conceptualizations of job performance on adverse impact, minority hiring, and predicted performance. *Journal of Applied Psychology, 82,* 656–664.

Hausknecht, J. P., Day, D. V., & Thomas, S. C. (2004). Applicant reactions to selection procedures: An updated model and meta-analysis. *Personnel Psychology, 57,* 639–683.

Heilman, M., Martell, R., & Simon, M. (1988). The vagaries of sex bias: Conditions regulating the undervaluation, equivaluation, and overvaluation of female job applicants. *Organizational Behavior & Human Decision Processes, 41,* 98–110.

Hellwig, B. (1985). The breakthrough generation: 73 women ready to run corporate America. *Working Woman,* 99.

Henle, C. (2004). Case review of the legal status of banding. *Human Performance, 17,* 415–432.

Herring, C. (2009). Does diversity pay? Race, gender, and the business case for diversity. *American Sociological Review, 74,* 208–224.

Highhouse, S., & Hoffman, J. R. (2001). Organizational attraction and job choice. In C. L. Cooper & I. T. Robertson (Eds.), *International review of industrial and organizational psychology* (Vol. 16, pp. 37–64). Manchester, UK: Wiley.

Hogler, R., Henle, C., & Bemus, C. (1998). Internet recruiting and employment discrimination: A legal perspective. *Human Resource Management Review, 8,* 149.

Holvino, E., & Kamp, A. (2009). Diversity management: Are we moving in the right direction? Reflections from both sides of the North Atlantic. *Scandinavian Journal of Management, 25*(4), 395–403.

Hough, L., Oswald, F., & Ployhart, R. (2001). Determinants, detection and amelioration of adverse impact in personnel selection procedures: Issues, evidence and lessons learned. *International Journal of Selection & Assessment, 9,* 152.

Howard, J., & Ferris, G. (1996). The employment interview context: Social and situational influences on interviewer decisions. *Journal of Applied Social Psychology, 26,* 112–136.

Huang, M. (2009). Race of the interviewer and the black-white test score gap. *Social Science Research, 38,* 29–38.

Huffcutt, A. I., Conway, J. M., Roth, P. L., & Stone, N. J. (2001). Identification and meta-analytic assessment of psychological constructs measured in employment interviews. *Journal of Applied Psychology, 86,* 897–913.

Huffcutt, A. I., & Roth, P. L. (1998). Racial group differences in employment interview evaluations. *Journal of Applied Psychology, 83,* 179–189.

Huffcutt, A. I., Roth, P. L., & McDaniel, M. A. (1996). A meta-analytic investigation of cognitive ability in employment interview evaluations: Moderating characteristics and implications for incremental validity. *Journal of Applied Psychology, 81,* 459–473.

Hurley-Hanson, A. E., & Giannantonio, C. M. (2006). Recruiters' perceptions of appearance: the stigma of image norms. *Equal Opportunities International, 25,* 450–463.

Hurtz, G., & Donovan, J. (2000). Personality and job performance: The five revisited. *Journal of Applied Psychology, 85,* 869–879.

Ibarra, H. (1992). Homophily and differential returns: sex differences in network structure and access in an advertising firm. *Administrative Science Quarterly, 37,* 422–447.

Johnson, N., & Droege, S. (2004). Reflections on the generalization of agency theory: Cross-cultural considerations. *Human Resource Management Review, 14,* 325–335.

Judge, T., & Ferris, G. (1992). The elusive criterion of fit in human resources staffing decisions. *Human Resource Planning, 15,* 47–67.

Kendall, P., & Ryan, E. (2009). Defined benefit plans: The quiet evolution. *Journal of Compensation & Benefits, 25,* 42–46.

Kim, S., & Gelfand, M. (2003). The influence of ethnic identity on perceptions of organizational recruitment. *Journal of Vocational Behavior, 63,* 396–116.

King, E. B., Mendoza, S. A., Madera, J. M., Hebl, M. R., & Knight, J. L. (2006). What's in a name? A multiracial investigation of the role of occupational stereotypes in selection decisions. *Journal of Applied Social Psychology, 36,* 1145–1159.

Kirnan, J. P., Farley, J. A., & Geisinger, K. F. (1989). The relationship between recruiting source, applicant quality, and hire performance; An analysis by sex, ethnicity, and age. *Personnel Psychology, 42,* 293–308.

Knouse, S. (2009). Targeted recruiting for diversity: Strategy, impression management, realistic expectations, and diversity climate. *International Journal of Management, 26,* 347–353.

Kravitz, D. (2007). Can we take the guesswork out of diversity practice selection? *Academy of Management Perspectives, 21,* 80–81.

Kravitz, D. A. (2008). The diversity-validity dilemma: Beyond selection—the role of affirmative action. *Personnel Psychology, 61,* 173–193.

Kravitz, D. A. (2010). The research-practice gap in diversity management. *Diversity Factor, 18*(1), 1–7.

Kuhn, P. & Skuterud, M. (2000) Job search methods: Internet versus traditional. *Monthly Labor Review, 123,* 3–11.

Larsen, D., & Phillips, J. (2002). Effect of recruiter on attraction to the firm: Implications of the elaboration likelihood model. *Journal of Business & Psychology, 16,* 347–364.

Le, H., Oh, I., Shaffer, J., & Schmidt, F. (2007). Implications of methodological advances for the practice of personnel selection: How practitioners benefit from meta-analysis. *Academy of Management Perspectives, 21*(3), 6–15

Lepak, D. P., Liao, H., Chung, Y., & Harden, E. E. (2006). A conceptual review of human resource management systems in strategic human resource management. *Research in Personnel and Human Resource Management, 25,* 217–271.

Lievens, F., Harris, M., Keer, E., & Bisqueret, C. (2003). Predicting cross-cultural training performance: The validity of personality, cognitive ability, and dimensions measured by an assessment center and a behavior description interview. *Journal of Applied Psychology, 88,* 476–489.

McDaniel, M. A., Morgeson, F. P., Finnegan, E. B., Campion, M. A., & Braverman, E. P. (2001). Use of situational judgment tests to predict job performance: A clarification of the literature. *Journal of Applied Psychology, 86,* 730–740.

McDaniel, M. A., Whetzel, D. L., Schmidt, F. L., & Maurer, S. D. (1994). The validity of employment interviews: A comprehensive review and meta-analysis. *Journal of Applied Psychology, 79,* 599–616.

McDonald, S. Lin, N., & Ao, D. (2009). Networks of opportunity: Gender, race, and job leads. *Social Problems, 56,* 385–402.

McKay, P. F., & Avery, D. R. (2006). What has race got to do with it? Unraveling the role of racioethnicity in job seekers' reactions to site visits. *Personnel Psychology, 59,* 395–429.

McKay, P. F., & Davis, J. L. (2007). Traditional selection methods as resistance to diversity in organizations. In K. M. Thomas (Ed.), *Diversity resistance in organizations: Manifestations and solutions* (pp. 151–174). Boca Raton, FL: Taylor & Francis.

McKay, P. F., & McDaniel, M. A. (2006). A reexamination of Black-White mean differences in work performance: More data, more moderators. *Journal of Applied Psychology, 91,* 538–554.

McPartland, C. (2009). Linklaters mulls ditching recruitment brochures. *Lawyer, 23,* 7.

Meyers, V., & Dreachslin, J. (2007). Recruitment and retention of a diverse workforce: challenges and opportunities. *Journal of Healthcare Management, 52,* 290–298.

Mor Barak, M. E., Cherin, D. A., & Berkman, S. (1998). Organizational and personal dimensions in diversity climate: Ethnic and gender differences in employee perceptions. *Journal of Applied Behavioral Science, 34,* 82–104.

Moser, K. (2005). Recruitment sources and post-hire outcomes: The mediating role of unmet expectations. *International Journal of Selection and Assessment, 13,* 188–197.

Murphy, K. R., & Shiarella, A. H. (1997). Implications of the multidimensional nature of job performance for the validity of selection tests: Multivariate frameworks for studying test validity. *Personnel Psychology, 50,* 823–854.

Newman, D., & Lyon, J. (2009). Recruitment efforts to reduce adverse impact: Targeted recruiting for personality, cognitive ability, and diversity. *Journal of Applied Psychology, 94,* 298–317.

Ng, E. S. W., & Burke, R. J. (2005). Person-organization fit and the war for talent: Does diversity management make a difference? *International Journal of Human Resource Management, 16,* 1195–1210.

Ones, D. S., Viswesvaran, C., & Schmidt, F. L. (1993). Comprehensive meta-analysis of integrity test validities: Findings and implications for personnel selection and theories of job performance [Monograph]. *Journal of Applied Psychology, 78,* 679–703.

O'Reilly, C. A., III, & Caldwell, D. F. (1980). Job choice: The impact of intrinsic and extrinsic factors on subsequent satisfaction and commitment. *Journal of Applied Psychology, 65,* 559–565.

Perkins, L. A., Thomas, K. M., & Taylor, G. A. (2000). Advertising and recruitment: Marketing to minorities. *Psychology & Marketing, 17,* 235–255.

Pfeffer, J. (1998). *The human equation: Building profits by putting people first.* Boston, MA: Harvard Business School Press.

Phillips, J. (1998). Effects of realistic job previews on multiple organizational outcomes: A meta-analysis. *Academy of Management Journal, 41,* 673–690.

Pitts, D. (2006). Modeling the impact of diversity management. *Review of Public Personnel Administration, 26,* 245–268.

Ployhart, R. E. (2006). Staffing in the 21st century: New challenges and strategic opportunities. *Journal of Management, 32*, 868–897.

Ployhart, R. E., & Holtz, B. C. (2008). The diversity-validity dilemma: Strategies for reducing racioethnic and sex subgroup differences and adverse impact in selection. *Personnel Psychology, 61*, 153–172.

Posthuma, R., Joplin, J., & Maertz Jr., C. (2005). Comparing the validity of turnover predictors in the United States and Mexico. *International Journal of Cross Cultural Management, 5*, 165–180.

Potosky, D., Bobko, P., & Roth, P. L. (2005). Forming composites of cognitive ability and alternative measures to predict job performance and reduce adverse impact: Corrected estimates and realistic expectations. *International Journal of Selection and Assessment, 13*, 304–315.

Pyburn, K. M., Jr., Ployhart, R. E., & Kravitz, D. A. (2008). The diversity-validity dilemma: Overview and legal context. *Personnel Psychology, 61*, 143–151.

Rafaeli, A., & Oliver, A. (1998) Employment ads: A configurational research agenda. *Journal of Management Inquiry, 7*, 342–358.

Rand, T. M., & Wexley, K. N. (1975). Demonstration of the effects, "similar to me," in simulated employment interviews. *Psychological Reports, 36*, 535–544.

Rau, B. L., & Hyland, M. M. (2003). Corporate teamwork and diversity statements in college recruitment brochures: Effects on attraction. *Journal of Applied Social Psychology, 33*, 2465–2492.

Reskin, B., McBrier, D., & Kmec, J. (1999). The determinants and consequences of workplace sex and race composition. *Annual Review of Sociology, 25*, 335–361

Riccucci, N. (1997). Cultural diversity programs to prepare for work force 2000: What's gone wrong? *Public Personnel Management, 26*(1), 35.

Richard, O. C. (2000). Racial diversity, business strategy, and firm performance: A resource-based view. *Academy of Management Journal, 43*, 164–177.

Roach, R. (2006). Corporate recruiting in the 21st century. *Diverse: Issues in Higher Education, 23*(18), 46–49.

Roberson, Q. M., & Park, H. J. (2007). Examining the link between diversity and firm performance: The effect of diversity reputation and leader racial diversity. *Group & Organization Management, 32*, 548–568.

Roth, P. L., BeVier, C. A., Bobko, P., Switzer, F. S., III., & Tyler, P. (2001). Ethnic group differences in cognitive ability in employment and educational settings: A meta-analysis. *Personnel Psychology, 54*, 297–330.

Roth, P. L., Bobko, P., McFarland, L. A., & Buster, M. (2008). Work sample tests in personnel selection: A meta-analysis of Black-White differences in overall and exercise scores. *Personnel Psychology, 61*, 637–662.

Roth, P. L., Van Iddekinge, C. H., Huffcutt, A. I., Edison, C. E., Jr., & Bobko, P. (2002). Corrections for range restriction in structured interview ethnic group differences: The values may be larger than researchers thought. *Journal of Applied Psychology, 87*, 369–376.

Rubaii-Barrett, N., & Wise, L. R. (2007). Language minorities and the digital divide. *Journal of Public Management and Social Policy, 12*, 5–27.

Ryan, A., Ployhart, R., & Friedel, L. (1998). Using personality testing to reduce adverse impact: a cautionary note. *Journal of Applied Psychology, 83*, 298–307.

Ryan, A., & Tippins, N. (2004). Attracting and selecting: What psychological research tells us. *Human Resource Management, 43*, 305–318.

Ryan, A. M., & Ployhart, R. E. (2000). Applicants' perceptions of selection procedures and decisions: A critical review and agenda for the future. *Journal of Management, 26*, 565–606.

Rynes, S. (1991). Recruitment, job choice, and post-hire consequences: A call for new research directions. In M. D. Dunnette & L. M. Hough (Eds.), *Handbook of industrial and organizational psychology* (2nd ed., pp. 419–489). Palo Alto, CA: Consulting Psychologists Press.

Rynes, S., & Barber, A. (1990). Applicant attraction strategies: An organizational perspective. *Academy of Management Review, 15*, 286–310.

Rynes, S., & Cable, D. M. (2003) Recruitment research in the twenty-first century. In: W. C. Borman & D. R. Ilgen (Eds.), *Handbook of psychology: industrial and organizational psychology* (pp. 55–76). New York: Wiley.

Rynes, S. L., Colbert, A. E., & Brown, K. G. (2002). HR professionals' beliefs about effective human resource practices: Correspondence between research and practice. *Human Resource Management, 41*, 149–174.

Rynes, S. L., Heneman, H. G., III, & Schwab, D. P. (1980). Individual reactions to organizational recruiting: A review. *Personnel Psychology, 33*, 529–542.

Sackett, P. R., & Ellingson, J. E. (1997). The effects of forming multi-predictor composites on group differences and adverse impact. *Personnel Psychology, 50*, 707–721.

Sackett, P., & Roth, L. (1996). Multi-stage selection strategies: A Monte Carlo investigation of effects on performance and minority hiring. *Personnel Psychology, 49*(3), 549–572.

Sackett, P. R., Schmitt, N., Ellingson, J. E., & Kabin, M. B. (2001). High-stakes testing in employment, credentialing, and higher education: Prospects in a post-affirmative-action world. *American Psychologist, 56*, 302–318.

Saks, A., & Uggerslev, K. (2010). Sequential and combined effects of recruitment information on applicant reactions. *Journal of Business & Psychology, 25*, 351–365.

Saks, A. M. (2005). The impracticality of recruitment research. In A. Evers, O. Smit-Voskuyl, & N. Anderson (Eds.), *Handbook of personnel selection* (pp. 47–72). Oxford, UK: Basil Blackwell.

Schmidt, F. L., & Hunter, J. E. (1998). The validity and utility of selection methods in personnel psychology: Practical and theoretical implications of 85 years of research findings. *Psychological Bulletin, 124*, 262–274.

Shah, P., & Kleiner, B. (2005). New developments concerning age discrimination in the workplace. *Equal Opportunities International, 24*(5/6), 15–23.

Singh, V., & Point, S. (2004). Strategic responses to the human resource diversity challenge: An on-line European top company comparison. *Long Range Planning, 37*, 295–318.

Singh, V., & Point, S. (2006). (Re)presentations of gender and ethnicity in diversity statements on European company websites. *Journal of Business Ethics, 68*, 363–379.

Smith, W., Wokutch, R., Harrington, K., & Dennis, B. (2004). Organizational attractiveness and corporate social orientation: Do our values influence our preference for affirmative action and managing diversity? *Business & Society, 43*, 69–96.

Stone, D., Stone-Romero, E., & Lukaszewski, K. (2007). The impact of cultural values on the acceptance and effectiveness of human resource management policies and practices. *Human Resource Management Review, 17*, 152–165.

Taber, M. E., & Hendricks, W. (2003). The effect of workplace gender and race demographic composition on hiring through employee referrals. *Human Resource Development Quarterly, 14*, 303–319.

Taylor, M. S., & Collins, C. J. (2000). Organizational recruitment: Enhancing the intersection of theory and practice. In C. L. Cooper & E. A. Locke (Eds.), *Industrial and organizational psychology: linking theory and practice* (pp. 304–334). Oxford, UK: Blackwell.

Thomas, K., & Wise, P. (1999). Organizational attractiveness and individual differences: Are diverse applicants attracted by different factors? *Journal of Business & Psychology, 13*, 375–390.

Thomas, K. M. (2008). *Diversity resistance in organizations*. Mahwah, NJ: Lawrence Erlbaum Associates.

Thompson, L., & Aspinwall, K. (2009). The recruitment value of work/life benefits. *Personnel Review, 38*, 195–210.

Toossi, M. (2006). A new look at long-term labor force projections to 2050. *Monthly Labor Review, 129*, 19–39.

Turban, D., & Cable, D. (2003). Firm reputation and applicant pool characteristics. *Journal of Organizational Behavior, 24*(6), 733–751.

Turban, D. B., & Dougherty, T. W. (1992). Influences of campus recruiting on applicant attraction to firms. *Academy of Management Journal, 35*, 739–765.

Van Hooft, E., Born, M., Taris, T., & Van der Flier, H. (2006). Ethnic and gender differences in applicants' decision-making processes: An application of the theory of reasoned action. *International Journal of Selection and Assessment, 14*, 156–166.

Van Hoye, G., & Lievens, F. (2007). Investigating Web-based recruitment sources: Employee testimonials vs. word-of-mouse. *International Journal of Selection and Assessment, 15*, 372–382.

Volpone, S. D., & Avery, D. R. (2010). I'm confused: How failing to value sexual identities at work sends stakeholders mixed messages. *Industrial and Organizational Psychology: Perspectives on Science and Practice, 3*, 90–92.

Von Bergen, C. W., Soper, B., & Foster, T. (2002). Unintended negative effects on diversity management. *Public Personnel Management, 31*, 239–252.

Walker, H. J., Feild, H. S., Giles, W. F., Armenakis, A. A., & Bernerth, J. B. (2009). Displaying employee testimonial on recruitment web sites: Effects of communication media, employee race, and job seeker race on organizational attraction and information credibility. *Journal of Applied Psychology, 94*, 1354–1364.

Whetzel, D. L., McDaniel, M. A., & Nguyen, N. T. (2008). Subgroup differences in situational judgment test performance: A meta-analysis. *Human Performance, 21*, 291–309.

Wiley, M., & Eskilson, A. (1985). Speech style, gender stereotypes, and corporate success: What if women talk more like men? *Sex Roles, 12*(9–10), 993–1007.

Williamson, I. O., Slay, H. S., Shapiro, D. L., & Shivers-Blackwell, S. L. (2008). The effect of explanations on prospective applicants' reactions to firm diversity practices. *Human Resource Management, 47*, 311–330.

Wise, L. R., & Tschirhart, M. (2000). Examining empirical evidence on diversity effects: How useful is diversity research for public sector managers? *Public Administration Review, 60*, 386–395.

Wright, P., Ferris, S. P., Hiller, J. S. & Kroll, M. (1995). Competitiveness through management of diversity: Effects on stock price valuations. *Academy of Management Journal, 38*, 272–287.

Zottoli, M. A., & Wanous, J. P. (2000). Recruitment source research: Current status and future directions. *Human Resource Management Review, 10*, 353–382.

CHAPTER
17 Career Development

Bryan L. Dawson, Kecia M. Thomas *and* Matthew J. Goren

Abstract

The benefits of career development may accrue throughout one's work life, from early career and vocational choice through to retirement. Yet are those benefits, and even career development itself, equally available to workers across various dimensions of demographic diversity—especially as we consider the informal and insidious nature of many career development options? This chapter explores the intersection of career development and workplace diversity. Specifically, we look at this intersection by asking (1) How can career development be an opportunity to promote diversity in organizations? and (2) How do career development disparities have a negative impact on the careers of marginalized workers and subsequently their employers? Special attention is paid to the subtle biases, ambient cues, and distancing behavior that may derail career development strategies, such as mentoring and networks for marginalized groups. We examine science, technology, engineering, and math (STEM) careers as an important and timely career path and case study in which to consider these issues.

Key Words: careers, STEM, mentoring, networks, bias

Introduction

The opportunity to develop in one's career is one of the greatest assets an organization can offer to recruit a new employee, likely second only to salary. Thomas (2005) defines career development as a lifelong process that includes the identification of one's career interests and needs, the development of the knowledge, skills, and abilities to enhance one's career, and the ongoing assessment of one's interests and skills in order to achieve career mobility. Mistakenly, career development is presumed to be an activity of junior workers, but increasingly organization scholars realize that career development is important throughout the lifespan, including retirement (Rhebergen & Wognum, 1997). The traditional concept of career development, in which an individual starts at the organization and moves up the hierarchy, is quickly disappearing with the advent of new technology, globalization, and organizational change. Individuals are now constructing their careers beginning with their vocational choice, and the use of mentoring is becoming even more important in one's career trajectory. Career development efforts are especially important for underrepresented workers or any workers who are new to organization life if they have not been socialized to understand the unique culture of professional career paths.

Career development is an important part of an organization's human resource strategy. Companies who engage in career development and mentoring are better able to educate their workforce and increase employee loyalty while fostering growth in their employees through training and mentoring relationships, which in return increase morale and reduce turnover (Allen, Eby, Poteet, Lentz, &

Lima, 2004). For employees, the benefits include increased flexibility of skills, ambition, and a sense of belonging and importance to the organization. Yet participating in career development may not be an equal opportunity (Thomas, 2005). Many of the best career development opportunities are informal—that is, they are not official or sanctioned or recognized by the organization. These informal career development mechanisms are frequently as powerful (if not more powerful) than the formal and sometimes artificial career development mechanisms developed and implemented by organizations. Informal career development mechanisms, such as some mentoring and networks, rely upon workplace relationships among peers or between superiors and subordinates.

Furthermore, subtle biases and stereotypes can sometimes prevent these developmental workplace relationships from forming and flourishing. When this occurs, informal sources of career development become unavailable for those who may need them the most. Understanding these potential inequities in career development helps us to better understand organizations' perceptions of diversity. Organizations may not be aware of the biases and barriers that affect marginalized group members' career development, while simultaneously believing they are embracing their diverse workforce.

There are multiple ways to think about the dynamics between diversity and career development. For example, organizational context, especially leadership, can create or limit opportunities for career development in a diverse work environment. Leadership behaviors and organization contextual factors reinforce career development as an equal opportunity regardless of worker demographic characteristics. Moreover, workplace policies, workplace programs, and accountability programs assist in creating a culture where diversity is valued and continued development is a norm.

When we consider the diversity and career development dynamic at a more individual level, the primary issues that emerge focus upon the career development experiences, or lack thereof, of marginalized group members. In other words, to what extent do women, people of color, sexual minorities, the disabled, and those who are economically struggling have the same career advice, support, and developmental opportunities as White, able-bodied, heterosexual, middle-class men? Subsequently, given career development disparities due to demographic characteristics like race and gender, what are the career costs for members of marginalized groups as well as for organizations and society overall? Ultimately, this discussion focuses on the importance of career development and mentoring and the persistence of career barriers in organizations and their outcomes.

External and internal barriers to career development for diverse employees
External barriers

Stereotypes are one form of external career barriers. Stereotypes are generalizations, typically negative, that limit the careers of many underrepresented workers. Negative stereotypes create opportunities for both access and treatment discrimination (Greenhaus, Parasuraman, & Worley, 1990). Access discrimination refers to the limitations for organizational/position entry or upward mobility to new higher-status roles. Treatment discrimination refers to the ways in which individuals or the organization itself treats its members differentially based upon their demographic status. Treatment discrimination in organizations may look like providing training or professional development opportunities for some workers and not others.

Internal barriers

Occupational segregation and demographic faultlines (Lau & Murnighan, 1998) present important internal barriers that depress some workers' career aspirations and expectations. Demographic faultlines occur when occupational roles and status are confounded by demographic group membership. Even in an organization that is high in gender diversity, for example, leaders are likely to be men while support staff are likely to be women. An observer could therefore accurately guess one's status in the organization by simply knowing a worker's gender. Working in this type of environment sends a message to workers about how far they could move up in an organization and where. For potential employees outside of the organization, faultlines are informative as well in that they provide similar messages regarding where one is most likely to be placed or fit in.

Moreover, social distancing occurs when colleagues (even leaders and followers) physically or psychologically distance themselves from one another. Social distancing in its physical form occurs when workers avoid and exclude one another. Psychological forms of social distancing occur when workers discount and discredit the presence and contributions of others. Many underrepresented workers therefore lack social integration

(Giscombe & Mattis, 2002), locking these workers out of key developmental relationships that we will discuss further.

This chapter will explore the dynamics between diversity and career development in organizations, especially as it relates to career development disparities. We will begin our discussion by reviewing the drivers of the first career development decision many make, that of vocational choice. We are especially concerned with those factors that attract women and people of color to certain career paths and deter them from choosing others. In this section we will deal with the career-related messages and information received by minority and majority group members and the outcome of those messages on vocational choice.

We then turn our attention to mentoring as a popular career development vehicle. Mentoring can be informal or formal, and it has the potential to benefit protégés instrumentally and psychosocially. Yet, women and people of color may not fully reap the benefits that mentoring may provide because they lack access to mentors, especially informal ones. Even when informal mentors are available to women and people of color, they may not be well positioned to provide both mentoring functions (Thomas, 2005; Thomas, Willis, & Davis, 2007).

Throughout this discussion, we take the liberty of examining these issues of career development and diversity within the context of organizations. There are times when career development is not an equal opportunity. Specifically, we look at "glass ceilings" and "sticky floors" as both potential career-derailing barriers and outcomes. We will also discuss what the outcomes are when career development is not an equal opportunity in organizations.

Vocational choice

The conscious decision to choose a career path for which one is suited is known as vocational choice. Perhaps the most influential theory regarding vocational choice is Holland's (1985), which postulates that vocational choice is an expression of one's personality. Holland offers a six-factor typology comprising different personality and work environment types: Realistic, Investigative, Artistic, Social, Enterprising, and Conventional. These six categories, referred to as RIASEC, are often used to classify an individual's interests and potential occupations (Armstrong, Rounds, & Hubert, 2008; Holland, 1997). Holland's (1985) theory does not make the assumption that people are tied to one type or that there are only six different ways to describe these people. Rather, any person can rank these six types in order of preference, leaving the most dominant factors to guide vocational choice (Holland, 1985, 1997). By matching an individual's interests to an occupation that shares similar characteristics, it is possible to identify potential career choices.

While there are a multitude of career development theories, many of them overlook the issues of race and gender (Lee & Armstrong, 1995). However, newer theoretical perspectives (i.e., social cognitive career theory) have been developed to address diverse issues surrounding culture, ethnicity, and gender that may influence career choices. Based on Bandura's (1986, 1997) general social cognitive theory, social cognitive career theory seeks to explain the factors that form vocational choices and interest (Lent, Brown, & Hackett, 1994; Sheu et al., 2010). According to the model, people develop goals to pursue career-related activities that are consistent with their interests and expected outcomes. However, many women and ethnic minorities may not have the same opportunities to pursue these career-related activities that match their interests, or may be dissuaded from pursuing such opportunities. These individuals may be receiving oppositional and limiting messages from as early as adolescence regarding which career choices are available and appropriate for them.

DRIVERS OF VOCATIONAL CHOICE

Women and people of color are represented more now than ever in higher education and the workforce. Indeed, in fields such as social science and law, women actually receive more new degrees than men do. Yet despite these gains, women and people of color remain numerical and representative minorities in the most prestigious jobs and in management—places where White men are still overrepresented (National Academy of Science, 2006). The longtime prevalence of this gender and ethnic disparity suggests a "glass ceiling," an invisible barrier that limits the opportunity for women and people of color to ascend the corporate ladder (e.g., Rosser, 2008). In a parallel process, women and people of color are sometimes given less meaningful or challenging work than their White male peers, leading to "sticky floors" that preclude advancement and career development.

Some explain this disparity as simply a "pipeline problem": well-educated senior employees are both more likely to obtain positions of power and, because of *past* injustice, be White men. If rates of advancement and attrition are the same across genders and ethnic groups, increasing the representation of women and people of color at the beginning of the pipeline (i.e., students) will eventually increase their representation at the end of the pipeline (i.e., managers and professors).

Yet even in fields that have reached numerical parity in degrees awarded, such as law, women and minorities make career decisions that lead them away from positions of greater power (Krakauer & Chen, 2003). More startlingly, some fields are becoming *less* diverse in recent years, such as computer science and science, technology, engineering, and mathematics (STEM) fields (National Science Foundation, 2008; Nelson, 2007). These same fields are even more likely to experience a "leaky pipeline," in which rates of advancement and attrition are higher for certain groups than others. For example, women receive 40 percent of STEM associates' degrees but only 20 percent of STEM doctoral degrees (National Science Foundation Science and Engineering Awards, 2005). Similarly, people of color are less likely to become university faculty in STEM fields as they are in the social sciences.

Women and ethnic minorities may be actively or passively discouraged from pursuing certain careers. A recent study of 1,226 female and underrepresented minority chemists and engineers found that 40 percent of minorities had been discouraged during their pursuit of a STEM career by faculty members in institutions of higher education. More than half of Latino women and Black men received some form of discouragement (Bayer Facts of Science Education XIV, 2010). For minority students, college professors were cited most frequently as the primary source of discouragement in pursuing technical-based careers. These perceptions, while prevalent in technology-related fields, are found throughout adolescence and in college-aged minority students. Moreover, negative perceptions of future career opportunities may be the consequences of the informal education that underrepresented students receive during their graduate training.

VOCATIONAL CHOICE AND IDENTITY

One important explanation for the leaky pipeline is self-selection away from certain fields. Often, the perceptions of these fields are inconsistent with the self-perceptions of people from underrepresented groups. For example, women in particular have difficulty identifying with the masculine or "nerdy" stereotypes of computer science (Cheryan et al., 2009; Margolis & Fisher, 2002; Schott & Selwyn, 2000). In other cases, people from underrepresented groups are directly and indirectly discouraged from participating in certain fields. In some cases, there are also negative stereotypes that people from underrepresented groups simply do not belong or cannot belong in certain fields (e.g., women are bad at math and African-Americans are poor students).

These stereotypes position underrepresented groups as lacking the knowledge, skills, and abilities needed to succeed in the workplace. Women face the additional negative stereotype that they lack the requisite drive and commitment to succeed. According to this view, non-work commitments such as family may take away women's time, focus, and investment in their careers, which subsequently derails their ability to move to the next level. People often internalize these negative stereotypes (Steele & Aronson, 1995) or psychologically disengage from the field entirely (e.g., Major & Schmader, 1998)—even when accounting for individual ability (Schmader, Major, & Gramzow, 2001) and past investment in the domain (Schmader, Johns, & Forbes, 2008; Shapiro & Neuberg, 2007).

People tend to avoid situations and goal pursuits that threaten their identity (Crocker & Major, 1989; Major & Schmader, 1998; Osborne, 1995, 1997; Steele, 1997). STEM fields, for example, may trigger identity threats for women and people of color because success in these fields means challenging powerful stereotypes of their groups. For people outside of STEM, identity threats may be powerful enough to keep them out. Yet even for some people already in the STEM fields, a desire to protect their identities may preclude them from engaging in important but challenging tasks to further their careers. This pattern is particularly true for people who endorse negative stereotypes about their groups. To the extent that women believe they lack math skills, they are unlikely to express interest in math-intensive fields, particularly computer science (Drybough, 2000). Moreover, the less interested women are in these fields, the less likely they are to pursue them as degree or career objectives (Cheryan et al., 2009).

Adolescents' expectations of vocational choices play an important role in career choice and occupational attainment (Diemer, 2009; Sewell & Hauser, 1975). Furthermore, projecting one's occupational self-concept represents a critical career development task for adolescents. This task, in turn, informs adolescents' vocational expectations—in other words, which jobs they expect to achieve in adulthood and which careers they aspire to have (Diemer, 2007). Importantly, adolescents' career aspirations predict their ultimate occupational attainment (Tangri & Jenkins, 1986).

The origins of the leaky pipeline, therefore, are found with an exploration of adolescent self-concept. Adolescents' occupational self-concept is informed by their social environment and social structure (Super, 1990). Adolescents learn of their possibilities through formal education, parental experience, jobs within their community, and other role models (Arbona, 1990; Constantine, Erickson, Banks, & Timberlake, 1998). However, not all children have the same opportunity for exposure to these influences. In particular, children from marginalized groups have fewer opportunities than their White counterparts.

RACE AND VOCATIONAL CHOICE

When we take marginalized groups into account, research has found that White youths and racial minority youths do not differ significantly in terms of initial career aspirations (Arbona, 1990; Fouad & Byars-Winston, 2005; Tomlinson & Evans-Hughes, 1991). However, meta-analysis reveals that minority youths have lower occupational expectations regarding possible career attainment (Fouad & Byars-Winston, 2005). These minority youths believe that they have fewer career choices and opportunities and that it will be difficult to attain a successful job (Constantine et al., 1998; Wang, Haertel, & Walberg, 1994). Their lowered expectations may be the result of a lack of exposure to job possibilities within their environments and the asymmetrical distribution of education among urban minority youths and their White counterparts. Moreover, the dearth of role models in their communities hinders the opportunities for minority children with lower socioeconomic status to develop healthy occupational self-concepts (Constantine et al., 1998).

Lowered vocational expectations influence perceptions of potential career choices and motivation to pursue prestigious occupations. While minority students may have the skills to compete in the workforce, many believe they will not be fully accepted (Fouad & Byars-Winston, 2005). Unfortunately, even when urban minority youths aspire to high-status occupations, they are less likely to believe that they can obtain such employment (Arbona, 1990).

GENDER AND VOCATIONAL CHOICE

Although people often choose their job based on their personal experiences and exposure to the workforce, studies have shown that gender plays a significant role in career choice (Adams & Walkerdine, 1986; Spender, 1982). Gender role stereotypes can be seen in adolescent girls' and college-aged women's choices to pursue a narrow range of stereotypically female occupations such as nursing and teaching (Betz, 1994; Krakauer & Chen, 2003). A recent study examining over 22,000 eighth and tenth graders found strong gender preferences in terms of career aspirations (Howard et al., 2011). In this study, girls selected jobs such as acting, fashion, cosmetology, photography, dancing, and elementary school teacher, while boys selected architect, police officer, professional athlete, and computer and mechanical engineer as their top careers. These gendered jobs demonstrate historically that occupations with a high female concentration are often paid less than those with concentrations of men, suggesting a societal devaluation of female-dominated fields (Howard et al., 2011).

These occupational stereotypes can limit aspirations of girls to fields in which they will be surrounded by others who look like them but will ultimately lower their potential long-term income. Therefore, relative to their male peers, female college students prefer less realistic and investigative occupations (Almiskry, Bakar, & Mohamed, 2009). Self-concepts, particularly self-efficacy, influence the development of gender differences in vocational interest (Betz, 1994).

AMBIENT CUES AND TRADITIONAL REPRESENTATION

Sometimes occupational stereotypes are communicated actively, but less obvious is the passive communication of these attitudes and biases through choice of dress, accessories, body language, and other environmental avenues, such as office or dorm decorations. People are very quick to use these ambient cues to make inferences about other people (e.g., Goslin, Ko, Mannarelli, & Morris, 2002) and organizations (Cheryan et al., 2009; Cheryan & Plaut, 2010). When these messages suggest that a person is unwelcome, they have deleterious effects on performance and turnover intentions. Not surprisingly, certain fields are more likely to offer an unwelcoming vibe. For example, over 40 percent of female and minority chemists and engineers perceived that STEM professionals did not communicate that women or minorities were wanted or needed in STEM fields (Bayer Facts of Science Education XIV, 2010).

Diversity climate is the cumulative result of intergroup interactions and organizational diversity policy. Interpersonal discrimination, exclusion, and a lack of interest in diversity all reflect a negative climate for diversity (Hall & Sandler, 1982; Morris & Daniel, 2008). The power of a diversity climate to shape performance and alter organizational functioning is profound. Compared to reducing prejudice among managers and directly trying to increase social fit among minority employees, improving the overall diversity climate was the most effective way to reduce subgroup differences in workplace performance as well as increasing perceptions of mentoring efficacy (Apospori et al., 2006; Kalev, Kelly, & Dobbins, 2006). While a positive diversity climate can help minority workers overcome their initial misgivings (Kalev et al., 2006; Konrad & Linnehan, 1995; Purdie-Vaughns et al., 2008; Walton & Cohen, 2007), a negative diversity climate can lead to decreased organization functioning and performance (Linnehan, Chrobot-Mason, & Konrad, 2006; McKay et al., 2007; Mitchell, Holtom, Lee,, Sablynski, & Erez, 2001; Plaut, Thomas, & Goren, 2009). In other words, a negative diversity climate can impede the career development of all employees, but especially those from underrepresented groups.

One of the most visible cues regarding organizational diversity climate is the traditional representation of gender and racial groups in an organization or field (Murphy, et. al., 2007; Purdie-Vaughns, et al., 2008; Sekaquaptewa & Thompson, 2003). People from underrepresented groups seem to be particularly aware of group representation as a cue. Actual organizational diversity (especially among managers) is an important indicator of climate (Linnehan et al., 2006). Even if organizational diversity is low, well-conceived diversity initiatives that adopt a multicultural, rather than colorblind, model of diversity have been associated with strong perceptions of organizational fit among employees from racial minority groups (Konrad & Linnehan, 1995; Plaut et al., 2009; Purdie-Vaughns et al., 2008). This effect is powerful enough to overturn the damage of a previously negative diversity climate (Walton & Cohen, 2007).

Even when information regarding group representation is absent, stereotypes about a field lead people to deduce that their group is unrepresented and therefore unwelcome (Cheryan et al., 2009; Margolis & Fisher, 2002; Schott & Selwyn, 2000; Turner, Hogg, Oakes, Reicher, & Wetherell, 1987). Changing these stereotypes is difficult but possible. For example, Murphy and colleagues (2007) had both men and women in computer science watch a video in which their field was presented as gender-balanced, dominated by women, or dominated by men. Men did not report feeling unwelcome, regardless of how computer science was presented. Because there is a stereotype against women performing well in computer science, however, women reported feeling as though they did not belong when computer science was presented as male-dominated. These women's feelings of exclusion in turn predicted a decreased desire to attend a professional conference to help develop their careers.

The absence of women and people of color in the top leadership levels of an organization can create and reinforce demographic faultlines (Lau & Murnighan, 1998). Although there may be women and people of color throughout the organization, their place is limited to certain levels or particular roles. Commonly, women and people of color are found at the lowest levels of the organization and in roles that are least critical to organizational health. This creates the image that the organization is open to diversity—but only to a certain point. When all leaders are White and male, and all their support staff are women and people of color, underrepresented groups get a message that they can be employed but not promoted. This certainly becomes a barrier to the recruitment, retention, and career development of underrepresented groups (Peterson, 2009).

PERCEIVED SIMILARITY

For people from underrepresented groups, there is inconsistency between beliefs about themselves and beliefs about the typical (or ideal) worker in certain fields. In other words, women and racial minorities are unlikely to perceive similarity between themselves and scientific workers (Cheryan et al., 2009; Diekman, Brown, Johnson, & Clark, 2010). People appear to have an innate need for belonging (Baumeister & Leary, 1995), and they try to satisfy this need by joining groups that seem similar to themselves (Heilman, 1983; Niedenthal, Cantor, & Kihlstrom, 1985; Walton & Cohen, 2007). On the other hand, people tend to avoid joining groups if they do not feel similar to the group members (Brewer & Weber, 1994; Brown, Novick, Lord, & Richards, 1992; Ledgerwood & Chaiken, 2007;

Mussweiler, 2003; Oyserman, Brickman, Bybee, & Celious, 2006; Walton & Cohen, 2007) or see their own traits, attributes, attitudes, and beliefs represented (Hannover & Kessels, 2004; Lee, 1998; Rommes et al., 2007). Perceptions of similarity between the self and the organization are important for predicting interest in the field (Hannover & Kessels, 2004) and anticipated success (Walton & Cohen, 2007) even when controlling for ability (Rommes et al., 2007).

Increasing the representation of women and racial minority groups can help increase perceptions of similarity (Murphy et al., 2007), but it is not always enough (Cheryan, Plaut, Davies, & Steele, 2009). Other aspects of the organization are also vital, including ambient cues (Cheryan et al., 2009), diversity climate, and organizational practices. Organizations that showcase their commitment to diversity by increasing racial diversity among recruiters (Avery, Hernandez, & Hebl, 2004; Thomas & Wise, 1999) and in recruitment advertisements are more attractive to racial minorities and just as attractive to Whites (Avery, 2003; Avery et al., 2004). Moreover, perceptions of fit within the organization predict voluntary turnover above and beyond job satisfaction, organizational commitment, or available job opportunities for people from underrepresented groups (Mitchell et al., 2001).

ONGOING VOCATIONAL CHOICE

Even after people from underrepresented groups are attracted to their current fields, various factors prompt them to leave their jobs or otherwise become psychologically disengaged more frequently than White men (McKay, Avery, Tonidandel, Morris, Hernandez, & Hebl, 2007). Compared to White men, women and racial minorities in organizations experience different and uneven expectations and opportunities for success, social pressures to conform, stereotyping, exclusion, and outright discrimination. In sum, these aspects of diversity climate affect people from underrepresented groups more than others and can lead to an unfulfilled need to belong (Cheryan et al., 2009), overburdened mental resources (Schmader & Johns, 2008), and negative health outcomes (Mendes, Gray, Mendoza-Denton, Major, & Epel, 2007). In other words, a negative diversity climate, stereotypes, and lack of access to mentoring can have disastrous consequences for the career development and well-being of people from underrepresented groups.

GENDER/RACE VALUATION

Unlike stereotypes of White men, stereotypes of women and racial minorities suggest that they are unfit for various work fields (e.g., science, engineering, and technology fields). These stereotypes create a host of negative outcomes both for the stereotyped employee and from the stereotyping colleague. People who are stereotyped to perform poorly in a certain domain tend to be aware of these stereotypes. The fear of being stereotyped can strain coworker relations and cause work-related and identity-related stresses (Davies, Spencer, Quynn, & Gerhardstein, 2002; Schmader et al., 2008; Shapiro & Neuberg, 2007; Steele, 1997; Steele & Aronson, 1995). Stereotype threat (Steele & Aronson, 1995) is the tendency for people to perform poorly on a task when they are aware of negative stereotypes and work especially hard to overcome these stereotypes. Unfortunately, in working to overcome the stereotypes, they overburden themselves and hinder their own performance (Schmader et al., 2008; Shapiro & Neuberg, 2007; Steele, 1997).

Stereotype threat is not the only way in which stereotypes harm the career development of women and racial minorities. When colleagues stereotype employees from underrepresented groups, they create an environment in which identity threats are more prevalent. These threats decrease performance, increase unwelcome social pressure to conform to more traditional expectations (Hartman & Hartman, 2008), and reduce retention—an issue that seems particularly problematic in technical fields (Crocker, Karpinski, Quinn, & Chase, 2003; Spencer, Steele, & Quinn, 1999).

EXPECTATIONS OF SUCCESS

To have successful career development, an employee must be assigned difficult but possible tasks that are considered important and central to the organization's mission. Women and racial minorities are not given these opportunities as frequently as White men (Maume, 1999; Williams, 1992). Because of lowered expectations (Bertrand & Mullainathan, 2004; Eagly & Karau, 2002), people from underrepresented groups are less likely to be assigned challenging or meaningful tasks. Over time, this leads to the "sticky floor" problem in which they cannot demonstrate their competency and fail to be promoted to more prestigious positions (Baker, 2003; Booth, Frankesconi, & Frank, 2003). Even when they are given challenging tasks, people from underrepresented groups are often assigned to roles not central to the organizational mission and become merely "diversity hires." Unable to prove their true worth to the central mission, these employees can hit the "glass ceiling" and never rise to upper management positions (Maume, 1999). Even when given the opportunity to succeed, however, people from underrepresented groups are often not evaluated evenly with their White male colleagues (Biernat & Manis, 1994). These issues can be alleviated by engaging in a mentoring relationship.

DISCRIMINATION AND ISOLATION

When a person is the only member of his or her group in an organization, he or she is a "solo" or "token." This experience is marginalizing for women and people of color and puts them at increased risk for discrimination and harassment (Rosser, 2008). This discrimination is experienced through the discrediting and devaluing of their work (Rosser, 2008) but also in the often subjective and arbitrary evaluation criteria that are used when they apply for promotion and tenure (National Academy of Science, 2006). For women, the bias that they confront exists in the organizational structure and rules that seem to underlie the informal mores and intentions of the organization (National Academy of Science, 2006). These biases may allow women to see potential career opportunities but never fully achieve them. Effectively combating these discriminatory practices and stereotypes may require a "critical mass" of people from underrepresented groups. In some cases, there are simply not enough women, people of color, or their allies to challenge or disprove stereotypes and question or confront discrimination.

In many fields, members of underrepresented groups such as women and people of color frequently encounter isolation and sometimes loneliness in their work (Rosser, 2008). If there are no influential role models and mentors, their isolation may be exacerbated. Therefore, the opportunity to advance might actually present an opportunity for greater responsibility and reward, but also the potential for greater isolation and even more visibility and critique. When senior women do take on positions of leadership and authority to create climates that are more inclusive for junior women and people of color, they are frequently faced with resentment (Rosser, 2008). At times, this resentment comes from the sources of support the senior woman had formerly relied upon throughout their career (Thomas, Johnson-Bailey, Phelps, Tran, & Johnson, 2012). The lack of diversity in leadership therefore limits the interest of more junior colleagues, creates a mentoring gap for younger colleagues, and keeps senior women confined to roles in which they cannot engage in meaningful organizational and structure change.

Across all organizations, people from underrepresented groups have higher rates of turnover than White men (McKay et al., 2007), and this is particularly true if they perceive that the organization is not committed to supporting diversity (McKay et al., 2007). Sometimes, women "opt out" when their workplaces and current career paths no longer meet their goals. Other times, they opt out because they perceive that goal attainment is not feasible in their environment (Thomas et al., in press). Corporate women suggest that the glass ceiling is a result of numerous issues, including the lack of developmental opportunity for women, especially with regard to having fiduciary responsibility, management experience, and global experience. Women also suggest that the male-dominated culture of many workplaces restricts their opportunity for development and career mobility. Systems of patriarchy in organizations likely lock women out of the developmental relationships with men that are necessary to understand the political culture of organizational life. Patriarchy therefore also limits the availability of the informal sources of information that women need to climb the corporate ladder, such as role models and mentors. Furthermore, when women (as well as people of color) do not see similar others succeeding in their workplace, they perceive that the organization will not permit them to succeed (Thomas, 2005).

Mentoring

Many organizations are seeking ways to reduce "opting out" along with perceived discrimination and isolation for their women and minority employees. Increasing mentoring opportunities for women and people of color is an important step toward creating a positive diversity climate and an equitable workplace. Mentoring is a developmental relationship through which a more experienced or knowledgeable individual (the mentor) shares skills, information, and perspective in an effort to maximize another individual's (the protégé's) personal and professional growth and potential. Mentoring is as a common form of career development and organizational investment in employees. Mentors provide two major functions to their protégés: career-related functions and psychosocial functions (Kram, 1985). Career-related functions focus on a protégé's success within a given organization and include coaching, exposure and visibility, sponsorship, protection, and the offering of challenging assignments. Psychosocial functions center on increasing competence and effectiveness through an enhanced sense of identity in the protégé's professional role through role modeling, acceptance and confirmation, counseling, and friendship (Chan, 2008; Kram 1985).

Social exchange theory provides a practical explanation for understanding the mentoring process (Eby, 2007; Ensher & Murphy, 1997, 2005). Social exchange theory purports that mentors provide certain resources to a protégé, such as increased connections, skills, and feedback, and the protégé can offer new skills and perspectives for the mentor. The key component to a successful mentoring relationship is that both parties view the relationship as valuable. The Eby (2007) mentoring investment model extends social exchange theory by suggesting that both mentors and protégés weigh the perceived costs and benefits of embarking on a mentoring relationship. In this model, when the perceived benefits (e.g., learning new skills) outweigh the costs (e.g., time investment), then the relationship will flourish.

Traditional mentoring relationships progress through four stages over time (Kram, 1985). In the first stage, *initiation*, the mentor and protégé are in the beginning of their relationship and spend time learning more about one another. In the second stage, *cultivation*, the protégé does most of their learning. This is the longest phase of the mentoring relationship and is expected to last from 2 to 5 years. During this time, the needs of the mentor and the protégé will inevitably evolve. This evolution leads to the third stage, *separation*, wherein the protégé begins the process of becoming independent from the mentor, leading the mentor to deem that he or she has no additional guidance to provide. The final stage, *redefinition*, occurs when the mentor–protégé relationship changes from a mentoring relationship to that of peers or colleagues.

Mentoring can take the form of a formal mentoring relationship or an informal relationship. Many organizations have developed a formal mentoring process to help develop and advance the careers of high-potential junior employees. Formal mentoring relationships are assigned or matched within the organization, whereas informal mentoring relationships develop naturally through mutual interaction.

Formal relationships are typically shorter, lasting 6 months to a year, compared to informal relationships, which can last from 3 to 6 years (Tran & Harrington, 2009). While different in the way they are created, both formal and informal mentoring relationships offer numerous benefits for both the protégé and the mentor.

More recently, newer approaches to mentoring have evolved, including group mentoring, peer mentoring, and step-ahead mentoring (Ensher & Murphy, 2010). A peer mentor is typically at the same level in the organization as the protégé. A step-ahead mentor is often one level above the protégé or in a position that represents the next logical step in the protégé's career path (Ensher, Thomas, & Murphy, 2001). While peer mentors may be easier for employees to obtain, they may lack the number and quality of connections that traditional mentors may possess. Therefore, peer mentors may offer a high degree of psychosocial support but may not offer the same degree of career support that traditional mentors provide (Allen, McManus, & Russell, 1999).

While formal mentoring is beneficial for an individual's career, informal mentoring can offer its own set of benefits to protégés as well. Even individuals who must seek mentors outside a formal organizational process still have experiences that are more positive that people without mentors (Apospori, Nikandrou, & Panayotopoulou, 2006). A recent meta-analysis assessing the effectiveness of formal/informal mentoring found that individuals in informal mentoring relationships have greater career support and higher salaries than those involved in formal mentoring relationships (Underhill, 2005). People without any mentor, however, fared worse than individuals in either formal or informal mentoring relationships.

MENTORING IMPORTANCE

By nature, mentoring relationships are developmental and therefore thought to be critical to career development. The guidance and advice from a mentor serves as a priceless resource for individuals in their early career years. Protégés have more effective socialization, lower turnover intentions, higher expectations for advancement within an organization, higher job and career satisfaction, higher compensation, and faster salary growth (Allen et al., 2004; Burke, Burgess, & Fallon, 2006; Eby, Allen, Evans, Ng, & DuBois, 2008). For mentors, providing mentoring is related to higher job satisfaction and organizational commitment as well as stronger perceptions of career success (Allen, Lentz, & Day, 2006; Collins, 1994).

More specifically, the act of serving as a mentor in later career years can provide a sense of contribution to future generations. Ultimately, mentoring provides employees with the resources, support, and visibility they require to advance in their organizations (Ragins, 1989). Organizations also benefit from mentoring as employees have an increased sense of loyalty and organizational commitment and are less likely to voluntarily leave. Beyond these benefits, mentoring has been shown to attract more employees and aid in the socialization of new employees (Ensher & Murphy, 2010). However, organizational climates can have an effect on the quality and willingness to mentor women and racial minorities. Negative organizational climates for diversity can derail the effectiveness of formal and informal mentoring relationships when senior workers fail to engage in mentoring relationships with women and people of color (Dreher & Cox, 2000; Valian, 1999).

White men are traditionally more integrated into organizational networks and therefore have greater access to mentoring opportunities, both as protégés and mentors, than women and people of color (Cocchiara, Kwesiga, Bell, & Baruch, 2010; Dreher & Cox, 2000; Valian, 1999). Perhaps due to these disparities, new female employees report less satisfaction with organizational support and greater turnover intentions than new male employees (Holton, 1995). Because men typically occupy both formal and informal positions of power within organizations, they can often secure better outcomes for their protégés. For example, having a White male mentor translated into a compensation advantage of roughly $15,000 a year for female MBAs on the job market (Dreher & Cox, 1996). Cultivating relationships with White men may therefore be a viable strategy for enhancing career development outcomes for minority and female workers (Dreher & Cox, 1996; Thomas, 1989). On the other hand, a recent meta-analysis examining gender and mentoring found that protégés with female mentors received more psychosocial and instrumental support than protégés with male mentors (O'Brien, Biga, Kessler, & Allen, 2010). Therefore, individuals may wish to consider gender differences in the mentoring relationship depending on their own expectations of the relationship.

CROSS-CULTURAL BARRIERS TO MENTORING

According to Byrnes' (1971) similarity-attraction theory, individuals are typically more comfortable around others who look like them. Furthermore, people who are at a place in their careers where they can serve as a mentor, such as upper-level executives, tend to be White males. These men are far more likely to choose other White men as their protégés rather than female, Black, or Hispanic professionals (Dreher & Cox, 1996). Moreover, studies have consistently found that minority protégés who are involved in a cross-cultural mentoring dyad receive less career and psychosocial support than protégés who have mentors similar to them (Feldman, Folks, & Turnley, 1999; Ortiz-Walters & Gilson, 2005).

Compounding this barrier, women and minorities tend to be more highly visible in organizations due to their token status. This status makes their potential success or failure as a protégé that much more likely to be observed. Because a protégé's outcome reflects a mentor's abilities and competency, White men are more hesitant to engage in a mentoring relationship with a woman or minority (Dreher & Cox, 1996). Facing the taboos these relationships create, minorities and Whites retreat to less intense ways of being together. Minority protégés are deprived of the mentoring relationships they need to develop and get ahead, and mentors are denied the experience of creativity, of generation, that they need in order to feel able to shape an institution's future and to create a personal legacy.

Thomas (1989) discusses some of the invisible and visible barriers to cross-gender and cross-race mentoring relationships. Within organizations, invisible pressures and dubious attributions may be placed on Black women who are perceived to be in career-enhancing relationships with White male superiors. These cross-race/cross-gender relationships can pose special challenges by triggering a triangle relationship among supervisors and subordinates. For instance, a Black man mentoring a White woman may be upsetting to White men who may believe the Black man's intentions are not pure. Alternatively, a White man mentoring a Black woman may illicit feelings of hostility from Black men. White men and Black men, however, have had few opportunities to develop non–race-based relationships and instead have remained opponents (Thomas, 1989). Because of this shared history, cross-race and cross-gender mentoring relationships are difficult (but not impossible) to foster. Having relatively less access to senior White male mentors limits the opportunities for career development for women and people of color.

Furthermore, the misinformed belief that minority students can be mentored only by faculty of color creates additional career development barriers for these students (Thomas, Willis, & Davis, 2007). Often, minority students are discouraged by well-intentioned White male professors, who may be genuinely concerned about the student's well-being but unable to recognize the influence of their own ingrained views of intellectual ability or group membership.

To alleviate these career development barriers, mentors must be willing to reflect upon their own experiences as graduate students and junior professionals and be open to ways in which the experiences of young minority professionals today may differ (Thomas et al., 2007). Mentors must be willing to seek out developmental challenges and understand that effective mentoring includes instrumental support beyond emotional support that can serve to patronize and overprotect protégés (Enomoto, Gardiner, & Grogan, 2002). Mentors must also be willing to develop their multicultural competency and receive training regarding feedback delivery, role modeling, and interpersonal communication (Chrobot-Mason & Ruderman, 2004).

Institutions should be aware of the tendency to overload new minority faculty members with minority-related service commitments to the extent that they cannot be effective mentors. Leadership must also consider the extent to which effective mentoring, especially of minority students, is a criterion in faculty evaluations and ultimately in tenure and promotion decisions. Leadership in businesses and universities should strive to create mutually rewarding diverse mentoring relationships through training on the stages of mentoring relationships, the development of mentoring contracts, the ethical responsibilities involved in mentoring, and the benefits and costs of mentoring for both racial and gender minority protégés and mentors themselves. Likewise, organizations should consider formal mentoring programs and networks to encourage intergroup socialization and foster developmental relationships across race and gender (Chrobot-Mason & Ruderman, 2004; Thomas et al., 2007). Indeed, organizations with formal mentoring programs—especially those that provide psychosocial support in addition to career support—are better at attracting talented people of color (Horvath, Wasko, & Bradley, 2008).

Conclusion and future directions

Developing the careers of diverse groups in organizations has implications not just for individual employees, but also for their organizations, entire industries, and society overall. Effective career development in organizations creates opportunities for workers to develop the knowledge, skills, and abilities needed to do their current jobs better as well as prepare for future opportunities. Importantly, effective career development also encourages workers to take on new, more visible, and more challenging assignments that unlock new work possibilities (Thomas, 2005). More challenging work promotes the development of skill sets that create career possibilities, mobility, and potentially higher salaries both within one's organization as well as outside of it. Effective career development may also allow migration into different work settings or industries.

Career development also creates an opportunity to learn through traditional classes, new experiences, advisement, or coaching. In addition to developing new knowledge and skills, career development helps to promote career self-efficacy, the belief that a worker can take on a new career challenge successfully. Career self-efficacy is especially important for workers who may be underrepresented in their career paths or workplaces and lack role models who have been successful in the same contexts. If workers lack career self-efficacy, they are less likely to engage in the challenging tasks necessary for career advancement.

Opportunities for learning, the development of career efficacy, as well as greater career mobility are also important personal and professional outcomes of career development. Unfortunately, career development is not always afforded to those who desire, require, or have earned it through past performance. Biases and stereotypes can undermine decisions regarding who is afforded career development. Stereotypes of women as not committed to work and ethnic minorities as being unintelligent create doubts that these workers are worth the financial and time investment required of both formal and informal career development efforts. Being locked out of opportunities to develop creates barriers for promotion, limited developmental opportunities, and limited access to career and support systems for underrepresented groups and especially for high-potential minority and female workers.

We have identified potentially fruitful future directions for research and practice related to career development opportunities for women and people of color. For example, in what ways can women and people of color receive more and better information so that they are employed in more diverse disciplines and careers? One potentially fruitful route is career development courses (e.g., Osborn,

Howard, & Leirer, 2007) that target dysfunctional and maladaptive thoughts. Moving further down the pipeline, it is important that educators work to deliver this information in ways that empower students to pursue careers in areas in which they are not tokens and can be effective. Furthermore, women and minorities may seek out new media such as social networking websites to help alleviate isolation, build networks, and create communities during post-secondary studies as well as in their professional lives. These efforts, combined with organizational commitment to comparable career paths for all workers that emphasize the value of diversity management, can help alleviate many of career development barriers experienced by women and minorities in the workforce.

Providing opportunities for career development can improve an organization's workforce, attract new hires, and retain talented employees. Career development begins when people make vocational choices, and continues as they are attracted to specific organizations, gain opportunities for mentoring, training, and promotion, and decide whether to stay at the organization or leave. Given the history and continuing realities of racial and gender discrimination, however, career development opportunities are not offered equally. Women and people of color, in comparison to White men, face barriers related to vocational choice, mentoring, training, promotion opportunities, and positive workplace climates. These barriers seem to be especially prevalent in STEM fields. Given their limited career development opportunities, people from underrepresented groups tend to have worse career outcomes than Whites, including lower workplace engagement, greater turnover, lower salaries, and fewer leadership positions. Organizations can help eliminate these barriers to career development by making commitment to diversity a core organizational policy and by increasing hiring, mentoring, and promotional opportunities for women and people of color.

References

Adams, C., & Walkerdine, V. (1986) *Investigating gender in the primary school: Activity-based INSET materials for primary teachers*. London: Inner London Education Authority.

Allen, T. D., Eby, L. T., Poteet, M. L., Lentz, E., & Lima, L. (2004). Career benefits associated with mentoring for protégés: A meta-analysis. *Journal of Applied Psychology, 89*(1), 127–136.

Allen, T. D., Lentz, E., & Day, R. (2006). Career success outcomes associated with mentoring others: A comparison of mentors and nonmentors. *Journal of Career Development, 32*(3), 272–285.

Allen, T. D., McManus, S. E., & Russell, J. E. A. (1999). Newcomer socialization and stress: Formal peer relationships as a source of support. *Journal of Vocational Behavior, 54*(3), 453–470.

Almiskry, A. S., Bakar, A. R., & Mohamed, O. (2009). Gender differences and career interest among undergraduates: Implications for career choices. *European Journal of Scientific Research, 26*, 465–469.

Apospori, E., Nikandrou, I., & Panayotopoulou, L. (2006). Mentoring and women's career advancement in Greece. *Human Resource Development International, 9*(4), 509–527.

Arbona, C. (1990). Career counseling research and Hispanics: A review of the literature. *Counseling Psychologist, 18*, 300–323.

Armstrong, P. I., Rounds, J., & Hubert, L. (2008). Re-conceptualizing the past: Historical data in vocational interest research. *Journal of Vocational Behavior, 72*(3) 284–297.

Avery, D. R. (2003). Reactions to diversity in recruitment advertising: Are differences black and white? *Journal of Applied Psychology, 88*, 672–679.

Avery, D. R., Hernandez, M., & Hebl, M. R. (2004). Who's watching the race? Racial salience in recruiting advertising. *Journal of Applied Social Psychology, 34*, 146–161.

Baker, J. G. (2003). Glass ceilings or sticky floors? A model of high-income law graduates. *Journal of Labor Research, 4*, 695–711.

Bandura, A. (1986). *Social foundations of thought and action: A social cognitive theory*. Englewood Cliffs, NJ: Prentice-Hall.

Bandura, A. (1997). *Self-efficacy: The exercise of control*. New York: Freeman.

Baumeister, R. F., & Leary, M. R. (1995). The need to belong: Desire for interpersonal attachments as a fundamental human motivation. *Psychological Bulletin, 117*, 497–529.

Bayer Facts of Science Education XIV. (2010). *Female and minority chemists and chemical engineers speak about diversity and underrepresentation in STEM*. Retrieved October 1, 2010 from http://bayerfactsofscience.online-pressroom.com/

Bertrand, M., & Mullainathan, S. (2004). Are Emily and Greg more employable than Lakisha and Jamal? A field experiment on labor market discrimination. *American Economic Review, 94*, 419–423.

Betz, N. E. (1994). Self-concept theory in career development and counseling. *Career Development Quarterly, 43*, 32–41.

Biernat, M., & Manis, M. (1994). Shifting standards and stereotype-based judgments. *Journal of Personality and Social Psychology, 66*, 5–20.

Booth, A. L., Francesconi, M., & Frank, J. (2003). A stick floor model of promotion, pay, and gender. *European Economic Review, 47*, 295–322.

Brewer, M. B., & Weber, J. G. (1994). Self-evaluation effects of interpersonal versus intergroup social comparison. *Journal of Personality and Social Psychology, 66*, 268–275.

Brown, J. D., Novick, N. J., Lord, K. A., & Richards, J. M. (1992). When Gulliver travels: Social context, psychological closeness, and self appraisals. *Journal of Personality and Social Psychology, 62*, 717–727.

Burke, R. J., Burgess, Z., & Fallon, B. (2006). Benefits of mentoring to Australian early career women managers and professionals. *Equal Opportunities International, 25*, 71–79.

Byrne, D. (1971). *The attraction paradigm*. New York: Academic Press.

Chan, A. W. (2008). Mentoring ethnic minority, pre-doctoral students: An analysis of key mentor practices. *Mentoring & Tutoring: Partnership in Learning, 16*, 263–277.

Cheryan, S., & Plaut, V. C. (2010). Explaining underrepresentation: A theory of precluded interest. *Sex Roles, 63*, 475–488.

Cheryan, S., Plaut, V. C., Davies, P. G., & Steele, C. M. (2009). Ambient belonging: how stereotypical cues impact gender participation in computer science. *Journal of Personality and Social Psychology, 97*, 1045–1060.

Chrobot-Mason, D., & Ruderman, M. N. (2004). Leadership in a diverse workforce. In M. S. Stockdale & F. J. Crosby (Eds.), *The psychology and management of workplace diversity* (pp. 100–121). Malden, MA: Blackwell Publishing.

Cocchiara, F. K., Kwesiga, E., & Bell, M. P., & Baruch, Y. (2010). Who benefits from graduate degrees? Effects of sex and perceived discrimination on human capital. *Career Development International, 15*(1), 39–58.

Collins, P. M. (1994). Does mentorship among social workers make a difference? An empirical investigation of career outcomes. *Social Work, 39*(4), 413–419.

Constantine, M. G., Erickson, C. D., Banks, R. W., & Timberlake, T. L. (1998). Challenges to the career development of urban racial and ethnic minority youth: Implications of vocational intervention. *Journal of Multicultural Counseling and Development, 26*, 83–95.

Crocker, J., Karpinski, A., Quinn, D. M., & Chase, S. K. (2003). When grades determine self-worth: Consequences of contingent self-worth for male and female engineering and psychology majors. *Journal of Personality and Social Psychology, 85*, 507–516.

Crocker, J., & Major, B. (1989). Social stigma and self-esteem: The self-protective properties of stigma. *Psychological Review, 96*, 608–630.

Davies, P. G., Spencer, S. J., Quinn, D. M., & Gerhardstein, R. (2002). Consuming images: How television commercials that elicit stereotype threat can restrain women academically and professionally. *Personality and Social Psychology Bulletin, 28*, 1615–1628.

Diekman, A. B., Brown, E., Johnston, A., & Clark, E. (2010). Seeking congruity between goals and roles: a new look at why women opt out of STEM careers. *Psychological Science, 21*, 1051–1057.

Diemer, M. A. (2007). Parental and school influences upon the career development of poor youth of color. *Journal of Vocational Behavior, 70*(3), 502–524.

Diemer, M. A. (2009). Pathways to occupational attainment among poor youth of color: The role of sociopolitical development. *Counseling Psychologist, 37*(1), 6–35.

Dreher, G., & Cox, T. H. (1996). Race, gender and opportunity: a study of compensation attainment and the establishment of mentoring relationships. *Journal of Applied Psychology, 81*(3), 297–308.

Dreher, G. F., & Cox, T. H. (2000). Labor market mobility and cash compensation: The moderating effects of race and gender. *Academy of Management Journal, 43*, 890–900.

Drybough, H. (2000). Underrepresentation of girls and women in computer science: classification of 1990s research. *Journal of Educational Computing Research, 23*, 181–202.

Eagly, A. H., & Karau, S. J. (2002). Role congruity theory and prejudice toward female leaders. *Psychological Review, 109*, 573–598.

Eby, L. T. (2007). Understanding relational problems in mentoring: a review and proposed investment model. In B. R. Ragins & K. E. Kram (Eds.), *The handbook of mentoring at work: Theory, research, and practice* (pp. 323–344). Thousand Oaks, CA: Sage Publications.

Eby, L. T., Allen, T. D., Evans, S. C., Ng, T., & DuBois, D. L. (2008). Does mentoring matter? A multidisciplinary meta-analysis comparing mentored and non-mentored individuals. *Journal of Vocational Behavior, 72*, 254–267.

Enomoto, E., Gardiner, M. & Grogan, M. (2002). Mentoring women in educational leadership. In F. Kochan (Ed.), *The organizational and human dimensions of successful mentoring programs and relationships* (pp. 207–220). Greenwich, CT: Information Age Publishing.

Ensher, E. A., & Murphy, S. (2005). *Power mentoring: How successful mentors and protégés get the most out of their relationships*. San Francisco, CA: Jossey-Bass.

Ensher, E. A., & Murphy, S. E. (1997). Effects of race, gender, perceived similarity, and contact on mentor relationships. *Journal of Vocational Behavior, 50*(3), 460–481.

Ensher, E. A., & Murphy, S. E. (2010). The Mentoring Relationship Challenges Scale: The impact of mentoring stage, type, and gender. *Journal of Vocational Behavior*.

Ensher, E. A., Thomas, C., & Murphy, S. E. (2001). Comparison of traditional, step-ahead, and peer mentoring on protégés' support, satisfaction, and perceptions of career success: A social exchange perspective. *Journal of Business and Psychology, 15*(3), 419–438.

Feldman, D. C., Folks, W. R., & Turnley, W. H. (1999). Mentor-protégé diversity and its impact on international internship experiences. *Journal of Organizational Behavior, 20*, 597–611.

Fouad, N., & Byars-Winston, A. (2005). Cultural context of career choice: Meta-analysis of race differences. *Career Development Quarterly, 53*, 223–233.

Giscombe, K., & Mattis, M. (2002). Leveling the playing field for women of color in corporate management: Is the business case enough? *Journal of Business Ethics. 37*(1), 103–119

Goslin, S. D., Ko, S. J., Mannarelli, T., & Morris, M. E. (2002). A room with a cue: Personality judgments based on offices and bedrooms. *Journal of Personality and Social Psychology, 82*, 379–398.

Greenhaus, J. H., Parasuraman, S., & Worley, W. M. (1990). Effects of race on organizational experience, job performance evaluations, and career outcomes. *Academy of Management Journal, 16*, 129–137.

Hall, R. M., & Sandler, B. R. (1982). *The classroom climate: A chilly one for women?* Washington, D.C.: Association of American Colleges.

Hannover, B., & Kessels, U. (2004). Self-to-prototype matching as a strategy for making academic choices: Why high school students do not like math and science. *Learning and Instruction, 14*, 51–67.

Hartman, H., & Hartman, M. (2008). How undergraduate engineering students perceive women's (and men's) problems in science, math and engineering. *Sex Roles, 58*, 251–265.

Heilman, M. E. (1983). Sex bias in work settings: the lack of fit model. *Research in Organizational Behavior, 5*, 269–298.

Holland, J. L. (1985). *Making vocational choices: A theory of vocational personalities and work environments* (2nd ed.). Englewood Cliffs, NJ: Prentice Hall.

Holland, J. L. (1997). *Making vocational choices: A theory of vocational personalities and work environments* (3rd ed.). Odessa, FL: Psychological Assessment Resources.

Holton, E. F., III. (1995). College graduates' experiences and attitudes during organizational entry. *Human Resource Development Quarterly, 6*, 59–78.

Horvath, M., Wasko, L., & Bradley, J. (2008). The effect of formal mentoring program characteristics on organizational attraction. *Human Resource Development Quarterly, 19*(4), 323–349.

Howard, K. A. S., Carlstrom, A. H., Katz, A. D., Chew, A. Y., Ray, G. C., Laine, L., & Caulum, D. (2011). Career aspirations of youth: Untangling race/ethnicity, SES, and gender. *Journal of Vocational Behavior*.

Kalev, A., Kelly, E., & Dobbin, F. (2006). Best practices or best guesses? Assessing the efficacy of corporate affirmative action and diversity policies. *American Sociological Review, 71*, 589–617.

Konrad, A. M., & Linnehan, F. (1995). Formalized HRM structures: Coordinating equal employment opportunity or concealing organizational practices? *Academy of Management Journal, 38*, 787–820.

Krakauer, L., & Chen, C. P. (2003). Gender barriers in the legal profession: Implications for career development of female law students. *Journal of Employment Counseling, 40*(2), 65–79.

Kram, K. E. (1985). *Mentoring at work: Developmental relationships in organizational life*. Glenview, IL: Scott, Foresman and Company.

Lau, D. C., & Murnighan, J. K. (1998). Demographic diversity and faultlines: The compositional dynamics of organizational groups. *Academy of Management Review, 23*, 325–340.

Ledgerwood, A., & Chaiken, S. (2007). Priming us and them: Automatic assimilation and contrast in group attitudes. *Journal of Personality and Social Psychology, 93*, 940–956.

Lee, C. C., & Armstrong, K. L. (1995). Indigenous models of mental health intervention: Lessons from traditional healers. In J. G. Ponterotto, J. M. Casas, L. A. Suzuki, & C. M. Alexander (Eds.), *Handbook of multicultural counseling* (pp. 441–456). Thousand Oaks, CA: Sage.

Lee, J. D. (1998). Which kids can "become" scientists? Effects of gender, self-concepts, and perceptions of scientists. *Social Psychology Quarterly, 61*, 199–219.

Lent, R. W., Brown, S. D., & Hackett, G. (1994). Toward a unifying social cognitive theory of career and academic interest, choice, and performance. *Journal of Vocational Behavior, 45*, 79–122.

Linnehan, F., Chrobot-Mason, D., & Konrad, A. M. (2006). Diversity attitudes and norms: The role of ethnic identity and relational demography. *Journal of Organizational Behaviour, 27*, 419–442.

Major, B., & Schmader, T. (1998). Coping with stigma through psychological disengagement. In J. K. Swim & C. Stangor (Eds.), *Prejudice: The target's perspective* (pp. 219–241). San Diego, CA: Academic Press.

Margolis, J., & Fisher, A. (2002). *Unlocking the clubhouse: Women in computing*. Cambridge: MIT.

Maume, D. J., Jr. (1999). Glass ceilings and glass escalators: Occupational segregation and race and sex differences in managerial promotions. *Work and Occupations, 26*, 483–509.

McKay, P. F., Avery, D. R., Tonidandel, S., Morris, M. A., Hernandez, M., & Hebl, M. R. (2007). Racial differences in employee retention: Are diversity climate perceptions the key? *Personnel Psychology, 60*, 35–62.

Mendes, W. B., Gray, H. M., Mendoza-Denton, R., Major, B., & Epel, E. S. (2007). Why egalitarianism might be good for your health: Physiological thriving during stressful intergroup encounters. *Psychological Science, 18*, 991–998.

Mitchell, T. R., Holtom, B. C., Lee, T. W., Sablynski, C. J., & Erez, M. (2001). Why people stay: Using job embeddedness to predict voluntary turnover. *Academy of Management Journal, 44*, 1102–1121.

Morris, L. K., & Daniel, L. G. (2008). Perceptions of a chilly climate: Differences in traditional and non-traditional majors for women. *Research in Higher Education, 49*, 256–273.

Murphy, M. C., Steele, C. M., & Gross, J. J. (2007). Signaling threat: How situational cues affect women in math, science, and engineering settings. *Psychological Science, 18*, 879–885.

Mussweiler, T. (2003). Comparison processes in social judgment: Mechanisms and consequences. *Psychological Review, 110*, 472–489.

National Academy of Science (2006). *Beyond bias and barriers: Fulfilling the potential of women in academic science and engineering*. Available at: www.nap.edu

National Science Foundation. (2008). *Women, minorities, and persons with disabilities in science and engineering*. Retrieved November 2, 2008, from http://www.nsf.gov/statistics/wmpd/pdf/tabc-4.pdf

National Science Foundation Science and Engineering Awards (2005): "Professional, etc. includes professional, unknown and other," Percent Female Among Doctorate Recipients.

Nelson, D. (2007). *A national analysis of minorities in science and engineering faculties at research universities. Top 40 departments in FY2007*. Retrieved from http://faculty-staff.ou.edu/N/Donna.J.Nelson-1/diversity/Faculty_Tables_FY07/07Report.pdf

Niedenthal, P. M., Cantor, N., & Kihlstrom, J. F. (1985). Prototype matching: A strategy for social decision making. *Journal of Personality and Social Psychology, 48*, 575–584.

O'Brien, K. E., Biga, A., Kessler, S. R., & Allen, T. D. (2010). A meta-analytic investigation of gender differences in mentoring. *Journal of Management, 36*, 537–554.

Ortiz-Walters, R., & Gilson, L. L. (2005). Mentoring in academia: An examination of the experiences of protégés of color. *Journal of Vocational Behavior, 67*, 459–475.

Osborn, D. S., Howard, D. K., & Leierer, S. J. (2007). The effect of a career development course on the dysfunctional career thoughts of racially and ethnically diverse college freshman. *Career Development Quarterly, 55*, 365–377.

Osborn, J. W. (1997). Race and academic disidentification. *Journal of Educational Psychology, 89*, 728–735.

Osborne, R. L. (1995). The continuum of violence against women in Canadian universities: Toward a new understanding of chilly campus climate. *Women's Studies International Forum, 18*, 637–646.

Oyserman, D., Brickman, D., Bybee, D., & Celious, A. (2006). Fitting in matters: Markers of in-group belonging and academic outcomes. *Psychological Science, 17*, 854.

Peterson, S. (2009). Career decision-making self-efficacy, integration, and the likelihood of managerial retention in governmental agencies. *Human Resource Development Quarterly, 20*, 451–475.

Plaut, V. C., Thomas, K. M., & Goren, M. J. (2009). Is multiculturalism or color blindness better for minorities? *Psychological Science, 20*, 444–446.

Purdie-Vaughns, V., Steele, C. M., Davies, P. G., Ditlmann, R., & Crosby, J. R. (2008). Social identity contingencies: How diversity cues signal threat or safety for African Americans in mainstream institutions. *Journal of Personality and Social Psychology, 94,* 615–630.

Ragins, B. (1989). Barriers to mentoring: the female manager's dilemma. *Human Relations, 42,* 1–22.

Rhebergen, B., & Wognum, I. (1997) Supporting the career development of older employees: an HRD study in a Dutch company. *International Journal of Training and Development, 3,* 191–198.

Rommes, E., Overbeek, G., Scholte, R., Engels, R., & De Kemp, R. (2007). "I'm not interested in computers": gender-based occupational choices of adolescents. *Information, Communication and Society, 10,* 299–319.

Rosser, S. V. (2008). *The science glass ceiling: Academic women scientists and their struggle to succeed.* Presentation made at Building Diversity in Higher Education, Charleston, WV.

Schmader, T., Johns, M., & Forbes, C. (2008). An integrated process model of stereotype threat effects on performance. *Psychological Review, 115,* 336–356.

Schmader, T., Major, B., & Gramzow, R. H. (2001). Coping with ethnic stereotypes in the academic domain: Perceived injustice and psychological disengagement. *Journal of Social Issues, 57,* 93–111.

Schott, G., & Selwyn, N. (2000). Examining the "male, antisocial" stereotype of high computer users. *Journal of Educational Computing Research, 23,* 291–303.

Sekaquaptewa, D., & Thompson, M. (2003). Solo status, stereotype threat, and performance expectancies: Their effects on women's performance. *Journal of Experimental Social Psychology, 39,* 68–74.

Sewell, W., & R. Hauser. (1975). *Education, occupation and earnings.* New York: Academic Press.

Shapiro, J. R., & Neuberg, S. L. (2007). From stereotype threat to stereotype threats: Implications of a multi-threat framework for causes, moderators, mediators, consequences, and interventions. *Personality and Social Psychology Review, 11,* 107.

Sheu, H., Lent, R. W., Brown, S. D., Miller, M. J., Hennessey, K. D., & Duffy, R. D. (2010). Testing the choice model of social cognitive career theory across Holland themes: A meta-analytic path analysis. *Journal of Vocational Behavior, 7,* 252–264.

Spencer, S. J., Steele, C. M., & Quinn, D. M. (1999). Stereotype threat and women's math performance. *Journal of Experimental Social Psychology, 35,* 4–28.

Spender, D. (1982), *Invisible women: the schooling scandal.* London: Writers and Readers Publishing Cooperative.

Steele, C. M. (1997). A threat in the air: How stereotypes shape intellectual identity and performance. *American Psychologist, 52,* 613–629.

Steele, C. M., & Aronson, J. (1995). Stereotype threat and the intellectual test performance of African Americans. *Journal of Personality and Social Psychology, 69,* 797–811.

Super, D. E. (1990). A life-span, life-space approach to career development. In D. Brown, L. Brooks, & Associates (Eds.), *Career choice and development* (2nd ed., pp. 197–261). San Francisco: Jossey-Bass.

Tangri, S. S., & Jenkins, S. R. (1986). Stability and change in role-innovation and life plans. *Sex Roles, 14,* 647–662.

Thomas, D. A. (1989). Mentoring and irrationality: The role of racial taboos. *Human Resource Management, 28,* 279–290.

Thomas, K. M. (2005). *Diversity dynamics in the workplace.* Belmont, CA: Thomson-Wadsworth.

Thomas, K. M., Johnson-Bailey, J., Phelps, R. E., Tran, N. M., & Johnson, L. (2012). Moving from pet to threat: narratives of professional Black women. In L. Comas-Diaz & B. Green (Eds.), *The psychological health of women of color.*

Thomas, K. M., Willis, L. A., & Davis, J. L. (2007). Mentoring minority graduate students: Issues and strategies for institutions, faculty, and students. *Equal Opportunities International, 26*(3), 178–192.

Thomas, K. M., & Wise, P. G. (1999). Organizational attractiveness and individual differences: Are diverse applicants attracted to different factors? *Journal of Business and Psychology, 13,* 375–390.

Tomlinson, S. M., & Evans-Hughes, G. (1991). Gender, ethnicity and college *students'* responses to the Strong-Campbell Interest Inventory. *Journal of Counseling & Development, 70*(1), 151–155.

Tran, N. M., & Harrington, M. (2009). *Cross-generational employee mentoring: A set of guidelines.* American Institute for Managing Diversity, Inc. Atlanta, GA.

Turner, J. C., Hogg, M. A., Oakes, P. J., Reicher, S. D., & Wetherell, M. S. (1987). *Rediscovering the social group: A self-categorization theory.* Cambridge: Basil Blackwell.

Underhill, C. M. (2005). The effectiveness of mentoring programs in corporate settings: A meta-analytical review of the literature. *Journal of Vocational Behavior, 68,* 292–307.

Valian, V. (1999). The cognitive bases of gender bias. *Brooklyn Law Review, 65,* 1037–1061.

Walton, G., & Cohen, G. (2007). A question of belonging: Race, social fit, and achievement. *Journal of Personality and Social Psychology, 92,* 82–96.

Wang, M. C., Haertel, G. D., & Walberg, H. J. (1994). What helps students learn? *Educational Leadership, 51,* 74–79.

Williams, C. L. (1992). The glass escalator: hidden advantages for men in the "female" professions. *Social Problems, 39,* 253–267.

CHAPTER
18

Leadership in a Diverse Workplace

Donna Chrobot-Mason, Marian N. Ruderman *and* Lisa H. Nishii

Abstract

Although there is a significant need to understand the implications of increasing demographic diversity for leadership, surprisingly little research has been conducted on the topic. In this chapter, we review the extant research in this area. We organize our review into three sections: how leaders lead themselves, others, and the organization. In the first section, we discuss issues related to social identity, and how leaders' social identities interact with those of their employees in influencing what may be required for effective leadership. In the second section, we discuss the qualities that leaders are likely to need when managing employees from diverse backgrounds. We focus on developing quality relationships, cultivating an inclusive climate, spanning boundaries, and framing of diversity initiatives. In the last section, we discuss research related to the role leaders play in setting their organization's diversity strategy, implementing diversity practices, managing conflict, responding to diversity crises, and measuring progress. We end with suggestions for future research.

Key Words: leader, diversity, inclusion, identity, affirming climate

Introduction

Traditionally, organizational leaders have worked with people who looked like them, shared the same culture, and worked in the same geographic location. Today's organizational leaders find themselves working across a vastly different landscape; workforces characterized by extreme homogeneity are an artifact of the past. With changing social customs and the growth of the Internet and its ability to reach all over the globe, the modern environment is asking people of all skin colors, backgrounds, and values to work together in organizations. A challenge to the current reality is that while technology has brought us together, humans still operate with the same stereotypes and mindsets that have torn groups apart throughout history. Thus, contemporary leadership requires the creation of direction, alignment, and commitment across workers who look, speak, and act differently (Drath, McCauley, Palus, Van Velsor, O'Connor, & McGuire, 2008; McCauley, Van Velsor, & Ruderman, 2010). Leaders in this current environment must engage and manage relationships across diverse coworkers, customers, and suppliers from around the globe. In short, to be successful, today's leader must encourage cooperation across a vast expanse of geographic, demographic, and functional boundaries (Ernst & Chrobot-Mason, 2011).

In this chapter, we examine the interface of existing research and theory on leadership with the literature on diversity in the workplace. Although the practical need for understanding the intersection of leadership and diversity is growing every day, this is a topic that hasn't received a great deal of attention from either leadership scholars or diversity scholars. Most discussions of leadership do not involve the heterogeneity of the workforce, and most discussions of diversity overlook the leadership capabilities needed to produce direction, alignment, and commitment in organizations responding to today's dynamic external environment. The two literatures have largely developed independently, with few attempts to bring them together.

In the future, we expect to see much more attention given to the interaction of diversity and leadership, reflecting both the rapidly changing demographics of the workforce (Eagly & Chin, 2010) and evolving leadership practices. Projections for the year 2018 suggest that the U.S. workforce will be undergoing significant change (Toosi, 2009). The United States is anticipating a large increase in the number of immigrants, and differential fertility rates will compound the rapid diversification of the working population.

At the same time that the workforce is shifting, so is the nature of leadership. People in leadership roles are faced with a highly complicated context. Revolutionary technological changes combined with economic challenges and a trend toward strategic alliances has changed the processes, boundaries, and structures of organizations. Delayering, downsizing, and outsourcing are common practices. Traditional bureaucratic organizations haven't completely gone away but have merged with newer, more flexible styles of organizations that allow for greater participation (Graetz & Smith, 2009). According to Ashkenas, Ulrich, Jick, and Kerr (2002), such changes in processes, boundaries, and structure have called for a new set of leadership capabilities that emphasize shared leadership across people and the ability to "connect" people who are very different from one another and separated by geography or culture. In an era of rapid change and expectations for greater employee participation, leaders must be able to remove the barriers that can inhibit innovation and power sharing within diverse groups. Indeed, with more and more organizations relying on diversity to generate the innovation that is required for survival, understanding and expanding upon the intersection of the diversity and leadership literatures is more important than ever.

Crossan, Vera, and Nanjad (2008) offer a cross-level framework for understanding leadership that is particularly useful for highlighting the many places where it is imperative to understand the intersection of diversity and leadership. They argue that in dynamic contexts, such as the 21st century, it is important that leadership requirements be understood in terms of both the micro and macro leadership elements. In addition to looking at leadership in terms of the interpersonal influence of a leader on a team, they incorporate two other levels of leadership—leadership of the self and leadership of the organization. This tri-level model offers a useful lens for examining leadership amid the growing diversity of the workforce because it acknowledges the differential impact of the dynamics of diversity on the individual (self), group, and organization. Leaders today must have the capacity to lead at all levels and understand the relationships between them. Transcendent leadership refers to the ability to lead at all three levels (Crossan et al., 2008).

At the level of self-management, we summarize what the literature tells us about how leaders manage their own identity, influence, and effectiveness as either a nontraditional, nondominant leader or a more traditional, dominant leader with greater privilege and power. We examine the role of identity in shaping both leaders and organizational members and some of the diversity-related barriers that have been found to exist. We also explore the literature on leader development and the skill set needed to lead effectively in today's diverse workplace.

Next, we examine the role of leaders in managing relationships with others in a diverse workplace. There is literature that suggests leaders play a critical role in leading across differences that exist both within and between organizational groups. To be able to integrate the perspectives of diverse others, leaders need to develop the capability to build effective relationships and workgroups, and to develop others. In relation to leading the organization, we explore how leading a diverse organization requires different strategies, organizational policies, and practices to leverage these differences and take full advantage of the potential that diversity may bring.

At all three levels, leaders are often the key lever in determining whether diversity becomes an organizational liability fraught with miscommunication, distrust, and conflict, or an organizational asset fueled by greater capacity for innovation and creativity. In reviewing current leadership theories about building and maintaining relationships in a diverse work context, we illustrate three key points.

First, research and theory examining leadership in the context of diversity, or at the intersection of diversity and leadership, remains sparse. In 1996, a two-part special issue on diversity leadership was published in *Leadership Quarterly*. At that time DiTomaso and Hooijberg (1996) argued that leaders within the diversity literature were conceived of "more as the targets of influence rather than as agents of influence" (p. 165). In other words, diversity literature at that time focused more on attempting to convince leaders that they should support diversity initiatives rather than focusing on how to accomplish this. As our review highlights, this stance has evolved and scholars are focusing more on how leaders can leverage differences rather than whether they should or should not support diversity. A recent special issue in the *American Psychologist* on diversity and leadership clarifies the importance of re-examining existing leadership theory and practice to incorporate issues of equity, diversity, social justice, and inclusion (Chin, 2010). Taken together, even though this literature remains sparse, we believe there is a growing recognition that these two topics are closely linked in the contemporary workplace and that additional research and theory in this area will emerge.

The second key point we will illustrate is that we believe leadership itself is evolving and changing both because of, and in response to, diversity. A heterogeneous workforce demands a different style of leadership and leaders must respond accordingly. Leadership in a diverse context must be more relational in nature than in the past (Chen & Van Velsor, 1996). As we explain below, both leadership theory and practice are evolving in such a way that emphasizes the development of quality relationships, consensual influence, and leadership as a socially constructed process.

The third key point we make throughout the chapter is that leadership plays a much more important role in the success or failure of a diverse workforce and diversity initiatives than previous research would suggest. There is a growing recognition in the literature that organizations can leverage differences to become a competitive advantage rather than a liability.

What is effective leadership?

Most research on leadership has addressed the question: what is effective leadership? Traditionally, leadership was thought of as a position in a hierarchical organization held by a manager or supervisor with set responsibilities, authorities, and spans of influence. For many years, the field responded to the question of effective leadership by looking at the characteristics of a leader either naturally in bureaucracies or more systematically in laboratories. According to McCauley (2010), answers took the form of personal attributes (e.g., personality and intelligence), roles and behaviors used by leaders (e.g., Mintzberg's [1973] ten management roles), competencies distinguishing the very best leaders from others (e.g., Boyatzis, 1982), expertise (e.g., tacit knowledge), and mastery of challenging experiences (McCall, 2010). Looking across many definitions of leadership, McCauley (2010) points out that those traditional approaches to leadership have three common elements: (1) they focus on influence as the key leadership process, (2) they examine the characteristics of individual leaders, and (3) they acknowledge that context matters. These models tend to emphasize the relationship between an organizational leader and his or her followers. McCauley also notes that these traditional models have common pitfalls, which have recently called them into question. These pitfalls include (1) an overemphasis on the individual at the expense of organizational processes, (2) confusing positional authority with influence, (3) expecting a single individual to have all the necessary capabilities, and (4) ignoring the particular demands of different situations, such as the heterogeneity of the workforce. Although there is evidence for all these different theories, they typically don't explain much variance in effectiveness, and there has been a realization that leadership as a force does not reside within single individuals in positions of authority.

More recently there has been a trend away from this positional approach to leadership with its emphasis on leader characteristics to a more modern approach that argues that leadership is a shared phenomenon constructed across people (DeRue & Ashford, 2010; Pearce & Conger, 2003). The concept of shared leadership means that there is a social process of group interaction and the development of a shared understanding of the goals and vision of the organization. As such, leadership requires social interactions that allow for the accomplishment of the work of a collective. Leadership is of the organization and not of individuals (Boal & Hooijberg, 2000). At a fundamental level, leadership can be understood as the social process for generating the direction, alignment, and commitment needed by a group to accomplish collective goals (Drath et al., 2008; McCauley et al., 2010). It has to do with leadership functions that encompass the actions of many people, processes, structures, and practices. Leadership also doesn't have to occur within the confines of a formal hierarchy; it can happen anywhere and anytime and is not limited to a particular setting. Over the years, the field has evolved from a focus on the individual to a focus on the actions of a collective. Leadership is now thought of as a relational property rather than as an individual ability. The field now looks at leadership embodied across people rather than a function located in a single individual with authority granted by a bureaucracy to direct a particular group.

It is the socially constructed nature of leadership that makes diversity an important consideration for both today and the future (Chen & Van Velsor, 1996). Leadership is in essence a consensual process endorsed by members of an organization where individuals mutually agree on who will be seen as having an identity as a leader (DeRue &Ashford, 2010). Even if an individual claims to be a leader, it is not so unless others reciprocate by granting or affirming a leader identity on the individual. Within the context of diversity, this framing of a leader identity is strongly affected by the attitudes and expectations associated with different social identities. This view of leadership as a socially constructed process influences how individuals manage themselves, how they operate when working with others, and how they lead in an organization.

Several different approaches to leadership focus on its shared or connected nature; these theories point to the importance of understanding the intersection of leadership and diversity. Social identity theory (see Chapter 5) helps to explain the importance of diversity at the self-management level by exploring how an identity as a leader is internalized. By explaining the dynamics of stereotyping and prejudice, social identity theory also has implications for leading others so that a group functions effectively. In addition, at the level of leading others, approaches such as leader–member exchange (LMX) theory, social identity conflict resolution, and boundary-spanning behaviors are also quite relevant to understanding how relationships can be best managed within the context of diversity. At the level of the organization, approaches that look at human resources practices, human capital strategies, and organizational learning have important implications for leadership in the context of diversity.

Leading self

Leadership of the self is one of the emerging areas of attention in the leadership literature. As mentioned above, traditional approaches looked at how demographic, behavioral, and background characteristics affect others. The shift to more contemporary approaches suggests that leaders need to understand the self in the context of a shared leadership environment where many are contributing to adaptive change. It requires being able to be aware of oneself amid growing diversity in the workplace.

Theoretical foundations
SELF-PERCEPTION

Leading oneself has to do with the internalization of an identity as a leader. There is a process through which individuals learn to think of themselves as a leader and look to claim leadership responsibilities. Social identity approaches to leadership offer a foundation for understanding what it means to lead oneself in the context of diversity and to internalize a leader identity.

Everyone has both a social identity and a personal identity. An individual's social identity involves group memberships such as nationality, race, gender, language, religion, generation, sexual orientation, and the like. Tajfel and Turner's (1979, 1986) theory of social identity and the associated self-categorization theory (Turner, 1982, 1985, 2004) suggest that these memberships are fundamental to the self, providing both a sense of belonging and a sense of distinctiveness. This distinctiveness means that people distinguish between people like them and people unlike them. Building upon this earlier theory, Hogg and his colleagues put forth a social identity theory of leadership (Hogg, 2001; Hogg & van Knippenberg, 2003; Hogg, Martin, Epitropaki, Mankad, Svensson, & Weeden, 2005) that emphasizes that social identity is important for understanding who will be accepted and perceived as a leader. In particular, research has established that various features of social identity such as gender, culture, and race influence others' acceptance of leadership behaviors, which is fundamental to developing an identity as someone who leads (Ayman, 1993; Eagly & Karau, 2002; Sy, Shore, Strauss, Shore, Tram, Whitely, & Ikeda-Muromachi, 2010; van Knippenberg, van Knippenberg, De Cremer, & Hogg, 2004).

Lord and Hall (2005) further suggest that the development of a leader identity requires the integration of one's social identities with one's professional and personal identities. In other words, leaders must understand themselves in terms of their organizational role, social identity, and personal traits. This idea of self-awareness is much broader than the traditional understanding of self-awareness as a function of personality and behaviors. Awareness of social identity suggests that leaders must understand how others react to them and be sensitive to the impact of the social identity of others. From a social identity point of view, leader development is a maturation process merging self and social knowledge with identification as a leader. For example, all three authors of this chapter have had to integrate their identities as leaders of research teams with their own sense of themselves as women and understand how gender may influence how others see and respond to them as leaders. As we have matured, our understanding of leadership has blended with what it means to be female in today's society. As maturity increases, it is easier to integrate different aspects of self. And, as a leader gains more experience, the leader identity grows more central to self-concept.

OTHERS' PERCEPTIONS

Developing as a leader requires claiming a leader identity, but this is only part of the process: as stated earlier, leadership roles must also be granted by others (DeRue & Ashford, 2010). A socially constructed view of leadership emphasizes that it is important to look at the processes by which people are recognized, accepted, and endorsed as leaders. Over the years, there has been substantial evidence that members of nondominant groups face identity-related obstacles in being granted an identity as a leader. There is a rich literature as to how prejudice seeps into the process of recognizing someone as a leader. For example, there have been volumes written about the scarcity of women in top leadership roles as a result of discrimination and bias resulting from the incompatibility of a feminine stereotype with the schemata of a leader. Starting with the work of Virginia Schein (1973, 1975), the "think manager, think male" phenomenon has been identified. Basically, this long line of research points to the fact that the dominant prototype of a leader is male, making it more difficult for perceivers to recognize women as leaders, as they simply do not fit one's schema of a leader. This tendency is robust; it has been documented repeatedly and in multiple countries (Schein, Mueller, Lituchy, & Liu, 1996). More recently, Eagly and Chin (2010) used meta-analytic techniques to account for the underrepresentation of women in the workforce as being the result of such discriminatory barriers (Eagly & Chin, 2010). Eagly and Karau (2002) reiterate that prejudice toward women is a function of the mismatch between femininity and expectations for prototypical leaders.

This subtle bias resulting from schema incongruity has received several different names by both scholars and the press over the years. Early on it was called a glass ceiling, or an invisible level above which women cannot rise due to discrimination. More recently, Eagly and Carli (2007) termed it a labyrinth to indicate that there are abrupt stops and turns throughout a woman's journey to the top. Ryan and Haslam (2005) have also identified the glass cliff—the appointment of women to precarious or no-win situations in which a single mishap can send them plummeting from the possibility of successful leadership. We don't mean to imply that these metaphors are all the same; however, they all make the point that discrimination—and not a lack of skills or abilities—is what holds women back. Regardless of the metaphor, the point is that a dominant masculine prototype blocks the recognition of women as leaders, hindering the route to the top.

Moreover, women are only one part of the population affected by these leader-recognition processes. Eagly and Chin (2010) point out that incongruent stereotypes have also created disadvantages for gay men (Madon, 1997), African-Americans (Bell & Nkomo, 2001; Livers & Caver, 2003), and Asian-Americans. Livers and Caver refer to the barrier facing African-American men and women as miasma, or a general fog that blurs their recognition in leadership positions and makes the path to the top more hazardous and circuitous. The point is that the process of claiming and being granted a leadership identity is much tougher for someone who is not of the dominant leader prototype. The dominant leader prototype may vary from society to society, but the ease of a person matching the dominant prototype claiming leadership is a constant. All else being equal, a candidate prototypical of the dominant group appears more qualified to others, regardless of the social identity of the perceiver (i.e., even among women, men appear to be more qualified as leaders than their female counterparts).

Prototypes of leaders are embedded in social systems in organizations and closely tied to power dynamics, with some social identity groups in a society having greater access to resources, status, and privileges than others. Research has pointed out that power differentials are intimately tied to how leadership is claimed and granted, with leadership experiences unfolding differently for people in different contexts (Oshry, 2010). In his discussion of the impact of power differentials on behavior, Oshry (2010) points out that people are often blind to the value of status in organizations—both those characterizing their own group and the characteristics of others. People know differences exist, but they are blind to the impact of these status differences. Applying a social identity lens to Oshry's work means that people are often blind to the impact of social identity in the context of leadership. This blindness occurs in two different ways: blindness to the context of others and blindness to one's own context.

When people are blind to the social identity of others, there is greater likelihood of misunderstanding and behaving in ways that undermine organizational effectiveness. Not understanding the impact of social hierarchies can make it difficult to provide coaching and mentoring. For example, the prototypical white male boss may not understand the frustration experienced by a female direct report who feels that she isn't granted the same opportunities as the men or may not be as readily accepted as a leader. And the White woman may not understand the difficulty her Asian colleague has in being seen as a leader rather than as an engineer. Despite accumulated research evidence about the deleterious effects of biases in leader categorization (Eagly & Karau, 2002; Ensari & Murphy, 2003; Rosette, Leondardelli, & Phillips, 2008; Schein, 1973; Sy et al., 2010), these dynamics are not always "seen" by members of dominant social identity groups. Rosette and colleagues (2008) point out that in the United States, members of dominant social identity groups give so much weight to individual skills, efforts, and abilities in workplace judgments that they are blind to social identity categories such as race. This can result in interactions that are characterized by attribution biases and misunderstandings.

The other type of blindness is to the impact of one's own identity. Ignorance to the impact of social identity can result in a response that is insensitive to the lack of privileges accorded by society to non-dominant groups. In her pioneering work on the "invisible knapsack of privilege," Peggy McIntosh (2007) argued that although individuals of dominant social identity groups might be able to recognize that others are disadvantaged, it is rare for them to recognize that they might be advantaged by their position of privilege. For example, someone from the dominant group may not be aware of the privileges they have had over the years and may be reluctant to create opportunities for others, attributing their own career progress solely to their own efforts rather than to a combination of effort and social identity-based privileges. Or someone from the dominant group may not be aware that colleagues view him or her as part of the privileged class and not know how to react when associated feelings come into play.

Strategies for enhancing leadership of self

A significant implication of a social identity approach to leadership is that it is important to understand social identity and recognize its impact. Effective management of oneself in a diverse environment requires self-awareness about social identity (Ferdman, 2008)—about how you see yourself and others, and how others perceive your social identity. Wasserman, Gallegos, and Ferdman (2008) point out that leaders have a responsibility to model the ways in which social identity blindness in themselves, and within organizations more generally, can be addressed. Pretending that organizations are gender, racially, or culturally neutral when they are not limits the effectiveness of leaders to be inclusive (Ayman & Korabik, 2010). As Brewer's well-known optimal distinctiveness theory (1991) has illustrated, people have a dual need for the validation of their uniqueness as well as their belongingness to groups that comprise individuals to whom they feel similar in some way. Indeed, a recent review of inclusion research (Shore, Randel, Chung, Dean, Ehrhart, & Singh, 2011) suggests that achieving both belongingness and uniqueness is key to experiences of inclusion. Thus, the failure of a leader to recognize the gender, racial, or cultural background of an employee potentially limits the employee's felt inclusion. Even if the employee feels a sense of belonging, if his or her unique identity is not acknowledged and accepted, the employee is forced to assimilate to the dominant social identity rather than be truly integrated or included. In situations characterized by heterogeneity it is important to assume that people may have different evaluations of the same experience; although a self-proclaimed leader may perceive assimilation among demographically different employees to be functional, the employees themselves may view their lack of felt belonging as the leader's responsibility, thereby limiting their acceptance of the individual as a leader.

Ferdman (2008) and Hannum (2007) offer similar methodologies for learning about identity, both one's own and that of others. Their approaches offer the opportunity for leaders to explore how much of their own identity comes from group membership and to appreciate the diversity within groups. They ask leaders to identify their own (multiple) sources of identity and to share them with others. It is followed by a large-group discussion about understanding the role of identities in interpersonal interactions (Ferdman, 2008). These self-awareness methods help people learn how much diversity there is in identity and the impact of identity on one's perceptions of others and in others' perceptions of oneself. Through this exercise, people consider which of their identities might be the most and least obvious to others at work. The assumption is that by being clear about their own identities and their importance, individuals can more easily avoid confusing their own lenses, feelings, and goals with projections from others. People are also able to see that when certain identities are relatively unimportant to them, they may overlook them in others; likewise, when certain identities are important to them, they may erroneously assume that those identities are important to and recognized by other people. The beauty of this exercise is that is unearths not just the differences across people's identities, but also the overlapping sources of identity among people who had previously assumed themselves to be different.

The identity awareness exercise described by both Ferdman (2008) and Hannum (2007) is useful because it helps people to become more aware of identity perception processes that otherwise often remain implicit. Extending this notion to perceptions of leadership, Rosette and colleagues (2008) suggest that people should be made aware of the cognitive biases that may lead them to favor people who match the prevailing leader prototype in terms of social identity. Although such awareness may not "correct" the bias, it can at least lead to a better understanding of the impact of social identity on perceptions of leadership. This is one way to address the issue of "blindness" to social identity, particularly on the part of the employees being led.

Leading self: Future research

Based on both research and theory highlighted in this section on leading the self, we offer the following research questions for consideration in future research:

- What is the process through which leaders evolve from a mindset in which they view a situation from their own identity and worldview to one in which they are able to view a situation from multiple views and lenses? Although Robert Kegan's work on adult development theory (1982, 1994) provides a framework for this, we still do not know much about what this process involves and, more importantly, how to incorporate this development into current leadership training and development activities.

- How can leaders overcome identity blindness? Throughout this chapter, we have illustrated how powerful issues of identity are in a diverse workplace. Effective leadership requires understanding one's own identity as well as the identity of others. While it seems clear that this involves recognition of privilege and social marking (Thomas & Chrobot-Mason, 2005), it is not clear what forms of training and development may be beneficial for helping leaders to overcome their blind spots. Growing research using the Implicit Association Test (e.g., Hofmann, Gawronski, Gschwendner, Le, & Schmitt, 2005) suggests that this may be a useful tool for helping individuals to recognize their implicit biases associated with social identity; however, less is known about the specific training interventions, incentives, and contextual cues that might help leaders to consciously overcome their biases and blind spots.

In the next section, we turn to looking at the literature discussing the impact of diversity on the act of leading others.

Leading others

In essence, the act of leadership is about guiding and influencing the behavior of others. Indeed, most leadership theory and research has to date focused on leading others. In the cross-level framework of Crossan, Vera, and Nanjad (2008), this level emphasizes the interpersonal influence of leaders. Leaders within organizations are responsible for setting goals and coordinating and managing the work of others to achieve these goals. However, the ability to influence and coordinate the work of others becomes more complex and more challenging within a diverse workplace. When the workgroup consists of diverse employees, collaboration and integrated efforts toward a common united vision are made more difficult because the leader and the other members of the workgroup often represent different social identity groups. Thus, the leader and those he or she is leading likely hold different perspectives, values, priorities, and opinions, perhaps speak different languages, and live in different parts of the world, and may hold very different positions and type of expertise within the organization. Until recently, leadership theory and research failed to address such complexities and assumed that workgroups were homogeneous and that leaders could fairly easily influence and exert power over employees. It is only recently that scholars have begun to acknowledge and study leadership within the context of diversity.

Theoretical foundations

In this section, we highlight two theories that have been examined in the literature from the lens of both leadership and diversity. Social identity and LMX theory have been used as a theoretical foundation to examine the relational and influence processes involved in leading diverse others.

SOCIAL IDENTITY THEORY OF LEADERSHIP

Although the social identity theory of leadership was described in the previous section as it applies to leading oneself and being aware of one's own identity, it is also important to consider the theory as a foundation for understanding how to effectively lead and influence others in the context of diversity. According to Hogg (2001; Hogg & van Knippenberg, 2003), groups more readily grant leadership to someone who is prototypical or representative of the group, and leaders have influence over others to the extent they embody the norms and prototype of the group. He describes how three social processes operate in conjunction to determine the level of influence and power a leader develops with respect to others.

The first process Hogg describes is prototypicality. Individuals who are perceived by others to occupy the most prototypical position of the group best embody the behaviors to which others conform. In other words, leaders emerge as having influence and power within a group because they best embody the values, beliefs, vision, etc., of the group as a whole. Also, the more prototypical a leader is, the more likely it is that he or she will be perceived as effective.

The second process involves social attraction. When leaders are well liked and fit with the prototype of the group, others are more likely to accept their ideas and direction.

Hogg suggests that the third process is attribution and information processing. When leaders are highly prototypical and socially attractive within a group, others are more likely to attribute their behavior to intrinsic leadership ability or charisma. Such leaders and their suggestions are intrinsically persuasive because they embody the norms of the group.

These three social processes combine to create a *cycle of influence*: when leaders embody the norms and prototype of the group, they are endorsed as leaders; their endorsement results in greater power to influence (Hogg, 2001).

The social identity theory of leadership suggests that leader influence and the ability to exert power are largely based on identity and the extent to which the leader embodies the group prototype. However, all three of the social processes described by Hogg are complicated when leaders and workgroup members are diverse and represent nontraditional or nondominant identities. In fact, Hogg (2001) suggests that one implication is that social minorities may find it more difficult to influence others because they fail to embody the group prototype. Typically, the social identity characteristics of the dominant group in society determine who is recognized as a potential leader. Leader recognition processes also work in reverse: those in top positions in the organization are thought to be characteristic of the organization, or exemplars of the organization. The more representative the person in a top hierarchical role is of the organization at large, the more likely others will identify with this leader and respond positively to leadership attempts. The less representative the person in a top organizational role, the more challenges the leader will face in influencing others. Another consideration is that as leaders and work teams become more diverse and the workplace itself becomes less homogeneous, the range of potential leaders who could embody group norms may actually increase. Thus, while social minorities may be at a disadvantage in assuming leadership roles when they fail to fit the group prototype, we are hopeful that this disadvantage will begin to disappear as the workplace becomes increasingly diverse and people become more aware of and sensitive to identity differences.

Viewing leadership through the lens of social identity suggests that leaders of diverse groups must be aware of their own identity as well as those around them to continually reshape and redefine the group prototype or, as Reicher and Hopkins (1996) suggest, become "entrepreneurs of identity." The important lesson here is that leaders who discover intersectionalities of identity, or identity similarities that cut across simple demographic boundaries (e.g., those defined by race and gender), are more likely to be effective, as the group prototype becomes less simplistic and more likely to capture the multiple identities represented in the group. Another benefit of highlighting cross-cutting identities is that doing so can help to reduce the salience of the demographic categories within the group that might mirror those that are socio-historically associated with status differences, since these are the ones that can drive negative intragroup dynamics unless actively counteracted (Ridgeway, 1991; Ridgeway & Correll, 2006).

In addition to blurring the distinctions across simple demographic boundaries by highlighting intersectionalities, leaders will also be more effective in leading diverse groups to the extent that their behavior and the norms that they establish delegitimize beliefs that exist in the broader society about the status differences between demographic groups (e.g., men are perceived to have higher status then women, Whites have higher status than non-Whites, etc.). As we describe more below, when leaders develop high-quality relationships with individuals of all backgrounds, they help to eliminate the potential salience of socio-historical status differences, thereby reducing stereotyping and biases related to cultural identities.

We now turn our attention to the LMX theory as it emphasizes the development of high-quality relationships and provides a strong theoretical foundation for understanding leading others in a diverse work environment.

LEADER–MEMBER EXCHANGE THEORY

LMX theory suggests that both leaders and their direct reports play a role in the quality of the relationship between each superior–subordinate dyad (Graen & Uhl-Bien, 1995). When the relationship is characterized by high levels of trust, interaction, and support (i.e., a "high-quality exchange"), the subordinates in those relationships enjoy positive work outcomes such as higher performance and lower turnover (Gerstner & Day, 1997). According to Graen and Uhl-Bien (1995), earlier LMX researchers suggested that due to limited time and social resources, workgroups would be best served by managers who focused their attention on the most promising of subordinates, whereas more recently researchers have recommended that managers offer all employees access to high-quality LMX relationships by extending an initial offer to develop LMX partnerships with each of them. The expectation was that by doing so, the LMX process would be perceived more equitably by employees, and would also expand the capability of the organization by developing the potential of more employees. Consistent with this, there is now growing empirical evidence to support the notion that when leaders develop quality relationships with each employee, they are more likely to foster high-quality relationships among their workgroup employees, as manifested in group cohesion, cooperation, and retention (e.g., Ford & Seers, 2006; Liden, Erdogan, Wayne, & Sparrowe, 2006; McClane, 1991; Schyns, Paul, Mohr, & Blank, 2005).

However, there is also evidence to suggest that leaders are more likely to develop high-quality relationships with those who are similar and belong to the same social identity group than with those who belong to another social identity group (Scandura & Lankau, 1996), and that such in-group bias has negative consequences. Scandura and Lankau (1996) describe the tentative nature of the development of a relationship involving cross-race and cross-gender leader–member dyads. Although the demonstration of mutual respect and development of trust are critical to the formation of a high-quality LMX relationship, identity differences often make this more difficult, as each member may have a different definition of respect and how it should be demonstrated. If mutual respect is demonstrated, then the next phase in development of the LMX relationship centers around trust. Again, the development of trust is more difficult in diverse dyads because even one violation of trust may destroy the relationship and reinforce negative stereotypes and expectations of discriminatory practices. For this reason, leaders must have a heightened sensitivity to the development of trust when leading diverse employees. Scandura and Lankau (1996) suggest this should be viewed as a fragile process "until norms emerge upon which both members can base expectations of the response and behaviors of the others" (p. 249).

Strategies for enhancing leadership

As research and theory on LMX suggests, successful leadership of diverse others requires a new set of skills and practices that were not required of leaders when the workplace was homogeneous. Contemporary leaders must create a cohesive team identity despite the fact that workgroup members vary greatly in their demographic, geographic, and professional identities. They also find themselves in the precarious position of attempting to bridge differences when they themselves may belong to a group that differs from the identity of at least some of their colleagues. Being different themselves can exacerbate the difficulty leaders face in attempting to create a cohesive group identity, as research shows that when leaders are a member of the out-group, this has a negative impact on workgroup member satisfaction, identification with the organization, and trust and support of leaders (Duck & Fielding, 1999, 2003). Thus, to be effective, leaders in a diverse workplace must first develop a different mindset that includes greater recognition of their own identity as well as the identity of others to understand the differences that exist within their team (as discussed in the previous section), and then develop a set of skills that facilitates the unification of a diverse group of individuals. This skill set needed to lead a diverse workforce may be considered under two broad areas: (1) individualized behaviors or strategies to enhance interactions with individual employees, which include transformational, relational, and inclusive leadership behaviors, and (2) intergroup behaviors or strategies focused on facilitating collaboration across diverse groups, which include creating shared goals, resolving conflict, and fostering collaboration through boundary-spanning leadership. We discuss strategies for leadership development in both areas in the following subsections.

INDIVIDUALIZED STRATEGIES

As described above, research on LMX has clearly shown that employees who enjoy high-quality relationships with their leader benefit from numerous positive outcomes (Gerstner & Day, 1997). Research on **transformational leadership** adds to our understanding of effective leadership by specifying the leader behaviors that help leaders to establish an emotional bond with workgroup members and motivate them to align with the leader's vision (Dvir, Kass, & Shamir, 2004). These behaviors differ significantly from transactional leadership behaviors. While transactional leaders are characterized as engaging in rational social exchange with others, transformational leaders provide inspirational motivation and intellectual stimulation and show individualized consideration (Bass, 1990; Bass & Avolio, 1994). Recent research suggests that transformational leadership behaviors may be critical for leveraging positive group outcomes like team identity and performance in diverse groups (Kearney & Gebert, 2009; Mitchell & Boyle, 2009). There are two reasons for this. First, transformational leadership behaviors enhance unity and a sense of commitment to the collective. Second, transformational leadership behavior seems to unleash the potential benefits that diversity may bring to the workplace, such as higher-quality decision making and greater innovation and creativity (Cox, 1991; Milliken & Martins, 1996; Page, 2007).

For example, when leaders communicate a compelling vision for the team and express confidence in members (i.e., inspirational motivation), they increase trust and commitment among diverse team members (Joshi, Lazarova, & Liao, 2009). When leaders are inspirational, team members begin to trust that their group has the collective skills, expertise, and achievements necessary to accomplish the mission, and they also begin to appreciate their team's accomplishments, thereby building the basis for identification and commitment to the team. When leaders engage in individualized consideration by considering and valuing the unique needs and skills of each employee, they foster mutual respect (Scandura & Lankau, 1996), a sense of collective identity, and trust among group members. As such, Howell and Shamir (2005) suggest that "charismatic leader–employee relationships" result in workgroup members who are willing to transcend their own self-interests for the sake of the collective team or organization and are highly committed to its vision and goals. Perhaps a key mechanism in this process is that by treating others with individualized consideration, a leader is able to signal that employees are valued.

Realizing the benefits of diversity seems to also be closely linked to transformational leadership behaviors characterized as intellectual stimulation. In particular, when leaders explicitly encourage questioning and challenging of accepted ideas, research shows that alternative views are more likely to be expressed and considered in the final solution (Mitchell & Boyle, 2009). When leaders show appreciation for employees' contributions and encourage them to provide input, their behaviors promote inclusion (Nembhard & Edmondson, 2006). Kearney and Gebert (2009) found that transformational leadership behaviors that facilitated the elaboration of task-relevant information within the diverse team were positively related to team performance. Their work suggests that leaders may be a key lever in unlocking the greater potential that exists in diverse groups when they engage in behaviors that facilitate the sharing and processing of task-relevant information. In other words, transformational leadership behaviors may account for the difference between a diverse team whose interactions are characterized by miscommunication, distrust, and conflict from one whose interactions lead to the emergence of innovative and creative ideas and solutions that come from a diverse team with varied perspectives, backgrounds, areas of expertise, and the like.

The LMX theory described earlier illustrates the importance of **developing high-quality relationships** in the workplace and the challenge leaders face in attempting to do so within a diverse work context in which there is a natural bias to favor in-group members. In a recent study, Nishii and Mayer (2009) argued that the development of LMX relationships of differential quality is likely to be more harmful for group processes and outcomes in diverse than homogeneous groups. This is because members of diverse groups are naturally more susceptible to demographically induced status hierarchies, power struggles, and in-group–out-group conflicts, and any differential treatment of employees on the part of leaders has the potential to reinforce and perpetuate such status hierarchies. In contrast, leaders who develop high-quality relationships with all of their employees delegitimize socio-historical status hierarchies by treating employees similarly rather than privileging a select few. As such, they help to establish a level playing field that facilitates positive group processes and lowers group conflict, as evidenced in lower turnover rates. In support of this, they found that when leaders facilitate high levels of inclusion and power sharing within their diverse groups by developing consistently high-quality relationships with employees, they help to attenuate and even reverse the positive relationship that is often observed between group diversity and turnover. However, when leaders are inclusive of only a select few employees, they may exacerbate the relationship between diversity and turnover.

An important implication of this research is that if leaders develop high-quality relationships with only demographically similar others, they will likely pay in the form of higher turnover, which in turn can be detrimental for group performance (Staw, 1980). Thus, leaders should be educated not just about how they can effectively develop high-quality relationships with employees, but also to think about the influence that the overall pattern of LMX relationships across employees (i.e., mean and variance of LMX relationships) may have on the relationship between group diversity and outcomes.

Indeed, developing high-quality relationships in a diverse workplace requires something beyond traditional individual leadership. According to Wasserman and colleagues (2008), it requires **relational leadership** and a new set of skills that includes flexibility, self-awareness, and the capacity to be vulnerable. Good leadership embodies relational interactions that are characterized by mutuality and equality (Fletcher, 2010) as well as coordination and shared responsibility with others in service of organizational goals (see Brickson, 2000, and Fletcher, 2010, for a discussion of relational identity orientation). Furthermore, it requires that leaders progress from achieving cultural competence to developing relational eloquence. Relational eloquence is achieved by "continuously attending to how one is making sense of or coordinating meaning with another or others in the relationship" (Wasserman et al., p. 184).

Similar conclusions can be drawn from theoretical work by Shore and her colleagues (2011), who suggest that leaders need to promote inclusion in information sharing and decision making and provide employees with voice in order to enhance inclusion. These inclusive leadership behaviors characterize high, but not low, LMX relationships. In the next section, we elaborate on inclusive behaviors as an effective strategy for enhancing leadership within a diverse work context.

It is important that leaders operating within a context of difference engage in a set of behaviors that contribute to the creation of an **inclusive work climate** that is inclusive, characterized as being high in respect and trust, and one in which all employees can fully contribute (Nishii, 2010). Although the topic of inclusion and diversity climate is covered extensively in Chapter 13, we refer to it here as well as we examine specific strategies for enhancing leadership within a diverse context that are well supported by research and theory. For purposes of our discussion, we will use Holvino, Ferdman, and Merrill-Sands's (2004) definition of inclusion, which is "equality, justice, and full participation at both the group and individual levels, so that members of different groups not only have equal access to opportunities, decision making, and positions of power, but they are actively sought out *because* of their differences" (p. 248). Leaders play a pivotal role in creating an environment in which diverse employees experience equality, justice, and full participation. At the heart of this lies respect.

In virtually any discussion of creating an inclusive climate, the issue of respect emerges. Therefore, leaders of a diverse workforce must strive to create an environment characterized by high levels of respect. Although the definition of what constitutes respectful behavior varies across cultures, the general concept appears across the literature as a key element in creating a work environment in which differences are valued. Hannum and Glover (2010) examined the role a leader plays in fostering respect in the workplace. They conclude that "at its core, respect is a continuous process of paying attention to someone" (p. 613). It involves understanding and accepting another's viewpoint as valid. They recommend that one demonstrable way leaders can foster a climate of respect is by exhibiting an interest in and appreciation of others' perspectives, knowledge, skills, and abilities. Similarly, Ferdman and his colleagues (Ferdman, Katz, Letchinger, & Thompson, 2009) suggest that leaders who wish to practice inclusion should focus on creating a safe space that invites people to engage and enable true dialogue to occur, showing respect by enabling people to have insight into why and how decisions are made, and being willing to understand and engage people's multiple perspectives. These views are supported by empirical research that has shown that leaders who solicit and appreciate employee input help to create climates that are high in psychological safety (Nembhard & Edmondson, 2006).

When leaders engage in and role model inclusive behavior, a number of positive outcomes are likely to accrue. In particular, there is some evidence to support the link between an inclusive work climate and employee outcomes of well-being, job satisfaction, and organizational commitment (Findler, Wind, & Mor Barak, 2007). There is also some evidence that leaders who facilitate inclusion by being interested in the ideas of employees, listening to them, giving them fair consideration, and taking action to address matters that have been raised create a climate within which employees are willing to speak up and participate fully in the workplace (Detert & Burris, 2007). Finally, research also suggests that inclusive climates are beneficial not only because they make the attainment of positive outcomes more likely, but because discrimination and harassment tend to be lower (Nishii, Langevin, & Bruyere, 2010).

INTERGROUP STRATEGIES

Leaders influence the satisfaction and productivity of a diverse workgroup not only by fostering high-quality relationships with individuals but also by fostering unity across divergent workgroups. At the intergroup level, leaders play an important role in creating or making salient a larger collective identity that encompasses and unites all subgroups (Hogg et al., 2005). This collective or superordinate identity is often the work team or organization itself. As discussed earlier in the section on transformational leadership behaviors, leaders form strong emotional ties with employees in part by communicating and fostering commitment to a vision and set of goals. Likewise, leaders play an important role in creating and strengthening ties between divergent subgroups by focusing on a common mission that serves to bind such groups together in service of **common goals**.

Along these lines, Pittinsky (2010) suggests that diversity calls for intergroup leadership that involves behaviors and practices that unite not just individuals but also subgroups in a common goal. He argues that leaders have traditionally attempted to create a collective identity across diverse individuals and groups by focusing on the elimination of negative attitudes and relationships. However, Pittinsky's work on a concept he calls "allophilia," from the Greek meaning love or liking of the other, suggests that leadership in a diverse context requires more than simply reducing negative attitudes; it requires increasing the positive attitudes different subgroups within the collective hold toward one another. He suggests that leadership behaviors that reduce negative attitudes are different from those that increase positive attitudes, and that leaders play an important role in facilitating both. Whereas negative attitudes toward members of certain groups are strongly influenced by social norms, positive attitudes represent an individual experience. Through their individual actions, leaders may role model behaviors that go beyond the absence of negative attitudes and treatment toward subgroups and include the development of high-quality positive relationships with all group members and emphasize values of equality (Pittinsky, 2010; Pittinsky & Maruskin, 2008; Pittinsky & Montoya, 2009).

Fiol, Pratt, and O'Connor (2009) also emphasize the importance of creating a superordinate identity while at the same time respecting subgroup identity differences. They too argue that organizational leaders are often a key lever in managing the tension that exists between subgroup identities and encouraging subgroups to focus instead on shared goals and a common mission. Leaders can actively counteract the pervasiveness of socio-historical biases and stereotypes by treating members of divergent subgroups in a noticeably egalitarian way. By eliminating any threats to subgroup identities by being egalitarian, the leader then makes it possible for group members to work collaboratively toward the accomplishment of shared group goals (Fiol et al., 2009), which is important for fostering positive group identities and outcomes (Brewer & Miller, 1984).

Sociological research on status characteristics theory would suggest that the key is for leaders to be aware of the demographic categories within the group that mirror those that are socio-historically associated with status differences, as these are the ones that can drive negative intragroup dynamics unless actively counteracted (Ridgeway, 1991; Ridgeway & Correll, 2006). To the extent that a leader's behavior and the norms that he or she establishes legitimize beliefs that exist in the broader society about the status differences between demographic groups (e.g., men are perceived to have higher status than women, Whites have higher status than non-Whites, etc.), the leader will perpetuate stereotyping and bias related to that cultural identity. When employees do not perceive leaders as promoting or perpetuating arbitrary status hierarchies based on demographic categories, subgroup identities are less likely to be perceived as threatened; this opens up the possibility for employees to transcend their own interests for the sake of the collective (Fiol et al., 2009) and trust the direction and goals the leader has set for the group.

Even within a highly collaborative work environment, at least some degree of conflict will arise, as this is a natural consequence of diversity. As the workplace becomes increasingly diverse, so too does the likelihood of identity-based conflict. Ruderman, Glover, Chrobot-Mason, and Ernst (2010) discuss the role of leaders in responding to **social identity conflict** in the workplace. They suggest that employees hold a strong expectation that someone in a leadership position will respond to situations in which conflict over identity differences emerges in the workplace. However, many leaders fail to act in such instances, likely due to a lack of confidence in their skills and ability to handle the situation effectively.

Based on their research with organizations across the globe, the authors suggest that the first critical step is for the leader to examine the whole picture and to develop an understanding of the many factors that influence collisions between social identity groups at work (e.g., cultural values, economic and political systems, organizational mission and infrastructure, history of conflict, etc.) and what role he or she plays within the larger picture. The second step is to clarify the message that the leader sends to the groups involved as well as to the organization as a whole. It is important that a leader's actions and words are aligned with his or her personal values as well as the firm's values and mission. Step three involves identifying realistic options for handling the conflict given available resources, and step four involves taking appropriate action. Leaders who intend to send the message that the group should learn from differences and value diversity must select a response to conflicts that conveys this message. In step five, leaders should monitor the situation to determine if the intended outcome has been achieved or if additional action may be needed. Finally, the last step involves reflection and learning once the conflict has been resolved. The authors emphasize the important role leaders play in helping the team reflect on the conflict and the resolution, to capture the learning that took place during the process, and to consider how this can be applied to future social identity difference conflicts that will inevitably arise within a diverse workplace.

Given that leaders cannot possibly be present to monitor and facilitate the resolution of every conflict that emerges, it is also important that they create norms that will operate in their absence. Earlier research focused on the possible benefits of highlighting norms of openness about conflict (Jehn, 1995) and encouraging collaborative strategies (De Dreu & Van Vianen, 2001) but found that neither strategy helps to improve conflict resolution. This may be because these strategies focus on conflict itself, and not the interpersonal context within which the conflicting parties are operating. Indeed, work by Brewer (1999) suggests that if the parties involved in a conflict are of different social status, then highlighting the need for cooperation can backfire since it makes the absence of mutual trust salient. More recent work by Nishii (2010) suggests that in inclusive climates, individuals are more likely to exhibit concern both for themselves and for others and to be committed to working through differences as a source of interpersonal learning. As a result, experiences of group conflict in diverse groups with inclusive climates do not have a negative impact on group morale, as is usually the case in diverse groups (De Dreu & Weingart, 2003). It appears that leaders play an important role in fostering expectations for relational eloquence and authenticity among employees by creating an inclusive climate within which they can forge meaningful relationships and foster dual concern for the self and other, both of which are critical for effective conflict resolution.

Leaders often engage in **boundary spanning** in an attempt to bridge differences and resolve conflict within their organization or team (Ernst & Chrobot-Mason, 2011). Differences in organizational level, area of expertise, demographic membership, and other boundaries between groups often emerge in the workplace as a border or constraint that limits effective communication and collaboration. However, research suggests that leaders can play an important role in transforming these differences or boundaries from a limitation into an opportunity. In a recent book based on data gathered as part of a multi-country study on leadership across differences conducted by the Center for Creative Leadership, Ernst and Chrobot-Mason (2011) examine six boundary-spanning leadership practices. Following an extensive review of the literature, they conclude that there are three overarching strategies leaders use in attempting to span boundaries.

The first, "managing boundaries," is based on work by Faraj and Yan (2009), who suggest that boundary management is challenging yet critical work that must be done to effectively manage cross-group interactions in the workplace. They argue that boundaries must be managed so that they are porous enough that resources and information can get in, but resistant enough to keep uncertainty and competing demands out. Leaders, therefore, may use strategies such as buffering and reflecting to define and clarify boundaries between groups (Ernst & Chrobot-Mason, 2011). Leaders buffer and protect their direct reports from external threats, competing demands, and other pressures by monitoring and managing the flow of resources, information, people, practices, and perceptions across boundaries. Leaders may also help groups better understand the boundaries and differences that exist between them by reflecting—enabling groups to see and understand the needs, goals, values, work styles, preferences, expertise, and experiences of other groups.

The second general strategy for boundary spanning identified by Ernst and Chrobot-Mason (2011) is "forging common ground." This was derived from research based in social identity theory that suggests that social identity differences, and the conflict they often create, may be mitigated by emphasizing one-on-one personal interactions rather than group-based interactions (to learn more about this strategy, known as decategorization, see Brewer & Miller, 1984) or by emphasizing a common identity that becomes superordinate to subgroup identities (to learn more about this strategy, known as recategorization, see Gaertner & Dovidio, 2007). Ernst and Chrobot-Mason (2011) recommend that leaders engage in practices such as connecting and mobilizing to forge common ground. Connecting may be accomplished by finding opportunities that allow employees to "step outside" of their boundaries into a neutral zone where people can interact as individuals rather than members who represent their social identity group. The strategy of mobilizing involves creating a common mission, vision, or goals that include all employees.

The third overarching strategy, "discovering new frontiers," focuses on ways to take advantage of both similarities and differences that exist at the boundary between groups to enhance creativity, innovation, and problem-solving capacity. It is largely based on research and theory on subcategorization (Haslam & Ellemers, 2005; Hewstone, & Brown, 1986) as well as cross-cutting (Brewer, 1995). Research has shown that when groups have distinct but complementary roles to contribute toward a common goal, both differences and commonalities are emphasized, and this leads to more positive intergroup attitudes and work outcomes (Eggins, Haslam, & Reynolds, 2002; Haslam, Eggins, & Reynolds, 2003). Brewer's (1995) work on cross-cutting suggests that it is important to carefully select team members so that intergroup conflict is minimized. She advocates systematically or randomly crossing workgroup roles with social identity group membership so that team composition cuts across organizational levels and functions. Based on this work, Ernst and Chrobot-Mason (2011) call out two practices leaders may use to tap into the potential that exists when diverse teams are created in the workplace—weaving and transforming. Leaders who engage in weaving integrate and draw out group differences within a larger whole or common vision. They find ways to capitalize on group differences in service of the larger whole such that subgroups all play an important and unique role in the mission of the entire group. Transforming involves leadership practices and activities that bring members of multiple groups together to create an entirely new social identity group or view a problem in an entirely new way. Both leadership practices attempt to take advantage of both the similarities and the differences that exist between groups to span boundaries and foster collaboration.

Leading others: Future research

In this section we focused on leading others. Overall, the results of our literature review suggest that leaders play a critically important role in creating a work climate that supports and retains a diverse workforce as well as leveraging the potential benefits that diversity may bring. The social identity theory of leadership and LMX theory provide a useful foundation for understanding key processes involved in the effective management of a diverse workforce. Also, research on transformational leadership, LMX and relational leadership, and inclusion provide evidence that specific leader behaviors affect the quality of workplace relationships, which ultimately affects employee satisfaction and productivity. Finally, research and theory on intergroup conflict and collaboration suggest that leaders also play an important role in resolving identity-based conflicts, fostering unity, and linking divergent groups in a common mission.

Despite the research and theory on leading diverse others presented here, it is evident that many research questions remain unanswered. We suggest the following questions may serve as a starting point for future research:

- What role do others play in monitoring and holding one another accountable for inclusive behavior? The literature is more informative about the role leaders play in creating an inclusive work environment than the role of other workgroup members, who may be just as important in creating an affirming climate. If leadership is to be viewed as a shared responsibility, then so too should the creation and maintenance of an inclusive climate. Thus, it is important that additional research explore the inclusive behavior and practices required of all workgroup members, and the implications this may have for diversity and team-building initiatives. Special attention needs to be paid to identifying the ways in which group members can formally and informally assess and monitor the inclusiveness of their workgroup and the nonthreatening actions they can take to enforce inclusive standards agreed upon by the group.

- How does the social identity theory of leadership and the cycle of influence manifest between the leader and workgroup members when social identity composition varies? Do the behaviors and strategies required for demonstrating inclusive leadership vary as a function of the demography of the group and the leader's own relational demography vis-à-vis group members? In other words, does or should leadership behavior vary depending on whether the leader is different in terms of identity from some group members versus different from all? It may be the case that leaders must behave or engage in a different set of practices to be recognized as a leader when they are demographically different from some or all other workgroup members.

Leading the organization

Diverse organizations face some unique and complex challenges. Organizations may face the challenge of operating in many different countries, employing and coordinating workers from many different cultures and regions of the world, providing a service or product for customers in all corners of the globe, and interacting with stakeholders and suppliers in every time zone. Successful leadership of multicultural organizations operating within a global market requires facilitation and coordination of diverse people, systems, and work. Thus, in this section, we examine leadership in a diverse workplace at the organizational level. In the model presented by Crossan and colleagues (2008), this involves leadership responsibilities such as strategy, structure, rules, and procedures.

Much of what we discussed in the previous section on leading others may also apply when leading a diverse organization. Senior leaders who engage in relational, transformational, inclusive, and boundary-spanning leadership behaviors serve as role models and encourage leaders at all levels of the organization to adopt a similar leadership style and approach to managing diversity. Their potential influence is significant as it becomes aggregated across leadership levels and across managers throughout the organization, which in turn shapes the organizational climate for diversity and inclusion. They often determine (or strongly influence) the diversity strategy and the narrative about why diversity matters. As Crossan and colleagues (2008) suggest, "leaders are not passive recipients of changes in strategy, organization, and environment, but rather can be dominant forces in affecting their change" (p. 572). In this next section, we summarize the literature that has examined leadership of a diverse organization and highlight some key practices leaders must pay particular attention to so they can influence the extent to which the organization is able to leverage differences.

Before doing so, however, we wish to clarify the potential costs to overlooking or mismanaging diversity at the organizational level of leadership. Munusamy, Ruderman, and Eckert (2010) identify the four types of capital that may be sacrificed if leaders of organizations discount the importance of diversity to leadership: human, identity, diversity, and social capital. At a very fundamental level, organizations can lose out by not paying attention to the many talented people who might not fit the prototype of the ideal leader. In these days of extreme competition, organizations that want to thrive need to take a highly inclusive approach to the development of the workforce.

Theoretical foundations

Diversity provides many potential advantages for organizations. It can help organizations to reach out to diverse customer groups and reach new markets. It can also allow for a variety of perspectives.

Paying attention to diversity allows a firm to be flexible and withstand changes in the markets and economy. These benefits are referred to as diversity capital (Munusamy, Ruderman, & Eckert, 2010). Below, we highlight two theoretical positions to explain how leaders accrue diversity capital. The first involves the process by which leaders create and then convey to others a meta-narrative or story about diversity within the organization, and the second involves various approaches to managing difference within the organization.

DEVELOPING A META-NARRATIVE

Leaders are unlikely to be successful at creating an inclusive climate for diversity unless they convey a convincing narrative that focuses on the opportunities afforded by successful management of diversity (Wasserman et al., 2008). Through their style, behaviors, and values, leaders shape and then convey a meta-narrative or story for diversity within their organization. Leaders serve as role models who both derive and implement diversity and inclusion policies and practices. Because of their position, expertise, and/or authority, leaders demonstrate for others the extent to which differences are valued, employee subgroups are treated in egalitarian ways, and collaboration is encouraged. Thus, their behavior creates a story for others in the organization to follow.

Nishii and Langevin (2010) adopt the view that leaders play an especially important role as "interpretive filters" of organizational practices (Bowen & Ostroff, 2004). The way that they "sensemake" about practices (Weick, 1979) and in turn provide meaning to their subordinates ("sensegive") influences the ultimate effectiveness of those practices (Pfeffer, 1981). They showed that managers who attribute the adoption of diversity practices to external compliance motives (like complying with legal standards, keeping up with what competitors are doing, and avoiding looking bad to external stakeholders) fail to implement diversity initiatives effectively, as seen in the high levels of discrimination related to gender, race, age, sexual orientation, and religion (Nishii & Langevin, 2010).

In comparison, managers who attribute the adoption of diversity practices to an internal belief in the opportunities afforded by diversity initiatives (e.g., achieving better strategic outcomes, promoting fairness, enhancing inclusion and well-being) more thoroughly enact change in their units, as seen in the significantly higher reports of inclusion and lower rates of discrimination. They explain their results in terms of the differences that arise from "coaching from compliance" versus "coaching with compassion": the former focuses on negative affect (e.g., the threat of noncompliance), arouses defensiveness, and induces individuals to achieve the minimum required for compliance, while the latter primes people's "ideal self" and enhances the motivational strength associated with pursuing desired behavioral changes (Boyatzis, 2006). It is also possible that leaders who believe in and are driven by internal motivations for managing diversity are better able to communicate a compelling vision to their employees and provide consistent, reliable diversity leadership; both sets of behaviors are consistent with the transformational leadership behaviors as described previously (Kearney & Gebert, 2009). Taken together, this study highlights the fact that the effectiveness of diversity initiatives depends in large part on the way that leaders perceive, make sense of, and implement such initiatives.

APPROACHES TO MANAGING DIFFERENCE

One of the primary ways leaders shape a meta-narrative with respect to diversity is in their approach to managing difference. Research championed by the Center for Creative Leadership reveals that leaders generally engage in one of three ways when addressing tension and conflict that emerges in the workplace as a result of identity differences (Ernst, Hannum, & Ruderman, 2010; Ruderman et al., 2010). Each approach represents underlying beliefs about the organization and its leaders' role in managing cross-group relationships. Some organizations take a "hands-off" or passive approach to managing differences. They may fail to act or intervene for a variety of reasons and beliefs. Many leaders choose to do nothing based on the belief that the workplace is not the appropriate venue for dealing with societal-level problems or that the organization is not responsible for intervening in such conflict. Others fail to see that a problem exists and deny the tension between groups. This is common particularly when the leader is a member of the dominant group and his or her own identity becomes a blind spot in the sense that the leader cannot see issues from other perspectives. Still other leaders may fail to act out of fear that they may make the situation worse by doing the wrong thing or calling too much attention to the differences that exist.

A second approach to managing differences is "direct and control." Leaders and organizations adopting this approach rely on both formal and informal authority, rewards, and punishments to manage relationships in such a way that the organizational mission and goals are protected. The intent behind the variety of leadership practices using this approach is to prevent or quickly extinguish conflict and tension based on group differences to maintain equilibrium in the organization. For example, some organizations rely on laws and regulations to address differences, while others emphasize a zero-tolerance approach to discrimination and harassment and include diversity policies in their employee handbook.

A third strategy for managing differences is the "cultivate and encourage" approach. The belief underlying this approach is that the organization should create the conditions that cultivate positive interactions among different groups and within which differences are valued. Leaders who adopt this type of approach actively manage differences and engage in, or support, a variety of practices that demonstrate the organization's commitment toward inclusion. Such practices may include diversity training, processes that encourage open dialogue, boundary-spanning behavior (as described earlier), and role modeling. Ruderman and colleagues (2010) report that the act of apologizing proved to go a long way in cultivating positive cross-group relationships. Recognizing and apologizing for some of the inevitable mistakes that occur when diverse groups interact with one another at work is very important for leaders to consider. Apologies demonstrate shared blame and responsibility, rather than the imposition of one group's interests over another's. They also help to communicate the idea that mistakes are a natural part of the learning process related to diversity. When leaders fail to recognize their own mistakes, they make it more likely that employees become preoccupied with avoiding mistakes rather than learning from them (Dragoni, 2005).

While these three approaches are descriptive both of leaders as they lead others in their workgroups and of more senior leaders who lead the organization, we believe that the approaches set by senior organizational leaders are particularly important because they help set the tone for the entire organization. When senior leaders role model the "cultivate and encourage" approach, they are more likely to cultivate climates for psychological safety, learning, and inclusion, all of which are necessary for optimizing the benefits of diversity. It is important that they guide other leaders throughout the organization to adopt the same approach, and to do so consistently. As Bowen and Ostroff (2004) suggest, intended diversity strategies and approaches need to be communicated by senior leaders in a way that is visible, understandable, and unambiguous, and perceived as relevant to individual employees, with the expected outcomes of diversity strategies being clearly explained. The importance of these messages being directed by senior leaders is underscored by Bowen and Ostroff's (2004) argument that communications originating from sources that are perceived as legitimate and authoritative are attended to more by employees. An important consideration, however, is the alignment between senior managers' communications and their behavior (Simons, 2002); the greater the agreement there is among senior leaders in their communications, the more likely it is that line managers and employees will also develop shared understandings of the organization's diversity strategy.

Strategies for enhancing leadership
MANAGING FAULTLINES

We learned about research on faultlines in Chapter 4. Just as the faultlines in the earth's crust may be dormant for some period and then crack apart as a result of tension and pressure underground, so too may differences within the workplace lie dormant until a triggering event brings differences to the forefront. This triggering event may cause a great divide between groups and create significant challenges for leaders who must encourage divergent and distrustful groups to work collaboratively to achieve the organization's mission (Chrobot-Mason, Ruderman, Weber, & Ernst, 2009).

Lau and Murnighan's work on faultlines and work in the area of relational demography suggest that workforce composition and the nature and quantity of differences that exist within a workgroup help determine the strength of a faultline and its potential for polarizing group members. To at least some degree, organizational leaders can influence the composition of their workforce through staffing and affirmative action practices and policies (see Chapters 15 &16). However, workforce composition is likely to ebb and flow, and workgroups may not always engender an ideal diversity mix. Some level of conflict and tension is perhaps inevitable within a diverse organization, and thus it behooves leaders to consider and then determine a strategy for handling the differences, disagreements, and conflict that result from diversity.

Gratton, Voigt, and Erickson (2007) examined the role of leaders in bridging faultlines within diverse teams. Based on their assessment of 55 teams from 15 European and American companies, they conclude that although there is a natural tendency when strong faultlines emerge for leaders to encourage team members to connect through meetings and social events, this approach may actually strengthen the faultline if it makes differences more apparent. What they suggest instead is that leading across a strong faultline initially requires a task-oriented style, but that the leader must make a switch to a more relationship-oriented style when the time is right. Beginning with a task-oriented leadership style is important so that the leader can focus on creating energy around the task itself such that collaboration and knowledge sharing are emphasized. In addition, this allows team members the chance to learn about one another's skills and competencies.

However, a relationship-oriented leadership style grows important as the need to deal with the tension and conflict that surround deeper levels of diversity, such as differences in values and priorities, emerges within the group. That is, to make the transition from an effective to an innovative organization, the leader must learn to bring to the surface and openly deal with intergroup tensions and create an environment of deep understanding and respect. Overall, these researchers conclude that although faultlines are a common hazard, there are significant differences between diverse teams in which a faultline leads to productivity declines versus teams that are productive and innovative despite strong faultlines. The determining factor, they argue, is the behavior of the leader.

DEALING WITH DIVERSITY CRISES

There is growing recognition of the fact that espoused strategy, practices, and climate do not always get implemented, and those that do may be implemented in ways that differ from the initial intention (Nishii, Lepak, & Schneider, 2008; Nishii & Wright, 2008). Particularly in the case of diversity management, employees may be looking for evidence of senior leaders' authentic commitment; thus, careful consideration of any misalignment between espoused and implemented strategy may be important for avoiding claims that management "doesn't walk the talk."

Diversity crises represent an opportunity and a challenge, in that how senior leaders respond to crises is very salient to employees and the external public (Bowen & Ostroff, 2004). Crises force leaders to examine the ways in which their espoused diversity strategy may be inappropriate, and/or how their espoused strategy may not be implemented as intended. James and Wooten (2005, 2006) found that when faced with a diversity crisis, many firms maintain a denial stance and demonstrate little openness to communication, while others engage in active organizational learning. Following settlement, these firms adopted change efforts to prevent or more effectively resolve future crises (James & Wooten, 2006). The difference between firms that thrive following crisis versus those that do not is the leadership displayed throughout the process (James & Wooten, 2005). Core competencies for crisis leadership include such things as (1) building a foundation of trust in which leaders communicate openly, honestly, and often; (2) creating a corporate mindset that takes a big-picture approach and considers multiple perspectives of the crisis; (3) making wise and rapid decisions rather than denying or avoiding the crisis; and (4) approaching crisis as an opportunity for growth and change.

IMPLEMENTING HUMAN RESOURCES PRACTICES

Although there are several chapters in the book that deal with human resources practices in the context of diversity, and we refer you to such chapters for a detailed discussion of each, we believe it is important to consider these practices with respect to leadership as well. Organizational practices that involve recruitment, hiring, development, and retention of diverse employees are all key "touchpoints" in which leaders play a significant role. At the organizational level, these are the mechanisms though which leaders may affect the extent to which diversity is present, valued, and leveraged. Leadership, defined in this chapter as the social process for generating the direction, alignment, and commitment needed by a group to accomplish collective goals, is enacted through the creation and execution of organizational practices and policies. Leaders throughout the organization, but particularly those at senior levels, serve as role models and provide cues for others about what type of behavior is expected and valued within the organization (Bowen & Ostroff, 2004). For example, senior leaders who fail to hire or promote diversity into the ranks of their senior management team send a strong message to the rest of the organization that they do not truly value diversity. Likewise, senior leaders who attend and fully participate in diversity training initiatives send a strong message to their subordinates that they too have something to learn when it comes to managing diversity (Chrobot-Mason, Hays-Thomas, & Wishik, 2008).

Another practice increasingly being used by senior leaders to communicate the importance of diversity is the establishment of employee resource groups. Research by Friedman and colleagues (Friedman & Holtom, 2002; Friedman, Kane, & Cornfield, 1998) has shown that employee network groups have a positive impact on career optimism and retention for minority workers. Network groups can provide nondominant group members with the opportunity to meet and exchange knowledge with others belonging to their own demographic group in the company, contributing to their sense of community and belonging. More recently, employee resource groups are taking on more strategic roles and are often "sponsored" by a senior leader who is held accountable for achieving goals associated with attracting talent, growing the business (e.g., by marketing more effectively to members of the identity group represented in the employee resource group), and the professional development of members of the particular identity group.[1] In this way, senior leaders become not just champions of the group, but help others to see the business value of diversity as reflected in the particular identity group by helping the organization to achieve recruiting and business growth goals. In other words, they play an active role in helping to support the business case for diversity.

PROMOTING A LEARNING CULTURE

Employees carefully observe the pattern of leaders' behaviors in an effort to interpret what priorities are valued by the leaders (Zohar & Luria, 2004). When leaders adopt an organizational diversity strategy that exemplifies a learning orientation, they are more likely to capitalize on the potential benefits that diversity brings. To the extent that leaders model, focus feedback efforts around, and reward learning-oriented behaviors, they help to create a learning-oriented organization. Learning-oriented leaders create opportunities for employees to engage in developmental and learning activities, encourage employees to transfer and apply learned skills to their work, model the importance of learning from mistakes, provide and accept constructive feedback on how to improve, and are genuinely open to learning from their interactions with coworkers and direct reports (Dragoni, 2005). By exhibiting these behaviors, leaders encourage organizational members to feel unthreatened by task challenges, value supportive relationships, and focus on organizational improvement (Dragoni, 2005), all of which may be critical for employees to integrate their diverse perspectives and leverage diversity to improve operational functioning.

Leaders also play a key role in fostering a culture of learning by serving in the role of mentor and encouraging others to do so as well (Chao, 2007). Research shows that mentoring for people of color and women helps such workers "break through" existing barriers to reach more senior levels within the organization (Blake-Beard, Murrell, & Thomas, 2007; Giscombe, 2007). Both formal and informal mentoring have potential benefits for employees, and in fact, recent research suggests that it behooves employees to take advantage of the possible benefits of both and foster a "constellation" of developmental relationships (Baugh & Fagenson-Eland, 2007). This may be particularly important for diverse employees who would benefit from having mentors from within their own demographic group as well as mentors from within the dominant group (Dreher & Cox, 1996; Ibarra, 1992). While not all leaders may be categorized as mentors, there is considerable overlap between these two roles in terms of the importance of developing high-quality relationships with direct reports (Godshalk & Sosik, 2007). For example, the LMX and transformational theories of leadership overlap with conceptualizations of supervisor mentoring. Thus, leaders may foster a learning culture and the career development of minority employees by developing mentoring relationships that facilitate learning by designing assignments and providing ongoing support and performance feedback (Kram, 1985).

Summary

Leading an organization that values diversity requires measuring progress toward diversity goals and rewarding intended behaviors and outcomes. Organizational leaders may measure progress toward diversity goals by measuring changes in things such as demographic representation, workforce flow that includes recruitment and retention data, employee opinion data derived from surveys, focus groups, and exit interviews, and litigation activity and costs (Jayne & Dipboye, 2004). When progress is made in these areas and diversity targets and goals are met, organizational leaders must find ways to reward such efforts to continue progress and ensure that attention toward diversity efforts is sustained over time.

An important consideration when evaluating the effectiveness of diversity management practices is recent work by Kalev and her colleagues (Kalev, Dobbins, & Kelly, 2006), which suggested that some of the practices that have historically been implemented to increase the representation of women and ethnic minorities in management (e.g., diversity training, mentoring, manager accountability for diversity goals) have not been as effective as hoped. This may be because these practices target moments of personnel decision making (e.g., hiring, promotion), but on their own fail to alter the everyday socio-relational sources of discrimination that inhibit the full engagement and advancement of members of historically marginalized groups. Thus, for organizational inclusion to be achieved, leaders must focus not just on the effective and fair implementation of human resources and diversity practices, but the creation of climates that are conducive to personalized interactions and learning from diversity.

Leading the organization: Future research

Based on both research and theory highlighted in this section on leading a diverse organization, we offer the following research questions for consideration in future research:

- What are the relative benefits of various diversity initiatives adopted by leaders for creating direction, alignment, and commitment in an organization? Although vitally important to understand the value proposition for investing resources into diversity programs, this is a research question that still has not been adequately addressed in the literature.

- How do organizational leaders learn from diversity crises or conflicts? Does the learning process differ following a positive versus a negative event? How important is it to actively engage in organizational change efforts following an event (such as a change in policy or practice) for learning to occur? Continuous learning is an important part of leading amid diversity. However, we know less about the situations that teach this than we do about leadership learning in general. It would be worthwhile to better understand how leaders acquire and express the self-understanding necessary to lead in a diverse context.

Summary, and setting the agenda for future research

Although research and theory devoted to the topic of leading within a diverse workplace is still underrepresented in the literature, we have provided an overview and summary of the extant literature at the intersection of diversity and leadership. We presented evidence of an evolving definition of effective leadership that is emerging both in response to, and in preparation for, an increasingly diverse workforce. This definition differs from the traditional one that viewed leadership as residing within an individual holding a formal position of authority. In contrast, leadership is increasingly now seen as a socially constructed process involving the entire group, and effective leadership is relational in nature. As such, we have argued that leaders now play a key role in the ultimate success or failure of a diverse workforce and the organization's ability to leverage differences as a competitive advantage.

By framing our review of the literature based on Crossan and colleagues' (2008) cross-level model involving leadership of self, others, and the organization, we have highlighted an important conclusion: effective leadership of a diverse workforce is not the responsibility of the person at the top, but of the entire organization. All employees need to understand the importance of self-leadership. Managers need to understand how this relates to demonstrating interpersonal influence in the leadership of others. And furthermore, executives need to understand issues of equality at the organizational level and that there is a real cost to the organization for overlooking diversity.

Because research on leadership and diversity remains sparse, we feel there are many research questions yet to be addressed and many opportunities for scholars to join this burgeoning research agenda. We suggest that future research in this area should focus on addressing three broad areas: (1) identifying a diversity-leadership mindset, (2) examining the implications of relational leadership in the context of diversity, and (3) exploring innovative and creative strategies for developing leaders with a diversity mindset who engage in relational leadership behavior.

Identifying a diversity-leadership mindset

Research is needed to understand what differentiates the leaders of organizations who are primarily motivated "from the head" to do what is good for their organization from leaders who are committed to real change "from the heart." Even though the number of organizations that have been recognized with corporate diversity awards has grown, these awards have done little to differentiate those organizations that are being led by leaders who believe that their work is done because they have adopted a wide variety of diversity practices and increased diverse representation, from organizations whose leaders have committed to going beyond the adoption of these practices to transforming their organizational cultures to be truly inclusive. Recent research by Catalyst (Prime & Moss-Racusin, 2009) suggests that leaders who are deeply committed to diversity initiatives may be driven by the ideal of equality in a way that is not true of less committed leaders, although more research is needed to bear this out. If a fundamental belief in equality sets effective diversity leaders apart from others, an important issue to understand is whether such beliefs can be cultivated in leaders by their organizations, and if so, how. Although laboratory research has shown that the activation of egalitarian goals can help to prevent the activation of implicit biases (Moskowitz, Gollwitzer, Wasel, & Schaal,1999), whether including egalitarian goals throughout performance management systems would be sufficient for instilling equality ideals among leaders—and a corresponding internal motivation to lead diversity effectively—remains to be seen.

Examining the implications of relational leadership in the context of diversity

Future research should consider whether more stereotypically feminine qualities may be what is needed for successful leadership in a diverse workplace. Recent research by Catalyst revealed that most organizations emphasize stereotypically masculine qualities among their leaders, such as being action-oriented, results-driven, skilled at problem solving, and assertive (Warren, 2009). However, our review of the existing literature suggests to us that more feminine, relational leadership styles may be better suited for leading diverse groups, as suggested by research on relational self-construal (Gelfand, Major, Raver, Nishii, & O'Brien, 2006). In contrast to a view of the self as largely independent of others, relational self-construal (RSC) reflects a self that is fundamentally connected to other individuals. Leaders who are high in RSC may be more effective at leading diverse groups for a number of reasons. Research suggests that their tendency to engage in perspective taking leads them to see the ways in which they are similar to others, and we see this as an important precondition for being a boundary-spanning leader. In addition, they work hard to develop and affirm connections with others since doing so is an important source of positive emotions and self-esteem, and they tend to adopt numerous tactics for fostering connections with others, such as engaging in personal self-disclosure and considering their actions in light of the implications for others' needs and feelings. In role modeling such behaviors for their employees and by prioritizing relationship building, they are more likely to create the conditions within which employees can see beyond stereotypes and interact with one another more authentically. Furthermore, leaders who are high in RSC are more likely to treat interactions with and among employees as being embedded within a broader temporal context; that is, to see their interactions as having important ramifications for their future relationships with others. As such, they are less likely to try to dominate others and/or leave conflict unresolved, and more likely to gather accurate information about others in an effort to understand their values and beliefs.

When exhibited by leaders, these behaviors are likely to help employees to believe that their voices are genuinely valued, or in other words to cultivate psychological safety and inclusion (Nembhard & Edmondson, 2006). Leaders who are intrinsically motivated to ask the right questions of others, rather than provide the right answers to others, are much more likely to create the kinds of environments in which employees feel safe to pursue the kind of interpersonal learning that is necessary for the benefits of diversity to emerge. In contrast, when leaders are assertive and overly results-driven, their employees are likely to become more concerned with proving their competence or avoiding failures than with learning from the challenges that may be introduced by diversity.

For organizations, the key is to understand the ways in which beneficial levels of RSC can be primed, or made temporally accessible, among leaders. When features of an organizational context send strong signals about the role appropriateness of behaving relationally, leaders will be induced to behave in the ways described above. According to work by Brickson (2000), who has similarly suggested that activating a relational orientation among individuals is critical for promoting the benefits and inhibiting the disadvantages associated with diversity, it is important for organizations to frame tasks and reward structures around dyads or groups rather than individuals and to promote integrated relationship networks within the organization. Thus, future research should examine how the organizational climate may improve if relational leadership became the norm and more feminine leadership characteristics were valued.

Exploring innovative and creative strategies for developing leaders of diversity

Development of leaders with a diversity mindset who understand the value of adopting a relational style of leadership to lead across differences effectively likely occurs not in the workplace, but rather much earlier. This type of leadership development must begin when children are first developing their leadership capacity and skill set. Research on leader development is clear in pointing out that development takes time, motivation, and effort and cannot be achieved solely by attending a half-day workshop. Developing leaders to successfully lead in a diverse workplace must begin in school and continue throughout an individual's professional career.

More explicit attention to diversity and inclusion within early childhood education is critical such that our leaders of tomorrow rise into their positions equipped with a belief in the ideal of equality. Although there is a relatively well-developed literature on diversity and inclusion within the education field, it has to date remained isolated from the organizational literature. In our future activities, it may behoove us to collaborate with educational researchers to try to understand which educational programs related to diversity and equality are effective not just at reducing diversity-related incidents in schools and enhancing the achievement outcomes of all students, but also in instilling lasting egalitarian ideals in the youth of today.

Future research must begin to view the development of such skills as a collaborative endeavor involving self, others, and organizations not only within the professional context, but also education and society at large. How do we as a society develop and foster leaders who are relational, span boundaries, engage differences and conflict constructively, and ultimately collaborate across differences to resolve society's most challenging issues? Is it outrageous to imagine that if we are successful, we could enjoy a world in which leaders battle less over territorial boundaries and instead collaborate more towards the achievement of global goals?

Note

1. We learned about the more strategic focus of employee resource groups through a series of focus groups with diversity executives from companies who belong to Cornell University's Center for Advanced Human Resource Studies (conducted in January 2009).

References

Ashkenas, R., Ulrich, D., Jick, T., & Kerr, S. (2002). *The boundaryless organization: Breaking the chains of organizational structure.* San Francisco: Jossey-Bass.

Ayman, R. (1993). Leadership perception: The role of gender and culture. In M. M. Chemers & R. Ayman (Eds.).*Leadership theory and research: Perspectives and Directions* (pp. 137–166). San Diego: Academic Press.

Ayman, R., & Korabik, K. (2010). Leadership: Why gender and culture matter. *American Psychologist, 65*(3), 157–170.

Bass, B. M. (1990). From transactional to transformational leadership: Learning to share the vision. *Organizational Dynamics, 18*(3), 19–31.

Bass, B. M., & Avolio, B.J. (1994). *Improving organizational effectiveness through transformational leadership.* Thousand Oaks, CA: Sage Publications.

Baugh, S. G., & Fagenson-Eland, E. A. (2007). Formal mentoring programs: A "poor cousin" to informal relationships? In B. R. Ragins & K. E. Kram (Eds.), *The handbook of mentoring at work* (pp. 249–272). Thousand Oaks, CA: Sage Publications.

Bell, E. L., & Nkomo, S. M. (2001). *Our separate ways: Black and White women and the struggle for professional identity.* Boston: Harvard Business School Press.

Blake-Beard, S. D., Murrell, A., & Thomas, D. (2007). Unfinished business: The impact of race on understanding mentoring relationships. In B. R. Ragins & K. E. Kram (Eds.), *The handbook of mentoring at work* (pp. 223–247). Thousand Oaks, CA: Sage Publications.

Boal, K. B., & Hooijberg, R. (2000). Strategic leadership research: Moving on. *Leadership Quarterly, 11*, 515–549.

Bowen, D. E., & Ostroff, C. (2004). Understanding HRM-firm performance linkages: The role of the "strength" of the HRM system. *Academy of Management Review, 29*(2), 203–221.

Boyatzis, R. E. (1982). *The competent manager: a model for effective performance.* New York: Wiley.

Boyatzis, R. E. (2006). Intentional change theory from a complexity perspective. *Journal of Management Development, 25*(7), 607–623.

Brewer, M. B. (1991). The social self: On being the same and different at the same time. *Personality and Social Psychology Bulletin, 17,* 475–482.

Brewer, M. B. (1995). Managing diversity: The role of social identities. In S. E. Jackson & M. N. Ruderman (Eds.), *Diversity in work teams* (pp. 47–68). Washington, DC: American Psychological Association.

Brewer, M. B. (1999). The psychology of prejudice: Ingroup love or outgroup hate? *Journal of Social Issues, 55*(3), 429–444.

Brewer, M. B., & Miller, N. (1984). Beyond the contact hypothesis: Theoretical perspectives on desegregation. In N. Miller & M. B. Brewer (Eds.), *Group in contact: The psychology of desegregation* (pp. 281–302). Orlando, FL: Academic Press.

Brickson, S. (2000). The impact of identity orientation on individual and organizational outcomes in demographically diverse settings. *Academy of Management Review, 25*(1), 82–101.

Chao, G. T. (2007). Mentoring and organizational socialization: Networks for work adjustment. In B. R. Ragins & K. E. Kram (Eds.), *The handbook of mentoring at work*(pp. 179–196). Thousand Oaks, CA: Sage Publications.

Chen, C. C., & Van Velsor, E. (1996). New directions for research and practice in diversity leadership. *Leadership Quarterly, 7*(2), 285–302.

Chin, L. L. (2010). Introduction to the special issue on diversity and leadership. *American Psychologist, 65*(3), 150–156.

Chrobot-Mason, D., Hays-Thomas, R., & Wishik, H. R. (2008). Understanding and defusing resistance to diversity training and learning. In K. Thomas (Ed)., *Diversity resistance in organizations* (pp. 23–54). New York: Lawrence Erlbaum Associates.

Chrobot-Mason, D., Ruderman, M. R., Weber, T., & Ernst, C. (2009). The challenge of leading on unstable ground: Triggers that activate social identity faultlines. *Human Relations, 62*(5), 1763–1794.

Cox, T., Jr. (1991). The multicultural organization. *Academy of Management Executive, 5,* 34–47.

Crossan, M., Vera, D., & Nanjad, L. (2008). Transcendent leadership: Strategic leadership in dynamic environments. *Leadership Quarterly, 19,* 569–581.

De Dreu, C. K. W., & Van Vianen, A. E. M. (2001). Managing relationship conflict and the effectiveness of organizational teams. *Journal of Organizational Behavior, 22,* 309–328.

De Dreu, C. K. W., & Weingart, L. R. (2003). Task versus relationship conflict, team performance, and team member satisfaction: A meta-analysis. *Journal of Applied Psychology, 88*(4), 741–749.

DeRue, D. S., & Ashford, S. J. (2010). Who will lead and who will follow? A social process of leadership identity construction in organizations. *Academy of Management Review, 35,* 627–647.

Detert, J. R., & Burris, E. R. (2007), Leadership behavior and employee voice: Is the door really open? *Academy of Management Journal, 50*(4), 869–884.

DiTomaso, N., &Hooijberg, R. (1996). Diversity and the demands of leadership. *Leadership Quarterly, 7,* 163–187.

Dragoni, L. (2005). Understanding the emergence of state goal orientation in organizational work groups: The role of leadership and multilevel climate perceptions. *Journal of Applied Psychology, 90,* 1084–1095.

Drath, W. H., McCauley, C. D., Palus, C. J., Van Velsor, E., O'Connor, P.M.G., & McGuire, J. B. (2008). Direction, alignment, commitment: Toward a more integrative ontology of leadership. *Leadership Quarterly, 19*(6), 635–653.

Dreher, G. F., & Cox. T. H. (1996). Race, gender and opportunity: A study of compensation attainment and the establishment of mentoring relationships. *Journal of Applied Psychology, 81*(3), 297–308.

Duck, J. M., & Fielding, K. S. (1999). Leaders and subgroups: One of us or one of them? *Group Processes & Intergroup Relations, 2,* 203–230.

Duck, J. M., & Fielding, K. S. (2003). Leaders and their treatment of subgroups: implications for evaluations of the leader and the superordinate group. *European Journal of Social Psychology, 33,* 387–401.

Dvir, T., Kass, N., & Shamir, B. (2004). The emotional bond: Vision and organizational commitment among high-tech employees. *Journal of Organizational Change Management, 17*(2), 126–143.

Eagly, A., & Chin, J. L. (2010). Diversity and leadership in a changing world. *American Psychologist, 65*(3), 216–224.

Eagly, A. H., & Carli, L. L. (2007). *Through the labyrinth: The truth about how women become leaders.* Boston: Harvard Business School Press.

Eagly, A. H., & Karau, S. J. (2002). Role congruity theory of prejudice toward female leaders. *Psychological Review, 109,* 573–598.

Eggins, R. A., Haslam, S. A., & Reynolds, K. J. (2002). Social identity and negotiation: Subgroup representation and superordinate consensus. *Personality and Social Psychology Bulletin, 28,* 887–899.

Ensari, N., & Murphy, S. (2003). Cross-cultural variations in leadership perceptions and attribution of charisma to the leader. *Organizational Behavior and Human Decision Processes, 92*(1–2), 52–66.

Ernst, C., & Chrobot-Mason, D. (2011). *Boundary spanning leadership: Six practices for solving problems, driving innovation and transforming organizations.* New York: McGraw-Hill.

Ernst, C., Hannum, K. M., & Ruderman, M. N. (2010). Developing intergroup leadership. In E. Van Velsor, C. D. McCauley, & M. N. Ruderman (Eds.), *Center for Creative Leadership handbook of leadership development* (3rd ed., pp. 375–404). San Francisco: Jossey-Bass.

Faraj, S., & Yan, S. (2009). Boundary work in knowledge teams. *Journal of Applied Psychology, 94,* 604–617.

Ferdman, B. M. (2008). Who perceives more discrimination? Individual difference predictors among Latinos and Anglos. *Business Journal of Hispanic Research, 2*(3), 71–75.

Ferdman, B. M., Katz, J., Letchinger, E., & Thompson, C. T. (2009). *Inclusive behavior and practices.* Unpublished manuscript prepared for the Institute for Inclusion.

Findler, L., Wind, L. H., & Mor Barak, M. E. (2007). The challenge of workforce management in a global society: Modeling the relationship between diversity, inclusion, organizational culture, and employee well-being, job satisfaction and organizational commitment. *Administration in Social Work, 31*(3), 63–94.

Fiol, C. M., Pratt, M. G., & O'Connor, E. J. (2009). Managing intractable identity conflicts. *Academy of Management Review, 34*(1), 32–55.

Fletcher, J. K. (2010). Leadership as relational practice. In K. A. Bunker, D. T. Hall, & K. E. Kram (Eds.), *Extraordinary leadership: Addressing the gaps in senior executive development.* San Francisco: Jossey-Bass.

Ford, L. R., & Seers, A. (2006). Relational leadership and team climates: Pitting differentiation versus agreement. *Leadership Quarterly, 17,* 258–270.

Friedman, R., Kane, M., & Cornfield, D. B. (1998). Social support and career optimism: Examining the effectiveness of network groups among black managers. *Human Relations, 51*(9), 1155–1177.

Friedman, R. A., & Holtom, B. (2002). The effects of network groups on minority employee turnover intentions. *Human Resource Management, 41*(4), 405–421.

Gaertner, S., & Dovidio, J. F. (2007). Addressing contemporary racism: The common intergroup identity model. In C. Willos-Esqueda (Ed.), *Motivational aspects of prejudice and racism* (pp. 111–133). New York: Springer.

Gelfand, M. J., Major, V. S., Raver, J. L., Nishii, L. H., & O'Brien, K. (2006). Negotiating relationally: The dynamics of the relational self in negotiations. *Academy of Management Review, 31*(2), 427–451.

Gerstner, C. R., & Day, D. V. (1997). Meta-analytic review of leader-member exchange theory: Correlates and construct issues. *Journal of Applied Psychology, 82,* 827–844.

Giscombe, K. (2007). Advancing women through the glass ceiling with formal mentoring. In B. R. Ragins & K. E. Kram (Eds.), *The handbook of mentoring at work* (pp. 549–572). Thousand Oaks, CA: Sage Publications.

Godshalk, V. M., & Sosik, J. J. (2007). Mentoring and leadership: Standing at the crossroads of theory, research, and practice. In B. R. Ragins & K. E. Kram (Eds.), *The handbook of mentoring at work* (pp. 149–178). Thousand Oaks, CA: Sage Publications.

Graen, G. B., & Uhl-Bien, M. (1995). Development of leader-member exchange (LMX) theory of leadership over 25 years: Applying a multi-level-multi-domain perspective. *Leadership Quarterly*, 6, 219–247.

Graetz, F., & Smith, A. C. T. (2009).Changing forms of organizing in Australian public companies. *Asia Pacific Journal of Human Resources*, 47(3), 340–360.

Gratton, L., Voigt, A., & Erickson, T. (2007). Bridging faultlines in diverse teams. *MIT Sloan Management Review*, 22–29.

Hannum, K. (2007). *Social identity—knowing yourself, leading others*. Greensboro, NC: Center for Creative Leadership.

Hannum, K. M., & Glover, S. L. (2010). Respect. In R. A. Couto (Ed.), *Political and civic leadership* (pp. 611–618). Thousand Oaks, CA: Sage.

Haslam, S. A., Eggins, R. A., & Reynolds, K. J. (2003). The ASPIRe model: Actualizing social and personal identity resources to enhance organizational outcomes. *Journal of Occupational and Organizational Psychology*, 76, 83–113.

Haslam, S. A., & Ellemers, N. (2005). Social identity in industrial and organizational psychology: Concepts, controversies, and contributions. In G. P. Hodgkinson & J. K. Ford (Eds.), *International review of industrial and organizational psychology* (Vol. 20, pp. 39–118). Chichester, UK: John Wiley & Sons, Ltd.

Hewstone, M., & Brown, R. (1986). Contact is not enough: An intergroup perspective on the contact hypothesis. In R. C. Hewstone & R. J. Brown (Eds.), *Contact and conflict in intergroup encounters* (pp. 1–44). Oxford: Blackwell.

Hofmann, W., Gawronski, B., Gschwendner, T., Le, H., & Schmitt, M. (2005). A meta-analysis on the correlation between the implicit association test and explicit self-report measures. *Personality and Social Psychology Bulletin*, 31(10), 1369–1385.

Hogg, M. A.(2001). A social identity theory of leadership. *Personality and Social Psychology Review*, 5, 184–200.

Hogg, M. A., Martin, R., Epitropaki, O., Mankad, A., Svensson, A., & Weeden, K. (2005). Effective leadership in salient groups: Revisiting leader-member exchange theory from the perspective of the social identity theory of leadership. *Personality and Social Psychology Bulletin*, 31(7), 991–1004.

Hogg, M. A., & van Knippenberg, D. (2003). Social identity and leadership processes in groups. *Advances in Experimental Social Psychology*, 35, 1–52.

Holvino, E., Ferdman, B. M., & Merrill-Sands, D. (2004). Creating and sustaining diversity and inclusion in organizations: strategies and approaches. In M. S. Stockdale & F. J. Crosby (Eds.), *The psychology and management of workplace diversity* (pp. 245–276). Malden, MA: Blackwell.

Howell, J. M., & Shamir, B. (2005). The role of followers in the charismatic leadership process: Relationships and their consequences. *Academy of Management Review*, 30, 96–112.

Ibarra, H. (1992). Homophily and differential returns: Sex differences in network structure and access in an advertising firm. *Administrative Science Quarterly*, 37(3), 422–447.

James, E. H., & Wooten, L. P. (2006). Diversity crises: How firms manage discrimination lawsuits. *Academy of Management Journal*, 49(6), 1103–1118.

James, E. H., & Wooten, L. P. (2005). Leadership as (Un)usual: How to display competence in times of crisis. *Organizational Dynamics*, 34(2), 141–152.

Jayne, M. E., & Dipboye, R. L. (2004). Leveraging diversity to improve business performance: Research findings and recommendations for organizations. *Human Resource Management*, 43, 409–424.

Jehn, K. A. (1995). A multimethod examination of the benefits and detriments of intragroup conflict. *Administrative Science Quarterly*, 40, 256–282.

Joshi, A., Lazarova, M. B., & Liao, H. (2009). Getting everyone on board: The role of inspirational leadership in geographically dispersed teams. *Organization Science*, 20, 240–252.

Kalev, A., Dobbin, F., & Kelly, E. (2006). Best practices or best guesses? Assessing the efficacy of corporate affirmative action and diversity policies. *American Sociological Review*, 71, 589–617.

Kearney, E., & Gebert, D. (2009). Managing diversity and enhancing team outcomes: The promise of transformational leadership. *Journal of Applied Psychology*, 94, 77–89.

Kegan, R. (1982). *The evolving self: Problem and process in human development*. Cambridge, MA: Harvard University Press.

Kegan, R. (1994). *In over our heads: The mental demands of modern life*. Cambridge, MA: Harvard University Press.

Kram, K. E. (1985). *Mentoring at work: Developmental relationships in organizational life*. Glenview, IL: Scott, Foresman.

Lau, D. C. & Murnighan, J. K. (1998). Demographic diversity and faultlines: The compositional dynamics of organizational groups. *Academy of Management Review*, 23, 325–340.

Liden, R. C., Erdogan, B., Wayne, S. J., & Sparrowe, R. T. (2006). Leader-member exchange, differentiation, and task interdependence: Implications for individual and group performance. *Journal of Organizational Behavior*, 27, 723–746.

Livers, A. B., & Caver, K. A. (2003). *Leading in black and white: working across the racial divide in corporate America*. San Francisco; Greensboro, NC: Jossey-Bass; Center for Creative Leadership.

Lord, R. G., & Hall, R. J. (2005). Identity, deep structure and the development of leadership skill. *Leadership Quarterly*, 16(4), 591–615.

Madon, S. (1997). What do people believe about gay males? A study of stereotype content and strength. *Sex Roles*, 37, 663–685.

McCall, M. W. (2010). Recasting leadership development. *Industrial and Organizational Psychology: Perspectives on Science and Practice*, 3(1), 3–19.

McCauley, C. D. (2010). Concepts of leadership. In Elaine Biech (Ed.), *ASTD leadership handbook* (pp. 1–11). Alexandria, VA: ASTD Press.

McCauley, C. D., Van Velsor, E., & Ruderman, M. N. (2010). Introduction: Our view of leadership development. In E. Van Velsor, C. D. McCauley, & M.N. Ruderman (Eds.), *Center for Creative Leadership handbook of leadership development* (3rd ed., pp. 1–26). San Francisco: Jossey-Bass.

McClane, W. E. (1991). Implications of member role differentiation: Analysis of a key concept in the LMX model of leadership. *Group and Organization Studies*, 16, 102–113.

McIntosh, P. (2007, February 15). White privilege: Unpacking the invisible knapsack. *Rachel's Democracy and Health News*.

Milliken, F. J., & Martins, L. L. (1996). Searching for common threads: Understanding the multiple effects of diversity in organizational groups. *Academy of Management Review, 21*(2), 402–433.

Mintzberg, H. (1973). *The nature of managerial work*. New York: Harper & Row.

Mitchell, R. J., & Boyle, B. (2009). A theoretical model of transformational leadership's role in diverse teams. *Leadership & Organization Development Journal, 30*(5), 455–474.

Moskowitz, G. B., Gollwitzer, P. M., Wasel, W., & Schaal, B. (1999). Preconscious control of stereotype activation through chronic egalitarian goals. *Journal of Personality and Social Psychology, 77*(1), 167–184.

Munusamy, V. P., Ruderman, M. N., & Eckert, R.H. (2010). Leader development and social identity. In E. Van Velsor, C. D. McCauley, & M.N. Ruderman (Eds.), *Center for Creative Leadership handbook of leadership development* (3rd ed., pp. 147–175). San Francisco: Jossey-Bass.

Nembhard, I. M., & Edmondson, A. C. (2006). Making it safe: The effects of leader inclusiveness and professional status on psychological safety and improvement efforts in health care teams. *Journal of Organizational Behavior, 27*(7), 941–966.

Nishii, L. H. (2010). *The benefits of climate for inclusion for diverse groups*. Unpublished manuscript.

Nishii, L. H., & Langevin, A. (2010). *Managers' diversity attributions: Why we should care*. Poster presented at the annual conference of the Society for Industrial and Organizational Psychology in Atlanta, GA.

Nishii, L. H., Langevin, A., & Bruyere, S. (2010). *Ageism and the retention of high performers: The positive impact of three forms of inclusion*. Technical report submitted to the SHRM Foundation.

Nishii, L. H., Lepak, D. P., & Schneider, B. (2008). Employee attributions of the "why" of HR practices: Their effects on employee attitudes and behaviors, and customer satisfaction. *Personnel Psychology, 61*, 503–545.

Nishii, L. H., & Mayer, D. M. (2009). Do inclusive leaders help to reduce turnover in diverse groups? The moderating role of leader-member exchange in the diversity to turnover relationship. *Journal of Applied Psychology, 94*(6), 1412–1426.

Nishii, L. H., & Wright, P. (2008). Variability within organizations: Implications for strategic human resource management. In D. B. Smith (Ed.), *The people make the place* (pp. 225–248). Mahwah, NJ: Lawrence Erlbaum Associates.

Oshry, B. (2010). People in context. In K. A. Bunker, D. T. Hall, & K. E. Kram (Eds.), *Extraordinary leadership: Addressing the gaps in senior executive development* (pp.175–196). San Francisco: Jossey-Bass.

Page, S. E. (2007). Making the difference: Applying the logic of diversity. *Academy of Management Perspectives, 21*(4), 6–20.

Pearce, C. L., & Conger, J. A. (2003). All those years ago: the historical underpinnings of shared leadership. In C. L. Pearce & J. A. Conger (Eds.), *Shared leadership: Reframing the hows and whys of leadership* (pp. 2–18). Thousand Oaks, CA: Sage.

Pfeffer, J. (1981). Management as symbolic action: The creation and maintenance of organizational paradigms. In B. B. Staw & L. L. Cummings (Eds.), *Research in organizational behavior* (Vol. 3, pp. 1–52). Greenwich, CT: JAI.

Pittinsky, T. L. (2010). A two-dimensional model of intergroup leadership. The case of national diversity. *American Psychologist, 65*(3), 194–200.

Pittinsky, T. L., & Maruskin, L. (2008). Allophilia: Beyond prejudice. In S. J. Lopez (Ed.), *Positive psychology* (Vol. 2, pp. 141–148). Westport, CT: Praeger.

Pittinsky, T. L., & Montoya, R. M. (2009). Is valuing equality enough? Equality values, allophilia, and social policy support for multiracial individuals. *Journal of Social Issues, 65*, 151–163.

Prime, J., & Moss-Racusin, C.A. (2009). *Engaging men in gender initiatives: What change agents need to know*. New York: A Catalyst Publication.

Reicher, S. D., & Hopkins, N. (1996). Seeking influence through characterizing self-categories: An analysis of anti-abortion rhetoric. *British Journal of Social Psychology, 35*, 297–311.

Ridgeway, C. L. (1991). The social construction of status value: Gender and other nominal characteristics. *Social Forces, 70*, 367–386.

Ridgeway, C. L., & Correll, S. J. (2006). Consensus and the creation of status beliefs. *Social Forces, 85*(1), 431–453.

Rosette, A. S., Leonardelli, G. J., & Phillips, K. W. (2008). The white standard: Racial bias in leader categorization. *Journal of Applied Psychology, 93*(4), 758–777.

Ruderman, M. N., Glover, S., Chrobot-Mason, D., & Ernst, C. (2010). Leadership practices across social identity groups. In K. Hannum, B. B. McFeeters, & L. Booysen (Eds.), *Leading across differences* (pp. 95–114). San Francisco: Pfieffer.

Ryan, M., & Haslam, A. (2005). The glass cliff: Evidence that women are over-represented in precarious leadership positions. *British Journal of Management, 15*, 1–10.

Scandura, T. A., & Lankau, M. J. (1996). Developing diverse leaders: A leader-member exchange approach. *Leadership Quarterly, 7*(2), 243–263.

Schein, V. E. (1973). The relationship between sex role stereotypes and requisite management characteristics. *Journal of Applied Psychology, 57*, 95–100.

Schein, V. E. (1975). The relationship between sex role stereotypes and requisite management characteristics among female managers. *Journal of Applied Psychology, 60*, 340–344.

Schein, V., Mueller, R., Lituchy, T., & Liu, J. (1996). Think manager—think male: A global phenomenon? *Journal of Organizational Behavior, 17*(1), 33–41.

Schyns, B., Paul, T., Mohr, G., & Blank, H. (2005). Comparing antecedents and consequences of leader-member exchange in a German working context to findings in the US. *European Journal of Work and Organizational Psychology, 14*, 1–22.

Shore, L. M., Randel, A. E., Chung, B. G., Dean, M. A., Ehrhart, K. H., & Singh, G. (2011). Inclusion and diversity in work groups: A review and model for future research. *Journal of Management, 37*(4), 1262–1289.

Simons, T. (2002). Behavioral integrity: The perceived alignment between managers' words and deeds as a research focus. *Organizational Science, 13*(1), 18–35.

Staw, B. M. (1980). The consequences of turnover. *Journal of Occupational Behavior, 1*, 253–273.

Sy, T., Shore, L., Strauss, J., Shore, T., Tram, S., Whiteley, P., & Ikeda-Muromachi, K. (2010). Leadership perceptions as a function of race-occupation fit: The case of Asian Americans. *Journal of Applied Psychology, 95*(5), 902–1010.

Tajfel, H., & Turner, J. C. (1979). An integrative theory of intergroup conflict. In W. S. Austin & S. Worchel (Eds.), *The social psychology of intergroup relations* (pp. 33–47). Monterey, CA: Brooks/Cole.

Tajfel, H., & Turner, J. C. (1986). The social identity theory of inter-group behavior. In S. Worchel & L. W. Austin (Eds.), *Psychology of intergroup relations*. Chicago: Nelson-Hall.

Thomas, K. M., & Chrobot-Mason, D. (2005). Group-level explanations of workplace discrimination. In R. L. Dipboye

& A. Colella (Eds.), *Discrimination at work: The psychological and organizational bases* (pp. 63–88). Mahwah, NJ: Lawrence Erlbaum Associates.

Toosi, M. (2009). Employment outlook: 2008–18. Labor force projections to 2018: older workers staying more active. *Monthly Labor Review*, November, 30–51.

Turner, J. C. (1982). Towards a cognitive redefinition of the group. In H. Tajfel (Ed.), *Social identity and intergroup relations*. Cambridge: Cambridge University Press.

Turner, J. C. (1985). Social categorization and the self-concept: A social cognitive theory of group behaviour. In E. J. Lawler (Ed.) *Advances in group processes* (2nd ed., pp. 77–122). Greenwich, CT: JAI Press.

Turner, J. C. (2004). Foreword, What the social identity approach is and why it matters. In S. A Haslam (Ed.), *Psychology in organizations: The social identity approach* (p. xvii). London: Sage.

Van Knippenberg, D., Van Knippenberg, B., De Cremer, D., & Hogg, M. A. (2004). Leadership, self, and identity: A review and research agenda. *Leadership Quarterly, 15,* 825–856.

Warren, A. K. (2009). *Cascading gender biases, compounding effects: An assessment of talent management systems*. New York: A Catalyst Publication.

Wasserman, I. C., Gallegos, P. V., & Ferdman, B. M. (2008). Dancing with resistance: Leadership challenges in fostering a culture of inclusion. In K. M. Thomas (Ed.), *Diversity resistance in organizations* (pp.175–200). New York: Taylor & Francis.

Weick, K. M. (1979). *The social psychology of organizing*. Reading, MA: Addison-Wesley.

Zohar, D., & Luria, G. (2004). Climate as a social-cognitive construction of supervisory safety practices: Scripts as proxy for behavioral patterns. *Journal of Applied Psychology, 89,* 322–333.

CHAPTER 19

Effective Diversity Training

Loriann Roberson, Carol T. Kulik *and* Rae Yunzi Tan

Abstract

Diversity training is an important and widely used component of organizational diversity management initiatives. This chapter reviews theory and research on diversity training design, delivery, evaluation, and effectiveness. The review suggests that in the past 10 to 15 years of research, advancements have been made on several fronts. The research literature on diversity training includes frameworks for pretraining needs assessment, learning models to guide diversity training design choices, and empirical evidence of diversity training's impact on training outcomes. However, the review also notes two major shortcomings. First, research has emphasized diversity training's effect on short-term changes in trainees' knowledge and attitudes, neglecting longer-term changes in their skills and behavior. Second, research has emphasized diversity training's effect on individual-level learning outcomes, neglecting its impact on team- and organization-level outcomes. These shortcomings are unlikely to be addressed unless scholars and practitioners engage in more collaborative field-based research on diversity training.

Key Words: diversity training, diversity training design, diversity training evaluation, diversity training effectiveness, diversity training research

Diversity training has been a key component of organizational diversity management initiatives for many years (Esen, 2005). Seventy-one percent of human resource (HR) professionals reported that diversity training was a part of their diversity management strategy in a recent survey, which reflected a slight increase from 67 percent found in a similar sample surveyed in 2005 (Society for Human Resource Management, 2010). Where diversity training is used it is often seen as essential: the study cited above further reported that 68 percent of these organizations offered mandatory diversity training to their top-level executives, with 70 percent requiring diversity training participation of nonmanagerial employees (Society for Human Resource Management, 2010). These numbers reflect managers' strong beliefs in the value of diversity training.

What do organizations want from diversity training? The objectives for diversity training span individual and organizational levels. Most immediately, diversity training is intended to increase diversity awareness in individuals, to promote positive intergroup attitudes, and to motivate positive behaviors among organizational members (Pendry, Driscoll, & Field, 2007). This training is believed to reduce prejudice and discrimination, facilitating positive intergroup interactions among coworkers and customers and enhancing organizational climate and morale (Cocchiara, Connerley, & Bell, 2010; Pendry et al., 2007; Wentling & Palma-Rivas, 1998). The "business case" further links these outcomes to an organization's competitive advantage: its flexibility and reputation, its ability to attract and retain talent, and its access to broader and more diverse markets (Cox & Blake, 1991; Jayne & Dipboye, 2004). When diversity training is linked to such an extensive set of organizational goals, it is no wonder that training is so enthusiastically embraced and so widely used.

The literature has documented the proliferation of diversity training across organizations and also noted that scholarly research on diversity training has lagged behind practice (Kulik & Roberson, 2008a). For years, writers called for more attention to research on diversity training (Chrobot-Mason & Quiñones, 2002; Kulik & Roberson, 2008a; Pendry et al., 2007). Research can play an important role in increasing the effectiveness of training by examining the outcomes and consequences of training efforts, indicating key factors needed to ensure training success, and identifying the most useful types of training (Aguinis & Kraiger, 2009). The past 10 to 15 years have witnessed a growth in scholarly interest and research on diversity training interventions. The purpose of this chapter is to summarize this literature. The chapter's structure reflects the full cycle involved in implementing effective diversity training—beginning with an assessment of the organization's needs, proceeding with the critical design and delivery decisions, and concluding with an evaluation of the training's effectiveness. In the final section, we offer conclusions about the effectiveness of diversity training and directions for future research.

Implementing effective diversity training

The instructional design model (Goldstein, 1993; Goldstein & Ford, 2002) serves as a standard for developing training and is commonly seen as key to improving the effectiveness of training (Goldstein & Ford, 2002; Noe, 1999). The model outlines a systematic approach, moving from the assessment of needs and employee pretraining states to training design and training evaluation. In the following sections we review theory and research on diversity training related to each of these stages.

Needs assessment

The instructional design model places needs assessment as the critical first step. It is used to determine what kind of training is needed, who should be trained, and whether organizational conditions will support training so that learning transfers to the job (Chrobot-Mason & Quiñones, 2002; Goldstein, 1993). One desired outcome of this assessment phase is a set of training goals and objectives that will guide program design and the choice of measures used to evaluate training success.

Another is evaluating trainees' readiness for training, which may also influence training design decisions and effectiveness (Salas & Cannon-Bowers, 2001). Needs assessment is seen as a prerequisite for successful training (Chrobot-Mason & Quiñones, 2002; Salas & Cannon-Bowers, 2001), and its omission is cited as a main cause of training failure (Bunch, 2007).

Training needs assessment consists of three related facets that together provide direction and guidance for the training program: organization analysis, task or operations analysis, and person analysis.

ORGANIZATION ANALYSIS

The purpose of an organization analysis is to identify aspects of the organizational context that could influence training delivery and results (Salas & Cannon-Bowers, 2001). In the diversity training literature, this phase of needs assessment has been viewed as the most important (Ford & Fisher, 1996) and has received the most research attention (Roberson, Kulik, & Pepper, 2003). The diversity training literature emphasizes the use of this phase for identifying the nature of diversity-related problems in the organization and gathering baseline data (Chrobot-Mason & Quiñones, 2002; King, Gulick, & Avery, 2009). One recommended framework for guiding organization analysis is Cox's (1991) six dimensions of a multicultural organization, suggested by Chrobot-Mason and Quiñones (2002). The use of Thomas and Ely's (1996) three paradigms for diversity in organization analysis has also been proposed (Chavez & Weisinger, 2008; Chrobot-Mason & Quiñones, 2002). Joplin and Daus (1997) present a model of organizational diversity integration that can be used as a needs assessment tool. Based on an individual-level developmental stage model of attitudes toward diversity (Baldwin & Hecht, 1995; Bennett, 1986), Joplin and Daus's (1997) model proposes three stages of organization-level diversity integration—intolerance, tolerance, and acceptance—with each stage having implications for training decisions.

Some specific measures useful for organizational analysis have also been presented in the literature. Larkey's (1996) Workforce Diversity Questionnaire assesses interactions in diverse groups as an indicator of diversity climate. Dahm, Willems, Ivancevich, and Graves (2009) built upon Larkey's work to develop the Organizational Diversity Needs Analysis Instrument to assess diversity climate and identify diversity-related problems. The Positive Climate for Diversity Scale (Chrobot-Mason & Aramovitch,

2004) is based on Cox's (1991) dimensions of a multicultural organization. Mor Barak, Chenin, and Berkman (1998) presented the Diversity Perceptions Scale, which assesses two organizational aspects of diversity climate (fairness and inclusion) and two personal attitudes (value of diversity and comfort with diversity). Soni (2000) provides two scales that assess perceptions of cross-group interactions (i.e., their quality and frequency) and perceived discrimination. Although several measures have been developed, Chrobot-Mason, Konrad, and Linnehan (2006) note that limited validity evidence is available. The usefulness of these measures for diversity training needs assessment has not yet been demonstrated.

In discussions of organization analysis, most of the literature emphasizes the analysis of diversity climate and identification of diversity-related problems. However, Roberson and colleagues (2003) suggest organization analysis can also be used to help answer more specific questions in the design and delivery of diversity training, such as the decision to use confrontation as a training method or the choice between awareness or skill training.

OPERATIONS OR TASK ANALYSIS

Organization analysis receives the most attention in the diversity training literature as a foundation for effective training. In contrast, the second aspect of training needs assessment, operations or task analysis, has been relatively ignored. This phase is used to specify the behaviors, knowledge, skills, and abilities needed for effective performance, typically using job analytic techniques (Goldstein, 1993; Salas & Cannon-Bowers, 2001). The importance of operations analysis is obvious when designing job skill training—operations analysis identifies the important tasks and the competencies that incumbents must learn to perform well. But in the diversity training literature, operations analysis has not always been viewed as relevant, since similar training content is usually provided to all employees regardless of their specific job responsibilities (Chrobot-Mason & Quiñones, 2002). Roberson and colleagues (2003) also did not identify operations analysis as particularly helpful in resolving five diversity training controversies. However, there is an important role for operations analysis in identifying the diversity competencies that will form the basis of training objectives. Diversity competencies define the knowledge, skills, and behaviors that characterize excellent performance. Some diversity competencies will be non–job-specific (e.g., ability to work effectively in a diverse team) and therefore relevant to all jobs. However, other competencies are likely to be specific for particular organizational roles, such as customer service or managerial jobs (e.g., ability to accommodate the needs of diverse clients or to deliver constructive performance feedback to diverse employees). As King and colleagues (2009) noted, focusing on behavioral competencies is a best practice in the general training literature that should be adopted in diversity training. Yet there has been little work in the literature to identify the nature of diversity competencies, and a generally accepted list of diversity competencies is not yet available (Day & Glick, 2000; Salas, Wilson, & Lyons, 2008).

Even though a taxonomy of diversity competencies has yet to gain wide acceptance, there has been some progress in this area. Garcia (1995) presented a set of objectives and skills for culturally competent communication. Joplin and Daus (1997) and Holmes (2004) also discussed attributes and skills required to effectively manage diversity initiatives. Day and Glick (2000) identified diversity skills important to HR managers, including team building, communication, and diversity management. Noting the vagueness of most definitions of diversity competence, Chrobot-Mason (2003) presented a list of 20 diversity competencies and associated behavioral indicators based on the diversity management and counseling psychology literatures. Work such as this will prove useful as a guide for diversity trainers and training design.

PERSON ANALYSIS

In the person analysis phase, the skill levels and readiness for training are assessed in individual trainees so that training can be tailored to their needs (Chrobot-Mason & Quiñones, 2002). Roberson and colleagues (2003) noted that person analysis has been largely ignored in the diversity training literature and suggested trainees' attitudes toward diversity, their previous experience with diversity, inconsistencies between attitude and behavior, and trust between trainers and trainees as individual differences that may influence training decisions and outcomes. Attitudes toward diversity can influence receptiveness to training (Chrobot-Mason & Quiñones, 2002) and guide the organization's choice of awareness or skill training (Roberson et al., 2003). To assess these diversity attitudes, King and colleagues (2009) suggested the Reaction-to-Diversity Inventory (DeMeuse & Hostager, 2001), which measures emotional reactions to diversity, behavioral intentions, and perceived personal consequences of diversity. The scale allows classification of respondents into Optimists, Realists, and Pessimists. Two other attitude measures are provided by Soni (2000): receptivity to diversity and receptivity to diversity management initiatives. Several instruments from counseling psychology have also been recommended. The Miville-Guzman Universality-Diversity Scale (Miville et al., 1999) assesses awareness and acceptance of both similarities and differences across national, regional, and racio-ethnic cultures. King and colleagues (2009) and Chrobot-Mason and colleagues (2006) recommend using this scale to identify training topics that require more or less attention. Racial or ethnic identity attitude measures (Helms, 1990; Phinney, 1992) can also indicate receptiveness and readiness for training, suggest training content, or influence training outcomes (Chrobot-Mason & Quiñones, 2002; Chrobot-Mason et al., 2006; King et al., 2009). For example, Linnehan, Chrobot-Mason, and Konrad (2006) found that ethnic identity achievement (the extent to which individuals have reflected on their ethnicity and its implications) was positively related to intentions to support diversity goals.

Wiethoff (2004) used the Theory of Planned Behavior (Ajzen, 1991) to analyze motivation to learn from diversity training. Her model includes three major determinants of intentions to learn from training: attitudes toward diversity training, perceived control (including beliefs that one has the resources to complete the program successfully and self-efficacy for learning from training), and subjective norms (beliefs about important others' perceptions of diversity training). Wiethoff recommends the use of this model in needs assessment for diversity training and suggests methods for collecting data on each of its components.

Finally, several writers have noted the value of assessing trainees' previous experience with diversity (Chrobot-Mason & Quiñones, 2002; King et al., 2009; Roberson et al., 2003). Chrobot-Mason and Quiñones (2002) suggest that previous experience may be related to training receptiveness and motivation to learn, and some evidence supports this. In Roberson and colleagues' (2001) study, the amount of previous diversity training experienced by trainees was positively related to cognitive and skill outcomes after diversity training. In research conducted by Kulik, Pepper, Roberson, and Parker (2007), trainees with previous diversity training reported greater interest in participating in further training.

Trainee experience may also influence the effectiveness of homogeneous or heterogeneous training groups (Roberson et al., 2001), with homogeneous training more effective for high-experience trainees.

SUMMARY

Although needs assessment is acknowledged as a best practice in the diversity training literature (Chrobot-Mason & Quiñones, 2002; Tan, Morris, & Romero, 1996), many organizations initiate training without conducting a needs assessment (Chavez & Weisinger, 2008; Hite & McDonald, 2006). Recent theoretical and empirical work on needs assessment is encouraging, with attention turning to operations and person analysis as well as organization analysis. These advances should encourage greater use of diversity training needs assessment.

Diversity training design

Program design refers to the organization and coordination of the training program (Noe, 1999). The design specifies the training content and the training activities for reaching the objectives. In this section we review the literature on diversity training design and delivery.

MODELS AND METHODS FOR DIVERSITY TRAINING DESIGN

While needs assessment ensures that the training program will be focused on critical knowledge, skills, or competencies and will be directed toward the appropriate trainee population, ideally a theory of learning also guides decisions about training content and methods (Ferdman, 2008; Sleezer, 2004). Diversity training has been heavily criticized as atheoretical and lacking models underlying training content (Paluck & Green, 2009; Pendry et al., 2007), but increasingly, theory and research are being used to suggest diversity training content and also to analyze existing diversity training methods. Models of diversity learning have been posited and elaborated, and evidence regarding their effectiveness is accumulating. Here, we organize our review of training methods around the two most common models for diversity training design.

Awareness first. A popular model of diversity learning proposes that diversity competency develops in stages, with diversity awareness developing first, before other learning. While this model is not new (Cox & Beale, 1997; Wentling & Palma-Rivas, 2000), recent work has continued to elaborate and refine it. For example, Chrobot-Mason (2003) and Chrobot-Mason and Quiñones (2002) propose a model based on developmental theories of cultural competency (Bennett, 1986) and racial or ethnic identity (Cross, 1978; Helms, 1990; Phinney, 1993), as well as Kraiger, Ford, and Salas's (1993) taxonomy of learning outcomes. Their model posits that diversity or multicultural competence develops in three stages: first diversity awareness, then behavioral learning, and finally action planning, in which behavioral intentions reflect earlier changes in values and attitudes. Variants of an "awareness first" model that differ in the number of stages have been put forward (e.g., Asburn-Nardo, Morris, & Goodwin, 2008; Avery & Thomas, 2004; Badhesha, Schmidtke, Cummings & Moore, 2008; Papadopoulos, Tilki & Lees, 2004; Ramsey, 1996); all of these models consistently place diversity awareness as the first stage of change. The obvious implication of these models for diversity training is that training should start with increasing awareness before addressing the other stages.

Diversity awareness is variously and loosely defined and typically refers to a combination of cognitive and affective outcomes (Chrobot-Mason, 2003; Chrobot-Mason & Quiñones, 2002). Cognitive outcomes included in awareness concern knowledge of facts, or declarative knowledge. In diversity training, relevant knowledge may refer to facts about different social identity groups (i.e., people with disabilities, Asians, Native Americans); facts about diversity in society (i.e., changing demographics, the business case for diversity, the continued existence of bias and discrimination); knowledge of social cognition theory and research (i.e., the stereotyping process and cognitive biases); and/or facts about diversity in the organization (i.e., the organization's stance on diversity, its diversity initiative, values, or mission).

The processes through which diversity knowledge influences attitudes and behavior have been proposed and discussed. Knowledge of the organization's diversity stance and initiatives is hoped to increase motivation and interest in programs, the perceived importance of diversity, and commitment to organizational diversity goals (Kulik & Roberson, 2008b; Pendry et al., 2007). This kind of knowledge can also influence beliefs about organizational diversity norms and expected standards of behavior (Dovidio et al., 2004). Knowledge of cognitive processes and biases is proposed to lead to increased attention to one's perceptions and less stereotyping, reducing differential treatment of other groups (Sanchez & Medkik, 2004). Information about minority groups and societal discrimination increases awareness of prejudice and factual knowledge of other social identity groups. Badhesha and colleagues (2008) argue that as valid knowledge of other groups increases, accurate information will replace false stereotypical information and reduce discriminatory behavior. Dovidio and colleagues (2004) propose that accurate information about social identity groups can also lead to the recognition of injustice and the realization that the prejudice and discrimination experienced by members of those groups are undeserved. In addition, knowledge of other social identity groups is often hoped to foster empathy through perspective taking (Dovidio et al., 2004; Pendry et al., 2007), which can lead to more positive attitudes toward other groups and increase altruistic motivation (Dovidio et al., 2004).

Traditional classroom methods are usually recommended for imparting factual knowledge (Chrobot-Mason & Quiñones, 2002; Holmes, 2004). Although this recommendation seems straightforward, even presenting facts about intergroup inequalities can be emotionally charged, triggering defensiveness and reactance (Chrobot-Mason & Quiñones, 2002; Pendry et al., 2007), or can inadvertently reinforce societal status differences among groups (Amoroso, Loyd, & Hoobler, 2009). Experienced trainers are needed to avoid these negative effects.

Another target of diversity awareness training is the organization of knowledge in memory, particularly social categorization. In the social psychology literature on intergroup relations, the categorization of people into in-groups and out-groups is viewed as a major cause of prejudice, resulting in in-group favoritism and out-group derogation (Brewer, 1997). Interventions using an intergroup approach are designed to change perceptions of group boundaries by reorganizing trainees' categorizations of their own and other groups (Paluck & Green, 2009). A substantial body of research in social psychology suggests that this reorganization can change attitudes and behaviors. Social identity and social categorization theories suggest four strategies for changing attitudes and improving group relations (Paluck & Green, 2009). One is decategorization, where individual identities are emphasized over group identities. A second is recategorization, where trainees are encouraged to think of all people as part of one large common group. In crossed categorization, the third method, two groups are made aware that they share membership in a third group. Finally, with integration methods, a common group identity is highlighted, but the value of sub-identities is simultaneously recognized and affirmed.

Some diversity training methods directly incorporate these strategies. Pendry and colleagues (2007) offer the commonly used "Who am I?" exercise, which involves trainees listing and discussing their important social identities, as an example of an intergroup strategy. This exercise can promote crossed categorization by increasing the awareness of common social identities (Pendry et al., 2007). In addition, Chavez and Weisinger (2008) present a "relational development" technique, which suggests an integration strategy.

Diversity training methods have also been analyzed using an intergroup framework. Dovidio and colleagues (2004) argue that giving factual knowledge about different identity groups can lead to decategorization by allowing trainees to see people as individuals rather than as undifferentiated out-group members. Sharing of personal stories and experiences by trainees and speakers can also facilitate decategorization (Amoroso et al., 2009). Pendry and colleagues (2007) examine other commonly used training exercises from an intergroup perspective, noting that under some circumstances, exercises that highlight group boundaries can serve to reinforce boundaries, not reduce them. Paluck (2006) also proposes ways in which intergroup contact research can inform decisions about diversity training methods and design.

Self-knowledge is a third aspect of diversity awareness. Self-knowledge refers to knowledge of one's own attitudes and biases and how they may influence one's perception and treatment of others. Research in social psychology has indicated that developing awareness and "owning" one's biases is a critical step toward learning to control them (Monteith, Voils, & Ashburn-Nardo, 2001). Self-knowledge is believed to lead to more "mindful" interactions (Gudykunst, 1998) and more questioning of one's initial impressions, which should reduce stereotyping and prejudiced behaviors. Increased self-knowledge may also increase dissonance and guilt, as trainees realize their perceptions and actions may not be consistent with their values (Pendry et al., 2007). This can heighten a sense of personal responsibility for inequalities and increase motivation to change (Dovidio et al., 2004).

Training methods for increasing self-knowledge all involve some level of confrontation, as they are meant to provoke trainees into examining their attitudes and the causes of their behavior. Recommended techniques range from simple self-assessments of attitudes (Holmes, 2004) to exercises or simulations that reveal trainees' underlying assumptions, attitudes, and biases. Szpara and Wylie (2005) describe exercises used to train teaching effectiveness assessors in which trainees list the words or characteristics they associate with various groups (e.g., Hispanic, urban) as well as the cues they used to make competence judgments when meeting another person or reading someone's work. These exercises were moderately effective in raising awareness of personal biases that could influence judgments. Pendry and colleagues (2007) describe several methods for demonstrating trainees' biases and provide an analysis of possible negative and positive effects of these techniques. One of these methods is the Implicit Association Test (IAT; Greenwald, McGhee, & Schwartz, 1998), which measures the strength of positive and negative associations in relation to social categories (e.g., Black/White, Muslim/Christian) at the automatic level. The IAT was not developed as a training tool. However, its use in diversity training has been discussed because it "provides a compelling demonstration of implicit bias" (Pendry et al., 2007, p. 38). Monteith and colleagues (2001), using the IAT with a racial (Black/White) comparison, found that a majority of participants could detect their own bias while completing the measure. If participants attributed the bias to racial stereotypes or prejudice, they experienced guilt. This suggests the IAT might be a useful training tool. However, Pendry and colleagues (2007) recommend caution. The IAT is difficult for trainees to understand and can generate a range of negative emotions. If the IAT is used, trainers need to thoroughly debrief trainees, explaining the meaning of the test and helping them to formulate next steps toward changing their attitudes and behavior (Pendry et al., 2007).

Higher levels of confrontation are involved in two frequently studied self-awareness exercises: Walking Through White Privilege (McIntosh, 1992), and Blue-eyes/Brown-eyes (Peters, 1987). Both involve simulations that dramatically illustrate group privilege, or the lack thereof. The Walking Through White Privilege exercise is based on McIntosh's (1992) realization of her own white privilege in the United States. In this exercise, as described in Pendry et al. (2007): "Participants...line up on one side of a room and respond to a number of statements (e.g., `I can easily find a doll for my child that represents his or her race') by taking a pace forward if they agree (i.e., have the privilege). Statements increase in severity regarding the consequences of the privilege. Typically, White participants take many more paces forward than participants of other ethnic or racial groups..., thereby providing a spatial demonstration of what happens in society" (p. 32). Laboratory research has examined some aspects of this exercise. Powell, Branscombe, and Schmitt (2005) found that, for White participants, reflecting on in-group (White) privilege instead of out-group (Black) disadvantage increased collective guilt, reducing prejudiced attitudes. In the 3- to 8-hour Blue-eyes/Brown-eyes simulation exercise, participants are categorized on the basis of eye color. Blue-eyed participants are subjected to overt discriminatory treatment from the trainer (and eventually from other participants), while brown-eyed participants are openly favored and privileged. Used with both children and adults, this exercise is meant to sensitize individuals to the experience of being stigmatized and the object of discrimination (Stewart et al., 2003). Evaluations of this exercise have found that it resulted in more positive attitudes toward other racio-ethnic groups and also increased participants' anger toward the self when they experienced prejudiced thoughts (Byrnes & Kiger, 1990; Stewart et al., 2003).

The use of confrontation in diversity training to increase self-awareness has been controversial (Roberson et al., 2003). These exercises are stressful for participants (Byrnes & Kiger, 1990; Pendry et al., 2007; Stewart et al., 2003). They are intended to influence attitudes and behavior through negative emotions—especially anger and guilt. Stewart and colleagues (2003), discussing the Blue-eyes/Brown-eyes exercise, suggest that anger may prompt self-examination and increase motivation to change. However, anger may also lead to more aggression toward the out-group. Reflecting on White privilege threatens Whites' social identity and self-esteem by challenging the legitimacy of their higher status. Those highly identified with being White may feel most threatened, as they are more motivated to protect their group's positive value (Branscombe, Schmitt, & Schiffhauer, 2007). Branscombe and colleagues (2007) found that reflecting on White privilege resulted in an increase in prejudice toward Blacks for participants highly identified with being White. The authors suggest that this type of exercise might be more effective for all participants if a superordinate identity is first made salient. Both Pendry and colleagues (2007) and Chrobot-Mason and Quiñones (2002) note that training creating anger and guilt needs to be accompanied by training that develops skills for dealing with these negative emotions and planning constructive action. These observations suggest that confrontation methods should not be used in one-shot training, but they might be effective when used by trainers who are familiar with the trainees and who can conduct follow-up sessions designed to help trainees work through negative emotions (Roberson et al., 2003).

Social learning theory. While "awareness first" is perhaps the most frequently mentioned model of learning noted in the diversity training literature, social learning theory (SLT; Bandura, 1986) is also frequently invoked as a theoretical basis for the design of diversity skill training. According to SLT, people learn when their own behavior results in positive consequences and also when they observe the actions of others and the consequences of their behavior, a process called "vicarious reinforcement" (Bandura 1982, 1986; Noe, 1999). Behaviors that are directly or vicariously rewarded are more likely to be recalled and reproduced by trainees. SLT further emphasizes the importance of self-efficacy—the belief that one can successfully learn—in the learning process. Trainees are more likely to attempt new behaviors when they feel they can be successful. This theory is the basis for behavior modeling training, which is widely and successfully used in organizational and educational settings to teach a variety of skills (Wexley & Latham, 2002). In behavior modeling training, the key behaviors to be taught are first identified. These are presented to trainees by a model during the training session. Opportunities for mastery through practice and feedback are provided, and transfer to the job setting is facilitated by goal setting and identifying situations on the job where new skills can be used (Noe, 1999).

In general, the diversity training literature recommends SLT as the preferred model for the design of any diversity skill training (Asburn-Nardo et al., 2008; Chrobot-Mason & Quiñones, 2002; Holmes, 2004), and some empirical studies of training based on SLT have appeared. The work of Combs and her colleagues (Combs, 2002; Combs & Griffith, 2007; Combs & Luthans, 2007) provides perhaps the most systematic and comprehensive application of this model to diversity training. In Combs and Luthans (2007), training was designed specifically to increase diversity efficacy, defined as confidence in promoting diversity goals and initiatives. The training program followed behavior modeling principles, incorporating video examples of appropriate and inappropriate actions and mastery experiences. Training had a significant effect on efficacy and behavioral intentions to value and promote diversity on the job. After one year, the training group scored significantly higher than the control group on ratings of the difficulty of diversity actions they attempted and their success in accomplishing diversity intentions.

Others have developed and evaluated more specific training methods or tools derived from a SLT perspective. Work on aversive racism (Dovidio & Gaertner, 1986) suggests that anxiety is a primary factor in intergroup bias. Avery, Richeson, Hebl, and Ambady (2009) found that, for White participants, the use of behavioral scripts reduced anxiety and increased self-efficacy in cross-racial interactions. The authors propose that this technique could be incorporated into diversity training with the script representing a model that trainees can follow, providing mastery experiences. Roberson, Kulik, and Pepper (2002) provided a procedure for generating critical diversity incidents that can be used for diversity skill training. The incidents can be used by trainers to model effective behaviors in diversity-related situations and provide opportunities for practice and feedback.

SUMMARY

Awareness training is the most common type of diversity training used in organizations (Hite & McDonald, 2006). Although evaluation studies of awareness training programs have shown some positive gains in knowledge (Kulik & Roberson, 2008a), the model that awareness leads to attitude and behavior change has rarely been empirically tested, and the available evidence is not encouraging. In Roberson, Kulik, and Pepper (2009), diversity knowledge measured immediately after training did not predict later transfer of diversity skills to the job. Sanchez and Medkik (2004) found that knowledge of social cognition and biases was not related to the extent to which trainees engaged in differential treatment of subordinates/coworkers after training.

However, these studies may not have provided a fair test of the "awareness first" model. In this model, awareness training is meant to be only a first step in the change process, laying the foundation for later learning. Yet in research and in practice, the recommendation for sequenced training efforts is rarely heeded. Most organizations do not provide much diversity training beyond an awareness component (Hite & McDonald, 2006; Johnson & Kravitz, 2008).

Evidence supporting SLT as a model for diversity training is stronger, although still limited. The studies on diversity training add to the already substantial evidence for the effectiveness of this approach in contexts other than diversity training. One prerequisite for using behavior modeling effectively is the identification of key behaviors: desired behaviors must be isolated so that a modeling display can be created and key points shown to trainees (Noe, 1999). The diversity literature has been slow in identifying behavioral competencies. More work on delineating specific diversity competencies should result in greater use of training based on SLT.

The two models are not contradictory and authors have recommended that the models be integrated and used together by presenting awareness training first, followed by behavior modeling training (Asburn-Nardo et al., 2008; Chrobot-Mason & Quiñones, 2002). The need for skill training after self-awareness methods that provoke negative emotions has been particularly emphasized (Chrobot-Mason & Quiñones, 2002; Pendry et al., 2007). Evaluations of training programs that adhere to these recommendations may result in stronger demonstrations of diversity training effectiveness.

Another important consideration in the design of training is the extent to which trainees' characteristics moderate the effectiveness of the training approaches. The importance of trainees' characteristics has most often been noted in relation to self-awareness training methods, particularly those involving higher levels of confrontation. Dovidio and colleagues (2004) suggest that techniques that highlight inconsistencies between trainees' values and their behavior or raise trainees' awareness of their personal biases will work best with trainees who have egalitarian standards. Pendry and colleagues (2007) and Roberson and colleagues (2003) note that confrontational methods may be more beneficial for more advanced or more diversity-competent participants who accept that discomfort is part of the change process. Others have proposed that trainees' characteristics should inform the choice between awareness and behavioral training. Nemetz and Christensen (1996) suggested that trainees with weak attitudes toward diversity will benefit most from awareness training, but those with strong negative attitudes will have unfavorable reactions to awareness training. For trainees with negative attitudes, teaching appropriate behaviors and providing clear contingencies for their on-the-job behavior will be more effective. Brief and Barsky (2000), focusing only on racial attitudes, made a similar argument. Only trainees who are motivated to avoid racial prejudice will benefit from diversity training, especially self-regulation training that helps trainees to monitor and control their reactions and increases self-efficacy in cross-racial interactions.

TRAINING DELIVERY DECISIONS

Research has also been conducted on characteristics of diversity training programs beyond the training content that can influence effectiveness.

Trainer demographics. A longstanding question in the diversity training literature concerns whether trainer demographics matter (Roberson et al., 2003). A survey of providers of diversity training by Bendick, Egan, and Lofhjelm (2001) found that a majority of trainers were female or people of color. Members of these groups are often preferred as diversity trainers under the assumption that they have greater experience and expertise with diversity issues than do white men, and a larger stake in the topic (Flynn, 1999; Karp & Sammour, 2000; Liberman, Block, & Uyekubo, 2010; Nice, n.d).

Liberman and colleagues (2010) provided some evidence for this assumption. In a laboratory study, they found that Black diversity trainers were perceived as more effective than White trainers (gender had no effect) and that the perceived expertise of the trainer partially mediated these results. In a second study, when White diversity trainers provided evidence of their knowledge of institutional discrimination, they were not perceived as less effective than Black trainers. These findings indicate that, in the absence of information about the trainer's background and experience, people use his or her race as a cue to his or her expertise about diversity and inclusion.

An alternative perspective on choice of diversity trainer suggests that the optimal trainer demographics depend on the characteristics of the trainees. Some have suggested that the trainer's demographics should match those of the trainees to enhance the trainer's credibility and promote the trainees' identification with the trainer (Mock & Laufer, 2001). Holladay and Quiñones (2005) examined trainer–trainee similarity based on national culture in a field study conducted in a multinational corporation. For trainees from individualist countries, the gender or culture of the diversity trainer had no impact on trainees' perceptions of the training's usefulness or the trainer's effectiveness. However, trainees from collectivist countries responded more positively to trainers from collectivist cultures. The authors suggest these results may reflect the tendency for collectivists to view out-group members less favorably. Trainees from collectivist countries also responded more favorably to male diversity trainers, perhaps reflecting stronger expectations in collectivist cultures that men will assume dominant roles (Holladay & Quiñones, 2005).

A third perspective argues that the trainer's demographics may interact with the content of the training to influence its effectiveness. Roberson and colleagues (2003) suggested that a diversity trainer who is demographically similar to trainees may be more effective than a dissimilar trainer for teaching behavioral skills, as similarity results in more effective modeling. Holladay and Quiñones (2008) examined interactions between the trainer's race and gender and the content of the diversity training course. Participants reported more favorable responses to female and minority trainers when the course content emphasized leveraging diversity by focusing on differences among people; however, no influence of trainer demographics was found when the course content emphasized a focus on similarities.

Demographic composition of the training group. Roberson and colleagues (2003) identified the demographic composition of the training group as a controversy in the diversity training literature. Some have recommended training groups that include a heterogeneous mix of social identity groups for their educational benefits (i.e., a wider range of experiences and opinions will be presented) and to reduce the possibility that some trainees will be viewed as tokens or feel pressured to act as a representative for their group (Chrobot-Mason & Quiñones, 2002; Johnson, 2008). Others have argued for the superiority of homogeneous training groups (Burkart, 1999; Kirkland & Regan, 1997; Kitfield, 1998). Homogeneous groups would facilitate discussion of within-group dynamics and allow trainees to express themselves freely while minimizing impression management concerns about appearing unprejudiced (Roberson et al., 2003). We found only one study examining this issue. Roberson and colleagues (2001) reported that the effects of group composition depended on the experience level of trainees. Trainees with prior diversity training gained greater knowledge and skill from the training program when they were assigned to training groups homogeneous in terms of race and nationality. However, the training outcomes of trainees with no prior diversity training were not influenced by group composition. The authors proposed that trainees with prior experience may be focused on learning behavioral skills, a more advanced diversity competency. Skill learning is enhanced in homogeneous groups, as the presence of similar others enhances the feelings of psychological safety needed to try new skills and behaviors, and also increases the opportunities to use other group members as models (Decker & Nathan, 1985; Roberson et al., 2001). This suggests that training group composition may be particularly important when diversity training focuses on skill development. While most writers have focused on race and gender when discussing group composition, trainee level (managerial or nonmanagerial) has also been noted as a variable to consider when assembling training groups. Chrobot-Mason and Quiñones (2002) suggest it may be useful to separate management and nonmanagement groups for diversity training to avoid discomfort and minimize risks when training requires self-disclosure. However, Cocchiara and colleagues (2010) argue that combining managerial and non-managerial employees within a training group is preferable because it underscores top-level commitment to diversity training.

Framing of training. The framing of training refers to how the training program is defined and communicated to trainees. The frame makes certain characteristics salient (Holladay, Knight, Paige, & Quiñones, 2003) and influences pretraining attitudes such as expectations about the course and motivation to learn (Quiñones, 1997). These pretraining attitudes have been shown to affect training outcomes (Noe, 1986; Tannenbaum, Mathieu, Salas, & Cannon-Bowers, 1991). Several aspects of framing have been discussed in the diversity training context. One issue concerns how diversity is defined: as narrow (focusing on one or two demographic variables—usually race or gender) or broad (including not only demographics, but also values, work styles, and personality). Many recommend using a broad definition, arguing that this frame acknowledges all employees, increases positive reactions, and reduces backlash (Chrobot-Mason & Quiñones, 2002; Mobley & Payne, 1992). Others argue that although a broad definition may make diversity training more "palatable," it diverts attention from historically excluded groups and key issues of prejudice and discrimination resulting from group inequalities. This will ultimately reduce the effectiveness of training as a vehicle for improving the status of women and people of color (Caudron & Hayes, 1997; Linnehan & Konrad, 1999). Rynes and Rosen (1995) reported that a broad definition of diversity was associated with greater perceived success of diversity training. Holladay and colleagues (2003) found that a broad or narrow definition of diversity alone had no impact on trainee reactions, but the combination of a broad definition of diversity with a traditional course title of "Diversity Training" resulted in the most positive reactions (e.g., greater perceived usefulness, more interest in attending, less perceived threat) from participants. Thus, the limited research tends to indicate that a broad definition of diversity does result in more positive reactions by trainees. However, arguments in favor of a narrow definition of diversity are not based on its effect on trainee reactions, but rather on the organizational effectiveness of training. Studies have not examined organizational outcomes in relation to definitions of diversity. We found one study examining individual training outcomes. Kulik, Perry, and Bourhis (2000) compared the effects of broadly focused (age, race, gender, and ethnicity) versus narrowly focused (age alone) diversity training on hiring decisions. Those who participated in the narrow program and who completed the subsequent hiring task under conditions of high cognitive load were less likely to recommend an older job candidate for hire. This suggests that attention focused on one dimension of diversity can have effects opposite to those intended.

Another framing issue discussed in the literature is the communicated reason for diversity training and trainees' perceptions of why they are being trained. Chrobot-Mason and Quiñones (2002) suggest that diversity training be framed as a part of the general skill set for managers so that the link between the knowledge and skills imparted in the training program and job requirements are clear. Two studies have reported effects of trainees' perceptions of reasons for being assigned to diversity training. In Holladay and colleagues (2003), participants reviewed a diversity course description that informed them either that the course was "remedial," due to below-average firm performance, or that the course was "advanced," due to superior performance. Men anticipated that the course would be the most threatening and generate the most backlash when training was framed with a narrow definition of diversity and remedial assignment. Women anticipated the least backlash and perceived threat when training was framed with a broad definition of diversity and advanced assignment. Sanchez and Medkik (2004) found an unintended framing effect in their field study. Their diversity training program generated more supervisory discriminatory behavior toward employees from different ethnic backgrounds, as rated by coworkers. Subsequent interviews to explore this unexpected outcome revealed that several supervisors believed they had been selected for training because of complaints from these employees, and after the training, supervisors' behavior towards the employees reflected their resentment.

Mandatory versus voluntary training. A final question in the literature concerns whether diversity training should be mandatory or voluntary. A 2007 poll found mandatory diversity training to be among the top ten diversity activities in organizations, as reported by a sample of 265 HR professionals and diversity specialists across a wide variety of industries (*New York Times*, 2007). Requiring training of organizational members sends a message about the importance of training and the organization's commitment to diversity (Bell, Connerley, & Cocchiara, 2009). Thus, mandatory training should increase the perceived valence of training, enhancing motivation to learn (Colquitt, LePine, & Noe, 2000). Supporting this argument, Rynes and Rosen (1995), in a survey of HR managers, found that mandatory diversity training for management-level employees was perceived as more successful. Mandatory training for nonmanagerial employees was not associated with perceived program success. However, organizations that require training may have other characteristics that support training success. For example, in Rynes and Rosen (1995), mandatory management diversity training was also associated with top management support for training and the use of post-training evaluations. Thus, the perceived success of mandatory diversity training may be due to greater organizational support for the training and the presence of additional HR structures that maximize training effectiveness (Aguinis & Kraiger, 2009) and not merely to the requirement to participate in training.

An alternative perspective argues that being forced to attend training may lower motivation to learn (Paluck, 2006) and generate greater backlash. Mandatory training for those with strong negative attitudes toward diversity can make their attitudes more extreme and increase stereotypic beliefs (Brief & Barsky, 2000; Joplin & Daus, 1997; Nemetz & Christensen, 1996). An example is found in Kaplan (2006), who presented several case studies in which mandatory diversity training including lesbian, gay, and bisexual content caused intense opposition from trainees with strong religious beliefs, leading to litigation. Kulik, Pepper, Roberson, and Parker (2007) concluded that voluntary diversity training was associated with more positive outcomes than mandatory training. Yet reliance on voluntary training may be insufficient for organizational change.

Kulik and colleagues (2007) found that those with greater diversity competence were more positive toward diversity training and more likely to attend training sessions. The authors argued that those with low competence may be unaware of their need for training and hence less likely to enroll in a class. Joplin and Daus (1997) suggest the choice between mandatory and voluntary training should be based on the organization's climate and history in dealing with diversity. In organizations with a negative diversity climate, mandatory training will be counterproductive because trainees' attitudes are negative and the organization culture will not support training transfer. Others suggest that individual trainee attitudes should guide the decision. If trainees have high levels of prejudice and strong commitment to their beliefs, mandatory training will backfire (Nemetz & Christensen, 1996).

SUMMARY

The limited research on these four delivery decisions makes clear conclusions difficult. There have been numerous evaluations of diversity training effectiveness, as we discuss in the following section. It is disappointing that more information is not available on the impact of these factors, since decisions regarding the factors must be made for any training program. It seems clear that the design and delivery characteristics interact to influence training effectiveness, and their interactive effects are further affected by other contextual factors (e.g., top management support, organizational diversity climate). Evaluations of diversity training should include a description of these design characteristics (trainer demographics, composition of training groups, framing of training, and whether training was mandatory or voluntary) when reporting results.

Training evaluation and transfer of training

Diversity training is likely to have several different impacts, and a comprehensive evaluation of an organization's training efforts should encompass as many potential impacts as possible. First, researchers and organizations are interested in understanding the extent to which trainee changes (e.g., changes in trainees' learning, motivation, or skill) can be attributed to the program (Grove & Ostroff, 1991). Second, researchers and organizations are interested in observing the extent to which any immediate changes resulting from the training affect the way trainees behave when they return to their work environment (Baldwin & Ford, 1988). Third, researchers and organizations are interested in learning whether changes in trainees have a downstream effect on the organization's effectiveness (Kirkpatrick, 1976).

TRAINEE CHANGES

At the individual level, the learning outcomes resulting from any organizational training program comprise three major categories: cognitive, skill-based, and affective (Kraiger, Ford, & Salas, 1993). Diversity training, in particular, is intended to increase knowledge about diversity, to improve attitudes about diversity, and to develop diversity skills. For example, Hayles (1996, p. 106) described diversity learning as involving "head (knowledge); hand (behaviors and skills); and heart (feelings and attitudes)," while Gudykunst, Guzley, and Hammer (1996) noted that most diversity training involves creating change in trainees' cognition, behavior, and affect. These three learning outcomes are essential components of a larger constellation of diversity competency (Avery & Thomas, 2004), and they are all important in developing people who can successfully interact with diverse others. Accordingly, evaluations of diversity training have largely focused on these outcomes.

Diversity knowledge. Workplace diversity training that is aimed at increasing trainees' diversity knowledge may entail learning about general intergroup differences, including differences associated with cultures (e.g., Hill & Augoustinos, 2001) or communication styles (e.g., Cornett-DeVito & McGlone, 2000) and social perception biases, which include group-based prejudice or discrimination (e.g., Armour, Bain, & Rubio, 2004). Diversity training may also involve more targeted education focusing on organization-specific content about workplace diversity issues (e.g., De Meuse, Hostager & O'Neil, 2007), diversity-related policies (Gutek, 1997), or strategic diversity initiatives (Kulik & Roberson, 2008a,b).

In general, diversity training is highly effective at increasing individuals' knowledge. Most evaluation studies on diversity training in organizational settings have consistently demonstrated short-term (i.e., immediately after training) increases in trainees' diversity knowledge (Abernethy, 2005; Anderson & Cranston-Gingras, 1991; Hebblethwaite, Woods, Stokie, Hames, Macha, Moss, & Wharton, 2006; Kracht, 1998; Krajic, Straßmayr, Karl-Trummer, Novak-Zezula, & Pelikan, 2005; Roberson, Kulik, & Pepper, 2001, 2002; Tan, Morris, & Romero, 1996). Krajic and colleagues (2005), for instance, found that hospital staff who attended 10 hours of cross-cultural training over 10 weeks reported higher levels of post-training knowledge in cross-cultural situations than their levels before training.

Studies assessing longer-term (e.g., 3 months after the intervention) training effects on diversity knowledge have also produced generally positive results (Armour, Bain, & Rubio, 2004; Brathwaite & Majumdar, 2006; Gany & Thiel de Bocanegra, 1996; Hill & Augoustinos, 2001; Law, 1998; Majumdar, Browne, Roberts, & Carpio, 2004; Nicholson, Hancock, & Dahlberg, 2007). For example, Armour, Bain, & Rubio, (2004) conducted a study to assess the effectiveness of a series of six 3-hour diversity training sessions provided to social work field instructors. They found that significant increases in cultural competence scores reported by participants were maintained 6 months later.

Attitudes about diversity. Training interventions designed to change attitudes generally fall into two categories: those that focus on changing overall attitudes toward diversity (e.g., Baba & Hebert, 2004; Bush & Ingram, 2001) and those that target attitudes or mindsets toward specific diversity dimensions, such as race, culture (Chudley, Skelton, Wall, & Jones, 2007), and sexual orientation (Finkel, Storaasli, Bandele, & Schaerfer, 2003), or diversity-related issues, such as prejudice (Choi-Pearson Castillo & Maples, 2004) and immigrant health concerns (Gany & Thiel de Bocanegra, 1996).

The evidence regarding diversity training effectiveness is less clear-cut for attitudes than for knowledge. Kulik and Roberson (2008a) concluded that diversity training was more effective in changing overall or global attitudes toward diversity than attitudes toward specific social groups. Several diversity training interventions have produced positive short-term effects on attitudes—for instance, reduced levels of modern racism (Choi-Pearson, Castillo & Maples, 2004) and higher levels of tolerance toward diversity (Edelstein, 2007). A handful of studies have also demonstrated positive longer-term effects of diversity training on attitudinal change, such as higher self-reported levels of diversity efficacy (Combs & Luthans, 2007), increased sensitivity to immigrant health concerns (Gany & Thiel de Bocanegra, 1996), and greater comfort with diversity (Armour, Bain, & Rubio, 2004).

Other studies have shown a negligible impact on attitudinal outcomes: Chrobot-Mason (2004) found no short-term effect of a manager-led diversity training workshop on White managers' levels of racial identity development; Finkel, Storaasli,

Bandele, and Schaerfer (2003) reported no immediate change in homophobic attitudes in graduate students and university staff following diversity training; Papadopoulos, Tilko, and Lees (2004) observed no post-training impact on cultural sensitivity among mental health service providers; Hill and Agoustinos (2001) assessed the impact of a cross-cultural training program administrated to 62 public service employees and found no significant decreases in modern racism, old-fashioned racism, or negative stereotyping 3 months after the intervention.

Negative effects of diversity training on attitudes have also occasionally been reported. Baba and Hebert (2004) found that a 32-hour mandatory cultural awareness program provided to prison inmates led to reports of lower comfort levels with culturally different others, even though participants became more aware of negative group relations after completing the training.

Diversity skills. Diversity training that is geared toward behavioral change or skill development provides trainees the opportunity to develop interpersonal competencies, such as cross-cultural communication skills (Bush & Ingram, 2001; Gany & Thiel de Bocanegra, 1996), conflict resolution skills (Kerka, 1998), relationship building skills (Ferguson, Keller, Haley & Quirk, 2003), and skills in handling cross-cultural situations (Krajic et al., 2005).

Evaluation of diversity skill training has received the least attention in the research literature. Among the small number of studies that assessed diversity skills, mixed findings are observed. Some diversity training interventions have demonstrated gains related to trainees' cross-cultural skills (Krajic et al., 2005) and their ability and confidence to communicate with culturally different others (Thomas & Cohn, 2006), as well as self-reported intentions to exhibit on-the-job diversity behaviors (Combs & Luthans, 2007).

There are also a handful of studies documenting a lack of diversity training impact on behavioral change. Chrobot-Mason (2004), for example, observed no effect of diversity training on participants' intentions to engage in behaviors that would support a diversity-friendly work environment. Papadopoulos and colleagues (2004) found no significant increases in self-reported cultural skills among participants after cultural competence training. Other studies have shown that diversity training is negatively associated with diversity skill development. For instance, Bush and Ingram (2001) found that diversity training was related to lower self-reported scores on relationship and communication skills. However, participants also indicated heightened awareness of their cultural diversity skill deficits following the training. The negative results on self-reported skills may have been an example of beta change (Golembiewski, Billingsley, & Yeager, 1976) in that training resulted in a recalibration of the skill measure: after training, with greater knowledge of their lack of skill, participants rated their skill levels more harshly than they did before training.

Transfer of training. For most organizational training efforts, successful performance during the training session is not the final goal. Instead, the primary concern is the positive *transfer* of training—the extent to which the learning generated during a training experience transfers to the job and leads to meaningful changes in work performance (Blume, Ford, Baldwin, & Huang, 2010; Goldstein & Ford, 2002). Similarly, a major goal of diversity training is to influence behavior in the work setting (Bendick et al., 2001).

Examination of transfer is not common in the diversity training literature. Results from the few existing studies report some positive news (e.g., Hanover & Cellar, 1998; Roberson, Kulik, & Pepper, 2009; Majumdar, Browne, Roberts, & Carpio, 2004; Wade & Bernstein, 1991). Hanover and Cellar (1998) found that 2 months after training, middle managers who participated in a diversity training workshop rated a series of diversity management practices (e.g., encourage open discussion of cultural differences; discourage comments or jokes that perpetuate stereotypes or prejudice) as more important than managers who did not participate. In addition, the trained managers reported that they engaged in these behaviors to a greater extent than the untrained managers.

Roberson, Kulik, and Pepper (2009) found support for the relationship between skill-based learning and use of transfer strategies (cognitive and behavioral tactics that trainees use to apply their training on the job, like talking with colleagues about diversity skills). Skill-based learning was positively related to trainees' use of transfer strategies measured four weeks after training. In a study conducted by Majumdar and colleagues (2004), patients of health-care providers who had undergone sensitivity training reported improved levels of overall functioning. Wade and Bernstein (1991) observed that clients of counselors who had attended cultural sensitivity training perceived their counselors as more credible and expressed greater satisfaction with their counseling sessions, compared to clients of counselors who did not attend training. These two studies suggest that trained counselors successfully transferred newly learned cultural sensitivity skills to their interactions with clients. However, Sanchez and Medkik (2004) noted negative effects of diversity training on job behaviors. In evaluating the effectiveness of cultural diversity awareness training among county government managerial employees, they found that coworkers of trainees observed more negative behavior toward individuals from other ethnic backgrounds compared to coworkers of those assigned to the matched comparison group.

Successful transfer depends in part on the content of diversity training (Baldwin & Ford, 1988). Linnehan, Chrobot-Mason, and Konrad (2006), for example, suggest that if the dominant focus of a diversity training program is on attitudes and awareness, the training program is unlikely to foster trainee skills that will generate on-the-job behavioral changes. The results of Roberson and colleagues (2009) support this, in that only diversity skill learning, not diversity knowledge or diversity attitudes, was related to the use of transfer strategies. However, successful transfer also depends on characteristics of the work environment that motivate trainees to learn during the training program and to use their acquired skills on the job (Kraiger, McLinden, & Casper, 2004; Tracey, Tannenbaum, & Kavanagh, 1995). Environmental characteristics are particularly important in transferring "open skills" of the type addressed by diversity training (Blume et al., 2010). With closed skills, trainees must behave in one particular way on the job according to the specified rules taught during training (Yelon & Ford, 1999). But with open skills, trainees have considerable choice in whether and how to apply trained principles and concepts to the job (Blume et al., 2010). For example, trainees who participate in a diversity training program might exhibit considerable variation in how often they seek out opportunities to interact with diverse colleagues or how they elicit diverse viewpoints during group discussions.

Two environmental characteristics appear to be particularly important in facilitating training transfer (Rouiller & Goldstein, 1993): situational cues and consequences. Situational cues are social and task stimuli in the work setting that remind trainees of the training context and provide opportunities to use newly acquired skills. Consequences refer to the positive and negative reactions of supervisors and peers when trainees use trained skills on the job. In combination, work environments that provide trainees with situational cues reminding them to use their trained skills and positive consequences for using trained skills provide a positive climate for transfer.

In diversity training, researchers have suggested that one of the most important situational cues facilitating transfer of training is the demographic composition of upper levels of the work unit (Herdman & McMillan-Capehart, 2010; Roberson et al., 2009). The demographic composition of people in powerful positions sends a message about the value of diversity in the organization (Roberson & Block, 2001), and diversity at upper levels provides more opportunities for trainees to exercise their new diversity skills due to more cross-group contact (Kossek & Zonia, 1993). Herdman and McMillan-Capehart (2010) found that the relationship between organizational diversity initiatives (initiatives that might include diversity training) and employees' perceptions of a positive diversity climate was stronger in hotels that had higher levels of minority representation in management. Roberson and colleagues (2009) found no evidence that the proportion of non-White faculty members in a trainee's department affected the transfer of training for teaching assistants participating in a university diversity training program. However, Roberson and colleagues (2009) did find a positive relationship between the proportion of non-White faculty members and trainees' skill-based learning, suggesting that situational cues might have influenced the trainees' motivation to learn during the training session rather than influencing their motivation to transfer that learning.

Further, diversity training transfer might be facilitated when management links positive and negative consequences to the appropriate and inappropriate diversity behaviors displayed by trainees (Gilbert & Ivancevich, 1999, 2000; Zhu & Kleiner, 2000). However, empirical evidence on the effectiveness of consequences for diversity training transfer is mixed. Roberson and colleagues (2009) and Herdman and McMillan-Capehart (2010) found that trainees' perceptions of consequences had positive effects on training transfer, but Hanover and Cellar (1998) found no effects. One challenge in facilitating diversity training transfer might be ensuring that trainees' managers have the skills they need to recognize and reward positive diversity behaviors (Beale, 1998). Successful diversity training transfer might therefore be facilitated by a top-down approach, in which the upper levels of an organizational hierarchy receive training that teaches them how to support subsequent training received by subordinates.

Situational cues and consequences might also operate in combination to influence diversity training transfer. For example, a visibly diverse management team might be a powerful signal of the organization's value for diversity (i.e., act as a situational cue). At the same time, a diverse management team might also be especially motivated to reward diversity skills displayed by trainees on the job (i.e., provide consequences) (Herdman & McMillan-Capehart, 2010).

SUMMARY

Cognitive, affective, and skill-based outcomes are all important in assessing the results of training. In practice, however, these three learning outcomes are rarely assessed in the same study. Most studies measure one, or at best two, of these dimensions, and diversity training is more likely to be assessed in relation to trainees' attitudes than in relation to their knowledge or behavior (Kulik & Roberson, 2008a). Post-training changes in skill and the transfer of diversity skill to the job have been the most neglected.

ORGANIZATIONAL IMPACT

The final objective of most organizational training programs is to influence organizational outcomes—to lower costs, improve efficiency, or enhance morale (Kirkpatrick, 1987). For diversity training programs, an organization might hope that trainees' enhanced diversity skills will help make the organization an employer of choice (with measurable effects on employee attraction and retention rates), will help diverse employees work together (with measurable effects on employee job satisfaction and employee grievances), and will better serve diverse customers and clients (with measurable effects on customer satisfaction). These "first-level" organizational effects might eventually generate "second-level" effects on organizational productivity or financial performance. These organizational outcomes are simultaneously distal from training and yet fundamental to judging training success (Alliger, Tannenbaum, Bennett, Traver, & Shotland, 1997). Increasingly, organizations are trying to judge their return on training investment, trying to calculate the performance value derived from every training dollar (Ramlall, 2003).

Unfortunately, it is difficult to identify exactly which results might be attributed directly to a specific training program (Kirkpatrick, 1987). As a result, few HR training programs, including diversity training programs, are assessed with regard to organization-level outcomes (Alliger et al., 1997). Few studies have examined the effectiveness of diversity training at the organizational (or workplace) level.

Kellough and Naff (2004) analyzed data from 137 public agencies and found that the use of diversity training was not associated with the promotion or quit ratios of either female or racial minority employees. Further analyses of the same dataset (Naff & Kellough, 2003) demonstrated that the use of diversity training was not associated with racial minority representation in the workforce, but diversity training was *negatively* associated with female representation. Since diversity training and workforce composition data were collected concurrently in this research, the causal relationship between the two variables is unclear. The results might indicate that the agencies that conduct diversity training are reluctant to hire women, or they might indicate that agencies with lower female representation are more motivated to initiate diversity training.

Kalev, Dobbin, and Kelly (2006) were able to make stronger causal inferences when they studied a random sample of 708 organizations using 1971–2002 federal data on workforce composition, coupled with survey data on the organizations' diversity training practices during that period. Diversity training did not increase the proportion of white women or black men working in these organizations, but it *decreased* the proportion of black women. Diversity training had only one positive effect on workforce composition: in organizations that simultaneously offered diversity training and established organizational responsibility for diversity through affirmative action plans or diversity task forces, the proportion of White women in the workforce increased.

Ely (2004) studied 486 bank branches. She looked at the relationship between the proportion of employees in the branch who either had participated or currently were participating in the firm's diversity education program and five indicators of branch performance (i.e., overall performance, revenue from new sales, customer satisfaction, customer referrals, sales productivity). She found no direct effects of employee participation on any of the performance measures.

Finally, Hirsh and Kmec (2009) studied 84 hospitals and related survey data on diversity training to discrimination charges filed in the subsequent year. They found that management participation in diversity training *reduced* the likelihood of discrimination charges. In fact, the probability of receiving any kind of discrimination was extremely low in the presence of managerial diversity training. However, employee participation in diversity *increased* the likelihood of discrimination charges. Hirsh and Kmec suggest these opposing effects occur because management diversity training reduces managers' discriminatory behavior, but employee diversity training raises employees' awareness of their rights.

SUMMARY

The small number of studies linking diversity training to organizational outcomes makes it difficult to draw firm conclusions about diversity training's effectiveness at the organizational level. Diversity training does appear to affect discrimination charges (Hirsh & Kmec, 2009), suggesting that participation in training changes the behavior of both managers and subordinates. But diversity training does not have any measurable effect on organizational sales performance (Ely, 2004). This lack of effect is consistent with findings in the broader training literature, where there is only a very weak association between any sort of training and organizational financial outcomes (Tharenou, Saks, & Moore, 2007). Workforce composition represents a more intermediate outcome. If diversity training was creating positive changes in trainees' knowledge, attitudes, or skills, we would expect these changes to have downstream effects on workforce composition (Kulik & Roberson, 2008b). Managers with more positive diversity attitudes would be more likely to hire diverse employees; coworkers with more positive diversity attitudes would create positive workgroup climates that help to retain diverse employees. The lack of effects reported by Naff and Kellough (2003) and the limited effects observed by Kalev and colleagues (2006) indicate that training *per se* does not affect workforce diversity. However, it is important to recognize that these studies are only examining the *presence* of diversity training and not its content. Skill-based diversity training, for example, might have more of an impact on workforce composition than awareness training. Further, Kalev and colleagues' (2006) results suggest that diversity training in isolation might be less effective than diversity training in combination with other diversity initiatives.

Conclusion

We opened this chapter noting the wide endorsement and use of diversity training in organizations. It has been estimated that organizations spend between $200 and 300 million annually on diversity training (Vedantam, 2008) in the hope that training will accomplish desired outcomes. Despite this emphasis, diversity training is also frequently criticized for failing to deliver expected benefits (Bennett, 2010; Cullen, 2007; Hansen, 2003). A recent study indicated that only 51 percent of U.S. employees viewed diversity education and training favorably, while 24 percent viewed them unfavorably (National Urban League, 2009). In particular, respondents found diversity training and education ineffective in enabling them to transfer skills back to their work environments (National Urban League, 2009). Other criticisms raised in the practice literature include "backlash" reactions from trainees belonging to majority groups (Dolezalek, 2008), insufficient emphasis on skills-based training (Gupta, 2009), and lack of employees' engagement and support for training (Nancherla, 2008).

Research has a particularly important role given this controversy over diversity training effectiveness, as it can provide evidence-based conclusions about effects and outcomes. The diversity training research we have reviewed offers some conclusions. Diversity training is effective for some individual trainee outcomes, most notably for increasing diversity knowledge and general attitudes about diversity in the short term. There is also some positive evidence on the effectiveness of diversity training for developing behavioral skills and the transfer of skills to the job setting, although few studies exist.

Recent research on diversity training has also addressed other concerns and criticisms. Analyses of trainee backlash and theory-based techniques to reduce it have been presented; trainees' motivation has been considered through research on needs assessment and framing; methods of skill training and the development of behavioral competencies have been given increased attention in the literature.

Yet there is still a long way to go before empirical research on diversity training can provide definitive answers to questions about how to make training most effective. Although a substantial body of literature on evaluations of diversity training exists, systematic evaluations of diversity training that measure the full range of expected individual-level outcomes—knowledge, attitudes, and behavior—remain few and far between. Behavioral skills and transfer are still relatively neglected even though they are among the most important desired outcomes of training. Because there has been very little research comparing different types of training, we can't really say what methods are most effective (Curtis & Dreachslin, 2008; Kulik & Roberson, 2008a). Because there has been little work on trainee characteristics or contextual effects on individual training outcomes, we can't really say under what conditions and for whom various types of training are most useful. Future research efforts must begin to build knowledge in these areas. Some critical directions for future research are:

1. What are the important trainee characteristics that influence training effectiveness or interact with training methods to influence outcomes? The literature has pointed to preexisting attitudes toward diversity and motivation to avoid prejudice as possible influences on the effectiveness of diversity training strategies (Brief & Barsky, 2000; Dovidio et al., 2004; King et al., 2009; Roberson et al., 2003). Training models that incorporate these trainee characteristics need to be developed and trainee characteristics need to be measured in evaluations of training effectiveness. Measuring pretraining individual differences may be controversial. Organizations may be reluctant to measure pretraining attitudes and motivation for fear of stigmatizing low-scoring trainees who are identified as needing "remedial" training. However, these concerns can be avoided if organizations conduct assessments that protect the anonymity of individual trainees while providing trainers with information about the overall level and variability of attitudes and motivations within training groups (e.g., via pretraining computerized self-tests; Perry, Kulik, & Field, 2009).

2. How can we evaluate diversity skill? One of the biggest challenges for diversity training evaluation of individual-level outcomes is designing good measures of diversity skill. Most research relies on trainee self-assessments of skills, but self-assessed diversity skills may be inflated due to social desirability (Constantine & Ladany, 2000), and people have difficulty accurately assessing their own skills, particularly at the low end of the skill continuum (Kruger & Dunning, 1999). One recommended strategy is to design situational interviews (Latham, Saari, Pursell, & Campion, 1980) or paper-and-pencil situational tests (Roberson, Kulik, & Pepper, 2002) that present participants with diversity challenges that the trainee is likely to encounter at work or in other real-world situations. Learners are asked what they would do in each situation, and their responses are scored against a standardized key.

3. What is the long-term impact of diversity training, including retention of knowledge and attitude gains, and transfer of skills to on-the-job behavior? Diversity training evaluations are usually conducted using a pretest–posttest design (Kulik & Roberson, 2008a), but this is a weak design with which to assess training effectiveness (Salas, Cannon-Bowers, Rhodenizer, & Bowers, 1999)—especially if the researchers' intent is to measure the effectiveness of training transfer. Participant changes resulting from diversity training might be delayed (not visible until after the posttest is administered) or short-lived (failing to be sustained until the posttest). Different learning outcomes (knowledge, attitudes, and skills) may have different change trajectories, and gains in one outcome may not appear until gains on another have stabilized (Holvino et al., 2004; Wentling & Palma-Rivas, 2000). Ideally, diversity training effectiveness would be assessed using repeated assessments during and after the diversity training intervention, so that researchers can track both immediate trainee changes and transfer of training.

The controversy over diversity training also concerns effectiveness at the organizational level. Organizations want more than individual outcomes from training—they want better team functioning, a more positive diversity climate, and enhanced morale and customer service, with ultimate effects on organizational effectiveness. But critics argue that diversity training has failed to accomplish this—worse, training may have negative effects on organizational outcomes (Cullen, 2007; Hansen, 2003). Research on diversity training has been less useful in addressing the controversy over organizational outcomes, although the role of research is still important. There is evidence that individual-level effects on trainees' knowledge, attitudes, and behavior affect some organizational outcomes (e.g., the probability of discrimination charges) but not others (e.g., organizational sales performance). Some critical directions for future research on higher-level outcomes are:

1. Researchers must define theoretically what higher-level outcomes might be influenced by diversity training and the processes that describe how those outcomes would be affected. If diversity training improves relationships among diverse sales employees, for example, coworkers might be more likely to help one another during sales "rushes" and jointly improve organizational sales performance. If

diversity training reduces the role that stereotypes play in organizational decision making, managers might be more open to hiring women and members of racial minorities, allowing the organization to make better use of the local labor market. If diversity training sensitizes health-care employees to the needs of different cultural groups, the employees might be better able to serve diverse patients, increasing patients' satisfaction with their health-care providers. But these three examples present unique pathways through which individual-level learning outcomes affect organization-level outcomes. Diversity training researchers need to continue to develop theories that directly link individual-level outcomes of diversity training with organizational-level outcomes (Cox, 1993; Avery & McKay, 2010). This theoretical work can help align expectations for what can reasonably be accomplished by diversity training, and specify the timeframe in which effects are likely to be observed. The development of such multilevel models would help to define important diversity competencies that training should address to maximize effectiveness, and could assist organizations in selecting appropriate measures for tracking diversity training outcomes.

2. We need to begin to consider the role of teams and team diversity training. One surprise in our review of the literature was the neglect of the team level in diversity training. In the general training literature, team training strategies have been developed and evaluated, with positive results (Aguinis & Kraiger, 2009; Salas & Cannon-Bowers, 2001). But we found no studies of team training in the diversity training literature—virtually all studies examine training for individual trainees. This neglect is even more surprising since the impact of diversity on team processes and performance has been a major focus of organizational research (e.g., Williams & O'Reilly, 1998). One productive area for future research regarding teams concerns investigating how individual-level diversity training outcomes influence outcomes at the team level. For example, Kochan and colleagues (2003) reported that training including communication skills reduced the negative effect of team racial diversity on group processes. Another productive area concerns the development and evaluation of diversity training methods targeting intact work teams. Jackson, Joshi, and Erhardt (2003) suggested that diversity training for teams might be more effective than individual training, yet this possibility has not been examined empirically. The literature provides possible directions for the design of team diversity training. Kochan and colleagues (2003) suggest that training on group process skills such as conflict management and communication would be useful. Chatman (2010) proposes that training diverse teams to create and enforce strong anti-bias and openness norms would increase a team's ability to capitalize on its diversity.

3. We need to recognize that diversity training may have different effects in different organizational contexts, and identify the contextual factors that are most likely to influence the effectiveness of diversity training. For example, the demographic composition of organizations may motivate employees to learn from diversity training (Roberson et al., 2009) and provide more opportunities to practice diversity skills on the job (Kossek & Zonia, 1993), resulting in greater training-to-job transfer of diversity competencies. However, understanding these contextual effects requires a greater emphasis in studying diversity training's effectiveness across organizations. We are beginning to see more meso-level research that examines diversity training across units or branches of a single organization (e.g., Ely, 2004), but cross-organization research on the effectiveness of diversity training is still rare (see Hirsh & Kmec, 2009; Kellough & Naff, 2003; Kalev et al., 2006, for notable exceptions). In addition, diversity training is often implemented as part of a larger diversity initiative. The particular "bundle" of diversity initiatives is likely to influence the effectiveness of diversity training, with some "sidecar" initiatives providing greater support for the changes initiated by diversity training. For example, Kalev and colleagues (2006) found that diversity training accompanied by accountability in the form of affirmative action plans or diversity taskforces increased the proportion of White women in the organization's workforce. Greater attention needs to be paid to the diversity practices that organizations bundle with diversity training. Kulik and Roberson (2008b) suggested that specific diversity initiatives solve some organizational diversity problems but simultaneously create new ones. Diversity training, in particular, may heighten employees' awareness about diversity challenges in the organization and motivate them to engage in voice or exit (Hirsh & Kmec, 2009). Therefore, an organization that implements diversity training as a standalone technique may experience short-term costs before it experiences longer-term benefits.

Faster progress would be made in pursuing this proposed research agenda if there were greater collaboration between diversity training scholars and diversity training practitioners, as field research is necessary for generating the most useful knowledge about diversity training (Kochan et al., 2003). The divide between scholarly research and organizational practice in diversity training has been noted (Ferdman, 2008). To some extent, this divide has resulted in two separate knowledge bases: one residing in scholarly literature, the other in organizational archives and practitioner memories. Here we reviewed the scholarly research literature, but little information on organizational practice is available. Organizations are actively engaged in diversity training, yet published research describing and evaluating these efforts is seldom found. One reason for this may be that organizations rarely evaluate their training efforts (Gutierrez, Kruzich, Jones, & Coronado, 2000; Hansen, 2003). Another reason is that organizations protect the details of their successful training programs to gain a competitive advantage in their efforts to become an employer of choice. Academic researchers and practitioners at other organizations tend to learn only about dramatic diversity training failures that receive extensive media coverage (e.g., the stereotyping exercise at Lucky Stores or the sexual harassment gauntlet at the Federal Aviation Agency; Sample, 2007). Yet our review of the scholarly literature revealed tantalizing hints of work being conducted behind organizational walls that would be of great interest to diversity scholars. For example, although the identification of competencies has received little attention in the scholarly literature, there is some evidence that organizations may be using defined competencies to design diversity training courses (e.g., Anand & Winters, 2008; King et al., 2009). Although we found no published studies of team diversity training, several articles mentioned team-based training initiatives developed and used in organizations (e.g., Anand & Winters, 2008; Salas et al., 2008).

In conclusion, advancements have been made in theory development and both the quality and quantity of empirical research on diversity training. Yet the research falls short of delivering robust recommendations about how to deliver effective diversity training in organizational settings. As we move forward, reciprocal relationships are desperately needed: diversity training research should reflect and influence practice, and diversity training practice should reflect and influence research.

References

Abernethy, A. D. (2005). Increasing the cultural proficiency of clinical managers. *Journal of Multicultural Counseling & Development, 33*(2), 81–93. Retrieved from Professional Development Collection database.

Aguinis, H., & Kraiger, K. (2009). Benefits of training and development for individuals and teams, organizations, and society. *Annual Review of Psychology, 60,* 451–474. doi:10.1146/annurev.psych.60.110707.163505

Ajzen, I. (1991). The theory of planned behavior. *Organizational Behavior and Human Decision Processes, 50,* 179–211. doi:10.1016/0749-5978(91)90020-T

Alliger, G. M., Tannenbaum, S. I., Bennett, W., Jr., Traver, H., & Shotland, A. (1997). A meta-analysis of the relations among training criteria. *Personnel Psychology, 50*(2), 341–358. Retrieved from Business Source Alumni Edition database.

Amoroso, L. M., Loyd, D. L., & Hoobler, J. M. (2009). The diversity education dilemma: Exposing status hierarchies without reinforcing them. *Journal of Management Education, 34*(6), 1–28. doi: 10.1177/1052562909348209

Anand, R., & Winters, M. (2008). A retrospective view of corporate diversity training from 1964 to the present. *Academy of Management Learning & Education, 7*(3), 356–372. Retrieved from Business Source Alumni Edition database.

Anderson, D. J., & Cranston-Gingras, A. (1991). Sensitizing counselors and educators to multicultural issues: An interactive approach. *Journal of Counseling & Development, 70*(1), 91–98. Retrieved from Professional Development Collection database.

Armour, M. P., Bain, B., & Rubio, R. (2004). An evaluation study of diversity training for field instructors: A collaborative approach to enhancing cultural competence. *Journal of Social Work Education, 40*(1), 27–38. Retrieved from Professional Development Collection database.

Asburn-Nardo, L., Morris, K. A., & Goodwin, S. A. (2008). The confronting prejudiced responses (CPR) model: Applying CPR in organizations. *Academy of Management Learning & Education, 7*(3), 332–342. Retrieved from Business Source Alumni Edition database.

Avery, D. R., & McKay, P. F., (2010). Doing diversity right: An empirically based approach to diversity management. In G. P. Hodgkinson & J. K. Ford (Eds.), *International review of industrial and organizational psychology* (Vol. 25, pp. 227–252). West Sussex: Wiley-Blackwell.

Avery, D. R., Richeson, J. A., Hebl, M. R., & Ambady, N. (2009). It does not have to be uncomfortable: The role of behavioral scripts in Black–White interracial Interactions. *Journal of Applied Psychology, 94*(6), 1382–1393. doi:10.1037/a0016208

Avery, D. R., & Thomas, K. M. (2004). Blending content and contact: The roles of diversity curriculum and campus heterogeneity in fostering diversity management competency. *Academy of Management Learning & Education, 3*(4), 380–396. Retrieved from Business Source Alumni Edition database.

Baba, Y., & Hebert, C. (2004). The effects of participation in a cultural awareness program on jail inmates. *Journal of Ethnic and Cultural Diversity in Social Work, 13*(3), 91–113. doi:10.1300/J051v13n03_05

Badhesha, R. S., Schmidtke, J. M., Cummings, A., & Moore, S. D. (2008). The effects of diversity training on specific and general attitudes toward diversity. *Multicultural Education & Technology Journal, 2*(2), 87–106. doi:10.1108/17504970810883360

Baldwin, J., & Hecht, M. (1995). The layered perspective of cultural (in)tolerance(s): The roots of multidisciplinary approach. In R. Wiseman (Ed.), *Intercultural communication* theory: International and intercultural communication annual (pp. 59–91). Thousand Oaks, CA: Sage.

Baldwin, T. T., & Ford, J. K. (1988). Transfer of training: A review and directions for future research. *Personnel Psychology, 41*(1), 63–105. doi: 10.1111/j.1744–6570.1988.tb00632.x

Bandura, A. (1982). Self-efficacy mechanism in human behavior. *American Psychologist, 37*(2), 122–147. doi: 10.1037/0003–066X.37.2.122

Bandura, A. (1986). *Social foundations of thought and action.* Englewood Cliffs, NJ: Prentice-Hall.

Beale, R. L., (1998). Invited reaction: Response to environmental factors and the effectiveness of workforce diversity training. *Human Resource Development Quarterly, 9*(2), 125–127. doi: 10.1002/hrdq.3920090204

Bell, M. P., Connerley, M. L., & Cocchiara, F. K. (2009). The case for mandatory diversity education. *Academy of Management Learning & Education, 8*(4), 597–609. Retrieved from Business Source Alumni Edition database.

Bendick, M., Egan, M. L., & Lofhjelm, S. M. (2001). Workforce diversity training: From anti-discrimination compliance to organizational development. *Human Resource Planning, 24*(2), 10–25. Retrieved from Business Source Alumni Edition database.

Bennett, D. (2010, March 7). Who's still biased? *The Boston Globe.* Retrieved from http://www.boston.com/bostonglobe

Bennett, M. J. (1986). A developmental approach to training for intercultural sensitivity. *International Journal of Intercultural Relations, 10*(2), 179–196. doi:10.1016/-0147–1767(86)90005–2

Blume, B. D., Ford, J. K., Baldwin, T. T., & Huang, J. L. (2010). Transfer of training: A meta-analytic review. *Journal of Management, 36*(4), 1065–1105. doi: 10.1177/0149206309352880

Branscombe, N. R., Schmitt, M. T., & Schiffhauer, K. (2007). Racial attitudes in response to thoughts of white privilege. *European Journal of Social Psychology, 37*(2), 203–215. doi:10.1002/ejsp.348

Brathwaite, A. C., & Majumdar, B. (2006). Evaluation of a cultural competence educational programme. *Journal of Advanced Nursing, 53*(4), 470–479. doi:10.1111/j.1365–2648.2006.03742.x

Brewer, M. B. (1997). The social psychology of intergroup relations: Can research inform practice? *Journal of Social Issues, 53*(1), 197–211. doi:10.1111/j.1540–4560.1997.tb02440.x

Brief, A. P., & Barsky, A. (2000). Establishing a climate for diversity: The inhibition of prejudiced reactions in the workplace. In G. Ferris (Ed.), *Research in personnel and human resources management* (pp. 91–129). New York: Elsevier.

Bunch, K. J. (2007). Training failure as a consequence of organizational culture. *Human Resource Development Review, 6*(2), 142–163. doi:10.1177/1534484307299273

Burkart, M. (1999, October). The role of training in advancing a diversity initiative. *Diversity Factor, 8*(1), 2–5. Retrieved from ABI/INFORM Global database.

Bush, V. D., & Ingram, T. N. (2001). Building and assessing cultural diversity skills: Implications for sales training. *Industrial Marketing Management, 30*(1), 65–76. doi:10.1016/S0019–8501(99)00089–9

Byrnes, D. A., & Kiger, G. (1990). The effect of a prejudice-reduction simulation on attitude change. *Journal of Applied Social Psychology, 20*(4), 341–356. doi:10.1111/j.1559–1816.1990.tb00415.x

Caudron, S., & Hayes, C. (1997). Are diversity programs benefiting African Americans? *Black Enterprise, 27*(7), 121–132. Retrieved from Academic Search Complete database.

Chatman, J. A. (2010). Norms in mixed sex and mixed race work groups. *Academy of Management Annals, 4*(1), 447–484. doi: 10.1080/19416520.2010.494826

Chavez, C. I., & Weisinger, J. Y. (2008). Beyond diversity training: A social infusion for cultural inclusion. *Human Resource Management, 47*(2), 331–350. doi:10.1002/hrm.20215

Choi-Pearson, C., Castillo, L., & Maples, M. F. (2004). Reduction of racial prejudice in student affairs professionals. *NASPA Journal (National Association of Student Personnel Administrators, Inc.), 42*(1), 132–148. Retrieved from Education Research Complete database.

Chrobot-Mason, D. (2003). Developing multicultural competence for managers: Same old leadership skills or something new? *Psychologist-Manager Journal, 6*(2), 3–16.

Chrobot-Mason, D. (2004). Managing racial differences. *Group & Organization Management, 29*(1), 5–31. doi:10.1177/1059601103252102

Chrobot-Mason, D., & Aramovitch, N. (2004). *Employee perceptions of an affirming climate for diversity and its link to attitudinal outcomes: A comparison of racial and gender groups.* Paper presented at the Annual Meeting of the Academy of Management, New Orleans, LA.

Chrobot-Mason, D., Konrad, A. M., & Linnehan, F. (2006). Measures for quantitative diversity scholarship. In A. M. Konrad, P. Prasad, & J. K. Pringle (Eds.), *Handbook of workplace diversity* (pp. 237–270). Thousand Oaks, CA: Sage.

Chrobot-Mason, D., & Quiñones, M. A. (2002). Training for a diverse workplace. In K. Kraiger (Ed.), *Creating, implementing, and managing effective training and development* (pp. 117–159). San Francisco, CA: Jossey-Bass.

Chudley, S., Skelton, J., Wall, D., & Jones, E. (2007). Teaching cross-cultural consultation skills: a course for UK and internationally trained general practice registrars. *Education for Primary Care, 18*(5), 602–615. Retrieved from Academic Search Complete database.

Cocchiara, F. K., Connerley, M. L., & Bell, M. P. (2010). "A GEM" for increasing the effectiveness of diversity training. *Human Resource Management, 49*(6), 1089–1106. doi:10.1002/hrm.20396

Colquitt, J. A., LePine, J. A., & Noe, R. A. (2000). Toward an integrative theory of training motivation: A meta-analytic path analysis of 20 years of research. *Journal of Applied Psychology, 85*(5), 678–707. doi:10.1037//0021–9010.85.5.678

Combs, G. M. (2002). Meeting the leadership challenge of a diverse and pluralistic workplace: Implications of self-efficacy for diversity training. *Journal of Leadership & Organizational Studies, 8*(4), 1–16. doi:10.1177/107179190200800401

Combs, G. M., & Griffith, J. (2007). An examination of interracial contact: The influence of cross-race interpersonal efficacy and affect regulation. *Human Resource Development Review, 6*(3), 222–244. doi:10.1177/1534484307303990

Combs, G. M., & Luthans, F. (2007). Diversity training: Analysis of the impact of self-efficacy. *Human Resource Development Quarterly, 18*(1), 91–120. doi:10.1002/hrdq.1193

Constantine, M. G., & Ladany, N. (2000). Self-report multicultural counseling competence scales: Their relation to social desirability attitudes and multicultural case conceptualization ability. *Journal of Counseling Psychology, 47*(2), 155–164. doi:10.1037/0022–0167.47.2.155

Cornett-DeVito, M. M., & McGlone, E. L. (2000). Multicultural communication training for law enforcement officers: A case study. *Criminal Justice Policy Review, 11*(3), 234–253. Retrieved from http://cjp.sagepub.com/content/11/3/234

Cox, T. H. Jr. (1993). *Cultural diversity in organizations: Theory, practice and research.* San Francisco, CA: Berrett-Koehler.

Cox, T. H. Jr. (1991). The multicultural organization. *Academy of Management Executive, 5*(2), 34–47. Retrieved from Business Source Alumni Edition database.

Cox, T. H. Jr., & Beale, R. (1997). *Developing competency to manage diversity: Readings, cases and activities.* San Francisco, CA: Berrett-Koehler.

Cox, T. H. Jr., & Blake, S. (1991). Managing cultural diversity: Implications for organizational competitiveness. *Academy of Management Executive, 5*(3), 45–56. Retrieved from Business Source Alumni Edition database.

Cross, W. E., Jr. (1978). The Thomas and Cross models of psychological nigrescence: A review. *Journal of Black Psychology, 5*(1), 13–31. doi:10.1177/009579847800500102

Cullen, L.T. (2007, April). Employee diversity training doesn't work. *Time.* Retrieved from http://www.time.com

Curtis, E. F., & Dreachslin, J. L. (2008). Integrative literature review: Diversity management interventions and organizational performance: A synthesis of current literature. *Human Resource Development Review, 7*(1), 107–134. doi:10.1177/1534484307311700

Dahm, M. J., Willems, E. P., Ivancevich, J. M., & Graves, D. E. (2009). Development of an organizational diversity needs analysis (ODNA) instrument. *Journal of Applied Social Psychology, 39*(2), 283–318. doi:10.1111/j.1559-1816.2008.00439.x

Day, N. E., & Glick, B. J. (2000). Teaching diversity: A study of organizational needs and diversity curriculum in higher education. *Journal of Management Education, 24*(3), 338–352. doi:10.1177/105256290002400305

Decker, P. J., & Nathan, B. R. (1985). *Behavior modeling training: Principles and applications.* New York: Praeger.

De Meuse, K. P., & Hostager, T. J. (2001). Developing an instrument for measuring attitudes toward and perceptions of workplace diversity: An initial report. *Human Resource Development Quarterly, 12*(1), 33–51. Retrieved from Business Source Complete database.

De Meuse, K. P., Hostager, T. J., & O'Neill, K. S. (2007). A longitudinal evaluation of senior managers' perceptions and attitudes of a workplace diversity training program. *Human Resource Planning, 30*(2), 38–46. Retrieved from ABI/INFORM Global database.

Dolezalek, H. (2008). The path to inclusion. *Training, 45*(4), 52–54. Retrieved from ABI/INFORM Global database.

Dovidio, J. F., & Gaertner, S. L. (1986). Prejudice, discrimination, and racism: Historical trends and contemporary approaches. In J. F. Dovidio, & S. L. Gaertner (Eds.), *Prejudice, discrimination, and racism* (pp. 1–34). New York: Academic Press.

Dovidio, J. F., Gaertner, S. L., Stewart, T. L., Esses, V. M., Ten Vergert, M., & Hodson, G. (2004). From intervention to outcome: Processes in the reduction of bias. In W. G. Stephan & P. Vogt (Eds.), *Education programs for improving intergroup relations: Theory, research, and practice* (pp. 243–265). New York: Teachers College Press.

Edelstein, S. (2007). Measurement of diversity tolerance of nutrition professionals using the Tolerance of Ambiguity Scale. *Topics in Clinical Nutrition, 22*(2), 130–136. doi: 10.1097/01.TIN.0000270132.25648.6f

Ely, R. (2004). A field study of group diversity, participation in diversity education programs, and performance. *Journal of Organizational Behavior, 25*(6), 755–780. doi: 10.1002/job.268

Esen, E. (2005). *2005 workplace diversity practices survey report.* Retrieved from Society for Human Resource Management website: http://www.shrm.org/Research/SurveyFindings/Articles/Pages/2005_20Workplace_20Diversity_20Practices_20Survey_20Report.aspx

Ferdman, B. M. (2008, July). *On the shoulders of giants? The role of scholarship and research in diversity teaching and training.* Keynote presentation at the 2nd Annual Teaching and Training Workplace Diversity Conference, George Mason University, Arlington, VA.

Ferguson, W. J., Keller, D. M., Haley, H., & Quirk, M. (2003). Developing culturally competent community faculty: A model program. *Academic Medicine, 78*(12), 1221–1228. Retrieved from the Journals@Ovid database.

Finkel, M. J., Storaasli, R. D., Bandele, A., & Schaefer, V. (2003). Diversity training in graduate school: An exploratory evaluation of the Safe Zone project. *Professional Psychology: Research and Practice, 34*(5), 555–561. doi:10.1037/0735-7028.34.5.555

Flynn, G. (1999). White males see diversity's other side. *Workforce, 78*(2), 52–55. Retrieved from Academic Search Complete database.

Ford, J. K., & Fisher, S. (1996). The role of training in a changing workplace and workforce: New perspectives and approaches. In E. E. Kossek & S. A. Lobel (Eds.), *Managing diversity: Human resource strategies for transforming the workplace* (pp. 164–193). Cambridge, MA: Blackwell.

Gany, F., & Thiel de Bocanegra, H. (1996). Maternal-child immigrant health training: changing knowledge and attitudes to improve health care delivery. *Patient Education and Counseling, 27*(1), 23–31. doi:10.1016/0738-3991(95)00786-5

Garcia, M. H. (1995). An anthropological approach to multicultural diversity training. *Journal of Applied Behavioral Sciences, 31*(4), 490–504. doi:10.1177/0021886395314013

Gilbert, J. A., & Ivancevich, J.M. (1999). Organizational diplomacy: The bridge for managing diversity. *Human Resource Planning, 22*(3), 29–39. Retrieved from Business Source Alumni Edition database.

Gilbert, J. A., & Ivancevich, J. M. (2000).Valuing diversity: A tale of two organizations. *Academy of Management Executive, 14*(1), 93–105. Retrieved from Business Source Alumni Edition database.

Goldstein, I. L. (1993). *Training in organizations* (3rd ed.). Pacific Grove, CA: Brooks-Cole.

Goldstein, I. L., & Ford, J. K. (2002). *Training in organizations* (4th ed.). Belmont, CA: Wadsworth.

Golembiewski, R. T., Billingsley, K., & Yeager, S. (1976). Measuring change and persistence in human affairs: types of change generated by OD designs. *Journal of Applied Behavioral Science, 12*(2), 133–157. doi: 10.1177/002188637601200201

Greenwald, A. G., McGhee, D. E., & Schwartz, J. L. K. (1998). Measuring individual differences in implicit cognition: The implicit association test. *Journal of Personality and Social Psychology, 74*(6), 1464–1480. doi:10.1037/0022-3514.74.6.1464

Grove, D. A., & Ostroff, C. (1991). Training program evaluation. In K. N. Wexley (Ed.), *Developing human resources* (pp. 5185–5220). Washington, DC: BNA Books.

Gudykunst, W. B. (1998). *Bridging differences: Effective intergroup communication* (3rd ed.). Thousand Oaks, CA: Sage.

Gudykunst, W. B., Guzley, R. M., & Hammer, M. R. (1996). Designing intercultural training. In D. Landis & R. S. Bhagat (Eds.), *Handbook of intercultural training* (2nd ed., pp. 61–80). Thousand Oaks, CA: Sage.

Gupta, S. R. (2009). Achieve cultural competency. *Training, 46*(2), 16–17. Retrieved from ABI/INFORM Global database.

Gutek, B. A. (1997). Sexual harassment policy initiatives. In W. O'Donohue (Ed.), *Sexual harassment: Theory, research and treatment* (pp. 185–198). Boston, MA: Allyn and Bacon.

Gutierrez, L., Kruzich, J., Jones, T., & Coronado, N. (2000). Identifying goals and outcome measures for diversity training: A multi-dimensional framework for decision-makers. *Administration in Social Work, 23*(3), 53–70. doi:10.1300/J147v24n03_04

Hanover, J. M., & Cellar, D. F. (1998). Environmental factors and the effectiveness of workforce diversity training. *Human Resource Development Quarterly, 9*, 105–124. doi:10.1002/hrdq.3920090203

Hansen, F. (2003, April). Diversity's business case doesn't add up. *Workforce*, 28–32. Retrieved from Academic Search Complete database.

Hayles, V. R. (1996). Diversity training and development. In R. L. Craig (Ed.), *The ASTD training and development handbook: A guide to human resource development* (3rd ed., pp. 104–123). New York: McGraw-Hill.

Hebblethwaite, A., Woods, A., Stokie, A., Hames, A., Macha, R., Moss, L., & Wharton, S. (2006). Access to community services for black and minority ethnic groups: Increasing staff awareness. *Learning Disability Practice, 9*(4), 10–14. Retrieved from Academic Search Complete database.

Helms, J. E. (1990). *Black and white racial identity*. New York: Greenwood Press.

Herdman, A. O., & McMillan-Capehart, A. (2010). Establishing a diversity program is not enough: Exploring the determinants of diversity climate. *Journal of Business and Psychology, 25*(1), 39–53. doi:10.1007/s10869-009-9133-1

Hill, M. E., & Augoustinos, M. (2001). Stereotype change and prejudice reduction: short- and long-term evaluation of a cross-cultural awareness programme. *Journal of Community & Applied Social Psychology, 11*(4), 243–262. doi:10.1002/casp.629

Hirsh, E., & Kmec, J. A. (2009). Human resource structures: Reducing discrimination or raising rights awareness? *Industrial Relations, 48*(3), 512–532. doi:10.1111/j.1468-232X.2009.00571.x

Hite, L. M., & McDonald, K. S. (2006). Diversity training pitfalls and possibilities: An exploration of small and mid-size US organizations. *Human Resource Development International, 9*(3), 365–377. doi:10.1080/13678860600893565

Holladay, C. L., Knight, J. L., Paige, D. L., & Quiñones, M. A. (2003). The influence of framing on attitudes toward diversity training. *Human Resource Development Quarterly, 14*(3), 245–263. doi:10.1002/hrdq.1065

Holladay, C. L., & Quiñones, M. A. (2008). The influence of training focus and trainer characteristics on diversity training effectiveness. *Academy of Management Learning & Education, 7*(3), 343–355. Retrieved from Business Source Alumni Edition database.

Holladay, C. L., & Quiñones, M. A. (2005). Reactions to diversity training: An international comparison. *Human Resource Development Quarterly, 16*(4), 529–545. doi:10.1002/hrdq.1154

Holmes, T. A. (2004). Designing and facilitating performance-based diversity training. *Performance Improvement, 43*(5), 13–20. doi:10.1002/pfi.4140430505

Holvino, E., Ferdman, B. M., & Merrill-Sands, D. (2004). Creating and sustaining diversity and inclusion in organizations: Strategies and approaches. In M. S. Stockdale & F. J. Crosby (Eds.), *The psychology and management of workplace diversity* (pp.245–276). Malden, MA: Blackwell.

Jackson, S., Joshi, A., & Erhardt, N. (2003). Recent research on team and organizational diversity: SWOT analysis and implications. *Journal of Management, 29*(6), 801–830. doi:10.1016/S0149-2063_03_00080-1

Jayne, M. E. A., & Dipboye, R. L. (2004). Leveraging diversity to improve business performance: Research findings and recommendations for organizations. *Human Resource Management, 43*(4), 409–424. doi:10.1002/hrm.20033

Johnson, C. D. (2008). It's more than the five to do's: Insights on diversity education and training from Roosevelt Thomas, a pioneer and thought leader in the field. *Academy of Management Learning & Education, 7*(3), 406–417. Retrieved from Business Source Alumni Edition database.

Johnson, C. D., & Kravitz, D. A. (2008). Atypical diversity teaching and training conference yields unique blend of offerings. *Equal Opportunities International, 27*(6), 559–565. doi:0.1108/02610150810897309

Joplin, J. R. W., & Daus, C. S. (1997). Challenges of leading a diverse workforce. *Academy of Management Executive, 11*(3), 32–46. Retrieved from Business Source Alumni Edition database.

Kalev, A., Dobbin, F., & Kelly, E. (2006). Best practices or best guesses? Assessing the efficacy of corporate affirmative action and diversity policies. *American Sociological Review, 71*(4), 589–617. doi:10.1177/000312240607100404

Kaplan, D. M. (2006). Can diversity training discriminate? Backlash to lesbian, gay, and bisexual diversity initiatives. *Employee Responsibilities and Rights Journal, 18*(1), 61–72. doi:10.1007/s10672-005-9005-4

Karp, H., & Sammour, H. (2000). Workforce diversity: Choices in diversity training programs and dealing with resistance to diversity. *College Student Journal, 34*(3), 451. Retrieved from Professional Development Collection database.

Kellough, J. E., & Naff, K. C. (2004). Responding to a wake-up call: An examination of federal agency diversity management programs. *Administration & Society, 36*(1), 62–90. doi:10.1177/0095399703257269

Kerka, S. (1998). Diversity training. *ERIC Trends and Issues Alerts*. Retrieved from http://www.calpro-online.org/eric/docs/tia00060.pdf

King, E. B., Gulick, L. M. V., & Avery, D. R. (2009). The divide between diversity training and diversity education: Integrating best practices. *Journal of Management Education, 34*(6), 891–906. doi:10.1177/1052562909348767

Kirkland, S. E., & Regan, A. M. (1997). Organizational racial diversity training. In C. E. Thompson & R. T. Carter (Eds.), *Racial identity theory: Applications to individual, group, and organizational interventions* (pp. 159–175). Mahwah, NJ: Erlbaum.

Kirkpatrick, D. L. (1976). Evaluation. In R. L. Craig (Ed.), *Training and development handbook: A guide to human resource development* (3rd ed., pp. 301–319). New York: McGraw-Hill.

Kirkpatrick, D. L. (1987). *More evaluating training programs*. Alexandria, VA: American Society for Training and Development.

Kitfield, J. (1998). Boot camp lite. *Government Executive, 30*(2), 45–49. Retrieved from ABI/INFORM Global database.

Kochan, T., Bezrukova, K., Ely, R., Jackson, S., Joshi, A., Jehn, K., Leonard, J., Levine, D., & Thomas, D. 2003. The effects of diversity on business performance: Report of the Diversity Research Network. *Human Resource Management, 42*(3), 1, 3–21. doi:10.1002/hrm.10061

Kossek, E. E., & Zonia, S. C. (1993). Assessing diversity climate: A field study of reactions to employer efforts to promote diversity. *Journal of Organizational Behavior, 14*(1), 61–81. doi:10.1002/job.4030140107

Kracht, D. W. (1998). *Diversity training among manufacturing companies: Reaction and learning in a for-profit and not-for-profit work environment* (Doctoral dissertation, University of Sarasota). Retrieved from Dissertations & Theses: Full Text. (Publication No. AAT 9900464)

Kraiger, K., Ford, J. K., & Salas, E. (1993). Application of cognitive, skill-based, and affective theories of learning outcomes to new methods of training evaluation. *Journal of Applied Psychology, 78*(2), 311–328. doi: 10.1037/0021–9010.78.2.311

Kraiger, K., McLinden, D., & Casper, W. J. (2004). Collaborative planning for training impact. *Human Resource Management, 43*(4), 337–351. doi: 10.1002/hrm.20028

Krajic, K., Straβmayr, C., Karl-Trummer, U., Novak-Zezula, S., & Pelikan, J. M. (2005). Improving ethnocultural competence of hospital staff by training: Experiences from the European "Migrant-friendly Hospitals" project. *Diversity in Health & Social Care, 2*(4), 279–290. Retrieved from SocINDEX with Full Text database.

Kruger, J., & Dunning, D. (1999). Unskilled and unaware of it: How difficulties in recognizing one's own incompetence lead to inflated self-assessments. *Journal of Personality and Social Psychology, 77*(6), 1121–1134. doi:10.1037/0022–3514.77.6.1121

Kulik, C. T., Pepper, M. B., Roberson, L., & Parker, S. K. (2007). The rich get richer: predicting participation in voluntary diversity training. *Journal of Organizational Behavior, 28*(6), 753–769. doi:10.1002/job.444

Kulik, C. T., Perry, E. L., & Bourhis, A. C. (2000). Ironic evaluation processes: Effects of thought suppression on evaluations of older job applicants. *Journal of Organizational Behavior, 21*(6), 689–711. Retrieved from Business Source Complete database.

Kulik, C. T., & Roberson, L. (2008a). Common goals and golden opportunities: Evaluations of diversity education in academic and organizational settings. *Academy of Management Learning & Education, 7*(3), 309–331. Retrieved from Business Source Alumni Edition database.

Kulik, C. T., & Roberson, L. (2008b). Diversity initiative effectiveness: What organizations can (and cannot) expect from diversity recruitment, diversity training, and formal mentoring programs. In A. P. Brief (Ed.), *Diversity at work* (pp. 265–317). New York: Cambridge University Press.

Larkey, L. K. (1996). The development and validation of the workforce diversity questionnaire: An instrument to assess interactions in diverse workgroups. *Management Communication Quarterly, 9*(3), 296–337. doi:10.1177/0893318996009003002

Latham, G. P., Saari, L. M., Pursell, E. D., & Campion, M. A. (1980). The situational interview. *Journal of Applied Psychology, 65*(4), 422–427. doi: 10.1037/0021–9010.65.4.422

Law, D. Y. (1998). *An evaluation of a cultural diversity training program*. Unpublished doctoral dissertation. Auburn University, Alabama.

Liberman, B. E., Block, C. J., & Uyekubo, S. M. (2010). *Diversity trainer preconceptions: The effects of trainer race and gender on perceptions of diversity trainer effectiveness*. Unpublished manuscript. Department of Organization and Leadership, Teachers College Columbia University, New York, United States.

Linnehan, F., Chrobot-Mason, D., & Konrad, A. M. (2006). Diversity attitudes and norms: The role of ethnic identity and relational demography. *Journal of Organizational Behavior, 27*(4), 419–442. doi:10.1002/job.382

Linnehan, F., & Konrad, A. M. (1999). Diluting diversity: Implications for intergroup inequality in organizations. *Journal of Management Inquiry, 8*(4), 399–414. doi:10.1177/105649269984009

Majumdar, B., Browne, G., Roberts, J., & Carpio, B. (2004). Effects of cultural sensitivity training on health care provider attitudes and patient outcomes. *Journal of Nursing Scholarship, 36*(2), 161–166. doi:10.1111/j.1547–5069.2004.04029.x

McIntosh, P. (1992). White privilege and male privilege: A personal account of coming to see correspondences through work in women's studies. In M. L. Anderson & P. H. Collins (Eds.), *Race, class and gender* (pp. 70–81). Belmont, CA: Wadsworth.

Miville, M. L., Gelso, C. J., Pannu, R., Liu, W., Touradji, P., Holloway, P., & Fuertes, J. (1999). Appreciating similarities and valuing differences: The Miville-Guzman Universality-Diversity scale. *Journal of Counseling Psychology, 46*(3), 291–307. doi:10.1037/0022–0167.46.3.291

Mobley, M., & Payne, T. (1992, December). Backlash! The challenge to diversity training. *Training and Development, 46*(12), 45–52. Retrieved from Professional Development Collection database.

Mock, K. R., & Laufer, A. S. (2001). *Race relations training in Canada: Toward the development of professional standards*. Toronto, Canada: The Canadian Race Relations Foundation.

Monteith, M. J., Voils, C. I., & Ashburn-Nardo, L. (2001). Taking a look underground: Detecting, interpreting, and reacting to implicit racial biases *Social Cognition, 19*(4), 395–417. doi:10.1521/soco.19.4.395.20759

Mor Barak, M. E., Charin, D. A., & Berkman, S. (1998). Organizational and personal dimensions in diversity climate: Ethnic and gender differences in employee perceptions. *Journal of Applied Behavioral Sciences, 34*(1), 82–104. doi:10.1177/0021886398341006

Naff, K. C., & Kellough, J. E. (2003). Ensuring employment equity: Are federal programs making a difference? *International Journal of Public Administration, 26*(12), 1307–1336. doi:10.1081/PAD-120024399

Nancherla, A. (2008, Nov). Why diversity training doesn't work... Right now. *Training and Development, 62*(11), 52–57. Retrieved from ABI/INFORM Global database.

National Urban League. (2009). *Diversity practices that work: The American worker speaks II*. Retrieved from http://www.nul.org/content/diversity-practices-work-american-worker-speaks

Nemetz, P. L., & Christensen, S. L. (1996). The challenge of cultural diversity: Harnessing a diversity of views to understand multiculturalism. *Academy of Management Review, 21*(2), 434–462. Retrieved from Business Source Alumni Edition database.

New York Times. (2007). *Looking around the corner: The view from the front line.* New York: The New York Times Company.

Nice, D. (n.d.). Can a middle aged White straight guy teach diversity classes? (The answer is: yes and no) [Online forum comment]. Retrieved from http://www.multiculturaladvantage.com/recruit/diversity/white-men-diversity/Can-a-Middle-Aged-White-Straight-Guy-Teach-Diversity.asp

Nicholson, K., Hancock, D., & Dahlberg, T. (2007). Preparing teachers and counselors to help under-represented populations embrace the information technology field. *Journal of Technology and Teacher Education, 15*(1), 123–143. Retrieved from Education Full Text database.

Noe, R. A. (1986). Trainees' attributes and attitudes: Neglected influences on training effectiveness. *Academy of Management Review, 11*(4), 736–749. Retrieved from Business Source Alumni Edition database.

Noe, R. A. (1999). *Employee training and development.* Boston, MA: Irwin/McGraw-Hill.

Paluck, E. L. (2006). Diversity training and intergroup contact: A call to action research. *Journal of Social Issues, 62*(3), 577–595. doi:10.1111/j.1540-4560.2006.00474.x

Paluck, E. L., & Green, D. P. (2009). Prejudice reduction: What works? A review and assessment of research and practice. *Annual Review of Psychology, 60*(1), 339–367. doi: 10.1146/annurev.psych.60.110707.163607

Papadopoulos, I., Tilki, M., & Lees, S. (2004). Promoting cultural competence in healthcare through a research-based intervention in the UK. *Diversity in Health and Social Care, 1*(2), 107–116. Retrieved from SocINDEX with Full Text database.

Pendry, L. F., Driscoll, D. M., & Field, S. C. T. (2007). Diversity training: Putting theory into practice. *Journal of Occupational and Organizational Psychology, 80*(1), 27–50. doi:10.1348/096317906X118397

Perry, E. L., Kulik, C. T., & Field, M. P. (2009). Sexual harassment training: Recommendations to address gaps between the practitioner and research literatures. *Human Resource Management, 48*(5), 817–837.

Peters, W. (1987). *A class divided: Then and now.* New Haven, CT: Yale University Press.

Phinney, J. S. (1993). A three-stage model of ethnic identity development in adolescence. In M. E. Bernal & G. P. Knight (Eds.), *Ethnic identity* (pp. 61–79). Albany, NY: University of New York Press.

Phinney, J. S. (1992). The multigroup ethnic identity measure. *Journal of Adolescent Research, 7*, 156–176. doi:10.1177/074355489272003

Powell, A. A., Branscombe, N. R., & Schmitt, M. T. (2005). Inequality as ingroup privilege or outgroup disadvantage: The impact of group focus on collective guilt and interracial attitudes. *Personality and Social Psychology Bulletin, 31*(4), 508–521.

Quiñones, M. A. (1997). Contextual influences on training effectiveness. In M. A. Quiñones & A. Ehrenstein (Eds.), *Training for a rapidly changing workplace: Applications of psychological research* (pp. 201–222). Washington, DC: American Psychological Association.

Ramlall, S. J. (2003). Measuring human resource management's effectiveness in improving performance, *Human Resource Planning, 26*(1), 51–62. Retrieved from ABI/INFORM Global database.

Ramsey, M. (1996). Diversity identity development training: Theory informs practice. *Journal of Multicultural Counseling and Development, 24*(4), 229–240. Retrieved from Academic Search Complete database.

Roberson, L., & Block, C. J. (2001). Racioethnicity and job performance: A review and critique of theoretical perspectives on the causes of group differences. *Research in Organizational Behavior, 23*, 247–325. doi:10.1016/S0191-3085(01)23007-X

Roberson, L., Kulik, C. T., & Pepper, M. B. (2002). Assessing instructor cultural competence in the classroom: An instrument and a development process. *Journal of Management Education, 26*(1), 40–55. doi:10.1177/105256290202600104

Roberson, L., Kulik, C. T., & Pepper, M. B. (2001). Designing effective diversity training: Influence of group composition and trainee experience. *Journal of Organizational Behavior, 22*(8), 871–885. doi:10.1002/job.117

Roberson, L., Kulik, C. T., & Pepper, M. B. (2009). Individual and environmental factors influencing the use of transfer strategies after diversity training. *Group and Organization Management, 34*(1), 67–89. doi:10.1177/1059601108329732

Roberson, L., Kulik, C. T., & Pepper, M. B. (2003). Using needs assessment to resolve controversies in diversity training design. *Group & Organization Management, 28*(1), 148–174. doi:10.1177/1059601102250028

Rouiller, J. Z., & Goldstein, I. L. (1993). The relationship between organizational transfer climate and positive transfer of training. *Human Resource Development Quarterly, 4*(4), 377–390. doi:10.1002/hrdq.3920040408

Rynes, S., & Rosen, B. (1995). A field survey of factor affecting the adoption and perceived success of diversity training. *Personnel Psychology, 48*(2), 247–270. doi:10.1111/j.1744-6570.1995.tb01756.x

Salas, E., & Cannon-Bowers, J. A. (2001). The science of training: A decade of progress. *Annual Review of Psychology, 52*(1), 471–499. doi:10.1146/annurev.psych.52.1.471

Salas, E., Cannon-Bowers, J. A., Rhodenizer, L., & Bowers, C. A. (1999). Training in organizations: Myths, misconceptions and mistaken assumptions. *Research in Personnel and Human Resources Management, 17*, 123–161.

Salas, E., Wilson, K. A., & Lyons, R. (2008). Designing and delivering training for multicultural interactions in organizations. In D. Stone & E. F. Stone-Romero (Eds.), *The influence of culture on human resource management processes and practices* (pp. 115–134). New York: Psychology Press.

Sample, J. (2007). The compelling argument for harassment prevention training: implications for instructional designers. *Performance Improvement, 46*(7), 18–26. Retrieved from ABI/INFORM Global database.

Sanchez, J. I., & Medkik, N. (2004). The effects of diversity awareness training on differential treatment. *Group & Organization Management, 29*(4), 517–536. doi:10.1177/1059601103257426

Sleezer, C. M. (2004). The contribution of adult learning theory to human resource development (HRD). *Advances in Developing Human Resources, 6*(2), 125–128. doi: 10.1177/1523422304263324

Society for Human Resource Management. (2010, October). *Workplace diversity practices: How has diversity and inclusion changed over time?* Retrieved from www.shrm.org/surveys

Soni, V. (2000). A twenty-first century reception for diversity in the public sector: A case study. *Public Administration Review, 60*(5), 395–408. doi: 10.1111/0033-3352.00103

Stewart, T. L., LaDuke, J. R., Bracht, C., Sweet, B. A. M., & Gamarel, K. E. (2003). Do the "eyes" have it? A program evaluation of Jane Elliott's "Blue-eyes/Brown-eyes" diversity training exercise. *Journal of Applied Social Psychology, 33*(9), 1898–1921. doi:10.1111/j.1559–1816.2003.tb02086.x

Szpara, M. Y., & Wylie, E. C. (2005). National Board for Professional Teaching Standards assessor training: Impact of bias reduction exercises. *Teachers College Record, 107*(4), 803–841. Retrieved from Education Full Text database.

Tan, D., Morris, L., & Romero, J. (1996). Changes in attitude after diversity training. *Training and Development, 50*(9), 54–55. Retrieved from Professional Development Collection database.

Tannenbaum, S. I., Mathiew, J. E., Salas, E., & Cannon-Bowers, J. A. (1991). Meeting trainees' expectations: The influence of training fulfillment on the development of commitment, self-efficacy, and motivation. *Journal of Applied Psychology, 76*(6), 759–769. doi:10.1037/0021–9010.76.6.759

Tharenou, P., Saks, A. M., & Moore, C. (2007). A review and critique of research on training and organizational-level outcomes. *Human Resource Management Review, 17*(3), 251–273. doi:10.1016/j.hrmr.2007.07.004

Thomas, D. A. & Ely, R. J. (1996). Making differences matter: A new paradigm for managing diversity. *Harvard Business Review, 74*(5), 79–90. Retrieved from Business Source Complete database.

Thomas, V. J., & Cohn, T. (2006). Communication skills and cultural awareness courses for healthcare professionals who care for patients with sickle cell disease. *Journal of Advanced Nursing, 53*(4), 480–488. doi:10.1111/j.1365–2648.2006.03741.x

Tracey, J. B., Tannenbaum, S. J., & Kavanagh, M. J. (1995). Applying trained skills on the job: The importance of the work environment. *Journal of Applied Psychology, 80*(2), 239–252. doi:10.1037/0021-9010.80.2.239

Vedantam, S. (2008, January). Most diversity training ineffective, study finds. *The Washington Post*, pp. A03.

Wade, P., & Bernstein, B. L. (1991). Culture sensitivity training and counselor's race: Effects on Black female clients' perceptions and attrition. *Journal of Counseling Psychology, 38*(1), 9–15. doi: 10.1037/0022–0167.38.1.9

Wentling, R. M., & Palma-Rivas, N. (1998). Current status and future trends of diversity initiatives in the workplace: Diversity experts' perspective. *Human Resource Development Quarterly, 9*(3), 235–253. doi: 10.1002/hrdq.3920090304

Wentling, R. M., & Palma-Rivas, N. (2000). Current status of diversity initiatives in selected multinational corporations. *Human Resource Development Quarterly, 11*(1), 35–60. Retrieved from Business Source Complete database.

Wexley, K. N., & Latham, G. P. (2002). *Developing and training human resources in organizations* (3rd ed.). Upper Saddle River, NJ: Prentice Hall.

Wiethoff, C. (2004). Motivation to learn and diversity training: Application of the theory of planned behavior. *Human Resource Development Quarterly, 15*(3), 263–278. doi:10.1002/hrdq.1103

Williams, K., & O'Reilly, C.A. (1998). Demography and diversity: A review of 40 years of research. *Research in Organizational Behavior, 20*, 77–140.

Yelon, S. L., & Ford, J. K. (1999). Pursuing a multidimensional view of transfer. *Performance Improvement Quarterly, 12*(3), 58–78. doi:10.1111/j.1937–8327.1999.tb00138.x

Zhu, J., & Kleiner, B. (2000). The failure of diversity training. *Nonprofit World, 18*(3), 12–14. Retrieved from Business Source Complete database. doi:10.1177/0146167204271713

CHAPTER 20

Work–Life Interface and Flexibility: Impacts on Women, Men, Families, and Employers

Alison M. Konrad

Abstract

Traditional organizational cultures pressure workers to prioritize the paid work role and to sacrifice participation in other life domains. However, performance in the paid work role affects and is affected by other roles the worker considers important. Multiple roles often conflict, but they also create positive synergies whereby workers utilize skills, ideas, and resources gained in different domains to enhance performance in all of them. Supportive organizational cultures and work–life flexibility practices help workers manage the interface between paid work and other life domains, and evidence suggests that they enhance work attitudes and performance. Given that multiple roles enhance workers' performance, commitment, and resilience, organizational structures and cultures that support employees' participation in multiple life domains are likely to generate positive benefits for firms as well as employees. The chapter ends with a theoretical model intended to stimulate future research in this area.

Key Words: work–life interface, work–life conflict, work–life facilitation, work–life flexibility benefits, gender ideology, gender role attitudes, division of household labor

Introduction

Work–life interface can be defined as the set of activities and experiences occurring at the intersections between paid work and other life domains (Frone, Russell, & Cooper, 1992a; Kinnunen, Feldt, Mauno, & Rantanen, 2010). It is the nexus within which the work role connects with other life roles and which individuals must navigate to successfully manage all the different activities and obligations of their lives. Authors in this area write of work–life interface variables (i.e., spillover between work and family, Moen, Kelly, & Hill, 2011), bridging the work–life interface, reconciling the work–life interface (Volpe & Murphy, 2011)—even work–life interface failure (Murphy & Kram, 2010). The construct of work–life interface asserts that paid workers have obligations to family, friends, community, and other activities that affect and are affected by the paid work role.

Research on the work–life interface can be traced to Kahn and colleagues (1964), who identified conflict between paid work and other major life roles as a significant source of strain for many men. Sixteen years later, Near, Rice, and Hunt (1980) published an article in the *Academy of Management Review* in which they painstakingly justified examining the relationship between work and nonwork (which they called "extra-work") by appealing to explanations by Weber, Durkheim, and Marx regarding the interdependence of work and other societal institutions. Near and colleagues posited that work and family are interdependent and possibly conflicting spheres of life. They based this conjecture on the findings of a study by Bailyn and Schein (1976) showing that for MIT graduates, work involvement loaded positively on the same scale with family involvement, which loaded negatively. By

1985, Greenhaus and Beutell (1985) had identified 18 studies of antecedents of work–family conflict, which they defined as "a form of interrole conflict in which the role pressures from the work and family domains are mutually incompatible in some respect" (p. 77). Reflecting the growth of the field, Kossek and Ozeki's (1998) meta-analysis included 32 studies linking work–family conflict to job satisfaction and 18 studies linking work–family conflict to life satisfaction. In 2005, a new meta-analysis included over 60 studies of the antecedents of work–family conflict (Byron, 2005).

Around the turn of the millennium, scholars began to develop the concept of enhancement or enrichment between work and other life roles, finding that while work and life are interrelated, they need not always be in conflict (Barnett & Hyde, 2001; Rothbard, 2001; Ruderman, Ohlott, Panzer, & King, 2002). By 2010, McNall, Nicklin, and Masuda (2010) identified over 50 studies examining the links between work–family enrichment and job-related outcomes for their meta-analysis.

The trajectory of work–life interface research coincides with the historical mass movement of married women and women with children into the paid labor force. For instance, in the United States, the labor force participation rate of married women with children under 6 years of age rose from 30.3 percent in 1970 to 61.6 percent in 2009 (U.S. Census Bureau, 2011). Table 20.1 shows labor force participation rates for women and men aged 30 to 34 in the early 1970s and in 2008 for 23 countries. In all cases except Poland, women show a substantial increase in labor force participation rate over that period.[1] The timing is not coincidental: work–family interface has become a considerably more important concern for employers since women have entered the workplace in large numbers (Greenhaus & Beutell, 1985) because women's lives do not fit the way organizations have traditionally structured the employment relationship.

That traditional organizational structure has favored the career development of what Joan Acker (1990) called "the disembodied worker." The disembodied worker brings no bodily limitations to the workplace, being hindered neither by the possibility of disability nor the demands of human reproduction. While the ideal disembodied worker does not exist in reality, the traditional organizational employment system rewards those employees who are able to most closely match the disembodied worker ideal. Hence, individuals who can make themselves available to the employer for longer hours at any time of the day or night, who are able to travel or relocate geographically at a moment's notice, and who never take time off for either positive events such as giving birth or negative events such as illness are the most likely to attain the highest earnings and the top organizational positions (Acker, 2006). Indeed, this idea lives on in many twenty-first-century organizations, where one of the most recent initiatives is the development of the "extreme job" (Hewlett & Luce, 2006).

The massive entry of women into the paid labor force around the world has created substantial variation in employee experiences, needs, and priorities at work. Increasingly, men live in dual-earner households, and their contributions to unpaid family labor have risen precipitously (Bianchi & Milkie, 2010), which means that they, too, have to combine paid work with substantial family demands (Moen et al., 2011). Furthermore, it has become illegal in most societies to bar women from tertiary education or to engage in discriminatory hiring (Konrad & Linnehan, 2003). As such, in most places, it is no longer possible to explicitly bar women from positions of power and responsibility in the workplace. Hence, although some employers might believe that women on average are less committed to the workplace and less able to make themselves available 24/7/365, they cannot use such claims to justify selecting and promoting only men.

Given these historic changes in the labor pool facing employers, most organizations acknowledge that work cannot be segmented away from other life domains and that work–life interface is a legitimate managerial concern (Coffey & Tombari, 2005). Furthermore, recent scholarship has mounted a formidable attack on the mythic ideal of the disembodied worker. The first prong of the attack has been a growing literature supporting the existence of work–life facilitation effects (Allis & O'Driscoll, 2008; Boyar & Mosley, 2007; Carlson, Witt, Zivnuska, Kacmar, & Grzywacz, 2008; Hill, 2005; Taylor, DelCampo, & Blancero, 2009; van Steenbergen & Ellemers, 2009; Voydanoff, 2005; Wiese & Salmela-Aro, 2008). This body of research provides evidence that workers who are more active in life domains outside of work tend to perform better in the paid work role. Given this evidence, the organizational pursuit of the disembodied worker appears to be misplaced because it causes organizational decision makers to prefer individuals who ultimately will perform less well and be less resilient over time.

Table 20.1 Labor Force Participation Rates of Women and Men Age 30 to 34

	Early 1970s		2008	
Country	% Men	% Women	% Men	% Women
Austria[b]	97.9	50.9	95.5	81.0
Canada[b]	93.3	41.4	92.8	81.1
Chile[a]	97.6	25.5	95.0	62.2
Costa Rica[d]	94.9	23.9	98.2	60.6
Cuba[a]	93.5	23.0	90.4	60.6
Denmark[a]	97.5	54.7	95.2	87.3
France[e]	97.2	54.6	96.4	82.9
Germany[a]	98.1	44.9	94.6	76.4
Greece[b]	95.5	31.9	97.2	72.9
Hong Kong[b]	98.8	36.3	96.6	80.0
Italy[b]	96.4	31.2	91.6	69.4
Japan[a]	98.6	47.3	96.5	65.1
Korea[a]	95.6	36.3	92.2	53.7
Mexico[a]	93.2	15.7	96.1	52.4
Pakistan[c]	87.1	8.0	97.6	22.6
Peru[c]	97.1	21.9	96.1	75.3
Poland[a]	97.1	77.7	93.7	77.8
Singapore[a]	98.3	22.7	98.1	80.5
Spain[a]	97.0	13.7	94.9	80.6
Sweden[a]	91.5	52.7	94.7	87.8
Switzerland[a]	98.8	42.9	97.9	80.9
Thailand[a]	96.5	78.7	96.1	85.0
United Kingdom[b]	98.0	44.9	94.1	75.7

[a]Data for early 1970s collected in 1970.
[b]Data for early 1970s collected in 1971.
[c]Data for early 1970s collected in 1972.
[d]Data for early 1970s collected in 1973.
[e]Data for early 1970s collected in 1975.

Source: ILO Department of Statistics, LABORSTA (http://laborsta.ilo.org)

The second prong of the attack on the myth of the disembodied worker is the increased scholarly focus on the "war for talent" and the desirability of becoming an "employer of choice." Basic demographic trends toward lower birth rates and increased cultural diversity in developed countries imply that the ability to attract, motivate, and retain high-quality workers is becoming a critical competitive advantage (Cox & Blake, 1991; Robinson & Dechant, 1997). During the careers of the baby boom generation, employers had the luxury of numbers in their favor, with a relatively large number of talented individuals available for each high-quality job opening (Hall & Richter, 1990). But with the maturing of the baby bust generation, the days when employers in developed countries enjoy a buyers' labor market are thought to be ending. The next generations of workers are relatively smaller and more culturally diverse than the baby boom generation, which means that employers can no longer rely upon a "one-size-fits-all" employment relationship. Rather, they must diversify their approach to worker attraction, motivation, and retention in order to build a workforce comprising the highest-ability individuals available in the new diverse pool of workers. The highest-ability members of the baby bust generations will be able to demand more supports from employers to fulfill their wishes for a more well-rounded and balanced life than that lived by their baby boomer parents (Beutell & Wittig-Berman, 2008; Twenge & Campbell, 2008). These developments mean that the traditional ideal of the disembodied worker is becoming more divorced from reality, and employers must change their traditional employment systems to fit the new environment.

The third prong on the attack of the myth of the disembodied worker is the substantial body of evidence suggesting that the work–life flexibility practices provided by employers result in positive outcomes for both employees and organizations (Arthur, 2003; Arthur & Cook, 2004; Glass & Finley, 2002; Konrad & Mangel, 2000; Ngo, Foley, & Loi, 2009; Perry-Smith & Blum, 2000). Work–life flexibility practices are defined as organizational actions aimed at supporting employees as they manage the interface between paid work and other aspects of their lives, including family (Lobel, 1999). They are "deliberate organizational changes" in policies, practices, or the target culture aimed at reducing work–family conflict and increasing support for employees' lives outside of work (Kelly et al., 2008, p. 310). In addition to documented increases in productivity (Konrad & Mangel, 2000), organizational performance (Perry-Smith & Blum, 2000), and positive employee attitudes (Allen, 2001; Hammer, Neal, Newsom, Brockwood, & Colton, 2005), Hall and Parker (1993) suggest that providing employees with flexibility options can help organizations cope with business cycles and downturns. Specifically, allowing workers to reduce paid work hours in recessionary times allows the employer to reduce labor costs without losing talent in the long term. In sum, if workers who use work–life flexibility practices are more committed, productive, and flexible, then organizations are likely to benefit from supporting employees with multiple role commitments instead of seeking individuals who resemble the mythic disembodied worker.

The goal of this chapter is to provide an overview of the extant scholarly research on work–life flexibility and the work–life interface experiences of paid workers. This field is vast and growing, with contributions from management, psychology, sociology, and organizational studies, and the task facing the chapter author is daunting. Fortunately, prior authors have provided extensive reviews of research examining work–family conflict (Allen, Herst, Bruck, & Sutton, 2000; Byron, 2005; Ford, Heinen, & Langkamer, 2007; Greenhaus & Beutell, 1985; Kossek & Ozeki, 1998; Madsen & Hammond, 2005; Mesmer-Magnus & Viswesvaran, 2005), the work–life interface (Bianchi & Milkie, 2010; Edwards & Rothbard, 2000; Greenhaus & Parasuraman, 1999; Grzywacz & Carlson, 2007; Lobel, 1999; Westman, 2001), work–family enrichment and facilitation (Greenhaus & Powell, 2006; Grzywacz, Carlson, Kacmar, & Wayne, 2007; McNall et al., 2010; Wayne, Grzywacz, Carlson, & Kacmar, 2007), and the impact of organizational work–life flexibility initiatives (Kelly et al., 2008; Kelly & Moen, 2007). This chapter draws extensively on their work as well as on work published in the past few years in an attempt to synthesize current knowledge and provide directions for future research.

Key constructs and models

Key constructs and relationships in the work–life interface field are depicted in Figure 20.1. Following Grzywacz and Carlson (2007), the figure shows the work–life interface as the combination of conflicts and facilitators between the paid work domain and other life domains. Scholars have identified situation and person effects on work–life interface, and these are indicated on the left-hand side of Figure 20.1 in the boxes labeled "environmental work–life flexibility supports" and "individual differences." The major outcomes identified in this body of research are shown on the right-hand side of Figure 20.1 and include work attitudes and performance, family attitudes and performance, and individual well-being.

Work–life conflict

As noted in the introduction to this chapter, work–life interface developed into a major research area as married women with children entered the labor force in increasing numbers (Bianchi, 2000).

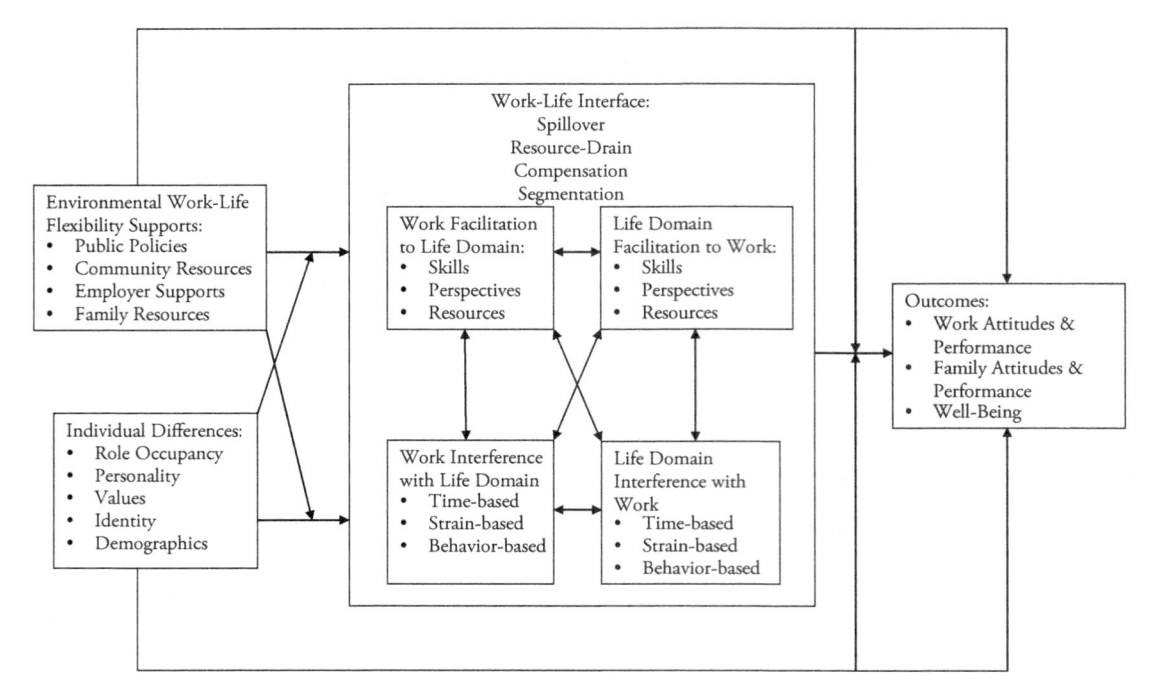

Figure 20.1. Antecedents and outcomes of work–life interface.

Women experienced numerous difficulties in work organizations designed by predominantly male management for a predominantly male labor force. An obvious difference between men's and women's experiences was the fact that women seemed to have more difficulty combining paid work with family responsibilities (Greenhaus & Beutell, 1985; Hall, 1972, 1975; Holahan & Gilbert, 1979a, b). Economists expressed concern that family obligations eroded women's productivity in the paid work role (Becker, 1985). Experts in child development researched concerns regarding the impact of women's paid work on young children and families (Desai, Chase-Lansdale, & Michael, 1989). In this context, not surprisingly, the field of work–life interface began with a rather narrow focus on the conflicts between the two domains of paid work and family (Frone et al., 1992a; Frone, Russell, & Cooper, 1992b; Greenhaus & Beutell, 1985).

Work–family conflict has been defined as "the frequency and intensity in which work interferes with family or family interferes with work" (Grzywacz & Carlson, 2007, p. 457) and "a form of interrole conflict in which work and family role demands are mutually incompatible so that meeting demands in one domain makes it difficult to meet demands in the other" (Edwards & Rothbard, 2000, p. 182). As these definitions imply, work–family conflict can arise from two directions, and state-of-the-art research utilizes measures that differentiate work-to-family conflict from family-to-work conflict (Gareis, Barnett, Ertel, & Berkman, 2009). Work-to-family conflict occurs when work interferes with family life, such as when paid work demands prevent workers from spending as much time with their family as they would like or reduce their ability to fulfill child-care and housework obligations (Carlson & Frone, 2003). Family-to-work conflict occurs when family life interferes with the paid work role, such as when family demands cause lateness and absenteeism or reduce the ability to accomplish job tasks (Carlson & Frone, 2003). Meta-analysis of 25 studies has shown that work-to-family conflict and family-to-work conflict are strongly positively correlated ($\rho = 0.48$) (Mesmer-Magnus & Viswesvaran, 2005).

Greenhaus and Beutell (1985) identified three forms of work–family conflict: (1) time-based conflicts, where time devoted to one domain consumes time needed to meet demands in another domain, (2) strain-based conflicts, where strains from one domain make it difficult to meet demands in another domain, and (3) behavior-based conflicts, where behaviors developed in one domain are incompatible with role demands in another domain. Meta-analytic results show that work–family conflict is negatively related to job and life satisfaction, although "family-to-work conflict appears to be less strongly related than bidirectional or work-to-family conflict" (Kossek & Ozeki, 1998, p. 145).

Work–life facilitation

More recently, authors have questioned the assumption, implicit in early work–family interface research, that the effects of paid work and family on each other can only be negative, and in 2001–02, scholars began to develop and marshal empirical support for the concept of *work–family* or *work–life facilitation* (Barnett & Hyde, 2001; Rothbard, 2001; Ruderman et al., 2002). Scholars have fostered the insight that people who have multiple life roles, such as paid worker, spouse, and parent, can be better performers at work because they bring resources and skills developed in other settings to the paid work role (Grzywacz, Carlson, Kacmar, & Holliday Wayne, 2007). People with multiple roles can also be more resilient to workplace stressors because supports and positive experiences in other life spheres either buffer or transfer to the workplace (Greenhaus & Powell, 2006).

Work–life facilitation effects occur due to the accumulation of a larger set of skills, perspectives, and resources due to active participation in multiple role domains (Greenhaus & Powell, 2006). "Skills refer to a broad set of task-related cognitive and interpersonal skills, coping skills, multitasking skills, and knowledge and wisdom derived from role experiences" (Greenhaus & Powell, 2006, p. 80). Perspectives are ways of perceiving individuals, situations, and events, and participating in multiple role domains expands the individual's understanding of different statuses (superior, peer, subordinate), contexts (solo, dyad, group), and cultures. Participating in multiple role domains also enhances personal access to resources, including psychological resources such as self-efficacy, social resources such as network ties and social capital, and material resources such as physical health or access to property. Work–family facilitation, like conflict, is bidirectional, and the global term includes both work-to-family and family-to-work facilitation (Gareis et al., 2009). Work-to-family facilitation occurs when the skills, perspectives, and resources acquired at work enhance performance in the family role. Family-to-work facilitation occurs when the skills, perspectives, and resources acquired in the family enhance performance in the paid work role.

Models of the work–life interface

Multiple models exist to predict the amount of conflict and facilitation occurring between paid work and other life domains (Edwards & Rothbard, 2000). *Spillover* refers to the extension or continuation of affect, values, skills, and behaviors from one domain into another. *Compensation* "represents efforts to offset dissatisfaction in one domain by seeking satisfaction in another domain" (Edwards & Rothbard, 2000, p. 180). *Segmentation* is separation between different life domains so that they do not affect each other. *Resource drain* "refers to the transfer of finite personal resources, such as time, attention, and energy, from one domain to another" (Edwards & Rothbard, 2000, p. 181).

Although the four models are conceptually distinct, testing these models against each other in empirical research has proven to be difficult. For instance, both the compensation model and the resource drain model predict a negative association between resources contributed to paid work and resources contributed to other life domains (Edwards & Rothbard, 2000). Longitudinal studies measuring satisfaction achieved and investments made in multiple domains at multiple points in time will be able to differentiate compensation effects, where investments in one domain are motivated by disappointment in another domain, from simple resource drain effects. To date, little such research has been conducted; however, a new study by Kinnunen, Feldt, Mauno, and Rantanen (2010) has found that high levels of family-to-work conflict resulted in increased levels of work-to-family conflict 1 year later for both husbands and wives and decreased job satisfaction 1 year later for wives. These findings support the spillover model, where strain in one domain leads to strain in the other. In another new study (Wiese, Seiger, Schmid, & Freund, 2010), researchers have developed a measure of perceived compensation between work and family to differentiate between these two models. Their findings indicate that perceptions of cross-domain compensation predicted domain-specific well-being—specifically, work-to-family compensation predicted job satisfaction and family-to-work compensation predicted family satisfaction. These findings supported the compensation model.

More recently, scholars are building models of the relationship between work–life conflict and work–life facilitation effects, adding complexity to the simple direct link between work–life balance and outcomes in Figure 20.1. Initial research in this area supports both the *independent-effects* model, where work-to-family conflict and facilitation show simple additive effects predicting personal well-being, and the *buffering* model, where family-to-work facilitation buffers the negative effects of family-to-work conflict (Gareis et al., 2009).

Research: Empirical findings

Scholars have conducted a substantial amount of research on the relationships depicted in Figure 20.1. Research on work–life conflict has generally supported the resource drain model of work–family interface. Research on work–life facilitation has generally supported the existence of positive spillover effects between work and other life domains. Both work–life conflict and work–life facilitation have substantive effects on attitudes, performance, and well-being in the workplace and in other life domains. Research on environmental work–life flexibility supports has focused on family and employer supports, and more work is needed to investigate the impact of public policies and supports available in the community. Research on individual difference effects has focused on role occupancy, values, and demographics, with less emphasis on personality and identity. Little research has examined the classical interaction between person and situation, and more research is needed to understand how individual and situational factors interact to affect the work–life interface and its outcomes.

Research findings on antecedents and outcomes of work–life conflict

Research on work–family conflict tends to support the resource drain model (Carlson & Perrewé, 1999; Halbesleben, Harvey, & Bolino, 2009; Nikandrou, Panayotopoulou, & Apospori, 2008), although few if any of these studies can rule out compensation effects (Kinnunen et al., 2010). For instance, Halbesleben, Harvey, and Bolino (2009) show that work engagement, or approaching work with high levels of energy and enthusiasm, is positively associated with work interference with family (WIF). They explain this finding with the argument from conservation of resources theory (Hobföll, 1989) that individuals have a limited amount of resources to invest in any given domain, so investments made in one domain are often offset by withholding investments in other life areas.

Meta-analytic findings on the antecedents of work–family conflict are consistent with the resource drain model. Combining the results of 60 empirical studies, Byron (2005) finds a pattern showing that work variables more strongly predict WIF, while family variables more strongly predict family interference with work (FIW). For instance, the number of hours spent at work is moderately positively correlated with WIF ($\rho = 0.26$) and uncorrelated with FIW ($\rho = 0.01$). Job stress is strongly positively correlated with WIF ($\rho = 0.48$) but only moderately correlated with FIW ($\rho = 0.29$). Importantly, job stress is more strongly associated with both WIF and FIW for parents than for others. Income is slightly positively correlated with WIF ($\rho = 0.10$) and uncorrelated with FIW ($\rho = 0.00$). Family stress is strongly positive correlated with FIW ($\rho = 0.47$) but only moderately correlated with WIF ($\rho = 0.30$). Family conflict is moderately positively correlated with both WIF ($\rho = 0.35$) and FIW ($\rho = 0.32$). Together, these findings show that investing resources in work results in interference in the family domain, while investing resources in family results in interference with the work domain.

Ford, Heinen, and Langkamer (2007) meta-analytically examined cross-domain relationships to assess "the permeability of the boundary between work and family domains and the extent to which positive and negative effects travel from one domain to the other" (p. 57). Their findings show generally small but significant effects of work variables and WIF on family satisfaction and of family variables and FIW on job satisfaction. The direction of these relationships indicates that job involvement, job stress, and WIF are negatively related to family satisfaction, while family stress, family conflict, and FIW are negatively related to job satisfaction. These findings support the resource drain model, indicating that resource investments or losses in one domain reduce satisfaction in the other.

Regarding outcomes, Kossek and Ozeki's (1998) meta-analysis showed that work–family conflict is moderately negatively associated with both job and life satisfaction. These findings also support a resource drain interpretation of work–family conflict: experiencing this conflict reduces one's capacity to generate satisfying outcomes in work and life. Also consistent with the resource drain model, Allen, Herst, Bruck, and Sutton's (2000) meta-analysis showed that WIF was moderately positively related to several stress outcomes, including general psychological strain, physical symptoms, depression, burnout, work-related stress, and family-related stress.

More recent research shows similarly negative effects of work–family conflict across a broader range of outcome variables. For instance, Wu, Chang, and Zhuang (2010) find that FIW reduces business success while WIF reduces marital satisfaction among Taiwanese co-preneurial women. Carlson and colleagues (2008) find that a supervisor's appraisal of an employee's level of work–family conflict negatively predicts the supervisor's ratings of interpersonal helping organizational citizenship behaviors (OCBs). van Steen Bergen and Ellemers (2009) show that work–family conflict increases cholesterol and body mass index, indicating negative health effects. Voydanoff (2005) finds that both WIF and FIW predict lower job and marital satisfaction and higher job stress and marital risk. Hill (2005) finds that WIF is negatively associated with job satisfaction, organizational commitment, family satisfaction, marital satisfaction, and life satisfaction and positively associated with individual stress. In the same study, FIW is negatively associated with family satisfaction and marital satisfaction and positively associated with individual stress.

Research findings on antecedents and outcomes of work–life facilitation

Many findings from the work–life facilitation research support the predicted positive spillover effect as people build and replenish their personal resources in multiple life areas, to the benefit of attitudes and performance in the work domain. A recent meta-analysis by McNall, Nicklin, and Masuda (2010) identifies 21 studies of work-to-family enrichment (WFE) and 25 studies of family-to-work enrichment (FWE). The findings for WFE indicate moderate positive relationships to job satisfaction ($\rho = 0.34$), affective commitment ($\rho = 0.35$), and life satisfaction ($\rho = 0.32$), a small positive relationship to health outcomes ($\rho = 0.21$), and no significant relationship to turnover intentions. The findings for FWE indicate a moderate positive relationship with family satisfaction ($\rho = 0.43$), small associations with job satisfaction ($\rho = 0.20$), affective commitment ($\rho = 0.24$), and health outcomes ($\rho = 0.21$), and no significant association with turnover intentions. These findings indicate positive attitudinal outcomes of WFE and FWE.

Other recent research has examined antecedents of WFE and FWE. For instance, Allis and O'Driscoll (2008) find that psychological involvement in family and personal activities predicts family-to-work facilitation, which in turn predicts positive well-being at work. Taylor Delcampo and Blancero (2009) report that a positive work climate for family, supervisor support, and intrinsically motivating job characteristics were positively associated with WFE. They also linked low levels of work–family conflict and high levels of WFE to the perceived fairness of the psychological contract.

Few studies have examined the link between WFE and FWE and work performance outcomes, and more research is needed in this area. Ruderman, Ohlott, Panzer, and King (2002) report that commitment to multiple roles was positively associated with 360-degree ratings of the effectiveness of managerial women. Carlson and colleagues (2008) find that a supervisor's appraisal of enrichment experienced by an employee predicted the supervisor's performance ratings for the employee.

Research findings on the impact of work–life flexibility supports

Environmental support for work–life interface potentially includes supports available from the family, the employer, and the larger community. Family and employer supports have been most commonly studied, and more work is needed to investigate the impact of public policies and supports available in the community. While the effect of supports on work–life conflict has been studied extensively, little research has examined the link between receipt of work–life supports from various sources and the experience of work–life facilitation (for exceptions, see Hill, 2005; Voydanoff, 2004, 2005).

Three meta-analyses have examined the link between receipt of **support from one's family** and the amount of work–life conflict experienced. Family support measures often focus on spousal support and sometimes differentiate emotional support from instrumental support. Byron (2005) identified 14 samples examining the relationship between family support and work–family conflict. She found that receipt of family support showed a small negative relationship with both WIF ($\rho = -0.11$) and FIW ($\rho = -0.17$). Ford, Heinen, and Langkamer (2007) identified 23 samples examining the link between family support and FIW and found a similarly small negative relationship ($\rho = -0.21$). Michel, Mitchelson, Pichler, and Cullen (2010) report a small negative meta-analytic correlation between family social support and FIW ($\rho = -0.21$, k = 31).

Three meta-analyses have examined the link between receipt of **support in the workplace** and the amount of work–life conflict experienced. Workplace support measures include support from supervisor, coworkers, and the organization itself (e.g., perceived organizational support [Eisenberger, Huntington, Hutchison, & Sowa, 1986]). Byron (2005) identified 17 samples examining the relationship between workplace support and work–family conflict. She found that receipt of workplace support showed a small negative relationship with both WIF (ρ = -0.19) and FIW (ρ = -0.12). Ford and colleagues (2007) identified 48 samples examining the link between workplace support and WIF and found a moderate negative relationship (ρ = -0.27). Michel and colleagues (2010) also found a moderate negative relationship between workplace social support and WIF (ρ = -0.27, k = 56).

The **organizational culture** for work–life interface can be defined as the set of values, beliefs, assumptions, and practices concerning employees who have important role responsibilities outside of the paid work domain. The organizational culture for work–life interface can be supportive when employees require flexibility at work in order to fulfill other roles effectively (Voydanoff, 2004), or it can indicate that work should have priority over other life domains (Mescher, Benschop, & Doorewaard, 2010). Climate for work and family is defined as employees' perception regarding how they are expected to manage the work–family interface (Kossek, Colquitt, & Noe, 2001). The climate for work and family can either support or discourage employees' attempts to be present and supportive when their family members need them.

Several studies have documented the importance of a supportive workplace culture or climate for helping employees manage the work–life interface (Hill, 2005; Holtzman & Glass, 1999; Kirchmeyer, 1995; Kossek et al., 2001; Lyness, Thompson, Francesco, & Judiesch, 1999; Mennino, Rubin, & Brayfield, 2005; Thompson, Beauvais, & Lyness, 1999; Voydanoff, 2004). For instance, both Voydanoff (2004) and Hill (2005) found that a supportive organizational culture had a significant negative effect on work–family conflict and a significant positive effect on work–family facilitation when several other significant predictors were statistically controlled.

Researchers have documented the positive effects on employees of a wide variety of **work–life flexibility practices**. A number of studies have combined practices into a single index and documented positive effects on employees, such as organizational citizenship behavior (Lambert, 2000), perceived productivity (Eaton, 2003), perceived family supportiveness of the organization (Allen, 2001), perceived organizational support (Lambert, 2000), increased work–family facilitation (Hill, 2005), increased job satisfaction (Behson, 2005; Breaugh & Frye, 2007; Cook, 2009; Frye & Breaugh, 2004; Hammer et al., 2005; Hill, 2005; Sahibzada, Hammer, Neal, & Kuang, 2005), increased organizational commitment (Eaton, 2003; Hill, 2005; Muse, Harris, Giles, & Feild, 2008; Thompson et al., 1999), increased psychological contract fairness (Taylor et al., 2009), and increased life satisfaction (Hill, 2005). Indices combining multiple work–life benefits have also been linked to reductions in negative outcomes for employees, specifically reduced work–family conflict (Allen, 2001; Frye & Breaugh, 2004; Hammer et al., 2005; Thompson et al., 1999), reduced role strain (Greenberger, Goldberg, Hamill, O'Neil, & Payne, 1989), reduced health symptoms (Greenberger et al., 1989), reduced turnover intentions (Allen, 2001; Behson, 2005; Cook, 2009; Thompson et al., 1999), and reduced burnout (Cook, 2009). These studies are useful for documenting the value of providing an array of work–life flexibility benefits.

Other studies have documented positive effects of work–life flexibility practices when examined separately. These studies are helpful for indicating the specific outcomes produced by particular practices. Positive effects have been documented for the provision of dependent care (Casper & Harris, 2008; Kossek & Nichol, 1992; Roehling, Roehling, & Moen, 2001), parental leaves (Grover & Crooker, 1995; Holtzman & Glass, 1999; Voydanoff, 2004), part-time work for professionals (Hill, Ferris, & Baker, 2004), and assistance with elder care (Sahibzada et al., 2005).

Byron's (2005) meta-analytic findings based on eight samples show that scheduling flexibility is moderately negatively related to WIF (ρ = -0.30) and has a small negative relationship with FIW (ρ = -0.17). Furthermore, the negative association between scheduling flexibility and WIF increases in magnitude as the proportion of the sample who are parents increases. Hence, scheduling flexibility is particularly effective for reducing WIF for parents.

Gajendran and Harrison's (2007) meta-analysis combines the results of 46 studies examining the effects of telecommuting, or working from home. Their findings show that telecommuting shows small positive relationships with several beneficial outcomes, including perceived autonomy (ρ = 0.22), relationship with supervisor (ρ = 0.12), job satisfaction (ρ = 0.10), and supervisor-rated performance (ρ = 0.19), reduced work–family conflict (ρ = -0.13), reduced role stress (ρ = -0.13), and reduced turnover intentions (ρ = -0.10). In addition, Nieminen and colleagues' (2011) meta-analysis found that telecommuting is moderately positively correlated with flexibility (ρ = 0.31), has a small positive correlation with work hours (ρ = 0.16), and is slightly negatively related to work–life balance (ρ = -0.03).

An important combined effect identified by authors is the **positive synergy between formal practices and managerial support**. Without managerial support, employees hesitate to use work–life flexibility benefits that are formally available in the organization (Breaugh & Frye, 2007). Lambert (2000) found that the perceived usefulness of the work–life flexibility benefits offered by the employer was a critical factor for predicting employee outcomes. Her index of perceived benefits usefulness was positively related to perceived organizational support, interpersonal helping, the provision of suggestions, and meeting attendance. Thompson, Beauvais, and Lyness (1999) emphasized the importance of managerial support for making benefits usage a realistic option for employees. They found that both managerial support and a supportive work–family culture were positively associated with benefits utilization. Cook (2009) found that supervisor support mediated the relationship between the availability of work–life flexibility benefits and reduced turnover. Together, these results indicate the importance of examining actual use of benefits when studying effects on employees. Examining the checklist of benefits provided by the employer does not take into consideration the possibility that employees might view the benefits as not useful or unattainable due to lack of supervisor support.

Authors are also starting to examine how different **practices might interact** with each other. For example, Golden, Veiga, and Simsek (2006) found that the combination of telecommuting and scheduling flexibility was more beneficial for reducing work interference with family than telecommuting alone. Wayne and Cordeiro (2003) found that lack of coworker support reduces the beneficial effect of leaves of absence. Foley, Ngo, and Lui (2005) found that the positive effect of role overload on work–family conflict was weaker when perceived organizational support was high. Findings reported by Sahibzada and colleagues (2005) suggest that different factors can serve as substitutes for each other. Specifically, they found that in a supportive work–family culture, work–life flexibility benefits were associated with reduced job satisfaction for those with elder-care responsibilities. In an unsupportive culture, however, work–life flexibility benefits were associated with increased job satisfaction for the same group.

Impact of individual differences

The most common individual differences examined as predictors of work–life interface have been role involvement and coping. According to Byron's (2005) meta-analytic findings, job involvement shows a small positive association with both WIF (ρ = 0.14) and FIW (ρ = 0.07), family involvement shows no association with WIF or FIW, and coping skills show a small negative association with WIF (ρ = -0.12) and FIW (ρ = -0.15).

Recent research examines individual trait differences for possible relationships to work–life interface outcomes. Nikandrou and colleagues (2008) find that self-esteem is negatively associated with WIF. Andreassi and Thompson (2007) find that the personality variable of internal locus of control is a negative predictor of WIF and FIW and a positive predictor of "positive spillover" between the work and family domains. Valcour (2007) finds that neuroticism is negatively associated with satisfaction with work–life balance. Halbesleben and colleagues (2009) find that negative affectivity is a positive predictor and conscientiousness is a negative predictor of both WIF and FIW. Conscientiousness also weakens the association between engaging in OCBs and both WIF and FIW. Judge, Ilies, and Scott (2006) find that trait negative affect and trait guilt are positively associated with FIW, while trait hostility is positively related to WIF. Lenaghan, Buda, and Eisner (2007) find that emotional intelligence buffers the impact of work–family conflict to weaken its negative impact on well-being.

Consistent with a social psychological perspective, Figure 20.1 indicates that individual factors potentially moderate the impact of environment on work–family interface and vice versa. But because the role of individual differences has only recently been investigated in work–life interface research, these potential interactions have yet to receive empirical attention. Examining the potential interactions between personal and situational variables is an important direction for future research.

Impact of gender, gender roles, and gender role attitudes

The disembodied worker ideal (Acker, 1990, 2006) is consistent with a gendered division of labor within families whereby men take the role of breadwinner and women take the role of homemaker (Eagly, 1987). This gendered division of labor creates a class of workers consisting of men who will never become pregnant, who will never nurse infants, and who have wives available at home full time to take care of their personal needs and those of their children and other family members. While men living this lifestyle can still fall ill or become disabled, they come as close as humanly possible to the ideal of the disembodied worker. As long as employers could count on an ample supply of these relatively homogeneous workers, human resource management (HRM) systems could construct a standardized set of work schedules, motivational techniques, and developmental processes all aimed at workers whose main priority is providing income to the family through paid work.

Gender roles are changing, and women now constitute almost half of the paid labor force in most countries. As a result, traditional HRM practices for the disembodied worker are becoming less effective for recruiting, motivating, and retaining high-quality workers. Changing gender roles are associated with attitudes and behavior in complex ways. Research on these changes is described in this section, with implications for managing the work–life interface.

Changing gender role behaviors in the family

Contemporary behavior in families is less tightly linked to traditional gender roles than in the past, and substantial variation exists between families in how paid work, homemaking, and caregiving tasks are distributed among adult family members. Women's entry into the paid labor force shows that participation in the breadwinner role has become less rigidly defined as masculine. Marriage, which used to be associated with women's withdrawal from the labor force, no longer shows any relationship to women's labor force participation or the number of hours they work per week (Bianchi, 2000). The arrival of children, however, continues to be significantly negatively associated with women's involvement in paid work, while showing a positive association with men's paid work involvement (Bianchi & Milkie, 2010). For instance, in-depth interviews with more than 100 members of dual-career couples showed that with the arrival of children, one of the partners, usually the woman, scales back her career efforts (Becker & Moen, 1999). Large-scale quantitative studies have replicated the finding that women reduce paid work involvement upon the arrival of children in the family, while men increase it (Hammer et al., 2005; Jacobs & Gerson, 2001; Moen & Yu, 2000). When their children are young, a substantial proportion of women work part time instead of full time (Bianchi, 2000). This pattern contrasts starkly to men's labor force responses to the arrival of children. Almost all new fathers continue to work full time, and fatherhood is associated with significant earnings benefits (Bianchi & Milkie, 2010; Glauber, 2008; Hodges & Budig, 2010; Lundberg & Rose, 2000). The earnings benefit of fatherhood implies that children increase men's motivation to generate income.

Like the breadwinner role, the homemaker role has become less rigidly gendered over time. In countries around the world, men have substantially increased their participation in child care and other homemaking activities over the past few decades (Bianchi, Robinson, & Milkie, 2006; Hook, 2006). Yet women continue to outperform men at unpaid labor in the family (Bianchi & Milkie, 2010): female employees combine more hours of unpaid work with their paid work responsibilities than their male counterparts do (Milkie, Raley, & Bianchi, 2009; Sayer, England, Bittman, & Bianchi, 2009).

As a result of the continued influence of traditional gender role expectations (Becker & Moen, 1999; Moen & Yu, 2000), mothers in general assume more parenting responsibility than fathers do, which means that the arrival of children creates more work–family conflict for women than it does for men (Beatty, 1996; Byron, 2005; Nelson & Burke, 2000). For instance, a study of white-collar workers showed that an increase in number of children is positively associated with women's but not men's perceptions of negative spillover from work to family (Maume & Houston, 2001). A large-scale quantitative study showed that for women but not for men, the number of both preschool-aged and school-aged children increased the likelihood of wishing one could reduce hours of paid work (Clarkberg & Moen, 2001).

Changing gender role attitudes

Gender role attitudes are associated with the extent to which people behave in ways that are consistent with traditional gender differences in family role participation. Brooks and Bolzendahl (2004) examined nationally representative data from the U.S. General Social Survey 1985–1998 and found evidence of increasing egalitarianism over time. Both age and year of data collection had significant unique effects, showing that younger cohorts are more egalitarian than older cohorts and that all cohorts show greater egalitarianism in more recent years.

Despite sweeping changes in the direction of egalitarianism, substantial variation in gender role attitudes exists within each nation globally (Treas & Widmer, 2000). Hakim (2002) argues that roughly 20 percent of women can be classified as "home-centered": family life and children are their main priorities in life, and they prefer not to work for pay. She classified another 20 percent of women as "work-centered": their main priority in life is their career. The remaining 60 percent were women who wish to combine paid work with family. Hakim's research documents significant links between women's work–life preferences and important behavioral outcomes, including fertility, labor force participation, and job choice.

Consistent with Hakim's (2002) view that preferences predict behavior in the domain of work and family roles, Stickney and Konrad (2007) found in a study of 28 countries that women with egalitarian attitudes earned significantly more money than women with traditional gender role attitudes. Similarly, Corrigall and Konrad (2007) reported that women with more traditional gender role attitudes in their early 20s worked shorter hours and earned less income in their late 20s than their counterparts with more egalitarian attitudes. Their longitudinal study also showed that for women, working longer hours at a younger age was positively associated with later gender egalitarianism. This latter finding shows that the relationship between gender role attitudes and behavior is more complex than suggested by Hakim. Gender role attitudes not only predict gender role participation, they also adjust in response to different experiences and situational constraints.

Men's attitudes also influence gender role behaviors in the family. Historically, men have been less likely than women to utilize the work–life flexibility options offered by employers (Greenberger et al., 1989). For instance, in Canada, new mothers (60 percent) are considerably more likely than new fathers (20 percent) to utilize paid parental leave benefits (Marshall, 2008). Research has shown that women consider the organizational provision of child-care programs (Frone & Yardley, 1996) and flexible work arrangements (Wiersma, 1990) to be more important and desirable (Haar & O'Driscoll, 2005) than men do.

Studies have also documented men's resistance to engaging in homemaking tasks. Bittman, England, Folbre, Sayer, and Matheson (2003) found that as men's incomes rise, their participation in household labor declines. Women are less able to reduce their participation in housework by earning more income, however. Bittman and colleagues found that women who make greater financial contributions to the family than their husbands also tend to assume more household responsibilities than their husbands do. Other research has shown that men's resistance to housework is negatively associated with their workplace authority, which suggests that men without authority in the workplace exercise authority in the home by refusing to engage in traditionally feminine homemaking tasks (Arrighi & Maume, 2000). Cha (2010) finds that having a spouse who works long hours for pay results in women but not men quitting their jobs, particularly among couples with children. Based on her findings, Cha argues that organizational cultures valorizing overwork exacerbate gender inequality. These latter findings illustrate that the relationships between gender role attitudes, behavior in families, and the management of people in the workplace are complex and represent an area worthy of more research attention.

Gender roles and the work–family interface

The gender role model of work–family interface (Gutek, Searle, & Klepa, 1991) argues that because women's traditional role of homemaker conflicts more with paid work than men's traditional role of income provider, working women more often than men face work–family conflict. As such, the work–life interface is more difficult for women to manage and affects their outcomes more strongly than the outcomes of men, who often have wives or partners who buffer the competing demands of paid work and family for them.

Byron's (2005) meta-analysis shows that gender as a main effect is unrelated to the amount of work–family conflict experienced (either WIF or FIW); however, among parents, mothers experience significantly more WIF and FIW than fathers do (table 4). This finding supports Gutek and colleagues' (1991) prediction that gender roles in the family make managing the work–family interface more difficult for women. The gender role view is also supported by Hill's (2005) findings that fathers experience less work–family conflict, less individual stress, and greater family and marital satisfaction than mothers even though they work long hours and experience a less supportive workplace culture for family life. Gajendran and Harrison's (2007) meta-analysis showing that telecommuting has a stronger positive association with supervisor-rated performance and self-perceived career prospects in samples that have higher percentages of women supports the gender role perspective, as does Dreher's (2003) finding that the presence of work–life flexibility programs is positively related to subsequent increases in the proportion of women in senior management positions. These latter findings show that employer supports for managing the work–family interface are particularly beneficial to women, which is consistent with the gender role perspective's argument that combining paid work and family is more difficult for women than for men.

Gender may also be a significant moderator of the relationship between work–family interface and other variables (e.g., Dentinger & Clarkberg, 2002; Posig & Kickul, 2004). Gutek and colleagues' (1991) gender role perspective suggests that work–family interface has stronger relationships with predictors and outcomes for women than for men, and some meta-analytic findings have supported this prediction. In her meta-analysis, Byron (2005) found that family involvement and hours of activity in the family domain are stronger predictors of FIW for women than for men. McNall and colleagues' (2010) meta-analysis shows that in samples composed of more women, FWE was a stronger predictor of job satisfaction and WFE was a stronger predictor of job satisfaction and family satisfaction.

Other meta-analytic findings, particularly those focused on job-related predictors of work–family conflict, show the opposite effect. Byron (2005) found that a number of variables are weaker predictors of WIF or FIW for women than for men, and Ford, Heinen, and Langkamer (2007) found that one of several relationships they examined was smaller for women than for men. The direction of these effects indicated that compared to men, women are less affected by both individual factors such as job involvement and coping skills as well as contextual factors such as scheduling flexibility and family support in their experiences of work–family conflict.

These meta-analytic findings suggest that research has been more successful at predicting men's experiences of work–family conflict than women's, with the implication that the models used to study work–family conflict have not included the most critical factors affecting women's experiences. Indeed, these models are based on the assumption that workers' experiences of work–family conflict are rational reactions to their work and family situation given their personal values and preferences. Factors unrelated to rationality and personal choice tend to be overlooked. The fact that women's work–family conflict experiences are relatively rigid in the face of different personal and situational factors suggests the existence of a construct outside of the domain of the job situation or personal choices regarding career and family.

Gender role attitude is a good candidate for this conceptual role. There is evidence that gender role attitudes are transmitted from parents to children, suggesting that to some extent people adopt their views at an early age, prior to making educational and career choices (Bjarnason & Hjalmsdottir, 2008). Religion is also significantly related to women's gender role views (Bang, Hall, Anderson, & Willingham, 2005) and is a cultural and societal factor that tends to be excluded from research on work–family conflict. Significant cohort effects indicate that broad societal changes influence gender role attitudes (Brooks & Bolzendahl, 2004). Recent research links gender role attitudes to government and public policy initiatives (Lachance-Grzela & Bouchard, 2010). Given that gender role attitudes are determined by societal and cultural factors, rational choice models are limited in their ability to explain their influence on work–family interface.

Little research has examined the role of gender role attitudes on the work–family interface. Minnotte, Minnotte, Pedersen, Mannon, and Kiger (2010) found that egalitarian women more than traditional women have reduced marital satisfaction when they experience more work–family conflict. Livingston and Judge's (2008) finding that traditional men feel more guilty while egalitarian men feel less guilty when they have high levels of FIW indicates that gender role attitudes are important predictors of outcomes for men in this area as well. Future research is needed to identify better predictors of work–family conflict for women, and research should also investigate the impact of gender role attitudes.

Theory: An integrated model of work–life interface

Previous authors have extended theory development in the work–life interface domain in several excellent prior reviews of the literature (Allen et al., 2000; Bianchi & Milkie, 2010; Byron, 2005; Edwards & Rothbard, 2000; Ford et al., 2007; Frone et al., 1992a; Frone, Yardley, & Markel, 1997; Greenhaus & Beutell, 1985; Greenhaus & Parasuraman, 1999; Greenhaus & Powell, 2006; Grzywacz & Carlson, 2007; Grzywacz, Carlson, Kacmar, & Wayne, 2007; Kelly et al., 2008; Kelly & Moen, 2007; Kossek & Ozeki, 1998; Madsen & Hammond, 2005; McNall et al., 2010; Mesmer-Magnus & Viswesvaran, 2005; Wayne et al., 2007; Westman, 2001). Based on and extending their work, Figure 20.2 shows an integrated model of work–life interface. This section describes the links between the constructs in the model and the contributions of the model to knowledge in this research domain.

The model in Figure 20.2 extends prior theorizing in two important ways. First, prior theorizing has often focused either on the person or on the organizational context as the primary factor affecting the work–life interface. A variety of work–life interface models have been developed that focus on the person to identify causal mechanisms linking role experiences in the paid work and other life domains. From the research inspired by these models, we know, for instance, that work and family roles can result in spillover (Kinnunen et al., 2010; Moen et al., 2011), compensation (Wiese et al., 2010), and buffering effects (Gareis et al., 2009). A separate set of models has focused on the effects of the situation, usually the organizational context. Kelly and colleagues' (2008) model, for example, shows how organizational work–life flexibility practices lead to positive individual-level outcomes for employees, which in turn aggregate to positive performance outcomes for the firm. Hence, although some within-person and cross-level theorizing has enhanced our understanding, extant theoretical models do not combine the person with the situation in a comprehensive way. In particular, the person-level models tend to ignore organizational context or relegate it to the status of a control variable, while models of organizational contextual factors leave out the psychological mechanisms through which work–life conflict and facilitation effects obtain. The model presented in Figure 20.2 overcomes the former limitation by incorporating the contextual factors affecting individual experiences in the form of role demands and environmental munificence. The model overcomes the latter limitation by incorporating the important psychological mechanisms linking experiences in different role domains, specifically role performance, allocation decisions, resource investments, and resource gains or losses.

Second, almost all previous theoretical models of work–life interface have been static rather than dynamic in that they indicate causal pathways from antecedents to outcomes without identifying any feedback loops. As an important exception, Edwards

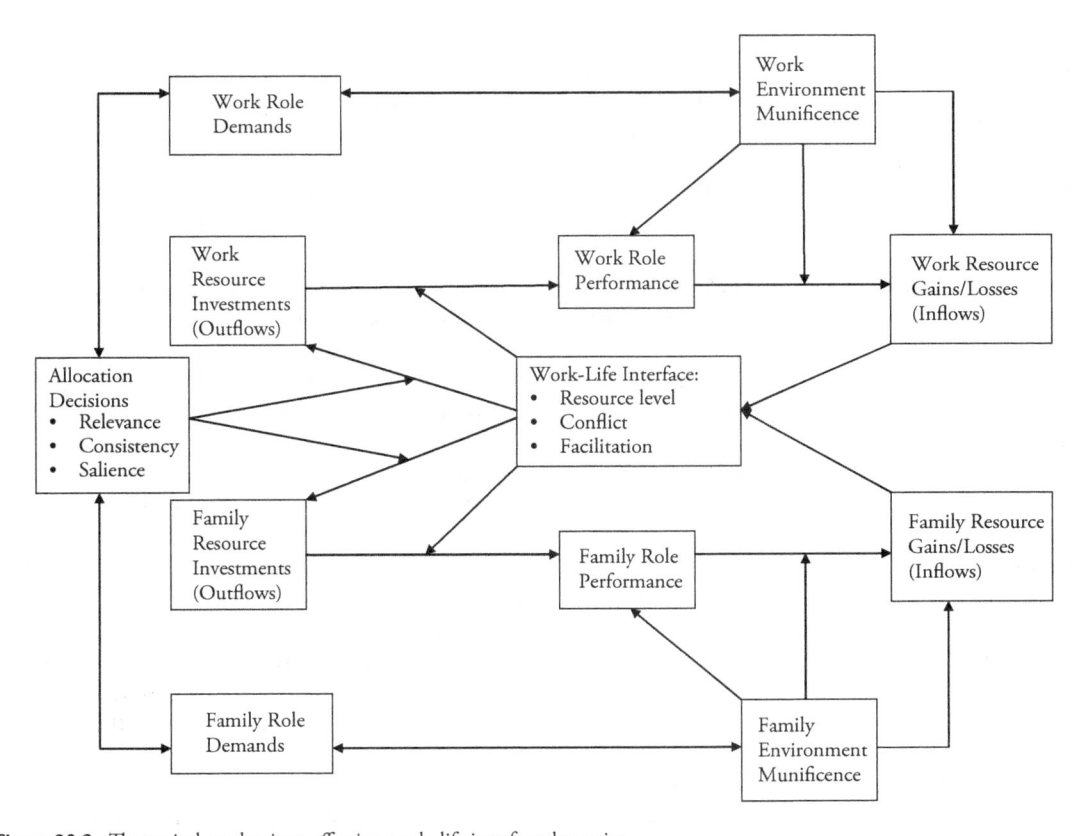

Figure 20.2. Theoretical mechanisms affecting work–life interface dynamics.

and Rothbard (2000, Fig. 7) indicate how moods generated as a result of level of performance and reward in the work and family domains feed back to affect performance in both domains. Their models are far from comprehensive, however, and they present them only as illustrations of how to utilize work–family linking mechanisms as building blocks to develop theories of work–life interface. The model presented in Figure 20.2 overcomes the limitations of prior models by incorporating dynamic feedback loops into a relatively comprehensive model.

Two limitations of the model in Figure 20.2 are obvious at first glance. First, the model focuses exclusively on paid work and family, ignoring the fact that for many people, there are other very important life domains, including religion, community, volunteerism, sports, arts, leisure, etc. The model could be extended fairly easily to other life domains, but Figure 20.2 depicts paid work and family because these domains have received the greatest amount of research attention.

The second obvious limitation of this model is the fact that it ignores the role of stable individual trait differences such as personality, values, beliefs, and attitudes. Individual difference variables could be added to the model as predictors, mediators, and moderators at several points, but for simplicity's sake, these factors have not been added to an already complex model. As stated above, gender role attitudes are likely to be significant predictors of behaviors and outcomes in the work–life interface domain, and the following text indicates a few places where they might enter the model.

Core work–life interface dynamic

The model depicts the relationship between paid work and family as a set of dynamic processes influenced by role demands, environmental munificence, and agentic decision making by individuals. The core of the model is based on conservation of resources theory (Hobföll, 1989), following Wayne and colleagues (2007). Hobföll's conservation of resources theory argues that people seek to maximize their store of resources in order to maintain readiness to face challenges in their environments. Resources are defined broadly as personal characteristics, objects, conditions, energies, and support that are valued by individuals as beneficial for navigating their lives effectively. People are motivated to increase their resources and experience stress when their store of resources becomes depleted or when investments they make fail to result in expected payoffs.

The integrated model of work–life interface shown in Figure 20.2 is based on the assumption from conservation of resources theory (Hobföll, 1989) that people will act to build and maintain their general store of personal resources. They can accomplish this goal by performing important life roles, such as paid work and family. Performing the work role results in work-related resource gains and losses, while performing the family role results in family-related resource gains and losses. Work and family resource losses and gains flow into the work–life interface, resulting in work–life conflict and facilitation effects, respectively. Conflict and facilitation make up part of the individual's general stock of personal resources available for investment in subsequent work and family activities.

The fact that work and family resources do not remain separate but instead flow into a general personal resource pool reflects the thinking of work–life conflict researchers, who argue that time constraints, strain, and behavioral habits arising in one domain affect one's actions and outcomes in the other. It is also consistent with the perspective of work–life facilitation researchers, who argue that performance in both roles generates skills, perspectives, and social capital, as well as material, psychological, and physiological resources that can be utilized in either or both domains (Greenhaus & Powell, 2006).

The model considers emotional reactions to work and family performance, core to Edwards and Rothbard's (2000, pp. 194–195, Fig. 7) model, as resource gains (or losses) that flow into the individual's general stock of personal resources capable of affecting investments in either or both domains. Similarly, the model places job attitudes, including satisfaction, commitment, and burnout, core to Kelly and colleagues' (2008) model, as work and family resource gains (or losses). The model considers time devoted to work and family, also core in Edwards and Rothbard's model, as part of the individual's resource investments. Table 20.2 shows how an admittedly partial list of constructs and variables cited as important by prior reviewers of this literature can fit into the general categories identified by each box shown in Figure 20.2.

Edwards and Rothbard (2000) argue that allocation decisions determine the extent to which investments in work and family conflict with each other. Following their model, Figure 20.2 indicates allocation decisions as moderators of the relationship between the individual's general stock of personal resources and investments in work and family roles. Following Greenhaus and Powell (2006),

Table 20.2 Examples of Variables Linked to Constructs Depicted in Figure 20.2

Work–Life Interface
- Resource levels:
  - Human capital
  - Social capital
  - Emotional energy
  - Physical and mental health
- Work–life conflict
- Work–life facilitation

Work Resource Investments
- Time, effort, energy
- Training
- Networking

Family Resource Investments
- Time, effort, energy
- Household labor, caregiving

Work Role Performance
- Job performance
- Extra-role performance
- Lateness, absenteeism

Family Role Performance
- Quality of caregiving
- Completion of needed household tasks

Work Resource Gains/Losses
- Gains
  - Compensation and benefits
  - Learning and development
  - Social support, social capital
- Losses
  - Physical/emotional exhaustion
  - Dissatisfaction

Family Resource Gains/Losses
- Gains
  - Learning and development
  - Social support, social capital
- Losses
  - Physical/emotional exhaustion
  - Dissatisfaction

Work Role Demands
- Role requirements, required hours
- Work overload
- Time pressure
- Emotional labor

Family Role Demands
- Marital status
- Number and ages of children
- Elder-care needs
- Household task needs

Allocation Decisions
- Relevance, consistency, salience of resources to role requirements
- Coping tactics and strategies

Work Environment Munificence
- Autonomy, control
- Authority, decision-making latitude
- Learning opportunities
- Respect
- Meaningful work, job complexity
- Job security
- Work–life flexibility benefits
- Supportive culture, climate

Family Environment Munificence
- Spouse or partner support
- Extended family support
- Health and disability status of family members
- Education, income, wealth
- Neighborhood, community characteristics

factors affecting these allocation decisions include the relevance of a particular resource to a particular role, the consistency between the resource and role requirements, and the salience of the resource for the individual when making allocation decisions. Gender role attitude is likely to be a significant determinant of allocation decisions, such that people with more traditional gender role attitudes allocate their resources in ways that fulfill the traditional gender assignments of women to homemaking tasks and men to income-generating tasks.

The general stock of personal resources is also depicted as moderating the link between work (family) resource investments and work (family) performance. In essence, this moderator effect indicates that the direct effect of investments (such as time) on performance is enhanced in the presence of other resources (such as a higher level of skills or being emotionally exhausted), which Wayne and colleagues call efficiency gains.

In summary, the dynamic process central to Figure 20.2 shows that individuals choose to invest resources in the paid work and family domains, which results in performance, which influences the subsequent level of resources available for further investment. Individual allocation decisions determine the extent to which resources flow between domains, and these decisions are moderated by the relevance, consistency, and salience of the resources for performing a particular role. Multiple resources have the potential to generate interactive effects generating either positive work–family facilitation synergies or negative work–family conflict dynamics.

External situational effects on the work–life interface dynamic

Figure 20.2 also shows external situational factors influencing the core work–life interface dynamic. The two types of situational factors emphasized in the model are role demands in each life domain and the munificence of each domain's environment.

Role theory is one of the basic theoretical foundations of the work–life interface field (Greenhaus & Beutell, 1985; Madsen & Hammond, 2005) and continues to guide contemporary research (e.g., Parasuraman & Simmers, 2001; Spector et al., 2004; Waumsley, Houston, & Marks, 2010). A role is defined as a set of expectations of a person occupying a particular structural position, such as manager, father, or daughter (Katz & Kahn, 1978). People occupy multiple roles, and Figure 20.2's model depicts the work–life interface as the set of relationships between inputs, behaviors, and outcomes of the different roles held by a single individual. Under the rubric of role theory, work and family role demands are communicated and reinforced to influence the behavior of the role occupant.

In Figure 20.2, work and family role demands influence the individual's investments in work and family activities through their impact on allocation decisions. As individuals become aware of work and family role demands, they make deliberate decisions to allocate their resources toward fulfilling those demands based on the relevance, consistency, and salience of the resource as it relates to the particular demand at hand. In addition, individuals have the agency to affect the work and family role demands placed upon them through the allocation decisions they make.

The work–life interface of each individual is embedded in a particular set of environments, which vary in their level of resource availability. Individuals in more munificent environments find it easier to build their store of personal resources, while individuals in more scarce environments find building and maintaining their stock of personal resources quite challenging. It is important to consider the munificence or scarcity of the environment(s) within which an individual is embedded when studying the work–life interface because the ease or difficulty of building and maintaining one's stock of personal resources affects individual outcomes.

Work environment munificence reflects the fact that some workplaces are more well resourced than others and provide employees with more rewards for their investments. Organizational work–family initiatives, central to Kelly and colleagues' (2008) model, constitute part of the workplace environment munificence, as does supervisor, coworker, and organizational support (Ford et al., 2007), scheduling control, and job autonomy, which are known to make combining work and family easier (Porter & Ayman, 2010; Valcour, 2007; Warner & Hausdort, 2009). Public policies supporting work–family interface for employees constitute work and family environment munificence at the national rather than the organizational level of analysis (Kelly et al., 2008).

In Figure 20.2, work environment munificence is posited as directly affecting individual work role performance because it is easier for workers to be productive if they have sufficient resources to perform their tasks. Work environment munificence is depicted as directly affecting work resource gains and losses to reflect the fact that many of the benefits of working for a munificent employer are received by employees regardless of their level of work performance. Work environment munificence is depicted as moderating the relationship between work role performance and work resource gains and losses because munificent employers are able to better reward employees for each increment of demonstrated performance. Finally, work environment munificence is indicated as influencing work demands, reflecting the positive impact of workplace resources on ease of accomplishing job tasks.

Family environment munificence reflects the fact that some families have greater resources while others have greater burdens. Positive relationships in the family, nearby relatives who provide high-quality child care, availability of high-quality educational institutions, and a positive partnership or marital relationship are examples of factors that add to family environment munificence. Chronic illness or disability of a family member, poor family relationships, low income, and living in a high-crime neighborhood are examples of factors that can detract from family environment munificence. Support from family members reduces work–family conflict, and family stress increases it (Ford et al., 2007).

In Figure 20.2, family environment munificence is depicted as directly affecting family resources gains or losses because many benefits accrue to family members regardless of how well they perform their designated family role. Family environment munificence is depicted as directly affecting family role performance because it is easier for individuals to perform their family role well if they have sufficient resources to do so. Family environment munificence is indicated as moderating the link between family role performance and family resource gains and losses because a more munificent family environment can provide richer rewards to individual members who perform their family roles well. Finally, family environment is indicated as affecting family demands, reflecting the fact that the presence of more resources in the family can reduce the burden of demands on family members.

Contributions of the integrated model

The integrated model of work–life interface shown in Figure 20.2 is not the only possible model for this domain, nor is it presented as the primary template upon which new research should be based. Rather, this model is intended to indicate the current state of theorizing and to draw attention to understudied areas in this domain.

The first contribution of the model in Figure 20.2 is that it brings together disparate theoretical models developed separately to explain work–life conflict, work–life facilitation, and the effects of work–life flexibility practices in organizations (Edwards & Rothbard, 2000; Frone et al., 1992a, 1997; Greenhaus & Beutell, 1985; Greenhaus & Powell, 2006; Kelly et al., 2008). Hence, it shows how these three research areas are related to each other and indicates that new research should take an integrative approach. Exemplary integrative research that considers work–life conflict, work–life facilitation, and work–life flexibility practices or other environmental factors together includes Hill (2005), Gareis and colleagues (2009), Taylor and colleagues (2009), and Voydanoff (2005).

A second contribution of the model is identifying the mechanisms linking demands from various life domains to work–life interface outcomes for individuals. By identifying resource inflows and outflows as a critical process (Edwards & Rothbard, 2000) and by applying the assumptions and propositions of conservation of resources theory (Hobfoll, 1989), the model outlines a dynamic set of processes linking demands in various life domains to experiences of conflict, facilitation, resource accumulation, and resource depletion. Increasingly, contemporary researchers are drawing upon conservation of resources theory to explain relationships in the work–life interface domain (e.g., Halbesleben et al., 2009), and the model in Figure 20.2 combines that theory with role theory to develop an integrated dynamic model.

A third contribution of the model is the addition of environmental munificence to the situational factors affecting individual behaviors and outcomes in the work–family interface domain. Much prior research has focused on role demands as situational factors affecting individuals in this domain (Madsen & Hammond, 2005); however, the roles occupied by individuals are situated within larger contexts that have substantial implications for people's ability to fulfill role demands and to garner personal resources as a result of high-quality role performance. The impact of environmental munificence on work–life interface has been underresearched, particularly at the neighborhood and community level of analysis (Bould, 2003). Voydanoff (2005) found that affective community resources, specifically a sense of community, neighborhood attachment, and support from friends, are positively related to both job and marital satisfaction beyond the impact of work–family conflict and work–family facilitation. This finding suggests that further research will identify significant effects of community environmental munificence on the work–life interface.

A final contribution of the model is the focus on the agency individuals have for choosing how to allocate their personal stock of resources (Edwards & Rothbard, 2000). Individual agency provides a moderator of the situational pressures people experience and recognizes resistance to situational determinism.

Directions for future research

A review of extant research and theorizing suggests several directions for future research in the work–life interface domain. This section provides a brief sketch of some possibilities.

First, while the term "work–life interface" implies an interest in the way a wide variety of possible life domains intersect with the paid work sphere, most research has focused on the relationship between paid work and experiences in the nuclear family. Some studies of elder care have broadened this research domain to the extended family (Kossek et al., 2001; Lee, Walker, & Shoup, 2001; MacDonald, Phipps, & Lethbridge, 2005; Sahibzada et al., 2005; Shoptaugh, Phelps, & Visio, 2004). Others are beginning to examine work–life interface for unmarried people without children (Hamilton, Gordon, & Whelan-Berry, 2006; Waumsley et al., 2010). Still more research is needed, however, on the experiences of people with different family structures, including a wider set of members of the extended family, same-sex couples, and single-parent families (Ciabattari, 2007).

Second, the intersection of paid work with other areas of life outside of the family, such as community, religion, arts, volunteerism, sports, and leisure, remains understudied. Studies examining three or more domains simultaneously can extend our knowledge considerably regarding the links between paid work and other life domains (Frone et al., 1992b), as well as different associations with mediators and moderators. A volunteer role might be particularly likely to enrich workplace performance through the development of skills, while participating in sports could be enriching for other reasons, perhaps the building of social capital. Leisure activities, particularly those conducted in solitude, could primarily enrich workplace performance by building or replenishing emotional energy. The interface among family, work, and community is particularly deserving of empirical exploration (Voydanoff, 2005). For instance, employer-provided work–life flexibility supports might be particularly beneficial to the outcomes of workers with relatively few supports available in their communities.

Third, considerably more research is needed on the relationships among different types of work–life flexibility supports. A strategic HRM perspective suggests the value of studying how various combinations of employer supports affect outcomes (Perry-Smith & Blum, 2000). Prior research indicates that the value of work–life flexibility benefits for improving employee outcomes depends upon the existence of managerial support for benefits usage (Breaugh & Frye, 2007; Cook, 2009; Thompson et al., 1999). A workplace culture of support of employees who require flexibility to perform roles outside of the paid work domain (Hill, 2005; Voydanoff, 2004) may interact with the provision of work–life flexibility benefits to enhance employee outcomes as well. As Kelly and colleagues (2008) noted, considerably more research is needed to identify which specific types of employer supports and which combinations of benefits are most beneficial for enhancing outcomes of employees and firms.

Fourth, a systems perspective (Katz & Kahn, 1978; Madsen & Hammond, 2005) suggests the value of examining how supports from different sources such as the family, the employer, the community, and government policy (Lachance-Grzela & Bouchard, 2010) combine to affect the processes and outcomes of the work–life interface. The relationships between behavior in families, workplace experiences, and outcomes for communities are complex. For instance, work–life flexibility supports are more often utilized by women than by men (McDonald, Brown, & Bradley, 2005), with the result that traditional gender differences in caregiving hours, paid work hours, earnings, and career development are maintained. Organizational practices beyond the provision of work–life flexibility benefits affect the work–life interface well, as illustrated by the link between men's subordination in the workplace and their resistance to housework (Arrighi & Maume, 2000). The impact of workplace experiences on families, communities, and gender equality deserves more study, particularly the relationship between people management practices and gender egalitarianism in the home. More research is also needed on the social psychological question of how situation and person interact to affect processes and outcomes, given that recent research is demonstrating the importance of both individual differences (Livingston & Judge, 2008; Nikandrou et al., 2008; Valcour, 2007) and environment (Kelly et al., 2008; Voydanoff, 2005; Warren, Fox, & Pascall, 2009).

Fifth, U.S. researchers and samples are overrepresented in this research domain. Kelly and colleagues (2008) note that a result of this bias is an emphasis on employer-provided work–family supports because U.S. public policy provides very little in the way of government supports for work–life interface. Hence, more research is needed on the effectiveness of various public policies for helping women, men, and families manage the work–life interface (Warren et al., 2009). Community supports also remain understudied (Bould, 2003; Voydanoff, 2005). Furthermore, the impact of various types of support, be it from employers or other sources, on work–life facilitation effects is worthy of further study.

Sixth, cross-cultural differences and similarities in experiences of the work–life interface require more research attention (Korabik, Lero, & Ayman, 2003). Hassan, Dollard, and Winefield (2010) argue that the relationships of WIF and FIW with outcome variables differ between Eastern and Western countries. In contrast, Hill, Yang, Hawkins, and Ferris (2004) report evidence from 48 countries supporting a universal work–family interface model where job flexibility is negatively associated with WIF and FIW and positively associated with work–family fit. The data from Hill and colleagues' study come from a single large multinational corporation, however, which suggests that organizational selection and socialization processes may have muted cultural differences among the 48 societies studied. These studies have not examined life domains outside of paid work and family and have ignored facilitation effects, among other limitations. Hence, considerable latitude exists for more cross-cultural research on the work–life interface.

Conclusion

Contemporary thinking and research suggest that organizations no longer serve themselves well by limiting career rewards to employees who fit the ideal of the disembodied worker. The concept of work–life facilitation argues that employees who are more involved in multiple roles are often better performers and more committed to the organization (McNall et al., 2010; Ruderman et al., 2002). The need to become an employer of choice in a more diverse sellers' labor market means that employers must provide more workplace supports in order to attract, motivate, and retain the highest-quality employees. In particular, a growing body of evidence suggests that providing work–life flexibility benefits (Gajendran & Harrison, 2007; Hill, 2005; Lambert, 2000) and developing a supportive organizational culture regarding work and family are valuable tools for managing the contemporary employment relationship (Kelly et al., 2008).

Despite the acknowledgement that work cannot be separated from other domains of life, organizations have been slow to change in this area (Mescher et al., 2010), and the disembodied worker ideal remains stubbornly embedded at the core of most HRM systems. The extreme job (Hewlett & Luce, 2006) is only one aspect of a much broader model that links career success to a willingness to give all to the employer at the expense of family and/or balance across other life domains. Consultants, investment bankers, lawyers, and top executives in large corporations of all kinds, as well as many leaders in government and the nonprofit world, spend 70, 80, 90 hours per week and more at their paid work roles. And these individuals are admired, held up as the supreme models of career success, and well remunerated for their one-sided commitments. Given the predominance of these images of success, it should not be surprising that organizational HRM systems continue to be based upon the disembodied worker ideal.

The integrated model of work–life interface presented in this chapter provides two clear routes toward change. First, individuals have choices regarding how to invest their time, effort, and talents and can refuse to fulfill the role demands of extreme jobs and occupations. The impact of this method of change is incremental and limited. Many individuals choose to replicate traditional patriarchal patterns whereby the role of income provider to the family is held by men, who then willingly take on extreme jobs in the pursuit of prestige and supreme material success (Cha, 2010; Hakim, 2002). Systemic factors such as lower pay in predominantly female occupations make following traditional patterns the "rational" choice for many families.

The second route toward change indicated in Figure 20.2's model is to enhance the munificence of the work and family environment in order to maintain sufficient resource flows to allow individuals to meet their role obligations. In the workplace, provision of work–life flexibility benefits provides workers with resources that can be allocated to both the work and family domains. Development of a supportive organizational culture for work and family creates the environment needed for employees to actually use flexibility benefits that might otherwise exist primarily only on paper (Eaton, 2003). Public policies can provide resources such as support for child and elder care, generous parental leaves, and tax relief for families (Warren et al., 2009). Investments in communities, including high-quality public education, neighborhood safety, and after-school programs for youths, provide families with resources and protection from resource drains. Organizational and public policies can increase the munificence of the work, family, and community environments in which individuals are embedded, with the result that women, men, and families experience greater satisfaction and reduced strain.

Note

1. Like other Eastern Bloc communist societies in 1970, Poland enforced a policy of mandatory full-time work regardless of gender, which resulted in a very high female labor force participation rate at that time.

References

Acker, J. (1990). Hierarchies, jobs, and bodies: A theory of gendered organizations. *Gender & Society, 4*(2), 139–158.

Acker, J. (2006). Inequality regimes: Gender, class, and race in organizations. *Gender & Society, 20*(4), 441–464.

Allen, T. D. (2001). Family-supportive work environments: The role of organizational perceptions. *Journal of Vocational Behavior, 58*, 414–435.

Allen, T. D., Herst, D. E. L., Bruck, C. S., & Sutton, M. (2000). Consequences associated with work-to-family conflict: A review and agenda for future research. *Journal of Occupational Health Psychology, 5*(2), 278–308.

Allis, P., & O'Driscoll, M. P. (2008). Positive effects of nonwork-to-work facilitation on well-being in work, family and personal domains. *Journal of Managerial Psychology, 23*, 273–291.

Andreassi, J. K., & Thompson, C. A. (2007). Dispositional and situational sources of control: Relative impact on work-family conflict and positive spillover. *Journal of Managerial Psychology, 22*(8), 722–740.

Arrighi, B. A., & Maume, D. J., Jr. (2000). Workplace subordination and men's avoidance of housework. *Journal of Family Issues, 21*(4), 464–487.

Arthur, M. M. (2003). Share price reactions to work-family human resource decisions: An institutional perspective. *Academy of Management Journal, 46*, 497–505.

Arthur, M. M., & Cook, A. (2004). Taking stock of work-family initiatives: How announcements of "family-friendly" human resource decisions affect shareholder value. *Industrial & Labor Relations Review, 57*, 599–613.

Bailyn, L., & Schein, E. H. (1976). Life/career considerations as indicators of quality of employment. In A. D. Biderman & T. F. Drury (Eds.), *Measuring work quality for social reporting* (151–168). New York: Wiley.

Bang, E., Hall, M. E. L., Anderson, T. L., & Willingham, M. M. (2005). Ethnicity, acculturation, and religiousity as predictors of female college students' role expectations. *Sex Roles, 53*(3/4), 231–237.

Barnett, R. C., & Hyde, J. S. (2001). Women, men, work, and family: An expansionist theory. *American Psychologist, 56*, 781–796.

Beatty, C. A. (1996). The stress of managerial and professional women: Is the price too high? *Journal of Organizational Behavior, 17*, 233–252.

Becker, G. S. (1985). Human capital, effort, and the sexual division of labor. *Journal of Labor Economics, 3*, S33–S58.

Becker, P. E., & Moen, P. (1999). Scaling back: Dual-earning couples' work-family strategies. *Journal of Marriage & Family, 61*(4), 995–1007.

Behson, S. J. (2005). The relative contribution of formal and informal organizational work-family support. *Journal of Vocational Behavior, 66*, 487–500.

Beutell, N. J., & Wittig-Berman, U. (2008). Work-family conflict and work-family synergy for generation X, baby boomers, and matures: Generational differences, predictors, and satisfaction outcomes. *Journal of Managerial Psychology, 23*, 507–523.

Bianchi, S. M. (2000). Maternal employment and time with children: Dramatic change or surprising continuity? *Demography, 37*, 401–414.

Bianchi, S. M., & Milkie, M. A. (2010). Work and family research in the first decade of the 21st century. *Journal of Marriage & Family, 72*(3), 705–725.

Bianchi, S. M., Robinson, J. P., & Milkie, M. A. (2006). *Changing rhythms of American family life*. New York: Russell Sage Foundation.

Bittman, M., England, P., Folbre, N., Sayer, L., & Matheson, G. (2003). When does gender trump money? Bargaining and time in household work. *American Journal of Sociology, 109*, 186–214.

Bjarnason, T., & Hjalmsdottir, A. (2008). Egalitarian attitudes towards the division of household labor among adolescents in Iceland. *Sex Roles, 59*(1), 49–60.

Bould, S. (2003). Caring neighborhoods: Bringing up the kids together. *Journal of Family Issues, 24*(4), 427–447.

Boyar, S. L., & Mosley, D. C., Jr. (2007). The relationship between core self-evaluations and work and family satisfaction: The mediating role of work-family conflict and facilitation. *Journal of Vocational Behavior, 71*, 265–281.

Breaugh, J. A., & Frye, N. K. (2007). An examination of the antecedents and consequences of the use of family-friendly benefits. *Journal of Managerial Issues, 19*, 35–52.

Brooks, C., & Bolzendahl, C. I. (2004). The transformation of US gender role attitudes: Cohort replacement, social-structural change, and ideological learning. *Social Science Research, 33*, 106–133.

Byron, K. (2005). A meta-analytic review of work-family conflict and its antecedents. *Journal of Vocational Behavior, 67*, 169–198.

Carlson, D. S., & Frone, M. R. (2003). Relation of behavioral and psychological involvement to a new four-factor conceptualization of work-family interference. *Journal of Business & Psychology, 17*(4), 515–535.

Carlson, D. S., & Perrewé, P. L. (1999). The role of social support in the stressor-strain relationship: An examination of work-family conflict. *Journal of Management, 25*(4), 513–540.

Carlson, D. S., Witt, L., Zivnuska, S., Kacmar, M. K., & Grzywacz, J. G. (2008). Supervisor appraisal as the link between family-work balance and contextual performance. *Journal of Business & Psychology, 23*, 37–49.

Casper, W. J., & Harris, C. M. (2008). Work–life benefits and organizational attachment: Self-interest utility and signaling theory models. *Journal of Vocational Behavior, 72*, 95–109.

Cha, Y. (2010). Reinforcing separate spheres: The effect of spousal overwork on men's and women's employment in dual-earner households. *American Sociological Review, 75*(2), 303–329.

Ciabattari, T. (2007). Single mothers, social capital, and work-family conflict. *Journal of Family Issues, 28*, 34–60.

Clarkberg, M., & Moen, P. (2001). The time-squeeze: Is the increase in working time due to employer demands or employee preferences? *American Behavioral Scientist, 44*, 1115–1136.

Coffey, C., & Tombari, N. (2005). The bottom-line for work/life leadership: Linking diversity and organizational culture. *Ivey Business Journal Online* (July-August).

Cook, A. (2009). Connecting work-family policies to supportive work environments. *Group & Organization Management, 34*, 206–240.

Corrigall, E. A., & Konrad, A. M. (2007). Gender role attitudes and careers: A longitudinal study. *Sex Roles, 56*(11–12), 847–855.

Cox, T., Jr., & Blake, S. (1991). Managing cultural diversity: Implications for organizational competitiveness. *Academy of Management Executive, 5*(3), 45–56.

Dentinger, E., & Clarkberg, M. (2002). Informal caregiving and retirement timing among men and women: Gender and caregiving relationships in late midlife. *Journal of Family Issues, 23*(7), 857–879.

Desai, S., Chase-Lansdale, L., & Michael, R. T. (1989). Mother or market? Effects of maternal employment on the intellectual ability of 4-year-old children. *Demography, 26*(4), 545–561.

Dreher, G. F. (2003). Breaking the glass ceiling: The effects of sex-ratios and work–life programs on female leadership at the top. *Human Relations, 56*, 541–562.

Eagly, A. H. (1987). *Sex differences in social behavior: A social-role interpretation*. Hillsdale, NJ: Erlbaum.

Eaton, S. C. (2003). If you can use them: Flexibility policies, organizational commitment, and perceived performance. *Industrial Relations, 42*, 145–167.

Edwards, J. R., & Rothbard, N. P. (2000). Mechanisms linking work and family: Clarifying the relationship between work and family constructs. *Academy of Management Review, 25*, 178–199.

Eisenberger, R., Huntington, R., Hutchison, S., & Sowa, D. (1986). Perceived organizational support. *Journal of Applied Psychology, 71*, 500–507.

Foley, S., Ngo, H.-Y., & Lui, S. (2005). The effects of work stressors, perceived organizational support, and gender on work-family conflict in Hong Kong. *Asia Pacific Journal of Management, 22*, 237–256.

Ford, M. T., Heinen, B. A., & Langkamer, K. L. (2007). Work and family satisfaction and conflict: A meta-analysis of cross-domain relations. *Journal of Applied Psychology, 92*(1), 57–80.

Frone, M. R., Russell, M., & Cooper, M. L. (1992a). Antecedents and outcomes of work-family conflict: Testing a model of the work-family interface. *Journal of Applied Psychology, 77*(1), 65–78.

Frone, M. R., Russell, M., & Cooper, M. L. (1992b). Prevalence of work-family conflict: Are work and family boundaries asymmetrically permeable? *Journal of Organizational Behavior, 13*, 723–729.

Frone, M. R., & Yardley, J. K. (1996). Workplace family supportive programs: Predictors of employed parents' importance ratings. *Journal of Occupational and Organizational Psychology, 69*, 351–366.

Frone, M. R., Yardley, J. K., & Markel, K. S. (1997). Developing and testing an integrative model of the work-family interface. *Journal of Vocational Behavior, 50*(2), 145–167.

Frye, N. K., & Breaugh, J. A. (2004). Family-friendly policies, supervisor support, work-family conflict, family-work conflict, and satisfaction: A test of a conceptual model. *Journal of Business & Psychology, 19*, 197–220.

Gajendran, R. A., & Harrison, D. A. (2007). The good, the bad and the unknown about telecommuting: Meta-analysis of psychological mediators and individual consequences. *Journal of Applied Psychology, 92*, 1524–1541.

Gareis, K. C., Barnett, R. C., Ertel, K. A., & Berkman, L. F. (2009). Work-family enrichment and conflict: Additive effects, buffering, or balance? *Journal of Marriage & Family, 71*(3), 696–707.

Glass, J. L., & Finley, A. (2002). Coverage and effectiveness of family-responsive workplace policies. *Human Resource Management Review, 12*, 313–337.

Glauber, R. (2008). Race and gender in families and work: The fatherhood premium. *Gender & Society, 22*, 8–30.

Golden, T. D., Veiga, J. F., & Simsek, Z. (2006). Telecommuting's differential impact on work-family conflict: Is there no place like home? *Journal of Applied Psychology, 91*, 1340–1350.

Greenberger, E., Goldberg, W. A., Hamill, S., O'Neil, R., & Payne, C. K. (1989). Contributions of a supportive work environment to parents' well-being and orientation to work. *American Journal of Community Psychology, 17*, 755–783.

Greenhaus, J. H., & Beutell, N. J. (1985). Sources of conflict between work and family roles. *Academy of Management Review, 10*(1), 76–88.

Greenhaus, J. H., & Parasuraman, S. (1999). Research on work, family, and gender: Current status and future directions. In G. N. Powell (Ed.), *Handbook of gender and work* (pp. 391–412). Thousand Oaks, CA: Sage.

Greenhaus, J. H., & Powell, G. N. (2006). When work and family are allies: A theory of work-family enrichment. *Academy of Management Review, 31*, 72–92.

Grover, S. L., & Crooker, K. J. (1995). Who appreciates family-responsive human resource policies: The imapct of family-friendly policies on the organizational attachment of parents and non-parents. *Personnel Psychology, 48*, 271–288.

Grzywacz, J. G., & Carlson, D. S. (2007). Conceptualizing work-family balance: Implications for practice and research. *Advances in Developing Human Resources, 9*(4), 455–471.

Grzywacz, J. G., Carlson, D. S., Kacmar, M. K., & Holliday Wayne, J. (2007). A multi-level perspective on the synergies between work and family. *Journal of Occupational and Organizational Psychology, 80*, 559–574.

Grzywacz, J. G., Carlson, D. S., Kacmar, M. K., & Wayne, J. H. (2007). A multi-level perspective on the synergies between work and family. *Journal of Occupational and Organizational Psychology, 80*, 559–574.

Gutek, B. A., Searle, S., & Klepa, L. (1991). Rational versus gender-role explanations for work-family conflict. *Journal of Applied Psychology, 76*, 560–568.

Haar, J. M., & O'Driscoll, M. P. (2005). Exploring gender differences in employee attitudes toward work-family practices and use of work-family practices. *Equal Opportunities International, 24*, 86–98.

Hakim, C. (2002). Lifestyles preferences as determinants of women's differentiated labor market careers. *Work & Occupations, 29*, 428–459.

Halbesleben, J. R. B., Harvey, J., & Bolino, M. C. (2009). Too engaged? A conservation of resources view of the relationship between work engagement and work interference with family. *Journal of Applied Psychology, 94*, 1452–1465.

Hall, D. T. (1972). A model of coping with role conflict: The role behavior of college-educated women. *Administrative Science Quarterly, 17*, 471–489.

Hall, D. T. (1975). Pressures from work, self, and home in the life stages of married women. *Journal of Vocational Behavior, 6*, 121–132.

Hall, D. T., & Parker, V. A. (1993). The role of workplace flexibility in managing diversity. *Organizational Dynamics, 22*(1), 5–18.

Hall, D. T., & Richter, J. (1990). Career gridlock: Baby boomers hit the wall. *Academy of Management Executive, 4*(3), 7–22.

Hamilton, E. A., Gordon, J. R., & Whelan-Berry, K. S. (2006). Understanding the work–life conflict of never-married women without children. *Women in Management Review, 21*(5), 393–415.

Hammer, L. B., Neal, M. B., Newsom, J. T., Brockwood, K. J., & Colton, C. L. (2005). A longitudinal study of the effects of dual-earner couples' utilization of family-friendly workplace supports on work and family outcomes. *Journal of Applied Psychology, 90*, 799–810.

Hassan, Z., Dollard, M. F., & Winefield, A. H. (2010). Work-family conflict in East v. Western countries. *Cross Cultural Management: An International Journal, 17*, 30–49.

Hewlett, S. A., & Luce, C. B. (2006). Extreme jobs: The dangerous allure of the 70-hour work week. *Harvard Business Review, 84*(12), 49–55, 58+.

Hill, E. J. (2005). Work-family facilitation and conflict, working fathers and mothers, work-family stressors and support. *Journal of Family Issues, 26*, 793–819.

Hill, E. J., Ferris, M., & Baker, R. Z. (2004). Beyond the mommy track: The influence of new-concept part-time work for professional women on work and family. *Journal of Family & Economic Issues, 25*, 121–136.

Hill, E. J., Yang, C., Hawkins, A. J., & Ferris, M. (2004). A cross-cultural test of the work-family interface in 48 countries. *Journal of Marriage & Family, 66*, 1300–1316.

Hobföll, S. E. (1989). Conservation of resources: A new attempt at conceptualizing stress. *American Psychologist, 44*, 513–524.

Hodges, M. J., & Budig, M. J. (2010). Who gets the daddy bonus?: Organizational hegemonic masculinity and the impact of fatherhood on earnings. *Gender & Society, 24*(6), 717–745.

Holahan, C. K., & Gilbert, L. A. (1979a). Conflict between major life roles: Women and men in dual-career couples. *Human Relations, 32*, 451–467.

Holahan, C. K., & Gilbert, L. A. (1979b). Interrole conflict for working women: Career versus jobs. *Journal of Applied Psychology, 64*, 86–90.

Holtzman, J., & Glass, J. (1999). Explaining changes in mothers' job satisfaction following childbirth. *Work & Occupations, 26*, 365–404.

Hook, J. L. (2006). Care in context: Men's unpaid work in 20 countries: 1965–2003. *American Sociological Review, 71*, 639–660.

Jacobs, J. A., & Gerson, K. (2001). Overworked individuals or overworked families? Explaining trends in work, leisure, and family time. *Work & Occupations, 28*, 40–63.

Judge, T. A., Ilies, R., & Scott, B. A. (2006). Work-family conflict and emotions: Effects at work and at home. *Personnel Psychology, 59*(4), 779–814.

Kahn, R. L., Wolfe, D. M., Quinn, R. E., Snoek, J. D., & Rosenthal, R. A. (1964). *Organizational stress.* New York: Wiley.

Katz, D., & Kahn, R. L. (1978). *The social psychology of organizations* (2nd ed.). New York: Wiley.

Kelly, E. L., Kossek, E. E., Hammer, L. B., Durham, M., Bray, J., Chermack, K., et al. (2008). Getting there from here: Research on the effects of work-family initiatives on work-family conflict and business outcomes. *Academy of Management Annals, 2*, 305–349.

Kelly, E. L., & Moen, P. (2007). Rethinking the clockwork of work: Why schedule control may pay off at work and at home. *Advances in Developing Human Resources, 9*(4), 487–506.

Kinnunen, U., Feldt, T., Mauno, S., & Rantanen, J. (2010). Interface between work and family: A longitudinal individual and crossover perspective. *Journal of Occupational and Organizational Psychology, 83*, 119–137.

Kirchmeyer, C. (1995). Managing the work-nonwork boundary: An assessment of organizational responses. *Human Relations, 48*, 515–536.

Konrad, A. M., & Linnehan, F. (2003). Affirmative action as a means of increasing workforce diversity. In M. J. Davidson & S. L. Fielden (Eds.), *Individual diversity and psychology in organizations* (pp. 95–111). Chichester: Wiley.

Konrad, A. M., & Mangel, R. (2000). The impact of work–life programs on firm productivity. *Strategic Management Journal, 21*(12), 1225–1237.

Korabik, K., Lero, D. S., & Ayman, R. (2003). A multi-level approach to cross cultural work-family research. *International Journal of Cross Cultural Management, 3*(3), 289–303.

Kossek, E. E., Colquitt, J. A., & Noe, R. A. (2001). Caregiving decisions, well-being, and performance: The effects of place and provider as a function of dependent type and work-family climate. *Academy of Management Journal, 44*(1), 29–44.

Kossek, E. E., & Nichol, V. (1992). The effects of on-site child care on employee attitudes and performance. *Personnel Psychology, 45*, 485–509.

Kossek, E. E., & Ozeki, C. (1998). Work-family conflict, policies, and the job-life satisfaction relationship: A review and directions for organizational behavior-human resources research. *Journal of Applied Psychology, 83*, 139–149.

Lachance-Grzela, M., & Bouchard, G. (2010). Why do women do the lion's share of housework? A decade of research. *Sex Roles, 63*(11–12), 767–780.

Lambert, S. J. (2000). Added benefits: The link between work–life benefits and organizational citizenship behavior. *Academy of Management Journal, 43*, 801–815.

Lee, J. A., Walker, M., & Shoup, R. (2001). Balancing elder care responsibilities and work: The impact on emotional health. *Journal of Business & Psychology, 16*(2), 277–289.

Lenaghan, J. A., Buda, R., & Eisner, A. B. (2007). An examination of the role of emotional intelligence in work and family conflict. *Journal of Managerial Issues, 19*(1), 76–94.

Livingston, B. A., & Judge, T. A. (2008). Emotional responses to work-family conflict: An examination of gender role orientation among working men and women. *Journal of Applied Psychology, 93*(1), 207–216.

Lobel, S. A. (1999). Impacts of diversity and work–life initiatives in organizations. In G. N. Powell (Ed.), *Handbook of gender & work* (pp. 453–476). Thousand Oaks, CA: Sage.

Lundberg, S., & Rose, E. (2000). Parenthood and the earnings of married men and women. *Labour Economics, 7*, 689–710.

Lyness, K. S., Thompson, C. A., Francesco, A. M., & Judiesch, M. K. (1999). Work and pregnancy: Individual and organizational factors influencing organizational commitment, timing of maternity leave, and return to work. *Sex Roles, 41*, 485–508.

MacDonald, M., Phipps, S., & Lethbridge, L. (2005). Taking its toll: The influence of paid and unpaid work on women's well-being. *Feminist Economics, 11*(1), 63–94.

Madsen, S. R., & Hammond, S. C. (2005). The complexification of work-family conflict theory: A critical analysis. *Tamara: Journal of Critical Postmodern Organization Science, 4*(1/2), 151–179.

Marshall, K. (2008). Fathers' use of paid parental leave. *Perspectives on Labour & Income, 20*, 5–14.

Maume, D. J., Jr., & Houston, P. (2001). Job segregation and gender differences in work-family spillover among white-collar workers. *Journal of Family & Economic Issues, 22*, 171–189.

McDonald, P., Brown, K., & Bradley, L. (2005). Explanations for the provision-utilisation gap in work–life policy. *Women in Management Review, 20*(1), 37–55.

McNall, L. A., Nicklin, J. M., & Masuda, A. D. (2010). A meta-analytic review of the consequences associated with work-family enrichment. *Journal of Business & Psychology, 25*, 381–396.

Mennino, S. F., Rubin, B. A., & Brayfield, A. (2005). Home-to-job and job-to-home spillover: The impact of company policies and workplace culture. *Sociological Quarterly, 46*, 107–135.

Mescher, S., Benschop, Y., & Doorewaard, H. (2010). Representations of work–life balance support. *Human Relations, 63*(1), 21–39.

Mesmer-Magnus, J. R., & Viswesvaran, C. (2005). Convergence between measures of work-to-family and family-to-work conflict: A meta-analytic examination. *Journal of Vocational Behavior, 67*, 215–232.

Michel, J. S., Mitchelson, J. K., Pichler, S., & Cullen, K. L. (2010). Clarifying relationships among work and family social support, stressors, and work-family conflict. *Journal of Vocational Behavior, 76,* 91–104.

Milkie, M. A., Raley, S., & Bianchi, S. M. (2009). Taking on the second shift: Time allocations and time pressures of U.S. parents of preschoolers. *Social Forces, 88,* 487–517.

Minnotte, K. L., Minnotte, M. C., Pedersen, D. E., Mannon, S. E., & Kiger, G. (2010). His and her perspectives: Gender ideology, work-to-family conflict, and marital satisfaction. *Sex Roles, 63,* 425–438.

Moen, P., Kelly, E. L., & Hill, R. (2011). Does enhancing work-time control and flexibility reduce turnover? A naturally occurring experiment. *Social Problems, 58*(1), 69–98.

Moen, P., & Yu, Y. (2000). Effective work/life strategies: Working couples, work conditions, gender, and life quality. *Social Problems, 47,* 291–326.

Murphy, W. M., & Kram, K. E. (2010). Understanding non-work relationships in developmental networks. *Career Development International, 15*(7), 637–663.

Muse, L., Harris, S. G., Giles, W. F., & Feild, H. S. (2008). Work–life benefits and positive organizational behavior: Is there a connection? *Journal of Organizational Behavior, 29,* 171–192.

Near, J. P., Rice, R. W., & Hunt, R. G. (1980). The relationship between work and nonwork domains: A review of empirical research. *Academy of Management Review, 5*(3), 415–429.

Nelson, D. L., & Burke, R. J. (2000). Women executives: Health, stress, and success. *Academy of Management Executive, 14*(2), 104–121.

Ngo, H.-Y., Foley, S., & Loi, R. (2009). Family-friendly work practices, organizational climate, and firm performance: A study of multinational corporations in Hong Kong. *Journal of Organizational Behavior, 30,* 665–680.

Nieminen, L. R. G., Nicklin, J. M., McClure, T. K., & Chakrabarti, M. (2011). Meta-analytic decisions and reliability: A serendipitous case of three independent telecommuting meta-analyses. *Journal of Business & Psychology, 26*(1), 101–121.

Nikandrou, I., Panayotopoulou, L., & Apospori, E. (2008). The impact of individual and organizational characteristics on work-family conflict and career outcomes. *Journal of Managerial Psychology, 23*(5), 576–598.

Parasuraman, S., & Simmers, C. A. (2001). Type of employment, work-family conflict, and well-being: A comparative study. *Journal of Organizational Behavior, 22,* 551–568.

Perry-Smith, J. E., & Blum, T. C. (2000). Work-family human resource bundles and perceived organizational performance. *Academy of Management Journal, 43,* 1107–1117.

Porter, S., & Ayman, R. (2010). Work flexibility as a mediator of the relationship between work-family conflict and intention to quit. *Journal of Management & Organization, 16,* 411–424.

Posig, M., & Kickul, J. (2004). Work-role expectations and work family conflict: Gender differences in emotional exhaustion. *Women in Management Review, 19*(7), 373–386.

Robinson, G., & Dechant, K. (1997). Building a business case for diversity. *Academy of Management Executive, 11*(3), 21–31.

Roehling, P. V., Roehling, M. V., & Moen, P. (2001). The relationship between work–life policies and practices and employee loyalty: A life course perspective. *Journal of Family & Economic Issues, 22,* 141–170.

Rothbard, N. P. (2001). Enriching or depleting? The dynamics of engagement in work and family roles. *Administrative Science Quarterly, 46,* 655–684.

Ruderman, M. N., Ohlott, P. J., Panzer, K., & King, S. N. (2002). Benefits of multiple roles for managerial women. *Academy of Management Journal, 45,* 369–386.

Sahibzada, K., Hammer, L. B., Neal, M. B., & Kuang, D. C. (2005). The moderating effects of work-family role combinations and work-family organizational culture on the relationship between family-friendly workplace supports and job satisfaction. *Journal of Family Issues, 20,* 820–839.

Sayer, L. C., England, P., Bittman, M., & Bianchi, S. M. (2009). How long is the second (plus first) shift? Gender differences in paid, unpaid and total work time in Australia and the United States. *Journal of Comparative Family Studies, 40,* 523–545.

Shoptaugh, C. F., Phelps, J. A., & Visio, M. E. (2004). Employee eldercare responsibilities: Should organizations care? *Journal of Business & Psychology, 19*(2), 179–196.

Spector, P. E., Cooper, C. L., Poelmans, S., Allen, T. D., O'Driscoll, M. P., Sanchez, J. I., et al. (2004). A cross-national comparative study of work-family stressors, working hours, and well-being: China and Latin America versus the Anglo world. *Personnel Psychology, 57*(1), 119–142.

Stickney, L. T., & Konrad, A. M. (2007). Gender-role attitudes and earnings: A multinational study of married women and men. *Sex Roles, 57*(11–12), 801–811.

Taylor, B., DelCampo, R., & Blancero, D. (2009). Work-family conflict/facilitation and the role of workplace supports for U.S. Hispanic professionals. *Journal of Organizational Behavior, 30,* 642–664.

Thompson, C. A., Beauvais, L. L., & Lyness, K. S. (1999). When work-family benefits are not enough: The influence of work-family culture on benefit utilization, organizational attachment, and work-family conflict. *Journal of Vocational Behavior, 54,* 392–415.

Treas, J., & Widmer, E. D. (2000). Married women's employment over the life course: Attitudes in cross-national perspective. *Social Forces, 78*(4), 1409–1436.

Twenge, J. M., & Campbell, S. M. (2008). Generational differences in psychological traits and their impact on the workplace. *Journal of Managerial Psychology, 23,* 862–877.

U.S. Census Bureau (2011). *Statistical abstract of the United States: Table 598.* Retrieved 11 April 2011 from http://www.census.gov/compendia/statab/2011/tables/11s0599.pdf.

Valcour, P. M. (2007). Work-based resources as moderators of the relationship between work hours and satisfaction with work-family balance. *Journal of Applied Psychology, 92,* 1512–1523.

van Steenbergen, E., & Ellemers, N. (2009). Is managing the work-family interface worthwhile? Benefits for employee health and performance. *Journal of Organizational Behavior, 30,* 617–642.

Volpe, E. H., & Murphy, W. M. (2011). Married professional women's career exit: Integrating identity and social networks. *Gender in Management: An International Journal, 26*(1), 57–83.

Voydanoff, P. (2004). The effects of work demands and resources on work-to-family conflict and facilitation. *Journal of Marriage & Family, 66,* 398–412.

Voydanoff, P. (2005). Social integration, work-family conflict and facilitation, and job and marital quality. *Journal of Marriage & Family, 67,* 666–679.

Warner, M. A., & Hausdort, P. A. (2009). Understanding work-to-family conflict: The role of organization and supervisor support for work–life issues. *Organization Management Journal, 6,* 130–145.

Warren, T., Fox, E., & Pascall, G. (2009). Innovative social policies: Implications for work–life balance among low-waged women in England. *Gender, Work & Organization, 16*(1), 126–150.

Waumsley, J. A., Houston, D. M., & Marks, G. (2010). What about us? Measuring the work–life balance of people who do not have children. *Review of European Studies, 2*(2), 3–17.

Wayne, J. H., & Cordeiro, B. L. (2003). Who is a good organizational citizen? Social perception of male and female employees who use family leave. *Sex Roles, 49,* 233–246.

Wayne, J. H., Grzywacz, J. G., Carlson, D. S., & Kacmar, M. K. (2007). Work-family facilitation: A theoretical explanation and model of primary antecedents and consequences. *Human Resource Management Review, 17,* 63–76.

Westman, M. (2001). Stress and strain crossover. *Human Relations, 54*(6), 717–751.

Wiersma, U. J. (1990). Gender differences in job attribute preferences: Work-home role conflict and job level as mediating variables. *Journal of Occupational and Organizational Psychology, 63,* 231–243.

Wiese, B. S., & Salmela-Aro, K. (2008). Goal conflict and facilitation as predictors of work-family satisfaction and engagement. *Journal of Vocational Behavior, 73,* 490–497.

Wiese, B. S., Seiger, C. P., Schmid, C. M., & Freund, A. M. (2010). Beyond conflict: Functional facets of the work-family interplay. *Journal of Vocational Behavior, 77,* 104–117.

Wu, M., Chang, C.-C., & Zhuang, W.-L. (2010). Relationships of work-family conflict with business and marriage outcomes in Taiwanese copreneurial women. *International Journal of Human Resource Management, 21*(5), 742–753.

PART 7

Systems Perspectives on Diversity

CHAPTER
21

Socioeconomic Trends: Broadening the Diversity Ecosystem

Michàlle E. Mor Barak *and* Dnika J. Travis

> **Abstract**
>
> Socioeconomic trends, such as worker and employer migration, increased life expectancy, and educational gaps, continue to magnify the numbers and kinds of people who work together in organizations. This chapter identifies 10 major socioeconomic trends affecting today's global workforce and reviews statistical data and research related to the effects of these trends on individual, group, and organizational outcomes. The authors examine the challenges and opportunities embedded in broadening the diversity ecosystem and offer future directions for research. Based on these socioeconomic trends, the authors conclude with a vision of inclusion for global diversity management.
>
> **Key Words:** global socioeconomic trends, workforce diversity, inclusion, social identity, systems justification

"Internal peace is an essential first step to achieving peace in the world. How do you cultivate it? It's very simple. In the first place by realizing clearly that all mankind is one, that human beings in every country are members of one and the same family."
—*The Dalai Lama*

Workforce diversity is not a transient phenomenon. Homogeneous societies are becoming, or have already become, heterogeneous, and this trend is irreversible. Changes in the global division of labor are blurring traditional geographic and corporate boundaries. At the same time, human rights advocates in countries around the world call for the inclusion of previously excluded and marginalized people in mainstream economic activities. These rapid changes in the composition of the workforce and the work environment continue to magnify the numbers and kinds of people who work together in organizations and to challenge our notion of the diversity ecosystem (Mor Barak, 2011).

An ecosystem in the context of a biological environment refers to "all the organisms living in a particular area, as well as the nonliving, physical components of the environment with which the organisms interact" (Reese et al., 2011, p. 4)). Applied to the workforce, the construct of diversity ecosystem refers to the amalgamation of people from different backgrounds (e.g., race, ethnicity, gender, ability, sexual orientation, educational and economic backgrounds, religious affiliations, and age), their individual attitudes and perceptions about diversity, their physical context (such as the work environment), and the social context (such as relevant laws and social policies) with which they interact.

Global changes in the composition of the workforce are so rapid that they defy categories and definitions previously developed to describe the phenomena of diversity in different countries. For example, Europe is becoming more heterogeneous and its new migrant populations cannot be described using population categorizations used in earlier decades. In a review of the term "Black" in both the United Kingdom and the United States, Agyemang, Bhopal, and Bruijnzeels (2005) stated that "in some circumstances, usually in politics or power struggles, the term Black signifies all non-white minority populations" (p. 1016). Similarly, the U.S. Census categories of race and ethnicity—in use since 1790—have long been inadequate to describe the rapidly changing population in the United States, let alone anywhere else in the world. These classifications, which were used in most of the early studies of diversity in the United States, have not varied much over the decades[1] (Office of Management and Budget, 1997). Even traditionally homogeneous societies such as Korea and Japan are seeing greater diversity, primarily in their major cities, and the categories used to describe their diversity are inadequate or underdeveloped (Cho & Mor Barak, 2008). The mixing of people from different cultures in the workplace is an increasingly salient concern for individuals, work organizations, and society as a whole. Across the globe, in addition to the more traditional diversity categories related to race, ethnicity, gender, and age, it is clear that other categories such as different abilities, social class, differential access to education, and sexual orientation should be included in describing the changing diversity landscape.

The dramatic socioeconomic trends of recent decades, such as worker and employer migration, increases in life expectancy and the widening of educational and economic gaps between diverse groups, have shifted the number and kinds of people who work together in organizations. In this chapter we examine the social and economic forces that have created a more diverse workforce worldwide. We first set the stage for these trends by discussing the broad range of definitions for diversity. Next, we examine 10 key socioeconomic trends, such as worker migration, employer migration, and education, that are affecting the global workforce, providing statistical and research evidence for each of the trends. We then examine the challenges and opportunities embedded in broadening the diversity ecosystem and offer future directions for research. Finally, based on these socioeconomic trends, we offer implications for diversity management with a focus on inclusion.

Setting the stage: Defining global workforce diversity

Conceptualizing workforce diversity within a global context helps set the stage for understanding the dynamics for broadening the diversity ecosystem. The initial definitions of workforce diversity were narrow and focused solely on people's membership in racial and ethnic groups (Kurowski, 2002; Mor Barak, 2011). The limited transferability of these conceptualizations required an expansion of the definitions to include more diversity categories. For example, Morning (2008) found that the United States' separation of ethnicity and race categories is unique and generally not found elsewhere in the world, stimulating the question of how ethnicity and race differ from each other and highlighting the fact that other countries often use race and ethnicity interchangeably (Morning, 2008). In addition, the conceptualization of diversity in many Asian countries that are perceived to be homogeneous societies (e.g., Korea, Japan) deserves special attention. As stated by Cho and Mor Barak (2008), "the scarcity in diversity research regarding ethnically homogenous countries such as Korea stems from a common misconception regarding diversity characteristics. Often, racial and ethnic homogeneity is misunderstood as a lack of diversity and, as a result, diversity characteristics such as gender, religion, and regional differences are overlooked" (p. 102).

In recent decades, scholars have made strides in providing alternative conceptualizations of diversity. To illustrate, Linda Larkey (1996) argued that diversity comprises "differences in worldviews or subjective culture, resulting in potential behavioral differences among cultural groups; and differences in identity among group members in relation to other groups" (p. 465). Definitions such as Larkey's highlight the importance of shared symbols, values, and norms that serve as a foundation for one's worldviews (Baugh, 1983; Collier & Thomas, 1988; Triandis, 2003) and in turn focus our attention on a sense of identity or belonging as the basis for understanding diversity (Ashforth & Mael, 1989; Giles & Coupland, 1991; Giles & Johnson, 1986; Konrad, 2003; Triandis, 2003; Mor Barak, 2011).

Other scholars have provided broader all-inclusive definitions of diversity. For example, Roosevelt Thomas' (1991) seminal work offered this definition of diversity: "Diversity includes everyone; it is not something that is defined by race or gender. It extends to age, personal and corporate background, education, function and personality. It includes life-style, sexual preference, geographic origin, tenure with the organization . . . and management or nonmanagement" (p. 10). These types of broader definitions, although meaningful in many contexts, have their limitations: they have the potential to dilute the gravity of prejudice, harassment, discrimination, and physical and emotional violence that are often associated with membership in a nondominant group (Linnehan & Konrad, 1999).

To overcome the limited applicability and transferability of previous definitions to the global context, in this chapter we employ the following definition:

> "Workforce diversity refers to the division of the workforce into distinction categories that (a) have a perceived commonality within a given cultural or national context, and that (b) impact potentially harmful or beneficial employment outcomes such as job opportunities, treatment in the workplace, and promotion prospects—irrespective of job-related skills and qualifications." (*Mor Barak*, 2011, p. 148)

This definition is useful because it (a) builds on people's shared experiences within any given cultural or national context, (b) provides openings for inclusion of culturally relevant categories (e.g., HIV status), and (c) highlights the magnitude the experiences of discrimination, prejudice, violence, harassment, and exclusion that marginalized and nondominant groups face within a specific cultural or national context (Mor Barak, 2011). As such, this definition serves as a foundation for understanding the socioeconomic trends and theoretical perspectives that inform the global diversity ecosystem.

Current socioeconomic trends

To focus our analysis of socioeconomic trends, we have identified 10 major trends that have affected, and continue to affect, the diversity composition of the global workforce. Contextually, societies have experienced a series of extraordinary economic crises in the early part of the twenty-first century that have reverberated throughout the global economy and have had a profound impact on the composition of the global workforce (ILO, 2011). Coupled with waves of regional political unrest and continued societal globalization, these events have reflected the historical context that undergirds the 10 key global socioeconomic trends featured in this chapter.

Trend 1: Advances in health care are generating an unprecedented growth in the world population, yet this trend is uneven and affects diversity differently across regions.

From 1.7 billion at the beginning of the twentieth century to an estimated 9 billion in 2050, the world's population is experiencing unprecedented growth (United Nations, 2009a) (Fig. 21.1). As such, "the world's population now grows by 1 billion about every 12 years" (Population Reference

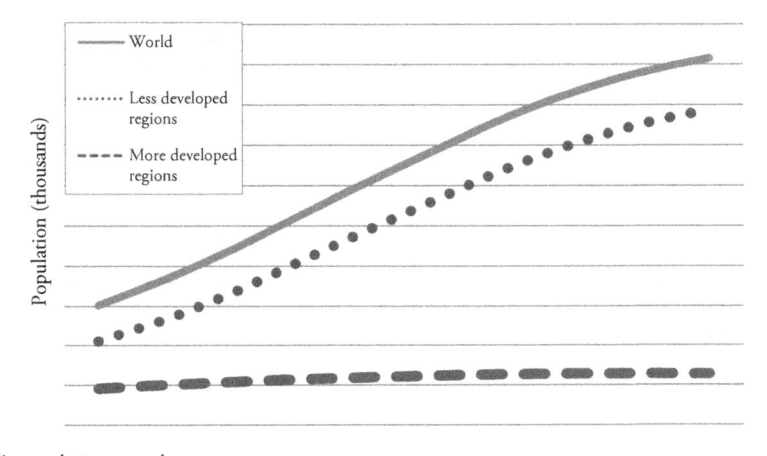

Figure 21.1. World's population growth.
Source: United Nations, Department of Economic and Social Affairs, Population Division (2009). *World population prospects: The 2008 revision*. Retrieved March 17, 2011, from www.un.org/esa/population/unpop.htm

Bureau, 2011, p. 3). Much of this growth can be attributed to advances in and access to improved health care in industrialized countries. These advances became more common in the 1960, when the world's population reached 3 billion. Gradually, these advances spread globally through the development and implementation of foreign aid programs, resulting in a rapid growth to 6 billion at the end of the century (Mor Barak, 2011). The projections are for continued growth, but perhaps at a somewhat slower pace (Bremner, Frost, Haub, Mather, Ringheim, & Zuehlke, 2010).

The rate of population growth or decline differs by age group and region (Table 21.1). Worldwide, estimates suggest a slight decline in the population between ages 0 and 14 from 28.4 percent in 2005 to 19.6 percent in 2050, as well as no change in the working-age population (15 to 64) in the same time period. Yet a steady increase is anticipated for those 65 and older, growing from 7.3 percent of the world's population in 2005 to 16.2 percent in 2050 (United Nations, 2009a).

In Africa, there is an expected increase the percentage of the population between ages 0 and 14, while other regions are expected to have decreases for that age group. For the working-age population, Africa is also slated for a considerable increase. Asia, Latin America, the Caribbean, and Oceania can expect to hold steady, whereas Europe and Northern America may experience a considerable decline in the percentage of the working-age population. Finally, all regions are expected to experience population growth of those 65 years and older. Thus, longer life expectancies are creating demographic shifts in the world's population, which is in turn increasing workforce diversity around the world.

Globally, advances in health care have a significant impact on survival, particularly in developing countries (for example, in Africa). Public health interventions, advancements in nutrition, and the use of vaccines and antibiotics have reduced the mortality of infants and children across the world (Bloom, 1993). Further, greater access to health care has complemented medical advances to increase life expectancy and survival rates. As an example, the polio vaccine had its 50th anniversary in 2005. This milestone marks other innovations that have dramatically affected the health and survival of people around the world, including the virtual eradication of smallpox and the elimination of polio, measles, and rubella in the United States (CDC, 2006). Also, vaccines for two sexually transmitted diseases (human papillomavirus [HPV] and hepatitis B) and continued research on HIV and genital herpes demonstrate the potential that continued medical advances have to affect health, survival, and longevity (College of Physicians of Philadelphia, 2011). Public health interventions (such as clean water technologies) have also had a major impact on health and well-being, thus improving survival rates in many developing countries (Cutler & Miller, 2005; Fielding, 1999).

Despite the historic growth, the continued spread of AIDS[2] as well as unexpected pandemics could slow population growth trends in all regions,

Table 21.1 The World's Population, by Age Group and Region

	0–14 (%)		15–64 (%)		65+ (%)	
	2005	2050	2005	2050	2005	2050
World	28.4	19.6	64.4	64.1	7.3	16.2
Africa	41.2	27.3	55.5	65.6	3.4	7.1
Asia	28.2	17.9	65.6	64.8	6.2	17.3
Europe	15.9	15	68.2	57.6	15.9	27.4
Latin America and the Caribbean	29.8	17	64	63.5	6.3	19.5
Northern America	20.5	16.9	67	61.1	12.5	22
Oceania	25	19.1	64.8	62.3	10.2	18.7

Source: United Nations, Department of Economic and Social Affairs, Population Division (2009a). *World population prospects: The 2008 revision*. Retrieved March 17, 2011, from www.un.org/esa/population/unpop.htm

particularly in Africa. In fact, "since the bubonic plague of the 14th century, no epidemic has had as strong an influence on population growth as HIV/AIDS" (Population Reference Bureau, 2011). An estimated 33.3 million people throughout the world are living with HIV/AIDS (Joint United Nations Programme on HIV/AIDS—UNAIDS, 2010). A staggering 71 percent of HIV/AIDS cases worldwide have been found in Africa, followed by Asia, with 14 percent of cases (Population Reference Bureau, 2011).

Yet there are some hopeful signs. Recent data from the UNAIDS *Report on the Global AIDS Epidemic* (2010) reveals that the number of new HIV cases has declined by 19 percent since 1999. In addition, "of the estimated 15 million people living with HIV in low- and middle-income countries who need treatment today, 5.2 million have access—translating into fewer AIDS-related deaths" (p. 7). Other significant milestones include the near-eradication of transmission of HIV from mother to infant, decreases in AIDS-related deaths, and fewer cases of HIV among young people.

The rise of obesity is also monumental, considering its potential adverse impact on the health and growth of the world's population. According to some estimates, almost 60 percent of the world's population will be overweight or obese by 2030 (Kelly, Yang, Chen, Reynolds, & He, 2008). Obesity as a public health problem is not limited to developed countries but extends to developing countries as well (Kelly et al.,, 2008). What is the impact of obesity on the world's population? Olshansky and colleagues (2005, p. 1143) declared that "unless effective population-level interventions to reduce obesity are developed, the steady rise in life expectancy observed in the modern era may soon come to an end and the youth of today may, on average, live less healthy and possibly even shorter lives than their parents." This is because obesity shortens life expectancy due to risks associated with diabetes, heart disease, and cancer (Kelly, et al., 2008; Olshansky et al., 2005).

Thus, a compelling case can be made that the world's population growth will slow down or even decline, depending on the extent to which public health concerns such as obesity and AIDS can be addressed systematically. Also relevant to workforce diversity, people with AIDS and those who are obese or overweight are often the target of workplace discrimination.

Conyers, Boomer, and McMahon (2005) suggest that the stigma associated with HIV/AIDS undergirds employment discrimination. They note that the discrimination experienced by people with HIV/AIDS at work is based on the stigma associated with the illness and its characteristics. In a cross-cultural comparison of 100 small business employers, Rao, Angell, Corrigan, and Lam (2008) found across the board that the study participants were apprehensive about hiring applicants with HIV/AIDS. They expressed fear of contamination, either by being infected or by being somehow negatively influenced by the mere connection with someone with HIV/AIDS. However, this varied by site, with those in Chicago reporting lower stigma-related attitudes than those in Hong Kong and Beijing. Notwithstanding the site differences, Rao and colleagues (2008) suggest that organizations should consider having culturally relevant strategies to help address HIV/AIDS-related stigma and employment discrimination.

Empirical evidence documenting the relationship between weight and employment discrimination is limited due to the lack of federal protections against obesity-related discrimination (Agerström & Rooth, 2011). Nonetheless, studies have documented discrimination based on weight. Building on a prior study of hiring managers in Sweden (Rooth, 2009), researchers found that automatic stereotypes related to obese individuals was directly related to hiring decisions such as receiving a callback for a job (Agerström & Rooth, 2011). In a review of empirical studies, Puhl and Heuer (2009) found that overweight and obese individuals are subject to stereotypes and discrimination at work, including wage penalty and bias in hiring decisions. Thus, more research is needed on the types of discriminatory practices targeting overweight and obese individuals. In particular, research is lacking related to the interrelationship between other diversity characteristics (e.g., gender, race, ethnicity) and weight bias in employment discrimination, as well as interventions to help deal with employment discrimination (Puhl & Heuer, 2009). This type of research can help inform public discourse on workforce diversity and inclusion.

Trend 2: The rising demand for migrant workers spurred by shifts in population growth, coupled with disparities in regional economic activities, contributes to the growing diversity of the workforce.

The uneven regional population growth noted earlier has fueled unprecedented waves of immigration across the globe. The aging population in the developed countries, coupled with low birth rates, serves as the main impetus for attracting immigrants from less-developed countries. As such, there has been a great influx of migrants into developed countries in recent decades (Table 21.2). A different picture emerges when looking at developing countries, where high birth rates and limited economic activities create pressure for emigration in search of jobs and livelihood (Mor Barak, 2011). Emigration pressures are expected to intensify due to the projected surge in the working-age populations in developing countries from 2.4 billion in 2005 to an estimated 3.6 billion in 2040, coupled with economies that are stagnant or growing at a slower rate (International Organization for Migration, 2010a). The sheer number of international migrants reflects this emerging trend. Approximately 214 million people migrated internationally in 2010, an increase from 195 million in 2005 (International Organization for Migration, 2010a; United Nations, 2009a). By 2050, this could swell to 405 million (International Organization for Migration, 2010a). This growing demand for migrant workers is spurred by shifts in population growth as well as worldwide environmental changes.

Migration (internal or international) is anticipated to continue due to environmental factors or natural catastrophes such as droughts, earthquakes, and climate change that affect the livelihood of local populations (International Organization for Migration, 2010a; Renaud, Bogardi, Dun, & Warner, 2008). This form of migration has been termed "environmental migration," although it has no standard definitions (International Organization for Migration, 2010a). Statistics show that over 20 million people were forced to relocate due to environmental factors (International Organization for Migration, 2010a).

With these type of trends, the "growing numbers of migrants from increasingly diverse backgrounds can increase diverse and cultural innovation, but can also make effective integration more difficult to achieve" (International Organization for Migration, 2010b, p. 5). Dialogue and research about the usefulness of mechanisms for effective implementation of interventions to deal with shifting trends can enhance the potential for greater workforce inclusion and the promotion of migrant rights.

Trend 3: Migration of employers generates new jobs in regions of low economic activity while at the same time infusing foreign culture into local communities.

A new approach to resolving national imbalances between labor supply and labor demand has emerged in the past few decades. Rather than attracting working-age immigrants, employers transfer existing facilities or open new ones overseas, where the working-age population needs jobs, giving rise to the *de facto* employer migration trend (Mor Barak, 2011). Essentially, in a liberalized trade environment, larger transnational corporations (mostly based in developed countries) export capital to reduce their labor costs and, indirectly, create new markets for their products. Even more midsized companies are outsourcing services (Kvedaraviciene & Boguslauskas, 2010). The transfer of capital and jobs is accompanied by an infusion of foreign culture into local economies (Fig. 21.2).

Most of the outsourced jobs have been going to India, where locally trained engineers and technicians write software, manage technical support, and provide customer service and other activities for U.S. corporations. By the year 2015, it is estimated that about 3.3 million service jobs in the United States will be outsourced overseas (Cook, 2004). Media reports about laid-off workers who had to train their replacements in India continue to produce negative public opinions, but the practice of outsourcing persists due to the compelling economic advantage it generates for multinational

Table 21.2 Inflows of Foreign Workers into Selected Countries (thousands)

Country	1999	2008
Australia	65.0	176.0
Austria	18.3	35.2
Belgium	8.7	25.0
Canada	107.1	192.5
France	12.1	32.6
Hungary	29.6	42.5
Japan	108.0	72.1
New Zealand	37.7	149.2
Norway	14.0	52.5
Switzerland	31.5	76.7
Sweden	2.4	11.0
United Kingdom	42.0	77.7
United States	360.4	677.5

Source: OECD. (2010a). Inflows of foreign workers. In *International migration outlook 2010*.

Globalization and liberalized world market

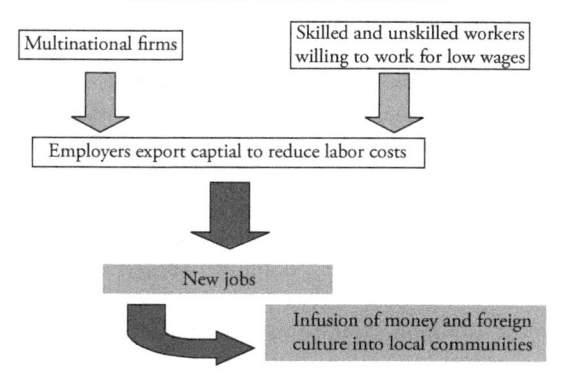

Figure 21.2. Migration of employers and global/local diversity.

and even midsized corporations (Kvedaraviciene & Boguslauskas, 2010). This is particularly relevant during difficult economic times, when cost savings are essential for a company's survival.

The economic benefits of outsourcing to developing countries are also quite obvious. In India, the IT business process outsourcing has grown "15 times to aggregate revenues of USD 69.4 billion in FY2009. In addition, as one of the largest employers in the organized private sector, it provides direct livelihood to 2.2 million people" (NASSCOM, 2010, p. 7). Although the pay may be low relative to the going rate in developed countries, in the context of the local economy these are considered very desirable jobs because the pay is good compared to other local jobs. In India, for example, these jobs are highly desired by young educated people, and often thousands of jobseekers show up for interviews when a new center opens.

In addition to providing jobs for unemployed or underemployed workers, such investment can support the development of the host economy by increasing access to technology and workforce training or increasing the host country's export potential. Concerns arise when the investment exploits and abuses the country, particularly its natural and human resources.

Another important yet often overlooked concern is related to the cultural challenges experienced by local communities related to imported jobs, particularly in call centers and support services communication industry (Kvedaraviciene & Boguslauskas, 2010). Western employers may demand that local employees replace their own cultural characteristics with the employer's cultural communication patterns and behaviors, such as adopting Western names and American accents to make communication more palatable for customers, mostly in the United States. Jones (2009) notes that "culture is an ambiguous, invisible force that people cannot see or fully explain, yet these invisible culture factors exert a powerful influence on work-related values and attitudes and on how people attempt to communicate meaning" (p. 191). For example, Jones describes differences in communication practices between individualistic and collectivist cultures such as the United States compared to China. U.S.-based organizations may use formalized communication such as memos or position papers to communicate policies or organizational practices, whereas in China communication may be more informal and dependent on interpersonal interaction, open communication, and consensus building. Forcing the employer's communication patterns on employees whose culture is tied to very different communication patterns could be a source of stress and misunderstandings that could affect the workers' well-being.

Imported jobs can have a profound impact on local traditional culture and authority patterns. Young adults who are earning more money than their elders and who are working long hours and night shifts in a context of the Westernized music and culture that proliferate in the call centers are more likely to rebel against their traditional community and upset traditional cultural structures. This cultural infiltration can destabilize the traditional family as well as the life in the local community.

Trend 4: Women's increased labor force participation around the world has had a simultaneous economic, cultural, and social impact on the workplace and on family life.

Women's increased participation in the labor force is arguably one of the most significant changes in diversity of the global workforce (Fig. 21.3). Globally, 1.2 billion women were employed or worked in some fashion (ILO, 2010b). This reflects an increase over the past 10 years, but regional differences exist (Table 21.3). Despite this, the share of women in the labor force has remained steady at around 40 percent globally since 2000 (ILO, 2010b).

Despite the current upswing in women's participation in the labor force, globally women have higher unemployment rates than men. The ILO stated that the 2009 unemployment rates were 7.0 percent for women and 6.3 percent for men (2010b). In Germany,

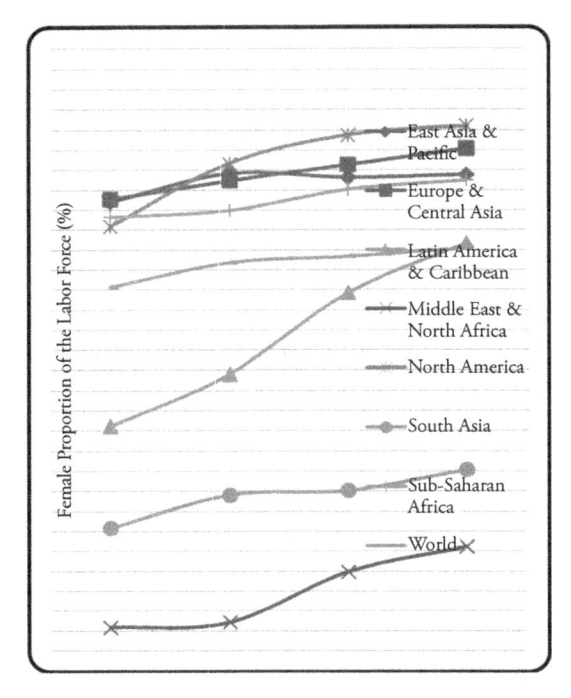

Figure 21.3. Female proportion of the labor force.
Source: World Bank (2011)

for example, there is an employment rate of 46 percent for women, yet women constitute 51 percent of the population (Statistisches Bundesamt, 2010). Nonetheless, this gap is narrowing (see Table 21.3)

(ILO, 2010a), which can be attributed to a combination of increased participation rates for women and decreased participation rates for men.

It is also noteworthy that 49 percent of women are international migrants (UN General Assembly, 2006). These women increasingly migrate independently. Nonetheless, female international migrants can face severe challenges. For example, for some women who emigrate to become domestic workers, life can be quite grim: "domestic workers typically work 15–18 hours a day, seven days a week. The most common complaints include unpaid wages for months or years, forced confinement in the workplace, and excessive workload. There are many complaints of verbal, physical, and sexual abuse and situations that amount to forced labor and trafficking" (Human Rights Watch, 2009, p. 3).

Women who work in jobs other than domestic employment also face barriers that hinder advancement, such as sexism, discrimination, harassment, and stereotyping. For example, "in the Korean context, women often face the cultural assumption that as newly hired employees they will soon marry, leave their jobs, and become full-time caregivers at home" (Cho & Mor Barak, 2008).

Why is there increased participation of women in the labor force? First, greater control over fertility increases a woman's opportunity to obtain an education and a job. Next, in countries with growing

Table 21.3 Women's and Men's Economic Activity Rates

	1999		2009 *(preliminary estimates)*	
	Women	**Men**	**Women**	**Men**
North Africa	26.6	76.4	27.4	76.4
Sub-Saharan Africa	60.4	81.4	62.6	81.2
Latin America and the Caribbean	46.6	80.7	51.7	79.7
East Asia	69.9	83.5	66.5	79.4
Southeast Asia and the Pacific	58.0	83.1	57.4	82.0
South Asia	34.3	82.9	34.9	81.6
Middle East	22.6	75.8	25.4	75.3
Developed economies and the European Union	51.8	70.4	52.9	68.6
Central and South-Eastern Europe (non-EU) and CIS	49.8	69.1	50.6	69.0
World	51.8	79.2	51.6	77.7

Source: ILO. (2010, January). *Global employment trends* (p. 50).

older populations, women may work more years than men because women have longer life expectancies than men, increasing the prospect of being employed for an extended duration. Finally, global economic development has created prospects for employment of women in developing countries (Mor Barak, 2011).

Around the world, women's increased labor force participation has had simultaneous economic, cultural, and social effects on the workplace and on family life. Indeed, the Centre for Development and Population Activities (2010) reports that: "There is a growing consensus among political and thought leaders that women play a critical role in any country's economic stability. Institutions including the World Bank have documented that promoting women's equal opportunity in the labor force and public life catalyzes a nation's growth. Investing in women also greatly enhances the well-being of children, who are more likely to survive and thrive if their mothers are healthy and educated, leading to a more stable future" (p. 1).

In a review of programs, the International Food Policy Research Institute (2005) discussed five key ways that women's participation can help secure access to food and nutrition. IFPI reports that agricultural technology efforts can make a greater impact on poverty than targeting men and can ensure access to human rights, all which can decrease poverty, improve the health of children, and lower the spread of HIV/AIDS. As such, women's ability to utilize agricultural technology and participate in the workforce can have a sustainable economic and social impact.

Trend 5: The growing presence of historically nondominant racial and ethnic groups in the workplace has increased the demand for equality and inclusion.

The number of racial and ethnic groups in the workplace is rapidly growing. For example, in Canada, visible minorities (Chinese, South Asians, and Blacks) are anticipated to increase from 13 percent of the population to 20 percent by 2016 (Banerjee, 2008). Similarly, the proportion of visible minorities (e.g., from China, South Africa, and India) in the Australian population has increased dramatically in the past several years (Australian Bureau of Statistics, 2008). The Australian Bureau of Statistics also noted that the number of ethnic group classification in the Australian census has risen (275 in 2006 vs. 191 in 2001), demonstrating the growing number of racial and ethnic groups.

These types of shifts can be attributed to major civil and human rights milestones in the latter part of the twentieth century that signaled widespread policy changes toward marginalized and nondominant racial and ethnic groups across the world. However, exclusion and discrimination of racial and ethnic minorities are still pervasive.

A major challenge relates to a lack of equal opportunities from the outset—creating a "sticky floor" rather than a "glass ceiling" effect (Bjerk, 2008). Arcand and d'Hombres' (2004) study of the relationship between ethnic discrimination and employment outcomes in a sample of 69,956 Brazilians serves as an example. The researchers found that Whites had twice the hourly wage and more years of education than Blacks and Browns. Although Blacks' and Browns' wages and education levels were significantly different from those of Whites, Blacks appeared to be more negatively affected by racial discrimination. The researchers attributed some of these disparities to the type of industry and the regions in which specific ethnic groups live.

The complicated process of enumerating race and ethnicity in national and global contexts is another challenge (Fearson, 2003; Morning, 2008). This challenge can limit the potential to develop comprehensive and cross-cultural perspectives on race and ethnic discrimination, prejudice, and bias in the workplace. For example, Fearson (2003) identified 882 ethnic groups in 160 countries in a study that sought to examine cross-national ethnicities. As another example, Arcand and d'Hombres (2004) noted 135 different terminologies used for ethnic and racial group classifications in Brazil.

An additional challenge relates to the multitude of diversity characteristics that any one person may hold (e.g., being a woman with a disability of Black and Latino heritage). Considering that more diverse groups are entering the workforce with multiple identities, experiences, and backgrounds, identifying inequality and discrimination will become increasingly more difficult. For instance, racial and ethnic diversity and immigration status may be inextricably linked in certain countries. Banerjee (2008) investigated perceived discrimination in this context. The researchers found that visible minorities (based on ethnicity) who were immigrants had a greater propensity to perceive that they experienced workplace discrimination compared to those who were native Canadian born.

When national, cultural, or personal values subscribe to colorblindness, challenges can emerge. In this, "the ideal of colorblindness is a major impediment to inclusion" (Davis & Travis, 2010) because potential constructive dialogues and recognitions of inequities or differences may be dampened (Apfelbaum, Sommers, and Norton, 2008). Arcand and d'Hombres (2004) discussed this challenge in their study of the employment-related based on ethnic discrimination in Brazil. The researchers started their article by stating that people in Brazil "virulently reject any possibility of racial difference because of the widespread belief that Brazilian social relationships are both harmonious and based on principles of equality" (Arcand & d'Hombres, 2004). However, Ciconello (2008) provided another perspective: "Racism in Brazil, albeit perceptible, is always blamed on other people and never on the daily practices of its agents, making it even more difficult to eliminate" (p. 1). These discussions of the extent of racism in Brazil are further complicated by the mobility of one's racial and ethnic group status whereby one's social position can be contextualized (Arcand & d'Hombres, 2004).

Finally, further challenges to understanding race and ethnic diversity trends can occur within a perceived homogeneous society. For example, language as a marker of ethnic identity in Africa shows great diversity, with over 400 languages represented in Nigeria, approximately 350 in Democratic Republic of Congo, and 100 in Sudan (UNECA, 2010). Also, in Korea, regional differences and prejudices show up as major diversity issues in work organizations (Cho & Mor Barak, 2008). For example, political conflicts as well as social and economic inequities exist between Kyoungsang and Cholla regions (of the nine regions in Korea). A majority of the companies are owned by those in the Kyongsang region, leaving the "indigenous people of Cholla to feel more excluded" (Cho & Mor Barak, 2008).

In all, identifying the racial and ethnic diversity trends in global context, though challenging, is critical to better understanding and fostering opportunities for diversity management. Perhaps as more empirical research and governmental initiatives surface, the current milestones in promoting racial and ethnic inclusion in the workplace will be exemplified. amplify.

Trend 6: Human rights efforts and national policies are sparking the potential for greater workforce inclusion based on sexual orientation and gender identity.

We know how controversial the issues surrounding sexual orientation can be. In the search for solutions, we recognize that there can be very different perspectives. And yet, on one point we all agree—the sanctity of human rights. As men and women of conscience, we reject discrimination in general, and in particular discrimination based on sexual orientation and gender identity. When individuals are attacked, abused or imprisoned because of their sexual orientation, we must speak out. We cannot stand by. We cannot be silent.
—United Nations Secretary-General *Ban Ki-moon*
(December 10, 2010, Human Rights Day)

Ban Ki-moon's remarks reflect global trends toward the eradication of laws, policies, and practices that hinder people's basic rights based on sexual orientation and gender identity. Globally, countries are making notable strides aligned with these international efforts.

In many countries some form of antidiscrimination legislation has been instituted in recent years to protect sexual orientation minorities from discrimination in the workplace and in other contexts. Examples include Australia, Canada, Denmark, Israel, Sweden, and South Africa (Mor Barak, 2011). Legislation in New Zealand, for example, has shifted from considering homosexuality illegal to prohibiting discrimination based on sexual orientation (in Section 21 of the Human Rights Act, 1993). Other laws, such as the Property Amendment Act of 2001, provide same-sex couples with property rights identical to those afforded to heterosexual married couples (Human Rights Commission, 2010).

In many countries the laws on sexual orientation and gender identity are a mix of some old laws that do not provide any protection in some areas and others that offer protection against discrimination in others. A case in point is the legislation in the United States. The Matthew Shepard and James Byrd Jr. Hate Crimes Prevention Act (HPCA) (Public Law No. 111–84) that was signed into law in 2009 by President Barack Obama identifies violent acts toward individuals because of their sexual orientation or gender identity as federal crimes. According to the U.S. ambassador to the UN, Susan Rice, this law is also significant because "for the first time, the words 'sexual orientation' and 'gender identity' became part of U.S. law to provide explicit protection to LGBT individuals" (U.S. Mission to the United Nations, 2010). Similarly, in 2010 a historic precedent was set when the "Don't ask, don't tell" policy (Public Law No. 103–160) was repealed by the U.S. Senate. For 17 years, this policy had prohibited gays and lesbians from serving openly in the U.S. military. On the other hand, the United States does not have a federal law that prohibits workplace discrimination against people because of their sexual orientation or gender identity (Fidas, 2010, 2011)—it is still "legal in 29 states to discriminate against job applicants and employees because of their sexual orientation, and in 38 states because of their gender identity" (Human Rights Campaign, 2010, p. 22). Nonetheless, precedents are being set in the private sector as antidiscrimination policies and practices are becoming more common in the United States.

A recent report from the Human Rights Campaign revealed that sexual orientation and gender identity are part of antidiscrimination policies in, respectively, 89 percent and 43 percent of Fortune 500 companies (Fidas, 2010). In addition, partner benefits are offered in 57 percent of Fortune 500 companies, and some form of transgender health benefits are provided in 41 percent of these companies.

These types of milestones are critical for the advancement of human rights based on sexual orientation and gender identity. However, profound obstacles exist in the United States and throughout the world. Many people experience physical and emotional violence, discrimination, and deep-rooted fear because of their sexual orientation or gender identity (United Nations Office of the High Commissioner for Human Rights). Most strikingly, the criminalization of homosexuality is still in effect in over 70 countries (United Nations Secretary-General, 2010). Even worse, 12 countries have laws dictating that individuals may be subject to the death penalty based on sexual orientation (Human Rights Education Association). In some areas, the lack of antidiscrimination laws may be explained by local traditions and religions. In Greece, for example, some individuals use "tradition and religious teachings to justify their active opposition to the enactment of current and forthcoming policies designed to protect gay people" (Drydakis, 2011, p. 89).

Actual and perceived discrimination based on one's sexual orientation is rampant around the world. In Thailand, for example, "visitors may mistake the 'land of smiles' as being a paradise for sexual minorities" (Noknoi & Wutthirong, 2010, p. 260), but discrimination, violence, and prejudice are pervasive. Gay people are banned from serving in the armed forces because homosexuality is seen as a "mental disorder" (Noknoi & Wutthirong, 2010).

In South Africa, Archbishop Emeritus Desmond Tutu reflected on the realities of gays and Lesbians in Africa (2010):

> "I am proud that in South Africa, when we finally won the chance to build a new Constitution, we included sexual orientation in our laws, because we knew from our bitter experience that an injury to one is an injury to all. Once again, however, people are being denied fundamental rights and freedoms. Gay men have been jailed and humiliated, transgender people attacked, lesbians raped. Our lesbian and gay brothers and sisters across Africa and elsewhere are living in fear. And they are living in hiding—away from care, away from the protection the State should offer to every citizen and away from health care, when all of us, especially Africans, need access to essential HIV services. This wave of hate must stop."

The lack of reliable and global data on sexual orientation is a key obstacle to identifying global trends related to sexual orientation and gender identity in the workplace. Any information on sexual orientation is mainly country-specific and collected through census data (although that is most likely not as reliable). For example, in the U.S. Census, data capture sexual orientation based on one's status in a cohabiting relationship but does not account for relationships outside of the home (Leppel, 2009). Obtaining accurate information can be a launching point to advancing greater acceptance and inclusion with respect to sexual orientation.

Trend 7: Different educational attainment between regions affects the types of desired and needed jobs and increases the movement of people and jobs around the world in search of a match.

> "The opportunities created by global processes will be actualized only if we continue to insist that education is a basic human right and to resist the tendency to reduce education into yet another market commodity. If we fail, I fear that our world will become increasingly unequal, competitive, polarized, conflicted and dangerous."
> —Power (2000)

In 2000, 164 governments convened at the World Education Forum in Dakar, South Africa, and pledged to achieve "Education For All" (World Education Forum, 2000). As a central part of the forum, the participants made a commitment to achieve six worldwide educational goals by 2015:

- Enhancing and expanding early childhood education
- Obtaining access to primary education for all children
- Meeting the learning needs of adults and young people through life skills programs
- Increasing adult literacy by 50 percent
- Achieving gender equality
- Ensuring opportunities for quality of education that facilitate learning needs in all areas, including life skills, literacy, and numeracy.

The need for international organizations and national institutions to work to advance the World Education Forum's goals is well depicted in the 2011 UNESCO report *The Hidden Crises: Armed Conflict and Education*. In this report, UNESCO chronicled significant and "hidden" barriers to education attainment. For example, 28 million people were prevented from attending school due to violent conflict, and one third (195 million) of the children under the age of 5 suffered from malnutrition, affecting their cognitive functioning and development (UNESCO, 2011).

While these statistics reflect severe challenges, trends in rising educational attainment around the world are also present. First, in most countries there is an 80 percent likelihood that a child will advance from primary to secondary education, although this is not true in about two thirds of African countries.[3] As such, enrollment into secondary education is so pervasive in developed countries that it is almost universally accepted (Mor Barak, 2011). Developing countries—even those that have traditionally excluded girls from education (e.g., sub-Saharan Africa, Southern Asia)—have also increasing enrollment rates for both women (albeit more gradually increasing) and men (Table 21.4).

Literacy rates are improving across all age levels (Table 21.5). Literacy rates in more developed countries were approximately above 80 percent in 2005–2008. In less developed countries, education rates are also on the rise—for example, increasing from 53 percent between 1985 and 1995 to 62 percent between 2005 and 2008 in sub-Saharan Africa. The statistics are also quite encouraging because youths have generally higher literacy rates than their adult counterparts.

In 2007, over 150 million students were enrolled in tertiary (higher) education, an increase from 28.6 million in 1970. This growth over the past four decades has been characterized by scholars as "explosive" (UNESCO Institute for Statistics, 2009). In a report prepared for the UNESCO 2009 World Conference on Higher Education, Altbach, Reisber, and Rumbley (2009) found that enrollment rates in higher education increased from 19 to 26 percent between 2000 and 2007, although to a far lesser extent in developing countries: "In low-income countries tertiary-level participation has improved only marginally, from 5% in 2000 to 7% in 2007. Sub-Saharan Africa has the lowest participation rate in the world (5%). In Latin America, enrolment is still less than half that of high-income countries" (p. iv). Over 2.5 million students are studying abroad, with an estimated increase to 7 million by 2020 (Altbach, Reisber, & Rumbley, 2009).

In the context of the global workforce, these trends (combined with population growth and greater inclusion of historically excluded or marginalized and nondominant groups) create an opportunity for building human capital and promoting workforce inclusion within a broadening diversity ecosystem.

Trend 8: Religious diversity presents unique challenges and opportunities to foster inclusion in a global labor force.

Figure 21.4 shows the proportion of the world's population who belong to various religions and indicates the extent to which religious diversity is reflected in the global labor force. This distribution varies by region. Countries such as Peru, Puerto Rico, and Portugal have over 85 percent Roman Catholics, while Afghanistan, Kuwait, and Mali are predominately Muslim. On the other hand, Lebanon is 60 percent Muslim and 39 percent Christian; Nigeria is 50 percent Muslim and 40 percent Christian (CIA World Fact Book, 2010).

Considering that the migration or workers and employers is a growing trend (see Trends 2 and 3), the potential for workplace inclusion within a context of religious diversity is quite compelling. However, social and governmental factors that hinder or even stifle the practice of religion pose a weighty challenge for global workforce inclusion. The Pew Forum on Religion & Public Life (2009) conducted a groundbreaking quantitative worldwide study on the extent to which government and social mechanisms hinder the practice of religious beliefs. This study found that 64 countries representing over 70 percent of the world's population "have high or very high restrictions on religions" (p. 1). The Pew Forum defined religious restrictions as those imposed by a combination of government policies, practices, and laws with other social acts

Table 21.4 Global Education Statistics (Select Countries)

Country	Reference year	Population (>= 25 yrs old)	No schooling (%) M	No schooling (%) F	Primary (ISCED 1) (%) M	Primary (ISCED 1) (%) F	Upper secondary (ISCED 3) (%) M	Upper secondary (ISCED 3) (%) F	Tertiary (ISCED 5-6) (%) M	Tertiary (ISCED 5-6) (%) F
Arab States										
Jordan	2008	2,699	5.5	15.8	12.0	10.3	14.0	14.3	19.1	12.7
Saudi Arabia	2004	10,678	15.6	32.5	17.4	12.3	15.9	12.8	15.0	14.8
United Arab Emirates	2005	2,620	11.3	10.9	13.1	7.5	23.2	28.7	15.7	25.1
Central and Eastern Europe										
Poland	2008	26,580	0.2	0.3	16.5	22.5	65.0	52.2	15.9	18.8
Turkey	2008	40,499	4.5	18.0	42.8	42.7	18.8	12.2	11.2	7.1
Ukraine	2001	32,860	x(8)	x(9)	6.4	10.4	42.2	31.1	35.8	39.7
Central Asia										
Azerbaijan	2008	4,775	0.8	1.8	2.7	6.0	48.0	51.1	17.5	10.8
Georgia	2002	2,946	0.2	0.5	6.1	8.0	37.1	33.8	26.7	25.1
Kazakhstan	2007	8,739	0.0	0.0	0.5	0.7	43.7	35.6	23.1	27.9
East Asia and the Pacific										
Australia	2008	14,142	–	–	7.3	8.0	37.2	24.4	32.7	38.9
Indonesia	2007	121,090	6.3	15.4	31.4	31.3	22.5	15.4	5.5	3.5
Philippines	2004	36,815	2.3	2.4	17.5	18.8	24.3	23.4	25.5	29.0
Republic of Korea	2005	31,635	2.7	9.5	9.4	15.5	38.7	36.8	38.6	25.2
Latin America and the Caribbean										
Brazil	2007	104,460	13.7	13.5	26.4	25.5	23.9	24.9	8.4	10.1

(continued)

Table 21.4 (Continued)

Country	Reference year	Population (>= 25 yrs old)	No schooling (%) M	No schooling (%) F	Primary (ISCED 1) (%) M	Primary (ISCED 1) (%) F	Upper secondary (ISCED 3) (%) M	Upper secondary (ISCED 3) (%) F	Tertiary (ISCED 5–6) (%) M	Tertiary (ISCED 5–6) (%) F
Mexico	2008	57,382	8.2	11.7	18.9	20.7	15.3	16.3	17.1	12.2
Panama	2000	1,466	8.3	9.8	30.4	27.0	21.4	23.5	9.4	11.4
North America and Western Europe										
Germany	2008	61,521	.	.	2.9	3.6	53.0	49.6	28.5	17.8
Israel	2007	3,907	1.9	4.2	10.2	10.2	36.6	33.0	39.3	43.4
Italy	2008	45,231	4.3	9.2	18.4	23.8	33.3	29.8	11.4	12.0
United States of America	2008	203,677	0.4	0.4	4.4	4.0	47.9	48.8	38.1	38.4
South and West Asia										
Bangladesh	2001	60,142	45.4	56.6	21.6	19.5	15.9	9.9	4.9	3.5
Bhutan	2005	280	13.1	12.5	12.8	15.1	5.7	5.1	9.2	8.1
Pakistan	2008	73,546	38.8	70.9	14.9	9.2	22.8	9.9	8.4	3.4
Sub-Saharan Africa										
Mali	2006	4,185	81.1	81.6	9.6	7.1	3.4	3.8	1.2	2.6
Senegal	2006	4,043	68.3	80.9	4.4	2.4	2.3	1.1	1.4	0.3
South Africa	2007	23,903	8.3	13.2	6.9	6.9	23.2	20.2	5.0	3.7

Source: UNESCO

Table 21.5 EFA (Education For All) Regional Literacy Rates

	Regional Adult Literacy Rate (%)			Regional Youth Literacy Rate (%)		
	1985–1994	1995–2004	2005–2008	1985–1994	1995–2004	2005–2008
Arab States	55.6	67.1	72.4	74.1	82.8	87.4
Central and Eastern Europe	95.9	97.3	97.6	98.3	98.7	98.8
Central Asia	97.9	99.0	99.4	99.8	99.8	99.7
East Asia and the Pacific	82.0	91.6	93.7	94.7	98.0	98.3
East Asia	81.8	91.5	93.7	94.7	98.1	98.4
The Pacific	93.2	93.5	93.0	91.8	92.1	91.2
Latin America and the Caribbean	84.4	89.7	91.0	91.8	96.2	96.9
Caribbean	62.6	68.3	70.7	74.3	80.8	80.1
Latin America	85.0	90.3	91.6	92.3	96.7	97.5
North America and Western Europe	98.7	98.9	99.0	99.7	99.7	99.7
South and West Asia	47.3	58.8	61.9	60.3	73.7	79.3
Sub-Saharan Africa	53.0	57.2	62.1	64.9	68.1	71.2

Source: UNESCO

of physical and emotional violence by individuals, groups, or organizations. As such, the Pew Forum study found that "among all regions, the Middle East-North Africa has the highest government and social restrictions on religion, while the Americas are the least restrictive on both measures. Among the world's 25 most populous countries, Iran, Egypt, Indonesia, Pakistan and India stand out as having the most restrictions when both measures are taken into account, while Brazil, Japan, the United States, Italy, South Africa and the United Kingdom have the least" (p. 2).

Even with these findings, the Pew Forum noted that government-imposed restrictions (e.g., laws, policies, or practices as part of governmental entities) do not necessarily coincide with the presence of hostile acts (i.e., hate crimes, public tensions, religiously motivated terrorism) toward religious groups. For example, China and Vietnam were classified as having many government restrictions, yet fewer hostile acts based on religion are committed there by people of different social groups (Grim, 2010). On the other hand, Bangladesh and Nigeria have more temperate governmental restrictions but appear to be high in hostile acts by social groups (Pew, 2009).

Hicks (2002) argues that religious differences as expressed by individuals' attire, speech, practices, and time off on holidays can contribute to conflicts in the contemporary, diverse workplace. Religious convictions are often deeply held and in many cases compel followers to adhere to certain rituals and behaviors that affect how people appear and act in the workplace. Religion is considered a form of invisible diversity due to the focus on one's belief system, but in many cases religious affiliation can be identified "on sight" by a person's attire, artifacts, or attendance (or actions) on days of religious observance (King, Bell, & Lawrence, 2009, p. 52). In addition, discussing or expressing spirituality and religiosity can be quite risky in today's global workforce due to the role that religious affiliation plays in social identity (Lips-Wiersma & Mills, 2002).

Despite these critical issues pertaining to religious diversity within the workplace, limited research exists detailing how religious diversity is experienced, perceived, and realized in work organizations (King, Bell, & Lawrence, 2009; Lips-Wiersma & Mills, 2002). Thus, research is needed on how religion is expressed and disclosed in the workplace, what aspects of diversity training can address religion as a key diversity factor, and how to prevent workplace-based religious discrimination (King, Bell, & Lawrence, 2009).

Trend 9: The rights, acceptance, and inclusion of the differently abled are creating emerging prospects for an expanded labor force.

The World Health Organization (WHO) (2011a) maintains that more than 1 billion individuals (15 percent of the world's population) have various forms of disabling conditions, including up to 190 million with notable challenges in functioning. Further, chronic medical conditions and the aging population are elevating the prevalence of disabilities around the world (WHO, 2011a). The International Classification of Functioning, Disability and Health (ICF) (2011) takes into account both individual conditions and environmental considerations in defining disability. Thus, ICF considers access, policies, negative attitudes, service delivery, and funding issues as critical factors that limit workplace participation of people with disabilities (WHO and World Bank, 2011).

With respect to mental health conditions, approximately 20 percent of children and adolescents globally have some form of mental disorder or problem. Focusing on children is critical because about 50 percent of mental disorders occur before the age of 14 years. Regional differences are also important to consider due to the limited access to mental health providers and resources in areas that have the "highest percentage of population under the age of 19" (WHO, 2011b).

According to WHO (2008), the most prevalent causes of disability are hearing loss, vision problems, and mental disorders (depression, substance use disorders, and psychoses). There are differences between high-income and low- and middle-income countries, as well as age differences (Table 21.6). WHO finds it particularly notable that disability conditions in low- and middle-income countries are largely due to preventable conditions.

People with disabilities experience barriers to employment that limit their active participation in the labor force. With increased access and removal of workplace barriers, participation of people with disabilities in the global labor force has the potential for a much-needed labor force expansion (RAND, 2004). However, challenges for workforce inclusion exist, as detailed in a 2010 study by the Organisation for Economic Co-operation and Development (OECD, 2010b):

• *Lack of opportunities for participation and integration in the labor force.* In the later part of the 2000s, those with disabilities or health problems had a 40 percent employment rate, in comparison to a 75 percent rate for those without a disability (the Nordic countries, Mexico, and Switzerland had the highest employment rates of those with disabilities). One in four of those with a disability work part time, as opposed to one in seven of those without a disability. Moreover, people with a disability are twice as likely to be unemployed than those without a disability.

• *Lower propensity to secure financial resources.* People with a disability have "15 percent lower disposable income than the national average" (p. 53). When looking at poverty thresholds in OECD countries, 22 percent of those with a

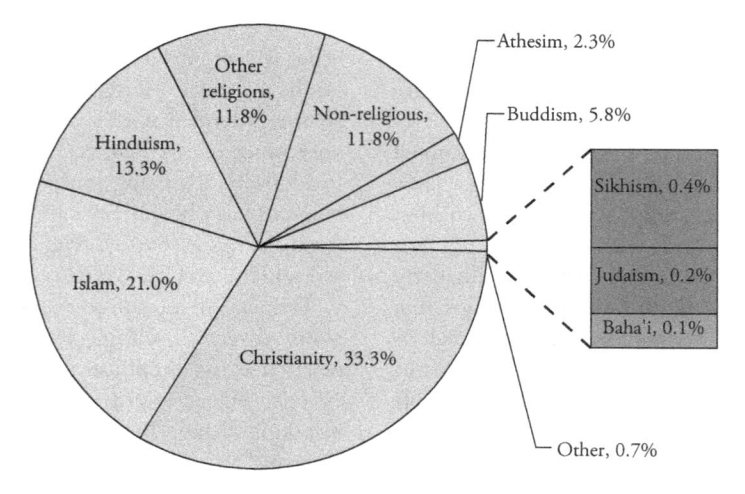

Figure 21.4. Religions worldwide.
Source: *CIA World Fact Book* (2010)

Table 21.6 2004 Disability Estimates, in millions (leading conditions)

	Low- and Middle-Income Countries		High-income countries		
	0–59 yrs	>60 yrs	0–59 yrs	>60 yrs	Total
Hearing loss	54.3	43.9	7.4	18.5	124.2
Vision problems (i.e., refractive errors)	68.1	39.8	7.7	6.4	121.9
Depression	77.6	4.8	15.8	0.5	98.7
Cataracts	20.8	31.4	0.5	1.1	53.8
Unintentional injuries	35.4	5.7	2.8	1.1	45.0
Osteoarthritis	14.1	19.4	1.9	8.1	43.4
Substance dependence and use—Alcohol	31.0	1.8	7.3	0.4	40.5
Infertility due to unsafe abortion and maternal sepsis	32.5	0.0	0.8	0.0	33.4
Macular degeneration	9.0	15.1	1.8	6.0	31.9
Chronic obstructive pulmonary disease	10.9	8.0	3.2	4.5	26.6
Ischemic heart disease	8.1	11.9	1.0	2.2	23.2
Bipolar disorder	17.6	0.8	3.3	0.4	22.2
Asthma	15.1	0.9	2.9	0.5	19.4
Schizophrenia	13.1	1.0	2.2	0.4	16.7
Glaucoma	5.7	7.9	0.4	1.5	15.5
Alzheimer and other dementias	1.3	7.0	0.4	6.2	14.9
Panic disorder	11.4	0.3	1.9	0.1	13.8
Cerebrovascular disease	4.0	4.9	1.4	2.2	12.6
Rheumatoid arthritis	5.9	3.0	1.3	1.7	11.9
Substance dependence and use—Drug	8.0	0.1	3.7	0.1	11.8

Source: Adapted from WHO's 2004 Global Health Update, 2008, p. 35.

household member with a disability are below the key threshold compared to 15 percent for national averages. There is also a lower propensity to have benefits that are part of having gainful employment.

• *Elevated costs associated with sickness and disabilities.* There are also economic costs across systems levels that affect the promotion of inclusion and job equality for the differently abled. This includes a greater financial impact on benefit systems (e.g., sickness absences, disability benefits). In OECD countries, 1.2 to 2 percent (when sickness is taken into consideration) of the GDP is spent on disability benefits (OECD, 2010b). An ILO report found that "economic losses related to disability are large and measurable, ranging from between 3 and 7 per cent of GDP" in low- and middle-income countries in Asia and Africa (Buckup, 2009, p. 51).

Despite these barriers, advances in modern medicine may simultaneously contribute to increased employability of those with disabilities due to improved survival rates and access to better health care. In developed countries, benefits to people with disabilities throughout the lifespan are more common.

However, these benefits may actually be a deterrent to securing paid employment due to the perceived or actual loss of benefits associated with obtaining employment (O'Reilly, 2004). Having said that, these benefits are probably not enough to replace the income from a paid job (Mor Barak, 2011).

Thus, advocates for people with disabilities have a strong interest in removing barriers to potential employment. In addition to doing the right thing from a civil rights perspective, there are economic benefits to expanding the employment rights of the differently abled. People with disabilities can enhance the labor supply in countries with little or no population growth. And longer life expectancies are likely to make governments less willing to provide lifetime support, however parsimonious, to people who incurred their disabilities as adults. These and other factors suggest that people with all types of abilities are likely to be a factor in increasing workforce diversity.

Trend 10: *Technological innovations accelerate the mix of workforce diversity in the virtual workplace, simultaneously bolstering inclusion and amplifying problems of miscommunication.*

Within the context of the socioeconomic trends highlighted in this chapter, the way people interact and perform in their workplaces is also being transformed by ever-changing technological advances (Dixon, 2000). For example, an examination of social media usage rates reveals a global picture of how technological innovations are broadening the diversity ecosystem and accelerating the mix of workforce diversity. The International Telecommunication Union (ITU) (2009), the United Nations' information and communication technology agency, tracks mobile phone and Internet usage based on data from countries all over the world:

- Throughout the world. 90 percent of the population (and 80 percent in rural areas) have some form of access to mobile networks. In developed countries, we have reached near-saturation points, with almost all people having cell phones. Developing countries (although the percentages vary) have increasing access to mobile phone networks: for example, 41 percent of people in Africa have cell phones.
- There are 2 billion Internet users worldwide (1.2 billion in developing counties). In some countries, having access to the Internet is considered a legal right, including Estonia, Finland, and Spain.
- Two hundred thousand text messages are sent each second. This represents an estimated increase from 1.8 trillion text messages sent in 2007 to 6.1 trillion in 2010.

Social media outlets such as Facebook and Twitter also illuminate how technological advances are shifting the way people work and interact in the diversity ecosystem. Social media forums broaden opportunities for users to build social networks, share information, and connect with current or potential consumers/clients in the modern workplace. For example, in 2010 Facebook estimated having over 750 million active users, who devoted over 700 billion minutes a month to the site. Translations into over 70 different languages are available on the site, more than 70 percent of users are located outside of the United States, and over 190 countries have business organizations that have Facebook platforms (Facebook, 2011). Further, upon Twitter's sixth anniversary in 2012, there were 140 million active Twitter users and 340 million tweets (brief messages) were sent per day, which was increased from 50 million daily tweets in 2010. (Twitter, 2012; 2011).

Social media has also changed the physical location of work, particularly the way teams and organizations conduct business. Technological advances provide new opportunities for greater interaction with people from different backgrounds (Qualman, 2011). However, this greater communication ease adds a level of complexity too. Communication via e-mail, for example, introduces additional opportunities for miscommunication. How do we figure out the exact meaning of the communication without any visual or audio clues (Is the other person joking? Is he angry?) And when the communication is cross-cultural, the opportunities for misunderstandings are multiplied. What might seem like an assertive request from the sender might come through to the receiver in another culture as an offensively aggressive one. Without the day-to-day interaction in a physical office, there are fewer opportunities to really get to know the other person and understand the cultural context of his or her work-related interactions.

In general, "technological advances are expected to continue to increase demand for a highly skilled workforce, support higher productivity growth, and change the organization of business and the nature of employment relationships" (RAND Corporation, 2010, p. 1). The implications for workforce diversity are all the more dramatic as individuals all over the world are gaining access to and adapting to using these new technologies. Despite these advances, many users lack skills or training and do not take full advantage of these technologies.. For example, in a study of women in Capetown, South Africa, Gitau, Marsden, and Donner (2010) found that among the challenges the participants faced in using technologies were dealing with security settings, establishing an e-mail account with a mobile phone with no computer access, and using passwords. As insignificant as these challenges may appear, "in much of the developing world, there are no alternatives; if you are unable to configure the handset yourself, you may never get on-line" (p. 2605). Therefore, such challenges limit the opportunities for individuals to engage in activities (such as e-mail) that are common in today's workforce.

Hence, cultivating diversity in contemporary work organizations using technological advances is wrought with potential challenges to full engagement. Kaplan and Haenlein (2010) suggest that work organizations need to ensure access for all employees by establishing structures to manage social media and to determine how and which employees are using these outlets. Combined with the nine previous trends, technological advancements such as mobile phones, the Internet, and social media is an vital component to broadening the diversity ecosystem and to including more individuals from diverse backgrounds, experiences, and ideas as well as the expansion of the contextual environment for it. As such, organizational leaders across the world are charged with maximizing the potential of technology and other organizational resources to promote greater workforce diversity and inclusion.

Broadening the diversity ecosystem: Challenges, opportunities, and future directions

Put together, the 10 socioeconomic trends presented in this chapter reflect global forces that make the workplace increasingly more diverse. The result of these trends is a growing worldwide mix of populations and an unprecedented increase in workforce diversity. These trends are not only a backdrop or context for organizations to consider; rather, they define the scope of what companies need to consider as their domain when they design diversity policies and programs. To avoid the pitfalls and reap the benefits of a diverse workforce, employers need to adopt a *broader vision of inclusion,* a vision that encompasses not only the organization itself but also its surrounding community and its national and international environment (Mor Barak, 2011).

Each of these trends presents specific challenges for diversity management that include increased intergroup miscommunication, cross-cultural misunderstanding, and intergroup conflicts. Yet these trends also present opportunities for expanding a vision of inclusion and using the multiple sources of talent embedded in the growing diversity of the workforce.

The juxtaposition of the first two trends is a case in point. From an economic perspective, it seems that there is a perfect match between the need of developed countries to attract immigrants because of their labor force shortages (due to low birthrates and increased longevity) and the economic needs of developing countries to export surplus workforce (due to high birthrates and high unemployment). These unprecedented waves of immigration have the potential to assist developed countries in maintaining levels of economic activity while at the same time reducing unemployment and economic hardship in developing countries. Yet the host country, the country of origin, work organizations, and the immigrants themselves are experiencing great challenges as a result of these population transfers. The host countries are often not ready to accept and fully include these immigrants with their "peculiar" cultures, resulting in resentment and animosity toward the newcomers. The sending countries are suffering from brain and talent drain that reduce their potential for economic development and growth. Work organizations are struggling to create policies that will foster an organizational culture of inclusion. The immigrants themselves are facing cross-cultural misunderstanding and sometimes even outright hostility.

It seems that employer migration, the third trend, might be the answer to these challenges. Instead of individuals and families uprooting and going through the difficulties of settling in new countries, employers export capital to developing countries, send management teams, and set up local branches that take advantage of the low labor costs and provide new jobs that alleviate the local pressures of unemployment. Yet these local branches typically are created in the image of the parent organization, superimposing a foreign culture onto local communities. Call centers in India, for example, require employees to work in an "Americanized" environment, go through a course to neutralize their accent, and adopt Western names to simulate a call center in the United States and make the customers feel more comfortable. These jobs often upset the traditional family and community age-based role and authority structures because these well-paying jobs go to younger adults who can more easily adapt to these demands.

Similarly, the fourth trend of women's increased labor force participation upsets traditional gender roles and challenges individuals, families, and communities to find new ways to fulfill work and family responsibilities. Although men share more of the household responsibilities than in previous generations, the burden of caring for children and of taking care of the home typically falls more on women than on men. More countries around the world have added legislation and social policies to combat discrimination in the workplace and to accommodate family leave. In addition to abiding by the laws, work organizations are experimenting with different ways to accommodate the changing family needs of employees by offering flexible work hours, paid family leave time, day care, and "off ramps" and "on ramps" allowing employees to take time off to care for family and then get back to work when they are ready to resume their full responsibilities. Yet despite these advancements and accommodations, women are still underrepresented in management and more lucrative jobs and are particularly underrepresented in executive and top management levels.

The presence of historically nondominant racial and ethnic groups in the workplace, the fifth trend, has remarkably increased, but, similar to women, these populations are still underrepresented in higher management levels and in lucrative positions. Racial and ethnic discrimination still exists in the workplace, but it is more subtle than before and, as a result, more difficult to combat. It is a barrier to promotion and fair compensation, and it limits individuals from expressing their talent as well as receiving fair compensation for their work. It also limits the organization's ability to fully benefit from the multifaceted talent pool.

Perhaps the widest global gap exists in recognizing the rights of sexual orientation and gender identity minorities (the sixth trend). While some countries provide full equal rights, including the right to legally marry, others tolerate open discrimination, and in some countries any behavioral expressions are criminalized and an openly gay or lesbian person could risk incarceration. Yet more people around the world are coming out to their families and communities and are demanding equal rights. As they continue to face misperceptions about their identity and discrimination and bigotry, sexual orientation minorities represent an important talent pool with often untapped potential.

Socioeconomic class remains a persistent barrier to economic progress of individuals, families, and communities around the world. Gaps in educational attainment (the seventh trend) sustain economic inequality and create barriers to social class mobility. Here the challenge for organizations is both intra-organizational (recruiting talent and providing training to close educational gaps) and extra-organizational (contributing to schools and other educational facilities at all levels in the community to help build a more educated workforce for the future).

One of the most emotionally charged areas of global diversity is that of religious diversity (the eighth trend). Strongly held religious beliefs are often tied to specific values, norms, and behaviors that may differ markedly from one religion to the next and may create animosity and strife between religious communities that could spill into the workplace. Religious traditions that prescribe gender roles and behaviors could pose a challenge to balancing religious accommodation with gender equality. Prayer schedules, dietary requirements, and other religiously tied behaviors that affect the workplace may require work organizations to institute policies that accommodate those religious needs in order to foster a culture of inclusion.

Recent advancements in legislation that require work organizations to adapt the workplace to the needs of people with disabilities have opened up more jobs for this population (the ninth trend). However, in many regions of the world such legislation does not exist and the employment opportunities for the differently abled are limited or nonexistent. In addition to discriminating against the differently abled, this lack of accommodation also prevents work organizations from accessing a growing talent pool of people with disabilities.

Technological advancements have shifted the workforce in ways that expand business functioning and bridge interpersonal work relationships across geographic distances (the 10th trend). Global businesses are applying these advances in managing information sharing and networking to reach diverse clients as well as to communicate with key stakeholders. Thus, unpacking the dynamics of communication (formal and informal; direct and indirect; written and oral) has the potential to promote workforce diversity and inclusion by bridging differences and enhancing interpersonal connections. However, sometimes these technological advances of the 21st century make global communication seem deceptively simple. Although electronic communication (e-mail, video conferencing, and social media) is accessible and can facilitate the *practice* of communicating across the globe, it does not make cross-cultural *understanding* any easier; in fact, these new communication methods often lack some of the essential ingredients of a face-to-face meeting that facilitate cross-cultural understanding. For example, e-mails lack the indicators of intention and mood that are present in a spoken conversation through tone of voice and facial expression. Video conferencing lacks the social context that exists in a face-to-face meeting as well as other essential human interaction activities such as sharing a meal ("breaking bread together") or going for a drink after working hours. These missing cues to social interaction can make cross-cultural communication even harder and may affect the way people feel about one another as well as their ability to trust and work with others harmoniously in a team. Work organizations cannot rely solely on electronic communications to facilitate important relationships. They need to foster cross-cultural understanding through investments in actual travel every once in a while (a periodic face-to-face meeting can lead to smoother ongoing e-mail and video conferencing communications) and to invest in workplace-based diversity and inclusion training.

Future directions

Current socioeconomic trends provide opportunities for people to interact in new ways, shift attitudes, as well as perhaps bridge differences, promote workplace inclusion, and advance human rights. They also trigger some questions that call for additional research and for testing new management practices to address the challenge of inclusion for the growing diversity in the global workforce. First, researchers need to focus on aggregate projections of global economic, demographic, and legislation trends that will affect the composition of the global workforce of the future. It is not enough to have demographic projections, however; these projections need to be grounded in an ecosystems perspective. They need to take into consideration shifting economic trends, given the volatility of the economic activities in different regions of the world, the shifting sentiments of populations within regions and countries with respect to legislation on immigration as well as discrimination against certain population groups, and shifting social policies regarding affirmative/positive action that, together, could affect workforce diversity both locally and globally. Second, it is important to understand the social-psychological context for the receptivity or rejection sentiments that affect a social and organizational culture of inclusion or exclusion. It is important to examine existing theories and see to what extent they are useful in explaining global diversity from an ecosystems perspective. Perhaps existing theories need to be updated or expanded, or perhaps new theoretical formulations need to be developed to provide more accurate explanations of these new realities. And, third, new organizational diversity initiatives need to be tested through field studies. These initiatives need to take into consideration not only the organizational intra-environment but also its contextual ecosystemic environment. In other words, it is not enough for organizations to examine the diversity of their own workforce; they also need to understand the contextual diversity of the communities within which they reside and direct their initiatives both internally and externally. For example, organizations could offer professional training programs to teenagers or young adults within the community to prepare them for future employment opportunities. Such initiatives could address both the educational gaps that overlap with socioeconomic status within the communities and the need to increase diversity within the organization. Field research of such initiatives could examine the costs and benefits of such initiatives and the potential outcomes of recruiting more diverse talent and creating a culture of inclusion within the organization.

Implications for global workforce diversity management: Toward a vision of inclusion

> "Perhaps travel cannot prevent bigotry, but by demonstrating that all peoples cry, laugh, eat, worry, and die, it can introduce the idea that if we try and understand each other, we may even become friends."
> —Maya Angelou

Maya Angelou's quote speaks to the potential of a broadened diversity ecosystem. The current socioeconomic trends offer challenges and opportunities for managing diversity, advancing human rights, and advancing a vision of inclusion in the workplace. Yet where do we start?

The 10 socioeconomic trends described in this chapter increase the representation of previously underrepresented groups in the workplace. These new realities could bring about negative feelings of resentment and animosity but could also expand social interactions between individuals who differ from one another and inspire positive collaborations. Increased interactions can put a new lens on individuals' social identities and challenge the status quo regarding the balance between groups with rights and privileges and those without. Individuals' ability to challenge their own assumptions about their identities and about "the way things are" and "the way things ought to be" can be enhanced by more frequent encounters and normalized work relationships with people whose appearance, background, and values may be drastically different from their own.

Quite compellingly, Maya Angelou's emphasis on the role of empathy and perspective taking in bridging differences can serve as a tangible and challenging starting point. Researchers share this sentiment (Latting & Ramsey, 2009). Engaging in empathy offers opportunities to hone in on the other's vantage point, thus increasing opportunities to consider other people's needs, experiences, and cultural backgrounds. This provides further opportunity to "disconfirm the negative stereotypes of members of out group distinctions…and thereby, reduce intergroup conflict" (Ensari & Miller, 2006, p. 593). Empathy and perspective taking are also fundamental to building inclusive workplaces across micro- and macro-systems.

Mor Barak's (Mor Barak, 2011; Mor Barak & Cherin, 1998)inclusive workplace model (see Fig. 21.1) takes the organization's diversity ecosystem into account in creating a framework for managing global diversity from the inside out and from the outside in. Inclusive workplaces value and maximize intra- and interpersonal differences in their workforce to achieve optimal organizational outcomes (Mor Barak, 2011; Mor Barak & Cherin, 1998). This includes greater opportunities for organizational advancement and promotion and involvement in decision making as well as other critical organizational processes (e.g., inclusion in formal and informal networks).

Building on Mor Barak's (2000, 2011) model, Davis and Travis (2010) recommended that organizations focus on taking stock on intra- and interorganizational processes and practices and on developing interpersonal skills for effective cross-cultural communication. According to Davis and Travis (2010), "taking stock" requires that work organizations do the following: (a) Revisit or create a vision of diversity and inclusion consistent with cultural contexts; (b) Assess formal and informal policies and practices to ensure that the diversity vision is realized in everyday situations; (c) Examine whether organizational processes and practices advocate and facilitate inclusion of community members and stakeholders; and (d) Assess whether diverse perspectives and experiences are leveraged in a way that builds effective organizational systems.

Conclusion

Workforces are becoming increasingly diverse, due largely to the interaction between economic forces and demographic trends and the advancements in antidiscrimination laws and equality initiatives resulting from the efforts of the international human rights movement. These trends should continue to promote diversity in the global workplace, although the social tensions they engender, along with potential broader economic or political failures, could set them back in the short term. Societies' tolerance and acceptance of diversity often lag behind economic necessity as well as human rights efforts and the implementation of national polices that foster inclusion. By and large, though, managing workforce diversity effectively will be necessary in a global workplace.

These trends for increased workforce diversity benefit national economies as well as national and international employers. For instance, countries welcoming foreign workers can enhance their economic success, particularly when these countries are experiencing tight labor markets. A case in point is Ireland. The Irish government helped create a comparative advantage for transnational firms' sales and support call centers. As a result, some companies concentrated their European operations under one Irish roof, bringing in native speakers from all over Europe to help their compatriots with their purchases—in their own language—when they dialed a toll-free number from home (Cowell, 2000). Where public policy deliberately creates diversity, managing it requires attention from both government and society, including help if economic conditions change and foreign workers need or want to return home.

Thanks to the Internet, information and entertainment are reaching virtually everywhere, promoting more encounters among diverse people. Young people are more likely to use these communication channels and thus take these encounters for granted, fostering a greater acceptance of diversity. As diversity becomes more widespread, workers of younger cohorts may become impatient with those from previous cohorts who might display reticence or even patterns of discrimination.

At the same time, traditionalists may find it difficult to change long-held attitudes and beliefs. This reluctance is more entrenched when it is rooted in religious beliefs that prescribe different roles for men and for women; this makes it difficult for some groups in society to accept gender equality in the workplace. Similarly, religion is cited by many to explain their reluctance in accepting workers who have diverse sexual orientations. And both governments and employers can be daunted by the financial costs of accommodating worker diversity, such as retooling the workplace to meet the needs of persons with different physical abilities.

Thus, part of the challenge of managing workforce diversity is managing the diversity of people's preconceived notions about those outside their own culture, especially those notions acquired when social norms and economic needs were different. In that sense, diversity management includes managing the demographics of past attitudes as well as future workforce trends.

To drive inherent, systemic change, organizations need to go beyond simply managing diversity within to creating a culture of inclusion both inside and out, with its ecosystemic environment. A culture of inclusion involves creating the conditions in which individuals can feel safe, valued, and fully engaged by bringing their unique characteristics into the workplace. To fully realize their potential, workers need to feel that they are recognized, honored, and appreciated in their full and most honest individual and social identity.

With a backdrop of the expanding diversity ecosystem, the inclusive workplace model offers a broad vision for managing diversity, one that includes individuals and groups that have a direct or indirect stake in the organization (Mor Barak, 2011). The model offers a comprehensive and multilevel approach that ensures fair and inclusive treatment of individuals who are different from the mainstream. It allows, encourages, and facilitates the inclusion of individual employees who are different from the mainstream in the organizational information networks and decision-making processes at each of the four levels—from the organization, through the community and state, to the international. Changing the organization's culture from merely "diversity tolerant" or "respectful of diversity" to *truly inclusive* can be done through deliberate actions at all four system levels included in the model.

Notes

1. For a complete listing of the U.S. Census Questionnaires since 1790, see: http://www.census.gov/history/www/through_the_decades/questionnaires/

2. For a more detailed review see the Global Report: UNAIDS report on the global AIDS epidemic 2010.

3. http://www.uis.unesco.org/TEMPLATE/pdf/ged/2004/GED2004_EN.pdf

References

Agerström, J., & Rooth, D.-O. (2011). The role of automatic obesity stereotypes in real hiring discrimination. *Journal of Applied Psychology, 96*(4), 790–805. doi:10.1037/a0021594

Agyemang, C., Bhopal, R., & Bruijnzeels, M. (2005). Negro, black, black African, African Caribbean, African American or what? Labelling African origin populations in the health arena in the 21st century. *Journal of Epidemiology and Community Health, 59*, 1014–1018.

Altbach, P. G., Reisber, L., & Rumbley, L. E. (2009). *Trends in global higher education: tracking an academic revolution (executive summary)*. A Report Prepared for theAmbassador Rice at U.N. event for Human Rights Day 2010. (2010, December 10, 2010). Press Release, America.gov. Retrieved from http://www.america.gov/st/texttrans-english/2010/December/20101210155326su0.7109905.html

Apfelbaum, E. P., Sommers, S. R., & Norton, M. I. (2008). Seeing race and seeming racist? Evaluating strategic colorblindness in social interaction. *Journal of Personality and Social Psychology, 95*, 918–932.

Arcand, J.-L., & d'Hombres, B. (2004), Racial discrimination in the Brazilian labour market: wage, employment and segregation effects. *Journal of International Development, 16*, 1053–1066. doi: 10.1002/jid.1116

Ashforth, B. E., & Mael, F. S. (1989). Social identity theory and the organization. *Academy of Management, 14*, 20–39.

Australian Bureau of Statistics. (2008). *The People of Australia: Statistics from the 2006 Census*. Retrieved online March 17, 2011 from http://www.immi.gov.au/media/publications/research/_pdf/poa-2008.pdf

Banerjee, R. (2008). An examination of factors affecting perception of workplace discrimination. *Journal of Labor Research, 29*, 380–401.

Baugh, J. (1983). *Black street speech: The history, structure, and survival*. Austin: University of Texas Press.

Bjerk, D. (2008). Glass ceilings or sticky floors? Statistical discrimination in a dynamic model of hiring and promotion. *Economic Journal, 118*, 961–982.

Bloom, D. E., & Brender, A. (1993). Labor and the emerging world economy. Population Bulletin, 48(2). Washington, DC: Population Reference Bureau.

Bremner, J., Frost, A., Haub, C., Mather, M., Ringheim, K., & Zuehlke, E. (2010). World Population Highlights: Key findings from PRB's 2010 world population data sheet *Population Bulletin* (Vol. 62).

Buckup, S. (2009). *The price of exclusion: The economic consequences of excluding people with disabilities from the world of work*. ILO Employment Sector Working Paper No. 43. GLADNET Collection. Paper 547. Retrieved from http://digitalcommons.ilr.cornell.edu/gladnetcollect/547. ILO, Geneva. ISBN 978–92–2-122921–6; 978–92–2-122922–3 (web); ISSN 1999–2939; 1999–2947 (web). PDF: http://www.ilo.org/disability.

Campbell, N. A., Reece, J. B., Taylor, M. R., Simon, E. J., & Dickey, J. L. (2006). *Biology: Concepts and connections* (6th ed.). San Francisco: BPearson/Benjamin Cummings.

CDC—National Center for Immunization and Respiratory Diseases (2006). *Vaccines timeline: 50 years of vaccine progress*.

Retrieved July 30, 2011 from http://www.cdc.gov/vaccines/pubs/vacc-timeline.htm.

Centre for Development and Population Activities (CEDPA). (2010). *From the ground up: profiles of women advancing economies.* Retrieved July 11, 2012 from http://www.cedpa.org/FromtheGroundUp/assets/pdf/global_women_report_final.pdf

Cho, S., & Mor Barak, M. E. (2008). Understanding of diversity and inclusion in a perceived homogeneous culture: A study of organizational commitment and job performance among Korean employees. *Administration in Social Work, 32*(4), 100–126.

CIA World Fact Book (2010). *Religions.* Retrieved July 31, 2011, from 9https://www.cia.gov/library/publications/the-world-factbook/fields/2122.html .

Ciconello, A. (2008). The challenge of eliminating racism in Brazil: the new institutional framework for fighting racial inequality. In: *From poverty to power: How active citizens and effective states can change the world.* Oxfam International. Retrieved March 2011July 11, 2012 from http://policy-practice.oxfam.org.uk/publications/the-challenge-of-eliminating-racism-in-brazil-the-new-institutional-framework-f-112382

College of Physicians of Philadelphia (2011). *Vaccines for sexually transmitted diseases.* Retrieved July 31, 2011, from http://www.historyofvaccines.org/content/articles/vaccines-sexually-transmitted-diseases.

Collier, M. J., & Thomas, M. (1988). Cultural identity: An interpretive perspective. In Y. Y. Kim & W. B. Gudykunst (Eds.), *Theories in intercultural communications* (pp. 99–122). Newbury Park, CA: Sage.

Conyers, L. M., Boomer, K. B., & McMahon, B., T. (2005). Workplace discrimination and HIV/AIDS: The national EEOC ADA research project. *Work: A Journal of Prevention, Assessment and Rehabilitation, 25,* 37–48.

Cook, J. (2004, February 12). Debate over outsourcing heats up, ignited by election year politics. *Seattle Post-Intelligencer.* Retrieved online September 29, 2004, from http://seattlepi.nwsource.com/business/160281_outsource12.html

Cowell, A. (2000, October 31). Dublin is a magnet for technology and young people. *New York Times,* p. C1.

Cutler, D. M., & Miller, G. (2005, February). The role of public health improvements in health advances: The 20th century United States. *Demography, 42*(1), 1–22.

Davis, K., & Travis, D. J. (2010).Culture and leadership. In G. Blau & P. Magrab (Eds.), *The Leadership Equation: Strategies for Individuals Who Are Champions for Children, Youth, and Families* (pp. 199–226). Baltimore, MD: Brookes Publishing.

Dixon, N. M. (2000). *Common knowledge: how companies thrive by sharing what they know.* Boston, MA: Harvard Business School Press.

Drydakis, N. (2011). Women's sexual orientation and labor market outcomes in Greece. *Feminist Economics, 17*(1), 89–117.

Ensari, N., & Miller, N. (2006). The application of the personalization model in diversity management. *Group Processes and Intergroup Relations, 9,* 589–607.

Facebook (2011). *Statistics.* Retrieved July 29, 2011, online from http://www.facebook.com/press/info.php?statistics.

Fearson, J. D. (2003). Ethnic and cultural diversity by country. *Journal of Economic Growth, 8*(2), 195–222.

Fidas, D. (2010). *Corporate Equality Index 2011: Rating American workplaces on lesbian, gay, bisexual and transgender equality* (9th ed). A Report of the Human Rights Campaign. Editor: Daryl Herrschaft. Retrieved March 2011 from http://www.hrc.org/documents/HRC-CEI-2011-Final.pdf

Fielding, J. E. (1999). Public health in the twentieth century: advances and challenges. *Annual Review of Public Health, 20,* xiii–xxx.

Giles, H., & Coupland, N. (1991). *Language: Contexts and consequences.* Bristol, PA: Open University Press.

Giles, W., & Johnson, P. (1986). Perceived threat, ethnic commitment and interethnic language behavior. In Y. Y. Kim (Ed.), *Interethnic communications: Current research* (pp. 91–116). Beverly Hills, CA: Sage.

Gitau, S., Marsden, G., & Donner, J. (2010) After access – challenges facing mobile-only internet users in the developing world. In: G. Fitzpatrick & S. Hudson (Eds.), *Proceedings of the 28th International Conference on Human Factors in Computing Systems* (CHI 2010) (pp. 2603–2606). New York: ACM.

Grim, B. J. (2010, November 4). Indonesia's place along the spectrum of global religious restriction [Electronic Version]. *The Pew Forum on Religion & Public Life.* Retrieved July 28, 2011, from http://pewforum.org/Government/Indonesias-Place-Along-the-Spectrum-of-Global-Religious-Restriction.aspx

Hicks, D. A. (2002). Spiritual and religious diversity in the workplace: Implications for leadership. *Leadership Quarterly, 13*(4), 379–396.

His Grace Archbishop Emeritus Desmond Tutu. (2010, September 17). *Video message for the United Nations panel: Ending violence and criminal sanctions based on sexual orientation and gender identity.* Retrieved January 2011 from http://geneva.usmission.gov/wp-content/uploads/2010/09/Tutu.pdf.

Human Rights Campaign (2010). *Corporate Equality Index 2011: Rating American workplaces on LGBT equality.* [Electronic Version]. Retrieved May 15, 2011, from http://www.hrc.org/documents/HRC-CEI-2011-Final.pdf

Human Rights Commission (2010). *Human rights in New Zealand.* Retrieved July 29, 2011, from http://www.hrc.co.nz/human-rights-environment/human-rights-in-new-zealand-2010/.

Human Rights Education Association. *Sexual orientation and human rights.* Retrieved July 11, 2012, from http://www.hrea.org/index.php?doc_id=432

Human Rights Watch. (2009). *Slow movement: Protection of migrants' rights in 2009.* Retrieved March 30, 2011, from http://www.hrw.org/node/87265

International Labour Office. (2010a). *Global employment trends.* Retrieved March 1, 2011, from www.ilo.org/public/libdoc/ilo/P/09332/09332(2010-January).pdf

International Labour Office (ILO). (2010b). *Women in labour markets: Measuring progress and identifying challenges.* Geneva: International Labour Organization. Retrieved July 10, 2012 from http://www.ilo.org/wcmsp5/groups/public/---ed_emp/---emp_elm/---trends/documents/publication/wcms_123835.pdf

International Labour Organization. (2011). *Global employment trends 2011: The challenge of a jobs recovery.* Retrieved online from http://www.ilo.org/wcmsp5/groups/public/---dgreports/---dcomm/---publ/documents/publication/wcms_150440.pdf.

International Organization for Migration. (2010a). *World migration report 2010: The future of migration building capacities for change.* Retrieved March 17, 2011, from http://publications.iom.int/bookstore/free/WMR_2010_ENGLISH.pdf

International Organization for Migration. (2010b). *World migration report 2010: The future of migration building capacities for change.* (Executive Summary). Retrieved Online March 17, 2011, from http://www.iom.int/jahia/webdav/shared/shared/mainsite/published_docs/wmr-2010/WMR-Executive-Summary.pdf

International Telecommunications Union. (2009) *The world in 2010: ICT facts and figures.* Retrieved July 28, 2011, from http://www.itu.int/ITU-D/ict/material/FactsFigures2010.pdf.

Jones, W. O. (2009). Outsourcing in China: opportunities, challenges, and lessons learned. *Strategic Outsourcing, 2*(2), 187–203.

Kaplan, A. M., & Haenlein, M. (2010). Users of the world, unite! The challenges and opportunities of Social Media. *Business Horizons, 53*(1), 59–68.

Kelly, T., Yang, W., Chen, C.-S., Reynolds, K., & He, J. (2008). Global burden of obesity in 2005 and projections to 2030. *International Journal of Obesity, 32*, 1431–1437. doi: 10.1038/ijto 2030.

King, J. E., Bell, M. P., & Lawrence, E. (2009). Religion as an aspect of workplace diversity: an examination of the US context and a call for international research. *Journal of Management, Spirituality & Religion, 6*(1), 43–57. doi:10.1080/14766080802648631

Konrad, A. M. (2003). Special issue introduction: Defining the domain of workplace diversity scholarship. *Group & Organization Management, 28*(4), 4–17.

Kurowski, L. (2002). Cloaked culture and veiled diversity: Why theorists ignored early US workforce diversity. *Management Decision, 40*(2), 183–191.

Kvedaraviciene, G., & Boguslauskas, B. (2010). Underestimated importance of cultural differences in outsourcing arrangements. *Inzinerine Ekonomika-Engineering Economics, 21*(2), 187–196.

Larkey, L. K. (1996). Toward a theory of communicative interactions in culturally diverse workgroups. *Academy of Management Review, 21*(2), 463–491.

Latting, J. K., & Ramsey, V. J. (2009). *Reframing change: how to deal with workplace dynamics, influence others, and bring people together to initiate positive change.* Santa Barbara, CA: ABC CLIO, LLC.

Leppel, K. (2009). Labour force status and sexual orientation. *Economica, 76*(301), 197–207.

Linnehan, F., & Konrad, A. M. (1999). Diluting diversity: Implications for intergroup inequality in organizations. *Journal of Management Inquiry, 8*(4), 399–414.

Lips-Wiersma, M., & Mills, M. (2002). Coming out of the closet: negotiating spiritual expression in the workplace. *Journal of Managerial Psychology, 17*(3), 183–202.

Mor Barak, M. E. (2011). *Managing diversity: Toward a globally inclusive workplace* (2nd ed.). Thousand Oaks, CA: Sage Publications, Inc.

Mor Barak, M. E., & Cherin, D. A. (1998). A tool to expand organizational understanding of workforce diversity: Developing a measure of Inclusion-Exclusion. *Administration in Social Work, 22*(1), 47–64.

Morning, A. (2008). Ethnic classification in global perspective: a cross-national survey of the 2000 Census Round. *Population Research and Policy Review, 27*(2), 239–272.

NASSCOM (2010, October 22). *Impact of IT-BPO industry in India: a decade in review.* (Executive Summary). Retrieved July 29, 2011, from http://www.nasscom.in/Nasscom/templates/LandingPage.aspx?id=4946

Noknoi, C., & Wutthirong, P. (2010). Leveraging diversity through raising awareness: sexual orientation discrimination in the Thailand workforce: implications for human resource management. *International Journal of Human Resources Development and Management, 10*(3), 254–271.

OECD. (2010a). Inflows of foreign workers. In *International migration outlook 2010.* OECD Publishing doi: 10.1787/migr_outlook-2010–47-en Retrieved online from http://www.oecd-ilibrary.org/social-issues-migration-health/international-migration-outlook-2010/inflows-of-foreign-workers_migr_outlook-2010–47-en

OECD. (2010b). *Sickness, disability and work: Breaking the barriers: A synthesis of findings across OECD countries.* OECD Publishing. doi: 10.1787/9789264088856-en

Office pf Management And Budget. (1997). *Revisions to the standards for the classification of federal data on race and ethnicity.* Retrieved March 15, 2011, from Http://Www.Whitehouse.Gov/Omb/Fedreg_1997standards

Olshansky, S. J., Passaro, D. J., Hershow, R. C., Lyden, J., Carnes, B., Brody, J., ... Ludwig, D. S. (2005). A potential decline in the life expectancy in the United States in the 21st century. *New England Journal of Medicine, 332*(11), 1138–1145.

Pew Research Center, Pew Forum on Religious and Public Life. (2009). *Global restrictions on religion.* Washington, DC: Pew Research Center, Pew Forum on Religious and Public Life.

Population Reference Bureau (2011). *Percent of world's HIV/AIDS cases, 2005.* Retrieved February 20, 2011, from http://www.prb.org/Educators/TeachersGuides/HumanPopulation/Health/QuestionAnswer.aspx

Power, C. N. (2000). Global trends in education. *International Education Journal, 1*(3), 152–163. Retrieved from: http://ehlt.flinders.edu.au/education/iej/articles/v1n3/power/power.pdf.

Puhl, R. M., & Heuer, C. A. (2009). The stigma of obesity: A review and update. *Obesity, 17*, 941–964.

Qualman, E. (2011). *Socialnomics: How social media transforms the way we live and do business.* Hoboken, NJ: John Wiley and Sons.

RAND Corporation. (2004). *The future at work—trends and implications* [Electronic Version]. Research Brief from http://www.rand.org/content/dam/rand/pubs/research_briefs/2005/RB5070.pdf.

Rao, D., Angell, B., Corrigan, P., & Lam, C. (2008). Stigma in the workplace: Employer attitudes about people living with HIV/AIDS in Beijing, Hong Kong, and Chicago. *Social Science and Medicine, 67*, 1541–1549.

Renaud, F., Bogardi, J. J., Dun, O., & Warner, K. (2008). *Environmental degradation and migration.* The Online-Handbook Demography of the Berlin-Institute. Retrieved March 2011 online from http://www.berlin-institut.org/online-handbookdemography/environmental-migration.html

Rooth, D. (2009). Obesity, attractiveness, and differential treatment in hiring: A field experiment. *Journal of Human Resources, 44*, 710–735.

Statistisches Bundesamt. (2010). *Current news: Occupations of women and men: Still in separate worlds?* Retrieved March 2011 from http://www.destatis.de/jetspeed/portal/cms/Sites/destatis/Internet/EN/Content/Statistics/Arbeitsmarkt/Aktuell,templateId=renderPrint.psml

Thomas, R. R., Jr. (1991). *Beyond race and gender*. New York: American Management Association.

Triandis, H. C. (2003). The future of workforce diversity in international organizations: A commentary. *Applied Psychology, 52*(3), 486–495.

Tutu, A. E. D. (Producer). (2010). *Ending violence and criminal sanctions based on sexual orientation and gender identity*. [Video message] Retrieved from http://geneva.usmission.gov/wp-content/uploads/2010/09/Tutu.pdf

Twitter (2011, March 14). *#Numbers*. Retrieved July 11, 2012 From http://blog.twitter.com/2011/03/numbers.html

UNAIDS. (2010) *Global Report: UNAIDS report on the global AIDS epidemic 2010*. Retrieved February 1, 2011, online from http://www.unaids.org/globalreport/documents/20101123_GlobalReport_full_en.pdf

UNDESA. (2009). *World population prospects: The 2008 revision*. Population Division of the Department of Economic and Social Affairs of the United Nations Secretariat. Retrieved March 17, 2011, from http://esa.un.org/unpp.

UNECA. (2010). *Diversity management in Africa: Findings from the African review mechanism and a framework for analysis and policy-making*. Retrieved July 11, 2012, from http://www.uneca.org/aprm/Documents/March082001/DiversityManagement-inAfrica.pdf

UNESCO. (2009). *World conference on higher education* [Electronic Version]. Retrieved July 1, 2011. from http://unesdoc.unesco.org/images/0018/001831/183168e.pdf .

UNESCO. (2011). *The hidden crisis: Armed conflict and education* (EFA Global Monitoring Report). [Electronic Version]. Retrieved July 27, 2011, from http://unesdoc.unesco.org/images/0019/001907/190743e.pdf

UNESCO Institute for Statistics. (2009). *Global Education Digest 2009: Comparing education statistics across the world* [Electronic Version]. Retrieved June 1, 2011, from http://www.uis.unesco.org/Library/Documents/ged09-en.pdf

UN General Assembly. (2006). *International migration and development. Report of the Secretary-General*, 18 May 2006, A/60/871. Retrieved April 1, 2011, from http://www.unhcr.org/refworld/docid/44ca2d934.html.

United Nations. (2009). World population prospects (2008 Revision), Retrieved February 17, 2011 from http://esa.un.org/unpp

United Nations Office of the High Commissioner for Human Rights. (n.d.). *Combating discrimination based on sexual orientation and gender identity*. Retrieved July 11, 2011 from http://www.ohchr.org/EN/Issues/Discrimination/Pages/LGBT.aspx

United Nations Secretary-General (2010, December 10). *Confront prejudice, speak out against violence, Secretary-General says at event on ending sanctions based on sexual orientation, gender identity*. Retrieved January 18, 2011, from Http://Www.Un.Org/News/Press/Docs/2010/Sgsm13311.Doc.Htm.

U.S. Mission to the United Nations (USUN). (2010, December 10). *Ambassador Rice at U.N. Event for Human Rights Day 2010* (Press Release). Retrieved March 2011 from http://www.america.gov/st/texttrans-english/2010/December/20101210155326su0.7109905.html

World Education Forum (2000). *The Dakar Framework for Action. Education for all: Meeting our collective commitments*. Retrieved May 1, 2011, from http://www.unesco.org/education/wef/en-conf/dakframeng.shtm

World Health Organization. (2008). *Global burden of disease 2004 update*. [Electronic Version]. Retrieved January 18, 2011, from http://www.who.int/healthinfo/global_burden_disease/2004_report_update/en/

World Health Organization. (2011a, June). *Disability and health*. Fact sheet 352. Retrieved July 10, 2012, from http://www.who.int/mediacentre/factsheets/fs352/en/

World Health Organization. (2011b. *10 facts on mental health* (Fact File). Retrieved July 29, 2011, from http://www.who.int/features/factfiles/mental_health/mental_health_facts/en/index.html

World Health Organization and World Bank (2011). *World report on disability*. [Electronic Version]. Retrieved July 29, 2011, from http://whqlibdoc.who.int/publications/2011/9789240685215_eng.pdf.

CHAPTER 22

Global Diversity Management

Mustafa Özbilgin, Karsten Jonsen, Ahu Tatli, Joana Vassilopoulou *and* Olca Surgevil

Abstract

With increased globalization of the competitive business environment, companies must adjust their operating practices to accommodate the cultural styles, norms, and preferences of the regions of the world in which they operate. This chapter reviews theories and research related to global diversity management (GDM). In addition, a framework for studying the meaning, operation, and management of diversity across national borders is presented. In particular, the shift of emphasis from normative and process-based approaches to a contextual and multifaceted understanding of GDM is explored. The chapter also explores key challenges and contradictions facing GDM. Finally, future directions in research and practice are discussed.

Key Words: diversity, global diversity management, equal opportunity, diversity research, organizational practices, processes and contexts

Introduction

In this chapter, we first trace the historical roots and meaning of global diversity management (GDM) and explain why a global approach to managing differences in the workforce is becoming increasingly important. Then we provide different models for theorizing about and practicing GDM. The chapter ends with a discussion of the challenges and contradictions facing GDM in relation to the question of responsibility, the challenge of translation, the role of global diversity managers, and organizational GDM philosophies.

Diversity management from domestic and national perspectives is often defined as recognizing and leveraging differences at work. Local approaches to diversity management originate from the North American context and date back to the late 1980s (Jonsen, Maznevski, & Schneider, 2011; Tatli & Özbilgin, 2009). Diversity management scholarship from domestic perspectives has reached a considerable level of maturity in recent years with publication of papers focusing on different dimensions of diversity, such as surface- and deep-level diversity (Harrison, Price, & Bell, 1998), readily detectable and less observable diversity (Webber & Donahue, 2001), job-related diversity (Pelled, 1996), informational, social category, and value diversity (Jehn, Northcraft, & Neale, 1999), social dominance theory and selection/attraction (Umphress et al., 2007), diversity of skills, abilities, and knowledge (Ashkanasy, Hartel, & Daus, 2002), and faultlines (Lau & Murnighan, 1998). Theorization of domestic diversity in the North American context promoted an understanding of priorities and salient strands of difference as well as the role of key institutions in effective diversity management in a way that captures the unique conditions of the North American context.

In the context of organizational practices, diversity management initiatives have become common among North American organizations: they actively advertise their achievements in managing diversity and attracting diverse talent. European and English-speaking countries followed the North American example in adoption of the term "diversity management." Common external forces, such as globalization, continuing post-industrial migration, demographic shifts, the decline of manufacturing, and the growth of the service sector, have played important roles in the diffusion of the diversity management philosophy (Wrench, 2005), and diversity interventions became part of the common language in organizations across the industrialized world (Ashkanasy, Hartel, & Daus, 2002). However, the transposition of diversity management practices even across industrialized countries has not been without complexity. There remain major variations in the interpretation and practice of equality and diversity across national borders (Özbilgin 2009). In fact, salient categories of difference such as ethnicity, disability, sexual orientation, and religion do not have the same historical, legal, and cultural legacies even between supposedly similar national settings of European countries (see Zanoni & Janssens, 2004, 2007, in Belgium; Risberg & Soederberg, 2008, in Denmark; Glastra et al., 2000; Subeliani & Tsogas, 2005, in the Netherlands; Ostendorp & Steyaert, 2009; Omanovic, 2009, in Sweden; Dereli, 2008, and Özbilgin et al., 2012, in Turkey). For instance, in Germany, the notion of diversity management largely ignores ethnicity as a category. Moreover, the majority of organizations are resistant to manage ethnic diversity, since organizations in Germany still do not view managing ethnic diversity as pertinent (Köppel et al., 2007). Vassilopoulou (2011, pp. 10–11) offers a possible explanation for this phenomenon in arguing that "the collective guilt after the Holocaust shaped the contemporary diversity management agenda in such a way that race-related issues are excluded from it." Resultantly, the topic of discrimination is marked by a collective silence, and terms such as race and racism are taboo in Germany. As evidenced in this example, and many others, diversity and equality concerns and patterns of disadvantage in the labor market are historically constructed, and historical constructions inform and shape the framework of the diversity agenda at the national, organizational, and individual levels (Özbilgin & Tatli, 2008; Prasad & Mills, 1997). For that reason, we need to develop a deeper appreciation of diversity management practices as contingent upon history and place.

Notwithstanding the difficulties in direct transposition of diversity across national borders, diversity management is now an internationally used term and is already recognized as a boon to international organizations, yet with internationally divergent theory and practice (Özbilgin, 2009). Divergence of practice and theory is evidenced in the way that GDM is a common field of management practice in global organizations, when the theorization of GDM is rather recent and still emerging in the literature. The trend toward effective management of diversity is predicted to continue in the next century, and firms that expand their operations abroad are likely to enjoy increasingly diverse pools of human resources in the global arena (Wright et al., 1995).

Domestic diversity scholars have tried to improve the framing of the diversity management literature through critical and inclusive perspectives (e.g., Barmes & Ashtiany, 2003; Dickens, 1999; Janssens & Zanoni, 2005; Lorbiecki & Jack, 2000; Roberson, 2006; Tatli, 2011). We have also witnessed a growing interest in managing diversity in regions outside North America in recent years (Klarsfeld, 2010; Özbilgin & Syed, 2010; Syed & Özbilgin, 2010). Today, the Anglo-Saxon domination of diversity management theorization (Jonsen, Schneider, & Maznevski, 2011) is challenged with expansion of the field with single-nation studies of diversity management outside this region. These studies demonstrated the ways in which the U.S.-originated diversity management approach has been modified as it travels to other countries (e.g., Glastra et al., 2000; Jones, Pringle, & Shepherd, 2000; Klarsfeld, 2009; Omanovic, 2009; Özbilgin, Syed, Ali, & Torunoglu, 2011; Risberg & Soderberg, 2008; Subeliani & Tsogas, 2005; Suss & Kleiner, 2008). In a recent edited collection, Klarsfeld (2010) brought together national perspectives on diversity management with chapters from all continents and traditionally underrepresented regions. Even in these national studies it is obvious that the degree of success in transposing diversity management efforts from North American models can be considered only partial (see chapters in Klarsfeld, 2010; D'Netto & Sohal, 1999; Tatli & Özbilgin, 2007; Vassilopoulou, 2011).

Although the expansion of the diversity management theorization to regions outside North America challenged what Dass and Parker (1999) termed as a best way to manage diversity in the literature, the expansion should come with some caveats. Most of the studies cited above remain limited to single national contexts, although they are falsely considered "international," from a North American and Eurocentric approach. In other words, single-country studies continue to dominate the new literature on diversity management. While diversity management theory is often presented as universally applicable, its key assumptions, evidence, and prescriptions remain limited to single countries in which the empirical data were gathered. In that sense, despite the stated geographic and conceptual expansion in diversity management research, academic studies on GDM continue to lag behind the practice because there is a dearth of comparative, international, multinational, and GDM research (Özbilgin & Tatli, 2008).

While single-country studies can serve to frame variation across cultural and national contexts, single-nation knowledge is insufficient to deal with the complexities of coordinating diversity management efforts across national borders (Özbilgin, 2008). As the Nigerian author Chimamanda Adichie (2010) warns us, there are dangers in telling a single story about social and economic life. The diversity management literature suffers from the danger of the single story in terms of its geographic focus and choice of strands and prescriptions. Despite the apparent rise of contextual research, which recognizes the significance of the unique history and established norms and institutions of varied countries, in exploring diversity management, there is still little in terms of comparative research that can help us transcend the deadlocks that are experienced in single-nation studies.

To reiterate, despite the aforementioned growth of the domestic diversity management theory and efforts to broaden the focus of diversity management and to make it more inclusive, there are only a handful of studies that cover international and comparative aspects of diversity management, including those by Healy and Oikelome (2007), Mor Barak (2000), Nishii and Özbilgin (2007), Özbilgin and Tatli (2008), Syed and Özbilgin (2010), and Klarsfeld (2010). These international studies demonstrate that diversity gains different meanings and has different salient strands and ways of effective management across national borders. The studies also highlight the inadequacy of direct transposition of diversity interventions; rather, effective diversity management warrants a nuanced and context-sensitive approach. Therefore, we argue that single-country studies are no longer enough for fostering innovation in diversity management and transcending path dependencies in national settings. International diversity management research can help us understand how and why diversity management is practiced differently in different national settings. Comparative studies of diversity can open up possibilities for innovation in domestic diversity management practices, which are often locked in path dependencies. Furthermore, much of the emphasis in domestic diversity theorization has been on individual differences rather than on similarities that bind people together (see, for example, Ayub & Jehn, 2010) or on actors, other than employers, that regulate the treatment of diversity at work (Tatli, 2011). We believe that GDM theory should transcend these limitations that the domestic variant of diversity management theory suffers from.

Defining global diversity management

Globalization, as one of the key drivers behind diversity, is to a large extent defined by its complexity; thus, managing globalization often means managing complexity (Lane et al., 2009), which includes interdependency, variety, and ambiguity. In fact, we may not progress much further if we do not accept that diversity is linked to complexity at many levels. Understanding this complexity requires us to explore the key drivers for organizations to adopt GDM policies, strategies, and practices. Unfortunately, for many, complexity easily leads to uncertainty and loss of control, which is exactly what our managerial and financial systems of today penalize. Complexity research holds that organizations need to match external variety by internal system variety (Ashby, 1956), as opposed to homogenization and centralization. This is conceptually and theoretically important as it also speaks to our current approach to diversity research and other sciences. However, we have yet to see research actually demonstrating this *law of requisite variety* in practice outside labs and student samples, especially at the organizational level. GDM as a field of study and management practice responds to a need to recognize that domestic diversity management approaches are not adequate to capture the demands of managing diversity in the global context.

GDM is a management philosophy that underpins a set of strategies, policies, initiatives, and training and development activities that seek to transcend national differences in diversity management policies and practices by recognizing and leveraging diverse sets of social and individual backgrounds, interests, beliefs, values, and ways of work across branch networks of organizations with international, multinational, global, and transnational workforces

(Özbilgin & Tatli, 2008). Seeking to explain the difference between domestic diversity management and GDM concepts, Stumpf, Watson, and Rustogi (1994) noted that while domestic diversity management is about leveraging individual differences to generate positive organizational outcomes, GDM is about transcending national differences to arrive at workable solutions for the international coordination of domestic diversity management initiatives. According to Nishii and Özbilgin (2007) GDM is about (1) gaining an understanding of contexts and meanings of domestic approaches to diversity management from a cross-national perspective and (2) management of diversity in multinational and global organizations from public, private, and voluntary sectors. In the former case, a comparative approach is taken with the aim of unpacking cross-national similarities and differences in terms of recognition and treatment of workforce diversity. The latter, on the other hand, corresponds to multinational, international, or global approaches that focus on devising strategies for coordinating diversity management in ways that can overcome the stalemate of national contexts.

Although there are overlaps, it is important to distinguish between possible approaches toward the research and practice of diversity management beyond domestic settings. Comparative diversity management research usually investigates and compares various dimensions, practices, and initiatives of diversity in different contexts (i.e., Risberg & Soderberg, 2008). Some of these studies also have international perspectives (i.e., Haq, 2004) and may explore diversity initiatives in organizations with a parent company in one country that manages and controls subsidiaries in different countries. Multinational research focuses on organizations that have operations across a wide range of countries and are managed through greater levels of localization, while research with a global focus is mainly interested in organizations that have centralized policies that transcend national differences and are usually managed by a team of managers from diverse locations (see Özbilgin & Tatli, 2008; Sippola & Smale, 2007; Wentling & Palma-Rivas, 2000). These different types of research with distinct focus are important to understand variants of diversity management in the global context. Against this backdrop, GDM has emerged as a response to a lack of translation of diversity management practices to suit the new national settings (Boxenbaum, 2006) and the observed failure of the ill-planned transposition of domestic diversity management approaches from one country to another (Cooke & Saini, 2010; Nishii & Özbilgin, 2007; Özbilgin, 2008; Sippola & Smale, 2007).

In terms of organizational diversity management practices and approaches, the increasing diffusion of GDM, particularly among U.S. multinational corporations (MNCs), can be understood as an answer to the growing impact of globalization on the workforce of organizations, making an international perspective to diversity management crucial (Shen, Chanda, & D'Netto, 2009; Wentling & Palma-Rivas, 2000). Numerous MNCs have workforces located outside the company's home country. In its core, GDM can be thought of as a tool relating the management of workforces across different countries (Mor Barak, 2005). Top management and human resource management (HRM) strategies are increasingly focused on capabilities and knowledge as drivers of competitive advantage (Evans, Pucik, & Björkman, 2011), which puts diversity and its global management in a central role. However, we know surprisingly little about how MNCs are responding to the increasing globalization of their workforces (Sippola & Smale, 2007). Most of the earlier works on GDM were motivated by organizations moving from developed countries to set up branch networks—that is, a network of national branches of an organization that operates in different countries around the globe. In recent years companies from developing countries such as China and India have started developing international branch networks. Thus, we need a revisioning of GDM with this new setting in mind.

Development of GDM theory and practice

There were multiple drivers for the development of GDM theory and practice, ranging from business and economic justifications to social and legal changes in the international context. Harvey and Buckley (1997) explain that global organizations pursue strategies to leverage differences among their employees so they can accrue competitive advantages in the international context. Besides the ambitions of global firms to gain strategic advantages, there are also contextual changes, such as the expansion of international law to cover issues of equality, in particular gender equality, in recent decades. The Convention on the Elimination of All Forms of Discrimination Against Women (CEDAW) has been ratified by an overwhelming majority of the countries in the world. There have also been promulgated legal protections against forms of discrimination, including those based on gender, ethnicity, age, disability, sexual orientation, and belief. As Acker (2006) noted, these legal changes have rendered visible different forms of discrimination and challenged their legitimacy. However, there is extensive national variation in the regulation of equality and diversity (Klarsfeld, 2010; Özbilgin, 2002).

International diversification of highly skilled workers (Al Ariss & Özbilgin, 2010) and increased competition for talent not only in the industrialized countries but also in emerging economies (Özbilgin & Vassilopoulou, 2010) have been other drivers for GDM theorization and practice. One of the key means for diffusion of the GDM approach internationally has been the role that professional bodies and learned organizations such as the Society for Human Resource Management (SHRM; United States) and the Chartered Institute of Personnel and Management (United Kingdom) have played in advocating for the necessity for GDM, in recognition of demands from their members from multinational organizations. The Global Compact held a conference in 2007 on GDM issues. In 2008 and 2010, SHRM organized the global diversity and inclusion summit, bringing 100 experts from around the globe to discuss how the global diversity and inclusion agenda can be pushed forward. In the second SHRM summit, an international resource, the Global Diversity and Inclusion Readiness Index, was introduced; it offers insights into the readiness of over 40 countries for the management of diversity and inclusion. Aside from these two vivid examples, the International Labor Organization, alongside other national bodies, promotes global labor standards. All these networked activities foster the diffusion of knowledge and sharing of best practices between a large number of international and national actors in the employment relations field, including trade unions, employers' associations, and government agencies of equality and diversity on the international stage.

Another reason for the emergence of GDM as distinct from the domestic variant has been the failures in transposing North American approaches to diversity management to other national contexts. Agocs and Burr (1996) explain that transposing diversity management approaches across national borders bodes ill for business success, as the usefulness and appropriateness of a specific approach to diversity management should be considered in the light of key national priorities. It should be assessed in terms of its contribution to core business objectives and its overall fit with the systems and structures in the workplace. Boxenbaum (2006) suggests that the dominant Nordic homogeneity, values, and democratic principles conflict with diversity management. Her study shows that a strategic reframing was necessary and possible, insofar as a translation from American diversity practices had to include legitimate local practices. Syed and Özbilgin (2009) find that cultural and contextual similarity between countries may be deceptive: institutions and structures may be imbued with different meanings and values, resulting in divergent requirements for the adoption of diversity management approaches. For example, when translated to the Scandinavian context, diversity management became entangled with migration concerns and integration of ethnic minorities into the labor force (de los Reyes, 2000; Omanovic, 2009). As a result, arguments based on corporate social responsibility, rather than the business case arguments, dominate the diversity debate in the region (Kamp & Hagedorn Rasmussen, 2004). Writing on the Swedish context, Kalonaityte (2010) observes that the diversity management approach in that country emphasized the role of the government rather than the private sector as the key stakeholder. Similarly, Klarsfeld (2009) argues that the unlike the original U.S. interpretation of presenting diversity management as an alternative to affirmative action, in France there is a simultaneous accommodation of these two approaches. In the case of Pakistan and Turkey, Syed and colleagues (2009) demonstrate that transposition of gender equality regimes between Muslim-majority countries is complicated by divergent historical legacies and different dominant ideologies, which instrumentally co-opt the message of equality but at the same time vacate its core meaning (i.e., real social change). These national studies demonstrate that diversity management takes different shapes and forms as it travels across national borders.

Still, as Özbilgin and Tatli (2008) point out, much of the diversity management literature tends not go beyond the national, organizational, and intergroup level. Jones and colleagues (2000) and Ferner and colleagues (2005) agree that diversity management approaches deriving, for instance, from the United States are often perceived as unsuitable when applied to other national contexts, leading to high levels of organizational resistance in terms of cultural and institutional aspects. Implementing GDM activities in foreign subsidiaries by means of an ethnocentric, host-country perspective brings with it a number of shortcomings and weaknesses (Ferner et al., 2005). In the same vein, Nishii and Özbilgin (2008) demonstrate that it is common to find ethnocentric assumptions jeopardizing the effective transposition of diversity management practices between countries. Instead, they recommend an approach that is sensitive to the needs and priorities of each national context. Egan and Bendick (2003) reveal in their research that the majority of the U.S. MNCs they investigated used a multi-domestic approach toward diversity management, with the corporate headquarters offering only rudimentary advice for diversity management to foreign subsidiaries in an attempt to avoid the perceived complexity involved in the development and enforcement of GDM initiatives. As a consequence, the diversity management activities differed significantly among foreign subsidiaries. However, this approach can also be problematic: differences across international practices of global firms expose them to reputational damage when practices that are legitimate in some countries are not considered legal or legitimate in others within the international branch network.

Chevrier (2003) studied three international project teams and identified four unique ways of managing cultural diversity. First, organizations can draw on general ethical notions such as tolerance and self-control at work; this approach welcomes individual differences but at the same time ignores them. Secondly, a more experiential approach may be adopted in which building positive personal and professional relationships at work may be encouraged. However, this approach may ignore the subjective nature of culture, leading to negative stereotypes being formed through regular interactions. The third choice for the management of cultural diversity is more transformational: the organization may foster a culture that is open to change as cultural differences are transcended through adoption of a more transnational culture. However, even in this third option, it would be naïve to assume that power imbalances between cultures can be transcended. Indeed, conflict and disagreement would surface even in this third case, which is supposed to be more open to dialogue among parties (see also the study of a specific MNC global culture by Erez & Shokef, 2008). Fourth, it is possible for organizations to adopt an *ad hoc* approach to cross-cultural management that supports the process of cross-cultural learning through a more managed and strategic process involving mediators. This fourth technique may overcome some of the assimilationist and integrationist tendencies that undermine principles of equality among parties with the use of informed actors who are trained to combat polarization (see, for example, the study by Vassilopoulou, 2011, which found that assimilationist and integrationist tendencies shape the notion of diversity management in the German context).

As the review of the literature and research evidence demonstrates, development of the GDM theory and practice is complex and varied. While GDM is theorized in terms of process in some cases, in others theorization focuses on context, and in still others GDM is studied as a set of contingent management interventions. As a result, the different models of GDM that are presented in the academic literature build on or emphasize different organizational drivers in attempting to overcome the complexities of cross-cultural and cross-national coordination of diversity management activities. The next section examines four key GDM models that we identified in the literature.

Models of global diversity management

Management of cultural diversity is often used as a proxy for global diversity management. However, culture is only one of the many criteria that may be considered under the broad umbrella of global differences. In fact, the GDM literature draws on a multidisciplinary base of knowledge across all fields of social sciences. It is possible to identify four models of GDM that are distinguishable in terms of theoretical loyalties, strengths, and limitations: strategic, process, context, and intervention models (Table 22.1).

The strategic model locates diversity management along the spectrum of localization and globalization, identifying when and how global firms choose to localize, centralize, or transcend such binary choices in their GDM strategies. The process model seeks to present the antecedents, correlates, and consequences of managing global diversity. The context model outlines the layered influences ranging from macro-international to meso-institutional and micro-agentic influences on the way global diversity is managed. The intervention model illustrates the choice of global diversity interventions, which vary according to the divergence in the branch network, the maturity of the global diversity program, and the leadership and resources afforded to the program.

Strategic model

The strategic model of GDM points to possibilities of localizing or centralizing GDM efforts. This model has its theoretical roots in Bartlett and

Table 22.1 Models of Global Diversity Management

Models of Global Diversity Management	Theoretical Foundation	Strength	Weakness
Strategic model	Global strategic management (e.g., Bartlett & Ghoshal, 1989)	Offers three distinct strategies of global diversity management: localized, universal, transversal	Matching approach, which relies on a single strategy, is not sophisticated enough due to the complexity of the GDM context, which may warrant multiple strategies.
Process model	Social psychology and identity theories (e.g., Byrne, 1971; Tajfel & Turner, 1986)	Focuses on global competencies and organizational/group identification	Ignores multiple stakeholders and does not consider conflict across different actors and contexts
Context model	Sociological theories (e.g., Layder, 1993)	Considers individual, organizational, sectoral, national, and international variations across time and place	GDM may also change context, rather than simply adapting organizations to contextual requirements
Intervention model	Theories of organizational change	Identifies a set of contingencies upon which an appropriate intervention model may be selected	Assumes a basic willingness to change within organizations

	Localised	*Universal*	*Transversal*
Policy focus	Local branch network policy	Global HQ policy	Global branch network/council policy
Practice	Locally specific	Globally prescribed	Global policy with national variation

Figure 22.1. Three strategies of GDM.
Source: Adapted from Özbilgin, 2009.

Ghoshal's (1989) distinction between global integration (i.e., transferring successful strategies and practices across borders) and local responsiveness (i.e., tailoring strategies and practices to fit the local context), and the tension between the two (see also Brock & Siscovick, 2007; Luo, 2001; Winter & Szulanski, 2001). As Figure 22.1 illustrates, global organizations may choose to localize, universalize, or transversalize their GDM strategies (Özbilgin & Tatli, 2008).

A localized strategy for GDM means that a local branch network can identify its own priorities without having them imposed by headquarters. Localized approaches are common when there are established mechanisms for dealing with diversity issues in the local context. However, such an approach may not be useful if diversity management is a new idea and there are blind spots regarding various strands in the local context. Localized strategy is underpinned by an assumption that local management would be interested in or keen on pursuing diversity issues. An outcome of the localized approach is that GDM presents a divergent profile across the branch network, as local branches pick and choose their own priorities and methods of managing diversity. In the localized strategy, activities are not coordinated from the center. Therefore, local branches may expose the global firm to reputational, legal, and financial risk due to the different branch approaches to diversity.

The universal strategy for GDM involves standardizing policies and practices of diversity management throughout a global firm (Rosenzweig, 1998). It eliminates regional and national variations in diversity management and by definition is insensitive to local context. If an organization adopts this "one-size-fits-all" strategy, it may fail to observe the legal, cultural, and social requirements and priorities for diversity management in that specific region, rendering diversity strategy irrelevant to some local branches.

Empirical GDM studies demonstrate that there is a tension between localized and universal strategies. Jonsen, Schneider and Maznevski's (2010) work on two large MNCs shows that the choice of a localized or universal strategy was largely influenced by the company's organizational structure. One company focused on ensuring that diversity and inclusion were well embedded into all of its main human resource systems and processes. As the other company was very decentralized in its structure and decision making, and its diversity initiatives echoed this: they varied widely between nations with different approaches to diversity.

In addition to the organizational structures, local branches are subject to and operate under unique national conditions, and this poses a challenge for GDM strategy. For example, Egan and Bendick (2003) presented two contrasting case studies that illustrated that despite cultural proximity, transposing diversity management approaches is challenging because other factors, such as institutional forces, laws, and social mores, may affect the choice of diversity approach in the local branch. Mor Barak's (2000) case study of a New York-based MNC operating in 170 countries, on the other hand, illustrates how an MNC may encounter challenges stemming from the tensions between globalization and localization. The main challenge that company faced was in translating its U.S.-based priorities for managing diversity to useable priorities in its global branch network, having realized that the concepts of race, gender, sexual orientation, and disability-based diversity do not readily translate into other cultures where ethnic diversity is not significant (for example, Japan) or religious strictures inform the logic of gender discrimination (for example, Saudi Arabia). The company adopted a dual strategy for recognizing unique elements of each country's context, incorporating this into the company policy, but at the same time, the company considered combating discrimination as a universal strategy despite divergent views from the branch network.

The transversal strategy seeks to overcome the traps of the local and universal strategies by adopting a negotiated approach to decision making with regard to diversity management across the branch network to get all branches to contribute to the shaping of the global approach. This negotiated process aims to ensure that the resulting policy and practices that emanate from it carry aspects of all cultural and national contexts of the branch network. Karabacakoglu and Özbilgin's (2010) case study of an MNC illustrates that the transnational approach bodes well for innovation in diversity management because it facilitates a platform for national approaches and priorities to be discussed and allows for some practices to be transposed effectively across the international network.

However, even this transversal approach suffers from a naïve assumption that power relations can be managed to create truly transversal settings. Instead, power inequities may become tacit and invisible in organizational discourses: they may call for equal voice without offering effective mechanisms for ensuring that everyone's voice matters.

Process model

Processes have been central to the study of diversity across the globe, especially in relation to work teams. There are, to name just a few, social processes, information and decision-making processes, task processes, and knowledge-sharing processes, each underpinned by numerous theories, mainly from psychology and social psychology. For example, social identity theory (Tajfel & Turner, 1986) has been a carrying basis for negative and positive effects, also addressing issues of power and legitimacy, and the similarity-attraction paradigm. Looking specifically at cultural diversity, a process framework was used to capture the effects of more than 100 diversity studies (Stahl, Maznevski, Voigt, & Jonsen, 2010). This model stipulates that cultural diversity tends to increase divergent processes (e.g., creativity and conflicts) and decrease convergent processes (e.g., communication, satisfaction with team, and social integration). At the organizational level, processes tend to systematically reduce rather than exploit the variety of perspectives that different people can bring (Brunsson, 1982). The similarity-attraction paradigm (Byrne, 1971) explains this, because people tend to be attracted to those whose attitudes and values are similar to their own, and to organizations with similar values

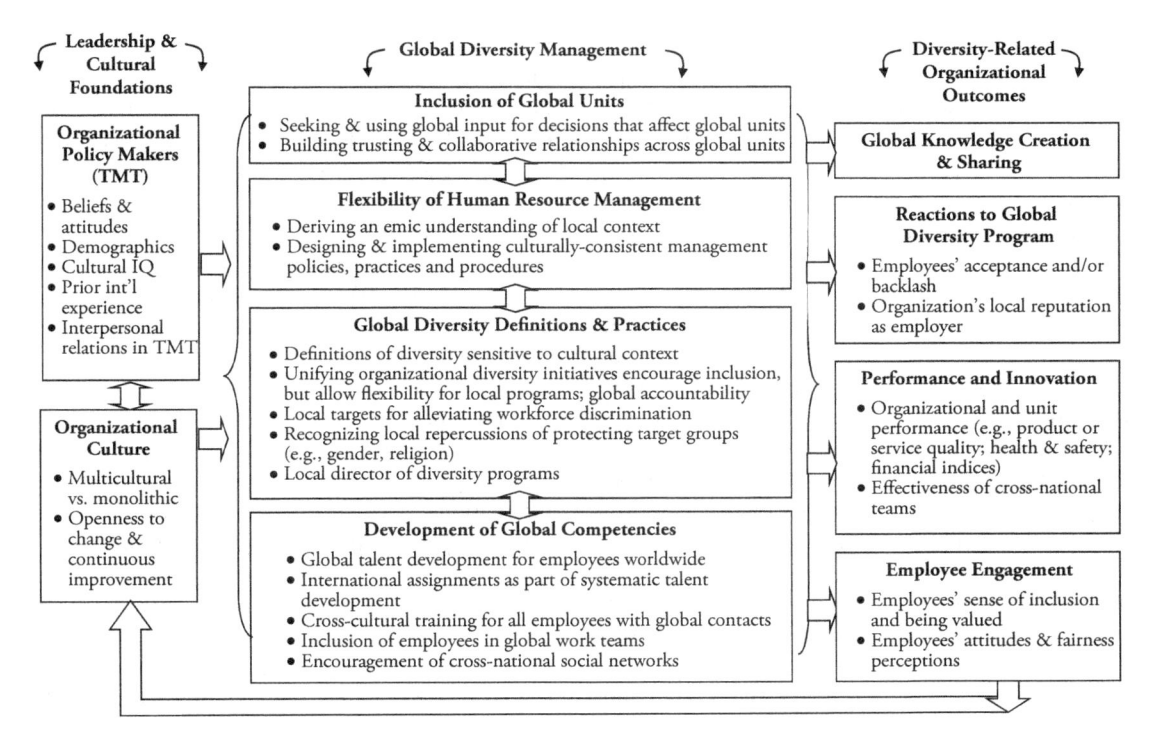

Figure 22.2. A process model of GDM.
Source: Nishii & Özbilgin, 2007.

```
┌─ Leadership & ─┐          ┌─ Global Diversity Management ─┐         ┌─ Diversity-Related ─┐
│    Cultural    │          │                                │         │   Organizational    │
│   Foundations  │          │                                │         │      Outcomes       │
```

Leadership & Cultural Foundations	Global Diversity Management	Diversity-Related Organizational Outcomes
Organizational Policy Makers (TMT) • Beliefs & attitudes • Demographics • Cultural IQ • Prior int'l experience • Interpersonal relations in TMT	**Inclusion of Global Units** • Seeking & using global input for decisions that affect global units • Building trusting & collaborative relationships across global units	**Global Knowledge Creation & Sharing**
	Flexibility of Human Resource Management • Deriving an emic understanding of local context • Designing & implementing culturally-consistent management policies, practices and procedures	**Reactions to Global Diversity Program** • Employees' acceptance and/or backlash • Organization's local reputation as employer
Organizational Culture • Multicultural vs. monolithic • Openness to change & continuous improvement	**Global Diversity Definitions & Practices** • Definitions of diversity sensitive to cultural context • Unifying organizational diversity initiatives encourage inclusion, but allow flexibility for local programs; global accountability • Local targets for alleviating workforce discrimination • Recognizing local repercussions of protecting target groups (e.g., gender, religion) • Local director of diversity programs	**Performance and Innovation** • Organizational and unit performance (e.g., product or service quality; health & safety; financial indices) • Effectiveness of cross-national teams
	Development of Global Competencies • Global talent development for employees worldwide • International assignments as part of systematic talent development • Cross-cultural training for all employees with global contacts • Inclusion of employees in global work teams • Encouragement of cross-national social networks	**Employee Engagement** • Employees' sense of inclusion and being valued • Employees' attitudes & fairness perceptions

and attitudes. Organizations then reinforce similarity by attracting, hiring, and retaining similar types of people (e.g., Jackson et al., 1991). The problem is that this has led to a perhaps negative view of diversity and its effects and potential across cultures (Brickson, 2008). Although these processes are assumed to be universal, we cannot take for granted that the same psychological mechanisms and processes are entirely universal and appropriate for other regions in the world (Magoshi & Chang, 2009; Markus & Kitayama, 2003). Recently, numerous scholars have started to look specifically for more positive processes. For example, Stahl, Mäkelä, Zander, and Maznevski (2010) highlight how cultural diversity and cultural differences can be viewed primarily as an asset rather than a liability. These authors argue that multicultural teams could act by "gluing different cultural contexts throughout organizations together" (p. 444) instead of measuring primarily the interpersonal complications. Also according to the information-processing and problem-solving approaches, diversities reinforce teamwork and help to provide more effective solutions to problems (Mannix & Neale, 2005).

A comprehensive process model of GDM is presented by Nishii and Özbilgin (2007). This model includes antecedents, correlates, and consequences of GDM (Fig. 22.2). Nishii and Özbilgin (2007) explain that supportive leadership and inclusive cultural foundations are precursors to setting up an effective GDM initiative. Including global units in decision-making processes, increasing the flexibility of HRM practices to accommodate and cater for individual differences, arriving at mutually agreed definitions and policies of global diversity, and fostering a set of key global competencies among staff are important activities that global diversity managers should set up in multinational firms. These competencies can be categorized into levels: systems skills, interpersonal skills, attitudes and orientation, and traits (Lane et al., 2009). The "highest" level, system skills, includes the ability to make ethical decisions. If the preconditions and effective management of GDM initiatives are ensured, a number of positive organizational outcomes can be expected, including improvements to knowledge sharing, creativity, and motivation, as well as employee engagement.

Although the process model is useful in integrating the contribution of the organizational psychology literature to our understanding of GDM processes, it suffers from inattention to context and the conflicting interests of diverse sets of influential actors within and outside organizations. Özbilgin and Tatli's recent study (2011) demonstrates that divergent interests of key stakeholders can stall progress toward equality. Therefore, an analysis of relations of power among key stakeholders is necessary to understand the process of change that GDM may inculcate in organizations.

Context model

While the positivist tradition (cf. Boone & Hendriks, 2009; Cannella, Park, & Lee, 2008) of GDM promotes process models, which explore antecedents, correlates, and consequences of diversity management, the interpretive tradition (cf. Bryan, 2010) of diversity management places more emphasis on the context and the role that institutional and individual stakeholders may have on the emergence of GDM policy. Joshi and Roh (2008) argued that there is a range of contextual explanations for the nonsignificant effects of diversity (organizational climate, country locations, virtuality, resource pressures on team members, etc.) and these are often neglected by researchers.

All GDM scholars, in the latter tradition, are embedded in a layered context ranging from macro-international to meso-national/sectoral and micro-institutional/individual. The context model of GDM is influenced by a sociologic approach that maintains that social phenomena are relationally constructed (Özbilgin, 2005) and generated through multilevel influences (Layder, 1993). As such, the final GDM approach is one that is negotiated through these levels with the influence of main actors. Diversity and equality concerns and patterns of disadvantage in the labor market are historically constructed, and they draw the framework of diversity agenda at the national, organizational, and individual levels (Özbilgin & Tatli, 2008). History can be understood as a major feature of social life that influences behavior and social activity in general. Moreover, history must be viewed as a primary feature in the relationship between social factors and institutional change, as it does generate organizational responses and practices. The contextual model of GDM is an outcome of the growth in GDM research in regions and countries outside North America (Dameron & Joffre, 2007; Nishii & Özbilgin, 2007; Sippola & Smale, 2007). Figure 22.3 illustrates the contextual model of GDM.

While there are global drivers due to changing demographics, and economic and legal forces at the international level encouraging adoption of diversity management principles, the legal, social, and economic conditions of countries account for some of the variation in adoption and implementation of practices. Institutional theory (Powell & DiMaggio, 1991) speaks to a confirmative homogeneity effect based on, for example, mimetic processes, and the authors claim startling similarity between organizational forms and practices (DiMaggio & Powell, 1983). However, this explanatory approach has proven to have cross-border limitations. Süss and Kleiner (2008) found that in Germany, societal expectations and benchmarking had only a weak influence on diversity management's implementation and the intensity by which it was practiced by German organizations, and normative isomorphism (such as trade associations, occupational networks, and education/training) had some influence on the adoption of diversity. The strongest influence they found was whether the company was a "foreign

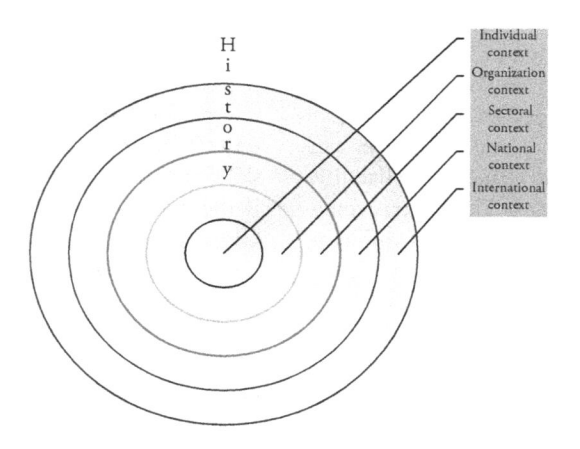

Figure 22.3. Contextual model of GDM.
Source: Adapted from Özbilgin & Tatli, 2008.

[American] entity" and "cooperation" (mimetic processes with either suppliers or clients). According to Süss and Kleiner (2008), laws and EU directives have almost no impact on diversity management's implementation among German organizations; the companies can choose to ignore them, presumably because such choices are not punished. Generally speaking, Europe has been claimed to have a less litigious atmosphere (Simons, 2002). Moreover, Europe as a region is very multicultural, but within borders countries tend to carry a monocultural mentality (Simons, 2002).

Discourse analyses (Bellard & Rühling, 2001) have shown differences between nations with regard to how diversity is legitimized. For example, German companies legitimized diversity concerns by a closer link to performance and related rationales. Whereas French companies took a more normative and holistic approach. Some of the underlying cultural assumptions behind such differences have been pointed out by several scholars (e.g. Ling, Floyd, & Baldridge, 2005; Schneider, 1989)—for example, uncertainty acceptance, individualism versus social orientation, and task orientation versus holistic and context-dependent view.

There are also sectoral and organizational drivers, particularly in relation to structures and systems of organizations being amenable to diversity concerns. Furthermore, the diversity management office at the national level plays a role in raising awareness and campaigning for global coordination of activities. The last but by no means the least significant issue is the role of individual agency in promoting the case for GDM offices. Opinion and decision leaders as well as individuals in strategic positions may see the significance of global coordination in diversity management issues. The potential link between global diversity initiatives and their positive impact on individual and group performance may also persuade senior managers to pay attention to GDM concerns.

The main weakness of the contextual approach is that often context is considered as something that affects GDM activities, but the other direction of the relationship between context and GDM is not explored: GDM activities are also known to change the social, economic, political, and technological landscape in which organizations operate.

Intervention model

GDM, like its domestic variant, aims to make organizations more welcoming of difference, and this requires the organization to change. Organizational change models for GDM appear to be underdeveloped, although we are not short of change models *per se* (e.g. Jick & Peiperl, 2010; Lane et al., 2009; Lewin, 1943) or values used as an instrumental management change tool (see Ogbonna & Harris, 2002, for a critical review). Many intervention models focus on reducing the barriers that create conflict, and other interpersonal issues based in social psychology (e.g., Brickson, 2008). The problem from the GDM perspective is that diversity is not a typical change issue. Although we can keep on pointing out relevant gaps (such as cognitive diversity), we must steer away from gap-filling approaches driven by traditional scholastic attitudes and traditions (cf. Alvesson & Sandberg, 2011; Sandberg & Tsoukas, 2011). Rather than predominantly relying on micro-models, more work is needed vis-à-vis holistic change models with the specific purpose of increasing diversity in organizations, other than geographic expansion. In fact, Martin and Meyerson (2008) point out the need to look at societal solutions because we have been trapped in incrementalism and institutional interlocks.

GDM initiatives and interventions that are required to achieve organizational changes may take various levels of engagement, such as informational, structural, and cultural levels. If the maturity of GDM is high, leadership support and resources are strong, and there are high levels of similarity among diversity priorities in the global branch network, we can expect GDM activities that lead to stronger transformational GDM activities, including organization development programs, setting of diversity councils, and cultural change programs. If these conditions are weak, however, then we see more surface-level global diversity activities, which are limited to awareness-raising and basic training. Figure 22.4 depicts how global diversity activities may vary across these three criteria.

GDM interventions may also take different forms depending on the organization's overall strategy for globalization. They may be centralized through a common strategy that is communicated to the branch network or localized at each national branch, where local branches identify their own priorities and relevant interventions. The former approach is a global approach that rests on a universal principle, whereas the latter approach resembles practices in MNCs that seek to localize their practices. In terms of diversity and globalization, one of the key markers of a global organization is its treatment of diversity (Hordes, Clancy, & Baddaley, 1995). Neither of these approaches is evident in

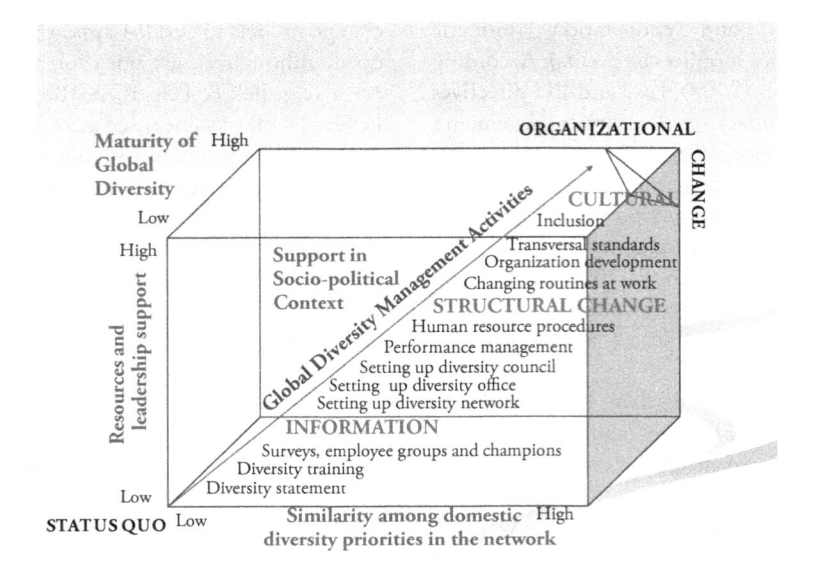

Figure 22.4. GDM activities in organizational change.

pure form in practice; instead, most organizations opt for a mixed approach.

Depending on the type, sector, and strategic direction of the organization, diversity management may be located in different parts of the organization hierarchy. The GDM office may be centralized in headquarters, or it may have a different headquarters on its own. It can also be decentralized, or it may assume a matrix structure with diffuse functions. While in many organizations the GDM function sits close to the HRM function or is even subsumed under it, more progressive firms have global diversity managers who are located in the strategic heart of the organization, independent of HRM, and who serve across the institution (Özbilgin & Tatli 2008). It is possible to centralize, localize, or adopt a more complex and distributed position for diversity management activities. There is also the option of outsourcing diversity management activities to management consultants, training organizations, or organizational development firms.

Cases and the challenges facing GDM and research

Despite the emergence of a number of models for GDM, there remain challenges in achieving effective global diversity strategies and practices. GDM remains a nebulous concept due to a number of complexities surrounding its philosophy and implementation. We identify three GDM challenges across the interconnected issues of translation, responsibility, and philosophy of GDM.

Responsibility and translation

One of the challenges in framing GDM is to decide whose responsibility it is to manage global diversity. The multilayered nature of the GDM literature makes it difficult to determine who has the primary responsibility for GDM. Depending on where we locate responsibility for management, we come up with different prescriptions for managing GDM. At the macro-level, GDM has become an industry in itself. There are international, national, and regional institutions in the public, private, and voluntary sectors, professional bodies and individuals whose main role is to serve as consultants, advisors, coaches, trainers, organization developers, managers, officers, executives, academics, professionals, and network, forum, and consortia members on diversity management policy and practices. Traditional actors in employment relations are also now party to the formulation and implementation of GDM policies and practices (e.g., Gilbert & Ivancevich, 2000).

While it is possible to identify a number of extra-organizational stakeholders at the macro-level, most of the GDM policy and practice is located at the meso-level—that is, within organizations (Tatli & Özbilgin, 2007). At the meso-level, the key challenge that organizations face is to reconcile demands for globalization and localization of GDM philosophies and practices. While global workforces need to be centrally coordinated to ensure a level of process and service standardization, the actual work often takes place in a specific national setting, which requires localization (Dunavant & Heiss, 2005). Managing global diversity requires reconciling the need for globally unified policies and locally embedded practices. Managing a diverse global workforce while sustaining consistency throughout the organization is seen as the major challenge in this regard (Rosenzweig, 1998). GDM initiatives need to be locally significant (Schneider & Barsoux, 2003). Therefore, MNCs have to pay attention to divergent national aspects such as legislation, languages spoken, religions, ethnicity, labor availability and composition, and industrial relations.

The question of responsibility is intertwined with the challenges of translating GDM policies and strategies across national borders. The process of expansion of the GDM literature and practice both geographically and functionally is imbued with tensions of power and dominance in terms of which country, region, culture, or function of management will have a greater voice in shaping the policies and practices of diversity. A significant challenge that ensues is linked to the translation of global diversity policies and practices across varied national, cultural, and organizational settings. A case showing the risks of a localized strategy for GDM can be found in Vassilopoulou's (2011) study of the practice of diversity management in the German branch of a North American MNC with more than 140 plants all over the world. The company adopted a localized diversity management strategy. As a result, there was a divergent diversity management profile between headquarters and the German plant. Unlike headquarters, the German branch did not consider ethnic diversity in its diversity management approach. The study revealed practices exposing the MNC to legal and financial risk. For example, the German branch violated legal obligations (i.e., the EU law) by not providing necessary information about employee rights and a contact person or unit in case a worker felt discriminated against. This happened without the knowledge of headquarters. This is an excellent example of the possible equality and organizational risks that companies expose themselves to if they fail to properly deal with the issues of how and in what scope diversity responsibilities are passed to different constituencies when diversity management is translated across borders.

A more positive example on how to translate diversity management policies globally through a well-defined strategy to distribute responsibilities is presented in Sucher and Corsi's (2010) study of a Dutch-based MNC with over 100,000 employees. The company has been driving diversity initiatives worldwide since 1997, and diversity management is framed as a change process taking place at three levels: personal, interpersonal, and organizational. The company's diversity management is formally driven by human resources but linked to and "owned" by other functional areas. This is done by linking diversity objectives and targets to both internal group priorities, such as core values and talent management, and external group priorities, such as social performance and sustainability. In translating the diversity management across multiple national settings, diversity targets are deemed universal and relevant across all branches across the globe but at the same time are adapted to local requirements and contexts (e.g., local labor market conditions and the skill and expertise composition of the local labor force).

Capacity of global diversity managers as change agents

Notwithstanding the issue of where to place responsibility for the practice of GDM, global diversity managers supposedly have a key role in designing, implementing, and overseeing the organizational GDM policy and strategy. Global diversity managers serve a different function than their domestic counterparts. They assume the role of coordinating the national policies and practices of diversity management, design and leadership of GDM strategy. The GDM role also involves building a structure that coordinates national diversity efforts, either through a more democratic method of setting up a diversity council or a diversity forum or by more directive means of communicating a diversity policy to the international network.

Similar to other managers, global diversity managers need to obtain buy-in from organizational actors for their diversity initiatives and interventions. Most importantly, diversity management initiatives need to be supported by key stakeholders, including organizational leaders, supervisors, functional and area managers, and other staff. The literature offers a number of prescriptions to achieve such acceptance by colleagues and leaders at work for diversity initiatives (e.g., Cox & Blake, 1991, offer an overview of six arguments that diversity managers could strategically use; see also Kirby and Richard, 2000).

However, Joplin and Daus (1997) earlier illustrated that diversity management has a number of challenges inherent in its take-up in organizations. These challenges include resistance by senior managers to share power; the complexity of tackling value-, belief-, and opinion-based differences; and the limited nature of diversity initiatives to change organizations beyond superficial concerns. French and Bell (1999) argue that resistance to change is mostly entrenched in fears concerning perceived loss of status, power, and influence. In the domestic diversity management context, managers show emotional and often negative reactions if existing organizational structures are subject to change, and this may derail or even sabotage change efforts (Thomas, 2008; Thomas & Ely, 1996). James and Wooten (2001) argue that a reflective perspective could help organizations to address resistance to change. Moving toward an institutionally and individually tailored change program could be a first step toward leveraging such reflective perspective for global diversity managers. As Joplin and Daus (1997) explained, using a "one-size-fits-all" approach to diversity management undermines the intelligence of participants in diversity interventions and ignores the intricate nature of vested interests and power relations at work. Such issues can be even more acute in the context of GDM due to the added cross-cultural and multinational complexity. Although some authors advocate the significance of learning as an important ingredient in diversity management activities (Flood & Romm, 1996; Iles, 1995), such learning-based approaches often falsely assume that learning alone can inculcate the changes that are necessary for transforming organizations; instead, such changes often require change agents to tackle entrenched and institutionalized forms of inequality, injustice, and discrimination.

Tatli and Özbilgin's (2009) work may offer clues on how global diversity managers may overcome the resistance to diversity policies and practices. They demonstrated that diversity managers may serve as change agents at work if they are endowed with a range of resources and if they have access to strategic processes of decision making and resource allocation at work. Global diversity managers, similar to their national counterparts, often operate under resource-poor conditions with limited access to economic resources (their budgets), social resources (membership in networks), cultural resources (their education, training, and experience), and symbolic capital (their ability to make use of these resources). Tatli and Özbilgin (2007) illustrate that diversity managers who enjoy resources, status, and power at work are able to deliver diversity initiatives that transform their organizations in deeper and more meaningful ways. Importantly, having a dedicated diversity office with a diversity budget helps to promote diversity processes (see Özbilgin & Tatli, 2008). In that sense, global diversity managers face some unique challenges in competition for resources. Although many global, multinational, and international organizations in the public, private, and voluntary sectors have set up GDM functions, there is also a reported shift of emphasis in some firms, where global corporate responsibility and global talent management functions compete for resources and inclusion in the corporate hierarchy.

Furthermore, global diversity managers have more limited opportunities for professional development and cultural and human capital accumulation compared to diversity managers who work at a national level. Much of the scholarship and education in the field of diversity management is embedded in domestic diversity practices (Bell, 2007; Freeman-Evans, 1994), and many universities now offer voluntary diversity training at the undergraduate and postgraduate levels, despite strong calls for compulsory education in the field (Bell, Connerley, & Cocchiara, 2009). Despite growing interest in the field of GDM, there is little formal education in this field by universities (Özbilgin & Tatli, 2008). Instead, many training and consultancy firms fill this void by offering training programs and professional networks. As global, multinational, and international organizations today are likely to have GDM functions, officers and directors who lead these functions can often turn to informal and commercial, rather than academic, sources of training. For that reason, new methods and comprehensive models for competencies that are necessary for managing global diversity are essential (Ashkanasy et al., 2002). Some researchers emphasize that diversity management competency consists of sorting various competencies, while others argue that this competency should be evaluated as a process (Cox & Beale, 1997). Diversity management competency is a learning process that enables managers to react effectively to opportunities and threats originating from sociocultural differences in a defined social system (Cox & Beale, 1997). The learning process composed of three stages as (a) creating awareness, (b) information and understanding development, (c) behavior and application. These three steps can be examined on the levels of both the individual and the organization. On the individual level, developing competency related to diversity means learning how to change personal behaviors while employees perform their daily tasks and responsibilities. Unfortunately, there is a lack of conceptual frames that address the unique challenges that global diversity managers encounter and unpack the competencies and expertise they may need in tackling these challenges. Therefore, there is a need for theoretical and empirical development in answering the question of "what does GDM competency include?"

Contradictions of the business case in the global context

Although the business case is widely scrutinized in the domestic context (Kelly & Dobbin, 1998; Noon, 2007; Wrench, 2005), GDM introduces new complexities regarding a focus on the business case. Therefore, there is a need to rethink the business case from the GDM perspective to advance both the practice and theory of managing global diversity. A few years ago a large company was investigating workforce diversity as a strategic issue (Jonsen, Schneider, & Maznevski, 2011). Diversity was broadly understood as differences such as nationality, education, gender, and personality. Based on a thorough analysis, including research literature, they reached the conclusion that there was *no compelling business case*, and thus diversity was not considered a topic of strategic importance (i.e., it was not on the strategic agenda). Moreover, it was pointed out by the CEO that there was *no burning platform*, as they perceived it. As a consequence, diversity did not increase, did not receive dedicated resources, and was not "managed" with particular initiatives. This successful white-male-manager engineering company made this decision in late 2006 and has had stellar financial performance since then, as they had before rejecting diversity as a strategic issue. Although some corporations in Europe consider diversity to be an important strategic issue, many are still not convinced, and the commitment of many European organizations has been summarized as "lukewarm" (Maxwell et al., 2003).

Corporations that do take on diversity as a strategic issue often cite the business case as a prime rationale, and the importance of diversity management has long been related to the business case (e.g., Dietz & Petersen, 2006). From a process perspective, this is logical and shows how an organization tends to operate and allocates resources in a liberal economic system. From a content perspective, it also makes sense to have a diverse workforce because it is most likely to increase creativity and subsequently innovation, and leads to a greater understanding of the customer base in an increasingly global world; this applies to many different kinds of organizations (e.g., social enterprises) (Bridgstock et al., 2010). These arguments were well established decades ago, as research took notice of the many diversity initiatives in the United States beginning in the 1980s. Equally well developed are the counterarguments about diversity being a double-edged sword because it creates tension and conflicts, elements that have been named a key task for future HR leaders (Evans, Pucik, & Björkman, 2011). Academics have been exploring this sphere for a long time. However, the concept and philosophy of diversity management have not been embraced by social science scholars, some of whom raised fundamental philosophical objections to the implicit assumptions of the diversity management concept for undermining the collective and solidaristic aspects of employment relations (Humphries & Grice, 1995) and for underplaying institutional and structural forms of disadvantage and discrimination in the workplace (Kersten, 2000). Yet some scholars were more cautious about creating false dichotomies and argued that diversity management does also include equality and ethical concerns (Gilbert, Stead, & Ivancevich, 1999; Tatli & Özbilgin, 2007; Tatli, 2011). While studies have identified a positive correlation between effective management of diversity and positive organizational outcomes (e.g., Barkema, Baum, & Mannix, 2002; Raatikainen, 2002), a recent meta-analysis found both positive and negative outcomes of workplace diversity (see Stahl et al., 2010a), equaling a zero net effect. This again suggests that although the potential has been well identified, the reality is somewhat different and daunting.

The business case rationale presents further challenges to the existing difficulties experienced in domestic settings. One such challenge is related to the tension between global integration and local responsiveness, as already discussed in this chapter. We sometimes have a great desire to allow context to become a decisive factor in a negative way instead of a positive way. For example, statements like, "in our industry it is different" or "in this particular country such diversity objectives are irrelevant/unachievable, are often made." In that sense, organizations may use local circumstances as excuses for having different diversity standards in different areas, leading to a "social dumping" effect. Özbilgin (2009) refers to a "tyranny of context" in cases where contextual differences are used to justify substandard diversity policies as opposed to using them in an enriching way to promote equality and inclusion. Similarly, Poster (2008) argues that different discourses in different countries (i.e., gender initiatives) are used to divert attention from overt forms of stratification and to avoid disruptions in employee relations.

Relying on the business case is imbued with potentially regressive equality and diversity outcomes for a number of reasons. First, in host countries where subsidiaries are located, antidiscrimination legislation may not be as sophisticated, and enforcement of laws and mechanisms to protect disadvantaged groups may be rather loose and weak compared to the home country. In such cases, diversity management may bring greater levels of costs than benefits. The business case is also contingent, as Noon (2007) suggests, and does not offer universal protection against discrimination (see Peng & Lin, 2008, for a similar discussion on global transfer of green management policies). In some countries, discriminatory practices may be common, socially accepted, and unquestioned. As a result, discrimination rather than diversity may make business sense. In other words, the business case depends on local labor market conditions. For example, in countries with high unemployment rates, competition for talent may offer a weak rationale. Similarly, in countries where the labor force is segregated and segmented along gender and ethnicity lines, it may be a common practice to keep the local internal workforce homogeneous. In such cultural contexts, diversity may receive resistance and diverse teams and workgroups may experience higher levels of conflict and communication problems due to the workers' lack of previous experience with such diverse scenarios. The unique challenges of persuasiveness of bottom-line rationales as drivers of diversity in the global context is largely due to the fact that the traditional business case is developed with a domestic, often Anglo-Saxon, context in mind (e.g. Johnston & Packer, 1987; Kandola & Fullerton, 1998). For that reason, a global strategy needs to be proactive and based on universal principles of equality and inclusion, and it should be enforced across all branches rather than being oriented toward locally contingent business case rationales (see Brock & Siscovick, 2007, for a discussion of maintaining basic ethical standards across subsidiaries).

The business case for diversity may be speaking the language of executives, but on its own—as a concept and a label—it is also a defeat in itself, as it has contributed to a crisis of perception regarding what diversity is all about. As Kulik and Roberson (2008) stated, the business case is not wrong but rather incomplete (cited in Dietz, Kleinlogel, & Chui, forthcoming). If the traditional business case is an inappropriate and perhaps even ineffective approach to the "selling" of workforce diversity, what, then, is a better one? What will move global organizations in the direction of increased diversity? Fundamentally there is a recognized need and trend for fairness in employment relations (Poster, 2008) and a radical *humanism* in business (Melé, 2009), as only then we will survive, flourish, and emancipate ourselves, collectively and individually (Aktouf & Holford, 2009). We must learn to relate business and society in a sensible way, and the core of our future market economy will contain rights, responsibilities, and citizenship (Steger, 2009). Thus, in a way we are seeking to civilize our economic system (Pirson et al., 2009), just as the economic system has been trying to civilize the state for the past few hundred years.

Concretely, in relation to workforce diversity and its management, we believe there are three key drivers for substantial change. The first driver is government and EU initiatives, such as quotas. This has already been put into place in some European countries, and the EU commissioner has recently stated that companies have only one last chance to get it right. The second driver is those champions who will pioneer top-down approaches. This movement has already been started by CEOs like Carlos Ghosn (Renault/Nissan), who has often advocated publicly for equality and has participated in debates, and Rene Obermann, who required a minimum of 30 percent women in middle and upper management by the end of 2015 at Deutsche Telekom. The German CEO not only speaks of competitiveness advantages but also uses the argument of social fairness. In his quest for achieving gender equality he is alert to many different kinds of social inequities, such as gender-balanced communication.

The third driver is perhaps an evolution of the old business case—the "new business case" or, preferably, rationale for diversity. Demographic changes and globalization mean that it is becoming increasingly important to increase the spectrum of employees. One reason is that the pool of "traditional" ethnic-majority male graduates is shrinking and cannot meet employers' demands in some countries, so companies need to hire from a variety of sources, such as recruiting women and employees from other countries. Another reason is that business models have dramatically changed in the past 20 years. Today's key stakeholders come from new heartlands. Their requirements and expectations are different. For example, requirements of trading partners and governments in many emerging markets (including BRIC countries) are more inclined to look at what the business can do to help improve the state and development of their nation. Technical knowledge alone is no longer enough, especially when more competition provides a larger choice. Instead, additional elements raise the game. For example, some countries in the Middle East and Africa are requiring "localization"—that is, more than 50 percent of leaders in a joint venture or subsidiary must be of national origin. In this case they bring respect and social justice into the equation of doing business.

Concluding remarks

Today, there is a wide range of alternative approaches to GDM. However, the expansion of this field of study has also brought about a level of divergence in theorization. Emergence of repertoires of GDM theory reflect the diversity of organizational forms as well as the historical and geographic contexts in which they are rooted. In this chapter we presented four models of GDM. The first model is strategic and refers to the choice of localized versus standardized GDM strategy and policy. An alternative is a transversal strategy. The second is a process model of GDM, which sets out the conditions for policies and practices of GDM as well as outcomes of effective implementation in a process format. The third model offers a contextual exposition, which reveals the layered and multifaceted influences on the choice of GDM interventions. The final model is an intervention model. Based on the four dimensions of GDM, it illustrates the range of global diversity interventions that an organization may choose.

Our database research of the articles listed in Social Science Citation Index found only six that use "global diversity management" in the title, abstract, key words, or text. This illustrates that the concept of GDM as a focus of research is yet to be established in the academic literature. We believe that as GDM grows and becomes a mature area of research, there are a number of areas that future studies need to pay specific attention to so that we can tackle the key challenges we identified in this chapter.

To start with, things are not progressing very quickly in many parts of the world, and practitioners are not helped by the fact that theory and research have been trailing behind in some areas. Diversity research has not "taken its own medicine," as it has largely been carried out by a homogeneous set of scholars. Jonsen, Schneider, and Maznevski (2011) found a low level of informational diversity in the field: heavily cited articles were from authors with only two educational backgrounds, and the field as such has been "cornered" by psychologists. This has implications for approaches and methodologies, as some areas and perspectives related to the macro-level have been underresearched, while team studies (especially laboratory studies with student samples) are overrepresented. Thus, perhaps as a consequence, we lack theoretical and empirical studies related to interventions and management of diversity at the organizational level. The key question is: *Which interventions actually work?* For example, Dietz, Kleinlogel, and Chui (forthcoming) provide thoughtful insights into how stereotypes and prejudices can lead to discrimination and intergroup conflict in organizational settings, but they also state that the literature does not provide evaluations of diversity management interventions. These authors conclude that after 20 years of diversity management research, we have advanced its science but are poorly equipped on how to inform management.

Interventions at a more holistic level are underresearched, not only at a global level but also at a local level. As pointed out earlier in this chapter, a fundamental weakness in this perspective has been an assumption of willingness to change. This is highly questionable, and Kanter's "uncertainty quotient" (1977, p. 49) may still explain a large part of the resistance, insofar as uncertainty reduction leads to conformity and homogenization. It also points to differences across borders, as national cultures have different levels of uncertainty avoidance (Hofstede, 2001). According to Thomas and Plaut (2008) there are many faces of diversity resistance in organizations, which do occur in different forms and at different levels. Therefore, there is a need to tailor global diversity programs in line with institutional and national concerns. This requires exploring societal issues as well as organizational ones. Some of the more fundamental discussions and assumptions concerning diversity in different cultural settings may simply have been suppressed or neglected. This can stem from a long period in which researchers try to explain diversity, or "sell it" as a strategic issue.

Authors such as Alvesson and Sandberg (2011) suggest more problematization methodology and reflective scholarship in an attempt to challenge the assumptions behind existing theories. There are, of course, a few exceptions. Matoba (2011) suggests the concept of a "third-culture building" approach, coming from the social constructionist view of the creative relationship between diversity and unity.

According to this perspective, diversity and unity are expressed in communication, and this communication, in turn, constructs or reconstructs diversity and unity. This view includes a commitment to leveraging human communication potential (competence) toward managing and performing the unification of diversity in organizations—that is, toward constructing and maintaining a new third culture. The resulting, constructed integration found embedded in third-culture building (unified diversity) is called bilateral integration. In such a construction process individuals from different cultures are integrated in a new hybrid culture that each of them can accept as a new part of their cultural identity. In this new culture individuals attain a new freedom: they are free to retrieve their original culture at any time, or they can get more distance from it. It is nevertheless possible and important for individuals to gain the competence to move freely and flexibly between their original cultural identity and the identity of the new culture.

One of the key barriers to increased diversity, seldom discussed specifically, is *how to engage people in power in discussions and activities that will lead to change.* In particular, how can ethnic majority men at all levels of management become change agents for diversity? Catalyst, the US based research organization, has undertaken a series of studies in this domain (e.g., Prime, Moss-Rascusin, & Foust-Cummings, 2009) and they provide relevant guidance, but this mindset has not yet penetrated organizations across the globe. Until it does, there is too much resistance from those who will encounter short-term losses if things change. It's simple math: if the total number of manager jobs is constant and current minorities in management jobs increase their numbers, then there will be fewer jobs for ethnic-majority male managers. We are not short of eloquent descriptions of how future organizations should look. For example, the chapter "The Coed Company" (Cronin & Fine, 2010) presents an inspirational vision of company cultures where gender is immaterial, integration is essential, and parity is paramount (pp. 207–236). Yet we must remember that although hope is a green blessing that we need a portion of every day, it is not a strategy. Thus, a main diversity management challenge in the global organization is to coordinate the interests among all the different groups and to facilitate a program that meets their different needs while diminishing conflicting agendas between them (cf. Dietz, Kleinlogel, & Chui, forthcoming; see also Kulik & Roberson, 2008).

A few studies (e.g., Maznevski, 1994) have shown how diverse teams can perform better when managed well, and the theoretical foundation for this claim is well known (e.g., Stahl, et al., 2010a). Other scholars, such as Ely and Thomas (2001), have contributed significantly, yet surprisingly little emphasis have been placed on researching how various managerial interventions and initiatives can positively moderate the diversity–performance relationship. Possibly this can be related to the complexity and nonlinearity of this matter, causing large corporations to apply different approaches (e.g., Dietz & Petersen, 2006) with similar results. But when managers ask what they should do to make diversity successful in their global organization, research should remain humble (and embarrassed) and ask them to offer feedback about their experiences. Or better, we should make an effort to be out there in the organizations following what goes on over time. A good example of this is the work of Aulikki Sippola and colleagues, who did an in-depth longitudinal study of a large European MNC (e.g., Sippola & Smale, 2007). They divide the design of the GDM into areas of philosophy, policies, and practices. The delivery itself was captured as "people-based integration," "information-based integration," "formalization-based integration," and "centralization-based integration." The authors concluded that the company was able to achieve global consistency at the level of diversity philosophy but had to rely more on multidomestic approaches to implementing diversity policies and practices.

Still, not many practitioners have the time or the patience to investigate what academics uncover and write about in scientific journals, but those who do may find out that the so-called business case for diversity is not as clear-cut as many advocates of diversity would like to make it. And here is a fundamental problem for global diversity: *What if there is no business case?* Does it mean that GDM is a dead duck? Pitching global diversity (and its management) only as a business case may well be the wrong path to take. First, for some companies there simply is not a business case for GDM. Major changes such as achieving effective management of equality and diversity in our global workforce and management are not made overnight by individuals, by single companies, or by governments alone. They require structural and institutional changes across all levels (micro, meso, and macro)—for example, support structures for child care, elder care, and other matters important to make a good work–family balance (e.g., changes in our schools and universities, let alone our own responsibilities as parents, friends, colleagues, spouses, and citizens). The task at hand will be to find approaches that challenge existing ways of thinking about diversity and inclusion without too blatantly undermining the people in power who are against such social progress and structural changes.

Human dignity is not being served when issues such as workplace diversity are assessed only in terms of return on investment. Was a business case ever presented for women participating in the Olympics? Was it a business case that gave Black people equal right to a seat on a bus in Alabama? Did a business case drive out apartheid in South Africa? The business-case approach may not pay off in the long run, and thus, eventually, the case may weaken the cause. As in many other aspects of business life today, the diversity "issue" is far too complex to address with a single rational approach. Looking at a spectrum of drivers and societal changes, we need to stop addressing diversity as a business case—and thereby as a choice—but rather focus on how we can make it work best. Diversity is here to stay on a global scale. We can celebrate it or hate it, but we cannot neglect it or postpone it.

First of all, we must understand GDM in action. In essence, we must start to ask the right questions, include the relevant contextual forces, and ask the right people (Jonsen et al., 2010; Özbilgin, 2010). We often refer to "experts in the field," but this can be interpreted as "desk experts" knowledgeable about an area of research, or practitioners doing it well. Both voices should be heard, and thus we need to apply a more holistic, context-dependent and cross-disciplinary approach in our quest for *scientific mindfulness*. We have learned from the literature that the theoretical progress of our field is still on the march, with a relatively small fraction focused on practical implications. Would it be too strong to state that during the past decade positivists got faultlines and asymmetry, and constructivists got intersectionality? But what did managers get? What did disadvantaged groups of employees get?

References

Acker, J. (2006). Inequality regimes: Gender, class, and race in organizations. *Gender & Society, 20*, 441–464.

Adichie, C. (2010). *The danger of a single story*. TED Talk. Available at http://www.youtube.com/watch?v=D9Ihs241zeg (accessed October 2010).

Agocs, C., & Burr, C. (1996). Employment equity, affirmative action and managing diversity: assessing the differences. *International Journal of Manpower, 17*(4–5), 30–45.

Aktouf, O., & Holford, W.D. (2009). The implications of humanism for business studies. In H. Spitzeck, M. Pirson, W. Amann, S. Khan, & E. V. Kimakowitz (Eds.), *Humanism in business* (pp. 101–122). Cambridge: Cambridge University Press.

Al Ariss, A., & Özbilgin, M. (2010). Understanding self-initiated expatriates: Career experiences of Lebanese self-initiated expatriates in France, *Thunderbird International Business Review, 52*(4), 275–285.

Alvesson, M., & Sandberg, J. (2011). Generating research questions through problematization. *Academy of Management Review, 36*(2), 247–271.

Ashby, W. R. (1956). *An introduction to cybernetics*. New York: J. Wiley.

Ashkanasy, N. M., Hartel, C. E. J., & Daus, C. S. (2002). Diversity and emotion: the new frontiers in organizational behaviour research. *Journal of Management, 28*, 307–338.

Ayub, N., & Jehn, K. A. (2010). The moderating influence of nationalism on the relationship between national diversity and conflict. *Negotiation and Conflict Management Research, 3*(3), 249–275.

Barkema, H. G., Baum, J. A. C., & Mannix, E. A. (2002). Management challenges in a new time. *Academy of Management Journal, 45*, 916–930.

Bartlett, C., & Ghoshal, S. (1989). *Managing across borders: The transnational solution*. Boston: Harvard Business School Press.

Barmes, L., & Ashtiany, S. (2003). The diversity approach to achieving equality: potential and pitfalls. *Industrial Law Journal, 32*, 274–296.

Bell, M. P. (2007). *Diversity in organizations*. Mason, OH: South-Western.

Bell, M. P., Connerley, M. L., & Cocchiara, F. (2009). The case for mandatory diversity education. *Academy of Management Learning and Education, 8*(4), 597–609.

Bellard, E., & Rüling, C.-C. (2001). *Importing diversity management: Corporate discourses in France and Germany*. Cahier de recherche de l'université de Genève, #13.

Boone, C., & Hendriks, W. (2009). Top management team diversity and firm performance: moderators of functional-background and locus-of-control diversity, *Management Science, 55*(2), 165–180.

Boxenbaum, E. (2006). Lost in translation? The making of Danish diversity management. *American Behavioral Scientist, 49*(7), 939–948.

Brickson, S. L. (2008). Re-assessing the standard: The expansive positive potential of a relational identity in diverse organizations. *Journal of Positive Psychology, 3*, 40–54.

Bridgstock, R., Lettice, F., Özbilgin, M. F., Tatli, A. (2010). Diversity management for innovation in social enterprises in the UK. *Entrepreneurship & Regional Development: An international journal, 22*(6), 557–574.

Brock, D. M., & Siscovick, I. C., (2007), Global integration and local responsiveness in multinational subsidiaries: Some strategy, structure, and human resource contingencies. *Asia Pacific Journal of Human Resources, 45*(3), 353–373.

Brunsson, N. (1982). The irrationality of action and action of rationality: Decisions, ideologies and organizational actions. *Journal of Management Studies, 19*(1), 29–44.

Bryan, A. (2010). Corporate multiculturalism, diversity management, and positive interculturalism in Irish schools and society. *Irish Educational Studies, 29*(3), 253–269.

Byrne, D. E. (1971). *The attraction paradigm*. New York: Academic Press.

Cannella, A. A., Park, J-H., & Lee, H-U. (2008). Top management team functional background diversity and firm performance: examining the roles of team member collocation and environmental uncertainty, *Academy of Management Journal, 51*(4), 768–784.

Chevrier, S. (2003). Cross-cultural management in multinational project groups. *Journal of World Business, 38,* 141–149.

Cooke, F. L., & Saini, D. S. (2010). Diversity management in India: a study of organizations in different ownership forms and industrial sectors. *Human Resource Management, 49*(3), 477–500.

Cox, T., & Beale, R. L. (1997). *Developing competency to manage diversity*. San Francisco: Berrett-Koehler Publishing.

Cox, T. H., & Blake, B. (1991). Managing cultural diversity: Implications for organizational competitiveness. *Academy of Management Executive, 5*(3), 45–56.

Cronin, L., & Fine, H. (2010). *Damned if she does, damned if she doesn't*. Amherst, NY: Prometheus Books.

D'Netto, B., & Sohal, M. S. (1999). Human resources practices and workforce diversity: an empirical assessment. *International Journal of Manpower, 20,* 530–547.

Dameron, S., & Joffre, O. (2007). The good and the bad: The impact of diversity management on cooperative relationships. *International Journal of Human Resource Management, 18*(11), 2037–2056.

Dass P., & Parker, B. (1999). Strategies for managing human diversity: from resistance to learning. *Academy of Management Executive, 13,* 68–80.

de los Reyes, P. (2000). Diversity at work: paradoxes, possibilities and problems in the Swedish discourse on diversity. *Economic and Industrial Democracy, 21,* 253–266.

Dereli, B. (Ed.) (2008). Kuresel Farklilik Yonetimi, Isgucundeki Farkliliklarin Yonetimi ["Management of Labour Diversity"]. Istanbul: Beta Kitap.

Dickens, L. (1999). Beyond the business case: a three-pronged approach to equality management. *Human Resource Management Journal, 5*(3), 45–56.

Dickens, L. (1999). Re-regulation for gender equality: from "either/or" to "both." *Industrial Relations Journal, 37,* 299–309.

Dietz, J., Kleinlogel, E. P., & Chui, C. (in press). Research on intergroup conflict: implications for diversity management. In G. K. Stahl & I. Björkman (Eds.), *Handbook of research in international human resource management* (2nd ed.). Cheltenham, UK: Edward Elgar.

Dietz, J., & Petersen, L. E. (2006). Diversity management. In G. K. Stahl & I. Björkman (Eds.), *Handbook of research in international human resource management* (pp. 223–243). Cheltenham: Edward Elgar.

DiMaggio, P. J., & Powell, W. (1983). The iron cage revisited. Institutional isomorphism and collective rationality in organizational fields. *American Sociological Review, 48,* 147–160.

Dunavant, B. M., & Heiss, B. (2005). *Global diversity 2005*. Diversity Best Practices. Washington, DC.

Egan, M. L., & Bendick Jr., M. (2003). Workforce diversity initiatives of U.S. multinational corporations in Europe. *Thunderbird International Business Review, 46,* 701–728.

Ely, R. J., & Thomas, D. A. (2001). Cultural diversity at work: the effects of diversity perspectives on work group processes and outcomes. *Administrative Science Quarterly, 46*(2), 229–273.

Erez, M., & Shokef, E. (2008). The culture of global organizations In P. Smith, M. Peterson, & D. Thomas (Eds.), *The handbook of cross-cultural management research* (pp. 285–300). Thousand Oaks, CA: Sage Publications, Inc.

Evans, P., Pucik, V., & Björkman, I. (2011). *The global challenge: international human resource management* (2nd ed.). New York: McGraw-Hill.

Ferner, A., Almond, P., & Colling, T. (2005). Institutional theory and the crossnational transfer of employment policy: The case of "workforce diversity" in US multinationals. *Journal of International Business Studies, 36*(3), 304–321.

Flood, R. L., & Romm, R. A. N. (1996). Contours diversity management and triple loop learning. *Kybernetes, 25,* 154–164.

Freeman-Evans, T. (1994). Benefiting from multiculturalism. *Association Management*, February, 52–56.

French, W. L., & Bell, C. H. (1999). *Organization development*. Upper Saddle River, NJ: Prentice-Hall.

Gilbert, J. A., & Ivancevich, J. M. (2000). Valuing diversity: A tale of two organizations. *Academy of Management Executive, 14*(1), 93–105.

Gilbert, J. A., Stead, B. A., & Ivancevich, J. M. (1999). Diversity management: A new organizational paradigm. *Journal of Business Ethics, 21,* 61–76.

Glastra, F., Meerman, M., Schedler, P., & de Vries, S. (2000). Broadening the scope of diversity management. Strategic implications in the case of the Netherlands. *Industrial Relations, 55,* 698–721.

Haq, R. (2004). International perspectives on workplace diversity. In M. Stockdale & F. Crosby (Eds.), *The psychology and management of workplace diversity* (pp. 277–298). USA and UK: Blackwell.

Harrison, D. A., Price, K. H., & Bell, M. P. (1998). Beyond relational demography: Time and the effects of the surface-and deep-level diversity on work group cohesion. *Academy of Management Journal, 41,* 96–107.

Harvey, M. G., & Buckley, M. R. (1997). Managing inpatriates: Building a global core competency. *Journal of World Business, 32,* 35–53.

Healy, G., & Oikelome, F. (2007). A global link between national diversity policies? The case of the migration of Nigerian physicians to the UK and USA. *International Journal of Human Resource Management, 18,* 1917–1933.

Hofstede, G. H. (2001). *Culture's consequences: Comparing values, behaviors, institutions, and organizations across nations* (2nd ed.). Thousand Oaks, CA: Sage Publications.

Hordes, M. W., Clancy, J. A., & Baddaley, J. (1995). A primer for global start-ups. *Academy of Management Executive, 9*(2), 7–11.

Humphries, M., & Grice, S. (1995). Equal employment opportunity and the management of diversity. *Journal of Organizational Change, 8,* 17–32.

Iles, P. (1995). Learning to work with difference. *Personnel Review, 24,* 44–60.

Jackson, S. E., Brett, J. F., Sessa, V. I., Cooper, D. M., Julin, J. A., & Peyronnin, K. (1991). Some differences make a difference: Individual dissimilarity and group heterogeneity as correlates of recruitment, promotions, and turnover. *Journal of Applied Psychology, 76*(5), 675–689.

James, E. H., & Wooten, L. P. (2001). Managing diversity. *Executive Excellence*, August, 17–18.

Janssens, M., & Zanoni, P. (2005). Many diversities for many services: theorizing diversity (management) in service companies. *Human Relations, 58,* 311–340.

Jehn, K., Northcraft, G., & Neale, M. (1999). Why differences make a difference: A field study of diversity, conflict, and performance in workgroups. *Administrative Science Quarterly, 44*(4), 741–763.

Jick, T. D., & Peiperl, M. A. (2010). *Managing change* (3rd ed.). New York: McGraw-Hill.

Johnston, W. B., & Packer, A. H. (1987). *Workforce 2000: Work and workers for the 21st century*. Washington, DC: Hudson Institute.

Jones, D., Pringle, J., & Shepherd, D. (2000). Managing diversity meets Aotearoa/New Zealand. *Personnel Review, 29*(3), 364–380.

Jonsen, K., Maznevski, M. L., & Schneider, S. C. (2010). Gender differences in leadership: believing is seeing. Implications for managing diversity. *Equality, Diversity and Inclusion, 29*(6), 549–572.

Jonsen, K., et al. (2010) (17 authors). Scientific mindfulness: a foundation for future themes in international business. In T. M. Devinney, T. Pedersen, & L. Tihanyi (Eds.), *Advances in international management: the past, present and future* (Vol. 23, pp. 43–69). New York: Emerald Publishing.

Jonsen, K. Schneider, S. C., & Maznevski, M. L. (2011). Diversity—a strategic issue? In S. Gröschl (Ed.), *Diversity in the workplace*. Stefan Ashgate, UK.

Joplin, J. R. W., & Daus, C. S. (1997). Challenges of leading a diverse workforce. *Academy of Management Executive, 11*(3), 32–47.

Joshi, A., & Roh, H. (2008). *Considering context in work team diversity research: a meta-analytic review*. Dorothy Harlow Distinguished Paper Award, Academy of Management Meeting, Anaheim, CA.

Kalonaityte, V. (2010). The case of vanishing borders: theorizing diversity management as internal border control. *Organization, 17*(1), 31–52.

Kamp, A., & Hagedorn-Rasmussen, P. (2004). Diversity management in a Danish context: towards a multicultural or segregated working life? *Economic and Industrial Democracy, 25*(4), 525–554.

Kandola, R., & Fullerton, J. (1998). *Managing the mosaic: Diversity in action* (2nd ed.). London: Institute of Personnel Development.

Kanter, R. M. (1977). *Men and women of the corporation*. New York: Basic Books.

Karabacakoğlu, F., & Özbilgin, M. (2010). Global diversity management at Ericsson: the business case. In L. Costanzo (Ed.), *Cases in strategic management*. London: McGraw-Hill.

Kelly, E., & Dobbin, F. (1998). How affirmative action became diversity management: Employer response to anti-discrimination law, 1961 to 1996. *American Behavioral Scientist, 41*, 960–984.

Kersten, A. (2000). Diversity management, dialogue, dialects and diversion. *Journal of Organizational Change Management, 13*, 235–248.

Kirby, S. L., & Richard, O. C. (2000). Impact of marketing work-place diversity on employee job involvement and organizational commitment. *Journal of Social Psychology, 140*, 367–377.

Klarsfeld, A. (2009). The diffusion of diversity management: The case of France. *Scandinavian Journal of Management, 25*, 363–373.

Klarsfeld, A. (2010). *International handbook on diversity management at work: country perspectives on diversity and equal treatment*. Cheltenham & New York: Edward Elgar.

Köppel, P., Yan, J., & Lüdicke, J. (2007). Cultural diversity management in Deutschland hinkt hinterher. Available at: www.bertelsmann-stiftung.de/cps/rde/xbcr/SID-0A000F14-5385B43A/bst/xcms_bst_Diversity managements_21374__2.pdf (Accessed 01.08.2008).

Kulik, C. T., & Roberson, L. (2008). Diversity initiative effectiveness: What organizations can (and cannot) expect from diversity recruitment, diversity training, and formal mentoring programs. In A. P. Brief (Ed.), *Diversity at work* (pp. 265–317). New York: Cambridge University Press.

Lane, H., Maznevski, M. L., Distefano, J. J., & Dietz, J. (2009). *International management behavior* (6th ed.). Chippenham, UK: Wiley.

Lau, D. C., & Murnighan, J. K. (1998). Demographic diversity and faultlines: The compositional dynamics of organizational groups. *Academy of Management Review, 23*, 325–340.

Layder, D. (1993). *New strategies in social research*. Cambridge: Polity Press.

Lewin, K. (1943). Defining the field at a given time. *Psychological Review, 50*, 292–310. Republished in *Resolving social conflicts & field theory in social science*. Washington, D.C.: American Psychological Association, 1997.

Ling, Y., Floyd, S. W., & Baldridge, D. C. (2005). Toward a model of issue-selling by subsidiary managers in multinational organizations. *Journal of International Business Studies, 36*(6), 637–654.

Lorbiecki, A., & Jack, G. (2000). Critical turns in the evolution of the diversity management. *British Journal of Management, 11*, 17–31.

Luo, Y. (2001). Determinants of local responsiveness: Perspectives from foreign subsidiaries in an emerging market. *Journal of Management, 27*(4), 451–477.

Magoshi, E., & Chang, E. (2009). Diversity management and the effects on employees' organizational commitment: evidence from Japan and Korea. *Journal of World Business, 44*(1), 31–40.

Mannix, E., & Neale, M. A. (2005). What differences make a difference: The promise and reality of diverse teams in organizations. *Psychological Science in the Public Interest, 6*(2), 31–55.

Markus, H. R., & Kitayama, S. (2003). Culture, self, and the reality of the social. *Psychological Inquiry, 14*(3), 277–283.

Martin, J., & Meyerson, D. (2008). Gender inequity and the need to study change. In D. Barry & H. Hansen (Eds.), *New approaches in management and organization* (pp. 552–553). Los Angeles: Sage.

Matoba, K. (2011). *Transformative dialogue for third culture building—Integrated constructionist approach for managing diversity*. Opladen & Farmington Hill: Budrich Unipress.

Maxwell, G., McDougall, M., Blair, S., & Masson, M. (2003). Equality at work in UK public-service and hotel organizations: Inclining towards managing diversity? *Human Resource Development International, 6*(2), 243.

Maznevski, M. L. (1994). Understanding our differences: Performance in decision-making groups with diverse members. *Human Relations, 47*(5), 531–552.

Melé, D. (2009). Current trends in humanism and business. In H. Spitzeck (Ed.), *Humanism in business* (pp. 123–140). Cambridge: Cambridge University Press.

Mor Barak, M. E. (2000). The inclusive workplace: An ecosystems approach to diversity management. *Social Work, 45*, 339–352.

Mor Barak, M. E. (2005). *Managing diversity: Toward a globally inclusive workplace*. Thousand Oaks, CA: Sage.

Nishii, L. H., & Özbilgin, M. F. (2007). Global diversity management: Towards a conceptual framework. *International Journal of Human Resource Management, 18*(11), 1883–1894

Noon, M. (2007). The fatal flaws of diversity and the business case for ethnic minorities. *Work, Employment and Society, 21*, 773–784.

Ogbonna, E., & Harris, L. C. (2002). Organizational culture. *Journal of Management Studies, 39*(5), 673–706.

Omanovic, V. (2009). Diversity and its management as a dialectical process: Encountering Sweden and the US. *Scandinavian Journal of Management, 25*, 352–362.

Ostendorp, A., & Steyaert, C. (2009). How difference can differences be(come)? Interpretative repertoires of diversity concepts in Swiss-based organizations. *Scandinavian Journal of Management, 25*, 374–384.

Özbilgin, M. (2002). The way forward for equal opportunities by sex in employment in Turkey and Britain. *International Management, 7*(1), 55–67.

Özbilgin, M. (2005). Relational methods in organization studies. In O. Kyriakidou & M. F. Özbilgin (Eds.), *Relational perspectives in organization studies* (pp. 244–264). Cheltenham: Edward Elgar Publisher.

Özbilgin, M. (Ed.) (2009). *Equality, diversity and inclusion at work*. Cheltenham and New York: Edward Elgar Press.

Özbilgin, M. (2010). Scholarship of consequence. *British Journal of Management, 21*, 1–6.

Özbilgin, M., & Syed, J. (2010). *Managing gender diversity in Asia: a research companion*. Cheltenham and New York: Edward Elgar Press.

Özbilgin, M., Syed, J., Ali, F., & Torunoglu, D. (2011). International transfer of policies and practices of gender equality in employment to and among Muslim majority countries: a study of Turkey and Pakistan. *Gender, Work and Organization*.

Özbilgin, M. F. (2008). Global diversity management. In P. Smith, M. F. Peterson, & D. C. Thomas (Eds.), *The handbook of cross-cultural management research* (pp. 379–396). London: Sage Press.

Özbilgin, M. F., Syed, J., Ali, F., & Torunoglu, D. (2012) International transfer of policies and practices of gender equality in employment to and among Muslim majority countries. *Gender, Work and Organization, 19*(4), 345–369.

Özbilgin, M. F., & Tatli, A. (2008). *Global diversity management: an evidence-based approach*. Basingstoke, UK: Palgrave.

Özbilgin, M. F., & Vassilopoulou, J. (2010). *Global talent management: the case of emerging economies*. London: Chartered Institute of Personnel and Development.

Özbilgin, M., & Tatli, A. (2011). Mapping out the field of equality and diversity: Rise of individualism and voluntarism. *Human Relations, 64*, 1229–1258.

Pelled, L. H. (1996). Demographic diversity, conflict, and work groups outcomes: An intervening process theory. *Organization Science, 7*(6), 615–631.

Peng, Y.-S., & Lin, S.-S. (2008), Local responsiveness pressure, subsidiary resources, green management adoption and subsidiary's performance: Evidence from Taiwanese manufactures. *Journal of Business Ethics, 79*(1–2), 199–212.

Pirson, M., Von Kimakowitz, E., Spitzeck, H., Aman, W., & Khan, S. (2009). Introduction: humanism in business. In H. Spitzeck (Ed.), *Humanism in business* (pp. 248–259). Cambridge: Cambridge University Press.

Poster, W. R. (2008) Filtering diversity: a global corporation struggles with race, class, and gender in employment policy. *American Behavioral Scientist, 52*, 307–341.

Powell, W. W. & DiMaggio, P. J. (Eds.) (1991). *The new institutionalism in organizational analysis*. Chicago: University of Chicago.

Prasad, P., & Mills, A. J. (1997). From showcase to shadow: understanding the dilemmas of managing workplace diversity. In P. Prasad, A. J. Mills, M. Elmes, & A. Prasad (Eds.), *Managing the organizational melting pot: Dilemmas of workforce diversity* (pp. 3–27). Thousand Oaks, CA: Sage.

Prime, J., Moss-Racusin, C., & Foust-Cummings, H. (2009). *Engaging men in gender initiatives: Stacking the deck for success*. New York: Catalyst.

Raatikainen, P. (2002). Contributions of multiculturalism to the competitive advantage of an organization. *Singapore Management Review, 24*, 81–88.

Risberg, A., & Soderberg, A. M. (2008). Translating a management concept: diversity management in Denmark. *Gender in Management, 23*, 426–441.

Roberson, Q. M. (2006). Disentangling the meanings of diversity and inclusion in organizations. *Group Organization Management, 31*(2), 212–236.

Rosenzweig, P. (1998). Managing the new global workforce: fostering diversity, forging consistency. *European Management Journal, 16*(6), 644–652.

Sandberg, J., & Tsoukas, H. (2011). Grasping the logic of practice: Theorizing through practical rationality. *Academy of Management Review, 36*(2), 338–360.

Schneider, S. C. (1989). Strategy formulation: The impact of national culture. *Organization Studies, 10*(2), 149–168.

Schneider, S. C., & Barsoux, J. (2003). *Managing across cultures*. Harlow, UK: Financial Times and Prentice Hall.

Shen, J., Chanda, A., & D'Netto, B. (2009). Managing diversity through human resource management: An international perspective and conceptual framework. *International Journal of Human Resource Management, 20*, 235–252.

Simons, G. F. (2002). *Eurodiversity: A business guide to managing difference*. Woburn: Butterworth-Heinemann.

Sippola, A., & Smale, A. (2007). The global integration of diversity management: A longitudinal case study. *International Journal of Human Resource Management, 18*(11), 1895–1916.

Stahl, G. K., Maznevski, M. L., Voigt, A., & Jonsen, K. (2010a). Unraveling the effects of cultural diversity in teams: a meta-analysis of res earch on multicultural work groups. *Journal of International Business Studies, 41*, 690–709.

Stahl, G. K., Mäkelä, K., Zander, L., & Maznevski, M. L. (2010b). A look at the bright side of multicultural team diversity. *Scandinavian Journal of Management, 26*(4), 439–447.

Steger, U. (2009). The ugly side of capitalism: What the young generation needs to combat. In H. Spitzeck (Ed.), *Humanism in business* (pp. 218–226). Cambridge: Cambridge University Press.

Stumpf, S. A., Watson, M. A., & Rustogi, H. (1994). Leadership in a global village: Creating practice fields to develop learning organizations. *Journal of Management Development, 13*, 16–25.

Subeliani, D., & Tsogas, G. (2005). Managing diversity in The Netherlands: a case study of Rabobank. *International Journal of Human Resource Management, 16*, 831–851.

Sucher, S. J., & Corsi, E. (2010). *Global diversity and inclusion at Royal Dutch Shell*. Harvard Business School, Case N2–610–056.

Suss, S., & Kleiner, M. (2008). Dissemination of diversity management in Germany: A new institutionalist approach. *European Management Journal, 26,* 35–47.

Syed, J., & Özbilgin M. (2009). A relational framework for international transfer of diversity management practices. *International Journal of Human Resource Management, 20*(12), 2435–2453.

Syed, J., Özbilgin, M., Torunoglu, D., & Ali, F. (2009). Rescuing gender equality from the false dichotomies of secularisim versus shariah in Muslim majority countries. *Women's Studies International Forum, 32*(2), 67–79.

Syed, J., & Özbilgin, M. (2010). *Managing cultural diversity in Asia: A research companion*. Cheltenham and New York: Edward Elgar Press.

Tajfel, H., & Turner, J. (1986). The social identity theory of intergroup behaviour. In S. Worchel & W. Austin (Eds.), *Psychology of intergroup relations* (pp. 7–24). Chicago: Nelson-Hall.

Tatli, A. (2011). A multi-layered exploration of the diversity management field: diversity discourses, practices and practitioners in the UK. *British Journal of Management, 22*(2), 238–253.

Tatli, A., & Özbilgin, M. (2009). Understanding diversity managers' role in organizational change: Towards a conceptual framework. *Canadian Journal of Administrative Sciences, 26*(3), 244–258.

Tatli, A., & Özbilgin, M. F. (2007). Diversity management as calling: Sorry, it's the wrong number! in I. Koall, V. Bruchhagen, & F. Höher (Eds.), *Diversity outlooks—managing diversity: zwischen ethik, business case und antidiskriminierung* (pp. 457–473).. Münster: LIT Verlag.

Thomas, D. A., & Ely, R.J. (1996). Making differences matter: A new paradigm for managing diversity. *Harvard Business Review, 74*(5), 79–90.

Thomas, K. M. (Ed.) (2008). *Diversity resistance in organizations*. New York: Lawrence Erlbaum Associates, Taylor and Francis Group.

Thomas, K. M., & Plaut, V. C. (2008). The many faces of diversity resistance in the workplace. In K. M. Thomas (Ed.), *Diversity resistance in organizations* (pp. 1–23). New York: Lawrence Erlbaum Associates, Taylor and Francis Group.

Umphress, E. E., Smith-Crowe, K., Brief, A. P., Dietz, J., & Watkins, M. B., (2007). When birds of a feather flock together and when they do not: Status composition, social dominance orientation, and organizational attractiveness. *Journal of Applied Psychology, 92*(2), 396–409.

Vassilopoulou, J. (2011). *Understanding the habitus of managing ethnic diversity in Germany. A multilevel relational study*. University of East Anglia, Norwich.

Webber, S. S., & Donahue, L. M. (2001). Impact of highly and less job-related diversity on work groups cohesion and performance: A meta-analysis. *Journal of Management, 27,* 141–162.

Wentling, R. M., & Palma-Rivas, N. (2000). Current status of diversity initiatives in selected multinational corporations. *Human Resource Development Quarterly, 11*(1), 35–60.

Winter, S., & Szulanski, G. (2001). Replication as strategy. *Organization Science, 12*(6), 730–743.

Wrench, J. (2005). Diversity management can be bad for you. *Race and Class, 46*(3), 73–84.

Wright, P., Ferris, S. P., Hiller, J. S., & Kroll, M. (1995). Competitiveness through management of diversity: Effects on stock price valuation. *Academy of Management Journal, 38*(1), 272–287.

Zanoni, P., & Janssens, M. (2004). Deconstructing difference: the rhetoric of human resource managers' diversity discourses. *Organization Studies, 25,* 55–74.

Zanoni, P., & Janssens, M. (2007). Minority employees engaging with (diversity) management: an analysis of control, agency and micro-emancipation. *Journal of Management Studies, 44,* 1371–1397.

CHAPTER 23

Law and Diversity: The Legal–Behavioral Science Divide in How to Define, Assess, and Counteract Bias

Evan P. Apfelbaum *and* Samuel R. Sommers

Abstract

Behavioral sciences and the law tend to approach issues of diversity from markedly different perspectives. The present chapter focuses on this divergence as it relates to the controversial issues of defining, assessing, and remedying racial bias. Our objective is not to offer a value judgment regarding the relative utility of either the legal or behavioral science perspective on bias, but rather to illuminate in balanced fashion the landscape of this institutional divide. For each of the three critical areas of divergence identified—how bias is defined, how bias is assessed, and how bias is remedied—we review seminal cases and standard legal practices alongside contemporary behavioral science research that offers a counterpoint to this perspective. We conclude with considerations for future work to bridge the legal–behavioral science divide.

Key Words: diversity, law, racial bias, employment discrimination, legal psychology

Not long ago, in a courtroom in the northeastern United States, the defense team in a capital murder trial assembled a diverse panel of experts to testify in a pretrial hearing. At issue was a motion to bar the death penalty in light of empirical evidence that death sentences in the United States are disproportionately handed down to Black defendants convicted of murdering White victims. Not only did the case in question involve a Black defendant accused of killing a White man, but it also took place in a state that had not executed anyone in more than half a century—a fact that, according to the defense, confirmed that capital punishment was not being applied in the unbiased, consistent manner required by Supreme Court precedent.

Testifying in the hearing were researchers representing a range of disciplines, including criminology, law, sociology, and psychology. Some expert witnesses described the results of archival analysis of actual trials spanning multiple U.S. jurisdictions—analyses that have demonstrated that cases are significantly more likely to end in death sentences when the defendant is Black and the victim is White (e.g., Baldus, Pulaski, & Woodworth, 1983; Baldus, Woodworth, Grosso, & Christ, 2002; Baldus, Woodworth, Zuckerman, Weiner, & Broffitt, 1998). Other researchers testified about the Capital Jury Project's interview studies with former jurors in death penalty cases, which have indicated, among other findings, that in deciding on a sentence, White jurors give less weight to mitigating factors when the defendant is Black versus White (e.g., Bowers & Foglia, 2003; Bowers, Steiner, & Sandys, 2001). And experimental psychologists—including the second author of this chapter—discussed mock juror simulations that identify the causal impact of race on jurors' perceptions and decision processes (e.g., Mitchell, Haw, Pfeifer, & Meissner, 2005; Sommers, 2007).

Taken together, this body of empirical findings derived from varied methodologies and researchers converged on a clear conclusion: The subset of capital cases involving a Black defendant and White victim were significantly more likely to end with a death sentence than other cases. This, of course, is quite the problematic conclusion for a system predicated on colorblindness and equal justice for all. Nonetheless, the trial judge remained unswayed by the mountain of empirical evidence attesting to this increased risk factor for bias. She denied the defense's motion, allowing the State to proceed with its pursuit of the death penalty, and, ultimately, the jury sentenced the defendant to death.

The purpose of this chapter is not to question whether the outcome of this motion was warranted, but rather to ask the broader question of why, in cases like this one, it is often true that even the most clear-cut empirical and theoretical conclusions offered by behavioral science fail to be persuasive in the eyes of the legal system. The answer in this trial—as evident in the judge's ruling and the questions she asked of the experts during the hearing—is that the scientific literature was discounted because it did not offer a definitive conclusion that bias was going to occur *in this particular case*. Indeed, other challenges to the death penalty on similar grounds have met a similar fate. For example, consider the U.S. Supreme Court's ruling in *McCleskey v. Kemp* (1987), in which the majority cited comparable concerns regarding the applicability of general research findings to the particulars of an individual case: "[the defendant] offers no evidence specific to his own case that would support an inference that racial considerations played a part in his sentence" (p. 279). The Court majority also cited the defendant's inability to "prove that the decision-makers in his case acted with discriminatory purpose" (p. 279).

Cases like these—in which behavioral scientists express confidence in the convergent reliability of empirical findings regarding racial bias, but courts fail to determine that actionable bias has occurred (or will occur) in a particular instance—are not uncommon. And they illustrate an undeniable reality, namely that behavioral science and the law approach issues regarding diversity from markedly different perspectives. There are undoubtedly a wide range of diversity-related questions that can be considered in terms of this apparent divergence, including, for instance, the assumptions that behavioral science and legal perspectives make about the effects of diversity on group performance, or questions of how organizations and institutions can best recruit and retain a diverse workforce. In the present chapter, though, we have elected to investigate a particularly important and divisive set of issues: how bias is conceived of, assessed, and remedied in behavioral science versus legal circles.

We target this specific set of issues for two central reasons. First, the gulf between legal and scientific perspectives is readily identifiable when it comes to these matters of bias in a way that makes it possible to delineate the basic logic and considerations driving these approaches to diversity. Second, issues of bias are of distinctive social, legal, and historical consequence in the United States. One need not look further than the jarring disparities that remain in hiring decisions, health outcomes, academic achievement, or criminal sentencing (e.g., Bertrand & Mullainathan, 2004; Krueger, Rothstein, & Turner, 2006; Spohn, 2000; Williams, 1999) to grasp the moral imperative of effectively addressing enduring forms of discrimination. And while both behavioral science and legal circles share a belief in the practical significance of eradicating bias, little consensus appears to exist in how to go about doing this, let alone how to define bias.

The objective of this chapter is to pinpoint key distinctions in the way these two camps conceptualize and treat bias, but not to make claims regarding which view of bias is "right" or "better." It is clear that legal institutions and behavioral scientists think of bias in different terms because they approach issues of human behavioral tendency from different angles with fundamentally different purposes. Generally speaking, legal entities focus on enforcing rules and determining culpability under a particular set of circumstances, whereas behavioral scientists focus more on discerning general patterns of human nature and less on predicting or assessing behavior in any single instance. So, for example, a behavioral scientist may be concerned with the question of what contextual factors render discrimination more likely in organizational settings. But even if research were to produce clear evidence that organizations with a particular incentive system or personnel structure were more likely to foster workplace discrimination, such evidence may be seen within legal circles as having little impact on the effort to adjudicate the particulars involved in any given discrimination lawsuit.

In short, our goal in the present chapter is not to offer a value judgment regarding the relative utility of either legal or behavioral science perspectives on bias, but rather to offer a balanced review of the central differences between these perspectives. We do so through a focus on three critical areas of divergence: how bias is defined, how it is assessed, and how it is counteracted.

How do we define bias?

At the foundation of the legal–behavioral science divide is the critical issue of how bias should be conceived of—that is, how do we define bias? As it turns out, the simplicity of this question belies the complexity of its answer. Both legal and behavioral science perspectives have long recognized lay conceptions of bias in which a single actor or group deliberately and openly perpetrates an observable form of prejudice. Consistent with this thinking, the longstanding tradition in legal circles has been to regard bias as a purposeful, plainly recognizable phenomenon.

Yet research developments over the past two decades by behavioral scientists have led the field to gradually move beyond this traditional conceptualization to a more expansive definition that includes subtler and less purposeful forms of prejudice (for reviews, see Blascovich & Mendes, 2010; Dovidio & Gaertner, 2010; Fazio & Olsen, 2003). Thus, in the present day, it is often the case that the legal system and behavioral scientists come to divergent conclusions regarding what constitutes bias, particularly when it comes to actions that do not fit squarely into the classic conceptualization of discrimination that draws on wholly conscious and deliberative processes. Here, we take a closer look at two central sticking points in the legal–behavioral science debate over what bias is: the degree to which actions are intentional and are explicit. We address these factors separately because they carry distinct implications for interpreting acts in the legal system, although they are not mutually exclusive characterizations of behavior in either arena.

Intentionality

One key point of departure between legal and behavioral science perspectives on bias is the issue of intentionality, and namely the question of whether actions must be deliberate to be considered discriminatory. Consider that a White manager's tendency to promote White rather than Black employees may or may not be intentional. If it is intentional, and can be corroborated by the proverbial "smoking gun" evidence (e.g., a recorded conversation in which the manager acknowledges that race has influenced his promotion decisions), then the determination of bias is straightforward. But in the absence of such overt, observable signs that the manager's pattern of offering promotions was motivated by race, what do we make of his behavior?

Behavioral scientists might determine the manager's practices to be biased even if he was not fully aware of his predisposition to promote White individuals. This is because researchers have increasingly turned to conceptualizations of bias that include less intentional, even nonconscious components. The assertion that biases may surface without intentionality or awareness may seem like a puzzling, if not dubious claim to some: unintentional biases are not generally discernable using the sort of methodologies that most nonresearchers would think of (e.g., attitude surveys), nor are they typically evident upon simple introspection. However, a host of recent investigations relying on clever alternatives to these measures (e.g., response-latency tasks, word completion and attribution exercises) confirm that such biases are real and prevalent and can predict important real-world outcomes. In response to these developments, the contemporary behavioral science perspective has expanded its interpretation of what bias is, no longer relying on the assumption that intentionality is a precondition for its existence. This conceptualization has been driven by empirical evidence demonstrating that individuals may unknowingly harbor racial preferences or associations that develop from a very early age and are perpetuated through various, seemingly innocuous socialization processes—biases that often show little relationship to their more explicit counterparts (Hofmann, Gawronski, Gschwendner, Le, & Schmitt, 2005).

For instance, some research examining the impact of media exposure has shown that simply viewing popular television programs can have the unforeseen consequence of fueling biases that conform to stereotypical depictions of Blacks (Weisbuch, Pauker, & Ambady, 2009). Importantly, accordingly to behavioral scientists, these biases can (and do) shape judgment and behavior despite the best intentions of those individuals who possess them. Consider that researchers who conduct experiments involving police shooting simulations have consistently found that Whites are significantly faster to pull the trigger when faced with a Black versus White target—an effect that persists even among police officers, but one that is not typically predicted by an individual respondent's level of personal prejudice or race-based animus (Correll, Park, Judd, & Wittenbrink, 2002; Correll, Park, Judd, Wittenbrink, Sadler, & Keesee, 2007).

Research findings like these demonstrate that individuals may exhibit bias in ways of which they are not fully aware or cannot easily recognize upon introspection. An individual exhibiting this sort of response, for example, may be characterized by a behavioral scientist as possessing a relatively high degree of unintentional, implicit racial bias, but a relatively low level (or the absence of) intentional, explicit bias. Behavioral scientists tend to describe the potential for such divergent preferences using a "dual-process" theoretical framework, which characterizes explicit and implicit processes as separate components (see Chaiken & Trope, 1999). In doing so, behavioral science separates intentionality as a precondition to more subtle forms of bias. From this perspective, that individuals often fail to recognize their susceptibility to bias or do not intend to fall victim to such tendencies does not necessarily render their actions less biased. But in the view of the legal system, asserting a lack of intentionality or awareness has traditionally placed such acts outside the boundaries of actionable bias.

For example, in *Washington v. Davis* (1976), the U.S. Supreme Court ruled against two Black men who claimed that their applications to become police officers in Washington D.C. had been denied in discriminatory fashion. The litigants had argued that the written personnel test used by the department was unfair given that its reliability had never been established, its relationship to job performance was tenuous, and a disproportionate number of Black applicants failed it. The Court majority dismissed these arguments, ruling that "Though the Due Process Clause of the Fifth Amendment contains an equal protection component prohibiting the Government from invidious discrimination, it does not follow that a law or other official act is unconstitutional solely because it has a racially disproportionate impact regardless of whether it reflects a racially discriminatory purpose" (p. 230). In other words, absent intent, there is no actionable discrimination; disparate impact need not be seen as evidence of discriminatory policy or behavior.

This definition of bias as requiring intentional discrimination can be observed in more recent cases as well (see Shin, 2010). Consider Justice Sandra Day O'Connor's unequivocal statement to this effect in a 2000 Supreme Court ruling: "The ultimate question in every employment discrimination case involving a claim of disparate treatment is whether the plaintiff was the victim of intentional discrimination" (*Reeves v. Sanderson Plumbing*, 2000, p. 153). The implications of this traditional legal view of bias are straightforward: the precondition of intentionality makes allegations of discrimination far more difficult to prove in the legal context, as determining intent in any given instance—particularly when the actors in question are unaware of or unwilling to admit to many of the influences on their behavior—is challenging to say the least.

At the same time, in recent decades some signs of an evolving legal conceptualization of bias have begun to emerge. For example, some Supreme Court opinions—often written in dissent—have included language that references the emerging prevalence of unconscious forms of bias:

> "Constitutional redress to racial discrimination has resulted primarily from judicial vigilance directed toward correcting overt and facially discriminatory legislation... toward blacks and other ethnic minorities. Remaining still is a more pernicious, albeit intangible, form of race discrimination in the individual's unconscious thoughts that influences the decision making process. As a result, individuals... ubiquitously attach a significance to race that is irrational and often used outside their awareness." *McCleskey v. Kemp,* 481 U.S. 279, 322, 95 L. Ed. 2d 262, 107 S. Ct. 1756 (1987) (Brennan, J. dissenting)

Overall, though, such changes in legal conceptions of bias have not been nearly as widespread or rapid as they have been in the behavioral sciences.

Explicitness

Related to the issue of intentionality is a second major point of divergence between legal and behavioral science conceptions of bias: the explicitness of the bias in question. This issue revolves around the question of whether actions must be overt and unambiguous to be considered discriminatory. As with issues of intentionality, there is clear consensus between the law and behavioral sciences when it comes to diagnosing bias in cases involving blatant acts of prejudice or explicit preference for members of one group over another. Consider, again, the example of a White manager's tendency to promote White versus Black employees. If a manager's behavior is egregiously inequitable (e.g., evidence indicating that the manager has never promoted a qualified Black employee despite countless opportunities to do so), then the determination of bias is plain and simple. But when observable markers of racial bias are subtler and ambiguous, the gulf between legal and behavioral science approaches to bias comes to light.

Admittedly, one may ask how frequently bias actually presents itself in clear-cut, prototypical terms. Surely, many individuals and institutions have come to think about racial bias through the lens of its most explicit instantiations (Sommers & Norton, 2006), colored by historical imagery of slavery in the United States, lynch mobs, segregated washrooms, and blatantly racist epithets. These events undoubtedly are invaluable to comprehending the sordid racial legacy of the United States, and they likely help crystallize the most overt forms of prejudice. However, they do not accurately capture the full range of forms in which racial bias can and does manifest in present-day society. For a variety of reasons, contemporary individuals—even ones harboring overtly racist attitudes—are far less likely to express their views in such outwardly identifiable forms. The emergence of powerful social norms that condemn overt prejudice has left some individuals who privately endorse bias to publicly deny such influences or to rationalize biased decisions with race-neutral justifications that support the same stance (Crandall, Eshleman, & O'Brien, 2002; Dovidio & Gaertner, 2004; Gaertner & Dovidio, 1986; Plant & Devine, 1998; Swim, Aiken, Hall, & Hunter, 1995). Such efforts allow bias to persist in ways that often are not easily detected (e.g., Norton, Vandello, & Darley, 2004; Sommers & Norton, 2008).

For example, people are remarkably good at coming up with neutral explanations to justify judgments that have been influenced by race. In one series of studies, Norton and colleagues (2004) presented White participants with information about two college applicants in which race was manipulated. When asked whom they would admit, respondents overwhelmingly selected the Black applicant, consistent with a motivation to appear unbiased. But in explaining these decisions, participants rarely mentioned race. Instead, when the Black applicant had the higher grade-point average, participants rated grades as most important. When the Black applicant had lower grades but more Advanced Placement classes than the White applicant, the number of advanced classes was described as more important. The ease with which people are able to generate such neutral explanations impedes identification of the influence of race on a wide range of judgments.

Illustrative of this shift in social conventions regarding issues of race are the measures used by contemporary behavioral scientists to assess its impact. Studies seeking to gauge bias are often no longer wholly reliant on the sort of self-report survey items that characterized the research of previous generations. Researchers have increasingly supplemented these methods with more indirect and less reactive indicators of bias, such as reaction time, physiological responses, nonverbal behavior, and desire for proximity (e.g., Amodio, Harmon-Jones, & Devine, 2003; Fazio, Jackson, Dunton, & Williams, 1995; Goff, Steele, & Davies, 2008; Greenwald, McGhee, & Schwartz, 1998; Mendes, Blascovich, Hunter, Lickel, & Jost, 2007).

Traditional legal conceptualizations of bias, on the other hand, tend to be more direct and straightforward. As alluded to above, employment discrimination lawsuits have historically hinged on the question of direct, "smoking gun" evidence in the determination of bias. For example, in its review of Ann Hopkins' (ultimately successful) gender bias claim against the accounting firm in *Price Waterhouse v. Hopkins* (1989), a plurality of Supreme Court justices based its opinion on the determination that Hopkins had "presented direct evidence that the employer placed substantial, though unquantifiable, reliance on a forbidden factor in making an employment decision" (p. 230).

At the same time, *Price Waterhouse v. Hopkins* (1989) was noteworthy in that it marked a departure from the traditional adjudication of discrimination claims. The ruling was the first time that the Court had determined that an employer could be found to have discriminated as long as it had taken an illegal criterion (such as race or gender) into account, even if other, legitimate factors had also influenced the employment action. Specifically, while the concerns that Price Waterhouse management had regarding Ann Hopkins' interpersonal style were legitimate under the law, the justices determined that she would not have been treated the same way (i.e., not promoted) had she been male. The *Price Waterhouse* case introduced the notion of "mixed-motives" discrimination, a concept that has been refined in subsequent rulings (see *Desert Palace v. Costa*, 2003; Norton, Sommers, Vandello, & Darley, 2006). This recent acknowledgment that employment decisions can be multiply (and simultaneously) determined by both legitimate and illegitimate factors—that discrimination is *not* always explicit and blatant—suggests the emergence of a more nuanced legal view of bias.

Differences in how bias is defined in legal and behavioral science circles can also be seen outside the realm of discrimination law. Consider, for example, how the legal system handles the question of the impact of race on the selection of juries. During jury selection, litigants are granted some say as to who sits in judgment of their case, principally through the use of peremptory challenges. Via peremptory challenges, a litigant may remove from the jury prospective jurors without providing any explanation. The only restrictions on peremptory use are that these challenges may not be used to exclude prospective jurors on the basis of their race or gender.

In the wake of a 1986 ruling reiterating this prohibition on race-based peremptories (*Batson v. Kentucky*), courts adopted a three-step procedure for investigating potential violations of the rule. First, the opposing attorney must make a *prima facie* case that the peremptory was based on the prospective juror's race, establishing at least a reasonable likelihood that such bias occurred. Second, the attorney in question must respond to this *Batson* challenge by providing a race-neutral explanation for the peremptory (or peremptories) in question. Third, the judge must make a determination as to whether the peremptory was, indeed, based on race (for more details, see Sommers & Norton, 2008). In short, enforcement of the *Batson* ruling and its progeny typically hinges on the self-reported responses given by attorneys to judicial questions regarding the impact of race. In other words, the very type of self-report measures that many behavioral scientists have abandoned in their empirical study of contemporary racial bias lies at the heart of the legal system's current definition of (and efforts to prevent) racial discrimination in jury selection.

In contemporary society at large, considerable confusion and controversy tends to surround questions of whether or not a particular ambiguous event constitutes racial bias. Therein lies the clear appeal of the perspective that discrimination is a strictly overt, transparent phenomenon: defining bias in explicit terms makes classifying—or refuting—bias straightforward. Moreover, for those individuals concerned with being labeled a "racist," living in a world that limits conceptions of bias to plainly observable actions makes for a considerably less stressful experience when it comes to dealing with issues of race (Sommers & Norton, 2006). Of course, the rewards of increased clarity may sometimes be outweighed by the risks of overlooking subtle forms of bias that fall outside the boundaries of traditional legal definitions.

Take, for example, the controversy surrounding the Support Our Law Enforcement and Safe Neighborhoods Act, recently passed into Arizona legislation. The stated goal of this law is to combat illegal immigration by requiring law enforcement officials to verify individuals' immigration status when there is reasonable suspicion of illegal entry into the United States. The prospect that such decisions would be susceptible to racial bias on the part of law enforcement was ostensibly addressed by the insertion of explicit language indicating that such determinations should not be made based on an individual's race. While such instructions offer straightforward parameters for compliance, in the absence of any other measures taken (e.g., assessment of policing behavior and outcomes for interactions involving Latino vs. non-Latino suspects), a behavioral science perspective would suggest that such admonishment is likely to fall short of addressing potential bias in the implementation of this law. Indeed, these explicit guidelines seem helpful only to the extent that law enforcement officials who *do* engage in racial profiling are willing to openly acknowledge as much when asked about the basis for their actions. Given the powerful social conventions proscribing overt bias in society, this prohibition against considering race and ethnicity in the enforcement of new immigration law—much like the prohibitions on race-based peremptory challenges reviewed above—seems less likely to influence actual behavior and more likely to inflate the perceived importance of ostensibly race-neutral explanations provided by police to justify their actions.

Summary

As illustrated throughout this section and in the example with which we began this chapter, the legal perspective on bias traditionally focuses on intentional, overt, and observable discrimination. This narrow view of bias is considerably more concrete and easier to enforce than the view that has emerged in the behavioral sciences. In behavioral scientific circles, by comparison, bias is often conceived of as manifesting in forms that are not wholly intentional or readily observable, and therefore much more difficult to identify conclusively. In this model, bias can be described as either conscious or nonconscious, overt or subtle, and explicit or implicit. Whereas it is true that legal conceptions of bias have begun in recent years to include some of these empirically driven behavioral science perspectives, the evolution of the legal perspective on discrimination has moved at a slower pace than it has in behavioral science circles.

How do we assess bias?

Among the most passionately debated issues surrounding the legal–behavioral science divide is the question of how bias ought to be assessed or measured. As alluded to above, the divergent approaches to this particular issue encapsulate one of the most challenging aspects of reconciling these two schools of thought: Because the legal system and the field of behavioral science seek to reveal bias for fundamentally different reasons, so, too, do their standard procedures for doing so differ.

Let us return, for instance, to the death penalty hearing described at the opening of this chapter, homing in on the differential methods by which behavioral scientists and legal professionals approached the task of assessing the potential for juror bias. The expert witnesses from the behavioral sciences described a wealth of empirical links between defendant and victim race in capital trial cases in making the argument that having a Black defendant and a White victim at trial significantly increases the likelihood of a death sentence. The evidence these scientists reported was neither based on subjective opinion nor idiosyncratic to one research method or laboratory. Rather, it consisted of a robust and converging pattern of results that was reflected in data collected from thousands of participants, across an assortment of study types, and independently corroborated by researchers unaffiliated with one another.

For example, David Baldus and colleagues (1983) examined over 2,000 capital trials from Georgia during the 1970s and found that race was a significant predictor of final outcome. Of the cases they examined, 3 percent involving a White defendant accused of killing a Black victim ended with a death sentence, and among Black defendants charged with killing a Black victim, a similarly low rate—just over 1 percent—were sentenced to death. These numbers looked very different when the victim was White, however. Among White defendants accused of killing a White victim, 8 percent were sentenced to die. For Black defendants with a White victim, the rate climbed to 21 percent. Such disparities persisted even after controlling for scores of nonracial differences between cases, and they are not confined to a particular state or time period, either: years later, Baldus examined death penalty cases in Philadelphia and came to similar conclusions (Baldus et al., 1998; see also Gross & Mauro, 1984; Paternoster, 1984).

But in the eyes of the trial judge in our opening example, these empirical data fell short of demonstrating bias because they could not conclusively predict whether or not it would occur in *this particular case*. Her ruling demonstrates the very real potential for evidence that meets the gold standard of statistical reliability and validity within the world of behavioral science to be viewed as ineffectual when transposed to a legal setting. In many respects, the legal system traditionally seeks a definitive answer when assessing bias that is antithetical to the most basic assumptions of the scientific approach, as behavioral scientists are rarely in the position to offer conclusions of certainty when it comes to the basis for a single data point.

The fact is that behavioral scientists are not typically driven by the goal of making ironclad predictions for individual cases. The scientific approach draws its strength from its ability to test the likelihood of generating one potential outcome (e.g., that jurors will hand down a death sentence) compared to any of a number of control conditions. These comparisons illuminate reliable and important biases that emerge over many observations, but they typically only go as far as to inform predictions about the probability of finding a similar outcome in the future. And therein lies the perception in some legal circles that this type of conclusion carries limited value.

Indeed, for individuals not familiar with the probabilistic assumptions inherent to the sciences, it is easy to see why the language behavioral scientists use to describe their conclusions often seems frustratingly vague or tentative. Even with the strongest of statistical tendencies, behavioral scientists will rarely use language more definitive than "significantly increases the likelihood" or "demonstrates a strong tendency." Such statements do not necessarily connote a lack of conviction, but rather the acknowledgment that human judgment and behavior are multiply determined outcomes, and that there is always unexplained variance or "noise" in a set of results. Even with clear support for a prediction, it is empirically inaccurate to claim that a single variable will operate in the same manner for every person across situations. As a result, it is often difficult for behavioral scientists to make the sort of assertions that the legal system seeks and values. This is true not only for isolated incidents of bias, but also for cases that seek to demonstrate a pattern of bias (e.g., class-action lawsuits).

For example, consider the 2005 class-action lawsuit filed against Merrill Lynch, a prominent financial management company, for allegedly engaging in systematic racial discrimination against Black financial advisors (*McReynolds v. Merrill Lynch*, 2005). At issue was the question of whether company-wide discrimination was to blame for the allegation that White financial advisors were hired, promoted, and compensated at disproportionate rates compared to Black financial advisors. A series of aggregate data analyses conducted by behavioral scientists clearly documented such race-based disparities: Black advisors were considerably less likely to be hired, and those who were hired were paid less and tended to be promoted into senior positions less frequently than their White counterparts (e.g., Bielby, 2008). Additional evidence revealed the infrequency with which Black advisors were included in organizational teams of advisors—teams that carried crucial benefits to their members, including the prospect of inheriting lucrative accounts from senior members.

Yet despite the preponderance of data consistent with discriminatory practices, and the scarcity of comparable evidence to support alternative explanations, the judge presiding over the case denied class-action status, siding with Merrill Lynch. Of note, the judge stated that

> "although statistical evidence may be a useful tool to prove discrimination, it is rarely sufficient in itself... Because plaintiffs' statistical evidence alone is insufficient to establish company-wide discrimination in a manner that affects each class member in the same way, each individual putative class member's claim for liability and damages will have to be tried to a jury." (*McReynolds et al. v. Merrill Lynch, Pierce, Fenner & Smith Inc*, U.S. District Court, Northern District of Illinois (2005), No. 05–06583)

Returning to the issue of race and jury selection, cases in this domain also illustrate the gulf that often exists between behavioral science's emphasis on aggregated data and the legal system's focus on the particular case at hand. Consider the most direct Supreme Court predecessor of the *Batson v. Kentucky* (1986) case reviewed above: the matter of *Swain v. Alabama* (1965). In *Swain*, the Court majority ruled that a systematic effort to remove from a jury selection panel prospective jurors of a particular racial group would violate the Constitutional rights of these individuals. While this ruling seems to indicate an acknowledgement that discrimination is often best assessed in the aggregate, in practice it remained nearly impossible to convince the Court that such systematic bias had occurred. In *Swain*, for instance, the Court majority was apparently unswayed by the fact that no African-American had gotten through jury selection and been empanelled as a criminal juror in Talladega County over the previous 15 years, even though the Black population rate of the region surpassed 25 percent.

Even in the wake of *Batson*'s more attainable standard for demonstrating racial bias in jury selection, efforts to identify such bias continue to focus primarily on close scrutiny of the details surrounding the case in question. Consider the more recent case of *Miller-El v. Dretke* (2005), in which the Supreme Court opinion provides an example of such careful analysis for the questioning of Billy Jean Fields, a Black prospective juror ultimately challenged by the prosecution. During jury selection, Fields expressed support for capital punishment, explaining that he thinks the government acts on God's behalf when it carries out the death penalty. Asked to justify his removal of Fields from the jury, the prosecutor expressed concerns about the prospective juror's religious attitudes and death penalty beliefs, and especially "the comment that any person could be rehabilitated if they find God." This explanation not only mischaracterizes Fields' statement but was also difficult to reconcile with the fact that several Whites who went unchallenged had expressed precisely such an ambivalent attitude toward rehabilitation.

Of course, pinpointing the existence of bias in any one instance or judgment is next to impossible—the decisions being made are subjective and the evidence on which they are based is ambiguous. Indeed, parsing the questions and answers from one jury selection *voir dire* can also produce support for the opposite conclusion: in this instance, the notion that the peremptory challenge used to remove Fields from the jury was not based on race. In his dissenting opinion in *Miller-El*, Justice Clarence Thomas suggested that the challenge was more ambiguous than first glance indicates. Using other excerpts, Thomas argued that Fields was, in many respects, an undesirable juror for the prosecution. His dissenting opinion also cited other factors—such as at what point during the *voir dire* each juror was questioned—as race-neutral considerations that could have been influential. To the extent that the competing *Miller-El* opinions offer a firm conclusion, it seems to be that peremptories are based on criteria too subjective to allow for definitive evidence that race has biased any one challenge in particular.

Taken together, cases like the ones described above demonstrate the general tendency for probabilistic evidence of racial bias gleaned from aggregated analyses to be viewed as less compelling and persuasive in legal circles than in the behavioral sciences. But while beliefs about the limited value of statistical evidence endure among many individuals in the legal system, recent legislation also signals growing interest in a more inclusive stance.

Consider, as one such example, the North Carolina Racial Justice Act signed into law in 2009. The law gives defendants facing the death penalty the right to present evidence—including statistics—that suggests that racial bias influenced their sentence or charges. Such statistical assessments may be used as a means to establish, among other biased practices, that "Death sentences were sought or imposed significantly more frequently upon persons of one race than upon persons of another race" (Senate Bill 461, Section 1, § 15A-2011). Should prospective defendants substantiate their claims of discrimination, their death sentences will be converted to life imprisonment without the possibility of parole.

The recently passed Fair Sentencing Act of 2010, which addressed the sentencing disparity for individuals arrested with crack versus powder cocaine, is similarly indicative of the increased impact of indirect, probabilistic depictions of racial bias. Prior to this law, the Anti-Drug Abuse Act of 1986 stipulated a mandatory 5-year prison sentence for individuals arrested with just 5 grams of crack cocaine, and a 10-year sentence for possessing 10 grams. When it came to powder cocaine, on the other hand, to receive prison sentences of the same severity, an individual would have to be caught with *500* and *1,000* grams, respectively—or literally 100 times the quantity required for crack. In the years following 1986, it became increasingly clear that this sentencing disparity was having a disproportionate impact on African-Americans. According to the Drug Enforcement Administration's 2005 records, 77 percent of the people arrested with crack cocaine were Black and a mere 10 percent were White; Blacks made up less than 29 percent of powder cocaine arrests (Bureau of Justice Statistics, 2005). With the Fair Sentencing Act of 2010, this disparity has finally been addressed. Under the new law, the crack-to-powder cocaine sentencing disparity has been reduced from 100-to-1 to 18-to-1 and the minimum threshold of crack possession that warrants a felony has been raised from 5 grams to 28 grams.

Summary

The historical divide in how bias is measured in the legal system and behavioral sciences has been shaped in large part by the different objectives driving each school of thought. In the legal system, the most central concern is usually the question of whether actionable bias has occurred or will occur in the specific case in question. In contrast, the primary impetus of behavioral science research is to determine whether bias is significantly more likely to emerge given the nature and context of the case at hand and its similarity to a sample of previous cases. As such, probabilistic assessments of bias—even when quite strong—tend to be far less persuasive to individuals in legal system than they are to behavioral scientists, a conclusion that poses serious challenges to behavioral science researchers who seek to apply their discipline's theory and method to the study of such issues.

How do we counteract bias?

That the legal system and behavioral sciences often take divergent approaches to defining and assessing racial discrimination carries implications for the measures taken by each to eradicate bias. Here, we begin by discussing standard practices that aim to remedy localized sources of bias in individual and group behavior, including efforts geared toward ensuring impartiality during procedural aspects of a given trial (e.g., jury selection and decision making). We then shift our attention to broader ideological and institutional differences amid the legal–behavioral science divide that are apparent in the overarching strategies taken to reduce bias and inequity.

Consistent with our focus throughout this chapter, we spotlight instances in which normative approaches in the legal system are at odds with conclusions offered by behavioral science research. One conclusion that becomes particularly clear when reviewing this content area is that behavioral scientists are more adept at identifying limitations of legal approaches to this issue and are less proficient at providing workable alternatives to these practices. We intend, however, for our discussion to direct attention to specific content areas in which legal standards and behavioral science diverge most dramatically—areas warranting priority in any broader effort to bridge the legal–behavioral science divide.

Individual- and group-based approaches to counteracting bias

How is racial bias typically counteracted in legal circles? Consider, once again, the illustrative example provided by jury selection. While there are several factors that may contribute to the relatively low percentage of racial minorities summonsed for jury service in the first place—perhaps the earliest phase at which systemic bias can infiltrate legal proceedings (see Sommers, 2008)—we begin by examining how the pool of potential jurors, already in the courtroom, are typically screened for bias via *voir dire*. At this stage of jury selection, the judge typically describes to the assembled panel of prospective jurors the nature of the current charges. So, for example, a judge may state that the purpose of the case is to evaluate objectively a plaintiff's claims that his employment was terminated due to racial discrimination. Prospective jurors would then be asked questions—by either the attorneys representing both sides and/or the judge, depending on courtroom and jurisdiction—regarding whether or not they would be able to act as impartial members of the jury.

The central assumption of this process is that one way to prevent bias when empanelling a jury is by simply asking prospective jurors to assess their own impartiality—or at the very least, asking for their honest responses to personal questions so that the judge may determine their impartiality. In some instances, a judge may follow up on an admission of potential bias by trying to "rehabilitate" that juror, inquiring as to whether she or he might be capable of putting these sentiments aside for the purposes of the present case. For many of the same reasons that behavioral scientists would consider it problematic to conceive of discrimination in wholly intentional, explicit terms, the contemporary behavioral scientist is likely to respond with skepticism to the notions that (a) jurors will be willing to openly self-report such biases and (b) jurors are fully aware of the nature and strength of their biases in the first place. Such questioning may weed out a few individuals who explicitly acknowledge that they cannot be objective, but on the whole, prospective jurors' responses to the question of "Can you be impartial given the nature of this case?" seem unlikely to be accurate or informative.

Indeed, multiple analyses have indicated that *voir dire* typically leads to juries with observable attitudes no different from those that are found among a group of 12 randomly selected individuals (Johnson & Haney, 1994; Zeisel & Diamond, 1978). More generally, and as referenced above, previous research findings have demonstrated that people are remarkably good at generating plausible, legitimizing justifications for decisions that carry the appearance of potential bias (Hodson, Dovidio, & Gaertner, 2002; Norton et al., 2004, 2006), as well as that people are notoriously inaccurate when it comes to identifying the true influences on their judgments and behaviors (see Nisbett & Wilson, 1977; O'Brien, Sommers, & Ellsworth, in press).

A similar analysis can be conducted of legal efforts during the actual course of a trial to neutralize testimony or statements with the potential to bias jurors' decision-making process—whether this bias is related somehow to race or takes a more general form. It is common practice for judges to explicitly instruct jurors to disregard a piece of prejudicial evidence or inadmissible testimony, but it is less clear whether, even with the best of intentions, individual jurors are capable of doing so. Steblay, Hosch, Culhane, and McWethy (2006) conducted a meta-analysis to examine the effectiveness of instructions to disregard inadmissible testimony by compiling data from 48 legal studies involving over 8,000 participants. Results revealed that inadmissible evidence typically leads to verdicts consistent with the content of that evidence, even when participants had been instructed to ignore such information. Some research has indicated that such evidence is particularly likely to have a lingering impact on jurors' perceptions when the defendant is Black versus White, even while jurors themselves report being *less* influenced by the inadmissible evidence when judging a Black defendant (see Johnson, Whitestone, Jackson, & Gatto, 1995).

Given the limitations of self-report and public questioning, behavioral scientists rarely rely on these methods alone, making use instead of additional tools for detecting racial bias. As detailed above, when faced with assessing bias in a given case, behavioral scientists often seek to identify patterns of outcomes across previous cases that are comparable in nature. So, for instance, the concern that an attorney is basing peremptory challenges on race is one that could be corroborated by examining the racial composition of other juries empanelled by the same attorney. In terms of the *type* of data collected, behavioral scientists also frequently go beyond self-report to include behavioral observation, physiological measures, and other more subtle markers of bias such as response times to certain stimuli, speed of categorization of relevant concepts, nonverbal behavior, and linguistic patterns. Of course, such measures make for less direct assessments of bias, and there is still healthy debate regarding the practical function and meaning of these measures when generalizing from the laboratory to the courtroom (see, e.g., Banaji, Nosek, & Greenwald, 2004; Kang & Banaji, 2006; Karpinski & Hilton, 2001; Krieger, 2004; Tetlock & Mitchell, 2009).

In short, one apparent point of departure in the perspectives taken by the law and behavioral sciences concerns the perceived utility of public questioning and individuals' self-reports for diagnosing and combating bias. Behavioral scientists tend to endorse the use of a range of methods to address the effects of race, whereas the legal system traditionally entrusts such matters to self-report data. While some behavioral scientific bias-assessment procedures could be adopted by the legal system relatively easily, it is clear that others face practical obstacles to implementation in the courtroom or in other legal venues.

Institutional and ideological approaches to counteracting bias

Beyond the enactment of focused measures intended to minimize bias in common legal procedures and practices, one can also think more abstractly about legal philosophies regarding how best to challenge issues of institutional bias. One particular ideology that has garnered considerable legal (and social) clout over the past several decades is that of colorblindness (see Apfelbaum, Norton, & Sommers, 2012 for a review). Colorblindness has come to represent an ideological position of managing issues of diversity that sees value in downplaying (or even ignoring altogether) race-based distinctions—the view that racial differences should not be considerations in a lawfully egalitarian society.

Colorblindness advanced to the forefront of legal rhetoric regarding racial equality on the shoulders of the Supreme Court's seminal ruling against racial segregation in schooling (*Brown v. Board of Education*, 1954) and the decisive legislation that followed, including the Civil Rights Act of 1964, the National Voting Rights Acts of 1965, and the Fair Housing Act of 1968, among other laws (see Plaut, 2010). During an era when the most proximate and salient concerns relating to bias were those regarding overt racial animosity and injustice, colorblindness became a legal and social calling for the type of fairness that could be achieved by embracing a shared American identity that overlooked differences in skin color and ethnicity.

In the decades following the civil rights movement, however, the legal applications of colorblindness have shifted. As noted by Plaut (2010), once emblematic of the fight for equal opportunity among racial minorities marginalized by openly discriminatory practices, contemporary legal arguments for colorblindness have become increasingly geared toward combating race-conscious policies (e.g., affirmative action; see Norton & Sommers, 2011). If racial minority status compels an advantage in hiring and school admissions and in the selection of voting districts and government subcontractors, the argument goes, then *Whites'* right for equal protection may be violated (*Adarand v. Peña*, 1995; *Bakke v. Board of Regents*, 1978; *Gratz v. Bollinger*, 2003; *Grutter v. Bollinger*; *Shaw v. Reno*, 1993; *Wygant v. Jackson Board of Education*, 1986).

The contemporary legal movement to equate colorblindness with impartiality is illustrated clearly by two recent U.S. Supreme Court rulings. In one, *Parents Involved in Community Schools v. Seattle School District No. 1* (2007), the perceived neutrality of a colorblind perspective was used to counter proposed race-based student diversification initiatives in school districts in Seattle, Washington, and Jefferson County, Kentucky. The court determined that states do not have a compelling interest to achieve a balance of students within schools operating solely on the basis of racial group membership. Chief Justice John Roberts crystallized the logic underlying this ruling when he declared "the way to stop discrimination on the basis of race is to stop discriminating on the basis of race."

A second recent case, *Ricci v. DeStefano* (2009), involved a claim of racial bias on behalf of 19 New Haven, Connecticut, firefighters whose passing scores on an entrance exam for management positions were invalidated. The unique aspect of this discrimination claim was that the plaintiffs alleging bias were mostly White. At issue was the fact that the exam yielded disproportionate results by race—namely, no Black firefighters had achieved passing scores, prompting city officials to abandon the exam and promotions altogether. The Supreme Court ultimately ruled in favor of the plaintiffs and their claim of discrimination, determining that invalidating the exam (and thus the plaintiffs' potential for promotion) was a race-based consideration at odds with the Equal Protection Clause and the spirit of a colorblind ideal.

Taken together, these rulings illustrate a belief system gaining steam in legal circles: Bias is best remedied by striving for colorblindness. But is there behavioral science evidence to support the notion that colorblindness achieves the goal of decreasing racial bias? As it turns out, review of the empirical literature does not yield much evidence for the beneficial properties of colorblindness—in fact, if anything, research suggests that colorblindness is associated with a variety of social and institutional costs.

Multiple studies have shown that a colorblind mindset leads to increases—not decreases—in levels of racial bias, as assessed via both explicit and subtle methods of attitude measurement (Richeson & Nussbaum, 2004; Wolsko, Park, Judd, & Wittenbrink, 2000). Richeson and Nussbaum (2004) placed participants in either a colorblind or multicultural mindset by asking participants to read and identify strengths in a statement that endorsed one of these approaches. The researchers then measured participants' level of racial bias, using both traditional self-report measures and a response-latency measure that assessed implicit bias. Results indicated the colorblind prompt produced higher levels of racial bias among participants, on both measures, as compared to participants exposed to the multicultural prompt.

Beyond shaping attitudes, recent work has indicated problematic effects of a colorblind ideology on the perception of racial progress and bias-related intervention. Apfelbaum, Pauker, Sommers, and Ambady (2010) demonstrated that children initially encouraged to view the pursuit of racial equality in colorblind (vs. value-diversity) terms were subsequently less likely to consider events depicting even overt forms of bias as constituting racial discrimination. Further, when teachers listened to children who had been primed with colorblindness describe these events, they were significantly less likely to see the need for intervention. Why? The data suggested that colorblindness led children to overlook the critical racial element when retelling these events. Given this finding, it is not difficult to understand why, for many individuals and institutions, colorblindness *appears* to be an effective tool for bias reduction—it creates the impression of a decline in racial discrimination. But these data demonstrate that colorblindness will lead individuals to be less likely to see and report bias, even when it clearly exists.

In total, legal endorsement of the remedial properties of colorblindness stand in contrast to conclusions emerging from behavioral science research on bias reduction. And in addition to the behavioral science conclusions reviewed above, a range of other negative consequences has been linked to colorblind approaches to managing diversity and addressing bias. Among White individuals, relying on colorblindness to guide interracial interaction tendencies (e.g., the tendency to avoid talking about race) can predict task underperformance, cognitive impairments, unfriendly nonverbal behavior, and the possibility of appearing *more* racially prejudiced in the eyes of Black observers (Apfelbaum, Sommers, & Norton, 2008). In organizational contexts, White employees' endorsement of colorblindness is associated with a decreased psychological investment and pride in their work among minority individuals (Plaut, Thomas, & Goren, 2009), as well as increased reservations about the potential for bias and exclusion (Purdie-Vaughns, Steele, Davies, Ditlmann, & Crosby, 2008). For instance, Plaut and her colleagues analyzed the responses of 3,758 employees at a large health-care organization to a diversity climate survey. Their results indicate that increases in White employees' endorsement of colorblindness were associated with decreases in psychological engagement among minority employees and increases in minorities' perceptions of bias in the organizational climate. White employees' endorsement of multiculturalism, on the other hand, demonstrated precisely the opposite pattern of results, predicting increases in minority engagement and decreases in perceptions of bias.

Summary

The law and behavioral sciences often take distinct approaches to achieving the common aim of counteracting racial bias. Such divergence is evident in both their response to bias in individual and group contexts and to remedying bias in institutional processes. A core legal–behavioral science distinction in the approach to counteracting bias in interpersonal contexts comes in the diversity of methods that are brought to bear. While behavioral scientists typically make use of a broad assortment of methods to detect and curtail racial bias, the legal system relies predominantly on the veridicality of public inquiry and information gathered from individuals' self-reports. At the institutional level, legal circles often regard a colorblind ideal—in which race-based considerations are deemphasized or altogether disregarded—to be synonymous with impartiality and justice. Yet emerging behavioral science research offers conclusions to the contrary, indicating that colorblindness carries with it various negative social, cognitive, and practical consequences. It is less clear from this research, however, which approach to bias reduction constitutes the most effective and practical alternative to colorblindness.

Conclusions

As many a contemporary controversy over race clearly demonstrates, "bias" means different things to different people. As detailed throughout this chapter, different institutions conceptualize, measure, and combat bias in different ways as well. These divergences evident between legal and behavioral science perspectives on bias complicate efforts for these two schools of thought to speak to one another on such matters, much less fruitfully integrate scientific theory and findings into the legal domain. The prototypical legal view of bias continues to focus on questions of intent and overt evidence; behavioral scientists continue to be better at identifying perceived flaws in legal efforts to curtail bias than they are at offering practical, legally feasible alternatives.

So are efforts to bridge this apparent gulf between legal and behavioral science perspectives on bias hopeless? Not necessarily. Although differences still exist, in many ways legal and behavioral science approaches to bias have grown closer in recent years. From rulings making it easier to bring mixed-motive allegations of discrimination to Supreme Court justices writing about unconscious forms of prejudice, there are signs that the law has begun to move away from a strict, narrow view of racism as obvious and wholly intentional. And of late, many scientists, too, seem to have started to appreciate more fully the benefits of triangulating research methods, collaborating with legal colleagues and professionals, and developing means of assessing bias in the here and now of the case at hand (see Kang & Banaji, 2006). While legal and behavioral science domains will always be predicated on different assumptions and driven by different objectives, in most respects opportunities for cross-talk and interdisciplinary investigation have never been greater.

Future directions

One particularly complex issue that emerges from our discussion of colorblindness and counteracting bias is the question of how race *should* be treated. If operating completely blind to racial differences brings with it problematic social and institutional outcomes, as demonstrated by mounting evidence from the behavioral sciences, then how *should* race be taken into consideration? There are no easy answers to this question, as demonstrated by the pair of Supreme Court rulings regarding affirmative action at the University of Michigan in 2003 (*Gratz v. Bollinger*, 2003; *Grutter v. Bollinger*, 2003). In the law school case, the Court ruled against Barbara Grutter, a rejected applicant, determining that the school's pursuit of diversity constituted a Constitutional and compelling state interest; but in the undergraduate case, Jennifer Gratz successfully challenged Michigan's undergraduate admissions policy that awarded 20 points to applicants from underrepresented minority groups (with 150 total points needed for admission). By some accounts, this attempt to clarify the ways in which race may be considered in admissions decisions only added to the confusion surrounding how to treat race (see Norton et al., 2006). How schools or organizations are supposed to operate in this gray area remains unclear, and increased sensitivity to the potential of unconscious or unintentional bias on the part of the legal system may only complicate matters further.

What are the implications for the practical value of behavioral science given that probabilistic evidence of racial bias is often seen as less persuasive in legal contexts? Given that analyses within the behavioral sciences are held to comparable standards of statistical reliability as scientific procedures that have been readily adopted in the courtroom (e.g., fingerprint analysis, DNA testing), why are there such stark differences in their perceived credibility? And what can be done to increase confidence in behavioral scientific analyses? Perhaps greater exposure to such measures will facilitate greater acceptance of such analyses. If so, in the short term, there are certain types of cases in which the conclusions from behavioral sciences may have greater potential for immediate impact. It seems quite likely, for example, that behavioral science data are viewed more skeptically through the *beyond a reasonable doubt* benchmark applied to criminal trials. It therefore seems plausible that probabilistic conclusions (often based on aggregated data) would carry more influence in noncriminal domains. But the specific question of what types of case are most amenable to application of behavioral science research remains an open and important one.

On the behavioral science side of the equation, an important lingering question growing out of the example with which we opened this chapter involves how experts can best try to portray and apply research findings to ongoing legal proceedings. Of note, researchers have been quite successful in effecting policy change and shaping trial outcomes in some domains (e.g., the extensive research literature regarding eyewitness memory that now informs a great deal of police practice and has influenced many a trial outcome; see Wells et al., 1998). But when it comes to the adjudication of bias, results have been far more modest. What accounts for the variable effectiveness and application of behavioral science research in legal contexts? Are there particular samples, methods, analyses, or other research-related considerations that can significantly increase the likelihood that important findings from behavioral sciences will find their way into legal realms? In short, what can behavioral scientists do to enhance the relevance and practical application of their work? These are the questions to which behavioral scientists would be wise to turn their future attention to the extent that they seek to inform and influence legal discourse.

Finally, in a global society that is becoming increasingly multicultural and diverse, how do the analyses in the present chapter extrapolate to manifestations of bias outside the White/Black binary focused on herein? Legal perspectives on racial bias are ostensibly comparable whether the target of discrimination is Black, Latino, Asian, or multiracial, but is this assumption of homogeneity warranted? Such questions also apply to issues of discrimination that fall outside the domain of race and ethnicity. There is reason to think that important differences may exist in how bias is conceived of and addressed with respect to these other groups. For instance, there is considerable variability in the degree to which individuals are able to physically conceal their membership in a stigmatized group (e.g., race vs. religion), in the extent to which individuals are perceived to have control over their stigmatized identity (e.g., gender vs. weight), and in the content of stereotypes associated with such groups. "Diversity" is not a construct that lends itself to a singular constellation of group members—it is (and has been) operationalized in myriad ways by behavioral scientists. Thus, one-size-fits-all prescriptions, diagnoses, and remedies for bias run the risk of portraying misleading oversimplifications of an inherently multifaceted issue.

References

Adarand v. Peña, 115 S. Ct. 2097 (1995).

Amodio, D. M., Harmon-Jones, E., & Devine, P. G. (2003). Individual differences in the activation and control of affective race bias as assessed by startle eyeblink responses and self-report. *Journal of Personality and Social Psychology, 84*, 738–753.

Apfelbaum, E. P., Norton, M. I., & Sommers, S. R. (2012). Racial colorblindness: Emergence, practice, and implications. *Current Directions in Psychological Science, 21*, 205–209.

Apfelbaum, E. P., Pauker, K., Sommers, S. R., & Ambady, N. (2010). In blind pursuit of racial equality? *Psychological Science, 21*, 1587–1592.

Apfelbaum, E. P., Sommers, S. R., & Norton, M. I. (2008). Seeing race and seeming racist? Evaluating strategic colorblindness in social interaction. *Journal of Personality and Social Psychology, 95*, 918–932.

Bakke v. Board of Regents, 438 U.S. 265 (1978).

Baldus, D. C., Pulaski, C. A., & Woodworth, G. (1983). Comparative review of death sentences: An empirical study of the Georgia experience. *Journal of Criminal Law and Criminology, 74*, 661–753.

Baldus, D. C., Woodworth, G., Grosso, C. M., & Christ, A. M. (2002). Arbitrariness and discrimination in the administration of the death penalty: A legal and empirical analysis of the Nebraska experience (1973–1999). *Nebraska Law Review, 81*, 486–775.

Baldus, D. C., Woodworth, G., Zuckerman, D., Weiner, N. A., & Broffitt, B. (1998). Racial discrimination and the death penalty in the post-Furman Era: An empirical and legal overview, with recent findings from Philadelphia. *Cornell Law Review, 83*, 1638–1770.

Banaji, M. R., Nosek, B. A., & Greenwald, A. G. (2004). No place for nostalgia in science: A response to Arkes & Tetlock. *Psychological Inquiry, 15*, 279–289.

Batson v. Kentucky, 476 U.S. 79 (1986).

Bertrand, M., & Mullainathan, S. (2004). Are Emily and Greg more employable than Lakisha and Jamal? *American Economic Review, 94*, 991–1013.

Bielby, W. T. (2008). Expert report submitted in *McReynolds v. Merrill Lynch*, United States District Court for the Northern District of Illinois, Eastern Division, Case No. 05-C-6583.

Blascovich, J. & Mendes, W. B. (2010). Social psychophysiology and embodiment. In S. T. Fiske, D. T. Gilbert, & G. Lindzey (Eds.), *The handbook of social psychology* (5th ed., pp. 194–227). New York: Wiley.

Bowers, W. J., & Foglia, W. D. (2003). Still singularly agonizing: Law's failure to purge arbitrariness from capital sentencing. *Criminal Law Bulletin, 39*, 51–86.

Bowers, W. J., Steiner, B. D., & Sandys, M. (2001). Death sentencing in Black and White: An empirical analysis of the role of jurors' race and jury racial composition. *University of Pennsylvania Journal of Constitutional Law, 3*, 171–274.

Brown v. Board of Education, 347 U.S. 483 (1954).

Bureau of Justice Statistics (2005). Federal Justice Statistics Resource Center, U.S. Department of Justice.

Chaiken, S., & Trope, Y. (1999). *Dual-process theories in social psychology*. New York: Guilford Press.

Correll, J., Park, B., Judd, C. M., & Wittenbrink, B. (2002). The police officer's dilemma: Using ethnicity to disambiguate potentially threatening individuals. *Journal of Personality and Social Psychology, 83,* 1314–1329.

Correll, J., Park, B., Judd, C. M., Wittenbrink, B., Sadler, M. S. & Keesee, T. (2007). Across the thin blue line: Police officers and racial bias in the decision to shoot. *Journal of Personality and Social Psychology, 92*, 1006–1023.

Crandall, C. S., Eshleman, A., & O'Brien, L. T. (2002). Social norms and the expression and suppression of prejudice: The struggle for internalization. *Journal of Personality and Social Psychology, 82*, 359–378.

Desert Palace Inc., v. Costa, 539 U.S. 90 (2003).

Dovidio, J. F., & Gaertner, S. L. (2004). Aversive racism. In M. P. Zanna (Ed.), *Advances in experimental social psychology* (pp. 1–52). San Diego, CA: Academic Press.

Dovidio, J. F., & Gaertner, S. L. (2010). Intergroup bias. In S. T. Fiske, D. T. Gilbert, & G. Lindzey (Eds.), *The handbook of social psychology* (5th ed., pp. 1084–1121). New York: Wiley.

Fazio, R., Jackson, J., Dunton, B., & Williams, C. (1995). Variability in automatic activation as an unobtrusive measure of racial attitudes: A bona fide pipeline? *Journal of Personality and Social Psychology, 69*, 1013–1027.

Fazio, R. H., & Olson, M. A. (2003). Implicit measures in social cognition: Their meaning and use. *Annual Review of Psychology, 54*, 297–327.

Gaertner, S. L., & Dovidio, J. F. (1986). The aversive form of racism. In J. F. Dovidio & S. L. Gaertner (Eds.), *Prejudice, discrimination, and racism* (pp. 61–89). Orlando, FL: Academic Press.

Goff, P. A., Steele, C. M., & Davies, P. G. (2008). The space between us: Stereotype threat and distance in interracial contexts. *Journal of Personality and Social Psychology, 94*, 91–107.

Gratz v. Bollinger, 539 U.S. 244 (2003).

Greenwald, A. G., McGhee, D. E., & Schwartz, J. K. L. (1998). Measuring individual differences in implicit cognition: The implicit association test. *Journal of Personality and Social Psychology, 74*, 1464–1480.

Gross, S., & Mauro, R. (1984). Patterns of death: An analysis of racial disparities in capital sentencing and homicide victimization. *Stanford Law Review, 37*, 27–153

Grutter v. Bollinger, 539 U.S. 306 (2003).

Hodson, G., Dovidio, J. F., & Gaertner, S. L. (2002). Processes in racial discrimination: Differential weighting of conflicting information. *Personality and Social Psychology Bulletin, 28*, 460–471.

Hofmann, W., Gawronski, B., Gschwendner, T., Le, H., & Schmitt, M. (2005). A meta-analysis on the correlation between the Implicit Association Test and explicit self-report measures. *Personality and Social Psychology Bulletin, 31*, 1369–1385.

Johnson, C., & Haney, C. (1994). Felony voir dire: An exploratory study of its content and effect. *Law and Human Behavior, 18*, 487–506.

Johnson, J. D., Whitestone, E., Jackson, L. A., & Gatto, L. (1995). Justice is still not colorblind: Differential racial effects of exposure to inadmissible evidence. *Personality and Social Psychology Bulletin, 21*, 893–898.

Kang, J., & Banaji, M. R. (2006). Fair measures: A behavioral realist revision of "affirmative action." *California Law Review, 94*, 1063–1118.

Karpinski, A., & Hilton, J. L. (2001). Attitudes and the implicit association test. *Journal of Personality and Social Psychology, 81*, 774–788.

Krieger, L. H. (2004). The intuitive psychologist behind the bench: Models of gender bias in social psychology and employment discrimination law. *Journal of Social Issues, 60*, 835–848.

Krueger, A., Rothstein, J., & Turner, S. (2006). Race, income, and college in 25 years: Evaluating Justice O'Connor's conjecture. *American Law and Economics Review, 8*, 282–311.

McCleskey v. Kemp, 481 U.S. 279 (1987).

McReynolds v. Merrill Lynch. (2005). United States District Court for the Northern District of Illinois, Eastern Division, Case No. 05-C-6583.

Mendes, W. B., Blascovich, J., Hunter, S. B., Lickel, B. & Jost, J. T. (2007). Threatened by the unexpected: Physiological responses during social interactions with expectancy-violating partners. *Journal of Personality and Social Psychology, 92*, 698–716.

Miller-El v. Dretke, 545 U.S. 231 (2005).

Mitchell, T. L., Haw, R. M., Pfeifer, J. E., & Meissner, C. A. (2005). Racial bias in mock juror decision-making: A meta-analytic review of defendant treatment. *Law and Human Behavior, 29*, 621–637.

Nisbett, R. E. & Wilson, T. D. (1977). Telling more than we can know. *Psychological Review, 84*, 231–259.

Norton, M. I., & Sommers, S. R. (2011). Whites see racism as a zero-sum game that they are now losing. *Perspectives in Psychological Science, 6*, 215–218.

Norton, M. I., Sommers, S. R., Vandello, J. A., & Darley, J. M. (2006). Mixed motives and racial bias: The impact of legitimate and illegitimate criteria on decision-making. *Psychology, Public Policy, and Law, 12*, 36–55.

Norton, M. I., Vandello, J. A., & Darley, J. M. (2004). Casuistry and social category bias. *Journal of Personality and Social Psychology, 87*, 817–831.

O'Brien, B., Sommers, S. R., & Ellsworth, P. C. (in press). Ask and what shall ye receive? A guide for using and interpreting what jurors tell us. *Journal of Law and Social Change.*

Parents Involved in Community Schools v. Seattle School District No. 1, 551 U.S. 701 (2007).

Paternoster, R. (1984). Prosecutorial discretion in requesting the death penalty: A case of victim-based racial discrimination. *Law and Society Review, 18*, 437–478.

Plant, E. A., & Devine, P. G. (1998). Internal and external motivation to respond without prejudice. *Journal of Personality and Social Psychology, 75*, 811–832.

Plaut, V. C. (2010). Diversity science: Why and how difference makes a difference. *Psychological Inquiry, 21*, 77–99.

Plaut, V. C., Thomas, K. M., & Goren, M. J. (2009). Is multiculturalism or color blindness better for minorities? *Psychological Science, 20*, 444–446.

Price Waterhouse v. Hopkins, 490 U.S. 228 (1989).

Purdie-Vaughns, V., Steele, C. M., Davies, P. G., Ditlmann, R., & Randall-Crosby, J. (2008). Social identity contingencies: How diversity cues signal threat or safety for African-Americans in mainstream institutions. *Journal of Personality and Social Psychology, 94*, 615–630.

Reeves v. Sanderson Plumbing Products, Inc. 530 U.S. 133 (2000).

Ricci v. DeStefano, 129 S. Ct. 2658 (2009).

Richeson, J. A., & Nussbaum, R. J. (2004). The impact of multiculturalism versus color-blindness on racial bias. *Journal of Experimental Social Psychology, 40*, 417–423.

Shaw v. Reno, 509 U.S. 630 (1993).

Shin, P. S. (2010). Liability for unconscious discrimination? A thought experiment in the theory of employment discrimination law. *Hastings Law Journal, 62*, 67–101.

Sommers, S. R. (2008). Determinants and consequences of jury racial diversity: Empirical findings, implications, and directions for future research. *Social Issues and Policy Review, 2*, 65–102.

Sommers, S. R. (2007). Race and the decision-making of juries. *Legal and Criminological Psychology, 12*, 171–187.

Sommers, S. R., & Norton, M. I. (2006). Lay theories about White racists: What constitutes racism (and what doesn't). *Group Processes and Intergroup Relations, 9*, 117–138.

Sommers, S. R., & Norton, M. I. (2008). Race and jury selection: Psychological perspectives on the peremptory challenge debate. *American Psychologist, 63*, 527–539.

Spohn, C. C. (2000). Thirty years of sentencing reform: The quest for a racially neutral sentencing process. In J. Horney (Ed.), *Criminal justice 2000: Vol. 3. Policies, processes, and decisions of the criminal justice system* (pp. 427–501). Washington, DC: U.S. Department of Justice, National Institute of Justice.

Steblay, N., Hosch, H. M., Culhane, S. E., & McWethy, A. (2006). The impact on juror verdicts of judicial instruction to disregard inadmissible evidence: A meta-analysis. *Law and Human Behavior, 30*, 469–542.

Swain v. Alabama, 380 U.S. 202 (1965).

Swim, J. K., Aiken, K. J., Hall, U. S., & Hunter, B. A. (1995). Sexism and racism: Old-fashioned and modern prejudices. *Journal of Personality and Social Psychology, 68*, 199–214.

Tetlock, P. E., & Mitchell, G. (2009). Implicit bias and accountability systems: What must organizations do to prevent discrimination? *Research in Organizational Behavior, 29*, 3–38.

Washington v. Davis, 426 U.S. 229 (1976).

Weisbuch, M., Pauker, K., & Ambady, N. (2009). The subtle transmission of race bias via televised nonverbal behavior. *Science, 326*, 1711–1714.

Wells, G. L., Smalls, M., Penrod, S., Malpass, R. S., Fulero, S. M, & Bimacombe, C. E. (1998). Eyewitness identification procedures: Recommendations for lineups and photospreads. *Law and Human Behavior, 22*, 1–39.

Williams, D. R. (1999). Race, socioeconomic status, and health: The added effects of racism and discrimination. *Annals of the New York Academy of Sciences, 896*, 173–188.

Wolsko, C., Park, B., Judd, C. M., & Wittenbrink, B. (2000). Framing interethnic ideology: Effects of multicultural and colorblind perspectives of judgments of groups and individuals. *Journal of Personality and Social Psychology, 78*, 635–654.

Wygant v. Jackson Board of Education, 476 U.S. 267 (1986).

Zeisel, H., & Diamond, S. S. (1978). The effect of peremptory challenges on jury and verdict: An experiment in a federal district court. *Stanford Law Review, 30*, 491–531.

PART 8

Conclusion/Integration

CHAPTER
24 Conclusion: Future Directions for Diversity Theory and Research

Quinetta M. Roberson

Abstract

The chapters in this handbook provide a comprehensive overview of the different approaches, perspectives and levels of analysis in diversity research. In doing so, they highlight the evolution of diversity as a science and practice, emphasizing existing conceptual and actionable knowledge on managing diverse workforces and capitalizing on the benefits of diversity in organizations. Each chapter offers suggestions for future research within specific topic areas that could help generate a broader and deeper understanding of diversity in organizations. The purpose of this chapter is to highlight points of intersection among the various topic areas and put forward meaningful areas of integration within the field. Specifically, I propose and discuss directions for a future research agenda including the conceptualization of diversity, mechanisms underlying diversity effects, contextual influences, diversity management and a more universal approach to the study of diversity.

Key Words: diversity as a science, future directions, scientific integration, diversity mechanisms, diversity context, diversity management, holistic perspective

The chapters in this handbook highlight the evolution of diversity as a science and practice, its foundational methods for generating knowledge, and the broad range of actionable knowledge created by researchers that can be applied to attracting, motivating, and retaining diverse workforces Within each chapter, the authors identify questions that remain to be addressed and provide agendas for continued scientific progress. While the pursuit of such agendas is critical for advancing our understanding of the meaning, operation, and effects of diversity, integration across topic areas is also needed to increase our knowledge of the phenomenon. Below, I identify and discuss possible areas of scientific integration including the conceptualization of diversity, mechanisms underlying diversity effects, the effects of context, diversity management, and a holistic approach to the study of diversity.

Conceptualization of diversity

In the section on the conceptualization of diversity, evolution in how researchers have explicated the definition of the theoretical construct is evident. What originated in equal employment opportunity legislation in the United States has now expanded to include a variety of attributes ranging from visible, or surface-level, characteristics to those that are not observable (deep-level characteristics). It is at this more entrenched level of identity that researchers have been able to capture a broader range of attributes, such as attitudes, values, and beliefs. However, further development of the construct may lead to a more comprehensive understanding of how diversity operates. As discussed throughout this volume, people identify similarities and differences between themselves and others based on any number of categories embedded in social environments. Given the variability in contextual features,

461

the attributes on which social categorization occurs in one environment may differ from those in another. Thus, by moving beyond a focus on traditional categories of diversity such as gender and race, researchers may gain greater insight into how cultural identity influences behavior. In Chapter 10, Jehn and Greer note that equivocal results regarding antecedents to conflict in groups and teams may be attributable, in part, to prior conceptualizations of social category that assume that most diversity is perceptible and/or task-related. Yet a number of scholars in this volume draw attention to the role of hidden, assumed, or invisible social identities and suggest that a consideration of such social categories may provide greater clarity on diversity processes and outcomes. Further, given that differences in socialization experiences and norms can distinguish people from different cultures and nations, as noted by Salas and colleagues (Chapter 3), expanding the concept of diversity to incorporate a broader range of objective and subjective aspects may increase the generalizability of the construct.

Multifaceted conceptualizations of diversity may also be useful for capturing the full range of differences that exist in global organizations. As noted by Roberts and Creary in Chapter 5, individuals' identities are a complex interaction of meanings that derive from group memberships, self-appraisals, interpersonal encounters, and beliefs. In addition, people's cultural profiles consist of multilayered value structures derived from the various social environments (e.g., team, department, organization, geographic location, culture, etc.) in which they work. Thus, to adequately capture and examine the effects of multiple identity structures within individuals, more research utilizing multidimensional conceptualizations of diversity is needed. Although faultline theory moves beyond a categorical approach to diversity to focus on alignment in individuals' attributes, this form of diversity depicts intragroup rather than intrapersonal identity. Therefore, the development of constructs to represent individuals' cultural profiles—specifically, facets of the profile and the relationships between them—may be useful for advancing the explanatory power of diversity as a construct and providing insight into how navigating the self influences interactions between diverse individuals.

Both throughout this volume and in the field as a whole, diversity has primarily been conceptualized as differences between individuals, with an investigative focus on how the number and diffusion of such differences within specific work contexts influence attitudes, behavior, and organizational outcomes. Given that a relatively large body of empirical research provides evidence of such effects, continued work on the consequences of within-unit differences is important. However, using more multifaceted views of diversity that include both observable and nonobservable characteristics, we can assume that units are not absolutely heterogeneous. In other words, because members of collectives may be characterized by some degree of sameness, a focus on diversity as dissimilarity may overlook an exegetic feature of group processes and outcomes. Accordingly, operationalizations of diversity are needed to capture and explore the effects of similitude, agreement, and/or equality. Following Thatcher's (Chapter 4) suggestions for evolving faultline definition and measurement, the development of measures to operationalize the homogeneity of a single subgroup or overlap across different types of attributes (e.g., categorical vs. nominal) may help researchers to more appropriately reflect the underlying mechanisms affecting group processes and outcomes.

Diversity research could also benefit from a more dynamic conceptualization of the construct. As noted by Lambert and Bell (Chapter 2) and Thatcher (Chapter 4), much of the research to date has assumed the characteristics of groups and their members to be immutable. However, as changes to individuals' identities and the composition of groups occur over time, mechanisms for accounting for such evolution are needed. For example, longitudinal research to assess movement in individuals' group memberships, the salience of such memberships, and their associated valences may provide insight into how changes in intraindividual identity structures influence group processes. Similarly, time-series research might be useful for examining how faultline endurance or trajectories alter group functioning and outcomes.

Mechanisms underlying diversity effects

As reviewed in the chapters on psychological and interactionist perspectives on diversity, researchers have relied upon different theoretical approaches to observing the effects of diversity in organizations. Some approaches discuss diversity from an intraindividual point of view, considering how individuals' perceptions and cognitive processes influence their reactions to and experiences with others, while other approaches study diversity from an interindividual standpoint with a focus on how social relations between individuals influence group-level processes and outcomes. Although these (and other) approaches have advanced our understanding of the various mechanisms through which diversity influences attitudes and behavior, developing more epistemological perspectives of diversity may help to propel the field forward. More simply, by synthesizing current theoretical foundations regarding the effects of diversity and adopting a broader view of the experience of diversity in the workplace, researchers may gain greater clarity into the interplay of diversity-related processes at various levels and the effects.

A review of the theoretical perspectives on diversity discussed in this volume highlights two dominant perspectives—social-categorization/similarity-attraction and information-processing/value-in-diversity—which have been instrumental in the articulation of the positive and negative effects of diversity on workgroup processes and performance. Researchers have also merged these perspectives to reconcile conflicting effects and propose that diverse groups may fail to recognize information processing benefits, given that the conflict they experience is likely to derive from intergroup biases stemming from categorization. Despite this theoretical integration, the evolution of diversity-related theory has been relatively stagnant. Beyond the aforementioned theories, which describe the intergroup processes through which diversity effects occur, much of the conceptual development in this area has centered on the gestation of the diversity construct (e.g., faultlines). Yet the study of diversity could be advanced by more theorizing on the lower-level processes that influence attitudes and behavior.

To further elucidate the psychological processes through which diversity effects occur, future research should explore connections between intraindividual mechanisms. For example, although few empirical studies have examined the relationship between stigma and stereotyping, Hebl and King (Chapter 7) note that researchers have argued that stigmatized individuals are typically targets of interpersonal rejection, negative stereotypes, and discrimination. However, as social categorization research suggests that implicit bias follows from general in-group/out-group distinctions, the development of a conceptual framework to differentiate the effects of depersonalization (as described by Ferguson and Porter in Chapter 6) and devaluation may clarify the circumstances under which members of certain groups will be negatively stereotyped versus stigmatized. As the devaluation of others has been posited as a tactic to reduce perceived threat to one's in-group, theory building on the role of stigmas in identity negotiation processes may guide future research on navigating the self. In addition, because stigmatization has been put forward as a means of system justification, integrating theory on stigma and ideology may offer an alternative explanation for prejudice and discrimination.

Although interactionist perspectives on diversity derive from a theoretical focus on social exchanges between members of different groups, the field could benefit from additional theorizing on relational processes that occur at a meso-level of analysis, or between individuals within groups. As research has envisaged diverse interactions as occurring between individuals who belong to different social groups or between the groups themselves, an obvious gap exists in connecting these levels of analysis. This point may be illustrated by a consideration of diversity and status. While status has been conceptualized within the sociological literature as a function of the amount of social influence conferred upon individuals by others within a group (as discussed by Phillips and colleagues, Chapter 9), insights into the mechanisms through which such social influence occurs are limited. In other words, we have little explanation of the processes through which individuals develop shared understandings of status in groups. However, researchers may draw upon complementary theoretical perspectives to explicate such processes. For example, Reagans (Chapter 11) discusses network formation processes by which diversity influences homophily, which might also be a useful lens through which to view the development of collective perceptions of power and status within groups. In particular, a focus on the structure and content of network connections may help to explicate how interrelationships between individuals belonging to different social categories influence social interaction and "sensemaking" about such categorizations. Similarly, building upon the findings of research reviewed by Jehn and Greer (Chapter 10) that highlight the influence of diversity on the level, amount, and type of conflict in groups, expanding the interactionist framework to consider the nature and quality of other types of social exchanges within groups may offer added insight into the process effects of diversity. For instance, theory development around the impact of diversity on other types of interaction, such as acculturation and negotiation, may highlight additional mechanisms underlying the relationship between diversity and group performance. Overall, greater theoretical attention to intragroup social dynamics is needed to provide a more comprehensive view of the social construction of diversity and its effects.

Despite the theoretical approach used to study diversity, multilevel perspectives on diversity are needed to fully examine the ways in which the effects of diversity unfold. This is not to suggest that such perspectives have not been taken in past research, as demonstrated in this volume. However, future research that integrates intra- and interindividual/group processes may provide novel insights into the operation and consequences of diversity. For example, how might different identity negotiation motives (e.g., alignment vs. emancipation) influence the creation of status hierarchies or the type and amount of conflict in diverse groups? Similarly, considering the divergent motives of hierarchy-enhancing versus hierarchy-attenuating ideologies, as noted by O'Brien and Gilbert (Chapter 8), what is the impact of ideology content and structure on information exchange, conflict, or the development of social capital in groups and teams? What is the relationship between stigma and status—specifically, are they similar constructs or causally related? If causally related, what are the mechanisms through which stigmatization affects status loss in groups? How does intergroup bias influence network formation processes? While these questions are not an exhaustive list for integrating psychological and interactionist perspectives on diversity, they are meant to stimulate thinking about other areas of intersection for diversity theory and research.

As noted by Roberts and Creary (Chapter 5), much of the diversity scholarship to date has assumed a latent perspective on interactions between members of diverse groups. Following this perspective, diversity-related attitudes and behavior are considered to be the result of relatively subconscious, psychological functions and their effects on the interrelationships between people. However, in their discussion of identity negotiation, they reflect on diversity processes from a more agentic viewpoint that involves personal involvement in forming and maintaining one's identity. This motivational approach to understanding identity may also be useful for further study of the psychology of diversity. For example, as negative reactions to diversity, such as discrimination and stigmatization, are the results of categorization processes based on attribute similarities/differences, individuals may engage in tactics to cultivate more positive, work-related identities. Volitional strategies, like self-disclosure and withholding information, may be used to respectively reveal or hide social identities, thus influencing others' perceptions and reactions. Accordingly, future research that examines the relationship between such individual-level processes and interactions between in-group/out-group members may bridge psychological and interactionist perspectives on diversity and facilitate understanding of diversity management at the individual level of analysis.

While directions for future research on firm-level diversity management practices are offered later in this chapter, the need for research that examines how such practices affect the psychological and social processes is considered here. As macro-level structures may influence individual cognitions and relational processes, investigations of their moderating influence may be important for facilitating effective interactions between diverse individuals. Obviously, diversity training initiatives (Roberson and colleagues, Chapter 19) may be effectual in reducing intergroup bias and stigmatization, dismantling power and status hierarchies, and diminishing conflict in teams. Similarly, career development programs, such as those described by Dawson and colleagues (Chapter 17), may aid diverse employees in navigating the self or generating effective social networks, while work–life programs, such as those described by Konrad (Chapter 20), may moderate hierarchy-enhancing ideologies related to gender roles in organizations. Because these programmatic effects are merely speculative without empirical study, research is needed to understand the effects of structural interventions on individual- and group-level diversity processes.

The effects of context

As further development of the diversity construct may lead to a more comprehensive understanding of how diversity operates, the research agenda may also be advanced by expanding the conceptualization of diversity context. As noted by Joshi and Roh (Chapter 12), demography, or the demographic composition of organizational units (e.g., divisions, branches, teams, etc.), may serve as an important structural feature of diversity context. At the same time, Roberts and Creary (Chapter 5) note that any one individual may have multiple sources of identity, which vary in salience across different social contexts. For example, in a 10-person executive team with two women, gender may be more salient than in an executive team of similar size that has an equal representation of men and women. Due to the social categorization and similarity-attraction processes discussed throughout this volume, cliques or subgroups may also be more likely to develop in the latter team, which is likely to affect information processing and other group processes. Thus, consistent with demography theory and research, diversity itself—both observable and nonobservable attributes and their alignment—may serve as an important contextual variable in research. Perceptions of such diversity may also be a key feature of context. In Chapter 13, van Knippenberg and colleagues highlight the consequences of diversity mindsets—in particular, individuals' own diversity attitudes and their perceptions of an organization's perspective on diversity. Given that such perceptions and attitudes along with other diversity cognitions, like those discussed by O'Brien and Gilbert (Chapter 8), may facilitate the creation and maintenance of diversity climates, future research should explore their interactive effects with diversity on organizational outcomes.

Although diversity researchers have conceptualized diversity climate as employees' shared perceptions of diversity policies, practices, and procedures, few studies have considered how variability in such perceptions might guide social behavior. In effect, research to date has incorporated a relatively narrow focus on diversity climate level, or the favorability of organizational diversity practices, rather than on diversity climate strength, or differences in employees' experiences and subsequent perceptions of the environment created by an organization's practices. Based on the findings of psychological climate research, variability in employees' perceptions of their work environment affects the availability and strength of cues for interpreting events and guiding behavior, and thus group-level outcomes. Because variance in employees' perceptions of an organization's diversity policies and procedures may serve as a signal for expectations about appropriate behavior as well as a filter through which to interpret diversity-related events, research is needed to examine the moderating influence on diversity climate strength on group processes and performance.

While a number of studies have examined how context shapes team diversity outcomes, limited attention has been given to contextual influences on individuals. However, some research suggests that structural, relational, and normative features of a diversity context may trigger psychological processes related to diversity. For example, Joshi and Roh (Chapter 12) discuss the findings of social network research showing that network closure elicits categorization processes by imposing a strong sense of common identity that distinguishes in-group from out-group members based on demographic attributes. Likewise, they refer to research that highlights the role of organizational history in the transference of hierarchy-enhancing ideologies from parent to subsidiary organizations. Although these are just two examples of the effects of diversity context, the findings highlight how specific features of a context can activate (or inhibit) diversity-related cognition. Accordingly, more research that adopts a situational approach to the psychology of diversity is needed to advance our understanding of how the context in which diversity is situated influences individual perceptions, attitudes, and behavior, and subsequently team outcomes.

As the relevant context for research on diversity in groups is the organization in which groups are nested, diversity researchers have begun to look at the influence of organizational design and strategic features on the diversity–performance relationship. However, as shown in the review by Richard and Charles (Chapter 14), additional research is needed to enhance the reliability of results in this area and our ability to draw strong conclusions regarding the relationship between diversity and organizational effectiveness. To move forward our understanding of diversity context, future research should concentrate on organizational outcomes directly affected by diversity. Within the current body of work, researchers have investigated the effects of diversity at various levels of organizations (e.g., workforce, management, top management teams, etc.) on a range of productivity, valuation, and financial outcomes. However, because such firm-level indicators are driven by a number of internal factors, such as strategic choices and accounting policies, and external factors, such as economic conditions and political factors, our ability to assume a causal relationship (even with time-series data) is restricted. Therefore, researchers should begin to examine the diversity–performance relationship with a focus on capabilities that have been shown to be driven by diversity. For example, as studies have shown that diversity enhances creativity and innovation, research is needed to associate heterogeneity (either as single attributes or faultlines) and measures of innovation, such as new products or patents, sales due to new products, or research-and-development spending. Similarly, as researchers have argued that more diverse organizations will be more agile and able to respond to environmental changes, future research should examine the association between diversity and decision outcomes, such as speed and comprehensiveness. While these are just a few examples of firm-level outcomes that might be directly affected by diversity, researchers should take an organizational capabilities perspective on its link to firm performance.

As future research expands the range of diversity outcomes studied to include meso-level outcomes directly influenced by heterogeneity, it should also encapsulate the variety in performance outcomes represented by organizational stakeholders. In addition to the sources of competitive advantage discussed above, marketing research suggests that diversity enhances a firm's cultural awareness and insight, and thus its ability to serve the needs of diverse consumer markets. Similarly, by matching the demographics of the workforce to those of the communities in which they operate or customer/client bases, firms may gain greater legitimacy with these stakeholders and an ability to understand them better. Along these lines, supply chain research suggests that greater diversity in an organization's supplier base improves resource access and acquisition, and subsequently operating performance. Given these potential effects, research that adopts a stakeholder perspective on diversity is needed. More specifically, diversity researchers should design studies that examine the effects of diversity on firms' capabilities related to different stakeholder groups, such as customer satisfaction, access to funding or other resources, and community impact.

The development of theory from a capabilities perspective is also needed. Currently, most organization-level diversity research invokes the resource-based view of the firm as the theoretical framework for how heterogeneity can serve as a source of competitive advantage. As discussed by Richard and Charles (Chapter 14), diversity is a strategic resource that is rare, difficult to imitate, and value-creating, with the basis for such value stemming from access to the unique combination of knowledge, skills, and abilities within diverse workforces. While the more recent knowledge-based view of the firm, which is similar to the information processing perspective discussed throughout this volume, more accurately captures the firm-level capabilities created by diversity, we have a limited understanding of processes through which such capabilities are cultivated or translate into different types of organizational performance. Empirical research has highlighted a number of endogenous and exogenous contextual variables that influence the relationship between diversity and firm performance (e.g., the firm's reputation, human resource policies, entrepreneurial orientation, environmental stability, etc.). Yet, beyond revealing the effects of such variables, little consideration has been given to why such variables are influential or how such influence occurs. Therefore, diversity researchers should attempt to synthesize meso- and macro-level theoretical perspectives and develop new theory on the strategic effects of diversity in organizations. More precisely, researchers should attempt to develop conceptual models of diversity that articulates the mechanisms through which diversity affects firms' strategic capabilities and subsequently performance outcomes.

From a contextual perspective, future diversity research should also use a temporal frame to explore how environmental changes influence the diversity–performance relationship. Although Chrobot-Mason and colleagues (Chapter 18) review research on diversity crises from a leadership perspective to understand firm-level responses to such events, these studies suggest that diversity-related events and firms' responses may represent an important contextual feature. For example, based on the findings of research showing that diversity awards and discrimination lawsuits affect a firm's reputation and investors' reactions, diversity events may alter the direction and magnitude of the effects of demography on firm financial performance. Similarly, as diversity achievements or crises (and leader responses) may affect diversity mindsets within organizations, there may be a respective enhancing or attenuating effect of diversity on organizational capabilities. While a static examination of such occurrences would not be effective for detecting resultant changes to organizational performance, an event perspective would allow diversity researchers to learn how the nature of changes in context moderate the firm-level effects of diversity.

Diversity management

As shown in the chapters that review research on diversity practices, there is evidence to support the effectiveness of different diversity management programs. For example, Dobbins and Kalev (Chapter 15) highlight the usefulness of targeted recruitment efforts in attracting women and minorities to workplaces and that of mentoring programs, which have facilitated the structural integration of members of underrepresented groups. Despite these compositional effects, additional research is needed on the impact of diversity programs on outcomes that drive organizational effectiveness. Following from the preceding discussion of organizational capabilities, a more precise input–process–output model of diversity and firm performance may be generated by investigating the effects of different programs on a firm's meso-level outcomes, such as innovation, resource acquisition, and system flexibility. However, researchers should focus on results that would be directly affected by specific diversity programs. For example, as Avery and colleagues (Chapter 16) highlight the impact of recruitment messages about an organization's value for diversity on applicant attraction, the operational value of such messages may be examined through research focused on talent management outcomes, such as employee engagement and retention. Similar effects of career development and work–life balance programs could be explored. Future research that combines managerial and interactionist perspectives on diversity might also be insightful. For instance, considering that few studies have examined the impact of diversity training on skill development or behavioral change, as noted by Roberson and colleagues (Chapter 19), studies are needed that observe training effects on coordination, cooperation, problem solving, and other unit-level processes that may improve organizational functioning and performance. To identify such effects, longitudinal research designs that allow researchers to attribute changes in unit processes and organizational outcomes to specific diversity programs are critical.

Also beyond the compositional effects of diversity programs, research should examine programmatic effects on inclusion. Conceptualized as the degree to which employees have access to and are involved in critical organizational processes, inclusion focuses on the participation of all employees and the incorporation of their diverse perspectives into operating processes. Accordingly, inclusion extends the concept of diversity to account for all culturally relevant differences within a given context. As an innumerable number of diversity attributes (both observable and nonobservable) may be present within a given context, inclusion considers those on which in-group/out-group distinctions may be made and subsequently affect group functioning. To provide guidance on leveraging differences to achieve organizational goals, Mor Barak and Travis (Chapter 21) highlight an inclusive workplace model. However, empirical research is needed to understand the role of diversity practices in this process. For example, as the authors recommend that people in organizations should develop interpersonal skills for cross-cultural communication so they can better collaborate across national and cultural boundaries, diversity training researchers could explore how the design and delivery of such training may facilitate these outcomes. Likewise, as they recommend that organizations cooperate with and contribute to their local communities, researchers could examine the effectiveness of employment equity and career development programs for including members of local communities in organizational workforces. Overall, while research has shown various diversity programs to be effective for increasing the overall heterogeneity of organizations, more attention to effects on structural integration (i.e., representation at higher levels) and involvement in critical processes is needed.

As noted in several chapters, greater integration of research and practice is needed. While such integration could happen, at a general level, through the pursuit of research questions generated from real diversity-related issues in organizations, there are several other ways to minimize the gap between research and practice. First, more field research on the design and outcomes of diversity programs would be beneficial for not only enhancing the external validity of diversity research findings, but also for understanding the challenges of implementation in organizations. Second, tests of the efficacy of a range of human resource management programs for increasing structural integration and facilitating group processes and performance may help to both link diversity research to other bodies of literature and identify potential sources of competitive advantage through diversity management. For example, as some organizations link managers' performance appraisal and/or compensation to their ability to engage and retain employees to facilitate accountability for diversity management, empirical examinations of the effects of these practices on diversity outcomes (e.g., cooperation, conflict, innovation, etc.) would facilitate a stronger association between scholarship and practice. Third, while much diversity research has concentrated on the consequences of single diversity practices (e.g., mentoring, training, recruitment), standalone practices are not typically used to increase and capitalize on the benefit of a diverse workforce. Instead, organizations rely upon a group, or bundle, of complementary and mutually reinforcing practices to achieve positive diversity outcomes. For example, rather than offer just paid time off, organizations will offer a range of work–life flexibility options, including flex-time, parental leave, and dependent care. Similarly, career development options may include not only training, but also mentoring, coaching, and networking opportunities. As the findings of research on human resource bundles suggest that sets of practices explain greater variance in organizational outcomes than do solitary practices, future research should examine the impact of bundled diversity practices in organizations.

As noted by Mor Barak and Travis (Chapter 21) and Ozbilgin and colleagues (Chapter 22), more research on diversity from a global perspective is needed to understand the operation and meaning of diversity across cultural contexts. While such research would inherently enhance the generalizability of findings outside of the United States, it would also help researchers and managers to identify diversity practices that are more or less effective in different cultures. For example, as some countries' legal systems do not allow tracking of employee demographic data, diversity practices targeted to members of specific demographic groups may not be effective or even lawful. Accordingly, organizations operating in such countries must devise more identity-blind practices to facilitate structural integration and/or inclusion. Research examining the usefulness of traditional diversity programs outside of the United States, as well as the tension between the global effectiveness and local responsiveness of such programs across different cultures, would move the field toward a more unified understanding of diversity and its management.

A universal approach to the study of diversity

While the necessity for research that considers contextual influences on the diversity–performance relationship and related processes was discussed earlier in this chapter, researchers must also recognize the embeddedness of this framework. As noted by both Mor Barak and Travis (Chapter 21) and Ozbiligin and colleagues (Chapter 22), the composition of workforces and subsequent effects of such heterogeneity are influenced by a range of exogenous factors that can alter the conceptualization and operation of diversity. For example, the history between members of different social groups, cultural profiles of different nations, and geographic location may establish nonobservable yet powerful faultlines on which social categorization and subsequently intergroup bias may be based. Similarly, features of the external environment, such as public policy or the volatility of economic trends, may shape the composition of international labor markets and subsequently of organizational workforces. Consequently, the representation of different social groups within workforces and the nature of interactions between them may differ depending on mixed features of the external environment. Further, strategies used by organizations to manage and capitalize upon such diversity may vary according to situational features at different levels. As diversity and diversity management occur within the local, national, and international contexts in which organizations operate, critical perspectives on diversity are needed to capture the embeddedness of the phenomenon.

To synthesize the findings of diversity research and move the field toward a more unified theory of diversity, future interdisciplinary work is critical. Considering that investigations of diversity have been conducted across a variety of fields, including psychology, sociology, anthropology, management, law, and social work (to name a few), there exists a wealth of theoretical perspectives and empirical results. However, because few comparative or integrative investigations between fields have been conducted, this expansive study of diversity has also given rise to several equivocalities. For example, Apfelbaum and Sommers (Chapter 23) draw attention to differences in the interpretation and measurement of racial bias from legal versus behavioral science perspectives, which has generated subsequent differences in the conclusions drawn about bias and its remediation. Likewise, although much diversity research across disciplines has relied upon social categorization and/or information processing explanations of diversity's effects, there has been little attention to the interrelatedness of these processes at different levels. For example, how might identity navigation processes simultaneously influence the construction of a group member's personal identity and the identity of the group to which he or she belongs? Might an organization's diversity climate represent a shared, hierarchy-enhancing ideology within an organization yet serve as a source of competitive advantage? Designing research to explore such questions would allow researchers to study the reciprocity of diversity-related phenomenon across theoretical perspectives and levels of analysis. In addition, such interdisciplinary work would provide an opportunity for the triangulation of results, thus increasing diversity researchers' ability to draw stronger conclusions about the meaning and operation of diversity in organizations.

Conclusion

As highlighted in this handbook, diversity yields both positive and negative effects on individuals, groups and teams, and organizations. Similarly, the study of diversity has yielded both negative and positive outcomes for the field. On the negative side, there is still much we do not know about diversity. On the positive side, there is still much we do not know about diversity. Thus, there is both the challenge that diversity research may remain stagnant by continuing along similar paths of investigation and the opportunity that evolution in research may advance our understanding of the meaning and operation of diversity. So, under what conditions can we avoid the potential challenges of diversity research yet capitalize on the opportunities? While this chapter and this handbook highlight areas ripe for theoretical development and empirical exploration, greater overall attention to the what, why, when, and how of diversity may provide insight into the complexities of the diversity phenomenon. Greater diversity in our conceptualizations, theoretical approaches, and methodologies may reveal more and varied information and expertise about diversity as well as ways that researchers can collaborate across disciplines. Such diversity in our research resources may subsequently enhance our problem solving around diversity research questions and stimulate even more creative ways of exploring diversity-related phenomena. Thus, the "value" in diversity research may also be in diversity.

INDEX

A
Access-and-legitimacy paradigm
Acculturation, 463
active faultlines, 55, 58–59, 63–64
adhocracy culture, organization, 245
adverse impact (AI), diversity selection, 289
affirmative action
    diversity, 144
    diversity programs, 254
    University of Michigan, 454
agents of influence, leadership, 316–317
age similarity, network connections, 197–198
agreeableness, personality factor, 227
alignment, faultlines, 53
allocation decisions, variables, 379, 381
allophilia, 326
ambivalence aversive racism, 104
American Psychological Association, 144
American Psychologist, 317
Analysis of Subjective Culture, Triandis, 34
analytical methods
    diversity research, 21–23
    perceived vs. actual diversity, 22–23
ancestry, cultural diversity, 35
antecedents, stigmatization, 123
antidiscrimination departments, 260
antidiscrimination legislation, 8, 253
Anti-Drug Abuse Act of 1986, 450
anti-harassment training, 272, 273
Asia, population by age, 396
assimilationism, hierarchy-enhancing ideology, 134, 141
asymmetry in conflict
    actual and perceived diversity, 186–187
    diversity and conflict, 183–187
    group-level conflict, 180, 184–185
    understudied types of conflict, 185–186
attitudes
    changing gender roles, 376–377
    diversity, 352–353
    diversity training, 343–344
    prejudice, 116
    pre-training, 350

attraction-selection-attrition framework, diversity research, 210
awareness, diversity training design, 344–345, 347, 348

B
Batson v. Kentucky (1986), 447, 449
behavior
    knowledge, 38
    norms and values, 38–39
    power differentials, 319–320
    role identity, 78
    values of individuals, 36, 37
behavioral sciences, approach to diversity, 10
behavioral scripts, 80
Belief in Just World (BJW)
    ideology, 133, 134, 140
    origin of ideology, 136
    structure, 138
bias
    anxiety, 348
    assessment, 10, 448–450
    categorization processes, 76
    counteracting, 450–453
    definition, 10, 444
    explicitness, 445–447
    individual- and group-based approaches to counteracting, 450–452
    institutional and ideological approaches to counteracting, 452–453
    intentionality, 444–445
    perception, 319
"Big Five," personality factors, 227–228, 290
bilateral integration, 436
biocultural approach, stigmatization, 122
blindness, social identity, 320, 321
body size discrimination, 26–27
bona fide occupational qualification (BFOQ), 257
bottom line, understanding, 275–276
boundary spanning, 327–328
breadwinner role, 376

Brown v. Board of Education (1954), 452
buffering model, work-life interface, 372
bureaucracy
    diversity, 263–265
    hiring and promotions, 261–263
Bureau of National Affairs (BNA), 255, 256
business case
    for diversity, 243, 333, 341, 345, 423
    global diversity, 433–435, 436
business strategy
    moderation model, 244
    workplace diversity, 243

C
campus recruiting, 284–285
career development
    ambient cues and traditional representation, 304–305
    cross-cultural barriers to mentoring, 309–310
    discrimination and isolation, 307
    disembodied worker, 367–369
    diversity, 8
    diversity climate, 305
    drivers of vocational choice, 302–303
    expectations of success, 306–307
    external barriers, 301
    future directions, 310–311
    gender and vocational choice, 304
    gender/race valuation, 306
    human resource strategy, 300–301
    identity, 303–304
    internal barriers, 301–302
    mentoring, 302, 307–310
    mentoring importance, 308–309
    ongoing vocational choice, 306
    opportunities, 310–311
    perceived similarity, 305–306
    race and vocational choice, 304
    social distancing, 301–302
    vocational choice, 302–307
categorization approach
    bias, 76
    diversity, 5–6

categorization-based outcomes
  context effects, 212
  normative context, 213–214
  relational context, 212–213
  structural context, 214–215
categorization-elaboration model (CEM)
  faultlines, 57
  information processing, 162
  workgroup diversity and performance, 224
categorization processes
  decategorization, 105–106
  future directions, 108–109
  intergroup bias in organizations, 103–108
  multiculturalism vs. colorblindness, 107–108
  mutual differentiation, 105, 107
  recategorization, 106–107
centralization-based integration, global diversity, 436
change agents, global diversity managers, 431–433
child-care programs, women's issues, 271, 274
Civil Rights Act, 126, 263, 269, 272, 452
civil rights movement, 253
claiming, identity, 87
clan culture, organization, 245
class, critical identity, 80–81
climate strength, shared diversity, 231, 235
closure, network, effect, 199
cocaine, racial bias, 450
cognitive ability tests (CATs), diversity selection, 289–291
cognitive accessibility, categorization, 57
cohesion
  social networks, 199
  team performance, 200–202
collaboration, cross-cultural, 41–42
collective cognition theory, cross-cultural research, 40
collective identity, politicized, 135
college recruitment, diversity climate, 231
colorblindness
  bias in organizations, 107–108
  counteracting bias, 452–453
  hierarchy-enhancing ideology, 134, 137, 141
  ideology research, 147–148
  inclusion, 401–402
  intergroup relations, 226
common goals, leaders, 326
communication, cross-cultural strategies, 34–35
communication technology use, faultlines, 61
comparative cross-national research, context, 216–217
comparative fit, categorization, 57
compensation, work-life interface, 371
competence expectations, workgroup interactions, 166

competition
  global, and workforce diversity, 239–240
  globalization, 4
competitive advantage
  diversity training, 341–342
  future research directions, 246–247
  high-quality workers, 368–369
  human capital, 282
competitive behaviors, social identity, 77–78
competitive diversity
  business strategy, 244
  human resource management practices, 245–246
  knowledge-based view (KBV), 242
  moderation model and current state of research, 243–246
  moderation model of diversity, 242–243
  organizational culture, 244–245
  resource-based view (RBV), 241–242
  value-in-diversity, 242
concealability, stigma, 116–117
conceptualization
  diversity beliefs and attitudes, 222–225
  diversity climate, 228–230
conceptualization of diversity, 4–5
conflict
  actual vs. perceived diversity, 186–187
  asymmetry, 183–187
  diversity faultlines, 182–183
  functional heterogeneity, 181–182
  group, 180–181, 187
  group-level, research, 184–185
  lifestyle heterogeneity and, 185–186
  power diversity, 186
  social category heterogeneity, 181
  understudied diversity, 185–186
confrontation, diversity training, 347
consequences, stigmatization, 124–125
construct dimensions, identification of, 27
contact hypothesis
  decategorization, 105–106
  stigmatization, 123
context
  categorization- and elaboration-based effects of normative, 212, 213–214
  categorization- and elaboration-based effects of relational, 212–213
  categorization- and elaboration-based effects of structural, 212, 214–215
  challenges in studying, 209–210, 217
  comparative cross-national research, 216–217
  cross-level research, 215–216
  defining diversity, 211–212
  diversity construct, 464–466
  future research, 215–217
  organizational research, 209
  qualitative research, 216

relational leadership, 335
temporal effects, 216
theoretical framework, 210–215
understanding, 275
context model, global diversity management, 425, 428–429
contextual perspectives, diversity, 7
contingency theory, diversity, 243
controllability, stigma, 117
cooperation, faultlines, 64
coping strategies, stigma, 120–121
Corning Glass Works v. Brennan (1974), 263
corporate diversity programs
  1960s and attack on Jim Crow, 256–259
  1970s and labor relations model, 259–265
  1980s: Reagan and rebranding equal opportunity, 265–269
  1990s and women's issues, 269–272
  anti-harassment programs, 272, 273
  bottom line, 275–276
  context, 275
  failure, 274
  nondiscrimination policies, 256–257
  origins and outcomes of, 254–255
  sociological approach, 255–256
  success, 274
  understanding diversity, 275
corporations, business case rationale, 433
creativity, faultlines, 64
critical identity theory, navigating the self, 75, 80–82
cross-categorization, 59
cross-cultural barriers, mentoring, 309–310
cross-cutting category theory, 59
cross-level research, context, 215–216
cultivate and encourage approach, managing difference, 331
cultivation, mentoring, 308
cultural diversity
  configuration of, within individuals, 37–38
  contextualizing, 42–43
  globalization, 32–33
  identity construction and navigating the self, 90–91
  individual-level, 37–39
  language systems, 34–35
  macrocomponents of, 34–36
  management, 424
  measurement, 45
  objective attributes of, 33, 34
  physical terrain and climate, 35
  political systems, 35
  research frontiers, 43–46
  situational triggers, 38–39
  social structures, 35
  sociodemographic cultural components, 35–36
  structure within individuals and teams, 45–46

student workgroups, 161
subjective attributes, 33, 36
team, 39–46
types of, 33–34
cultural identities, situational triggers, 38–39
cultural intelligence, teams, 42
culture, 167
  defined, 33–36
  diversity, 5
  learning, 333
customer markets, internationalization, 3–4
cycle of influence, social identity, 322, 329

D

death penalty hearing, 448
decategorization, prejudice reduction, 105–106
decision making, information and opinions, 159
deep-level diversity
  conceptualization, 14, 15, 16–17
  cultural components, 41–42
demographic attributes (DEM), 17–19, 23
demographic dissimilarity, diversity vs., 233
demographic diversity. *See also* network connections
  double-edged sword of, 221–222
  informational resource, 222
  organization of work processes, 192
  social categorization, 221
  United States, 283
demographic faultlines
  active faultlines and faultline triggers, 58–59, 63–64
  career development barrier, 301–302
  categorization-elaboration model (CEM), 57
  conflict, 182–183
  consequences, 59–60, 64
  definition, 52–53
  direct vs. moderating effects, 65
  diversity forms, 54, 55–56
  diversity types and, 54–55
  faultline composition and antecedents, 57–58, 63
  faultline definition and measurement, 65–66
  faultline endurance, 61–62, 65
  gaps in the study of faultlines, 63–66
  latent and active, 58–59
  moderators of faultlines-outcomes relationship, 60–61, 65
  relationship between diversity and, 53–56, 67n.1
  research, 57–62, 66
  role in capturing demographic complexity, 62–63
  term, 53
  theoretical underpinnings, 56–57
  women and people of color, 305
demographic similarity
  network connections, 193–195
  propinquity, 196–198
deregulation, globalization and competition, 4
Desert Palace v. Costa (2003), 446
design. *See* diversity training design
design features, moderation model, 246
desk experts, 437
devaluation threats, identity work, 85
developmental perspective, positive identity, 91
differences, 13
differential power approach, workgroup model, 17–19
direct and control, managing difference, 330–331
disabilities in workplace, socioeconomic trend, 408–410, 412
disagreement. *See also* conflict; group conflict
disclosure dilemmas, 120
discourse, navigating the self, 81–82
discrimination
  assessing bias, 448–450
  career development, 307
  career development barrier, 301
  employment, 445, 446
  global diversity, 434
  organizations, 119
  Ricci v. DeStafano (2009), 452
  sexual orientation, 228
  stigmatizers, 124
  Washington v. Davis (1976), 445
Discrimination-and-fairness paradigm
disembodied worker
  career development, 367–369
  focus on "war for talent," 368–369
  impact of gender, 375–378
  work-life facilitation, 367
  work-life flexibility, 369
disparity, 13
  diversity, 19–21, 55–56, 67n.2
  measurement, 22, 45
dispelling, negative stereotypes, 85–86
disruption, stigma, 117
distance, 13, 34
distancing, threats, 85
diversity, 167. *See also* context; ideologies
  advantages in organizations and teams, 98–99
  bureaucracy and, 263–265
  categorization approach, 5–6
  conceptualization of, 4–5, 461–462
  conflict, 181–182
  contingency theory, 243
  as culture, 5
  defining, 158–159
  double-edged sword of, 221–222
  effects of context, 464–466
  equal opportunity and antidiscrimination legislation, 8
  equal opportunity programs, 266
faultline theory, 62–63
holistic approach to study of, 468
ideologies, 132–133
ideology, 6
interactionist perspectives, 6–7
legal-behavioral science divide, 10
management, 466–468
mechanisms underlying effects, 462–464
perceived vs. actual, 22–23
performance benefits and process, 7
phenomenon, 4, 5
relationship to demographic faultlines, 53–56
social networks, 199–202
strategies for developing leaders of, 336
systems perspectives on, 9
team performance, 202–203
term, 28, 115
understanding, 275
variations of traits, 13
diversity advantage
  design features, 246
  future research directions, 246–247
  human resource management, 245–246
  moderation model, 242–243
  value-in-diversity, 240–241
diversity attitudes
  affirmative action, 144
  categorization-elaboration model (CEM), 224
  conceptualization and measurement of, 222–225
  consequences of, 225–226
  decision-making groups, 224–225
  determinants of, 226–228
  discrimination scales, 223
  future directions, 233–235
  ideology, 144–145
  immigration, 145
  individual, 222–228
  intergroup biases, 224–225
  labels, 223
  learning from experience, 227
  outcomes, 220–221
  psychological climates, 233, 234
  value of diversity, 226
  women in workplace, 144–145
  workplace, 146
diversity attributes, cross-national research, 216–217
diversity beliefs
  attribute-specific beliefs, 223
  categorization-elaboration model (CEM), 224
  conceptualization and measurement of, 222–225
  consequences of, 225–226
  decision-making groups, 224–225
  determinants of, 226–228
  future directions, 233–235
  individual, 222–228
  intergroup biases, 224–225

INDEX | 473

diversity beliefs (cont.)
    labels, 223
    outcomes, 220–221
    value of diversity, 226
diversity climate
    career development, 305
    conceptualization and measurement, 228–230
    consequences of perceived, 230
    definition, 228
    determinants of perceptions of, 231
    diversity attitudes and, 234
    holistic approach to study of diversity, 468
    individual perceptions, 228–231
    organizational climate, 229
    racio-ethnic and gender diversity, 244
    shared, 231–233
    team diversity-performance relationship, 229
    team diversity perspectives, 229–230
diversity cognition
    climate and, 235
    diversity and demography, 233
    outcome ratings, 225
    personality factors, 227–228
diversity crises, dealing with, 332
diversity culture audits, from attitude surveys to, 267
diversity disadvantage, social identity theory, 240
diversity ecosystem, challenges, opportunities and future, 411–413
diversity forms, demographic faultlines, 54, 55–56
diversity hires, expectations of success, 307
diversity-leadership mindset, 8
diversity management, 7, 266, 284, 466–468. See also corporate diversity programs; global diversity management
    domestic diversity in North America, 419–420
    global, 9–10
    global, managers as change agents, 431–433
    integration of research and practice, 467–468
    moderation model, 243
    women's issues, 273–274
Diversity Perceptions Scale, 343
diversity-performance debate, network connections, 198–199
diversity-performance research, 7
    diversity climate of team, 229
    diversity in groups, 465–466
diversity programs, 8. See also corporate diversity programs
    management effects, 269
diversity recruitment, literature, 292, 293
diversity research
    analytical methods and measures, 21–23
    challenges, 14
    cultural diversity, 43–46
    deep-level diversity, 14, 15, 16–17
    differential power approach, 17–18
    diversity as separation, variety and disparity, 19–21
    diversity types, 16–21
    early theories, 14–16
    expectations approach, 17, 18
    future, 23–27
    hidden traits approach, 23–26
    identifying construct dimensions, 27
    integrative multicultural approach, 18–19
    invisible social identities, 23–26
    multicultural approach, 18–19, 25
    mutable traits, 26
    perceived vs. actual diversity, 22–23
    similarity-attraction paradigm, 14–15
    social identity theory (SIT), 15–16
    surface-level diversity, 15, 16
    trait approach, 17, 18
    trait self-disclosure, 26
    weight and body size, 26–27
    workgroup models, 17–19
diversity scholarship, navigating the self, 73–74
diversity skills, evaluation of training, 353, 357
diversity staffing
    future directions, 293–294
    how to select for diversity, 289–291
    literature review, 283–291
    recruiting and retaining diverse workforce, 291–293
    what messages organizations should be sending, 285–286
    when the time is right for, 287
    where organizations should be recruiting, 287–289
    who should be recruiting applicants, 284–285
    why organizations should have, 283–284
diversity taskforces, 267, 268
diversity training
    academic research and practitioners, 358–359
    attitudes, 352–353
    choice of diversity trainer, 349
    communicated reason for, 350–351
    delivery decisions, 349–351
    demographics of training group, 349–350
    design, 344–351
    directions for future research, 357–358
    diversity skills, 353
    fair employment, 267
    framing of training, 350
    from race relations workshops to, 266–267
    management linking consequences, 354–355
    mandatory vs. voluntary, 351
    mentoring, 268–269
    models and methods for design, 344–348
    needs assessment, 342–344
    networking programs, 268
    operations analysis, 343
    organizational impact, 355–356
    organization analysis, 342–343
    person analysis, 343–344
    task analysis, 343
    teams, 358
    trainee changes, 352–355
    trainer demographics, 349
    training evaluation and transfer of training, 351–356
    transfer of training, 353–355
    workforce diversity, 268–269
diversity training design
    awareness first, 344–345, 347, 348
    confrontation, 347
    diversity knowledge, 345
    diversity trainer, 349
    Implicit Association Test (IAT), 346
    models and methods, 344–348
    self-awareness exercises, 346–347
    self-knowledge, 346
    social categorization, 345–346
    social learning theory, 347–348
    theory of learning, 344
    trainees' characteristics, 348–349
diversity types, demographic faultlines, 65–66
diversity-validity dilemma, selection, 291
double minorities, information processing, 163
dual identification, hyphenations, 88
Due Process Clause of the Fifth Amendment, 445
education
    diversity mindset, 336
    diversity training, 356–357
    literacy rates, 404, 407
    socioeconomic trend, 403–404, 412

E

Education For All (EFA), literacy rates, 407
egalitarianism
    hierarchy-attenuating ideology, 135
    structure, 137, 139
elaboration-based outcomes
    context effects, 212
    normative context, 213–214
    relational context, 212–213
    structural context, 214–215
embedded intergroup relations approach, 216
employee resource groups (ERGs)
employee staffing, competitive advantage, 282

employer antidiscrimination policies, women and minorities, 256
employer migration, socioeconomic trend, 398–399, 411–412
employment cycle, stigma, 119
employment discrimination, 445, 446
employment interview, selection, 290
endurance, faultlines, 61–62, 65
entitlement. *See* team entitlement
entrepreneurs of identity, 322
environmental munificence
   family, 379, 381, 382–383
   integrated model, 383
   work, 379, 381, 382
environmental support, work-life flexibility, 373
equal employment opportunity, 8
   attitude surveys, 254, 267
   diversity culture audits, 267
   diversity mission statements, 266
   diversity programs and workforce diversity, 268–269
   diversity taskforces, 267
   job descriptions, 262–263, 264
   job ladders, 262, 264
   job posting, 262, 264
   job tests, 261, 264
   mentoring and networking programs, 267–268
   monitoring individual managers, 260
   organizational responsibility, 259–260
   performance evaluations, 263, 264–265
   Reagan and rebranding, 265–269
   responsibility and diversity, 260–261
   salary classification, 263, 265
Equal Employment Opportunity Commission (EEOC), 255
equal opportunity policies, targeted recruitment and training, 258–259
equal opportunity taskforces, 267
Equal Pay Act, 263
equal protection, court cases, 452
Equal Protection Clause, 452
ethnic, 167
ethnic diversity
   socioeconomic trend, 401–402, 412
   team performance, 210
ethnicity
   communication media, 170–171
   cultural diversity, 35
   diversity programs and management effects, 269
   diversity research, 14
   faultline activation, 64
ethnic minorities
   colorblindness, 147–148
   self-esteem, 118
   status, 171
Europe, population by age, 396
European Union (EU), women's and men's economic activity, 400
evaluative perspective

positive identity, 90–91
positive relational identity, 92
expectations approach, workgroup model, 17–19
experience, diversity and learning from, 227
experts in the field, 437
explicit attitudes, intergroup bias, 103–104
explicitness, bias, 445–447

F

factions, faultline trigger, 58
failure, understanding, 274
Fair Housing Act of 1968, 452
fairness perception, selection, 286
Fair Sentencing Act of 2010, 450
family, changing gender role behaviors, 376
family environment munificence
   integrated model, 383
   variables, 379, 381
   work-life interface, 382–383
family interference with work (FIW), 372, 377–378
family resource gains/losses, variables, 379, 381
family resource investments, variables, 379, 381
family role demands, variables, 379, 381
family role performance, variables, 379, 381
family support, work-life flexibility, 373
family-to-work enrichment (WFE), 373
faultlines. *See also* demographic faultlines
   active, 55, 63–64
   bridging, 331–332
   composition and antecedents of, 57–58
   consequences, 59–60, 64
   definition and measurement, 65–66
   direct vs. moderating effects, 65
   diversity, and conflict, 182–183
   endurance, 61–62, 65
   latent, 55
   leadership managing, 331–332
   potential sources in organizational groups, 57–58
   social category, 54
   strength, 53, 54
   term, 53, 65–66
faultline theory
   demographic complexity, 62–63
   identity groups, 5
   performance of group, 59–60
faultline trigger, active, 58–59
feigning indifference, threats, 85, 86
female leaders, role congruity, 78–79
The Feminist Case Against Bureaucracy, Ferguson, 263
firm performance, diversity and, 7
flextime programs, women's issues, 270–271, 273
formalization-based integration, global diversity, 436

Fortune 100, teams, 166
framing, diversity training, 350
France, 368, 398
functional heterogeneity, conflict, 181–182

G

gays, lesbians, and transgender. *See also* lesbian, gays, bisexual and transgender (LGBT)
gender, 167
   changing role attitudes, 376–377
   changing role behaviors in family, 376
   critical identity, 80–81
   cultural diversity, 35–36
   disembodied worker ideal, 375–378
   role congruity, 78–79
   stereotype threat, 306
   vocational choice, 304
   work-family interface, 377–378
gender diversity
   attitudes, 226–227
   beliefs in value, 226
   diversity climate, 244
   group outcomes, 210
   information elaboration, 232
gender identity
   socioeconomic trend, 402–403, 412
   structural context, 215
geography, faultline trigger, 58
glass ceiling
   equal opportunities, 401
   expectations of success, 307
   perception, 319
   vocational choice, 302
Glass Ceiling Commission, 253, 259
Global Compact, 423
global competition, workforce diversity, 239–240
Global Diversity and Inclusion Readiness Index, 423
global diversity management
   activities in organizational change, 430
   business case rationale, 433–435
   capacity of managers as change agents, 431–433
   context model, 425, 428–429
   database research, 435
   definition, 421–422
   development of, theory and practice, 422–424
   domestic diversity in North America, 419–420
   expansion of diversity management outside North America, 420–421
   human resources, 422, 423
   intervention model, 425, 429–430, 435
   models of, 424–430
   national borders, 9–10
   process model, 425, 426–428
   responsibility and translation, 430–431
   strategic model, 424–426

globalization
  cultural diversity, 32–33
  driving diversity, 421–422
  workforce diversity, 239–240, 399
  world economies, 3–4
granting, identity, 87
Gratz v. Bollinger 2003, 452, 454
Greece, labor force participation, 368
grievance procedures, sexual harassment, 272, 273
Griggs v. Duke Power (1971), 259, 261
group approach, counteracting bias, 450–452
group composition, demographic diversity and faultlines, 54
group conflict. *See also* conflict
  asymmetry, 180, 183–187
  conflict and group effectiveness, 180–181
  types of intra-, 180
  workgroup outcomes, 179–180
group consciousness, 135
group diversity
  faultline theory, 62–63
  organizational success, 52
group effectiveness
  conflict and, 180–181
  diversity, 6
group identity, culture, 36
group-level organizational citizenship behaviors (GOCB), 64
group memberships
  identity performance, 84–85
  social identity, 76–77
  stigma, 116
group mentoring, 308
group outcomes, faultlines, 64
group processes
group size, faultline composition, 63
growth, narrative-as-identity, 83
Grutter v. Bollinger (2003), 452, 454

H

hands-off approach, managing difference, 330
health care, socioeconomic trend, 395–397
heterogeneity, 13, 98
hidden diversity, social identities, 23–26
hierarchical organization, leadership, 317
hierarchy-attenuating ideologies, 6, 135–136, 139–140, 146–147
hierarchy culture, organization, 245
hierarchy-enhancing ideologies, 6, 133–134, 139–140
HIV/AIDS, socioeconomic trend, 396–397
holistic approach, study of diversity, 468
homemaker role, 376
homophily
  demographic diversity and, 196
  network connections, 193–195
  social interactions, 160

social networks, 201
Hudson Institute, Workforce 2000, 3
human capital perspective
  global diversity management, 432
  value-in-diversity, 242
  workplace diversity, 241
human dignity, workplace diversity, 437
humanitarianism, hierarchy-attenuating ideology, 135
human resources. *See also* diversity training
  career development, 300–301
  disembodied worker, 376
  diversity climate, 228
  diversity staffing, 287
  diversity training, 341
  global diversity management, 422, 423
  implementing practices, 332–333
  mandatory vs. voluntary training, 351
  organizational diversity, 232–233
  service organizations, 243
  surveys, 255
  workforces, 4
  workplace diversity, 242
human rights, socioeconomic trend, 402–403, 412
Human Rights Campaign, 403
Hurricane Katrina, 147, 216
hyphenation, dual identification, 88

I

identity-as-self perspective, 5
identity awareness, perception, 320–321
identity construction
  critical identity, 81
  narrative-as-identity, 82
identity groups
  faultline theory, 5
  negative views of themselves, 118
  positive views of themselves, 118
  vocational choice, 303–304
identity narratives, narrative-as-identity, 83
identity negotiation, identity work, 84, 86–87
identity performance, identity work, 84–87
identity regulation, critical identity, 81
identity work
  claiming, 87
  devaluation threats, 85
  granting, 87
  identity negotiation, 84, 86–87
  identity performance, 84–87
  legitimacy threats, 85–87
  navigating the self, 75, 83–87
  social validation, 87
  threat, 84, 85
ideological approach, counteracting bias, 452–453
ideologies
  Belief in Just World (BJW), 133, 134, 136, 140
  classes, 133–136
  colorblindness, 107–108, 147–148

definition, 133
diversity attitudes, 144–145
diversity in workplace, 6, 132
future research, 146–148
hierarchy-attenuating ideologies, 135–136
hierarchy-enhancing ideologies, 133–134
implications for workplace, 139–140, 145–146
intergroup relations, 141–144
malleability, 147
multiculturalism, 107–108, 148
Protestant Work Ethic (PWE), 133, 134, 136, 137, 140
psychological origins and functions of, 136–137
self, 140–141
structure of, 137–139
system justification, 148*n*.2
ignorance, social identity, 320
immigration
  ideologies and attitudes, 145
  socioeconomic trend, 397–398, 411
Implicit Association Test (IAT), 103–104, 109, 346
implicit attitudes, intergroup bias, 103–104, 109
implicit egalitarianism, 109
inclusion
  belongingness and uniqueness, 320
  diverse workforce, 411
  diversity mindset, 336
  global diversity management, 427
  racial and ethnic groups in workplace, 401–402
  workforce diversity, 413–414
inclusive climate, developing a meta-narrative, 330
inclusive work climate, 325–326
inclusive workplace model, 414
inclusivity effect, context, 216
independent-effects model, work-life interface, 371–372
individual approach, counteracting bias, 450–452
individual behavior, role identity, 78
individual differences, 4–5
individualism-collectivism, faultlines, 65
individualism vs. collectivism, culture, 36
individual-level cultural diversity
  configuration, 37–38
  situational triggers, 38–39
individuals, faultline triggers, 64
informal integration
informational/opinion diversity, 159, 163
informational resource perspective, 222
information-based integration, global diversity, 436
information elaboration
  decision-making groups, 224–225
  shared diversity climates, 232
information-processing perspective

beyond double minorities, 163–164
categorization elaboration model, 162
categorization of articles, 168
diversity, 6, 463
double minorities, 163
expansion of, 162–164
explicit status/explicit, 172
explicit status/tacit, 170–172
group effectiveness, 6–7
integrating social categorization with, 162
minority influence, 163
no status/explicit, 168–169
no status/tacit, 169–170
social category perspective, 163, 172–173
tacit status/tacit, 170
teams, 41
theory, 210
understanding diversity, 159, 161–162
inhibition, stereotypes, 109
initiation, mentoring, 308
innovation
institutional approach, counteracting bias, 452–453
institutions, minority-focused recruiting, 288
integration
dual identification, 88
role identity, 79–80
integration and learning perspective, 230
intentionality, bias, 444–445
interactional model of cultural diversity (IMCD)
interactionist perspectives, 6–7, 463
interests, faultline trigger, 58
intergroup bias, 99
decategorization, 105–106
diversity beliefs and attitudes, 224–225
future directions, 108–109
mutual differentiation, 107
organizations, 103–108
recategorization, 106–107
intergroup emotions theory, stigmatization, 121
intergroup relations
high status perceivers/high status targets, 142–143
high status perceivers/low status targets, 141–142
ideological asymmetries, 147
ideologies, 141–144
low status perceivers/high status targets, 143–144
low status perceivers/low status targets, 143
workplace, 145–146
International Classification of Functioning, Disability and Health (ICF), 408
International Food Policy Research Institute (IFPI), 401
internationalization, customer markets, 3–4

International Organization for Migration, 398
International Telecommunication Union (ITU), 410
Internet
recruiting, 287–289
technological advance, 411, 414
interpersonal dynamics, team performance, 6–7
interpersonal experiences, stigma, 119–120
intersectionality, critical identity, 80–81
intervention model, global diversity management, 425, 429–430, 435
interviews, recruiting applicants, 285
intragroup conflict
faultlines, 59
perceived and actual, 186–187
types, 180
intrapersonal experiences, stigma, 117–118
invisible identities, identity performance, 86
invisible social identities, future research, 23–26
isolation, career development, 307

J

Jim Crow. *See also* corporate diversity programs
attack on, 256–259
corporate nondiscrimination policies, 256–257
recruitment programs, 257–258
targeted recruitment and training, 258–259
training for opportunity, 258
job descriptions, 262–263, 264
job ladders, 262, 264
job posting, 262, 264
job-relatedness
job tests, 261, 264
job type, faultline moderator, 65
jury selection, counteracting bias, 450–451
justification-suppression model (JSM), 122

K

knowledge
diversity, 352
diversity training design, 345
driving behavior, 38
knowledge, skills, and abilities (KSA), 17–19, 25, 157
knowledge exchange, 6
categorization elaboration model, 162
communication media and ethnicity, 170–171
competence expectations, 166
database searches, 167–168
expanding information processing, 162–164

expectations states theory, 165
explicit status/explicit information processing, 172
explicit status/tacit information processing, 170–172
future directions, 167–172
globalization, 4
information processing perspective, 161–162, 172–173
integrating information processing with social categorization, 164
minorities, 163–164, 171
minority influence and social categorization, 163
no status/explicit information processing, 168–169
no status/tacit information processing, 169–170
performance expectations, 165
similarity-attraction perspective, 160–161
social category perspective, 159, 160–161, 172–173
status and power, 165
status characteristics theory, 165–166
status differences in diverse groups, 164–167
status violations' influencing information processing, 166–167
tacit status/tacit information processing, 170
task experience, 166
understanding diversity through, 158
knowledge transfer
group effectiveness, 6–7
network connections, 192–193

L

labor force
entry of women into paid, 367–369
female proportion, 400
participation rates by country, 368
women's participation in global, 399–401, 412
labor market, international, 4
labor market shortages, diversity staffing, 287
labor relations model
antidiscrimination departments, 260
bureaucracy and diversity, 263–265
bureaucratic hiring and promotion, 261–263
creating organizational responsibility, 259–260
expanding, 259–265
monitoring individual managers, 260
responsibility and diversity, 260–261
language, objective culture, 34–35
latent faultlines, 55, 58–59
Latin America, 396, 400, 405–406, 407
law and diversity. *See also* legal-behavioral science

INDEX | 477

law and diversity (cont.)
  assessment of bias, 448–450
  bias, 444–447
  counteracting bias, 450–453
  future directions, 454–455
law of requisite variety, 421
leader-member exchange (LMX) theory, 318, 323
  developing high-quality relationships, 324–325
  inclusive work climate, 325–326
  relational leadership, 325
  transformational leadership, 324
leadership
  accountability
    boundary spanning, 327–328
    concept of shared, 317
  diversity, 8
  diversity-leadership mindset, 334–335
  diversity management, 247
  effective, 317–318
  intersection of, and diversity, 315–317
  leading others, 321–329
  leading self, 318–321
  leading the organization, 329–334
  managing relationships, 316
  power differentials, 319–320
  relational, in context of diversity, 335
  research and theory, 316–317
  self-management, 316
  setting agenda for future research, 334–336
  social identity conflict, 327
  social identity theory of, 322–323
  socially constructed nature of, 318
  strategies for developing, 336
  strategies for enhancing, 323–328, 331–333
leaky pipeline, vocational choice, 303–304
learning
  career development, 310
  culture of, in organizations, 333
  diversity training design, 344
  global diversity management, 432
learning-and-effectiveness paradigm
legal approach, diversity, 10
legal-behavioral science. *See also* law and diversity
  assessing bias, 448–450
  bias, 444
  colorblindness, 452–453
  counteracting bias, 450–453
  future directions, 454–455
  jury selection, 450–451
  voir dire, 451
legitimacy threats, identity work, 85–87
lesbian, gays, bisexual and transgender (LGBT)
  gender identity, 402–403
  self-affirming, 82
  social change, 78
  workers, 28
lifestyle heterogeneity, conflict, 185–186

line-management, diversity, 247
literacy rates, education, 404, 407
looking-glass self, 119

M

McCleskey v. Kemp (1987), 443, 445
McReynolds v. Merrill Lynch (2005), 449
majority influence, 167
manageable, diversity, 220
management
  bureaucratic hiring and promotion, 261–263
  diversity training impact, 355–356
  workforce diversity, 413–414
managing difference, organizational leadership, 330–331
mandatory training, diversity, 351
manifestations, stigmatization, 123–124
market culture, organization, 245
marketing
masculinity vs. femininity, culture, 36
maternity leaves, 270
Matthew Shepard and James Byrd Jr. Hate Crimes Prevention Act (HPCA), 402
maximum separation diversity, 55
maximum variety diversity, 55
measurement
  cultural diversity, 45
  diversity beliefs and attitudes, 222–225
  diversity climate, 228–230
  faultline, 65–66
  separation, variety, and disparity, 22
  shared climates, 231
membership
  beliefs and behaviors, 37–38
  culture, 36
mentoring
  career development, 8, 302, 307–310
  cross-cultural barriers to, 309–310
  diversity management, 267–268
  importance of, 308–309
  stages, 308
  workforce diversity, 268–269
meritocracy
  hierarchy-enhancing ideology, 134
  structure, 137–138
Merrill Lynch, class-action lawsuit against, 448–449
meta-stereotypes, meta-perceptions, 119
Mexico, 368, 406
Miller-El v. Dretke (2005), 449
minorities
  antidiscrimination policies, 256
  career development, 310–311
  discrimination and isolation, 307
  diversity attitudes, 226–227
  diversity staff and evaluation, 261
  firms with training programs, 258
  human resources, 228
  identity development, 83
  mentoring, 309–310

program effects on management diversity, 269
  recruitment of, 284–285, 294
  similarity perceptions, 305–306
  status, 171
  stereotype threat, 306
  vocational choice, 304
  work-family programs and opportunities, 271–272
minority influence, 163, 167
minority recruiters, 285, 286
mission statements, 266
Miville-Guzman Universality-Diversity Scale, 344
moderate variety diversity, 55
moderation model
  business strategy, 244
  current research, 243–246
  design features, 246
  diversity advantage, 242–243
  human resource management, 245–246
  organizational culture, 244–245
moderators, faultlines-outcomes relationship, 60–61, 65
monolithic organizations
motherhood, 167
Multi-City Study of Urban Inequality, 258–259
multicultural approach, workgroup model, 18–19, 25
multiculturalism, 167
  bias in organizations, 107–108
  hierarchy-attenuating ideology, 135, 141
  ideology research, 148
  intergroup relations, 226
  structure, 139
multicultural teams
  collaboration, 41–42
  cultural intelligence, 42
  information processing perspective, 41
  international relations between countries, 42–43
  potential, 46
  status of nations, 43
  task, 42
  team conflict, 43
multinational corporations (MNCs), diversity management, 422, 424, 426, 431
multinational teams
  cultural diversity salience, 40–42
  deep-level components, 41–42
  social categorization, 41
  social distance perceptions, 41
mutable traits, 26
mutual differentiation, categorization, 105, 107

N

narrative-as-identity, navigating the self, 75, 82–83
National Association for the Advancement of Colored People (NAACP), 257

nationality, cross-cultural teams, 45
National Longitudinal Survey
 of Youth, 276
National Organization for Women,
 257, 269
National Organizations Survey (1997),
 161, 275
national origin, 44–45, 167
National Voting Rights Acts of 1965, 452
navigating the self
 critical identity theory, 75, 80–82
 cultural diversity influence, 90–91
 future inquiry, 87–92
 identity conflicts, 73–74
 identity work, 75, 83–87
 implications for actors, observers and
  intergroup relations, 88–90
 narrative-as-identity, 75, 82–83
 performance on work-related tasks,
  89–90
 phrase, 74
 positive relational identities, 91–92
 proactive identity construction, 73
 psychological well-being, 89
 role identity theory, 75, 78–80
 segmentation and integration, 79–80
 social identity theory, 74, 76–78
 theoretical perspectives on, 74, 75
 understanding complex identities, 88
needs assessment, diversity training,
 342–344
negative stereotypes, strategy of dispelling,
 85–86
negative views, identity group, 118
network connections
 age similarity, 197–198
 demographic diversity, 196
 demographic similarity, 193–195,
  196–197
 diversity and team performance,
  202–203
 diversity as connections, 193–195
 diversity-performance debate, 198–199
 future directions, 195–198
 homophily, 193–195, 196
 knowledge management, 192–193
 propinquity, 195, 196–198
 social networks, 199–202
 structural hole research, 200
 team performance, 198–199
 transactive memory system (TMS),
  202–203
networking programs, 267, 268
niche markets, globalization, 4
normative diversity context
 categorization- and elaboration-based
  effects, 212, 213–214
 conceptualization, 211
norms, behavior, 38–39
North America
 diversity management theorization
  outside, 420–421
 domestic diversity, 419–420

education, 406, 407
population by age, 396
North Carolina Racial Justice Act, 450

O

Office of Federal Contract Compliance
 Programs, 266
openness to diversity, climate, 229
openness to experience, 61, 227
operations analysis, diversity training, 343
oppressed minority ideology, 135
optimal distinctiveness theory, 56
optimism
 diversity-performance debate, 199
 network connections, 199–201
Organisation for Economic Co-operation
 and Development (OECD),
 408–409
organizational capital resources, 241
organizational citizenship behaviors
 (OCBs), 373
organizational climate, 228, 229, 234
organizational culture
 learning, 333
 moderation model, 244–245
 normative diversity context, 213–214
 work-life interface, 374
organizational demography, 13
 diversity, 230, 233–234
 structural context, 212, 214–215
organizational diversity, 240
Organizational Diversity Needs
 Analysis, 342
organizational groups, faultlines, 57–58
organizational success, group
 diversity, 52
organizations
 advantages of diversity, 98–99
 attitudes, 103–104
 decategorization, 105–106
 design features, 246
 developing a meta-narrative, 330
 discrimination, 119
 diversity crises, 332
 diversity training impact, 355–356
 foundations of leadership, 329–331
 future research, 334
 globalization, 4
 implementing human resources
  practices, 332–333
 intergroup bias, 103–108
 leadership of, 329–334
 managing difference, 330–331
 managing faultlines, 331–332
 mentoring importance, 308–309
 messages of, during staffing, 285–286
 multiculturalism vs. colorblindness,
  107–108
 mutual differentiation, 107
 needs assessment of diversity training,
  342–343
 recategorization, 106–107
 recruiting applicants, 284–285

research vs. practice of diversity
 training, 358–359
staffing for diversity, 283–284
teams and diversity, 157–158
organization status (ORG), 17–19
outcomes
 positive vs. negative, 233
 reward systems, 245–246
outsourced jobs, socioeconomic trend,
 398–399, 411

P

*Parents Involved in Community Schools
 v. Seattle School District No. 1*
 (2007), 452
peer mentoring, 308
people-based integration, global
 diversity, 436
perceived surface-level dissimilarity, 38
perception
 actual vs. perceived diversity, 184,
  186–187
 diversity training, 350–351
performance. *See also* identity performance
 evaluations, 263, 264–265
 expectations, 165
 faultlines, 59, 60
 outcomes, 44
 work-related tasks, 89–90
personal identity, self-perception, 318
personality and cognitive behavior styles
 (PCB), 17–19, 25
personality diversity, beliefs in value, 226
personality factors, diversity beliefs and
 attitudes, 227–228
person analysis, diversity training,
 343–344
personnel selection
 competitive advantage, 282
 diversity, 289–291
pessimism
 diversity-performance debate, 198–199
 network connections, 200–201
Pew Forum on Religion & Public Life,
 404, 407
phenotypes
philosophy, global diversity
 management, 433
physical capital resources, 241
physical environment, cultural
 diversity, 35
pipeline program, vocational choice,
 302–303
Plans for Progress, 256, 266
Pluralistic organizations
political conservatism, hierarchy-
 enhancing ideology, 133–134,
 136, 138
political liberalism, hierarchy-attenuating
 ideology, 135, 138, 139
political systems, cultural diversity, 35
politicized collective identity, 135
population growth, world, 395, 396

Positive Climate for Diversity Scale, 342
positive identity
  developmental perspective, 91
  evaluative perspective, 90–91
  structural perspective, 91
  virtue perspective, 90
positive identity construction, cultural diversity influence, 90–91
positive relational identities, navigating the self, 91–92
positive views, identity group, 118
power
  critical identity, 80, 82
  definitions, 165
  differentials, 319–320
  distance, 36, 44, 65
  diversity, 186
  dynamics, 82
  global diversity management, 432
practice perspectives, diversity, 7
Pregnancy Discrimination Act of 1978, 126
prejudice
  attitudes, 116
  decategorization, 105–106
  existence, 109
  justification-suppression model (JSM), 122
  social categorization, 99
Price Waterhouse v. Hopkins (1989), 446
prisoners' dilemma situations, 161
problem solving, network connections, 199–202
process conflict, team, 180, 181
process model, global diversity management, 425, 426–428
propinquity, network connections, 195, 196–198
protean careers
  proactivity and resilience, 83
  self-directed career models, 79
protégés, mentoring importance, 308–309
Protestant Work Ethic (PWE)
  ideology, 133, 134, 140, 147
  origin of ideology, 136, 137
  structure, 138
proximity, demographic similarity, 195, 197–198
psychological diversity, climates, 233–234
psychological perspectives on diversity, 5
psychology, competence expectations, 166

Q
qualitative research, context, 216

R
race, 167
  Batson v. Kentucky (1986), 447
  critical identity, 80–81
  cultural diversity, 35
  faultline activation, 64
  socially constructed term, 14
  vocational choice, 304

racial diversity, socioeconomic trend, 401–402, 412
racio-ethnic diversity
  diversity climate, 244
  socioeconomic trend, 401–402, 412
racio-ethnicity, applicant recruiting, 284–285, 287
racioethnic research, 14
racism, ambivalence aversive, 104
rational choice theory, network closure, 199
Reaction-to-Diversity Inventory, 343
realistic, investigative, artistic, social, enterprising, and conventional (RIASEC), vocational choice, 302
recategorization, group-level thinking, 106–107
recruiters
  campus, 284–285
  minority, 284–285
recruiting, Internet, 287–289
recruitment
  definition, 282
  diversity, 287–289
  diversity staffing, 283–284
  integration with selection, 294
  locations, 287–289
  messages, 285–286
  programs, 257–258
  recruiters, 284–285
  sources, 287–289
redefinition, mentoring, 308
Reeves v. Sanderson Plumbing (2000), 445
relational demography, 13
  diversity, 230, 232, 233–234
  faultlines, 331
relational diversity context
  categorization- and elaboration-based effects, 212–213
  conceptualization, 211
relational leadership, 325, 335
relational self-construal (RSC), 335
relationship conflicts
  demographic faultlines, 182, 183
  intragroup, 180
  team viability, 181
relations-oriented diversity, 158
religious diversity, 167, 404, 407–408, 412
religious minorities, recruiting, 286
remediation, stigmatization, 125–126
research, cultural diversity, 43–46
resistance
  affirming identities, 82
  global diversity management, 431–432
  uncertainty quotient, 435
resource acquisition
resource-based view (RBV), competitive advantage, 241–242
resource drain, work-life interface, 371
responsibility, global diversity management, 430–431
reward structures, faultline trigger, 58

reward systems, outcome interdependence, 245–246
Ricci v. DeStafano (2009), 452
Robbers Cave study, 15–16
role congruity research, 78–79
role identity theory
  navigating the self, 75, 78–80
  segmentation and integration, 79–80
Rowe v. General Motors Corp. (1972), 263

S
salary classification, 263, 265
satisfaction, faultlines, 59, 60
schools, diversity mindset, 336
science, technology, engineering, and mathematics (STEM), vocational choice, 303
segmentation
  role identity, 79–80
  work-life interface, 371
selection process
  integration with recruitment, 294
  literature, 293–294
  recruiting for diversity, 285–286, 289–291
self. *See also* navigating the self
  individuals navigating, 5
  psychology well-being, 140–141
  workplace, 145
self-awareness, social identity, 320–321
self-categorization theory, 15, 56
self-concept, structural perspective, 91
self definition, critical identity, 81
self-disclosure, trait, 26
self-enhancement, social identity, 76–77
self-esteem, stigma, 118
self-knowledge, training design, 346
self-management, 316
  others' perceptions, 319–320
  self-perception, 318–319
  strategies for enhancing, 320–321
  theoretical foundations, 318–320
separation
  definition, 55
  diversity, 19–21, 55–56, 67n.2
  measurement, 22, 45
  mentoring, 308
September 11, 2001, 216
service organizations, human resources, 243
sexual harassment, 253, 272, 273
sexual orientation, 167
  discrimination, 228
  socioeconomic trend, 402–403, 412
shared cognition, climate strength, 231, 235
shared diversity climate
  assessment, 234–235
  climate strength, 231, 235
  consequences, 232
  determinants of, 232–233
  information elaboration, 232
  inter-subgroup sharedness, 235

measurement, 231
relational demography, 232
shared leadership, concept of, 317–318
Shultz v. Wheaton Glass Co. (1970), 263
similarity-attraction paradigm
   diversity research, 14–15, 38
   recruitment, 285, 293
   social identity, 76
   subgroups, 56
similarity-attraction perspective
   context, 464–465
   understanding diversity, 159, 160–161
similarity perception, vocational choice, 305–306
situational judgment tests (SJTs), 290
situational strength perspective, normative diversity context, 212, 213–214
situational triggers, cultural identities, 38–39
skills, evaluation of diversity, 353
"smoking gun" evidence, 444, 446
social behavior, role identity, 78
social capital theory, relational context, 212–213
social categorization perspective
   categorical thinking, 99–103
   consequences, 100–102
   context, 464–465
   diversity, 159, 463
   diversity training design, 345–346
   faultlines, 54, 56–57
   grouping of people, 99–100
   heterogeneity, 181
   integrating with information processing, 162, 172–173
   intergroup bias, 102–103
   minority influence, 163
   subgroupings, 221
   teams, 41
   theory, 159, 160–161, 210
social competition, social identity, 77–78
social creativity, social identity, 77
social distance, 56–57, 301–302
social dominance theory
   hierarchy-enhancing ideologies, 143, 147
   structure of ideology, 138
social exchange theory, mentoring, 308
social identity theory
   conflict, 327
   cycle of influence, 322, 329
   diversity disadvantage, 240
   diversity of groups, 160
   diversity research, 15–16
   future research, 87–88
   invisible, 23–26
   leadership, 322–323
   navigating the self, 74, 75, 76–78
   self-leadership, 318, 320–321
   subgroups, 56
social justice
social learning theory, training, 347–348
social media, innovations, 410, 411

social minorities, information processing, 162
social mobility, social identity, 77
social networks
   brokerage and creative problem solving, 199–202
   career development, 311
   closure and collective action, 199
   diversity, 199–202
   diversity-performance relationship, 6–7
social psychological distance theory, in-group/out-group, 56–57
social structures, cultural diversity, 35
Society for Human Resource Management (SHRM), 423
sociodemographics, cultural diversity, 35–36
socioeconomic status (SES), 167
socioeconomic trends
   disability estimates, 409
   education, 403–404, 412
   Education For All (EFA), 407
   employer migration, 398–399, 411–412
   global education statistics, 405–406
   health care, 395–397
   HIV/AIDS, 396–397
   human rights based on sexual orientation and gender identity, 402–403, 412
   immigration, 397–398, 411
   inflows of foreign workers, 398
   innovations for virtual workplace, 410–411
   outsourcing jobs, 398–399
   people with disabilities, 408–410
   racial and ethnic groups in workplace, 401–402
   religious diversity, 404, 407–408, 412
   women's and men's economic activity rates, 400
   women's labor force participation, 399–401, 412
   world's population growth, 395, 396
sociofunctional approach, stigmatization, 122
sociological approach, diversity programs, 255–256
sociology, competence expectations, 166
South and West Asia, education, 406, 407
Southeast Asia and Pacific, 400
spillover, work-life interface, 371
spirals of silence, 23
staffing. *See* diversity staffing
status, 167
   categorization of articles, 168
   competition within group, 195
   definitions, 165
   diverse groups, 164–167
   expectations states theory, 165
   information processing, 166
   multicultural teams, 43, 44
   performance expectations, 165

status characteristics theory, 165–166
   violations influencing information processing, 166–167
   vs. power, 165
status characteristics theory, 165–166
status hierarchies, dominance and submission, 89
step-ahead mentoring, 308
stereotype content model (SCM), stigmatization, 121–122
stereotypes
   beliefs, 116
   career development barrier, 301, 304
   coping strategies, 120–121
sticky floors
   equal opportunities, 401
   expectations of success, 306
   vocational choice, 302
stigma
   aesthetics, 117
   antecedents, 123
   concealable, 116–117
   consequences, 124–125
   controllability, 117
   coping strategies, 120–121
   definition, 116
   devalued differences, 115
   dimensions, 116–117
   disruption, 117
   future research directions, 126–127
   hereditary-based, 116
   intergroup emotions theory, 121
   interpersonal experiences, 119–120
   intrapersonal experiences, 117–118
   justification-suppression model (JSM), 122
   managing impressions, 119–120
   manifestations, 123–124
   remediation, 125–126
   stereotype content model (SCM), 121–122
   stigmatizers' perspectives, 121–126
   system justification, 122
   targets' perspectives, 117–121
   targets' self-esteem, 118
   theories, 5–6, 115–116, 121–122
strategic human resource management (SHRM), 294
strategic model, global diversity management, 424–426
strategy theory, diversity, 7
strength, faultline, 53, 54
structural diversity context
   categorization- and elaboration-based effects, 212, 214–215
   definition, 211–212
structural integration
structural perspective, self-concept, 91
subgroup categorization, faultline, 59, 62–63
subgroup climate, demography, 232
subgroup thinking, demographic diversity, 221

INDEX | 481

sub-Saharan Africa, 400, 406, 407
success, understanding, 274
superordinate categorization, social identity, 77, 88
Support Our Law Enforcement and Safe Neighborhoods Act, 447
suppression, justification-, model (JSM), 122
Supreme Court, 442, 443, 445, 452
surface-level display cues, identity work, 84–85
surface-level diversity
 conceptualization, 15, 16
 mapping, 20–21
 teams, 40–41
Swain v. Alabama (1965), 449
system justification, 122, 148*n*.2
systems perspectives, diversity, 9

T

targeted recruitment programs
 Blacks and women, 257
 gender and racial diversity, 273–274
targets of influence, leadership, 316–317
task, cultural diversity, 42
task analysis, diversity training, 343
task conflicts
 demographic faultline, 59–60
 intragroup, 180
 performance, 181
 team viability, 181
task content, faultline, 58, 61
task experience, status hierarchy, 166
task-oriented, diversity, 158
team diversity
 beliefs in value, 226
 cross-level context, 215–216
 diversity training, 358
 perspectives, 229–230
 structural context, 214–215
team entitlement, faultline, 59, 60–61
team performance
 diversity and, 202–203
 diversity climate, 232
 ethnic diversity, 210
 information elaboration, 224–225
 multiple teams, 203
 network connections, 198–199
 social networks, 200
teams
 advantages of diversity, 98–99
 communication, 34–35
 cultural differences within, 40–42
 cultural diversity, 39–46
 deep-level cultural components, 41–42
 diversity-performance debate, 198–199
 Fortune 100 companies, 166
 multinational, and cultural diversity salience, 40–42
 national differences across, 39–40
 performance of multiple, 203
 surface-level diversity, 40–41

top management teams (TMT), 241, 242
turnover, 65
viability, 180–181
work of organizations, 157–158
technological innovations, workplace, 410–411, 412–413
temporal effects, diversity context, 216
terrorists attacks, 216
Theory of Planned Behavior, 344
"think manager, think male" phenomenon, 319
third-culture building, diversity and unity, 435–436
Threats, identity work, 84, 85–87
Top management teams (TMTs)
trainer demographics, diversity training, 349
training. *See also* diversity training
 demographics of group, 349–350
 design, 8–9
 sexual harassment grievance, 272, 273
 targeted recruitment programs, 258
trait approach, workgroup model, 17–19
traits, 26
transactive memory system (TMS), 202–203
transfer, diversity training, 353–355
transformational leadership, 247, 324
translation, global diversity management, 430–431
triggers, active faultline, 58–59, 63–64
Turkey, gender equality, 423
turnover rates
 high-quality relationships, 325
 team, 65
 women and people of color, 307

U

UNAIDS *Report on the Global AIDS Epidemic*, 397
uncertainty avoidance, culture, 36
uncertainty quotient, resistance, 435
University of Michigan, affirmative action, 454
upper-echelons theory, 241
Urban League, 257
U.S. General Social Survey, 376
U.S. Office of Personnel Management, outreach, 288

V

value-in-diversity
 diversity advantage, 240–241
 human capital, 242
value-in-diversity hypothesis, 161
values
 behavior, 38–39
 beliefs, and attitudes (VBA), 17–19, 25
 cultural diversity, 36
 driving behavior, 37
 national origin, 44–45
variation, 13

cultural diversity, 32–33
measurement, 45
variety
 diversity, 19–21, 55–56, 67*n*.2
 measurement, 22
virtual workplace, technological innovations, 410–411, 412–413
virtue perspective
 positive identity, 90
 positive relational identity, 91–92
visible attributes, diversity advantage, 240–241
vocational choice
 ambient cues and traditional representation, 304–305
 discrimination and isolation, 307
 drivers of, 302–303
 expectations of success, 306–307
 gender and, 304
 gender/race valuation, 306
 identity, 303–304
 ongoing, 306
 perceived similarity, 305–306
 race and, 304
 Realistic, Investigative, Artistic, Social, Enterprising, and Conventional (RIASEC), 302
voir dire, counteracting bias, 451
voluntary training, diversity, 351

W

Walking Through White Privilege, self-awareness, 346–347
"war for talent," disembodied worker, 368–369
Washington v. Davis (1976), 445
weight discrimination, 26–27, 28
Western Europe, education, 406, 407
women
 antidiscrimination policies, 256
 career development, 310–311
 discrimination and isolation, 307
 diversity attitudes, 226–227
 diversity staff and evaluation, 261
 entry into paid labor force, 367–369
 firms with training programs, 258
 labor force participation, 399–401, 412
 mentoring, 309–310
 program effects on management diversity, 269
 recruitment, 294
 similarity perceptions, 305–306
 stereotype threat, 306
 targeted recruitment programs, 257
 work-family programs and opportunities, 271–272
 workplace ideologies and attitudes, 144–145
women's issues
 child-care programs, 271
 diversity management, 273–274
 flextime programs, 270–271
 grievance procedures and training, 272

maternity leaves, 270
opportunities for women and minorities, 271–272
rise of, in 1990s, 269–272
sexual harassment grievance systems, 272, 273
work-family programs, 270–271
work environment munificence
  integrated model, 383
  variables, 379, 381
  work-life interface, 382
work-family facilitation, 371
work-family interface. *See also* work-life interface
  gender roles, 377–378
work-family programs, women's issues, 270–271, 273–274
Workforce 2000, Hudson Institute, 3
workforce diversity
  definition, 395
  diversity programs and, 268–269
  drivers for change, 434
  ecosystem, 393–394
  global, 9, 394–395
  globalization and global competition, 239–240
  inclusion, 413–414
  leadership, 315–317
  recruiting and selecting diverse, 291–292
  sociological approach, 255–256
  top management teams (TMTs), 242
Workforce Diversity Questionnaire, 342
workgroup models, diversity research, 17–19
workgroup outcomes, conflict, 179–180
work interference with family (WIF), 372, 377–378
work-life conflict
  antecedents and outcomes of, 372–373
  definition, 370

work-life interface, 369–371
work-life facilitation
  antecedents and outcomes of, 373
  disembodied worker, 367
  interface research, 371
work-life flexibility
  disembodied worker, 369
  environmental support, 373
  impact of supports, 373–375
  interacting practices, 375
  practices, 374–375
  synergy between formal practices and managerial support, 375
work-life interface
  antecedents and outcomes of, 370
  buffering model, 372
  changing gender role attitudes, 376–377
  compensation, 371
  conflict, facilitation, flexibility, 9
  cross-cultural differences and similarities, 384–385
  definition, 366
  entry of women in paid labor force, 367–369
  external situational effects, 382–383
  future research, 383–385
  gender impact, 375–378
  gender role behaviors in family, 376
  gender roles and, 377–378
  independent-effects model, 371–372
  individual differences, 375
  integrated model of, 378–383, 385
  intersection of paid work with outside areas, 384
  key constructs and models, 369–372
  labor force participation rates, 368
  models of, 371–372
  organizational culture, 374
  research, 367, 372–375
  resource drain, 371

segmentation, 371
spillover, 371
term, 383
theoretical mechanisms affecting, dynamics, 379
variables linked to constructs, 379, 381
work-life conflict, 369–371, 372–373
work-life facilitation, 371, 373
work-life flexibility supports, 373–375, 384
workplace. *See also* corporate diversity programs
  ideologies, 139–140
  implications of ideologies, 145–145
  stigmatized or devalued attributes, 115
  technological innovations for virtual, 410–411, 412–413
  women in, 144–145
workplace diversity, 167, 220
  diversity advantage, 240–241
  diversity disadvantage, 240
  human capital perspective, 241
  human dignity, 437
  human resources, 242
  United States, 44
workplace support, 373–374
work resource gains/losses, variables, 379, 381
work resource investments, variables, 379, 381
work role demands, variables, 379, 381
work role performance, variables, 379, 381
work styles, culture-specific, 39–40
work-to-family enrichment (WFE), 373
work values, faultline composition, 63
World Education Forum, 403–404
World Health Organization (WHO), disabled individuals, 408
worldview, ideology, 133